CADE'S
CAMPIN
TOURING
MOTOR CAF
SITE GUIDE

GW00501906

2 0 0 2

Compiled and Edited by
Reg Cade and Barry Gallafent

Published by
Marwain Publishing Limited,
Marwain House, Clarke Road, Mount Farm, Milton Keynes MK1 1LG
Tel: 01908 643022

Design and Administration
Vicky Jones

Advertisement Manager
Derek Inall

Colour Reproduction by
Pepberry Limited, Aspley Guise, Milton Keynes, MK17 8HF

Printed by
Acorn Web Offset, Normanton, West Yorkshire, WF6 1TW

Distributed by (Booktrade)
Bravo Limited
311 Ballards Lane, London, N12 8LY

(Camping and Caravan Trade)
Marwain Publishing Limited

ISBN 0 - 905377 - 88 - 5

Caravan & Camping
Haven
BRITISH HOLIDAYS

We've come together to offer you more
Where great family holidays are made!

Prices start from

*£4
Per night

*Based on nights in Spring or Autumn and includes the 2 for 1 offer.

SCOTLAND, THE NORTH WEST AND NORTHUMBERLAND
1. Craig Tara
2. Seton Sands - See Page 270
3. Haggerston Castle - See Page 166
4. Blue Dolphin
5. Primrose Valley
6. Reighton Sands
7. Lakeland - See Page 54
8. Marton Mere - See Page 137

THE EAST OF ENGLAND
9. Thorpe Park - SeePage 145
10. Golden Sands
11. Cherry Tree
12. Wild Duck
13. Orchards - See Page 116

DORSET
14. Rockley Park - See Page 108
15. Seaview
16. Weymouth Bay
17. Littlesea

DEVON, SOMERSET AND CORNWALL
18. Devon Cliffs
19. Perran Sands
20. Doniford Bay
21. Burnham on Sea - See Page 178

WALES
22. Kiln Park - See Page 248
23. Greenacres - See Page 239
24. Presthaven Sands

What A Perfect Mix...

- Freedom to choose from even more coastal locations throughout the UK
- Freedom to enjoy on-Park life
- Freedom to relax with the familiarity of your own touring caravan, motorhome, tent or trailer

We Welcome...

✓ Touring Caravans, Motorhomes

✓ Trailer Tents and Tents

For Haven or British Holidays call now on:

08705 13 44 02

or see your local travel agent quoting CADES

Haven Holidays/British Holidays, 1 Park Lane, Hemel Hempstead, Herts. HP2 4YL.

ear Reader

s our pleasure to welcome you to the thirtieth edition of Cade's Camping, Touring & otor Caravan Site Guide.

ie information we provide is updated annually and is supplied to us directly by the vners or operators of each individual park. This way we ensure that we provide only e most current details so that you may more easily find the right park for *your* oliday.

'e include a complete variety of parks, from individual privately owned parks with :commodation for just a few units to those owned by some of the largest names in e Caravan Holiday business. Somewhere between these covers you will find just nat you are looking for.

; always we would like to point out that we are not agents of the parks listed, nor ey of us and we only publish such information as is supplied to us by them, in good ith. Parks are however aware of their obligation under the Trade Descriptions Act to ovide only true and accurate information. Many parks included in our listings and ose with advertisements have been with Cade's for a considerable number of years, emonstrating our continuing faith in each other.

nother important point to mention is that on some parks, certain facilities may only e available in the high season. You should always check directly with the park efore travelling, that any facility you particularly require will be available at the time your visit.

t the request of many of our readers, we have added an index to parks catering for dults' only and also an index of parks featuring 'fishing on site' or 'lakes' in their tractions. We hope the inclusion of these new features will make the guide even ore useful for everyone. To find the whereabouts of these, please refer to the main dex.

II that remains for me now is to thank you for choosing Cade's and wish you all the ery best of Touring Holidays in 2002.

Barry M Gallafent

arry M Gallafent
anaging Director - Marwain Publishing Limited

3

INDEX

4

5

SYMBOLS

SYMBOLS

- ♠ Tents
- 🚐 Motor Caravans
- 🚙 Touring Caravans
- ⇌ Nearest Station
- ♿ Facilities for Disabled
- 🏍 No Motorcycles
- ƒ Electricity Hook-ups
- ▣ Fully Serviced Pitches
- 🅗 Hard Standings
- 🚽 Flush Toilets
- ⚲ Water
- ⌐ Showers
- ☉ Shaver Points
- 🖐 Washing Facilities
- ▭ Ironing Facilities
- 🔲 Launderette
- ♻ Chem. Toilet Disposal
- S🏪 Site Shop
- M🏪 Mobile Shop
- l🏪 Local Shop
- ⊡ Gas
- ☎ Public Telephone
- ✕ Café Restaurant
- ♈ Licensed Club
- 📺 T.V.
- ✦ Games Room
- ⩍ Childs Play Area
- ⬎ Outdoor Pool
- ⬏ Indoor Pool
- ✳ Sports Area
- ⋈ Pets Welcome
- ▣ Parking by Unit
- ▣ Credit Cards Accepted
- ▣ Money-Off Vouchers
  Accepted
- A Adults Only Park

Nearby Facilities
- ⌐ Golf
- ✦ Fishing
- ⚓ Sailing
- ⚓ Boating
- ∪ Riding
- ⌐ Water Ski-ing
- ℛ Tennis
- ⋌ Climbing

SYMBOLES FRANÇAIS

- ♠ Tentes
- 🚐 Auto-Caravanes
- 🚙 Caravanes
- ⇌ Gare Locale
- ♿ Handicapés
- ƒ Branchments Electrique Pour Caravanes
- ▣ Emplacement Service Complet
- 🅗 Emplacement Surface Dure
- 🏍 Motorcyclettes Non-Admises
- 🚽 Toilettes
- ⚲ Eau
- ⌐ Douches
- ☉ Prises Electrique pour Rasoirs
- 🖐 Bains
- ▭ Repassage
- 🔲 Laverie Automatique
- ♻ Décharge pour W.C. Chemique
- S🏪 Magasin du Terrain
- M🏪 Magasin Mobile
- l🏪 Magasin du Quartier
- ⊡ Gaz
- ☎ Cabines Téléphoniques
- ✕ Café
- ♈ Club/Bar Patenté
- 📺 Salle de Télévision
- ✦ Salle de Jeux
- ⩍ Terrain de Jeux Enfants
- ⬎ Piscine du Terrain
- ⬏ Piscine a l'interieur
- ✳ Terrain de Sports et de Jeux
- ▣ Stationment à côté de la caravane permis
- ▣ Carte Credit Accepter
- ▣ Bon Remise 'Cades' Accepter
- A Camping Seulment Adulte

Nearby Facilities
- ⌐ Golf
- ✦ Pêche
- ⚓ Voile
- ⚓ Canotage
- ∪ Equitation
- ⌐ Ski Nautique
- ℛ Tennis
- ⋌ Ascension

6

Discover Britain with us...

Three Cliffs Bay near Gowerton Club Site

THE CARAVAN CLUB

So much more to enjoy

Here's what our visitors say

"A beautiful unspoiled site – one night 'en route' was transformed into 10 days of delight by helpful and knowledgeable Wardens"

Grummore, Scottish Highlands

"What a gem of a site – well kept, with birds, views and walks – we'll be back"

Dockray Meadow, Lake District

"This is our first time with The Club – if all sites are as good, we're in for a real treat"

Daleacres, Kent

You can expand your choice of sites with our **'Site Collection 2002'** *brochure featuring over 200 quality Club Sites in Britain and Ireland. All welcome tourer and motor caravanners and trailer tenters and many are open to non-members and tent campers.*

For your FREE copy complete the coupon and return to the address below (or write to this address quoting ref. CAD7)

**The Caravan Club, Dept DC,
FREEPOST WD3000,
EAST GRINSTEAD, RH19 1BR**

*Brochure publication date end November 2001.
All Caravan Club members will automatically
receive this brochure.*

www.caravanclub.co.uk

Mr, Mrs, Miss, Ms	Initials	Surname
Address		
	Post Code	
Tel. No.		

OR CALL US *FREE* ON 0800 521161

QUOTING REFERENCE **CAD7**

The best of the
outdoors
indoors

The Caravan and
Holiday Home Show

24-27 January 2002
23-26 January 2003

THE CARAVAN
& OUTDOOR
LEISURE SHOW
EARLS COURT
LONDON

27 November - 2 December 2001
5-10 November 2002

TEL **020 7370 8203** FAX **020 7370 8142**
www.caravanshows.com E-MAIL **info@caravanshows.com**

A free gift, we know you want (because you're already holding it)

Tourer Select is the only insurance recommended by Practical Caravan Magazine. By taking out a policy with Tourer Select you can effectively obtain your CADE'S Guide for free. Anybody taking out a policy as a result of this advertisement will receive a discount equivalent to the price of the CADE'S Guide (£5.25).

Policy benefits

- Choice of cover options to suit all budgets and any age of caravan
- Comprehensive "all year round" cover, at home, in storage or in transit
- "New-for-old" cover for caravans up to 5 years of age
- No claims bonus
- Discount for approved security devices/storage
- Easy payment options by Direct Debit Switch or Credit Card

Call for a no obligation quotation:

01452 511480

stating CG01

JLT Leisure. A division of JLT Corporate Risks Limited. Lloyd's broker. Regulated by the General Insurance Council. A member of Jardine Lloyd Thompson Group.

Safety comes first with CaSSOA

Secure storage of your caravan means peace of mind for you and lower insurance costs. Now the Caravan Storage Site Owners' Association (CaSSOA) can help you choose a site that assures your prize possession will be safe and secure.

It's estimated that there are currently 300,000 caravans in the UK today, of which a startling 5,000 are stolen each year. Two thirds of these thefts occur at storage sites.

At the same time, caravan owners are increasingly required under insurance conditions to ensure their vehicles are stored securely. Caravan owners storing their caravan at home are concerned because the caravan's presence - or lack of it - is seen as a "calling card" to would-be burglars.

High levels of security are offered by sites members of the Caravan Storage Site Owners Association

Meanwhile, police admit the problem of caravan theft is difficult for them to treat as a priority. They record a stolen caravan in the same manner as they record a stolen pint of milk.

The dilemma for caravan owners is: "I need to use a caravan storage site, but how do I choose a safe one?" CaSSOA decided that the situation for caravan owners was simply unacceptable. With the backing of police forces and other insurers loss adjusters the association started a major project to inspect and assess caravan storage sites across the UK.

In total, over 2000 sites were visited. There are now 106 members of the association.

For further information please contact
The Caravan Storage Site Owners' Association
Call 0115 9349826 for more help

www.oakwood-village.co.uk

Visit over 2000 holiday parks at www.ukparks.com

ukparks.com

Plan your stay on Britain's biggest site!
Find the perfect pitch for your tourer or tent, or discover where you can rent or buy a luxury holiday home.

Easy and quick to use, plus regular updates including special deals and offers.

NGLAND

EDFORDSHIRE
IDGMONT
se & Crown, 89 High Street,
dgmont, Bedfordshire, MK43 0TY.
d: 01525 **Tel:** 280245
earest Town/Resort Woburn/Ampthill
rections Midway between Ampthill and
oburn on A507 2 miles south of junc 13
.

creage 3 **Open** All Year
ccess Good **Site** Level
tes Available ⋏ ⊕ ⊖ **Total** 20
acilities ⨍ 🚽 ▲ ☺ ⛟
🏪 🛒 ⚡ 🕂 🔲 🔲 🔲
earby Facilities ⌐ ✔ ⚓ ✗ ∪ ♨ ♬
 Ridgmont
jacent to Woburn Safari Park and 4 miles
m Woburn Abbey.

ERKSHIRE
ORNEY REACH
nerden Caravan Site, Off Old Marsh
ne, Dorney Reach, Nr. Maidenhead,
rkshire, SL6 0EE.
d: 01628 **Tel:** 627461
earest Town/Resort Maidenhead
rections Leave M4 junc 7, Slough West,
en A4 towards Maidenhead. Third turn
t signposted Dorney Reach and caravan
e, then first turn right.
creage 3 **Open** April **to** October
ccess Good **Site** Level
tes Available ⋏ ⊕ ⊖ **Total** 60
acilities ⚹ ⨍ 🚽 ▲ ⌐ ☺ ⤵ 🔲 ⛟
 ⊕ ▲ 🕂 🔲 🔲
earby Facilities ⌐ ✔ ✗ ∪
 Taplow
ear River Thames.

URLEY
urley Farm Caravan & Camping Park,
epherds Lane, Hurley, Nr. Maidenhead,
rkshire, SL6 5NE.
d: 01628 **Tel:** 823501/824493
d: 01628 **Fax:** 825533
ebsite: www.hurleyfarm.co.uk
earest Town/Resort Maidenhead/
enley-on-Thames.
rections Maidenhead, A4130 west
wards Henley. 3¼ miles turn right, ¾
le past East Arms PH into Shepherds
ne. Entrance 200 yards on left.
creage 15 **Open** March **to** October

Access Good **Site** Level
Sites Available ⋏ ⊕ ⊖ **Total** 200
Facilities ⚹ ⨍ 🚽 🚽 ▲ ⌐ ☺ ⤵ 🔲 ⛟
🏪 🛒 ⚡ ❄ 🕂 🔲 🔲 ⛟
Nearby Facilities ⌐ ✔ ✗ ∪ ♬
 🚉 Maidenhead
On picturesque River Thames. Ideal touring
centre for Henley, Windsor (Legoland),
Oxford and London. Launching ramp. Walks
along riverside and into nearby forest. Site
shop in peak season only. Disabled toilet
facilities. David Bellamy Gold Award.

NEWBURY
Oakley Farm Caravan Park, Oakley
Farm House, Penwood Road, Wash
Water, Newbury, Berkshire, RG20 0LP.
Std: 01635 **Tel:** 36581
Nearest Town/Resort Newbury.
Directions From the A34 south of Newbury
take the exit marked Highclere and Wash
Common. Turn left onto the A343 towards
Newbury, turn right after ¼ mile (by car sales
garage) into Penwood Road. Site is then 400
metres on your left.
Acreage 3 **Open** March **to** October
Access Good **Site** Gentle Slope
Facilities ⨍ 🚽 🚽 ▲ ⌐ ☺ 🔲 ⛟
🏪 🛒 ⚡ 🕂 🔲 🔲 🔲
Nearby Facilities ⌐ ♬
 🚉 Newbury

RISELEY
Wellington Country Park, Riseley, Nr
Reading, Berkshire, RG7 1SP.
Std: 01189 **Tel:** 326444
Std: 01189 **Fax:** 326445
Nearest Town/Resort Reading
Directions Between Reading and
Basingstoke. Signposted from the A33,
approx. 4 miles south of the M4 junction 11
and 5 miles north of the M3 junction 5.
Acreage 350 **Open** March **to** October
Access Good **Site** Level
Sites Available ⋏ ⊕ ⊖ **Total** 60
Facilities ⨍ 🚽 🚽 ▲ ⌐ ☺ 🔲 ⛟
🏪 🛒 ⚡ 🕂 🔲 🔲 ⛟
Nearby Facilities ⌐ ✔ ✗ ∪ ♬
 🚉 Reading
In part of the Duke of Wellingtons estate.
Childrens animal farm, adventure
playground, nature trails, crazy golf, boating
and a gift shop.

A COLOUR MAP SECTION STARTS ON PAGE 281

BRISTOL (County of)
BRISTOL
**Brook Lodge Touring Caravan &
Camping Park,** Brook Lodge Farm,
Cowslip Green, Bristol, BS40 5RD.
Std: 01934 **Tel:** 862311
Email: info.under.bristol.for.park
Nearest Town/Resort Bristol/Bath
Directions From the historic city of Bristol
take the A38 south west for 7 miles, park is
signposted on the left. From the M5 junction
19 take the A369, then the B3129, then the
B3130, then right onto the A38. 6 miles from
the A368 at Churchill take the A38 north,
park is on the right in 3½ miles.
Acreage 3½ **Open** March **to** October
Access Good **Site** Mostly Level
Sites Available ⋏ ⊕ ⊖ **Total** 29
Facilities ⨍ 🚽 🚽 ▲ ⌐ ☺ ⤵ 🔲 ⛟
🏪 🛒 ⚡ 🕂 🔲 🔲
Nearby Facilities ⌐ ✔ ∪ ♬
Beautiful grounds with trees, lawns and
garden. Historic hamlet of Cowslip Green,
recognised internationally as a heritage area
of significant importance relating to the early
works in the Abolition of Slavery, W
Wilberforce/H More. Trout fishing at Blagdon
Lake 2 miles, hot air ballooning by
arrangement nearby and a dry ski slope 3
miles. Bird life and walks. Swimming pool
available in July and August (unheated).
Rural non-tourist area. Ideal for touring. ETB
Graded 3 Stars, AA 3 Pennants and ANWB
Approved Park.

BUCKINGHAMSHIRE
BEACONSFIELD
Highclere Farm Country Touring Park,
Newbarn Lane, Seer Green, Near
Beaconsfield, Bucks, HP9 2QZ.
Std: 01494 **Tel:** 874505
Std: 01494 **Fax:** 875238
Nearest Town/Resort Beaconsfield
Directions Leave the M40 at junction 2, go
into Beaconsfield and take the A355 towards
Amersham. After 1 mile turn right to Seer
Green and follow tourist signs.
Acreage 6 **Open** March **to** January
Access Good **Site** Level
Sites Available ⋏ ⊕ ⊖ **Total** 60
Facilities ⚹ ⨍ 🚽 🚽 ▲ ⌐ ☺ ⤵ 🔲 ⛟
🏪 🛒 ⚡ 🕂 🔲 🔲 🔲
Nearby Facilities ⌐ ∪ ♬
 🚉 Seer Green
Near to Legoland, Chiltern Air Museum,
Miltons Cottage, Odds Farm (Rare Breeds),
Bekonscot, Milton Keynes and London.

Wheelhome Motorcaravans

The (seven times) award winning specialists in converting cars and M.P.V.s such as Ford Galaxy, Suzuki Wagon R+, Suzuki Carry etc. into compact, garageable campers from only £12,550 to £29,500 that can be used as every-day cars with Automatic transmission, Power steering and Air conditioning etc etc.
Winners of the "Motorcaravan of the Year" award seven times!

Established 1986 — *S.V.A. approved vehicles*

Cars taken in part exchange, demonstrations anytime *by appointment*.
Used Wheelhomes are available. Tel; 01277 372241 or 01245 421875.
25. Stocks Lane Doddinghurst, Brentwood, Essex, CM15 0BN.
Email; sales@wheelhome.co.uk   Web site; www.wheelhome.co.uk

COSGROVE leisure park

Cosgrove Leisure park is situated on the Buckinghamshire & Northamptonshire border just north of Milton Keynes.

The park is based around twelve lakes situated in 180 acres of beautiful parkland with both the River Tove and the River Great Ouse passing through the grounds.

Why not join the majority of touring caravan owners at the park and keep your caravan here all season, enjoying full use of the facilities whenever you wish.

Alternatively, why not bring your touring caravan, tent or motor home and stay for a weekend.

We will have a reduced number of pitches available for the 2002 season therefore pre-booking is essential.

Please note we accept family groups only.

- 350+ Electrical Hook Ups
- Excellent Coarse Fishing
- Modern Toilet & Shower Facilities
- Swimming Pool & Paddling Pool
- Large Children's Play Area
- Grocery & Accessories Shop
- Poolside Cafe & Fish & Chip Shop
- Amusement Arcade
- Mini Golf & Tennis
- Water Skiing

Cosgrove Leisure Park, Cosgrove, Milton Keynes, MK19 7JP
Find us just off the A508 near Old Stratford, Milton Keynes and through the village of Cosgrove
Telephone 01908 563360 Fax 01908 263615 Web: www.cosgrovepark.co.uk

VINGHOE

Iver Birch Campsite, Silver Birch Café, Ivinghoe, Near Leighton Buzzard, Beds, LU7 9EN.
Std: 01296 **Tel:** 668348
Nearest Town/Resort Tring
Directions From Tring take the B488 towards Dunstable, go through Bulbourne and we are 2 miles on the left hand side, near Ivinghoe Village.
Acreage 1 **Open** April **to** October
Access Good **Site** Level
Sites Available ▲ � ➡ **Total** 12
Facilities ▥☉⌓ ➡✖⊡
Nearby Facilities ↾ ⌿ ∪
≠ Tring
Near to Whipsnade Zoo, Woburn Safari Park, Ridgeway Footpath (1 mile), Ivinghoe Beacon and Asheridge Park. Indoor swimming pool nearby.

NEWPORT PAGNELL

Lovat Meadow Caravan Park, London Road, Newport Pagnell, Buckinghamshire, MK16 9BQ.
Std: 01908 **Tel:** 610858
Email: newportptc@aol.com
Website: www.members.aol.com/newportptc/
Nearest Town/Resort Newport Pagnell
Directions 1½ miles from the M1 junction 14. Follow signs to Newport Pagnell along the A509, cross the roundabout onto the B526, park is 500 yards on the left.
Open March **to** January
Access Good **Site** Lev/Slope
Sites Available � ➡ **Total** 40
Facilities ƒ ➡🚿⊡
Nearby Facilities ⌿
≠ Milton Keynes
Riverside location, ideal for fishing. Adjacent to our own indoor heated swimming pool. Dogs welcome if kept on leads.

STONY STRATFORD

Cosgrove Leisure Park, Cosgrove, Milton Keynes, MK19 7JP.
Std: 01908 **Tel:** 563360
Std: 01908 **Fax:** 263615
Email: enquiries@cosgrovepark.co.uk
Website: www.cosgrovepark.co.uk
Nearest Town/Resort Stony Stratford
Directions Off the A508 north of Milton Keynes, through the village of Cosgrove.
Acreage 180 **Open** 1 April **to** 1 Nov
Access Good **Site** Level
Sites Available ▲ � ➡ **Total** 906
Facilities ƒ ▥ ♨ ⌓ ☉ ⬚ ➡
🏪🍴✕♨☉❄✖⊡
Nearby Facilities ↾ ⌿ ⚓ ✠ ∪ ⋇ ⌖
≠ Wolverton
180 acres featuring twelve lakes and two rivers. Please see our advertisement under Northamptonshire.

CAMBRIDGESHIRE

BURWELL

Stanford Park, Weirs Road, Burwell, Cambridgeshire, CB5 0BP.
Std: 01638 **Tel:** 741547
Nearest Town/Resort Cambridge/Newmarket
Directions From Cambridge take B1102 to Burwell from Newmarket take B1103 to Burwell.
Acreage 20 **Open** All Year
Access Good **Site** Level
Sites Available ▲ � ➡ **Total** 150

Facilities ⅙ ƒ ▥ ▯ ♨ ⌓ ☉⬚➡ 🗗 ➡
🏪☉🏪❄✖⊡
Nearby Facilities ↾ ⌿ ⚓ ✠ ∪ ⌖
≠ Newmarket
Near to rivers, on the Fens for birdwatching etc., Newmarket Horse Racing, Cambridge and historic houses. RAC appointed and AA 4 Pennants. You can also call us on Mobile 07802 439997.

CAMBRIDGE

Appleacre Park, London Road, Fowlmere, Royston, Hertfordshire, SG8 7RU.
Std: 01763 **Tel:** 208354/208229
Nearest Town/Resort Cambridge
Directions 9 miles south of Cambridge on the B1368 through Fowlmere Village.
Acreage 3 **Open** All Year
Access Good **Site** Level
Sites Available ▲ �▯ **Total** 20
Facilities ƒ ▥ ▯ ♨ ⌓ ☉⬚➡ 🗗 ➡
🏪 🗗 ⊡
Nearby Facilities ↾ ⌿
≠ Shepreth
A small pleasant park at the southern end of a village with trees and shade. Within easy reach of Duxford Imperial War Museum.

CAMBRIDGE

Highfield Farm Touring Park, Highfield Farm, Long Road, Comberton, Cambridge, CB3 7DG.
Std: 01223 **Tel:** 262308
Std: 01223 **Fax:** 262308
Website: www.highfieldfarmtouringpark.co.uk
Nearest Town/Resort Cambridge
Directions From Cambridge - Leave A1303/A428 (Bedford) after 3 miles, follow camping signs to Comberton. From M11 - Leave junction 12, take A603 (Sandy) for ½ mile then B1046 to Comberton (2 miles).
Acreage 8 **Open** April **to** October
Access Good **Site** Level
Sites Available ▲ � ➡ **Total** 120
Facilities ƒ ▥ ▯ ♨ ⌓ ☉⬚➡ 🗗 ➡
🏪🍴▯☉🏪❄✖⊡➡
Nearby Facilities ↾ ⌿ ∪
≠ Cambridge
Well maintained, long established family run Touring Park. Close to the historic University City of Cambridge, and the Imperial War Museum, Duxford. Awarded AA camp site of the year 1991/92 Midlands winner.

EARITH

Westview Marina, High Street, Earith, Huntingdon, Cambridgeshire, PE28 3PN.
Std: 01487 **Tel:** 841627
Email: lesfiduk@yahoo.com
Nearest Town/Resort St. Ives (Cambs)
Directions 5 miles from St. Ives and 12 miles from Cambridge.
Acreage 2 **Open** March **to** October
Access Good **Site** Level
Sites Available ▲ � ➡ **Total** 28
Facilities ƒ ▥ ♨ ⌓ ⏚ ☉➡
Nearby Facilities ↾ ⌿ ✠ ⌖
≠ Huntingdon
River frontage. Ideal touring.

ELY

Riverside Caravan & Camping Park, 21 New River Bank, Littleport, Ely, Cambridgeshire, CB7 4TA.
Std: 01353 **Tel:** 860255
Nearest Town/Resort Ely
Directions Site is signposted off the A10 (Ely/Littleport By-Pass). Please telephone for further details.
Acreage 4 **Open** March **to** October
Access Good **Site** Level
Sites Available ▲ � ➡ **Total** 50

Facilities ƒ ▥ ▯ ♨ ⌓ ☉⬚➡ 🗗 ➡
Nearby Facilities ↾ ⌿ ⚓ ✠
≠ Littleport
Alongside the Great Ouse River. Ideal for touring Cambridgeshire and Norfolk.

ELY

Two Acres Caravan Park, Ely Road, Little Thetford, Ely, Cambridgeshire, CB6 3HH.
Std: 01353 **Tel:** 648870
Std: 01353 **Fax:** 648870
Nearest Town/Resort Ely
Directions On the A10 to Cambridge, 2 miles south of Ely on the left hand side.
Acreage 2 **Open** 1 March **to** 8 February
Access Good **Site** Level
Sites Available ▲ � ➡ **Total** 36
Facilities ⅙ ƒ ▥ ▯ ♨ ⌓ ☉⬚➡ ➡
Nearby Facilities ↾ ⌿
≠ Ely
On the edge of the Fens. Ideal for visiting Cambridge and Newmarket.

GRAFHAM

Old Manor Caravan Park, Church Road, Grafham, Huntingdon, Cambridgeshire, PE18 0BB.
Std: 01480 **Tel:** 810264
Std: 01480 **Fax:** 819099
Email: camping@old-manor.co.uk
Website: www.old-manor.co.uk
Nearest Town/Resort Huntingdon
Directions From the A1 at Buckden roundabout follow caravan park signs. From the A14 leave at Ellington and follow caravan park signs from the village.
Acreage 6½ **Open** February **to** November
Access Good **Site** Level
Sites Available ▲ � ➡ **Total** 80
Facilities ⅙ ƒ ▥ ♨ ⌓ ☉⬚➡ 🗗 ➡
♨ ☉ 🏪 🗗 ❄✖⊡➡
Nearby Facilities ↾ ⌿ ⚓ ✠ ∪ ⌖
≠ Huntingdon
Near to Grafham Water.

GREAT SHELFORD

Camping & Caravanning Club Site, 19 Cabbage Moor, Great Shelford, Cambs, CB2 5NB.
Std: 01223 **Tel:** 841185
Website:
www.campingandcaravanningclub.co.uk
Directions Leave the M11 at junction 11 onto the B1309 signposted Cambridge. At the first set of traffic lights turn right, after ½ mile you will see the site sign on the left hand side pointing down the lane.
Open March **to** October
Site Level
Sites Available ▲ � ➡ **Total** 120
Facilities ⅙ ƒ ▥ ♨ ⌓ ☉⬚➡ 🗗 ➡
▯ ☉ 🏪 🗗 ⊡
Nearby Facilities ↾ ⌿
≠ Great Shelford
On the outskirts of the city of Cambridge. 6 miles from Duxford Imperial War Museum and the American Cemetery. BTB Graded and AA 4 Pennants. Non members welcome.

HUNTINGDON

Burleigh Hill Farm, Somersham Road, St. Ives, Huntingdon, Cambridgeshire, PE27 3LY.
Std: 01480 **Tel:** 462173
Std: 01480 **Fax:** 462173
Nearest Town/Resort St. Ives
Directions From St. Ives take the B1040 to Somersham, this takes you past St. Ives Industrial Estate, at small roundabout turn right for Somersham. After a third of a mile the farm is on the left, continue down the private tarmac drive.

15

Acreage 4 **Open** All Year
Access Good **Site** Level
Sites Available ♫ ⚎ **Total** 15
Facilities ƒ ⚑ ⚒ ┌ ⊙ ⛱ ⚐ ⚑┐⚑ 🖰
Nearby Facilities ┌ ⚲ ⚓ ⚔ ⚲ ∪ ⚲ ♬
≈ Huntingdon
Parkland setting in Cromwell Country and historic town. Links to footpath walks and good fishing. Historic barn for use with large groups and rallies. Ideal touring stop for the M11 and A14. You can also contact us on Mobile 07855 286238.

HUNTINGDON

Huntingdon Boathaven & Caravan Park, The Avenue, Godmanchester, Huntingdon, Cambridgeshire, PE18 8AF.
Std: 01480 **Tel:** 411977
Email: boathavenhunts@virgin.net
Nearest Town/Resort Cambridge
Directions From the A14 turn off to Godmanchester and travel towards Huntingdon. Turn left before the fly-over to Huntingdon Boathaven.
Acreage 2 **Open** March **to** October
Access Good **Site** Level
Sites Available ♫ ⚎ ⚎ **Total** 23
Facilities ⚒ ƒ ⚑ ⚒ ⚑ ┌ ⊙ ⛱ ⚐
⚑ ⚒ ⚑┐⚑
Nearby Facilities ┌ ⚲ ⚓ ⚔
≈ Huntingdon
Marina and caravan park situated on the Great River Ouse. Near to many tourist attractions.

HUNTINGDON

Quiet Waters Caravan Park, Hemingford Abbots, Huntingdon, Cambridgeshire, PE28 9AJ.
Std: 01480 **Tel:** 463405
Nearest Town/Resort St Ives/Huntingdon
Directions West of Cambridge on the A14, after 12 miles look for Hemingford Abbots, we are 1 mile into the village. 3 miles east of Huntingdon on the A14.
Acreage ½ **Open** April **to** October
Access Good **Site** Level
Sites Available ♫ ⚎ ⚎ **Total** 20
Facilities ƒ ⚒ ⚑ ┌ ⊙ ⛱ ⚐ ⚑ ⚒ ⚑
⚑ ⚒ ⚑┐⚑ 🖰
Nearby Facilities ┌ ⚲ ⚔ ∪
≈ Huntingdon
In the centre of a riverside village, good for fishing and boating.

HUNTINGDON

The Willows Caravan Park, Bromholme Lane, Brampton, Huntingdon, Cambs, PE18 8NE.
Std: 01480 **Tel:** 437566
Std: 01480 **Fax:** 432828
Email: willows@willows33.freeserve.co.uk
Nearest Town/Resort Huntingdon
Directions Brampton is situated on the A1 and the A14 (formerly A604). Follow the B1514 through Brampton towards Huntingdon, taking right hand signposted turning into Bromholme Lane.
Acreage 4 **Open** All Year
Access Good **Site** Level
Sites Available ♫ ⚎ ⚎ **Total** 55
Facilities ⚒ ƒ ⚑ ⚒ ⚑ ┌ ⊙ ⛱ ⚐
⚑ ⚒ ⚔ ⚑┐⚑ 🖰
Nearby Facilities ┌ ⚲ ⚓ ⚔ ∪ ♬
≈ Huntingdon
Situated on Ouse Valley Way, attractive walks. Launching area for boats and canoes. Fishing and boating available. Resident wardens on site. Country park, Grafham Water and sports facilities nearby. Site is Caravan Club, Camping & Caravanning Club and AA Listed.

MARCH

Floods Ferry Touring Park, Staffurths Bridge, March, Cambridgeshire, PE15 0YP.
Std: 01354 **Tel:** 677302
Website: www.floodsferrytouringpark.co.uk
Nearest Town/Resort March
Directions 4 miles from March. Take the A141 from March towards Chatteris, look for Floods Ferry and golf course sign and take this turn, continue for 3 miles and look for park sign on the right, single lane road to the park.
Acreage 7 **Open** All Year
Access Good **Site** Level
Sites Available ♫ ⚎ ⚎ **Total** 100
Facilities ƒ ⚑ ⚒ ⚑ ⚒ ⚑ ┌ ⊙ ⛱ ⚐
⚑ ⚒ ⚑ ⚒ ⚑ ⚑┐⚑
Nearby Facilities ┌ ⚲ ⚓ ⚔
≈ March
Relaxed, remote location adjacent to the Old Nene River. Slipway for boating and a ramp for disabled access. Ideal for walking, fishing (on site) and bird watching. Cycle route. Facilities for assited disabled. Disabled fishing access. Views across Fenland.

ST. IVES

Crystal Lakes Touring & Fishing Site, Crystal Lakes, The Low Road, Fenstanton, St. Ives, Cambridgeshire, PE18 9HU.
Std: 01480 **Tel:** 497728
Nearest Town/Resort St. Ives
Directions Turn off the A14 at Fenstanton and follow signs.
Acreage 10 **Open** March **to** October
Access Good **Site** Level
Sites Available ♫ ⚎ ⚎ **Total** 76
Facilities ƒ ⚑ ⚒ ⚑ ┌ ⊙ ⛱ ⚐ ⚑ 🖰 🖰
⚑ ⚒ ⚑ ⚒ ⚑ ⚑┐⚑
Nearby Facilities ┌ ⚲ ⚓ ⚔ ∪ ♬
≈ Huntingdon
Horse riding, fishing lakes and car boot sales. Sunday Markets open all year.

WISBECH

Orchard View Caravan & Camp Park, 100 Broadgate, Sutton St Edmund, Near Spalding, Lincs, PE12 0LT.
Std: 01945 **Tel:** 700482
Email: raymariaorchardview@btinternet.com
Nearest Town/Resort Wisbech/Crowland
Directions A47 Peterborough to Wisbech road, at Guyhirn turn at signpost for Guyhirn/ Wisbech St Mary, turn left at T-Junction signposted Parson Drove, over Clough Bridge into Lincolnshire. Take the second right signposted Sutton St Edmund.
Acreage 2½ **Open** 31 March **to** October
Access Good **Site** Level
Sites Available ♫ ⚎ ⚎ **Total** 37
Facilities ⚒ ƒ ⚑ ⚒ ⚑ ┌ ⊙ ⛱ ⚐ ⚑ 🖰
⚑ ⚒ ⚑ ⚒ ⚑ ⚑ ⊛ ⚑┐⚑
Nearby Facilities ┌ ⚲ ⚔ ∪ ♬
≈ Peterborough
Rural site, peace and quiet. Waterways and cycling. Fenland touring centre. 6 berth statics available for hire.

WISBECH

Virginia Lake & Caravan Park, Virginia House, St John's Fen End, Wisbech, Cambridgeshire, PE14 8JF.
Std: 01945 **Tel:** 430332
Std: 01945 **Fax:** 430128
Nearest Town/Resort Wisbech/Kings Lynn
Directions On the A47 7 miles from Wisbech and 7 miles from Kings Lynn. Follow tourist board signs from the A47.

Acreage 5 **Open** All Year
Access Good **Site** Level
Sites Available ♫ ⚎ ⚎ **Total** 40
Facilities ⚒ ƒ ⚑ ⚒ ⚑ ⚑ ┌ ⊙ ⛱ ⚐ ⚑ 🖰
⚑ ⚒ ⚑ ⚒ ⚑ ⚑ ⚑ ⚑┐⚑
Nearby Facilities ┌ ⚲ ∪ 🖰
≈ Kings Lynn
2 acre course fishing lake on site. 30 minutes from Sandringham and 45 minutes from the coast.

YARWELL

Yarwell Mill Caravan Park, Mill Lane, Yarwell, Peterborough, Cambridgeshire, PE8 6PS.
Std: 01780 **Tel:** 782344
Nearest Town/Resort Peterborough/ Stanford
Acreage 55 **Open** March **to** October
Access Good **Site** Level
Sites Available ⚎ ⚎ **Total** 124
Facilities ⚒ ♫ ƒ ⚑ ⚒ ⚑ ┌ ⊙ ⛱ ⚐
⚑ ⚒ ⚑ ⚑┐⚑
Nearby Facilities ┌ ⚲ ⚔ ∪
≈ Peterborough
Many pretty stone villages and towns near. Fishing in the River Nene or lake.

CHANNEL ISLES

GUERNSEY

Fauxquets Valley Farm Camping Site, Fauxquets de Bas, Catel, Guernsey, Channel Islands, GY5 7QA.
Std: 01481 **Tel:** 255460
Std: 01481 **Fax:** 251797
Email: fauxquets@campguernsey.freeserve.co.
Website: www.welcome.to/ fauxquetsvalleycampsite
Nearest Town/Resort St. Peter Port
Directions Follow sign for Catel, turn l onto Queens Road. Turn right at the sit for the German Underground Hospital
Acreage 3 **Open** Easter **to** 20 September
Site Level
Sites Available ♫ **Total** 90
Facilities ƒ ⚑ ⚒ ⚑ ┌ ⊙ ⛱
⚑ ⚒ ⚑ ⚒ ⚑ ⚑ ⚑ ⚑ ⚑ ⊛ ⚑┐⚑ 🖰 🖰
Nearby Facilities ┌ ⚲ ⚓ ⚔ ∪ ♬ ♬
1½ miles from sea, beautiful countrysid quiet site. Fully equipped tents available hire. Licensed bar.

JERSEY

Beuvelande Camp Site, Beuvelande, St Martin, Jersey, Channel Islands, JE3 6EZ
Std: 01534 **Tel:** 853575
Std: 01534 **Fax:** 857788
Nearest Town/Resort St. Martin
Directions From the harbour take the A to St. Martin Church then follow signs camp site.
Acreage 6 **Open** 1 May **to** 15 Sept
Site Level
Sites Available ♫ **Total** 150
Facilities ⚒ ƒ ⚑ ⚒ ⚑ ┌ ⊙ ⛱ ⚐ 🖰
⚑ ⚒ ⚑ ⚒ ⚑ ⚑ ⚑ ⚑ ⚑┐⚑
Nearby Facilities
Caravans are not allowed on the Channel Islands.

JERSEY

Rozel Camping Park, Summerville, St Martin, Jersey, Channel Islands, JE3 6AX
Std: 01534 **Tel:** 856797
Std: 01534 **Fax:** 856127
Email: rozelcamping@jerseyhols.co
Nearest Town/Resort St. Helier
Directions 5 miles from St. Helier. A6 Martin's Church then B38 to Rozel.

Acreage 3 **Open** May **to** Mid Sept
Site Level
Sites Available ⋏ **Total** 80
Facilities ♿ ✦ 🚽 ♨ Ր ⊙ ⌿ 🔌 🍴
🔧 🗖 🛈 ♠ ⚘ ⏧ 🖭
Nearby Facilities Ր ✓ ⚓ ⚐ ⌇
Hire tents available, own tents welcome.
Nearby a picturesque beach and harbour
aswell as Gerald Durrell's Zoo.

CHESHIRE
CHESTER
Birch Bank Farm, Stamford Lane,
Christleton, Chester, Cheshire, CH3
7QD.
Std: 01244 **Tel:** 335233
Nearest Town/Resort Chester
Directions From Chester take the A51
east for 3 miles, turn right after the Little
Chef.
Acreage 1 **Open** 1 May **to** 31 October
Access Good **Site** Level
Sites Available ⋏ ⚘ ☕ **Total** 10
Facilities ⌿ 🚽 ✦ Ր ⊙ ♨ 🖭⚘🖭
Nearby Facilities
⚐ Chester
A small farm site with good facilities.
Close to Chester yet free from traffic
noise.

CHESTER
Netherwood Touring Site,
Netherwood House, Whitchurch Road,
Nr. Chester, Cheshire, CH3 6AF.
Std: 01244 **Tel:** 335583
Std: 01244 **Fax:** 336066/335583
Email: broaddavies@btinternet.com
Website: www.netherwoodtouringsite
Nearest Town/Resort Chester
Directions On A41, approx. 1 mile from
Chester bypass.
Acreage 1½ **Open** March **to** October
Access Good **Site** Level
Sites Available ⚘ ☕ **Total** 15
Facilities ⌿ 🚽 ✦ Ր ⊙ 🍴
🔧 🗖 ♠⚘🖭A
Nearby Facilities Ր ✓ ⚓ ⚘
⚐ Chester
On Shropshire Union Canal. 5 miles from
Zoo.

CHESTER
**Northwood Hall Country Touring
Park,** Dog Lane, Kelsall, Chester,
Cheshire, CW6 0RP.
Std: 01829 **Tel:** 752569
Std: 01829 **Fax:** 751157
Email: enquiries@northwood-hall.co.uk
Website: www.northwood-hall.co.uk
Nearest Town/Resort Chester
Directions 7 miles east of Chester off the
A54, adjacent to Delamere Forest.
Acreage 5 **Open** All Year
Access Good **Site** Level
Sites Available ⋏ ⚘ ☕ **Total** 30
Facilities ⌿ 🔌 🚽 ✦ Ր ⊙ ♨ 🗖 🖭
🔧 🗖 ♨⚘🖭
Nearby Facilities Ր ✓ ⚘ U
⚐ Chester
Delamere Forest and the walled city of
Chester.

KNUTSFORD
Woodlands Park, Wash Lane, Allostock,
Cheshire, WA16 9LG.
Std: 01565 **Tel:** 723429
Std: 01332 **Fax:** 810818
Nearest Town/Resort Holmes Chapel
Directions Take the A50 North for approx.
3 miles, turn left just by Boundary Water Park
into Wash Lane and travel for ¼ mile, park
is on the left hand side.
Open 1 March **to** 6 January
Access Good **Site** Level
Sites Available ⋏ ⚘ ☕ **Total** 40
Facilities ⌿ 🚽 ✦ Ր ⊙⌿ 🔌 🗖 🍴 🐾
Nearby Facilities Ր ✓
⚐ Goostrey
Quiet woodland park with lovely local walks
and fishing on site.

MACCLESFIELD
Strawberry Wood Caravan Park, Home
Farm, Farm Lane, Lower Withington,
Macclesfield, Cheshire, SK11 9DU.
Std: 01477 **Tel:** 571407
Nearest Town/Resort Macclesfield
Directions Leave the M6 at junction 18 and
take the A54 to Holmes Chapel. Then take
the A535 to Macclesfield, after 4 miles turn
right onto the B5392 and Farm Lane is 700
yards on the right hand side.
Acreage 5 **Open** March **to** October
Access Good **Site** Level
Sites Available ⋏ ⚘ ☕ **Total** 25
Facilities ⌿ 🚽 ✦ Ր ⊙ 🍴 🖭
Nearby Facilities Ր ✓
⚐ Goostrey
Large coarse fishing pond adjacent to the
site.

WARRINGTON
Holly Bank Caravan Park, Warburton
Bridge Road, Rixton, Warrington,
Cheshire, WA3 6HU.
Std: 0161 **Tel:** 775 2842
Nearest Town/Resort Warrington
Directions 2 miles from M6 junction 21 on
A57 (Irlam) turn right at lights into Warburton
Bridge Road entry on left, Warrington 5
miles.
Open All Year
Access Good **Site** Level
Sites Available ⋏ ⚘ ☕ **Total** 85.
Facilities ♿ ⌿ 🚽 ✦ Ր ⊙⌿ 🔌 🗖 🍴
🔧 🔲 🗖 ♠ ❋ 🖭
Nearby Facilities Ր ✓ ⚘ U
⚐ Irlam
Dunham Park, Tatton Park, and ideal touring
North Cheshire.

WINSFORD
**Lamb Cottage Camping & Caravan
Park,** Dalesford Lane, Whitegate, Nr.
Northwich, Cheshire, CW8 2BN.
Std: 01606 **Tel:** 888491/882302
Std: 01606 **Fax:** 882302
Email: Awalker40@compuserve.com
Nearest Town/Resort Northwich/
Winsford
Directions Leave the M6 at Junction 19 onto
the A556 to Chester, turn at lights by
Sandiway Post Office into Dalesford Lane,
site is located 1 mile on the right, past garage
on the left.

Acreage 4 **Open** March **to** October
Access Good **Site** Level
Sites Available ⋏ ⚘ ☕ **Total** 70
Facilities ♿ ⌿ 🚽 ✦ Ր ⊙ ⌿ 🍴
🔧 🗖 ♠⚘🖭
Nearby Facilities Ր ✓ ⚓ ⚘ U
⚐ Cuddington
Ideal touring, walks in Delamere Forest, 45
mins to Chester, Manchester Airport etc..
Discounts for rallies and club outings.

CORNWALL
BODMIN
Camping & Caravanning Club Site, Old
Callywith Road, Bodmin, Cornwall, PL31
2DZ.
Std: 01208 **Tel:** 73834
Website:
www.campingandcaravanningclub.co.uk
Directions From the north stay on the A30
until signpost 'Bodmin', turn right crossing
over the dual carriageway in front of
industrial estate, then turn immediately left
at international sign. Site is on the left down
Old Callywith Road.
Acreage 11 **Open** April **to** October
Site Lev/Slope
Sites Available ⋏ ⚘ ☕ **Total** 175
Facilities ⌿ 🚽 Ր ⊙ ⌿ 🔌 🗖 🍴
🔧 🗖 ♠ ♨⚘🖭
Nearby Facilities Ր ✓ ⚓ ⚘ U
⚐ Bodmin Parkway
On the edge of Bodmin Moor. Within easy
reach of the coast and close to many places
of interest. BTB Graded. Non members
welcome.

BODMIN
Glenmorris Park, Longstone Road, St.
Mabyn, Cornwall, PL30 3BY.
Std: 01208 **Tel:** 841677
Std: 01208 **Fax:** 841677
Website: www.glenmorris.cornwall.eu.org
Nearest Town/Resort Bodmin/
Wadebridge
Directions South of Camelford on the A39,
turn left after BP Garage onto the B3266 to
Bodmin. 6 miles to Longstone, turn right at
crossroads signposted St. Mabyn, site is
approx 400 metres on the right.
Acreage 10 **Open** Easter **to** End October
Access Good **Site** Level
Sites Available ⋏ ⚘ ☕ **Total** 80
Facilities ⌿ 🚽 ✦ Ր ⊙ ⌿ 🔌 🗖 🍴
🔧 🗖 ♠ ♨⚘🖭
Nearby Facilities Ր ✓ ⚓ ⚘ U ⌇ ♪
⚐ Bodmin Parkway
Ideal for the North and South coast, Bodmin
Moor, the Eden Project and the Camel Trail.

BODMIN
Lanarth Hotel & Caravan Park, St. Kew
Highway, Bodmin, Cornwall, PL30 3EE.
Std: 01208 **Tel:** 841215
Nearest Town/Resort Wadebridge
Directions On the A39 at St. Kew Highway,
approx 4 miles east of Wadebridge and 8
miles west of Camelford.
Acreage 10 **Open** April **to** October
Access Good **Site** Lev/Slope
Sites Available ⋏ ⚘ ☕ **Total** 86

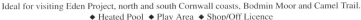

Facilities
Nearby Facilities
⇌ Bodmin
Beautiful rural setting, conveniently situated for beaches and moor. Ideal for touring Cornwall and Devon.

BODMIN
Ruthern Valley Holiday Park,
Ruthernbridge, Nr. Bodmin, Cornwall, PL30 5LU
Std: 01208 **Tel:** 831395
Email: ruthernvalley@hotmail.com
Website: www.self-catering-ruthern.co.uk
Nearest Town/Resort Bodmin
Directions Through Bodmin on A389 towards St. Austell, on outskirts of Bodmin Ruthernbridge signposted right. Follow signs for Ruthern or Ruthernbridge.
Acreage 2 **Open** April **to** October
Access Good **Site** Level
Sites Available ▲ ⊕ ⊞ **Total** 30
Facilities
Nearby Facilities
⇌ Bodmin Parkway
Quiet peaceful wooded location centrally based for touring.

BODMIN
South Penquite Farm, South Penquite, Blisland, Bodmin, Cornwall, PL30 4LH.
Std: 01208 **Tel:** 850296
Email: thefarm@bodminmoor.co.uk
Website: www.southpenquite.co.uk
Nearest Town/Resort Bodmin
Directions Enter Cornwall on the A30 and drive for approx. 18 miles, take right turn signposted St. Breward, farm lane will be on the right after 3 miles.
Acreage 5 **Open** May **to** September

Access Good **Site** Level
Sites Available ▲ ⊞ **Total** 25
Facilities
Nearby Facilities
⇌ Bodmin Parkway
South Penquite is a 200 acre organic sheep farm set high on Bodmin Moor. Farm walk and bike hire available.

BOSCASTLE
Lower Pennycrocker Farm, St. Juliot, Boscastle, Cornwall, PL35 0BY.
Std: 01840 **Tel:** 250257
Website: www.pennycrocker.co.uk
Nearest Town/Resort Boscastle
Directions 2½ miles north of Boscastle on B3263, turn left signposted Pennycrocker.
Acreage 4 **Open** Easter **to** September
Access Good **Site** Level
Sites Available ▲ ⊕ ⊞ **Total** 40
Facilities
Nearby Facilities
⇌ Bodmin
Scenic views, ideal touring.

BOSCASTLE
St. Tinney Farm Holidays, St. Tinney Farm, Otterham, North Cornwall, PL32 9TA.
Std: 01840 **Tel:** 261274
Email: info@st-tinney.co.uk
Website: www.st-tinney.co.uk
Nearest Town/Resort Boscastle
Directions Take the A39 south from Bude, after 10 miles signposted Otterham. 1 mile from the A39 signposted St. Tinney Farm.
Acreage 5 **Open** Easter **to** October
Access Good **Site** Level
Sites Available ▲ ⊕ ⊞ **Total** 25
Facilities
Nearby Facilities
⇌ Bodmin

Two lakes for coarse fishing on site. Free pony rides, pony trekking and an adventure playground. David Bellamy Gold Award for Conservation.

BUDE
Budemeadows Touring Holiday Park,
Poundstock, Bude, Cornwall, EX23 0NA.
Std: 01288 **Tel:** 361646
Std: 01288 **Fax:** 361646
Email: wendyjo@globalnet.co.uk
Website: www.budemeadows.com
Nearest Town/Resort Bude
Directions From Bude take A39 south for 3 miles.
Acreage 9 **Open** All Year
Access Good **Site** Level
Sites Available ▲ ⊕ ⊞ **Total** 140
Facilities
Nearby Facilities
⇌ Exeter
1 mile from sandy beaches, cliff walks and rolling surf of Widmouth Bay. Spectacular coastal scenery. Licenced Bar.

BUDE
Camping & Caravanning Club Site,
Gillards Moor, St Gennys, Bude, Cornwall, EX23 0BG.
Std: 01840 **Tel:** 230650
Website:
www.campingandcaravanningclub.co.uk
Directions Going south on the A39 the site is on the right in lay-by 9 miles from Bude. Going north on the A39 the site is on the left in lay-by 9 miles from Camelford, approx. 3 miles from the B3262 junction. Brown camping signs ½ mile either side of the site, also on both ends of the lay-by.
Acreage 6 **Open** April **to** Sept
Site Lev/Slope

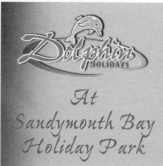

Sites Available ⋏ ⊕ ⊜ Total 105
Facilities ⅍ ⨍ ◲ Ⅶ ◪ ⎚ ⊙ ↯ ⊿ ▢ ☞
◪ ⓞ ◈ Ⅶ ♠ ⋔ ☜◲ ◳
Nearby Facilities ◲ ⚘ ⬆ ↘ ∪ ♠ ⋎
⇻ Exeter
Near the coastal paths in the heart of King Arthur's Country. Table tennis on site. BTB Graded. Non members welcome.

BUDE
Cornish Coasts Caravan Park, Middle Penlean, Poundstock, Bude, Cornwall, EX23 0EE.
Std: 01288 **Tel:** 361380
Email: ccoasts@aol.com
Website: www.cornishcoasts.co.uk
Nearest Town/Resort Bude/Widemouth Bay
Directions On seaward side of A39 Bude to Camelford road, 5 miles south of Bude.
Acreage 3 **Open** Easter **to** October
Access Good **Site** Lev/Slope
Sites Available ⋏ ⊕ ⊜ **Total** 45
Facilities ⨍ Ⅶ ◪ ⎚ ⊙ ↯ ⊿ ▢ ☞
◪ ⓞ ◈ ⋔ ☜◲ ◳
Nearby Facilities ◲ ⚘ ⬆ ↘ ∪ ♠ ⋎
⇻ Exeter
Peaceful, friendly site. Superb views over countryside and coast line. Ideal touring location with many beaches nearby. Good base for spectacular coastal path, walking groups transport arranged. Holiday caravans to let.

BUDE
Coxford Meadow, Crackington Haven, Bude, Cornwall, EX23 0NS.
Std: 01840 **Tel:** 230707
Nearest Town/Resort Bude
Directions Take the A39 from Bude and turn right at Wainhouse Corner to Crackington, take second turning right by the chapel.
Acreage 1 **Open** Easter **to** Oct

Access Good Site Level
Sites Available ⋏ ⊕ ⊜ Total 15
Facilities Ⅶ ⅍ ◲ ⊙ ◪⋔◲
Nearby Facilities ◲ ⚘
⇻ Bodmin/Exeter
Rural position with sea views. Near the coastal path.

BUDE
Ivyleaf Camping Park, Ivyleaf Hill, Bush, Near Bude, Cornwall, EX23 9LD.
Std: 01288 **Tel:** 321442
Nearest Town/Resort Bude
Directions From Bideford take the A39 south, go past Kilkhampton and in approx. 2 miles, at sharp right hand bend, continue into lane, site is on the left below the summit of the hill. From Bude take the A39 north, go past Stratton and in approx. 1 mile turn right at Ivyleaf sign, steep ascent to the site on the right.
Acreage 3 **Open** All Year
Access Good **Site** Lev/Slope
Sites Available Total 5
Facilities ⨍ ◲ ◲ Ⅶ ◪ ⎚ ⊙ ↯ ☞
Ⅶ◪ ◈ ❀
Nearby Facilities ◲ ⚘ ⬆ ↘ ∪ ♠ ⋎
⇻ Barnstaple
Good views from the site. East access to the North Cornwall coast.

BUDE
Penhalt Farm Holiday Park, Widemouth Bay, Bude, Cornwall, EX23 0DG.
Std: 01288 **Tel:** 361210
Std: 01288 **Fax:** 361210
Website: www.holidaybank.co.uk/penhaltfarmholidaypark
Nearest Town/Resort Bude
Directions From the A39 travelling south from near Bude, 4½ miles down take the second turn right to Widemouth Bay. Turn left at the bottom, about two thirds of a mile

along windy hilly road on the left.
Acreage 8 **Open** Easter **to** October
Access Good **Site** Lev/Slope
Sites Available ⋏ ⊕ ⊜ **Total** 100
Facilities ⅍ ⨍ ◲ ⎚ ⅍ ◲ ⊙ ↯ ⊿ ▢ ☞
◪ ⓞ ◈ Ⅶ ♠ ⋔◲
Nearby Facilities ⚘ ⬆ ↘ ∪
⇻ Exeter
Stunning sea views of the dramatic North Cornish coastline. Close to coastal footpath. Ideal for walking, surfing and touring. Very good surf and sandy beach.

BUDE
Penstowe Caravan & Camping Park, Penstowe Park Holiday Village, Kilkhampton, Bude, Cornwall, EX23 9QY.
Std: 01288 **Tel:** 321354
Std: 01288 **Fax:** 321273
Email: info@penstoweleisure.co.uk
Website: www.penstoweleisure.co.uk
Nearest Town/Resort Bude
Directions 4 miles north of Bude on the A39 at Kilkhampton.
Acreage 6 **Open** April **to** October
Access Good **Site** Sloping
Sites Available ⋏ ⊕ ⊜ **Total** 80
Facilities ⅍ ⨍ ◲ Ⅶ ◪ ⅍ ◲ ⊙ ↯ ⊿ ▢ ☞
◪ ⓞ ◈ ✕ ⓨ Ⅶ ♠ ⋔ ↯ ⊛ ☜◲ ◳ ◲
Nearby Facilities ◲ ⚘ ⬆ ↘ ∪ ♠ ⋎
⇻ Barnstaple/Exeter
New touring caravan site attached to an established, highly rated holiday village with excellent facilities. Quiet site with lovely views.

BUDE
Red Post Inn Holiday Park, Launcells, Bude, Cornwall, EX23 9NW.
Std: 01288 **Tel:** 381305
Email: redpostinn@aol.com
Nearest Town/Resort Bude
Directions 4 miles from Bude on the A3072 road to Holsworthy.

19

CORNWALL

Site 200yds along road on right hand side.
Acreage 12 **Open** April to October
Access Good **Site** Lev/Slope
Sites Available 人 ⌖ ⊟ **Total** 160
Facilities & / ⌂ ⊞ ⌖ ❄ ⌢ ⊙ ↲ ▤ ◻ ☎
☎ ⌘ ☓ ⌖ ▥ ⛝ ⌂ ⊛ ⌦ ⊡ ◳
Nearby Facilities ⌐ ✦ ⚓ ⚡ ∪ ♪ ⚘
 ≠ Exeter
Overlooks sea and coastline, woodland
walks, coarse fishing, large childrens play
area, dog exercise field, short golf course.
Sandy beaches 1½ miles. Licensed farm
restaurant. Contact Mrs Q. Colwill.

CAMELFORD

Inny Vale Holiday Village, Davidstow,
Camelford, Cornwall, PL32 9XN.
Std: 01840 **Tel:** 261248
Std: 01840 **Fax:** 261740
Email: jn.c@which.net
Website: www.innyvale.co.uk
Nearest Town/Resort Camelford/Tintagel
Directions On the A30 3 miles west of
Launceston turn right onto the A395. After
approx. 9 miles turn left at the crossroads
just after Davidstow sign, Inny Vale is 300
yards on the left hand side.
Acreage 6 **Open** All Year
Access Good **Site** Level
Sites Available 人 ⌂ ⊟ **Total** 27
Facilities / ⌂ ⊞ ⊞ ❄ ⌢ ⊙ ↲ ▤ ◻ ☎
☎ ⌘ ☓ ⌖ ❄ ⛝ ◪ ↲ ⌦ ⊡ ◳
Nearby Facilities ⌐ ✦ ⚓ ⚡ ∪ ♪ ♪ ⚘
 ≠ Bodmin Parkway
Alongside the River Inny. Bar/restaurant and
tennis court. 5 miles from Tintagel, 6 miles
from Boscastle and 15 miles from Bude.

CAMELFORD

Lakefield Caravan Park, Lower
Pendavey Farm, Camelford, Cornwall,
PL32 9TX.
Std: 01840 **Tel:** 213279
Std: 01840 **Fax:** 213279
Email: lakefield@pendavey.fsnet.co.uk
Nearest Town/Resort Camelford/Tintagel
Directions 1¼ miles north of Camelford on
the B3266 Boscastle road.
Acreage 5 **Open** Easter to October
Access Good **Site** Level
Sites Available 人 ⌂ ⊟ **Total** 40
Facilities / ⊞ ⊞ ❄ ⌢ ⊙ ↲ ◻ ☎
☎ ⊙ ⌂ ◪ ⊛ ↲ ⊟
Nearby Facilities ⌐ ✦
 ≠ Bodmin
Scenic views, own lake. Ideal for touring
Cornwall. Full equestrian facilities providing
lessons, site rides and hacks for all the
family. British Horse Society Qualified
Instruction. Pets Corner and Tea Shop on
site.

Acreage 4 **Open** March to October
Access Good **Site** Level
Sites Available 人 ⌂ ⊟ **Total** 50
Facilities & / ⌂ ⊞ ⊞ ❄ ⌢ ⊙ ↲ ▤ ◻ ☎
☎ ⌘ ☓ ⌖ ▥ ↲ ⊟ ◳
Nearby Facilities ⌐ ✦ ⚓ ⚡ ∪ ♪
 ≠ Barnstaple
Ideal for touring, easy access. Adventure
playground and a public house on site. AA
3 Pennants.

BUDE

Sandymouth Bay Holiday Park, Stibb,
Bude, Cornwall, EX23 9HW.
Std: 01288 **Tel:** 352563
Std: 01288 **Fax:** 354822
Email: sandymouthbay@aol.com
Website: www.sandymouthbay.co.uk
Nearest Town/Resort Bude
Directions Just off the A39 4 miles north of
Bude.
Acreage 20 **Open** April to October
Access Good **Site** Lev/Slope
Sites Available 人 ⌂ ⊟ **Total** 150
Facilities & / ⊞ ❄ ⌢ ⊙ ↲ ▤ ◻ ☎
☎ ⊙ ⌂ ☓ ⌖ ❄ ⛝ ↲ ⊟ ◳
Nearby Facilities ⌐ ✦ ⚡ ∪
 ≠ Barnstaple
Graded Park. Set in meadowland
overlooking the bay.

BUDE

**Upper Lynstone Camping & Caravan
Park,** Upper Lynstone Farm, Bude,
Cornwall, EX23 0LP.
Std: 01288 **Tel:** 352017
Std: 01288 **Fax:** 359034
Email: reception@upperlynstone.co.uk
Website: www.upperlynstone.co.uk
Nearest Town/Resort Bude
Directions ½ mile south of Bude on
Widemouth Bay road.
Acreage 5 **Open** Easter to October
Access Good **Site** Lev/Slope
Sites Available 人 ⌂ ⊟ **Total** 90
Facilities / ⊞ ❄ ⌢ ⊙ ↲ ▤ ◻ ☎
☎ ⊙ ⌂ ◪ ↲ ⊟ ◳
Nearby Facilities ⌐ ✦ ∪ ♪
 ≠ Exeter
Within easy reach of good surfing beaches.
Access to cliff walks. Families and couples
only, no groups.

BUDE

Wooda Farm Park, Poughill, Bude,
Cornwall, EX23 9HJ.
Std: 01288 **Tel:** 352069
Std: 01288 **Fax:** 355258
Email: enquiries@wooda.co.uk
Website: www.wooda.co.uk
Nearest Town/Resort Bude
Directions Take road to Poughill 1¼ miles,
go through village. At crossroads turn left.

CARLYON BAY

Carlyon Bay Camping Park, Cypress
Avenue, Carlyon Bay, St. Austell,
Cornwall, PL25 3RE.
Std: 01726 **Tel:** 812735
Std: 01726 **Fax:** 815496
Nearest Town/Resort St. Austell
Directions Take the A30 to Bodmin then the
A391 to St Austell. Turn left onto the A390
and follow signs.
Acreage 32 **Open** April to October
Access Good **Site** Level
Sites Available 人 ⌂ ⊟ **Total** 180
Facilities & / ⌂ ⊞ ⊞ ❄ ⌢ ⊙ ↲ ▤ ◻ ☎
☎ ⌘ ☓ ⌖ ⌂ ◪ ❄ ⊛ ↲ ⊟ ◳
Nearby Facilities ⌐ ✦ ⚓ ⚡ ∪ ♪
 ≠ St. Austell/Par
Only 2½ miles from the Eden Project.
Footpath to the beach, Bein Playworld and
Cornish Market World. Ideal for touring
Cornwall.

COVERACK

Little Trevothan Caravan Park,
Coverack, Helston, Cornwall, TR12 6SD.
Std: 01326 **Tel:** 280260
Std: 01326 **Fax:** 280260
Email: trevothan@connexions.co.uk
Website: www.connexions.co.uk/
trevothan/index.htm
Nearest Town/Resort Helston
Directions A39 to Helston, follow B3083 to
Culdrose, turn left B3293 signposted to
Coverack. Go past BT Goonhilly, turn right
before Zoar Garage, third turning on left,
300yds on the right.
Open April to October
Access Good **Site** Level
Sites Available 人 ⌂ ⊟ **Total** 60
Facilities / ⊞ ⊞ ❄ ⌢ ⊙ ↲ ▤ ◻ ☎
☎ ⌘ ⊙ ⌂ ⛝ ❄ ⊛ ↲ ⊟ ◳
Nearby Facilities ⌐ ✦ ⚓ ⚡ ∪
 ≠ Redruth
Beach nearby, flat meadows, off road.

COVERACK

Penmarth Farm Camp Site, Coverack,
Helston, Cornwall.
Std: 01326 **Tel:** 280389
Nearest Town/Resort Helston
Directions 10 miles from Helston.
Acreage 2 **Open** March to October
Access Good **Site** Level
Sites Available 人 ⌂ ⊟ **Total** 28
Facilities ⚡ ⊞ ❄ ⌢ ⊙ ↲ ⌖ ⊙ ↲
Nearby Facilities ⌐ ✦ ⚓ ⚡ ∪
 ≠ Cambourne
¼ mile to beach and walks. Milk, cream and
eggs at farm. Woodland walk to the sea and
beach.

CRACKINGTON HAVEN

Hentervene Caravan & Camping Park, Crackington Haven, Nr. Bude, Cornwall, EX23 0LF.
Std: 01840 **Tel:** 230365
Nearest Town/Resort Bude
Directions 10 miles southwest of Bude, turn off A39 opposite Otterham Garage, signed Crackington Haven. After 2½ miles turn left onto Crackington Road at Hentervene sign, park is ½ mile on right - 2 miles from beach.
Acreage 8¼ **Open** All Year
Access Good **Site** Level
Sites Available A ⊕ ⊕ **Total** 35
Facilities ⚡ 🏠 ⛎ ♨ ⌂ ⊙ ⇨ 🕭 ⬛ ▣ ☎
🖫 🎱 🄶 ⊙ ⚌ 🛆 🞓 🛒 ⊞ 🎇 ⬛ ⊟
Nearby Facilities � ✔ ⚓ ❄ ∪ ⌖ ♪ ⚘
⌖ Bodmin
Sands, swimming and surfing. Ideal touring centre - 2 miles from the beach. All year parking, tourers caravans sales. Take-away meals available in season. Closed for camping only end of October to 1st April. Statics available all year.

CRANTOCK

Quarryfield Caravan & Camping Park, Crantock, Nr. Newquay, Cornwall, TR8 5RJ.
Std: 01637 **Tel:** 872792
Std: 01637 **Fax:** 872792
Nearest Town/Resort Newquay
Directions Signposted off the A392, turn right to Crantock.
Acreage 5 **Open** April **to** October
Access Good **Site** Level
Sites Available A ⊕ ⊕ **Total** 125
Facilities ⚡ 🏠 ⛎ ♨ ⌂ ⊙ ⇨ ⚌
🖫 🎱 🄶 ⊙ ⚌ 🝙 🞓 ♨ ⤳ ⊞
Nearby Facilities ✔ ⚓ ❄ ∪ ♪
⌖ Newquay
Very close to the beach and a river.

FALMOUTH

Menallack Farm, Treverva, Falmouth, Cornwall, TR10 9BP.
Std: 01326 **Tel:** 340333 **Fax:** 340333
Email: menallack@fsb.dial.co.uk
Nearest Town/Resort Falmouth
Directions From Truro take the A39 to the "Asda" roundabout and turn right to Mabe. In the village turn left at the crossroads 1½ miles, turn right at crossroads signposted Gweek. Go through Treverva and site is ¾ mile on the left hand side.
Acreage 1½ **Open** Easter **to** October
Access Good **Site** Lev/Slope
Sites Available A ⊕ ⊕ **Total** 30
Facilities ⚡ ⛎ ♨ ⌂ ⊙ ⚌ 🖫 🎱 ⊙ ⤳ ⊟
Nearby Facilities ✔ ⚓ ∪ ⚘
⌖ Penryn
Quiet site with lovely views over a wooded valley towards Helford River area.

FALMOUTH

Pennance Mill Farm Chalets & Camping, Pennance Mill Farm, Maenporth, Falmouth, Cornwall, TR11 5HJ
Std: 01326 **Tel:** 317431 **Fax:** 317431
Nearest Town/Resort Falmouth
Directions Take the A39 from Truro to Falmouth, follow the brown international camping signs to Hillhead roundabout and turn right. Straight across at the next crossroads, site is 2 miles from Falmouth to Maenporth at the bottom of the hill on the left.
Acreage 5 **Open** Easter **to** October
Access Good **Site** Level
Sites Available A ⊕ ⊕ **Total** 75
Facilities ⚡ 🏠 ⛎ ♨ ⌂ ⊙ ⇨ ⚌ ⬛ ☎
🖫 🎱 🄶 ⊙ ⚌ 🝙 🞓 🛆 ⊞ 🎇 ⬛
Nearby Facilities � ✔ ⚓ ❄ ∪ ♪ ⚘
⌖ Falmouth
Set in a sheltered valley on a working dairy farm. See the cows being milked. ½ mile to

Maenporth beach. National Trust gardens and Helford River within 2½ miles.

FALMOUTH

Retanna Holiday Park, Edgcumbe, Helston, Cornwall, TR13 0EJ.
Std: 01326 **Tel:** 340643
Email: retannaholpark@lineone.net
Website: www.retanna.co.uk
Nearest Town/Resort Falmouth/Helston
Directions Situated midway between Falmouth and Helston on the A394, on the right hand side immediately after Edgcumbe.
Acreage 8 **Open** March **to** October
Access Good **Site** Lev/Slope
Sites Available A ⊕ ⊕ **Total** 24
Facilities ⚡ 🏠 ⛎ ♨ ⌂ ⊙ ⇨ ⚌ ⬛ ☎
🖫 🎱 🄶 ⊙ ⚌ 🝙 🞓 🛆 ⊞ ⬛ ⊟
Nearby Facilities � ✔ ⚓ ❄ ∪ ♪ ⚘
⌖ Falmouth
Helford River area, close to a number of tourist attractions.

FALMOUTH

Tregedna Farm Touring Park, Tregedna Farm, Maenporth, Falmouth, Cornwall, TR11 5HL.
Std: 01326 **Tel:** 250529
Nearest Town/Resort Falmouth
Directions Take the A39 from Truro to Falmouth, turn off right at Hillhead roundabout and continue straight for 2½ miles.
Acreage 10 **Open** May **to** September
Access Good **Site** Sloping
Sites Available A ⊕ ⊕ **Total** 40
Facilities ⚡ 🏠 ⛎ ♨ ⌂ ⊙ ⇨ ⚌ ⬛ ☎
🖫 🄶 ⚌ ⊞ ⊟
Nearby Facilities � ✔ ⚓ ∪ ♪
⌖ Penmere
½ mile to Maenporth beach. Close to all well known NT Gardens. Ideal for touring South and West Cornwall.

FOWEY

Penhale Caravan & Camping Park,
Fowey, Cornwall, PL23 1JU.
Std: 01726 **Tel:** 833425 **Fax:** 833425
Email: penhale@farmersweekly.net
Nearest Town/Resort Fowey
Directions 1 mile west of Lostwithiel on the
A390, turn left onto the B3269. After 3 miles
turn right at the roundabout onto the A3082.
Penhale is 500yds on the left.
Acreage 5 **Open** April **to** October
Access Good **Site** Lev/Slope
Sites Available ▲ ♦ ⊞ **Total** 56
Facilities / ⅏ ♨ ⌐ ⊙ ᵈ ◿
◫ ⅃◎ ◙ ♣ ✕ ⊡
Nearby Facilities ⌐ ✓ ⚓ ⅄ ∪ ⊅ ♞
⇌ Par
Splendid views, close to sandy beaches with
many lovely walks nearby. Central for touring.

FOWEY

Penmarlam Caravan & Camping,
Bodinnick-by-Fowey, Cornwall, PL23 1LZ.
Std: 07900 **Tel:** 221457 Daytime
Email: fhc@foweyharbour.co.uk
Website: www.foweyharbour.co.uk
Nearest Town/Resort Fowey
Directions A38 Liskeard by-pass, fork left
A390. Left at East Taphouse B3359 follow
signs to Bodinnick. Site on right of Bodinnick
ferry road.
Acreage 1 **Open** April **to** October
Access Good **Site** Level
Sites Available ▲ ♦ ⊞ **Total** 30
Facilities ⚿ / ⅏ ♨ ⌐ ⊙ᵈ ◿ ⅃◎ ✕ ⊡
Nearby Facilities ✓ ⚓ ⅄ ∪
⇌ Par/Lostwithiel
Private quay, slip and storage for small
boats. Good walks over mainly National
Trust Land. You can also call us in the
Evenings on 01726 870164.

FOWEY

**Polruan Holidays - Camping &
Caravanning,** Polruan-by-Fowey,
Cornwall, PL23 1QH.
Std: 01726 **Tel:** 870263 **Fax:** 870263
Email: polholiday@aol.com
Nearest Town/Resort Fowey.
Directions From Plymouth A38 to Dobwalls,
left onto A390 to East Taphouse, then left
onto B3359. After 4¼ miles turn right
signposted Polruan.
Acreage 2 **Open** April **to** September
Access Good **Site** Lev/Slope
Sites Available ▲ ♦ ⊞ **Total** 32
Facilities / ⅃ ⅏ ⅌ ♨ ⌐ ⊙ᵈ ◿ ◙ ☎
⅃◎ ◙ ♣ ꕔ ⊡
Nearby Facilities ✓ ⚓ ⅄ ∪
⇌ Par
Coastal park surrounded by sea, river and
National Trust farmland.

GORRAN HAVEN

Trelispen Caravan & Camping Park,
Gorran, St. Austell, Cornwall, PL26 6HT.
Std: 01726 **Tel:** 843501 **Fax:** 843501
Email: trelispen@care4free.net
Nearest Town/Resort Gorran Haven
Directions From the A390 at St. Austell take

B3293 for Mevagissey. Nearing Mevagissey
take the road for Gorran Haven, nearing
Gorran Haven look for Trelispen Camping
Park signs.
Acreage 1½ **Open** April **to** October
Access Good **Site** Level
Sites Available ▲ ♦ ⊞ **Total** 40
Facilities / ⅏ ⌐ ⊙ᵈ ◿ ◙ ☎ ⅃ ⊞ ⊡
Nearby Facilities ✓ ⚓ ⅄ ∪ ⊅
⇌ St. Austell
Small site in pleasant rural surroundings,
near impressive cliff scenery and several
safe sandy beaches.

HAYLE

Atlantic Coast Park, 53 Upton Towans,
Gwithian, Hayle, Cornwall, TR27 5BL.
Std: 01736 **Tel:** 752071
Email: enquiries@atlanticcoast-
caravanpark.co.uk
Website: www.atlanticcoast-
caravanpark.co.uk
Nearest Town/Resort Hayle
Directions When entering Hayle from
Camborne by-pass (A30), turn right at the
double roundabout onto the B3301, Atlantic
Coast Park is approx. 1 mile on the left.
Acreage 4½ **Open** April **to** October
Access Good **Site** Level
Sites Available ▲ ♦ ⊞ **Total** 32
Facilities / ⅏ ♨ ⌐ ⊙ᵈ ◿ ◙ ☎
⅃ ◎ ♣ ꕔ ⊡
Nearby Facilities ⌐ ✓ ⚓ ⅄ ∪ ⊅ ♞
⇌ Hayle
Situated in sand dunes close to a bathing
and surfing beach, excellent walks.

HAYLE

Beachside Holiday Park, Hayle,
Cornwall, TR27 5AW.
Std: 01736 **Tel:** 753080
Std: 01736 **Fax:** 757252
Email:
reception@beachside.demon.co.uk
Website: www.beachside.co.uk
Nearest Town/Resort Hayle
Directions Leave the A30 at Hayle and
follow brown tourist signs to 'Beachside'.
Acreage 20 **Open** Easter **to** 30 Sept
Access Good **Site** Lev/Slope
Sites Available ▲ ♦ ⊞ **Total** 90
Facilities / ⅏ ♨ ⌐ ⊙ᵈ ◿ ◙ ☎
⅃ ◎ ⅌ ♣ ꕔ ✕ ⊡
Nearby Facilities ⌐ ✓ ⚓ ⅄ ∪ ♞
⇌ Hayle
Right beside a golden sandy beach.

HAYLE

**Higher Trevaskis Caravan & Camping
Park,** Gwinear Road, Connor Downs,
Hayle, Cornwall, TR27 5JQ.
Std: 01209 **Tel:** 831736
Nearest Town/Resort Hayle/St Ives
Directions At Hayle roundabout (Little Chef)
on A30 take the first exit (signposted Connor
Downs). After 1 mile turn right to Carnhell
Green. Park is on the right in ¾ of mile.
Acreage 5¼ **Open** April **to** October
Access Good **Site** Level
Sites Available ▲ ♦ ⊞ **Total** 75
Facilities / ⅃ ⅏ ♨ ⌐ ⊙ᵈ ◿ ◙ ☎
⅃ ⅃ ◎ ♣ ꕔ ⊡
Nearby Facilities ⌐ ✓ ⚓ ⅄ ∪ ⊅ ♞

⇌ Hayle
Friendly, secluded, family run, countryside
park. Spacious, level pitches in small
enclosures. Designated play areas and our
renowned spotlessly clean facilities.

HAYLE

Parbola Holiday Park, Wall, Gwinear,
Cornwall, TR27 5LE.
Std: 01209 **Tel:** 831503
Std: 01209 **Fax:** 831503
Email: bookings@parbola.co.uk
Website: www.parbola.co.uk
Nearest Town/Resort Hayle
Directions Travel on A30 to Hayle, at
roundabout leave first exit to Connor Downs.
At end of village turn right to Carnhell Green,
right at T-Junction, Parbola is 1 mile on the
left.
Acreage 17 **Open** April **to** September
Access Good **Site** Level
Sites Available ▲ ♦ ⊞ **Total** 115
Facilities ⅃ / ⅏ ♨ ⌐ ⊙ᵈ ◿ ◙ ☎
⅃ ⅃ ◎ ♣ ꕔ ꕔ ✕ ⊡ ⊡
Nearby Facilities ⌐ ✓ ⚓ ⅄ ∪ ⊅ ♞
No dogs allowed during July and August.

HAYLE

Sunny Meadow Holiday Park, Lelant
Down, Hayle, Cornwall, TR27 6LL.
Std: 01736 **Tel:** 752243
Email:
sunnymeadowcornwall@hotmail.com
Nearest Town/Resort Hayle/St Ives
Directions Take the Hayle by-pass, turn off
for St Ives to the mini roundabout. Take the
first left onto the B3311. We are ¼ mile up
on the left.
Acreage 1 **Open** March **to** 31 Jan
Access Good **Site** Level
Sites Available ▲ ♦ ⊞ **Total** 3
Facilities ⅃ / ⅏ ♨ ⌐ ⊙ᵈ ◿ ◙ ☎
⅃ ◎ ⊞ ꕔ ⊡ ⊡
Nearby Facilities ⌐ ✓ ⅄ ∪ ⊅ ♞
⇌ St Erth
A few miles from both north and south coasts
offering ideal opportunity to tour the
Peninsula.

HELSTON

Boscrege Caravan Park, Ashton,
Helston, Cornwall, TR13 9TG.
Std: 01736 **Tel:** 762231
Std: 01736 **Fax:** 762231
Website: www.caravanparkcornwall.com
Nearest Town/Resort Praa Sands
Directions From Helston follow Penzance
road (A394) to Ashton, turn right by post
office along road signposted to Godolphin
and continue about 1½ miles to Boscrege
Park.
Acreage 7 **Open** Easter/1 April **to** Oct
Access Good **Site** Level
Sites Available ▲ ♦ ⊞ **Total** 50
Facilities / ⅏ ♨ ⌐ ⊙ᵈ ◿ ◙ ☎
◎ ◙ ⊞ ♣ ꕔ ✕ ⊡ ⊡
Nearby Facilities ⌐ ✓ ⚓ ⅄ ∪ ⊅ ♞
⇌ Penzance
Quiet family park in garden setting. No club.
Near sandy beaches. Ideal for exploring
West Cornwall. Microwave for campers.

RAC Selected Site **Hedley Wood Caravan & Camping Park** **AA**
Bridgerule, Holsworthy, Devon EX22 7ED Tel **(01288) 381404** Fax **(01288) 381644**
16 acre woodland family run site with outstanding views, where you can enjoy a totally relaxing holiday with a 'laid back' atmosphere. Sheltered & open camping areas. Just 10 minutes drive from the beaches, golf courses, riding stables & shops. **On Site facilities include:** Children's adventure centre, Bars, Clubrooms, Shop, Laundry, Meals & all amenities. Free hot showers and water. Nice dogs/pets **are** welcome. Daily kennelling facility, Dog walks/Nature trail. Clay pigeon shoot. Static caravans for hire, **caravan storage** available. **Open All Year.** Why not visit our Website: www.hedleywood.co.uk

HELSTON

Gunwalloe Caravan Park, Gunwalloe, Helston, Cornwall, TR12 7QP.
Std: 01326 **Tel:** 572668
Nearest Town/Resort Helston
Directions Take the A3083 from Helston towards Lizard for 2 miles, turn right to Gunwalloe for 1 mile, on the right signposted.
Acreage 2½ **Open** Easter **to** October
Access Good **Site** Level
Sites Available ▲ ⊞ ⊟ **Total** 40
Facilities ✦ ⑭ ♨ ┌ ⊙ ┙ 🏪 🛍 🌭 ⊟
Nearby Facilities ┌ ✦ ∪
➤ Redruth
Central for the Lizard Peninsula. 1 mile from coastal walks.

HELSTON

Lower Polladras Touring Park, Carleen, Nr. Helston, Cornwall, TR13 9NX.
Std: 01736 **Tel:** 762220 **Fax:** 762220
Email: polladras@hotmail.com
Web: www.caravancampingsites.co.uk/cornwall/lowerpolladras.htm
Nearest Town/Resort Helston
Directions From Helston take the A394 to Penzance and turn right at the Hilltop Garage along the B3302. After ½ mile turn left to Carleen village. From the A30 turn left in Camborne along the B3303, then take the first right turning after junction of 3303 and 3302.
Acreage 4 **Open** April **to** October
Access Good **Site** Level
Sites Available ▲ ⊞ ⊟ **Total** 60
Facilities ✦ ⑭ ♨ ┌ ⊙ ┙ 🗑 🍴 🛍 🌭 ⊟
Nearby Facilities ┌ ✦ ∆ ≽ ∪ ⊿
➤ Camborne
Pleasant views of surrounding hills. Ideal touring situation.

HELSTON

Poldown Caravan & Camping Site, Carleen, Breage, Helston, Cornwall, TR13 9NN
Std: 01326 **Tel:** 574560 **Fax:** 574560
Email: poldown@poldown.co.uk
Website: www.poldown.co.uk
Nearest Town/Resort Helston
Directions Take A394 (signed Penzance) from Helston. At top of the hill on outskirts of Helston take the B3303 signed Hayle/St Ives. Take the second left on this road and we are ¼ mile along.
Acreage 1¼ **Open** May **to** Sept
Access Good **Site** Level
Sites Available ▲ ⊞ ⊟ **Total** 13
Facilities ✦ ⑭ ♨ ┌ ⊙ ┙ 🗑 🛍 🏪 🌭 🛍 ⊟
Nearby Facilities ┌ ✦ ∆ ≽ ∪ ⊿
➤ Penzance
Small, secluded, pretty site. Ideal for touring West Cornwall. ETB 4 Star Graded.

HELSTON

Trelowarren Caravan & Camping Park, Mawgan, Helston, Cornwall, TR12 6AF.
Std: 01326 **Tel:** 221637 **Fax:** 221427
Nearest Town/Resort Helston/Truro
Directions Take the A3083 Helston to Lizard road, at the end of Culdrose Air Base take the B3293 to St. Kevern. Follow signposts to Trelowarren.
Acreage 22 **Open** April **to** Sept
Access Good **Site** Lev/Slope

Sites Available ▲ ⊞ ⊟ **Total** 250
Facilities ♿ ✦ ⑭ ♨ ┌ ⊙ ┙ 🗑 🛍 🌭
🍴 🏪 ⓘ ⚶ ♨ ☂ 🔒 ▲ 🌭 ⊟
Nearby Facilities ┌ ✦ ∆ ≽ ∪ ⊿ ⅋
➤ Redruth/Camborne
1000 acre estate grounds with woodland walks, craft centres, bistro and Lizard Project Centre. Surrounded by beaches.

ISLES OF SCILLY

Jenford, Bryher, Isles of Scilly, Cornwall.
Std: 01720 **Tel:** 422886 **Fax:** 423092
Nearest Town/Resort Penzance
Acreage 1 **Open** April **to** October
Site Level
Sites Available ▲ **Total** 37
Facilities ⑭ ♨ ┌ ⊙ ┙ 🛍 ⓘ ⚶
Nearby Facilities ┌ ✦ ∆ ≽ ∪ ⊿

ISLES OF SCILLY

St. Martin's Campsite, Middle Town, St. Martin's, Isles of Scilly, Cornwall, TR25 0QN
Std: 01720 **Tel:** 422888 **Fax:** 422888
Email:
chris@stmartinscampsite.freeserve.co.uk
Directions Take a ferry, plane or helicopter from Penzance to St. Mary's. Launch from St. Mary's to St. Martin's.
Acreage 2½ **Open** Easter **to** End Oct
Site Level
Sites Available ▲ **Total** 50
Facilities ✦ ⑭ ♨ ┌ ⊙ ┙ 🛍 ⓘ ⚶
Nearby Facilities ┌ ✦ ∆ ≽ ∪ ⊿
➤ Penzance
Adjacent to a south facing, white sandy beach on a peaceful, idyllic island.

JACOBSTOW

Edmore Tourist Park, Edgar Road, Wainhouse Corner, Jacobstow, Bude, Cornwall, EX23 0BJ.
Std: 01840 **Tel:** 230467
Email: edmore@touristpark.freeserve.co.uk
Website: www.cornwallvisited.co.uk
Nearest Town/Resort Bude
Directions 8 miles south of Bude on the A39.
Acreage 2 **Open** Easter **to** October
Access Good **Site** Level
Sites Available ▲ ⊞ ⊟ **Total** 28
Facilities ✦ ⑭ ♨ ┌ ⊙ ┙ 🗑 🛍 ⓘ 🌭 ⊟
Nearby Facilities ┌ ✦ ∪
➤ Bodmin
3 miles from the beach. Ideal touring.

LANDS END

Cardinney Caravan & Caravan Park, Main A30, Lands End Road, Crows-An-Wra, Lands End, Cornwall, TR19 6HJ.
Std: 01736 **Tel:** 810880 **Fax:** 810998
Email: cardinney@btinternet.com
Website: www.cardinney-camping-park.co.uk
Nearest Town/Resort Sennen Cove
Directions From Penzance follow Main A30 to Lands End, approx 5¼ miles. Entrance on right hand side on Main A30, large name board at entrance.
Acreage 5 **Open** 1 Feb **to** End Nov
Access Good **Site** Level
Sites Available ▲ ⊞ ⊟ **Total** 105
Facilities ✦ 🍴 ⑭ ♨ ┌ ⊙ ┙ 🛍 ⓘ ⚶ 🛍 🏪

⚒ ⑭ ♨ 🛍 🛍 ┙ 🏪 🛍 🛍
Nearby Facilities ┌ ✦ ∆ ≽ ∪ ⊿ ♨ ⅋
➤ Sennen Cove Blue Flag, scenic coastal walks, ancient monuments, scenic flights, Minack Ampitheatre, trips to the Isles of Scilly. Ideal for touring Lands End Peninsula. AA 3 Pennants and West Country Tourist Board Graded 4 Ticks.

LANDS END

Lower Treave Caravan Park, Crows-an-Wra, St. Buryan, Penzance, Cornwall, TR19 6HZ.
Std: 01736 **Tel:** 810559 **Fax:** 810559
Email: camping@lowertreave.demon.co.uk
Website: www.lowertreave.demon.co.uk
Nearest Town/Resort Penzance
Directions On A30 Penzance/Lands End road, ½ mile west of Crows-an-Wra.
Acreage 4½ **Open** April **to** October
Access Good **Site** Level
Sites Available ▲ ⊞ ⊟ **Total** 80.
Facilities ✦ ⑭ ♨ ┌ ⊙ ┙ 🗑 🛍 🏪 🌭 ⊟
Nearby Facilities ┌ ✦ ∆ ≽ ∪ ⅋
➤ Penzance
Quiet family site in the heart of Lands End peninsular with panoramic rural views to the sea. Sheltered, level grass terraces. Blue Flag beach 2½ miles. AA 3 Pennants, Camping & Caravan Club Listed and Caravan Club Listed.

LAUNCESTON

Chapmanswell Caravan Site, St. Giles on the Heath, Launceston, Cornwall, PL15 9SG
Std: 01409 **Tel:** 211382
Nearest Town/Resort Launceston
Directions Chapmanswell Caravan Park is situated 6 miles from Launceston along the A388 on your left hand side going towards Holsworthy, just past the pub and garage in Chapmanswell.
Acreage 12 **Open** 15 March **to** 15 Nov
Access Good **Site** Level
Sites Available ▲ ⊞ ⊟ **Total** 81
Facilities ✦ ⑭ ♨ ┌ ⊙ ┙ 🗑 🛍 ⓘ ⚶
🏪 ☀ 🌭 🛍 ⊟
Nearby Facilities ┌ ✦ ∆ ≽ ∪ ⊿
Very central for Cornwall and Devon, easy reach of North Devon beaches, Dartmoor and Cornish resorts. Village pub meals 200 yards. Caravan storage available.

LISKEARD

Great Trethew Manor Camp Site, Horningtops, Liskeard, Cornwall, PL14 3PY
Std: 01503 **Tel:** 240663 **Fax:** 240695
Email: great_trethew_manor@yahoo.com
Website: www.great-trethew-manor.co.uk
Nearest Town/Resort Looe
Directions From Liskeard follow the A38 for approx. 3 miles, turn right onto the B3251. After ¼ mile turn left into drive entrance.
Acreage 30 **Open** March **to** September
Access Good **Site** Level
Sites Available ▲ ⊞ ⊟ **Total** 55
Facilities ✦ ⑭ ♨ ┌ ⊙ ┙ 🗑 🛍 ⓘ ⚶ ☂ ▲ 🌭 ⊟
Nearby Facilities ┌ ✦ ∆ ≽ ∪ ⊿ ♨ ⅋ ⅌
On site features include fishing, tennis, woodland walks, beautiful gardens and hotel facilities. Near to beaches, moorland, sea sports and many historic buildings.

LISKEARD

Pine Green Caravan Park, Double Bois, Liskeard, East Cornwall, PL16 6LE.
Std: 01579 **Tel:** 320183
Email: maryruhleman@btinternet.com
Website: www.jpr1994.sagehost.co.uk
Nearest Town/Resort Liskeard
Directions 3 miles from Liskeard towards Bodmin. Just off the main A38 at Double Bois.
Acreage 3 **Open** All Year
Access Good **Site** Level
Sites Available Λ ⊕ ⊕ **Total** 50
Facilities ∮ ⊞ ⅏ ♨ ┌ ⊙ ⊸ ⚇ ⊡ ☎
☺ ⓑ ❄ 🖃
Nearby Facilities ┌ ✓ ⊥ ❄ U ⊅ �
❄ Liskeard
Overlooking beautiful wooded valley and open countryside.

LISKEARD

Trenant Chapel House, Trenant Caravan Park, St Neot, Liskeard, Cornwall, PL14 6RZ.
Std: 01579 **Tel:** 320896
Nearest Town/Resort Liskeard
Directions Take St Cleer road off A38 at Dobwalls, 1 mile left signposted St. Neot, 1 mile right SP Trennant, ½ mile right signposted Trennant.
Acreage 1 **Open** April to October
Site Level
Sites Available Λ ⊕ ⊕ **Total** 8
Facilities ∮ ⅏ ♨ ┌ ⊙ ⊸ ⚇ ⊡ ☎
⅏❄🖃
Nearby Facilities ✓ ⊥ ❄ U
❄ Liskeard
Siblyback and Colliford Reservoirs close, fishing, boardsailing and bird watching. Site in sheltered corner upper Fowey valley bounded by tributary of Fowey river, close Bodmin moor, ideal walking, touring.

LIZARD

Chy-Carne Holiday Park, Kuggar, Kennack Sands, Ruan Minor, Helston, Cornwall, TR12 7LX.
Std: 01326 **Tel:** 290200
Email: chy-carne@hotmail.com
Website: www.cornwall.online.co.uk/chy-carne
Nearest Town/Resort Helston
Directions From Helston follow the A3083 for approx. 2 miles, at mini roundabout turn left onto the B3293 signposted St Keverne. Approx. 1 mile past Goonhilly Earth Satellite Station turn right, onto T-Junction turn left, site is on the left.
Open Easter to October
Access Good **Site** Level
Sites Available Λ ⊕ ⊕ **Total** 65
Facilities ∮ ⅏ ♨ ┌ ⊙ ☎
⅏ ☺ ⅏ ⅏ ╫ ⊡ 🖃
Nearby Facilities ┌ ✓ ⊥ ❄
❄ Penzance
¼ mile from the beach, ideal for touring. Some sea views.

LIZARD

Gwendreath Farm Caravan Park,
Kennack Sands, Helston, Cornwall, TR12 7LZ.
Std: 01326 **Tel:** 290666
Email: tom.gibson@virgin.net
Website: www.tomandlinda.co.uk
Nearest Town/Resort The Lizard
Directions A3083 from Helston, left on B3293 after R.N.A.S. Culdrose. After Goonhilly Earth Station, take the first right then first left. At end of lane go through Seaview Caravan Site to second reception.
Acreage 3 **Open** Easter
Access Good **Site** Level
Sites Available Λ ⊕ ⊕ **Total** 30
Facilities ∮ ⅏ ♨ ┌ ⊙ ⊸ ⚇ ⊡ ☎
⅏ ⅏ ☺ ⅏ ⅏ ⊛ ╫ ⊡ 🖃
Nearby Facilities ┌ ✓ ⊥ ❄ U
❄ Redruth
Attractive, peaceful family site overlooking the sea in an area of outstanding natural beauty. Short woodland walk to safe sandy beaches.

LIZARD

Henry's Campsite, Caerthillian Farm, The Lizard, Helston, Cornwall, TR12 7NX.
Std: 01326 **Tel:** 290596
Nearest Town/Resort Helston
Directions Take the main A3083 Helston to Lizard road, enter the village and take the first turn right across the village green, then turn second right.
Acreage 1½ **Open** All Year
Access Good **Site** Lev/Slope
Sites Available Λ ⊕ ⊕ **Total** 30
Facilities ∮ ⅏ ┌ ⊙ ☎ ⅏ ⅏ ⊡ 🖃
Nearby Facilities ┌ ✓ ⊥ ❄ U ⋉ ⋊
❄ Redruth
Outstanding views. Close to secluded or popular beaches and near coastal footpaths.

LIZARD

Silver Sands Holiday Park, Kennack Sands, Gwendreath, Ruan Minor, Helston, Cornwall, TR12 7LZ.
Std: 01326 **Tel:** 290631
Std: 01326 **Fax:** 290631
Email: enquiries@silversandsholidaypark.co.uk
Website: www.silversandsholidaypark.co.uk
Nearest Town/Resort Helston
Directions On entering Helston take the A3083 Lizard road, pass R.N.A.S. Culdrose then turn left at roundabout onto the B3293 signposted St Keverne. In 4 miles, immediately past Goonhilly Satellite Station, turn right to Kennack. After 1 mile turn left.
Acreage 9 **Open** May to September
Access Good **Site** Lev/Slope
Sites Available Λ ⊕ ⊕ **Total** 34
Facilities ∮ ⅏ ♨ ┌ ⊙ ⊸ ⚇ ⊡ 🖃
⅏ ☺ ⅏ ⅏ ⊛ ╫ ⊡ 🖃
Nearby Facilities ┌ ✓ ⊥ ❄ U
❄ Redruth
800mts to safe sandy beach, ideal touring and walking. Quiet, family site in area of outstanding natural beauty.

LONGDOWNS

Calamankey Campsite, Calamankey Farm Campsite, Longdowns, Penryn, Cornwall, TR10 9DL.
Std: 01209 **Tel:** 860314
Email: calamankey@cwcom.net
Website: www.calamankey.cwc.net
Nearest Town/Resort Falmouth
Directions A394 from Penryn, 2½ miles.
Acreage 2½ **Open** Easter to October
Access Good **Site** Sloping
Sites Available Λ ⊕ ⊕ **Total** 60
Facilities ⊞ ⅏ ┌ ⊙ ⊸ ☎ ⅏❄🖃🖃
Nearby Facilities ┌ ✓ ⊥ ❄ U ⋊
❄ Penryn
Farming area. Beach 4½ miles. Ideal touring.

LOOE

Camping Caradon Touring Park,
Trelawne, Looe, Cornwall, PL13 2NA.
Std: 01503 **Tel:** 272388
Std: 01503 **Fax:** 272388
Website: www.campingcaradon.co.uk
Nearest Town/Resort Looe
Directions From Looe t\ake the A38 towards Polperro. After 2 miles turn right onto the B3359. Take the next turning right and Camping Caradon is clearly signposted.
Acreage 3½ **Open** Easter to End Oct
Access Good **Site** Level
Sites Available Λ ⊕ ⊕ **Total** 85
Facilities ∮ ⊞ ⅏ ♨ ┌ ⊙ ⊸ ⚇ ⊡ ☎
⅏ ⅏ ✕ ♀ ♠ ⅏ ╫ ⊡ 🖃
Nearby Facilities ┌ ✓ ⊥ ❄ U ⋉ ⋊
❄ Looe
Quiet countryside site on a local bus route. Ideal base for touring.

LOOE

Looe Valley Touring Park, Polperro Road, Looe, Cornwall, PL13 2JS.
Std: 01503 **Tel:** 262425
Std: 01503 **Fax:** 265411
Email: bookings@looevalley-park.demon.co.uk
Nearest Town/Resort Looe
Directions From Tideford turn left onto the A374, then turn right onto the A387 signposted Looe. Follow the road through Looe and Polperro, after 2½ miles we are on the right.
Acreage 23 **Open** April to September
Access Good **Site** Lev/Slope
Sites Available Λ ⊕ ⊕ **Total** 500
Facilities ∮ ⊞ ⅏ ♨ ┌ ⊙ ⊸ ⚇ ⊡ ☎
⅏ ⅏ ☺ ✕ ♀ ⅏ ♠ ⅏ ⅏ ╫ ⊡ 🖃
Nearby Facilities ┌ ✓ ⊥ ❄ U ⋉ ⋊
❄ Looe
Close to Cornwall's beautiful countryside, coastline, superb attractions and charming villages.

LOOE

Polborder House Caravan & Camping Park, Bucklawren Road, St. Martin, Looe, Cornwall, PL13 1QR.
Std: 01503 **Tel:** 240265
Std: 01503 **Fax:** 240700
Email: rlf.polborder@virgin.net
Website: www.peaceful-polborder.co.uk
Nearest Town/Resort Looe

Set in glorious countryside between Looe & Polperro, two of the most beautiful fishing villages in Cornwall.

Close to safe sandy beaches and secluded coves.

Quote: CP

- Level, well drained pitches with electric hook-ups
- FREE entertainment & Children's club
- Eurotents, Caravan & Camping & Holiday Homes
- FREE heated swimming pool
- Shop, Takeaway & Launderette
- Semi seasonal pitches & winter storage available
- Rallies welcome

Looe Valley
TOURING PARK

01503 262425

bookings@looevalley-park.demon.co.uk

Directions 2¼ miles east of Looe off B3253, follow signs for Polborder and Monkey Sanctuary.
Acreage 3 **Open** April **to** October
Access Good **Site** Level
Sites Available ⚠ ♙ ⛺ **Total** 36
Facilities ♿ ⚭ ☐ ⊞ 🅿 ♨ ⌂ ⊙ ⊿ 🔲 ◻ ▽
⛵ 🔲 ❷ 🔺 ✈ ☐ 🄳
Nearby Facilities ⌿ ✓ 🛝 ⚓ U ℛ
⛴ Looe
Small, select, award winning park set in beautiful countryside, 1¼ miles from the sea.

LOOE

Talland Barton Caravan Park, Talland Bay, Looe, Cornwall, PL13 2JA.
Std: 01503 **Tel:** 272715
Std: 01503 **Fax:** 272224
Nearest Town/Resort Looe
Directions Take A387 from Looe towards Polperro. After 1 mile turn left. Follow this road for 1½ miles. The site is on the left hand side by Talland Church.
Acreage 10 **Open** Easter **to** October
Access Poor **Site** Lev/Slope
Sites Available ⚠ ♙ ⛺ **Total** 60
Facilities ♿ ⚭ ☐ 🅿 ♨ ⌂ ⊙ ⊿ 🔲 ▽
Nearby Facilities ⌿ ✓ 🛝 ⚓ U ℛ
⛴ Looe
Between Looe and Polperro, near a beach. Peaceful countryside, ideal touring.

LOOE

Tregoad Farm Camping & Caravanning Park, St. Martins, Looe, Cornwall, PL13 1PB.
Std: 01503 **Tel:** 262718
Std: 01503 **Fax:** 264777
Email: tregoadfarmccp@aol.com
Website: www.cornwall-online.co.uk/tregoad
Nearest Town/Resort Looe.
Directions Situated approx. 1½ miles from Looe and 200yds off the Plymouth to Looe road (B3253).
Acreage 10 **Open** April **to** October
Access Good **Site** Level
Sites Available ⚠ ♙ ⛺ **Total** 150
Facilities ♿ ⚭ ☐ 🅿 ♨ ⌂ ⊙ ⊿ 🔲 ▽
⛵ 🔲 ❷ 🔺 ✈ ☐ 🄳
Nearby Facilities ⌿ ✓ 🛝 ⚓ U ℛ
⛴ Looe/Liskeard
Ideally situated on southerly slopes with magnificent views to Looe Bay and the rolling Cornish Hinterland.

LOOE

Trelay Farmpark, Pelynt, Looe, Cornwall, PL13 2JX.
Std: 01503 **Tel:** 220900
Std: 01503 **Fax:** 220900

Nearest Town/Resort Looe/Polperro
Directions From Looe take the A387 towards Polperro. After 2 miles turn right onto the B3359. Trelay Farmpark is clearly signed ¾ mile on the right.
Acreage 3 **Open** Easter **to** October
Access Good **Site** Level
Sites Available ⚠ ♙ ⛺ **Total** 55
Facilities ♿ ⚭ 🆚 🅿 ♨ ⌂ ⊙ ⊿ 🔲 ◻ ▽
⛵ 🔲 ❷ 🔺 ☐ 🄳
Nearby Facilities ⌿ ✓ 🛝 ⚓ U ℛ
⛴ Looe
A quiet, uncommercialised park surrounded by farmland. Wide views over open countryside. Large pitches on a gentle south facing slope. Immaculate facilities.

LOSTWITHIEL

Powderham Castle Tourist Park, Lanlivery, Nr. Fowey, Cornwall, PL30 5BU.
Std: 01208. **Tel:** 872277
Nearest Town/Resort Fowey/St. Austell
Directions 1½ miles southwest Lostwithiel on A390, turn right at signpost, up road 400 yards.
Acreage 10 **Open** April **to** October
Access Good **Site** Level
Sites Available ⚠ ♙ ⛺ **Total** 75
Facilities ⚭ 🄷 🆚 🅿 ⌂ ⊙ ⊿ 🔲 ◻ ▽
⛵ 🔲 ❷ 🔺 ✡ 🄷 🄳 🄵
Nearby Facilities ⌿ ✓ 🛝 ⚓ U ℛ ✠
⛴ Lostwithiel
Quiet spacious site, uncommercialised. Ideal for touring all of Cornwall and near the Eden Project. Battery charging, freezer pack service. Dish washing and vegetable preparation facilities. Indoor Badminton and soft tennis court, putting green and a multiactivity games area. Seasonal pitches/storage. Winner AA Award for Sanitation and Environmental Facilities.

MARAZION

Trevair Touring Site, South Treveneague Farm, St. Hilary, Penzance, Cornwall, TR20 9BY.
Std: 01736 **Tel:** 740647
Nearest Town/Resort Marazion
Directions 3 miles from Marazion, B3280 through Goldsithney signposted South Treveneague.
Acreage 3½ **Open** End March **to** October
Access Good **Site** Level
Sites Available ⚠ ♙ ⛺ **Total** 35
Facilities ⚭ 🆚 🅿 ⌂ ⊙ ⊿ 🔲 ◻ ▽ 🄷 🄳
Nearby Facilities ⌿ ✓ 🛝 U
⛴ St. Erth
Everyone is welcome at our clean and friendly site. Set in the peace and quiet of the countryside, yet within 2/3 miles of beaches, shops and pubs.

MARAZION

Wheal Rodney, Marazion, Cornwall, TR17 0HL.
Std: 01736 **Tel:** 710605
Std: 01736 **Fax:** 710605
Nearest Town/Resort Marazion
Directions ½ mile north Marazion.
Acreage 4¼ **Open** 1 April or Easter **to** Oct
Access Good **Site** Level
Sites Available ⚠ ♙ ⛺ **Total** 45
Facilities ⚭ 🆚 🅿 ⌂ ⊙ ⊿ 🔲 ◻ ▽
⛵ 🔲 ❷ 🔺 🄷 🄳
Nearby Facilities ⌿ ✓ 🛝 ⚓ U ℛ ℛ ✠
⛴ Penzance
½ mile from safe beach. Sauna, solarium, spa bath on site.

MAWGAN PORTH

Magic Cove Touring Park, Mawgan Porth, Newquay, Cornwall, TR8 4BZ.
Std: 01637 **Tel:** 860263
Email: magic@redcove.co.uk
Website: www.redcove.co.uk
Nearest Town/Resort Newquay
Directions Take the A30 to Bodmin, 4 miles from the end of the dual carriageway, iron bridge ½ mile turn right onto the A3059. At the roundabout take the second left to Newquay, ¾ mile turn right to the airport, T-Junction turn right to Mawgan Porth.
Acreage 1 **Open** Easter **to** Oct
Access Good **Site** Level
Sites Available ⚠ ♙ ⛺ **Total** 26
Facilities ⚭ 🆚 🅿 ⌂ ⊙ ⊿ 🔲 ▽ ⛵ 🔺 🄳
Nearby Facilities ⌿ ✓ ℛ
⛴ Newquay
300yds from a sandy beach. Ideal centre for North Cornwall coast. Water adjacent to each pitch and TV points.

MAWGAN PORTH

Marver Touring Park, Marver Chalets, Mawgan Porth, Near Newquay, Cornwall, TR8 4BB.
Std: 01637 **Tel:** 860493
Std: 01637 **Fax:** 860493
Email: familyholidays@aol.com
Nearest Town/Resort Newquay
Directions From Newquay take the B3276 coast road to Padstow. After 6 miles, on entering Mawgan Porth, turn right at the filling station, park is 300 yards on the left.
Acreage 2½ **Open** Easter **to** October
Access Good **Site** Level
Sites Available ⚠ ♙ ◻ **Total** 25
Facilities ⚭ 🆚 🅿 ⌂ ⊙ ⊿ 🔲 ▽ ⛵ ❷ 🔺 🄳
Nearby Facilities ⌿ ✓ 🛝 ⚓ U ℛ
⛴ Newquay
Peaceful location in a valley with superb views. 300 yards to the beach, excellent coastal walks. Ideal base for touring Cornwall.

MAWGAN PORTH

Sun Haven Valley Holiday Park,
Mawgan Porth, Near Newquay, Cornwall,
TR8 4BQ.
Std: 01637 **Tel:** 860373
Std: 01637 **Fax:** 860373
Email: traceyhealey@hotmail.com
Website: www.sunhavenvalley.co.uk
Nearest Town/Resort Newquay/Padstow
Directions From the A30 4 miles after
Bodmin turn right signposted Newquay and
Airport. Continue to follow signs for the Airport
and after 1½ miles turn right to St. Mawgan.
Turn right at Mawgan Porth Garage.
Acreage 7 **Open** April **to** October
Access Good **Site** Level
Sites Available A ⚏ ⚐ **Total** 118
Facilities ⚒ ✦ ⊞ Ⅲ ⚏ ⚓ ⌐ ⊙ ⚋ ⚐ ☎
⚑ ⚒ ⚙ ⚏ ☒ ⚑ ⊣ ⊡ ☐
Nearby Facilities ⌐ ✦ ⚑ ⚘ U
⚓ Newquay

¾ miles from Mawgan Porth beach,
surrounded by countryside. Family
bathrooms available.

MEVAGISSEY

Seaview International, Boswinger,
Gorran, St. Austell, Cornwall, PL26 6LL.
Std: 01726 **Tel:** 843425
Std: 01726 **Fax:** 843358
Email: enquiries@seaviewinternational.com
Website: www.seaviewinternational.com
Nearest Town/Resort Mevagissey
Directions From St. Austell take B3273 to
Mevagissey, prior to village turn right. Then
follow signs to Gorran.
Acreage 28 **Open** April **to** September
Access Good **Site** Level
Sites Available A ⚏ ⚐ **Total** 165
Facilities ⚒ ✗ ✦ ⊞ Ⅲ Ⅲ ⚏ ⚓ ⌐ ⊙ ⚋ ⚋
⚐ ☎ ⚑ ⚒ ⚙ ⚏ Ⅶ ⚑ ⚘ ☒ ⚑ ⊣ ⊡ ☐
Nearby Facilities ✦ ⚑ ⚘ ⚓ ⚘
⚓ St Austell

England's TOP PARK. Beautiful level park
overlooking the sea, surrounded by sandy
beaches, nearest ½ mile. Free sports and
pastimes on site. All facilities are centrally
heated including under floor heating. Holiday
caravans also for hire. AA Best Campsite
of the Year 1995/6 and AA 5 Pennant
Premier Park.

MEVAGISSEY

Tregarton Park, Gorran, Near
Mevagissey, St. Austell, Cornwall, PL26
6NF.
Std: 01726. **Tel:** 843666
Std: 01726 **Fax:** 844481
Email: enquiries@tregartonpark.co.uk
Website: www.tregartonpark.co.uk
Nearest Town/Resort Mevagissey
Directions From St Austell take the B3273
signposted Mevagissey. At the top of
Pentewan Hill turn right signposted Gorran.
Park is 3 miles on the right (signposted).
Acreage 12 **Open** April **to** October
Access Good **Site** Lev/Slope
Sites Available A ⚏ ⚐ **Total** 130
Facilities ⚒ ⊞ Ⅲ ⚏ ⚓ ⌐ ⊙ ⚋ ⚐ ☎
⚑ ⚒ ⚙ ⚏ ⚘ ☒ ⚑ ⊣ ⊡ ☐
Nearby Facilities ⌐ ✦ ⚑ ⚘ U ⚓ ⚘
⚓ St. Austell

Beautiful sheltered park with glimpses of the
sea through the valley. Nearest beach is 1½
miles. Lost Garden of Heligan only a 2
minute drive away and Eden Project 20
minutes.

MULLION

Franchis, Cury Cross Lanes, Mullion,
Helston, Cornwall, TR12 7AZ.
Std: 01326 **Tel:** 240301
Email: franchis@lineone.net
Website: www.franchis.co.uk
Nearest Town/Resort Mullion
Directions On the A3083, 5 miles south of
Helston and 2 miles north of Mullion.
Acreage 4 **Open** Easter **to** October
Access Good **Site** Lev/Slope
Sites Available A ⚏ ⚐ **Total** 70
Facilities ⚒ Ⅲ ⚏ ⚓ ⌐ ⊙ ⚋ ☎
⚑ ⚒ ⚙ ⚑ ⊣ ⊡ ☐
Nearby Facilities ⌐ ✦ ⚑ ⚘ U
⚓ Redruth

Set in 17 acres of woodland and fields. Near
to beaches and Helford River.

MULLION

Mullion Holiday Park, Mullion, Near
Helston, Cornwall, TR12 7LJ.
Std: 01326 **Tel:** 240000
Std: 01326 **Fax:** 241141
Email: sid@weststarholidays.co.uk

Website: www.weststarholidays.co.uk
Nearest Town/Resort Helston
Directions From the A30 take the A39 to
Truro and continue on the Falmouth road.
Take the A394 to Helston then the A3083 to
The Lizard. After 7 miles we are on the left.
Acreage 49 **Open** May **to** September
Access Good **Site** Level
Sites Available A ⚏ ⚐ **Total** 150
Facilities ⚒ ⊞ Ⅲ Ⅲ ⚏ ⚓ ⌐ ⊙ ⚋ ⚐ ☐
⚑ ⚒ ⚙ ☒ ⚑ Ⅶ ⚏ ⚓ ⊙ ⚋ ⊣ ⊡ ☐
Nearby Facilities ⌐ ✦ ⚑ ⚘ U ⚘ ⚓
⚓ Redruth

Close to safe, sandy beaches with splendid
scenery and a dramatic coastline. Near to
many superb attractions including The Eden
Project. Ideal for touring.

MULLION

Teneriffe Farm Caravan Site, A.B.
Thomas, Teneriffe Farm, Mullion, Helston,
Cornwall, TR12 7EZ.
Std: 01326 **Tel:** 240293
Std: 01326 **Fax:** 240293
Nearest Town/Resort Helston
Directions 10 miles Helston to The Lizard,
turn right for Mullion. Take Mullion Cove
road, turn left Predannack.
Acreage 3 **Open** Easter **to** October
Access Good **Site** Lev/Slope
Sites Available A ⚏ ⚐ **Total** 20
Facilities ⚒ ⚏ ⚓ ⌐ ⊙ ⚋ ⚐ ☒ ⚑ ⊣ ⊡ ☐
Nearby Facilities ⌐ ✦ ⚑ ⚘ U ⚘
⚓ Redruth

Views of sea. Tumble drying facility. S.A.E.
required for brochure.

NEWQUAY

Cottage Farm Touring Park,
Treworgans, Cubert, Newquay, Cornwall,
TR8 5HH.
Std: 01637 **Tel:** 831083
Nearest Town/Resort Newquay
Directions Newqauy to Redruth road
A3075, turn right onto High Lanes. Follow
signs to Cubert, before Cubert Village turn
right signposted Crantock-Wesley road.
Down the lane for ¼ mile then turn left
signposted Tresean and Treworgans.
Acreage 2 **Open** April **to** October
Access Good **Site** Level
Sites Available A ⚏ ⚐ **Total** 45

Mullion
in Cornwall

beautiful spaces
in breathtaking places!

Mullion Holiday Park is situated in an area of outstanding natural beauty close to glorious sandy beaches.

★ Plenty of space for your touring caravan, motorhome or tent.

★ All the convenience of restaurant, takeaway, bars, supermarket & launderette.

★ Enjoy bowling, multi-sports courts and great live entertainment or sit back and relax around the indoor and outdoor pools.

★ Electric & Super Hook-ups.

WESTSTAR
Holiday Parks

www.weststarholidays.co.uk

01326 240 000

Quote CP

27

Facilities ✦ 🏠 📺 ♨ ℓ ☉ 🍴 🛒 🔲 ☎ 🅿 🛈 🛒 📪

Nearby Facilities ℾ ✈ ⚓ ⚒ ◡ ♪
≈ Newquay

Within easy reach of three National Trust beaches. Small, family site, peaceful and in a rural location.

NEWQUAY

Hendra Holiday Park, Newquay, Cornwall, TR8 4NY.
Std: 01637 **Tel:** 875778
Std: 01637 **Fax:** 879017
Email: hendra.cornwall@dial.pipex.com
Website: www.hendra-holidays.com
Nearest Town/Resort Newquay
Directions A30 to Cornwall to Indian Queens, take the Newquay road to Quintrell Downs. Hendra is 1¼ miles before Newquay Town Centre.
Acreage 36 **Open** February **to** October
Access Good **Site** Lev/Slope
Sites Available ⚠ ⚏ 🚐 **Total** 600
Facilities ♨ ✦ 🏠 📺 🅿 ♨ ℓ ☉ 🍴 🛒 🔲 ☎
🛒 🅿 🛈 🛒 ✕ ♀ 📶 🌲 🔥 ⚒ ☉ 📪 📺
Nearby Facilities ℾ ✈ ⚓ ⚒ ◡ ♪
≈ Newquay

Scenic country views. Train rides. Oasis indoor fun pool with 3 sensational water slides. Short breaks welcome. Brochure Line - FREEPHONE 0500 242523.

NEWQUAY

Holywell Bay Holiday Park, Holywell Bay, Near Newquay, Cornwall, TR8 5PR.
Std: 01637 **Tel:** 871111
Std: 01637 **Fax:** 850818
Email: bookings@newquay-hol-park.demon.co.uk
Website: www.newquay-holiday-parks.co.uk
Nearest Town/Resort Newquay
Directions From Newquay take the A3075

towards Goonhavern until you reach a sign for Cubert/Holywell, turn right.
Acreage 10 **Open** Mid May **to** Mid Sept
Access Good **Site** Level
Sites Available ⚠ ⚏ **Total** 75
Facilities ✦ 📺 🅿 ♨ ℓ ☉ 🍴 🛒 🔲 ☎
🛒 🅿 🛈 🛒 ✕ 📶 🌲 ⚒ ☉ ☀ 📪
Nearby Facilities ℾ ✈ ⚓ ⚒ ◡ ♪ ♪
≈ Newquay

A short walk to the beach. FREE entertainment.

NEWQUAY

Monkey Tree Holiday Park, Scotland Road, Rejerrah, Newquay, Cornwall, TR8 5QR.
Std: 01872 **Tel:** 572032/571298
Std: 01872 **Fax:** 572602
Email: walker.group@virgin.net
Website: www.chycor.co.uk/monkey-tree
Nearest Town/Resort Newquay/ Perranporth
Directions From the A30 take the turning onto the B3285 to Perranporth. Take the second turning on the right signposted Monkey Tree Holiday Park. The park can be found 1 mile on the left hand side.
Acreage 19 **Open** April **to** Oct
Access Good **Site** Level
Sites Available ⚠ ⚏ 🚐 **Total** 295
Facilities ♨ ✦ 📺 🅿 ♨ ℓ ☉ 🍴 🛒 🔲 ☎
🛒 🅿 🛈 🛒 ✕ ♀ 📶 🌲 🔥 ⚒ ❄ 📪 📺
Nearby Facilities ℾ ✈ ⚓ ⚒ ◡ ♪ ♪ ✗
≈ Truro

Within 3 miles of sandy beaches with surfing (tuition). 4 miles from Newquay and 8 miles from Truro. Easily accessible to all parts of Cornwall with its location adjacent to the A30.

NEWQUAY

Newperran Tourist Park, Rejerrah, Newquay, Cornwall, TR8 5QJ.
Std: 01872 **Tel:** 572407
Website: www.newperran.co.uk
Nearest Town/Resort Newquay
Directions Take A30 turn right 2½ mile past the village of Mitchell. On reachin A3075 at Goonhaven turn right and after mile, sign on righthand side turning on le
Acreage 25 **Open** Mid May **to** Mid Sept
Access Good **Site** Level
Sites Available ⚠ ⚏ 🚐 **Total** 270
Facilities ♨ ✦ 🏠 📺 🅿 ♨ ℓ ☉ 🍴 🛒 🔲 ☎
🛒 🅿 🛈 🛒 ✕ 📶 🌲 ⚒ ☉ ☀ 📪
Nearby Facilities ℾ ✈ ⚓ ⚒ ◡ ♪ ♪
≈ Newquay

Concessionary green fees, own fishing lak nearby, scenic views and central to nir golden beaches. AA 5 Pennants.

NEWQUAY

Newquay Holiday Park, Newquay, Cornwall, TR8 4HS.
Std: 01637 **Tel:** 871111
Std: 01637 **Fax:** 850818
Email: bookings@newquay-ho-park.demon.co.uk
Website: www.newquay-holiday-parks.co.uk
Nearest Town/Resort Newquay
Directions East of Newquay on the A305 towards St Columb.
Open Mid May **to** Mid Sept
Access Good **Site** Sloping
Sites Available ⚠ ⚏ 🚐 **Total** 350
Facilities ✦ 📺 🅿 ♨ ℓ ☉ 🍴 🛒 🔲
🛒 🅿 🛈 🛒 ✕ ♀ 📶 🌲 🔥 ⚒ ☉ 📪
Nearby Facilities ℾ ✈ ⚓ ⚒ ◡ ♪ ♪
≈ Newquay

South facing park, 2 miles outside Newquay. FREE entertainment.

A Warm Welcome to

Parkdean Holidays

EMAIL: enquiries@parkdean.com
www.parkdeanholidays.com

BROCHURE HOTLINE
HOLIDAY HOMES & TOURING · ALL PARKS
01637 871111

Newquay
HOLIDAY PARKS

EMAIL: enquiries@newquay-hol-park.demon.co.uk
www.newquay-holiday-parks.co.uk

Fantastic Locations & Great Value for Money

---

olywell Bay
Holiday Park

2001 SILVER

Next to glorious sandy beach
- Touring/Camping Facilities • Marked Pitches
- Electric Hook-Ups • Free Showers
- Refurbished Club • Sky TV★ • Entertainment
- Maxi Million Club★ • Themed Play Area★
- Heated Pool • Amusements • Shop
- Take-Away • Launderette • Full Facilities
- Holiday Homes also available

 AA

HOLIDAY PARK

Newquay
Holiday Park

2001 GOLD

Superb location in south facing parkland
- Touring/Camping Facilities • Marked Pitches
- Electric Hook-Ups • Free Showers • Shop
- Refurbished Club • Sky TV★ • Entertainment
- Maxi Million Club★ • Heated Pool
- Themed Play Area★ • Restaurant★
- Take-Away • Launderette • Amusements
- Pool • Snooker • Crazy Golf • Pitch n' Putt
- Full Facilities • Holiday Homes available

 AA
HOLIDAY PARK

★ NEW IN 2001   ★ NEW FOR 2002

St Minver
Holiday Park

Set in grounds of old manor house
- Touring/Camping Facilities • Electric Hook-Ups
- Club & Bar • Sky TV • Entertainment
- Maxi Million Club • Indoor Pool
- Play Area for under 5's • Pool Tables
- Adventure Playground • Amusements
- Take-Away & Snack Bar • Crazy Golf
- Shop • Launderette • Full Facilities
- Holiday Homes available

 AA
HOLIDAY PARK

29

NEWQUAY

Resparva House Touring Park, Summercourt, Newquay, Cornwall, TR8 5AH.
Std: 01872 **Tel:** 510332
Email: touringpark@resparva.co.uk
Website: www.resparva.co.uk
Nearest Town/Resort Newquay
Directions From east on A30, ¼ mile west of Summercourt turn left signposted Chapel Town/ Summercourt. Site entrance is on the right.
Acreage 1 **Open** May **to** September
Access Good **Site** Level
Sites Available ⅄ ⚘ ⚑ **Total** 15
Facilities ∮ ⬛ ♨ ⌐ ⊙ 🛁 ⅃𝄪 ⊙┿🗐A
Nearby Facilities ⌐ ✔ ⌃ ↘ Ụ ⌇
ADULTS ONLY, secluded touring site with views over farm meadows. Pitches are separated by hedges. In the centre of Cornwall, near the A30.

NEWQUAY

Riverside Holiday Park, Gwills, Lane, Newquay, Cornwall, TR8 4PE.
Std: 01637 **Tel:** 873617
Std: 01637 **Fax:** 877051
Email: info@riversideholidaypark.co.uk
Website: www.riversideholidaypark.co.uk
Nearest Town/Resort Newquay
Directions Approx. 2½ miles from Newquay town centre, situated 1 mile off the A392 Newquay road.
Acreage 7 **Open** Easter **to** October
Access Good **Site** Level
Sites Available ⅄ ⚘ ⚑ **Total** 120
Facilities ∮ ⬛ ♨ ⌐ ⊙ 🛁 ⚑ ⊙ ☎
♐ Ợ ⊙ ⚑ ✕ ⛽ ⛩ ♠ ⌂ ⌐ ⊡ ⊟
Nearby Facilities ⌐ ✔ Ụ ⌇
♐ Newquay
In a peaceful position, beside the River Gannel. Only 2½ miles from the spectacular coastline and sandy beaches.

NEWQUAY

Rosecliston Park, Trevemper, Newquay, Cornwall, TR8 5JT.
Std: 01637 **Tel:** 830326
Email: enquiries@rosecliston.prestel.co.uk
Website: www.3mc.co.uk/rosecliston
Nearest Town/Resort Newquay
Directions Take A3075 from Newquay, Rosecliston is 1 mile on left.
Acreage 8 **Open** Whitsun **to** September
Access Good **Site** Lev/Slope
Sites Available ⅄ ⚘ ⚑ **Total** 130
Facilities ∮ ⬛ ♨ ⌐ ⊙ 🛁 ⚑ ⊡ ☎
♐ Ợ ⊙ ⚑ ✕ ⛽ ♠ ↘⊦⊟ ⊡ ⊟
Nearby Facilities ⌐ ✔ Ụ ⌇
♐ Newquay
Entertainment in July and August. All ages welcome.

NEWQUAY

Summer Lodge Holiday Park, Whitecross, Newquay, Cornwall, TR8 4LW.
Std: 01726 **Tel:** 860415
Std: 01726 **Fax:** 861490
Email: reservations@summerlodge.co.uk
Nearest Town/Resort Newquay
Directions A30 turn right at onto the A392. Approx 2 miles along the A392 you come to Whitecross, holiday park signposted left.
Acreage 10 **Open** Easter **to** September
Access Good **Site** Level
Sites Available ⅄ ⚘ ⚑ **Total** 50
Facilities ♿ ∮ ⬛ ♨ ⌐ ⊙ 🛁 ⚑ ⊡ ☎
♐ Ợ ⊙ ⚑ ✕ ⛽ ⛩ ♠ ⌂ ↘ ⊡ ⊟
Nearby Facilities ⌐ ✔ ⌃ Ụ
♐ Newquay
Set in beautiful countryside and ideally situated for touring. Short distance from beach and main town of Newquay.

NEWQUAY

Sunnyside Holiday Park, Quintrell Downs, Newquay, Cornwall, TR8 4PD.
Std: 01637 **Tel:** 873338
Std: 01637 **Fax:** 851403
Email: info@sunnyside.co.uk
Website: www.sunnyside.co.uk
Nearest Town/Resort Newquay
Directions From Newquay take the A392. Site is situated at Quintrell Downs, 2¼ miles from the town centre.
Acreage 11 **Open** April **to** 30 October
Sites Available ⅄ ⚑ **Total** 100
Facilities ⬛ ♨ ⌐ ⊙ 🛁 ⚑
⊡ ♐ Ợ ⊙ ⚑ ✕ Ụ ⛽ ♠ ⊛ ⊟A
Nearby Facilities ⌐ ✔ ⌃ ↘ Ụ ⌇
♐ Quintrell Downs
Cornwalls leading site for 18-35 age group. On site night club plus a minibus service to town.

NEWQUAY

The Meadow, Holywell Bay, Newquay, Cornwall, TR8 5PP.
Std: 01872 **Tel:** 572752
Website: www.holywellbeachholidays.co.uk
Nearest Town/Resort Newquay
Directions From Newquay take the A3075, after 3 miles turn right heading towards Redruth.
Acreage 1½ **Open** Easter **to** October
Access Good **Site** Level
Sites Available ⚘□ **Total** 6
Facilities ∮ ⬛ ♨ ⌐ ⊙ 🛁 ⚑ ☎ ⅃ Ợ ⊟
Nearby Facilities ⌐ ✔ Ụ
♐ Newquay
Sheltered site by the beach and a stream, in a small village.

Treloy Tourist Park *The Friendly Tourist Park*

Family site for touring caravans, tents and motorcaravans. Convenient for beaches & beauty spots.
We cater for Families and Couples only.

Facilties Include:
- Heated Swimming Pool • Licenced Club Family Room
- Free Entertainment • TV and Games Room • Shop
- Cafe/Takeaway • Laundry • FREE Showers
- Private Washing Cubicles • Baby Rooms
- Indoor Dishwashing Sinks • Adventure Playground
- Public Telephones • Electric Hook-ups (16 amp)
- Course Fishing nearby
- 15 miles from the Eden Project

Our own superb 9 HOLE PAR 32 GOLF COURSE is just 400 yards from the Park, with sculptured American style greens.
• Golf Shop • Clubs & Buggy for hire • Licenced Clubhouse •
• Concessionary green fees for golfers staying at the Park •

Please Write or Telephone for a Free Colour Brochure *Treloy Tourist Park*
NEWQUAY • CORNWALL • TR8 4JN • Telephone: 01637 872063 or 876279
E-mail: holidays@treloy.co.uk • Website: www.treloy.co.uk

NEWQUAY

Trebarber Farm, St. Columb Minor, Newquay, Cornwall, TR8 4JT.
Std: 01637 **Tel:** 873007
Std: 01637 **Fax:** 873007
Nearest Town/Resort Newquay
Directions 3 miles from Newquay on A3059, Newquay to St. Columb Major road.
Acreage 5 **Open** May to October
Access Good **Site** Level
Sites Available ▲ ♦ ⊞
Facilities ⊞ ♨ ⌐ ⊙ ⌿ ◢ ☐ ☎ ⓢ ⌸ ⊟ ▣
Nearby Facilities ⌐ ✓ ⊥ ⊀ U ⊅
⚓ Newquay
Quiet, ideal family centre for touring and beaches. Within walking distance of Porth reservoir (coarse fishing) and a golf course.

NEWQUAY

Treloy Tourist Park, Newquay, Cornwall, TR8 4JN.
Std: 01637 **Tel:** 872063/876279
Std: 01637 **Fax:** 872063/876279
Email: holiday@treloy.co.uk
Website: www.treloy.co.uk
Nearest Town/Resort Newquay
Directions 5 minutes from Newquay on the A3059 Newquay to St Columb Major Road
Acreage 11¼ **Open** April to September
Access Good **Site** Level
Sites Available ▲ ♦ ⊞ **Total** 141
Facilities ⌿ ⊟ ⊞ ⊞ ♨ ⌐ ⊙ ⌿ ◢ ☐ ☎ ⓢ ⊘ ♨ ⌷ ♠ ⚘ ⊟ ▣
Nearby Facilities ⌐ ✓ ⊥ ⊀ U ⊅
⚓ Newquay
Ideal site for touring the whole of Cornwall. Coarse fishing nearby. Own golf course ½ mile, concessionary Green Fees. Free entertainment.

NEWQUAY

Trenance Caravan & Chalet Park, Edgcumbe Avenue, Newquay, Cornwall, TR7 2JY.
Std: 01637 **Tel:** 873447
Std: 01637 **Fax:** 852677
Email: tony.hoyte@virgin.net
Website: www.mywebpage/nettrenance
Nearest Town/Resort Newquay
Directions On the main A3075 Newquay to Truro road, approx. 1 mile from Newquay town centre.
Acreage 12 **Open** April to 11 October
Access Good **Site** Sloping
Sites Available ▲ ♦ ⊞ **Total** 50
Facilities ⌿ ⊞ ♨ ⌐ ⊙ ⌿ ◢ ☐ ☎ ⓢ ⊘ ♨ ⌷ ♠ ⊟ ▣
Nearby Facilities ⌐ ✓ ⊥ ⊀ U ⊅
⚓ Newquay

NEWQUAY

Trencreek Holiday Park, Trencreek, Newquay, Cornwall, TR8 4NS.
Std: 01637 **Tel:** 874210
Website: www.trencreekholidaypark.co.uk
Nearest Town/Resort Newquay
Directions A392 to Quintrell Downs, turn right Newquay East/Porth, at Porth crossroads, ¾ mile outside Newquay, turn left to Trencreek.
Acreage 10 **Open** April to September
Access Good **Site** Level
Sites Available ▲ ♦ ⊞ **Total** 150
Facilities ♨ ⌿ ⊟ ⊞ ⊞ ♨ ⌐ ⊙ ⌿ ◢ ☐ ☎ ⓢ ⌷ ⊙ ♨ ⌷ ♠ ⊟ ⊟
Nearby Facilities ⌐ ✓ ⊥ ⊀ U ⊅ ⊿ ⚹
⚓ Newquay
Coarse fishing on site, 15 minutes footpath walk to Newquay, 1 mile by road.

NEWQUAY

Trethiggey Touring Park, Quintrell Downs, Newquay, Cornwall, TR8 4LG.
Std: 01637 **Tel:** 877672
Email: enquiries@trethiggey.co.uk
Website: www.trethiggey.co.uk
Nearest Town/Resort Newquay
Directions Follow main route signposted to Newquay and turn left onto the A3058 at Quintrell Downs, the site is in ¼ mile.
Acreage 15 **Open** 1st March to 1st January
Access Good **Site** Level
Sites Available ▲ ♦ ⊞ **Total** 157
Facilities ⌿ ⊟ ⊞ ♨ ⌐ ⊙ ⌿ ◢ ☐ ☎ ⓢ ⌷ ⊙ ♨ ⌷ ♠ ⊛ ⌸ ⊟ ▣
Nearby Facilities ⌐ ✓ ⊥ ⊀ U ⊅ ⊿
⚓ Quintrell Downs
Peaceful location with scenic views, close to several sandy beaches. NO overcrowding. Caravan storage. Touring caravans to let. Take-away food available and an off licence on site. Just 15 miles from the Eden Project.

NEWQUAY

Trevarrian Holiday Park, Mawgan Porth, Newquay, Cornwall, TR8 4AQ.
Std: 01637 **Tel:** 860381
Email: holidays@trevarrian.co.uk
Website: www.trevarrian.co.uk
Nearest Town/Resort Newquay
Directions Follow the A30 to Bodmin, continue until you go under a railway bridge then turn right. At the next roundabout take the Newquay road, pass the petrol station on the right and turn next right, continue to the T-Junction and turn right, Park is ½ a mile on the right.
Acreage 7 **Open** Easter to 1 October
Access Good **Site** Level
Sites Available ▲ ♦ ⊞ **Total** 180

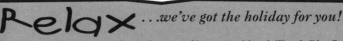

Trevella & Newperran

CARAVAN AND CAMPING PARK

TOURIST PARK

Both parks have spotless facilities including modern toilet and shower blocks with individual wash cubicles, razor points, babies room, hairdressing room, hairdriers, launderette, crazy golf, games room, TV room, cafe, shop and off licence, free heated swimming pools and adventure play areas.

DAVID BELLAMY CONSERVATION AWARD GOLD

THE FAMILY RUN HOLIDAY PARKS

Our parks are renowned for their cleanliness and hygiene and we spare no effort to maintain this reputation.
- Concessionary green fees at Perranporth's excellent links golf course.
- Nature reserve and well stocked lake at Trevella offers Free Fishing (no closed season).

VOTED TWO OF THE TOP 10 TOURING PARKS IN CORNWALL

TREVELLA PARK
20 CRANTOCK, NEWQUAY, CORNWALL TR8 5EW.   **TEL: 01637 830308**
www.trevella.co.uk

English Tourism Council
★★★★★
HOLIDAY PARK

Trevella just outside Newquay and its seven golden beaches. A breathtakingly beautiful secluded family park. As well as touring pitches there are holiday caravans for hire with toilet, shower and colour Satellite TV.

NEWPERRAN TOURIST PARK
20 REJERRAH, NEWQUAY, CORNWALL TR8 5QJ.   **TEL: 01872 572407**
www.newperran.co.uk

English Tourism Council
★★★★
TOURING PARK

Newperran has been developed from a small Cornish farm in a picturesque, beautifully cared for setting. It is a level park with perimeter pitching ideal for caravans, tents, motor homes and the perfect family holiday.

TELEPHONE FOR COLOUR BROCHURES OR WRITE FOR BROCHURE TO THE SITE OF YOUR CHOICE.

acilities ⚊ ♿ ☎ ⌂ ⊙ ⛃ ▣ ◻ ☕
▯ ◨ ⚌ ✗ ▽ ⑪ ♨ ∧ ☀ ✈ ▣ ⊡
Nearby Facilities ┌ ✈ ⚓ ↖ ∪ ⇃ ♪ ✳
✈ Newquay
Near the beach, surfing and the Eden
Project.

NEWQUAY
Trevella Park, Crantock, Newquay,
Cornwall, TR8 5EW.
Std: 01637 Tel: 830308
Website: www.trevella.co.uk
Nearest Town/Resort Newquay
Directions 2 miles south of Newquay on the
A3075, turn right signposted Crantock.
Acreage 15 Open Easter to October
Access Good Site Level
Sites Available ▲ ⊕ ⊟ Total 270
Facilities ⚊ ♿ ☎ ⌂ ⊙ ⛃ ▣ ◻ ☕
▯ ◨ ⚌ ✗ ▽ ⑪ ♨ ∧ ☀ ✈ ▣
Nearby Facilities ┌ ✈ ⚓ ↖ ∪ ⇃ ♪
✈ Newquay
¼ mile from the beach, concessionary green
fees, own fishing lake. AA 5 Pennants.

NEWQUAY
Trevornick Holiday Park, Holywell Bay,
Newquay, Cornwall, TR8 5PW.
Std: 01637 Tel: 830531
Std: 01637 Fax: 831000
Email: info@trevornick.co.uk
Website: www.trevornick.co.uk
Nearest Town/Resort Newquay
Directions Take Newquay to Perrenporth
A3075 road. Take turning for Cubert/
Holywell.
Acreage 30 Open Easter to September
Access Good Site Level
Sites Available ▲ ⊕ ⊟ Total 500
Facilities ⚊ ♿ ☎ ⌂ ⊙ ⛃ ▣ ◻ ☕
▯ ◨ ⚌ ✗ ▽ ⑪ ♨ ∧ ☀ ✈ ▣ ⊡
Nearby Facilities ┌ ✈ ⚓ ↖ ∪ ♪

✈ Newquay
Next to the beach, stunning sea views.
Tourers and static tents. Golf and fishing on
site.

NEWQUAY
Watergate Bay Holiday Park, Watergate
Bay, Newquay, Cornwall, TR8 4AD.
Std: 01637 Tel: 860387
Std: 01637 Fax: 860387
Email: watergatebay@email.com
Website: www.watergatebay.co.uk
Nearest Town/Resort Newquay
Directions 4 miles north of Newquay on the
B3276 Coast Road to Padstow. Follow
directions shown from Watergate Bay.
Acreage 30 Open March to November
Access Good Site Level
Sites Available ▲ ⊕ ⊟ Total 171
Facilities ⚊ ♿ ☎ ⌂ ⊙ ⛃ ▣ ◻ ☕
▯ ◨ ⚌ ✗ ▽ ⑪ ♨ ∧ ☀ ✈ ▣ ⊡ ◻
Nearby Facilities ┌ ✈ ↖ ∪ ♪
✈ Newquay
½ mile from Watergate Bay in a rural location
in an area of outstanding natural beauty.

NEWQUAY
White Acres Country Park, Whitecross,
Newquay, Cornwall, TR8 4LW.
Std: 01726 Tel: 860220
Std: 01726 Fax: 860877
Email: reception@whiteacres.co.uk
Website: www.whiteacres.co.uk
Nearest Town/Resort Newquay
Directions Turn off the A30 onto the A392
in the direction of Newquay. Park is 6 miles
outside Newquay at Whitecross Junction.
Acreage 120 Open 23 March to 26
October
Access Good Site Level
Sites Available ▲ ⊕ ◻ Total 100
Facilities ⚊ ♿ ☎ ⌂ ⊙ ⛃ ▣ ◻ ☕
▯ ◨ ⚌ ✗ ▽ ⑪ ♨ ∧ ☀ ✈ ▣ ⊡

Nearby Facilities ┌ ✈ ⚓ ↖ ∪ ⇃
✈ Newquay
Fifteen coarse fishing lakes. Six beaches
within 8 miles. 10 miles from the Eden
Project.

PADSTOW
Carnevas Farm Holiday Park, Carnevas
Farm, St. Merryn, Padstow, Cornwall,
PL28 8PN.
Std: 01841. Tel: 520230
Std: 01841 Fax: 520230
Nearest Town/Resort Padstow
Directions Take Newquay coast road from
Padstow, turn right at Tredrea Inn just before
getting to Porthcothan Bay. Site ¼ mile up
road on right.
Acreage 8 Open April to October
Access Good Site Lev/Slope
Sites Available ▲ ⊕ ⊟ Total 198
Facilities ⚊ ♿ ☎ ⌂ ⊙ ⛃ ▣ ◻ ☕
▯ ◨ ⚌ ✗ ▽ ⑪ ♨ ∧ ☀ ✈ ▣
Nearby Facilities ┌ ✈ ↖ ∪ ⇃ ♪
✈ Newquay
Near numerous sandy beaches in lovely
rural position, ideal touring, well run family
park. AA 3 Pennants and ETB 4 Star Park.

PADSTOW
Dennis Cove Camping, Dennis Cove,
Padstow, Cornwall, PL28 8DR.
Std: 01841 Tel: 532349
Nearest Town/Resort Padstow
Directions Signposted off A389 on outskirts
of Padstow Town.
Acreage 5 Open April to September
Access Fair Site Lev/Slope
Sites Available ▲ ⊕ ⊟ Total 62
Facilities ⚊ ♿ ☎ ⌂ ⊙ ⛃ ▣ ◻ ☕
▯ ◨ ⚌ ▽ ☀ ✈ ▣
Nearby Facilities ┌ ✈ ⚓ ↖ ∪ ⇃ ♪
✈ Bodmin Parkway
Site adjoins Camel Estuary and town of

Padstow's top rated caravan site. Easy access to this quiet rural setting of 13½ acres for 100 units. Panoramic views over the Camel Estuary and countryside. Footpath to Padstow. Assessed 'Excellent', clean shower blocks with some individual cubicals. En-suite pitches with private WC and hand basin. Picnic tables. Food and gas accessory shop. Doggy area. Many sandy beaches from 1½ miles.
Friendly Welcoming from the resident proprietor.

**Padstow, Cornwall PL28 8LE
Tel/Fax: 01841 532061**

Padstow. Scenic views and ideal base for variety of watersports. 5 Touring caravan pitches only. No large groups without prior reservation.

PADSTOW
Maribou Holiday Park, St. Merryn, Padstow, Cornwall, PL28 8QA.
Std: 01841 Tel: 520520
Std: 01841 Fax: 521154
Nearest Town/Resort Padstow
Directions Signposted off the B3274 4 miles from Padstow.
Open Easter **to** October
Access Good **Site** Level
Sites Available ▲ ⊕ □ **Total** 100
Facilities ∤ ▥ ♨ ୮ ⊙ ᵴ ᵹ ◻ ☜
♨ ⛱ ✕ ♀ ⚑ ▯ ᵹ ▤ ⬛
Nearby Facilities ୮ ✓ ⚓ ↘ ∪ ⋡
⇌ Bodmin Parkway
Family run site near to seven beaches. Ideal touring.

PADSTOW
Mother Ivey's Bay Caravan Park, Trevose Head, Padstow, Cornwall, PL28 8SL.
Std: 01841 **Tel:** 520990
Std: 01841 **Fax:** 520550
Email: info@motheriveysbay.com
Website: www.motheriveysbay.com
Nearest Town/Resort Padstow
Directions Signposted from the B3276 Padstow to Newquay coast road.
Acreage 30 **Open** April **to** October
Access Good **Site** Lev/Slope
Sites Available ▲ ⊕ ⚘ **Total** 350
Facilities ∤ ▥ ☷ ♨ ୮ ⊙ ᵴ ᵹ ◻ ☜
♨ ⚅ ⛱ ▯ ᵹ ▤ ⬛
Nearby Facilities ୮ ✓ ⚓ ∪
⇌ Newquay
Stunning coastal setting overlooking the beach.

PADSTOW
Music Water Touring Park, Rumford, Wadebridge, Cornwall, PL27 7SJ.
Std: 01841 Tel: 540257
Std: 01841 Fax: 540257
Nearest Town/Resort Padstow
Directions Wadebridge A39 to roundabout take B3274 signposted Padstow. Turn left after 2 miles, park is 500yds on the right.
Acreage 7 **Open** April **to** October
Access Good **Site** Level
Sites Available ▲ ⊕ ⚘ **Total** 145
Facilities ∤ ▥ ♨ ୮ ⊙ ᵴ ᵹ ◻ ☜
♨ ⊙ ⛱ ♀ ⚑ ▯ ↘ ▤ ⬛
Nearby Facilities ୮ ✓ ∪ ⋡
⇌ Bodmin
Clean, friendly, family site with scenic views. Splash pool. Ideal walking.

PADSTOW
Old MacDonald's Farm, Porthcothan Bay, Padstow, Cornwall, PL28 8LW.
Std: 01841 **Tel:** 540829
Email: karen@old-macdonalds-farm.co.uk
Website: www.old-macdonalds-farm.co.uk
Nearest Town/Resort Padstow/Newquay
Directions Just off the B3276 coast road. 5 miles south of Padstow and 9 miles north of Newquay.
Acreage 3½ **Open** All Year
Access Good **Site** Level
Sites Available ▲ ⊕ ⚘ **Total** 40
Facilities ⚅ ∤ ▥ ♨ ୮ ⊙ ♨ ✕ ▯ ↘ ⬛
Nearby Facilities
½ mile to the beach. Campers have free access to old MacDonald's Farm Park and can help feed the animals. Pony rides, crazy golf and a miniature railway on site. Dutch speaking owners.

PADSTOW
Padstow Holiday Park, Cliffdowne, Padstow, Cornwall, PL28 8LB.
Std: 01841 **Tel:** 532289
Website: www.padstowholidaypark.co.uk
Nearest Town/Resort Padstow
Directions From Wadebridge take the A38 to Padstow, site is on the right 1 mile before Padstow.
Acreage 3 **Open** All Year
Access Good **Site** Level
Sites Available ▲ ⊕ ⚘ **Total** 50
Facilities ∤ ▥ ☷ ♨ ୮ ⊙ ᵹ ᵴ ◻
♨ ⊙ ⛱ ᵹ ⬛
Nearby Facilities ୮ ✓ ⚓ ↘ ∪ ⋡
⇌ Bodmin
Quiet location with no club or bar. 1 mile from a sandy cove. Footpath to Padstow (1 mile). ½ mile from a Tesco store.

PADSTOW
Seagull Tourist Park, St Merryn, Padstow, Cornwall, PL28 8PT.
Std: 01841 **Tel:** 520117
Nearest Town/Resort Padstow
Acreage 8 **Open** Easter/1 April **to** End Oct
Access Good **Site** Level
Sites Available ▲ ⊕ ⚘ **Total** 100
Facilities ∤ ▥ ♨ ୮ ⊙ ᵴ ᵹ ◻
♨ ⊙ ⛱ ✕ ▯ ⬛
Nearby Facilities ୮ ✓ ⚓ ↘ ∪ ⋡ ♞
⇌ Bodmin Parkway
Seven golden sandy beaches within 10 minutes drive. Small family park, quiet farmland. Coastal walks, golf, fishing, boating, surf and cycle hire.

DSTOW

ethern Touring Park, Padstow,
nwall, PL28 8LE.
: 01841 **Tel:** 532061
01841 **Fax:** 532061
ail: camping.trerethern@btinternet.com
osite: www.btinternet.com/
mping.trerethern
rest Town/Resort Padstow
ctions On A389 1 mile south south west
adstow.
eage 13¼ **Open** April to October
ess Good **Site** Level
s Available ⚠ ⚎ ⚎ **Total** 100
ilities ⚐ ⚐ ▯ ▯ ▯ ⚐ ⚐ ⚐ ⚐ ⚐ ⚐
⚐ ⚐ ⚐ ⚐ ⚐
rby Facilities ▶ ✦ ⚐ ✦ ∪ ⚐ ⚐
oramic views, several sandy beaches
in 3 miles. Extra large pitches, footpath
adstow. En-suite pitches. No statics.
arate dog exercise area. Free brochure.

R

Sands Holiday Park, Par Beach, St.
tell Bay, Cornwall, PL24 2AS.
01726. **Tel:** 812868 **Fax:** 817899
ail: holidays@parsands.co.uk
bsite: www.parsands.co.uk
rest Town/Resort St. Austell/Fowey
ctions 4 miles east of St Austell on road
owey A3082.

Acreage 12 **Open** April to October
Access Good **Site** Level
Sites Available ⚠ ⚎ ⚎ **Total** 200
Facilities ⚐ ⚐ ▯ ▯ ⚐ ⚐ ⚐ ⚐ ⚐ ⚐
▯ ⚐ ⚐ ▯ ⚐ ⚐ ⚐ ⚐ ⚐ ⚐ ⚐
Nearby Facilities ▶ ✦ ⚐ ✦ ∪ ⚐
⚐ Par
Alongside safe sandy beach and freshwater
wildlife lake. Indoor heated swimming pool
with aquaslide. Luxury extra wide caravan
for hire. Rose Award. Please see our colour
advertisement.

PENTEWAN

Pengrugla Caravan Park, Pentewan, St.
Austell, Cornwall, PL26 6BT.
Std: 01726 **Tel:** 843485
Std: 01726 **Fax:** 844142
Email: info@pentewan.co.uk
Website: www.pentewan.co.uk
Nearest Town/Resort Mevagissey
Directions From the A390 at St. Austell take
the B3273 towards Mevagissey. After 5 miles
at the top of a long hill turn right and follow
brown tourism signs. Entrance is on the left.
Acreage 12 **Open** April to October
Access Good **Site** Level
Sites Available ⚠ ⚎ ⚎ **Total** 89
Facilities ⚐ ⚐ ▯ ⚐ ⚐ ⚐ ⚐ ⚐ ⚐
⚐ ⚐ ⚐ ⚐ ⚐
Nearby Facilities ▶ ✦ ⚐ ✦ ∪ ⚐ ⚐
⚐ St. Austell

Large individual pitches. Ideal base for visits
to the beautiful and famous Lost Gardens
of Heligan and The Eden Project. A peaceful
and tranquil site with arrangement to allow
customers full use of all the facilities of
nearby sister site Pentewan Sands.

PENTEWAN

Pentewan Sands Holiday Park,
Pentewan, St. Austell, Cornwall, PL26
6BT.
Std: 01726 **Tel:** 843485
Std: 01726 **Fax:** 844142
Email: info@pentewan.co.uk
Website: www.pentewan.co.uk
Nearest Town/Resort Mevagissey
Directions From A390 at St. Austell take
B3273 south towards Mevagissey. Entrance
is 4 miles on left.
Acreage 32 **Open** April to October
Access Good **Site** Level
Sites Available ⚠ ⚎ ⚎ **Total** 480
Facilities ⚐ ⚐ ▯ ▯ ⚐ ⚐ ⚐ ⚐ ⚐ ⚐
⚐ ▯ ⚐ ⚐ ⚐ ⚐ ⚐ ⚐ ⚐ ⚐ ⚐ ⚐
Nearby Facilities ▶ ✦ ⚐ ✦ ∪ ⚐ ⚐
⚐ St. Austell
Large individual marked pitches (many with
electric hook-ups) on well equipped site with
own safe sandy beach. Ideal for water sports
and a convenient base for visits to The Eden
Project and Lost Gardens of Heligan. NO
dogs, NO single sex parties and NO jetskis.

PENZANCE

eigh Farm Site, Boleigh Farm,
horna, St. Buryan, Penzance,
nwall, TR19 6BN.
l: 01736 **Tel:** 810305
arest Town/Resort Penzance
ections On the B3315 5 miles from
nzance, first farm house after Lamorna
ve turning.
en April **to** October
cess Good **Site** Sloping
es Available ▲ ⊞ ⌂ **Total** 30
cilities ⅏ ♨ ⌐ ☉ ☎ ⅋ ⅃ ⌖ ⊡
arby Facilities
Penzance

PENZANCE

rris Farm, Gulval, Penzance, Cornwall,
20 8XD.
l: 01736 **Tel:** 365806
l: 01736 **Fax:** 365806
arest Town/Resort Penzance
ections Leave A30 turning right at
owlas on road to Luogvan B3309 to
stlegate. Follow road to Chysauster
cient village.
reage 8 **Open** May **to** October
cess Good **Site** Sloping
es Available ▲ ⊞ ⌂
cilities ⅏ ♨ ☎ ⌖ ⊡
arby Facilities ⚓ ⚲ ∪
Penzance

PENZANCE

nneggy Cove Holiday Park, Higher
nneggy, Rosudgeon, Penzance,
nwall, TR20 9AU.
l: 01736 **Tel:** 763453
l: 01736 **Fax:** 763453
ail: enquiries@kenneggycove.co.uk
bsite: www.kenneggycove.co.uk
arest Town/Resort Penzance
ections Midway between Penzance and
ston on the A394, turn south onto signed
e, go down ½ mile.
reage 4 **Open** Easter **to** End October
cess Good **Site** Level
es Available ▲ ⊞ ⌂ **Total** 70
cilities ⅀ ⅏ ♨ ⌐ ☉ ⅃ ⌂ ◻ ☎
⅋ ☉ ⚑ ✕ ⊓ ♠ ⊞ ✳ ⌖ ⊡
arby Facilities ⚓ ⚲ ⚖ ∪ ↗
Penzance

Sea views. Near the South West Coastal
Path and a safe secluded beach. Centrally
situated for West Cornwall attractions.

PENZANCE

River Valley Country Park, Relubbus,
Penzance, Cornwall, TR20 9ER.
Std: 01736 **Tel:** 763398
Std: 01736 **Fax:** 763398
Email: rivervalley@surfbay.dircon.co.uk
Website: www.rivervalley.co.uk
Nearest Town/Resort Penzance
Directions From the A30 at St. Michaels
Mount roundabout, take the A394 towards
Helston. Turn left at the next roundabout
onto the B3280 to Relubbus, after approx.
3 miles turn left after the small bridge to River
Valley.
Acreage 18 **Open** March **to** October
Access Good **Site** Level
Sites Available ▲ ⊞ ⌂ **Total** 150
Facilities ⅃ ⌐ ⅏ ♨ ⌐ ☉ ⅃ ⌂ ◻ ☎
⅀ ☉ ⚑ ⌖ ⊡
Nearby Facilities ⌐ ⚲ ⚖ ∪
⚓ Penzance
Partly wooded park, situated in one of the
most picturesque valleys in Cornwall.
Alongside a small trout stream. Beaches
nearby. Ideal touring base.

PENZANCE

Wayfarers Caravan & Camping Park, St.
Hilary, Penzance, Cornwall, TR20 9EF.
Std: 01736 **Tel:** Penzance 763326
Email: wayfarers@eurobell.co.uk
Website: www.cornwall-online.co.uk/
wayfarers
Nearest Town/Resort Marazion
Directions 2 miles east of Marazion on
B3280.
Acreage 4 **Open** March **to** January
Access Good **Site** Level
Sites Available ▲ ⊞ ⌂ **Total** 60
Facilities ⅃ ⅏ ♨ ⌐ ☉ ⅃ ⌂ ◻ ☎
⅀ ☉ ⚑ ✕ ⊓ ⌖ ⊡
Nearby Facilities ⌐ ⚲ ⚖ ∪ ↗ ↗ ✕
⚓ Penzance
Select, peaceful holiday park. Couple only
£42.50 per week including EHU. Discount
in holiday homes. Short breaks. Immaculate
facilities. Take-away food available. AA 3
Pennant. Members of Cornwall Tourist
Board.

PERRANPORTH

Penrose Farm Touring Park,
Goonhavern, Truro, Cornwall, TR4 9QF.
Std: 01872 **Tel:** 573185
Email: penrosefarm2001@hotmail.com
Website: www.members.xoom.com/
penrosefarm/
Nearest Town/Resort Perranporth
Directions Leave A30 onto the B3285
signed Perranporth, site 1½ miles on the left.
Acreage 9 **Open** April **to** September
Access Good **Site** Level
Sites Available ▲ ⊞ ⌂ **Total** 100
Facilities ⚫ ⅃ ⅏ ⅏ ♨ ⌐ ☉ ⅃ ◻ ☎
⅀ ☉ ⚑ ⊓ ⌖ ⊡ ⊡
Nearby Facilities ⌐ ⚲ ⚖ ∪ ↗ ↗ ↗
⚓ Newquay/Truro
Quiet, clean and sheltered park with animal
centre and adventure play area. Good
spacing. Close to Perranporth beach. Award
winning private 'Superloos'.

PERRANPORTH

Perran Sands Holiday Park,
Perranporth, Cornwall, TR6 0AQ.
Std: 01872 **Tel:** 573742
Std: 01872 **Fax:** 571158
Email: admin_perran_sands@rank.com
Website: www.havenholidays.com
Nearest Town/Resort Perranporth
Directions Take the A30 through Cornwall.
3 miles after Mitchell turn right onto the
B3285 towards Perranporth. Perran Sands
is on the right just before Perranporth.
Acreage 25 **Open** 30 April **to** 28 Oct
Access Good **Site** Level
Sites Available ▲ ⊞ ⌂ **Total** 450
Facilities ⚫ ⅃ ⅏ ♨ ⌐ ☉ ⅃ ◻ ☎
⅀ ☉ ⚑ ✕ ⊓ ♠ ⊓ ⚑ ✳ ⌖ ⊡ ⊡
Nearby Facilities ⌐ ⚲ ⚖ ∪ ↗ ↗ ✕
⚓ Truro
On a cliff top amid dunes and grassland. A
short walk from the beach.

PERRANPORTH

Perran Springs Touring Park,
Goonhavern, Truro, Cornwall, TR4 9QG.
Std: 01872 **Tel:** 540568
Std: 01872 **Fax:** 540568
Email: perransprings@cwcom.net
Website: www.perransprings.co.uk
Nearest Town/Resort Perranporth

Directions Leave the A30 and turn right onto the B3285 signposted Perranporth. Follow the brown tourism signs marked 'Perran Springs' for 1½ miles. Entrance and flags will then be clearly seen.
Acreage 21 **Open** April **to** October
Access Good **Site** Level
Sites Available ▲ � ⊟
Facilities ⌂ ⏚ 🆖 ⚓ ┌ ☉ ❑ 🍴
🎾 🎮 ⓪ ❀ ✗ ▥ 📶 ⛁
Nearby Facilities ┌ ✦ ⚓ ∪ ♪
≈ Truro
Award winning, friendly, quiet family park offering: FREE FISHING on our Coarse Fishing Lake, Take-away, Eurotents, Caravan Holiday Homes, Spacious Level Pitches and Panoramic Countryside Views.

PERRANPORTH
Perranporth Camping & Touring Park, Budnick, Perranporth, Cornwall, TR6 0DB.
Std: 01872 **Tel:** 572174
Nearest Town/Resort Perranporth
Directions ½ mile north east of Perranporth town centre off the B3285 Perranporth to Newquay road.
Acreage 6½ **Open** Easter **to** End Sept
Access Good **Site** Lev/Slope
Sites Available ▲ � ⊟ **Total** 180
Facilities ⌂ ⏚ 🆖 ⚓ ┌ ☉ ❑ 🍴
🎾 ⓪ ❀ ▥ 📶 ⛁ ⓐ
Nearby Facilities ┌ ∪ ♪
≈ Truro/Newquay
In a sheltered, well drained valley. ½ mile to the town and beach. Adjacent to a golf course. Take-away food available.

POLPERRO
Killigarth Manor Caravan Park, Polperro, Looe, Cornwall, PL13 2JQ.
Std: 01503. **Tel:** 272216
Std: 01503 **Fax:** 272065

Website: www.killigarth.co.uk
Nearest Town/Resort Polperro
Directions From Looe take the A387, after approx 4 miles turn left, signposted Killigarth. Park is about 400yds on the left.
Acreage 7 **Open** Easter **to** October
Access Good **Site** Level
Sites Available ▲ � ⊟ **Total** 202
Facilities ⌂ ⏚ 🆖 ⚓ ┌ ☉ ❑ 🍴
🎾 ⓪ ❀ ✗ ▥ ⚓ ⁂ ❀ 📶 ⛁ ⓐ
Nearby Facilities ┌ ✦ ⚓ ∪ ♪ ♪
≈ Looe
Set in an area of outstanding natural beauty. AA Holiday Centre.

POLZEATH
South Winds Camping & Caravan Park, Old Polzeath Road, Polzeath, Near Wadebridge, Cornwall, PL27 6QU.
Std: 01208 **Tel:** 863267
Std: 01208 **Fax:** 862080
Website: www.rockinfo.co.uk
Nearest Town/Resort Polzeath
Acreage 7 **Open** Easter **to** October
Access Good **Site** Level
Sites Available ▲ � ⊟ **Total** 100
Facilities ⌂ ⏚ 🆖 ⚓ ┌ ☉ ❑ 🍴
▥ ⓪ ❀ ⚓ ❀ 📶 ⛁ ⓐ
Nearby Facilities ┌ ✦ ⚓ ∪ ♪ ♪ ⚲
≈ Bodmin Road
Outstanding views of countryside and sea.

POLZEATH
Tristram Caravan & Camping Park, Polzeath, Nr Wadebridge, Cornwall, PL27 6SR.
Std: 01208 **Tel:** 863267/862215
Std: 01208 **Fax:** 862080
Website: www.rockinfo.co.uk
Nearest Town/Resort Wadebridge
Acreage 5 **Open** Easter **to** November
Access Good **Site** Level

Sites Available ▲ � ⊟ **Total** 130
Facilities ⌂ ⏚ 🆖 ⚓ ┌ ☉ ❑ 🍴 ⓐ ⛁
🎾 ▥ ⓪ ❀ ✗ ♀ ⚓ ❀ 📶 ⛁ ⓐ
Nearby Facilities ┌ ✦ ⚓ ∪ ♪ ♪
≈ Bodmin Parkway
Cliff top site. Direct access onto Polze
beach.

PORTHTOWAN
Porthtowan Tourist Park, Mile Hill, Porthtowan, Truro, Cornwall, TR4 8TY.
Std: 01209 **Tel:** 890256
Std: 01209 **Fax:** 890256
Nearest Town/Resort Porthtowan/Trur
Directions Take signpost off A30 Redr
Porthtowan. Cross the A30, through no
country to T-Junction, right up the hill, p
Woodlands Restaurant, park is on the le
Acreage 5½ **Open** Easter **to** October
Access Good **Site** Level
Sites Available ▲ � ⊟ **Total** 50
Facilities ⌂ ⏚ 🆖 ⚓ ┌ ☉ ❑ ⓐ
🎾 ⓪ ❀ ⚓ ❀ 📶 ▥ ⛁ ⓐ
Nearby Facilities ┌ ✦ ⚓ ∪ ♪ ♪
≈ Redruth
A level site with spacious pitches in an a
of outstanding natural beauty. Just ½ a r
from sandy, surf beach. Ideal touring ba

PORTHTOWAN
Rose Hill Touring Park, Porthtowan, Truro, Cornwall, TR4 8AR.
Std: 01209 **Tel:** 890802
Email: reception@rosehillcamping.co.u
Website: www.rosehillcamping.co.uk
Nearest Town/Resort St. Agnes
Directions From the A30 take the B3²
signposted St. Agnes and Porthtowan, a
1 mile turn left signed Porthtowan. Site
100 yards past beach road.
Acreage 3 **Open** April **to** October
Access Good **Site** Level

STUNNING LOCATIONS CORNWALL

POLZEATH

EXCELLENT FACILITIES

One of the most spectacular, safest and best surfing beaches in Cornwall. Visitors return each year to enjoy the beauty and safety of its golden sands and clear blue sea.

Tristram

South Winds

We have two prime sites at Polzeath. Tristram above right and shown on the aerial picture is on the gently sloping cliff overlooking the beach with direct access to the beach. The site is private and safe for children. It also has its own shop, restaurant and take away on site. South Winds above left is different, families like the peace and quiet with beautiful sea and panoramic rural views yet only half a mile from the beach. Both sites have modern toilets, showers and laundry facilities.

01208 863267 (South Winds)
01208 862215 (Tristram)
Fax: **01208 862080**   **www.rockinfo.co.uk**

South Winds, Polzeath, Cornwall PL27 6QU

AA

APPROVED Cornwall ACCOMMODATION

MasterCard   VISA

41

PORTHTOWN TOURIST PARK

Mile Hill, Porthtowan, Truro, Cornwall TR4 8TY

(01209) 890256

A QUIET, FAMILY RUN SITE SET IN AN AREA OF OUTSTANDING NATURAL BEAUTY. WE OFFER SPACIOUS LEVEL PITCHES WITHIN FOUR FIELDS COVERING 5 ACRES. IDEAL FOR FAMILIES, WITH ADVENTURE PLAYGROUND AND PLAY AREA, JUST ½ A MILE FROM A SANDY SURFING BEACH, COASTAL FOOTPATH AND MINERAL TRAMWAY TRAILS. CENTRAL FOR TOURING CORNWALL.

WRITE OR PHONE FOR A BROCHURE

Sites Available ▲ ⊟ ⊞ **Total** 50
Facilities & ╱ ⊟ ⓊⒷ ▲ ℾ ☉ ⌣ ⤵ ◢ ▢ ☎
♨ ⓪ ☎ ✕ ▢ ⓓ
Nearby Facilities ┏ ╱ ⌕ ⤶ U ⌗
⇌ Redruth
Friendly family run site, sheltered and situated in the coastal village of Porthtowan. Just 4 minutes level walk to the beach, pubs, restaurants and coastal path. 5 Star immaculate toilet block. Fresh crusty bread and croissants baked daily. No clubhouse or games room, just a bit of paradise surrounded by trees and bird song. Close to a sandy beach.

PORTREATH

Tehidy Holiday Park, Harris Mill, Redruth, Cornwall, TR16 4JQ.
Std: 01209 **Tel:** 216489
Std: 01209 **Fax:** 216489
Nearest Town/Resort Portreath
Directions Take Redruth Porthtowan exit from A30. Take Porthtowan North Country exit from double roundabout, turn left at first crossroads. Cross next two crossroads Tehidy Holiday Park 200 yards on left pass Cornish Arms Public House.
Acreage 1 **Open** Easter **to** October
Access Good **Site** Level
Sites Available ▲ ⊟ ⊞ **Total** 18
Facilities ╱ ⓊⒷ ▲ ℾ ☉ ⌣ ⤵ ◢ ▢ ☎
♨ ℞ ⓪ ☎ ▥ 🏃 ⋀ ⊛ ⤶ ▢ ⓓ
Nearby Facilities ┏ ╱ ⌕ ⤶ U ⌗
⇌ Redruth
Near beach, scenic views, ideal touring.

PORTSCATHO

Trewince Touring, Trewince Manor, Portscatho, Truro, Cornwall, TR2 5ET.
Std: 01872 **Tel:** 580289
Std: 01872 **Fax:** 580694
Email: touring@trewince.co.uk
Website: www.trewince.co.uk
Nearest Town/Resort Portscatho
Directions From Portscatho take the road to St. Anthony Head, Trewince is ¾ miles past the church.
Acreage 3 **Open** July **to** September
Access Good **Site** Lev/Slope
Sites Available ▲ ⊟ ⊞ **Total** 25
Facilities ╱ ⓊⒷ ▲ ℾ ☉ ⌣ ⤵ ◢ ▢ ☎
℞ ☎ ✕ ▥ 🏃 ⌕ ⤶ ▢ ⓓ
Nearby Facilities ┏ ╱ ⌕ ⤶ U ⌗ ♠
⇌ Truro
Near the beach with sea views. Own quay and moorings.

PRAA SANDS

Lower Pentreath, Lower Pentreath Farm, Praa Sands, Penzance, Cornwall, TR20 9TL.
Std: 01736 **Tel:** 763221
Email: andrew.wearne@tinyworld.co.uk
Nearest Town/Resort Penzance

Directions From Penzance take the A394 towards Helston. Go through Rosudgeon, take Pentreath Lane immediately before the garage on the right hand side, we are at the bottom of the hill.
Acreage 1 **Open** April **to** October
Access Good **Site** Lev/Slope
Sites Available ▲ ⊟ ⊞ **Total** 15
Facilities ⓊⒷ ▲ ℾ ☉ ⌣ ⤵ ◢ ☎ ⤶ ▢
Nearby Facilities ┏ ╱ ⌕ ⤶ U
⇌ Penzance
Small friendly site, 400 yards from the beach.

REDRUTH

Globe Vale Caravan Park, Radnor, Redruth, Cornwall, TR16 4BH.
Std: 01209 **Tel:** 891183
Email: globe@ukgo.com
Website: www.globe.ukgo.com
Nearest Town/Resort Portreath
Directions Take the Portreath and Porthtowan exit off the A30, at the double roundabout take the third exit to North Country. At the crossroads turn right signposted Radnor and the site.
Acreage 9 **Open** Feb **to** November
Access Good **Site** Lev/Slope
Sites Available ▲ ⊟ ⊞ **Total** 28
Facilities ╱ ⓊⒷ ▲ ℾ ☉ ⌣ ⤵ ◢ ▢ ☎
♨ ☎ ✕ ▢ ▥ ⋀ ⤶ ▢ ⓓ
Nearby Facilities ┏ ╱ ⌕ U
⇌ Redruth
6 minutes from Portreath and Porthtowan beach. Ideal base for touring the whole of Cornwall. Surfing beach of Newquay only 20 minutes away.

REDRUTH

Lanyon Holiday Park, Loscombe Lane, Four Lanes, Near Redruth, Cornwall, TR16 6LP.
Std: 01209 **Tel:** 313474
Std: 01209 **Fax:** 313422
Email: jamierielly@supanet.com
Website:
www.lanyoncaravanandcampingpark.co.uk
Nearest Town/Resort Redruth
Directions From Redruth take the B3297 towards Helston for approx. 2 miles, as you enter the small village of Four Lanes park is 400 yards.
Acreage 14 **Open** February **to** January
Access Good **Site** Level
Sites Available ▲ ⊟ ⊞ **Total** 50
Facilities ╱ ⊟ ⊟ ⓊⒷ ▲ ℾ ☉ ⌣ ▢ ☎
℞ ☎ ✕ ▥ 🏃 ⋀ ⊛ ⤶ ▢ ⓓ
Nearby Facilities ┏ ╱ ⌕ ⤶ U ⌗ ♠ ♪
⇌ Redruth
Surrounded by open countryside. Ideal touring base with Falmouth, Helston, Truro and Newquay only a short drive away. 6 miles to the nearest beach.

REDRUTH

Tresaddern Holiday Park, St. Day, Redruth, Cornwall, TR16 5JR.
Std: 01209 **Tel:** 820459
Email: gillroberts53@yahoo.com
Website: www.tresaddern.co.uk
Nearest Town/Resort Redruth
Directions From A30 2 miles east of Redruth take A3047 Scorrier, in 400yds B3298 Falmouth, site 1½ miles on right.
Acreage 3 **Open** Easter **to** October
Access Good **Site** Level
Sites Available ▲ ⊟ ⊞ **Total** 25
Facilities ╱ ⓊⒷ ▲ ℾ ☉ ⌣ ◢ ▢ ☎
℞ ⓪ ☎ ⋀ ⊛ ⤶ ▢
Nearby Facilities ┏ ╱ U
⇌ Redruth
Quiet rural site, central for touring south Cornwall.

REDRUTH

Wheal Rose Caravan & Camping Park, Wheal Rose, Scorrier, Redruth, Cornwall, TR16 5DD.
Std: 01209 **Tel:** 891496
Std: 01209 **Fax:** 891496
Email: les@whealrosecaravanpark.co.uk
Website:
www.whealrosecaravanpark.co.uk
Nearest Town/Resort Porthtowan/Redruth
Directions From the A30 take the Scorrier slip road and turn right at the Plume of Feathers, turn next left and the park is 100 yards on the left.
Acreage 6½ **Open** March **to** December
Access Good **Site** Level
Sites Available ▲ ⊟ ⊞ **Total** 50
Facilities & ╱ ⊟ ⓊⒷ ▲ ℾ ☉ ⌣ ⤵ ◢ ▢ ☎
♨ ℞ ⓪ ☎ ▥ 🏃 ⋀ ⊛ ⤶ ▢ ⓓ
Nearby Facilities ┏ ╱ U
⇌ Redruth
Central for all West Cornwall attractions. 12 miles from Newquay, 8 miles from Truro and 30 miles from Lands End.

RUAN MINOR

The Friendly Camp, Tregullas Farm, Penhale, Ruan Minor, Helston, Cornwall, TR12 7LJ.
Std: 01326 **Tel:** 240387
Nearest Town/Resort Mullion
Directions 7 miles south of Helston on left hand side of A3083, just before junction of B3296 to Mullion which is 1 mile.
Acreage 1¼ **Open** April **to** November
Access Good **Site** Level
Sites Available ▲ ⊟ ⊞ **Total** 18
Facilities ⓊⒷ ▲ ℾ ☉ ⌣ ▢ ℞ ⓪ ⤶ ▢
Nearby Facilities ┏ ╱ ⤶ U
⇌ Redruth
Nice views, ideal touring, nice moorland walks.

SALTASH

Dolbeare Caravan & Camping Park,
Landrake, Saltash, Cornwall, PL12 5AF.
Std: 01752 **Tel:** 851332
Email: dolbeare@compuserve.com
Website: www.dolbeare.co.uk
Nearest Town/Resort Saltash
Directions 4 miles west of Saltash, turn off
A38 at Landrake immediately after
footbridge into Pound Hill, signposted.
Acreage 9 **Open** All Year
Access Good **Site** Lev/Slope
Sites Available A ⊕ ⊕ **Total** 60.
Facilities ƒ 🖰 🚽 ♨ ⌇ ⊙ ᵴ 🛒 ⊒ 🖾 ☎
🏲 🖰 🛇 🗚 ⬅🖸🖻
🚆 Saltash
Quality touring park in magnificent
countryside. Free, plentiful hot water. Level
hard standings and large grass areas.
Please telephone for a brochure.

SALTASH

**Notter Bridge Caravan & Camping
Park,** Notter Bridge, Saltash, Cornwall,
PL12 4RW.
Std: 01752 **Tel:** 842318
Email: holidays@notterbridge.co.uk
Website: www.notterbridge.co.uk
Nearest Town/Resort Plymouth
Directions A38, 3½ miles west of Tamar
Bridge, Plymouth, signposted Notter Bridge.
Acreage 6¼ **Open** April/Easter **to**
September
Access Good **Site** Level
Sites Available A ⊕ ⊕ **Total** 29
Facilities ƒ 🖰 🚽 ♨ ⌇ ⊙ ᵴ 🛒 ⊒ 🖾 ☎
🏲 🖰 🛇 🗚 ⬅🖸
🚆 Plymouth
Sheltered, level site in a picturesque wooded
valley with river frontage. Fishing, pub food
opposite. Indoor swimming pool nearby.
Ideal centre for Plymouth, Cornwall and
Devon.

ST. AGNES

Beacon Cottage Farm Touring Park,
Beacon Drive, St. Agnes, Cornwall, TR5
0NU.
Std: 01872 **Tel:** 552347/553381
Nearest Town/Resort St. Agnes
Directions From A30, take B3277 to St.
Agnes, take road to the Beacon. Follow
signs to site.
Acreage 2 **Open** April **to** September
Access Good **Site** Level
Sites Available A ⊕ ⊕ **Total** 50
Facilities ƒ 🖰 🚽 ♨ ⌇ ⊙ ᵴ 🛒 ⊒ 🖾 ☎
🏲 🖰 🛇 🗚 ⬅🖸🖻
🚆 Truro

On working farm, surrounded by National
Trust land. Sandy beach 1 mile, beautiful
sea views.

ST. AGNES

**Presingoll Farm Caravan & Camping
Park,** St. Agnes, Cornwall, TR5 0PB.
Std: 01872 **Tel:** 552333
Website:
www.presingollfarm.fsbusiness.co.uk
Nearest Town/Resort St. Agnes
Directions Leave the A30 at Chiverton
Cross roundabout and take the B3277 for
St. Agnes. Site is 3 miles on the right.
Acreage 3½ **Open** Easter **to** End October
Access Good **Site** Level
Sites Available A ⊕ ⊕ **Total** 90
Facilities & ƒ 🖰 🚽 ♨ ⌇ ⊙ ᵴ 🛒 ⊒ 🖾 ☎
🏲 🖰 🛇 🗚 ⬅🖸🖻
🚆 Truro
Working farm overlooking the North
Cornwall coastline. Near the Cornish
Coastal Path and surf beaches within 2
miles. Ideal for walking. Dogs must be kept
on a lead.

ST. AUSTELL

Croft Farm Holiday Park, Luxulyan,
Bodmin, Cornwall, PL30 5EQ.
Std: 01726 **Tel:** 850228
Std: 01726 **Fax:** 850498
Email: lynpick@globalnet.co.uk
Website: www.croftfarm.co.uk
Nearest Town/Resort St. Austell
Directions From A390 (Liskeard to St
Austell) turn right past the level crossing in
St Blazey (signposted Luxulyan). In ¼ mile
turn right at T-Junction, continue to next T-
Juntion and turn right. The park is on the
left within ½ mile. N.B. DO NOT take any
other routes signposted Luxulyan/Lux Valley.
Acreage 4 **Open** End March **to** End Oct
Access Good **Site** Level
Sites Available A ⊕ ⊕ **Total** 56
Facilities ƒ 🖰 🚽 ♨ ⌇ ⊙ ᵴ 🛒 ⊒ 🖾 ☎
🏲 🖰 🛇 🗚 ⬅🖸🖻
🚆 Luxulyan
David Bellamy Gold Conservation Award
winners.

ST. AUSTELL

Penhaven Touring Park, Pentewan
Road, St. Austell, Cornwall, PL26 6DL.
Std: 01726 **Tel:** 843687
Std: 01726 **Fax:** 843870
Email: penhaven.camon@virgin.net
Website: www.penhaventouring.co.uk
Nearest Town/Resort Mevagissey
Directions 3 miles south of St Austell on
the B3273 Mevagissey road, 1 mile after the

village of London Apprentice.
Acreage 13 **Open** Easter/1 April **to** 31
October
Access Good **Site** Level
Sites Available A ⊕ ⊕ **Total** 105
Facilities & ƒ 🖰 🚽 ♨ ⌇ ⊙ ᵴ 🛒 ⊒ 🖾 ☎
🏲 🖰 🛇 🗚 ⬅🖸🖻
🚆 St Austell
Situated between Heligan Gardens and the
Eden Project, this sheltered valley site is of
outstanding natural beauty. With either an
off-road cycle or walk to the village, beach
and Mevagissey. Central for exploring all of
Cornwall.

ST. AUSTELL

River Valley Holiday Park, London
Apprentice, St Austell, Cornwall, PL26
7AP.
Std: 01726 **Tel:** 73533
Std: 01726 **Fax:** 73533
Email: johnclemo@aol.com
Website: www.cornwall-holidays.co.uk
Nearest Town/Resort St Austell
Directions Take the B3273 from St Austell
to Mevagissey, 1 mile to London Apprentice,
site is on the left hand side.
Acreage 9 **Open** April **to** September
Access Good **Site** Level
Sites Available A ⊕ ⊕ **Total** 40
Facilities ƒ 🖰 🚽 ♨ ⌇ ⊙ ᵴ 🛒 ⊒ 🖾 ☎
🏲 🖰 🛇 🗚 ⬅🖸🖻
🚆 St Austell
Alongside a river with woodland walk and
cycle trail to the beach.

ST. AUSTELL

Sun Valley Holiday Park, Pentewan
Road, St. Austell, Cornwall, PL26 6DJ.
Std: 01726 **Tel:** 843266
Email:
reception@sunvalleyholidays.co.uk
Website: www.sunvalleyholidays.co.uk
Nearest Town/Resort Mevagissey
Directions Take B3273 from St. Austell, site
1 mile past 'London Apprentice', on right.
Acreage 20 **Open** April **to** October
Access Good **Site** Level
Sites Available A ⊕ ⊕ **Total** 22
Facilities ƒ 🖰 🚽 ♨ ⌇ ⊙ ᵴ 🛒 ⊒ 🖾 ☎
🏲 🖰 🛇 🗙 🛇 🖰 🗚 ⬅🖸🖻
🚆 St. Austell
Site situated in woodland and pasture
surrounding. 1 mile from sea. Ideal touring
centre. Tennis on site. Close to Eden Project.

ST. AUSTELL
Trencreek Farm Holiday Park,
Hewaswater, St. Austell, Cornwall, PL26 7JG.
Std: 01726 **Tel:** 882540
Std: 01726 **Fax:** 883254
Email: trencreekfarm@aol.com
Website: www.trencreek.co.uk
Nearest Town/Resort St. Austell
Acreage 56 **Open** Easter **to** End October
Access Good **Site** Level
Sites Available A ⊞ ⌖ **Total** 198
Facilities ...
Nearby Facilities ...
⚲ St. Austell
Kids Club in main season and 4 fishing lakes on site.

ST. AUSTELL
Treveor Farm Caravan & Camping Park,
Gorran, St Austell, Cornwall, PL26 6LW.
Std: 01726 **Tel:** 842387
Std: 01726 **Fax:** 842387
Nearest Town/Resort Gorran Haven
Directions Take the B2373 from St Austell. After Pentewan beach at top of hill turn right to Gorran. Approx 4 miles on turn right at signboard.
Acreage 4 **Open** April **to** October
Access Good **Site** Level
Sites Available A ⊞ ⌖ **Total** 50
Facilities ...
Nearby Facilities ...
⚲ St Austell
Near to beach, coastal path, Lost Gardens of Heligan and only 12 miles from Eden Project.

ST. AUSTELL
Trewhiddle Holiday Estate, Pentewan Road, St. Austell, Cornwall, PL26 7AD.
Std: 01726 **Tel:** 67011
Std: 01726 **Fax:** 67010
Email: mcclelland@btinternet.com
Website: www.trewhiddle.co.uk
Nearest Town/Resort St. Austell
Directions From St Austell take the B3273 towards Mevagissey. Trewhiddle is ¾ miles from the roundabout on the right.
Acreage 16½ **Open** All Year
Access Good **Site** Lev/Slope
Sites Available A ⊞ ⌖ **Total** 105
Facilities ...
Nearby Facilities ...
⚲ St. Austell
Only 15 minutes from Eden Project and Heligan Gardens. Three beaches within four miles.

ST. BURYAN
Tower Park Caravans & Camping, St. Buryan, Penzance, Cornwall, TR19 6BZ.
Std: 01736 **Tel:** 810286
Email: caravans+camping@towerpark97.freeserve.co.uk
Website: www.towerpark97.freeserve.co.uk
Nearest Town/Resort Penzance
Directions From the A30 Lands End road turn left onto the B3283 towards St. Buryan. In the village turn right then right again and the park is 300 yards on the right.
Acreage 12 **Open** March to January
Access Good **Site** Level
Sites Available A ⊞ ⌖ **Total** 102
Facilities ...

Nearby Facilities ...
⚲ Penzance
Quiet, rural park located midway between Penzance and Lands End. Ideal touring and walking in West Cornwall.

ST. IVES
Balnoon Camping Site, Balnoon, Near Halsetown, St. Ives, Cornwall, TR26 3JA.
Std: 01736 **Tel:** 795431
Email: nat@balnoon.fsnet.co.uk
Nearest Town/Resort St. Ives
Directions From the A30 take the A3074 for St. Ives, at the second mini-roundabout turn first left signposted St. Ives Day Visitors (B3311), turn second right signposted Balnoon. Approx. 3 miles from the A30.
Acreage 1 **Open** Easter **to** October
Access Good **Site** Level
Sites Available A ⊞ ⌖ **Total** 24
Facilities ...
Nearby Facilities ...
⚲ St. Ives
Situated in the countryside with views of adjacent rolling hills. Equidistant from the beautiful beaches of Carbis Bay and St. Ives, approx. 2 miles.

ST. IVES
Higher Chellew Touring Caravan & Camping Site, Higher Chellew, Nancledra, Penzance, Cornwall, TR20 8BD.
Std: 01736 **Tel:** 364532
Email: camping@higherchellew.co.uk
Website: www.chycor.co.uk/camping/higherchellew
Nearest Town/Resort St Ives
Directions Take the A30 to the village of Crowlas, turn right onto the B3309 signposted Ludgvan and Nancledra. After 2 miles at the T-Junction turn right onto the B3311, turn right after ¾ mile into a private

e signed Higher Chellew.
reage 1¼ **Open** March **to** October
cess Good **Site** Level
tes Available ▲ ⚏ ⚐ **Total** 30
cilities ...
arby Facilities ...
  Penzance/St Ives
iet, rural site with spectacular panoramic,
untryside views. Immaculate facilities.
sy access to all that makes West Cornwall
ecial.

T. IVES

ttle Trevarrack Tourist Park, Laity
ne, Carbis Bay, St. Ives, Cornwall,
26 3HW.
d: 01736 **Tel:** 797580
d: 01736 **Fax:** 797580
mail: littletrevarrack@hotmail.com
ebsite: www.littletrevarrack.com
earest **Town/Resort** St. Ives
rections Turn off the A30 onto the A3074
wards St. Ives. After 3 miles at Carbis Bay
e site is signposted left opposite the
nction to the beach, turn left and follow for
0 yards to the crossroads, go straight
ross and the site is directly on the right.
reage 20 **Open** April **to** October
ccess Good **Site** Lev/Slope
tes Available ▲ ⚏ ⚐ **Total** 254
acilities ...
earby Facilities ...
  Carbis Bay
ar the beach. Bus service to St. Ives in
gh season only. Ideal for touring West
ornwall. 2 dogs allowed per pitch.

ST. IVES

Penderleath Caravan & Camping Park,
Towednack, St. Ives, Cornwall, TR26 3AF.
Std: 01736 **Tel:** 798403 **Fax:** 798403
Website: www.penderleath.co.uk
Nearest Town/Resort St. Ives
Directions From the A30 take the A3074
signposted St. Ives. At the second mini
roundabout turn left, at the end of the road
turn left then immediately right, turn left at
next fork.
Acreage 10 **Open** May **to** October
Access Good **Site** Lev/Slope
Sites Available ▲ ⚏ ⚐ **Total** 75
Facilities ...
Nearby Facilities ...
  ⚓ St. Ives
Set in a classified area of outstanding natural
beauty, with fabulous views over countryside
to the sea. Very peaceful and tranquil. Adults
Only period.

ST. IVES

Polmanter Tourist Park, Halsetown, St.
Ives, Cornwall, TR26 3LX.
Std: 01736 **Tel:** 795640 **Fax:** 795640
Email: phillip_osborne@hotmail.com
Website: www.polmanter.com
Nearest Town/Resort St. Ives
Directions Take the A3074 to St. Ives from
the A30. First left at the mini-roundabout
taking Holiday Route to St. Ives (Halsetown).
Turn right at the Halsetown Inn, then first left.
Acreage 20 **Open** March **to** October
Access Good **Site** Level
Sites Available ▲ ⚏ ⚐ **Total** 240
Facilities ...
Nearby Facilities ...
  ⚓ St. Ives

Just 1½ miles from St. Ives and beaches.
Central for touring the whole of West
Cornwall. Tennis on park.

ST. IVES

St. Ives Bay Holiday Park, Upton
Towans, Hayle, Cornwall, TR27 5BH.
Std: 01736 **Tel:** Hayle 752274
Std: 01736 **Fax:** 754523
Email: stivesbay@dial.pipex.com
Website: www.stivesbay.co.uk
Nearest Town/Resort Hayle
Directions A30 from Camborne to Hayle,
at roundabout take Hayle turn-off and then
turn right onto B3301, 600yds on left enter
park.
Acreage 12 **Open** May **to** September
Access Good **Site** Lev/Slope
Sites Available ▲ ⚏ ⚐ **Total** 200
Facilities ...
Nearby Facilities ...
  ⚓ Hayle
Park adjoining own sandy beach, onto St.
Ives Bay. Children very welcome. Sea views.
Dial-a-Brochure 24 hours, Mr R. White. (See
our display advertisment).

ST. JUST

Kelynack Caravan & Camping Park,
Kelynack, St. Just, Nr. Penzance,
Cornwall, TR19 7RE.
Std: 01736 **Tel:** 787633
Email: steve@kelynackholidays.co.uk
Website: www.ukparks.co.uk/kelynack
Nearest Town/Resort St. Just in Penwith
Directions From Penzance take A3071 St.
Just road, then after 6 miles turn left onto
the B3306 Lands End coast road, ½ mile to
site sign.
Acreage 2 **Open** April **to** October
Access Good **Site** Level

Sites Available ▲ ⊕ ⊟ **Total** 20
Facilities ♿ ✦ ⅏ ⊞ ⤐ ↑ ⊙ ⬎ ⛴ ◻ ▣
⅏ ¡⧆ ⊙ ⊟ ★ ⋒ ⦿ ✻⊬⊡ ◻
Nearby Facilities ↑ ✔ ⚓ ⋆ ✗
≉ Penzance
¾ mile beach, on coast road. Sheltered site alongside a stream in valley setting. Ideal for touring.

ST. JUST

Levant House, Levant House, Levant Road, Pendeen, Penzance, Cornwall, TR19 7SX.
Std: 01736 Tel: 788795
Nearest Town/Resort St. Just-in-Penwith.
Directions From St. Just-in-Penwith take the B3306 towards St. Ives. At Trewellard turn left. Site is in two fields 200yds on the left.
Acreage 2½ **Open** April **to** October
Access Good **Site** Lev/Slope
Sites Available ▲ ⊕ ⊟ **Total** 43
Facilities ✦ ⅏ ⊞ ⤐ ↑ ⊙ ⬎ ⛴ ◻ ▣
Nearby Facilities ↑ ✔ ⚓ ✗
≉ Penzance.
Approx. 8 minutes wlak to the Coastal Path. Rock climbing at Bosegran.

ST. JUST

Roselands Caravan Park, Dowran, St. Just, Penzance, Cornwall, TR19 7RS.
Std: 01736 Tel: 788571
Std: 01736 Fax: 788571
Email: camping@roseland84.freeserve.co.uk
Website: www.roselands.co.uk
Nearest Town/Resort Penzance
Directions From the A30 Penzance by-pass take the A3071 to St. Just for 5 miles, turn left at sign and park is 800 yards.
Acreage 3 **Open** January **to** October
Access Good **Site** Level
Sites Available ▲ ⊕ ⊟ **Total** 30
Facilities ✦ ⅏ ⊞ ⤐ ↑ ⊙ ⬎ ⛴ ◻ ▣
⅏ ⊙ ⊟ ✗ ⋒ ★ ⤐⊬⊡ ◻
Nearby Facilities ↑ ✔ ⚓ ⋆ ∪ ⚲ ℛ ✗
≉ Penzance
Close to the sea. Ideal for walking and bird watching. All attractions nearby. 5 miles from Lands End.

ST. JUST

Secret Garden Caravan Park, Bosavern House, St. Just, Penzance, Cornwall, TR19 7RD.
Std: 01736 Tel: 788301
Std: 01736 Fax: 788301
Email: marcol@bosavern.u-net.com
Website: www.bosavern.u-net.com
Nearest Town/Resort St. Just/Penzance
Directions Take the A3071 from Penzance towards St. Just. Approximately 550yds

before St. Just turn left onto the B3306 signposted Lands End and airport. Bosavern Garden Caravan Park is 500yds from the turn off, behind Bosavern House.
Acreage 2¼ **Open** March **to** October
Access Good **Site** Level
Sites Available ⊕ ⊟ **Total** 12
Facilities ♿ ✦ ⅏ ⊞ ↑ ⊙ ⬎ ⛴ ◻ ▣
⊟ ✗ ⊞⊬⊡ ◻ ▣
Nearby Facilities ↑ ✔ ⚓ ⋆ ⚲ ℛ ✗
≉ Penzance
Walled garden site surrounded by trees and flowers. Excellent walking country, good beaches nearby. Local authorities licensed site.

ST. JUST

Trevaylor Caravan & Camping Park, Botallack, St Just, Cornwall, TR19 7PU.
Std: 01736 Tel: 787016
Email: bookings@trevaylor.com
Website: www.trevaylor.com
Nearest Town/Resort Penzance
Directions Situated on the B3306 Lands End to St Ives road, approx 1 mile to the north of St Just.
Acreage 5 **Open** Mid March **to** October
Access Good **Site** Level
Sites Available ✦ ⅏ ⊞ ↑ ⊙ ⬎ ⛴ ◻ ▣ **Total** 85
Facilities ✦ ⅏ ⊞ ↑ ⊙ ⬎ ⛴ ◻ ▣
⅏ ⊙ ⊟ ✗ ⟊ ⋒ ★ ⦿⊬⊡ ◻ ▣
Nearby Facilities ↑ ✔ ⚓ ⋆ ⚲ ✗
≉ Penzance
Easy access to the golden sands, white surf from the Atlantic Ocean, rugged cliffs and coastal paths. Off License, bar and bar food and take-away on site.

ST. MAWES

Trethem Mill Touring Park, St. Just-in-Roseland, Truro, Cornwall, TR2 5JF.
Std: 01872 Tel: 580504
Std: 01872 Fax: 580968
Email: reception@trethem-mill.co.uk
Website: www.trethem-mill.co.uk
Nearest Town/Resort St. Mawes
Directions From Tregony follow the A3078 to St. Mawes. Approx. 2 miles after passing through Trewithian look out for caravan and camping sign.
Acreage 4 **Open** April **to** October
Access Good **Site** Lev/Slope
Sites Available ▲ ⊕ ⊟ **Total** 84
Facilities ✦ ⅏ ⊞ ↑ ⊙ ⬎ ⛴ ◻ ▣
⅏ ⊙ ⊟ ⊞ ★ ⤐⊬⊡ ◻ ▣
Nearby Facilities ↑ ✔ ⚓ ⋆ ∪ ⚲ ℛ
≉ Truro

ST. MERRYN

Tregavone Farm Touring Park, St. Merryn, Padstow, Cornwall, PL28 8JZ.
Std: 01841 Tel: 520148

Nearest Town/Resort Padstow
Directions Turn right off A39 (Wadebridge to St. Columb) onto A389 (Padstow) come to a T-junction and turn right, in 1 mile turn ▶ entrance on left after 1 mile.
Acreage 4 **Open** March **to** October
Access Good **Site** Level
Sites Available ♿ ✦ ⅏ ⊞ ↑ ⊙ ⬎ ⛴ ◻ ▣ **Total** 40
Facilities ♿ ✦ ⅏ ⊞ ↑ ⊙ ⬎ ⛴ ⤐ ◻ ▣⊬
Nearby Facilities ↑ ✔ ⚓ ⋆ ∪ ⚲ ℛ
≉ Newquay
Quiet family run site situated near san surfing beaches, country views, w maintained and grassy. AA 2 Pennants.

ST. MERRYN

Trethias Farm Caravan Park, St. Merry Padstow, Cornwall, PL28 8PL.
Std: 01841 Tel: 520323
Nearest Town/Resort Padstow
Directions From Wadebridge follow sig to St. Merryn, go past Farmers Arms, th turning right (our signs from here).
Acreage 12 **Open** April **to** September
Access Good **Site** Level
Sites Available ▲ ⊕ ⊟ **Total** 62
Facilities ✦ ⅏ ⊞ ↑ ⊙ ⬎ ⛴ ◻
⅏ ⊙ ⊟ ⤐⊡
Nearby Facilities ↑ ✔ ⚓ ⋆ ∪ ⚲
≉ Bodmin Parkway
Near beach, scenic views. Couples a family groups only.

ST. MERRYN

Trevean Farm Caravan & Camping Park, St. Merryn, Padstow, Cornwall, PL28 8PR.
Std: 01841 Tel: 520772
Website: www.bhhpa.org.uk/ treveanfarmc+cpark
Nearest Town/Resort Padstow
Directions From St. Merryn village take ▶ B3276 Newquay road for 1 mile. Turn for Rumford, site ¼ mile on the right.
Acreage 2 **Open** April **to** October
Access Good **Site** Level
Sites Available ▲ ⊕ ⊟ **Total** 36
Facilities ✦ ⅏ ⊞ ↑ ⊙ ⬎ ⛴ ◻
⅏ ¡⧆ ⊙ ⊟ ⊞⊬⊡ ◻
Nearby Facilities ↑ ✔ ⚓ ⋆ ∪ ⚲ ℛ
≉ Newquay
Situated near several sandy, surfi beaches. ETC 3 Star Grading.

ST. MERRYN

Treyarnon Bay Caravan Park, Treyarno Bay, Padstow, Cornwall, PL28 8JR.
Std: 01841 Tel: 520681
Website: www.treyarnonbay.co.uk
Nearest Town/Resort Padstow
Directions Follow road for Treyarnon fro B3276 Newquay to Padstow road. Follo

...he and into car park at the bottom of the ...age. (Holiday park adjoins car park).
...reage 4 **Open** April **to** September
...e Level
...tes Available ▲ ⌂ ➔ **Total** 60
a c i l i t i e s 🆅 ♿ ↑ ⊙ ⌫ ⚌ ◻ ☂
⚊ 📶 ◱ ➘ ⊡
...earby Facilities ⌐ ✦ ⚓ ⤳ ∪
Newquay
...verlooking bay. Ideal for touring, surfing, ...olf, swimming or just lazing by the sea. ...afé/restaurant and a licenced hotel/pub ...arby.

...T. MINVER

...nham Farm Caravan & Camping ...rk, St. Minver, Wadebridge, Cornwall, ...27 6RH.
...d: 01208 **Tel:** 812878
...ail: info@dinhamfarm.co.uk
...ebsite: www.dinhamfarm.co.uk
...earest Town/Resort Rock
...rections 3 miles west of Wadebridge on ...e B3314.
...creage 2½ **Open** April **to** October
...ccess Good **Site** Lev/Slope
...tes Available ▲ ⌂ ➔ **Total** 40
a c i l i t i e s ⌂ ↑ 🆅 ♿ ↑ ⊙ ⌫ ⚌ ◻ ☂
⚊ ◱ ⊡ ⚐ ✦ ➘ ➘ ⊡ ⊡
...earby Facilities ⌐ ✦ ⚓ ⤳ ∪ ⚲ ♪
⚊ Bodmin Parkway
...vely secluded park, overlooking the River ...amel and surrounded by trees and shrubs. ...wn heated swimming pool. Near golden ...ndy beaches.

INTAGEL

...ossiney Farm Caravan Site, Tintagel, ...ornwall, PL34 0AY.
...d: 01840 **Tel:** 770481
...ebsite: www.bossineyfarm.co.uk
...earest Town/Resort Tintagel
...rections ¾ miles from centre of Tintagel ...n main Boscastle road.
...creage 2 **Open** April **to** October
...ccess Good **Site** Lev/Slope
...tes Available ⌂ ↑ 🆅 ➔ **Total** 20
a c i l i t i e s ⌂ ↑ 🆅 ♿ ↑ ⊙ ⌫ ⚌ ◻ ☂
⚊ ⊙ ➘ ⊡ ⊡
...earby Facilities ⌐ ✦ ⚓ ∪ ♪
...eal touring centre, near beach, inland ...ews.

INTAGEL

...he Headland Caravan & Camping ...ark, Atlantic Road, Tintagel, Cornwall, ...L34 0DE.
...td: 0184. **Tel:** 770239
...td: 01840 **Fax:** 770925
...mail: headland.cp@virgin.net
...'ebsite: www.headlandcp-tintagel.co.uk
...earest Town/Resort Tintagel

Directions Follow camping/caravan signs from B3263 through village to Headland.
Acreage 4 **Open** Easter **to** October
Access Good **Site** Lev/Slope
Sites Available ▲ ⌂ ➔ **Total** 60
Facilities ⌐ 🆅 ♿ ↑ ⊙ ⌫ ⚌ ◻ ☂
⚊⚐ ◱ ⊙ ◱ ➘ ➘ ⊡
Nearby Facilities ⌐ ✦ ⚓ ⤳ ∪ ♪
⚊ Bodmin Parkway
Three beaches walking distance. Scenic views. Ideal touring centre.

TORPOINT

Whitsand Bay Holiday Park, Millbrook, Torpoint, Cornwall, PL10 1JZ.
Std: 01752 **Tel:** 822597
Std: 01752 **Fax:** 823444
Email: enquiries@whitsandbayholidays.co.uk
Website: www.whitsandbayholidays.co.uk
Nearest Town/Resort Plymouth
Directions From Plymouth take the A38 to Trerulefoot, at roundabout turn left. After 3 miles turn right to Millbrook, after 1 mile turn left to Millbrook. After 2 miles turn right to Whitsand Bay and after 2½ miles turn left into the park.
Acreage 27 **Open** All Year
Site Lev/Slope
Sites Available ▲ ⌂ ➔ **Total** 120
Facilities ↑ 🆅 ♿ ↑ ⊙ ⌫ ⚌ ◻ ☂
⚊⚐ ◱ ⊙ ✕ ⚐ ◱ ♣ ◻ ⊙ ➘ ⊡ ⊡ ⊡
Nearby Facilities ⌐ ✦ ⚓ ⤳ ∪ ⚲ ♪
⚊ Plymouth
Hilltop location with stunning sea and country views. Just minutes walk to sandy beaches. In an ancient monument. Only 8 miles from Plymouth.

TRURO

Carnon Downs Caravan & Camping Park, Carnon Downs, Truro, Cornwall, TR3 6JJ.
Std: 01872 **Tel:** 862283
Email: park@carnon-downscaravanpark.co.uk
Website: www.carnon-downs-caravanpark.co.uk
Nearest Town/Resort Truro
Directions On the A39 Falmouth road, 3 miles West of Truro.
Acreage 20 **Open** April **to** October
Access Good **Site** Level
Sites Available ▲ ⌂ ➔ **Total** 110
Facilities ⌂ ↑ 🄵 🆅 ♿ ↑ ⊙ ⌫ ⚌ ◻ ☂
⚊⚐ ◱ ⊙ ◱ ♣ ➘ ⊡ ⊡
Nearby Facilities ⌐ ✦ ⚓ ⤳ ∪ ⚲ ♪
⚊ Truro
Quiet, family run park with good quality facilities. Ideally central for touring. Excellent location for sailing and water sports. David Bellamy Gold Award for Conservation and ETB 5 Star 'Exceptional' Graded.

TRURO

Chacewater Camping & Caravan Park, Coxhill, Chacewater, Truro, Cornwall, TR4 8LY.
Std: 01209 **Tel:** 820762
Std: 01209 **Fax:** 820544
Email: chacepark@aol.com
Nearest Town/Resort Truro
Directions From A30 take the A3047 to Scorrier. Turn left at Crossroads Hotel onto the B3298. 1½ miles left to Chacewater ½ mile sign directs you to the park.
Acreage 6 **Open** May **to** End September
Access Good **Site** Level
Sites Available ▲ ⌂ ➔ **Total** 94
Facilities ⚒ ↑ 🄵 🆅 ♿ ↑ ⊙ ⌫ ⚌ ◻ ☂
⚊⚐ ◱ ⊙ ◱ ◱ ➘ ⊡ ⊡ A
Nearby Facilities ⌐ ✦ ∪
⚊ Truro
Exclusively for Adults. The ideal holiday base for the Over 30's.

TRURO

Cosawes, Perranarworthal, Truro, Cornwall, TR3 7QS.
Std: 01872 **Tel:** 863724
Std: 01872 **Fax:** 870268
Nearest Town/Resort Falmouth
Directions Midway between Truro and Falmouth on the A39.
Acreage 100 **Open** All Year
Access Good **Site** Level
Sites Available ▲ ⌂ ➔ **Total** 50
Facilities ↑ 🆅 ♿ ↑ ⊙ ⌫ ⚌ ◻ ☂
⚊⚐ ◱ ⊙ ➘ ⊡
Nearby Facilities ⌐ ✦ ⚓ ⤳ ∪ ⚲ ♪
⚊ Perranwell
Situated in a 100 acre wooded valley, an area of outstanding natural beauty.

TRURO

Liskey Holiday Park, Greenbottom, Truro, Cornwall, TR4 8QN.
Std: 01872 **Tel:** 560274
Std: 01872 **Fax:** 560274
Email: enquiries@liskeyholidaypark.co.uk
Website: www.liskeyholidaypark.co.uk
Nearest Town/Resort Truro
Directions 3½ miles west of Truro, off A390 between Threemilestone and Chacewater.
Acreage 8 **Open** March **to** October
Access Good **Site** Lev/slope
Sites Available ▲ ⌂ ➔ **Total** 68
Facilities ↑ 🄵 🆅 ♿ ↑ ⊙ ⌫ ⚌ ◻ ☂
⚊⚐ ◱ ⊙ ◱ ♣ ⊙ ➘ ⊡ ⊡
Nearby Facilities ⌐ ✦ ⚓ ⤳ ∪ ♪
⚊ Truro
Small family site, central for exploring Cornwall. Adventure play barn, games field, heated toilet block, family bathroom and dishwashing sinks. 10 minutes to the sea.

TRURO

Summer Valley Touring Park, Shortlanesend, Truro, Cornwall, TR4 9DW.
Std: 01872 **Tel:** 277878
Email: res@summervalley.co.uk
Website: www.summervalley.co.uk
Nearest Town/Resort Truro
Directions 2 miles out of Truro on Perranporth road (B3284). Sign on left just past Shortlanesend.
Acreage 3 **Open** April **to** October
Access Good **Site** Level
Sites Available ▲ ⊕ ⊞ **Total** 60
Facilities ⌁ ⊞ ☇ ⌂ ⊙ ⌐ ◢ ▢ ☛
♨ ⧫ ⊙ ☎ ⌸ ⤵ ▣ ⊡ ⬚
Nearby Facilities ⌂ ✦ ⚓ ⚘ U ₽
✦ Truro
Ideal centre for touring Cornwall.

TRURO

Treloan Coastal Farm Holidays, Treloan Lane, Portscatho, The Roseland, Truro, Cornwall, TR2 5EF.
Std: 01872 **Tel:** 580899
Std: 01872 **Fax:** 580989
Email: holidays@treloan.freeserve.co.uk
Website: www.coastalfarmholidays.co.uk
Nearest Town/Resort Portscatho/Truro
Directions From Truro take the A390 through Tresillian and onto the by-pass, take second right turn onto the A3078 signposted Tregony and St. Mawes. At Trewithian turn left signposted Portscatho and follow signs.
Acreage 35 **Open** All Year
Access Good **Site** Level
Sites Available ▲ ⊕ ⊞ **Total** 57
Facilities ⌁ ⌁ ⎌ ⊞ ⊞ ☇ ⌂ ⊙ ⌐ ◢ ▢ ☛
⧫ ⊙ ☎ ⊛ ⤵ ⊡
Nearby Facilities ✦ ⚓ ⚘ U
✦ Truro/St. Austell
A working museum and organic farm on the coastal path offering self catering, touring and camping in beautiful surroundings. Access to three secluded beaches. Close to shops, pubs, etc.. Squash courts nearby. Shire horses.

TRURO

Trevarth Holiday Park, Blackwater, Truro, Cornwall, TR4 8HR.
Std: 01872 **Tel:** 560266
Std: 01872 **Fax:** 560379
Email: trevarth@lineone.net
Nearest Town/Resort St. Agnes
Directions Take the A30 to Chiverton roundabout, take the Blackwater exit and we are 300 yards on the right.
Acreage 2 **Open** April **to** October
Access Good **Site** Level
Sites Available ▲ ⊕ ⊞ **Total** 30
Facilities ⌁ ⊞ ☇ ⌂ ⊙ ⌐ ◢ ▢ ☛
⧫ ⊙ ☎ ⚘ ⊞ ⊛ ⤵ ▣ ⊡ ⬚
Nearby Facilities ⌂ ✦ U
✦ Truro
Rural park in an excellent location for touring north and south coast resorts.

WADEBRIDGE

Gunvenna Caravan & Camping Park, St. Minver, Wadebridge, Cornwall, PL27 6QN.
Std: 01208 **Tel:** 862405
Std: 01208 **Fax:** 862405
Nearest Town/Resort Wadebridge
Directions Take the A30 to Bodmin then the A389 to Wadebridge. Take the A39 to Polzeath then the B3314, remain on this road and Gunvenna Caravan Park is on the right hand side.
Acreage 10 **Open** Easter **to** October
Access Good **Site** Lev/Slope
Sites Available ▲ ⊕ ⊞ **Total** 75
Facilities ⌁ ⎌ ☇ ⌂ ⊙ ⌐ ◢ ▢ ☛
♨ ⧫ ⊙ ☎ ✕ ⚘ ⊞ ⤵ ⊛ ⤵⤵
Nearby Facilities ⌂ ⚓ ⚘ U ₽ ₽
✦ Bodmin
Polzeath and rock beaches. Good sandy beaches.

WADEBRIDGE

Little Bodieve Holiday Park, Bodieve Road, Wadebridge, Cornwall, PL27 6EG.
Std: 01208 **Tel:** 812323
Website: www.littlebodieve.co.uk
Nearest Town/Resort Wadebridge
Directions 1 mile north of Wadebridge Town centre off the A39 trunk road. 1/3rd mile on the B3314 road to Rock and Port Isaac.
Acreage 22 **Open** Late March **to** October

Access Good **Site** Level
Sites Available ▲ ⊕ ⊞ **Total** 195
Facilities ⌁ ⌁ ⎌ ☇ ⌂ ⊙ ⌐ ◢ ▢
♨ ⊙ ☎ ✕ ⏚ ⊞ ⚘ ⌸ ⤵ ▣ ⊡
Nearby Facilities ⌂ ✦ ⚓ ⚘ U ₽ ₽
✦ Bodmin Parkway
Nearest park to the Camel Trail, close superb beaches. Ideal touring centre. 6 g courses within a 20 minute drive. Cl Rallies welcome.

WADEBRIDGE

Lundynant Caravan Site, Polzeath, Nr. Wadebridge, Cornwall, PL27 6QX.
Std: 01208 **Tel:** 862268
Nearest Town/Resort Polzeath
Directions From Wadebridge take tʰ B3314 to Polzeath, 7 miles.
Acreage 3 **Open** April **to** October
Access Fair **Site** Lev/Slope
Sites Available ▲ ⊕ ⊞ **Total** 49
Facilities ⌁ ⎌ ☇ ⌂ ⊙ ⌐ ◢ ▢
♨ ⧫ ⊙ ☎ ⤵ ▣ ⊡ ⬚
Nearby Facilities ⌂ ✦ ⚓ ⚘ U ₽ ₽
✦ Bodmin Parkway
Alongside a public footpath to the beach a village (with several shops) a 5-10 minu walk. Ideally situated for coastal walking.

WADEBRIDGE

The Laurels Holiday Park, Whitecross, Wadebridge, Cornwall, PL27 7JQ.
Std: 01208 **Tel:** 813341
Std: 01208 **Fax:** 813341
Email: anicholson@thelaurels-park.freeserve.co.uk
Website: www.thelaurels-park.freeserve.co.uk
Nearest Town/Resort Padstow
Directions From Wadebridge take the Aˀ south west, turn onto the A389 towarᵈ Padstow, The Laurels is on the right.
Acreage 2½ **Open** Easter **to** End Octobᵉ
Access Good **Site** Level
Sites Available ▲ ⊕ ⊞ **Total** 30
Facilities ⌁ ⎌ ☇ ⌂ ⊙ ⌐ ◢ ▢
♨ ☎ ⤵ ▣ ⊡ ⬚
Nearby Facilities ⌂ ✦ ⚓ ⚘ U ₽
✦ Newquay/Bodmin
In an area of outstanding natural beauⁱ Close to sandy Atlantic beaches. Ideʲ touring centre for Cornwall and North Devᵒ ETC 4 Star Grading and AA 3 Pennants.

WADEBRIDGE

Trewince Farm Holiday Park, St. Issey, Wadebridge, Cornwall, PL27 7RL.
Std: 01208 **Tel:** 812830
Std: 01208 **Fax:** 812835
Nearest Town/Resort Padstow
Directions Take the A39 from Wadebridge and turn right onto the A389 to Padstow, signposted 1 mile on the left.
Open Easter **to** October
Access Good **Site** Level
Sites Available ▲ ⚏ ⚑ **Total** 120
Facilities ⚓ ⨍ ⊞ ⊡ ♨ ⌐ ⊙ ⊐ ▱ ◨ ☎
♨ ◨ ⊙ ♣ ⋀ ⟲ ⤳ ⊞ ⊡
Nearby Facilities ⌐ ∪
✈ Bodmin Parkway
Award winning park, only 4 miles from picturesque Padstow and the Camel Trail - Ideal for cycling and walking.

WHITSTONE

Keywood Caravan Park, Whitstone, Holsworthy, Devon, EX22 6TW.
Std: 01288 **Tel:** 341338
Email: info@keywoodholidays.co.uk
Website: www.keywoodholidays.co.uk
Nearest Town/Resort Bude
Directions Take the A30 from Launceston then take the B3254 Bude road and follow to the village of Whitstone, signposted on the left.
Acreage 12 **Open** 31 March **to** 31 October
Access Poor **Site** Level
Sites Available ▲ ⚏ ⚑ **Total** 50
Facilities ⨍ ⊡ ♨ ⌐ ⊙ ⊐ ▱ ◨ ☎
♨ ◨ ⊙ ♣ ⋀ ⟲ ⊞ ⤳ ⊡
Nearby Facilities ⌐ ∪ ☡ ✗
✈ Bodmin
10 minute drive to the beaches and Bude. Many places of interest to visit within a 30 mile radius. Ideal base for touring.

CUMBRIA

ALLONBY

Manor House Caravan Park, Edderside Road, Allonby, Nr Maryport, Cumbria, CA15 6RA.
Std: 01900. **Tel:** 881236
Std: 01900 **Fax:** 881160
Email: holidays@manorhousepark.co.uk
Website: www.manorhousepark.co.uk
Nearest Town/Resort Allonby
Directions B5300 from Maryport, through Allonby, 1 mile turn right, park 1 mile on right. Signposted on main road.
Acreage 2 **Open** March **to** 15th Nov
Access Good **Site** Level
Sites Available ▲ ⚏ ⚑ **Total** 30
Facilities ⨍ ⊡ ♨ ⌐ ⊙ ⊐ ▱ ◨ ☎
◨ ⊡ ♣ ⋀ ⊛ ⤳ ⊞ ⊡

Nearby Facilities ⌐ ∕ ⚓ ⤳ ∪ ✗
✈ Maryport
1 mile from beach, quiet park. Ideal for touring North Lakes.

ALSTON

Hudgill Caravan Park, South Hudgill, Alston, Cumbria, CA9 3LG.
Std: 01434 **Tel:** 381731
Nearest Town/Resort Alston
Directions 2 miles from Alston on the A689.
Acreage 12 **Open** March **to** 14 November
Access Good **Site** Level
Sites Available ▲ ⚏ ⚑ **Total** 15
Facilities ⨍ ⊞ ⊡ ♨ ⌐ ▱ ◨ ☎
♨ ⓄⓍ ⊙ ⋀ ⤳
Nearby Facilities ⌐ ∕ ∪ ☡ ✗
✈ Penrith
Highest market town of Alston, golf club, Kilhope Mines & Museum, high force waterfall, near the Lake District and Nenthead Mines. Static caravans for hire and sale with 2 or 3 bedrooms.

APPLEBY

Hawkrigg Farm, Colby, Appleby-in-Westmorland, Cumbria, CA16 6BB.
Std: 017683 **Tel:** 51046
Nearest Town/Resort Appleby
Directions From Appleby take the B6260 turn west onto the Colby road. In Colby turn left onto Kings Meaburn Road, take the first turning right.
Open All Year
Access Good **Site** Level
Sites Available ▲ ⚏ ⚑ **Total** 15
Facilities ⨍ ⊡ ♨ ⌐ ⊙ ⤳ ⤹
Nearby Facilities ⌐ ∕
✈ Appleby
Good views of the Pennines. Ideal for touring and walking. Near to the Lake District. Swimming pool nearby. Two hard standings available.

APPLEBY

Silverband Park, Silverband, Knock, Nr Appleby, Cumbria, CA16 6DL.
Std: 017683 **Tel:** 61218
Nearest Town/Resort Appleby
Directions Turn right off the A66 Brough to Penrith at Kirkby Thore. After 2 miles turn left at the T-Junction, then turn right after 100yards, site is on the right in 1 mile.
Acreage ½ **Open** All Year
Access Good **Site** Sloping
Sites Available ⚏ ⚑ **Total** 12
Facilities ⨍ ⊡ ♨ ⌐ ⊙ ♨ ⊙ ⤳ ⊡
Nearby Facilities ⌐ ∕ ∪
✈ Appleby
Ideal for touring the lakes and Penines. Penine Way 4 miles. Off license on site. Fell walking.

APPLEBY

Wild Rose Park, Ormside, Appleby, Cumbria, CA16 6EJ.
Std: 017683 **Tel:** 51077
Std: 017683 **Fax:** 52551
Email: cad@wildrose.co.uk
Website: www.wildrose.co.uk
Nearest Town/Resort Appleby
Directions Centre Appleby take B6260 Kendal for 1½ miles. Left Ormside and Soulby 1½ miles left, ½ mile turn right.
Acreage 40 **Open** All Year
Access Good **Site** Lev/Slope
Sites Available ▲ ⚏ ⚑ **Total** 184
Facilities ⚓ ⨍ ⊞ ⊡ ♨ ⌐ ⊙ ⊐ ▱ ◨ ☎
♨ ◨ ⊙ ⓍⓂ ♣ ⋀ ⟲ ⊛ ⤳ ⊞ ⊡
Nearby Facilities ⌐ ∕
✈ Appleby
Quiet park in unspoilt Eden Valley, superb views. Midway between Lakes and Yorkshire Dales.

ARNSIDE/SILVERDALE

Fell End Caravan Park, Slackhead Road, Hale, Near Milnthorpe, Cumbria, LA7 7BS.
Std: 015395 **Tel:** 62122
Email: slcar@freenetname.co.uk
Nearest Town/Resort Arnside/Silverdale
Directions Leave the M6 at junction 35, take the A6 north and turn left at Wildlife Oasis after driving past Esso Fuel Station and follow caravan tourism signs.
Acreage 12 **Open** All Year
Access Good **Site** Lev/Slope
Sites Available ▲ ⚏ ⚑ **Total** 68
Facilities ⚓ ⨍ ⨯ ⨍ ⊞ ⊡ ♨ ⌐ ⊙ ⊐ ▱ ◨ ☎
◨ ⊙ ♨ ◨ ⓄⓍ ⊙ ⓂⒶ ⤳ ⊞ ⊡
Nearby Facilities ⌐ ∕ ⚓ ⤳ ∪ ✗
✈ Arnside
In an area of outstanding natural beauty, Fell End is a meticulously kept site with mature gardens and a country inn. Close to Lakes and Dales. Open all year to tourers. Please telephone for special offers.

ARNSIDE/SILVERDALE

Hall More Caravan Park, Field House, Hall More, Hale, Nr. Milnthorpe, Cumbria, LA7 7BP.
Std: 015395 **Tel:** 63383
Std: 015395 **Fax:** 63810
Email: slcar@freenetname.co.uk
Nearest Town/Resort Arnside/Milnthorpe
Directions Leave the M6 at junction 35, take the A6 north and turn left at Wildlife Oasis (after passing Esso fuel station). Follow signs to Fell End Caravan Park and Hall More is signposted from there.
Acreage 5 **Open** March **to** October
Access Good **Site** Level
Sites Available ▲ ⚏ ⚑ **Total** 50

Ormside, Appleby-in-Westmorland, Cumbria CA16 6EJ

Excellence in Eden

Friendly family park in beautiful countryside with magnificent views of the Pennines. Ideal base for exploring the LAKE DISTRICT and YORKSHIRE DALES, or simply relax and enjoy the peace and tranquillity of the Eden Valley.

Superb facilities for tourers and tents including super clean loos, laundry, special play facilities for under fives, play ground and sports areas for older children, heated outdoor swimming pools, TV rooms and games for all the family to enjoy.

Well stocked mini-market and licenced restaurant with take-away.

Seasonal and monthly rates for tourers, also Luxury Holiday Homes for sale - Seasonal or all year use.

Sorry, No Letting, No Bar, No Club.

Brochure with pleasure - Telephone: 017683 51077

Email: cad@wildrose.co.uk   Internet: www.wildrose.co.uk

Facilities ♿ ∤ 🖶 🖵 🆎 ⚓ ☊ ⊙ ⊣ ◪ 🖵 📞
🏮 🛉 🚻 🔁
Nearby Facilities Ⴑ ✔ ∪ ⊀
⇌ Arnside
Rural location, excellent for walking, rambling, etc.. Next to a Trout Fishery and Riding Centre. Easy access to the Lake District.

BASSENTHWAITE
Herdwick Croft Caravan Park, Ouse Bridge, Bassenthwaite, Keswick, Cumbria, CA12 4RD.
Std: 017687 **Tel:** 76605
Nearest Town/Resort Keswick
Directions Take the A66 from Keswick to Cockermouth, turn right onto the B5291. 1 mile from the A66.
Acreage 2 **Open** Easter **to** October
Access Good **Site** Level
Sites Available Å ⇞ ⊜ **Total** 10
Facilities ∤ 🆎 ⚓ ☊ ⊙ ⊣ ◪ 📞 🏮 🛉
Nearby Facilities ✔ ⚓ ⊀ ∪ ⊀
⇌ Carlisle

BOTHEL
Skiddaw View Holiday Park, Bothel, Wigton, Cumbria, CA7 2JG.
Std: 016973 **Tel:** 20919
Website: www.skiddawview.co.uk
Nearest Town Keswick/Cockermouth
Directions From Keswick travel north on the A591, take the last turning left before the T-Junction with the A595.
Acreage 3 **Open** March **to** 5 November
Site Level
Sites Available Å ⇞ ⊜ **Total** 20
Facilities ∤ 🖶 🆎 ⚓ ☊ ⊙ ⊣ ◪ 🖵 📞
🏮 🅿 🖰 🛉 🔁 🖵 🖵
Nearby Facilities Ⴑ ✔ ⚓ ∪
⇌ Aspatria
Panoramic views. 5 miles from Bassenthwaite Lake and 5 miles from Allonby beach.

BRAMPTON
Irthing Vale Caravan Park, Old Church Lane, Brampton, Cumbria, CA8 2AA.
Std: 016977 **Tel:** 3600
Nearest Town/Resort Brampton
Directions From the M6 junction 43 take the A69 to Brampton, then the A6071 signposted Longtown for ½ mile. Turn into Old Church Lane, site is on the left in 400yds (signposted).
Acreage 4 **Open** March **to** October
Access Good **Site** Level
Sites Available Å ⇞ ⊜ **Total** 40
Facilities ∤ 🆎 ⚓ ☊ ⊙ ⊣ ◪ 🖵 📞
🏮 🅿 🖰 🔁 🖵
Nearby Facilities Ⴑ ✔ ⚓ ⊀ ∪
⇌ Brampton Junction
Ideal location for Hadrians (Roman) Wall, days out and visiting Carlisle and the romantic Border country. Near Gretna Green and South West Scotland.

BROUGHTON IN FURNESS
Birchbank Farm, Birchbank, Blawith, Ulverston, Cumbria, LA12 8EW.
Std: 01229 **Tel:** 885277
Email: birchbank@btinternet.com
Nearest Town/Resort Coniston Water
Directions A5092 ¼ mile west of Gawthwaite turn for Woodland. Site is 2 miles on the right along an unfenced road.
Acreage ½ **Open** Mid May **to** October
Access Good **Site** Level
Sites Available Å ⇞ ⊜ **Total** 8
Facilities ∤ 🆎 ⚓ ☊ ⊙ ⊣ 🛉 🔁 🖵
Nearby Facilities ⊀ ∪
⇌ Kirkby in Furness
Small farm site. Next to open Fell, good walking area.

CARLISLE
Dandy Dinmont Caravan & Camping Site, Blackford, Carlisle, Cumbria, CA6 4EA
Std: 01228 **Tel:** 674611
Email: dandydinmont@btopenworld.com
Website: www.caravan-camping-carlisle.itgo.com
Nearest Town/Resort Carlisle
Directions On A7 at Blackford, 4¼ miles north of Carlisle. Leave M6 at intersection 44, take the A7 Galashiels road (site approx 1½ miles on the right). After Blackford sign, follow road directional signs to site.
Acreage 4 **Open** March **to** October
Access Good **Site** Level
Sites Available Å ⇞ ⊜ **Total** 47
Facilities ∤ 🖵 🆎 ⚓ ☊ ⊙ ◪ 📞
🖰 🏮 🔁 🖵
Nearby Facilities ✔ ∪ ℛ
⇌ Carlisle
Historic Carlisle-Castle, Cathedral, Roman Wall, Border Country only 45 minutes to Lake District.

CARLISLE
Green Acres Caravan Park, High Knells, Houghton, Carlisle, Cumbria, CA6 4JW.
Std: 01228 **Tel:** 675418
Nearest Town/Resort Carlisle
Directions Leave the M6 at junction 44 (North Carlisle). Take the A689 for 1 mile, turn left signposted Scaleby. Site is 1 mile on the left.
Acreage 1 **Open** Easter **to** October
Access Good **Site** Level
Sites Available Å ⇞ ⊜ **Total** 30
Facilities ∤ 🖵 🆎 ⚓ ☊ ⊙ ⊣ ◪ 🔁 🖵
Nearby Facilities Ⴑ ✔ ℛ
⇌ Carlisle
Ideal touring base for Hadrians Wall, Carlisle City, Lake District and Scottish Borders. AA 3 Pennant Graded.

CARLISLE

Orton Grange Caravan Park, Wigton Road, Carlisle, Cumbria, CA5 6LA.
Std: 01228 **Tel:** 710252
Email: diane@ortongrange.flyer.co.uk
Nearest Town/Resort Carlisle
Directions 4 miles west of Carlisle on A595.
Acreage 6 **Open** All Year
Access Good **Site** Level
Sites Available A ⚏ ⊞ **Total** 50
Facilities ⅃ ⚏ ⅏ 🚿 ⌕ ⊙ ⤵ ⬜ 🍴
⚏ 🅿 🚻 🅿
Nearby Facilities ⌐ ✓ U
⮬ Dalston
Ideal for touring, north lakes, the Roman Wall plus Border country. Camping shop/ Tent sales.

COCKERMOUTH

Violet Bank Holiday Home Park,
Simonscales Lane, off Lorton Road, Cockermouth, Cumbria, CA13 9TG.
Std: 01900 **Tel:** 822169 **Fax:** 822169
Nearest Town/Resort Cockermouth
Directions From Cockermouth town centre take Lorton Street (B5292), after ¼ mile turn right into Vicarage Lane which leads onto Simonscales Lane and then onto a country lane to the caravan park.
Open 1 March **to** 15 Nov
Access Good **Site** Level
Sites Available A ⚏ ⊞
Facilities ⅃ ⅏ ⚏ ⌕ ⊙ ⤵ ⬜ 🍴
⚏ 🅿 🚻 🅿
Nearby Facilities ⌐ ✓ ⚓ ⤱ U ⌀
⮬ Workington
Quiet, peaceful site with excellent views.

COCKERMOUTH

Wheatsheaf Inn Caravan Park, Low Lorton, Cockermouth, Cumbria, CA13 9UW.
Std: 01900 **Tel:** 85268

Nearest Town/Resort Cockermouth
Directions 4 miles from Cockermouth on the Buttermere and Loweswater road.
Open March **to** 1 Nov
Access Good **Site** Level
Sites Available A ⚏ ⊞ **Total** 15
Facilities ⅃ ⚏ ⅏ ⌕ ⊙ ⤵ 🍴
⚏ 🅿 🚿 ⌕ ⬜ 🅿
Nearby Facilities ⌐ ✓ ⚓ ⤱ U ⌀ ⌀ ✻
⮬ Penrith

COCKERMOUTH

Whinfell Camping, Lorton, Nr Cockermouth, Cumbria, CA13 0RQ.
Std: 01900 **Tel:** 85260/85057
Nearest Town/Resort Cockermouth
Directions Take the A66 then the B5292 at Braithwaite into Low Lorton, follow caravan and camping signs. Or take the 5289 from Cockermouth.
Acreage 5 **Open** 15 March **to** 15 Nov
Access Good **Site** Level
Sites Available A ⚏ ⊞ **Total** 40
Facilities ⅃ ⚏ ⅏ ⚏ ⅏ ⌕ ⊙ ⤵ 🍴
⚏ ⊙ ⤱ 🅿
Nearby Facilities ⌐ ✓ ⚓ ⤱ U ⌀ ✻
⮬ Workington
Ideal touring and walking. Near to many attractions including Whinlatter Visitor Centre, Sellafield Visitor Centre, Ravenglass Miniature Steam Railway, Muncaster Castle & Gardens and an Owl centre.

COCKERMOUTH

Wyndham Holiday Park, Old Keswick Road, Cockermouth, Cumbria, CA13 9SF.
Std: 01900 **Tel:** 822571/825238
Website: www.wyndhamholidaypark.co.uk
Nearest Town/Resort Cockermouth
Directions ¼ of an hours drive from Keswick on the A66 or 3 minutes from Cockermouth town centre.
Acreage 12 **Open** March **to** November
Access Good **Site** Lev/Slope

Sites Available A ⚏ ⊞ **Total** 30
Facilities ⅃ ⚏ ⅏ ⅏ ⚏ ⌕ ⊙ ⤵ ⬜ 🍴
⚏ ⊙ ⅏ 🚿 ⌀ ⌕ ⤱ 🅿 🅿
Nearby Facilities ⌐ ✓ ⚓ ⤱ U ⌀ ⌀ ✻
⮬ Workington
Cockermouth is the birthplace of Wordsworth also Fletcher Christian of Mutiny on the Bounty. Next door to an indoor swimming pool.

CONISTON

Coniston Hall Camping Site, Coniston, Cumbria, LA21 8AS.
Std: 015394 **Tel:** 41223
Nearest Town/Resort Coniston
Directions 1 mile south of Coniston.
Acreage 200 **Open** March **to** October
Site Level
Sites Available A ⊞
Facilities ⅏ ⚏ ⌕ ⊙ ⤵ ⬜ 🍴 ⚏ ⅏ ⊙ ⤱ 🅿
Nearby Facilities ✓ ⚓ ⤱ U ⌀ ✻
⮬ Windermere
Lake access. Dogs to be kept on leads.

CONISTON

Hoathwaite Farm Caravan & Camping Site, Torver, Coniston, Cumbria, LA21 8AX
Std: 015394 **Tel:** 41349
Nearest Town/Resort Coniston
Directions A593 to Torver, after 3 miles turn left at green railings. After 100yds turn left over first farm cattlegrid, follow road to farm.
Acreage 30 **Open** All Year
Access Good **Site** Lev/Slope
Sites Available A ⊞
Facilities ⬜ ⤱ 🅿
Nearby Facilities ✓ ⚓ ⤱ U ✻
⮬ Ulverston
Scenic, ideal for touring and walking. Lake access from the site for boating etc.. Touring Caravans are Caravan Club Members only.

Dandy Dinmont Caravan & Camping Park

Phone for our new FREE colour brochure

Dandy Dinmont Caravan & Camping Park
Blackford
Carlisle
CA6 4EA
Tel/Fax: 01228 674611
dandydinmont@btopenworld.com
www.caravan-camping-carlisle.itgo.com

A quiet Countryside Park situated 1.5 miles North of the M6 Junction 44, on the right of Galashiels road at Blackford. Ideal for an overnight halt or as a base for visiting historic Carlisle, the Scottish Borders or Roman Hadrian's Wall. Lake District only a short drive away, Beside the Reivers cycle route.

52

ONISTON

er Cottage Caravan Park, Pier
ottage, Coniston, Cumbria, LA21 8AJ.
d: 01539 Tel: 441497
earest Town/Resort Coniston
rections 1 mile east of Coniston off the
285 Hawkshead road.
creage 1 Open March to October
ccess Good Site Level
tes Available ⊕□ Total 10
cilities ⒰ ⚹ ↾ ⊙ ☀ ⌕⇥⌷
earby Facilities ✔⚒⊥✦∪♪✻
  Windermere
keside site with boating, fishing and
lwalking.

ROOK

atherheath Lane Camping & Caravan
rk, Chain House, Bonningate, Kendal,
mbria, LA8 9BZ.
d: 01539 Tel: 821154
mail:
therheath@lakedistrictcaravans.co.uk
ebsite: www.lakedistrictcaravans.co.uk
earest Town/Resort Bowness on
ndermere
rections From Kendal A591 take B5284
Crook, turn right at sign to Burneside.
creage 1 Open March to 15 Nov
ccess Good Site Level
tes Available ⚹ ⊕ ⚌ Total 20
a c i l i t i e s ∮ ⒰ ⚹ ↾ ⊙ ☀ ⚌ ☀
  ☎⒲⇥⌷
earby Facilities ✔⚒⊥✦∪♪✻
  Burneside
ke District National Park. Pool table on
e.

UMWHITTON

airndale Caravan Park, Cumwhitton,
eadsnook, Brampton, Near Carlisle,
mbria, CA8 9BZ.
d: 01768 Tel: 896280
earest Town/Resort Carlisle
rections Follow A69 to Warwick Bridge
d then follow unclassified road through
eat Corby to Cumwhitton, approx. 9 miles.
creage 2 Open March to October
ccess Good Site Level
tes Available ⊕ ⚌ Total 5
cilities ∮ ⒰ ⒲ ⚹ ↾ ⊙ ☀ ☀⇥⌷⒲
earby Facilities ✔⚒⊥✦
  Carlisle
cenic views, ideal touring, quiet site, water
d electricity to individual touring sites.
indsurfing nearby.

ENT

wegales Farm, Cowgill, Dent,
edbergh, Cumbria, LA10 5RH.
d: 01539 Tel: 625440
earest Town/Resort Sedbergh
rections Leave the M6 at junction 37 and
ead towards Sedbergh then Dent, park is
½ miles east of Dent Village.
creage 11½ Open All Year
ccess Good Site Level
tes Available ⚹ ⊕ ⚌ Total 60
acilities ⒰ ↾ ⊙ ☀⇥⌷
earby Facilities ✔⚒✻
 Dent
ongside a river. Ideal for children.

ENT

igh Laning Farm Caravan & Camping
ark, High Laning Farm, Dent, Nr.
edbergh, Cumbria, LA10 5QJ.
d: 01539 Tel: 625239
d: 01539 Fax: 625116
mail:
argarettaylor4@compuserve.com
eb: www.caravancampingsites.co.uk/
mbria/dent

Nearest Town/Resort Sedbergh
Directions Leave the M6 at junction 37 and
take the A684 to Sedbergh, Dent is 5 miles
from Sedbergh. Take the A1 then exit onto
the A684 to Leyburn, Bainbridge and
Hawes, Dent is 15 miles from Hawes.
Open All Year
Access Good Site Level
Sites Available ⚹ ⊕ ⚌
Facilities ⚹ ∮ ⌷ ⒰ ⒲ ⚹ ↾ ⊙ ⇥ ⚌ ⌷ ☀
  ⚻ ⒰⚌⌷⒲
Nearby Facilities ↾ ✔⊥✦∪♪♫✻
  ⇥ Dent
Dent is quaint and peaceful with lovely walks
and beautiful scenery. Ideal for birdwatching.
Historical attractions, cobbled village and
The Three Peaks.

EGREMONT

Home Farm Caravan Park, Home Farm,
Rothersyke, Egremont, Cumbria, CA22 2US
Std: 01946 Tel: 824023
Nearest Town/Resort Egremont
Directions From the south on the A595 to
Calderbridge, take the first right after
Blackbeck roundabout and follow St Bees
signs on the B5345. 3 miles from St. Bees
and 2 miles from Egremont.
Acreage 2 Open March to November
Access Good Site Lev/Slope
Sites Available ⊕ ⚌ Total 18
Facilities ∮ ⒰ ⒲ ⚹ ↾ ⊙ ⇥⌷ ☀ ☀⇥⌷
Nearby Facilities ↾ ✔∪
  ⇥ St. Bees
Near beaches, lakes and mountains. Self
owned tourers only.

EGREMONT

Tarnside Caravan Park, Braystones,
Near Beckermet, Cumbria, CA21 2YL.
Std: 01946 Tel: 841308
Email: ann@hotmail.com
Nearest Town/Resort Egremont
Directions 2 miles south of Egremont,
follow brown tourist signs on the B5345.
Acreage 10 Open All Year
Access Narrow Roads Site Level
Sites Available ⚹ ⊕ ⚌ Total 20
Facilities ⚹ ∮ ⌷ ⒰ ⒲ ⚹ ↾ ⊙ ⌐ ⌷ ☀
  ⒰☎⚹♀⒲⚻⇥⌷
Nearby Facilities ↾ ✔∪✻
  ⇥ Braystones (On Site)
Overlooking the sea and West Lake District
Fells. Ideal base for touring the Lake District.

ESKDALE

Fisherground Farm, Eskdale, Cumbria,
CA19 1TF.
Std: 019467 Tel: 23319
Email: camping@fisherground.co.uk
Website: www.fishergroundcamping.co.uk
Nearest Town/Resort Broughton in
Furness
Directions ¾ mile past Broughton on A595
turn RT. up Duddon Valley (signed Ulpha).
4 miles to Ulpha, then turn LT., (signed
Eskdale). 6 miles over Birker Moor, descend
to Eskdale turn RT. at King George IV Inn.
Fisherground is first farm on LT.
Acreage 3 Open March to November
Access Good Site Level
Sites Available ⚹ ⚌ Total 100
Facilities ⒰ ⚹ ↾ ⊙ ⌐ ⌷ ⚌ ⌷ ☀
  ⒰☎⚹Λ⊛⇥⌷
Nearby Facilities ✔⊥✦∪✻
  ⇥ Ravenglass
Quiet family site in the heart of the Lake
District. 7 mile miniature railway 100yds
(private station). Adventure playground,
pond and laundry. Camp fires allowed. Voted
Northern Campsite of the Year 1997 by
Camping Magazine and AA Award for
Excellence. Brochure on request.

GOSFORTH

Seven Acres Caravan Park & Camping
Site, Holmrook, Cumbria, CA19 1YD.
Std: 019467 Tel: 25480
Nearest Town/Resort Whitehaven
Directions Half way between Gosforth and
Holmrook on the A595 (Broughton-in-
Furness to Workington road) west coast
road.
Acreage 3 Open March to Mid November
Access Good Site Level
Sites Available ⚹ ⊕ ⚌ Total 103
Facilities ∮ ⒰ ⒲ ⚹ ↾ ⊙ ⌷ ☀
  ⒰☎⚹Λ⇥⌷
Nearby Facilities ↾ ✔⊥✦∪♪♫✻
  ⇥ Seascale
Family owned and run site at the foot of
Wasdale Valley, 3 miles from the coast. Ideal
for touring the Western Lake District,
walking, golf, fishing, riding and relaxing.

GRANGE-OVER-SANDS

Cartmel Caravan & Camping Park,
Wells House Farm, Cartmel, Grange-
Over-Sands, Cumbria, LA11 6PN.
Std: 015395 Tel: 36270
Std: 015395 Fax: 36270
Website: www.ukparks.co.uk/cartmel
Nearest Town/Resort Grange-over-
Sands
Directions Enter Cartmel from the A590,
turn right at the Pig & Whistle, turn next left
and the entrance is shortly on the right hand
side.
Acreage 3 Open March to October
Site Level
Sites Available ⚹ Total 55
Facilities ⚹ ∮ ⒲ ⚹ ↾ ⊙ ☀ ⚌ ☀
  ⒰☎⚹Λ⇥⌷
Nearby Facilities ↾ ✔∪
  ⇥ Grange-over-Sands
Tranquil park set in picturesque
surroundings, yet only 2 minutes from the
village square. Cartmel, one of South
Lakelands oldest and prettiest villages, has
grown up around its famous 12th Century
Priory.

GRANGE-OVER-SANDS

Greaves Farm Caravan Park, c/o
Prospect House, Barber Green, Grange-
over-Sands, Cumbria, LA11 6HU.
Std: 015395 Tel: 36329/36587
Website: www.ukparks.co.uk/greaves
Nearest Town/Resort Grange-over-
Sands
Directions Come off the A590 approx 1 mile
south of Newby Bridge at the sign "Cartmel
4 miles". Proceed 1½ miles to sign for
caravan park.
Acreage 3 Open March to October
Access Good Site Level
Sites Available ⚹ ⊕ ⚌ Total 10
Facilities ∮ ⒲ ⚹ ↾ ⊙ ☀ ⒰☎⇥⌷
Nearby Facilities ↾ ✔⊥✦∪✻
  ⇥ Grange-over-Sands
Quiet, select, family run park. Ideal base for
exploring the Lake District.

GRANGE-OVER-SANDS

High Fell Gate Caravan Park, High Fell
Gate, Grange-over-Sands, Cumbria, LA11
7QA.
Std: 015395 Tel: 36231
Nearest Town/Resort Grange-over-
Sands
Directions Between Grange-over-Sands
and Cartmel, next to Grange Fell Golf Club.
Acreage 6 Open 15 Feb to 15 Nov
Access Good Site Sloping
Sites Available ⚹ ⊕ ⚌ Total 20
Facilities ∮ ⒰ ⒲ ⚹ ↾ ⊙ ⌐ ⌷ ☀
  ⒰☎⚹⇥⌷⒲

Nearby Facilities ⌐ ✒ ⊰ ∪ ♪ ⫟
≉ Grange-over-Sands
Next to a golf club and near the beach and six pubs.

GRANGE-OVER-SANDS

Lakeland Leisure Park, Moor Lane, Flookburgh, Nr. Grange-over-Sands, Cumbria, LA11 4LT.
Std: 015395 **Tel:** 58556
Std: 015395 **Fax:** 58559
Website: www.british-holidays.co.uk
Nearest Town/Resort Grange-over-Sands

Directions Leave the M6 at junction 36 onto the A590, turn left onto the A6/A590 for Barrow-in-Furness. Then take the B5277 through Grange-over-Sands, then Allithwaite and into Flookburgh. Turn left at the village square and travel 1 mile down this road to the Park.
Open March **to** October
Access Good **Site** Level
Sites Available ⋏ ⌖ ⌷ **Total** 125
Facilities ⅍ ≀ ⏆ ≛ ⌐ ⊙⊰ ⊿ ⌷ ⌹
⌾ ⌘ ⏀ ⊟ ✗ ⊻ ⑪ ⋏ ⊓ ⋡ ⌖ ⁂⫟⏥⏢ ⊟
Nearby Facilities ⌐ ✒ ⊿ ⊰ ∪ ⇗ ♪ ⫟
≉ Cark
Less than 10 miles from Lake Windermere. Ideal for touring and exploring.

GRANGE-OVER-SANDS

Oak Head Caravan Park, Ayside, Grange-over-Sands, Cumbria, LA11 6JA.
Std: 015395 **Tel:** Newby Bridge 31475
Nearest Town/Resort Grange-over-Sands

Directions M6 junction 36 follow signs for Newby Bridge, site is signposted on left hand side of A590, 2 miles from Newby Bridge, 13 miles from M6.
Acreage 2½ **Open** March **to** October
Access Good **Site** Lev/slope
Sites Available ⋏ ⌖ ⌷ **Total** 90
Facilities ≀ ⏆ ≛ ⌐ ⊙⊰ ⊿ ⌷ ⌹
⏀ ⊟ ⌂ ⫟⏢
Nearby Facilities ⌐ ✒ ⊿ ⊰ ∪ ⇗ ♪ ⫟
≉ Grange-over-Sands
Scenic views, ideal touring. Within easy reach of all lakes.

GRANGE-OVER-SANDS

Old Park Wood Caravan Park, Holker, Cark-in-Cartmel, Grange-over-Sands, Cumbria, LA11 7PP.
Std: 015395 **Tel:** 58266
Std: 015395 **Fax:** 58101
Email: pobatopw@aol.com
Nearest Town/Resort Grange-over-Sands
Directions Take the A590 to Grange-over-Sands then onto the B5278. Head for Holker Hall, ½ mile past the main gates turn left and follow the road for 1 mile, signposted.

Open March **to** October
Access Good **Site** Level
Sites Available ⌖ ⌷
Facilities ≀ ⏆ ⏶ ⌐ ⊙⊰ ⊿ ⌷ ⌹
⌾ ⏀ ⊟ ⑪ ⋡⫟⏥
Nearby Facilities ⌐ ✒
≉ Cark-in-Cartmel
Alongside an estuary with views of the mountains.

GREYSTOKE

Hopkinsons Whitbarrow Hall Caravan Park, Berrier, Penrith, Cumbria, CA11 0XB.
Std: 017684 **Tel:** 83456
Nearest Town/Resort Keswick
Directions Leave M6 at junction 40, A66 towards Keswick after 8 miles turn right at signpost Hutton Roof site ½ mile from A66. NEW tourist signs "Hopkinsons".
Acreage 8 **Open** March **to** October
Access Good **Site** Level
Sites Available ⋏ ⌖ ⌷ **Total** 80
Facilities ≀ ⏆ ⏶ ⌐ ⊙⊰ ⊿ ⌷ ⌹
⌾ ⏀ ⊟ ♀ ⋏ ⑪ ⌖⫟⏢
Nearby Facilities ⌐ ✒ ⊿ ⊰ ∪ ⇗ ⫟
≉ Penrith
Views. 5 miles from Ullswater, 10 miles from Keswick and 8 miles from Penrith. Lake District. AA 3 Pennants.

HAWKSHEAD

Hawkshead Hall Farm, Near Ambleside, Cumbria, LA22 0NN.
Std: 015394 **Tel:** 36221
Nearest Town/Resort Hawkshead
Directions 5 miles south of Ambleside on the B5286.
Acreage 5 **Open** March **to** October
Access Good **Site** Lev/Slope
Sites Available ⋏ ⌖ ⌷ **Total** 50
Facilities ⏆ ⏆⊙⌹ ⌹ ⏀
Nearby Facilities
≉ Windermere

HAWKSHEAD

The Croft Caravan & Camp Site, North Lonsdale Road, Hawkshead, Nr. Ambleside, Cumbria, LA22 0NX.
Std: 015394 **Tel:** 36374
Std: 015394 **Fax:** 36544
Email: enquiries@hawkshead-croft.com
Website: www.hawkshead-croft.com
Nearest Town/Resort Hawkshead
Directions From Ambleside 5 miles on the B5286 at village of Hawkshead.
Acreage 5 **Open** March **to** November
Access Good **Site** Level
Sites Available ⋏ ⌖ ⌷ **Total** 100
Facilities ⌿ ≀ ⏆ ≛ ⌐ ⊿ ⌷ ⌹
⏀ ⌂ ⏀ ⊟ ⌂
Nearby Facilities ✒ ∪
≉ Windermere

KENDAL

Camping & Caravanning Club Site, Millcrest, Shap Road, Kendal, Cumbria, LA9 6NY.
Std: 01539 **Tel:** 741363
Website: www.campingandcaravanningclub.co.uk
Directions On the A6, 1½ miles north Kendal, site entrance is 100 yards north the nameplate 'Skelsmergh'.
Acreage 3 **Open** March **to** October
Site Lev/Slope
Sites Available ⋏ ⌖ ⌷ **Total** 50
Facilities ≀ ⏆ ⏆ ≛ ⌐ ⊙⊰ ⊿ ⌹
⏀ ⏀ ⋏⫟⏢ ⊟
Nearby Facilities ⌐ ✒ ∪ ♪
≉ Kendal
Right in the middle of the Lake Distric Tumble drier and spin drier on site. B Graded. Non members welcome.

KENDAL

Lambhowe Caravan Park, Crosthwaite, Near Kendal, Cumbria, LA8 8JE.
Std: 015395 **Tel:** 68483
Nearest Town/Resort Bowness on Windermere
Directions Leave the M6 at junction 36 ai take the A590, then take the A5074 towar Bowness. Lambhowe is opposite th Damson Dene Hotel.
Acreage 20 **Open** 1 March **to** 16 Nov
Access Good **Site** Level
Sites Available ⌖ ⌷ **Total** 14
Facilities ≀ ⏆ ⏆ ≛ ⌐ ⊙ ⌹
⏀ ⌂ ♀⫟⏢
Nearby Facilities ⌐ ♪
≉ Windermere
Set in the delightful Lyth Valley. Just a 1 minute drive to Lake Windermere.

KENDAL

Pound Farm Caravan Park, Crook, Kendal, Cumbria, LA8 8JZ.
Std: 01539 **Tel:** 821220
Nearest Town/Resort Bowness-on-Windermere
Directions Leave the M6 junction 36, tu onto the A591. After 10 miles at larg roundabout take the B5284 to Crook, ar Pound Farm is 2 miles on the left.
Acreage 4 **Open** 1 March **to** 14 Nov
Access Good **Site** Sloping
Sites Available ⋏ ⌖ ⌷ **Total** 20
Facilities ≀ ⏆ ⏆ ≛ ⌐ ⊙⊰ ⌷ ⏀⫟⏢
Nearby Facilities ⌐ ✒
≉ Kendal
Ideal for touring the Lake District.

KENDAL

Limpool Caravan Park, Levens, Kendal, Cumbria, LA8 8EQ.
Std: 015395 **Tel:** 52265
Nearest Town/Resort Kendal
Directions 6 miles south of Kendal on the A6, at Levens Bridge turn right onto the A590, Park is 500 metres on the left.
Acreage 2½ **Open** 15 March **to** 31 October
Access Good **Site** Level
Sites Available ♫ ⊞ **Total** 15
Facilities ∮ 🕮 🅵 🎇 ⌂ ⊙ ↻ 🗑 🛡
🍴 ☖ 🕮 ⊛ ⛻🖃
Nearby Facilities ┌ ✦ ⚓ ┶ ∪ ⊅ ♫ ⚹
‡ Oxenholme
Alongside the River Kent and near the south lakes. Easy access from the M6 motorway (5 minutes).

KESWICK

Burns Farm Caravan Site, St. Johns-in-the-Vale, Keswick, Cumbria, CA12 4RR.
Std: 017687 **Tel:** 79225
Nearest Town/Resort Keswick
Directions Turn left off the A66 (Penrith to Keswick road) ½ mile past B5322 junction signposted Castlerigg Stone Circle. Site is on the right, farm is on the left. 2¼ miles from Keswick.
Acreage 1¼ **Open** Easter **to** October
Access Good **Site** Level
Sites Available ▲ ♫ ⊞ **Total** 40
Facilities ∮ 🕮 🎇 ⊙ ↻ 🛡 ☖ ⊛⛻🖃🖃
Nearby Facilities ┌ ✦ ┶ ∪ ♫ ⚹
‡ Penrith
Ideal touring, walking and climbing. Beautiful views, quiet family site.

KESWICK

Camping & Caravanning Club Site, Derwentwater, Keswick, Cumbria, CA12 5EP.
Std: 01768 **Tel:** 772392
Website:
www.campingandcaravanningclub.co.uk
Nearest Town/Resort Keswick
Directions From the A66 roundabout at Keswick take the Carlisle road and turn sharp right, then right again onto the site, signposted.
Acreage 14 **Open** February **to** Nov
Access Good **Site** Level
Sites Available ▲ ♫ ⊞ **Total** 250
Facilities & ∮ 🕮 🅵 🕮 🎇 ⊙ ↻ 🗑 🛡
🍴 ☖ ⊛⛻🖃
Nearby Facilities ┌ ✦ ⚓ ┶ ∪ ⊅ ♫ ⚹
‡ Penrith
Situated on the banks of Derwentwater, ideal for fishing and water sports. Boat launching for small boats. Good hillwalking area. Close to the centre of Keswick. BTB Graded. Non members welcome.

KESWICK

Dalebottom Farm Caravan & Camping Park, Naddle, Keswick, Cumbria, CA12 4TF.
Std: 017687 **Tel:** 72176
Nearest Town/Resort Keswick
Directions 2 miles south of Keswick on the A591 Windermere road.
Acreage 6 **Open** 1 March **to** 1 Nov
Sites Available ▲ ♫ ⊞
Facilities ∮ 🕮 🎇 ⊙ ↻ 🛡 ☖
🍴 ☖ ⊛🖃
Nearby Facilities ┌ ✦ ⚓ ┶ ∪ ♫ ⚹
‡ Penrith
In the heart of lakeland.

KESWICK

Lakeside Holiday Park, Off Crowpark Road, Keswick, Cumbria, CA12 5EW.
Std: 017687 **Tel:** 72878
Std: 017687 **Fax:** 72017
Email:
welcome@lakesideholidaypark.co.uk
Website: www.lakesideholidaypark.co.uk
Nearest Town/Resort Keswick
Directions Leave the M6 at junction 40 and take the A66 west. Follow signs for town centre past Lakes Supermarket and turn next right passing Keswick Rugby Club, signposted 150 metres.
Acreage 6 **Open** March **to** November
Access Good **Site** Level
Sites Available ♫ ⊞ **Total** 64
Facilities ∮ 🕮 🅵 🕮 🎇 ⊙ ↻ 🗑 🛡 🖃
☖ ⊛🖃
Nearby Facilities ┌ ✦ ⚓ ∪ ♫ ⚹
‡ Penrith
Lake frontage. Just a 7 minute flat walk to the market square. David Bellamy Gold Conservation Award and ETB 4 Star Graded.

KESWICK

Scotgate Camping & Touring Site, Braithwaite, Keswick, Cumbria, CA12 5TF.
Std: 017687 **Tel:** 78343
Std: 017687 **Fax:** 78099
Website: www.scotgateholidaypark.co.uk
Nearest Town/Resort Keswick
Directions 2 miles from Keswick, just off the A66 at the junction for Braithwaite B5292.
Acreage 9 **Open** March **to** Mid Nov
Access Good **Site** Level
Sites Available ▲ ♫ ⊞ **Total** 165
Facilities ∮ 🕮 🅵 🕮 🎇 ⊙ ↻ 🗑 🛡 🖃
🎱 ☖ ☖ ✕ ⛻🖃
Nearby Facilities ┌ ✦ ⚓ ┶ ∪ ♫ ⚹
‡ Penrith
Central for all lakes. Ideal for walking.

KESWICK

Thirlspot Farm Caravan Park, Thirlmere, Keswick, Cumbria, CA12 4TW.
Std: 01768 **Tel:** 772551
Nearest Town/Resort Keswick
Directions Situated on the A591 between Keswick and Grasmere.
Open June **to** September
Access Good **Site** Level
Sites Available ▲ ☐
Facilities 🕮 🎇 ⊙ ↻ 🛡 ☖🖃
Nearby Facilities ┌ ✦ ⚓ ┶ ∪ ⊅ ♫ ⚹
‡ Penrith
Close to mountains and a lake, ideal for walkers.

KIRKBY LONSDALE

New House Caravan Park, Kirkby Lonsdale, Cumbria, LA6 2HR.
Std: 015242 **Tel:** 71590
Nearest Town/Resort Kirkby Lonsdale/Kendal
Directions From Kirkby Lonsdale take the A65 towards Settle, after approx. 1½ miles site is on the right 300 yards past Whoop Hall Inn.
Acreage 3½ **Open** March **to** End Oct
Access Good **Site** Lev/Slope
Sites Available ♫ ⊞ **Total** 50
Facilities ∮ 🕮 🅵 🕮 🎇 ⊙ ↻ 🗑 🛡 🖃
🎱 ☖ ☖ ⛻🖃
Nearby Facilities ┌ ✦ ∪
‡ Carnforth
Situated near to the historic town of Kirkby Lonsdale and Devils Bridge. An ideal location to visit lakes and Yorkshire Dales.

KIRKBY STEPHEN

Bowberhead Caravan Site, Bowberhead Farm, Ravenstonedale, Kirkby Stephen, Cumbria, CA17 4NL.
Std: 015396 **Tel:** 23254
Std: 015396 **Fax:** 23254
Email:
hols@cumbriaclassiccoaches.co.uk
Website:
www.cumbriaclassiccoaches.co.uk
Nearest Town/Resort Kirkby Stephen
Directions 4½ miles south of Kirkby Stephen off the A683 road to Sedgbergh.
Acreage 1¼ **Open** All Year
Access Good **Site** Lev/Slope
Sites Available ▲ ♫ ⊞ **Total** 7
Facilities ∮ 🕮 🎇 ⊙ ↻ 🗑 🛡 🖃
☖ ☖ ⊛🖃
Nearby Facilities ┌ ✦ ∪ ♫
‡ Kirkby Stephen
Settle to Carlisle Line, beautiful views, best fell walking. TV hook-ups. Vintage coach excursions from the site.

KIRKBY STEPHEN

Pennine View Caravan & Camping Park, Pennine View, Station Road, Kirkby Stephen, Cumbria, CA17 4SZ.
Std: 017683 **Tel:** 71717
Nearest Town/Resort Kendal
Directions On the A685, approx. 1 mile from Kirkby Stephen town centre.
Acreage 2½ **Open** Beg March **to** End Oct
Access Good **Site** Level
Sites Available ▲ ∮ ⊞ **Total** 43
Facilities & ∮ 🕮 🅵 🎇 ⊙ ↻ 🗑 🛡
☖ ☖ ⊛🖃
Nearby Facilities ┌ ✦ ∪ ♫
‡ Kirkby Stephen
On the edge of the River Eden. On the outskirts of the small market town of Kirkby Stephen. Ideal for walking and touring, the Yorkshire Dales and the Lake District.

KIRKBY THORE

Low Moor, Kirkby Thore, Penrith, Cumbria, CA10 1XG.
Std: 017683 **Tel:** 61231
Nearest Town/Resort Appleby
Directions On the A66 7 miles south east of Penrith, between Temple Sowerby and Kirkby Thore villages.
Acreage 1½ **Open** April **to** October
Access Good **Site** Level
Sites Available ▲ ♫ ⊞ **Total** 12
Facilities ∮ 🕮 🎇 🅵 ⊙ 🛡 🖃
🍴 🎱 ☖ 🕮 ⛻🖃
Nearby Facilities ✦
‡ Penrith
Open country.

LAMPLUGH

Inglenook Caravan Park, Lamplugh, Workington, Cumbria, CA14 4SH.
Std: 01946 **Tel:** 861240
Std: 01946 **Fax:** 861240
Nearest Town/Resort Cockermouth
Directions Leave A66 road at Cockermouth and take A5086 road (Egremont). 7 miles on turn left at caravan sign.
Acreage 3½ **Open** All Year
Access Good **Site** Level
Sites Available ▲ ♫ ⊞ **Total** 30
Facilities ∮ 🕮 🎇 🅵 ⊙ 🛡
🎱 ☖ ☖ 🕮 ⛻🖃🖃
Nearby Facilities ┌ ✦ ∪
‡ Workington
Scenic surroundings and an attractive environment. Golf 4C. 10 miles to beach. Ideal touring and walking area. Luxury holiday homes for hire. A.A. Recommended 3 Pennant site, A.A. Award for Excellence and Rose Award 2000.

LONGTOWN

Camelot Caravan Park, Sandysike, Longtown, Carlisle, Cumbria, CA6 5SZ.
Std: 01228 **Tel:** 791248
Nearest Town/Resort Longtown
Directions On left 1¼ miles south of Longtown on A7, northbound leave M6 at exit 44, take A7 (Longtown) site on right in 4 miles.
Acreage 1¼ **Open** March **to** October
Access Good **Site** Level
Sites Available ▲ ⌖ ⊟ **Total** 20
Facilities ⨍ ⎈ ⟲⊙⌁ ⛺ ♒ ⌗⊡
Nearby Facilities ⌖ ⫽ ∪
⚇ Carlisle
Ideal for Solway coast, Carlisle Settle railway, romantic Gretna Green, base for Hadrians Wall and border towns, Carlisle Castle. AA 3 Pennants.

LONGTOWN

High Gaitle Caravan Park, Gaitle Bridge, Longtown, Cumbria, CA6 5LU.
Std: 01228 **Tel:** 791819
Std: 01228 **Fax:** 791819
Nearest Town/Resort Carlisle
Directions From Carlisle travel north on the A7 to Longtown, then take the A6071 north towards Gretna. Approx. 10 miles from Carlisle.
Acreage 6 **Open** All Year
Access Good **Site** Level
Sites Available ▲ ⌖ ⊟ **Total** 30
Facilities ⨍ ⎈ ⟲⊙⌁ ♒ ⊡
Nearby Facilities ⌖ ⫽
⚇ Carlisle
Ideal touring location for the Lake District, Borders region, Gretna Green and Hadrians Wall.

LONGTOWN

Oakbank Lakes, Longtown, Near Carlisle, Cumbria, CA6 5NA.
Std: 01228 **Tel:** 791108
Std: 01228 **Fax:** 791108
Email: oakbank@nlaq.globalnet.co.uk
Nearest Town/Resort Longtown
Directions Take the A7 from Longtown towards Hawick, signposted second left.
Open All Year
Access Good **Site** Level
Sites Available ▲ ⌖ ⊟ **Total** 24
Facilities ⨍ ⎈ ⟲⌁ ⊙ ♒
Nearby Facilities ⫽
3 coarse fishing lakes, plus under 16's practice pools.

MARYPORT

Spring Lea Caravan Park, Allonby, Maryport, Cumbria, CA15 6QF.
Std: 01900 **Tel:** 881331
Std: 01900 **Fax:** 881209
Nearest Town/Resort Maryport
Directions 5 miles north of Maryport on the B5300 coast road.
Acreage 5 **Open** March **to** October
Access Good **Site** Level
Sites Available ▲ ⌖ ⊟ **Total** 35
Facilities ⨍ ⎈ ⟲⊙⌁ ♒
Nearby Facilities ⌖ ⫽ ⚓ ∪
⚇ Maryport

300 yards from the beach with views of Lakeland and Scottish hills. Leisure centre for sauna etc.. Bar/restaurant on site.

MARYPORT

Westville Caravan Park, Allonby, Maryport, Cumbria, CA15 6QA.
Std: 01900 **Tel:** 881392
Nearest Town/Resort Allonby
Directions From Maryport take the A596 north, then take the B5300 signposted Allonby, on the edge of town.
Acreage 2½ **Open** 1 March **to** 14 November
Access Good **Site** Level
Sites Available ⌖ ⊟ **Total** 8
Facilities ⨍ ⎈ ⟲⌁ ♒
Nearby Facilities ⌖ ⫽ ⚓ ∪ ⚇
⚇ Maryport
Near the beach and Lake District National Park. You can also call us on 01772 339490.

MEALSGATE

The Larches Caravan Park, Mealsgate, Wigton, Cumbria, CA7 1LQ.
Std: 016973 **Tel:** 71379/71803
Std: 016973 **Fax:** 71782
Nearest Town/Resort Wigton
Directions From the north take the A57/A74/A7/A69 to Carlisle, follow the A595 to Mealsgate. From the south leave the M6 at junction 41, take the B5305 Wigton road as far as the A595. Turn left and follow the A595 to Mealsgate.
Acreage 17 **Open** March **to** October
Access Good **Site** Lev/slope
Sites Available ▲ ⌖ ⊟ **Total** 73
Facilities ⨍ ⎈ ⟲⊙⌁ ♒
Nearby Facilities ⌖ ⫽ ⚓ ∪ ⫽
⚇ Wigton
ADULTS ONLY SITE. Ideal for couples, peace and quiet in the countryside with beautiful views. Excellent toilets. ADAC Yellow Award.

MELMERBY

Melmerby Caravan Park, Melmerby, Penrith, Cumbria, CA10 1HE.
Std: 01768 **Tel:** 881311
Std: 01768 **Fax:** 881311
Nearest Town/Resort Penrith
Directions Situated in Melmerby Village on the A686, 10 miles north east of Penrith.
Open Mid-March **to** November
Access Good **Site** Level
Sites Available ⌖ ⊟ **Total** 5
Facilities ⨍ ⎈ ⟲⌁
Nearby Facilities ⌖ ⫽
Excellent walking country, ideal base for touring North Pennines, Eden Valley and Lake District.

MILNTHORPE

Waters Edge Caravan Park, Crooklands, Near Kendal, Cumbria, LA7 7NN.
Std: 015395 **Tel:** 67708
Std: 015395 **Fax:** 67610
Nearest Town/Resort Kendal
Directions A65 Crooklands, ¾ mile from M6 motorway junction 36.

Acreage 3 **Open** March **to** November
Access Good **Site** Level
Sites Available ▲ ⌖ ⊟ **Total** 35
Facilities ⨍ ⎈ ⟲⌁ ♒
Nearby Facilities ⌖ ⫽ ∪ ⫽
⚇ Oxenholme
Set in quiet and pleasant countryside. Lake, Yorkshire Dales and Morecambe Bay with easy reach.

PENRITH

Beckes Caravan Site, Penruddock, Penrith, Cumbria, CA11 0RX.
Std: 017684 **Tel:** 83224
Nearest Town/Resort Penrith
Directions 7 miles from Penrith, 11 miles from Keswick. Turn right off the A66 onto the B5288, 400 yards on the right.
Acreage 3½ **Open** Easter **to** October
Access Good **Site** Lev/Slope
Sites Available ▲ ⌖ ⊟ **Total** 23
Facilities ⨍ ⎈ ⟲⌁ ♒
Nearby Facilities ⌖ ⫽ ⚓ ∪ ⫽
⚇ Penrith
Ideal touring for Lakes. Discounted rates for O.A.P.s.

PENRITH

Cross Dormont Camp Site, Dunroamin, Cross Dormont, Howtown, Penrith, Cumbria, CA10 2NA.
Std: 017684 **Tel:** 86537
Email: cola@zoom.co.uk
Nearest Town/Resort Penrith
Directions From Penrith follow the main road for approx. 5 miles then turn left into Howtown road. We are approx. 1½ mile along on the left hand side.
Acreage 5 **Open** March **to** November
Access Good **Site** Level
Sites Available ▲ ⌖ ⊟ **Total** 10
Facilities ⎈ ⌁ ⟲⌁ ⫽
Nearby Facilities ⫽ ⚓ ∪ ⫽
⚇ Penrith
Quiet family run site, overlooking a lake with lake access. Near to a yacht club.

PENRITH

Flusco Wood Caravan Park, Flusco, Penrith, Cumbria, CA11 0JB.
Std: 01768 **Tel:** 480020
Email: fluscowood@btclick.com
Website: www.fluscowood.co.uk
Nearest Town/Resort Penrith
Directions Leave the M6 at junction 40 and travel west on the A66 for 4 miles.
Acreage 14 **Open** Easter **to** November
Access Good **Site** Sloping
Sites Available ⌖ ⊟ **Total** 47
Facilities ⨍ ⎈ ⟲⊙⌁
Nearby Facilities ⌖ ⫽ ⚓ ∪ ⫽
⚇ Penrith
Grassed, serviced pitches set in woodland clearings. 1 mile from the Lake District. Last Year: Prices held for 2002. ETB 4 Star Graded.

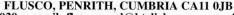

LOWTHER HOLIDAY PARK

Lowther Holiday Park Limited
Eamont Bridge, Penrith, Cumbria CA10 2JB
Tel: (01768) 863631   www.lowther-holidaypark.co.uk

*We would like to extend an invitation to all those who have not
yet discovered the charm and beauty of Lowther Holiday Park.
A haven of peace and tranquillity, set in 50 acres of natural
parkland on the banks of the River Lowther. Home of the
rare and facinating Red Squirrel.*

PENRITH

Gillside Caravan & Camping Site,
Glenridding, Penrith, Cumbria, CA11 0QQ.
Std: 017684 **Tel:** 82346
Email: gillside@uk.packardbell.org
Nearest Town/Resort Penrith
Directions A592 signposted Ullswater, 14
miles from Penrith. In Glenridding turn right,
follow sign for Gillside.
Acreage 8 **Open** March **to** Mid Nov
Access Good **Site** Level
Sites Available A ⊕ ⊕ **Total** 65
Facilities ⚡ ⬛ ⚓ ⌐ ⊙ ⊶ ◻ ⬤
⬛ ☺ ⊛ ⊡
Nearby Facilities ⌐ ✓ ⊥ ⌁ U ♙ ⅄
⚓ Penrith
Foot of Helvellyn, 5 minutes walk from Lake
Ullswater.

PENRITH

Lowther Holiday Park, Eamont Bridge,
Penrith, Cumbria, CA10 2JB.
Std: 01768 **Tel:** 863631
Std: 01768 **Fax:** 868126
Email: holiday.park@lowther.co.uk
Website: www.lowther-holidaypark.co.uk
Nearest Town/Resort Penrith
Directions 1 mile south of Penrith on the
A6.
Acreage 50 **Open** March **to** November
Access Good **Site** Lev/Slope
Sites Available A ⊕ ⊕ **Total** 225
Facilities ⚡ ⚡ ⬛ ⚓ ⌐ ⊙ ⊶ ◻ ⬤
⬛ ☺ ⊛ ✗ ⬛ ⚑ ⊶ ⊡ ◻ ⊡
Nearby Facilities ⌐ ✓ ⊥ ⌁ U ♙ ♙ ⅄
A haven of peace and tranquility in natural
parkland on the banks of the River Lowther,
home of the rare and fascinating red squirrel.
AA Campsite of the Year for Northern
England 1998/1999.

PENRITH

Park Foot Caravan & Camping Park,
Howtown Road, Pooley Bridge, Penrith,
Cumbria, CA10 2NA.
Std: 017684 **Tel:** Pooley Bridge 86309
Std: 017684 **Fax:** 86041
Email: park.foot@talk21.com
Website: www.parkfootullswater.co.uk
Nearest Town/Resort Pooley Bridge
Directions 5 miles southwest of Penrith.
Leave M6 at junction 40, then take A66 for
Ullswater, next roundabout take A592 then
road for Pooley Bridge and 1 mile on
Howtown Road to site.
Acreage 40 **Open** March **to** October
Access Good **Site** Lev/Slope
Sites Available A ⊕ ⊕ **Total** 323
Facilities & ⚡ ⬛ ⚓ ⌐ ⊙ ⊶ ◻ ⬤
⬛ ☺ ⊛ ✗ ⚑ ⬛ ⚑ ⊛ ⊶ ⊡ ◻ ⊡
Nearby Facilities ⌐ ✓ ⊥ ⌁ U ♙ ⅄

⚓ Penrith
Family run park beside Lake Ullswater with
boat and car launching access. Licensed
bar, restaurant and takeaway. Pony trekking,
mountain bike hire, tennis and table tennis
on site.

PENRITH

Side Farm Camp Site, Side Farm,
Patterdale, Penrith, Cumbria, CA11 0NP.
Std: 017684 **Tel:** 82338
Nearest Town/Resort Penrith
Directions On the A592 Penrith to
Windermere road.
Open Easter **to** End Oct
Site Lev/Slope
Sites Available A ⊕
Facilities ⬛ ⚓ ⌐ ⊙ ⊶ ⬛ ☺ ✗ ⊶ ⊡
Nearby Facilities ✓ ⊥ ⌁ U ♙ ⅄
⚓ Penrith
On the edge of Lake Ullswater. Families
welcome. New Tea Room at the farm. Ideal
touring and walking.

PENRITH

Stonefold, Newbiggin, Stainton, Penrith,
Cumbria, CA11 0HP.
Std: 01768 **Tel:** 866383
Website: www.stonefold.co.uk
Nearest Town/Resort Penrith
Directions Leave the M6 at junction 40 and
take the A66 Keswick road. Turn right at the
sign for Newbiggin and Stonefold is one
minutes drive on the left.
Acreage 2 **Open** March **to** November
Access Good **Site** Level
Sites Available A ⊕ ⊕ **Total** 15
Facilities ⚡ ⬛ ⌐ ⊙ ⊶ ⬤ ⊶ ⊡
Nearby Facilities ⌐ ✓ ⊥ ⌁ U ♙ ♙ ⅄
⚓ Penrith
Family run site with a panoramic position
overlooking Eden Valley. An ideal base for
exploring and enjoying the lakes. 5 miles
from Ullswater.

PENRITH

Thacka Lea Caravan Site, Thacka Lea,
Penrith, Cumbria, CA11 9HX.
Std: 01768. **Tel:** 863319
Nearest Town/Resort Penrith
Directions From south, left off A6, past Shell
Station north end of town. From north, turn
right Grey Bull.
Acreage 1 **Open** March **to** October
Access Good **Site** Level
Sites Available ⊕ ⊕ **Total** 25
Facilities ⚡ ⚡ ⬛ ⚓ ⌐ ⊙ ⊶ ⬤ ⊶ ⊡
Nearby Facilities ⌐
⚓ Penrith
Ten minutes town centre walking. Good
touring.

PENRITH

Thanet Well Caravan Park, Greystoke,
Penrith, Cumbria, CA11 0XX.
Std: 017684 **Tel:** 84262
Nearest Town/Resort Penrith
Directions M6 junction 41 onto B5305 for
Wigton, approx 6 miles turn left for Lamonby,
follow caravan signs for approx 2 miles to
park.
Acreage 3 **Open** March **to** October
Access Good **Site** Lev/Slope
Sites Available A ⊕ ⊕ **Total** 20
Facilities ⚡ ⬛ ⚓ ⌐ ⊙ ⊶ ⬛ ◻ ⊡
⬛ ⬛ ☺ ⊛ ⊡ ⊶ ⊡
Nearby Facilities ⌐ ⊥ ⌁ U ♙ ⅄
⚓ Penrith
Scenic views, Fell walking, touring and
cycling. AA 3 Pennants.

PENRITH

**The Cross Fell Camping & Caravan
Park,** The Fox Inn, Ousby, Penrith,
Cumbria, CA10 1QA.
Std: 01768 **Tel:** 881374
Std: 01768 **Fax:** 881152
Email: sue@fox-ousby.co.uk
Website: www.fox-ousby.co.uk
Nearest Town/Resort Penrith
Directions From Penrith take the A686
towards Alston, after 6 miles turn right at the
crossroads signposted Ousby. The Fox Inn
is in the centre of the village.
Acreage 3 **Open** 1 March **to** 10 Jan
Access Good **Site** Level
Sites Available A ⊕ ⊕ **Total** 9
Facilities ⚡ ⬛ ⚓ ⌐ ⊙ ⊶ ⬛ ⬤
⬛ ☺ ✗ ⊽ ⊶ ⊡
Nearby Facilities ✓ ⅄
⚓ Langwathby
Peaceful park in quiet countryside. 3 static
caravans also available for hire.

PENRITH

Waterside Farm Campsite, Waterside
Farm, Howtown Road, Pooley Bridge,
Penrith, Cumbria, CA10 2NA.
Std: 017684 **Tel:** 86332
Std: 017684 **Fax:** 86332
Website: www.watersidefarm-
campsite.co.uk
Nearest Town/Resort Ullswater
Directions Leave the M6 at junction 40 and
take the A66 for 1 mile, turn left onto the
A592 for Ullswater and after 4 miles turn left
to Pooley Bridge. Go through the village and
turn right at the church then right again, we
are 1 mile on the right past the other sites.
Open March **to** October
Site Lev/Slope
Sites Available A ⊕
Facilities ⬛ ⚓ ⌐ ⊙ ⊶ ⬤ ◻ ⬤
⬛ ☺ ⊛ ⊡ ⊛ ⊶

Nearby Facilities ⚲ ⚓ ⚒ ∪ ⚓
⚞ Penrith
Genuine lakeside location with beautiful views of a lake and fells. Boat, canoe and mountain bike hire available.

RAVENGLASS

Walls Caravan Camping Park, Ravenglass, West Cumbria, CA18 1SR.
Std: 01229 **Tel:** 717250
Email:
wallscaravanpark@ravenglass98.freeserve.co.uk
Website:
www.ravenglass98.freeserve.co.uk
Nearest Town/Resort Ravenglass/Whitehaven
Directions A595 into Ravenglass. Site at entrance to village.
Acreage 5 **Open** March **to** October
Access Good **Site** Sloping
Sites Available ⚑ ⛺ ⛟ **Total** 60
Facilities ⚒ ⛺ ⏍ ⚓ ⌒ ⊙ ↵ ⚆ ◻ ☎
⚏ ⏃ ⚆ ⛺ ⚒ ⊞
Nearby Facilities ⌐ ⚲ ⚓ ⚒ ∪ ⚓ ⚲
⚞ Ravenglass
Muncaster castle, Ravenglass and Eskdale miniature Railway, Ravenglass Gullery and Nature Reserve, Muncaster Watermill, Roman sites in area. AA 3 Pennants.

SEDBERGH

Pinfold Caravan Park, Garsdale Road, Sedbergh, Cumbria, LA10 5JL.
Std: 01539 **Tel:** 620576
Std: 01539 **Fax:** 620576
Email: slcar@freenetname.co.uk
Nearest Town/Resort Sedbergh
Directions Take A684 through Sedbergh, caravan park 450 yds from village, over Dales Bridge, on left hand side of road.
Acreage 3 **Open** March **to** October
Access Good **Site** Level
Sites Available ⚑ ⛺ ⛟ **Total** 38
Facilities ⚒ ⛺ ⏍ ⚓ ⌒ ⊙ ↵ ⚆ ◻ ☎
⚏ ⏃ ⚆ ⛺ ⚒ ⊞
Nearby Facilities ⌐ ⚲ ⚓ ⚒ ∪
⚞ Oxenholme
Alongside river Rawthey below the Howgill Fells, ideal fell walking and touring. Fishing on the site. Motorcycles are permitted but no groups please.

SEDBERGH

Yore House Farm Caravan Park, Yore House Farm, Lunds, Sedbergh, Cumbria, LA10 5PX.
Std: 01969 **Tel:** 667358
Nearest Town/Resort Hawes
Directions On the A684 10 miles from Sedbergh and 6 miles from Hawes, near the Moorcock Pub. On the North Yorkshire and Cumbria border.
Open Easter **to** End Sept

Access Good **Site** Level
Sites Available ⚑ ⛺ ⛟ **Total** 7
Facilities ⏍ ⛺ ⚒
Nearby Facilities
⚞ Garsdale
Quiet, farm site beside the River Ure. In sight of the famous Settle to Carlisle railway.

SILECROFT

Silecroft Caravan Park, Silecroft, Millom, Cumbria, LA18 4NX.
Std: 01229 **Tel:** 772659
Std: 01229 **Fax:** 772659
Email: silecroftpark@aol.com
Website: www.caravanholidayhomes.com
Nearest Town/Resort Silecroft
Directions Turn off the A595 7 miles west of Broughton-in-Furness.
Acreage 6 **Open** March **to** October
Access Good **Site** Level
Sites Available ⚑ ⛺◻ **Total** 60
Facilities ⚒ ⛺ ⏍ ⚓ ⌒ ⊙ ↵ ⚆ ◻ ☎
⚏ ⚆ ⚓ ⏃ ⚆ ⊗ ↵ ⊞ ⚲
Nearby Facilities ⌐ ⚲ ⚓ ⚒ ∪ ⚓ ⚲
⚞ Silecroft
Next to the beach and 1 mile from mountains.

SILLOTH

Hylton Caravan Park, Eden Street, Silloth, Cumbria, CA7 4AY.
Std: 016973 **Tel:** 31707
Email: stanwix.park@btinternet.com
Website: www.stanwix.com
Nearest Town/Resort Silloth
Directions This park is off Eden Street. Entering Silloth on the B5300 follow signs for ½ a mile.
Acreage 18 **Open** 1 March **to** 15 Nov
Access Good **Site** Level
Sites Available ⚑ ⛺ ⛟ **Total** 92
Facilities ⚒ ⏍ ⛺ ⏍ ⚓ ⌒ ⊙ ↵ ⚆ ◻ ☎
⚆ ⚏ ⏃ ⚆ ⊞
Nearby Facilities ⌐ ⚲ ⚓ ∪ ⚲
⚞ Carlisle
Quiet site convenient for the town centre. 213 holiday home pitches and 92 camping/touring pitches with mains service hook-ups. New luxury amenity block with toilets, bathrooms, launderette and disabled facilities. Sister park to Stanwix Park Holiday Centre with lots of super facilities which are free to Hylton residents.

SILLOTH

Moordale Park, Blitterlees, Silloth, Cumbria, CA7 4JZ.
Std: 016973 **Tel:** 31375
Nearest Town/Resort Silloth
Directions From Silloth take the B5300 Silloth to Maryport road. Moordale is about 2 miles on the right hand side.
Acreage 7 **Open** March **to** October

Access Good **Site** Level
Sites Available ⚑ ⛺ ⛟ **Total** 12
Facilities ⚒ ⛺ ⏍ ⚓ ⌒ ⊙ ↵ ⚆ ◻ ☎
⚏ ⚆ ⏃ ↵ ⊞
Nearby Facilities ⌐ ⚲ ⚓ ∪ ⚲ ⚓
⚞ Wigton
A quiet and spacious site adjacent to the beach and a golf course. Convenient for the Lake District and Scotland. Holiday homes for hire.

SILLOTH

Seacote Caravan Park, Skinburness Road, Silloth, Cumbria, CA5 4QJ.
Std: 016973 **Tel:** 31121
Std: 016973 **Tel:** 31031
Nearest Town/Resort Carlisle
Directions From Carlisle take the A595, then the A596 and finally the B5302 to Silloth.
Acreage 5½ **Open** 1 March **to** 15 Nov
Access Good **Site** Level
Sites Available ⛺ ⛟ **Total** 20
Facilities ⚐ ⚒ ⛺ ⏍ ⚓ ⌒ ⊙ ↵ ⚆ ◻ ☎
⏃ ⚆ ⚓ ⏃ ↵ ⊞
Nearby Facilities ⌐ ⚲ ∪ ⚲ ⚓
⚞ Carlisle
Peace and tranquility, adjacent to Solway. Central to the Lake District and Scottish Borders.

SILLOTH

Solway Holiday Village, Skinburness Drive, Silloth, Wigton, Cumbria, CA7 4QQ.
Std: 016973 **Tel:** 31236
Std: 016973 **Tel:** 32553
Nearest Town/Resort Silloth
Directions Drive into Silloth, turn right at the Raffa Club and follow road for ½ mile. Turn right at signpost for holiday village.
Open March **to** October
Access Good **Site** Level
Sites Available ⚑ ⛺ ⛟
Facilities ⚒ ⛺ ⏍ ⚓ ⌒ ↵ ⚆
⚆ ⚏ ⚆ ⊗ × ⚲ ⚔ ⏃ ⚓ ↵ ⊞ ⚲
Nearby Facilities ⌐ ⚲ ∪ ⚲
⚞ Wigton
Near the beach.

SILLOTH

Stanwix Park Holiday Centre, Silloth (West), Cumbria, CA7 4HH.
Std: 016973 **Tel:** 32666
Std: 016973 **Fax:** 32555
Email: stanwix.park@btinternet.com
Website: www.stanwix.com
Nearest Town/Resort Silloth
Directions Enter Silloth on B5302, turn left at sea front, 1 mile to West Silloth on B5300. Site on right.
Acreage 18 **Open** All Year
Access Good **Site** Level
Sites Available ⚑ ⛺ ⛟ **Total** 121

Facilities [icons]
Nearby Facilities [icons]
⚡ Carlisle
Large holiday centre with full range of facilities for all the   family, indoor and outdoor, including pony trekking. Sunbeds, water shoot. Indoor leisure complex. See our display advertisment.

SILLOTH

Tanglewood Caravan Park,
Causewayhead, Silloth, Cumbria, CA7 4PE.
Std: 016973 **Tel:** 31253
Nearest Town/Resort Silloth
Directions Take B5302, 1 mile inland from town on Wigton road.
Acreage 2 **Open** Easter **to** October
Access Good **Site** Level
Sites Available ▲ ♦ ⬛ **Total** 31
Facilities [icons]
Nearby Facilities [icons]
⚡ Wigton
Tree sheltered site, ideal for touring lakes and borders. Pets free of charge.

ST. BEES

Seacote Park, The Beach, St. Bees, Cumbria, CA27 0ES.
Std: 01946 **Tel:** 822777
Std: 01946 **Fax:** 824442
Email: reception@seacote.com
Website: www.seacote.com
Nearest Town/Resort Whitehaven
Directions Take the A525 to West Cumbria, follow signs to St. Bees then to the beach.
Acreage 4 **Open** All Year
Access Good **Site** Level
Sites Available ▲ ♦ ⬛ **Total** 40

Facilities [icons]
Nearby Facilities [icons]
⚡ St. Bees
Adjoining a lovely beach, in a historic award winning village, on the fringe of the Lake District. Hotel adjacent.

TEBAY

Westmorland Caravan Site Tebay, Tebay
Westmorland Services M6 Northbound, Cumbria, CA10 3SB.
Std: 015396 **Tel:** 24511 **Fax:** 24511
Website: www.wms.com
Nearest Town/Resort Penrith/Kendal
Directions M6 Motorway 1 mile north of junction 38, take the Westmorland Tebay Services exit and follow signs for Tebay Caravan Site. Access also from Tebay East Services M6 south, follow signs.
Acreage 3½ **Open** Mid-March **to** October
Access Good **Site** Level
Sites Available ♦ ⬛ **Total** 70
Facilities [icons]
Nearby Facilities [icon]
⚡ Penrith/Oxenholme
Ideal base for the Lake District and the Yorkshire Dales.

TROUTBECK

Gill Head Farm, Troutbeck, Penrith, Cumbria, CA11 0ST.
Std: 017687 **Tel:** 79652
Email: gillhead@talk21.com
Website: www.gillheadfarm.co.uk
Nearest Town/Resort Keswic
Directions Just off A66 on A5091 9 miles Keswick, 5 miles Ullswater.
Acreage 10 **Open** April **to** October
Access Good **Site** Level

Sites Available ▲ ♦ ⬛ **Total** 54
Facilities [icons]
Nearby Facilities [icons]
⚡ Penrith
Ideal touring, scenic views.

TROUTBECK

Hutton Moor End Caravan & Camping Site, Moor End, Troutbeck, Penrith, Cumbria, CA11 0SX.
Std: 01768 **Tel:** 779615
Email: moorend.csjdb@virgin.net
Nearest Town/Resort Keswick
Directions On A66 9 miles west of junc 40 M6. Turn left for Wallthwaite.
Acreage 2½ **Open** Easter/1st Apr **to** Nov
Access Good **Site** Sloping
Sites Available ▲ ♦ ⬛ **Total** 50
Facilities [icons]
Nearby Facilities [icons]
⚡ Penrith

ULLSWATER

Sykeside Camping Park, Brotherswater, Patterdale, Cumbria, CA11 0NZ.
Std: 017684 **Tel:** 82239 **Fax:** 82558
Website: www.sykeside.co.uk
Nearest Town/Resort Ambleside
Directions From Windermere take the A592 for 9 miles, go over Kirkstone Pass and Park is next to the Brotherswater Inn.
Acreage 5 **Open** All Year
Site Level
Sites Available ▲ ♦ ⬛ **Total** 100
Facilities [icons]
Nearby Facilities [icons]
⚡ Windermere
Mountains and lakes for walking, fishing and sailing.

ULLSWATER

The Quiet Caravan & Camping Site,
Ullswater, Nr. Penrith, Cumbria, CA11
0LS.
Std: 0176 84 **Tel:** 86337
Std: 0176 84 **Fax:** 86610
Nearest Town/Resort Pooley Bridge
Directions Take A592 from Penrith, turn
right at lake and right again at Brackenrigg
Hotel follow road for 1½ miles, site on right
hand side of road.
Acreage 6 **Open** March **to** November
Access Good **Site** Lev/Slope
Sites Available ▲ ⌂ ⊞ **Total** 83
Facilities ⌇ ⊞ ⊞ ⚓ ↾ ⊙ ⊿ ⊿ ⊡ ❤
℁ ⊘ ⊠ ⋔ ♠ ⊛ ⊬⊟
Nearby Facilities ↾ ✓ ⚓ ⊿ ∪ ♪ ⋟
⊯ Penrith
Idyllic setting amongst the fells, voted Best
Campsite in Britain by Camping Magazine,
AA Northern Campsite of the Year. Large
adventure playground and Olde Worlde Bar
(probably the best campsite bar in Britain!)
Top 100 Park and ETB 'Exceptional'
Graded.

ULLSWATER

**Ullswater Caravan Camping & Marine
Park,** Watermillock, Penrith, Cumbria,
CA11 0LR.
Std: 0176 84 **Tel:** 86666
Std: 0176 84 **Fax:** 86095
Email: info@uccmp.co.uk
Website: www.uccmp.co.uk
Nearest Town/Resort Penrith
Directions A592 from Penrith, turn right at
lake and right again at telephone kiosk,
signposted Watermillock Church.
Acreage 7 **Open** March **to** 14 November
Access Good **Site** Lev/Slope

Sites Available ▲ ⌂ ⊞ **Total** 155
Facilities ⊘ ⌇ ⊞ ⊞ ⚓ ↾ ⊙ ⊿ ⊿ ⊡ ❤
℁ ⊘ ⊠ ✗ ♥ ⋔ ♠ ⋏⊬⊟⊞ ⊡
Nearby Facilities ↾ ✓ ⚓ ⊿ ∪ ♪
⊯ Penrith
Lake District National Park. Scenic views.
Boat launching and moorings 1 mile.

ULVERSTON

Bardsea Leisure, Priory Road, Ulverston,
Cumbria, LA12 9QE.
Std: 01229 **Tel:** 584712
Std: 01229 **Fax:** 580413
Nearest Town/Resort Ulverston
Directions Leave the M6 at junction 36 and
take the A590 then the A5087.
Acreage 10 **Open** All Year
Access Good **Site** Lev/Slope
Sites Available ▲ ⌂ ⊞ **Total** 83
Facilities ⌇ ⊞ ⊞ ⚓ ↾ ⊙ ⊿ ⊿ ⊡ ❤
⊘ ⊠ ✗ ⋔⊬⊟
Nearby Facilities ↾ ✓ ⊿
⊯ Ulverston
Ideal for touring.

ULVERSTON

Black Beck Caravan Park, Bouth, Nr.
Ulverston, Cumbria, LA12 8JN.
Std: 01229 **Tel:** 861274
Std: 01229 **Fax:** 861041
Email: ribble@netcomuk.co.uk
Website: www.partingtons.com
Nearest Town/Resort Ulverston
Directions On the A590 5 miles from
Ulverston.
Open 1 March **to** 15 Nov
Access Good **Site** Level
Sites Available ▲ ⌂ ⊞ **Total** 25
Facilities ⋌ ⌇ ⊞ ⊞ ⚓ ↾ ⊙ ⊿ ⊿ ⊡ ❤
℁ ⊘ ⊠ ⊟ ⊞ ⊡
Nearby Facilities ↾ ✓ ⚓ ⊿ ∪ ♪ ⋟

⊯ Ulverston
Beck through the centre of the park. Lake
Windermere is easuly accessible.

ULVERSTON

Crake Valley Holiday Park, Water Yeat,
Blawith, Near Ulverston, Cumbria, LA12
8DL.
Std: 01229 **Tel:** 885203
Nearest Town/Resort Ulverston
Directions Take the A590, at Greenodd turn
right onto the A5902 Workington road. After
2 miles fork right onto the A5084 for
Coniston, park is 3 miles on the left hand
side.
Acreage ¼ **Open** April **to** October
Site Lev/Slope
Sites Available ▲ **Total** 6
Facilities ⊞ ⚓ ↾ ⊙ ⊿ ⊡ ⊞ ⊠⊬⊟
Nearby Facilities ↾ ✓ ⚓ ⊿ ∪
⊯ Ulverston
400 metres from Coniston Water and open
to Blawith Common.

WALNEY ISLAND

South End Caravan Park, Walney,
Barrow in Furness, Cumbria, LA14 3YQ.
Std: 01229 **Tel:** 472823
Nearest Town/Resort Barrow in Furness
Directions A590 to Barrow, then follow
Walney signs. Turn left after crossing bridge
to Walney, 4 miles south from there.
Acreage 7 **Open** March **to** October
Site Sloping
Sites Available ▲ ⌂ ⊞ **Total** 60
Facilities ⋌ ⌇ ⊞ ⚓ ↾ ⊙ ⊿ ⊿ ⊡ ❤
℁ ⊘ ⊠ ♥ ⋔ ♠ ⊛ ⋏⊬⊟ ⊡
Nearby Facilities ↾ ✓ ∪
⊯ Barrow
Close to beach, good views.

Ashes Lane Caravan & Camping Park   01539 821119

Ashes Lane is a family run, four star park situated within beautiful open and undulating countryside with lovely panoramic views. Excellent facilities on site including a cosy and welcoming bar. **See under Windermere for details.**

Staveley, Kendal, Cumbria LA8 9JS • Tel: 01539 821119 • Fax: 01539 821282
E-mail: asheslanepark@avmail.co.uk • Web Site: www.asheslane.com

ATERMILLOCK

otts Hill Caravan Chalet Site,
termillock, Penrith Cumbria, CA11 0JR.
: 017684 **Tel:** 86328
arest Town/Resort Penrith
ections A592 from Penrith turn off at
wbarrow Lodge Grill approx 8 miles from
nrith, entrance ½ mile on right.
cess Good **Site** Lev/Slope
cilities ƒ ⊞ ▯ ⌐ ⊙ ☎ ⛾ ⛾ ▯ ◌ ⛾⊬⊟
arby Facilities ┌ ↗ ⚓ ↘ ∪ ⚡
Penrith

NDERMERE

hes Lane Caravan & Camping Park,
aveley, Kendal, Cumbria, LA8 9JS.
: 01539 **Tel:** 821119 **Fax:** 821282
ail: vans@asheslanepark.freeserve.co.uk
bsite: www.asheslane.com
arest Town/Resort Windermere
ections From Kendal take the A591
yards Windermere for 1½ miles, follow
nposts.
reage 22 **Open** 14 March **to** 14 Jan
cess Good **Site** Level
es Available ▲ ♀ ☗ **Total** 250
cilities ♿ ƒ ⊞ ▯ ☎ ⌐ ⊙ ☐ ◌ ⛾
▯ ◌ ☗ ✕ ⛾ ⊞ ☚ ⚘⊬⊟☐
arby Facilities ┌ ↗ ⚓ ↘ ∪ ⚡ ⚡ ⚡
Staveley/Kendal
en aspect with panoramic views. Family
om and a cosy bar with a log fire.

Adventure playground on site. Take-away.
Close to all Lake District attractions.

WINDERMERE
Fallbarrow Park, Rayrigg Road,
Windermere, Cumbria, LA23 3DL.
Std: 015394 **Tel:** 44422 ext 42
Std: 015394 **Fax:** 88736
Email: Via Web Site
Website: www.fallbarrow.co.uk
Nearest Town/Resort Windermere
Directions Just north of Bowness village on
A592.
Acreage 32 **Open** 8 March **to** 8
November
Access Good **Site** Level
Sites Available ♀ ☗ **Total** 38
Facilities ♿ ƒ ⊞ ▯ ☎ ⌐ ⊙ ☐ ◌ ⛾
▯ ◌ ☗ ✕ ⛾ ⊞ ☚ ⚘⊬⊟☐
Nearby Facilities ┌ ↗ ⚓ ↘ ∪ ⚡ ⚡
⚡ Windermere
On shore of Lake Windermere. Boating
facilities. ETC 5 Star Graded, AA 5 Pennant
Premier Park and AA Campsite of the Year
1996/97. Tourers have direct connections to
water, waste, TV and electric. Please refer
to our colour advertisement.

WINDERMERE
Limefitt Park, Windermere, Cumbria,
LA23 1PA.
Std: 015394 **Tel:** 32300 ext 42
Email: Via Web Site.
Website: www.camping-windermere.co.uk

Nearest Town/Resort Windermere
Directions In Lakeland valley 4 miles north
of Windermere on A592 to Ullswater.
Acreage 25 **Open** 1 week before Easter
to End Oct
Access Good **Site** Lev/Slope
Sites Available ▲ ♀ ☗ **Total** 165
Facilities ♿ ƒ ⊞ ▯ ☎ ⌐ ⊙ ☐ ◌ ⛾
▯ ◌ ☗ ✕ ⛾ ⊞ ☚ ⚘⊟☐
Nearby Facilities ┌ ↗ ⚓ ↘ ∪ ⚡ ⚡
⚡ Windermere
Spectacular Lakeland valley location with
fishing on site. Ten minutes drive to Lake
Windermere. Tourers and family campers
welcome. Friendly Lakeland pub with bar
meals. 'Do-it-Yourself' Camper's kitchen,
shop, plus a full range of award winning
facilities. AA 5 Pennant Premier Park.
Luxurious holiday caravans for hire. No
dogs. Please see our colour advertisement.

WINDERMERE
Park Cliffe Camping & Caravan Estate,
Birks Road, Tower Wood, Windermere,
Cumbria, LA23 3PG.
Std: 015395 **Tel:** 31344
Std: 015395 **Fax:** 31971
Email: info@parkcliffe.co.uk
Website: www.parkcliffe.co.uk
Nearest Town/Resort Windermere
Directions M6 junction 36, A590 to Newby
Bridge. Turn right onto A592, in 4 miles turn
right into Birks Road. Park is roughly ½ mile
on the right.

Acreage 25 **Open** March **to** October
Access Good **Site** Lev/Slope
Sites Available ▲ ⊕ ⊟ **Total** 250
Facilities ⚷ ∮ ⊟ ℕ ⅏ ♨ ┌ ⊙ ⥂ ⛟ ⚑ ▣ ☎
♨ ☺ ⚐ ✗ ⛾ ♠ ⊛ ⊬⊟ ▣ ☺ ☎
Nearby Facilities ┌ ✓ ⊥ ⅃ ∪ ⋺ ♫ ⅌
✈ Windermere
Near to Lake Windermere with outstanding views of lakes and mountains, ideal touring. AA 4 Pennants and RAC.

WINDERMERE

White Cross Bay Leisure Park & Marina, Ambleside Road, Windermere, Cumbria, LA23 1LF.
Std: 015394 **Tel:** 43937
Std: 015394 **Fax:** 88704
Email: wxb@windermere.uk.com
Website: www.windermere.uk.com
Nearest Town/Resort Windermere/Ambleside
Directions Leave the M6 at junction 36 and follow direction signs to Windermere on the A591. Following signs for Ambleside, park is on the left hand side after approx. 2 miles.
Acreage 2 **Open** 1 March **to** 14 Nov
Access Good **Site** Level
Sites Available ⊕ ⊟
Facilities ♨ ∮ ⊟ ℕ ⅏ ♨ ┌ ⊙ ⥂ ⛟
▣ ♨ ☺ ⚐ ✗ ⛾ ♠ ⊬⊟ ▣ ☺
Nearby Facilities ┌ ✓ ⊥ ⅌ ⅃ ♫ ⅌
✈ Windermere
Natural woodland setting right on the shores of Lake Windermere. Restaurant, mini market, bar, ski school, lake access and marina. Excellent base to explore.

DERBYSHIRE
AMBERGATE

The Firs Farm Caravan & Camping Park, Crich Lane, Nether Heage, Ambergate, Belper, Derbys, DE56 2JH.
Std: 01773 **Tel:** 852913
Email: thefirsfarmcaravanpark@btinternet.com
Nearest Town/Resort Ambergate
Directions 1½ miles south of Ambergate turn left off the A6 onto Broad Holme Lane. At top of lane turn left, park is 500yds on the left.
Acreage 3 **Open** All Year
Access Good **Site** Level
Sites Available ▲ ⊕ ⊟ **Total** 60
Facilities ∮ ⊟ ℕ ⅏ ♨ ┌ ⊙ ⥂ ⛟
ℕ ⅃ ♠⊬▣A
Nearby Facilities ┌ ✓ ⊥ ⅌ ∪ ♫
✈ Ambergate
Magnificent views, well maintained, quiet, landscaped site. Friendly, family run park with a sauna. Host of local attractions. Gas, launderette, pub and restaurant nearby.

ASHBOURNE

Bank Top Farm, Fenny Bentley, Ashbourne, Derbyshire, DE6 1LF.
Std: 01335. **Tel:** 350250
Nearest Town/Resort Ashbourne
Directions Take A515 from town 2 miles. Take B5056, site 200 yards opposite Bentley Brook Inn.
Acreage 2½ **Open** Easter **to** End Sept
Access Good
Sites Available ▲ ⊕ ⊟
Facilities ⚷ ∮ ⊟ ℕ ♨ ┌ ⊙ ⥂ ⛟ ♨ ℕ ⊬▣
Nearby Facilities ┌ ⅌ ∪ ⅌ ♫
✈ Derby
Scenic views from site. Area ideal for touring Dovedale and other Dales, also pretty little villages. Viewing gallery to watch the milking of the cows. Washing machine and spin dryer available. Dogs to be kept on leads. Prices available on request. AA 3 Pennants.

ASHBOURNE

Callow Top Holiday Park, Buxton Road, Ashbourne, Derbyshire, DE6 2AQ.
Std: 01335 **Tel:** 344020
Std: 01335 **Fax:** 343726
Email: callowtop@talk21.com
Website: www.callowtop.co.uk
Nearest Town/Resort Ashbourne
Directions The access to Callow Top is only ¼ mile from Ashbourne on the A515 Buxton road. The entrance is directly opposite Sandybrook Garage, follow the private road for ½ mile to the end.
Acreage 15 **Open** Easter **to** November
Access Good **Site** Level
Sites Available ▲ ⊕ ⊟ **Total** 150
Facilities ⚷ ∮ ⊟ ℕ ♨ ┌ ⊙ ⥂ ⛟ ⚑ ▣ ☎
♨ ☺ ⚐ ✗ ⛾ ⛾ ⊬⊟ ☺
Nearby Facilities ┌ ✓ ⊥ ⅌ ∪ ⅌ ♫
✈ Derby
Alton Towers only 20 minutes away, Tissington Trail cycle path is adjacent, Carsington Reservoir 5 miles. Many footpaths. Fishing on site.

ASHBOURNE

Gateway Caravan Park, Osmaston, Near Ashbourne, Derbyshire, DE6 1NA.
Std: 01335 **Tel:** 344643
Email: karen@gatewaypark.fsnet.co.uk
Website: www.ashbourne-accommodation.co.uk
Nearest Town/Resort Ashbourne
Directions 1 mile south of Ashbourne turn right off the A52, park is 400 metres on the right hand side.
Acreage 15 **Open** All Year
Access Good **Site** Level
Sites Available ▲ ⊕ ⊟ **Total** 200
Facilities ⚷ ∮ ⊟ ℕ ⅏ ♨ ┌ ⊙ ⥂ ⛟ ⚑ ▣ ☎
♨ ☺ ⚐ ⛾ ⛾ ⊬▣
Nearby Facilities ┌ ✓ ⊥ ⅌ ∪ ♫

✈ Derby
Entertainment on Saturday nights during school holidays and Bank Holiday weekends. The Peak District and only minutes to Alton Towers.

ASHBOURNE

Highfields Farm Caravan Park, Fenny Bentley, Ashbourne, Derbyshire, DE6 1LF.
Std: 0870 **Tel:** 741 8000
Std: 0870 **Fax:** 741 2000
Email: ca@highfieldsfarmcaravanpark.co.uk
Website: www.highfieldsfarmcaravanpark.co.uk
Nearest Town/Resort Ashbourne
Directions 3 miles north of Ashbourne on the A515 towards Buxton.
Acreage 30 **Open** March **to** October
Access Good **Site** Level
Sites Available ▲ ⊕ ⊟ **Total** 105
Facilities ∮ ⊟ ℕ ♨ ┌ ⊙ ⥂ ⛟ ⚑
♨ ℕ ☺ ⚐ ♠ ⊛ ⊬▣ ☺
Nearby Facilities ┌ ✓ ⊥ ⅌ ∪ ⅌ ♫
✈ Derby
Next to the Tissington Trail. Ideal touring.

ASHBOURNE

Newton Grange Caravan Site, Newton Grange, Ashbourne, Derbyshire, DE6 1NJ.
Std: 01335 **Tel:** 310214
Nearest Town/Resort Ashbourne
Directions On the A515 4½ miles north of Ashbourne.
Acreage 1 **Open** Mid March **to** End October
Access Good **Site** Level
Sites Available ▲ ⊕ ⊟ **Total** 15
Facilities ⚷ ∮ ⊟ ⊬▣
Nearby Facilities ✓ ⊥ ∪
✈ Derby
Close to Buxton, Matlock and Alton Towers. Tissington Trail adjacent for cycling and walking. Ideal touring.

ASHBOURNE

Rivendale Caravan & Leisure Park, Buxton Road, Alsop-en-le-Dale, Ashbourne, Derbyshire, DE6 1QU.
Std: 01332 **Tel:** 843000
Std: 01332 **Fax:** 842311
Email: alsopdale@aol.com
Website: www.ukparks.co.uk/rivendale
Nearest Town/Resort Hartington
Directions 6½ miles north of Ashbourne directly accessed from the A515 (Buxton road).
Acreage 35 **Open** March **to** January
Access Good **Site** Level
Sites Available ▲ ⊕ ⊟ **Total** 80
Facilities ⚷ ∮ ⊟ ℕ ⅏ ♨ ┌ ⊙ ⥂ ⛟ ⚑
♨ ☺ ⚐ ✗ ⛾ ⛾ ♠ ⅏ ⊬▣ ☺ ☎

Rivendale

Peak District
Tel (01332) 843000

Surrounded by famous Peak District scenery with footpaths and trails from site, convenient for Chatsworth, Alton Towers, Dove Dale and Carsington Water.

* Licensed Cafe & Bar
* Open all year except Feb.
* 10 acre amenity field
* Disabled Facilities.
* Hard-standing pitches
* Central-heated buildings
* Open Xmas & New Year
* Holiday Homes for sale

E-mail: rivendale@fsmail.net
www.RivendaleCaravanPark.co.uk

...arby Facilities ┌ ╱ ⚓ ↘ ∪ ⭑
Buxton
...rrounded by scenic countryside, ideal for
...lking, cycling and outdoor hobbies.
...nvenient for Chatsworth, Alton Towers
...d many other attractions.

...SHBOURNE

...ndybrook Country Park, Buxton
...ad, Ashbourne, Derbyshire, DE6 2AQ.
...d: 01335 **Tel:** 300000
...d: 01335 **Fax:** 342679
...nail: admin@sandybrook.co.uk
...ebsite: www.sandybrook.co.uk
...earest **Town/Resort** Ashbourne
...rections From Ashbourne take the A515
...wards Buxton, Sandybrook is approx. 1
...le on the right hand side.
...reage 3 **Open** April **to** October
...ccess Poor **Site** Sloping
...tes Available ▲ ⌂ **Total** 30
...cilities ┌ ⓌⒸ ╤ ┌ ⊙ ┘ ⚓ ⊠ ⚓ ∪
...earby Facilities ┌ ╱ ⚓ ↘ ∪
Derby
...ry close to Dovedale and the Tissington
...ail and 15 minutes from Alton Towers.

...AKEWELL

...mping & Caravanning Club Site, c/o
...opping Farm, Youlgreave, Bakewell,
...rbyshire, DE45 1NA.
...d: 01629 **Tel:** 636555
...ebsite:
...ww.campingandcaravanningclub.co.uk
...rections Take the A6 Bakewell to Matlock
...ad, turn onto the B5056 Ashbourne road.
...ter ½ mile take the right hand branch to
...ulgreave, turn sharp left after the church
...to Bradford Lane opposite The George
...tel. Continue ½ mile to club sign then turn
...ht into Farmers Lane for ¼ mile.
...creage 14 **Open** March **to** Sept
...te Sloping
...tes Available ▲ ⌂ **Total** 100
...cilities ┌ ╱ ⚓ ↘ ∪ ♪ ⭑
...Matlock
...eally situated for the Peak District. Near
...Haddon Hall and Chatsworth House. Non
...embers welcome.

...AKEWELL

...reenhills Caravan & Camping Park,
...ow Hill Lane, Buxton Road, Bakewell,
...rbyshire, DE45 1PX.
...d: 01629 **Tel:** 813052
...d: 01629 **Fax:** 815131

Email: greenhills@talk21.com
Website: www.greenhillsleisure.com
Nearest Town/Resort Bakewell
Directions 1 mile north west of Bakewell
turn left into Crow Hill Lane, turn first right
over the cattle grid.
Acreage 8 **Open** March **to** October
Access Good **Site** Lev/Slope
Sites Available ▲ ⌂ ⌂ **Total** 150
Facilities ┌ Ⓦ Ⓒ ╤ ┌ ⊙ ┘ ⚓ ⊠ ◻ ⚓
⚓ Ⓘ Ⓖ ⊕ ☂ ♈ ⛅ ⚓ ♦ Ⓟ Ⓔ Ⓑ
Nearby Facilities ┌ ╱ ∪ ℛ ⭑
⚓ Buxton/Matlock
Close to Chatsworth House and Haddon
Hall.

BAKEWELL

Peakland Caravans, High Street, Stoney
Middleton, Hope Valley, S32 4TL.
Std: 01433 **Tel:** 631414
Email: peakland2000@aol.com
Nearest Town/Resort Bakewell
Directions Stoney Middleton is on the A623,
3 miles west of Baslow. Approaching from
Baslow turn left by the Moon Inn and Village
Cross. Continue up the hill for a third of a
mile, park is on the right.
Open Easter **to** End October
Site Level
Sites Available ▲ ⌂ ⌂ **Total** 12
Facilities ┌ Ⓦ ╤ ┌ ⊙ ┘ ◻ ⛅ ♈ ▣
Nearby Facilities ┌ ╱ ∪ ℛ ⭑
⚓ Grindleford
Ideal for touring, walking and climbing.
STATICS ALSO FOR HIRE.

BAKEWELL

Stocking Farm Caravan & Camp Site,
Stocking Farm, Calver Bridge, Calver,
Hope Valley, S32 3XA.
Tel: Hope Valley 630516
Nearest Town/Resort Bakewell
Directions Out of Bakewell on the A619 fork
left onto the B6001 to traffic lights. Turn right
then first left, after Derbyshire Craft Centre
first left again.
Acreage 1½ **Open** April **to** October
Access Good **Site** Level
Sites Available ▲ ⌂ ⌂ **Total** 10
Facilities ⚓ Ⓦ ╤ ┌ ⊙ ┘ ◻ ⛅ ♈
Nearby Facilities ∪ ⭑
⚓ Grindleford
Scenic views, idea touring. Married couples
and families only. Dogs must be kept on a
lead.

BRADWELL

Eden Tree Caravan Park, Eccles Lane,
Bradwell, Hope Valley, Derbyshire, S33
9JT.
Std: 01433 **Tel:** 620873
Nearest Town/Resort Bakewell
Directions On the outskirts of the village of
Bradwell, 10 miles from Bakewell.
Open March to October
Access Good **Site** Sloping
Sites Available ▲ ⌂□ **Total** 20
Facilities ┌ Ⓦ Ⓒ ╤ ┌ ⊙ ┘ ⚓ ⚓ Ⓘ Ⓖ ▣
Nearby Facilities ┌ ╱ ⚓ ∪ ℛ ⭑
⚓ Hope
In the heart of the Peak District National
Park. Close to Chatsworth House,
Castleton, Buxton and many other
attractions.

BUXTON

Cottage Farm Caravan Park, Blackwell
in the Peak, Derbyshire, SK17 9TQ.
Std: 01298 **Tel:** 85330
Email: mail@cottagefarmsite.co.uk
Website: www.cottagefarmsite.co.uk
Nearest Town/Resort Buxton
Directions From Buxton, 6 miles east on
the A6. Take an unclassified road north,
signposted.
Acreage 3 **Open** March **to** October
Access Good **Site** Level
Sites Available ▲ ⌂ ⌂ **Total** 30
Facilities ⚓ ┌ Ⓦ Ⓒ ╤ ┌ ⊙ ⚓
⚓ Ⓖ ♈ ▣
Nearby Facilities
⚓ Buxton
Centre of a National Park, ideal for walking
and touring by car.

BUXTON

Endon Cottage, Hulme End, Buxton,
Derbyshire, SK17 0HG.
Std: 01298 **Tel:** 84617
Nearest Town/Resort Leek/Buxton
Directions From the main A roads take the
B5054 into Hulme End and follow Beresford
Lane signs. 10 miles from Leek, Buxton and
Ashbourne.
Acreage 2 **Open** 1 April **to** 15 Oct
Access Good **Site** Sloping
Sites Available ▲ ⌂ ⌂ **Total** 30
Facilities Ⓦ ♈ ⛅ ♈
Nearby Facilities ╱
⚓ Buxton
Ideal for walking and touring.

BUXTON

Lime Tree Park, Dukes Drive, Buxton,
Derbyshire, SK17 9RP.
Std: 01298 **Tel:** 22988
Website: www.ukparks.co.uk/limetree
Nearest Town/Resort Buxton

Directions From Buxton proceed south on the A515 for ½ mile, sharp left after Buxton Hospital, ½ mile along on the right.
Open March **to** October inc.
Access Good **Site** Lev/Slope
Sites Available ▲ ⊕ ⊞ **Total** 100
Facilities ⚿ �ℓ ⊞ ⚷ ↑ ⊙ ⊣ ▰ ⊡ ☎
⚹ ⍾ ⊛ ♨ ⚶ ↦ ⊟ ⊡
Nearby Facilities ↑ ✓ ⚓ ⚲ ∪ ♞ ⚡
⚉ Buxton
Ideal location for touring the Peak District. TV room.

BUXTON

Newhaven Caravan & Camping Park, Newhaven, Nr. Buxton, Derbyshire, SK17 0DT.
Std: 01298 **Tel:** 84300
Nearest Town/Resort Buxton
Directions Midway between Ashbourne and Buxton on A515. At the junction with A5012.
Acreage 27 **Open** March **to** October
Access Good **Site** Level
Sites Available ▲ ⊕ ⊞ **Total** 125
Facilities ℓ ⍾ ⊞ ⚷ ↑ ⊙ ⊣ ▰ ⊡ ☎
⚹ ⊛ ♨ ⚶ ↦ ⊟ ⊡
Nearby Facilities ↑ ✓ ⚓ ⚲ ∪ ♞
⚉ Buxton
Ideal centre for touring Peak District, National Park and Derbyshire Dales. Café/restaurant opposite site.

BUXTON

Pomeroy Caravan & Camping Park, Street House Farm, Pomeroy, Nr. Flagg, Buxton, Derbyshire, SK17 9QG.
Std: 01298 **Tel:** 83259
Nearest Town/Resort Buxton
Directions From Buxton take the A515 towards Ashbourne, site is 5 miles on the right, go over the cattle grid, 200 yard tarmac drive to the site.
Acreage 2 **Open** Easter/1 April **to** 31 October
Access Good **Site** Level
Sites Available ▲ ⊕ ⊞ **Total** 40
Facilities ⚿ ⊞ ⚷ ↑ ⊙ ⊣ ▰ ⊡ ☎
⊛ ↦ ⊟ ⊡
Nearby Facilities ↑ ∪ ♞
⚉ Buxton
Site adjoins the northern end of Cromford High Peak Trail. Cycle hire centre 3 miles. Ideal walking and cycling.

BUXTON

Shallow Grange, Chelmorton, Near Buxton, Derbyshire, SK17 9SG.
Std: 01298 **Tel:** 23578
Std: 01298 **Fax:** 78242
Email: holland@shallowgrangefarm.freeserve.co.uk
Nearest Town/Resort Buxton
Directions From Buxton take the A515 Ashbourne road and travel for 2 to 3 miles. Turn left onto the A5270 and Shallow Grange is ½ mile on the left.
Acreage ¾ **Open** April **to** October
Access Good **Site** Sloping
Sites Available ▲ ⊕ ⊞ **Total** 20
Facilities ⚿ ℓ ⊟ ⊞ ⚷ ↑ ⊙ ⊣ ▰ ⊡ ☎
⚹ ⊛ ♨ ↦ ⊟
Nearby Facilities ↑ ✓ ⚓ ⚲ ∪ ♞ ⚡
⚉ Buxton
Walking in the SSSI Dale. Chatsworth House, Haddon Hall and Bakewell nearby.

BUXTON

Thornheyes Farm, Longridge Lane, Peak Dale, Buxton, Derbyshire, SK17 8AD.
Std: 01298 **Tel:** 26421
Nearest Town/Resort Buxton
Directions From Buxton take the A6 towards Stockport, after 1½ miles turn right

---

for Peakdale. Go to the top of the hill and turn right, first on the right.
Acreage 1½ **Open** Easter **to** Oct
Access Good **Site** Sloping
Sites Available ▲ ⊕ ⊞ **Total** 15
Facilities ℓ ⊞ ↑ ⊣ ⊙ ↦
Nearby Facilities ↑
⚉ Buxton
Ideal for touring the Peak District. Children must be kept under strict control. No ball games, no frizbys and no kites allowed. No bike riding on field. Pets are welcome if kept on leads.

BUXTON

Waterloo Inn Caravan & Camping Site, The Waterloo Inn, Main Street, Biggin, Buxton, Derbyshire, SK17 0DH.
Std: 01298 **Tel:** 84284
Nearest Town/Resort Buxton
Directions From Buxton take the A515 towards Ashbourne, signposted.
Acreage 2 **Open** All Year
Access Good **Site** Sloping
Sites Available ▲ ⊕ ⊞
Facilities ⚿ ℓ ⊞ ⚷ ↑ ⊙ ⊣ ▰ ☎
⍾ ⊛ ✕ ♀ ⍾ ↦ ⊡
Nearby Facilities ↑ ✓ ⚓ ⚲ ∪ ♞
⚉ Buxton
Ideal walking country, Peak Park, Tissington and High Peak Cycle Trail.

CASTLETON

Rowter Farm, Castleton, Hope Valley, Derbyshire, S33 8WA.
Std: 01433 **Tel:** 620271
Nearest Town/Resort Castleton
Directions Off the B6061 near the top of Winnats Pass. 2½ miles west of Castleton through Winnats Pass.
Acreage 4 **Open** April **to** End Oct
Access Good **Site** Level
Sites Available ▲ ⊕ ⊞ **Total** 30
Facilities ⊞ ⚷ ↑ ☎ ↦
Nearby Facilities ↑ ∪ ♞
⚉ Hope
Ideal for walking, biking, sight seeing and touring.

CHESTERFIELD

Millfield Camping & Touring Park, Mill Lane, Old Tupton, Chesterfield, Derbyshire, S42 6AE.
Std: 01246 **Tel:** 861082
Std: 01246 **Fax:** 861082
Email: millfieldpark@hotmail.com
Nearest Town/Resort Chesterfield
Directions Leave the M1 at junction 29 and take the A6175 to the centre of Clay Cross and the junction with the A61, turn right then left between the Trustees Savings Bank and the Post Office, Millfield is situated directly 1 mile on the right hand side.
Open All Year
Access Good **Site** Level
Sites Available ▲ ⊕ ⊡ **Total** 20
Facilities ⊞ ⚷ ↑ ⊙ ⊣ ⊛ ✕ ↦ ⊟ ⊡
Nearby Facilities ↑ ✓ ∪
⚉ Chesterfield
The Peak District National Park, Sherwood Forest and Meadenhall.

DERBY

Beechwood Park, Main Road, Elvaston, Thulston, Derby, Derbyshire, DE72 3EQ.
Std: 01332 **Tel:** 751938
Nearest Town/Resort Derby
Directions From Derby take the A6 south and turn left onto the B5010 (Elvaston, Thulston and Borrowash), park is on the right hand side just past Elvaston road sign.
Acreage 5 **Open** All Year
Access Good **Site** Level
Sites Available ▲ ⊕ ⊞ **Total** 50

Facilities ⚿ ℓ ⊞ ⚷ ↑ ⊙ ⊣
⚹ ⍾ ⊛ ♨ ⚶ ↦ ⊟ ⊡
Nearby Facilities ✓ ⚓ ⚲ ∪
⚉ Derby
Lakes and a children's Go-Kart track. 3 yards from Elvaston Castle and Coun Park.

DOVERIDGE

Cavendish Cottage Camping & Cara **Site,** Doveridge, Ashbourne, Derbys, D 5JR.
Std: 01889 **Tel:** 562092
Nearest Town/Resort Uttoxeter
Directions On the main road in Doveri take the sign posts for (Doveridge).
Acreage 2 **Open** All Year
Access Good **Site** Level
Sites Available ▲ ⊕ ⊞ **Total** 15
Facilities ℓ ⊞ ⊙ ☎ ⍾ ⊛ ↦
Nearby Facilities
⚉ Uttoxeter
Alton Towers, Dovedale, Sudbury Hall a many pleasant walks. Owner Mr G Woo

EDALE

Fieldhead Campsite, Edale, Hope Vall Derbyshire, S33 7ZA.
Std: 01433 **Tel:** 670386
Website: www.fieldhead-campsite.co.uk
Nearest Town/Resort Castleton
Directions 4½ miles from Castleton.
Acreage 3 **Open** All Year
Site Level
Sites Available ▲ **Total** 50
Facilities ⊞ ⚷ ↑ ⊙ ⊣ ☎ ⍾ ↦
Nearby Facilities ↑ ✓ ⚓ ⚲ ∪ ♞ ♞
⚉ Edale
Alongside a river, next to Peak District Vis Centre. 6 fields, 2 of which are by the ri All superb views of Mamtor Ridge a Kinder Scout. At the start of Pennine Wa

EDALE

Highfield Farm, Upper Booth, Edale, Hope Valley, S33 7ZJ.
Std: 01433 **Tel:** 670245
Nearest Town/Resort Buxton/Castleton
Directions Turn right off the A625 oppos Hope Church, take minor road to Eda Follow the road up the valley, pass ↑ turning for Edale Village, at bottom of hill turn right, go past the viaduct and pa picnic area, round the corner and the hou is up ahead.
Acreage 30 **Open** Easter **to** October
Access Good **Site** Lev/Slope
Sites Available ▲ ⊕ ⊞
Facilities ⊞ ☎ ⍾ ⊟ ⊡
Nearby Facilities ∪ ♞
⚉ Edale
Good walking country, ideal for climbing a caves nearby.

EDALE

Upper Booth Campsite, Upper Booth Farm, Edale, Hope Valley, S33 7ZJ.
Std: 01433 **Tel:** 670250
Email: helliwell@farming.co.uk
Nearest Town/Resort Chapel-en-le-Frith
Directions 2 miles from Edale Village, miles east of Chapel-en-le-Frith. Midw between Sheffield and Manchester.
Open All Year
Site Level
Sites Available ▲ **Total** 30
Facilities ⊞ ⍾ ↑ ⊙ ⊣ ☎ ⍾ ⊟
Nearby Facilities ↑ ✓ ∪ ♞
⚉ Edale
Ideal base for walkers, outdoor enthusias exploring the Peak District or just relaxi in beautiful countryside.

COOPER'S CAMP & CARAVAN SITE
Newfold Farm, Edale, Hope Valley, Derbyshire S33 7ZD

Located in the centre of the Peak District National Park, the small hamlet of Edale marks the beginning of the Pennine Way. Ideal base for hill walking and touring the Peak District. AA Approved Site. Facilities include: Toilet block with hot water and showers. Post Office and shop. Cafe/Restaurant. Gas supplied. Village pub within 100 yards. Free hot water in hand basins and dishwashing facilities. Caravans for hire. Open all year.

Proprietors - Roger & Penny Cooper.
Tel: (01433) 670372

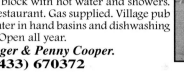

DALE
Waterside Camp Site, Waterside, Barber Booth Road, Edale, Hope Valley, S33 7ZL.
Std: 01433 **Tel:** 670215
Std: 01433 **Fax:** 670293
mail: jenn.cooper@cw.com
Nearest **Town/Resort** Buxton
Open Easter to End Sept
Access Good **Site** Level
Sites **Available** Total 50
Facilities
Nearby Facilities
Edale
Near to the Pennine Way, Blue John Caverns, Chatsworth House (18 miles) and Bakewell. Café ½ mile.

EYAM
Brosterfield Caravan Park, Brosterfield Farm, Foolow, Eyam, Hope Valley, S32 QB.
Std: 01433 **Tel:** 630958
Nearest **Town/Resort** Bakewell
Directions From Bakewell take the A6/A6465 north west for 5½ miles, turn east onto the A623, turn first left and site is on the left.
Open All Year
Access Good **Site** Level
Sites **Available** Total 50
Facilities
Nearby Facilities
Bamford
Ideal touring, walking and climbing.

HARTINGTON
Barracks Farm Caravan & Camping Site, Beresford Dale, Hartington, Buxton, Derbyshire, SK17 0HQ.
Std: 01298 **Tel:** 84261
Nearest **Town/Resort** Buxton
Directions Buxton A515 approx 10 miles. After leaving Buxton go on for 7 miles, turn

right for Hartington B5054. Go through village for 1½ miles, turn left for Beresford Dale, continue for ¼ mile then turn left again signposted Beresford Dale. The site is second on the left.
Acreage 5 **Open** Easter to End Oct
Access Good **Site** Level
Sites Available Total 40
Facilities
Nearby Facilities
Buxton
Alongside river, scenic views and ideal touring.

HATHERSAGE
Swallow Holme Caravan Park, Station Road, Bamford, Hope Valley, S33 0BN.
Std: 01433 **Tel:** 650981
Directions A6013 12 miles west of Sheffield.
Acreage 2¼ **Open** April to October
Access Good **Site** Level
Sites Available Total 60
Facilities
Nearby Facilities
Bamford
Scenic views and ideal touring.

HAYFIELD
Camping & Caravanning Club Site, Kinder Road, Hayfield, High Peak, Derbyshire, SK22 2LE.
Std: 01663 **Tel:** 745394
Website:
www.campingandcaravanningclub.co.uk
Directions On the A624 Glossop to Chapel-en-le-Frith road, the Hayfield by-pass. Well signed to the village, follow wooden carved signs to the site.
Acreage 7 **Open** March to October
Site Level
Sites Available Total 90
Facilities
Nearby Facilities

New Mills
On the banks of the River Sett. Ideal for fell and moorland walkers. 6 miles from a Victorian style swimming pool. 12 miles from Granada Studios. BTB Graded. Non members welcome.

HOPE
Hardhurst Farm Camping & Caravan Site, Hardhurst Farm, Parsons Lane, Aston, Hope Valley, Derbyshire, S33 6RB.
Std: 01433 **Tel:** 620001
Nearest Town/Resort Sheffield/Buxton/Castleton
Directions Take the A625 west from Sheffield, travel for 12 miles.
Acreage 3 **Open** All Year
Access Good **Site** Level
Sites Available Total 37
Facilities
Nearby Facilities
Hope
Ideal area for walking, touring and climbing.

HOPE
Laneside Caravan Park, Hope, Hope Valley, Derbyshire, S33 6RR.
Std: 01433 **Tel:** 620215
Std: 01433 **Fax:** 620214
Nearest Town/Resort Hope
Directions Camp site borders river/bridge on the Hope Village boundary.
Open April to October
Access Good **Site** Level
Sites Available
Facilities
Nearby Facilities
Hope
Alongside the River Noe. Just a few minutes walk to the village shops, pubs and restaurant.

The Perfect Setting For
Your Caravan Holiday in
in the heart of the
Derbyshire Peak District

FOR A FREE BROCHURE CALL 01629 732428

HOPE

Pindale Farm Camp Site, Pindale Farm, Pindale Road, Hope, Hope Valley, S33 6RN.
Std: 01433 **Tel:** 620111
Std: 01433 **Fax:** 620729
Nearest Town/Resort Hope
Directions Follow signs for Pindale then caravan signs.
Acreage 1 **Open** March **to** October
Site Level
Sites Available ▲ ☐ **Total** 60
Facilities 🚿 🛁 ♿ �🅿️ ⊙ 🍴 🍼 🛒 ⚡
Nearby Facilities ✓ ∪ ✗
≈ Hope

MATLOCK

Birchwood Farm Caravan Park, Wirksworth Road, Whatstandwell, Matlock, Derbyshire, DE4 5HS.
Std: 01629 **Tel:** 822280
Std: 01629 **Fax:** 822280
Nearest Town/Resort Matlock Bath
Directions Leave to A6 at Whatstandwell, take the B5035 towards Wirksworth, about 1 mile.
Acreage 4 **Open** April **to** October
Access Good **Site** Lev/Slope
Sites Available ▲ ♿ 🚐 **Total** 70
Facilities 🚿 🛁 ♿ 🚻 ⚡ ⊙ 🍴 🛒 ⚡
🏪 ⊙ ⏏️ ⏏️
Nearby Facilities ⌐ ✓ ⚓ ✗ ✗
≈ Whatstandwell
Near High Peak Trail, ideal touring area. Carsington Water 20 minutes. Table Tennis on site.

MATLOCK

Darwin Forest Country Park, Darley Moor, Two Dales, Matlock, Derbyshire, DE4 5LN.
Std: 01629 **Tel:** 732428
Std: 01629 **Fax:** 735015
Email: info@darwinforest.co.uk
Website: www.darwinforest.co.uk
Nearest Town/Resort Matlock
Directions From Chesterfield take the A632 for Matlock, turn onto the B5057 for Darley Dale. Park is on the right hand side.
Open March **to** November
Access Good **Site** Level

Sites Available 🚐 🚐 **Total** 50
Facilities 🛁 🚿 🔲 🚻 ⚡ 🍴 ⊙ 🍼 ⚡ ⊡ ⚡
🏪 ⊙ 🛒 ✗ ⊙ ♿ 🏢 ♿ 🍴 🏪 ⊡ ⊡
Nearby Facilities ⌐ ✓ ⚓ ✗ ∪ ✗ ✗
≈ Matlock
Set in superb woodland, excellent touring area with many attractions. Tennis on site.

MATLOCK

Haytop Country Park, Whatstandwell, Matlock, Derbyshire, DE4 5HP.
Std: 01773 **Tel:** 852063
Nearest Town/Resort Matlock
Directions Heading north on the A6, immediately after crossing the bridge in Whatstandwell turn left.
Acreage 65 **Open** All Year
Site Lev/Slope
Sites Available ▲ 🚐 🚐 **Total** 60
Facilities 🛁 🔲 🚻 ⚡ ⌐ ⊙ 🍴 ⚡ ⚡
🏪 ⊙ 🛒 ⊡
Nearby Facilities ∪ ✗
≈ Whatstandwell
Fishing and boating on park. Some pets are welcome.

MATLOCK

Hollybush Camp Site, The Old Toll Bar, Grangemill, Matlock, Derbyshire, DE4 4HU
Std: 01629 **Tel:** 650577
Nearest Town/Resort Matlock
Directions Situated on the A5012 2 miles from Matlock, opposite Hollybush Public House. 9 miles from Bakewell and Ashbourne on the B5056 and 14 miles from Derby on the A6.
Acreage 2 **Open** All Year
Access Good **Site** Level
Sites Available ▲ 🚐 🚐 **Total** 50
Facilities 🛁 🔲 🚻 ⚡ ⊙ 🍼 ♿ 🏪 🏪 🏪
✗ ⚡ ⊛ 🛒 ⊡ ⊡
Nearby Facilities ⌐ ✓ ⚓ ∪ ⊙ ✗ ✗
≈ Matlock
Peak National Park, Carsington Water and Peak Rail.

MATLOCK

Merebrook Caravan Park, Derby Road, Whatstandwell, Derbyshire, DE4 5HH.
Std: 01773 **Tel:** 852154
Nearest Town/Resort Matlock/Belper
Directions A6, 5¼ miles either way.

Acreage 2½ **Open** All Year
Access Good **Site** Level
Sites Available ▲ 🚐 🚐 **Total** 75
Facilities 🛁 🚿 🛁 🚻 ⚡ ⌐ ⊙ 🍴 ⚡
🏪 🏪 🛒 ⊡
Nearby Facilities ⌐ ✓ ⚓ ∪ ⚓ ✗
≈ Whatstandwell
Alongside river, scenic views. Ideal for loc attractions. Open for tents March to Octobe Tourers all year. Fishing on site.

MATLOCK

Pinegroves Caravan Park, High Lane, Tansley, Matlock, Derbys, DE4 5BG.
Std: 01629 **Tel:** 534815
Nearest Town/Resort Matlock.
Directions From the M1 junction 28, ta the A38 then the A615 towards Matlock. miles past Wessington, turn left crossroads into High Lane. Site is 600y on the left.
Acreage 7 **Open** April **to** 30 October
Access Good **Site** Level
Sites Available ▲ 🚐 🚐 **Total** 60
Facilities 🛁 🛁 🚿 🚻 ⚡ ⌐ ⊙ 🍴 ⚡
🛒 ⊡ ⊡
Nearby Facilities ⌐ ✓ ⚓ ✗ ∪ ⚓ ✗
≈ Matlock
Quiet site in woodland and ope countryside. Static caravans for sal Seasonal pitches available for couple without children.

MATLOCK

Sycamore Country Park, Lant Lane, Tansley, Matlock, Derbyshire, DE4 5LF.
Std: 01629 **Tel:** 55760
Email: info@sycamore-park.co.uk
Website: www.sycamore-park.co.uk
Nearest Town/Resort Matlock
Directions From the roundabout in th centre of Matlock take the A615 to Tansle Turn left into Church Street and follow 1½ miles, Park is on the left after th bungalows.
Acreage 8 **Open** 15 March **to** 31 Octobe
Access Good **Site** Level
Sites Available ▲ 🚐 🚐 **Total** 35
Facilities 🛁 🚻 ⚡ ⌐ ⊙ 🍴
🏪 ♿ ⊙ 🏪 ✗ ⊡ ⊡
Nearby Facilities ⌐ ✓ ⚓ ✗ ∪ ⚓ ✗
≈ Matlock

ently screened, level site on a quiet country
ne, very well maintained. Chatsworth,
ddon Hall, Tramway Village, Matlock and
th all within 8 miles.

TAVELEY

verdale Park, 'Riverdale', Bent Lane,
aveley, Near Chesterfield, Derbyshire,
3 3UG.
d: 01246 Tel: 473373
ebsite: www.ukparks.co.uk/
erdalemph
earest Town/Resort Staveley
rections 2 miles off the M1 junction 30
the A619.
en All Year
cess Good Site Level
tes Available ♥□ Total 4
cilities ⚡ 🚻 🔥 ♿ 🅿 🟦 ⓘ 🛒 🔲
arby Facilities 🏌 🚶 ⚓ 🚣
  Chesterfield

HALEY BRIDGE

ngstones Caravan Park, Yeardsley
ne, Furness Vale, Whaley Bridge,
erbyshire, SK23 7EB.
d: 01663 Tel: 732152
earest Town/Resort Whaley Bridge
rections From Whaley Bridge take A6
wards Stockport, in Furness Vale turn left
Pelican crossing (Cantonese resturant on
rner).
reage 3 Open March to October
ccess Good Site Lev/Slope
tes Available ⚠ ♥ 🚐
cilities ⚡ 🔥 🛒 🟦 ⓘ 🔲 🛒 🔲
arby Facilities 🏌 🚶 ⚓ 🚣 🎣 ✈
  Furness Vale

▶EVON

SHBURTON

shburton Caravan Park, Waterleat,
shburton, Devon, TQ13 7HU.
d: 01364 Tel: 652552 Fax: 652552
ail:
o@ashburtondevon.freeserve.co.uk
ebsite:
ww.ashburtoncaravanpark.co.uk
earest Town/Resort Ashburton
rections From the A38 Plymouth to
eter road, turn into North Street and
oceed past the shops. Before the bridge
n off signposted Waterleat.
reage 2 Open March to October
te Level
tes Available ⚠ ♥ Total 35
cilities ⚡ 🚻 🔥 🔥 ♿ 🅿 ⚡ 🛒 🔲 🛒
  🟦 🔲 🚻 🟦
arby Facilities 🏌 🚶 ⚓ 🚣 🎣 🚶
  Newton Abbot
ongside the River Ashburn.

ASHBURTON

Parkers Farm Holiday Park, Higher
Mead Farm, Ashburton, Devon, TQ13
7LJ.
Std: 01364 **Tel:** 652598
Std: 01364 **Fax:** 654004
Email: parkersfarm@btconnect.com
Website: www.parkersfarm.co.uk
Nearest Town/Resort Ashburton
Directions Take the A38 to Plymouth, when
you see the sign 26 miles Plymouth take
second left at Alston Cross marked
Woodland - Denbury. The site is behind the
bungalow.
Acreage 10 **Open** April **to** October
Access Good **Site** Level Terrace
Sites Available ⚠ ♥ 🚐 **Total** 60
Facilities 🚻 ⚡ 🔥 🔥 🔥 ♿ ⊙ 🛒 🔲 🛒 🟦
  🟦 🔲 🚻 🟦 ✖ 🛒 ♿ 🏍 🔲 🔲
Nearby Facilities 🏌 🚶 ⚓ 🚣 🎣 🚶
  ✈ Newton Abbot
A real working farm enviroment with goats,
sheep, pigs, cows, ducks and rabbits set
amidst beautiful countryside.

ASHBURTON

The River Dart Country Park, Holne
Park, Ashburton, Devon, TQ13 7NP.
Std: 01364 **Tel:** 652511
Std: 01364 **Fax:** 652020
Nearest Town/Resort Ashburton
Directions A38 Devon expressway to
Exeter/Plymouth. Follow brown signs from
Ashburton.
Acreage 90 **Open** Easter/1 April **to** Sept
Access Good **Site** Level
Sites Available ⚠ ♥ 🚐 **Total** 170
Facilities 🚻 ⚡ 🔥 🔥 🔥 ♿ ⊙ 🛒 🔲 🛒 🟦
  🟦 🔲 🚻 🟦 ✖ 🛒 ♿ 🏍 🔲 🔲
Nearby Facilities 🏌 🚶 ⚓ 🚣 🎣 🚶
  ✈ Newton Abbot
Magnificent site alongside the River Dart.
Ideal touring site for Dartmoor and the South
Devon coast.

AXMINSTER

Andrewshayes Caravan Park, Dalwood,
Axminster, Devon, EX13 7DY.
Std: 01404 **Tel:** 831225 **Fax:** 831893
Email: enquiries@andrewshayes.co.uk
Website: www.andrewshayes.co.uk
Nearest Town/Resort Seaton.
Directions Just off the A35 3 miles from
Axminster and 6 miles from Honiton. Turn
north at Taunton Cross and the site entrance
is 100 yards.
Acreage 10 **Open** March **to** 31 January
Access Good **Site** Sloping
Sites Available ⚠ ♥ 🚐 **Total** 90
Facilities 🚻 ⚡ 🔥 🔥 🔥 ♿ ⊙ 🛒 🔲 🛒 🟦
  🟦 🔲 🚻 ✖ 🛒 ♿ 🏍 🔲 🔲
Nearby Facilities 🏌 🚶 ⚓ 🚣 🚶

✈ Axminster.
Peaceful, clean park in beautiful countryside.
Ideal for family holiday. Easy reach of
resorts. New toilet building with family rooms
and disabled room.

AXMINSTER

Hunters Moon Holiday Park,
Hawkchurch, Axminster, Devon, EX13
5UL.
Std: 01297 **Tel:** 678402
Std: 01297 **Fax:** 678402
Nearest Town/Resort Lyme Regis
Directions From Axminster take A35
towards Dorchester for 3 miles. At main
crossroads take left B3165 towards
Crewkerne. Follow for 2¼ miles turn left to
Hunters Moon.
Acreage 12 **Open** 15 March **to** 14 Nov
Access Good **Site** Level
Sites Available ⚠ ♥ 🚐 **Total** 149
Facilities 🔥 🚻 🚻 🔥 ♿ ⊙ 🛒 🔲 🛒 🟦
  🟦 🔲 🚻 ✖ 🛒 🟦 🏍 🔲 🔲
Nearby Facilities 🏌 🚶 ⚓ 🚣 🚶
  ✈ Axminster
Super views over Axe Valley. Pitch & putt.
Ideal for family holidays and exploring
Devon, Dorset and Somerset.

BARNSTAPLE

**Brightlycott Farm Caravan & Camping
Site,** Brightlycott Farm, Barnstaple,
Devon, EX31 4JJ.
Std: 01271 **Tel:** 850330
Email: friend.brightlycott@virgin.net
Nearest Town/Resort Barnstaple
Directions Leave Barnstaple on the A39
towards Lynton, turn right 1½ miles after the
hospital signposted Brightlycott and
Roborough.
Acreage 4 **Open** 15 March **to** 15 Jan
Access Good **Site** Sloping
Sites Available ⚠ ♥ 🚐 **Total** 20
Facilities 🔥 🚻 🔥 ♿ ⊙ 🛒 🛒
  🟦 🔥 🔲 🚻 🔲 🟦
Nearby Facilities 🏌 🚶 🚣 🚶
  ✈ Barnstaple
Extremely peaceful, small, friendly, family
run site situated on a 200 acre farm with
panoramic views.

BARNSTAPLE

**Greenacres Farm Touring Caravan
Park,** Bratton Fleming, Barnstaple, North
Devon, EX31 4SG.
Std: 01598 **Tel:** 763334
Nearest Town/Resort Barnstaple
Directions From North Devon link road
(A361), turn right at Northaller roundabout
(by Little Chef). Take the A399 to Blackmoor
Gate, approx 10 miles. Park signed (300yds
from the A399).
Acreage 4 **Open** April **to** October

Access Good **Site** Level
Sites Available ♫ ⛟ **Total** 30
Facilities 👤 ƒ 🅷 🆄🅲 ⚓ ⌐ ⊙ ☕ ⛟ 🍽
🅻 🅾 🏠 🛆 ❋ 🔌🅿🄲 🅴
Nearby Facilities 🥾 ∪
⇥ Barnstaple
Moors and coast 5 miles, towns 10 miles. Peaceful, secluded park with scenic views. Ideal for touring, walking and cycling.

BARNSTAPLE

Midland Holiday Park, Braunton Road, Ashford, Barnstaple, North Devon, EX31 4AU.
Std: 01271 **Tel:** 343691
Std: 01271 **Fax:** 326355
Website: www.midlandpark.co.uk
Nearest Town/Resort Barnstaple
Directions Take the A361 from Barnstaple signposted Braunton and Ilfracombe. The park is on the right 3 miles out of Barnstaple.
Acreage 8 **Open** Easter **to** Mid-Nov
Access Good **Site** Level
Sites Available 🛆 ♫ ⛟ **Total** 95
Facilities ƒ 🆄🅲 ⚓ ⌐ ⊙ ☕ ⛟ 🍽
🅻 🅾 🏠 ❋ 🍴 🛆 ⚐ ❋ 🔌🅿🄲 🅴
Nearby Facilities ⌐ 🥾 ⚓ ⚡ ∪ ♪
⇥ Barnstaple
On the River Taw Estuary. Ideally situated for all beaches, shops, attractions and all sports. Exmoor and The Tarka Trail.

BERRYNARBOR

Watermouth Cove Holiday Park,
Berrynarbor, Nr. Ilfracombe, North Devon, EX34 9SJ.
Std: 01271 **Tel:** 862504
Email:
info@watermouthcoveholidays.co.uk
Website:
www.watermouthcoveholidays.co.uk
Nearest Town/Resort Ilfracombe/Combe Martin

Directions Leave the M5 at junction 27 and join the North Devon link road. Leave the link road at North Aller roundabout and follow signs for Combe Martin. Go through Combe Martin and Watermouth is 2 miles on.
Acreage 27 **Open** Easter **to** End October
Access Good **Site** Level
Sites Available 🛆 ♫ ⛟ **Total** 90
Facilities ƒ 🅷 🆄🅲 ⚓ ⌐ ⊙ ☕ ⛟ 🍽 🅾 🍽
🅻 🅻 🅾 🏠 ❋ 🍴 🛆 ❋ 🔌🅿🄲 🅴
Nearby Facilities ⌐ 🥾 ⚓ ⚡ ∪ ♪
⇥ Barnstaple
Picturesque views and private sandy beach. Headland walks. Adjacent to small craft harbour.

BIDEFORD

Steart Farm Touring Park, Horns Cross, Bideford, Devon, EX39 5DW.
Std: 01237 **Tel:** 431836
Email: steartcamping@tinyworld.co.uk
Nearest Town/Resort Bideford
Directions From Bideford follow the A39 west (signed Bude). Pass through Fairy Cross and Horns Cross, 2 miles after Horns Cross site will be on the right. 8 miles from Bideford.
Acreage 10¼ **Open** Easter **to** October
Access Good **Site** Lev/Slope
Sites Available 🛆 ♫ ⛟ **Total** 60
Facilities ƒ 🆄🅲 ⚓ ⌐ ⊙ ☕ ⛟ 🍽
🅻 🅾 🏠 🛆 ❋ 🔌🅿🄲 🅴
Nearby Facilities ⌐ 🥾 ∪ ♪
⇥ Barnstaple
Set in 17 acres overlooking Bideford Bay, 1 mile from the sea. 2¼ acre dog exercise area and daytime dog kenelling. 2 acre childrens play area.

BRAUNTON

Chivenor Caravan Park, Chivenor Cross Braunton, Barnstaple, North Devon, EX 4BN.
Std: 07071 **Tel:** 228478
Email: chivenorcp@lineone.net
Nearest Town/Resort Braunton
Directions On the A361 Barnstaple Braunton road, on the only roundabo between the two.
Acreage 3 **Open** March **to** November
Access Good **Site** Level
Sites Available 🛆 ♫ ⛟ **Total** 40
Facilities ƒ 🅵 🅷 🆄🅲 ⚓ ⌐ ⊙ 🅾
🅻 🅾 🏠 🛆 ❋ 🔌🅿🄲 🅴
Nearby Facilities ⌐ 🥾 ⚓ ⚡ ∪ ♪ ♪
⇥ Barnstaple
100 yards from the Tarka Trail. Saunt Sands 3 miles. Central for touring No Devon.

BRAUNTON

Lobb Fields Caravan & Camping Park Saunton Road, Braunton, Devon, EX33 1EB.
Std: 01271 **Tel:** 812090
Std: 01271 **Fax:** 812090
Email: lobbfields@compuserve.com
Website: www.lobbfields.com
Nearest Town/Resort Braunton
Directions Take the A361 to Braunton, th take the B3231. The park entrance is 1 m from Braunton centre on the right.
Acreage 14 **Open** 16 March **to** 28 Oct
Access Good **Site** Gentle Slope
Sites Available 🛆 ♫ ⛟ **Total** 180
Facilities ƒ 🆄🅲 ⚓ ⌐ ⊙ ☕ 🅾
🅻 🅾 🏠 🛆 ❋ 🔌🅿🄲 🅴
Nearby Facilities ⌐ 🥾 ⚓ ⚡ ∪ ♪ ♪
⇥ Barnstaple
1½ miles from the beach. 1 mile from t Tarka Trail.

BRIXHAM

Centry Touring Caravans & Tents, Cudberry House, Centry Road, Brixham, Devon, TQ5 9EY.
Std: 01803 **Tel:** 853215 **Fax:** 853261
Email: jlacentry.touring@talk21.com
Website: www.ukparks.co.uk/centry
Nearest Town/Resort Brixham
Directions Entering Brixham on the A3022, bear right at the first set of traffic lights and follow signs to Berry Head.
Acreage 2 **Open** March **to** November
Access Good **Site** Level
Sites Available ▲ ⬥ ⬤ **Total** 30
Facilities ⟍ ⬛ ⟌ ⬤ ⟍ ⬤ ⬛ ⟍ ⬜
Nearby Facilities ⟍ ⟍ ⬥ ⟍ ⟍ ⬥ ⟍ ✕
 ⟍ Paignton
next to the coastal footpath and adjacent to Berry Head Country Park.

BRIXHAM

Galmpton Touring Park, Greenway Road, Galmpton, Brixham, Devon, TQ5 0EP.
Std: 01803 **Tel:** 842066
Std: 01803 **Fax:** 844458
Email: galmptontouringpark@hotmail.com
Website: www.galmptontouringpark.co.uk
Nearest Town/Resort Brixham
Directions Signposted right off the A379 Brixham road ¼ mile past the end of the A380 Torbay ring road.
Acreage 10 **Open** Easter **to** September
Access Good **Site** Lev/Slope
Sites Available ▲ ⬥ ⬤ **Total** 120
Facilities ⬥ ⟍ ⬛ ⬛ ⟍ ⟍ ⬤ ⟍ ⬛ ⬜ ⬤
 ⟍ ⬤ ⬛ ⟍ ⬜ ⬜ ⬜
Nearby Facilities ⟍ ⟍ ⬥ ⟍ ⟍ ⟍ ⟍
 ⟍ Paignton
Terraced site with stunning River Dart views, in a central Torbay location. Pets are welcome but not in peak season (mid July to August).

BUCKFAST

Churchill Farm, Buckfastleigh, Devon, TQ11 0EZ.
Std: 01364 **Tel:** 642844
Email: apedrick@farmersweekly.net
Nearest Town/Resort Buckfastleigh/Buckfast
Directions Exit A38 at Dartbridge, follow signs for Buckfast Abbey, proceed up hill to crossroads. Turn left into no-through road towards church. Farm entrance is opposite the church 1½ miles from the A38.
Acreage 2 **Open** Easter **to** October
Access Good **Site** Lev/Slope
Sites Available ▲ ⬥ ⬤ **Total** 25
Facilities ⟍ ⬛ ⟍ ⬤ ⟍ ⬤ ⬜ ⬜
Nearby Facilities ⟍ ⟍ ⬥ ⟍ ⟍ ⬥ ⟍ ✕
 ⟍ Totnes

Stunning views of Dartmoor and Buckfast Abbey, the latter being within easy walking distance as are the Steam Railway, Butterfly Farm, Otter Sanctuary and local inns. Seaside resort 10 miles.

BUCKFASTLEIGH

Beara Farm Camping Site, Colston Road, Buckfastleigh, Devon, TQ11 0LW.
Std: 01364 **Tel:** 642234
Nearest Town/Resort Buckfastleigh
Directions Coming from Exeter take first left after passing South Devon Steam Railway and Butterfly Centre at Buckfastleigh, signpost marked Beara, fork right at next turning then 1 mile to site, signposted on roadside and junctions.
Acreage 3¼ **Open** All Year
Access Good **Site** Level
Sites Available ▲ ⬥ ⬤ **Total** 30
Facilities ⟍ ⬛ ⬛ ⟍ ⬤ ⟍ ⬤ ⟍ ⬜ ⬜
Nearby Facilities ⟍ ⟍ ⬥ ✕
 ⟍ Totnes
Quiet, select, sheltered site adjoining River Dart. Within easy reach of sea and moors and 1½ miles southeast of Buckfastleigh.

CHAGFORD

Woodland Springs Touring Park, Venton, Near Chagford, Devon, EX6 6PG.
Std: 01647 **Tel:** 231695
Nearest Town/Resort Okehampton
Directions From Exeter take the A30, after 17 miles turn left at Merrymeet roundabout onto the A382 towards Moretonhampstead, after 1½ miles the park is on the left, signpost Venton.
Acreage 4 **Open** 14 March **to** 14 Nov
Access Good **Site** Level
Sites Available ▲ ⬥ ⬤ **Total** 85
Facilities ⟍ ⬛ ⬛ ⟍ ⬤ ⟍ ⬤ ⬛ ⬜ ⬜ A
Nearby Facilities ⟍ ⟍ ⬥
 ⟍ Exeter
Quiet, secluded site within the Dartmoor National Park, surrounded by wood and farmland. Good access for the larger units and large all-weather pitches. Off season breaks.

CHUDLEIGH

Holmans Wood Tourist Park, Harcombe Cross, Chudleigh, Devon, TQ13 0DZ.
Std: 01626 **Tel:** 853785
Nearest Town/Resort Chudleigh
Directions From Exeter take the A38 Towards Plymouth. Go past the racecourse and after 1 mile take the B3344 for Chudleigh. We are on the left at the end of the sliproad.
Acreage 11 **Open** March **to** End October
Access Good **Site** Level
Sites Available ▲ ⬥ ⬤ **Total** 144
Facilities ⬥ ⟍ ⬛ ⬛ ⬛ ⟍ ⬤ ⟍ ⬤ ⬜ ⬤
 ⬛ ⬤ ⬛ ⬛ ✳ ⟍ ⬜ ⬜

Nearby Facilities ⟍ ⟍ ⬥ ⟍ ⬤ ⟍ ⟍ ✕
 ⟍ Newton Abbot
Ideal touring for Dartmoor, Haldon Forest, Exeter and Torbay.

CLOVELLY

Dyke Green Farm Camping Site, Dyke Green Farm, Clovelly, Bideford, Devon, EX39 5RU.
Std: 01237 **Tel:** 431279
Email: edwardjohns2@hotmail.com
Nearest Town/Resort Clovelly
Directions From Bideford or Bude (West) take the A39, at roundabout Clovelly Cross.
Acreage 3½ **Open** Easter **to** October
Access Good **Site** Level
Sites Available ▲ ⬥ ⬤ **Total** 40
Facilities ⟍ ⬛ ⬤ ⟍ ⬤ ⬤
 ⬛ ⬛ ⬛ ⬤ ✕ ⟍ ⬜ ⬜
Nearby Facilities ⟍ ⟍ ⬥ ⟍ ⟍ ⬥ ⟍ ✕
 ⟍ Barnstaple
Clovelly village and beach. Ideal walking. Milky Way, Kilarney Springs and The Big Sheep.

COMBE MARTIN

Newberry Farm, Woodlands, Combe Martin, North Devon, EX34 0AT.
Std: 01271 **Tel:** 882334
Email: enq@newberrycampsite.co.uk
Website: www.newberrycampsite.co.uk
Nearest Town/Resort Combe Martin/Ilfracombe
Directions Leave the M5 at junction 27 and take the A361 to Aller Cross Roundabout. A399 to Combe Martin.
Acreage 20 **Open** Easter **to** October
Access Good **Site** Level
Sites Available ▲ ⬥ ⬤ **Total** 110
Facilities ⬥ ⟍ ⬛ ⬤ ⟍ ⬤ ⟍ ⬤ ⬤
 ⬛ ⬛ ⬛ ⬤
Nearby Facilities ⟍ ⟍ ⬥ ⟍ ⬤ ⟍
 ⟍ Barnstaple
Beautiful countryside valley site. Combe Martin beach and village within 5 minutes walk. Coarse fishing lake. Woodland walks. ETC 3 Star Touring Park. Sorry, no dogs.

COMBE MARTIN

Stowford Farm Meadows, Combe Martin, Devon, EX34 0PW.
Std: 01271 **Tel:** 882476 **Fax:** 883053
Email: enquiries@stowford.co.uk
Website: www.stowford.co.uk
Nearest Town/Resort Combe Martin
Directions Situated on the A3123 Combe Martin/Woollacombe Road at Berry Down.
Acreage 140 **Open** Easter **to** October
Access Good **Site** Lev/Slope
Sites Available ▲ ⬥ ⬤ **Total** 570
Facilities ⬥ ⟍ ⬛ ⬤ ⟍ ⬤ ⟍ ⬤ ⬤ ⬤
 ⬛ ⬤ ⬛ ✕ ⬤ ⬛ ⬤ ✳ ✳ ⟍ ⬜ ⬜
 ⬛ ⬤ ⬛ ⬤ ✳ ⟍ ⬜ ⬜
Nearby Facilities ⟍ ⟍ ⬥ ⟍

71

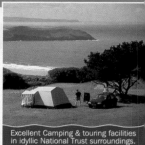

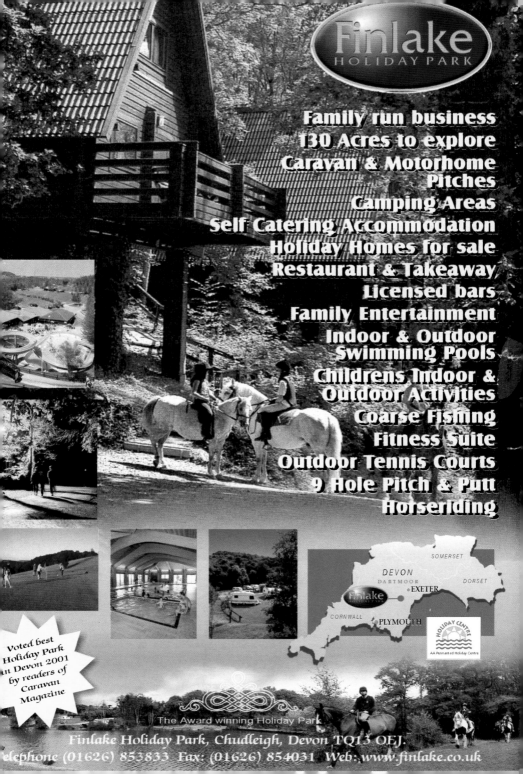

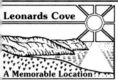
* Barnstaple
et in 450 acres of beautiful countryside.
eal touring site at the heart of North Devon.
enowned for our extensive range of
cilities at excellent value. Caravan repair
orkshop and caravan accessories shop.

ROYDE BAY
ay View Farm Holidays, Bay View
arm, Croyde, Devon, EX33 1PN.
td: 01271 Tel: 890501
ebsite: www.bayviewfarm.co.uk
earest Town/Resort Croyde
irections At Braunton on A361 turn west
main road B3231 towards Croyde Village
creage 10 Open Easter to September
te Level
tes Available ▲ ⌂ ☻
acilities
arby Facilities
Barnstaple
ear beach, 5 mins walking, Scenic views,
eal touring, booking advisable peak
ason. S.A.E. for information.

ROYDE BAY
uda Holiday Park, Croyde Bay, North
evon, EX33 1NY.
td: 01271 Tel: 890671
td: 01271 Fax: 890656
mail: enquiries@ruda.co.uk

Website: www.ruda.co.uk
Nearest Town/Resort Barnstaple
Directions From Barnstaple take the A361 to Braunton. In the centre of Braunton at the traffic lights turn left onto the B3231 and follow signs to Croyde.
Acreage 200 **Open** 15 March **to** 31 October
Access Good **Site** Level
Sites Available ▲ ⌂ ☐ **Total** 330
Facilities
Nearby Facilities
Barnstaple
Our own beach, Croyde Bay is immediately adjacent to camping and touring pitches. Excellent surfing and walking.

CULLOMPTON
Forest Glade Holiday Park, Cullomptom, Devon, EX15 2DT.
Std: 01404 **Tel:** 841381 **Fax:** 841593
Email: forestglade@cwcom.net
Website: www.forestglade.mcmail.com
Nearest Town/Resort Cullompton
Directions A373 Cullompton/Honiton, turn for Sheldon at Keepers Cottage Inn, 2½ miles east of Cullompton. Touring caravans via Dunkeswell Road only.
Acreage 10 **Open** Mid March to End Oct
Access See Directions **Site** Level
Sites Available ▲ ⌂ ☻ **Total** 80

Facilities
Nearby Facilities
Honiton/Tiverton Parkway
Central for southwest twixt coast and moors. Large flat sheltered camping pitches. Caravans for hire. Free heated indoor swimming pool and Paddling pool, riding, gliding and tennis on site.

DARTMOUTH
Little Cotton Caravan Park, Dartmouth, South Devon, TQ6 0LB.
Std: 01803 **Tel:** 832558 **Fax:** 834887
Website:
www.littlecottoncaravanpark.co.uk
Nearest Town/Resort Dartmouth
Directions Take the A38 ta Buckfastleigh, A384 to Totnes, from Totnes to Halwell on the A381. At Halwell take the A3122 Dartmouth road, park is on the right at entrance to town.
Acreage 7½ **Open** 15 March **to** October
Access Good **Site** Lev/Slope
Sites Available ▲ ⌂ ☻ **Total** 95
Facilities
Nearby Facilities
Totnes
Scenic views, ideal touring. Park and ride service in the next field. Luxurious new toilet and shower facilities.

DARTMOUTH

Start Bay Caravan Park, Strete, Nr. Dartmouth, South Devon, TQ6 0RU.
Std: 01803 **Tel:** 770535 **Fax:** 770535
Nearest Town/Resort Dartmouth
Directions 5 miles from Dartmouth on the coast road to Kingsbridge, turn right at Strete Post Office for Halwell.
Acreage 1¼ **Open** April (Easter) **to** End Sept
Access Good **Site** Level
Sites Available ▲ ⚏ ⚐ **Total** 25
Facilities ⚅ 🚿 🎮 🍴 ⊙ 🍽 ▤ ▣ 🍺 ⚑ 🎣 ⏣ ⊡ ▣
Nearby Facilities ⌐ ✓ ⚓ ∪ ⅃ ⋩
⇌ Totnes
In the countryside, near the sea. Black Pool Sands and Slapton Ley.

DARTMOUTH

Woodlands Leisure Park, Blackawton, Totnes, Devon, TQ9 7DQ.
Std: 01803 **Tel:** 712598 **Fax:** 712680
Email: enquiries@woodlandspark.com
Website: www.woodlandspark.com
Nearest Town/Resort Dartmouth
Directions 4 miles from Dartmouth on main road A3122 (formally B3207).
Acreage 16 **Open** Easter **to** Nov
Access Good **Site** Level
Sites Available ▲ ⚏ ⚐ **Total** 210
Facilities ⚅ 🚿 🎮 🍴 ⊙ 🍽 ▤ ▣ 🍺 ⚑ 🚿 ✖ ♨ ⊡ ▣
Nearby Facilities ⌐ ✓ ⚓ ∪
⇌ Totnes
'The Best Site We've Stayed In' say so many of our customers, be sure to book early. Experience the highest standard facilities from beautiful bathrooms to large, level pitching lawns, set in tranquil terraces. Enjoy our famous Leisure Park for free with two nights stay, a sparkling combination of indoor and outdoor attractions. Three watercoasters, 500m Toboggan Run and biggest indoor venture centre in the UK.

DAWLISH

Cofton Country Holidays, Starcross, Near Dawlish, Devon, EX6 8RP.
Std: 01626 **Tel:** 890111
Std: 01626 **Fax:** 891572
Email: info@coftonholidays.co.uk
Website: www.coftonholidays.co.uk
Nearest Town/Resort Dawlish Warren
Directions On the A379 Exeter to Dawlish road, ½ mile after the fishing village at Cockwood.
Acreage 16 **Open** Easter **to** October
Access Good **Site** Level
Sites Available ▲ ⚏ ⚐ **Total** 450
Facilities ⚅ ✖ 🚿 🎮 🍴 ⊙ 🍽 ▤ ▣ 🍺 ⚑ 🚿 ✖ ♨ ⊡ ▣
Nearby Facilities ⌐ ✓ ⚓ ∪ ⅃ ⋩
⇌ Dawlish
In beautiful rural countryside near to sandy Dawlish Warren beach. Clean and tidy family run park. Superb complex and swimming pool. Swan Pub with family lounge and meals. See our advert on the back cover.

DAWLISH

Golden Sands Holiday Park, Week Lane, Dawlish, South Devon, EX7 0LZ.
Std: 01626 **Tel:** 863099
Email: info@goldensands.co.uk
Website: www.goldensands.co.uk
Nearest Town/Resort Dawlish
Directions From M5 junction 30 take the A379 Dawlish, through Starcross. After 2 miles Week Lane is the second left opposite the filling station, on the right.
Acreage 2¼ **Open** Easter **to** October
Access Good **Site** Level
Sites Available ⚏ ⚐ **Total** 60

Facilities ⚅ 🚿 🎮 🍴 ⊙ 🍽 ▤ ▣ 🍺 ⚑ ✖ 🚿 🎣 ♨ ⊡ ▣
Nearby Facilities ⌐ ✓ ⚓ ∪ ⅃ ⋩
⇌ Dawlish
Family run for family fun! Small touring park 2/3rds of a mile from Dawlish Warren beach with free nightly, family entertainment in the licensed club. Unique indoor/outdoor swimming pool. Pets are welcome during low and mid season only.

DAWLISH

Lady's Mile Holiday Park, Exeter Road, Dawlish, Devon, EX7 0LX.
Std: 01626 **Tel:** 863411
Std: 01626 **Fax:** 888689
Email: info@ladysmile.co.uk
Website: www.ladysmile.co.uk
Nearest Town/Resort Dawlish
Directions On A379 road 1 mile north of Dawlish and 10 miles south of Exeter.
Acreage 20 **Open** Mid March **to** End Oct
Access Good **Site** Level
Sites Available ▲ ⚏ ⚐ **Total** 485
Facilities ⚅ 🚿 🎮 🍴 ⊙ 🍽 ▤ ▣ 🍺 ⚑ 🚿 ✖ ♨ ⊡ ▣
Nearby Facilities ⌐ ✓ ⚓ ∪ ⅃ ⋩
⇌ Dawlish
Very close to a Blue Flag Beach and near to Dartmoor National Park. Ideal base for exploring Devon.

DAWLISH

Leadstone Camping, Warren Road, Dawlish, Devon, EX7 0NG.
Std: 01626 **Tel:** 872239/864411
Std: 01626 **Fax:** 873833
Email: info@leadstonecamping.co.uk
Website: www.leadstonecamping.co.uk
Nearest Town/Resort Dawlish
Directions Leave the M5 at junction 30 and take signposted road A379 to Dawlish. As you approach Dawlish, turn left on brow

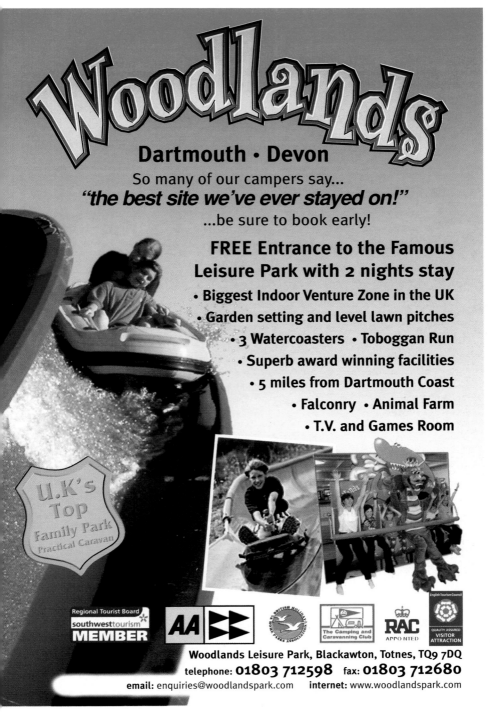

Woodlands

Dartmouth • Devon

So many of our campers say...

"the best site we've ever stayed on!"

...be sure to book early!

FREE Entrance to the Famous Leisure Park with 2 nights stay

- Biggest Indoor Venture Zone in the UK
- Garden setting and level lawn pitches
- 3 Watercoasters • Toboggan Run
- Superb award winning facilities
- 5 miles from Dartmouth Coast
- Falconry • Animal Farm
- T.V. and Games Room

U.K's Top Family Park
Practical Caravan

Regional Tourist Board
southwesttourism
MEMBER

AA

The Camping and Caravanning Club

RAC APPOINTED

English Tourism Council
QUALITY ASSURED VISITOR ATTRACTION

Woodlands Leisure Park, Blackawton, Totnes, TQ9 7DQ
telephone: **01803 712598**   fax: **01803 712680**
email: enquiries@woodlandspark.com   internet: www.woodlandspark.com

hill, signposted Dawlish Warren. Our site is ½ mile on right.
Acreage 7 **Open** 21 June to 9 Sept
Access Good **Site** Lev/Slope
Sites Available ⚠ ⊞ ⊞ **Total** 160
Facilities ⸹ ⊞ ⚑ ⌑ ⊙ ⥴ ⊿ ⊠ ⊡ ☕
⬙ ⍯ ⊙ ⊛ ⚑ ⨉⊞⊡ ⊡
Nearby Facilities ⌑ ⌇ ⚓ ⚲ ∪ ⚐ ⚑
⇌ Dawlish Warren
Rolling grassland in a natural secluded bowl within ½ mile of sandy 2 mile Dawlish Warren Beach and nature reserve. Ideally situated for discovering Devon.

DAWLISH WARREN
Peppermint Park, Warren Road, Dawlish Warren, Devon, EX7 0PQ.
Std: 01626 **Tel:** 863436
Email: info@peppermintpark.co.uk
Website: www.peppermintpark.co.uk
Nearest Town/Resort Dawlish
Directions Leave M5 at junction 30 and take the A379 Dawlish road. Approx. 2½ miles after Starcross take sharp left for Dawlish Warren. Park is approx. 1¼ miles down the hill on the left.
Acreage 16 **Open** Easter to September
Access Good **Site** Lev/Slope
Sites Available ⚠ ⊞ ⊞ **Total** 300
Facilities ⸹ ⊞ ⚑ ⌑ ⊙ ⥴ ⊿ ⊠ ⊡ ☕
⬙ ⍯ ⊙ ⊛ ⨉ ⚐ ⚑ ⚲ ✳⊞⊡ ⊡
Nearby Facilities ⌑ ⌇ ⚓ ⚲ ⚐
⇌ Dawlish Warren
Closest touring park to Dawlish Warren beach (600 metres). The only 4 Star Graded touring park at Dawlish Warren. Grassland park sheltered by mature trees. Coarse fishing. Free nightly entertainment. David Bellamy Silver Award and AA 4 Pennants.

DOLTON
Dolton Caravan Park, The Square, Dolton, Winkleigh, Devon, EX19 8QF.
Std: 01805 **Tel:** 804536
Nearest Town/Resort Great Torrington
Directions From the A3124 turn at the Beacon Garage signposted Dolton. Go into the village and turn right at the Union Inn, the site is at the rear of Royal Oak Inn.
Acreage 2¼ **Open** Mid March to October
Access Good **Site** Level
Sites Available ⚠ ⊞ ⊞ **Total** 25

Facilities ⸹ ⊞ ⚑ ⌑ ⊙ ⥴ ⊿ ⊠ ⊡ ☕
⬙ ⊙ ⊞ ⊡
Nearby Facilities ⌑ ⌇ ∪
Scenic views. Ideal for touring Exmoor and Dartmoor. Walking on the Tarka Trail.

EXETER
Barley Meadow Caravan & Camping Park, Crockernwell, Exeter, Devon, EX6 6NR
Std: 01647 **Tel:** 281629
Nearest Town/Resort Okehampton/Exeter
Directions 10 miles from Exeter on the A30 to Okehampton, turn left signposted Crockernwell, 3 miles site is on the left. From Okehampton travel for 7 miles towards Exeter, at large roundabout turn left, 3 miles site is on the right.
Acreage 4½ **Open** March to November
Access Good **Site** Level
Sites Available ⚠ ⊞ ⊞ **Total** 40
Facilities ⸹ ⊞ ⊞ ⚑ ⌑ ⊙ ⥴ ⊿ ⊠ ⊡ ☕
⬙ ⊙ ⊞ ⊞ ✳⊞⊡
Nearby Facilities ⌑ ⌇ ∪
Very clean facilities on this quiet site on the edge of Dartmoor with superb views. 150 yards from Two Moors Way walk. Heated shower blocks. No charge for dogs. Excellent access for touring Dartmoor.

EXETER
Haldon Lodge Farm Caravan & Camping Park, Kennford, Nr. Exeter, Devon, EX6 7YG.
Std: 01392 **Tel:** 832312
Nearest Town/Resort Exeter
Directions 4¼ miles South of Exeter, ½ mile from the end of M5 turn off A38 at Kennford Services. Follow signs for Haldon Lodge turning left through Kennford Village past the Post Office. Proceed to Motorway bridge turning left to Dunchideock, 1 mile to site.
Open All Year
Access Good **Site** Lev/Slope
Sites Available ⚠ ⊞ ⊞
Facilities ⸹ ⊞ ⊞ ⚑ ⌑ ⊙ ⥴ ⊿ ⊠ ⊡ ☕
⬙ ⍯ ⊙ ⊞ ⊛ ⊞⊡
Nearby Facilities ⌑ ⌇ ⚓ ⚲ ∪ ⚐ ⚑ ⚲
⇌ Exeter
Peaceful family site with beautiful forest scenery, nature walks, fishing lakes, riding holidays and barbeques. Excellent touring centre. Sea and Exeter 15 minutes.

EXETER
Kennford International Caravan Park
Kennford, Exeter, Devon, EX6 7YN.
Std: 01392 **Tel:** 833046
Std: 01392 **Fax:** 833046
Email: ian@kennfordint.fsbusiness.co.u
Website: www.kennfordint.co.uk
Nearest Town/Resort Exeter
Directions From the M5 join the A towards Plymouth and Torquay. Exi Kennford Services, pass the garage, go c the bridge and we are on the left. App 10 minutes from Exeter.
Acreage 15 **Open** All Year
Access Good **Site** Level
Sites Available ⚠ ⊞ ⊞ **Total** 137
Facilities ⸹ ⸹ ⊞ ⊞ ⚑ ⌑ ⊙ ⥴ ⊿ ⊠ ⊡
⬙ ⊙ ⊞ ⊛ ⨉ ⚐ ⚑ ⚲✳⊞⊡ ⊡
Nearby Facilities ⌑ ⌇ ∪
⇌ Exeter
Kennford International is close to beac and the city of Exeter. Fishing and villages of Kenn and Kennford nearby.

EXMOUTH
Castle Brake, Castle Lane, Woodbury, Near Exeter, Devon, EX5 1HA.
Std: 01395 **Tel:** 232431
Email: reception@castlebrake.co.uk
Website: www.castlebrake.co.uk
Nearest Town/Resort Exmouth
Directions M5 junction 30 take the A3 to Halfway Inn. Turn right onto the B31 after 2 miles turn right to Woodbury. The p is 500yds on the right.
Acreage 10 **Open** March to October
Access Good **Site** Level
Sites Available ⚠ ⊞ ⊞ **Total** 42
Facilities ⸹ ⊞ ⚑ ⌑ ⊙ ⥴ ⊿ ⊠
⊙ ⊞ ⊛ ⨉ ⚐ ⊞ ⚑ ✳⊞⊡ ⊡
Nearby Facilities ⌑ ⌇ ⚓ ⚲ ∪ ⚐
⇌ Exmouth
Beautiful views of the River Exe. Exmo beach 6 miles. Good touring centre for E Devon and beyond.

EXMOUTH
Devon Cliffs Holiday Park, Sandy Bay Exmouth, Devon, EX8 5BT.
Std: 01395 **Tel:** 226226
Std: 01395 **Fax:** 223111
Website: www.havenholidays.com

Nearest Town/Resort Exmouth
Directions Turn off the M5 at exit 30 and take the A376 for Exmouth. Clear directions from Exmouth to Devon Cliffs, follow brown tourism signs.
Open March **to** October
Access Good **Site** Sloping
Sites Available ▲ ⊞ ⊟ **Total** 145
Facilities ⚫ ⚫ ⚫ ⚫ ⚫ ⚫ ⚫ ⚫ ⚫ ⚫ ⚫ ⚫ ⚫ ⚫ ⚫ ⚫ ⚫
Nearby Facilities ⚫ ⚫ ⚫ ⚫ ⚫ ⚫ ⚫
⚫ Exmouth
Spectacular hillside setting, on top of the cliffs, overlooking the beautiful Sandy Bay, with access to our very own sandy beach.

EXMOUTH

Webbers Farm Caravan & Camping Park, Castle Lane, Woodbury, Near Exeter, Devon, EX5 1EA.
Std: 01395 **Tel:** 232276
Std: 01395 **Fax:** 233389
Email: reception@webbersfarm.co.uk
Website: www.webbersfarm.co.uk
Nearest Town/Resort Exmouth
Directions Leave the M5 at junction 30 (Exeter Services) and follow the A376, at the second roundabout take the B3179 (5 miles) to Woodbury. In the village follow the brown and white tourism signs.
Acreage 10 **Open** April **to** End Sept
Access Good **Site** Lev/Slope
Sites Available ▲ ⊞ ⊟ **Total** 115
Facilities ⚫ ⚫ ⚫ ⚫ ⚫ ⚫ ⚫ ⚫ ⚫
Nearby Facilities ⚫ ⚫ ⚫ ⚫ ⚫ ⚫ ⚫
⚫ Exmouth
Relaxing family site on a working farm. Lots of space. Easy access from the M5 and the A30. 15 minutes from the seaside and historic Exeter. Endless choice of local activities, walks and places to visit. Please telephone for a brochure.

HOLSWORTHY

Hedley Wood Caravan & Camping Park, Bridgerule, Holsworthy, Devon, EX22 7ED.
Std: 01288 **Tel:** 381404
Std: 01288 **Fax:** 381644
Email: alan@hedleywood.co.uk
Website: www.hedleywood.co.uk
Nearest Town/Resort Bude/Holsworthy
Directions From Holsworthy take the A3072 towards Bude, at Red Post crossroads turn south onto the B3254 to Launceston. After 2¼ miles turn right to Titson, site entrance is 500 yards on the right.
Acreage 16½ **Open** All Year
Access Good **Site** Lev/Slope
Sites Available ▲ ⊞ ⊟ **Total** 120
Facilities ⚫ ⚫ ⚫ ⚫ ⚫ ⚫ ⚫ ⚫ ⚫ ⚫ ⚫
Nearby Facilities ⚫ ⚫ ⚫ ⚫ ⚫
⚫ Exeter
Open and sheltered camping areas with a 'laid back' atmosphere. Dog kennelling facility and a dog walk/nature trail.

HOLSWORTHY

Newbuildings, Brandis Corner, Holsworthy, Devon, EX22 7YQ.
Std: 01409 **Tel:** 221305
Nearest Town/Resort Bude/Bideford/ Dartmoor
Directions Take the A30 to Okehampton then the A3079 through Halwill Junction to Dunsland Cross. Go straight across the A3072, and Newbuildings is on the left 200 yards down Farm Lane.
Acreage 4 **Open** All Year
Access Good **Site** Level
Sites Available ▲ ⊞ ⊟ **Total** 10
Facilities ⚫ ⚫ ⚫ ⚫ ⚫ ⚫ ⚫ ⚫
Nearby Facilities ⚫ ⚫ ⚫ ⚫ ⚫ ⚫ ⚫ ⚫
⚫ Exeter
Central rural position, excellent for walking. 12 miles from beaches and the Moors. Licensed pub within ¼ mile. Open all year, ground conditions permitting.

HONITON

Camping & Caravanning Club Site, Otter Valley Park, Honiton, Devon, EX14 8ST.
Std: 01404 **Tel:** 44546
Website:
www.campingandcaravanningclub.co.uk
Directions From the A30 leave at the first exit for Honiton, keep left off the slip road and keep going left. (Road skirts the perimeter of the site).
Acreage 5 **Open** April **to** Sept
Site Lev/Slope
Sites Available ▲ ⊞ ⊟ **Total** 90
Facilities ⚫ ⚫ ⚫ ⚫ ⚫ ⚫ ⚫ ⚫ ⚫ ⚫
⚫ ⚫ ⚫ ⚫ ⚫ ⚫ ⚫
Nearby Facilities ⚫
⚫ Honiton
In the valley of the River Otter, a great start for a visit to the South West. 1 mile from Allhallows Museum. AA 3 Pennants and BTB Graded. Non members welcome.

ILFRACOMBE

Big Meadow Touring Caravan & Camping Park, Watermouth, Ilfracombe, Devon, EX34 9SJ.
Std: 01271 **Tel:** 862282
Website: www.big-meadow.co.uk
Nearest Town/Resort Ilfracombe
Directions Situated on the A399 coastal road approximately 2 miles from Ilfracombe, opposite Watermouth Castle Tourist Attraction.
Acreage 9 **Open** Easter **to** 31 October
Access Good **Site** Level
Sites Available ▲ ⊞ ⊟ **Total** 125
Facilities ⚫ ⚫ ⚫ ⚫ ⚫ ⚫ ⚫ ⚫ ⚫ ⚫
⚫ ⚫ ⚫ ⚫ ⚫ ⚫ ⚫ ⚫ ⚫ ⚫ ⚫
Nearby Facilities ⚫ ⚫ ⚫ ⚫ ⚫ ⚫ ⚫
⚫ Barnstaple
Sheltered family site with stream running through. Near Weymouth Harbour and two beaches within walking distance.

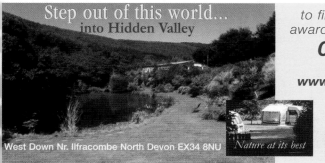

ILFRACOMBE

Hele Valley Holiday Park, Dept C, Hele Bay, Ilfracombe, North Devon, EX34 9RD.
Std: 01271 **Tel:** 862460 **Fax:** 867926
Email: holidays@helevalley.co.uk
Website: www.helevalley.co.uk
Nearest Town/Resort Ilfracombe
Directions Take A399 to Ilfracombe turn at signpost Hele village, to bottom of lane, take righthand turning into Holiday Park.
Acreage 4 **Open** Easter **to** End October
Access Good **Site** Level
Sites Available A ⊕ ⊜ **Total** 50
Facilities ...
Nearby Facilities ...
≉ Barnstaple
Only camping park in Ilfracombe. Beach only a few minutes walk. Tranquil secluded valley, alongside a stream with scenic views.

ILFRACOMBE

Hidden Valley Touring & Camping Park, West Down, Nr Ilfracombe, North Devon, EX34 8NU.
Std: 01271 **Tel:** 813837
Std: 01271 **Fax:** 814041
Email: hvpdevon@aol.com
Website: www.hiddenvalleypark.com
Nearest Town/Resort Ilfracombe
Acreage 25 **Open** All Year
Access Good **Site** Level
Sites Available A ⊕ ⊜ **Total** 134
Facilities ...
Nearby Facilities ...
≉ Barnstaple
Beautiful park with a stream running through it, woodland walks and a lovely garden. Within easy reach of our famous Golden Coast and Exmoor National Park.

ILFRACOMBE

Little Meadow Camp Site, Watermouth, Ilfracombe, Devon, EX34 9SJ.
Std: 01271 **Tel:** 866862
Email: info@littlemeadow.co.uk
Website: www.littlemeadow.co.uk
Nearest Town/Resort Ilfracombe
Directions On A399 between Ifracombe and Combe Martin.
Acreage 5 **Open** Easter **to** September
Access Good **Site** Terraced
Sites Available A ⊕ ⊜ **Total** 50
Facilities ...
Nearby Facilities ...
≉ Barnstaple
Quiet and peaceful and the best view in Devon.

ILFRACOMBE

Mill Park Touring Site, Berrynarbor, Nr. Ilfracombe, Devon, EX34 9SH.
Std: 01271 **Tel:** 882647
Email: millpark@globalnet.co.uk
Website: www.millpark.co.uk
Nearest Town/Resort Ilfracombe
Directions Situated on the A399 coast road between Combe Martin and Ilfracombe near Watermouth Castle. Take the turning opposite the Sawmills Inn signposted to Berrynarbor.
Acreage 30 **Open** 15 March **to** 15 Nov
Access Good **Site** Level
Sites Available A ⊕ ⊜ **Total** 165
Facilities ...
Nearby Facilities ...
≉ Barnstaple
Well sheltered site with woodland walks. Coarse fishing lake. Well stocked shop, take away food, off licence, laundry, etc..

ILFRACOMBE

Mullacott Cross Caravan Park, Mullacott Cross, Ilfracombe, Devon, EX34 8NB.
Std: 01271 **Tel:** 862212
Std: 01271 **Fax:** 862979
Email: info@mullacottcaravans.co.uk
Website: www.mullacottcaravans.co.uk
Nearest Town/Resort Ilfracombe
Directions On A361 1½ miles south of Ilfracombe.
Acreage 5 **Open** Easter **to** Mid Oct
Access Good **Site** Lev/Slope
Sites Available A ⊕ ⊜ **Total** 110
Facilities ...
Nearby Facilities ...
≉ Barnstaple
Excellent centre for touring North Devon.

ILFRACOMBE

Napps Caravan Site, Napps, Old Coast Road, Berrynarbor, Ilfracombe, North Devon, EX34 9SW.
Std: 01271 **Tel:** 882557
Std: 01271 **Fax:** 882557
Email: bookings@napps.fsnet.co.uk
Website: www.napps.co.uk
Nearest Town/Resort Ilfracombe
Directions On A399, 1¼ miles west of Combe Martin, turn right onto Old Coast Road (signposted). Site 400yds along Old Coast Road.
Acreage 11 **Open** March **to** November
Access Good **Site** Level
Sites Available A ⊕ ⊜ **Total** 250
Facilities ...
Nearby Facilities ...
≉ Barnstaple
Probably the most beautiful coastal setting you will see. Beach 200yds. Popular family

site with woodland and coastal walks, tennis on site. Summer parking and Winter storage available.

IVYBRIDGE

Cheston Caravan & Camping Park, Folly Cross, Wrangaton Road, South Brent, Devon, TQ10 9HF.
Std: 01364 **Tel:** 72586
Std: 01364 **Fax:** 72586
Nearest Town/Resort Ivybridge
Directions From Exeter, after by-passing South Brent, turn left at Wrangaton Cross slip road then right A38. From Plymouth take South Brent (Woodpecker) turn, at end of slip road turn right, go under A38 and rejoin A38 and follow directions from Exeter.
Acreage 1¼ **Open** 15th March **to** 15th Jan
Access Good **Site** Level
Sites Available A ⊕ ⊟ **Total** 23
Facilities ⚿ ∮ ▥ ▥ ≗ ┌ ⊙ ⊖ ⊒ ⊡ ⊡ ☎
▯ ⊙ ⊜ ▥ ⊬ ⊟
Nearby Facilities ┌ ⏐ ⚓ ⋟ ∪ ⋡ ⅋
Set in beautiful Dartmoor. Perfect for touring, walking and bird watching. Nearest beach 9 miles. Pets welcome. Easy access from A38.

KINGSBRIDGE

Karrageen Caravan & Camping Site, Bolberry, Malborough, Kingsbridge, Devon, TQ7 3EN.
Std: 01548 **Tel:** 561230
Std: 01548 **Fax:** 560192
Email: phil@karrageen.co.uk
Website: www.karrageen.co.uk
Nearest Town/Resort Salcombe
Directions Take the A381 Kingsbridge to Salcombe road, turn sharp right into Malborough Village. In 0.6 miles turn right

(signposted Bolberry), after 0.9 miles the site is on the right and reception is at the house on the left.
Acreage 7½ **Open** 15 March **to** 15 Nov
Access Good **Site** Lev/slope
Sites Available A ⊕ ⊟ **Total** 75
Facilities ⚿ ∮ ▥ ≗ ┌ ⊙ ⊖ ⊒ ⊡ ☎
⊠ ▯ ⊙ ⊜ ⊬ ⊟
Nearby Facilities ┌ ⏐ ⚓ ⋟ ∪ ⋡ ⅋
⇌ Totnes/Plymouth
Nearest and best park to Hope Cove, beaches 1 mile away. Situated in beautiful, scenic countryside and surrounded by superb National Trust coastline. Terraced, level, tree lined pitches. Parents and baby room and family shower room. Hot take-away food. Superb cliff top walking. A site with a view. See our advertisement under Salcombe.

KINGSBRIDGE

Mounts Farm Touring Park, The Mounts, Nr. East Allington, Kingsbridge, South Devon, TQ9 7QJ.
Std: 01548 **Tel:** 521591
Email: mounts.farm@lineone.net
Website: www.mountsfarm.co.uk
Nearest Town/Resort Kingsbridge
Directions On the A381 Totnes/ Kingsbridge. 3 miles north of Kingsbridge. Entrance from A381 - DO NOT go to East Allington Village.
Acreage 6 **Open** April **to** October
Access Good **Site** Level
Sites Available A ⊕ ⊟ **Total** 50
Facilities ∮ ▥ ≗ ┌ ⊙ ⊖ ⊒ ⊡ ☎
⊠ ⊜ ⊬ ⊛ ⊬ ⊟ ⊟
Nearby Facilities ┌ ⏐ ⚓ ∪ ⅋
⇌ Totnes
In an area of outstanding natural beauty. Ideal for touring all South Devon.

KINGSBRIDGE

Parkland, Sorley Green Cross, Salcombe, Devon, TQ7 4AF.
Std: 01548. **Tel:** 852723
Nearest Town/Resort Kingsbridge
Directions From Totnes follow the A381, main Kingsbridge road, to Sorley Green Cross. Go straight ahead and the site is 100 yards on the left.
Acreage 3 **Open** All Year
Access Good **Site** Level
Sites Available A ⊕ ⊟
Facilities ∮ ▥ ▥ ≗ ┌ ⊙ ⊖ ⊒ ⊡ ☎
▯ ⊙ ⊜ ⊬ ⊟
Nearby Facilities ┌ ⏐ ⚓ ⋟ ∪ ⋡ ⅋ ⊁
Central for beaches, nearest beach Bantham Sands 2½ miles. Also central for touring (river 1 mile). Well sheltered site with views over Salcombe. One pitch with hard standing, hook-up water point and T.V. point (Super Pitch). Out of season package prices available. Pub within 1 mile. Safe walking to the town of Kingsbridge. Sorley Adventure Park ¼ mile away.

LYDFORD

Camping & Caravanning Club Site, Lydford, Near Okehampton, Devon, EX20 4BE.
Std: 01822 **Tel:** 820275
Website: www.campingandcaravanningclub.co.uk
Nearest Town/Resort Lydford
Directions A30 take the A386 signposted Tavistock and Lydford Gorge. Pass the Fox Hounds Public House on the left, turn right signposted Lydford. At the war memorial turn right, right fork, site is on the left.
Acreage 7½ **Open** March **to** October
Access Good **Site** Lev/Slope
Sites Available A ⊕ ⊟ **Total** 70
Facilities ∮ ▥ ≗ ┌ ⊙ ⊖ ⊒ ⊡ ☎
▯ ⊙ ⊜ ⊠ ⊬ ⊬ ⊟ ⊟

earby Facilities ✓ ⚓ ⌕ ∪ ♁ ⚲
⚓ Lydford
tuated in a quiet rural setting, overlooking river. On the edge of Dartmoor, close to e moors, Lydford Gorge and castle. BTB raded. Non members welcome.

YNTON
hannel View Caravan & Camping ark, Manor Farm, Barbrook, Lynton, orth Devon, EX35 6LD.
d: 01598 Tel: 753349
d: 01598 Fax: 752777
mail: channelview@bushinternet.com
ebsite: www.channel-view.co.uk
earest Town/Resort Lynton/Lynmouth
rections 2 miles south east of Lynton on e A39.
creage 6 Open Easter to October
ccess Good Site Level
tes Available ⚑ ⌂ ⚐ Total 110
acilities ⚒ ⚘ ☎ ⚓ ⌂ ⊙ ⚙ ⚑ ⚐ ⚏
⚏ ⚐ ⚏ ⚏ ✦⚐ ⚏ ⚏
earby Facilities ⌁ ✓ ⚓ ⌕ ∪ ♁ ♃ ⚲
⚓ Barnstaple
anoramic views, on the edge of Exmoor erlooking Lynton/Lynmouth. ETB 4 Star raded.

YNTON
loud Farm Campsite, Cloud Farm, are, Lynton, Devon, EX35 6NU.
td: 01598 Tel: 741278
td: 01598 Fax: 741278
mail: lornadoonefarm@aol.com
earest Town/Resort Porlock/Minehead
rections Take the A39 from Porlock and llow signs for Lorna Doone Farm. Turn left Cloud Farm entrance just before the river.
creage 6 Open All Year
ccess Reasonable Site Level
tes Available ⚑ ⌂ ⚐ Total 35
acilities ⚏ ☎ ⚓ ⌂ ✕⚐⚏
earby Facilities ⌁ ✓ ⚓ ∪ ♁ ⚲
⚓ Taunton
eautiful, safe, family site in the heart of the mous Doone Valley. Alongside a river for shing, swimming or paddling. No roads her than private drive. Horse riding for all vels on site.

YNTON
illsford Bridge Camping Site, Hillsford ridge, Lynton, Devon.
td: 01598 Tel: 741256
earest Town/Resort Lynmouth
rections A39 from Minehead.
creage ½ Open Easter to Oct
ccess Good Site Level
tes Available ⚑ ⌂ ⚐
acilities ⚏ ⌂
earby Facilities ⌁ ✓ ⌕ ∪ ♁ ⚲

⌕ Barnstaple
Alongside a river.

MODBURY
Camping & Caravanning Club Site,
California Cross, Modbury, Devon, PL21 0SG.
Std: 01548 Tel: 821297
Website: www.campingandcaravanningclub.co.uk
Nearest Town/Resort Ivybridge
Directions On the A38 travelling south west take the A3121 to the crossroads, straight across to the B3196 to California Cross Hamlet. Turn left after California Cross Hamlet but before the petrol station, site is on the right.
Acreage 3¾ Open April to October
Access Good Site Lev/Slope
Sites Available ⚑ ⌂ ⚐ Total 80
Facilities ⚒ ⚏ ⚘ ☎ ⚓ ⌂ ⊙ ⚙ ⚑ ⚐ ⚐
⚏ ⚐ ⚏ ⚏ ✦⚐ ⚏
Nearby Facilities ✓ ∪ ♁
⚓ Ivybridge
Rural setting centrally situated in the South Hams. Close to the beaches of Salcombe and Torbay. Take-away food available two nights a week. 5 miles from Sorley Tunnel Childrens Adventure Park. BTB Graded. Non members welcome.

MODBURY
Moor View Touring Park, California
Cross, Near Modbury, South Devon, PL21 0SG.
Std: 01548 Tel: 821485
Email: moorview@tinyworld.com
Website: www.ukparks.co.uk/moorviewtouring
Nearest Town/Resort Modbury
Directions 3 miles east of Modbury on the B3207. From the A38 westbound leave at Wrangaton Cross signed Ermington A3121, turn left at the top of sliproad and follow Moor View camping signs.
Acreage 6 Open Easter to Mid Oct
Access Good Site Level
Sites Available ⚑ ⌂ ⚐ Total 68
Facilities ⚒ ⚏ ⚘ ☎ ⚓ ⌂ ⊙ ⚙ ⚑ ⚐ ⚐
⚏ ⚐ ⚏ ⚏ ⚏ ✦⚐ ⚏
Nearby Facilities ⌁ ✓ ∪ ♁
⚓ Ivybridge
6 miles to Bigbury Bay, 15 miles to Plymouth, 5 miles to Dartmoor and 15 miles to Dartmouth.

MODBURY
Pennymoor Caravan Park, Modbury,
Devon, PL21 0SB.
Std: 01548 Tel: 830269/830542
Nearest Town/Resort Kingsbridge/Salcombe

Directions Approx 30 miles West of Exeter, leave A38 at Wrangaton Cross. Turn left, then straight across at next crossroads and continue for approx 4 miles. Pass petrol garage on left, then take second left, site is 1 mile on the right.
Acreage 6 Open 15 March to 15 Nov
Access Good Site Level
Sites Available ⚑ ⌂ ⚐ Total 155
Facilities ⚒ ⚘ ⚏ ☎ ⚓ ⌂ ⊙ ⚙ ⚑ ⚐ ⚐
⚏ ⚐ ⚏ ⚏ ✦⚐ ⚏
Nearby Facilities ⌁ ✓ ⚓ ⌕ ∪ ♁
⌕ Plymouth
Peaceful rural site. Ideal touring base. Central to towns, moors, beaches. Bigbury-on-Sea only 5 miles. Holiday caravans to let. New superb toilet/shower block. Free colour brochure.

MORETONHAMPSTEAD
Clifford Bridge Park, Nr. Drewsteignton,
Exeter, Devon, EX6 6QE.
Std: 01647 Tel: 24226
Email: info@clifford-bridge.co.uk
Website: www.ukparks.co.uk/cliffordbridge
Nearest Town/Resort Moretonhampstead
Directions Leave A30 Dual carriage way to Cheriton Bishop, off Dual Thatch 2 miles to crossroads turn right, 1 mile to Clifford.
Acreage 8 Open Easter to September.
Access Good Site Level
Sites Available ⚑ ⌂ ⚐ Total 65
Facilities ⚒ ⚏ ⚘ ☎ ⚓ ⌂ ⊙ ⚙ ⚑ ⚐ ⚐
⚏ ⚐ ⚏ ⚏ ⚏ ✦⚐ ⚏
Nearby Facilities ⌁ ✓ ∪
⌕ Exeter
The upper Teign Valley and Gorge is noted for it's outstanding natural beauty, superb viewpoints and magnificent woodland tracks, its location in Dartmoor National Park makes it a unique touring centre for walking fishing, riding and golf.

MORTEHOE
Easewell Farm Holiday Park, Mortehoe,
Woolacombe, North Devon, EX34 7EH.
Std: 01271 Tel: 870225
Std: 01271 Fax: 870225
Nearest Town/Resort Woolacombe
Directions Leave the M5 at junction 27 and take the A361 via Barnstaple. At Braunton turn left at Mullacott Cross to Mortehoe Village. Easewell is signposted on the right.
Acreage 16 Open Easter to End Sept
Access Good Site Level
Sites Available ⚑ ⌂ ⚐ Total 150
Facilities ⚒ ⚏ ⚘ ☎ ⚓ ⌂ ⊙ ⚙ ⚑ ⚐ ⚐
⚏ ⚏ ⚐ ⚏ ✕ ⚑ ⚐ ⚏ ⚐ ✦⚐ ⚏
Nearby Facilities ⌁ ✓ ∪ ♁
⌕ Barnstaple
Within walking distance of the beach.

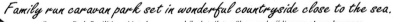

MORTEHOE

North Morte Farm Caravan & Camping Park, North Morte Road, Mortehoe, Woolacombe, North Devon, EX34 7EG.
Std: 01271 **Tel:** 870381
Std: 01271 **Fax:** 870115
Email: info@northmortefarm.co.uk
Website: www.northmortefarm.co.uk
Nearest Town/Resort Woolacombe
Directions 14 miles from Barnstaple on the A361 take the B3343 and follow signs to Mortehoe. In the village turn right at the Post Office, park is 500 yards on the left.
Open Easter **to** End Sept
Access Narrow **Site** Lev/Slope
Sites Available ▲ ⊕ ⊞ **Total** 175
Facilities & ∱ ⊞ ⊞ ♨ ╭ ⊙ ⊸ ⬛ ◱ ●
⠀⠀♁ ℤ ☐ ☎ ◫ ♨ ⊞ ☐ ●
Nearby Facilities ╭ ✓ ⊀ ∪
⊭ Barnstaple
500 yards from Rockham Beach. Adjoining National Trust land. Ideal walking country.

MORTEHOE

Warcombe Farm Camping Park, Mortehoe, Near Woolacombe, North Devon, EX34 7EJ.
Std: 01271. **Tel:** 870690
Std: 01271 **Fax:** 871070
Nearest Town/Resort Barnstaple
Directions Turn left off the A361, Barnstaple to Ilfracombe road at Mullacott Cross roundabout signposted Woolacombe. After 2 miles turn right towards Mortehoe. Site is first on the right in less than a mile.
Acreage 19 **Open** 15 March **to** 31 Oct
Access Good **Site** Level
Sites Available ▲ ⊕ ⊞ **Total** 145
Facilities ∱ ⊞ ♨ ╭ ⊙ ⊸ ⬛ ◱ ●
⠀⠀♁ ℤ ☐ ☎ ⊞ ☐
Nearby Facilities ╭ ✓ ⊥ ⊀ ∪
⊭ Barnstaple
1¼ miles to Woolacombe beach. Panoramic sea views. Well drained level land, family run. Fishing on site.

NEWTON ABBOT

Dornafield, Two Mile Oak, Newton Abbott, Devon, TQ12 6DD.
Std: 01803 **Tel:** 812732
Std: 01803 **Fax:** 812032
Website: www.dornafield.com

Nearest Town/Resort Newton Abbot
Directions Take the A381 (Newton Abbott to Totnes), in 2 miles at Two Mile Oak Inn turn right. In ½ mile turn first left, site is 200 yards on the right.
Acreage 30 **Open** 20th March **to** October
Access Good **Site** Level
Sites Available ▲ ⊕ ⊞ **Total** 135
Facilities & ∱ ⊞ ⊞ ♨ ╭ ⊙ ⊸ ⬛ ◱ ●
⠀⠀♁ ℤ ☐ ☎ ◫ ♨ ⊞ ☐ ●
Nearby Facilities ╭ ✓ ⊥ ⊀ ∪ ♪ ⅄
⊭ Newton Abbot
Beautiful 14th Century farmhouse location with superb facilities to suit discerning caravanners and campers.

NEWTON ABBOT

Lemonford Caravan Park, Bickington, Newton Abbot, Devon, TQ12 6JR.
Std: 01626 **Tel:** 821242
Email: mark@lemonford.co.uk
Website: www.lemonford.co.uk
Nearest Town/Resort Ashburton
Directions From Exeter along A38 take A382 turnoff, on roundabout take 3rd exit and follow signs to Bickington. From Plymouth take A383 turnoff, follow road for ¼ mile and turn left into site.
Acreage 7 **Open** Mid March **to** End October
Access Good **Site** Level
Sites Available ▲ ⊕ ⊞ **Total** 90
Facilities ∱ ⊞ ⊞ ♨ ╭ ⊙ ⊸ ⬛ ◱ ●
⠀⠀♁ ℤ ☐ ☎ ⊞ ♨ ⊞
Nearby Facilities ╭ ✓ ⊥ ⊀ ∪ ♪ ⅄
⊭ Newton Abbot
In a beautiful setting and scrupulously clean. Close to Torbay and the Dartmoor National Park.

NEWTON ABBOT

The Dartmoor Halfway, Bickington, Newton Abbot, Devon, TQ12 6JW.
Std: 01626 **Tel:** 821270
Std: 01626 **Fax:** 821820
Nearest Town/Resort Newton Abbot
Directions From Newton Abbot take the A383 towards Ashburton and Plymouth, site is 3 miles on the right hand side.
Acreage 1½ **Open** All Year
Access Good **Site** Level
Sites Available ⊕ ⊞ **Total** 22

Facilities & ∱ ⊞ ⊞ ♨ ╭ ⊙ ⊡ ●
⠀⠀⊞ ✗ ◫ ♨ ⊞ ☐
Nearby Facilities ╭ ✓ ⊥ ⊀ ∪ ♪ ⅄
⊭ Newton Abbot
ETB 4 Star Graded Park. A family run site nestling on the edge of Dartmoor, beside the River Lemon in Bickington, 'Halfway' between Newton Abbot and Ashburton.

NEWTON ABBOT

Twelveoaks Farm Caravan Park, Twelveoaks Farm, Teigngrace, Newton Abbot, Devon, TQ12 6QT.
Std: 01626 **Tel:** 352769
Std: 01626 **Fax:** 352769
Nearest Town/Resort Newton Abbot
Directions Take the A38 towards Exeter and Plymouth, take turning off le signposted Teigngrace (before Drumbridge roundabout). Continue for approx. 1½ mile through the village and Twelveoaks is on the left hand side.
Acreage 2 **Open** All Year
Access Good **Site** Sloping
Sites Available ▲ ⊕ ⊞ **Total** 25
Facilities & ∱ ⊞ ♨ ╭ ⊙ ⊸ ⬛ ◱
⠀⠀♁ ℤ ☐ ☎ ⅄ ⊞
Nearby Facilities ╭ ✓ ⊥ ⊀ ∪ ♪ ⅄
⊭ Newton Abbot
We have a walk running alongside a river and to a country park which is called Templer Way. Approx. 8 miles from the beach and Dartmoor. Heated swimming pool.

NEWTON FERRERS

Briar Hill Caravan & Camping Park, Briar Hill Farm, Newton Ferrers, Plymouth Devon, PL8 1AR.
Std: 01752 **Tel:** 872252
Std: 01395 **Fax:** 568374
Nearest Town/Resort Newton Ferrers
Open March **to** November
Access Good **Site** Lev/Slope
Sites Available ▲ ⊕ ⊞ **Total** 50
Facilities ∱ ⊞ ♨ ╭ ⊙ ⊸ ⬛ ◱
⠀⠀◨ ⅄ ⊞ ☐
Nearby Facilities ╭ ✓ ⊥ ⊀ ∪ ♪ ⅄
⊭ Plymouth
Near the beach and coastal walk. Only miles from the city of Plymouth. Boat hire and riding locally. Dogs must be kept on short lead.

OKEHAMPTON

Bridestowe Caravan Park, Bridestowe,
r. Okehampton, Devon, EX20 4ER.
td: 01837 **Tel:** 861261
earest Town/Resort Bude
irections Leave M5 for A30 to
kehampton 3 miles west of Okehampton
rn off A30 to Bridestowe village, follow
amping signs to site.
pen March **to** December
ccess Good **Site** Level
ites Available ⚠ ⌂ 🚐 **Total** 53
acilities ⨍ 🚻 🎱 ☏ ☺ ⌁ 🛒 ⊡ ☎
♨ 🅿 🏪 🛒 ⛽🚻🖼🄿🄴
earby Facilities ⌐ ✗ U
artmoor National Park 2 miles, ideal for
alking, horse riding and fishing and touring
evon and Cornwall. Within easy reach of
astal resorts.

OKEHAMPTON

Bundu Camping & Caravan Park,
ourton Down, Okehampton, Devon,
X20 4HT.
td: 01837 **Tel:** 861611
mail: bundusargent@aol.com
ebsite: www.bundu.co.uk
earest Town/Resort Okehampton
irections Slip road off the A30 dual
arriageway to the A386 Tavistock/Sourton.
rn left then left again after 100yds, site is
t the top of the road on the right.
creage 4 **Open** March **to** November
ccess Good **Site** Level
ites Available ⚠ ⌂ 🚐 **Total** 38
acilities ⨍ 🚻 🎱 ☏ ☺ ⌁ 🛒 ⊡ ☎
♨ 🏪🖼🄿🄴
earby Facilities ⌐ ✗ U
⇌ Exeter
ituated on Dartmoor, ideal for walking.
entrally based for touring Devon and
ornwall.

OKEHAMPTON

Dartmoor View Holiday Park, Whiddon
Down, Okehampton, Devon, EX20 2QL.
Std: 01647 **Tel:** 231545
Std Fax: 231654
Email: anyone@dartmoorview.co.uk
Website: www.dartmoorview.co.uk
Nearest Town/Resort Okehampton
Directions Take the A30 from Exeter (17
miles), turn left at Whiddon Down
roundabout, park is ½ mile on the right.
Acreage 5 **Open** March **to** 9th November
Access Good **Site** Level
Sites Available ⚠ ⌂ 🚐 **Total** 75
Facilities ⨍ 🚻 🎱 ☏ ☺ ⌁ 🛒 ⊡ ☎
♨ 🅿 🏪🍴🎱⚓ ✗ ⊛🖼🄿🄴
Nearby Facilities ⌐ ✗ U ♘ ✈
⇌ Exeter
Excellent facilities, close to Dartmoor
National Park. Letterboxing centre. Ideal for
touring.

OKEHAMPTON

Olditch Holiday Park, Olditch Farm,
Sticklepath, Okehampton, Devon, EX20 2NT
Std: 01837 **Tel:** 840734
Std Fax: 840877
Email: info@olditch.co.uk
Website: www.olditch.co.uk
Nearest Town/Resort Okehampton
Directions From Okehampton travel
towards Exeter following signs to
Sticklepath, go through the village and camp
site is on the right hand side.
Acreage 5 **Open** Mid March **to** Mid Nov
Access Good **Site** Sloping
Sites Available ⚠ ⌂ 🚐 **Total** 32
Facilities ⨍ 🚻 🎱 ☏ ☺ ⌁ 🛒 ⊡ ☎
♨⚓🏪🖼🄿🄴
Nearby Facilities ⌐ ✗ U ♘ ✈
⇌ Okehampton/Exeter
A quiet, peaceful site with direct walking

access to Dartmoor National Park. Horse
riding, cycling and walking. Ideal base for
touring the West Country.

OKEHAMPTON

Yertiz Caravan & Camping Park, Exeter
Road, Okehampton, Devon, EX20 1QF.
Std: 01837 **Tel:** 52281
Email: yertiz@dial.pipex.com
Website: www.dialspace.dial.pipex.com/
yertiz
Nearest Town/Resort Okehampton
Directions From Okehampton town centre
take the Exeter road, Yertiz is ¾ mile on the
right hand side.
Acreage 3½ **Open** All Year
Access Good **Site** Lev/Slope
Sites Available ⚠ ⌂ 🚐 **Total** 30
Facilities ♿ ⨍ 🚻 🎱 ☏ ☺ ⌁ 🛒 ⊡ ☎
♨🅿🏪🖼🄿🄴
Nearby Facilities ⌐ ✗ U ✈
⇌ Exeter
Small, friendly site with lovely views of
Dartmoor. Good for local walking and touring
the West Country. Easy access to the town.

PAIGNTON

Beverley Park Holiday Centre,
Goodrington Road, Paignton, Devon, TQ4
7JE.
Std: 01803 **Tel:** 843887 **Fax:** 845427
Email: info@beverley-holidays.co.uk
Website: www.beverley-holidays.co.uk
Nearest Town/Resort Paignton
Directions 2 miles south of Paignton (ring
road) A3022. Turn left into Goodrington
Road.
Acreage 9½ **Open** February **to** December
Access Good **Site** Level
Sites Available ⚠ ⌂ 🚐 **Total** 194
Facilities ⨍ 🚻 🎱 ☏ ☺ ⌁ 🛒 ⊡ ☎
♨ 🅿 🏪🍴✗ 🎱⚓🎱⊡🄴
Nearby Facilities ⌐ ✗ ⚓ 🐟 U ⊿ ♠

HIGHER WELL FARM HOLIDAY PARK

We welcome tourers, tents and motor caravans. A quiet secluded park in lovely Devon countryside. Central for touring south Devon, 4 miles from Torbay beaches and 1 mile from River Dart and Stoke Gabriel.
NEW TOILET/SHOWER BUILDING OPENED IN 2001 with family and disabled rooms. Electric hook-ups, hard standings, launderette, shop and payphone. Families and couples only. Dogs on leads welcome.
Also HOLIDAY CARAVANS FOR HIRE
JOHN & LIZ BALL, Higher Well Farm Holiday Park,
Stoke Gabriel, Totnes, Devon TQ9 6RN.   Stoke Gabriel (01803) 782289

⚊ Paignton
Views across Torbay. Indoor heated swimming pool, tennis court. Sauna.

PAIGNTON

Byslades International Camping & Touring Park, Totnes Road, Paignton, Devon, TQ4 7PY.
Std: 01803 **Tel:** 555072
Std: 01803 **Fax:** 555072
Email: bysladesitp@lineone.net
Website: www.bysladestouringpark.co.uk
Nearest Town/Resort Paignton
Directions 2¼ miles west of Paignton on the A385.
Acreage 23 **Open** April to October
Access Good **Site** Level
Sites Available ▲ ⊞ ⊞ **Total** 190
Facilities & ∮ ⊞ ⊞ ♨ ┌ ⊙ ┘ ▵ ☐ ♥
№ ☐ ⊠ ✗ ♀ 周 ♠ 瓜 ⚓ ※ ▤ ☐ ☐
Nearby Facilities ┌ ✓ ⏛ ⚘ ∪ ⌗
⚊ Paignton
The site is overlooking a beautiful valley and is centrally situated to visit all parts of Devon. Tennis court on site.

PAIGNTON

Higher Well Farm Holiday Park, Stoke Gabriel, Totnes, Devon, TQ9 6RN.
Std: 01803 **Tel:** 782289
Nearest Town/Resort Paignton
Directions From Paignton take A385 towards Totnes, turn off left at Parkers Arms

Pub. Go 1½ miles then turn left again, site is 200 yards down road.
Acreage 8 **Open Easter to** October
Access Good **Site** Lev/Slope
Sites Available ▲ ⊞ ⊞ **Total** 80
Facilities & ∮ ∮ ⊞ ⊞ ♨ ┌ ⊙ ┘ ▵ ☐ ☐
№ ☐ ⊠ ┿ ☐
Nearby Facilities ┌ ✓ ⏛ ⚘ ∪
⚊ Paignton
Within 4 miles Torbay beaches, 1 mile village Stoke Gabriel and River Dart.

PAIGNTON

Hoburne Torbay, Grange Court, Grange Road, Goodrington, Paignton, Devon, TQ4 7JP.
Std: 01803 **Tel:** 558010
Std: 01803 **Fax:** 696286
Email: enquiries@hoburne.com
Website: www.hoburne.com
Nearest Town/Resort Paignton
Directions From junc 31 of M5, travel south for approx 20 miles on A380 to junction with A385. Continue south on A380 (Paignton Ring Road) for 1 mile, turn left into Goodrington Road by Esso Filling Station. After ¾ mile turn left into Grange Road and follow signs to park.
Acreage 20 **Open** Mid Feb **to** End Oct
Access Good **Site** Sloping
Sites Available ⊞ ⊞ **Total** 157
Facilities ∮ ⊞ ⊞ ♨ ┌ ⊙ ┘ ▵ ☐ ♥
№ ☐ ⊠ ✗ ♀ 周 ♠ 瓜 ⚓ ※ ▤ ☐

Nearby Facilities ┌ ✓ ⏛ ⚘ ∪ ⌗ ♣ ⚘
⚊ Paignton
Panoramic views over Torbay, close Goodrington beach.

PAIGNTON

Lower Yalberton Holiday Park, Long Road, Paignton, Devon, TQ4 7PQ.
Std: 01803 **Tel:** 558127
Std: 01803 **Fax:** 558127
Nearest Town/Resort Paignton
Directions Travelling towards Brixham on the A3022, at the traffic lights at North Factory turn right, park is 1 mile on the right
Acreage 25 **Open** May to September
Access Good **Site** Lev/Slope
Sites Available ▲ ⊞ ⊞ **Total** 543
Facilities ∮ ⊞ ♨ ┌ ⊙ ┘ ▵ ☐ ♥
№ ☐ ⊠ ✗ ♀ 周 ♠ 瓜 ⚓ ┿ ☐ ☐
Nearby Facilities ┌ ✓ ⏛ ⚘
⚊ Paignton
Family run site set in the countryside yet close to the town. Only 3 miles from three lovely beaches. Ideal touring centre.

PAIGNTON

Marine Park Holiday Centre, Grange Road, Paignton, Devon, TQ4 7JR.
Std: 01803 **Tel:** 843887
Std: 01803 **Fax:** 845427
Email: info@beverley-holidays.co.uk
Website: www.beverley-holidays.co.uk
Nearest Town/Resort Paignton

A beautifully landscaped Touring and Camping Park and a wide range of luxury Caravan Holiday Homes.

For free brochure:
Tel: 01803 550504
(24hr answer 01803 521684)

or write to Paignton Holiday Park, Dept. CC, Totnes Rd, Paignton, S.Devon TQ4 7PW

Set in an area of outstanding natural beauty and close to the beaches & attractions of the English Riviera. There is a full range of facilities for you to enjoy including a licensed club with entertainment & dancing, 15th Century Thatched Pub, large heated swimming pool, shop, cafe, children's activity & play area, laundry & shower facilities.

Lower Yalberton

Holiday Park
Long Road, Paignton, Devon TQ4 7P(
Tel / Fax: (01803) 558127

Facilities for Touring Caravans, Tents and Dormobiles.
Static Holiday Caravans for Hire. Electric Hook-ups.

In the heart of the country yet only 2½ miles from three beaches. Paignton, Goodrington and Broad Sands. Paignton town centre just 2 miles. Great touring area. 20 miles from Dartmoor National Park. We have a lounge bar (family entertainment during Whitsun, July/August), swimming pool (heated), launderette, colour TV room, children's play area, amusement room, disco and cafe. What more do you need? Spend your holiday with us at Lower Yalberton. Open May to September.

Please send SAE for brochure.

Directions 2 miles south of Paignton off A379.
Acreage 4 **Open** May to September
Access Good **Site** Lev/Slope
Sites Available ⚏ ⛺ **Total** 22
Facilities 🚿 🚽 ⚓ ⌂ ⊙ 🍴 ▱ ◻ ☎
🏪 ⊙ 🏊 ♨ ▱ 🅿
Nearby Facilities ┏ ✓ ⚓ ⤧ ∪ ≈ ♗
✈ Paignton

PAIGNTON

Paignton Holiday Park, Totnes Road, Paignton, Devon, TQ4 7PW.
Std: 01803 **Tel:** 550504
Std: 01803 **Fax:** 529909
Nearest Town/Resort Paignton
Directions 1½ miles west of Paignton on the A385.
Acreage 20 **Open** March to October
Access Good **Site** Lev/Slope
Sites Available ⚏ ⛺ ⚓ **Total** 250
Facilities 🚿 🚽 ⛲ 🚽 ⌂ ⊙ 🍴 ▱ ◻ ☎
🏪 ⊙ 🏊 ✕ 🍴 ♨ ♨ ⤧ ▱ 🅿
Nearby Facilities ┏ ✓ ⚓ ⤧ ∪ ≈ ♗
✈ Paignton
Ideal touring site near beaches yet convenient for Dartmoor National Park. 16th Century pub and restaurant adjacent to the park.

PAIGNTON

Ramslade Touring Park, Stoke Road, Stoke Gabriel, Paignton, Devon, TQ9 6QB.
Std: 01803 **Tel:** 782575
Std: 01803 **Fax:** 782828
Email: ramslade@compuserve.com
Website: www.ramslade.co.uk
Nearest Town/Resort Paignton
Directions From Paignton take A385, turn left at Parkers Arms, site 1½ miles on right.
Acreage 9 **Open** 30 March to 27 October
Access Good **Site** Lev/Slope
Sites Available ⚏ ⛺ ⚓ **Total** 135
Facilities ⚏ 🚿 🚽 ⛲ 🚽 ⌂ ⊙ 🍴 ▱ ◻ ☎
🏪 ⚐ ⊙ 🏊 ▱ ♨ ♨ ⤧ ▱ 🅿
Nearby Facilities ┏ ✓ ⚓ ⤧ ♗
✈ Paignton
Quiet site. No dogs in high season. Babies bathroom, logland play areas and paddling pool with waterfall.

PAIGNTON

Whitehill Holiday Park, Stoke Road, Paignton, South Devon, TQ4 7PF.
Std: 01803 **Tel:** 782338
Std: 01803 **Fax:** 782722
Email: enquiries@whitehillfarm.co.uk
Website: www.whitehillfarm.co.uk
Nearest Town/Resort Paignton
Directions Turn off the A385 at Parkers

Arms Pub, ½ mile from Paignton Zoo, signposted Stoke Gabriel. Park is 1 mile along this road.
Acreage 30 **Open** 10th May to End September
Access Good **Site** Lev/Slope
Sites Available ⚏ ⛺ ⚓ **Total** 400
Facilities 🚿 🚽 ⛲ 🚽 ⌂ ⊙ 🍴 ▱ ◻ ☎
🏪 ⊙ 🏊 ✕ 🍴 ♨ ♨ ⤧ ⊛ ▱ ◻ ▣
Nearby Facilities ┏ ✓ ⚓ ⤧ ∪ ≈ ♗
✈ Paignton
Beautifully situated in rolling Devon countryside yet within easy reach of the sea, Torquay and the Dartmoor National Park.

PAIGNTON

Widend Touring Park, Berry Pomeroy Road, Marldon, Paignton, Devon, TQ3 1RT.
Std: 01803 **Tel:** 550116
Std: 01803 **Fax:** 550116
Nearest Town/Resort Paignton/Torquay
Directions Turn into Five Lanes Road towards Berry Pomeroy off the main Torquay ring road (A380) new duel carriageway at Marldon. Singmore Hotel is on the corner.
Acreage 22 **Open** Easter to October
Access Good **Site** Level
Sites Available ⚏ ⛺ ⚓ **Total** 185
Facilities ⚏ 🚿 🚽 ⛲ 🚽 ⌂ ⊙ 🍴 ▱ ◻ ☎
🏪 ⊙ 🏊 ✕ 🍴 ♨ ♨ ⤧ ⊛ ▱ ◻ ▣
Nearby Facilities ┏ ✓ ⚓ ⤧ ∪ ≈ ♗ ♗
✈ Torquay
Quiet, family run park for families and mixed couples only. A most central site for most of the sea and country amenities in South Devon. Dogs not allowed from Mid-July to the end of August. Seasonal pitches available.

PLYMOUTH

Pilgrims Rest, 41 Knighton Road, Wembury, Plymouth, Devon, PL9 0EA.
Std: 01752 **Tel:** 863429
Nearest Town/Resort Plymstock/Plymouth
Directions From Plymouth take the road to Kingsbridge, go through Elburton Village and turn left towards Wembury, site is on the left.
Acreage 1 **Open** May to September
Site Gentle Slope
Sites Available ⚏ ⛺ ⚓ **Total** 20
Facilities ⚓ 🚿 🚽 ⊙ 🍴 ♨ ⤧ ▱
Nearby Facilities ∪ ♗
✈ Plymouth
Just a 5 minute drive to the beach. Coastal walks, surfing, Post Office, pub serving food, two churches and gas available nearby. Bus stop at park entrance.

PLYMOUTH

Riverside Caravan Park, Longridge Road, Marsh Mills, Plymouth, Devon, PL 8LD.
Std: 01752 **Tel:** 344122 **Fax:** 344122
Email: info@riversidecaravanpark.con
Website: www.riversidecaravanpark.cor
Nearest Town/Resort Plymouth
Directions From the A38 take the slip ro to Plymouth, at the roundabout take the th exit onto Plympton road, at trafficlights tu left, then first right.
Acreage 10½ **Open** All Year
Access Good **Site** Level
Sites Available ⚏ ⛺ ⚓ **Total** 220
Facilities 🚿 🚽 ⛲ 🚽 ⌂ ⊙ 🍴 ▱ ◻ ☎
🏪 ⊙ 🏊 ✕ 🍴 ♨ ⤧ ⊛ ✣ ▱ ◻ ▣
Nearby Facilities ┏ ✓ ⚓ ⤧ ∪ ≈ ♗
✈ Plymouth
Alongside the River Plym.

PUTSBOROUGH

Putsborough Sands Caravan Park, Th Anchorage, Putsborough, Georgeham, North Devon, EX33 1LB.
Std: 01271 **Tel:** 890230/890121
Std: 01271 **Fax:** 890208
Email: rob@putsborough-sands.co.uk
Website: www.putsborough-sands.co.uk
Nearest Town/Resort Ilfracombe/Barnstaple
Directions Directions given upon bookir
Open April to October
Access Poor **Site** Sloping
Sites Available ⚏ **Total** 25
Facilities ⚓ 🚿 🚽 ⌂ ⊙ 🍴 ♨ ▱
Nearby Facilities ┏ ✓ ⚓ ⤧ ∪ ≈ ♗ ♗
✈ Barnstaple
Adjacent to Multi Award Winning beach, t beach in North Devon. Unique positi sloping with level pitches. Booking essential, please contact Park Manageme

SALCOMBE

Alston Farm Camping & Caravan Site Nr. Salcombe, Kingsbridge, Devon, TQ7 3BJ.
Std: 01548 **Tel:** 561260
Std: 01548 **Fax:** 561260
Email: alston.campsite@ukgateway.net
Website: www.welcome.to/alstonfarm
Nearest Town/Resort Salcombe
Directions Signposted on left of A3 between Kingsbridge and Salcom towards Salcombe.
Acreage 15 **Open** Easter to October
Access Good **Site** Level
Sites Available ⚏ ⛺ ⚓ **Total** 200
Facilities 🚿 🚽 ⌂ ⊙ 🍴 ▱ ◻
🏪 ⊙ 🏊 ♨ ⤧ ▱

SALCOMBE

Bolberry House Farm Camping & Caravanning Park, Bolberry, Malborough, Kingsbridge, Devon, TQ7 3DY.
Std: 01548 **Tel:** 561251/560926
Email: bolberry.house@virgin.net
Website: www.bolberryparks.co.uk
Nearest Town/Resort Salcombe
Directions Take the A381 from Kingsbridge to Malborough. Turn right through the village, follow signs to Bolberry ¾ mile.
Acreage 6 **Open** March to October
Access Good **Site** Level
Sites Available A ⊕ ⊟ **Total** 70
Facilities ƒ ⓌⒸ ♿ ⌐ ⊙ ⊣ ⚫ ▣ ♥
Nearby Facilities ┌ ✦ ⚓ ⌂ Ư ⊅ ♟
≉ Totnes
Friendly and peaceful, family run park on coastal farm. Mostly level. Wonderful sea views and stunning cliff top walks. Safe sandy beaches 1 mile at the quaint old fishing village of Hope Cove. Salcombe's scenic and pretty estuary, a boating paradise 3½ miles. AA 3 Pennants and ETC 3 rosettes.

SALCOMBE

Higher Rew Caravan & Camping Park, Malborough, Kingsbridge, Devon, TQ7 3DW.
Std: 01548 **Tel:** 842681
Std: 01548 **Fax:** 843681
Email: enquiries@higherrew.co.uk
Website: www.higherrew.co.uk
Nearest Town/Resort Salcombe
Directions When approaching from Kingsbridge on the A381 to Salcombe, turn right at Malborough and follow signs to Soar approx. 1 mile then turn left at Rew Cross. Higher Rew is then the first turning on the right.
Acreage 5 **Open** Mid March to End Oct
Access Good **Site** Terraced
Sites Available A ⊕ ⊟ **Total** 80
Facilities ƒ ⓌⒸ ♿ ⌐ ⊙ ⊣ ⚫ ▣ ♥
Nearby Facilities ⚓ ✦ ♟
≉ Totnes
Family run park in an area of outstanding natural beauty on a farm. 1 mile from beaches and beautiful cliff walks.

SALCOMBE

Sun Park, Soar, Malborough, Nr. Kingsbridge, Devon, TQ7 3DS.
Std: 01548 **Tel:** 561378
Website: www.sun-park.co.uk

Nearest Town/Resort Salcombe.
Directions A381 fron Kingsbridge to Malborough, turn right through village, follow sign Soar Mill Cove for 1¼ miles, site on right.
Acreage 3¼ **Open** Easter to End Sept
Site Level
Sites Available A ⊕ ⊟ **Total** 70
Facilities ƒ ⊞ ♿ ⌐ ⊙ ⊣ ⚫ ▣ ♥
& ⊞ ⓘ ♨ ⚫ ♥ ▣ ▣
Nearby Facilities ┌ ✦ ⚓ ⌂ Ư ♟
≉ Totnes.
Within walking distance of Soar Mill Cove, in an area of outstanding natural beauty. Ideal centre for touring.

SEATON

Ashdown Caravan Park, Colyton Hill, Colyton, Near Seaton, Devon, EX24 6HY.
Std: 01297 **Tel:** 21587/22052
Nearest Town/Resort Seaton/Beer/Colyton
Directions 3 miles north west of Seaton. Situated ½ a mile off the A3052, signposted.
Acreage 7 **Open** April to October
Access Good **Site** Level
Sites Available A ⊟ **Total** 90
Facilities ƒ ⓌⒸ ♿ ⌐ ⊙ ⊣ ⚫ ♨ & ⊙ ♥ ▣
Nearby Facilities ┌ ✦ ⚓ ⌂ Ư ♟
≉ Axminster/Honiton
Quiet and spacious site.

SEATON

Berry Barton Caravan Park, Berry Barton, Branscombe, Seaton, Devon, EX12 3BD.
Std: 01297 **Tel:** 680208
Std: 01297 **Fax:** 680108
Nearest Town/Resort Sidmouth
Directions From the M5 at Exeter take the A3052 to Branscombe turning, go to Fountain Head and turn right just after the pub, Berry Barton is at the top of the hill on the right.
Acreage 16 **Open** 15 March to 15 Nov
Access Good **Site** Level
Sites Available A ⊕ ⊟ **Total** 71
Facilities ⊟ ⓌⒸ ♿ ⌐ ⊙ ⊣ ⚫ ▣ ⓘ ⊙ ⓘ ♥ ▣
Nearby Facilities ┌ ✦ ⌂ Ư ♟
≉ Honiton
Near the beach and a river for fishing. Good pub food. Riding school on site.

SEATON

Leacroft Touring Park, Colyton Hill, Colyton, Devon, EX24 6HY.
Std: 01297 **Tel:** 552823
Std: 01297 **Fax:** 552823
Nearest Town/Resort Seaton/Beer
Directions A3052 Sidmouth to Lyme Regis road, 2 miles west of Seaton. Turn left at

---

Stafford Cross international caravan sign, site is 1 mile on the right.
Acreage 10 **Open** End March to October
Access Good **Site** Lev/Slope
Sites Available A ⊕ ⊟ **Total** 138
Facilities & ƒ ⊞ ⓌⒸ ♿ ⌐ ⊙ ⊣ ⚫ ▣ ♥
⓯ & ⚫ ♨ ⌂ ♥ ▣ ♥
Nearby Facilities ┌ ✦ ⚓ ⌂ Ư
≉ Axminster
Quiet, peaceful site in open countryside. Picturesque villages to explore and woodland walks nearby.

SEATON

Manor Farm Caravan Site, Seaton Down Hill, Seaton, Devon, EX12 2JA.
Std: 01297 **Tel:** 21524
Nearest Town/Resort Seaton
Directions From Lyme Regis A3052, left at Tower Cross, ½ mile entrance on left.
Acreage 22 **Open** April to 15th Nov
Access Good **Site** Lev/Slope
Sites Available A ✕ ⊕ ⊟ **Total** 274
Facilities & ✕ ƒ ⊞ ♿ ⌐ ⊙ ⊣ ⚫ ▣ ♥
⓯ & ⌂ ♥
Nearby Facilities ┌ ✦ ⚓ ⌂ Ư ♟
≉ Axminster
Glorious scenic views of valley and Lyme Bay. Farm animals, rare breeds. A quiet site only 1 mile from beach. Ideal touring centre for glorious East Devon. Gas available nearby.

SIDMOUTH

Kings Down Tail Caravan & Camping Park, Salcombe Regis, Sidmouth, Devon, EX10 0PD.
Std: 01297 **Tel:** 680313
Std: 01297 **Fax:** 680313
Email: info@kingsdowntail.co.uk
Website: www.uk.parks.co.uk./ kingsdowntail
Nearest Town/Resort Sidmouth
Directions On the A3052 3 miles east of Sidmouth, opposite Branscombe Water Tower. Please note that we are NOT in Salcombe Regis Village.
Acreage 5 **Open** 15 March to 15 Nov
Access Good **Site** Level
Sites Available A ⊕ ⊟ **Total** 100
Facilities ƒ ⊞ ⓌⒸ ♿ ⌐ ⊙ ⊣ ⚫ ▣ ♥
⓯ & ⚫ ♨ ⌂ ♥ ▣ ♥
Nearby Facilities ┌ ✦ Ư ♟
≉ Honiton
Site shop also has an off license. Heated shower block. Local fishermen are happy to take people out on boat trips. Ideal centre for East Devon and West Dorset. Two static caravans also available for hire. Pets are welcome if kept on a lead.

SALCOMBE REGIS CAMPING AND CARAVAN PARK

Sidmouth, Devon

Award Winning Family Park in an area of outstanding natural beauty. Excellent facilities including hard standing pitches with electric hook-ups. Taps available on perimeter pitches at no extra cost. Children's playground, putting green, dog walking area, shop/off licence, battery charging and gas supplies. BBQ's permitted/also for hire, heated amenity block/free hot water. **The discerning camper's choice.**

Open Easter to October. FREE Colour brochure
Tel/Fax: 01395 514303
www.salcombe-regis.co.uk   E-mail: info@salcombe-regis.co.uk

SIDMOUTH

Oakdown Touring & Holiday Home Park, Weston, Sidmouth, Devon, EX10 0PH.
Std: 01297 **Tel:** 680387
Std: 01297 **Fax:** 680541
Email: oakdown@btinternet.com
Website: www.bestcaravanpark.co.uk
Nearest Town/Resort Sidmouth
Directions 1½ miles east of Sidford on A3052, take the second Weston turning at the Oakdown sign. Site 50 yards on left. Also signposted with international Caravan/ Camping signs.
Acreage 13 **Open** April **to** October
Access Good **Site** Level
Sites Available ▲ ⊕ ♛ **Total** 120
Facilities ⅃ ∮ 🖻 🗓 🕮 ⚓ ┌ ⊙ ⊖ ⌫ ▣ ♥
🖸 ⚒ 🗓 ⚘ ✳ 🄿 ⊟ 🖭
Nearby Facilities ┌ ✔ ⚓ ⚓ ∪ ⫞ ♬
⇌ Honiton
Sidmouths Award Winning park set in glorious East Devon Heritage coast, near beautiful Weston Valley owned by National Trust, lovely cliff walks. Caravan storage. Field trail to nearby world famous Donkey Sanctuary. Caravan holiday homes to let. Awards for 1997 - England for Excellence Silver Award. Awards for 2000 - ETB 5 Star Grading, AA 4 Pennant De-Luxe Park, David Bellamy Gold Conservation Award, Loo of the Year Award, Calor Gas Best Park in England 1999, Devon & Cornwall Police Award for Security.

SIDMOUTH

Salcombe Regis Camping & Caravan Park, Salcombe Regis, Sidmouth, Devon, EX10 0JH.
Std: 01395 **Tel:** 514303
Std: 01395 **Fax:** 514303
Email: info@salcombe-regis.co.uk
Website: www.salcombe-regis.co.uk
Nearest Town/Resort Sidmouth
Directions Signposted 1½ miles east of Sidmouth. ½ mile off the A3052 Exeter to Lyme Regis coast road. ½ mile down the lane on the left hand side.
Acreage 16 **Open** Easter **to** October
Access Good **Site** Lev/Slope
Sites Available ▲ ⊕ ♛ **Total** 100
Facilities ∮ 🗓 🕮 ⚓ ┌ ⊙ ⊖ ⌫ ▣ ♥
⚒ 🖸 ⚘ 🗓 ✳ 🄿 ⊟
Nearby Facilities ┌ ✔ ⚓ ∪ ♬
⇌ Honiton
Situated in an area of outstanding natural beauty, within walking distance of the sea and famous Donkey Sanctuary. Own water supply available for motor caravans and tourers. Heated amenity block. Quiet, "Excellent" Graded Park with David Bellamy Gold Environmental Award.

SLAPTON

Newlands Farm Camping & Caravan Site, Newlands Farm, Slapton, Nr. Dartmouth, Devon, TQ7 2RB.
Std: 01548 **Tel:** 580366
Email: cades@devon-camping.co.uk
Website: www.devon-camping.co.uk
Nearest Town/Resort Dartmouth
Directions From Totnes take the A381 towards Kingsbridge, after Halwell Village take the fourth left signposted Slapton. Go 4 miles to Buckland Cross, proceed for ¼ mile, site is on the left hand side.
Acreage 10 **Open** 23 May **to** September
Access Good **Site** Level
Sites Available ▲ ⊕ ♛ **Total** 45
Facilities ∮ 🕮 ⚓ ┌ ⊙ ⊖ 🖩 🄿 ✳ 🖭
Nearby Facilities ┌ ✔ ⚓ ⚓ ∪ ⫞ ♬
We have a friendly, uncommercialised, quiet site overlooking beautiful countryside and sea. Within 1 mile of glorious beaches, cliff walks and a nature reserve. Woodlands Leisure Centre is close by with fun for all the family.

SOUTH BRENT

Great Palstone Caravan Park, Exeter Road, South Brent, Devon, TQ10 9JP.
Std: 01364 **Tel:** 72227
Nearest Town/Resort Totnes
Directions From Marley Head junction on the Devon expressway follow signs for South Brent and brown tourist signs for Great Palstone.
Open 15 March **to** 15 Nov
Access Good **Site** Level
Sites Available ▲ ⊕ ♛ **Total** 25
Facilities ∮ 🗓 🕮 ⚓ ┌ ⊙ ⊖ 🄿 ♥
🛈 🖸 ⚒ 🗓 ✳ 🖭
Nearby Facilities ┌ ✔ ⚓ ⚓ ∪ ⫞ ♬ ✱
⇌ Totnes
Situated within Dartmoor National Park. 8 miles from the coast. Seasonal pitches.

SOUTH BRENT

Webland Farm Holiday Park, Avonwick, Nr. South Brent, Devon, TQ10 9EX.
Std: 01364 **Tel:** 73273
Nearest Town/Resort Totnes
Directions Leave the A38 at Marley Head A385 exit. Follow Webland signs from the roundabout and along lane for about 1¼ miles.
Acreage 5 **Open** 15th March **to** 15th Nov
Access Good **Site** Lev/Gentle Slope
Sites Available ▲ ⊕ ♛ **Total** 35
Facilities ⚒ ∮ 🕮 ⚓ ┌ ⊙ ⊖ 🄿 ♥
⚘ 🗓 ✳ 🖭
Nearby Facilities ┌ ✔ ∪
⇌ Totnes
Overlooked by Dartmoor Hills, very quiet country park, well placed for touring the coast and Dartmoor and the many tourist attractions in the area.

SOUTH MOLTON

Romansleigh Holiday Park, Odam Hill, South Molton, North Devon, EX36 4NB.
Std: 01769 **Tel:** 550259
Nearest Town/Resort Barnstaple
Directions Take the B3137 South Molton to Witheridge road. Site is signposted right approximately 4 miles from South Molton and 2 miles past Alswear.
Acreage 2 **Open** 15 March **to** 31 October
Access Good **Site** Level
Sites Available ▲ ⊕ ♛ **Total** 20
Facilities ∮ 🕮 ⚓ ┌ ⊙ ⊖ ⌫ ▣
🖸 ⚒ 🗓 ⚘ 🗓 ✳ 🄿 ♬
Nearby Facilities ┌ ✔ ∪ ✱
⇌ Umberleigh
Secluded, wooded valley with grounds of 10 acres. Easy access to Exmoor and the North Devon coast. Magnificent views.

SOUTH MOLTON

Yeo Valley Holiday Park, c/o Blackcock Inn, Molland, South Molton, North Devon, EX36 3NW.
Std: 01769 **Tel:** 550297 **Fax:** 550101
Email: info@yeovalleyholidays.com
Website: www.yeovalleyholidays.com
Nearest Town/Resort South Molton
Directions Signposted clearly from A361 just east of South Molton.
Acreage 7 **Open** 15 March **to** 15 Oct
Access Good **Site** Gently Sloping
Sites Available ▲ ⊕ □ **Total** 65
Facilities ∮ 🗓 🕮 ⚓ ┌ ⊖ ⌫ ▣
⚒ 🛈 🖸 ✳ 🖭
Nearby Facilities
⇌ Tiverton Parkway/Barnstaple
Quiet secluded valley on the edge of Exmoor. Ideal for walking, cycling and outdoor pursuits.

STOKENHAM

Old Cotmore Farm, Old Cotmore Farm, Stokenham, South Devon, TQ7 2LR.
Std: 01548 **Tel:** 580240 **Fax:** 580875
Email: graham.bowsher@btinternet.com
Nearest Town Kingsbridge/Salcombe
Directions Take the A379 Kingsbridge/ Dartmouth road, at the Carehouse Cross Stokenham turn right signposted Beesands. Farm is 1 mile on the right and is signposted.
Acreage 10 **Open** March **to** November
Access Good **Site** Lev/Slope
Sites Available ▲ ⊕ ♛ **Total** 30
Facilities ⅃ ∮ 🗓 🕮 ⚓ ┌ ⊙ ⊖ ⌫ ▣
⚒ 🛈 🖸 ⚘ 🗓 ✳ 🄿 ⊟
Nearby Facilities ┌ ✔ ⚓ ⚓ ∪ ⫞ ♬
⇌ Totnes
Small, family run, picturesque, peaceful, with views over farms and fields. Cliff walks, beaches, diving, fishing and bird watching. Excellent pubs.

AVISTOCK

rford Bridge Holiday Park, Peter Tavy,
istock, Devon, PL19 9LS.
: 01822 **Tel:** 810349
: 01822 **Fax:** 810349
ail: enquiry@harfordbridge.co.uk
bsite: www.harfordbridge.co.uk
arest Town/Resort Tavistock
ections A386 Okehampton road 2 miles
th of Tavistock.
reage 16½ **Open** March to November
ess Good **Site** Level
es Available ⚊ ⊞ ⊟ **Total** 120
cilities ⊞ ⊞ ⊞ ⚒ ⌐ ☺ ⌐ ⊡ ☻
⊞ ⊞ ⚒ ⊞ ⊡ ⊟ ⊟
arby Facilities ⌐ ✔ ∪ ♪
⚐ Plymouth
autiful, family run park with scenic views,
ʳrside pitches, fishing and tennis. Ideal
touring Dartmoor National Park. Rose
ard.

AVISTOCK

ʰher Longford, Moorshop, Tavistock,
ⱽon, PL19 9LQ.
: 01822 **Tel:** 613360
ail: stay@higherlongford.co.uk
bsite: www.higherlongford.co.uk
arest Town/Resort Tavistock
ections Tavistock/Princetown road, 2
es from Tavistock on the B3357.
reage 6 **Open** All Year
ess Good **Site** Level
es Available ⚊ ⊞ ⊟ **Total** 52
cilities ⊞ ⊞ ⊞ ⚒ ⌐ ☺ ⌐ ⊡ ☻
⊞ ⚒ ✕ ⊞ ⚒ ⊞ ⊡ ⊟
arby Facilities ⌐ ✔ ∪
Plymouth.
uated in the Dartmoor National Park,
ⁿtral for touring Devon and Cornwall.
ᵒor swimming pool nearby. David
ᵃmy Gold Award for Conservation.

AVISTOCK

ⁿgstone Manor Caravan & Camping
ʳk, Langstone Manor, Moortown,
ⁱstock, Devon, PL19 9JZ.
: 01822 **Tel:** 613371
: 01822 **Fax:** 613371
ail: web@langstone-manor.co.uk
bsite: www.langstone-manor.co.uk
arest Town/Resort Tavistock
ections Take the B3357 from Tavistock
ⱽards Princetown, after approx. 2 miles
ⁿ right at crossroads, pass over the cattle
d, continue up the hill then turn left
ᵒwing signs for Langstone Manor. We are
mile on the right.
reage 5½ **Open** 15 March to 15 Nov
ess Good **Site** Level
es Available ⚊ ⊞ ⊟ **Total** 40

Facilities ⌐ ⊞ ⚒ ⌐ ☺ ⌐ ⌐ ⊡ ☻
⊞ ⚐ ⊞ ⚒ ✕ ⚒ ⚒ ⊞ ⊞ ⊡ ⊟
Nearby Facilities ⌐ ✔ ∪ ♪ ✈
⚐ Plymouth
Direct access onto Dartmoor. Only 6 miles
from Cornwall. Beaches within 12 miles.
ETB 3 Star Graded and AA 3 Pennant
Luxury Site.

TAVISTOCK

Woodovis Park, Tavistock, Devon, PL19
8NY.
Std: 01822 **Tel:** 832968
Std: 01822 **Fax:** 832948
Email: info@woodovis.com
Website: www.woodovis.com
Nearest Town/Resort Tavistock
Directions Take A390 Liskeard road from
Tavistock. Site signposted right in 3 miles.
Acreage 14 **Open** March to October
Access Good **Site** Lev/Slope
Sites Available ⚊ ⊞ ⊟ **Total** 50
Facilities ⚒ ⌐ ⊞ ⊞ ⚒ ⌐ ☺ ⌐ ⊡ ☻
⊞ ⚐ ⊞ ⚒ ✕ ⚒ ⚒ ⊞ ⊡ ⊟
Nearby Facilities ⌐ ✔ ⚒ ⚒ ∪ ♪ ♪ ✈
⚐ Plymouth/Gunnislake
BTB Graded Park. Quiet, rural site with
outstanding views. Near to Dartmoor, coasts
and Cornwall. Excellent facilities, free
showers, laundry/washing-up room. Shop,
off-license, farm produce, bread/croissants
baked on site. Heated indoor pool, sauna
and jacuzzi. Pitch and putt.

TEDBURN ST MARY

Springfield Holiday Park, Tedburn Road,
Tedburn St. Mary, Exeter, Devon, EX6
6EW.
Std: 01647 **Tel:** 24242
Std: 01647 **Fax:** 24131
Email: springhol@aol.com
Website:
www.springfieldholidaypark.co.uk
Nearest Town/Resort Exeter
Directions Leave the M5 at junction 31
(Okehampton) and take the A30. Leave at
the third exit signposted Tedburn St. Mary
and Cheriton Bishop and follow signs.
Acreage 9 **Open** 15 March to 15 Nov
Access Good **Site** Level
Sites Available ⚊ ⊞ ⊟ **Total** 88
Facilities ⚒ ⊞ ⊞ ⚒ ⌐ ☺ ⌐ ⊡ ☻
⊞ ⚐ ⊞ ⚒ ✕ ⚒ ⚒ ⊞ ⊞ ⊟
Nearby Facilities ⌐ ✔ ⚒ ⚒ ∪ ♪ ✈
⚐ Exeter
On the fringe of Dartmoor National Park.
Central for beaches and ideal for touring.

TEIGNMOUTH

Coast View Holiday Park, Torquay Road,
Teignmouth, Shaldon, South Devon, TQ14
0BG.
Std: 01626 **Tel:** 872392

Website: www.coastviewpark.co.uk
Nearest Town/Resort Teignmouth.
Directions Follow A38 from Exeter, take left
fork A380 to Torquay. Proceed along the
A380 for about 6 miles taking the A381
towards Shaldon. Turn right at traffic lights,
cross Shaldon bridge and follow main road.
Camp is on the right hand side.
Acreage 21 **Access** Good **Site** Level
Sites Available ⚊ ⊞ ⊟ **Total** 100
Facilities ⚒ ⚒ ⊞ ⊞ ⊞ ⚒ ⌐ ☺ ⌐ ⊡ ☻
⊞ ⚐ ⊞ ⚒ ✕ ⚒ ⚒ ⊞ ⊞ ⊡ ⊟
Nearby Facilities ⌐ ✔ ⚒ ⚒ ∪ ♪ ♪ ✈
⚐ Teignmouth
Scenic views across the sea to the South
Devon coastline, Devon coast. Ideal for
touring.

TEIGNMOUTH

Wear Farm Caravan Site, E. S. Coaker &
Co., Newton Road, Bishopsteignton, Nr.
Teignmouth, Devon, TQ14 9PT.
Std: 01626 **Tel:** 775249/779265/775015
Std: 01626 **Fax:** 775249
Nearest Town/Resort Teignmouth
Directions Off the A380 take the A381
towards Teignmouth, Wear Farm can be
found ¼ a mile on the right from the dual
carriageway.
Acreage 15 **Open** Easter to End October
Access Good **Site** Level
Sites Available ⚊ ⊞ ⊟ **Total** 147
Facilities ⚒ ⊞ ⚒ ⌐ ☺ ⌐ ⊡ ☻
⊞ ⚐ ⊞ ⚒ ⊞ ⊟
Nearby Facilities ⌐ ✔ ⚒ ⚒ ∪ ♪ ♪
⚐ Newton Abbot
Alongside a river, scenic views and ideal
touring.

TIVERTON

Minnows Caravan Park, Sampford
Peverell, Tiverton, Devon, EX16 7EN.
Std: 01884 **Tel:** 821770
Std: 01884 **Fax:** 821770
Website: www.ukparks.co.uk/minnows
Nearest Town/Resort Tiverton
Directions Leave the M5 at junction 27 and
take the A361 signposted Tiverton and
Barnstaple. After 600 metres take the slip
road signposted Sampford Peverell, turn
right at the mini roundabout, straight on.
Acreage 5½ **Open** 8 March to 11 Nov.
Access Good **Site** Level
Sites Available ⚊ ⊞ ⊡ **Total** 45
Facilities ⚒ ⚒ ⚒ ⊞ ⊞ ⊞ ⚒ ⌐ ⊡ ☻
⊞ ⊞ ⚒ ⊞ ⊡ ⊟
Nearby Facilities ⌐ ✔ ⚒ ∪ ♪
⚐ Tiverton Parkway
Alongside the Grand Western Canal
Countryside Park, ideal for walking, cycling
and fishing. Village with pub and shops ½
mile along the canal. Discount for Caravan
Club Members.

IT'S FUN FOR ALL THE FAMILY

WOOLACOMBE SANDS HOLIDAY PARK

NEAREST HOLIDAY PARK TO THE BEACH

Heated Indoor Swimming Pool, Licensed Club-Nightly Entertainment, Children's Games Room & Play Area.

TOURING & CAMPING

Designated areas for Tents and Tourers,
Showers, Toilets, Wash basins, Hair dryers, Launderette.
Electric Hook Ups available.

CHALETS / CARAVANS / COTTAGES

Up to 8 people, ALL facilities including Colour TV, Private Bathroom,
set in beautiful countryside overlooking the sea & miles of golden sands.

01271 870569
www.woolacombe-sands.co.uk

Woolly Bear Club:- www.woolly-bear.co.uk

Beach Rd, Woolacombe,
N. Devon EX34 7AF

TIVERTON
West Middlewick Farm, Nomansland, Nr. Tiverton, Devon, EX16 8NP.
Std: 01884 **Tel:** 860286
Nearest Town/Resort Tiverton
Directions Take the old A373 (now the B3137) W.N.W.from Tiverton, farm is beside road one mile beyond Nomansland, on right 9 miles from Tiverton).
Acreage 3 **Open** All Year
Access Good **Site** Level
Sites Available A 母 ⊕ **Total** 15
Facilities 𝄞 🛈 🏪 ┌ ⊙ ⊴ 🍴 ▮* ⊁ ⌂
Nearby Facilities ┌ ✓ U ⏚
≠ Tiverton Parkway
Panoramic view towards Exmoor, quiet surroundings, children welcome. Genuine farm with the same family management since 1933.

TIVERTON
Zeacombe House Caravan Park, East Anstey, Near Tiverton, Devon, EX16 9JU.
Std: 01398 **Tel:** 341279
Nearest Town/Resort Tiverton
Directions Leave the M5 at junction 27 and take the A361 to Tiverton. At the roundabout turn right signposted the A396 to Minehead and Dulverton. After 5 miles turn left at the Exeter Inn, after 1¾ miles turn left at the Black Cat onto the B3227, 5 miles to Knowstone and the site is on the left.
Acreage 4½ **Open** 31 March **to** 31 October
Access Good **Site** Level
Sites Available A 母 ⊕ **Total** 70
Facilities 𝄞 🛈 🏪 ┌ ⊙ ⊴ 🍴 ▮ ⌂
Nearby Facilities ┌ ✓ U
≠ Tiverton
Near to Exmoor, Tarr Steps, National Trust properties, Tarka Trail and Rosemoor Gardens. Ideal for walking.

TORQUAY
Manor Farm Camp Site, Manor Farm, Daccombe, Nr Torquay, Devon, TQ12 4ST.
Std: 01803 **Tel:** 328294
Nearest Town/Resort Torquay
Directions From Newton Abbot take the A380 for Torquay. Go through roundabout at Kerswell Gardens to next set of traffic lights, turn left into Kingskerswell Road, follow camp signs.
Acreage 4 **Open** 20 May **to** 20 Sept
Site Lev/Slope
Sites Available A 母 ⊕ **Total** 75
Facilities 🛈 🏪 ┌ ⊙ ⊴ 🍴 ▮ 🆀 ⊕ ⊁
Nearby Facilities ┌ ✓ ⏚ ⌖ U ⏚ ♫ ⊁
≠ Torquay
Near the beach, scenic views, ideal touring. Bed & Breakfast available all year round.

TORQUAY
Widdicombe Farm Touring Park, The Ring Road (A380), Compton, Marldon, Torquay, Paignton, Devon, TQ3 1ST.
Std: 01803 **Tel:** 558325
Std: 01803 **Fax:** 559526
Email: enq@torquaytouring.co.uk
Website: www.torquaytouring.co.uk
Nearest Town/Resort Torquay/Paignton
Directions From Exeter take the A380 to Torquay, at the large roundabout controlled by traffic lights follow signs for Torquay. At next roundabout turn right into Hamlyn Way, go to the top of the hill and at the next roundabout go straight on. Look to the right to see our park, proceed to the next roundabout and double back to Widdicombe Farm.
Acreage 8 **Open** Mid March **to** Mid Nov
Access Good **Site** Level
Sites Available A 母 ⊕ **Total** 160
Facilities 𝄞 🛈 🏪 ┌ ⊙ ⊴ 🍴 ▮ 🆀 ⌂
Nearby Facilities ┌ ✓ ⏚ ⌖ U ⏚ ♫
≠ Torquay/Paignton
A very friendly family run park. Lovely countryside setting, yet so near to Torquay. Restaurant serving home cooked food. Country Stye Club House with good entertainment, mid and high season. No narrow country lanes. Bargain Breaks from £40.00 per week. Luxury at the right price.

TORRINGTON
Greenways Valley, Torrington, Devon, EX38 7EW.
Std: 01805 **Tel:** 622153
Std: 01805 **Fax:** 622320
Nearest Town/Resort Torrington/Westward Ho!
Directions Site is just one mile from Torrington town centre. Take B3227 (to South Molton) turn right into Borough Road then 3rd left to site entrance.
Acreage 8 **Open** Mid March **to** October
Access Good **Site** Level
Sites Available A 母 ⊕ **Total** 10
Facilities 𝄞 🛈 🏪 ┌ ⊙ ⊴ 🍴 ▮ ⌂
Nearby Facilities ┌ ✓ ⏚ ⌖ U ♫
≠ Barnstaple
Peaceful well tended site with a southerly aspect overlooking a beautiful wooded valley. Tennis and heated pool on park.

TORRINGTON
Smytham Manor Leisure, Smytham Manor, Little Torrington, Devon, EX38 8PU.
Std: 01805 **Tel:** 622110
Email: info@smytham.fsnet.co.uk

Nearest Town/Resort Gt Torrington/Westward Ho!
Directions 2 miles south Torrington on A386 to Okehampton.
Acreage 25 **Open** Mid March **to** October
Access Good **Site** Level
Sites Available A 母 ⊕ **Total** 30
Facilities 𝄞 🛈 🏪 ┌ ⊙ ⊴ 🍴 ▮ 🆀 ⌂
Nearby Facilities ┌ ✓ ⏚ ⌖ U ⏚ ♫ ⊁
≠ Barnstaple
Attractive landscaped grounds, close to moors and beach with direct access to the Tarka Trail. Good base for exploring Devon.

TOTNES
Edeswell Farm Country Caravan Park, Edeswell Farm, Rattery, South Brent, Devon, TQ10 9LN.
Std: 01364 **Tel:** 72177
Std: 01364 **Fax:** 72177
Email: welcome@edeswellfarm.co.uk
Website: www.edeswellfarm.co.uk
Nearest Town/Resort Totnes
Directions Fron Exeter follow the A38 approx 22 miles ignore Rattery signs leave at Marley Head Junction signposted Paignton, Totnes A358. Site ½ mile on right.
Acreage 6 **Open** February **to** November
Access Good **Site** Terraced
Sites Available 母 ⊕ **Total** 46
Facilities 𝄞 🛈 🏪 ┌ ⊙ ⊴ 🍴 ▮ 🆀 ⌂
Nearby Facilities ┌ ✓ ⏚ ⌖ U ⏚ ♫ ⊁
≠ Totnes
Dartmoor, country site for quiet family holidays but with all facilities. Indoor heated swimming pool and cycle hire on site.

WOOLACOMBE
Damage Barton, Mortehoe, Woolacombe, North Devon, EX34 7EJ.
Std: 01271 **Tel:** 870502
Std: 01271 **Fax:** 870712
Website: www.damagebarton.co.uk
Nearest Town/Resort Woolacombe
Directions Take the A361 from Barnstaple and turn left at the Mullacott Cross roundabout onto the B3343 signposted Woolacombe and Mortehoe. After 1¾ miles turn right signposted Mortehoe, site is on the right after approx. 1 mile.
Acreage 16 **Open** 20 March **to** 5 November
Access Good **Site** Lev/Slope
Sites Available A 母 ⊕ **Total** 145
Facilities ⅙ 𝄞 🛈 🏪 ┌ ⊙ ⊴ 🍴 ▮ 🆀 ⌂
Nearby Facilities ┌ ✓ U ♫
≠ Barnstaple
Peaceful site with good views, wild flowers and birds. Access to a network of footpaths including the coastal path.

WOOLACOMBE

Europa Holiday Village, Station Road, Woolacombe, Devon, EX34 7AN.
Std: 01271 **Tel:** 870159
Nearest Town/Resort Woolacombe
Directions Less than a mile from and above Woolacombe on the right hand side of the main road leading into the resort.
Acreage 11 **Open** Easter **to** October
Access Good **Site** Lev/slope
Sites Available A ⌂ ⊟ **Total** 100
Facilities ⌂ ⬛ ⬛ ♨ ↄ ⊙ ⌷ ☺
⧊ ⬛ ⬛ ♀ ⬛ ⬛ ⬛ ⬛ ⬛ ⊕ ⬛ ⬛ ⬛
Nearby Facilities ↄ ✓ ⚓ ⤢ U ⌇ ⚲ ⚹
⇌ Barnstaple
Panoramic views of surrounding countryside and Woolacombe Bay. Quietly situated informal site where well behaved animals (and children!) are welcome.

WOOLACOMBE

Golden Coast Holiday Village, Woolacombe, Devon, EX34 7HW.
Std: 01271 **Tel:** 870343
Std: 01271 **Fax:** 870089
Email: goodtimes@woolacombe.com
Website: www.woolacombe.com
Nearest Town/Resort Woolacombe
Directions Take the A361 to Barnstaple and follow Ilfracombe signs, take the Woolacombe junction from Mullacott Cross.
Open March **to** January
Access Good **Site** Lev/Slope
Sites Available A ⌂ ⊟ **Total** 300
Facilities ⌂ ⬛ ⬛ ♨ ↄ ⊙ ⌷ ☺
⧊ ⬛ ⬛ ☺ ✗ ♀ ⬛ ♨ ⬛ ⬛ ⊕ ⬛ ⬛ ⬛
Nearby Facilities ↄ ✓ ⚓ ⤢ U ⌇ ⚲ ⚹
⇌ Barnstaple
Close to the Blue Flag beach of Woolacombe, free bus service to the beach. Choice of three parcs and their facilities, entertainment and accommodation.

WOOLACOMBE

Little Roadway Farm, Woolacombe, North Devon, EX34 7HL.
Std: 01271 **Tel:** 870313
Std: 01271 **Fax:** 871085
Nearest Town/Resort Woolacombe
Directions Take the A361 to Mullacott Cross roundabout and turn left towards Woolacombe, follow tourism signs and turn left onto the B3231, Little Roadway Farm is on this road.
Acreage 20 **Open** March **to** November
Access Good **Site** Lev/Slope
Sites Available A ⌂ ⊟ **Total** 200
Facilities ⌂ ⬛ ♨ ↄ ⊙ ⌷ ☺
⧊ ⬛ ⬛ ☺ ✗ ⬛ ⬛
Nearby Facilities ↄ ✓ ⚓ ⤢ U ⌇ ⚲ ⚹
⇌ Barnstaple
Within 1 mile of Woolacombe beach. Easy access to Putsborough, Croyde, Saunton and Exmoor.

WOOLACOMBE

Twitchen Parc, Mortehoe, Woolacombe, North Devon, EX34 7ES.
Std: 01271 **Tel:** 870343
Std: 01271 **Fax:** 870089
Email: goodtimes@woolacombe.com
Website: www.woolacombe.com
Nearest Town/Resort Woolacombe
Directions From Barnstaple/Ilfracombe road (A361) to junction with B3343 at Mullacott Cross, first left signposted Woolacombe for 1¾ miles, then right signposted Mortehoe. Park is 1¼ miles on left.
Acreage 20 **Open** March **to** October
Access Good **Site** Sloping
Sites Available A ⌂ ⊟ **Total** 300
Facilities ⌂ ⬛ ⬛ ♨ ↄ ⊙ ⌷ ☺
⧊ ⬛ ☺ ✗ ♀ ⬛ ♨ ⬛ ⬛ ⬛ ⬛ ⬛
Nearby Facilities ↄ ✓ ⚓ ⤢ U ⌇ ⚲

⇌ Barnstaple
Rural, scenic setting, close t Woolacombe's glorious sandy beach an spectacular coastal walks.

WOOLACOMBE

Woolacombe Sands Holiday Park, Beach Road, Woolacombe, North Devon, EX34 7AF.
Std: 01271 **Tel:** 870569
Std: 01271 **Fax:** 870606
Email: lifesabeach@woolacombe-sands.co.uk
Website: www.woolacombe-sands.co.uk
Nearest Town/Resort Woolacombe
Directions Take the A361 Barnstaple t Ilfracombe road, at Mullacott Cros roundabout turn onto the B3343 t Woolacombe. Park is on the left on the las bend before the village of Woolacombe.
Open April **to** October
Access Good **Site** Level
Sites Available A ⌂ ⊟ **Total**
Facilities ⌂ ⬛ ♨ ↄ ⊙ ⌷ ☺ ⬛ ⬛ ☺
⧊ ☺ ✗ ♀ ⬛ ♨ ⬛ ⬛ ⬛ ⬛ ⬛ ⬛
Nearby Facilities ↄ ✓ U
⇌ Barnstaple
Nearest site to Woolacombe's 3 mile beach Set in beautiful countryside with sceni views overlooking the sea.

DORSET

BERE REGIS

Rowlands Wait Touring Park, Rye Hill, Bere Regis, Dorset, BH20 7LP.
Std: 01929 **Tel:** 472727
Std: 01929 **Fax:** 472727
Email: info@rowlandswait.co.uk
Website: www.rowlandswait.co.uk
Nearest Town/Resort Wareham
Directions At Bere Regis take road signposted to Wool/Bovington, about ¾ mile at top of Rye Hill turn right. Site 300yds.
Acreage 8 **Open** March **to** January
Access Good **Site** Lev/Slope
Sites Available A ♛ ⬛ **Total** 71
Facilities ⎰ 🚽 ⬛ 🔥 ⌐ ⊙ ⤵ ⬛ ⬛ 🍽
🏊 🏤 🐕 ⬛ 🐾 🅰 ⊛ ⤒ 🅿 🖂 ⬛
Nearby Facilities ⌐ ✔ ⚓ 🜨 U ⩗ ₽
➾ Wool
Situated in area of outstanding natural beauty. Within easy reach of coast, direct access from site into heath and woodland. Ideal walking, touring and the quiet family holiday. Club Rallies welcome. Open Winter by arrangement. Countryside Discovery Member. David Bellamy Gold Conservation Award. A warm welcome awaits you.

BLANDFORD

The Inside Park, Blandford, Dorset, DT11 9AD.
Std: 01258 **Tel:** 453719
Std: 01258 **Fax:** 459921
Email: inspark@aol.com
Website: www.members.aol.com/inspark/inspark
Nearest Town/Resort Blandford Forum
Directions 1¼ miles south west of Blandford on the road to Winterborne Stickland. Signposted from junction of A350 and A354 on Blandford bypass.
Acreage 13 **Open** Easter **to** October
Access Good **Site** Lev/Slope
Sites Available A ♛ ⬛ **Total** 100
Facilities ⎰ 🚽 ⬛ 🔥 ⌐ ⊙ ⤵ ⬛ ⬛ 🍽
🏊 ⬛ 🐕 🅰 ⊛ ⤒ 🅿 🖂
Nearby Facilities ⌐ ✔ U ₽
Rural environment with extensive wildlife. Ideal for touring. Caravan storage available.

BOURNEMOUTH

St. Leonards Farm, Ringwood Road, West Moors, Ferndown, Dorset, BH22 0AQ.
Std: 01202 **Tel:** 872637
Std: 01202 **Fax:** 855683
Website: www.st-leonardsfarm.co.uk
Nearest Town/Resort Bournemouth
Directions On the A31 4 miles west of Ringwood, opposite West Moors Garage.

Acreage 12 **Open** April **to** September
Access Good **Site** Level
Sites Available A ♛ ⬛
Facilities ⎰ 🚽 ⬛ 🔥 ⌐ ⊙ ⤵ ⬛ ⬛ 🍽
🏊 🏤 🐕 🅰 ⤒ 🅿 🖂
Nearby Facilities ⌐ ✔ ⚓ 🜨 U ⩗ ₽
➾ Bournemouth Central

BRIDPORT

Binghams Farm Touring Caravan Park, Binghams Farm, Melplash, Bridport, Dorset, DT6 3TT.
Std: 01308 **Tel:** 488234
Email: binghamsfarm@hotmail.com
Website: www.binghamsfarm.co.uk
Nearest Town/Resort West Bay/Bridport.
Directions Turn off A35 in Bridport at the roundabout onto A3066, signposted Beaminster. In 1¼ miles turn left into Farm Road.
Acreage 5 **Open** All Year
Access Good **Site** Level
Sites Available A ♛ ⬛ **Total** 60
Facilities ⎰ 🚽 ⬛ 🔥 ⌐ ⊙ ⤵ ⬛ ⬛ 🍽
🏊 ⬛ 🐕 ⊛ ⤒ 🅿 🅰
Nearby Facilities ⌐ ✔ ⚓ 🜨 U ⩗ ₽
➾ Dorchester
EXCLUSIVELY FOR ADULTS. An Award Winning Park set in an area of outstanding natural beauty yet only 3 miles from the coast. An ideal base to explore Dorset. All modern heated facilities.

BRIDPORT

Coastal Caravan Park, Annings Lane, Burton Bradstock, Bridport, Dorset, DT6 4QP.
Std: 01308 **Tel:** 422139
Std: 01308 **Fax:** 425672
Email: holidays@wdlh.co.uk
Website: www.wdlh.co.uk
Nearest Town/Resort Burton Bradstock
Directions In Burton Bradstock turn at the Anchor Inn, take the second turn right into Annings Lane, park is 1½ miles down the lane.
Acreage 5 **Open** March **to** October
Access Good **Site** Level
Sites Available A ♛ ⬛ **Total** 35
Facilities 🚽 ⬛ 🔥 ⌐ ⊙ ⤵ ⬛ ⬛ 🍽 🐾
Nearby Facilities ⌐ ✔
Quiet location in the countryside, surrounded by active farm land.

BRIDPORT

Eype House Caravan Park, Eype, Bridport, Dorset, DT6 6AL.
Std: 01308 **Tel:** 424903
Std: 01308 **Fax:** 424903
Email: enquiries@eypehouse.co.uk
Website: www.eypehouse.co.uk
Nearest Town/Resort Bridport

Directions Signposted Eyes Mouth off the A35.
Acreage 4 **Open** Easter **to** 30 October
Site Sloping
Sites Available A ♛ ⬛ **Total** 20
Facilities ⎰ 🚽 🔥 ⌐ ⊙ ⤵ ⬛ ⬛ 🍽
🏊 ⬛ 🐕 ⤒ 🅿
Nearby Facilities ⌐ ✔ ⚓ 🜨 U
➾ Crewkerne/Weymouth
On a coastal path only 200 yards from the beach. Sorry, NO touring caravans.

BRIDPORT

Freshwater Beach Holiday Park, Burton Bradstock, Bridport, Dorset, DT6 4PT.
Std: 01308 **Tel:** 897317
Std: 01308 **Fax:** 897336
Email: enquiries@fbhp.co.uk
Website: www.fbhp.co.uk
Nearest Town/Resort Bridport
Directions From Bridport take B3157 towards Weymouth site 2 miles on right.
Acreage 40 **Open** Easter **to** October
Access Good **Site** Level
Sites Available A ♛ ⬛ **Total** 500
Facilities ⎰ 🚽 ⬛ 🔥 ⌐ ⊙ ⤵ ⬛ ⬛ 🍽
🏊 🏤 🐕 ⬛ ⤒ 🅿 🖂
Nearby Facilities ⌐ ✔ ⚓ 🜨 U
➾ Dorchester
Own private beach. Free family entertainment. Good cliff walks. Golf course adjoining park.

BRIDPORT

Highlands End Farm Holiday Park, Eype, Bridport, Dorset, DT6 6AR.
Std: 01308. **Tel:** 422139
Std: 01308 **Fax:** 425672
Email: holidays@wdlh.co.uk
Website: www.wdlh.co.uk
Nearest Town/Resort Bridport
Directions On approach to Bridport from east (Dorchester) on A35 turn left at roundabout, follow Bridport By-pass. Second roundabout take third exit signposted A35 West 1 mile turn left to Eype and follow signposts.
Acreage 8 **Open** March **to** October
Access Good **Site** Level
Sites Available A ♛ ⬛ **Total** 195
Facilities ⎰ 🚽 🖸 ⬛ ⬛ 🔥 ⌐ ⊙ ⤵ ⬛ ⬛ 🍽
🏊 ⬛ 🐕 🅰 ⊛ ⤒ 🅿 🖂
Nearby Facilities ⌐ ✔ 🜨 U ₽
➾ Axminster
Exceptional views across Lyme Bay, 500 metres from the beach. Heated swimming pool, steam room and sauna. Tennis and Pitch & Putt on site. All weather awning areas.

BRIDPORT

Home Farm Caravan & Campsite,
Rectory Lane, Puncknowle, Near
Dorchester, Dorset, DT2 9BW.
Std: 01308 **Tel:** 897258
Nearest Town/Resort Weymouth
Directions Take the A35 towards Bridport,
before entering the dual carriageway turn
left to Litton Cheney and follow the road to
Puncknowle. 12 miles from Dorchester.
Acreage 5 **Open** 1 April **to** 14 October
Access Good **Site** Lev/Slope
Sites Available Å ⊕ ⊟ **Total** 42
Facilities ƒ ⊞ ⅏ ⅃ ⌐ ⊙ ┙ ▱ ☎
⅊ ⌂ ⊛ ╬ ⊡
Nearby Facilities ⌐ ✓ U
✸ Weymouth/Dorchester
In a beautiful area, 1½ miles from the
Heritage Coast. Ideal touring.

BRIDPORT

West Bay Holiday Park, West Bay,
Bridport, Dorset, DT6 4HB.
Std: 01308 **Tel:** 422424
Std: 01308 **Fax:** 421371
Website: www.parkdeanholidays.com
Nearest Town/Resort Weymouth
Directions A35 from Dorchester. West Bay
is towards the harbour.
Open Easter **to** End Oct
Access Good **Site** Level
Sites Available Å ⊕ ⊟ **Total** 131
Facilities ⅊ ƒ ⅏ ⅃ ⌐ ⊙ ┙ ▱ ☎
⅊ ⅊ ⌂ ⊛ ✗ ♀ ⊡ ♠ ⋔ ⌂ ✸ ╬ ⊡ ⊡ ⊡
Nearby Facilities ⌐ ✓ ⚓ U
✸ Dorchester
Riverside, next to the harbour.

CHARMOUTH

Manor Farm Holiday Centre, Manor
Farm, Charmouth, Bridport, Dorset, DT6
6QL.
Std: 01297 **Tel:** 560226
Std: 01297 **Fax:** 560429
Email:
enq@manorfarmholidaycentre.co.uk
Website:
www.manorfarmholidaycentre.co.uk
Nearest Town/Resort Charmouth.
Directions Come off the Charmouth bypass
at east end Manor Farm is ¾ mile on right,
in Charmouth.
Acreage 30 **Open** All Year
Access Good **Site** Lev/Slope
Sites Available Å ⊕ ⊟ **Total** 345
Facilities ⅊ ƒ ⊞ ⅏ ⅃ ⌐ ⊙ ┙ ▱ ☎
⅊ ⌂ ⊛ ✗ ♀ ♠ ⋔ ✸ ⊛ ╬ ⊡ ⊡ ⊡
Nearby Facilities ⌐ ✓ ⚓ ✗ U ⚲ ♪
✸ Axminster.
Ten minutes level walk to beach, alongside
river. In area of outstanding natural beauty.
Ideal touring.

CHARMOUTH

Monkton Wyld Farm, Charmouth, Dorset,
DT6 6DB.
Std: 01297 **Tel:** 34525
Email: holidays@monktonwyld.co.uk
Website: www.monktonwyld.co.uk
Nearest Town/Resort Charmouth
Directions Take the A35 from Axminster
towards Charmouth, cross the county
boundary into Dorset and almost
immediately turn left down an unmarked
lane. Brown tourist sign only.
Acreage 6 **Open** Easter **to** 30 Oct
Access Good **Site** Level
Sites Available Å ⊕ ⊟ **Total** 60

Facilities ⅊ ƒ ⊡ ⅏ ⅃ ⌐ ⊙ ┙ ▱ ☎
⅊ ⅊ ⌂ ⊛ ♠ ╬ ⊡ ⊡
Nearby Facilities ⌐ ✓ ⚓ ✗ U ⚲ ♪
✸ Axminster
Beautifully landscaped pitches with room to
relax, and space for children to play. Friendly
helpful wardens offer every assistance
Spotless shower block.

CHARMOUTH

Newlands Holidays, Charmouth, Dorset,
DT6 6RB.
Std: 01297 **Tel:** 560259
Email: enq@newlandsholidays.co.uk
Website: www.newlandsholidays.co.uk
Nearest Town/Resort Charmouth/Lyme
Regis
Directions Turn off the A35 at the eastern
exit for Charmouth, Newlands is situated a
short distance on the left hand side.
Acreage 23
Access Good **Site** Terraced
Sites Available Å ⊕ ⊟ **Total** 200
Facilities ⅊ ƒ ⊞ ⅏ ⅃ ⌐ ⊙ ┙ ▱ ☎
⅊ ⅊ ⌂ ⊛ ✗ ♀ ♠ ⋔ ⅃ ✸ ╬ ⊡ ⊡ ⊡
Nearby Facilities ⌐ ✓ ⚓ ✗ U ♪
✸ Axminster
Situated in the Heritage Coast village o
Charmouth, near Lyme Regis. Wonderfu
views and walks through National Trust land
A short stroll to the village centre and safe
beach.

CHARMOUTH

Wood Farm Caravan & Camping Park,
Axminster Road, Charmouth, Bridport,
Dorset DT6 6BT.
Std: 01297. **Tel:** 560697
Std: 01297 **Fax:** 560697
Email: holidays@woodfarm.co.uk
Website: www.woodfarm.co.uk
Nearest Town/Resort Charmouth

Family Seaside Fun at Freshwater Beach
HOLIDAY PARK

Own Private BEACH!

Club Membership FREE! Entertainment *

Fun filled days on privately-owned family park next to our own private beach. Large Camping & Touring fields and Self Catering Holiday Caravans.

- Heated outdoor swimming pools
- Club Complex with licensed restaurant and bars
- Nightly Entertainment (*Whitsun-Mid Sept.)
- Children's activities and amusements
- Beach fishing and wind-surfing
- Horse/Pony Rides
- Supermarket and take-away foods
- Fine country and cliff walks
- Golf course adjoining park
- Caravan sales
- High level of facilities and amenities

FRESHWATER BEACH HOLIDAY PARK
Burton Bradstock, Near Bridport, Dorset DT6 4PT
Tel: 01308 897317 · Fax: 01308 897336
Email: info@freshwaterbeach.co.uk · www.freshwaterbeach.co.uk

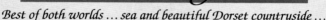

Directions On A35, ½ mile west Charmouth.
Acreage 12
Access Good **Site** Terraced
Sites Available ▲ ⊕ ⊜ **Total** 216
Facilities & ↑ ⊞ ⊞ ⅏ ♨ Γ ⊙ ⌿ ⚄ ⊡ ☎
⅏ ⊡ ⊜ ⚲ ⋔ ⊡ ▣
Nearby Facilities Γ ⌿ ⊿ ⋎ ∪ ⋕ ℛ
⚓ Axminster
Beach ¾ mile. Country setting. Tennis and coarse fishing ponds on site. Indoor heated swimming pool.

CHIDEOCK

Golden Cap Holiday Park, Seatown, Chideock, Nr. Bridport, Dorset, DT6 6JX.
Std: 01308 **Tel:** 422139
Std: 01308 **Fax:** 425672
Email: holidays@wdlh.co.uk
Website: www.wdlh.co.uk
Nearest Town/Resort Bridport
Directions On approach to Bridport from east (Dorchester) follow A35 signs around Bridport by-pass. After 2 miles west of Bridport turn left for Seatown, at Chideock park is signposted.
Acreage 10 **Open** March **to** October
Access Good **Site** Level
Sites Available ▲ ⊕ ⊜ **Total** 120
Facilities & ↑ ⊞ ⊞ ⅏ ♨ Γ ⊙ ⌿ ⚄ ⊡ ☎
⅏ ⊡ ⊜ ⚲ ⋔ ▣
Nearby Facilities Γ ⌿ ℛ
⚓ Axminster
100 metres from beach, overlooked by the famous Golden Cap cliff top. Indoor swimming pool available 5 minutes travelling time. All weather awning areas. Unique location on the Heritage Coastline.

CHRISTCHURCH

Heathfield Caravan & Camping Park, Forest Road, Holmsley, Near Bransgore, Dorset, BH23 8LA.
Std: 01425 **Tel:** 672397
Std: 01425 **Fax:** 672397
Email:
office@heathfieldcaravanpark.co.uk
Nearest Town/Resort Bournemouth
Directions From the traffic lights at Lyndhurst drive 9 miles towards Christchurch on the A35. Turn right signposted Godwinscroft, then first right and the site is 200 yards on the left. From Christchurch turn left after the East Close Hotel, then first right and the site is 200 yards on the left.
Acreage 14 **Open** 1st Weds in March **to** End Oct
Access Good **Site** Level
Sites Available ▲ ⊕ ⊜ **Total** 200
Facilities & ↑ ⊞ ⅏ ♨ Γ ⊙ ⌿ ⚄ ☎
⅏ ⅃⅃ ⊡ ⊜ ⚲ ⋔ ▣
Nearby Facilities Γ ⌿ ∪ ⋕ ℛ
⚓ Hinton Admiral
Well appointed site on the edge of the New Forest. Ideal walking and cycling.

CHRISTCHURCH

Holmsley Caravan & Camping Site - Forestry Commission, Forest Road, Holmsley, Christchurch, Dorset, BH23 7EQ.
Std: 0131 **Tel:** 314 6505

Email: fe.holidays@forestry.gsi.gov.uk
Website: www.forestholidays.co.uk
Nearest Town/Resort Christchurch
Directions Turn west 8 miles southwest of Lyndhurst off the A35 and follow Holmsley Camp Site signs.
Acreage 89 **Open** 21 March **to** 31 October
Access Good **Site** Level
Sites Available ▲ ⊕ ⊜ **Total** 700
Facilities & ↑ ⅏ ♨ Γ ⊙ ⌿ ⚄ ⊡ ☎
⅏ ⊡ ⊜ ⚲ ▣ ▣
Nearby Facilities ∪
⚓ New Milton
Coast within 5 miles. Shop and fast food takeaway on site.

CHRISTCHURCH

Longfield, Matchams Lane, Hurn, Christchurch, Dorset, BH23 6AW.
Std: 01202 **Tel:** 485214
Nearest Town/Resort Christchurch/Bournemouth
Directions A338 into Bournemouth. Hurn road, Christchurch, Wessex Way.
Acreage 2½ **Open** All Year
Access Good **Site** Level
Sites Available ⊕ ⊜ **Total** 20
Facilities ↑ ⅏ ♨ Γ ⊙ ⌿ ⚄ ☎ ⊡ ⊜ ⚲ ⋔
Nearby Facilities Γ ⌿ ⊿ ⋎ ∪
⚓ Christchurch

CHRISTCHURCH

Meadowbank Holidays, Stour Way, Christchurch, Dorset, BH23 2PQ.
Std: 01202 **Tel:** 483597
Std: 01202 **Fax:** 483878
Email: enquiries@meadowbank-holidays.co.uk
Website: www.meadowbank-holidays.co.uk
Nearest Town/Resort Bournemouth
Directions From Ringwood take the A338 towards Bournemouth and turn off for Christchurch, follow caravan signs.
Acreage 2 **Open** March **to** October
Access Good **Site** Level
Sites Available ⊕ ⊜ **Total** 41
Facilities & ↑ ⊞ ⅏ ♨ Γ ⊙ ⌿ ⚄ ⊡ ☎
⅏ ⊡ ⊜ ⚲ ⋔ ▣ ▣
Nearby Facilities Γ ⌿ ⊿ ⋎ ∪ ℛ
⚓ Bournemouth
Riverside setting. Close to Bournemouth, Christchurch and the New Forest.

CHRISTCHURCH

Mount Pleasant Touring Park, Matchams Lane, Hurn, Christchurch, Dorset, BH23 6AW.
Std: 01202 **Tel:** 475474
Email: enq@mount-pleasant-cc.co.uk
Website: www.mount-pleasant-cc.co.uk
Nearest Town/Resort Bournemouth
Directions From Ringwood take the A338, exit at the Christchurch/Airport signs. Follow signs for the Airport until you reach a mini roundabout, then follow camping signs.
Acreage 10 **Open** March **to** October
Access Good **Site** Level
Sites Available ▲ ⊕ ⊜ **Total** 150
Facilities & ↑ ⊞ ⊞ ⅏ ♨ Γ ⊙ ⌿ ⚄ ⊡ ☎
⅏ ⅃⅃ ⊡ ⊜ ✕ ⋔ ⊡ ▣
Nearby Facilities Γ ⌿ ⊿ ⋎ ∪ ⋕ ℛ

⚓ Christchurch
Exceptionally clean, "Excellent Graded" park. Closest camping to Bournemouth. Near to lovely forest walks.

CORFE CASTLE

Burnbake Campsite, Rempstone, Corfe Castle, Dorset, BH20 5JJ.
Std: 01929 **Tel:** 480570 **Fax:** 480626
Email: info@burnbake.com
Website: www.burnbake.com
Nearest Town/Resort Swanage
Directions Between Corfe Castle and Studland just off the B3351. From Wareham take the A351 to Corfe Castle, turn left under the castle onto the Studland road, through the old railway arches, and take the third turning left signposted Rempstone.
Acreage 12 **Open** April **to** September
Site Lev/Slope
Sites Available ▲ ⊜ **Total** 130
Facilities ⅏ ♨ Γ ⊙ ⌿ ⊡ ☎
⅏ ⊡ ⊜ ⊛ ⋔ ⅃
Nearby Facilities Γ ⌿ ⊿ ⋎ ∪ ⋕ ℛ ⋇
⚓ Wareham
A quiet, secluded site in woodlands with a stream. 4 miles from Studland with its three miles of sandy beach and excellent safe bathing. 4 miles from Swanage.

CORFE CASTLE

Knitson Tourers Site, Knitson Farm, Corfe Castle, Dorset, BH20 5JB.
Std: 01929 **Tel:** 425121
Nearest Town/Resort Swanage
Directions Take the A351 to Swanage outskirts, turn first left into Wash Pond Lane. Continue until the lane finishes at a T-Junction turn left. Site is approx. ½ mile further on, on the left hand side.
Acreage 5½ **Open** Easter **to** October
Site Lev/Slope
Sites Available ▲ ⊕ ⊜ **Total** 60
Facilities ☎ ⅏ ⅃⅃ ⊡ ⊜ ⊛ ⋔ ⅃
Nearby Facilities Γ ⌿ ⊿ ⋎ ∪ ⋕ ℛ ⋇
⚓ Wareham
Set in very beautiful countryside with many walks radiating from the field, including Swanage and Studland beaches.

CORFE CASTLE

The Woodland Camping Park, The Glebe, Bucknowle Farm, Wareham, Dorset, BH20 5PQ.
Std: 01929 **Tel:** 480280/480315
Nearest Town/Resort Swanage/Wareham
Directions Take Church Knowle and Kimmeridge road off the A351 at Corfe Castle ruins, site is ½ mile on the right.
Acreage 20 **Open** Easter **to** October
Site Lev/Slope
Sites Available ▲ ⊕ ⊜ **Total** 65
Facilities ↑ ⅏ ♨ Γ ⊙ ☎
⅏ ⊡ ⊜ ⋔ ⊡ ▣
Nearby Facilities Γ ⌿ ⊿ ⋎ ∪ ⋕ ℛ ⋇
Direct access onto Purbeck Hills by public footpath. 3 beaches within 5 miles. A quiet family site. SAE for full information.

CORFE CASTLE

Woodyhyde Camp Site, Valley Road, Corfe Castle, Dorset, BH20 5HT.
Std: 01929 **Tel:** 480274
Email: woodyhydefarm@aol.com
Website: www.woodyhyde.co.uk
Nearest Town/Resort Swanage
Directions From Wareham take the A351 towards Swanage, site is approx. 1 mile past Corfe Castle on the right hand side.
Acreage 13 **Open** April **to** October
Sites Available ▲ ⚏ **Total** 160
Facilities ∮ ⬛ ⚡ ⌐ ⊙ ☎ 𝄞 ⊟ ⬛
Nearby Facilities ⌐ ⚓ ⊁ U ⊿ ⅄
⇌ Wareham
Swanage Steam Railway runs through the site.

DORCHESTER

Giants Head Caravan & Camping Park, Old Sherborne Road, Dorchester, Dorset, DT2 7TR.
Std: 01300 **Tel:** 341242
Nearest Town/Resort Dorchester
Directions From Dorchester avoiding bypass, at top of town roundabout take Sherborne Road approx 500 yards fork right at Loaders Garage signposted. From Cerne Abbas take the Buckland Newton road.
Acreage 3 **Open** March **to** October
Access Good **Site** Lev/Slope
Sites Available ▲ ⚏ ⚏ **Total** 50
Facilities ∮ ⬛ ⚡ ⌐ ⊙ ⊣ ⚊ ⊠ ☎ ⬛ ⊙ ✦ ⊟ ⬛
Nearby Facilities ⌐ ⋗ U
⇌ Dorchester
Ideal touring, wonderful views, good walking. Car is essential. Chalets available for hire.

DORCHESTER

Morn Gate Caravan Park, Bridport Road, Dorchester, Dorset, DT2 9DS.
Std: 01305 **Tel:** 889284
Std: 01202 **Fax:** 669595
Email: morngate@ukonline.co.uk
Nearest Town/Resort Dorchester/Weymouth
Directions 3 miles west of Dorchester on the A35.
Acreage 6¼ **Open** 16 March **to** 12 January
Access Good **Site** Level
Sites Available ▲ ⚏ **Total** 42
Facilities ⬛ ⬛ ⚡ ⌐ ⊙ ⬛ ⚊ 𝄞 ⊟ ⬛ ⬛
Nearby Facilities ⌐ ⋗ ⚓ ⋗ U ⊿
⇌ Dorchester
Quiet select park, near to Weymouth offering a superb beach and eight watersports.

DORCHESTER

Warmwell Country Touring Park, Warmwell, Nr. Dorchester, Dorset, DT2 8JD.
Std: 01305 **Tel:** 852313 **Fax:** 851824
Email: touring@warmwell.fsbusiness.co.uk
Website: www.warmwell.touring.20m.com
Nearest Town/Resort Weymouth
Directions From the A35 Dorchester to Poole road take the B3390 signposted Warmwell.
Acreage 15 **Open** All Year
Access Good **Site** Level
Sites Available ▲ ⚏ ⚏ **Total** 190
Facilities ∮ ⬛ ⬛ ⚡ ⌐ ⊙ ⊣ ⚊ ⊠ ☎ 𝄞 ⬛ ⊙ ☎ ⬛ ⟟ ✦ ⚑ ⊢ ⊟ ⬛
Nearby Facilities ⌐ ⋗ ⚓ ⋗ U ⊿ ℛ
⇌ Moreton
Opposite major leisure attractions. Rallies welcome. Seasonal and storage facilities.

GILLINGHAM

Thorngrove Camping & Caravan Site, Thorngrove House, Common Mead Lane, Gillingham, Dorset, SP8 4RE.
Std: 01747 **Tel:** 821221
Std: 01747 **Fax:** 826386
Nearest Town/Resort Gillingham
Directions Situated off the B3081 Gillingham to Wincanton road, 1 mile from the town, follow caravan signs.
Acreage 2+ **Open** All Year
Access Good **Site** Level
Sites Available ▲ ⚏ ⚏ **Total** 34
Facilities ⚗ ⌐ ⬛ ⬛ ⚡ ⌐ ⊙ ⊣ ☎
𝄞 ⬛ ⊙ ✦ ⊟ ⬛ ⬛
Nearby Facilities ⋗
⇌ Gillingham
Beautiful countryside. Ideal touring.

LULWORTH COVE

Durdle Door Holiday Park, Lulworth Cove, Wareham, Dorset, BH20 5PU.
Std: 01929 **Tel:** 400200
Std: 01929 **Fax:** 400260
Email: durdle@lulworth.com
Website: www.lulworth.com
Nearest Town/Resort Wareham
Directions Take the B3077 Wool to West Lulworth road, fork right in West Lulworth Village, entrance is at the top of the hill.
Acreage 45 **Open** March **to** October
Access Good **Site** Lev/Slope
Sites Available ▲ ⚏ ⚏ **Total** 193
Facilities ∮ ⬛ ⬛ ⚡ ⌐ ⊙ ⊣ ⚊ ⊠ ☎
𝄞 ⬛ ⊙ ☎ ⟟ ⚑ ⊢ ⊟ ⬛
Nearby Facilities ⌐ ⋗ ⚓ ⋗ U
⇌ Wool
Unique cliff top position overlooking the famous landmark of Durdle Door.

Shrubbery
Touring Park
Caravans & Camping

- Electrical Hook Ups
- New Toilet & Shower Block
- Disabled Facilities
- Laundry
- New Play Area
- Quiet Level Site

OFF PEAK SPECIAL OFFERS

Rousdon, Lyme Regis, Dorset. DT7 3XW. Tel: 01297 442227

LYME REGIS

Cummins Farm, Penn Cross, Charmouth, Bridport, Dorset, DT6 6BX.
Std: 01297 **Tel:** 560898
Nearest Town/Resort Lyme Regis
Directions Midway between Charmouth and Lyme Regis, 200 metres from the A3052.
Acreage 5½ **Open** Easter **to** End Sept
Access Good **Site** Level
Sites Available A ⚕ ⛺ **Total** 30
Facilities Ⓤ ☂ ⓁⒺ⅋⊡
Nearby Facilities ⌐ ✓ ⚓ U
⚡ Axminster
Quiet farm site in a rural setting.

LYME REGIS

Shrubbery Touring Park, Rousdon, Lyme Regis, Dorset, DT7 3XW.
Std: 01297 **Tel:** 442227
Nearest Town/Resort Lyme Regis
Directions 3 miles west of Lyme Regis on the A3052.
Acreage 10 **Open** March **to** November
Access Good **Site** Level
Sites Available A ⚕ ⛺ **Total** 120
Facilities ⚒ ∮ ⓊⒺ ⚓ ⌐ ⊙ ⊣ ⬛ ⊡ ☂
⚴ ⓧ ⚙ ⚙ Ⓐ ⌐ ⊟ ⊟ ⊡
Nearby Facilities ⌐ ✓ ⚓ ✕ U ⚓ ℛ
⚡ Axminster
Quiet, level, sheltered site.

LYME REGIS

Westhayes Caravan Park, Rousdon, Nr. Lyme Regis, Dorset, DT7 3RD.
Std: 01297 **Tel:** 23456 **Fax:** 625079
Website: www.welcome.to/westhayes.co.uk
Nearest Town/Resort Lyme Regis/Seaton
Directions Leave Axminster on A358 Seaton road, 3 miles turn left at Boshill Cross signposted Lyme Regis, site 1 mile

on left.
Acreage 7½ **Open** All Year
Access Good **Site** Level
Sites Available A ⚕ ⛺ **Total** 150
Facilities ⚒ ∮ ⓊⒺ ⚓ ⌐ ⊙ ⊣ ⬛ ⊡ ☂
⚴ ⒾⒺ ⓧ ⚙ ⚙ Ⓐ ⚓ ⊬ ⊟ ⊟ ⊡
Nearby Facilities ⌐ ✓ ⚓ ✕ ⚓
⚡ Axminster
Rallies welcome. Storage facilities. Static caravans for sale. Seasonal tourers.

OWERMOIGNE

Sandyholme Holiday Park, Moreton Road, Owermoigne, Nr. Dorchester, Dorset, DT2 8HZ.
Std: 01305 **Tel:** 852677
Email: smeatons@sandyholme.co.uk
Website: www.sandyholme.co.uk
Nearest Town/Resort Dorchester/Weymouth
Directions Situated off the A352 Dorchester/Wareham Road - 1 mile through the pretty village of Owermoigne.
Acreage 6 **Open** Easter **to** October
Access Good **Site** Level
Sites Available A ⚕ ⛺ **Total** 60
Facilities ⚒ ∮ ⓊⒺ ⚓ ⌐ ⊙ ⊣ ⬛ ⊡ ☂
⚴ ⓧ ⚙ ⚙ Ⓐ ⚓ ⊬ ⊟ ⊟ ⊡
Nearby Facilities ⌐ ✓
⚡ Moreton
Quiet family park in Hardy countryside, ideal touring spot with all facilities, situated between Lulworth Cove and Weymouth. Swimming pool nearby.

POOLE

Beacon Hill Touring Park, Blandford Road North, Poole, Dorset, BH16 6AB.
Std: 01202 **Tel:** 631631 **Fax:** 625749
Email: bookings@beaconhilltouringpark.co.uk
Website: www.beaconhilltouringpark.co.uk

Nearest Town/Resort Poole/Bournemouth
Directions Situated on the A350 ¼ mile north of the junction with the A35, between Poole and Blandford.
Acreage 30 **Open** Easter **to** October
Access Good **Site** level
Sites Available A ⚕ ⛺ **Total** 170
Facilities ⚒ ∮ ⓊⒺ ⚓ ⌐ ⊙ ⊣ ⬛ ⊡ ☂
⚴ ⓧ ⚙ ✕ ⓂⒺ ⚙ Ⓐ ⚵ ⊛ ⊬ ⊡
Nearby Facilities ⌐ ✓ ⚓ ✕ U ⚓ ℛ
⚡ Poole
Partly wooded, lovely peaceful setting, scenic views. Proximity main routes. Ideal touring base for Bournemouth, New Forest and Dorset. Coarse fishing, tennis and childrens play areas on site. Take away meals and coffee shop in high season. Proximity to main routes. ETB 3 Star Graded, Bellamy Conservation Award Park, AA 4 Pennants and ANWB Listed.

POOLE

Huntick Farm Caravans, Huntick Farm, Lytchett Matravers, Poole, Dorset, BH16 6BB
Std: 01202 **Tel:** 622222
Nearest Town/Resort Poole
Directions Off the A350 Blandford to Poole road. Take the turning for Lytchett Matravers and at the Rose & Crown Pub turn down Huntick Road. The site is approx. ¾ miles on the right.
Acreage 3 **Open** April **to** October
Access Good **Site** Level
Sites Available A ⚕ ⛺ **Total** 30
Facilities ∮ ⓊⒺ ⚓ ⌐ ⊙ ⊣ ⬛ ⚕ ☂
⊟ Ⓐ ⊛ ⊬
Nearby Facilities ⌐ ✓ ⚓ ✕ U ⚓
⚡ Poole/Wareham
Small, quiet, level grassed site in wooded surroundings. Within 6 miles of a sandy beach. 10% reduction for O.A.P's.

Westhayes
CARAVAN PARK

In an ideal touring location on the borders of Dorset & Devon. The characterful resort of Lyme Regis, three miles, famous for "The French Lieutenants Woman." Seaton, three miles, with its long sea-front & adjoining picturesque village of Beer.

ROUSDON, NR LYME REGIS, DORSET DT7 3RD
www.welcome.to/westhayes

For a colour brochure tel: (01297) 23456

Facilities include:
- OUTDOOR HEATED SWIMMING POOL
- Shop • Bar
- Childrens Playground
- Launderette
- Modern toilet facilities including disabled toilet & family washroom
- Electric hook-ups
- Caravan storage
- Static caravans for sale
- Rallies welcome
- Horse Riding, Golf, fishing, boating & water sports are close by

POOLE

Merley Court Touring Park, Merley, Wimborne, Nr Poole, Dorset, BH21 3AA.
Std: 01202 **Tel:** 881488
Std: 01202 **Fax:** 881484
Email: holidays@merley-court.co.uk
Website: www.merley-court.co.uk
Nearest Town/Resort Poole
Directions Direct access from the A31 Wimborne bypass and the A349 Poole junction.
Acreage 20 **Open** March 1st **to** Jan 7th
Access Good **Site** Level
Sites Available **Total** 160
Facilities
Nearby Facilities
Poole
AA 5 Pennant Premier park. Bournemouth 8 miles, Poole 4 miles, Purbeck and New Forest 7 miles. Caravan Magazine 'Readers' Site of the Year 2001, AA Campsite of the Year 1999, Practical Caravan Magazine 'Best Family Park' 1993 and 1997. Includes a Leisure Garden set in a beautifully landscaped walled garden, with croquet, petanque, beach volleyball, crazy golf and attractive gardens to explore. Pets are welcome but not between 15th July and 1st September.

POOLE

Organford Manor Caravans & Holidays, Organford, Poole, Dorset, BH16 6ES.
Std: 01202 **Tel:** 622202
Email: organford@lds.co.uk
Nearest Town/Resort Poole
Directions Approaching from the Poole direction on the A35. At the Lytchett roundabout/junction of the A35/A351 continue on the A35 (signposted Dorchester) for ¼ mile. Take the first left, site first entrance on right.
Acreage 3 **Open** 15 March **to** October
Access Good **Site** Level
Sites Available **Total** 70
Facilities
Nearby Facilities
Poole/Wareham
Quiet, secluded site in wooded grounds of 11 acres. Seasonal site shop. Site within 10 miles of good beaches, Bournemouth to Swanage. Facilities for the disabled limited, few motorcycles accepted at Proprietors discretion.

POOLE

Pear Tree Touring Park, Organford Road, Holton Heath, Poole, Dorset, BH16 6LA.
Std: 01202 **Tel:** 622434
Std: 01202 **Fax:** 631985
Email: info@visitpeartree.co.uk
Website: www.visitpeartree.co.uk
Nearest Town/Resort Poole
Directions Take A35 Poole/Dorchester road. Turn onto A351 to Wareham at Lytchett Minster. Turn right within 1 mile signposted Organford. Second site on left hand side ½ mile.
Acreage 7½ **Open** April **to** October
Access Good **Site** Level
Sites Available **Total** 125
Facilities
Nearby Facilities
Wareham/Poole
Quiet, family, country park, centrally situated for Bournemouth, Poole and Swanage. The New Forest, the Purbeck Hills and the lovely sandy beaches at Sandbanks and Studland Bay are all within easy reach. Mobile fish and chip van.

POOLE

Rockley Park, Napier Road, Hamworthy, Poole, Dorset, BH15 4LZ.
Std: 08457 **Tel:** 753753
Website: www.british-holidays.co.uk
Nearest Town/Resort Poole
Directions From town centre go over lifting bridge and follow road to traffic lights. Turn left and follow signs for the park.
Open March **to** October
Access Good **Site** Sloping
Sites Available **Total** 75
Facilities
Nearby Facilities
Poole
Direct access to the beach. Kids Club and a full family entertainment programme. Watersports, bowling, multisports court and a Burger King on park. Boat storage facilities. Rose Award.

POOLE

Sandford Holiday Park, Holton Heath, Poole, Dorset, BH16 6JZ.
Std: 01202 **Tel:** 631600
Std: 01202 **Fax:** 625678
Email: sid@weststarholidays.co.uk
Website: www.weststarholidays.co.uk
Nearest Town/Resort Poole
Directions Located on the A351 (signposted Wareham) which branches off the A35 approx. 5 miles west of Poole. Turn right at Holton Heath traffic lights by Texaco Petrol Station, park is on the left.
Acreage 64 **Open** April **to** November
Access Good **Site** Level
Sites Available **Total** 500
Facilities
Nearby Facilities
Wareham

BEACON HILL TOURING PARK,
POOLE, DORSET. TEL: 01202 631631
www.beaconhilltouringpark.co.uk
AA
TOURING PARK
SILVER

SANDFORD *in Dorset*

beautiful spaces *in breathtaking places!*

Four Star award winning Holiday Park in an area of outstanding natural beauty, set in 64 acres of secluded woodland. Close to superb sandy beaches, Poole, Bournemouth and the New Forest.

- ☆ Spacious Level Private Pitches
- ☆ Electric & Super Electric Hook-up
- ☆ **Free** Indoor & Outdoor Heated Pools
- ☆ **Free** Live Nightly Entertainment
- ☆ **Free** Children's Clubs
- ☆ On Park Restaurant, Supermarket, Off Licence, Bars and Take-Away

WESTSTAR *Holiday Parks*

☎ **01202 631 600**

🖥 **www.weststarholidays.co.uk/ca**

@ **touring@weststarholidays.co.uk**

Quote CP

Visit the beautiful Purbeck Hills, Poole Harbour and other superb attractions. Ideal for touring Dorset.

SHAFTESBURY
Blackmore Vale Caravan Park, Sherborne Causeway, Shaftesbury, Dorset, SP7 9PX.
Std: 01747 **Tel:** 852573/851523
Std: 01747 **Fax:** 851671
Website: www.caravancampingsites.co.uk
Nearest Town/Resort Shaftsbury
Open All Year
Access Good **Site** Level
Sites Available A ♥ ♠ **Total** 50
Facilities ♪ ⌂ ⑩ ♣ ♠ ⌐ ⊙ ⌐ ♥
🖰 ♨ ⛝ ⊡ 🖃
Nearby Facilities U
➤ Gillingham
Scenic views, ideal touring.

ST. LEONARDS
Camping International, 229 Ringwood Road, St. Leonards, Nr. Ringwood, Hants, BH24 2SD.
Std: 01202 **Tel:** 872817
Std: 01202 **Fax:** 893986
Email: campint@globalnet.co.uk
Website: www.users.globalnet.co.uk/~campint
Nearest Town/Resort Bournemouth
Directions 2¼ miles west of Ringwood on A31.
Acreage 8 **Open** March to October
Access Good **Site** Level
Sites Available A ♥ ♠ **Total** 205
Facilities ♪ ⌂ ⑩ ♣ ♠ ⌐ ⊙ ⌐ ♣ ⌐ ▣ ♥
🖰 ♨ ♣ ✕ ♬ ⑪ ♠ ⋀ ⟡ ✿ ⊬ ▣ 🖃 ⛝
Nearby Facilities ⌐ ✓ ∪ ₽
➤ Bournemouth.
New Forest, Bournemouth and coast, ideal touring.

ST. LEONARDS
Oakhill Farm Caravan Park, 234 Ringwood Road, St. Leonards, Ringwood, Hampshire, BH24 2SB.
Std: 01202 **Tel:** 876968
Nearest Town/Resort Ringwood
Directions 2½ miles west of Ringwood on A31.
Acreage 36 **Open** 1 April to 31 October
Access Good **Site** Level
Sites Available A ♥ ♠ **Total** 80
Facilities ♪ ⑩ ♣ ⌐ ⊙ ⌐ ▣ ♥ 🖰 ♨ ♣✕🖃
Nearby Facilities
➤ Bournemouth
Within easy reach of the New Forest.

ST. LEONARDS
Shamba Holiday Park, 230 Ringwood Road, St. Leonards, Ringwood, Dorset, BH24 2SB.
Std: 01202 **Tel:** 873302
Email: holidays@shamba.co.uk
Website: www.shamba.co.uk
Nearest Town/Resort Ringwood
Directions Just off the A31 midway between Ringwood and Wimborne.
Acreage 7 **Open** March to October
Access Good **Site** Level
Sites Available A ♥ ♠ **Total** 150
Facilities ♪ ⌂ ⑩ ♣ ⌐ ⊙ ⌐ ♣ ▣ ♥
🖰 ♨ ♣ ♡ ♬ ♠ ⋀ ✿ ✕ ⛝
Nearby Facilities ⌐ ✓ ∆ ✕ ∪
➤ Bournemouth
Close to the New Forest and Bournemouth. AA 3 Pennants.

SWANAGE
Cauldron Barn Farm Caravan Park, Cauldron Barn Road, Swanage, Dorset, BH19 1QQ.
Std: 01929 **Tel:** 422080
Std: 01929 **Fax:** 427870

Email: cauldronbarn@fsbdial.co.uk
Nearest Town/Resort Swanage
Directions Turn left off Victoria Avenue into Northbrook Road, take the third left into Cauldron Barn Road.
Acreage 5 **Open** Mid March **to** Mid Nov
Access Good **Site** Level
Sites Available A ♥ ♠ **Total** 20
Facilities ♪ ⌂ ⑩ ♣ ⌐ ⊙ ⌐ ♣ ▣ ♥
🖰 ♨ ⑩ ♠ ⋀ 🖃 A
Nearby Facilities ⌐ ✓ ∆ ✕ ∪ ₽ ✗
➤ Wareham
A rural site only 800 yards from the beach.

SWANAGE
Downshay Farm, Haycrafts Lane, Swanage, Dorset, BH19 3EB.
Std: 01929 **Tel:** 480316
Email: downshay.pike1@farmersweekly.net
Nearest Town/Resort Swanage
Directions From Corfe Castle take the A351 towards Swanage, at Harmans Cross turn right, ½ mile up the hill, second right.
Acreage 6 **Open** 20 July to 31 August
Site Sloping
Sites Available A □ **Total** 40
Facilities ⑩ ♣ ⌐ ⊙ ⌐ ♥ ✕ 🖃
Nearby Facilities ⌐ ✓ ∆ ✕ ∪ ₽ ✗
➤ Wareham
Beaches, walks and a steam railway.

SWANAGE
Flower Meadow Caravan Park, Haycrafts Lane, Swanage, Dorset, BH19 3EB.
Std: 01929 **Tel:** 480035
Email: hobbs@fmcp.freeserve.co.uk
Nearest Town/Resort Swanage
Directions Take the A351 Wareham to Swanage road, at Harmans Cross crossroads turn south towards the steam railway. Park is 200 yards on the left hand side.

Acreage 2 **Open** April **to** October
Access Good **Site** Lev/Slope
Sites Available ▲ ⊞ ⊟ **Total** 30
Facilities ⅃ ⬚ ⬚ ⬚ 𝄐 ⊙ ⬚ ▣
Nearby Facilities
�³⁵ Wareham
Near a steam railway station that goes to Swanage or Corfe Castle. 3½ miles from the beaches at Swanage.

SWANAGE
Priestway Holiday Park, Priestway, Swanage, Dorset, BH19 2RS.
Std: 01929 **Tel:** 422747/424154
Std: 01929 **Fax:** 421822
Nearest Town/Resort Swanage
Directions Take the A351 from Wareham, 1 mile past 'Welcome to Swanage' sign take the right hand fork into High Street, then the second right into Steer Road and continue up the hill. 5 minute drive from the town and beach.
Acreage 15 **Open** April **to** October
Access Good **Site** Lev/Slope
Sites Available ▲ ⊞ ⊟ **Total** 62
Facilities ⬚ ⅃ ⬚ ⬚ ⬚ 𝄐 ⊙ ⬚ ⬚ ▣ ⬚
𝄞 ⬚ ⬚ ⊞ ⬚
Nearby Facilities ⌐ ✓ ⚓ ⌇ ∪ ⫶ ♝
➳ Wareham
Views of the sea and the Purbeck Hills, lovely cliff walks. 1 mile from the beach. Next door to a public indoor swimming pool.

SWANAGE
Tom's Field Camping & Shop, Tom's Field Road, Langton Matravers, Swanage, Dorset, BH19 3HN.
Std: 01929 **Tel:** 427110
Std: 01929 **Fax:** 427110
Email: tomsfield@hotmail.com
Website: www.tomsfieldcamping.co.uk

Nearest Town/Resort Swanage
Acreage 4½ **Open** Mid March **to** End Oct
Site Lev/Slope
Sites Available ▲ ⊟ **Total** 100
Facilities ⬚ ⬚ ⬚ 𝄐 ⊙ ⬚ ⬚
𝄞 ⬚ ⬚ ⬚ ⊞ ⬚
Nearby Facilities ⚓ ⫶ ♝
➳ Wareham
Set in beautiful countryside, an area of outstanding natural beauty. Coastal walk can br reached in 15 minutes. Pets are welcome if kept on leads.

SWANAGE
Ulwell Cottage Caravan Park, Ulwell, Swanage, Dorset, BH19 3DG.
Std: 01929 **Tel:** 422823
Std: 01929 **Fax:** 421500
Email: enq@ulwellcottagepark.co.uk
Website: www.ulwellcottagepark.co.uk
Nearest Town/Resort Swanage
Directions 1½ miles from Swanage on Studland Road. Turn left by telephone box (left hand side) on side of road.
Open March **to** 7 January
Access Good **Site** Lev/Slope
Sites Available ▲ ⊞ ⊟ **Total** 70
Facilities ⬚ ⅃ ⬚ ⬚ ⬚ 𝄐 ⊙ ⬚ ⬚ ▣ ⬚
𝄞 ⬚ ⬚ ✕ ⬚ ⬚ ⬚ ✳ ⊞ ▣ ▣
Nearby Facilities ⌐ ✓ ⚓ ⌇ ∪ ⫶ ♝
➳ Wareham
Near sandy beaches, scenic walks and ideal for all water sports. Rose Award.

SWANAGE
Ulwell Farm Caravan Park, Ulwell, Swanage, Dorset, BH19 3DG.
Std: 01929 **Tel:** 422825
Website: www.ukparks.co.uk/ulwellfarm
Nearest Town/Resort Swanage
Directions Approx. 1½ miles from Swanage

on the road towards Studland and Sandbanks Chain Ferry. Park entrance is on the right 150 metres after the end of 30mph limit.
Acreage 2½ **Open** April **to** September
Access Good **Site** Sloping
Sites Available ▲ ⊞ ⊟ **Total** 5
Facilities ⅃ ⬚ ⬚ 𝄐 ⊙ ⬚ ⬚ ▣ ⬚
⬚ ⬚ ⬚ ⊞ ▣
Nearby Facilities ⌐ ✓ ⚓ ⌇ ∪ ⫶ ♝
➳ Wareham
Situated in an area of outstanding varied countryside and coastal scenery. Safe bathing and water sports nearby.

WAREHAM
Birchwood Tourist Park, North Trigon, Wareham, Dorset, BH20 7PA.
Std: 01929 **Tel:** 554763
Std: 01929 **Fax:** 556635
Nearest Town/Resort Wareham
Directions Located 3 miles north-west of Wareham in Wareham Forest. From Wareham Railway Station roundabout follow signs for Bere Regis. After 2¼ miles park is on the right.
Acreage 25 **Open** March **to** October
Access Good **Site** Level
Sites Available ▲ ⊞ ⊟ **Total** 175
Facilities ⅃ ⬚ ⬚ 𝄐 ⊙ ⬚ ▣ ⬚
𝄞 ⬚ ⬚ ⬚ ✳ ⊞ ▣ ▣
Nearby Facilities ⌐ ✓ ⚓ ⌇ ∪ ⫶ ♝
➳ Wareham
Situated in Wareham Forest with direct access to forest walks. Ideal for touring the whole of Dorset.

WAREHAM
East Creech Farm Caravan & Camping Site, East Creech Farm, East Creech, Wareham, Dorset, BH20 5AP.

Std: 01929 **Tel:** 480519
Std: 01929 **Fax:** 481312
Email: debbie.best@euphony.net
Website: www.pages.euphony.net/debbie.best/holiday
Nearest Town/Resort Wareham
Directions Take the Wareham bypass, at the Stoborough roundabout take the Blue Pool road. Site is on the right ½ mile past The Blue Pool entrance.
Acreage 2½ **Open** 31 March **to** 31 Oct
Access Good **Site** Lev/Slope
Sites Available ▲ ⊕ ⊕ **Total** 60
Facilities ƒ ⬚ ⬚ ⊙ ⊙ ♥ ⋔ ⊬ ⊡
Nearby Facilities ✔
✦ Wareham
Quiet family site, ideal for walking.

WAREHAM

Lookout Holiday Park, Stoborough, Wareham, Dorset, BH20 5AZ.
Std: 01929 **Tel:** 552546
Std: 01929 **Fax:** 556662
Email: enquiries@caravan-sites.co.uk
Website: www.caravan-sites.co.uk
Nearest Town/Resort Wareham
Directions 1 mile south of Wareham on the Swanage road.
Acreage 15 **Open** April **to** October
Access Good **Site** Level
Sites Available ▲ ⊕ ⊕ **Total** 150
Facilities ƒ ⬚ ⬚ ⚲ ⊙ ⊙ ⊣ ♥ ⚑ ⊡ ⬚
⊠ ⊙ ⊠ ⚵ ⊡ ⊡
Nearby Facilities ⊢ ✔ ⚓ ⚘ ∪ ♣
✦ Wareham
Ideal for touring the Purbecks and Studland Bay. For Touring Caravans we are open All Year, Static Caravans February to the end of November.

WAREHAM

Luckford Wood Caravan & Camping Park, Luckford Wood House, East Stoke, Wareham, Dorset, BH20 6AW.
Std: 01929 **Tel:** 463098
Std: 01929 **Fax:** 405715
Email: info@luckfordleisure.co.uk
Website: www.luckfordleisure.co.uk
Nearest Town/Resort Wareham/Lulworth Cove
Directions From Wareham take the A352 to Wool, turn left onto the B3070 to Lulworth Cove. At West Holme crossroads turn right to Wool, entrance is 1 mile on the right hand side.
Acreage 6 **Open** April **to** September
Access Good **Site** Level
Sites Available ▲ ⊕ ⊕ **Total** 100
Facilities ƒ ⬚ ⬚ ⚲ ⊙ ⊙ ⊣ ♥ ⬚ ⊬ ⊡
Nearby Facilities ⊢ ✔ ⚓ ⚘ ∪ ♪ ♣ ♣
✦ Wool
Family run park with a personal service. Wooded and shaded areas, stream and ancient droveway. Camp fires allowed in designated areas. Boule pitch and picnic area. Adult Only areas available. Caravan storage available. Closest site to Durdle Door and Lulworth Cove in the area.

WAREHAM

Manor Farm Caravan Park, 1 Manor Farm Cottage, East Stoke, Wareham, Dorset, BH20 6AW.
Std: 01929 **Tel:** 462870 **Fax:** 462870
Email: info@manorfarmcp.co.uk
Website: www.manorfarmcp.co.uk
Nearest Town/Resort Wareham/Lulworth Cove
Directions From Wareham take the A352 to East Stoke. Turn left by redundant church and the park is ½ mile along the lane, third drive on the right. Or take the B3070 and

turn into Holme Lane, at the crossroads turn right signposted Manor Farm CP. Or from Wool turn down Bindon Lane, at the crossroads turn left signposted Manor Farm CP, site is 300 yards on the left.
Acreage 2½ **Open** Easter **to** September
Access Good **Site** Level
Sites Available ▲ ⊕ ⊕ **Total** 50
Facilities ⚹ ⚸ ƒ ⬚ ⬚ ⚲ ⊙ ⊣ ♥
⊠ ⊙ ⬚ ⬚ ⚑ ⊡ ⊡
Nearby Facilities ⊢ ✔ ⚓ ⚘ ∪ ♪ ♣
✦ Wool/Wareham
Flat, grass touring park on a working farm in a rural area of outstanding natural beauty, central for most of Dorset. Family run park with clean facilities. Resident Proprietors David & Gillian Topp. A.A. 3 Pennant, RAC Appointed - Alan Roger Good Sites Guide. No groups or singles. No motorcycles or rallies. Bed & Breakfast also available.

WAREHAM

Ridge Farm Camping & Caravan Park, Barnhill Road, Ridge, Wareham, Dorset, BH20 5BG.
Std: 01929 **Tel:** 556444 **Fax:** 556222
Email: ridge.farm@u.genie.co.uk
Website: www.ridgefarm.co.uk
Nearest Town/Resort Wareham
Directions Approx. 1½ miles south of Wareham turn left in the village of Stoborough towards Ridge. Follow signs down Barnhill Road to Ridge Farm at the end of the lane.
Acreage 3½ **Open** Easter **to** October
Access Good **Site** Level
Sites Available ▲ ⊕ ⊕ **Total** 60
Facilities ƒ ⬚ ⚲ ⊙ ⊙ ⊣ ♥ ⚑ ⊡ ⬚ ♥
⊠ ⊙ ⬚ ⊡
Nearby Facilities ⊢ ✔ ⚓ ⚘ ∪ ♪ ♣ ♣
✦ Wareham
Peaceful, family run site adjacent to a

WAREHAM FOREST TOURIST PARK

Family Site, set in 40 acres of woodlands.
Open grassy spaces. Direct access to Forest Walks.

☆ Heated Swimming Pool (Peak)
☆ Children's Paddling Pool (Peak)
☆ Indoor Games Room
☆ Children Adventure Playground
☆ Individual Cubicles in Toilets
☆ Fully Serviced Pitches
☆ Launderettes
☆ Shop & Off Licence (Peak)
☆ Snack Bar/Takeaway (Peak)
☆ Disabled Facilities
☆ Toilet Block Heated During Winter

Credit Cards Accepted

OPEN ALL YEAR

For further details and free colour brochure
write or phone: **Peter & Pam Savage**
Wareham Forest Tourist Park
North Trigon, Wareham, Dorset BH20 7NZ

Tel & Fax: (01929) 551393
E-mail: holiday@wareham-forest.co.uk
Website: www.wareham-forest.co.uk

working farm and RSPB Reserve. In an area of outstanding natural beauty and ideally situated for the Purbeck Hills, Poole Harbour and the coast. Boat launching nearby.

WAREHAM

Wareham Forest Tourist Park, North Trigon, Wareham, Dorset, BH20 7NZ.
Std: 01929 **Tel:** 551393
Std: 01929 **Fax:** 551393
Email: holiday@wareham-forest.co.uk
Website: www.wareham-forest.co.uk
Nearest Town/Resort Wareham
Directions Located midway between Wareham and Bere Regis (off the A35).
Open All Year
Access Good **Site** Level
Sites Available ▲ ⚌ ⚌ **Total** 200
Facilities ...
Nearby Facilities ┌ ✔ ⚓ ≗ ∪ ♪
≉ Wareham
Forest and wild life. Heated toilet block during the winter period.

WAREHAM

Woodlands Camping Park Ltd., Bindon Lane, East Stoke, Wareham, Dorset, BH20 6AS.
Std: 01929 **Tel:** 462327 **Fax:** 462327
Email: woodlandscamping@zoom.co.uk
Website: www.resort-guide.co.uk/woodlands
Nearest Town/Resort Wareham
Directions At Wareham take the A352 to Wool. In Wool go over the railway crossing and turn immediately left past station. On a right hand bend turn left, site is approx 1½ miles on the right.
Acreage 2 **Open** All Year
Site Level
Sites Available ▲ **Total** 40

Facilities ...
Nearby Facilities ┌ ✔ ⚓ ∪
≉ Wool
Situated on the Purbeck Cycle Way. Near to Lulworth Cove and Durdle Door.

WEYMOUTH

Bagwell Farm Touring Park, Bagwell Farm, Chickerell, Weymouth, Dorset, DT3 4EA.
Std: 01305. **Tel:** 782575
Email: enquiries@bagwellfarm.co.uk
Website: www.bagwellfarm.co.uk
Nearest Town/Resort Weymouth
Directions 4 miles from Weymouth, take the Bridport road, site entrance 500 yards past Victoria Inn on B3157.
Acreage 14 **Open** All Year
Access Good **Site** Lev/Slope
Sites Available ▲ ⚌ ⚌ **Total** 320
Facilities ...
Nearby Facilities ┌ ✔ ⚓ ≗ ∪ ♪ ♫ ⚡
≉ Weymouth
Views of The Fleet and Chesil Beach. New bar with restaurant on site. Take-away food available.

WEYMOUTH

East Fleet Farm Touring Park, Fleet Lane, Chickerell, Weymouth, Dorset, DT3 4DW.
Std: 01305 **Tel:** 785768
Email: enquiries@eastfleet.co.uk
Website: www.eastfleet.co.uk
Nearest Town/Resort Weymouth
Directions 3 miles west of Weymouth on the B3157, left at Chickerell T.A. Camp.
Acreage 20 **Open** 16 March **to** 15 Jan
Access Good **Site** Lev/Slope
Sites Available ▲ ⚌ ⚌ **Total** 210

Facilities ...
Nearby Facilities ┌ ✔ ⚓ ≗ ∪ ♪ ♫
≉ Weymouth
On edge of Fleet Water. Area of outstanding natural beauty.

WEYMOUTH

Littlesea Holiday Park, Lynch Lane, Weymouth, Dorset, DT4 9DT.
Std: 01305 **Tel:** 774414
Std: 01305 **Fax:** 760038
Website: www.havenholidays.co.uk
Nearest Town/Resort Weymouth
Directions Leave the M5 and follow signs for Weymouth, very well signposted.
Open Beg April **to** End Oct
Access Good **Site** Lev/Slope
Sites Available ▲ ⚌ ⚌ **Total** 150
Facilities ...
Nearby Facilities ┌ ✔ ⚓ ≗ ∪ ♪ ♫
≉ Weymouth
Overlooking Chesil Beach.

WEYMOUTH

Pebble Bank Caravan Park, 90 Camp Road, Wyke Regis, Weymouth, Dorset, DT4 9HF.
Std: 01305 **Tel:** 774844
Std: 01305 **Fax:** 774844
Email: info@pebblebank.co.uk
Website: www.pebblebank.co.uk
Nearest Town/Resort Weymouth
Directions From harbour roundabout up hill to mini roundabout, turn right onto Wyke Road. Camp Road is 1 mile at the apex of a sharp right hand bend, at the bottom of hill.
Acreage 7½ **Open** Easter/1 April **to** 4 Oct
Access Good **Site** Lev/Slope
Sites Available ▲ ⚌ ⚌ **Total** 140

Facilities ⚹ 🆔 🛉 ⌂ ☺ 🚿 🍴 🛒 🍽
🏧 🐕 ⚓ 🔥 🛉 🚃
Nearby Facilities ⌂ 🚴 ⚓ 🛶 ∪ 🎣 ♠ 🏇
🏊 Weymouth
You can also call us on: FREE PHONE 0500 242656. Debit Cards accepted.

WEYMOUTH

Portesham Dairy Farm Camp Site,
Bramdon Lane, Portesham, Weymouth,
Dorset, DT3 4HG.
Std: 01305 **Tel:** 871297 **Fax:** 871297
Nearest Town/Resort Weymouth
Directions 7 miles from Weymouth on
B3157 Coast road.
Acreage 3 **Open** 16 March **to** 31 Oct
Access Good **Site** Level
Sites Available ▲ 🚐 🚃 **Total** 60
Facilities ⚹ ⚹ 🆔 🛉 ⌂ ☺ 🚿 🍴 🛒 🍽
🏊 🐕 🚿 🔥 🛒
Nearby Facilities 🚴 ♠
🏊 Weymouth
Ideal touring for Chesil area.

WEYMOUTH

Sea Barn Farm, Fleet, Weymouth,
Dorset, DT3 4ED.
Std: 01305 **Tel:** 782218 **Fax:** 775396
Email: wib@seabarn.fsnet.co.uk
Website: www.weymouth.gov.uk/
tour3.htm
Nearest Town/Resort Weymouth
Directions From Weymouth take the B3157
towards Bridport. After 2½ miles at the mini
roundabout turn left, after 1 mile towards the
sea Sea Barn Farm is signposted left.
Acreage 12 **Open** Easter **to** 31 October
Sites Available ▲ ☐ **Total** 250
Facilities ⚹ 🆔 🛉 ⌂ ☺ 🚿 🍴 🛒 🍽
🏊 🐕 🚿 ✕ 🍴 🛒 ♠ 🔥 ☀ 🛒
Nearby Facilities ⌂ 🚴 ⚓ 🛶 ∪ 🏇

🏊 Weymouth
A beautiful situation with panoramic sea and
countryside views, overlooking Portland
Chesil Beach and The Fleet Nature Reserve.

WEYMOUTH

Seaview Holiday Park, Preston,
Weymouth, Dorset, DT6 6DZ.
Std: 01305 **Tel:** 833037
Website: www.havenholidays.com
Nearest Town/Resort Weymouth
Directions Take the A353 from the centre
of Weymouth, along the seawall to Preston.
Seaview is ½ mile beyond the village, up
the hill on the right.
Open Easter **to** October
Site Sloping
Sites Available ▲
Facilities ⚹ 🆔 🛉 ⌂ ☺ 🚿 🍴 🛒 🍽
🏊 🎱 🐕 🚿 ✕ 🍴 🛒 ♠ 🔥 🛒 🛒
Nearby Facilities ⌂ 🚴 ∪
🏊 Weymouth
Nestles on a hillside looking out over the
charming Bowleaze Cove.

WEYMOUTH

Waterside Holiday Park, Bowleaze Cove,
Weymouth, Dorset, DT3 6PP
Std: 01305 **Tel:** 833103 **Fax:** 832830
Email: info@watersideholidays.co.uk
Website: www.watersideholidays.co.uk
Nearest Town/Resort Weymouth
Directions 1½ miles from Weymouth town
centre heading east on the A353.
Acreage 35 **Open** 1 April **to** 3 Nov
Access Good **Site** Level
Sites Available ▲ 🚐 🚃 **Total** 120
Facilities & ⚹ ⚹ 🆔 🛉 ⌂ ☺ 🚿
🛒 🏊 🐕 🚿 ✕ 🍴 🛒 ♠ 🔥 ☀ 🛒 🛒
Nearby Facilities ⌂ 🚴 ⚓ 🛶 ∪ 🎣 ♠ 🏇
🏊 Weymouth
Situated in Bowleaze Cove, alongside the
edge of Weymouth Bay.

WEYMOUTH

West Fleet Holiday Farm, Fleet,
Weymouth, Dorset, DT3 4ED.
Std: 01305 **Tel:** 782218 **Fax:** 775396
Email: wib@seabarn.fsnet.co.uk
Website: www.weymouth.gov.uk/
tour3.htm
Nearest Town/Resort Weymouth
Directions From Weymouth take the B3157
towards Bridport. After 2½ miles at the ONLY
mini roundabout turn left, after 1 mile turn
right at the sign.
Acreage 12 **Open** Easter **to** 31 October
Access Good **Site** Level
Sites Available ▲ 🚃 **Total** 250
Facilities ⚹ 🆔 🛉 ⌂ ☺ 🚿 🍴 🛒 🍽
🏊 🐕 🚿 ✕ 🍴 🛒 ♠ 🔥 ☀ 🛒
Nearby Facilities ⌂ 🚴 ⚓ ∪ 🏇
🏊 Weymouth
Beautiful Dorset countryside. Countryside
walks, links to the coastal path. Children's
favourite with heated swimming pool,
clubhouse and plenty of space.

WEYMOUTH

Weymouth Bay Holiday Park, Preston,
Weymouth, Dorset, DT3 6BQ.
Std: 01305 **Tel:** 832271 **Fax:** 825101
Website: www.havenholidays.com
Nearest Town/Resort Weymouth
Directions On the A353 Weymouth to
Preston road, on the right about 10 minutes
drive from Weymouth.
Open Easter **to** October
Access Good **Site** Level
Sites Available 🚐 🚃 **Total** 50
Facilities & 🚿 ⚹ 🆔 🛉 ⌂ ☺ 🚿 🛒 🍽
🏊 🐕 🚿 ✕ 🍴 🛒 ♠ 🔥 ☀ 🛒 🛒
Nearby Facilities ⌂ 🚴 ⚓ ∪
🏊 Weymouth
Excellent indoor and outdoor swimming
pools.

WIMBORNE

Charris Camping & Caravan Park,
Candy's Lane, Corfe Mullen, Wimborne,
Dorset, BH21 3EF.
Std: 01202 **Tel:** 885970
Email: jandjcharris@iclway.co.uk
Website: www.charris.co.uk
Nearest Town/Resort Wimborne
Directions A31 Wimborne bypass 1 mile
west of Wimborne. Signs for entrance.
Acreage 3 **Open** March **to** January
Access Good **Site** Lev/Slope
Sites Available A ♏ ♐ **Total** 45
Facilities ƒ ⅋ ♏ ♐ ♐ ⊙ ⊐ ⚐ ▣ ▦
♏ ▯♐ ♐ ♐ ▤ ▤
Nearby Facilities ♐ ✓ ⚓ ⚡ ∪ ♐ ♐
✈ Poole.
4 Star Graded Park, Caravan Club listed,
Caravan and Camping Club listed. Good
central site convienient for coast and New
Forest. Poole 7½ miles, Bournemouth 8¼
miles. Good overnight stop for Cherbourg
ferry. Cafe/restaurant close by.

WIMBORNE

Springfield Touring Park, Candys Lane,
Corfe Mullen, Wimborne, Dorset, BH21
3EF.
Std: 01202 **Tel:** 881719
Nearest Town/Resort Wimborne
Directions 1¼ miles west of Wimborne just
off main A31.
Acreage 3½ **Open** Mid March **to** October
Access Good **Site** Lev/Slope
Sites Available A ♏ ♐ **Total** 45
Facilities ♐ ƒ ♏ ♐ ♐ ⊙ ⊐ ⚐ ▣ ▦
♏ ▯♐ ♐ ♐ ♐ ▤
Nearby Facilities ♐ ✓ ⚓ ⚡ ∪ ♐ ♐
✈ Poole
Family run park, overlooking the Stour
Valley. Free showers and awnings.
Convenient for the coast, New Forest also
ferry. Low Season Offers - £40.00, any 7
days for 2 adults plus electric. Members of
the BH & HPA.

WIMBORNE

Wilksworth Farm Caravan Park,
Cranborne Road, Wimborne, Dorset,
BH21 4HW.
Std: 01202 **Tel:** 885467
Website:
www.wilksworthfarmcaravanpark.co.uk
Nearest Town/Resort Wimborne Minster
Directions Take the B3078 from Wimborne
towards Cranborne, we are 1 mile north of
Wimborne on the left hand side.
Acreage 11 **Open** March **to** October
Access Good **Site** Level
Sites Available A ♏ ♐ **Total** 85
Facilities ♐ ƒ ♏ ♏ ♐ ♐ ⊙ ⊐ ⚐ ▣ ▦
♏ ▯♐ ♐ ⚑ ♐ ⚙ ✖ ▦ ▣
Nearby Facilities ♐ ✓ ⚓ ⚡ ∪ ♐ ♐ ♐
✈ Poole
Rural location on a working farm. Park
surrounds a Grade II listed house that once
belonged to Henry VIII.

WOOL

Whitemead Caravan Park, East Burton
Road, Wool, Dorset, BH20 6HG.
Std: 01929 **Tel:** 462241 **Fax:** 462241
Email: nadinechurch@aol.com
Website:
www.whitemeadcaravanpark.co.uk
Nearest Town/Resort Wareham
Directions Off the A352 Wareham to
Weymouth road. 5 miles west of Wareham
and 5 miles north of Lulworth Cove.
Acreage 5 **Open** April **to** End October
Access Good **Site** Level
Sites Available A ♏ ♐ **Total** 95

Facilities ƒ ♏ ♐ ♐ ♐ ⊙ ⊐ ⚐ ▣ ▦
♏ ▯♐ ♐ ⚑ ♐ ♐ ⊛ ⚙ ▣ ▣
Nearby Facilities ♐ ✓ ⚓ ∪ ♐ ♐ ♐ ♐
✈ Wool
Woodland site with several secluded
pitches. Off licence and take-away food
available on site.

DURHAM

BARNARD CASTLE

Bendholm Farm Caravan Park,
Eggleston, Barnard Castle, Co. Durham,
DL12 0AX.
Std: 01833 **Tel:** 650457
Email: bendholm@lineone.net
Nearest Town/Resort Barnard Castle
Directions On the B6278 from Barnard
Castle.
Open March **to** October
Access Good **Site** Level
Sites Available A ♏ ♐
Facilities ƒ ▣ ♏ ♏ ♐ ♐ ⊙ ⊐ ⚐
♏ ▯♐ ⊙ ♐
Nearby Facilities ♐ ✓ ⚓ ⚡ ∪ ♐
✈ Darlington

BARNARD CASTLE

Camping & Caravanning Club Site,
Dockenflatts Lane, Lartington, Barnard
Castle, Co. Durham, DL12 9DG.
Std: 01833 **Tel:** 630228
Website:
www.campingandcaravanningclub.co.uk
Directions On approach from Scotch
Corner take the second turn right for
Middleton in Teesdale and Barnard Castle.
On approach from Penrith take the B6277
to Middleton in Teesdale. In approx 1 mile
take turn off left signposted Raygill Riding
Stables. The site is 500 metres on the left.
Acreage 10 **Open** March **to** October
Site Level
Sites Available A ♏ ♐ **Total** 90
Facilities ♐ ƒ ♏ ♐ ♐ ⊙ ⊐ ⚐ ▣ ▦
▯♐ ⊙ ♐ ▦ ⚑ ▣ ▣
Nearby Facilities ♐ ✓ ∪ ♐
✈ Darlington
Well placed for exploring the Pennines and
the city of Durham. AA 4 Pennants and BTB
Graded. Non members welcome.

BARNARD CASTLE

Cote House Caravan Park, Middleton-in-
Teesdale, Barnard Castle, Co. Durham,
DL12 0PN.
Std: 01833 **Tel:** 640515
Nearest Town/Resort Middleton-in-
Teesdale
Directions From Middleton-in-Teesdale
travel south to Mickleton, turn towards
Grassholme Reservoir, site entrance is
adjacent.
Acreage 16 **Open** March **to** October
Access Good **Site** Level
Sites Available A ♏ ♐ **Total** 20
Facilities ♏ ♐ ♐ ⊙ ⊐
Nearby Facilities ♐ ✓ ⚓ ⚡ ∪ ♐
✈ Darlington
By the River Lune.

BARNARD CASTLE

Hetherick Caravan Park, Marwood,
Barnard Castle, County Durham, DL12
8QX.
Std: 01833 **Tel:** 631173
Std: 01833 **Fax:** 690426
Nearest Town/Resort Barnard Castle
Directions 3 miles from Barnard Castle.
Take the B6278 towards Eggleston and

Middleton-in-Teesdale, take second right
turn towards Kinninvie and Woodland.
Acreage 15 **Open** March **to** October
Access Good **Site** Level
Sites Available A ♏□ **Total** 41
Facilities ♏ ƒ ♏ ♏ ♐ ♐ ⊙ ⊐ ⚐ ▣ ▦
♏ ▯ ⊙ ♐ ♏ ▦ ▣
Nearby Facilities ♐ ✓ ∪ ♐
✈ Darlington
Pleasant park situated on a working farm,
in the heart of beautiful Teesdale. 3 miles
from the pretty market town of Barnard
Castle.

BARNARD CASTLE

Pecknell Farm Caravan Site, Pecknell
Farm, Lartington, Barnard Castle, Co.
Durham, DL12 9DF.
Std: 01833 **Tel:** 638357
Nearest Town/Resort Barnard Castle
Directions 1½ miles from Barnard Castle
on the B6277 to Lartington, we are the first
farm on the right.
Acreage 1½ **Open** March **to** October
Access Good **Site** Level
Sites Available A ♏ ♐ **Total** 15
Facilities ƒ ▣ ♏ ♐ ♐ ⊙ ⊐ ▣ ⚑ ▦
Nearby Facilities ♐ ✓ ∪ ♐
✈ Darlington
Ideal walking area, very attractive walk into
historic Barnard Castle. Within easy reach
of many attractions.

BARNARD CASTLE

Thorpe Hall, Wycliffe, Barnard Castle, Co.
Durham, DL12 9TW.
Std: 01833 **Tel:** 627230
Std: 01833 **Fax:** 627471
Nearest Town/Resort Barnard Castle
Directions From Barnard Castle take the
Whorlton road, at the T-junction turn right,
go over the bridge, up the hill and turn right,
site entrance is ¼ mile on the left.
Open March **to** October
Access Good **Site** Level
Sites Available A ♏ ♐ **Total** 10
Facilities ƒ ▣ ♏ ♐ ♐ ⊙ ⊐ ⚐ ▣ ▦
▣ ▦ ▯ ▣
Nearby Facilities ♐ ✓ ∪ ♐
✈ Darlington
In a quiet location, near a river, in the
grounds of a country house. Excellent
walking.

BARNARD CASTLE

Winston Caravan Park, The Old Forge,
Winston, Darlington, Co. Durham, DL2
3RH.
Std: 01325 **Tel:** 730228
Std: 01325 **Fax:** 730228
Email: m.willetts@ic24.net
Website: www.touristnetuk.com/ne/
winston
Nearest Town/Resort Darlington
Directions From Darlington take the A67
west for 10 miles, turn left onto the B6274
into Winston Village, site is 400 yards on
the right hand side.
Open March **to** October
Access Good **Site** Level
Sites Available A ♏ ♐ **Total** 21
Facilities ƒ ♏ ♏ ♐ ♐ ⊙ ⊐ ⚐ ▣ ▦
♏ ⊙ ♐ ▣
Nearby Facilities ♐ ✓ ⚡ ∪ ♐
✈ Darlington
Ideally situated for exploring the many
attractions in County Durham.

BEAMISH

Bobby Shafto Caravan Park, Cranberry Plantation, Beamish, Co. Durham, DH9 0RY.
Std: 0191 **Tel:** 370 1776
Std: 0191 **Fax:** 370 1776
Nearest Town/Resort Chester-le-Street
Directions Leave the A1(M) at junction 63 (Chester-le-Street) and follow signs for 4 miles along the A693 to Stanley. From the North West take the A68 heading south to Castleside and follow the signs along the A692 and the A693 via Stanley.
Acreage 9 **Open** March **to** October
Access Good **Site** Lev/Slope
Sites Available A ⊕ ⊕ **Total** 40
Facilities ⌖ ⬚ ⬚ ♨ ⌐ ⊙ ➘ ⬚ ☎
⬚ ⬚ ⬚ ♀ ⬚ ⬚ ⬚ ⬚
Nearby Facilities ⌐ ✔ ∪ ⋆
➤ Durham
Adjacent to the World famous Beamish Museum.

BISHOP AUCKLAND

Witton Castle Caravan & Camping Site, Witton Le Wear, Bishop Auckland, Co. Durham, DL14 0DE.
Std: 01388 **Tel:** 488230
Std: 01388 **Fax:** 488008
Website: www.wittoncastle.com
Nearest Town/Resort Bishop Auckland
Directions On A68 signposted between Toft Hill and Witton le Wear.
Acreage 30 **Open** March **to** October
Access Good **Site** Lev/Slope
Sites Available ⌖ A ⊕ ⊕ **Total** 280
Facilities ⌖ ⬚ ♨ ⌐ ⊙ ➘ ⬚ ☎
⬚ ⬚ ⬚ ✕ ♀ ⬚ ⬚ ⬚ ⬚ ⬚
Nearby Facilities ⌐ ✔ ∪ ⋆
➤ Bishop Auckland
Set in central Co Durham in an area of outstanding natural beauty.

CONSETT

Manor Park, The Caravan Park, Broadmeadows, Castleside, Consett, Co. Durham, DH8 9HD.
Std: 01207 **Tel:** 501000
Std: 01207 **Fax:** 590271
Website: www.manor-park-caravan-site.co.uk
Nearest Town/Resort Consett
Directions Just off the A68, 3¼ miles south of Castleside (signposted Broadmeadows).
Acreage 7 **Open** April **to** October
Access Good **Site** Lev/Slope
Sites Available A ⊕ ⊕ **Total** 40
Facilities ♿ ⌖ ⬚ ♨ ⌐ ⊙ ➘ ⬚ ☎
⬚ ⬚ ⬚ ⬚ ⬚ ⬚
Nearby Facilities ⌐ ✔ ⬚
➤ Durham
Bordering a designated area of outstanding natural beauty.

DURHAM

Finchale Abbey Farm, Finchale Abbey (Priory), Co. Durham, DH1 5SH.
Std: 0191 **Tel:** 386 6528
Std: 0191 **Fax:** 386 8593
Email: godricawatson@hotmail.com
Website: www.finchaleabbey.co.uk
Nearest Town/Resort Durham City
Directions Off the A1M north of Durham and head south onto the A167, over four roundabouts and at the fifth roundabout turn left (Arnison Centre) and follow signs for Finchale Priory.
Open All Year
Access Good **Site** Lev/Slope
Sites Available A ⊕ ⊕ **Total** 80
Facilities ♿ ⌖ ⬚ ⬚ ♨ ⌐ ⊙ ➘ ⬚ ☎
⬚ ⬚ ✕ ♀ ⬚ ⬚ ⬚ ⬚
Nearby Facilities ⌐ ✔ ⋆

➤ Durham
Historic Site situated in a meander of the River Wear. Surrounded by beautiful countryside, overlooking the ruins of the Priory.

HARTLEPOOL

Ash Vale Holiday Park, Ash Vale, Easington Road, Hartlepool, Co. Durham, TS24 9RF.
Std: 01429 **Tel:** 862111
Std: 01429 **Fax:** 862111
Email: ashvale@compuserve.com
Website: www.ashvalepark.com
Nearest Town/Resort Hartlepool
Directions Take the A179 off the A19, at the third roundabout turn first left, across the next roundabout and we are 300 yards on the left.
Acreage 6
Access Good **Site** Level
Sites Available A ⊕ ⊕ **Total** 30
Facilities ⌖ ⬚ ♨ ⌐ ⊙ ➘ ⬚ ☎
⬚ ⬚ ⬚ ⬚ ⬚ ⬚
Nearby Facilities ⌐ ✔ ⬚ ⋆ ∪ ⋆
➤ Hartlepool
1 mile from a long sandy beach. 3 miles from Historic Ships Museum.

MIDDLETON-IN-TEESDALE

Mickleton Mill Caravan Park, The Mill, Mickleton, Barnard Castle, Co. Durham, DL12 0LS.
Std: 01833 **Tel:** 640317
Std: 01833 **Fax:** 640317
Email: mickletonmill@aol.com
Nearest Town/Resort Barnard Castle
Directions From Barnard Castle take the B6277. In Mickleton take the first turn right past Blacksmiths Arms, go down the bank and bear left at the bottom of the hill.
Acreage 7½ **Open** April **to** October
Access Poor **Site** Level
Sites Available ⊕ ⊕ **Total** 75
Facilities ⌖ ⬚ ⬚ ♨ ⌐ ⊙ ➘ ⬚ ☎
⬚ ⬚ ⬚ ⬚ ⬚
Nearby Facilities ⌐ ✔ ⬚ ∪ ⬚
➤ Darlington
Set on the banks of the River Lune, with free fishing on site.

WOLSINGHAM

Bradley Mill Caravan Park, Wolsingham, Bishop Auckland, County Durham, DL13 3JJ.
Std: 01388 **Tel:** 527285
Std: 01388 **Fax:** 527285
Email: stay@bradleyburn.co.uk
Website: www.bradleyburn.co.uk
Nearest Town/Resort Wolsingham
Directions 2 miles east of Wolsingham on the A689 and 2 miles west of the A68/A689 junction.
Open April **to** October
Access Good **Site** Lev/Slope
Sites Available A ⊕ ⊕ **Total** 12
Facilities ⌖ ⬚ ♨ ⌐ ⊙ ⬚ ☎ ⬚ ⬚ ⬚ ⬚
Nearby Facilities ⌐ ✔ ∪ ⬚
➤ Bishop Auckland
N.B. This is a STATIC holiday park with a few pitches available for tourers.

**IT IS ALWAYS
ADVISABLE TO
BOOK DURING
PEAK SEASON**

ESSEX

BRENTWOOD

Camping & Caravanning Club Site, Warren Lane, Frog Street, Kelvedon Hatch, Near Brentwood, Essex, CM15 0JG.
Std: 01277 **Tel:** 372773
Website:
www.campingandcaravanningclub.co.uk
Nearest Town/Resort Brentwood
Directions Leave the M25 at junction 28 and take the A1023 towards Brentwood. Turn left onto the A128 to Ongar, the site is 3 miles on the right, signposted.
Acreage 12 **Open** March **to** October
Access Good **Site** Level
Sites Available A ⊕ ⊕ **Total** 90
Facilities ⌖ ⬚ ♨ ⌐ ⊙ ➘ ⬚ ⬚ ☎
⬚ ⬚ ⬚ ⬚ ⬚ ⬚ ⬚
Nearby Facilities ⌐ ✔ ⬚
➤ Brentwood
Peaceful site, good for country walks. 20 miles from the centre of London. Plenty of sporting activities within easy reach. BTB Graded. Non members welcome.

BURNHAM-ON-CROUCH

Creeksea Place Caravan Park, Ferry Road, Burnham-on-Crouch, Essex, CM0 8PJ.
Std: 01621 **Tel:** 782387
Nearest Town/Resort Burnham-on-Crouch
Directions Entering Burnham-on-Crouch on the B1010, you will see a tourism sign on the right pointing down Ferry Road.
Acreage 10 **Open** March **to** Nov
Access Good **Site** Level
Sites Available A ⊕ ⊕ **Total** 60
Facilities ⌖ ⬚ ♨ ⌐ ⊙ ➘ ⬚
⬚ ⬚ ⬚ ⬚ ⬚ ⬚ ⬚ ⬚
Nearby Facilities ⌐ ✔ ⬚ ⬚ ∪
➤ Burnham-on-Crouch
¾ miles from the River Crouch. Fishing facilities on site.

CANVEY ISLAND

Thorney Bay Park, Thorney Bay Road, Canvey Island, Essex, SS8 0DB.
Std: 01268 **Tel:** 691500
Std: 01268 **Fax:** 682167
Nearest Town/Resort Southend-on-Sea
Directions Take the A13 Southend bound then take the A130 to Canvey Island. Follow signs to the sea front and Thorney Bay Road, we are on the right.
Acreage 3 **Open** March **to** October
Access Good **Site** Level
Sites Available A ⊕□ **Total** 30
Facilities ⌖ ⌖ ⬚ ♨ ⌐ ⊙ ➘ ⬚ ☎
⬚ ⬚ ⬚ ⬚ ✕ ⬚ ⬚
Nearby Facilities ⌐ ✔
➤ Benfleet
Near to the beach, local cinema, golf course and leisure centre.

CLACTON-ON-SEA

Highfield Holiday Park, London Road, Clacton-on-Sea, Essex, CO16 9QY.
Std: 01255 **Tel:** 4429287
Std: 01255 **Fax:** 689805
Email:
enquiries@highfield.gbholidayparks.co.uk
Nearest Town/Resort Clacton-on-Sea
Directions From the M25 take the A12 then the A120 leading to the A133 directly to Clacton. Situated on the B1441 approx. 2 miles from the town centre on the left hand side (well signposted).
Open March **to** October
Access Good **Site** Level
Sites Available ⊕ ⊕ **Total** 315

acilities ⚡ 🏠 🏕 ☕ 🎣 🍴 🚿 💷
🏪 🚻 🅿 🚃 ✕ 🛒 🎾 🎡 ♿ 🔥 ☎
Nearby Facilities 🏇 🥾 ⛵ ↔ 🛶 ⚓ ♪
⚓ Clacton-on-Sea
Near the beach, great for family activities,
sensational fun in the evening. Local
attractions including the pier, Colchester
Zoo, Seaquarium and more.

CLACTON-ON-SEA
Sacketts Grove, Jaywick Lane, Clacton-
on-Sea, Essex, CO16 7BD.
Std: 01255 **Tel:** 427765
Std: 01255 **Fax:** 428752
Nearest Town/Resort Clacton-on-Sea
Directions Take the A12 from London or
join the A120 at Colchester, A133 at Frating
and follow signs for Sacketts Grove.
Acreage 6 **Open** Easter **to** Early October
Access Good **Site** Level
Sites Available ▲ 🚐 🚍 **Total** 120
Facilities ⚡ 🏠 ☕ 🎣 🍴 🚿 ♿ 🍴 ☎
🏪 🚻 ✕ 🛒 🎾 🎡 ♿ 🔥
Nearby Facilities 🏇 🥾 ⛵ ↔ ♪ ♪
⚓ Clacton
1 mile from the beach. Riding school on site.
Ideal for touring and camping.

CLACTON-ON-SEA
Silver Dawn Touring Park, Jaywick Lane,
Clacton-on-Sea, Essex, CO16 8BB.
Std: 01255 **Tel:** 421856
Nearest Town/Resort Clacton-on-Sea
Directions Take the A12 then the A120 to
Clacton.
Acreage 3 **Open** April **to** October
Access Good **Site** Level
Sites Available 🚐 🚍 **Total** 38
Facilities ⚡ 🎣 🍴 🚿 ♿ 🔥 🍴 ☕ 🛒
Nearby Facilities 🏇 🥾 ⛵ ↔ 🛶 ♪ ♪
⚓ Clacton-on-Sea

CLACTON-ON-SEA
Tower Holiday Park, Jaywick, Clacton-
on-Sea, Essex, CO15 2LF.
Std: 0870 **Tel:** 442 9290 **Fax:** 820060
Email: tower@gbholidayparks.co.uk
Website: www.gbholidayparks.co.uk
Nearest Town/Resort Clacton-on-Sea
Directions From the A12 take the A120 then
the A133 to Clacton seafront. Turn right and
follow signs through Jaywick.
Open March **to** October
Access Good **Site** Level
Sites Available 🚐 🚍 **Total** 100
Facilities ⚡ 🎣 🏠 🍴 🚿 ♿ 🔥 🍴 ☎
🏪 🚻 ✕ 🛒 🎾 🔥 🎡 🎾 🎡 🔥
Nearby Facilities 🏇 🥾 ⛵ ↔ 🛶 ♪
⚓ Clacton-on-Sea
Next to the beach and only 3 miles from
Clacton town. Ideal base for touring East
Anglia.

COLCHESTER
Colchester Camping & Caravan Park,
Cymbeline Way, Lexden, Colchester,
Essex, CO3 4AG.
Std: 01206 **Tel:** 545551 **Fax:** 710443
Email: enquiries@colchestercamping.co.uk
Website: www.colchestercamping.co.uk
Nearest Town/Resort Colchester
Directions From the A12 in any direction,
follow tourist signs for caravan park into
Colchester on the A133 Colchester central
slip road.
Acreage 12 **Open** All Year
Access Good **Site** Level
Sites Available ▲ 🚐 🚍 **Total** 251
Facilities ⚡ 🎣 🏠 🏕 🏠 🍴 🚿 ♿ 🔥 🍴 ☎
🏪 🚻 🛒 🚃 🎡 🎾 🔥
Nearby Facilities 🏇 🥾 ⛵ ↔ 🛶 ♪
⚓ Colchester
Close to Britains oldest town, convenient for
ferry ports. Ideal for touring East Anglia.

HALSTEAD
Gosfield Lake Resort, Church Road,
Gosfield, Nr Halstead, Essex, CO9 1UE.
Std: 01787 **Tel:** 475043
Std: 01787 **Fax:** 478528
Email: turps@gosfieldlake.co.uk
Website: www.gosfieldlake.co.uk
Nearest Town/Resort Halstead
Directions A120, A131 and A1017 from
Braintree, 5 miles A1024, Sible Hedingham
A1017.
Acreage 7 **Open** All Year
Access Good **Site** Level
Sites Available Total 25
Facilities ⚡ 🏠 🍴 ⊙ ♿ ✕ 🔥 🛒
Nearby Facilities 🏇 🥾 ⛵ ↔
⚓ Braintree
Near a lake for water-skiing.

MALDON
Barrow Marsh Caravan Park,
Goldhanger Road, Heybridge, Maldon,
Essex, CM9 4RA.
Std: 01621 **Tel:** 852859
Std: 01621 **Fax:** 853593
Nearest Town/Resort Maldon
Directions From Maldon travel towards
Heybridge and turn onto the B1026
Goldhanger Road to Mill Beach. Site is 3
miles on the left hand side.
Acreage 14 **Open** 1 April **to** 30 Oct
Access Good **Site** Level
Sites Available ▲ 🚐 🚍 **Total** 15
Facilities ⚡ 🏠 🍴 🎣 🍴 🚿 ♿ 🍴 ☎
🚻 🅿 🛒 🚃 🔥
Nearby Facilities 🥾 ⛵ ↔
⚓ Witham
Situated by Blackwater Estuary. 16 miles
from the historic town of Colchester.

MANNINGTREE

The Strangers Home Inn & Camping Site, The Street, Bradfield, Nr. Manningtree, Essex, CO11 2US.
Std: 01255 **Tel:** 870304
Nearest Town/Resort Manningtree
Directions Take the A12 from Colchester then the A120 to Harwich/Clacton, stay on the A120 past Clacton turn off and turn left at Horsley Cross to Manningtree. Take the first turn right to Bradfield.
Acreage 2½ **Open** March **to** October
Access Good **Site** Level
Sites Available Λ � ♟ **Total** 70
Facilities ✦ 🅿 ♨ ☏ ☉ 🚿 ⛟
🏪 🛒 🏐 ✕ 🎱 🍴 🅰 🌳 ⊟
Nearby Facilities ┏ ✓ 🏊 ⟲ U ♪
⊀ Mistley
Near the beach at the River Stour. 9 miles from Harwich International port and 10 miles from historic Colchester. 10 miles from the seaside resorts of Clacton, Walton and Frinton. 12 miles from Ipswich.

MERSEA ISLAND

Fen Farm Camping & Caravan Site, Fen Farm, East Mersea, Colchester, Essex, CO5 8UA.
Std: 01206 **Tel:** 383275
Std: 01206 **Fax:** 386316
Email: fenfarm@talk21.com
Website: www.fenfarm.co.uk
Nearest Town/Resort West Mersea
Directions Take the B1025 from Colchester, take the left fork onto Mersea Island. Take the first turn right past the Dog & Pheasant Public House, signposted.
Acreage 5 **Open** March **to** September
Access Good **Site** Level
Sites Available Λ ♟ ♠ **Total** 45
Facilities ♿ ✦ 🅿 🅿 ♨ ☏ ☉ 🚿 ⛟
🏪 🛒 🏐 🍴 🅰 🌳 ⊟

Nearby Facilities ✓ 🏊 🦆 ♪
⊀ Colchester
Quiet, rural, family site by the beach and on an estuary. Close to a country park.

MERSEA ISLAND

Waldegraves Holiday & Leisure Park, Mersea Island, Colchester, Essex, CO5 8SE.
Std: 01206 **Tel:** 382898
Std: 01206 **Fax:** 385359
Email: holidays@waldegraves.co.uk
Website: www.waldegraves.co.uk
Nearest Town/Resort Mersea
Directions From Colchester take B1025, 10 miles to West Mersea. Take left fork to East Mersea, second road to right.
Acreage 45 **Open** March **to** November
Access Good **Site** Level
Sites Available Λ ♟ ♠ **Total** 200
Facilities ♿ ✦ 🅿 🅿 🅿 ♨ ☏ ☉ 🚿 ⛟ 🔲 ☎
🏪 🛒 🏐 ✕ 🎱 🍴 🅰 🌳 ⊛ ✕ 🅿 ⊟ 🔲
Nearby Facilities ┏ ✓ 🏊 ⟲ U ♪
⊀ Colchester
Grass park, surrounded by trees and lakes. Safe private beach, fishing and golf. Ideal family park. New swimming pool. Holiday homes for hire and sale.

SOUTHEND-ON-SEA

Riverside Village Holiday Park, Wallasea Island, Rochford, Essex, SS4 2EY
Std: 01702 **Tel:** 258297 **Fax:** 258555
Nearest Town/Resort Southend
Directions From A127 through Rochford, follow caravan signs for Ashingdon then Wallasea Island. From Chelmsford left at Battlesbridge, past Hullbridge for Ashingdon then Wallasea.
Acreage 25 **Open** March **to** October
Access Good **Site** Level
Sites Available Λ ♟ ♠ **Total** 60

Facilities ✦ 🅿 ♨ ☏ ☉ 🚿 ⛟ 🔲 ☎
🏪 🛒 🏐 🏐 🍴 🅰 🅿 🔲
Nearby Facilities ┏ ✓ 🏊 🦆 U
⊀ Rochford
Alongside River Crouch, Nature reserve picturesque inns with excellent food Country walks. Boule pitch. Licensed bar and restaurant nearby.

SOUTHMINSTER

Waterside Holiday Park, St. Lawrence Bay, Southminster, Essex, CM0 7LP.
Std: 01621 **Tel:** 779248 **Fax:** 778106
Email: waterside@gbholidayparks.co.uk
Website: www.gbholidayparks.co.uk
Nearest Town/Resort Southminster
Directions Head south from Maldon on the B1018, go through Mundon to Latchingdon then bear left towards St Lawrence Bay, site is signposted.
Acreage 45 **Open** April **to** October
Access Good **Site** Lev/Slope
Sites Available Λ ♟ ♠ **Total** 60
Facilities ♿ ✦ 🅿 🅿 ♨ ☏ ☉ 🚿 ⛟ 🔲 ☎
🏪 🛒 🏐 ✕ 🎱 🍴 🅰 🅿 🔲
Nearby Facilities ✓ 🏊 🦆 ♪
Situated on the Black Water Estuary with own slipway and beach. Beautiful green park with great views. Bird watching (SSSI). Ideal for water sports, subject to weather.

ST. OSYTH

The Orchards Holiday Village, Point Clear, St. Osyth, Clacton-on-Sea, Essex, CO16 8LJ.
Std: 01255 **Tel:** 820651 **Fax:** 820184
Website: www.british-holidays.co.uk
Nearest Town/Resort Clacton
Directions From Clacton-on-Sea take the B1027 (signposted Colchester). Turn left after Pumphill Station, over crossroads in St Osyth, 3 miles on to the park.

Open March to October
Access Good Site Level
Sites Available ⚏ ☵ Total 45
Facilities ⚙ ⚡ ∮ ⊟ ⊞ ⊌ ⚑ ⌯ ⊙ ⚒ ⚏
⚏
⚏ ⚏ ⊟ ⚒ ✗ ⚐ ⊞ ⚑ ⚐ ☰ ⚒ ※ ☵ ⊟ ⊡ ⚏ ♨
Nearby Facilities ⌯ ✓ ⚓ ⌣ ∪ ⚘ ♪
⚞ Clacton
Close to Colchester historic town. Kids Club and a full family entertainment programme. Beach access, water sports, golf, pitch'n'putt, fishing lakes, bars and take-away. Dogs are allowed but not in peak season. Bike hire available nearby.

WALTON-ON-THE-NAZE
Naze Marine Holiday Park, Hall Lane, Walton-on-the-Naze, Essex, CO14 8HL.
Std: 0870 **Tel:** 442 9292
Std: 01255 **Fax:** 682427
Email:
nazemarine@gbholidayparks.co.uk
Website: www.gbholidayparks.co.uk
Nearest Town/Resort Walton-on-the-Naze
Directions From the main A12 to Colchester. Take the main A120 Harwich road as far as the A133, then take the A133 to Weeley. As you approach Weeley take the B1033 all the way to Walton sea front, Naze Marine is situated on the left.
Open March to October
Access Good Site Level
Sites Available ⚏ ☵ **Total** 44
Facilities ⚙ ∮ ⊞ ⚑ ⌯ ⊙ ⚒ ⚏ ♨
⚏ ⚏ ⊟ ⚒ ✗ ⚐ ⊞ ⚑ ☰ ⚒ ※ ♪
Nearby Facilities ⌯ ✓ ⚓ ♪
Attractive touring park offering access to sandy beaches, country walks on the adjacent nature reserve and popular restaurants in the nearby town.

GLOUCESTERSHIRE
CIRENCESTER
Hoburne Cotswold, Broadway Lane, South Cerney, Cirencester, GL7 5UQ.
Std: 01285 **Tel:** 860216
Std: 01285 **Fax:** 868010
Email: enquiries@hoburne.com
Website: www.hoburne.com
Nearest Town/Resort Cirencester
Directions 4 miles south of Cirencester on the A419, follow signs to Cotswold Hoburne, in the Cotswold Water Park.
Acreage 70 **Open** March to October
Access Good Site Level
Sites Available ⚏ ⚏ ☵ **Total** 302
Facilities ∮ ⊞ ⚑ ⌯ ⊙ ⚒ ⚏ ⚏ ♨
⚏ ⚏ ⊟ ⚒ ✗ ⚐ ☰ ⚑ ☰ ⚒ ※ ⊞ ♪
Nearby Facilities ⌯ ✓ ⚓ ⌣ ∪ ⚘ ♪

⚞ Swindon
In the centre of the Cotswold Water Park - and ideal base for all watersports and nature lovers. Tennis on site.

CIRENCESTER
Mayfield Touring Park, Cheltenham Road, Perrotts Brook, Cirencester, GL7 7BH.
Std: 01285 **Tel:** 831301
Std: 01285 **Fax:** 831301
Nearest Town/Resort Cirencester
Directions On A435, 13miles Cheltenham and 2miles Cirencester. From Cirencester by-pass A419/A417 take the Burford Road exit then follow camping and caravan signs.
Acreage 10 **Open** All Year
Access Good Site Lev/Slope
Sites Available ⚏ ⚏ ☵ **Total** 76
Facilities ∮ ⊟ ⊞ ⚑ ⌯ ⊙ ⚒ ⚏ ♨
⚏ ⚏ ⊟ ⚒ ※ ⊞ ⊡ ⚏
Nearby Facilities ⌯ ✓ ⚓ ⌣ ∪ ⚘ ♪
⚞ Kemble
Touring Cotswolds, castles, Abbey, Wildlife park, Local pub is five minutes walk - food suitable for children. 16 hard standing/grass pitches. Boar 6 acres of ground for recreation. Some 16 amp electric points.

CIRENCESTER
Second Chance Caravan Park, Nr. Marston Meysey, Wiltshire, SN6 6SN.
Std: 01285 **Tel:** 810675
Nearest Town/Resort Castle Eaton/Fairford
Directions Between Swindon and Cirencester on the A419. Turn off at the Fairford/Marston Meysey exit and follow the caravan park signs. Proceed approx. 3 miles then turn right at the Castle Eaton signpost. We are on the right.
Acreage 2 **Open** March to November
Access Good Site Level
Sites Available ⚏ ⚏ ☵ **Total** 26
Facilities ∮ ⊟ ⊞ ⚑ ⌯ ⊙ ⚒ ⚏ ⚏ ♨ ⊟ ⊞ ⊡
Nearby Facilities ⌯ ✓ ⚓ ⌣
⚞ Swindon
Riverside location, private fishing and access for your own canoe, to explore upper reaches of Thames. Ideal base for touring the Cotswolds. A.A. 2 Pennants and RAC.

COLEFORD
Bracelands - Forestry Commission Caravan & Camping Site, Christchurch, Forest of Dean, Coleford, Gloucestershire, GL16 7NN.
Std: 01594 **Tel:** 833376
Email: fe.holidays@forestry.gsi.gov.uk
Website: www.forestholidays.co.uk
Nearest Town/Resort Coleford
Directions At the crossroads of the A4136 and minor road at the Pike House Inn (1 mile

north of Coleford), go north for ½ mile following campsite signs. Reception for Bracelands is at the Christchurch site.
Acreage 14 **Open** 21 March **to** 31 October
Access Good Site Level
Sites Available ⚏ ⚏ ☵ **Total** 520
Facilities ⚙ ∮ ⊞ ⚑ ⌯ ⊙ ⚒ ⚏
⚏ ⚏ ☰ ⊞ ⊡
Nearby Facilities ✓ ∪ ♪
⚞ Gloucester
Panoramic views over the magnificent countryside, Highmeadow Wood and the Wye Valley. Watch Peregrines at Symonds Yat, plus a host of outdoor activities.

COLEFORD
Christchurch - Forestry Commission Caravan & Camping Site, Christchurch, Coleford, Gloucestershire, GL16 7NN.
Std: 01594 **Tel:** 833376
Email: fe.holidays@forestry.gsi.gov.uk
Website: www.forestholidays.co.uk
Nearest Town/Resort Coleford
Directions At the crossroads of the A4136 1 mile north of Coleford, go north for ½ mile following signs to the campsite. Reception is on the left.
Open 21 March **to** 3 November
Access Good Site Sloping
Sites Available ⚏ ⚏ ☵ **Total** 280
Facilities ⚙ ∮ ⊞ ⚑ ⌯ ⊙ ⚒ ⚏
⚏ ⚏ ⊟ ☰ ⊞ ⊡
Nearby Facilities ⌯ ✓ ⚓ ∪ ♪ ♪
⚞ Gloucester
Situated high above the beautiful Wye Valley, with waymarked walking routes down to the river through the surrounding woodland. Near to Clearwell Caves ancient iron mines. Laundry service. Barbecue area. Pets are welcome but not between 16 March and 27 October. SITE RE-OPENS 20 December to 5 January 2003.

COLEFORD
Woodlands - Forestry Commission Caravan Site, Christchurch, Forest of Dean, Coleford, Gloucestershire, GL16 7NN.
Std: 01594 **Tel:** 833376
Email: fe.holidays@forestry.gsi.gov.uk
Website: www.forestholidays.co.uk
Nearest Town/Resort Coleford
Directions At the crossroads of the A4136 and a minor road at Pike House Inn, 1 mile north of Coleford, go north for ½ mile following campsite signs. Reception for Woodlands is at Christchurch site.
Acreage 22 **Open** 21 March **to** 31 October
Access Good Site Level
Sites Available ⚏ ☵ **Total** 90
Facilities ⊟ ⚑ ⊞ ⊡

Nearby Facilities
⚊ Gloucester

A superbly wooded site with pitches set amongst trees. Ideal for a peaceful, tranquil break. Note : This site has NO toilets.

COLEFORD

Woodlands View Caravan Park, Sling, Near Coleford, Gloucestershire, GL16 8JA.
Std: 01594 **Tel:** 835127
Std: 01594 **Fax:** 835127
Nearest Town/Resort Coleford
Directions From Coleford take the B4228 towards Chepstow, after ½ a mile you will pass Puzzle Wood on the right hand side, we are signposted ¼ mile on the left.
Acreage 1½ **Open** April to October
Access Good **Site** Level
Sites Available ⚊ ⚊ ⚊ **Total** 20
Facilities ⚊ ⚊ ⚊ ⚊ ⚊ ⚊ ⚊ ⚊
⚊ ⚊ ⚊ ⚊
Nearby Facilities ⚊ ⚊ ⚊ ⚊ ⚊
⚊ Lydney
Near to Clearwell Caves and Puzzle Wood.

DURSLEY

Hogsdown Farm Caravan & Camping Site, Lower Wick, Dursley, GL11 6OX.
Std: 01453 **Tel:** 810224
Website: www.mywebpage.net/hogsdown
Nearest Town/Resort Gloucester
Directions Between junctions 13 & 14 of M5, 1mile off A38, 2miles from Berkeley.
Acreage 4 **Open** All Year
Access Good **Site** Level
Sites Available ⚊ ⚊ ⚊ **Total** 40
Facilities ⚊ ⚊ ⚊ ⚊ ⚊ ⚊ ⚊ ⚊ ⚊
⚊ ⚊ ⚊ ⚊ ⚊ ⚊
Nearby Facilities ⚊ ⚊ ⚊ ⚊
⚊ Stroud
Ideal stopover north, south and touring Cotswolds Edge and Way Country, Severn Vale. Slimbridge Wild Fowl Trust, Berkeley castle, Jenner Museum, Western Burt Arboretum. Cotswold & Severn Way within 2miles. Oldbury power station, butterfly farm and rare animal farm. Also B+B.

GLOUCESTER

Red Lion Caravan & Camping Park, Wainlode Hill, Norton, GL2 9LW.
Std: 01452 **Tel:** 730251
Nearest Town/Resort Gloucester
Directions Off A38 at Norton, signposted Wainlode Hill, 5 miles Gloucester.
Acreage 12½ **Open** All Year
Access Good **Site** Level
Sites Available ⚊ ⚊ ⚊ **Total** 90
Facilities ⚊ ⚊ ⚊ ⚊ ⚊
⚊ ⚊ ⚊ ⚊ ⚊ ⚊ ⚊ ⚊ ⚊
Nearby Facilities ⚊ ⚊ ⚊ ⚊
⚊ Gloucester
Licensed Inn, hot and cold snacks. On banks of River Severn. Good fishing on site.

LECHLADE

Bridge House Campsite, Bridge House, Lechlade, GL7 3AG.
Std: 01367 **Tel:** 252348
Nearest Town/Resort Lechlade
Directions Lechlade A361 to Swindon. Opposite Riverside car park.

Acreage 3½ **Open** April to October
Site Level
Sites Available ⚊ ⚊ ⚊ **Total** 51
Facilities ⚊ ⚊ ⚊ ⚊ ⚊ ⚊ ⚊ ⚊ ⚊
⚊ ⚊ ⚊ ⚊
Nearby Facilities ⚊ ⚊
⚊ Swindon
Ideal for touring Cotswolds and Upper Thames.

MORETON VALENCE

Gables Farm Caravan & Camping Site, Moreton Valence, GL2 7ND.
Std: 01452 **Tel:** 720331
Std: 01452 **Fax:** 720331
Nearest Town/Resort Gloucester
Directions On A38 6 miles from Gloucester. 2 miles from M5 junction 13.
Acreage 3 **Open** March to Nov
Access Good **Site** Level
Sites Available ⚊ ⚊ ⚊ **Total** 40
Facilities ⚊ ⚊ ⚊ ⚊ ⚊ ⚊ ⚊ ⚊ ⚊
Nearby Facilities ⚊
⚊ Gloucester
Overnight or local touring. Wetlands Trust 6 miles. S.A.E. Gloucester docks and museums.

MORETON-IN-MARSH

Cross Hands Inn Caravan Park, Moreton-in-Marsh, GL56 0SP.
Std: 01608 **Tel:** 643106
Nearest Town/Resort Chipping Norton
Directions From Chipping Norton take the Worcester road A44. After 3 miles you will see the Inn on your right on the main A44 at the junction of A436.
Acreage 1¼ **Open** All Year
Access Good **Site** Level
Sites Available ⚊ ⚊
Facilities ⚊ ⚊ ⚊ ⚊ ⚊ ⚊ ⚊ ⚊ ⚊ ⚊ ⚊
Nearby Facilities ⚊ ⚊ ⚊
⚊ Moreton-in-Marsh
Ideal touring site for the Cotswolds and only about 20 miles to Stratford-On-Avon.

SLIMBRIDGE

Tudor Caravanning & Camping Park, Shepherds Patch, Slimbridge, Gloucestershire, GL2 7BP.
Std: 01453 **Tel:** 890483
Email: info@tudorcaravanpark.co.uk
Website: www.tudorcaravanpark.co.uk
Nearest Town/Resort Dursley/Gloucester
Directions Leave the M5 at junction 13 and follow signs for 'Wildfowl Trust, Slimbridge'. 1¼ miles off the A38 at the rear of the Tudor Arms Pub.
Acreage 7¼ **Open** All Year
Access Good **Site** Level
Sites Available ⚊ ⚊ ⚊ **Total** 75
Facilities ⚊ ⚊ ⚊ ⚊ ⚊ ⚊ ⚊ ⚊ ⚊
⚊ ⚊ ⚊ ⚊
Nearby Facilities ⚊ ⚊
⚊ Dursley
Sharpness Canal next property to Wildfowl Trust. AA 4 Pennants.

TEWKESBURY

Croft Farm Leisure & Water Park, Brendons Hardwick, Tewkesbury, GL20 7EE.
Std: 01684 **Tel:** 772321
Std: 01684 **Fax:** 773379
Email: alan@croftfarmleisure.co.uk
Website: www.croftfarmleisure.co.uk
Nearest Town/Resort Tewkesbury
Directions 1½ miles north-east of Tewkesbury on B4080.
Acreage 10 **Open** 1 March to 1 January
Access Good **Site** Level
Sites Available ⚊ ⚊ ⚊ **Total** 76
Facilities ⚊ ⚊ ⚊ ⚊ ⚊ ⚊ ⚊ ⚊ ⚊
⚊ ⚊ ⚊ ⚊ ⚊ ⚊ ⚊ ⚊ ⚊
Nearby Facilities ⚊ ⚊ ⚊ ⚊ ⚊
⚊ Ashchurch
Lakeside location with own watersports lake for sailing, windsurfing and canoeing.

TEWKESBURY

Dawleys Caravan Park, Owls Lane, Shuthonger, Tewkesbury, GL20 6EQ.
Std: 01684 **Tel:** 292622
Std: 01684 **Fax:** 292622
Nearest Town/Resort Cheltenham/ Gloucester
Directions A38 north from Tewkesbury approimately 2 miles on the left hand side. Or 1¼ miles south on A38 from M50 junction 1.
Acreage 3 **Open** 15 March to October
Access Fair **Site** Sloping
Sites Available ⚊ ⚊ ⚊ **Total** 20
Facilities ⚊ ⚊ ⚊ ⚊ ⚊ ⚊ ⚊
⚊ ⚊ ⚊ ⚊ ⚊ ⚊
Nearby Facilities ⚊ ⚊ ⚊ ⚊ ⚊
⚊ Cheltenham
Near ar river, secluded rural site, close to M5 and M50.

HAMPSHIRE

ANDOVER

Wyke Down Touring Caravan & Camping Park, Picket Piece, Andover, Hampshire, SP11 6LX.
Std: 01264 **Tel:** 352048 **Fax:** 324661
Email: wykedown@wykedown.co.uk
Website: www.wykedown.co.uk
Nearest Town/Resort Andover.
Directions International Camping Park Signs from a303 Trunk Road, follow signs to Wyke Down.
Acreage 7 **Open** All Year
Access Good **Site** Level
Sites Available ⚊ ⚊ ⚊ **Total** 150
Facilities ⚊ ⚊ ⚊ ⚊ ⚊ ⚊ ⚊
⚊ ⚊ ⚊ ⚊ ⚊ ⚊ ⚊ ⚊ ⚊ ⚊
Nearby Facilities ⚊ ⚊
⚊ Andover.
Ideal touring area. Golf driving range Country pub and restaurant.

ASHURST

Ashurst Caravan & Camping Site - Forestry Commission, Lyndhurst Road, Ashurst, Hampshire, SO4 2AA.
Std: 0131 **Tel:** 314 6505
Email: fe.holidays@forestry.gsi.gov.uk
Website: www.forestholidays.co.uk
Nearest Town/Resort Lyndhurst

Kingfisher Park
Tel: (02392) 502611
Browndown Road, Gosport.

A family run park very close to the sea. Club, restaurant, launderette, children's games room. Caravans for hire and for sale. We have several empty holiday home pitches available.

Directions 5 miles southwest of Southampton on the A35, signposted.
Acreage 23 **Open** 21 March **to** 24 Sept
Access Good **Site** Level
Sites Available ∧ ⊕ ⇔ **Total** 280
Facilities & ⚏ ⇸ ⌂ ⊙ ⌴ ▣ ◻ ♥ ☎ ▣ ◻
Nearby Facilities ⌆ ∪
⚓ Ashurst
Lightweight area on site for walkers and cyclists. 10 minutes walk to the shops in Ashurst Village.

BEAULIEU
Decoy Pond Farm, Beaulieu Road, Beaulieu, Brockenhurst, Hampshire, SO42 7YQ.
Std: 023 **Tel:** 8029 2652
Nearest Town/Resort Lyndhurst
Directions From Lyndhurst take the B3056, after crossing railway bridge, first on the left.
Acreage 5 **Open** March **to** October
Access Good **Site** Level
Sites Available ∧ ⊕ ⇔ **Total** 4
Facilities ⚏ ⇸ ⌂ ♥ ⚒
Nearby Facilities ⌆ ⚓ ∪
⚓ Beaulieu Road
Ideal for the New Forest.

BRANSGORE
Harrow Wood Farm Caravan Park, Poplar Lane, Bransgore, Nr. Christchurch, Dorset, BH23 8JE.
Std: 01425 **Tel:** 672487 **Fax:** 672487
Email: harrowwood@caravan-sites.co.uk
Website: www.caravan-sites.co.uk
Nearest Town/Resort Christchurch/ Bournemouth
Directions On the A35, 11 miles south-west of Lyndhurst turn right at the Cat & Fiddle Public House. Go 2 miles to Bransgore and turn first right after the school into Poplar Lane.
Acreage 6 **Open** 1 March **to** 6 January
Access Good **Site** Level
Sites Available ⊕ ⇔ **Total** 60
Facilities ⚐ ⚏ ⌴ ⇸ ⌂ ⊙ ⇸ ⌴ ◻ ♥
⚏ ⬡ ☎ ▣
Nearby Facilities ⌆ ⚓ ⚓ ⚒ ∪
⚓ Hinton Admiral
Within easy reach of the New Forest and the sea.

BRANSGORE
Heathfield Caravan & Camping Park, Forest Road, Holmsley, Bransgore, Hampshire, BH23 8LA.
Std: 01425 **Tel:** 672397
Email:
office@heathfieldcaravanpark.co.uk
Nearest Town/Resort Christchurch
Directions From the traffic lights at Lyndhurst drive for 9 miles towards Christchurch on the A35. Turn right signposted Godwinscroft, then turn first right and the site is 200 yards on the left. From Christchurch turn left after the East Close Hotel, turn first right and the site is 200 yards on the left.
Acreage 14 **Open** March **to** End Oct
Access Good **Site** Level
Sites Available ∧ ⊕ ⇔ **Total** 200
Facilities & ⚐ ⚏ ⌴ ⇸ ⌂ ⊙ ⇸ ⌴
⚏ ▣ ⊙ ☎ ⬡ ▣
Nearby Facilities ⌆ ⚓ ∪ ⚓ ℛ
⚓ Hinton Admiral

BROCKENHURST
Aldridge Hill - Forestry Commission Caravan & Camping Site, Brockenhurst, Hampshire, SO42 7QD.
Std: 0131 **Tel:** 314 6505
Email: fe.holidays@forestry.gsi.gov.uk
Website: www.forestholidays.co.uk
Nearest Town/Resort Brockenhurst
Directions At the Ford in Brockenhurst turn right, the site is 1 mile on the right.
Acreage 22 **Open** 22 May **to** 03 June
Access Good **Site** Level
Sites Available ∧ ⊕ ⇔ **Total** 200
Facilities ♥ ☎ ⬡ ▣ ◻
Nearby Facilities ∪
⚓ Brockenhurst
In a heathland clearing in the heart of the New Forest, on the edge of Blackwater Stream. Note : This site has NO toilets. SITE RE-OPENS 19 June 2002 to 02 September 2002.

BROCKENHURST
Hollands Wood Caravan & Camping Site - Forestry Commission, Lyndhurst Road, Brockenhurst, Hampshire, SO42 7QH.

Std: 0131 **Tel:** 314 6505
Email: fe.holidays@forestry.gsi.gov.uk
Website: www.forestholidays.co.uk
Nearest Town/Resort Brockenhurst
Directions ½ mile north of Brockenhurst on the A337, signposted.
Acreage 168 **Open** 26 March **to** 27 Sept
Access Good **Site** Level
Sites Available ∧ ⊕ ⇔ **Total** 600
Facilities & ⚏ ⇸ ⌂ ⊙ ⇸ ⌴ ◻
⚏ ⬡ ▣ ◻
Nearby Facilities ⌆ ∪
⚓ Brockenhurst
Sheltered site in an oak woodland. Special 'dog free' area. Brockenhurst Village nearby.

BROCKENHURST
Roundhill Caravan & Camping Site - Forestry Commission, Beaulieu Road, Brockenhurst, Hampshire, SO46 7QL.
Std: 0131 **Tel:** 314 6505
Email: fe.holidays@forestry.gsi.gov.uk
Website: www.forestholidays.co.uk
Nearest Town/Resort Brockenhurst
Directions On the B3055, 2 miles south east of Brockenhurst off the A337, signposted.
Acreage 156 **Open** 24 March **to** 27 September
Access Good **Site** Level
Sites Available ∧ ⊕ ⇔ **Total** 500
Facilities & ⚏ ⇸ ⊙ ♥ ☎ ⬡ ▣ ◻
Nearby Facilities ⌆ ⚓ ∪
⚓ Brockenhurst
Wide open heathland site in the heart of the New Forest.

CADNAM
Ocknell/Longbeech Caravan & Camping Sites - Forestry Commission, Fritham, Nr. Lyndhurst, Hampshire, SO43 7NH.
Std: 0131 **Tel:** 314 6505
Email: fe.holidays@forestry.gsi.gov.uk
Website: www.forestholidays.co.uk
Nearest Town/Resort Lyndhurst
Directions From the A31 at Cadnam take the B3079, then the B3078 via Brook and Fritham (signposted).
Acreage 48 **Open** 24 March **to** 27 September
Access Good **Site** Level

Select Fishery Creek, a delightful, tranquil setting adjoining a tidal creek of Chichester harbour. Short walk to beaches, bars, restaurants, etc.. Free slipway and fishing. Modern toilet blocks. Free showers. Shop. Children's play area. Storage space all year round. Pets welcome. Electric hook-ups.

Fishery Lane, Hayling Island, Hampshire PO11 9NR   Tel: 023 9246 2164   Fax: 023 9246 0741   E-mail: camping@fisherycreek.fsnet.co.uk

ites Available ▲ ⊕ 🚐 Total 480
acilities 🚽 ♨ 🅿🚿🏪⊟🔌
earby Facilities ┌ ✓ ∪
wo contrasting sites. Ocknell has pectacular views over the surrounding ountryside and Longbeech is set in an ncient oakwood. Toilets at Ocknell only.

AREHAM

ibles Park, Dibles Road, Warsash, outhampton, Hants, SO31 9SA.
td: 01489 **Tel:** 575232
earest Town/Resort Fareham
irections Turn left off the A27 (Portsmouth Southampton) opposite Lloyds Bank into ocks Road (sinposted Warsash). In about ½ miles at the T-Junction turn right into Varsash Road, in about 300yds turn left into eet End Road. Take the second right and e are on the right.
creage ¾ **Open** All Year
ccess Good **Site** Level
ites Available ▲ ⊕ 🚐 **Total** 14
acilities ♨ 🅒 🛒 ┌ ⊙ ↻ 🍴 🔲 🚿
🕿 🛇 🏪🔌
earby Facilities ┌ ✓ ⚓ ↖ ∪ ℛ
hingle beach 1½ miles.

AREHAM

llerslie Touring Caravan & Camping ark, Down End Road, Fareham, ampshire, PO16 8TS.
td: 01329 **Tel:** 822248
earest Town/Resort Fareham
irections Take the A27 into Fareham, 1 ile.
creage 2½ **Open** March **to** October
ccess Good **Site** Sloping
ites Available ▲ ⊕ ☐ **Total** 30
acilities ♨ 🅒 🛇 🛒 ┌ ⊙ ↻ 🍴 🔲 🚿
🔌⊟
earby Facilities ┌ ✓ ⚓ ↖ ∪ ℛ
⚓ Fareham

AREHAM

outh Hants Country Club (Natursit), lackhouse Lane, North Boarhunt, areham, Hampshire, PO17 6JS.
td: 01329 **Tel:** 832919 **Fax:** 834506
mail: contact@southhants.swinternet.co.uk
ebsite: www.naturistholidays.co.uk
earest Town/Resort Fareham
irections Take the A32 north to Wickham, t the church turn right onto the B2177 and avel for 1¾ miles to Boarhunt filling station. ork right, then turn right, right again to barrier.
creage 2½ **Open** Easter **to** End Oct
ccess Good **Site** Level
ites Available ▲ ⊕ ☐ **Total** 53
acilities ♨ ♨ 🛒 ┌ ⊙ ↻ 🍴 🔲 🚿
🕿 🛇 🏪🔌 ⚓ 🌳 🔌
earby Facilities ┌ ✓ ∪ ℛ
⚓ Fareham
ear to historic ships, Southsea, Marwell oo, Poultons Park and the New Forest.

ORDINGBRIDGE

andy Balls, Godshill, Fordingbridge, ampshire, SP6 2JZ.
td: 01425 **Tel:** 653042 **Fax:** 653067
mail: post@sandy-balls.co.uk
ebsite: www.sandy-ball.co.uk
earest Town/Resort Fordingbridge

Directions Take the B3078 east from Fordingbridge, 1½ miles to Godshill.
Acreage 120 **Open** All Year
Access Good **Site** Level
Sites Available ▲ ⊕ 🚐 **Total** 256
Facilities ⅃ ♨ ┌ 🅒 🛒 ┌ ⊙ ↻ 🍴 ▯ 🔲 🚿
🕿 🛇 🛇 🏪 🛒 🔌 ⚓ 🌳🔌 🔲 🚿
Nearby Facilities ┌ ✓ ∪
⚓ Salisbury
Situated between the Hampshire Avon and the New Forest, ideal for exploring the New Forest and surrounding area.

GOSPORT

Kingfisher Caravan Park, Browndown Road, Stokes Bay, Gosport, Hampshire, PO13 9BE.
Std: 023 **Tel:** 9250 2611 **Fax:** 9258 3583
Email: info@kingfisher-caravan-park.co.uk
Web: www.kingfisher-caravan-park.co.uk
Nearest Town/Resort Gosport
Directions Exit 11 off the M27, take the A32 to Gosport. After approx. 3 miles at Fort Brockhurst follow caravan signs to Stokes Bay.
Acreage 14 **Open** All Year
Access Good **Site** Level
Sites Available ▲ ⊕ 🚐 **Total** 100
Facilities ♨ 🅒 🛒 ┌ ⊙ ↻ 🍴 🔲 🚿
🕿 🛇 🛇 🛒 ✕ ▯ 🛒 🏪 🛒 🌳🔌
Nearby Facilities ┌ ✓ ⚓ ℛ
⚓ Portsmouth Hard
Within easy reach of Portsmouth with ferries to the Continent and the Isle of Wight.

HAMBLE

Riverside Park, Satchell Lane, Hamble, Hampshire, SO31 4HR.
Std: 023 **Tel:** 8045 3220 **Fax:** 8045 3611
Email: enquiries@riversideholidays.co.uk
Website: www.riversideholidays.co.uk
Nearest Town/Resort Southampton
Directions Leave the M27 at junction 8, follow signs for Hamble Village on the B3397 for approx. 2 miles, then turn left into Satchell Lane. Riverside is on the left hand side of Satchell Lane above Mercury Marina.
Acreage 2 **Open** March **to** October
Access Good **Site** Lev/Slight Slope
Sites Available ▲ ⊕ 🚐 **Total** 45
Facilities ♨ 🅒 🛒 ┌ ⊙ ↻ 🍴 🔲 🚿
▯🛇 🛇 🏪🔌 🔲 🚿
Nearby Facilities ┌ ✓ ⚓ ↖ ∪
⚓ Hamble
Overlooking the River Hamble with a marina below the park. In the very pretty village of Hamble.

HAYLING ISLAND

Fishery Creek Caravan & Camping Park, Fishery Lane, Hayling Island, Hampshire, PO11 9NR.
Std: 023 **Tel:** 9246 2164 **Fax:** 9246 0741
Email: camping@fisherycreek.fsnet.co.uk
Nearest Town/Resort Hayling Island
Directions Turn off the A27 at Havant, take the A3023 to Hayling Island. Turn left at the first roundabout and follow brown tourism signs to Fishery Creek, left after Mengham Town, left into Fishery Lane, park is at the end of the lane.
Acreage 8 **Open** March **to** October
Access Good **Site** Level

Sites Available ▲ ⊕ 🚐 **Total** 165
Facilities ♨ ⅃ 🅒 🛒 ┌ ⊙ ↻ 🍴 🔲 🚿
🕿 🛇 🛇 🛒 ▯🏪🔌 🔲 🚿
Nearby Facilities ┌ ✓ ⚓ ↖ ∪ ℛ ℛ
⚓ Havant
Alongside a beautiful tidal creek, offering peace and tranquility. Own slipway, short path to beach. Fishing on site. Caravan storage available all year round.

HAYLING ISLAND

Fleet Park, Yew Tree Road, Hayling Island, Hampshire, PO11 0QF.
Std: 02392 **Tel:** 463684
Website: www.haylingcampsites.co.uk
Nearest Town/Resort Havant/Southsea
Directions Follow A3023 from Havant. Approx. 2 miles on Island turn left into Copse Lane then first right into Yew Tree Road.
Acreage 3 **Open** March **to** October
Access Good **Site** Level
Sites Available ▲ ⊕ 🚐 **Total** 75
Facilities ♨ ⅃ 🅒 🛒 ┌ ⊙ ↻ 🍴 🔲 🚿
🕿 🛇 🛇 🛒 ▯🏪🔌 🔲 🚿
Nearby Facilities ┌ ✓ ⚓ ↖ ∪ ℛ ℛ
⚓ Havant
Quiet family site on a creek. Near Ferry Port. Portsmouth/Southsea, Isle of Wight. Easy touring for New Forest and Beaulieu.

HAYLING ISLAND

Lower Tye Camp Site, Copse Lane, Hayling Island, Hants, PO11 0QB.
Std: 023 **Tel:** 9246 2479 **Fax:** 9246 2479
Website: www.haylingcampsites.co.uk
Nearest Town/Resort Havant
Directions Exit the M27 or the A3M motorway at Havant. Follow the A3023 from Havant, turn left into Copse Lane. You will see the sign after being on Hayling Island for approx 1¼ miles.
Acreage 5 **Open** March **to** November
Access Good **Site** Level
Sites Available ▲ ⊕ 🚐 **Total** 150
Facilities ♨ 🅒 🛒 ┌ ⊙ ↻ 🍴 🔲 🚿
🕿 🛇 🛇 ✕ 🛒 ▯🏪🔌 🔲 🚿
Nearby Facilities ┌ ✓ ⚓ ↖ ∪ ℛ ℛ
⚓ Havant
Plunge pool on site. Near Portsmouth, Isle of Wight, Singlton Open Air Museum, Chichester, excellent Blue Flag beach, all water sports. Storage available and caravan parking with full use on site.

HAYLING ISLAND

Oven Camping Site, Manor Road, Hayling Island, Hampshire, PO11 0QX.
Std: 02392 **Tel:** 464695 **Fax:** 462479
Website: www.haylingcampsites.co.uk
Nearest Town/Resort Havant
Directions Exit M27 or the A37 at Havant. Take the A3023 from Havant, approx 3 miles after crossing bridge onto Hayling Island bear right at the roundabout. Site is on the left in 450yds.
Acreage 10 **Open** March **to** Dec Incl.
Access Good **Site** Level
Sites Available ▲ ⊕ 🚐 **Total** 330
Facilities ♨ ⅃ 🅒 🛒 ┌ ⊙ ↻ 🍴 🔲 🚿
🕿 🛇 🛇 ✕ 🛒 ▯🏪🔌 🔲 🚿
Nearby Facilities ┌ ✓ ⚓ ↖ ∪ ℛ ℛ
⚓ Havant
Heated swimming pool. Excellent touring

area for Portsmouth, Chichester, New Forest etc. Safe, clean, Blue Flag beaches, excellent for water sports. Caravan storage and on-site caravan parking. Rallies - special price. We accept motorcycles at our discretion.

LYNDHURST

Denny Wood - Forestry Commission Caravan & Camping Site, Near Lyndhurst, Hampshire, SO43 7PZ.
Std: 0131 **Tel:** 314 6505
Email: fe.holidays@forestry.gsi.gov.uk
Website: www.forestholidays.co.uk
Nearest Town/Resort Lyndhurst
Directions Take the B3056 from Lyndhurst, the site is 2½ miles on the right.
Acreage 27 **Open** 24 March **to** 27 Sept
Access Good **Site** Level
Sites Available A ♣ ⚏ **Total** 170
Facilities ♥ ♨ ♨ �ℙ ⊡
Nearby Facilities ✓ U
⚲ Brockenhurst
Peaceful, grassland site among scattered oaks. New Forest ponies roam free around the site. Note : This site has NO toilets.

LYNDHURST

Matley Wood - Forestry Commission, Near Lyndhurst, Hampshire, SO43 7FZ.
Std: 0131 **Tel:** 314 6505
Email: fe.holidays@forestry.gsi.gov.uk
Website: www.forestholidays.co.uk
Nearest Town/Resort Lyndhurst
Directions Take the B3056 from Lyndhurst, the site is 2 miles on the left. Reception for Matley Wood is at Denny Wood.
Acreage 5 **Open** 24 March **to** 27 Sept
Access Good **Site** Level
Sites Available A ♣ ⚏ **Total** 70
Facilities ♥ ⚲ ⊡ ⊡
⚲ Brockenhurst
A small, secluded site within the natural woodland of the New Forest. Note : This site has NO toilets.

MILFORD-ON-SEA

Lytton Lawn, Lymore Lane, Milford-on-Sea, Hants, SO41 0TX.
Std: 01590 **Tel:** 648331 **Fax:** 645610
Email: holidays@shorefield.co.uk
Website: www.shorefield.co.uk
Nearest Town/Resort Lymington
Directions From Lymington take the A337 towards Everton. Turn left onto the B3058 towards Milford-on-Sea and take the second left into Lymore Lane.
Acreage 4 **Open** 1 February **to** 5 January
Access Good **Site** Lev/Slope
Sites Available A ♣ ⚏ **Total** 135
Facilities ♿ ⚲ ∮ ⌂ ⊞ ⚏ ♨ ⅌ ⊙ ↵ ♨
⚏ ♥ ♨ ◳ ⚏ ♨ ♧ ↴ ⊡ ⊡
Nearby Facilities ⌐ ✓ ⚓ ↘ U ⚞
⚲ New Milton
Views of the Isle of Wight. 1 mile from the beach and 2 miles from the New Forest. FREE membership to the leisure club, restaurant, licensed club, colour TV, games room, indoor/outdoor swimming pools and tennis are available at our sister site Shorefield Country Park (2½ miles).

NEW MILTON

Hoburne Bashley, Sway Road, New Milton, Hampshire, BH25 5QR.
Std: 01425 **Tel:** 612340 **Fax:** 632732
Email: enquiries@hoburne.com
Website: www.hoburne.com
Nearest Town/Resort New Milton
Directions From the A35 Lyndhurst/ Bournemouth road, take the B3055 signposted Sway. Over crossroads at 2¼ miles. Park is ½ mile on left.
Open March **to** October
Access Good **Site** Level
Sites Available A ♣ ⚏ **Total** 400
Facilities ♿ ⚲ ∮ ⌂ ⊞ ⚏ ♨ ⅌ ⊙ ↵ ♨
⚏ ♥ ♨ ◳ ⚏ ♧ ⚑ ⊞ ♨ ❀ ⚞ ⚏ ⊡ ⊡
Nearby Facilities ✓ ⚓ ↘ U ⚞

⚲ New Milton
New Forest - 2 miles from beach, 10 mile[s] Bournemouth. Own golf course and tennis Many facilities. Rose Award for Excellence and England for Excellence Silver Award.

NEW MILTON

Setthorns Caravan & Camping Site - Forestry Commission, Wootton, New Milton, Hampshire, BH25 5WA.
Std: 0131 **Tel:** 314 6505
Email: fe.holidays@forestry.gsi.gov.uk
Website: www.forestholidays.co.uk
Nearest Town/Resort New Milton
Directions Take the A35 from Lyndhurst signposted 7 miles south west of Lyndhurst[.]
Acreage 60 **Open** All Year
Access Good **Site** Level
Sites Available A ♣ ⚏ **Total** 320
Facilities ∮ ♥ ♨ ⊡ ⊡
Nearby Facilities ⌐ U
⚲ New Milton
Open woodland site with pitches nestlin[g] among pine and oak trees. This site has NO toilet facilities.

OWER

Green Pastures Farm, Ower, Romsey, Hampshire, SO51 6AJ.
Std: 023 **Tel:** 8081 4444
Email: enquiries@greenpasturesfarm.com
Website: www.greenpasturesfarm.com
Nearest Town/Resort Romsey
Directions Site is signposted from the A3[1] and the A3090 at Ower (exit 2 off M27[)] follow directions for Salisbury for ½ mil[e] then follow our own signs.
Acreage 5 **Open** 15 March **to** 31 October
Access Good **Site** Level
Sites Available A ♣ ⚏ **Total** 45
Facilities ♿ ∮ ⊞ ⚏ ♨ ⅌ ⊙ ↵ ⊙ ♨
⚏ ◳ ⚏ ⊡ ⊡
Nearby Facilities ⌐ ✓ U ⚞
⚲ Romsey

Red Shoot Camping Park

LINWOOD, NEAR RINGWOOD, HAMPSHIRE BH24 3QT
TELEPHONE: (01425) 473789   FAX: (01425) 471558
APPROVED SITE FOR TENTS, CARAVANS AND MOTOR HOMES

Beautifully situated in the NEW FOREST, with lovely walks from the camp site gate. Ideal centre for walking, touring and for nature lovers, yet only half hours drive from Bournemouth and the sea.
❑ Excellent Toilet/Shower Facilities ❑ Electric Hook-ups ❑ Well Stocked Shop & Off Licence
❑ Children's Play Area ❑ Laundry Room ❑ Facilities for the Disabled ❑ Mountain Bike Hire
❑ Special Off Peak Tariff ❑ Owner supervised to high standard.

'Red Shoot Inn' lies adjacent to the camp site, and is an attractive old pub serving real ales, good food and welcoming families.

For Details and Brochure send a S.A.E. to:
Nick & Jaqui Oldfield at the above address.

This popular little site has been owned and managed by the same family for over 30 years.

South Coast
and New Forest

With two high quality destinations to choose from, Shorefield Holidays offers you the best of both worlds in touring locations

LYTTON LAWN
TOURING PARK

OAKDENE
FOREST PARK

Set in beautiful natural parkland close to Milford beach and the historic New Forest with views to the Isle of Wight. Peaceful, unspoilt and relaxing. Electricity hook-up, showers, laundrette, shop, 'Premier Pitches' and a children's area. Optional Leisure Club facilities 2¹/₂ miles away.

Over 55 acres of beautiful parkland giving direct access to the Avon Forest, and only 9 miles from Bournemouth's sandy beaches. New 'Premier Pitches', indoor and outdoor pools, sauna, steam room, spa bath, flume, gym, adventure playground, club with entertainment, cafeteria, takeaway, general store and launderette.

SHOREFIELD
HOLIDAYS LIMITED

RALLIES WELCOME AT BOTH SITES

2000 DAVID BELLAMY CONSERVATION AWARD GOLD

For further details telephone
01590 648331 Ref. CADT

Oakdene Forest Park, St. Leonards, Ringwood, Hants BH24 2RZ
Lytton Lawn, Lymore Lane, Milford on Sea, Hants SO41 0TX
e-mail: holidays@shorefield.co.uk   **www.shorefield.co.uk**

ENGLAND FOR EXCELLENCE
THE ENGLISH TOURIST BOARD
AWARDS FOR TOURISM

A grassy site on family run farm, within easy reach of the New Forest. Paultons Park 1 mile. Convenient for ferries. Ample space for children to play in full view of units. Separate toilet/shower room for the disabled. Day-kennelling available.

RINGWOOD

Oakdene Forest Park, St. Leonards, Ringwood, Hampshire, BH24 7RZ.
Std: 01590 **Tel:** 648331 **Fax:** 645610
Email: holidays@shorefield.co.uk
Website: www.shorefield.co.uk
Nearest Town/Resort Ringwood/ Bournemouth
Directions 3 miles west of Ringwood off the A31 just past St Leonards Hospital.
Acreage 55 **Open** 1 Feb **to** 5 Jan
Access Good **Site** Level
Sites Available A ⊕ ⊜ **Total** 200
Facilities ⅃ ⌨ ♨ ⌐ ⊙ ⅃ ⊿ ⊡ ☏
♨ ⊙ ⊜ ✕ ⋀ ⋒ ⫯ ✈ ⬛ ⊡
Nearby Facilities ↾ ✓ ∪
☈ Bournemouth
Bordering Avon Forest, surrounded by parkland and Forestry Commission land. 9 miles from Bournemouth beaches. NEW indoor and outdoor swimming pools, plus flume, gym, sauna and steam room.

RINGWOOD

The Red Shoot Camping Park, Linwood, Nr. Ringwood, Hampshire, BH24 3QT.
Std: 01425 **Tel:** 473789 **Fax:** 471558
Email: enquiries@redshoot-campingpark.com
Website: www.redshoot-campingpark.com
Nearest Town/Resort Ringwood.
Directions Fron Ringwood take A338, 2

miles north of Ringwood take right turn signed Moyles Court and Linwood. Follow signs to Linwood.
Acreage 4 **Open** March **to** October
Access Good **Site** Lev/Slope
Sites Available A ⊕ ⊜ **Total** 105
Facilities ⅃ ♨ ⌨ ♨ ⌐ ⊙ ⅃ ⊿ ⊡ ☏
♨ ⊙ ⊜ ✕ ⋀ ⊡
Nearby Facilities ↾ ✓ ⊥ ∪ ⌓ ☇
☈ Brockenhurst.
Situated in a beautiful part of the New Forest. Half hour drive to Bournemouth coast, Salisbury and Southampton. Good pub adjacent. Mountain bike hire. Off peak tariff early and late season.

RINGWOOD

Tree Tops Touring Caravan Park, Hurn Road, Avon Castle, Matchams, Ringwood, Hampshire, BH24 2BP.
Std: 01425 **Tel:** 475848
Nearest Town/Resort Ringwood
Directions Take the A31, at Ringwood filter left and follow signs to Matchams, site is 2 miles on the left.
Open Easter **to** Sept
Access Good **Site** Level
Sites Available A ⊕ ⊜
Facilities ✖ ♨ ⌨ ♨ ⌐ ⊙ ⅃ ⊿ ☏
⊙ ⊜ ⊟ A
Nearby Facilities ↾ ✓ ⊥ ☇
☈ Bournemouth
Ideal for touring Dorset and Hampshire.

ROMSEY

Hill Farm Caravan Park, Branches Lane, Sherfield English, Romsey, Hampshire, SO51 6FH.
Std: 01794 **Tel:** 340402 **Fax:** 342358
Email: gjb@hillfarmpark.com

Website: www.hillfarmpark.com
Nearest Town/Resort Romsey
Directions From Romsey take the A30▮ west, turn right onto the A27 toward▮ Salisbury. In Sherfield English at the fir▮ crossroads turn right into Branches Lan▮ site is approx. 1 mile.
Acreage 11 **Open** March **to** October
Access Good **Site** Lev/Slope
Sites Available A ⊕ ⊜ **Total** 150
Facilities ⅃ ♨ ⌨ ♨ ⌐ ⊙ ⅃ ⊿ ⊡ ☏
♨ ⊙ ⊜ ⋀ ✳ ⫯ ⊡
Nearby Facilities ↾ ✓ ∪ ☇
☈ Romsey
Set in beautiful Hampshire countryside w▮ offer a quiet, rural location. Just 3 miles no▮ of the New Forest and only 20 minutes fro▮ Salisbury, Winchester and Southampton.

SOUTHSEA

Southsea Leisure Park, Melville Road, Southsea, Hampshire, PO4 9TB.
Std: 023 **Tel:** 9273 5070 **Fax:** 9282 1302
Email: info.scs@btinternet.com
Website: www.southsea-caravans-ltd.co.uk
Nearest Town/Resort Portsmouth
Directions From M27/A27/A3M tak▮ southbound A2030 for 4 miles, turn left on▮ the A288 and follow signs.
Acreage 12 **Open** All Year
Access Good **Site** Level
Sites Available A ⊕ ⊜ **Total** 216
Facilities ⅃ ♨ ⌨ ♨ ⌐ ⊙ ⅃ ⊿ ⊡ ☏
♨ ⏦ ⊙ ⊜ ✕ ⑆ ⋀ ⊠ ⫯ ⊡ ⊡
Nearby Facilities ↾ ✓ ⊥ ⋆ ☇
☈ Portsmouth Harbour
Located beside the beach at the quieter e▮ of historic Portsmouth. Only 10 minute▮ from cross-channel ferries. Fully equippe▮ modern touring facilities.

HEREFORDSHIRE
BROMYARD

Joyce Caravan Park, Stanford Bishop,
Bringsty, Near Worcester, WR6 5UB.
Std: 01886 **Tel:** 884248
Nearest Town/Resort Bromyard
Directions 3 miles east of Bromyard off the
A4220. Follow official signs from the A44/
A4220 junction.
Acreage 1½ **Open** March **to** October
Access Good **Site** Level
Sites Available ⊞ ⊞ **Total** 18
Facilities & f ⬚ ♨ ∩ ⊙ ⌿ ⚿ ⊠ ⊡
⬚ ⬚ ⌇ ⊞
Nearby Facilities ⌿
Ideal for exploring the heart of England and
the Welsh Marches etc.. Dogs are welcome
by arrangement. Booking is advisable.

CRASWALL

Old Mill Caravan Park, Old Mill, Craswall,
Herefordshire, HR2 0PN.
Std: 01981 **Tel:** 510226
Nearest Town/Resort Hereford.
Directions 8 miles off the A465 at Pandy.
Acreage 2 **Open** Easter **to** October
Access Good **Site** Level
Sites Available ⊞ ⊞ ⊞
Facilities ⬚ & ⊙ ⌇ ⌇ ⊞
Nearby Facilities ⌿ ⌿ ∪
≠ Hereford.
Near Offas Dyke path, alongside river.
Scenic views of the Black Mountains.

HAY-ON-WYE

Penlan Caravan Park, Penlan, Brilley,
Hay-on-Wye, Herefordshire, HR3 6JW.
Std: 01497 **Tel:** 831485
Std: 01497 **Fax:** 831485
Nearest Town/Resort Hay-on-Wye
Directions From Kington Church follow the
Brilley to Whitney-on-Wye road for 4 miles.
Look for National Trust signs on the left, turn
sharp left into Apostles Lane, Penlan is first
on the right.
Acreage 2½ **Open** Easter **to** October
Access Fair **Site** Lev/Slope
Sites Available Total 12
Facilities ⌿ f ⬚ ♨ ∩ ⊙ ⚿ ⚿ ⌇
Nearby Facilities ⌿ ⌿ ⚿ ⌇ ∪
≠ Hereford
Peaceful and relaxing site. Ideal for exploring
Mid Wales and the black and white villages
of Herefordshire. National Trust small holding.

HEREFORD

Cuckoo's Corner, Moreton-on-Lugg,
Herefordshire, HR4 8AH.
Std: 01432 **Tel:** 760234
Email: cuckoos.corner@ic24.net
Website: www.geocities.com/cuckooscorner
Nearest Town/Resort Hereford
Directions 4 miles north of Hereford on the
A49, 100 yards beyond signpost Village
Centre and Marden. Or 10 miles south of
Leominster opposite advance sign Village
Centre and Marden.
Acreage 1½ **Open** All Year
Access Good **Site** Level
Sites Available ⊞ ⊞ ⊞ **Total** 10
Facilities & f ⬚ ⬚ ⬚ ∩ ⊙ ⚿
Nearby Facilities ⌿ ⌿ ⚿ ∪
Friendly family site with pleasant views.
Archery and croquet on site. Farm animals
and pet exercise area. Good touring area.

HEREFORD

The Millpond, Little Tarrington,
Herefordshire, HR1 4JA.
Std: 01432 **Tel:** 890243 **Fax:** 890243
Email: enquiries@millpond.co.uk
Website: www.millpond.co.uk

Nearest Town/Resort Hereford/Ledbury
Directions Leave the M50 at junction 2 and
take the A417 to Ledbury, go around the by-
pass and drive west on the A438/A417 to
Trumpet crossroads. Take the A438 toward
Hereford and turn second right to Millpond.
Open March **to** October
Access Good **Site** Level
Sites Available ⊞ ⊞ ⊞ **Total** 30
Facilities & f ⬚ ∩ ⊙ ⚿ ⚿ ⬚ ⬚
Nearby Facilities ⌿
≠ Hereford/Ledbury
Alongside a picturesque lake, coarse fishing.

HEREFORD

Upper Gilvach Farm, St. Margarets,
Vowchurch, Hereford, Herefordshire, HR2 0QY
Std: 01981 **Tel:** 510618
Nearest Town/Resort Hereford.
Directions 4 miles off the B4348.
Open Easter **to** October
Access Good **Site** Level
Sites Available ⊞ ⊞ ⊞ **Total** 20
Facilities ⬚ ⬚ ⚿ ⬚ ⬚
Nearby Facilities ⌿ ⌿ ∪ ⚿ ⚿
≠ Hereford.

LEOMINSTER

Arrow Bank Caravan Park, Nun House
Farm, Eardisland, Near Leominster,
Herefordshire, HR6 9BG.
Std: 01544 **Tel:** 388312 **Fax:** 388312
Nearest Town/Resort Leominster
Directions 6 miles west of Leominster, off
the A44 Rhayadr/Brecon road.
Acreage 5 **Open** March **to** October
Access Good **Site** Level
Sites Available ⊞ ⊞ ⊞ **Total** 34
Facilities f ⬚ ⚿ ∩ ⊙ ⚿ ⚿ ⬚ ⊠ ⬚
⬚ ⬚ ⌇ ⊞
Nearby Facilities ⌿ ⌿ ∪ ⚿
≠ Leominster
Peaceful, landscaped park with very
spacious and level pitches, set in a beautiful
"Black and White" village. Ideal holiday base.

LEOMINSTER

Nicholson Farm, Docklow, Near
Leominster, Herefordshire, HR6 0SL.
Std: 01568 **Tel:** 760346
Nearest Town/Resort Leominster/Bromyard
Directions On the A44 between Bromyard
and Leominster.
Open Easter **to** October
Access Good **Site** Level
Sites Available ⊞ ⊞ ⊞ **Total** 7
Facilities f ⬚ ⚿ ∩ ⚿
Nearby Facilities ⌿ ⌿ ∪ ⚿
≠ Leominster
A working dairy farm with carp fishing on
site. ½ hour away from two cathedral cities.

LEOMINSTER

Pearl Lake Leisure Park, Shobdon,
Leominster, Herefordshire, HR6 9NQ.
Std: 01568 **Tel:** 708326 **Fax:** 708408
Email: enquiries@pearl-lake.freeserve.co.uk
Website: www.pearl-lake.co.uk
Nearest Town/Resort Leominster
Directions Take the A44 from Leominster
for 2 miles, turn right onto the B4529, then
take the A4110 to Mortimers Cross and turn
left onto the B4362, park is on the right as
you are leaving Shobdon Village.
Acreage 80 **Open** March **to** 30 November
Access Good **Site** Level
Sites Available ⊞ ⊞ ⊞ **Total** 15
Facilities & f ⬚ ⬚ ⬚ ⚿ ∩ ⊙ ⚿ ⬚ ⊠ ⬚
⚿ ⬚ ⬚ ⬚ ⚿ ⚿ ⊞
Nearby Facilities ⌿ ⌿ ⚿ ∪
20 acres of woodland, outstanding park in a
beautiful setting. 15 acre lake, golf course.
bowling green.

PETERCHURCH

Poston Mill Park, Peterchurch, Golden
Valley, Herefordshire, HR2 0SF.
Std: 01981 **Tel:** 550225 **Fax:** 550885
Email: enquiries@poston-mill.co.uk
Website: www.ukparks.co.uk/postonmill
Nearest Town/Resort Hereford
Directions On B4348. 11 miles from
Hereford and 11 miles from Hay on Wye.
Acreage 33 **Open** All Year
Access Good **Site** Level
Sites Available ⊞ ⊞ ⊞ **Total** 64
Facilities & f ⬚ ⬚ ⬚ ⚿ ∩ ⊙ ⚿ ⬚ ⊠ ⬚
⚿ ⬚ ⬚ ⬚ ⬚ ⚿ ⬚ ⬚ ⬚ ⚿ ⚿ ⊞ ⊞ ⊞
Nearby Facilities ⌿ ⌿ ∪ ⚿
≠ Hereford
Highly recommended, beautiful, well
maintained park with electric, water and T.V.
(inc. Satellite) connections on all pitches. Set
on the banks of the River Dore. Adjacent to
an excellent restaurant/bar.

PETERCHURCH

The Bridge Inn, Michaelchurch Escley,
Hereford, HR2 0JW.
Std: 01981 **Tel:** 510646 **Fax:** 510646
Email: lisabridge@tesco.net
Nearest Town/Resort Hereford
Directions From Hereford take the A465
towards Abergavenny, turn right onto the
B4348 for Hay-on-Wye, turn left onto
unclassified road for Michaelchurch and
Vowchurch. In the village at the T-Junction turn
left, 300 yards past the church turn left again.
Acreage 1 **Open** All Year
Access Good **Site** Level
Sites Available ⊞ ⊞ ⊞ **Total** 12
Facilities f ⬚ ⬚ ⚿ ∩ ⊙ ⚿ ⬚ ⬚ ⬚ ⚿ ⚿ ⬚ ⊞ ⊞
Nearby Facilities ⌿ ⌿ ∪ ⚿
≠ Hereford
Riverside location, adjacent to a pub and
restaurant. Ideal walking and cycling area.

ROSS-ON-WYE

Broadmeadow Caravan Park,
Broadmeadows, Ross-on-Wye,
Herefordshire, HR9 7BH.
Std: 01989 **Tel:** 768076 **Fax:** 566030
Email: broadm4811@aol.com
Nearest Town/Resort Ross-on-Wye
Directions Adjacent to the A40 Ross relief
road. Access from Pancake roundabout off
relief road turning onto Ross. Take the first
right opposite Wolf Tools into Ashburton
Estate Road, then turn right by Safeway
Supermarket.
Acreage 16 **Open** Easter/1st Apr **to** Sept
Access Good **Site** Level
Sites Available ⊞ ⊞ ⊞ **Total** 150
Facilities & f ⬚ ⬚ ⬚ ⚿ ∩ ⊙ ⚿ ⬚ ⊠ ⬚
⚿ ⬚ ⬚ ⚿ ⚿ ⊞
Nearby Facilities ⌿ ⚿ ∪ ⚿ ⚿
≠ Gloucester
Lake walks. Fishing on site. Only 10 minutes
to the centre of Ross-on-Wye. Ideal touring
and walking in the Wye Valley. ETB 5 Star
Graded.

ROSS-ON-WYE

Lion House, Fawley, Kings Caple,
Herefordshire, HR1 4UQ.
Std: 01432 **Tel:** 840524
Nearest Town/Resort Ross-on-Wye
Directions Take the A49 off Wilton
roundabout, turn second right, in Hoarwithy
turn right after the The New Harp. Bear right,
go over the bridge and continue for 1¾
miles, British Lion is on the left hand side.
Acreage 2 **Open** March **to** November
Access Good **Site** Sloping
Sites Available ⊞ ⊞ ⊞ **Total** 5
Facilities f ⬚ ∩ ⚿ ⬚ ⚿ ⊞
≠ Hereford

ROSS-ON-WYE

Lower Ruxton Farm, Kings Caple, Herefordshire, HR1 4TX.
Std: 01432 **Tel:** 840223
Nearest Town/Resort Ross-on-Wye
Directions A49 from Ross-on-Wye, 1 mile turn right follow signs for Hoarwithy (Kings Caple 4 miles) across river bridge ½ mile sign to Ruxton second farm on right.
Acreage 8 **Open** Mid July **to** End Aug
Site Level
Sites Available ▲ **Total** 20
Facilities 𝕗 ⚿ ⊟
Nearby Facilities ✈ Hereford
Alongside a river.

SYMONDS YAT

Symonds Yat Caravan & Camping Limited, Symonds Yat West, Near Ross-on-Wye, Herefordshire, HR9 6BY.
Std: 01600 **Tel:** 890883/891069
Std: 01600 **Fax:** 890883
Email: geoff@camping&caravan.com
Website: www.camping&caravan.com
Nearest Town/Resort Monmouth
Directions A40, 7 miles to Ross-on-Wye and 4 miles to Monmouth. Park is ¼ mile from the A40.
Acreage 1 **Open** March **to** October
Access Good **Site** Level
Sites Available ▲ ⚏ ⚐ **Total** 35
Facilities 𝕗 ▥ ▨ ♨ ℯ ⊙ ⊒ ⚐
🏋 🛒 ✖ ⊟ ⊟
Nearby Facilities ┌ ✔ ➴ ⚲
✈ Hereford
In an area of outstanding natural beauty, adjacent to the River Wye which is ideal for walking, canoeing and fishing. Good for touring the Forest of Dean.

SYMONDS YAT WEST

Doward Park Camp Site, Great Doward, Symonds Yat West, Near Ross-on-Wye, Herefordshire, HR9 6BP.
Std: 01600 **Tel:** 890438
Email: dowardpark@ntlworld.com
Website: www.dowardparkfree-online.co.uk
Nearest Town/Resort Monmouth
Directions On the A40 between Ross-on-Wye and Monmouth. Turn off at Symonds Yat West and follow signs for The Doward.
Acreage 4 **Open** Easter **to** October
Access Good **Site** Level
Sites Available ▲ ⚏ ⚐ **Total** 40
Facilities 𝕗 ▥ ▨ ♨ ℯ ⊙ ⊒ 🏋 🛒 ✖ ⊟
Nearby Facilities ┌ ✔ ➴ ⚲
✈ Hereford
Very scenic and peaceful site with excellent, clean facilities. Close to the River Wye with woodland and river walks. Ideal base for touring the Wye Valley and the Forest of Dean.

WHITCHURCH

Sterrett's Caravan Park, Symonds Yat (West), Near Ross-on-Wye, Herefordshire, HR9 6BY.
Std: 01594 **Tel:** 832888
Website: www.ukparks.co.uk/sterretts
Nearest Town/Resort Ross-on-Wye
Directions Take the A40 from Ross-on-Wye or Monmouth to Whitchurch. ½ mile from the A40 to Symonds Yat (West).
Acreage 5 **Open** March **to** October
Access Good **Site** Level
Sites Available ▲ ⚏ ⚐ **Total** 8
Facilities 𝕗 ▥ ▨ ♨ ℯ ⊙ ⊒ 🛒 ▣ ☎
🏋 🛒 ✖ ⋀ ✖ ⊟
Nearby Facilities ┌ ✔ ➴ ∪ ⚲
✈ Hereford
Flat and grassy site, close to a river.

HERTFORDSHIRE
BALDOCK

Radwell Mill Lake, Radwell Mill, Baldock, Herts, SG7 5ET.
Std: 01462 **Tel:** 730253
Std: 01462 **Fax:** 733421
Nearest Town/Resort Baldock
Directions Junction 10 A1(M) then the A507, ½ mile towards Baldock take a lane signed "Radwell Only" to the lake and site.
Acreage 3 **Open** Easter **to** November
Access Good **Site** Level
Sites Available ▲ ⚏ ⚐ **Total** 20
Facilities ▨ ⊒ ☎ ✖
Nearby Facilities ✈ Baldock
Quiet site with a lake and orchard. Good for bird watching. New Motorway Services, ½ mile away, with café/restaurant, shops and take-away food.

HERTFORD

Camping & Caravanning Club Site, Mangrove Road (Not Ball Park), Hertford, Hertfordshire, SG13 8QF.
Std: 01992 **Tel:** 586696
Website:
www.campingandcaravanningclub.co.uk
Directions From the A10 follow the A414 Hertford signs to the next roundabout (Foxholes) and go straight across, after 200 yards turn left signposted Balls Park and Hertford University. Turn left at the T-Junction into Mangrove Road, go past Simon Balle School, University and Cricket Ground, site is 400 yards past the cricket club on the left.
Open March **to** October
Site Level
Sites Available ▲ ⚏ ⚐ **Total** 250
Facilities ♿ 𝕗 ▥ ▨ ♨ ℯ ⊙ ⊒ ☎ ▣ ☎
🏋 🛒 ❈ ✖ ⊟ ⊟
Nearby Facilities ┌ ✔ ∪ ⚲
✈ North & East Hertford
Set in acres of meadowland. 5 miles from Hatfield House and 20 miles from London. BTB Graded. Non members welcome.

HODDESDON

Lee Valley Caravan Park, Dobbs Weir, Charlton Meadows, Essex Road, Hoddesdon, Hertfordshire, EN11 0AS.
Std: 01992 **Tel:** 462090
Std: 01992 **Fax:** 462090
Email: info@leevalleypark.org.uk
Website: www.leevalleypark.com
Nearest Town/Resort Hoddesdon
Directions From the A10 take the Hoddesdon turn off, at the second roundabout turn left signposted Dobbs Weir. The caravan park is on the right within a mile.
Open 31 March **to** 31 October
Access Good **Site** Level
Sites Available ▲ ⚏ ⚐ **Total** 100
Facilities ♿ 𝕗 ▨ ♨ ℯ ⊙ ⊒ 🛒 ☎
🏋 🛒 ⋀ ✖ ⊟
Nearby Facilities ✔ ➴ ⚲
✈ Broxbourne
Alongside the River Lea.

ISLE OF MAN
DOUGLAS

Glen Dhoo Camping Site, Hillberry, Onchan, Nr. Douglas, Isle of Man, IM4 5BJ.
Std: 01624 **Tel:** 621254
Std: 01624 **Fax:** 621254
Email: glenghoo@m.c.b.net
Website: www.caravancampingsites.co.u
Nearest Town/Resort Douglas
Directions 2½ miles from Douglas seafro on the A18 road and TT Course. 1 mile fro Onchan, 100 yards before Hillberry Corne
Acreage 3 **Open** April **to** September
Site Lev/Slope
Sites Available ▲ ⚏ ⚐ **Total** 50
Facilities 𝕗 ▥ ▨ ♨ ℯ ⊙ ⊒ 🛒 ▣ ☎
🏋 ⊙ 🛒 ⊟
Nearby Facilities ┌ ✔ ⚓ ∪

PEEL

Peel Camping Park, PTC6, Derby Road Peel, Isle of Man, IM5 1RG.
Std: 01624 **Tel:** 842341
Std: 01624 **Fax:** 844010
Email: ptc@mc6.net
Nearest Town/Resort Peel
Directions A20 edge of town signposted
Acreage 4 **Open** Mid April **to** End Sept
Access Good **Site** Level
Sites Available ▲ ⚏ ⚐ **Total** 100
Facilities 𝕗 ▨ ♨ ℯ ⊙ ⊒ 🛒 🏋 🛒 ▥ ▨ [
Nearby Facilities ┌ ✔ ⚓ ➴ ∪ ⚲
3 miles T.T. course, near sea, central island, cars and motorcycles free.

ISLE OF WIGHT
ATHERFIELD

Chine Farm Camping Site, Military Roa Atherfield Bay, Isle of Wight, PO38 2JH.
Std: 01983 **Tel:** 740228
Nearest Town/Resort Freshwater
Directions East of Freshwater 8 miles o the A3055 Coast Road.
Acreage 5 **Open** May **to** September
Access Good **Site** Level
Sites Available ▲ ⚏ ⚐ **Total** 80
Facilities ▨ ♨ ℯ ⊙ ⊒ ⊙ ⋀ ❈ ✖ ⊟
Nearby Facilities ┌ ✔
Footpath to beach. Sea view. 3¼ mile Blackgang Chine.

BEMBRIDGE

Whitecliff Bay Holiday Park, Hillway, Whitecliff Bay, Bembridge, Isle of Wight, PO35 5PL.
Std: 01983 **Tel:** 872671
Email: holiday@whitecliff-bay.com
Website: www.whitecliff-bay.com
Nearest Town/Resort Sandown
Directions B3395 road to Sandown, follc signposts.
Acreage 15 **Open** April **to** October
Access Good **Site** Lev/Slope
Sites Available ▲ ⚏ ⚐ **Total** 450
Facilities ♿ 𝕗 ▥ ▨ ♨ ℯ ⊙ ⊒ 🛒 ▣
🏋 ⊙ 🛒 ✖ ▽ 🛒 ⋀ 🐾 ❈ ✖ ⊟
Nearby Facilities ┌ ✔ ⚓ ➴ ∪ ⚲ ⚲
✈ Brading
Situated in pleasant countryside adjoini Whitecliff Bay with sandy beach. Indoor pc and leisure centre, family owned ar managed.

BRIGHSTONE BAY

Grange Farm Caravan & Camping Site, Military Road, Brighstone Bay, Brighstone, Isle of Wight, PO30 4DA.
Std: 01983 **Tel:** 740296 **Fax:** 741233
Email: grangefarm@brighstonebay.fsnet.co.uk
Website: www.brighstonebay.fsnet.co.uk
Nearest Town/Resort BrighstoneNewport
Directions On coastal road A3055 midway from Freshwater to Chale (approx 5mls).
Acreage 2 **Open** March **to** End October
Access Good **Site** Level
Sites Available Å ♀ ☐ **Total** 60
Facilities ♦ ₩ ♣ ╷ ⊙ ┙ ┛ ☐ ☜
♀☌ ╏☌ ⊙ ☎ ⁄⊟⊡
Nearby Facilities ┣ ✓ ⚓ ✈ ⊅
Family run park on a small working farm with unusual farm animals. Situated right by the sea, just a minute walk to the beach. South facing. Self catering accommodation also available. No motorcycle groups. Fossil hunting and fishing, a walkers paradise.

COWES

Waverley Park Holiday Centre, 51 Old Road, East Cowes, Isle of Wight, PO32 6AW.
Std: 01983 **Tel:** 293452 **Fax:** 200494
Email: waverleypark@netscapeonline.co.uk
Nearest Town/Resort Cowes
Directions Signposted from Red Funnel Ferries, only 500 yards from the East Cowes Terminal.
Acreage 10½ **Open** March **to** October
Access Good **Site** Sloping
Sites Available Å ♀ ☐ **Total** 45
Facilities ♦ ₩ ♣ ╷ ⊙ ┙ ┛ ☐ ☜
♀☌ ╏☌ ⊙ ☎ ✗ ▽ ☐ ↳ ⊞ ☐ ☐
Nearby Facilities ┣ ✓ ⚓ ✈ ⊙ ⊅ ⊿
⚓ Ryde
Panoramic views over the Solent.

NETTLESTONE

Pondwell Camping & Chalets, Pondwell Hill, Nettlestone, Isle of Wight, PO34 5AQ.
Std: 01983 **Tel:** 612330 **Fax:** 613511
Nearest Town/Resort Ryde

Directions Signposted from Wightlink Fishbourne. Take A3054 to Ryde then A3055 turning left along B3350 to Seaview. Site is next to Wishing Well Pub.
Acreage 14 **Open** May **to** September
Access Good **Site** Level
Sites Available Å ♀ ☐ **Total** 200
Facilities ♣ ♦ ₩ ♣ ╷ ⊙ ┙ ┛ ☐ ☜
♀☌ ⊙ ☎ ☍ ♣ ⁄⊟ ☐ ☐
Nearby Facilities ┣ ✓ ⚓ ✈ ⊙ ⊿
⚓ Ryde
Set in countryside with scenic views, walking distance to sea.

NEWCHURCH

Southland Camping Park, Winford Road, Newchurch, Isle of Wight, PO36 0LZ.
Std: 01983 **Tel:** 865385 **Fax:** 867663
Email: info@southland.co.uk
Website: www.southland.co.uk
Nearest Town/Resort Sandown/Shanklin
Directions Newport to Sandown road A3056/A3055 through Arreton, after Fighting Cocks Public House take the second left. Continue along road for 1 mile, site is on the left.
Acreage 5¾ **Open** Easter **to** September
Access Good **Site** Level
Sites Available Å ♀ ☐ **Total** 120
Facilities ♦ ₩ ♣ ╷ ⊙ ┙ ┛ ☐ ☜
♀☌ ╏☌ ⊙ ☎ ☍ ⁄⊟ ☐ ☐
Nearby Facilities ┣ ✓ ⚓ ✈ ⊙ ⊿ ⊅
⚓ Lake
Sheltered, secluded touring park, generous level pitches. Far reaching views over Arreton Valley.

RYDE

Beaper Farm Camping & Caravan Park, Near Ryde, Isle of Wight, PO33 1QJ.
Std: 01983 **Tel:** 615210/875184
Email: beaper@btinternet.com
Nearest Town/Resort Ryde
Directions On the main A3055 Ryde to Sandown road, go past Tesco roundabout for ½ mile, Beaper Farm is second on the left.

Acreage 13 **Open** April **to** October
Access Good **Site** Level
Sites Available Å ♀ ☐ **Total** 150
Facilities ♦ ♣ ₩ ♣ ╷ ⊙ ┙ ┛ ☐ ☜
♀☌ ⊙ ⁄⊟ ☐
Nearby Facilities ┣ ✓ ⚓ ✈ ⊙ ⊿
⚓ Ryde
Near to beaches, golf, water sports, fishir trips, horse riding, ice skating, ten p bowling and nightclubs, plus Isle of Wigl Steam Railway.

RYDE

Kite Hill Farm Caravan & Camping Park, Kite Hill Farm, Wootton Bridge, Near Ryde, Isle of Wight, PO33 4LE.
Std: 01983 **Tel:** 882543
Email: barry@kitehillfarm.freeserve.co.uk
Nearest Town/Resort Ryde
Directions Take the A3054, Ryde is 3 miles from Newport and 3½ miles fro Firestone, Copse Road.
Acreage 12½ **Open** All Year
Access Good **Site** Lev/Slope
Sites Available Å ♀ ☐ **Total** 50
Facilities ♦ ♣ ₩ ♣ ╷ ⊙ ┙ ┛ ☐
♀ ⊙ ☎ ⁄⊟ ☐
Nearby Facilities ┣ ✓ ⚓ ✈ ⊙ ⊅
⚓ Ryde
Graded Park. Ideal for touring, stea railway, walking, beaches, local attraction sailing and local pubs.

SANDOWN

Cheverton Copse Caravan & Camping Park, Newport Road, Near Lake, Sandown, Isle of Wight, PO36 0JP.
Std: 01983 **Tel:** 403161 **Fax:** 402861
Nearest Town/Resort Sandown
Directions On the A3056 Newpor Sandown road, 1¼ miles west of Sandown
Acreage 1 **Open** May **to** September
Access Good **Site** Sloping
Sites Available Å ♀ ☐ **Total** 26
Facilities ♣ ♦ ₩ ♣ ╷ ⊙ ┙ ┛ ☐ ☜
╏☌ ⊙ ☎ ▽ ⁄⊟ ☐ ☐
Nearby Facilities ┣ ✓ ⚓ ✈ ⊙ ⊅ ⊿
⚓ Lake
Near to all amenities, ideal for touring wit superb views.

SANDOWN

Fairway Holiday Park, The Fairway, Sandown, Isle of Wight, PO36 9PS.
Std: 01983 **Tel:** 403462 **Fax:** 405713
Email: janice@hg-london.demon.co.uk
Nearest Town/Resort Sandown
Directions Off Sandown/Shanklin road, into Fairway at Manor House Pub, Lake. Approx ½ mile from centre of Sandown.
Acreage 5½ **Open** March to September
Access Good **Site** Level
Sites Available ▲ ⬤ ⬤ **Total** 150
Facilities ⨍ ▥ ▥ ♨ ⌐ ⊙ ⊣ ⬛ ▣ ☎
⛻ ▯ ⬤ ✗ ♉ ▥ ♠ ⋀ ◄ ▣ ◻ ☎
Nearby Facilities ⌐ ✔ ⚓ ↖ ∪ ⋒ ⚞
≈ Sandown
Picturesque location, with many facilities, relaxed, family atmosphere.

SANDOWN

Old Barn Touring Park, Cheverton Farm, Newport Road, Sandown, Isle of Wight, PO36 9PJ.
Std: 01983 **Tel:** 866414 **Fax:** 865988
Email: oldbarn@weltinet.com
Website: www.oldbarntouring.co.uk
Nearest Town/Resort Sandown
Directions From Newport take the A3056, Park is on the right ½ mile after Apse Heath mini roundabout.
Acreage 5 **Open** 1 May to 25 Sept
Access Good **Site** Level
Sites Available ▲ ⬤ ◻ **Total** 60
Facilities ⨍ ▥ ▥ ♨ ⌐ ⊙ ⊣ ⬛ ▣ ☎
⛻ ⬤ ⬛ ♠ ⋀ ◄ ▣ ◻
≈ Lake
½ miles from the seaside towns of Sandown and Shanklin. Grade II Listed Barn used as a TV and games room.

SANDOWN

Queen Bower Dairy Caravan Park, Alverstone Road, Queen Bower, Sandown, Isle of Wight, PO36 0NZ.
Std: 01983. **Tel:** 403840
Email: qbdcaravanpark@aol.com
Website: www.iow.org.uk/qbdcaravanpark
Nearest Town/Resort Sandown
Directions On the A3056 Newport to Sandown road, turn into Alverstone Road at Apse Heath crossroads. Park is 1 mile on the left.
Acreage 2¼ **Open** May to October
Access Good **Site** Level
Sites Available ⬤ ⬤ **Total** 20
Facilities ⨍ ▥ ▥ ♨ ⛻ ◄ ▣
Nearby Facilities ⌐ ✔ ⚓ ↖ ⋒ ⚞
≈ Sandown
Scenic views, ideal touring. Sell our own produced Dairy products (milk and cream). Public telephone ¼ mile.

SANDOWN

Village Way Caravan & Camping Park, Newport Road, Apse Heath, Sandown, Isle of Wight, PO36 9PJ.
Std: 01983 **Tel:** 863279
Nearest Town/Resort Sandown
Directions From Newport take the A22 to Blackwater then the A3056 to Apse Heath. We are on the main A3056.
Open All Year
Access Good **Site** Level
Sites Available ▲ ⬤ ⬤ **Total** 14
Facilities ⨍ ▥ ▥ ♨ ⌐ ⊙ ⊣ ⬛ ▣ ☎
▯ ⬤ ⬛ ◻
Nearby Facilities ⌐ ⚓ ↖ ∪ ⋒ ⚞ ⚞
≈ Sandown
Near the beach. Free carp fishing on site. Beautiful country walks to the woods and within walking distance of a garden centre and Safeways. The Heights Leisure Centre is only a mile away.

SHANKLIN

Landguard Camping Park, Landguard Manor Road, Shanklin, Isle of Wight, PO37 7PH.
Std: 01983 **Tel:** 867028 **Fax:** 865988
Email: landguard@fsbdial.co.uk
Website: www.landguard-camping.co.uk
Nearest Town/Resort Shanklin
Directions A3056 from Newport, ½ mile before Lake Town sign turn right up Whitecross Lane. 400 yards to site.
Acreage 7 **Open** May to September
Access Good **Site** Level
Sites Available ▲ ⬤ ⬤ **Total** 150
Facilities ♿ ⨍ ▥ ▥ ♨ ⌐ ⊙ ⊣ ⬛ ◻ ☎
⛻ ▯ ⬤ ✗ ♉ ▥ ♠ ⋀ ⋇ ⊛ ▣ ◻
Nearby Facilities ⌐ ✔ ⚓ ↖ ∪
≈ Shanklin
Marked pitches.

SHANKLIN

Ninham Country Holidays, Shanklin, Isle of Wight, PO37 7PL.
Std: 01983 **Tel:** 864243 **Fax:** 868881
Email: office@ninham-holidays.co.uk
Website: www.ninham-holidays.co.uk
Nearest Town/Resort Shanklin
Directions Signposted off Newport/Sandown road (A3056). Site entrance is ¼ mile west of Safeway's on the left.
Acreage 10 **Open** May to September
Access Very Good **Site** Level
Sites Available ▲ ⬤ ⬤ **Total** 98
Facilities ⨍ ▥ ♨ ⌐ ⊙ ⊣ ⬛ ◻ ☎
▯ ⬤ ⬛ ♠ ⋀ ⋇ ⊛ ▣ ◻
Nearby Facilities ⌐ ✔ ⚓ ↖ ∪ ⋒ ⚞
≈ Shanklin
Country park setting close to Islands premier seaside resort. Ferry inclusive "Package" holidays.

ST. HELENS

Carpenters Farm Camp Site, Carpenters Farm, St. Helens, Ryde, Isle of Wight, PO33 1YL.
Std: 01983 **Tel:** 872450
Nearest Town/Resort Sandown
Directions On the B3330, 3 miles from Sandown or Ryde.
Acreage 12½ **Open** End May **to** Oct
Access Good **Site** Sloping
Sites Available ⚠ ⌂ ☝ **Total** 70
Facilities ☇ ⬚ ☏ ☺ ⬛ ⌂ ☕
⬚⬛☕⬛
Nearby Facilities ⚓ ≈ ∪
≠ Brading

VENTNOR

Appuldurcombe Gardens Caravan & Camping Park, Wroxall, Ventnor, Isle of Wight, PO38 3EP.
Std: 01983 **Tel:** 852597 **Fax:** 856225
Email: appuldurcombe@freeuk.com
Website:
www.appuldurcombe.freeuk.com
Nearest Town/Resort Ventnor
Directions From Newport take the A3020 and turn off towards Shanklin. Go through Godshill, turn right at Whiteley Bank roundabout towards Wroxall.
Acreage 4 **Open** April **to** October
Access Good **Site** Lev/Slope
Sites Available ⚠ ⌂ ☝ **Total** 100
Facilities ☇ ⬚ ☏ ☺ ⬛ ⌂ ☕
⬚⬛☕⬛⬛⬛
Nearby Facilities ⚓ ☇ ⚓ ∪ ⚐ ♁
≠ Shanklin
Very pretty family site, just minutes by car from lovely beaches.

YARMOUTH

The Orchards Holiday Caravan & Camping Park, Newbridge, Yarmouth, Isle of Wight, PO41 0TS.
Std: 01983 **Tel:** 531331 **Fax:** 531666
Email: info@orchards-holiday-park.co.uk
Website: www.orchards-holiday-park.co.uk
Nearest Town/Resort Yarmouth
Directions 4 miles east of Yarmouth and 6 miles west of Newport on B3401. Entrance opposite Newbridge Post Office.
Acreage 8 **Open** 20 February **to** 2 January
Access Good **Site** Lev/Slope
Sites Available ⚠ ⌂ ☝ **Total** 175
Facilities ⬛ ☇ ⬚ ⬛ ⬛ ☏ ☺ ⬛ ⌂ ☕
⬚⬛⬚⬛⬛⬛☇⬛☀☀⬛⬛⬛
Nearby Facilities ⚓ ☇ ⚓ ∪ ♁
≠ Lymington
Good views of the Downs and Solent. Bookings inclusive of car ferries throughout season. Outdoor swimming pool from late May to early September, indoor swimming pool all season. Take-away food, self-service shop and coarse fishing on site. Battery charging, small function/meeting room. Small rallies welcome. Ideal for rambling and cycling.

PLEASE
MENTION CADE'S
WHEN REPLYING
TO ADVERTISERS

KENT
ASHFORD

Broadhembury Caravan & Camping Park, Steeds Lane, Kingsnorth, Ashford, Kent, TN26 1NQ.
Std: 01233 **Tel:** 620859 **Fax:** 620859
Email: holidays@broadhembury.co.uk
Website: www.broadhembury.co.uk
Nearest Town/Resort Ashford
Directions Leave the M20 at junction 10 take the A2070 following signs fo Kingsnorth. Turn left at the secon crossroads in the village.
Acreage 7 **Open** All Year
Access Good **Site** Level
Sites Available ⚠ ⌂ ☝ **Total** 80
Facilities ☇ ⬛ ⬛ ⬛ ☏ ☺ ⬛ ⌂ ☕
⬚⬛⬚⬛⬛⬛☇⬛☀⬛⬛⬛
Nearby Facilities ⚓ ☇ ∪ ♁
≠ Ashford
Quiet, Award Winning park in Kentis countryside with every modern amenity Central to many places of interes Convenient for all Channel crossings.

ASHFORD

Dunn Street Farm, Westwell, Ashford, Kent, TN25 4NJ.
Std: 01233 **Tel:** 712537
Nearest Town/Resort Ashford
Directions Travel west on the A20 t Hothfield, turn right into Watery Lane, 2 mile to Westwell Village. Site is on North Down Way, ½ mile north of the village.
Acreage 5 **Open** April **to** October
Access Fair **Site** Level
Sites Available ⚠ ⌂ ☝ **Total** 40
Facilities ☇ ⬛ ☏ ☺ ⬛ ☕ ⬛
Nearby Facilities ⚓ ∪ ♁
Ideal for walking and cycling. Central fo Canterbury, Sissinghurst, Weald of Kent an general touring of the North Downs.

BROADHEMBURY HOLIDAY PARK

Caravanning & Camping in the lovely village of Kingsnorth in beautiful Kentish countryside.

FROM BROADHEMBURY ...
- ☆ Walk the famous footpaths through areas of outstanding natural beauty
- ☆ Cycle signposted routes through country lanes to picturesque villages and ancient towns
- ☆ Shop-shop-shop in Ashford's new vast outlet village, designer names at discounted prices
- ☆ Golf; Homeland Bettergolf only one mile
- ☆ Visit castles, gardens, sandy beaches and hundreds of places of interest
- ☆ Sail across the Channel. Broadhembury is one of the nearest and conveniently sitused 5 Star Parks for the Channel Tunnel and all ferry crossings

Full details of all places to visit are available in our comprehensive Tourist Information Centre at our reception.

OPEN ALL YEAR ~ Broadhembury is an attractive, level, landscaped park with every convenience and amenity, where young and old alike will enjoy a holiday to remember and repeat.

❄ ***SPECIAL*** - **Extra 15% Discount (from second night onwards) for:-**
- ☆ Best of British brochure holders. Visit www.bob.org.uk and request yours.
- ☆ Caravan Club and Camping & Caravanning Club members.
- ☆ Carnet Card holders.

Keith & Jenny, proprietors since 1969, look forward to welcoming ***YOU*** *this season.*

Visit www.broadhembury.co.uk or phone **01233 620859** for a brochure
Broadhembury Holiday Park, Steeds Lane, Kingsnorth, Ashford, Kent TN26 1NQ

WOODLANDS PARK, BIDDENDEN, KENT

A friendly park set in the beautiful Kent countryside, with numerous castles, gardens and pretty villages nearby, Woodlands offers tranquil and peaceful holidays. We are situated in an excellent central location for visiting all tourist attractions around East Sussex and Kent.

- ♦ Modern Toilet/Shower block (free showers)
- ♦ Washing Up Facilities
- ♦ Launderette
- ♦ Electrical Hook-ups (must be pre-booked)
- ♦ Site Shop
- ♦ Camping Accessories
- ♦ Gas Sales
- ♦ Children's Play Area
- ♦ Tents, Motorhomes and Caravans all welcome
- ♦ Disabled Facilities
- ♦ Finalist 1998 Welcome to Kent Awards
- ♦ Finalist 1998 Loo of the Year Award

Tenterden Road, Biddenden, Kent, TN27 8BT   Tel/Fax: 01580 291216
Email:- woodlandsp@aol.com   Web site:- www.campingsite.co.uk
Park open March to October (weather permitting).
Please call for tourist brochure.
Situated along the A262, 3 miles north of Tenterden, 1.5 miles south of Biddenden

BIDDENDEN

Spilland Farm Holiday & Tourist Park,
Benenden Road, Biddenden, Kent, TN27
8BX.
Std: 01580 **Tel:** 291379
Std: 01580 **Fax:** 291379
Nearest Town/Resort Biddenden/
Tenterden
Directions A262 from Biddenden, 1 mile
fork right, park ¼ mile on right.
Acreage 6 **Open** April **to** September
Access Good **Site** Sloping
Sites Available ⌂ ⌂ **Total** 65
Facilities ♦ ⊞ ♨ ⌐ ⊙ ╝ ☎ ⌯ ⊙ ⊕ ⊬ ▣
Nearby Facilities ⌐ ✈ ⚓ ∪
⊭ Headcorn
Centre for tourists, castles etc., yet 15 miles
to coast at Rye. No motor caravans
accepted.

BIDDENDEN

Woodlands Park, Tenterden Road,
Biddenden, Ashford, Kent, TN27 8BT.
Std: 01580 **Tel:** 291216
Std: 01580 **Fax:** 291216
Email: woodlandsp@aol.com
Nearest Town/Resort Tenterden/Leeds
Castle
Directions On A262, 3 miles north of
Tenterden. 15 miles south of Maidstone.
Acreage 10 **Open** March **to** October
Access Good **Site** Level
Sites Available ⌂ ⌂ ⌂ **Total** 200
Facilities ⚿ ♦ ⊞ ♨ ⌐ ⊙ ╝ ▱ ⌷ ☎
⌯ ⌯ ⊙ ⚧ ⌷ ⊛ ⊬ ▣
Nearby Facilities ⌐ ✈ ∪ ♪
⊭ Headcorn
Quiet, country site. Ideal for tourist centre.

BIRCHINGTON

Quex Caravan Park, Park Road,
Birchington, Kent, CT7 0BL.
Std: 01843 **Tel:** 841273 **Fax:** 740585
Email: info@keatfarm.co.uk
Website: www.keatfarm.co.uk
Nearest Town/Resort Margate/Ramsgate
Directions Follow road signs to Margate.
When in Birchington turn right at mini
roundabout (signposted Margate).
Approximately 100yds after roundabout take
the first turning on the right and then right
again as directed by Tourist Board signs.
Acreage 3 **Open** 7 March **to** 7 November
Access Good **Site** Level
Sites Available ⌂ ⌂ **Total** 50
Facilities ⚿ ♦ ⊞ ♨ ⌐ ⊙ ╝ ▱ ⌷ ☎
⌯ ⌯ ⊙ ⊕ ⌷ ▣ ⊟
Nearby Facilities ⌐ ✈ ⚓ ∪ ♪
⊭ Birchington
Ideal base for touring Thanet and
Canterbury areas.

BIRCHINGTON

St. Nicholas Camping Site, Court Road,
St. Nicholas at Wade, Nr. Birchington,
Kent, CT7 0NH.
Std: 01843 **Tel:** 847245
Nearest Town/Resort Birchington
Directions Off the A299, turn left at St.
Nicholas signpost, go over bridge into Court
Road. Off the A28 turn into the village.
Acreage 3 **Open** 1 April **to** 1 October
Access Good **Site** Level
Sites Available ⌂ ⌂ ⌂ **Total** 70
Facilities ♦ ⊞ ♨ ⌐ ⊙ ╝ ☎ ⌯ ⌯ ⊙ ▱ ⊬ ▣
Nearby Facilities ⌐ ✈ ∪
⊭ Birchington
On the outskirts of the village, near to a
sandy beach and two pubs. Central to five
major towns.

BIRCHINGTON

Thanet Way Caravan Co., Frost Farm,
Frost Lane, St. Nicholas-at-Wade,
Birchington, Kent, CT7 0NA.
Std: 01843 **Tel:** 847219
Nearest Town/Resort Minis Bay
Directions From the M2 take the A299 for
17 miles to St Nicholas roundabout, turn
back on the A299, ¼ mile signposted.
Open March **to** October
Access Good **Site** Lev/Slope
Sites Available ⌂ ⌂ **Total** 10
Facilities ⌐ ♦ ⊞ ♨ ⌐ ⊙ ☎ ⌯ ⌯ ⊙ ⊛ ⊬ ▣
Nearby Facilities ⌐ ✈ ⚓ ∪ ♪
⊭ Birchington
Quiet country site, 1½ miles from beach.
Walking.

BIRCHINGTON

Two Chimneys Caravan Park,
Shottendane Road, Birchington, Kent,
CT7 0HD.
Std: 01843 **Tel:** 841068/843157
Std: 01843 **Fax:** 843157/848676
Email: info@twochimneys.co.uk
Website: www.twochimneys.co.uk
Nearest Town/Resort Margate
Directions 1½ miles Birchington, turn right
into park lane at Birchington Church, left fork
"RAF Manston". First left onto B2049 site ½
mile on right.
Acreage 10 **Open** March **to** October
Access Good **Site** Level
Sites Available ⌂ ⌂ ⌂ **Total** 90
Facilities ⚿ ♦ ⊞ ♨ ⌐ ⊙ ╝ ▱ ⌷ ☎
⌯ ⌯ ⊙ ☎ ⚧ ⌷ ⊬ ▣
Nearby Facilities ⌐ ✈ ⚓ ∪ ♪ ♪
⊭ Birchington
Country site, ideal touring centre, 3 miles
Margate, 13 miles Canterbury. Sauna and
spa bath. Tennis court on site.

CANTERBURY

Ashfield Farm Caravan & Camping Site,
Asgfield Farm, Waddenhall, Petham,
Canterbury, Kent, CT4 5PX.
Std: 01227 **Tel:** 700624
Email:
mpatterson@ashfieldfarm.freeserve.co.uk
Nearest Town/Resort Canterbury
Directions From Canterbury take the
B2068, site is approx. 6 miles on the right.
Or leave the M20 at junction 11 and take
the B2068, site is approx. 8 miles on the
left.
Acreage 4 **Open** April **to** November
Access Good **Site** Level
Sites Available Å ⊕ ⊕ **Total** 20
Facilities ⭕ ∮ 🚽 ╤ ℙ ⊙ ⊖ ♨
🏪 ⓪ 🌀🕈🖭
Nearby Facilities ⌐ ✒ ∪
✈ Canterbury
Situated in an area of outstanding natural
beauty. Close to Canterbury and the Kent
coast.

CANTERBURY

Camping & Caravanning Club Site,
Bekesbourne Lane, Canterbury, Kent, CT3
4AB.
Std: 01227 **Tel:** 463216
Website:
www.campingandcaravanningclub.co.uk
Directions From Canterbury follow the
A257 towards Sandwich, turn right opposite
the golf course.
Acreage 20 **Open** All Year
Site Lev/Slope
Sites Available Å ⊕ ⊕ **Total** 210
Facilities ⭕ ∮ 🎲 🚽 ╤ ℙ ⊙ ⊖ ♨
🔘 🏪 🕈 ⓪ 🌀🕈🖭
Nearby Facilities ⌐
✈ Canterbury
Close to Canterbury and within easy reach
of the Channel ports. 2 miles from
Canterbury Cathedral and Howletts Wildlife
Park. BTB Graded. Non members welcome.

CANTERBURY

Red Lion Caravan Park, Old London
Road, Dunkirk, Canterbury, Kent, ME13
9LL.
Std: 01227 **Tel:** 750661
Nearest Town/Resort Canterbury

Directions Take the A2 London bound and
slip off after Gate Services for Dunkirk and
Boughton, park is ½ mile. Signposted from
the A2.
Acreage 1 **Open** Easter **to** Nov
Access Good **Site** Level
Sites Available ⊕ ⊕ **Total** 25
Facilities ⭕ ∮ 🚽 ╤ ℙ ⊙ ⊖ 🕈 ╳ 🕈🖭 🖭
Nearby Facilities ⌐ ∪
✈ Canterbury
Only 15 miles from Dover Port and the
Channel Tunnel. 4 miles from the City of
Canterbury.

CANTERBURY

Rose & Crown, The Minnis, Stelling
Minnis, Canterbury, Kent, CT4 6AS.
Std: 01227 **Tel:** 709265
Nearest Town/Resort Canterbury/
Folkestone
Directions On the B2068, 6 miles from
Canterbury, 4 miles from the M20 junction
11 and the Channel Tunnel.
Acreage 3 **Open** All Year
Access Good **Site** Level
Sites Available Å ⊕ ⊕ **Total** 30
Facilities 🚽 ╤ ∮ 🚽 ╤ ℙ 🎲 ╳ ⓪ 🕈 🖭 🖭
Nearby Facilities ⌐ ✒ △ ⅃ ∪
✈ Canterbury/Folkestone
Adjacent to Minnis for lots of walks and
cycling. Next to a pub and shop.

CANTERBURY

Royal Oak Camping & Caravan, 114
Sweech Gate, Broad Oak, Canterbury,
Kent, CT2 0QP.
Std: 01227 **Tel:** 710448
Email: kiki@royaloak29.freeserve.co.uk
Nearest Town/Resort Canterbury/Herne
Bay
Directions From Canterbury take the A28
towards Margate and Herne Bay for 3 miles.
Go through Sturry and turn left at the top of
the hill.
Acreage 1 **Open** March **to** October
Access Good **Site** Level
Sites Available Å ⊕ ⊕ **Total** 20
Facilities ∮ 🎲 🚽 ╤ ℙ 🎲 ╳ 🎲 🖭 🕈 🖭
Nearby Facilities ⌐ ✒ ∪
✈ Sturry
Centrally located for the City of Canterbury,
Herne Bay, Margate and Dover for ferries to
France.

CANTERBURY

Yew Tree Caravan Park, Stone Street,
Petham, Canterbury, Kent, CT4 5PL.
Std: 01227 **Tel:** 700306
Std: 01227 **Fax:** 700306
Email: info@yewtreepark.com
Website: www.yewtreepark.com
Nearest Town/Resort Canterbury
Directions 4 miles south of Canterbury o
the B2068, turn right by the Chequers Publ
House, park entrance is on the left han
side.
Acreage 2 **Open** March **to** October
Access Good **Site** Lev/Slope
Sites Available Å ⊕ ⊕ **Total** 45
Facilities ⭕ ∮ 🎲 🚽 ╤ ℙ ⊙ ⊖ ♨ 🖭 🖭
🏪 ⓪ 🌀🕈🖭🖭
Nearby Facilities ⌐ ✒ ∪
✈ Canterbury East
Small picturesque park overlooking th
Chartham Downs. Scenic views, larg
swimming pool, ideal touring base.

CHATHAM

Woolmans Wood Tourist Caravan Park
Rochester Road (B2097), Chatham, Kent
ME5 9SB.
Std: 01634 **Tel:** 867685
Std: 01634 **Fax:** 867685
Email: woolmans.wood@currantbun.com
Nearest Town/Resort Rochester
Directions Take the A229 to Maidstone, a
the roundabout take the B2097 signposte
Bridgewood Borstal. After ¼ of a mi
'Woolmans Wood' is on the right hand sid
Acreage 5 **Open** All Year
Access Good **Site** Level
Sites Available Å ⊕ ⊕ **Total** 60
Facilities ∮ 🎲 🚽 ╤ ℙ ⊙ ⊖ ♨ 🖭 🖭 🕈
🏪 ⓪ 🌀🕈🖭
Nearby Facilities ⌐ ✒ △ ⅃ ∪ ⅃ ♪
✈ Chatham
Rochester Castle and Cathedral, an
Chatham Naval Base.

DEAL

Clifford Park Caravans, Clifford Park,
Thompson Close, Walmer, Deal, Kent,
CT14 7PB.
Std: 01304 **Tel:** 373373
Nearest Town/Resort Deal
Directions A258, Deal 1 mile and Dover

miles.
Acreage ¼ **Open** March **to** 30 October
Access Good **Site** Level
Sites Available ▲ ⬕ ⬕ **Total** 15
Facilities ⚡ ⚿ 🛢 ⬕ 🛢 🌂 ⊙ ⬕ 🖤 🛢 🛒 🏪 🗜
Nearby Facilities ⟍ ⟋ ⟍ ⟍ U ⚲ ℛ
⚓ Walmer
Ideal touring area for day trips to France or the beaches.

DOVER

Hawthorn Farm, Martin Mill, Dover, Kent, CT15 5LA.
Std: 01304 **Tel:** 852658
Std: 01304 **Fax:** 853417
Email: info@keatfarm.co.uk
Website: www.keatfarm.co.uk
Nearest Town/Resort Dover
Directions Martin Mill is approx. 3 miles from Dover, signposted along the main A258 towards Deal.
Acreage 27 **Open** March **to** October
Access Good **Site** Level
Sites Available ▲ ⬕ ⬕ **Total** 250
Facilities ⚡ ⬕ 🛢 ⌐ ⊙ ⬛ 🛢 ⬕ 🛒
🏪 🗜 🛢 🛒 🏪 🗜
Nearby Facilities ⟍ ⟋ ⚓ U
⚓ Martin Mill
Beautiful Award Winning park in a quiet and peaceful location. Superb toilet and shower facilities.

DYMCHURCH

New Beach Holiday Village, Hythe Road, Dymchurch, Kent, TN29 0JX.
Std: 01303 **Tel:** 872234
Std: 01303 **Fax:** 872939
Nearest Town/Resort Folkestone
Directions From Maidstone take the M20 to Folkestone, turn off at junction 11 and follow signs to Hythe. Then take the A259 coast road to Hastings and New Beach is 4 miles from Hythe.
Open 1 March **to** 11 January
Access Good **Site** Level
Sites Available ▲ ⬕ ⬚ **Total** 200
Facilities ⚡ ⬕ 🛢 ⌐ ⊙ ⬛ 🛢 ⬕ 🛒
🏪 🗜 🛢 🌂 🛒 🏪 🚍 🗜 🛒 🏪 🗜
Nearby Facilities ⟍ ⟋ ⚓ ⟍ U
⚓ Folkestone

EASTCHURCH

Warden Springs Caravan Park, Warden Point, Eastchurch, Sheppey, Kent, ME12 4HF.
Std: 01795 **Tel:** 880216
Std: 01795 **Fax:** 880218
Email: jackie@wscp.freeserve.co.uk
Website: www.wardensprings.co.uk
Nearest Town/Resort Sheerness
Directions M20 junction 7 or M2 junction 5 to the A249. A249 to Sheppey, B2231 to Eastchurch.

Acreage 2 **Open** March **to** October
Access Good **Site** Sloping
Sites Available ▲ ⬕ ⬕ **Total** 48
Facilities ⚿ ⚡ ⬕ ⬛ 🛢 ⌐ ⊙ ⬛ 🛢 ⬕ 🛒
🏪 🗜 🛢 🛒 🌂 🛒 🏪 🚍 🛢 ⟍ 🛒 🏪 🗜
Nearby Facilities ⟍ ⟋ ⚓ U ⚲
⚓ Sheerness
Near beach, scenic views, fishing. ETB 4 Star Graded.

FAVERSHAM

Painters Farm Caravan & Camping Site,
Painters Forstal, Ospringe, Faversham, Kent, ME13 0EG.
Std: 01795 **Tel:** 532995
Nearest Town/Resort Faversham
Directions Turn south off the A2 at Faversham signposted Painters Forstal/Eastling. 1½ miles down a No Through road at Forstal.
Acreage 3 **Open** March **to** October
Access Good **Site** Level
Sites Available ▲ ⬕ ⬕ **Total** 50
Facilities ⚡ ⬕ 🛢 ⌐ ⊙ ⬛ 🛢 ⬕ 🛒 🏪 🗜
Nearby Facilities ⟍
⚓ Faversham
Pleasant orchard setting. Convenient for the coast and Channel Ports.

FOLKESTONE

Camping & Caravanning Club Site, The Warren, Folkestone, Kent, CT19 6PT.
Std: 01303 **Tel:** 255093
Website:
www.campingandcaravanningclub.co.uk
Directions From the M2 and Canterbury on the A260 take a left turn at the roundabout into Hill Road, Folkestone. Go straight over the crossroads into Wear Bay Road, turn second left past Martello Tower, site is ½ mile on the right.
Open April **to** Sept
Site Level
Sites Available ▲ ⬕ **Total** 80
Facilities ⬕ 🛢 ⌐ ⊙ ⬛ 🛢 🏪 🗜 🛢 🛒 🏪 🗜
Nearby Facilities ⟍ ⟋ ⟍ ℛ ⚲
⚓ Folkestone
Just a short walk to the beach. On a clear day you can see France. Fishing off the site on the sea front, 50 yards. BTB Graded. Non members welcome.

FOLKESTONE

Little Satmar Holiday Park, Winehouse Lane, Capel-le-Ferne, Nr. Folkestone, Kent, CT18 7JF.
Std: 01303 **Tel:** 251188
Std: 01303 **Fax:** 251188
Email: info@keatfarm.co.uk
Website: www.keatfarm.co.uk
Nearest Town/Resort Folkestone
Directions Travelling towards Folkestone on the A20 from Dover, exit left signposted

---

Capel-le-Ferne onto the B2011. After 1 mile turn right into Winehouse Lane.
Acreage 6 **Open** March **to** October
Access Good
Sites Available ▲ ⬕ ⬕ **Total** 40
Facilities ⚡ ⬕ 🛢 ⌐ ⊙ ⬛ 🛢 ⬕ 🛒 🏪 🗜
🏪 🛒 🛢 🌂 🛒 🏪 🚍 🗜
Nearby Facilities ⟍ ⟋ ⚓ U
⚓ Folkestone
Quiet, secluded park. Convenient for Channel ports and Tunnel.

FOLKESTONE

Little Switzerland Caravan & Camping Park, Little Switzerland, Wear Bay Road, Folkestone, Kent, CT19 6PS.
Std: 01303 **Tel:** 252168
Email: littleswitzerland@lineone.net
Website: www.caravancampingsites.co.uk
Nearest Town/Resort Folkestone
Directions From Dover follow Folkestone signs then Country Park signs.
Open March **to** October
Access Good **Site** Level
Sites Available ▲ ⬕ ⬕
Facilities ⚡ ⬕ 🛢 ⌐ ⊙ ⬛ 🛢 ⬕ 🛒
⬛ 🏪 🗜 🛢 🛒 🌂 🛒 🏪 🚍 🗜
Nearby Facilities ⟍ ⟋ ⚓ ⟍ U ⚲ ℛ ⚹
⚓ Folkestone

FOLKESTONE

Varne Ridge Holiday Park, 145 Old Dover Road, Capel-le-Ferne, Nr. Folkestone, Kent, CT18 7HX.
Std: 01303 **Tel:** 251765
Email: vrcp@varne-ridge.freeserve.co.uk
Website: www.varne-ridge.co.uk
Nearest Town/Resort Dover/Folkestone
Directions Approx. 5 miles from both Folkestone and Dover on the B2011, situated in the Old Dover Road.
Acreage 1½ **Open** March **to** October
Access Good **Site** Level
Sites Available ⬕ ⬕ **Total** 6
Facilities ⚡ ⬕ 🛢 ⌐ ⊙ ⬛ ⬕ 🛢 🏪 🛒
Nearby Facilities ⟍ ⟋ ⚓ ⟍ U ⚲ ℛ
⚓ Dover/Folkestone
Overlooking the North Downs and the English Channel. Cliff top walks and cycle rides following paths to either Folkestone or Dover. All bookings must be made in advance, 3 night minimum stay.

HERNE BAY

Southview Camping, Southview, Maypole Lane, Hoath, Canterbury, Kent, CT3 4LL.
Std: 01227 **Tel:** 860280
Email: southviewcamping@aol.com
Nearest Town/Resort Canterbury
Directions Well signed from the A299 at Herne Bay or the A28 near Canterbury.
Acreage 3 **Open** March **to** October

Access Good **Site** Level
Sites Available ⚠ ⛺ 🚐 **Total** 45
Facilities ♿ ♀ 🚻 🚾 🔥 🏪 ☉ 🍴 🛒 🖲 ☎
🍴 🛈 🚲 🍴 🏕
Nearby Facilities 🏍 ✓ ⚓ 🛈 ∪ ⚒ 🎣
☀ Herne Bay
Very central location for Canterbury and the beautiful beaches of Thanet. Public telephone 100yds. Dogs by appointment only.

LEYSDOWN-ON-SEA

Priory Hill Holiday Park, Wing Road, Leysdown-on-Sea, Isle of Sheppey, Kent, ME12 4QT.
Std: 01795 **Tel:** 510267
Std: 01795 **Fax:** 510267
Email: philip@prioryhill.co.uk
Website: www.prioryhill.co.uk
Nearest Town/Resort Leysdown-on-Sea
Directions From the M2 or M20 onto the A249 then the B2231 to Leysdown, follow tourism signs to Priory Hill.
Acreage 15½ **Open** March **to** October
Access Good **Site** Level
Sites Available ⚠ ⛺ 🚐 **Total** 50
Facilities ♿ ♀ 🚾 🔥 🏪 ☉ 🍴 🛒 🖲 ☎
🍴 🍴 🚲 🍴 ✕ 🍴 🏕 🎣 🍴 📞 🖲 🖃
Nearby Facilities 🏍 ✓ ⚓ 🛈 ∪ ⚒ 🎣
☀ Sheerness
Seaside park with a clubhouse, indoor heated swimming pool and entertainment on site. Please see our Web Site for details.

MAIDSTONE

Cold Blow Camping, Cold Blow Farm, Cold Blow Lane, Thurnham, Kent, ME14 3LR.
Std: 01622 **Tel:** 735038
Std: 01622 **Fax:** 735038
Email: coldblowcamping@btconnect.com
Website: www.coldblow-camping.co.uk
Nearest Town/Resort Maidstone
Directions Leave the M20 at junction 7 onto the A249 towards Detling. After 300 yards turn right into Detling, turn right opposite Cock Horse along Pilgrims Way. At the second crossroads turn left towards Hucking, we are at the top of the hill on the right.
Acreage 7 **Open** All Year
Access Good **Site** Level
Sites Available ⚠ ⛺ 🚐 **Total** 15
Facilities ♿ ♀ 🚻 🚾 🔥 🏪 ☉ 🍴 🛒 🖲 ☎
🍴 ✕ 📞 🖃 🖲
Nearby Facilities 🏍 ✓ ⚓ ✕ ∪ 🎣
☀ Bearsted
Adjacent to North Downs Way. Excellent walking and pubs. Detling Church, Maidstone, Leeds Castle, Rochester, Chatham and Kent County Showground all nearby. Camping barn available. Affiliated to the Camping & Caravanning Club.

MAIDSTONE

Hogbarn Caravan Park, Hogbarn Lane, Stede Hill, Harrietsham,Maidstone, Kent, ME17 1NZ.
Std: 01622 **Tel:** 859648
Std: 01622 **Fax:** 859912
Email: mail@hogbarn.fsnet.co.uk
Website: www.fitt-caravans.co.uk
Nearest Town/Resort Maidstone
Directions Leave the M20 at junction 8 and take the A20 for Lenham. After Harrietsham Village railway bridge turn second left across the A20.
Open Easter **to** October
Access Good **Site** Level
Sites Available ⚠ ⛺ 🚐 **Total** 45
Facilities ♿ ♀ 🚻 🚾 🔥 🏪 ☉ 🍴 🛒 🖲 ☎
🍴 🍴 🚲 🍴 🏕 ✕ 🍴 📞 🖃
Nearby Facilities 🏍
☀ Harrietsham
Near to Leeds Castle.

MAIDSTONE

Pine Lodge Touring Park, Ashford Road, Hollingbourne, Kent, ME17 1XH.
Std: 01622 **Tel:** 730018
Std: 01622 **Fax:** 734498
Website: www.ukparks.co.uk/pinelodge
Nearest Town/Resort Maidstone
Directions Leave the M20 at junction 8, onto the A20 roundabout, turn off towards Bearsted and Maidstone. Pine Lodge is on the left after approx. ½ mile.
Acreage 7 **Open** All Year
Access Good **Site** Level
Sites Available ⚠ ⛺ 🚐
Facilities ♿ ♀ 🚻 🚾 🔥 🏪 ☉ 🍴 🛒 🖲 ☎
🍴 🍴 🚲 📞 🖃 🖲
Nearby Facilities 🏍 ✓ ∪ 🎣
☀ Bearsted
Ideal for exploring the Kent countryside. Leeds Castle. Only 1 hour from London and convenient for ferries and The Channel Tunnel.

MARDEN

Tanner Farm Touring Caravan & Camping Park, Tanner Farm, Goudhurst Road, Marden, Kent, TN12 9ND.
Std: 01622 **Tel:** 832399 **Fax:** 832472
Email: tannerfarmpark@cs.com
Website: www.tannerfarmpark.co.uk
Nearest Town/Resort Maidstone/ Tunbridge Wells
Directions From the A262 or A229 onto the B2079. Midway between the village of Marden and Goudhurst.
Acreage 15 **Open** All Year
Access Good **Site** Level
Sites Available ⚠ ⛺ 🚐 **Total** 100
Facilities ♿ ♀ 🚻 🚾 🔥 🏪 ☉ 🍴 🛒 🖲 ☎
🍴 🍴 🚲 🍴 📞 🖃 🖲

Nearby Facilities 🥾
☀ Marden
Peaceful, secluded park in the centre of a 150 acre farm, shire horses kept.

NEW ROMNEY

Marlie Farm Holiday Village, Dymchurch Road, New Romney, Kent, TN28 8UE.
Std: 01797 **Tel:** 363060
Nearest Town/Resort New Romney
Directions ¼ mile east of New Romney on the A259.
Open Easter **to** October
Access Good **Site** Level
Sites Available ⚠ ⛺ 🚐 **Total** 250
Facilities ♿ ♀ 🚻 🚾 🔥 🏪 ☉ 🍴 🛒 🖲 ☎
🍴 🍴 🚲 🍴 ✕ 🍴 🏕 🍴 ✕ 🍴 📞 🖃 🖲
Nearby Facilities 🏍 ✓ ⚒
☀ Fishford International

RAMSGATE

Manston Caravan & Camping Park, Manston Court Road, Manston, Ramsgate, Kent, CT12 5AU.
Std: 01843 **Tel:** 823442
Email: roy@manston-park.co.uk
Website: www.manston-park.co.uk
Nearest Town/Resort Ramsgate
Directions From the M2 follow the A299 and join the A253 towards Ramsgate. Turn left onto the B2048 then first right onto the B2190 towards KIA. Turn right onto the B2050 across the airfield passing the entrance to KIA. Take the first turning left into Manston Court Road, park is 500 yards on the right.
Acreage 7 **Open** April **to** October
Access Good **Site** Level
Sites Available ⚠ ⛺ 🚐 **Total** 100
Facilities ♀ 🚾 🔥 🏪 ☉ 🍴 🛒 🖲 ☎
🍴 🍴 🚲 🍴 📞 🖃 🖲
Nearby Facilities 🏍 ✓ ⚓ ✕ ∪ ⚒ 🎣
☀ Ramsgate
Quiet, family park. Motorcycles are sometimes accepted.

RAMSGATE

Nethercourt Touring Park, Nethercourt Hill, Ramsgate, Kent, CT11 0RX.
Std: 01843 **Tel:** 595485
Std: 01843 **Fax:** 595485
Email: suepsb@aol.com
Nearest Town/Resort Ramsgate
Directions Off the main London road on the outskirts of the town.
Acreage 2 **Open** April **to** October
Access Good **Site** Level
Sites Available ⚠ ⛺ 🚐 **Total** 52
Facilities ♿ ♀ 🚻 🚾 🔥 🏪 ☉ 🍴 🛒 🖲 ☎
🍴 🍴 🏕 🍴 🍴 📞 🖃 🖲
Nearby Facilities 🏍 ✓ ⚓ ∪ 🎣
☀ Ramsgate
1¼ miles from the beach and harbour.

Welcome to the garden of England

Set in semi-woodland. Modern centrally heated toilet, shower and laundry building. Swimming Pool. Fully licenced "Welcome Bar".

Thriftwood CARAVAN & CAMPING PARK
* WROTHAM HILL * PLAXDALE GREEN ROAD *
* STANSTED * NR WROTHAM * KENT TN15 7PB *
TEL: (01732) 822261   FAX: (01732) 824636

Easy access to London, only 30 minutes by train. Holiday caravans for hire. Many local Stately Homes and Castles to visit.

Call for Free Colour Brochure.

SEVENOAKS

East Hill Farm Caravan Park, East Hill, Near Otford, Sevenoaks, Kent, TN15 6YD.
Std: 01959 **Tel:** 522347
Nearest Town/Resort Sevenoaks
Directions Please telephone for directions.
Acreage 6 **Open** April **to** October
Access Good **Site** Level
Sites Available ⚤ ⚤ ⚤ **Total** 30
Facilities 🔲 🚻 ⊙ ⚽ 🅗 🅜 🖭
Nearby Facilities ⚓ ∪
⚆ Otford

SEVENOAKS

Gate House Wood Touring Park, Ford Lane, Wrotham Heath, Sevenoaks, Kent, TN15 7SD.
Std: 01732 **Tel:** 843062
Nearest Town/Resort Maidstone/ Sevenoaks
Directions From Maidstone take the M20 and exit at junction 3 onto the M26, within ½ mile take junction 2A. At the roundabout take the A20 signposted Paddock Wood, continue straight through the traffic lights at Wrotham Heath and take the first turn left signposted Trottiscliffe. After 50 yards turn left into Ford Lane and the park is 100 yards on the left.
Acreage 3½ **Open** April **to** November
Access Good **Site** Level
Sites Available ⚤ ⚤ ⚤ **Total** 60
Facilities ⚤ 🔲 🚻 ⚤ ⚓ ⊙ ⚽ 🖭
🅖 ⊙ 🅐 🖭
Nearby Facilities ⚓ ∪
⚆ Borough Green
Conveniently situated for Channel ports and sightseeing in South East London (45 minutes by train). Many country pubs, restaurants and take-away nearby.

SHEERNESS

Seacliff Holiday Estate Ltd., Oak Lane, Minster, Sheerness, Kent, ME12 3QS.
Std: 01795 **Tel:** 872262
Nearest Town/Resort Sheerness
Directions Take the A2/M2 then the A249 and follow signs to Minster. Go through the village and look for a tourist sign on the left at Oak Lane.
Open March **to** October
Access Good **Site** Sloping
Sites Available ⚤ ⚤ ⚤ **Total** 40
Facilities ⚤ 🔲 🚻 ⊙ 🖭 🅖 ⚤ ✕ ⚤ 🅐 🖭
Nearby Facilities ⚓ ✔ ⚓ ∪ ⚤ ₽
⚆ Sheerness
Quiet location with panoramic sea views.

WHITSTABLE

Primrose Cottage Caravan Park, Golden Hill, Whitstable, Kent, CT5 3AR.
Std: 01277 **Tel:** 273694
Nearest Town/Resort Whitstable
Directions On A2990, 1 mile east of Whitstable roundabout.
Acreage ½ **Open** March **to** October
Access Good **Site** Level
Sites Available ⚤ ⚤ ⚤ **Total** 10
Facilities ⚤ 🔲 🚻 ⊙ ⚤ 🅖 ⊙ ⚤ 🖭
Nearby Facilities ⚓ ✔ ⚓ ∪ ⚤ ₽
⚆ Whitstable

WROTHAM

Thriftwood Caravan Park, Plaxdale Green Road, Stansted, Nr. Wrotham, Kent, TN15 7PB.
Std: 01732 **Tel:** 822261
Std: 01732 **Fax:** 824636
Nearest Town/Resort Sevenoaks
Directions On A20 on top of Wrotham Hill, 3¼ miles south of Brands Hatch, exit 2 off M20 signposted with international camping signs.

Acreage 10 **Open** March **to** January
Access Good **Site** Level
Sites Available ⚤ ⚤ ⚤ **Total** 150
Facilities ⚤ ⚤ 🔲 🚻 ⚤ ⚓ ⊙ ⚤ 🅐 🖭 ⚤
🅢 🅖 ⊙ ⚤ 🅐 ⚤ ✕ 🅐 🖭 ⚤
Nearby Facilities ⚓ ✔ ∪ ₽
⚆ Borough Green
35 minutes by train to London, convenient for southern ports. Free colour brochure on request.

LANCASHIRE
BENTHAM

Riverside Caravan Park, High Bentham, Lancaster, Lancashire, LA2 7LW.
Std: 015242 **Tel:** 61272
Std: 015242 **Fax:** 62163
Website: www.riversidecaravanpark.co.uk
Nearest Town/Resort High Bentham
Directions Follow caravan signs off the B6480 at the Black Bull Hotel in Bentham.
Acreage 10 **Open** March **to** October
Access Good **Site** Level
Sites Available ⚤ ⚤ ⚤ **Total** 60
Facilities ⚤ 🔲 ⚤ ⚓ ⊙ ⚤ 🅐 🖭 ⚤
🅢 ⊙ ⚤ 🅣 🅐 🅐 ⚤ ✕ 🖭
Nearby Facilities ⚓ ✔ ₽
⚆ Bentham
Free fishing for trout and sea trout adjacent to the site. Electric points for tourers.

BLACKPOOL

Gillett Farm Caravan Park, Peel Road, Nr. Blackpool, Lancs, FY4 5JU.
Std: 01253 **Tel:** 761676
Nearest Town/Resort Blackpool
Directions Blackpool junction 4 on M55 turn left to Kirkham 400yds, straight on at the roundabout to traffic lights. Turn right and immediate left into Peel Road. 350yds second site on the right.

UNDERHILL
Touring Caravan & Camping Park
Penny Farm, Peel, Blackpool

An ideal location for a caravan or camping holiday, with panoramic views of the Fylde countryside and easy access to Blackpool beach and entertainment centre.

You are assured of a warm welcome from the resident site wardens who maintain the grounds and the facilities to a high standard.

Under Hill is managed by the International League for the Protection of Horses and is situated adjacent to one of its Equine Centres where abused and neglected horses, ponies and donkeys are rehabilitated before being re-homed.

Everyone enjoying a holiday at Under Hill is contributing to the ILPH's work for Equines worldwide. (Registered Charity No. 206658). For a free site brochure write to:
Under Hill Caravan & Camping Site, New Preston Road, Peel, Blackpool, Lancs FY4 5JS
Phone: 01253 763107   Email: hq@ilph.org   Website www.ilph.org

Acreage 12 **Open** March **to** October
Access Good **Site** Slightly Sloping
Sites Available ▲ ⬛ 🚐 **Total** 76
Facilities ∮ 🛁 🚻 ♨ ⌂ ⊙ ⌿ ▣ ⊙ ☎
🏊 🎮 ⊙ ⬛ ▥ ♠ Ⓜ ➡ ▣ ⊡
Nearby Facilities ▶ ✓ ⚓ ☂ ∪ ⋡ ♪
🚲 Blackpool
Within easy reach of Blackpool, Lytham St Annes and Fleetwood.

BLACKPOOL
Mariclough - Hampsfield, Preston New Road, Peel, Blackpool, Lancs, FY4 5JR.
Std: 01253 **Tel:** 761034
Nearest Town/Resort Blackpool
Directions M55 junction 4, first left onto the A583. Go through traffic lights, site 200yds on the left.
Acreage 2 **Open** Easter **to** November
Access Good **Site** Level
Sites Available ▲ ⬛ 🚐 **Total** 50
Facilities ∮ 🛁 🚻 ♨ ⌂ ⊙ ⌿
🏊 🎮 ⊙ ⬛ ▥ ➡ ▣
Nearby Facilities ▶ ✓ ⚓ ☂ ∪ ♪
🚲 Blackpool/Kirkham
Flat, mowed grass, sheltered park. Off license. Please telephone before 8pm.

BLACKPOOL
Marton Mere Holiday Village, Mythop Road, Blackpool, Lancashire, FY4 4XN.
Std: 08457 **Tel:** 660188
Website: www.british-holidays.co.uk
Nearest Town/Resort Blackpool
Directions Take the A583 towards Blackpool, turn right at Clifton Arms traffic lights onto Mythop Road, park is 150 yards on the left.
Acreage 93 **Open** March **to** October
Access Good **Site** Level
Sites Available ⬛ 🚐 **Total** 431
Facilities ♿ ∮ 🛁 🚻 ♨ ⌂ ⊙ ⌿ ▣ ⊙ ☎
🏊 🎮 ⊙ ⬛ ☓ ▥ ♨ ♠ ⌂ ⊙ ➡ ▣ ▣
Nearby Facilities
A sanctuary for birds and wildlife with spectacular views. Kids Club, family entertainment, bowling, tennis, amusements and crazy golf.

BLACKPOOL
Pipers Height Caravan & Camping Park, Peel Road, Peel, Blackpool, Lancashire, FY4 5JT.
Std: 01253 **Tel:** 763767

Nearest Town/Resort Blackpool
Directions Exit M55 junction 4 take the first turning left on the A583. At the first set of lights turn right then sharp left. Site is first on the right. Site ½ mile from the M55.
Acreage 11 **Open** March **to** November
Access Good **Site** Level
Sites Available ▲ ⬛ 🚐 **Total** 150
Facilities ♿ ∮ ✗ 🛁 🚻 ♨ ⌂ ⊙ ⌿ ▣ ⊙ ☎
🏊 🎮 ⊙ ⬛ ☓ ♨ ♠ ➡ ▣
Nearby Facilities ▶ ✓ ⚓ ☂ ∪ ♪
🚲 Blackpool
Static caravan sales.

BLACKPOOL
Redleigh Orchard Touring Caravan Park, Cropper Road, Blackpool, Lancashire, FY4 5LB.
Std: 01253 **Tel:** 691459/691266
Nearest Town/Resort Blackpool
Directions Leave the M55 at junction 4, at the roundabout turn left, proceed to the next roundabout and take second exit, proceed to second roundabout and take the fourth exit, Park is 100 yardson the right.
Acreage 1¾ **Open** 1 March **to** 1 Nov
Access Good **Site** Level
Sites Available ⬛▢ **Total** 21
Facilities ∮ 🛁 🚻 ♨ ⌂ ⊙ ⬛ ⊙ ➡ ▣ ▣
Nearby Facilities ▶ ✓ ⚓ ☂ ∪ ♪
🚲 Blackpool South
Quiet site near a garden centre, pub and equestrian centre. Only 2 miles to the beach and 4 miles from the famous Blackpool Tower and centre.

BLACKPOOL
Richmond Hill Caravan Park, 352 St. Anne's Road, Blackpool, Lancashire, FY4 2QN.
Std: 01253 **Tel:** 344266
Website: www.richmondhill.free-online.co.uk
Nearest Town/Resort Blackpool/Lytham St. Annes
Directions We are situated near the Airport. Approach from the M55 following signs to the airport and Southshore, turn right at the traffic lights by the Halfway House Pub, 200 yards on the right.
Acreage 1 **Open** March **to** End October
Access Good **Site** Level
Sites Available ⬛ 🚐 **Total** 15

Facilities ∮ 🛁 🚻 ♨ ⌂ ⊙ ⌿ ▣
🎮 ⊙ ⬛ ▥ ➡ ▣
Nearby Facilities ▶ ✓ ⚓ ☂ ∪ ⋡ ♪
🚲 Blackpool
Quiet site, 'the countryside in the town'. Near to all the amenities of Blackpool, frequent bus service.

BLACKPOOL
Sunset Park, Sower Carr Lane, Hambleton, Poulton-le-Fylde, Blackpool, Lancashire, FY6 9EQ.
Std: 01253 **Tel:** 700222 **Fax:** 701756
Email: sunset@caravans.com
Web: www.caravans.com/parks/sunset
Nearest Town/Resort Blackpool
Directions M55 junction 3 onto the A585 First traffic lights turn left, second traffic lights bear right, next set of traffic lights turn right onto the A588. After village of Hambleton turn right.
Acreage 2 **Open** April **to** October
Access Good **Site** Level
Sites Available ▲ ⬛ 🚐 **Total** 30
Facilities ∮ 🛁 🚻 ♨ ⌂ ⊙ ⌿ ▣ ☎
🏊 ⊙ ⬛ ☓ ♀ ♨ ➡ ▣ ▣ ♠
Nearby Facilities ▶ ✓ ⚓ ☂ ♪
🚲 Poulton-le-Fylde
Rural site. Sunset Club with a licensed bar. Sauna and spa, coarse fishing. Blackpool and Fleetwood nearby.

BLACKPOOL
Under Hill Caravan & Camping Site, New Preston Road, Peel, Blackpool, Lancashire, FY4 5JS.
Std: 01253 **Tel:** 763107
Email: hq@ilph.org
Website: www.ilph.org
Nearest Town/Resort Blackpool
Directions 3 miles east of Blackpool on the A583 and ½ mile from the M55 junction 4.
Acreage 4 **Open** April **to** End Nov
Access Good **Site** Sloping
Sites Available ▲ ⬛ 🚐 **Total** 40
Facilities ∮ 🛁 🚻 ♨ ⌂ ⊙ ⌿ ▣ 🎮 ⬛ ➡ ▣
Nearby Facilities
🚲 Blackpool
Near the beach and Pleasure Beach attractions. Adjacent to and managed by the International League for the Protection of Horses. Ideal touring. Free brochure.

CARNFORTH

Bolton Holmes Farm, Bolton-le-Sands, Carnforth, Lancashire, LA5 8ES.
Std: 01524 **Tel:** 732854
Nearest Town/Resort Lancaster/Morecambe
Directions Travel north on A6. Take first left after Royal Hotel, Mill Lane, Bolton-le-Sands.
Open April to September
Access Good **Site** Sloping
Sites Available ▲ ⊞ ⊟ **Total** 30
Facilities
Nearby Facilities
⇌ Carnforth
Scenic views. On shore side.

CARNFORTH

Capernwray House, Capernwray, Carnforth, Lancs, LA6 1AE.
Std: 01524 **Tel:** 732363
Std: 01524 **Fax:** 732363
Email: thesmiths@capernwrayhouse.com
Website: www.capernwrayhouse.com
Nearest Town/Resort Carnforth/Kirby Lonsdale
Directions Leave the M6 junction 35 and follow signs for Over Kellet. At the village green turn left signposted Capernwray. Site is 2 miles on the right.
Acreage 18 **Open** March to October
Access Good **Site** Lev/Slope
Sites Available ▲ ⊞ ⊟ **Total** 60
Facilities
Nearby Facilities
⇌ Carnforth
Near a canal, beautiful scenery and good walking. Seasonal pitches available.

CARNFORTH

Detron Gate, Bolton-le-Sands, Carnforth, Lancashire, LA5 9TN.
Std: 01524 **Tel:** 732842
Nearest Town/Resort Morecambe
Acreage 10 **Open** April to October
Access Good **Site** Lev/Slope
Sites Available ⊞ ⊟ **Total** 150
Facilities
Nearby Facilities
⇌ Carnforth

CARNFORTH

Holgate's Caravan Parks Ltd., Cove Road, Silverdale, Nr. Carnforth, Lancashire, LA5 0SH.
Std: 01524 **Tel:** 701508
Std: 01524 **Fax:** 701580
Email: caravan@holgates.co.uk
Website: www.holgates.co.uk
Nearest Town/Resort Morecambe
Directions 5 miles northwest of Carnforth, between Silverdale and Arnside.
Acreage 10 **Open** 22 Dec to 3 Nov
Access Good **Site** Lev/Slope
Sites Available ▲ ⊞ ⊟ **Total** 70
Facilities
Nearby Facilities
⇌ Silverdale
On Morecambe Bay. In area of outstanding natural beauty. Spa bath, sauna, steam room, licensed lounge bar. Restricted facilities during Winter months. AA Campsite of the Year Award 1995/96, Regional Winner for Northern England.

CARNFORTH

Old Hall Caravan Park, Capernwray, Carnforth, Lancashire, LA6 1AD.
Std: 01524 **Tel:** 733276
Std: 01524 **Fax:** 734488
Email: oldhall@charis.co.uk
Website: www.oldhall.uk.com
Nearest Town/Resort Carnforth
Directions Leave the M6 at junction 35, go to Over Kellet. Turn left in the village of Over Kellet and the park is 1½ miles on the right.
Open 1 March to 10 January
Access Good **Site** Level
Sites Available ⊞ ⊟ **Total** 38
Facilities
Nearby Facilities
⇌ Carnforth
Quiet, peaceful, woodland retreat.

CARNFORTH

Red Bank Farm, The Shore, Bolton-le-Sands, Carnforth, Lancashire, LA5 8JR.
Std: 01524 **Tel:** 823196
Std: 01524 **Fax:** 824981
Nearest Town/Resort Morecambe
Directions From the A6 at Bolton-le-Sands, take the A5105 to Morecambe. After 500yds sharp right and right again at the railway bridge, turn left along the shore into the farm.
Acreage 3 **Open** Easter to October
Site Lev/Slope
Sites Available ▲ ⊟ **Total** 50
Facilities
Nearby Facilities
⇌ Lancaster/Morecambe
On the shore side of Morecambe Bay. Camp on our organic field and see our organically fed animals, (ie milking cows and sheep).

CLITHEROE
Camping & Caravanning Club Site,
Edisford Road, Clitheroe, Lancashire, BB7 3LA.
Std: 01200 **Tel:** 425294
Website:
www.campingandcaravanningclub.co.uk
Directions Nearest main road is the A59. From the west follow the A671 into Clitheroe. Look for the signpost indicating a left turn to Longridge/Sports Centre, turn into Greenacre Road approx 25 metres beyond the pelican crossing. Continue until the T-Junction at Edisford Road, turn left and continue past the church on the right, look for the Sports Centre on the right and car park opposite.
Acreage 6 **Open** March **to** October
Site Lev/Slope
Sites Available A ⚏ ⛺ **Total** 80
Facilities ⌁ ⚏ ⟟ ⊙⟲ 🖳 ⛿ 🟊 🖭 🅰🗜🖷
Nearby Facilities ┣ ✏ 🏊 U ⚲
⇌ Clitheroe
In the Ribble Valley, on the banks of a river. Local ghost walks on a weekly basis. Near Clitheroe Castle. BTB Graded. Non members welcome.

CLITHEROE
Shireburne Park, Waddington Road, Edisford Bridge, Clitheroe, Lancashire, BB7 3LB.
Std: 01200 **Tel:** 423422 **Fax:** 442383
Nearest Town/Resort Clitheroe
Directions Leave the M6 at junction 31 and take the A59 towards Clitheroe. Turn onto the A671 at Clitheroe signpost, then turn left onto the B6243 Moor Lane and follow signs for Edisford Bridge. After crossing Edisford Bridge turn right into Waddington Road following caravan signs, park is approx. 1 mile on the left.
Open March **to** October
Access Good **Site** Level
Sites Available A ⚏ ⛺ **Total** 10
Facilities ⚏ ⟟ ⛿ ⟟ ⊙⟲ 🟊 ⛿ ⚱ 🖳🗜🖷
Nearby Facilities ┣ ✏
⇌ Clitheroe
Picturesque woodland park, adjacent to the River Ribble in the Forest of Bowland, an area of outstanding natural beauty.

CLITHEROE
Three Rivers Country Park, Eaves Hall Lane, West Bradford, Clitheroe, Lancs, BB7 3JG.
Std: 01200 **Tel:** 423523
Std: 01200 **Fax:** 442383
Email: hol@three-rivers.co.uk
Website: www.three-rivers.co.uk
Nearest Town/Resort Clitheroe
Directions A59 'Clitheroe North' turning, through the village to a T-Junction and turn left for West Bradford. Go past the Three Millstones Pub on the left, go round the s-bend and take the first turn right. ½ mile along this lane on the right is Three Rivers.
Acreage 45 **Open** All Year
Access Good **Site** Level
Sites Available A ⚏ ⛺ **Total** 80
Facilities ⚏ ⟟ 🖳 ⟟ ⊙⟲ 🖳 ⛿ ⚱ 🟊 ⟟ 🅰🗜🖷
Nearby Facilities ┣ ✏ U
⇌ Clitheroe
Forest and the Trough of Boland. Explore picturesque villages, Clitheroe Castle and Ingleton Waterfalls. Easy driving distance to the Yorkshire Dales and Skipton.

CROSTON
Royal Umpire Caravan Park, Southport Road, Croston, Preston, Lancashire, PR26 9JB.
Std: 01772 **Tel:** 600257
Std: 01772 **Fax:** 600662
Nearest Town/Resort Chorley
Directions Approx. 3-4 miles from the A581.
Acreage 60 **Open** All Year
Access Good **Site** Level
Sites Available A ⚏ ⛺ **Total** 200
Facilities ⌁ ⚏ ⟟ 🖳 ⟟ ⊙⟲ 🖳 ⛿ 🟊 🖭 ⚱ ⟟ 🗜🖷
Nearby Facilities ┣ ✏ U
⇌ Croston
Nice and quiet park, alongside the River Lostock. Ideal touring.

GARSTANG
Claylands Caravan Park, Cabus, Garstang, Nr. Preston, Lancashire, PR3 1AJ.
Std: 01524 **Tel:** 791242 **Fax:** 792406
Email: alan@claylands-caravan-park.co.uk

Website: www.claylands-caravanpark.co.uk
Nearest Town/Resort Blackpool
Directions Leave the M6 at junction 32, miles north by-pass Garstang. Signpost off the A6, 2 miles north of Garstang traffic lights.
Acreage 10 **Open** March **to** November
Access Good **Site** Level
Sites Available A ⚏ ⛺ **Total** 60
Facilities ⌁ ⚏ ⟟ 🖳 ⛿ ⟟ ⊙⟲ 🖭 ⟟ 🟊 ⛿ ⚱ ⊙🖳✗ ⟟ 🅰 ⟟ 🗜🖷🖷
Nearby Facilities ┣ ✏ 🏊 U ⚲
⇌ Preston
Well stocked fishing lakes for coarse fishing

GARSTANG
Smithy Caravan Park, Cabus Nook Lane, Winmarleigh, Garstang, Lancashire, PR3 1AA.
Std: 01995 **Tel:** 606200
Std: 01995 **Fax:** 606444
Email:
sue@smithycaravans.freeserve.co.uk
Nearest Town/Resort Lancaster/ Morecambe
Acreage 4 **Open** March **to** 4 January
Access Good **Site** Lev/Slope
Sites Available A ⚏ ⛺ **Total** 30
Facilities ⚏ ⟟ 🖳 ⟟ ⊙⟲ 🖭 ⟟ 🗜
Nearby Facilities ┣ ✏ 🏊 U ⚲
⇌ Lancaster
Alongside the Preston to Lancaster Canal. Private fishing lake. 50 minute drive to the Lakes.

GARSTANG
Wyreside Farm Park, Allotment Lane, St Michael's-on-Wyre, Garstang, Lancashire, PR3 0TE.
Std: 01995 **Tel:** 679797
Email: wyresidefarm@riverparks.co.uk
Website: www.ukparks.co.uk/ wyresidefarm
Nearest Town/Resort Garstang/ Blackpool
Directions Leave the M6 at junction 32 and take the A6 north for 3½ miles. West at Guy Thatch hamlet into St. Michael's Road, 3 miles to the mini roundabout on the A586, north over the bridge, past grapes, first right after right hand bend.

Acreage 4½ **Open** March **to** October
Access Good **Site** Level
Sites Available ⚠ ⊞ ☗ **Total** 10
Facilities ♿ ♂ 🚿 🚽 ⚡ ☎ ⊙ ⊒ ☕ ☂ ⌂ ➡ 🛒 ⊞
Nearby Facilities ► ✔ ⚓ ⤭ ∪ ♣
 ⇌ Preston
On the banks of the River Wyre. Central for Blackpool, the Lakes and the Trough of Bowland. Canoeing nearby.

HEYWOOD
Gelder Wood Park, Ashworth Road, Rochdale, Lancashire, OL11 5UP.
Std: 01706 Tel: 364858
Std: 01706 Fax: 364858
Nearest Town/Resort Heywood
Directions Leave the M62 at junction 18 onto the M66 (signposted Bury). After 3 miles turn off via slip road and roundabout onto the A58 (signposted Heywood). After 1 miles in Heywood centre, at the end of one way system turn left into Bamford Road. After ¾ miles at the T-Junction turn left onto the B6222 (signposted Bury). After 20 yards turn right at site sign into Ashworth Road (care required, steep and narrow in places). Site is on the right in ¾ miles.
Acreage 4 **Open** March **to** October
Access Good **Site** Sloping
Sites Available ⚠ ⊞ ☗ **Total** 34
Facilities ♿ ♂ 🚿 🚽 ☎ ⊙ ➡⊞
Nearby Facilities ► ✔ ∪
 ⇌ Rochdale/Bury
ADULTS ONLY. Central for Manchester City with all its attractions and Lancaster.

LANCASTER
Cockerham Sands Country Park, Cockerham, Lancaster, Lancashire, LA2 0BB.
Std: 01524 Tel: 751387
Std: 01524 Fax: 752275
Nearest Town/Resort Lancaster
Directions Leave M6 at Junction 33, take the A6 signposted Garstang/Glasson Dock for 1¼ miles. Turn right onto Cockerham Road and follow signs for Glasson/Glasson Dock. Proceed for 2 miles into Cockerham Village, turn right following signs for Glasson/Thurnham Hall. After 2¼ miles turn left at Thurnham Hall and follow lane to the end, 3 miles.
Open March **to** October
Access Good **Site** Level
Sites Available ⊞ ☗ **Total** 9
Facilities ♿ ♂ 🚿 🚽 ☎ ⊙ ⊒ ☕ ☂ ⌂ 🛒 ⊙ 🍴 ➡ ⚓ ➡ 🛒
Nearby Facilities ► ✔ ∪
 ⇌ Lancaster

LANCASTER
Laundsfield, Stoney Lane, Galgate, Near Lancaster, Lancashire, LA2 0JZ.
Std: 01524 Tel: 751763
Nearest Town/Resort Lancaster
Directions ½ a mile from the M6 junction 33, 1½ miles from Lancaster University and 4 miles from Lancaster.
Open March **to** October
Access Good **Site** Level
Sites Available ⚠ ⊞ ☗ **Total** 20
Facilities 🚿 ☎ ⊙ ⊒ ☕ 🍴 ➡
Nearby Facilities ► ✔ ⚓ ⤭ ∪
 ⇌ Lancaster
Near to a canal marina.

LANCASTER
Mosswood Caravan Park, Crimbles Lane, Cockerham, Lancaster, Lancashire, LA2 0ES.
Std: 01524 Tel: 791041 Fax: 792444
Email: enquiries@mosswood.co.uk
Website: www.mosswood.co.uk
Nearest Town/Resort Lancaster
Directions Leave the M6 at junction 33, take the A6 heading south then the second right to Cockerham. Follow the A588 west for 1 mile and there is a Mosswood sign at the top of Crimbles Lane.
Acreage 25 **Open** March **to** October
Access Good **Site** Level
Sites Available ⚠ ⊞ ☗ **Total** 30
Facilities ♿ ♂ 🚿 🚽 ☎ ⊙ ⊒ 🍴 ☕ 🏐 ⊙ 🛒 ⌂ ➡ ⊞
Nearby Facilities ► ✔ ∪
 ⇌ Lancaster
Ideal location midway between Blackpool & Morecambe. Fishing, parachuting and microlight flying are all available near to our park which abounds wildlife. ETB 5 Star Graded & David Bellamy Gold Award for Conservation.

LANCASTER
New Parkside Farm Caravan Park, Denny Beck, Caton Road, Lancaster, Lancashire, LA2 9HH.
Std: 01524 Tel: 770123
Email: new-parkside@hotmail.com
Website: www.ukparks.co.uk/newparkside
Nearest Town/Resort Lancaster
Directions Leave the M6 at junction 34 and take the A683 towards Kirkby Lonsdale. Park is situated 1 mile on the right.
Acreage 4 **Open** March **to** October
Access Good **Site** Lev/Slope
Sites Available ⚠ ⊞ ☗ **Total** 40
Facilities ♿ ♂ 🚿 ☎ ⊙ ⊒ ☕ ➡⊞
Nearby Facilities ► ✔ ∪
 ⇌ Lancaster
A working farm with beautiful views of Lune Valley. On the edge of Forest of Bowland and close to historic Lancaster and Morecambe Bay. Central for lakes and dales.

LYTHAM ST. ANNES
Eastham Hall Caravan Park, Saltcoates Road, Lytham St. Annes, Lancashire, FY8 4LS.
Std: 01253 Tel: 737907
Nearest Town/Resort Lytham St. Annes
Directions Leave Lytham centre on the A584 coast road towards Preston. Through traffic lights at the junction with Dock Road and Lorne Street and at the mini roundabout turn left. Go over the railway bridge, turn right at the next mini roundabout and the site is ½ mile on the right.
Acreage 20 **Open** March **to** October
Access Good **Site** Level
Sites Available ⊞ ☗ **Total** 120
Facilities ♂ 🚿 🚽 ☎ ⊙ ⊒ ☕ ➡ 🛒 ⊞ 🏐 ⊙ 🍴 ⌂ ➡ ⊞
Nearby Facilities ► ✔ ⚓ ⤭ ∪ ♣
 ⇌ Lytham
Quiet, rural site yet close to lovely Lytham St Annes, miles of beach with bustling Blackpool only 15 minutes away. Dogs allowed on leads.

MORECAMBE
Bungalow Camp Site, 272 Oxcliffe Road, Morecambe, Lancashire, LA3 3EH.
Std: 01524 Tel: 411273
Nearest Town/Resort Morecambe
Directions Leave the M6 at junction 34, 3 miles.
Open 1 March **to** 3 Jan
Access Good **Site** Level
Sites Available ⊞ ☗
Facilities ♂ 🚿 ☎ ⊙ ⊒ 🍴 ☕ ➡ 🛒 ⊞
Nearby Facilities
 ⇌ Morecambe
1 mile from the beach. Ideal for touring the Lakes.

MORECAMBE
Glen Caravan Park, Westgate, Morecambe, Lancashire, LA3 3EL.
Std: 01524 Tel: 423896
Nearest Town/Resort Morecambe
Directions In Morecambe itself close to promenade, Regent Road and Westgate.
Acreage ½ **Open** March **to** October
Access Good **Site** Level
Sites Available ⊞ ☗ **Total** 10
Facilities ♂ 🚿 ☎ ⊙ ⊒ 🍴 ☕ ➡ 🛒 ⊞ ⊙ 🛒➡⊞
Nearby Facilities ► ✔ ⚓ ∪ ♣
15 minutes walk Morecambe Promenade.

MORECAMBE
Greendales Farm, Carr Lane, Middleton, Morecambe, Lancashire, LA3 3LH.
Std: 01524 Tel: 852616
Email: kenneth.owen/@ntcworld.com
Nearest Town/Resort Morecambe

Directions Junction 34 off the M6, follow signs for Morecambe then Middleton. Turn down Carr Lane, site is on the left ½ mile down road to house and site is at the rear.
Acreage 2 Open All Year
Access Good Site Lev/Slope
Sites Available ▲ ♣ ⊕ Total 20
Facilities ⓕ 🄷 🅆 ♨ ⌐ ⊙ ⌐ ⓖ 🅰 ▾🄴
Nearby Facilities ⌐ ✓ ⚓ ⚘ U ⚲ ⚡ 🕴
≈ Morecambe
Near Middleton Sands with its large beach. Close to the Lake District, Blackpool and Morecambe.

MORECAMBE

Melbreak Camp Site, Carr Lane, Middleton, Nr. Morecambe, Lancashire, LA3 3LH.
Std: 01524 Tel: 852430
Nearest Town/Resort Morecambe
Directions Leave the M6 at junction 34 and take the A683 for 3 miles, at the second roundabout turn left, after 4 miles turn left for Middleton. Turn right by the church and site is ½ mile on the left.
Acreage 1½ Open March to October
Access Good Site Level
Sites Available ▲ ♣ ⊕ Total 50
Facilities ⓕ 🅆 ♨ ⌐ ⊙ ⌐ ⚌ 🄾 ▾
🕾 ⊙ ▾🄴
Nearby Facilities ⌐ ✓ U ⚡
≈ Morecambe
Site is ½ mile from Middleton Sands and 3 miles from seaside attractions of Morecambe.

MORECAMBE

Morecambe Lodge Caravan Park, Shore Lane, Bolton-le-Sands, Carnforth, Lancs, LA5 8JP.
Std: 01524 Tel: 823260/824361
Nearest Town/Resort Morecambe/ Lancaster
Directions A6 north from Lancaster, 4 miles to Bolton-le-Sands, turn left onto coastal road A5105 at traffic lights. 200yds turn right by the first house and follow this road to the beach. Site is on the left before the beach.
Acreage 1¼ Open March to October
Access Good Site Level
Sites Available ♣ ⊕ Total 25
Facilities ⚡ ⓕ 🄵 🄷 🅆 ♨ ⌐ ⊙ 🄾 ▾
🄸🄲 🅰▾🄴
Nearby Facilities ⌐ ✓ ⚓ ⚘ U ⚲
≈ Carnforth
Direct access to the beach, peaceful with beautiful views of lakes, hills. Noted for spectacular sunsets. Pressure reduced water and sewage hook-ups.

MORECAMBE

Ocean Edge Leisure Park, Moneyclose Lane, Heysham, Lancashire, LA3 2XA.
Std: 01524 Tel: 855657
Std: 01524 Fax: 855884
Email: slcar@freenetname.co.uk
Nearest Town/Resort Morecambe/ Lancaster
Directions M6 junction 34, follow signs for Port of Heysham, site signed from 2 miles.
Acreage 20 Open March to October
Access Good Site Level
Sites Available ▲ ♣ ⊕ Total 100+
Facilities ⓕ 🄵 🄷 🅆 ♨ ⌐ ⊙ ⌐ ⚌ 🄾 ▾
🕾 🄸 ⚌ 🗙 🝙 🝨 🄭 🄫 ❀ ▾🄴 🄴
Nearby Facilities ⌐ ✓ ⚓ ⚘ U ⚡
≈ Morecambe
Coastal park with bars, entertainment and cabaret, kiddies disco, amusements and day-time activities. Indoor pool and sauna, mini-market, indoor and outdoor play areas. A complete family park. Ideal touring centre. Holiday Home hire and sales.

MORECAMBE

Regent Leisure Park, Westgate, Morecambe, Lancashire, LA3 3DF.
Std: 01524 Tel: 413940
Std: 01524 Fax: 832247
Email: slcar@freenetname.co.uk
Nearest Town/Resort Morecambe
Directions Leave the M6 at junction 34 and follow the A589 over the River Lune. Turn left at the third roundabout and the park is approximately 1 mile on the left.
Acreage 15 Open March to 1 January
Access Good Site Level
Sites Available ♣ ⊕ Total 11
Facilities ⚓ ⓕ 🄵 🄷 🅆 ♨ ⌐ ⊙ ⌐ ⚌ 🄾 ▾
🕾 🄸 🄲 ⚌ 🗙 🝙 🝨 🄭 ▾🄴🄴
Nearby Facilities ⌐ ✓ ⚓ U ⚲ ⚡
≈ Lancaster
½ mile from the promenade with magnificent views over Morecambe Bay. 3 outdoor pools, Sportsmans Bar, cabaret lounge, mini-market, indoor and outdoor play areas and a café with take-away. Hard standing only - No awnings. Holiday home hire. ETB 5 Star Park and Rose Award.

MORECAMBE

Riverside Caravan Park, Heaton-with-Oxcliffe, Morecambe, Lancashire, LA3 3ER.
Std: 01524 Tel: 844193
Std: 01524 Fax: 383437
Email: info@riverside-morecambe.co.uk
Website: www.riverside-morecambe.co.uk
Nearest Town/Resort Morecambe/ Lancaster
Directions From Lancaster take the A589 towards Morecambe. At the second roundabout take the A683, at next roundabout turn left, second 100 yards at the roundabout turn right, ½ mile Lancaster Road.
Acreage 2¼ Open 1 March to 1 Jan
Access Good Site Level
Sites Available ▲ ♣ ⊕ Total 50
Facilities ⚓ ⓕ 🅆 ♨ ⌐ ⊙ ▾
🄸🄲 🄾 ⚌ ❀ ▾🄴
Nearby Facilities ⌐ ✓ ⚓ ▾
≈ Lancaster
Alongside the Lune Estuary and a very old pub. Road can be subject to tidal flooding.

MORECAMBE

Venture Caravan Park, Langridge Way, Westgate, Morecambe, Lancashire, LA4 4TQ.
Std: 01524 Tel: 412986
Std: 01524 Fax: 422029
Email: mark@venturecaravanpark.co.uk
Website: www.venturecaravanpark.co.uk
Nearest Town/Resort Morecambe
Open All Year
Access Good Site Level
Sites Available ▲ ♣ ⊕
Facilities ⚓ ⓕ 🄵 🄷 🅆 ♨ ⌐ ⊙ ⌐ ⚌ 🄾 ▾
🕾 🄸 🄲 ⚌ 🗙 🝙 🝨 🄭 🄫 ❀ ▾🄴
Nearby Facilities ⌐ ✓ ⚓ ▾ ⚲ ⚡
≈ Morecambe

ORMSKIRK

Abbey Farm Caravan Park, Dark Lane, Ormskirk, Lancashire, L40 5TX.
Std: 01695 Tel: 572686
Std: 01695 Fax: 572686
Email: abbeyfarm@yahoo.com
Nearest Town/Resort Southport
Directions From the M6 junction 27 onto the A5209 to Newburgh and Parbold. After 4½ miles turn left onto the B5240 and turn immediate right into Hobcross Lane. Site is 1½ miles on the right.
Acreage 6 Open All Year
Access Good Site Level

Sites Available ▲ ♣ ⊕ Total 104
Facilities ⚓ ⓕ 🄵 🄷 🅆 ♨ ⌐ ⊙ ⌐ ⚌ 🄾 ▾
🕾 🄸 ⊙ ⚌ 🄭 ❀ ▾🄴🄲 🄴
Nearby Facilities ⌐ ✓ U ⚡
≈ Ormskirk
Peace and quiet in a rural setting. Idea touring centre. Family bathroom available. Off license on site. A Countryside Discover Park, David Bellamy Environment Awar and Merseyside Caravan Park of the Yea 1995.

ORMSKIRK

Hurlston Hall Country Caravan Park, Southport Road, Scarisbrick, Ormskirk, Lancashire, L40 8HB.
Std: 01704 Tel: 841064
Std: 01704 Fax: 841700
Nearest Town/Resort Southport
Directions Leave the M6 at junction 26 an join the M58. Leave the M58 at junction and follow the A570 towards Southport, g through Ormskirk, Hurlston Hall is 3 mile outside Ormskirk.
Acreage 6 Open Easter to October
Access Good Site Level
Sites Available ▲ ♣ ⊕ Total 60
Facilities ⚓ ⓕ ♣ ⊕ ⌐ ⊙ ⌐ ⚌ 🄾 ▾
⊙ 🄸 🗙 ▾🄴
Nearby Facilities ⌐ ✓
≈ Ormskirk
Hurlston Hall sits beside a coarse fishin lake available to visitors. It also has an 1 hole golf course with driving range an clubhouse on site.

PILLING

Glenfield Caravan Park, Smallwood Hey Road, Pilling, Nr. Blackpool, Lancashire, PR3 6HE.
Std: 01253 Tel: 790782
Nearest Town/Resort Blackpool
Directions In the village of Pilling just o the A588 Lancaster to Blackpool main road 10 miles from Lancaster and Blackpool.
Acreage 8 Open March to October
Access Good Site Level
Sites Available ♣ ⊕ Total 8
Facilities ⓕ 🅆 ♨ ⌐ ⊙ ⌐ ⚌ 🄾 ▾
🄸⊙ ▾🄴
Nearby Facilities ⌐ ✓ ⚓ U ⚡
≈ Poulton-le-Fylde
Flat site on the coast. Ideal for walking an cycling.

PREESALL

Maaruig Caravan Park, 71 Pilling Lane, Preesall, Poulton-le-Fylde, Lancashire, FY6 0HB.
Std: 01253 Tel: 810404
Nearest Town/Resort Blackpool
Directions Leave the M55 at junction 3 onto the A585 towards Fleetwood. At th third set of traffic lights turn right onto th A588. Follow Knott End (B5377) up to th T-Junction, turn left then the first right int Pilling Lane.
Acreage 1 Open 1 March to 4 January
Access Good Site Level
Sites Available ▲ ♣ ⊕ Total 28
Facilities ⓕ 🄵 🄷 🅆 ♨ ⌐ ⊙ ⌐ ⚌ 🄾 ▾ 🄸▾🄴
Nearby Facilities ⌐ ✓ ⚓ U
≈ Poulton-le-Fylde
Quiet site, near the beach.

SOUTHPORT

Willowbank Holiday Home & Touring Park, Coastal Road, Ainsdale, Southport, Lancashire, PR8 3ST.
Std: 01704 Tel: 571566
Std: 01704 Fax: 571566
Email: info@willowbankcp.co.uk
Website: www.willowbankcp.co.uk
Nearest Town/Resort Southport

irections From Liverpool take the A565
Formby for 16 miles, turn left into Coastal
oad (signposted Ainsdale Beach), we are
50 yards on the left. From Southport take
oastal Road for 4 miles and turn right into
te.
creage 4½ Open 1 March to 10 Jan
ccess Good Site Level
ites Available ⋏ ⚏ ▢ Total 54+
acilities ⬗ ∮ ⚏ 🆖 ⚓ ⌐ ⊙ ⊷ ▱ ▢ ●
🛒 ▢ 🅐 🅟 ▢ 🅒 🅔
earby Facilities 𝄽 ✔ ⚓ ∪ ℛ
⚐ Ainsdale

uiet family park, close to the beach. Near
nature reserve and National Trust Red
quirrel Reserve. Good area for walking and
ycling. ETB 4 Star Graded, David Bellamy
ilver Award for Conservation and NW
ourist Board Silver Award.

HORNTON

neps Farm Holiday Park, River Road,
tanah, Thornton-Cleveleys, Blackpool,
ancashire, FY5 5LR.
td: 01253 Tel: 823632
td: 01253 Fax: 863967
Vebsite: www.kneps-farm.co.uk
earest Town/Resort Blackpool
irections 5 miles north north east of
lackpool. From the M55 junction 3 take the
585 Fleetwood road to the River Wyre
otel on the left, turn right at the roundabout
nto the B5412 signposted Little Thornton.
urn right at the mini-roundabout after the
chool onto Stanah Road, go straight over
e next roundabout leading to River Road.
creage 3½ Open March to Mid Nov
ccess Good Site Level
ites Available ⋏ ⚏ ∮ ⚏ 🆖 ⚓ ⌐ ⊙ ⊷ ▱ ▢ ●
🛒 ▢ 🅐 🅟 ▢
earby Facilities 𝄽 ✔ ⚓ ⚓
⚐ Poulton-le-Fylde

ituated adjacent to the Stanah Amenity and
icnic Area, forming part of the River Wyre
stuary Country Park. A rural retreat close
⊳ Blackpool.

VARTON

ank Lane Caravan Park, Bank Lane,
Varton, Near Preston, Lancashire, PR4
TB.
td: 01772 Tel: 633513
td: 01772 Fax: 633513
earest Town/Resort Blackpool
irections Leave the M6 at junction 32 onto
e M55, leave at junction 3 and take the
584, follow signs to Warton.
creage 3 Open March to October
ccess Good Site Level
ites Available ⋏ ⚏ ▢ Total 45
acilities ∮ ⚏ 🆖 ⚓ ⌐ ⊷ ▢ ●
⚐ ❘⚏ ▢ 🅐 🅟 ▢
earby Facilities 𝄽 ✔ ⚓ ⚓ ∪ ℛ
⚐ Kirkham

airhaven Lakes and Blackpool Pleasure
each.

VARTON

aklands Caravan Park, Lytham Road,
Varton, Preston, Lancashire, PR4 1AH.
td: 01772 Tel: 634459
earest Town/Resort Lytham St. Annes

Directions Leave the M6 at junction 31 and
follow the A583 towards Blackpool, then take
the A584 towards Lytham St. Annes.
Acreage 9 Open 1 March to 1 Nov
Access Good Site Lev/Slope
Sites Available ⋏ ⚏▢ Total 30
Facilities ⬗ ∮ ⚏ 🆖 ⚓ ⌐ ⊙ ⊷ ● ⚏ 🅐 ⚓
Nearby Facilities 𝄽 ✔ ⚓ ∪
⚐ St. Annes

LEICESTERSHIRE
CASTLE DONINGTON
Donington Park Farmhouse Hotel,
Melbourne Road, Isley Walton, Near
Castle Donington, Leicestershire, DE74
2RN.
Std: 01332 Tel: 862409
Std: 01332 Fax: 862364
Email: info@parkfarmhouse.co.uk
Website: www.parkfarmhouse.co.uk
Nearest Town/Resort Castle Donington
Directions Leave the M1 at junction 24, go
past East Midlands Airport on the A453. 1½
miles after the airport take the Melbourne
Road at Isley Walton, site is ½ mile on the
right hand side.
Acreage 7 Open All Year to Except Xmas
Access Good Site Lev/Slope
Sites Available ⋏ ⚏ ▢ Total 60
Facilities ⬗ ∮ ⚏ 🆖 ⚓ ⌐ ⊙ ▢ ●
▢ 🅐 ✕ 🅐 ⊷ 🅔 ▢
Nearby Facilities 𝄽 ⚓ ∪
⚐ Derby
At Donington Motor Racing Circuit. Ideal for
Southern Derbyshire and the Peak District.

LOUGHBOROUGH
Proctors Pleasure Park, Proctors Park
Road, Barrow-on-Soar, Leicestershire,
LE12 8QF.
Std: 01509 Tel: 412434
Std: 01509 Fax: 412747
Nearest Town/Resort Loughborough
Directions 2 miles south of Loughborough
on the A6. Travel from the south on the A6
until you see signs for both Barrow and
Quorn, follow signs to Barrow. As you enter
Barrow the site is immediately on the right
after the traffic lights on the bridge.
Acreage 150 Open All Year
Access Good Site Level
Sites Available ⋏ ⚏ ●
Facilities ∮ 🆖 ⚓ ⌐ ⊙ ● ❘⚏ 🅐 ▢ ⚓ ⊷ ▢
Nearby Facilities 𝄽 ✔ ⚓ ⚓
⚐ Barrow-on-Soar
Alongside a river and surrounded by
attractive countryside. River and private lake
for fishing. Shops nearby. You can also
contact us on Mobile 07976 284919.

MARKET BOSWORTH
Bosworth Water Trust, Far Cotton Lane,
Market Bosworth, Leicestershire, CV13
6PD.
Std: 01455 Tel: 291876
Std: 01455 Fax: 291876
Email: info@bosworth-water-
trust.freeserve.co.uk

Website: www.bosworth-water-
trust.freeserve.co.uk
Nearest Town/Resort Market Bosworth
Directions From Hinckley A447, left onto
the B585 to Market Bosworth. From
Nuneaton A444 and cross the A5, right onto
the B585 to Market Bosworth.
Acreage 50 Open All Year
Access Good Site Level
Sites Available ⋏ ⚏ ● Total 20
Facilities ⬗ ∮ ⚏ 🆖 ⚓ ⌐ ⊙ ⊷ ●
⚐ ❘⚏ ▢ 🅐 🅐 ⊷ 🅔
Nearby Facilities 𝄽 ✔ ⚓ ⚓ ∪ ℛ ⚓
⚐ Hinckley
50 acre park with a 5 acre caravan park. £2
per car to enter. Battlefields of Market
Bosworth, Twycross Zoo and steam railway.

LINCOLNSHIRE
BARTON-UPON-HUMBER
Silver Birches Tourist Park, Silver
Birches, Waterside Road, Barton-Upon-
Humber, North Lincolnshire, DN18 5BA.
Std: 01652 Tel: 632509
Nearest Town/Resort Hull/Cleethorpes
Directions From the A15 or A1077, follow
Humber Bridge Viewing Area signs to
Waterside Road, site is just past the Sloop
public house.
Acreage 1¼ Open April to November
Access Good Site Level
Sites Available ⋏ ⚏ ● Total 24
Facilities ⬗ ∮ ⚏ 🆖 ⚓ ⌐ ⊙ ⊷ ●
❘⚏ ▢ 🅐 🅐 ❋ ⊷ 🅔
Nearby Facilities ✔ ℛ
⚐ Barton-Upon-Humber
Next to Barton Clay Pits Nature Reserve.
Ideal for touring.

BOSTON
Orchard Park, Frampton Lane, Hubberts
Bridge, Boston, Lincolnshire, PE20 3QU.
Std: 01205 Tel: 290328
Std: 01205 Fax: 290247
Website: www.orchardpark.co.uk
Nearest Town/Resort Boston
Directions Take the A52 from Boston, in 3
miles 'Four Cross Roads' Pub turn right
onto the B1192. Park is on the right in about
¼ mile.
Acreage 36 Open All Year
Access Good Site Level
Sites Available ⋏ ⚏ ● Total 60
Facilities ⬗ ∮ ⚏ 🆖 ⚓ ⌐ ⊙ ⊷ ▱ ▢ ●
⚐ ▢ 🅐 ✕ 🅐 🅐 ⊷ 🅔 ▢
Nearby Facilities 𝄽 ✔ ∪
⚐ Hubberts bridge
Angling lake on site.

BOSTON
Pilgrims Way Camping Park, Church
Green Road, Fishtoft, Boston,
Lincolnshire, PE21 0QY.
Std: 01205 Tel: 366646
Website: www.pilgrims-way.co.uk
Nearest Town/Resort Boston/Skegness
Directions Take the A52 Boston to
Skegness road, 1 mile out of town turn right
at Ball House Pub, follow signs to camping
park.
Acreage 1 Open Easter to End
September

LINCS

Access Good **Site** Level
Sites Available ⚠ ⬛ **Total** 20
Facilities ⬛ ⬛ ⬛ ⬛ ⬛ ⬛ ⬛ ⬛ ⬛ ⬛ ⬛ ⬛
Nearby Facilities ⬛ ⬛ ⬛ ⬛ ⬛ ⬛
 ≈ Boston
Quiet park. 20 minutes from Skegness.
Close to Bowling, swimming and historical
sites. AA 4 Pennants De Lux.

BOSTON

Plough Caravan Site, Station Road,
Swineshead Bridge, Boston,
Lincolnshire, PE20 3PS.
Std: 01205 **Tel:** 820300
Nearest Town/Resort Boston
Directions 8 miles from Sleaford on the
A17.
Acreage 2 **Open** 1 April **to** 31 October
Access Good **Site** Level
Sites Available ⬛ ⬛ **Total** 14
Facilities ⬛ ⬛ ⬛ ⬛ ⬛ ⬛ ⬛ ⬛
Nearby Facilities ⬛ ⬛
 ≈ Swineshead Bridge
Alongside a river for fishing.

BOSTON

White Cat Caravan & Camping Park,
Shaw Lane, Old Leake, Boston,
Lincolnshire, PE22 9LQ.
Std: 01205 **Tel:** 870121
Email: mkibby@whitecat.freeserve.co.uk
Website: www.whitecatpark.com
Nearest Town/Resort Boston/Skegness
Directions 8 miles from Boston on the
A52 Skegness road. At Old Leake follow
signs to a right turn into Shaw Lane, site
is 300 yards on the left.
Acreage 2½ **Open** Mid March **to** Mid Nov
Sites Available ⚠ ⬛ **Total** 40
Facilities ⬛ ⬛ ⬛ ⬛ ⬛ ⬛ ⬛ ⬛
⬛ ⬛ ⬛ ⬛ ⬛ ⬛ ⬛
Nearby Facilities ⬛

 ≈ Boston
Ideal touring for Fens, wild life marshes,
Skegness resort. Permanent tourer sites
available.

CAISTOR

Nettleton Park, Moortown Road, Near
Caistor, North Lincolnshire, LN7 6JQ.
Std: 01472 **Tel:** 851501 **Fax:** 852967
Nearest Town/Resort Grimsby/
Mablethorpe
Directions From the A46 Grimsby to Lincoln
road, at Nettleton take the Moortown Road
opposite The Salutation Inn, Park is 1½
miles on the right.
Acreage 66 **Open** Early March **to** End Oct
Access Good **Site** Level
Sites Available ⬛ ⬛ **Total** 12
Facilities ⬛ ⬛ ⬛ ⬛ ⬛ ⬛ ⬛ ⬛
⬛ ⬛ ⬛ ⬛ ⬛ ⬛ ⬛
Nearby Facilities ⬛ ⬛ ⬛ ⬛
 ≈ Cleethorpes/Grimsby
Set in acres of Pine forests and beautifully
manicured gardens. Limited touring pitches,
early booking is advisable.

CHAPEL ST. LEONARDS

The Beeches Caravan Park, Trunch
Lane, Chapel St. Leonards, Lincolnshire,
PE24 5UA.
Std: 01754 **Tel:** 871877 **Fax:** 871870
Nearest Town/Resort Skegness
Directions From Skegness take the A52
signposted Chapel St. Leonards.
Open March **to** October
Access Good **Site** Level
Sites Available ⚠ ⬛ ⬛
Facilities ⬛ ⬛ ⬛ ⬛ ⬛ ⬛ ⬛ ⬛ ⬛ ⬛
Nearby Facilities ⬛ ⬛ ⬛
 ≈ Skegness
Very quiet, greenfield site for families and
couples.

CLEETHORPES

Thorpe Park Holiday Centre, Thorpe
Park, Humberston, Cleethorpes, North
East Lincolnshire, DN36 4HG.
Std: 01472 **Tel:** 813395
Website: www.british-holidays.co.uk
Nearest Town/Resort Cleethorpes
Directions From the M180 take the A18
and follow signs for Grimsby and
Cleethorpes. In Cleethorpes town centre
follow signs for the park.
Open March **to** September
Access Good **Site** Level
Sites Available ⚠ ⬛ **Total** 85
⬛ ⬛ ⬛ ⬛ ⬛ ⬛ ⬛ ⬛ ⬛ ⬛ ⬛ ⬛ ⬛
Nearby Facilities ⬛ ⬛ ⬛ ⬛
 ≈ Cleethorpes
Next to Pleasure Island. Near the beach.
Kids Club and a full family entertainment
programme. Fishing lake, pets corner, go
crazy golf and a mini park train.

CONINGSBY

Orchard Caravans, Witham Bank,
Chapel Hill, Coningsby, Lincs, LN4 4PZ.
Std: 01526 **Tel:** 342414
Directions 1½ miles along Riverbank Road
off the A153 Sleaford to Horncastle road.
Near Tattershall Bridge.
Acreage 2½ **Open** March **to** October
Access Good **Site** Level
Sites Available ⚠ ⬛ ⬛ **Total** 45
Facilities ⬛ ⬛ ⬛ ⬛ ⬛ ⬛ ⬛ ⬛ ⬛ ⬛ ⬛ ⬛ ⬛
Nearby Facilities ⬛ ⬛ ⬛ ⬛ ⬛
Secluded site running alongside the River
Witham. Ideal base for touring.

HORNCASTLE

Ashby Park, West Ashby, Near
Horncastle, Lincs, LN9 5PP.
Std: 01507 **Tel:** 527966
Website: www.ukparks.co.uk/ashby

Thorpe Park
Cleethorpes, Lincolnshire

Caravan & Camping

BRITISH HOLIDAYS

WE WELCOME: ✓ Motor Homes ✓ Trailer Tents ✓ Touring Vans

Prices start from **£5** *per pitch, per night

*Based on a basic Tourer, Tent or Motor Home pitch per family at Thorpe Park between 11 and 24 May 2002. Subject to supplements.

2 FOR 1
Book 2 nights for the price of 1 night during April, May, June, September or October 2002.
Applies to new bookings only. Only one offer per booking. Subject to limited availability. Prices refer to Standard Pitches and are subject to the terms, conditions and supplements of the current touring brochure.

Great Touring Facilities and Amenities on Park

Call For Details
Information correct as of date of print

To book call the park on: **01472 813395**
or see your local travel agent quoting: Cades

Thorpe Park Holiday Centre, Cleethorpes, North East Lincolnshire. DN35 0PW

Visit Our Website at: www.british-holidays.co.uk

---

earest Town/Resort Horncastle
irections 1¾ miles north of Horncastle etween the A153 and the A158.
creage 54 **Open** All Year
ccess Good **Site** Level
ites Available ▲ ⌂ ⊟ **Total** 80
acilities ⌂ ∮ ▯ ▯ ⚓ ⌐ ☉ ⊣ ☐ ☎
⛢ ⊙ ☒ ✦ ▯ ⊟
earby Facilities ⌐ ∕ ∪
≈ Lincoln
ix fishing lakes, pub and restaurant ½ mile, wimming pool 1¾ miles. 23 miles to the east. Holiday caravans for sale. David ellamy Gold Award for Conservation.

UTTOFT
olly Common Caravan Park, Jolly ommon Lane (Via Sea Lane), Huttoft, ford, Lincolnshire, LN13 9RW.
td: 01507 **Tel:** 490236
earest Town/Resort Mablethorpe/ kegness
irections Take the A52 Sutton to kegness road, turn first left in the village of uttoft. After ¾ miles turn right, site is 200 ards on the left.
creage 9 **Open** 15 March **to** October
ccess Good **Site** Level
tes Available ⌂ ⊟ **Total** 55
acilities ∮ ▯ ⚓ ⌐ ⊣ ☎ ✦ ⊟
earby Facilities ⌐ ∕ ⊥ ∪ ♁
≈ Skegness
eaceful countryside site with spacious tches. 1 mile from the beach and a golf ourse. Private coarse fishing. Suitable for ature couples.

MMINGHAM
llingholme Caravan Site, Church End, ast Halton, North Lincolnshire, DN40 NX.
td: 01469 **Tel:** 540594

Nearest Town/Resort Grimsby/ Cleethorpes
Directions From the A180 take the A160 towards Killingholme, turn left at the roundabout, Site is approx. 1½ miles on the right opposite the church.
Open All Year
Access Good **Site** Level
Sites Available ⌂ ⊟
Facilities ∮ ▯ ▯ ⌐ ☎ ⛢ ☉ ⚓ ✦ ⊟
Nearby Facilities ∕ ∪
Near Cleethorpes. Under New Management.

INGOLDMELLS
Country Meadows Holiday Park, Anchor Lane, Ingoldmells, Skegness, Lincs, PE25 1LZ.
Std: 01754 **Tel:** 874455
Std: 01754 **Fax:** 874125
Email: geoff@countrymeadows.co.uk
Website: www.countrymeadows.co.uk
Nearest Town/Resort Skegness
Directions On the A52 4 miles north of Skegness. ¾ mile out of Ingoldmells Village turn right into Anchor Lane, go 1 mile down toward the sea and the site is on the left hand side.
Acreage 10 **Open** March **to** October
Access Good **Site** Level
Sites Available ▲ ⌂ ⊟ **Total** 200
Facilities ∮ ▯ ▯ ⚓ ⌐ ☉ ⊣ ⚓ ☐ ☎ ⛢ ☉ ⚓ ▯ ✦ ⊟
Nearby Facilities ⌐ ∕ ⚓ ∪ ♁ ♁
≈ Skegness
5 minutes walk from the beach. Fishing on site.

INGOLDMELLS
Hardy's Touring Site, Sea Lane, Ingoldmells, Skegness, Lincs, PE25 1PG.
Std: 01754 **Tel:** 874071

Nearest Town/Resort Skegness/ Ingoldmells
Directions Take the A52 north from Skegness to Ingoldmells. At the Ship Inn in Ingoldmells turn right down Sea Lane, towards the sea. Site is ½ mile on the right.
Acreage 5 **Open** Easter **to** October
Access Good **Site** Level
Sites Available ⌂ ⊟ **Total** 112
Facilities ∮ ▯ ⚓ ⌐ ☉ ⚓ ▯ ◎ ☎ ⛢ ☉ ⚓ ✕ ▯ ✦ ⊟
Nearby Facilities ⌐ ∕ ∪ ♁ ♁
≈ Skegness
5 minutes walk from the beach. 10 minutes from an animal farm and near Fantasy Island.

INGOLDMELLS
Valetta Farm Caravan Site, Mill Lane, Addlethorpe, Skegness, Lincolnshire, PE24 4TB.
Std: 01754 **Tel:** 763758
Nearest Town/Resort Skegness
Directions Turn left off the A158 (Horncastle to Skegness road) in Burgh-le-Marsh at the signpost Ingoldmells and Addlethorpe. Follow signposts for Ingoldmells for 3 miles, turn right by disused mill into Mill Lane. Site is on the left in 150yds.
Acreage 2 **Open** 25 March **to** 20 October
Access Good **Site** Level
Sites Available ▲ ⌂ ⊟ **Total** 35
Facilities ⚓ ∮ ▯ ⚓ ⌐ ☉ ⚓ ☎ ⚓
Nearby Facilities ⌐ ∕ ⊥ ∪ ♁
≈ Skegness
1 mile from the beach, quite a pretty site in the country.

LINCOLN
Hartsholme Country Park,
Skellingthorpe Road, Lincoln, Lincolnshire, LN6 0EY.
Std: 01522 **Tel:** 873578

LINCS

Nearest Town/Resort Lincoln
Directions 2½ miles south west of Lincoln city centre. Signposted from the A46 on the B1378.
Acreage 2½ **Open** March **to** October
Access Good **Site** Level
Sites Available ⚊ ⚋ ⚌ **Total** 50
Facilities ⚊ ⚋ 🚽 ⚌ ⚊ ☺ ⚊
⚊ ⚊ ⚊ ⚊ ⚊ ⚊
Nearby Facilities
⚊ Lincoln
Set amongst mature woodland with a large picturesque lake, as well as open grassland. Adjacent to Swanholme Lakes local nature reserve. Also open for Lincoln's Christmas Market.

LINCOLN

Shortferry Caravan Park, Ferry Road, Fiskerton, Lincoln, Lincolnshire, LN3 4HU.
Std: 01526 **Tel:** 398021
Std: 01526 **Fax:** 398102
Email: kay@shortferry.co.uk
Website: www.shortferry.co.uk
Nearest Town/Resort Lincoln
Directions From the A46 Lincoln ring road take the A158 towards Skegness. After approx. 5 miles turn right at Shortferry sign, continue to follow signs for approx. 5 miles.
Acreage 80 **Open** All Year
Access Good **Site** Level
Sites Available ⚊ ⚋ ⚌ **Total** 50
Facilities ⚊ ⚋ ⚌ ⚊ ⚊ ⚊ ⚊ ⚊
⚊ ⚊ ⚊ ⚊ ⚊ ⚊ ⚊
Nearby Facilities ⚊ ⚋ ⚌
⚊ Lincoln
Situated by a river with 2 fishing ponds. Fishing tackle and bait shop. Entertainment most weekends. Bar meals and take-away in our public house. Tennis on site. Seasonal outdoor heated swimming pool.

LONG SUTTON

Silverhill Caravan Park, Roman Bank, Lutton Gowts, Long Sutton, Lincolnshire, PE12 9LQ.
Std: 01406 **Tel:** 365673
Std: 01406 **Fax:** 364406
Nearest Town/Resort Hunstanton
Directions From Kings Lynn take the A17 and follow signs to Butterfly Park, site is ½ a mile on the left opposite Monmouth Lane. From Sleaford take the A17 and follow signs for Butterfly Park.
Acreage 6-7 **Open** All Year
Access Good **Site** Level
Sites Available ⚊ ⚋ ⚌ **Total** 45+
Facilities ⚊ ⚋ ⚌ ⚊ ⚊ ⚊ ⚊
Nearby Facilities ⚊ ⚋
⚊ Kings Lynn
Flat terrain, ideal for walking and cycling. Near Butterfly & Falconry Park, Long Sutton market town and Hunstanton seaside resort. 30mph zone all the way to Long Sutton, 15-20 minute walk.

MABLETHORPE

Denehurst Guest House & Camping Touring Site, Alford Road, Mablethorpe, Lincolnshire, LN12 1PX.
Std: 01507 **Tel:** 472951
Std: 01507 **Fax:** 472951
Website:
www.denehurstguesthouse.co.uk
Nearest Town/Resort Mablethorpe
Directions On the A1104 Alford road, west of Mablethorpe ¾ mile. A157 from Louth.
Acreage 1 **Open** March **to** December
Access Good **Site** Level
Sites Available ⚊ ⚋ ⚌ **Total** 20
Facilities ⚋ ⚌ ⚊ ⚊ ☺ ⚊ ⚊ ⚊ ⚊ ⚊ ⚊ ⚊
Nearby Facilities ⚊ ⚋
⚊ Skegness
One mile to the beach and shops.

MABLETHORPE

Dunes Holivan Estate, Quebec Road, Mablethorpe, Lincolnshire, LN12 1QH.
Std: 01507 **Tel:** 473327
Std: 01507 **Fax:** 473327
Email: holivans@enterprise.net
Website: www.holivans.co.uk
Nearest Town/Resort Mablethorpe
Directions Go into Mablethorpe on the A1104, up to the pullover and turn left into Quebec Road. After ¾ mile turn into the caravan park.
Acreage 10 **Open** Easter **to** October
Access Good **Site** Level
Sites Available ⚊ ⚋ ⚌ **Total** 25
Facilities ⚋ ⚌ ⚊ ☺ ⚊
⚊ ⚊ ⚊ ⚊ ⚊ ⚊ ⚊ ⚊ ⚊
Nearby Facilities ⚋
⚊ Skegness/Grimsby
Adjacent to dunes and beaches.

MABLETHORPE

Golden Sands Holiday Park, Quebec Road, Mablethorpe, Lincs, LN12 1QJ.
Std: 01507 **Tel:** 477871
Std: 01507 **Fax:** 472066
Website: www.havenholidays.com
Nearest Town/Resort Mablethorpe
Directions From Mablethorpe town centre follow the sea front road to the north end for Golden Sands.
Acreage 10 **Open** Easter **to** October
Access Good **Site** Level
Sites Available ⚊ ⚋ ⚌ **Total** 365
Facilities ⚊ ⚋ ⚌ ⚊ ⚊ ☺ ⚊ ⚊
⚊ ⚊ ⚊ ⚊ ⚊ ⚊ ⚊ ⚊ ⚊ ⚊ ⚊ ⚊ ⚊ ⚊
Nearby Facilities ⚊ ⚋ ⚌
⚊ Skegness
Situated close to a fine sandy beach, with excellent facilities for all the family, providing a fun packed holiday.

MABLETHORPE

Grange Farm Leisure Ltd., Alford Road, Mablethorpe, Lincolnshire, LN12 1NE.
Std: 01507 **Tel:** 472814
Nearest Town/Resort Mablethorpe
Directions Situated on the A1104 between Mablethorpe and Maltby-le-Marsh. Approx. ½ miles from the centre of Mablethorpe.
Open March to November
Access Good **Site** Level
Sites Available ⚠ ♨ ♿ **Total** 35
Facilities ...
Nearby Facilities ✓
⚆ Skegness
Set in open farmland. 4 coarse fishing lakes, carp lake and fly fishing lake. Tackle shop. Public Bar on premises with food available. Pets are welcome by arrangement.

MABLETHORPE

Willows Caravan Park, Maltby le Marsh, Near Mablethorpe, Lincolnshire, LN13 ...JS.
Std: 01507 **Tel:** 450244
Std: 01507 **Fax:** 450450
Email: lakeside@donamott.com
Website: www.donamott.com
Nearest Town/Resort Mablethorpe
Directions On the A1104 Mablethorpe to Alford road, 1 mile from Mablethorpe Town Centre.
Acreage 32 **Open** 15 March to 30 November
Access Good **Site** Level
Sites Available ... **Total** 40
Facilities ...
Nearby Facilities ...
⚆ Skegness
Quiet, secluded, well maintained park set in 32 acres, yet only 1 mile from the town centre. Large, well-stocked fishing lake and hole golf course. Good central location for local resorts and activities.

MARKET DEEPING

Tallington Lakes, Barholm Road, Tallington, Stamford, Lincolnshire, PE9 ...RJ.
Std: 01778 **Tel:** 347000
Std: 01778 **Fax:** 346213
Email: info@tallington.com
Website: www.tallington.com
Nearest Town/Resort Stamford
Directions Off the A1 at Stamford, through the centre following signs. A16 Spalding/Market Deeping for 6 miles. Go through the village of Tallington, over the level crossing and take the first left (garden centre on the corner). Entrance is 600yds on the right.
Acreage 250 **Open** All Year
Access Good **Site** Level
Sites Available ... **Total** 135
Facilities ...
Nearby Facilities ...
⚆ Stamford
Tallington Lakes is a watersports centre offering some of the best water-skiing, jetskiing, sailing and wind-surfing in the country.

MARKET DEEPING

The Deepings Caravan Park, Outgang Road, Market Deeping, Lincolnshire, PE6 ...LQ.
Std: 01778 **Tel:** 344335
Std: 01778 **Fax:** 344394
Nearest Town/Resort Market Deeping
Directions Park is 2 miles from Market Deeping on the B1525. Take the first left after the Goat Inn.

Open February to December
Access Good **Site** Level
Sites Available ... **Total** 45
Facilities ...
Nearby Facilities ...
⚆ Peterborough
Fishing on park.

MARKET RASEN

Manor Farm Caravan & Camping Site, Manor Farm, East Firsby, Market Rasen, Lincolnshire, LN8 2DB.
Std: 01673 **Tel:** 878258
Std: 01673 **Fax:** 878258
Email: info@lincolnshire-lanes.com
Website: www.lincolnshire-lanes.com
Nearest Town/Resort Market Rasen/Lincoln
Directions Take the A15 north from Lincoln, 2½ miles past RAF Scampton turn right signposted Spridlington. In Sprid Village turn left signposted Normanby, site is ¾ miles on the left.
Acreage 3 **Open** All Year
Access Good **Site** Level
Sites Available ... **Total** 21
Facilities ...
Nearby Facilities ...
⚆ Market Rasen/Lincoln

MARKET RASEN

The Rother Camp Site, Gainsborough Road, Middle Rasen, Nr. Market Rasen, Lincolnshire, LN8 3JU.
Std: 01673 **Tel:** 842433
Email: ken.a.@steed40.freeserve.co.uk
Nearest Town/Resort Market Rasen
Directions 1½ miles west of Market Rasen, on east side of A631/A46 junction. Site at rear of Rother.
Acreage 2 **Open** March to October
Access Good **Site** Level
Sites Available ... **Total** 45
Facilities ...
Nearby Facilities ...
⚆ Market Rasen
Tree and hedge screened. Natural, relaxed country site. Good overnight stop and touring centre.

MARKET RASEN

Walesby Woodland Caravan Park, Walesby Road, Market Rasen, Lincolnshire, LN8 3UN.
Std: 01673 **Tel:** 843285
Nearest Town/Resort Market Rasen
Directions In Market Rasen, take the B1203 to Tealby. After ¾ mile, turn left onto unclassified road to Walesby. ¼ mile on the left, enter lane. Site entrance 150 yards on right, signposted.
Acreage 2½ **Open** March to 1st November
Access Good **Site** Level
Sites Available ... **Total** 60
Facilities ...
Nearby Facilities ...
⚆ Market Rasen
Ideal sight seeing. Lincoln 16 miles. Set in forestry land, many walks. Total peace yet close to town. 20 miles from beach. AA 3 Pennant, RAC Appointed, Calor Gas Runner-up Green Award 1993 and EMTB Best of Tourism Awards 1995 Caravan Park of the Year Winner.

NORTH SOMERCOTES

Lakeside Park, North Somercotes, Near Louth, North Lincolnshire, LN11 7RB.
Std: 01507 **Tel:** 358428
Std: 01507 **Fax:** 358135
Nearest Town/Resort Grimsby/Mablethorpe
Directions Situated on the A1031 Grimsby to Mablethorpe coast road. Continue through the village of North Somercotes and Park is ½ mile on the left.
Acreage 110 **Open** Early March to End November
Access Good **Site** Level
Sites Available ... **Total** 125
Facilities ...
Nearby Facilities ...
⚆ Grimsby
Th perfect location for exploring Skegness, Mablethorpe, the market town of Louth and The Lincolnshire Wolds.

SALTFLEET

Sunnydale Holiday Park, Sea Lane, Saltfleet, Lincolnshire, LN11 7RP.
Std: 0870 **Tel:** 442 9293
Std: 01507 **Fax:** 339100
Nearest Town/Resort Louth
Directions Head towards Louth on the A16, take the B1200 through Manby and Saltfleetby. Drive through Saltfleet and turn off along Sea Lane, the park is 400 yards on the left.
Open March to November
Access Good **Site** Level
Sites Available ... **Total** 40
Facilities ...
Nearby Facilities ...
⚆ Cleethorpes
Attractive touring park ideal for exploring the beauty of Lincolnshire. Quality on park facilities. Close to summer seaside attractions and picturesque market towns.

SCUNTHORPE

Brookside Caravan & Camping Park, Stather Road, Burton-Upon-Stather, Scunthorpe, Lincolnshire, DN15 9DH.
Std: 01724 **Tel:** 721369
Nearest Town/Resort Scunthorpe
Directions B1430 from Scunthorpe Town centre to Burton-Upon-Stather (4 miles) turn left in front of Sheffield Arms public house. Down the hill past the Ferry Boat Inn, entrance to park 100yds further on right - signposted.
Acreage 6 **Open** All Year
Access Good **Site** Level
Sites Available ... **Total** 35
Facilities ...
Nearby Facilities ...
⚆ Scunthorpe
Set in an area of outstanding beauty, enjoying scenic views over the River Trent, ideal base for touring, fishing, walking and cycling.

SKEGNESS

Herons Mead Fishing Lake & Touring Park, Marsh Lane, Orby, Near Ingoldmells, Skegness, Lincolnshire, PE24 5JA.
Std: 01754 **Tel:** 873357
Email: watercolours@freeuk.com
Website: www.ukparks.co.uk/herons
Nearest Town/Resort Ingoldmells/Skegness
Directions Take the A158 Lincoln to Skegness road, turn left just after Gunby roundabout for Orby and Ingoldmells. 1 mile after Orby look for brown tourism signs.

Ronam Cottage ☆ Open All Year ☆
Pinfold Lane, Anderby, Nr. Skegness, Lincolnshire PE24 5YA

Quiet park with beautiful views of open countryside. Good facilities and a high standard of cleanliness. We look forward to seeing you.

Tel: 01507 490750

Acreage 15 **Open** April to November
Access Good **Site** Level
Sites Available ⚠ ⌑ ⛺ **Total** 50
Facilities ✦ 🆆🅲 ♨ ⌑ ⊙ ⌿ 🔥 ▣ ☎ 🏪 ✕ 🅿 ♨
Nearby Facilities ⌑ ✓ ⚓ ↝ ∪ ♪ ♫
✈ Skegness
Excellent fishing on site. 4 miles from beaches and attractions. David Bellamy Gold Award for Conservation. 3 miles from a shop and 2 miles from gas supplies.

SKEGNESS
Hill View Fishing Lakes & Touring Caravan Park, Skegness Road (A52), Hogsthorpe, Nr. Skegness, Lincs, PE24 5NR.
Std: 01754 **Tel:** 872979
Directions On the A52, 7 miles from Skegness towards Mablethorpe.
Acreage 16 **Open** 15 March to 30 Oct
Access Good **Site** Level
Sites Available ⌑ ⛺ **Total** 90
Facilities ♿ ⚡ ✦ 🆆🅲 ♨ ⌑ ⊙ ⌿ ☎ ▣ 🏪 ✕ ▣ 🅿 ▣
Nearby Facilities ⌑ ✓ ⚓ ♪
✈ Skegness
Ideal touring, three well stocked fishing lakes.

SKEGNESS
Homelands Caravan Park, Sea Road, Anderby, Skegness, Lincolnshire, PE24 5YB.
Std: 01507 **Tel:** 490511
Website: www.caravancampingsites.co.uk
Nearest Town/Resort Skegness/Mablethorpe
Directions From Skegness take the A52 coast road to Mablethorpe, approx. 10-12 miles from Skegness.
Acreage 1 **Open** March to November
Access Good **Site** Level
Sites Available ⚠ ⌑ ⛺ **Total** 10
Facilities ⚡ ✦ 🆆🅲 ♨ ⌑ ⊙ ⌿ ☎ 🏪 ✕ ▣
Nearby Facilities ⌑ ✓
✈ Skegness/Mablethorpe
Quiet, friendly site in the countryside. 4/6 Berth Static Van also available for hire.

SKEGNESS
North Shore Holiday Centre, Roman Bank, Skegness, Lincolnshire, PE25 1SL.
Std: 01754 **Tel:** 763815
Std: 01754 **Fax:** 761323
Email: info@holidaycentre.fsnet.co.uk
Website: www.skegness-resort.co.uk/northshore
Nearest Town/Resort Skegness
Directions A52 towards Mablethorpe, 500yds from the A158 junction.
Open March to October
Access Good **Site** Level
Sites Available ♿ ⚡ ⛺ **Total** 250
Facilities ♿ ✦ 🆆🅲 ♨ ⌑ ⊙ ⌿ 🔥 ▣ ☎ 🏪 ⊙ 🏪 ✕ ▣ 🅿 ▣
Nearby Facilities ⌑ ✓ ⚓ ↝ ∪ ♪ ♫
Near the beach. Pitch & Putt and Miniature Golf on site. New all weather pitches now available.

SKEGNESS
Retreat Farm, Croft, Skegness, Lincolnshire, PE24 4RE.
Std: 01754 **Tel:** 762092
Nearest Town/Resort Skegness
Directions South of Skegness on the A52.
Acreage 2 **Open** Easter to End Oct
Access Good **Site** Level
Sites Available ⚠ ⌑ ⛺ **Total** 35
Facilities ✦ 🆆🅲 ♨ ⊙ ☎
Nearby Facilities ⌑ ✓
✈ Skegness

SKEGNESS
Richmond Holiday Centre, Richmond Drive, Skegness, Lincolnshire, PE25 3TQ.
Std: 01754 **Tel:** 762097
Std: 01754 **Fax:** 765631
Email: richmond.leisure1@virgin.net
Website: www.richmondholidays.com
Nearest Town/Resort Skegness
Directions Follow signs to the coach park on Richmond Drive, we are located approx. ½ a mile past the coach park on the right hand side.
Acreage 50 **Open** March to November
Access Good **Site** Level
Sites Available ♿ ⌑ ⛺ **Total** 173
Facilities ♿ ✦ 🆆🅲 ♨ ⌑ ⊙ ⌿ 🔥 ▣ ☎ 🏪 ⊙ 🏪 ✕ ▣ 🏪 ⛲ ☀ ↝ ▣ ▣
Nearby Facilities ⌑ ✓ ↝ ∪
✈ Skegness
Close to the town and the beach. Nightly entertainment during peak weeks.

SKEGNESS
Riverside Caravan Park, Wainfleet Bank, Wainfleet, Skegness, Lincolnshire, PE24 4ND.
Std: 01754 **Tel:** 880205
Nearest Town/Resort Skegness
Directions A52 Boston to Skegness. Turn left onto the B1195 to Wainfleet All Saints and follow brown signs.
Acreage 1.4 **Open** 15th March to October
Access Good **Site** Level
Sites Available ⚠ ⌑ ⛺ **Total** 30
Facilities ✦ ▣ 🆆🅲 ♨ ⌑ ⊙ ⌿ 🔥 ☎ ▣
Nearby Facilities ⌑ ✓ ⚓ ↝
✈ Wainfleet
Alongside a river for fishing and boating. Beach 6 miles.

SKEGNESS
Ronam Cottage, Pinfold Lane, Anderby, Skegness, Lincolnshire, PE24 5YA.
Std: 01507 **Tel:** 490750
Nearest Town/Resort Skegness/Mablethorpe
Directions From Alford take the A1104 and turn onto the A1111 to Bilsby. Turn right onto the B1449 then left onto the A52, turn first right to Anderby. After 1½ miles turn left on the bend, site entrance is 50 yards on the right.
Acreage 1½ **Open** All Year
Access Good **Site** Level
Sites Available ⚠ ⌑ ▣ **Total** 15
Facilities ✦ 🆆🅲 ♨ ⌑ ⊙ ▣ ✕
Nearby Facilities ⌑ ✓
✈ Skegness
Near to Anderby Creek and beach. Countryside walks.

SKEGNESS
Skegness Water Leisure Park, Walls Lane, Skegness, Lincolnshire, PE25 1JF.
Std: 0500 **Tel:** 821963
Std: 01754 **Fax:** 612511
Nearest Town/Resort Skegness/Ingoldmells
Directions Conveniently situated 3 miles north of Skegness just off the A52, 400 yards from Butlins. Once you reach the outskirts of Skegness follow the brown information signs.
Acreage 133 **Open** 6 March to 30 October
Access Good **Site** Level
Sites Available ⚠ ⌑ ⛺ **Total** 200
Facilities ✦ 🆆🅲 ♨ ⌑ ⊙ ⌿ 🔥 ▣ ☎ 🏪 ⊙ 🏪 ✕ ▣ 🏪 ▣ ▣ ▣
Nearby Facilities ⌑ ✓ ∪
✈ Skegness
Near the beach and a fishing lake. Water skiing lake on site. Near Funcoast World (Butlins).

SKEGNESS
Top Yard Farm Caravan Park, Croft Bank, Croft, Skegness, Lincolnshire, PE24 4RL.
Std: 01754 **Tel:** 880189
Website: www.skegness-resort.co.uk/topyard
Nearest Town/Resort Skegness
Directions On the A52 Skegness to Boston road, 2 miles south of Skegness on the left hand side.
Acreage 2 **Open** March to October
Access Good **Site** Level
Sites Available ⚠ ⌑ ⛺ **Total** 35
Facilities ✦ 🆆🅲 ♨ ⌑ ⊙ ⌿ 🔥 ☎ 🏪 ⊙ 🏪 ✕ ▣ 🏪 ▣
Nearby Facilities ⌑ ✓
✈ Skegness
Near to Butlins and Fantasy Island.

SLEAFORD
Low Farm Touring Park, Spring Lane, Folkingham, Sleaford, Lincolnshire, NG34 0SJ
Std: 01529 **Tel:** 497322
Nearest Town/Resort Sleaford
Directions 9 miles south of Sleaford on the A15. Go through village, turn right opposite the petrol station.
Acreage 2¼ **Open** Easter to October
Access Good **Site** Lev/Slope
Sites Available ⚠ ⌑ ⛺ **Total** 36
Facilities ✦ 🆆🅲 ♨ ⌑ ⊙ ▣ 🏪 ⊙ ☀ ↝ ▣ ▣
Nearby Facilities ✓
✈ Sleaford

SPALDING
Delph Bank Touring Caravan & Camping Park, Old Main Road, Fleet Hargate, Holbeach, Nr. Spalding, Lincs, PE12 8LL.
Std: 01406 **Tel:** 422910
Website: www.ukparks.co.uk/delphbank
Nearest Town/Resort Holbeach
Directions From Kings Lynn take the A17. Turn left in the village of Fleet Hargate on the right, site is on the left. From Spalding take the A151 to Holbeach, continue a further miles to Fleet Hargate, turn right into the

148

llage and look for our sign on the right.
creage 3 **Open** 1 March **to** 30
ovember
ccess Good **Site** Level
ites Available ⋏ ♿ ⊞ **Total** 45
acilities ⌁ 🚽 ♨ 🌣 ⊙ 🛒 🔌 ◻ ☎
🔯 ⊙ ☕🔌◻🅰
earby Facilities ⌁ ✈
☞ Kings Lynn
ADULTS ONLY PARK. An attractive, quiet,
ee lined site, convenient for touring the
ens and Lincolnshire/Norfolk coastal
esorts. Pubs and eating places within
alking distance. BH & HPA Member. ETB
Star Graded and AA 3 Pennants.

SPALDING

oremans Bridge Caravan Park, Sutton
t James, Nr. Spalding, Lincolnshire,
E12 0HU.
td: 01945 **Tel:** 440346
td: 01945 **Fax:** 440346
mail: foremansbridge@btinternet.com
Website: www.foremans-bridge.co.uk
earest Town/Resort Spalding/Kings
ynn/Wisbech
irections From the A17 take the B1390
☞ Sutton St James, site is on the left after 2
iles.
creage 2¼ **Open** March **to** November
ccess Good **Site** Level
ites Available ♿ ⌁ 🚽 ⊞ ♨ ♨ ⊙ 🌣 🔌 ◻ ☎
♨ 🔯 ⊙ ☕🔌 ◻ ☎
earby Facilities ⌁ ∪
☞ Spalding/Kings Lynn
0 minutes away from the beach, fishing
ongside park. Ideal for touring the Fens.
ix holiday statics and 2 holiday cottages
open all year) also available for hire. 2 miles
a restaurant. NEW cycle hire centre. ETB
Star Grading and David Bellamy Silver
ward for Conservation.

STAMFORD

oad End Farm Caravan Park, Road
nd Farm, Great Casterton, Stamford,
ncolnshire, PE9 4BB.
td: 01780 **Tel:** 763417
td: 01780 **Fax:** 489212
earest Town/Resort Stamford
irections 1 mile north of Stamford on the
1081, turn right at sign for Little Casterton,
te is 100 yards on the right.
creage 4 **Open** All Year
ccess Good **Site** Lev/Slope
ites Available ⋏ ♿ ⊞ **Total** 12
acilities ⌁ 🚽 ♨ 🔌 ▯♨ ⊙ 🔌◻
earby Facilities ⌁ ✈ ⚓ ⚒
☞ Stamford
lose to Rutland Water which is the largest
an-made lake in Europe.

SUTTON-ON-SEA

Cherry Tree Site, Huttoft Road, Sutton-
on-Sea, Lincs, LN12 2RU.
Std: 01507 **Tel:** 441626
Email: murray.cherrytree@virgin.net
Website: www.ukparks.co.uk/
cherrytreesite
Nearest Town/Resort Sutton-on-Sea
Directions Take the A52 south from Sutton-
on-Sea, 1¼ miles on the left hand side.
Entrance via a lay-by. Tourist Board signs
on road.
Acreage 3 **Open** March **to** October
Access Good **Site** Level
Sites Available ⋏ ♿ ⊞ **Total** 60
Facilities ⌁ 🚽 ♨ ♨ 🌣 ⊙ 🔌 ◻ ☎
▯♨ ⊙ ☕🅰🔌◻
Nearby Facilities ⌁ ✈ ∪ ⚒
☞ Skegness
Beach, golf course and Lincolnshire Wolds.

SUTTON-ON-SEA

Kirkstead Holiday Park, North Road,
Trusthorpe, Sutton-on-Sea, Lincolnshire,
LN12 2QD.
Std: 01507 **Tel:** 441483
Email: mark@kirkstead.force9.co.uk
Website: www.kirkstead.force9.co.uk
Nearest Town/Resort Sutton-on-Sea
Directions Take the A52 coast road from
Sutton to Mablethorpe, turn off left at
Trusthorpe. Signposted from the A52.
Acreage 6 **Open** March **to** 1 December
Access Good **Site** Level
Sites Available ⋏ ♿ ⊞ **Total** 60
Facilities ⌁ 🚽 ♨ ♨ 🌣 ⊙ 🔌 ◻ ☎
▯♨ ⊙ ☕ ▯ 🔯⚓🔌◻
Nearby Facilities ⌁ ✈ ∪ ⚒
☞ Skegness
10 minute walk to the beach. Clubhouse,
new shower block. Familys welcome.

TATTERSHALL

Willow Holt Caravan & Camping Park,
Lodge Road, Tattershall, Lincolnshire, LN4
4JS.
Std: 01526 **Tel:** 343111
Std: 01526 **Fax:** 345391
Email: willowholt@gofree.co.uk
Website: www.willowholt.co.uk
Nearest Town/Resort Lincoln/Boston
Directions Take the A153 Sleaford/
Skegness road, in Tattershall turn at the
market place onto country road signposted
Woodhall Spa. In 1½ miles site is on the
left. Good wide entrance.
Acreage 25 **Open** 15 March **to** 31
October
Access Good **Site** Level
Sites Available ⋏ ♿ ⊞ **Total** 100
Facilities ⌁ 🚽 ♨ ♨ 🌣 ⊙ ▯♨ ⊙ ☕🔌◻
Nearby Facilities ⌁ ✈ ⚓⚒∪ ⚒ ⚒

Peaceful site, all level pitches, abundant
wildlife. Ten acres of fishing lakes on site,
free to site occupants for 2002.

WAINFLEET ALL SAINTS

Swan Lake Caravan Park, Culvert Road,
Wainfleet, Skegness, Lincolnshire, PE24
4NJ.
Std: 01754 **Tel:** 881456
Email: swan.lake@talk21.com
Website: www.swan-lake.co.uk
Nearest Town/Resort Skegness
Directions Follow brown tourism signs from
the A52, between Skegness and Boston.
Acreage 7 **Open** March **to** November
Access Good **Site** Level
Sites Available ⋏ ♿ ⊞ **Total** 25
Facilities ⌁ 🚽 ♨ ♨ 🌣 ⊙ 🔌 ◻ ☎
▯♨ ☕ 🔯◻
Nearby Facilities ⌁ ✈
☞ Thorpe Culvert
Near the River Steeping. Fishing on park.
Caravans available for hire. Ideal touring.
Sorry, no dogs allowed.

WOODHALL SPA

Bainland Country Park, Horncastle
Road, Woodhall Spa, Lincolnshire, LN10
6UX.
Std: 01526 **Tel:** 352903 **Fax:** 353730
Email: bookings@bainland.com
Website: www.bainland.com
Nearest Town/Resort Woodhall Spa
Directions Situated on the B1191, 1½ miles
from Woodhall Spa towards Horncastle. Just
before petrol station.
Acreage 12 **Open** All Year
Access Good **Site** Level
Sites Available ♿ ⌁ ⊞ **Total** 150
Facilities ♿ ⌁ 🚽 ♨ ♨ 🌣 ⊙ 🔌 ◻ ☎
▯♨ 🔯 ⊙ ☕ ▯ 🔯⚓✈🔯⚒🔌◻
Nearby Facilities ⌁ ✈ ⚓⚒∪ ⚒ ⚒
☞ Metheringham
Situated on the edge of the Wolds,
surrounded by woodland. Ideally central for
touring this delightful county. Golf and tennis
on site.

WOODHALL SPA

**Jubilee Park Camping & Caravanning
Park,** Stixwould Road, Woodhall Spa,
Lincolnshire, LN10 6QH.
Std: 01526 **Tel:** 352448
Nearest Town/Resort Horncastle
Directions 6 miles from Horncastle on the
B1191 Sleaford road.
Open April **to** October
Access Good **Site** Level
Sites Available ⋏ ♿ ⊞▯ **Total** 88
Facilities ♿ ⌁ 🚽 ♨ 🔌 ⊙ ☕☎⊙✕▯⚒⚒
Nearby Facilities ⌁ ✈ ⚒ ⚒
☞ Lincoln
Ideal touring centre.

Classified as one of the top parks
in Lincolnshire, Bainland is
situated on the edge of the Wolds,
surrounded by woodland,
1½ miles from the centre of
Woodhall Spa.

The Park of over 40 acres, caters
for caravans, motorhomes and
campers alike with Super and
Standard pitches,
electric hook - ups and satellite
T.V. points.

TOP AWARD WINNING PARK

Bainland
Country Park

18 hole Par 3
Golf Course
Practice Putting Green
All weather Bowling Green
Indoor/Outdoor Tennis
Crazy Golf
Trampoline
Table Tennis
Indoor Swimming Pool
Childrens Adventure
Playground
Sauna
Jacuzzi
Sunbeds
Childrens
'Poachers Den'
soft playroom
Bar
Restaurant
Rallies Welcome

Tel: Woodhall Spa (01526) 352903
Horncastle Road, Woodhall Spa, Lincolnshire, LN10 6UX   www.bainland.com   email: bookings@bainland.com

WOODHALL SPA

Kirkstead Bridge Holiday Park, c/o Croft Bank Holiday Park, Croft Bank, Skegness, Lincolnshire, PE24 4RE.
Std: 01754 **Tel:** 763887
Nearest Town/Resort Woodhall Spa
Directions Off the B1293 1 mile south of Woodhall Spa.
Acreage 1 **Open** 10 March **to** 31 October
Access Good **Site** Level
Sites Available ▲ ⊞ □ **Total** 20
Facilities ⨍ ⊞ ♨ ⌐ ⌣ ☐ ☎ ⊟ ▣
Nearby Facilities ⌐ ⏌
⚓ Sleaford
On the banks of the River Witham and only 1 mile from the ancient town of Woodhall Spa.

LONDON
CHINGFORD

Lee Valley Campsite, Sewardstone Road, Chingford, London, E4 7RA.
Std: 020 **Tel:** 8529 5689
Std: 020 **Fax:** 8559 4070
Email: info@leevalleypark.org.uk
Website: www.leevalleypark.com
Nearest Town/Resort Chingford
Directions Leave the M25 at junction 26 and take the A112 south, follow signs. Site is between Chingford and Waltham Abbey.
Open March **to** October
Access Good **Site** Lev/Slope
Sites Available ▲ ⊞ ⊟
Facilities ⅍ ⨍ ⊞ ♨ ⌐ ⌣ ⌣ ⊿ ☐ ☎
⅋ ☐ ☎ ⚕ ⊬ ▣ ▣
Nearby Facilities ⌐ ⏌
⚓ Chingford

LEYTON

Lee Valley Cycle Circuit Campsite, Quartermile Lane, Stratford, London, E15 2EN.
Std: 020 **Tel:** 8534 6085
Std: 020 **Fax:** 8536 0959
Email: info@leevalleypark.org.uk
Website: www.leevalleypark.com
Nearest Town/Resort Stratford/Leyton
Directions Take the A102[M] and follow signs for Spitalfields.
Open April **to** October
Sites Available ▲ ⊞ ⊟
Facilities ⅍ ⊞ ♨ ⌐ ⌣ ⌣ ☐ ☎ ☎ ✕ ▣
Nearby Facilities ♪
⚓ Leyton

MANCHESTER
HYDE

Camping & Caravanning Club Site, Crowden, Hadfield, Hyde, Greater Manchester, SK13 1HZ.
Std: 01457 **Tel:** 866057
Website: www.campingandcaravanningclub.co.uk
Directions On the A628 Manchester to Barnsley road, in Crowden follow signs for car park, Youth Hostel and camp site. Camp site is approx. 300 yards from the main road.
Acreage 2½ **Open** March **to** Nov
Site Sloping
Sites Available ▲ **Total** 45
Facilities ⊞ ♨ ⌐ ⌣ ⌣ ☎ ⅋ ☐ ☎ ⊟ ▣ ▣
Nearby Facilities ♪ ⚒
⚓ Hadfield/Glossop
In the heart of the Peak District National Park, close to the Pennine Way. BTB Graded. Non members welcome.

LITTLEBOROUGH

Hollingworth Lake Caravan Park, Round House Farm, Rakewood, Littleborough, OL15 0AT.
Std: 01706 **Tel:** 378661
Nearest Town/Resort Rochdale
Directions Leave the M62 at junction 21, Milnrow B6255. Follow Hollingworth Lake Country Park signs to the Fish Pub. Take Rakewood Road, then the second on the right.
Acreage 3 **Open** All Year
Access Good **Site** Level
Sites Available ▲ ⊞ ⊟ **Total** 45
Facilities ⅍ ⨍ ⊞ ⊞ ♨ ⌐ ⌣ ⌣ ☐ ☎
⅋ ☐ ☎ ▣
Nearby Facilities ⌐ ♪ ⚔ ⚒ ∪
⚓ Littleborough
Near a large lake that covers 120 acres.

STOCKPORT

Elm Beds Caravan Park, Elm Beds Road, Poynton, Stockport, Cheshire, SK12 1TG.
Std: 01625 **Tel:** 872370
Website: www.ukparks.co.uk/elmbeds
Nearest Town/Resort Stockport
Directions Take the A6 from Stockport and join the A523 to Poynton, at traffic lights turn east, straight on for 2 miles.
Acreage 2 **Open** March **to** October
Access Uneven **Site** Lev/Slope
Sites Available ▲ ⊞ ⊟ **Total** 20
Facilities ⨍ ⊞ ♨ ⌐ ⌣ ⌣ ⅋ ☐ ☎ ⊟ ▣
Nearby Facilities ⌐ ♪ ⚒ ∪
⚓ Poynton
Adjacent to Macclesfield Canal. Near the Peak District National Park.

WIGAN

Gathurst Hall Farm, Gathurst Lane, Shevington, Near Wigan, Greater Manchester, WN6 8JA.
Std: 01257 **Tel:** 253464
Nearest Town/Resort Southport
Directions Leave the M6 at junction 26 or 27 and take the B5206 to Shevington. We are near the Navigation Public House on the canal side.
Open March **to** October
Access Good **Site** Level
Sites Available ▲ ⊞ ⊟ **Total** 16
Facilities ⨍ ⊞ ♨ ⌐ ⌣ ⌣ ☎ ⚒
Nearby Facilities ♪ ⚒ ∪
Alongside the Liverpool Leeds Canal.

NORFOLK
ACLE

Broad Farm Trailer Park, Fleggburgh, Burgh St. Margaret, Great Yarmouth, Norfolk, NR29 3AF.
Std: 01493 **Tel:** 369273
Nearest Town/Resort Great Yarmouth
Directions Situated midway between Acle and Caister-on-Sea on the A1064.
Acreage 25 **Open** Easter **to** 30 Sept
Access Good **Site** Level
Sites Available ▲ ⊞ ⊟ **Total** 400
Facilities ⅍ ⚕ ⨍ ⊞ ♨ ⌐ ⌣ ⌣ ☎ ⅃ ☐ ☎
⅋ ⅋ ☐ ☎ ✕ ⍦ ♬ ⚲ ⊬ ▣ ▣ ☎
Nearby Facilities ⌐ ♪ ⚒ ∪
⚓ Acle
Ideally situated for visiting the Norfolk Broads. Only 7 miles from Great Yarmouth and 15 miles from the historic city of Norwich.

ATTLEBOROUGH

Oak Tree Caravan Park, Norwich Road Attleborough, Norfolk, NR17 2JX.
Std: 01953 **Tel:** 455565
Email: oaktree.cp@virgin.net
Website: www.oaktree-caravan-park.co.uk
Nearest Town/Resort Attleborough
Directions Turn right off the A11 (Thetford to Norwich road) signposted Attleborough in 2 miles continue through Attleborough passing Sainsburys, fork left immediately past the church at T-junction, site is on the right in ½ mile.
Acreage 5 **Open** All Year
Access Good **Site** Level
Sites Available ▲ ⊞ ⊟ **Total** 30
Facilities ⨍ ⊞ ♨ ⌐ ⌣ ⅋ ⅃ ☐ ⊬ ⊟ A
Nearby Facilities ⌐ ♪ ∪
⚓ Attleborough

BURGH ST. PETER

Waveney River Centre, Burgh St. Peter Staithe, Burgh St. Peter, Norfolk, NR34 0BT.
Std: 01502 **Tel:** 677217
Std: 01502 **Fax:** 677566
Nearest Town/Resort Beccles
Directions From Beccles take the A146 towards Great Yarmouth, follow signs from Haddiscoe.
Acreage 4 **Open** April **to** October
Access Good **Site** Level
Sites Available ▲ ⊞ ⊟ **Total** 20
Facilities ⨍ ⊟ ⊞ ♨ ⌐ ⌣ ⌣
⅋ ☐ ☎ ✕ ♨ ⍦ ♩ ⌣
Nearby Facilities ♪ ⚔ ⚒
⚓ Beccles
Riverside site with a public house.

CAISTER-ON-SEA

Grasmere Caravan Park, Bultitudes Loke, Yarmouth Road, Caister-on-Sea, Great Yarmouth, Norfolk, NR30 5DH.
Std: 01493 **Tel:** 720382
Nearest Town/Resort Great Yarmouth
Directions Enter Caister from roundabout near Yarmouth Stadium at Yarmouth end of bypass. After ½ mile turn sharp left just before the bus stop.
Acreage 2 **Open** April **to** Mid October
Access Good **Site** Level
Sites Available ⊞ ⊟ **Total** 46
Facilities ⅍ ⨍ ⊟ ⊞ ♨ ⌐ ⌣ ⌣ ⊿ ☐ ☎
⅋ ⅋ ☐ ☎ ▣ ▣
Nearby Facilities ⌐ ♪ ⚔ ⚒ ∪ ♪
⚓ Great Yarmouth
½ mile from beach, 3 miles to centre of Great Yarmouth. Advance bookings taken for touring site pitches. Each pitch with it's own electric, water tap and foul water drain. Some hard standings.

CAWSTON

Haveringland Hall Park, Cawston, Norwich, Norfolk, NR10 4PN.
Std: 01603 **Tel:** 871302
Std: 01603 **Fax:** 879223
Email: haveringland@claranet.com
Website: www.haveringlandhall.co.uk
Nearest Town/Resort Norwich
Directions Leave Norwich on the A140 towards Cromer, turn left onto the B1149 Holt. Leaving Horsford turn left (Haveringland (as per caravan and camping sign) and follow road for 4 miles until Park Lodge gate on the right hand side. Turn right as per sign and follow concrete road for 800 yards until reception on the left.
Acreage 110 **Open** March **to** October
Access Good **Site** Level
Sites Available ▲ ⊞ ⊟ **Total** 65
Facilities ⨍ ⊞ ⊞ ♨ ⌐ ⌣ ⌣ ☐ ⅋ ☐ ☎ ⅋ ▣ ▣ ☎

Nearby Facilities ┌ ✗ ✦ U
✈ Norwich

Haveringland Hall Park is set in over 100 acres of a former country house estate. For the quiet enjoyment of the guests there are a 12 acre fishing lake, a 2 acre ornamental wildlife lake and 50 acres of woodland. The touring park is conveniently placed on the levelled, terraced gardens of the former hall. Ideal countryside location close to the Norfolk Broads, the sea and the convenience and amenities of the city of Norwich.

CLIPPESBY

Clippesby Holidays, Clippesby Hall, Clippesby, Norfolk, NR29 3BL.
Std: 01493 **Tel:** 367800
Std: 01493 **Fax:** 367809
Email: holidays@clippesby.com
Website: www.clippesby.com
Nearest Town/Resort Acle
Directions Turn down the lane opposite the Clippesby Village sign which is on the B1152 between Acle (A1064) and Potter Heigham (A149). Then turn into the first drive on the right, 500yds signposted.
Acreage 34 **Open** Easter W/end & May **to** September
Access Good **Site** Level
Sites Available ▲ ⬛ ➡ **Total** 100
Facilities 🚽 ⛽ ⬜ ♨ ┌ ⊙ 🍴 ▣ 🛒
🏪 🐟 🎣 ✗ ♀ ▦ 🛒 ❖ ✦ ▣ 🔲 🔲 🗑
Nearby Facilities ┌ ✗ ⚓ ✦ U
✈ Acle

A quiet family-owned park in the grounds of Clippesby Hall in Broadlands National Park - great cycling country! Its sheltered glades provide a haven both for birds and for campers. Attractive lodges and woodland cottages (up to ETB 2-3 Star Rating). Lots of family things to do including tennis and putting. ETB 4 Star Graded and David Bellamy Gold Award for Conservation. Send for colour brochure of camping and touring and for lodges/cottages.

CROMER

Forest Park Caravan Site Limited, Northrepps Road, Cromer, Norfolk, NR27 0JR.
Std: 01263 **Tel:** 513290
Std: 01263 **Fax:** 511992
Nearest Town/Resort Cromer
Directions Take coast road B1159 south, in approx 1 mile fork right onto Northrepps Road. Site entrance is approx ½ mile on the left.
Acreage 85 **Open** 15 March **to** 15 January
Access Good **Site** Sloping
Sites Available ▲ ⬛ ➡ **Total** 330
Facilities 🚽 ⬜ ♨ ┌ ⊙ 🍴 ▣ 🔲 🛒
🏪 🐟 🎣 ✗ ♀ ▦ 🛒 ❖ ✦ ▣ 🔲
Nearby Facilities ┌ ✗ ⚓ ✦ U ⚑ ♪
✈ Cromer

Park is at the apex of a fabulous touring area, with beach close to hand and golf club adjoining.

CROMER

Ivy Farm Holiday Park, 1 High Street, Overstrand, Nr. Cromer, Norfolk, NR27 0PS.
Std: 01263 **Tel:** 579239
Website: www.ivy-farm.co.uk
Nearest Town/Resort Cromer
Directions Take the coast road from Cromer towards Mundesley and Overstrand is the next village. Pass the church on the left, pass the garden centre on the right, turn next left into Carr Lane. Entrance is half way down on the right.

Acreage 4 **Open** 20 March **to** 31 October
Access Good **Site** Lev/Slope
Sites Available ▲ ⬛ ➡ **Total** 43
Facilities 🚽 ⬜ ♨ ┌ ⊙ 🍴 ▣ 🔲 🛒
🏪 🐟 🎣 ❖ ✦ ▣
Nearby Facilities ┌ ✗ ⚓ ✦ U ♪
✈ Cromer

Just a 2 minute walk to the beach. Country walks.

CROMER

Laburnum Caravan Park, Water Lane, West Runton, Cromer, Norfolk, NR27 9QP.
Std: 01263 **Tel:** 837473
Email: laburnum@primax.co.uk
Website: www.ukparks.co.uk/laburnum
Nearest Town/Resort Sheringham
Directions 1½ miles from Sheringham turn left by the Village Inn.
Acreage 13 **Open** March **to** October
Sites Available ⬛ ➡ **Total** 180
Facilities 🚽 ⬜ ♨ ┌ ⊙ 🍴 ▣ 🔲 🛒
🏪 🐟 🎣 ▦ ✦ ▣
Nearby Facilities ┌ ✗ U ⚑ ♪
✈ West Runton

Gently sloping, cliff top site.

CROMER

Little Haven Caravan & Camping Park, The Street, Erpingham, Norwich, Norfolk, NR11 7QD.
Std: 01263 **Tel:** 768959
Std: 01263 **Fax:** 768959
Email: patl@haven30.fsnet.co.uk
Nearest Town/Resort Cromer
Directions From Norwich take the A140 to Cromer, 5 miles before Cromer turn left at the sign for Erpingham, after 2 miles the site is signposted 175 yards.
Acreage 3½ **Open** March **to** October
Access Good **Site** Lev/Slope

PEACEFUL AND FRIENDLY

WoodHill Park

**SET BETWEEN
CROMER & SHERINGHAM
IN PRETTY NORTH NORFOLK**

Award winning **Woodhill** is one of Norfolk's finest parks. Set in countryside overlooking the sea, you will find **peace and tranquillity**. Developed to the highest standards our peaceful park specialises in touring and camping, with **multi-service and electric hook-up pitches**, superb toilet and cleansing facilities.

We also hire **luxurious caravan holiday homes**, which overlook the sea, boasting **central heating, satellite TV, barbecue** & many other extras.

WE THINK YOU'LL FIND, AS MANY DO – THAT YOU WILL RETURN.

WOODHILL PARK

CROMER ROAD, EAST RUNTON, CROMER, NORFOLK NR27 9PX.

Telephone: 01263 512242

E-mail: info@woodhill-park.com

www.woodhill-park.com

English Tourism Council

ROSE AWARD CARAVAN HOLIDAY PARKS

BLUE SKY LEISURE
A Blue Sky Leisure Park

153

Sites Available ▲ ⊞ Total 25
Facilities ∮ 🖵 🕽 🥄 ↺ ⊙ 🗑 ↜⊞A
Nearby Facilities ↾ ✔ ⚓ ❄ ∪
⇌ Cromer
Ideal for touring North Norfolk and Norfolk Broads.

CROMER
Manor Farm Caravan & Camping Site,
Manor Farm, East Runton, Cromer,
Norfolk, NR27 9PR.
Std: 01263 **Tel:** 512858
Std: 01263 **Fax:** 512858
Email: caravansite@manor-farm.sagehost.co.uk
Website: www.manor-farm.sageweb.co.uk
Nearest Town/Resort Cromer
Directions 1½ miles west of Cromer, turn off the A148 at signpost 'Manor Farm'.
Acreage 16 **Open** Easter to October
Access Good **Site** Lev/Slope
Sites Available ▲ ⊞ ⊟ Total 130
Facilities ♿ 🥄 ∮ 🖵 🥄 ↺ ⊙ 🥄 🗑 ⚓
🕽 🛁 ⋔⊞
Nearby Facilities ↾ ✔ ∪ ⚓
⇌ Cromer
Panoramic sea and woodland views. Spacious, quiet, family run farm site. Ideal for families. Separate field for dog owners.

CROMER
Seacroft Camping & Caravan Park,
Runton Road, Cromer, Norfolk, NR27 9NJ.
Std: 01263 **Tel:** 511722
Email: seacroft@ic24.net
Website: www.seacroftcamping.co.uk
Nearest Town/Resort Cromer
Directions 1 mile west of Cromer on A149 coast road.
Acreage 5 **Open** 20 March to 31 October
Access Good **Site** Gently Sloping
Sites Available ▲ ⊞ ⊟ Total 118
Facilities ♿ 🥄 ∮ 🖵 🥄 ↺ ⊙ 🥄 🗑 ⚓
🕽 ↺ 🛁 ✗ ▽ 🖵 🛋 🍴 ↜⊞🕽
Nearby Facilities ↾ ✔ ⚓ ❄ ∪ ⚓
⇌ Cromer
Well screened camping area divided by rows of shrubs. Fine sea views.

CROMER
Woodhill Camping & Caravan Park,
Cromer Road, East Runton, Cromer,
Norfolk, NR27 9PX.
Std: 01263 **Tel:** 512242
Std: 01263 **Fax:** 515326
Email: info@woodhill-park.com
Website: www.woodhill-park.com
Nearest Town/Resort Cromer
Directions Set between East and West Runton on the seaside of the A149 Cromer to Sheringham road.
Acreage 32 **Open** April to October
Access Good **Site** Lev/Slope
Sites Available ▲ ⊞ ⊟ Total 390
Facilities ♿ 🥄 ∮ 🖵 🥄 ↺ ⊙ ⚓ 🗑 ⚓
🕽 🛢 ↺ 🛁 🛋 ⊛↜⊞🕽🖵
Nearby Facilities ↾ ✔ ⚓ ❄ ∪ ⚓
⇌ West Runton
Peaceful and tranquil, set in countryside overlooking the sea, developed to highest standards. Multi-service and super size hook-up pitches. Rose Award.

CROMER
Woodland Leisure Park, Trimingham,
Norfolk, NR11 8AL.
Std: 01263 **Tel:** 579208
Std: 01263 **Fax:** 576477
Email: info@woodland-park.co.uk
Website: www.woodland-park.co.uk
Nearest Town/Resort Cromer
Directions From Cromer take the B1159 coast road towards Mundesley, Trimingham is approx. 4 miles.
Acreage 50 **Open** Mid March to End October
Access Good **Site** Level
Sites Available ⊞□ Total 120
Facilities ♿ ∮ 🖵 🥄 ↺ ⊙ 🥄 🗑 ⚓
🕽 ↺ 🛢 ✗ ▽ 🖵 🛋 🍴 ↜⊞🕽🖵
Nearby Facilities ↾ ✔ ⚓ ❄ ∪ ⚓ ⚓
⇌ Cromer
Near the beach. Ideal base for North Norfolk.

DISS
Applewood Caravan & Camping Park,
Banham Zoo, The Grove, Banham,
Norwich, Norfolk, NR16 2HE.
Std: 01953 **Tel:** 888370
Std: 01953 **Fax:** 888427
Nearest Town/Resort Diss

Directions Banham is situated between Attleborough and Diss on the B1113 Norwich to Bury St Edmunds road. Follow the brown tourist signs.
Acreage 13 **Open** All Year
Access Good **Site** Level
Sites Available ▲ ⊞ ⊟ Total 113
Facilities ♿ ∮ 🖵 🥄 ↺ ⊙ 🥄 🗑 ⚓
🕽 🕽🛢 ↺ 🛁 ✗ 🖵 🛋 ↜⊞🕽🖵
Nearby Facilities ↾
⇌ Diss
Banham Zoo.

DISS
The Willows Camping & Caravan Park,
Diss Road, Scole, Norfolk, IP21 4DH.
Std: 01379 **Tel:** 740271
Std: 01379 **Fax:** 740271
Nearest Town/Resort Diss
Directions 1½ miles from Diss Railway Station. Turn right out of the station and turn left onto the A1066 towards Scole.
Acreage 4 **Open** April to October
Access Good **Site** Level
Sites Available ▲ ⊞ ⊟ Total 35
Facilities ∮ 🖵 🥄 ↺ ⊙ 🥄 🗑 ⚓ ⚓
🕽🛢 🛁 ↜⊞🕽
Nearby Facilities ↾ ✔
⇌ Diss

FAKENHAM
Crossways, Holt Road (A148), Little Snoring, Fakenham, Norfolk, NR21 0AX.
Std: 01328 **Tel:** 878335
Std: 01328 **Fax:** 878335
Nearest Town/Resort Fakenham
Directions On A148 3 miles from Fakenham towards Cromer.
Acreage 1¼ **Open** All Year
Access Good **Site** Level
Sites Available ▲ ⊞ ⊟ Total 27
Facilities ∮ 🖵 🕽 🥄 ↺ ⊙ 🥄 🗑 🕽🛢 ↺↜⊞🕽
Nearby Facilities ↾ ✔ ⚓ ❄ ∪ ⚓
⇌ Kings Lynn
8 miles from coast. Ideal for touring North Norfolk.

FAKENHAM

Fakenham Racecourse Caravan & Camping Site, The Racecourse, Fakenham, Norfolk, NR21 7NY.
Std: 01328 **Tel:** 862388
Std: 01328 **Fax:** 855908
Nearest Town/Resort Fakenham
Directions On approaching Fakenham from all directions, follow "Campsite" and international caravan/camping signs, they all refer to this site.
Acreage 11½ **Open** All Year
Access Good **Site** Level
Sites Available A ⊕ ⊟ **Total** 115
Facilities ⅃ ✉ 🐕 ⚿ 📶 🅐 🖕🏻 ⊙ ↩ 🔌 🔲 🍽
🎿 🅾 🎣 ✗ 🍴 🗼 🛒 ➗🖕🏻 🔲
Nearby Facilities ⌐ 🚶 🏊 🅿
⚓ King's Lynn
Immaculate facilities in beautiful countryside. Heated toilets. Ideally situated for visiting Norfolk's stately homes, bird and wildlife sanctuaries, rural life museums, coastal resorts and other attractions too numerous to mention. There is something for EVERYONE in the Fakenham area.

FAKENHAM

Manor Park, Manor Farm, Tattersett, Kings Lynn, Norfolk, PE31 8RS.
Std: 01485 **Tel:** 528310
Nearest Town/Resort Fakenham
Directions From Kings Lynn take the A148, 5 miles from Tattersett Coxford.
Acreage 4 **Open** March **to** October
Access Good **Site** Lev/Slope
Sites Available A ⊕ ⊟ **Total** 30
Facilities ⅃ 🐕 ✉ 📶 🅐 ⊙ 🔲 🍽
🎿 🅾 🛒 ➗🖕🏻 🔲
Nearby Facilities ⌐ 🚶
⚓ Kings Lynn
15 minutes from beaches, Wells-Next-the-Sea, etc..

FAKENHAM

The Garden Caravan Site, Barmer Hall, Syderstone, Kings Lynn, Norfolk, PE31 8SR.
Std: 01485 **Tel:** 578220/178
Std: 01485 **Fax:** 578178
Email: nigel@mason96.fsnet.co.uk
Nearest Town/Resort Fakenham
Directions From Fakenham or Kings Lynn take the A148, then take the B1454 towards Hunstanton, 4 miles on the right hand side.
Open March **to** November
Access Good **Site** Lev/Slope
Sites Available A ⊕ ⊟ **Total** 30
Facilities ⅃ 🐕 📶 🅐 🖕🏻 ⊙ ↩ 🔌 🍽
🎿 🅾 ➗🖕🏻 🔲
Nearby Facilities ⌐ 🚶 🏊 🛶 🅿
A lovely secluded and sheltered site in a walled garden. Close to the famous North Norfolk coast.

FAKENHAM

The Old Brick Kilns, Little Barney Lane, Barney, Fakenham, Norfolk, NR21 0NL.
Std: 01328 **Tel:** 878305
Std: 01328 **Fax:** 878948
Email: enquire@old-brick-kilns.co.uk
Website: www.old-brick-kilns.co.uk
Nearest Town/Resort Fakenham
Directions From Fakenham take the A148 to Cromer, after 6 miles turn right onto the B1354 (Aylsham). After 300 yards turn right to Barney then left to Little Barney.
Acreage 6 **Open** 20 Feb **to** 6 Jan
Access Good **Site** Lev/Slope
Sites Available A ⊕ ⊟ **Total** 60
Facilities ⅃ 🐕 ✉ 📶 🅐 🖕🏻 ⊙ ↩ 🔌 🔲 🍽
🎿 🅾 ✗ 🗼 🛒 ➗🖕🏻 🔲
Nearby Facilities 🚶
⚓ Norwich
Fishing on site. Central for north Norfolk facilities and attractions.

GREAT HOCKHAM

Puddledock Farm Camp Site, Puddledock Farm, Great Hockham, Thetford, Norfolk, IP24 1PA.
Std: 01953 **Tel:** 498455
Nearest Town/Resort Thetford
Directions Midway between Thetford and Watton on the A1075. Turn left at 83 past Forestry Commission picnic site, no roadside sign.
Acreage 5 **Open** All Year
Access Good **Site** Level
Sites Available A ⊕ ⊟ **Total** 30
Facilities 🐕 📶 🅐 ⊙ 🗼 ➗🖕🏻 🔲
Nearby Facilities 🚶 🛶
⚓ Thetford
Very quiet site with an abundance of birds and wildlife. Backs onto the forest for walks. Putting green on site.

GREAT YARMOUTH

Bureside Holiday Park, Boundary Farm, Oby, Nr. Great Yarmouth, Norfolk, NR29 3BW.
Std: 01493 **Tel:** 369233
Nearest Town/Resort Great Yarmouth
Directions From Acle take the A1064 over the bridge, then first left after Acle Bridge and follow caravan and tent signs to Oby.
Acreage 12 **Open** Spring Bank End May **to** Mid Sept
Access Good **Site** Level
Sites Available A ⊕ ⊟ **Total** 170
Facilities ✐ ⅃ 🐕 ✉ 📶 🅐 ⊙ ↩ 🔌 🔲 🍽
🎿 🅾 🎣 🍴 🛒 ➗🖕🏻 🔲
Nearby Facilities 🚶 🛶 🏊 🛶
⚓ Acle
Situated in unspoilt broadland, launching slipway, ¾ mile of river fishing, carp and tench lake. Heated swimming pool and play area.

GREAT YARMOUTH
Burgh Castle Marina & Caravan Park, Nr. Great Yarmouth, Norfolk, NR31 9PZ.
Std: 01493 **Tel:** 780331
Std: 01493 **Fax:** 780163
Email: burghcastlemarin@cs.com
Nearest Town/Resort Gorleston-on-Sea
Directions A143. At 2 miles southwest from Gorleston roundabout fork right for Belton and Burgh Castle then ¾ mile turn right and entrance ¾ mile on the left.
Acreage 15 **Open** All Year
Access Good **Site** Level
Sites Available A ⊕ ⊜ **Total** 45
Facilities & ⨍ ⌂ 🏠 🄼 ⚓ ♁ ⊙⌦ ⊿ ⊡ 🐾
🕿 🄶 🍴 ✕ 🏪 🛢 🞂 🗗🄳🄴
Nearby Facilities ┌ ✔ ⚓ ⟲ ∪ ⦿ 𝓡
⇥ Great Yarmouth
Own salt water harbour with slipway, pontoons and boat park. Free public house with restaurant. Exhibition and information centre. David Bellamy Gold Award for Conservation.

GREAT YARMOUTH
Cherry Tree Holiday Park, Mill Road, Burgh Castle, Near Great Yarmouth, Norfolk, NR31 9QR.
Std: 01493 **Tel:** 780024
Std: 01493 **Fax:** 780457
Email: admin.cherrytree@bourne-leisure.co.uk
Website: www.havenholidays.com
Nearest Town/Resort Great Yarmouth
Directions From Great Yarmouth take the A143 Beccles/Diss road. After Bradwell take the turning for Belton and Burgh Castle & Marina, turn first right into Stepshort and follow signs for Cherry Tree.
Acreage 1 **Open** April to October
Access Good **Site** Level
Sites Available ⊕ ⊜ **Total** 17

GREAT YARMOUTH
Facilities & ♣ ⨍ 🄼 ⚓ ♁ ⊙ ⊿ ⊡ 🐾
🕿 🄶 🍴✕ 🏪🛢 🄼 ♁ ⟲ ⇥ 🗗🄳🄴
Nearby Facilities ┌ ✔
⇥ Great Yarmouth
Close to the beautiful Norfolk Broads, Great Yarmouth and Gorleston Beach.

GREAT YARMOUTH
Drewery Caravan Park, California Road, California, Great Yarmouth, Norfolk, NR29 3QW.
Std: 01493 **Tel:** 730845
Std: 01493 **Fax:** 731968
Nearest Town/Resort Great Yarmouth
Directions Take the A149 from Great Yarmouth, at the Greyhound Stadium roundabout turn left, at next roundabout take the second exit onto the B1159. Go to roundabout and take the second exit, after ¼ mile turn right into California Road and follow to the end. Site is opposite California Tavern. 6 miles from Great Yarmouth.
Acreage 4 **Open** Easter to October
Access Good **Site** Level
Sites Available A ⊕ ⊜ **Total** 135
Facilities & ⨍ 🄼 ⚓ ♁ ⊙⌦ 🄶 🛢 🞂 🞀
Nearby Facilities ┌ ✔ ⚓ ⟲ ∪ 𝓡
⇥ Great Yarmouth
Near the beach. Ideal for Norfolk Broads and Great Yarmouth.

GREAT YARMOUTH
Liffens Holiday Park, Burgh Castle, Great Yarmouth, Norfolk, NR31 9QB.
Std: 01493 **Tel:** 780357
Std: 01493 **Fax:** 782383
Website: www.liffens.co.uk
Nearest Town/Resort Great Yarmouth
Directions From Great Yarmouth follow signs for Lowestoft A12. After third roundabout look for sign for Burgh Castle. Follow for 2 miles to T-junction turn right, follow tourist signs to Liffens.

GREAT YARMOUTH
Acreage 12 **Open** Easter to October
Access Good **Site** Level
Sites Available A ⊕ ⊜ **Total** 150
Facilities & ⨍ ⌂ 🏠 🄼 ⚓ ♁ ⊙⌦ ⊿ ⊡ 🐾
🕿 🄶 🍴✕ 🏪 🞂 🄼 ♁ ⟲ ⇥ 🗗🄳🄴
Nearby Facilities ┌ ✔ ⚓ ⟲ ∪ 𝓡
⇥ Great Yarmouth
Family holiday park close to old Roman fortress yet 10 minutes from Gt. Yarmouth. 2 bars/restaurant/cabaret. 2 heated pools, NEW water slide. Play area amusements. Free colour brochure. Booking is advisable.

GREAT YARMOUTH
Liffens Welcome Holiday Centre, Butt Lane, Burgh Castle, Great Yarmouth, Norfolk, NR31 9PY.
Std: 01493 **Tel:** 780481
Std: 01493 **Fax:** 781627
Nearest Town/Resort Great Yarmouth
Directions From Great Yarmouth follow signs for Lowestoft A12. After the third roundabout look for the sign for Burgh Castle. Follow for 2 miles to the T-junction and turn left, at the next T-junction turn right site is on the right.
Acreage 12 **Open** April to October
Access Good **Site** Lev/Slope
Sites Available A ⊕ ⊜ **Total** 150
Facilities & ⨍ 🄼 ⚓ ♁ ⊙⌦ ⊿ ⊡ 🐾
🕿 🄶 🄻⊙ 🏪✕ 🞂 🄼 ♁ 🛢 ✱⊛⇥🗗🄳🄴
Nearby Facilities ┌ ✔ ⚓ ⟲ 𝓡
⇥ Great Yarmouth
Family holiday park in beautiful Broadland countryside, yet only 10 minutes from Great Yarmouth. Bars, entertainment and indoor heated swimming pool. Free colour brochure. Booking is advisable.

The best choice in self-catering, tenting & touring holidays for Great Yarmouth and the Norfolk Broads

Your holiday choice!

The decision is yours.
There's a fun-packed holiday at...

LIFFENS
THE FAMILY OWNED HOLIDAY PARK

Set in picturesque countryside offering superb accommodation, daytime and evening entertainment including cabaret and live music – open-air heated pool with waterslide, tennis courts, crazy golf, amusements, kids club, bars, restaurant and take-away.*

24HR BROCHURE LINE
01493 780357

One brochure for both parks
www.liffens.co.uk

Liffens Holiday Park, Burgh Castle, Gt. Yarmouth, Norfolk NR31 9QB

There's a slightly quieter pace of holiday to choose at...

LIFFENS
WELCOME
HOLIDAY CENTRE

Just a strole away from Liffens and offering the same quality and value, you'll find Welcome. Our excellent facilities include – covered heated pool, gym, solarium, bar with evening entertainment, table tennis, kids play area and a shop.*

24HR BROCHURE LINE
01493 780481

One brochure for both parks
www.liffens.co.uk

Liffens Welcome Holiday Centre, Burgh Castle, Gt. Yarmouth, Norfolk NR31 9PY

* EACH PARK OFFERS: Luxury self-catering caravans with shower & colour TV.
Grassed area for tents, tourers and motor homes. (FREE showers and hot water.) – Electric hook-ups available.
ALL FACILITIES AVAILABLE TO GUESTS STAYING AT EITHER PARK.

NORFOLK

GREAT YARMOUTH

Rose Farm Touring & Camping Park, Stepshort, Belton, Great Yarmouth, Norfolk, NR31 9JS.
Std: 01493 **Tel:** 780896
Std: 01493 **Fax:** 780896
Nearest Town/Resort Gorleston
Directions From Great Yarmouth on new bypass take the A143 to Beccles, through Bradwell up to the small dual carriageway. Turn right into new road signposted Belton and Burgh Castle. Down new road first right at Stepshort, site is first on right.
Acreage 6 **Open** All Year
Access Good **Site** Level
Sites Available A ⊕ ⊕ **Total** 80
Facilities & ⅃ ⚏ ♨ ⌐ ⊙ ➔ ⊿ ⊠ ☎
⊙ ⊞ ⚑ ⋔⊕⊞⚏
Nearby Facilities ⌐ ✓ ⚑ ➤ ∪ ⋺ ♪
✦ Great Yarmouth
A clean site in peaceful surroundings.

GREAT YARMOUTH

The Grange Touring Park, Yarmouth Road, Ormesby St. Margaret, Great Yarmouth, Norfolk, NR29 3QG.
Std: 01493 **Tel:** 730306
Std: 01493 **Fax:** 730188
Email: long-beach@fsnet.co.uk
Website: www.norfolkbroads.com/longbeach/
Nearest Town/Resort Great Yarmouth
Directions 3 miles north of Great Yarmouth off the A149 at Caister bypass roundabout (north end).
Acreage 3½ **Open** Easter **to** October
Access Good **Site** Level
Sites Available A ⊕ ⊕ **Total** 70
Facilities & ⅃ ⚏ ♨ ⌐ ⊙ ➔ ⊿ ⊠ ☎
⚏ ⅋⊙⚏ ♈ ⊠ ⋔⊕⊞
Nearby Facilities ⌐ ✓ ⚑ ➤ ∪ ♪
✦ Great Yarmouth
First class facilities. Very convenient for Great Yarmouth. BTA 4 Star Graded.

GREAT YARMOUTH

Vauxhall Holiday Park, Acle New Road, Great Yarmouth, Norfolk, NR30 1TB.
Std: 01493 **Tel:** 857231
Std: 01493 **Fax:** 331122
Email: vauxhall.holidays@virgin.net
Website: www.vauxhall-holiday-park.co.uk
Nearest Town/Resort Great Yarmouth
Directions Situated on the A47 as you approach Great Yarmouth from Norwich. ¾ miles from the town centre.
Acreage 48 **Open** Easter **to** Sept
Access Good **Site** Level
Sites Available A ⊕ ⊕ **Total** 256
Facilities & ⅃ ⚏ ⚏ ♨ ⌐ ⊙ ➔ ⊿ ⊠ ☎
⚏ ⅋⊙⚏ ♈ ⊠ ⋔ ⚑ ⊕ ➤ ⊞ ⚏
Nearby Facilities ⌐ ✓ ⚑ ➤ ∪ ⋺ ♪
✦ Great Yarmouth
Ideal centre for attractions of Great Yarmouth and for exploring the famous Norfolk Broads. Health and fitness centre including sauna, solarium and gym. ALSO OPEN from May to October half term.

GREAT YARMOUTH

Wild Duck Holiday Park, Howards Common, Belton, Great Yarmouth, Norfolk, NR31 9NE.
Std: 01493 **Tel:** 780268
Std: 01493 **Fax:** 782308
Website: www.havenholidays.com
Nearest Town/Resort Great Yarmouth
Directions 3 miles outside Great Yarmouth on the A143, turn rightoff the dual carriageway and follow brown tourism signs through Belton Village.
Open March **to** End Oct

GREAT YARMOUTH

Access Good **Site** Level
Sites Available A ⊕ ⊕ **Total** 230
Facilities & ⅃ ⚏ ♨ ⌐ ⊙ ➔ ⊠ ☎
⚏ ♈ ⊙ ⊠ ✗ ⊡ ⅋ ⊞ ⚑ ➤ ⋔⊕⊞ ⚏
Nearby Facilities ⌐ ✓ ⚑ ➤ ∪ ♪
✦ Great Yarmouth
5/10 minutes drive to the nearest beach. Close to Great Yarmouth, Norwich, Norfolk Broads, Bygone Village, Lowestoft and Suffolk Wildlife Park.

GREAT YARMOUTH

Willowcroft Camping & Caravan Park, Staithe Road, Repps with Bastwick, Potter Heigham, Norfolk, NR29 5JU.
Std: 01692 **Tel:** 670380
Std: 01692 **Fax:** 670380
Email: camping@willowcroft4.freeserve.co.uk
Website: www.willowcroft4.freeserve.co.uk
Nearest Town/Resort Potter Heigham
Directions 10 miles from Great Yarmouth on the Potter Heigham road, into Church Road, then Staithe Road.
Acreage 2 **Open** All Year
Access Good **Site** Level
Sites Available A ⊕ ⊕ **Total** 44
Facilities ⅃ ⚏ ♨ ⌐ ➔ ☎ ♈ ⊙ ⋔⊕⊞
Nearby Facilities ✓ ⚑ ➤
✦ Acle
Quiet park, just a two minute walk to a river for fishing. Excellent for canoeing, bird watching, walking and cycling etc..

HADDISCOE

Pampas Lodge Camping & Caravanning Park, The Street, Haddiscoe, Norwich, Norfolk, NR14 6AA.
Std: 01502 **Tel:** 677265
Std: 01502 **Fax:** 677265
Email: pampas@globalnet.co.uk
Nearest Town/Resort Beccles/Great Yarmouth
Directions On the A143 midway between Beccles and Great Yarmouth. Main road frontage.
Acreage 3 **Open** All Year
Access Good **Site** Level
Sites Available A ⊕ ⊕ **Total** 36
Facilities ⅃ ⚏ ⚏ ♨ ⌐ ⊙ ➔ ⊿ ☎
⚏ ✗ ⋔⊕⊞
Nearby Facilities ⌐ ✓ ⚑ ➤ ∪
✦ Haddiscoe
1 mile from a river and 4 miles from the sea. Ideal for touring Norfolk and Suffolk.

HARLESTON

Little Lakeland Caravan Park, Wortwell, Harleston, Norfolk, IP20 0EL.
Std: 01986 **Tel:** 788646
Std: 01986 **Fax:** 788646
Email: information@littlelakeland.co.uk
Website: www.littlelakeland.co.uk
Nearest Town/Resort Harleston
Directions Turn off A143 (Diss to Lowestoft) at roundabout signposted Wortwell. In village turn right about 300 yards after Bell P.H. at bottom of lane turn right into site.
Acreage 4 **Open** March **to** October
Access Good **Site** Level
Sites Available A ⊕ ⊕ **Total** 40
Facilities & ⅃ ⚏ ♨ ⌐ ⊙ ➔ ⊿ ⊠ ☎
⚏ ♈ ⊙ ⋔⊕⊞
Nearby Facilities ⌐ ✓ ⚑ ➤ ∪
✦ Diss
Half acre fishing lake, site library.

HARLESTON

Waveney Valley Lakes. Wortwell, Norfo IP20 0EJ.
Std: 01986 **Tel:** 788676
Std: 01986 **Fax:** 788129
Email: enquiries.wvl@talk21.com
Website: www.waveneyvalleylakes.com
Nearest Town/Resort Harleston
Directions From Diss take the A14 towards Bungay, turn right at the seco roundabout into Wortwell, site is 200 metr past the garage on the right hand side.
Acreage 60 **Open** March **to** November
Access Good **Site** Level
Sites Available A ⊕ ⊕ **Total** 15
Facilities ⅃ ⚏ ♨ ⌐ ⊙ ➔ ⊠
⚏ ⊙ ✗ ⋔⊕⊞ ⚏
Nearby Facilities
✦ Diss
9 lakes and an abundance of wildlife. Fishi on site.

HEMSBY

Long Beach Caravan Park, Hemsby, Great Yarmouth, Norfolk, NR29 4JD.
Std: 01493 **Tel:** 730023
Std: 01493 **Fax:** 730188
Email: long-beach@fsnet.co.uk
Website: www.norfolkbroads.com/longbeach/
Nearest Town/Resort Great Yarmouth
Directions Take the A149 north from Gre Yarmouth, at the roundabout on Caist Bypass take the B1159. At Hemsby turn ea onto Beach Road, then turn second left King's Loke signposted Long Beach.
Acreage 5 **Open** Mid March **to** 5 Nov
Access Good **Site** Level
Sites Available A ⊕ ⊕ **Total** 50
Facilities ⅃ ⚏ ♨ ⌐ ⊙ ➔ ⊿ ⊠
⚏ ♈ ⊙ ⊠ ✗ ⋔⊕ ∪
Nearby Facilities ⌐ ✓ ⚑ ➤ ∪
✦ Great Yarmouth
Park includes 30 acres of sandy beach a dunes. Very convenient for Great Yarmou and the Norfolk Broads.

HEMSBY

Newport Caravan Park (Norfolk) Ltd., Newport Road, Hemsby, Great Yarmouth Norfolk, NR29 4NW.
Std: 01493 **Tel:** 730405
Email: enquiries@newportcaravanpark.co.uk
Website: www.newportcaravanpark.co.u
Nearest Town/Resort Great Yarmouth
Directions Take the A149 from Great Yarmouth, B1159 follow signs for Hemsb Winterton-on-Sea, turn right to Newpo Road.
Open Easter **to** End October
Access Good **Site** Level
Sites Available A ⊕ ⊕ **Total** 90
Facilities ⅃ ⚏ ♨ ⌐ ⊙ ➔ ⊿ ⊠
⚏ ♈ ⊙ ⊠ ✗ ⋔⊕ ∪
Nearby Facilities ⌐ ✓ ⚑ ➤ ∪
✦ Great Yarmouth
500yds from the beach, 6 miles from Gre Yarmouth. Convenient base for visiting th Broads, North Norfolk and Norwich.

HORSEY

Waxham Sands Holiday Park, Warren Farm, Horsey, Norfolk, NR29 4EJ.
Std: 01692 **Tel:** 598325
Std: 01692 **Fax:** 598325
Nearest Town/Resort Great Yarmouth
Directions Situated on the B1159 ma coast road, 12 miles north of Gre Yarmouth.
Acreage 25 **Open** Spring Bank Holiday t 30 Sept
Access Good **Site** Level

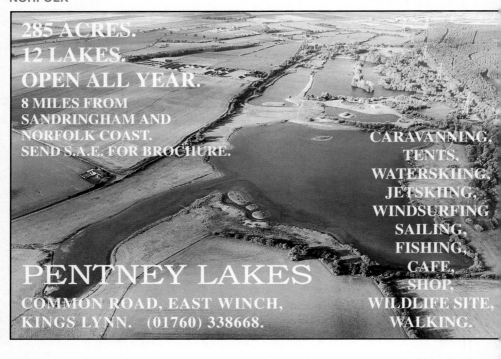

285 ACRES.
12 LAKES.
OPEN ALL YEAR.
8 MILES FROM SANDRINGHAM AND NORFOLK COAST. SEND S.A.E. FOR BROCHURE.

CARAVANNING, TENTS, WATERSKIING, JETSKIING, WINDSURFING SAILING, FISHING, CAFE, SHOP, WILDLIFE SITE, WALKING.

PENTNEY LAKES

COMMON ROAD, EAST WINCH, KINGS LYNN. (01760) 338668.

acilities ⬡ ✦ 🅼 ♨ ⌂ ☉ 🍴 ▨ ▢ ☎
🛆 ▢ 🕿 🅰 ➤◧
earby Facilities ⌐ ✦ ⚓ ⤫ ∪
➤ Great Yarmouth
/e have our own beach and are adjacent
» a nature reserve. Good location for
.tractions of Norfolk. Close to the Norfolk
.roads.

HUNSTANTON
Manor Park Holiday Village, Manor
.oad, Hunstanton, Norfolk, PE36 5AZ.
td: 01485 **Tel:** 532300
td: 01485 **Fax:** 533881
mail: info@manor-park.co.uk
Jebsite: www.manor-park.co.uk
•pen March **to** October
.ccess Good **Site** Level
.ites Available ⊕ 🚐 **Total** 64
a c i l i t i e s ⬡ ✦ 🅼 ♨ ⌂ ☉ 🍴 ▨ ▢ ☎
🛆 ▢ 🕿 ✕ ⛾ 🅰 ◸➤◧▢
Nearby Facilities
➤ Kings Lynn

KINGS LYNN
Gatton Water Touring Caravan &
Camping Site, Hillington, Nr.
.andringham, Kings Lynn, Norfolk, PE31
.BJ.
td: 01485 **Tel:** 600643
mail: gatton.waters@virgin.net
Jebsite: www.caravan-sitefinder.co.uk
Jearest Town/Resort Kings Lynn
•irections 8 miles from Kings Lynn on the
.148 (Kings Lynn/Cromer road).
Acreage 24 **Open** April **to** October
.ccess Good **Site** Level
.ites Available ⚲ ⊕ 🚐 **Total** 90
a c i l i t i e s ✦ 🅼 ♨ ⌂ ☉ 🍴 ☎
🛆 ▢ 🕿 ✕ ⛾➤◧🅰
Nearby Facilities
➤ Kings Lynn
.DULTS ONLY SITE. Most pitches overlook
. lake. Fishing on site.

KINGS LYNN
.ings Lynn Caravan & Camping Park,
`arkside House, New Road, North
.unction, Kings Lynn, Norfolk, PE33 0QR.
td: 01553 **Tel:** 840004
mail: klynn.campsite@tesco.net
Nearest Town/Resort Kings Lynn
•irections 1½ miles from the A17, A47, A10
.nd A149 main Kings Lynn Hardwick
.oundabout. Take the A47 towards
.waffham and take the first right at North
.unction.
.creage 3½ **Open** All Year
.ccess Good **Site** Level
.ites Available ⚲ ⊕ 🚐 **Total** 35

Facilities ✦ 🅼 ♨ ⌂ ☉ 🍴 ☎ ▨✦◧▢ ▣
Nearby Facilities ⌐ ✦ ⚓ ⤫ ∪ ⚗ ♬
➤ Kings Lynn
Situated in a beautiful parkland setting with
mature trees. Well situated for Kings Lynn,
inland market towns, the North Norfolk
coast, watersports and good pubs. Tesco's
nearby. Rallies welcome.

KINGS LYNN
Pentney Lakes Caravan & Leisure Park,
Common Road, East Winch, Kings Lynn,
Norfolk, PE32 1NN.
Std: 01760 **Tel:** 338668
Std: 01760 **Fax:** 338668
Email: pentneylakes@aol.com
Website: www.pentneylakes.co.uk
Nearest Town/Resort Kings Lynn
Directions From Kings Lynn take the A47
towards Swaffam. When you reach East
Winch look for Carpenters Arms Pub on the
left, turn right opposite the pub into Common
Road.
Acreage 300 **Open** All Year
Access Good **Site** Level
Sites Available ⚲ ⊕ 🚐 **Total** 100
Facilities ⬡ ✦ ▤ 🅷 🅼 ♨ ⌂ 🍴 ▢ ☎
🛆 ▢ ✕ ☉ ⛾ 🅰
Nearby Facilities ⌐ ∪
➤ Kings Lynn
Leisure Park including fishing, water skiing,
jet skiing, sailing and boating. Ideal for
touring.

MUNDESLEY
Sandy Gulls Cliff Top Touring Park,
Cromer Road, Mundesley, Norfolk, NR11
8DF.
Std: 01263 **Tel:** 720513
Nearest Town/Resort Cromer.
Directions South along the coast road for
4 miles.
Acreage 2½ **Open** Easter **to** October
Access Good **Site** Level
Sites Available ⊕ 🚐 **Total** 40
Facilities ⬡ ✦ 🅼 ♨ ⌂ 🍴 ▨ 🎲 🅳 ◧▢ ▣
Nearby Facilities ⌐ ✦ ⚓ ⤫ ∪ ♬
➤ Cromer
Cliff top location, overlooking the beach.
Near to the Broads National Park. ETB 3
Star Graded Park

NORTH WALSHAM
Two Mills Touring Park, Yarmouth Road,
North Walsham, Norfolk, NR28 9NA.
Std: 01692 **Tel:** 405829
Std: 01692 **Fax:** 405829
Email: enquiries@twomills.co.uk
Website: www.twomills.co.uk
Nearest Town/Resort North Walsham
Directions Follow Hospital signs passing

the Police Station on route. 1 mile on the
left from the town centre.
Acreage 6 **Open** 1 March **to** 3 January
Access Good **Site** Level
Sites Available ⚲ ⊕ 🚐 **Total** 59
Facilities ⬡ ✦ 🅷 🅼 ♨ ⌂ ☉ 🍴 ▨ ▢ ☎
🛆 ▢ 🕿✦◧▢ ▣ 🅰
Nearby Facilities ⌐ ✦ ⚓ ⤫ ∪
➤ North Walsham
ADULTS ONLY.

NORWICH
Swans Harbour Caravan & Camping
Park, Barford Road, Marlingford, Norwich,
Norfolk, NR9 4BE.
Std: 01603 **Tel:** 759658
Nearest Town/Resort Norwich
Directions Turn off the B1108 (Norwich to
Watton road). 3 miles past Southern Bypass
turn right signposted Marlingford. Follow
brown tourist signs to the site.
Acreage 4 **Open** All Year
Access Good **Site** Level
Sites Available ⚲ ⊕ 🚐 **Total** 30
Facilities ✦ 🅼 ♨ ⌂ ☉ 🍴 ☎ 🅰➤
Nearby Facilities ⌐ ✦
➤ Wymondham
Alongside a river with own fishing rights.

NORWICH
The Willows, Woodland View, Stratton
Strawless, Norwich, Norfolk, NR10 5LT.
Std: 01603 **Tel:** 754315
Nearest Town/Resort Aylsham/Norwich
Directions 5 miles from Norwich Airport on
the A140 Cromer road. Enter into Stratton
Strawless Hall.
Open All Year
Access Good **Site** Level
Sites Available ⊕ 🚐 **Total** 5
Facilities ✦ 🅼 ♨ ⌂ 🍴 ☎ 🅰➤◧
Nearby Facilities
➤ Norwich
The Norfolk Broads, seaside resorts and a
good bus service. You can also call us on
Mobile 07760 362364.

POTTER HEIGHAM
Causeway Cottage Caravan Park,
Bridge Road, Potter Heigham, Nr. Great
Yarmouth, Norfolk, NR29 5JB.
Std: 01692 **Tel:** 670238
Nearest Town/Resort Great Yarmouth
Directions Potter Heigham is between
Great Yarmouth and Norwich. Turn off the
A149 at Potter Heigham, we are 250yds
from the river and old bridge.
Acreage 1 **Open** March **to** October
Access Good **Site** Level
Sites Available ⚲ ⊕ 🚐 **Total** 5
Facilities ⬡ ✦ ▤ 🅷 🅼 ♨ ⌂ ☉🍴 🎲 ▢ ❋ ▣

Beeston Regis Caravan Park

"The King of the Clifftop View"

**Cromer Road, Beeston Regis,
West Runton, Norfolk NR27 9NG
Tel: 0700 BEESTON (2337866)
www.beestonregis.co.uk
e-mail: enquiries@beestonregis.co.uk**

Nearby Facilities
⚞ Great Yarmouth
250yds from river, shops and hotels. Fishing, boating and walking. 6 miles from Golden Sands beach.

PULHAM ST. MARY
Waveney Valley Holiday Park, Airstation Farm, Pulham St Mary, Diss, Norfolk, IP21 4QF.
Std: 01379 **Tel:** 741228
Std: 01379 **Fax:** 741228
Website: www.caravanparksnorfolk.co.uk
Nearest Town/Resort Harleston
Directions Take A140 at Scole, travel north for 3 miles. Turn right into Dickleborough and at the church turn right, 2 miles on take the first turn left then first left again.
Open April **to** October
Access Good **Site** Level
Sites Available A ⌂ ⊟ **Total** 25
Facilities
Nearby Facilities
⚞ Diss
Licensed pub on site.

REEDHAM
Reedham Ferry Touring Park, Reedham Ferry, Norwich, Norfolk, NR13 3HA.
Std: 01493 **Tel:** 700429
Std: 01493 **Fax:** 700999
Nearest Town/Resort Acle
Directions Turn off the A47 (Norwich to Great Yarmouth road) at Acle follow the Reedham road out of Acle. Go all the way to Reedham, over the railway bridge, large road sign to Reedham Ferry.
Acreage 4 **Open** Easter **to** End October
Access Good **Site** Level
Sites Available A ⌂ ⊟ **Total** 20
Facilities
Nearby Facilities
⚞ Reedham
Quietness and tranquility. Tumble dryer available.

SCRATBY
Green Farm Caravan Park, Scratby, Great Yarmouth, Norfolk, NR29 3NW.
Std: 01493 **Tel:** 730440
Website: www.greenfarm-holidays.co.uk
Nearest Town/Resort Great Yarmouth
Directions 4 miles north of Great Yarmouth on the B1159.
Acreage 20 **Open** 26 March **to** October
Access Good **Site** Level
Sites Available A ⌂ ⊟ **Total** 200
Facilities
Nearby Facilities
⚞ Great Yarmouth
Near the beach.

SCRATBY
Scratby Hall Caravan Park, Scratby, Great Yarmouth, Norfolk, NR29 3PH.
Std: 01493 **Tel:** 730283
Nearest Town/Resort Great Yarmouth
Directions Approx. 5 miles north of Great Yarmouth, off the B1159, signed.
Acreage 4½ **Open** Easter **to** Mid October

Access Good **Site** Level
Sites Available A ⌂ ⊟ **Total** 108
Facilities
Nearby Facilities
⚞ Great Yarmouth
Quiet, rural site. Approx. ½ mile from the beach.

SEA PALLING
Golden Beach Holiday Centre, Beach Road, Sea Palling, Norwich, Norfolk, NR12 0AL.
Std: 01692 **Tel:** 598269
Std: 01692 **Fax:** 598693
Nearest Town/Resort Stalham
Directions Follow the coast road to Stalham then follow caravan and camping signs to Sea Palling. Turn down Beach Road, site is on the left 200 yards from the beach.
Acreage 7 **Open** March **to** 1 November
Access Good **Site** Level
Sites Available A ⌂ ⊟ **Total** 50
Facilities
Nearby Facilities
⚞ Wroxham
Family site with a family atmosphere, 200 yards from the beach. New toilets.

SHERINGHAM
Beeston Regis Caravan Park Limited, Cromer Road, West Runton, Cromer, Norfolk, NR27 9NG.
Std: 01263 **Tel:** 823614
Email: beestonregiscp@btinternet.com
Website: www.beestonregis.co.uk
Nearest Town/Resort Sheringham
Directions From Sheringham take the A149 coast road towards Cromer. After ¾ mile you will see the main entrance to the park on the left hand side, opposite Beeston Hall School.
Acreage 44 **Open** March **to** October
Access Good **Site** Level
Sites Available A ⌂ ⊟ **Total** 440
Facilities
Nearby Facilities
⚞ West Runton
Cliff top position in an area of outstanding natural beauty. Direct access to a sandy beach.

SHERINGHAM
Kelling Heath Holiday Park, Weybourne, Holt, Norfolk, NR25 7HW.
Std: 01263 **Tel:** 588181
Std: 01263 **Fax:** 588599
Email: info@kellingheath.co.uk
Website: www.kellingheath.co.uk
Nearest Town/Resort Sheringham
Directions Turn north at site sign at Bodham on the A148 or turn south off the A149 at Weybourne Church.
Acreage 250 **Open** 19 March **to** December
Access Good **Site** Level
Sites Available A ⌂ ⊟ **Total** 300
Facilities
Nearby Facilities
⚞ Sheringham

A 250 acre estate of woodland and heath with magnificent views of the Weybou coastline. Rose Award.

SNETTISHAM
Diglea Caravan & Camping Park, 32 Beach Road, Snettisham, Kings Lynn, Norfolk, PE31 7RA.
Std: 01485 **Tel:** 541367
Nearest Town/Resort Hunstanton
Directions From Kings Lynn take the A1 towards Hunstanton, after approx. 1 miles turn left at the sign marked Snettish Beach.
Acreage 9 **Open** April **to** October
Access Good **Site** Level
Sites Available A ⌂ ⊟ **Total** 200
Facilities
Nearby Facilities
⚞ King's Lynn
500 yards from the beach. Bird reserve clo by.

STANHOE
The Rickels Caravan & Camping Site, Bircham Road, Stanhoe, Kings Lynn, Norfolk, PE31 8PU.
Std: 01485 **Tel:** 518671
Std: 01485 **Fax:** 518969
Nearest Town/Resort Hunstanton
Directions From Kings Lynn take the A1 to Hillington, turn left onto the B1153 to Gre Bircham. Fork right onto the B1155 to t crossroads, straight over. Site is 100yds the left.
Acreage 2¼ **Open** March **to** October
Access Good **Site** Lev/Slope
Sites Available A ⌂ ⊟ **Total** 30
Facilities
Nearby Facilities
⚞ Kings Lynn
Local beaches, stately homes, Sandringha and market towns. Childrens Televisic Dogs 50p per night, short dog walk.

SWAFFHAM
Breckland Meadows Touring Park, Ly Road, Swaffham, Norfolk, PE37 7PT.
Std: 01760 **Tel:** 721246
Email: info@brecklandmeadows.co.uk
Website: www.brecklandmeadows.co.uk
Nearest Town/Resort Kings Lynn/ Hunstanton
Directions Take the A47 from Kings Ly to Swaffham, approx 15 miles. Take the fi exit off the dual carriageway, site is ¼ m before Swaffham town centre.
Acreage 3 **Open** All Year
Access Good **Site** Level
Sites Available A ⌂ ⊟ **Total** 45
Facilities
Nearby Facilities
⚞ Kings Lynn
Small, friendly and very clean park. Cent for touring Norfolk. Ideal for walking a cycling. NOTE: Strictly bookings only fro 1 Nov to 28 February.

A Unique Holiday Experience

AMONGST 250 ACRES OF WOODLAND & HEATHLAND CLOSE TO THE

North Norfolk
COASTLINE AT WEYBOURNE

AN AWARD WINNING ENVIRONMENT
- Winner of the **British Airways Tourism for Tomorrow** award for protection of the environment.
- A **David Bellamy "Gold"** conservation award.
- Winner of the **TOURFOR** award for sound environmental management of a tourism destination.

TOURING PITCHES
Set amongst open heathland enjoying backdrops of mature pine and other species of trees. Electric hook-up points and fully equipped amenity buildings with diasbled facilities are available.

LUXURY HOLIDAY HOMES
Enjoy short breaks or longer stays in luxurious holiday homes set amongst mixed woodland and heathland. Sleeping up to eight each home has full central heating and uPVC double-glazing.

RELAX AND ENJOY
- Nature trails and woodland walks with magnificent views of the Weybourne coastline
- Tutored rambles, pond dipping and other activities at certain times of the year
- A range of environmental activity using self-guided leaflets available
- Cycle routes on park, or the quiet country lanes surrounding Kelling Heath
- Tennis courts, trim trail, orienteering course and petanque

KELLING VILLAGE SQUARE with:-
- Health & Fitness Club with indoor pool, sauna and steam rooms and gym
- Village Store
- The Forge Bar, a choice of two bars with meals available and entertainment if you choose
- The Folly with traditional entertainment in the open air from jazz bands to folk at selected times of the year

KELLINGHEATH
WEYBOURNE, HOLT, NORFOLK NR25 7HW
E-mail: info@kellingheath.co.uk
☎ 01263 588181
www.kellingheath.co.uk

A Blue Sky Leisure Park

GOLD

THETFORD

Lowe Caravan Park, Ashdale, 134 Hills Road, Saham Hills (Near Watton), Thetford, Norfolk, IP25 7EW.
Std: 01953 **Tel:** 881051
Nearest Town/Resort Watton
Directions Take the A11 from Thetford then take the road to Watton. Go through the high street and take second turn into Saham Road (past the golf club). Take the second turning on the right, at T-Junction turn right and site is first on the right.
Acreage 2 **Open** All Year
Access Good **Site** Level
Sites Available Å �btⁱ ⊟ **Total** 20
Facilities ƒ ⅍ ⬚ ⌐ ⊙ ⌣ ☂ ⊙ ⊁ ⬚ ⬚
Nearby Facilities ⌐
➤ Thetford/Norwich
Quiet, relaxing site in the countryside.

THETFORD

The Dower House Touring Park, East Harling, Norwich, Norfolk, NR16 2SE.
Std: 01953 **Tel:** 717314 **Fax:** 717843
Email: info@dowerhouse.co.uk
Website: www.dowerhouse.co.uk
Nearest Town/Resort Norwich
Directions From Thetford take A1066 East for 5 miles, fork left at camping sign onto unclassified road, site on left after 2 miles signposted.
Acreage 20 **Open** 20th March **to** October
Access Good **Site** Level
Sites Available Å �btⁱ ⊟ **Total** 160
Facilities ♿ ƒ ⅍ ⬚ ⬚ ⌐ ⊙ ⌣ ⬚ ◻ ☂
⅍ ⊙ ⬚ ✗ ♚ ⬚ ⬚ ❈ ⬚ ⊟ ⬚
Nearby Facilities ✔
➤ Harling Road
Set in Thetford Forest, the site is spacious and peaceful. Although we have a bar, we have no amusement arcade or gaming machines.

THETFORD

Thorpe Woodlands - Forestry Commission, Shadwell, Thetford, Norfolk, IP24 2RX.
Std: 01842 **Tel:** 751042
Email: fe.holidays@forestry.gsi.gov.uk
Website: www.forestholidays.co.uk
Nearest Town/Resort Thetford
Directions Take the A1066 from Thetford, after 5 miles bear left to East Harling. The

site is ¼ mile on the left.
Open End March **to** End Oct
Access Good **Site** Level
Sites Available Å �btⁱ ⊟ **Total** 138
Facilities ƒ ☂ ⅍ ⬚ ↦ ⬚
Nearby Facilities
➤ Thetford
In Thetford Forest Park, on the banks of the River Thet. A good base for visiting the Norfolk Broads. Note : This site has NO toilets.

WELLS-NEXT-THE-SEA

Pinewoods Holiday Park, Beach Road, Wells-Next-the-Sea, Norfolk, NR23 1DR.
Std: 01328 **Tel:** 710439
Std: 01328 **Fax:** 711060
Email: holiday@pinewoods.co.uk
Website: www.pinewoods.co.uk
Nearest Town/Resort Wells-Next-the-Sea
Directions Follow brown tourism signs for Pinewoods, ¾ miles from Wells.
Open 15 March **to** October
Access Good **Site** Level
Sites Available Å �btⁱ ⊟
Facilities ♿ ƒ ⬚ ⬚ ⬚ ⌐ ⊙ ⌣ ⬚ ◻ ☂
⅍ ⊙ ⬚ ✗ ♚ ⬚ ⬚ ✦ ⬚ ⊟ ⬚
Nearby Facilities ⌐ ✔ ⌣ ∪ ⨾
➤ Kings Lynn
Next to the beach in an area of outstanding natural beauty. Adjacent to Halkham Nature Reserve.

WELLS-NEXT-THE-SEA

Stiffkey Campsite, The Greenway, Vale Farm, Stiffkey, Wells-Next-the-Sea, Norfolk, NR23 1QP.
Std: 01328 **Tel:** 830235 **Fax:** 830119
Nearest Town/Resort Wells-Next-the-Sea
Directions Take the A149 east towards Cromer, Stiffkey is the next village 3½ miles from Wells.
Acreage 6 **Open** April **to** October
Site Lev/Slope
Sites Available Å �btⁱ ⊟ **Total** 80
Facilities ⬚ ⬚ ⌐ ⊙ ⌣ ⅍ ⊙ ↦
Nearby Facilities ⌐ ⚓ ⌣ ∪ ⨾
➤ Kings Lynn/Cromer
Adjoining marsh saltings and the beach. Near to steam and miniature railway. Good shop and pub in the village.

NORTHAMPTONSHIRE
KETTERING

Kestrel Caravan Park, Windy Ridge, Warkton Lane, Kettering, Northamptonshire, NN16 9XG.
Std: 01536 **Tel:** 514301
Std: 01536 **Fax:** 514301
Email: kestrelcaravans@freeserve.co.uk
Nearest Town/Resort Kettering
Directions Leave the A14 at junction 10 ▪ Kettering, go straight on at the first set ◂ traffic lights and turn next right into Warkto Lane.
Acreage 1 **Open** All Year
Access Good **Site** Level
Sites Available Å �btⁱ ⊟ **Total** 20
Facilities ♿ ƒ ⬚ ⬚ ⌐ ⊙ ☂ ⅍ ⊙ ⬚ ⬚ ⬚
Nearby Facilities ⌐ ✔ ⌣ ⨾
➤ Kettering
Near Wickstead Park.

NORTHAMPTON

Billing Aquadrome Ltd., Crow Lane, Great Billing, Northampton, Northamptonshire, NN3 9DA.
Std: 01604 **Tel:** 408181
Std: 01604 **Fax:** 784412
Email: brochures@aquadrome.co.uk
Website: www.aquadrome.co.uk
Nearest Town/Resort Northampton
Directions Leave the M1 at junction 15, full AA signposted from there.
Acreage 235 **Open** March **to** November
Access Good **Site** Level
Sites Available Å �btⁱ ⊟ **Total** 755
Facilities ♿ ƒ ⬚ ⬚ ⬚ ⌐ ⊙ ⌣ ⬚ ◻ ☂
⅍ ⊙ ⬚ ✗ ⌣ ⬚ ↦ ⊟
Nearby Facilities ⌐ ✔
➤ Northampton
Funfair at times during the year, bar restaurants, boating and fishing.

THRAPSTON

Mill Marina, Midland Road, Thrapston, Kettering, Northants, NN14 4JR.
Std: 01832 **Tel:** 732850
Nearest Town/Resort Kettering
Directions Approx. 1 mile from the A14 an A605 junction. Take directions to Thrapsto then follow tourism signs.
Acreage 10 **Open** Easter **to** 31 Oct
Access Good **Site** Level

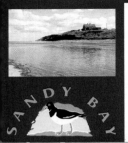
Sites Available ▲ ⬛ 🚐 Total 75
Facilities ⌗ 🅿 ♨ ❓ ⊙ 🛏 ⬛ 🔲 ☎
⬛ ⊙ 🛒 🍴 📶 🔲 🔲
Nearby Facilities ⌐ ✎ ⚓ ⚲ ∪ ♪
🚉 Kettering
Riverside pitches. 25 boat moorings and good coarse fishing. Rallies possible. Rural setting but easy walk to local shops.

NORTHUMBERLAND

ALNWICK

Alnwick Rugby Football Club, Greenfield, Alnwick, Northumberland, NE66.
Std: 01665 **Tel:** 602870
Nearest Town/Resort Alnwick
Directions On the south side of Alnwick, visible from the A1. Approach by turning left off the slip road onto Willowborn Avenue.
Acreage 9 **Open** May to August
Access Good **Site** Level
Sites Available ⬛ ⊙ Total 72
Facilities 🔲 ♨ 🅿 ⬛ 🔲 ⬛ 🔲
Nearby Facilities ⌐ ⚓ ∪ ♪
🚉 Alnwick

AMBLE

Rose Cottage Camp Site, Rose Cottage, Birling, Warkworth, Morpeth, Northumberland, NE65 0XS.
Std: 01665 **Tel:** 711459
Nearest Town/Resort Alnwick
Directions On the A1068 7 miles south of Alnwick.
Open April to September
Site Level
Sites Available ▲ 🚐 Total 14
Facilities 🔲 ♨ 🅿 ⊙ 📶 🔲 🔲
Nearby Facilities

🚉 Alnmouth
Near the beach. Ideal touring.

ASHINGTON

Sandy Bay Holiday Park, North Seaton, Ashington, Northumberland, NE63 9YD.
Std: 01670 **Tel:** 815055
Std: 01670 **Fax:** 812705
Email: sandybay@gbholidayparks.co.uk
Website: www.gbholidayparks.co.uk
Nearest Town/Resort Ashington/Newbiggin-by-Sea
Directions From the A1 take the A19, at the roundabout turn onto the A189 heading north. At next roundabout turn right onto the B1334 towards Newbiggin-by-Sea, Sandy Bay is on the right.
Acreage 2 **Open** March to November
Access Good **Site** Level
Sites Available ⬛ 🚐 Total 50
Facilities ⌗ 🅿 ♨ 🅿 ⊙ ⬛ 🔲 ☎
🍴 🔲 ⊙ 🛒 ✕ 🍷 ♠ 🎣 📶 🔲
Nearby Facilities ⌐ ✎ ∪
🚉 Morpeth
Located next to the beach and on the mouth of the River Wansbeck. A perfect holiday haven offering something for the whole family.

BAMBURGH

Glororum Caravan Park, Glororum, Bamburgh, Northumberland, NE69 7AW.
Std: 01668 **Tel:** 214457/214205
Std: 01668 **Fax:** 214622
Email: info@glororum-caravanpark.co.uk
Website: www.glororum-caravanpark.co.uk
Nearest Town/Resort Bamburgh
Directions Situated 1 mile from Bamburgh on the B1341 Adderstone road. From the A1 take the B1341 at Adderstone Garage and continue for 4 miles.

Acreage 22 **Open** April to October
Access Good **Site** Level
Sites Available ▲ ⬛ 🚐 Total 100
Facilities ✕ ⌗ 🅿 ♨ 🅿 ⊙ ⬛ 🔲 ☎
🈂 🔲 ⊙ ♠ 📶 🔲
Nearby Facilities ⌐ ✎ ⚓ ∪ ♪ ✈ ✗
🚉 Berwick-upon-Tweed
1 mile from the beach. Water sports, hill walking, pony trekking and many historic castles nearby. Fishing and boat trips to Farne Island.

BEADNELL

Beadnell Links Ltd., Beadnell Harbour, Beadnell, Chathill, Northumberland, NE67 5BU.
Std: 01665 **Tel:** 720526
Email: b.links@talk21.com
Website: www.ukparks.co.uk/beadnell
Nearest Town/Resort Beadnell
Directions B1340 to Beadnell, thereafter signed.
Open April to October
Access Good **Site** Level
Sites Available ▲ 🚐 Total 20
Facilities ⌗ 🅿 ♨ 🅿 ⊙ ⬛ 🔲 ☎
🈂 🔲 ⊙ 📶 🔲
Nearby Facilities ⌐ ✎ ⚓ ∪ ♪
🚉 Chathill
Site near beach.

BEADNELL

Camping & Caravanning Club Site, Beadnell, Chathill, Northumberland, NE67 5BX.
Std: 01665 **Tel:** 720586
Website:
www.campingandcaravanningclub.co.uk
Directions From south leave the A1 and follow the B1430 signposted Seahouses. At Beadnell ignore signs for Beadnell Village, site is on the left after the village, just beyond

the left hand bend. From north leave the A1 and follow the B1342 via Bamburgh and Seahouses, site is on the right just before Beadnell Village.
Acreage 14 **Open** April **to** Sept
Site Level
Sites Available Λ ⚌ **Total** 150
Facilities ▥ ♨ ♏ ⊙ ⌣ ⚊ ▢ ☎ ℟ ☺ ⚍ ⊁ ♿ ▣ ▣
Nearby Facilities ┍ ✔ ⚓ ⚲ ∪ ♪
2 miles of sandy beach just over the road. 6 miles from Bamburgh Castle. BTB Graded. Non members welcome.

BELLINGHAM
Brown Rigg Caravan & Camping Park, Tweed House, Brown Rigg, Bellingham, Hexham, Northumberland, NE48 2JY.
Std: 01434 **Tel:** 220175
Std: 01434 **Fax:** 220175
Email: enquiries@northumberlandcaravanparks.com
Website: www.northumberlandcaravanparks.com
Nearest Town/Resort Hexham
Directions Take the A69, after Hexham in ½ mile turn right signposted Acomb, Chollerford and Bellingham. At Chollerford turn left onto the B6318, go over the river and turn second left onto the B6320 signposted Wark and Bellingham.
Acreage 5 **Open** 31 March **to** 31 Oct
Access Good **Site** Level
Sites Available Λ ⚌ ⚌ **Total** 60
Facilities ∮ ▥ ▥ ♨ ♏ ⊙ ⌣ ⚊ ▢ ☎ ℟ ☺ ⚍ ⊡ ♿ ⚠ ╋▣
Nearby Facilities ┍ ✔ ⚓ ⚲ ∪
≉ Hexham
Ideal for touring Hadrians Wall, Kielder Water and Forest and the Borders region.

BERWICK-UPON-TWEED
Beachcomber Campsite, Goswick, Berwick-upon-Tweed, Northumberland, TD15 2RW.
Std: 01289 **Tel:** 381217
Nearest Town/Resort Berwick-upon-Tweed
Directions From Berwick-upon-Tweed take the A1 south, after approx. 1 mile take a left turn signposted Goswick and Cheswick. Follow this country road for approx. 4 miles to the Campsite.
Acreage 4 **Open** Easter **to** End September
Access Good **Site** Level
Sites Available Λ ⚌□ **Total** 50
Facilities ∮ ▥ ♨ ♏ ⊙ ⌣ ▢ ☎ ℟ ☺ ✗ ⚠ ╋▣
Nearby Facilities ┍ ⚲
≉ Berwick-upon-Tweed
Quiet, family run site situated behind the dunes (50 metre walk) of a very large sandy

beach. Horse riding on site. Golf within ½ mile.

BERWICK-UPON-TWEED
Haggerston Castle, Beal, Northumberland, TD15 2PA.
Std: 01289 **Tel:** 381333
Email: becky.roberts@british-holidays.co.uk
Website: www.british-holidays.co.uk
Nearest Town/Resort Berwick-upon-Tweed
Directions On A1, 7 miles south of Berwick-upon-Tweed.
Open March **to** October
Access Good **Site** Level
Sites Available Λ ⚌ ⚌ **Total** 159
Facilities ↧ ♏ ∮ ▥ ▥ ♨ ♏ ⊙ ⌣ ⚊ ▢ ☎ ℟ ☺ ⚍ ✗ ♐ ⚠ ❋ ⊁ ✈▣ ▣ ▣
Nearby Facilities ┍ ✔ ∪ ♪
≉ Berwick
Situated in an area of great heritage interest. Lots of on park facilities. Kids Club and farm. A full family entertainment programme. Golf, horse riding, tennis, bowls, boating, bikes and heated swimming pools. Rose Award and David Bellamy Conservation Award.

BERWICK-UPON-TWEED
Marshall Meadows Farm, Berwick-upon-Tweed, Northumberland, TD15 1UT.
Std: 01289 **Tel:** 307375
Nearest Town/Resort Berwick-upon-Tweed
Directions Approx. 1½ miles north of Berwick.
Open March **to** October
Access Good **Site** Level
Sites Available Λ ⚌ ⚌ **Total** 40
Facilities ↧ ∮ ▥ ▥ ♨ ♏ ⊙ ⌣ ☎ ℟ ☺ ⚠ ╋▣
Nearby Facilities ┍ ✔ ⚓ ⚲ ∪
≉ Berwick-upon-Tweed

BERWICK-UPON-TWEED
Ord House Country Park, East Ord, Berwick-upon-Tweed, Northumberland, TD15 2NS.
Std: 01289 **Tel:** 305288
Std: 01289 **Fax:** 330832
Email: enquiries@ordhouse.co.uk
Website: www.ordhouse.co.uk
Nearest Town/Resort Berwick-upon-Tweed
Directions Take East Ord road from bypass, follow caravan signpost.
Acreage 42 **Open** All Year
Access Good **Site** Lev/Slope
Sites Available Λ ⚌ ⚌ **Total** 60
Facilities ↧ ∮ ▥ ▥ ♨ ♏ ⊙ ⌣ ⚊ ▢ ☎ ℟ ☺ ✗ ⚠ ⚍ ❋✈▣ ▣ ▣
Nearby Facilities ┍ ✔ ⚓ ⚲ ∪
≉ Berwick-upon-Tweed

Award Winning park with an 18th century mansion house containing a licenced club.

EMBLETON
Camping & Caravanning Club Site, Dunstan Hill, Dunstan, Alnwick, Northumberland, NE66 3TQ.
Std: 01665 **Tel:** 576310
Website: www.campingandcaravanningclub.co.uk
Directions Travelling north on the A1 take the B1340 signposted Seahouses, follow to the T-Junction at Christon Bank and turn right, take the next right signpost Embleton, turn right at the crossroads then first left signposted Craster. Travelling south on the A1 take the B6347 through Christon Bank, take a right turn to Embleton, turn right at the crossroads, then first left signposted Craster, site is 1 mile on the left.
Acreage 14 **Open** March **to** Nov
Site Level
Sites Available Λ ⚌ ⚌ **Total** 150
Facilities ↧ ∮ ▥ ♨ ♏ ⊙ ⌣ ⚊ ▢ ☎ ℟ ☺ ⚍ ⊡ ♿ ▣ ▣
Nearby Facilities ✔ ∪
≉ Ashington
1 mile from the coast. Access to Dunstanburgh Castle from the site. BTB Graded. Non members welcome.

HALTWHISTLE
Camping & Caravanning Club Site, Burnfoot Park Village, Haltwhistle, Northumberland, NE49 0JP.
Std: 01434 **Tel:** 320106
Website: www.campingandcaravanningclub.co.uk
Directions Follow signs from the new by-pass.
Open March **to** October
Site Level
Sites Available Λ ⚌ ⚌ **Total** 60
Facilities ↧ ∮ ▥ ♨ ♏ ⊙ ⌣ ⚊ ▢ ☎ ℟ ☺ ⚍ ⊡ ▣ ▣
Nearby Facilities
≉ Haltwhistle
On the banks of the River South Tyne for fishing on site. Close to the Pennine Way. BTB Graded. Non members welcome.

HALTWHISTLE
Seldom Seen Caravan Park, Haltwhistle, Northumberland, NE49 0NE.
Std: 01434 **Tel:** 320571
Website: www.ukparks.com
Nearest Town/Resort Haltwhistle
Directions Off the A69 east of Haltwhistle, signposted.
Open March **to** January
Access Good **Site** Level
Sites Available Λ ⚌ ⚌ **Total** 20
Facilities ∮ ▥ ▥ ♨ ♏ ⊙ ℟ ☺ ♐ ▢ ☎ ⚠ ╋▣

CRESSWELL TOWERS HOLIDAY PARK
A Charming Location close to the Northumbria Coastline

The woodland setting gives Cresswell Towers a magical quality and helps create a relaxed and informal atmosphere. This area of Northumberland is renowned for its interesting walks, stunning views and for the abundance of exciting things to see and do.

- Outdoor heated swimming pool • Norseman Club • Multi-sports court
- Well stocked mini-market • Adventure play area • Cafe and take-away
- Beautiful sandy beaches • Sea fishing and watersports opportunities locally

Fantastic rates available - Phone **01670 860411** *for details*
Visit our website **www.gbholidayparks.co.uk**
Cresswell Towers Holiday Park, Nr. Morpeth, Northumberland NE61 5JT

Nearby Facilities ⌐ ✔ ∪ ♟
⚓ Haltwhistle
Central touring area, Roman wall. David Bellamy Gold Award for Conservation.

HAYDON BRIDGE

Ashcroft Farm, Bardon Mill, Hexham, Northumberland, NE47 7JA.
Std: 01434 **Tel:** 344409
Nearest Town/Resort Haltwhistle
Directions Take the A69 to Bardon Mill and follow signs.
Acreage 2 **Open** Easter **to** November
Access Good **Site** Level
Sites Available ⇞ ⇆ **Total** 5
Facilities ☂ ⫯ ⚑ ⌕ ⊡
Nearby Facilities ⌐ ✔ ∪
⚓ Bardon Mill
Alongside a river and just off the Roman Wall.

HAYDON BRIDGE

Poplars Riverside Caravan Park,
Eastland Ends, Haydon Bridge, Hexham, Northumberland, NE47 6BY.
Std: 01434 **Tel:** 684427
Nearest Town/Resort Hexham
Directions Take the A69 Newcastle to Carlisle road, follow signs from the bridge in the village.
Acreage 2½ **Open** March **to** October
Access Good **Site** Level
Sites Available ⇞ ⇆ **Total** 14
Facilities ⚒ ⫯ ⎙ ⯐ ⚡ ⌐ ⊙ ⤴ ◪ ⊡ ☎
⚷ ⬮ ⚑ ⋔ ⊡
Nearby Facilities ⌐ ✔ ∪ ♟
⚓ Haydon Bridge
Small, peaceful site close to the village. Fishing on site.

HEXHAM

Barrasford Park Caravan & Camping Site, 1 Front Drive, Barrasford Park, Nr. Hexham, Northumberland, NE48 4BE.
Std: 01434 **Tel:** 681210
Email: barrasfordsite@hotmail.com
Nearest Town/Resort Hexham
Directions Take the A69 to Corbridge, turn onto the A68 to Jedburgh. Barrasford Park is signposted 8 miles north of Corbridge on the A68.
Acreage 2 **Open** April **to** October
Access Good **Site** Sloping
Sites Available ⇞ ⇆ **Total** 30
Facilities ⫯ ⎙ ⯐ ⚡ ⌐ ⊙ ☎
⚷ ⬮ ⚑ ⋔ ⊡
Nearby Facilities ⌐ ✔
⚓ Hexham
Set in a 60 acre woodland park, 6 miles from Hadrian's Wall.

HEXHAM

Causey Hill Caravan Park, Causey Hill, Hexham, Northumberland, NE46 2JN.
Std: 01434 **Tel:** 604647
Nearest Town/Resort Hexham
Directions On the racecourse road at High Yarridge.
Open April **to** October
Access Good **Site** Level
Sites Available ⇞ ⇆ **Total** 35
Facilities ⫯ ⎙ ⯐ ⚡ ⌐ ⊙ ⤴ ◪ ⊡ ☎
⚷ ⬮ ⚑ ⋔ ⊡
Nearby Facilities ⌐ ✔ ⚓ ⚲ ∪ ♟ ♞ ↟
⚓ Hexham

HEXHAM

Fallowfield Dene Caravan Park, Acomb, Hexham, Northumberland, NE46 4RP.
Std: 01434 **Tel:** 603553
Std: 01434 **Fax:** 601252
Website: www.tynedale.gov.uk
Nearest Town/Resort Hexham
Directions From Hexham Bridge take the A69 west, after 250 yards turn north onto the A6079 for Acomb. After 250 yards turn right signposted caravan park and follow signs, after 1½ miles turn left into Fallowfield Dene.
Acreage 17½ **Open** 23 March **to** 28 Oct
Access Good **Site** Level
Sites Available ⇞ ⇆ **Total** 155
Facilities ⚒ ⫯ ⎙ ⯐ ⚡ ⌐ ⊙ ⤴ ◪ ⊡ ☎
⚷ ⬮ ⚑ ⊡ ⊡
Nearby Facilities ⌐ ✔ ⚓ ⚲ ∪ ♟
⚓ Hexham
Near Hadrians Wall, Kielder Water and Forest and the Metro Centre. Easy access to the East coast, the Lake District and Scotland.

HEXHAM

Hexham Racecourse Caravan Site, High Yarridge, Hexham, Northumberland, NE46 2JP.
Std: 01434 **Tel:** 606881
Std: 01434 **Fax:** 605814
Email: hexrace@aol.com
Website: www.hexham-racecourse.co.uk
Nearest Town/Resort Hexham
Directions 1½ miles from the centre of Hexham, leave the A69 at Bridge End roundabout and follow signs south through the town.
Acreage 8 **Open** 1 May **to** 1 Oct
Access Good **Site** Level
Sites Available ⇞ ⇆ **Total** 60
Facilities ⫯ ⎙ ⯐ ⚡ ⌐ ⊙ ⤴ ◪ ⊡ ☎
⬮ ⬮ ⚑ ⋔ ↟
Nearby Facilities ⌐ ✔ ⚓ ⚲ ∪ ♟
⚓ Hexham
Set in beautiful, unspoilt countryside. Ideal touring.

HEXHAM

Springhouse Farm Caravan Park, Slaley, Hexham, Northumberland, NE47 0AW.
Std: 01434 **Tel:** 673241
Email: springhouse.cp@btinternet.com
Nearest Town/Resort Hexham
Open March **to** October
Access Good **Site** Sloping
Sites Available ⇞ ⇆ **Total** 20
Facilities ⫯ ⎙ ⯐ ⚡ ⌐ ⊙ ⤴ ◪ ⊡ ☎
⚷ ⬮ ⬮ ⚑ ✳ ⋔ ⊡ ⊡
Nearby Facilities ⌐ ⚲ ∪
⚓ Hexham Station
Quiet, surrounded by forest. Panoramic views, excellent country walks.

MORPETH

Cresswell Towers Holiday Park, Cresswell, Morpeth, Northumberland, NE61 5JT.
Std: 01670 **Tel:** 860411
Std: 01670 **Fax:** 860226
Email: cresswelltowers@gbholidayparks.co.uk
Website: www.gbholidayparks.co.uk
Nearest Town/Resort Ashington
Directions Take the A189 towards Morpeth and Ashington, follow signs for Ellington/Alnwick. A1068 coastal route, Cresswell is signposted from there.
Open March **to** October
Access Good **Site** Level
Sites Available ⇞ ⇆ **Total** 20
Facilities ⫯ ⎙ ⯐ ⌐ ⤴ ◪ ☎
⚷ ⬮ ⬮ ⚑ ⚒ ✕ ∪ ⛱ ⋔ ✳ ⌕ ⊡ ⊡ ⊡
Nearby Facilities ⌐ ✔ ⚓ ∪ ♟
⚓ Morpeth
Woodland park, approx. a 5 minute walk to the nearest beach. Short drive to the nearest town of Ashington.

MORPETH

Forget-Me-Not Caravan Park, Croftside, Longhorsley, Morpeth, Northumberland, NE65 8QY.
Std: 01670 **Tel:** 788364
Email: info@forget-me-notcaravanpark.co.uk
Website: www.forget-me-notcaravanpark.co.uk
Nearest Town/Resort Morpeth
Directions From the A1 take the A697 to Longhorsley, turn left in Longhorsley towards Netherwitton, park is 1¼ miles on the right.
Acreage 20+ **Open** March **to** October
Access Good **Site** Level
Sites Available ⇞ ⇆ **Total** 60
Facilities ⚒ ⫯ ⎙ ⯐ ⚡ ⌐ ⊙ ⊙ ☎ ⚷ ⬮ ⚒ ✕ ⯑ ⛱ ⋔ ↟ ⊡
Nearby Facilities ⌐ ✔ ⚓ ⚲
⚓ Morpeth
On the edge of a national park, ideal touring. 7 miles from the beach.

Percy Wood Caravan Park

Swarland, Nr. Morpeth, Northumberland NE65 9JW   Tel: (01670) 787649

The park which is set in 60 acres of mixed woodland, 2 miles from the A1, 3 miles from the A697 and adjacent to a golf corse, is ideally placed for touring coast and country.
The touring and holiday home pitches are generously spaced giving peaceful holidays. Centrally heated toilet block. Laundry.
All pitches with electric hook-ups, some with water and drainage. 12ft wide caravans for hire or sale.

MORPETH

Percy Wood Caravan Park, Swarland, Nr. Morpeth, Northumberland, NE65 9JW.
Std: 01670 **Tel:** 787649
Std: 01670 **Fax:** 787034
Email:
enquiries@percywood.freeserve.co.uk
Website: www.ukparks.co.uk/percywood
Nearest Town/Resort Alnwick
Directions From the A1 turn off to Swarland and follow caravan signs.
Acreage 60 **Open** March **to** Janurary
Access Good **Site** Lev/Slope
Sites Available ▲ ⊕ ⊕ **Total** 80
Facilities f ⊞ ⊞ ⊞ ⅃ ⌐ ⊙ ⊿ ⊡ ☎
⊠ ⅃⊠ ⊙ ⊜ ⊜ ⋒ ※ ⊬⊟ ⊟ ☐
Nearby Facilities ⌐ ✓ ∪ ☌
✈ Morpeth
Ideal base for touring coast and country. Adjacent to a golf course and forest walks. Rose Award..

OTTERBURN

Border Forest Caravan Park,
Cottonshope Burnfoot, Nr. Otterburn, Northumberland, NE19 1TF.
Std: 01830 **Tel:** 520259
Website:
www.borderforestcaravanpark.co.uk
Nearest Town/Resort Jedburgh/Hexham
Directions Adjacent to A68 - 17 miles to Jedburgh, 28 miles to Hexham, 38 miles to Newcastle.
Acreage 3 **Open** 1st March **to** 31st October
Access Good **Site** Level
Sites Available ▲ ⊕ ⊕ **Total** 36
Facilities f ⊞ ⌐ ⊙ ⊿ ⊕ ⊿ ☎
Nearby Facilities ⌐ ✓ ⊥ ⅃ ∪ ⅃ ☌
✈ Hexham
Surrounded by Cottonshope, Burn and River Rede. Ideal walking and touring base. 6 miles south of the Scottish Border at Carter Bar. Situated in Kielder Forest Park.

OVINGHAM

The High Hermitage Caravan Park, The Hermitage, Ovingham, Prudhoe, Northumberland, NE42 6HH.
Std: 01661 **Tel:** 832250
Std: 01661 **Fax:** 834848
Nearest Town/Resort Prudhoe
Directions Take the A69 from Newcastle or Hexham and take exit to Wylam. Go straight ahead at first crossroads to Wylam, follow road and turn right at the bottom to Ovingham, site entrance is 1½ miles down this river road opposite water intake area.
Acreage 2½ **Open** April **to** October
Access Good **Site** Gently Sloping
Sites Available ⊕ ⊕ **Total** 33

Facilities f ⊞ ⊞ ⊞ ⅃ ⌐ ⊙ ⊿ ☐ ☎
⅃⊠ ⊙ ⊜ ⊟
Nearby Facilities ⌐ ✓ ⊥ ⅃ ∪ ☌
✈ Wylam/Prudhoe
Quiet, rural, riverside site with extensive wildlife. Grassy slope sheltered by trees on north, east and west sides. Giant chess and draughts. Ideal for touring the Roman Wall and associated sites plus gorgeous Northumberland countryside and beaches.

ROTHBURY

Coquetdale Caravan Park, Whitton, Rothbury, Morpeth, Northumberland, NE65 7RU.
Std: 01669 **Tel:** 620549
Email:
enquiry@coquetdalecaravanpark.co.uk
Website:
www.coquetdalecaravanpark.co.uk
Nearest Town/Resort Rothbury
Directions ½ mile southwest of Rothbury on road to Newtown.
Acreage 1½ **Open** Easter **to** October
Access Good **Site** Level
Sites Available ▲ ⊕ ⊕ **Total** 50
Facilities f ⊞ ⅃ ⌐ ⊙ ⊿ ⊿ ⊡ ☎
⅃⊠ ⊙ ⊜ ⋒ ※ ⊬⊟ ⊟
Nearby Facilities ⌐ ✓ ∪ ☌ ⅃
✈ Morpeth
Beautiful views. Ideal situation for touring Borders and coast. All units are strictly for families and couples only.

SEAHOUSES

Seafield Caravan Park, Seafield Road, Seahouses, Northumberland, NE68 7SP.
Std: 01665 **Tel:** 720628
Std: 01665 **Fax:** 720088
Email: info@seafieldpark.co.uk
Website: www.seafieldpark.co.uk
Nearest Town/Resort Seahouses
Directions B1340 east off the main A1 to the coast.
Acreage 1 **Open** March **to** January
Access Good **Site** Level
Sites Available ⊕ ⊕ **Total** 20
Facilities ⊞ ⊞ ⊞ ⊞ ⅃ ⌐ ⊙ ⊿ ⊿
⊡ ☎ ⅃⊠ ⊙ ⊜ ⋒ ※ ⊬⊟ ⊟
Nearby Facilities ⌐ ✓ ⊥ ⅃ ∪ ☌
✈ Chathill
In the centre of the village, near to a beach, scenic views and the harbour.

WOOLER

Highburn House Caravan & Camping Park, Wooler, Northumberland, NE71 6EE.
Std: 01668 **Tel:** 281344/281839
Email: relax@highburn-house.co.uk
Nearest Town/Resort Wooler

Directions Off A1 take A697 to Wooler town centre, at the top of Main Street take left turn, 400 metres on left is our site.
Acreage 12 **Open** April **to** December
Access Good **Site** Level
Sites Available ▲ ⊕ ⊕ **Total** 100
Facilities ⊕ ⊁ f ⊞ ⊞ ⅃ ⌐ ⊙ ⊿ ⊿ ⊡ ☎
⅃⊠ ⊙ ⊜ ⋒ ※ ⊬⊟ ⊟
Nearby Facilities ⌐ ✓ ∪ ☌ ⅃
✈ Berwick
Stream runs through middle of site, beautiful view over hills and valley.

NOTTINGHAMSHIRE
CARLTON-ON-TRENT

Carlton Manor Caravan Park, Ossington Road, (off A1), Carlton-on-Trent, Nr. Newark, Nottinghamshire, NG23 6NU.
Std: 01530 **Tel:** 835662
Nearest Town/Resort Newark
Directions A1 north towards Doncaster. Site is 7 miles north of Newark. Signposted on the A1.
Acreage 2 **Open** April **to** October
Access Good **Site** Level
Sites Available ▲ ⊕ ⊕ **Total** 22
Facilities f ⊞ ⊞ ⅃ ⌐ ⊙ ☎ ⅃⊠ ⊜ ⋒ ⊬⊟
Nearby Facilities ✓
✈ Newark Village
We do allow individual motor cyclists, but not groups. Spotless toilets and clean site. Warden on site at all times. Emergency phone on site at Wardens. Hotel opposite open all day for food and drink etc.. Doctor in village. Train spotting on site. Shops and fishing in village. Pubs, library, hairdressers etc. all nearby. Shop (Co-Op) open between 8am and 8pm. 10 miles from Robin Hood country. You can also contact Mrs Goodman on MOBILE 07870 139256.

HOLME PIERREPONT

Holme Pierrepont Caravan & Camping Park, National Water Sports Centre, Adbolton Lane, Nottingham, NG12 2LU.
Std: 0115 **Tel:** 982 4721
Std: 0115 **Fax:** 945 5213
Nearest Town/Resort Nottingham
Directions Follow brown National Water Sports signs. 1½ miles from Trent Bridge off the A52 to Grantham.
Acreage 28 **Open** April **to** October
Access Good **Site** Level
Sites Available ▲ ⊕ ⊕ **Total** 330+
Facilities ⅙ ∮ ⬚ ⬚ ⌐ ⬚ ⬚ ⬚
⬚ ⬚ ⬚ ⬚ ⬚ ⬚
Nearby Facilities ✓ ⚤ ⅍ ⚲
⚓ Nottingham
Next to the River Trent in 270 acres of parkland with a Nature Reserve. 100 pitches available on the Rally field.

NEWARK

Milestone Caravan Park, North Road, Cromwell, Newark, Notts, NG23 6JE.
Std: 01636 **Tel:** 821244
Std: 01636 **Fax:** 822256
Email: milestone.cp@pgen.net
Nearest Town/Resort Newark
Directions A1 south take the signpost for Cromwell, site is ½ mile on the left. A1 north take the signpost for Cromwell Doll Museum, over the flyover and the site is on the left in 100 yards.
Acreage 8 **Open** All Year
Access Good **Site** Level
Sites Available ▲ ⊕ ⊕ **Total** 60
Facilities ⅙ ∮ ⬚ ⬚ ⬚ ⌐ ⊙ ⬚
⬚ ⬚ ⬚ ⬚
Nearby Facilities ⌐ ✓ ∪ ⚲
⚓ Newark
Level, grass site with a lake and picnic area. Specialist fishing lakes in the village. A short distance to Sherwood Forest, Nottingham and Lincoln.

NOTTINGHAM

Manor Farm, Thrumpton, Nottinghamshire, NG11 0AX.
Std: 0115 **Tel:** 983 0341
Std: 0115 **Fax:** 983 0341
Nearest Town/Resort Nottingham
Directions From M1 junction 24, take the A453 Nottingham south, in 3 miles turn left. In 100 yds turn right. At next junction turn left, site immediately on right.
Acreage 3 **Open** All Year
Access Good **Site** Level
Sites Available ▲ ⊕ ⊕ **Total** 12
Facilities ∮ ⬚ ⬚ ⬚ ⌐ ⊙ ⬚ ⬚
Nearby Facilities ⌐ ✓ ⚤ ∪ ⚲
⚓ Nottingham
Good walks, fishing in the village on River Trent. We charge a small extra fee for electric and awnings. New toilets and showers. We are able to cater for very large mobile homes as our gateways are so wide.

NOTTINGHAM

Moor Farm Holiday & Home Park, Moor Lane, Calverton, Nottingham, Notts, NG6 8UJ.
Std: 0115 **Tel:** 965 2426/965 5351
Std: 0115 **Fax:** 965 5351
Nearest Town/Resort Nottingham/Newark
Directions Leave the M1 at junction 26 and take the A610 then the A60 towards Mansfield and Nottingham. Take the A614 towards Doncaster and follow signs to Calverton.
Acreage 60 **Open** All Year

Access Good **Site** Level
Sites Available Total 70
Facilities ∮ ⬚ ⬚ ⬚ ⬚ ⬚ ⬚ ⬚
Nearby Facilities ⌐ ✓ ∪
⚓ Lowdham/Nottingham
Set in Robin Hood countryside, across the road from a pub. Fishing on site.

NOTTINGHAM

Thornton's Holt Camping Park, Stragglethorpe, Radcliffe-on-Trent, Notts, NG12 2JZ.
Std: 0115 **Tel:** 933 2125
Std: 0115 **Fax:** 933 3318
Email: camping@thorntons-holt.co.uk
Website: www.thorntons-holt.co.uk
Nearest Town/Resort Nottingham
Directions 3 miles east of Nottingham turn south of A52 towards Cropwell Bishop. Park is ¼ mile on left.
Acreage 15 **Open** All Year
Access Good **Site** Level
Sites Available ▲ ⊕ ⊕ **Total** 90
Facilities ⅙ ∮ ⬚ ⬚ ⬚ ⌐ ⊙ ⬚ ⬚ ⬚ ⬚
⬚ ⬚ ⬚ ⬚ ⬚ ⬚ ⬚ ⬚ ⬚
Nearby Facilities ⌐ ✓ ⚤ ⅍ ∪ ⚲ ⚲
⚓ Radcliffe-on-Trent
Only 3 miles from Nottingham. Ideal base for touring Sherwood Forest and the Vale of Belvoir. Pub and restaurant nearby.

OLLERTON

Shannon Caravan & Camping Park, Wellow Road, Ollerton, Nottinghamshire, NG22 9AP.
Std: 01623 **Tel:** 869002
Website: www.caravan.sitefinder.co.uk
Nearest Town/Resort Newark
Directions On the A616 between Wellow and Ollerton.
Open All Year
Access Good **Site** Level
Sites Available ▲ ⊕ ⊕ **Total** 34
Facilities ⅙ ∮ ⬚ ⬚ ⬚ ⬚ ⌐ ⊙ ⬚
⬚ ⬚ ⬚
Nearby Facilities ⌐ ✓ ∪
⚓ Newark
Set in Robin Hood countryside. Close to Sherwood Forest, museums and historic sites.

RATCLIFFE ON SOAR

Red Hill Marina, Ratcliffe-on-Soar, Nottinghamshire, NG11 0EB.
Std: 01509 **Tel:** 672770
Nearest Town/Resort Nottingham
Directions Leave the M1 at junction 24 and take the A453, 1½ miles on the left hand side.
Open All Year
Access Good **Site** Level
Sites Available ▲ ⊕ ⊕ **Total** 5
Facilities ∮ ⬚ ⬚ ✕ ⬚ ⬚
Nearby Facilities ✓
⚓ Loughborough
By a river.

SUTTON-IN-ASHFIELD

Shardaroba Caravan Park, Silverhill Lane, Teversal, Near Sutton-in-Ashfield, Nottinghamshire, NG17 3JJ.
Std: 01623 **Tel:** 551838
Std: 01623 **Fax:** 552174
Email: stay@shardaroba.co.uk
Website: www.shardaroba.co.uk
Nearest Town/Resort Sutton-in-Ashfield
Acreage 6 **Open** All Year
Access Good **Site** Lev/Slope
Sites Available ▲ ⊕ ⊡ **Total** 100
Facilities ⅙ ∮ ⬚ ⬚ ⬚ ⌐ ⊙ ⬚ ⬚ ⬚ ⬚
⬚ ⬚ ⬚ ⬚ ⬚
Nearby Facilities ⌐ ✓ ∪

⚓ Mansfield

TUXFORD

Greenacres Touring Park, Lincoln Road, Tuxford, Newark, Nottinghamshire, NG22 0JN.
Std: 01777 **Tel:** 870264
Std: 01777 **Fax:** 872512
Email: bailey-security@freezone.co.uk
Website: www.freezone.co.uk/bailey-security/
Nearest Town/Resort Retford
Directions From A1 (north or south) follow signs. Park is on the left 250yds after Fountain Public House.
Acreage 4½ **Open** Mid March **to** End Oct
Access Good **Site** Level
Sites Available ▲ ⊕ ⊕ **Total** 67
Facilities ⅙ ∮ ⬚ ⬚ ⬚ ⌐ ⊙ ⬚ ⬚ ⬚ ⬚
⬚ ⬚ ⬚ ⬚ ⬚ ⬚ ⬚ ⬚ ⬚
Nearby Facilities ✓
⚓ Retford
Ideal for night halt or for touring Robin Hood country. Static caravans for sale and hire.

TUXFORD

Orchard Park, Marnham Road, Tuxford, Near Newark, Nottinghamshire, NG22 0PY.
Std: 01777 **Tel:** 870228
Std: 01777 **Fax:** 870320
Website:
www.caravanparksnottinghamshire.com
Nearest Town/Resort Retford
Directions Turn off the A1 dual carriageway at Tuxford via the slip road onto the A6075 signposted Lincoln A57. After 1½ miles turn right into Marnham Road, site is on the right in ¾ miles.
Acreage 7 **Open** Mid March **to** End October
Access Good **Site** Level
Sites Available ▲ ⊕ ⊕ **Total** 65
Facilities ⅙ ∮ ⬚ ⬚ ⬚ ⌐ ⊙ ⬚ ⬚ ⬚
⬚ ⬚ ⬚ ⬚ ⬚ ⬚ ⬚ ⬚ ⬚ ⬚
Nearby Facilities ✓ ∪ ⚲
⚓ Retford
Peaceful location. Ideal for touring Robin Hood country.

WORKSOP

Camping & Caravanning Club Site, The Walled Garden, Clumber Park, Worksop, Nottinghamshire, S80 3BD.
Std: 01909 **Tel:** 482303
Website:
www.campingandcaravanningclub.co.uk
Nearest Town/Resort Worksop
Directions From the A1 turn onto the A614 southbound, in ¼ mile take the first entrance into Clumber Park and follow signs.
Acreage 2½ **Open** March **to** October
Access Good **Site** Level
Sites Available ▲
Facilities ∮ ⬚ ⬚ ⌐ ⊙ ⬚ ⬚
⬚ ⬚ ⬚ ⬚ ⬚
Nearby Facilities ⌐ ✓
⚓ Retford
Quiet, sheltered site set in the 400 acres of Clumber Park estate. Cycling, walking and fishing are available on the estate. Many places of interest nearby. MEMBERS CARAVANS ONLY. Non members welcome.

WORKSOP

Riverside Caravan Park, Central Avenue, Worksop, Notts, S80 1ER.
Std: 01909 **Tel:** 474118
Nearest Town/Resort Nottingham
Directions Follow signs for Worksop town centre and turn left into Stobbins Lane, turn

right into Central Avenue and left again into site.
Open All Year
Access Good **Site** Level
Sites Available ▲ ⊞ ⊞ **Total** 60
Facilities ⨍ 🏠 📰 🚰 ⌢ ⊙ ☂ 🛇 🏪 ⊟
Nearby Facilities ⌐ ✓
⇌ Worksop
Alongside a canal for fishing and walks.

OXFORDSHIRE
ABINGDON
Bridge House Caravan Site, Clifton Hampden, Abingdon, Oxfordshire, OX14 3EH.
Std: 01865 **Tel:** 407725
Nearest Town/Resort Abingdon
Directions On the A415 from Abingdon.
Open April to October
Access Good **Site** Level
Sites Available ▲ ⊞ ⊞
Facilities ⨍ 📰 🚰 ⌢ ⊙ 🛇 ☂ 🛇⇥⊟A
Nearby Facilities ✓
⇌ Culham
On the banks of the Thames River.

BANBURY
Anita's Touring Caravan Park, (Formerly Mollington Caravan Park), The Yews, Mollington, Banbury, Oxfordshire, OX17 1AZ.
Std: 01295 **Tel:** 750731
Nearest Town/Resort Banbury/Oxford
Directions From Banbury head north on the A423 for 4 miles, or leave the M40 at junction 11 onto the A423. Site is 200 metres past the Mollington turn on the left, signposted.
Acreage 2 **Open** All Year
Access Good **Site** Lev/Slope
Sites Available ▲ ⊞ ⊞ **Total** 24
Facilities ⚹ ⨍ 🏠 📰 🚰 ⌢ ⊙ ⌢ ☂
🅿 ⊛⇥⊟🖪
Nearby Facilities ⌐ ✓ ∪
⇌ Banbury
On a working farm at the edge of a village, just a short walk to a country pub. Lovely walks and cycling. Near many National Trust properties such as Blenheim Palace and Warwick Castle, also near Oxford, Stratford and the Cotswolds.

BANBURY
Barnstones Caravan Site, Barnstones, Main Street, Great Bourton, Nr Banbury, Oxon, OX17 1QU.
Std: 01295 **Tel:** 750289
Nearest Town/Resort Banbury
Directions Leave Banbury on the A423 to Southam, in 3 miles turn right signposted Great Bourton. Site entrance is 100yds on

the right.
Acreage 3 **Open** All Year
Access Good **Site** Level
Sites Available ▲ ⊞ ⊞ **Total** 50
Facilities ⨍ 🖪 📰 🚰 ⌢ ⊙ ⌢ 🛇 🛇 ☂
🅿 🛇 🛇 🛇 🛇 ⊛⇥⊟🖪
Nearby Facilities ⌐ ✓ ⚓ ⤳ ∪ ℛ
⇌ Banbury
Cotswolds, Oxford, Stratford-upon-Avon and Warwick Castle. 40 pitches are hard standing with a grass area for awnings. 20 pitches are fully serviced. Food now available on site.

BANBURY
Bo Peep Farm Caravan Park, Aynho Road, Adderbury, Near Banbury, Oxon, OX17 3NP.
Std: 01295 **Tel:** 810605
Std: 01295 **Fax:** 810605
Email: warden@bo-peep.co.uk
Website: www.bo-peep.co.uk
Nearest Town/Resort Banbury
Directions Take the A4260 south from Banbury for 3 miles. At Adderbury turn left onto the B4100 towards Aynho, site is ½ mile on the right.
Acreage 12 **Open** March to November
Access Good **Site** Level
Sites Available ▲ ⊞ ⊞ **Total** 88
Facilities ⨍ 🖪 🚰 ⌢ ⊙ ⌢ 🛇 ☂
🅿 🛇 🛇 ☂⇥⊟A
Nearby Facilities ⌐ ✓ ∪ ℛ
⇌ Banbury
Quiet, elegant and restful park with a ½ mile driveway. Farm walks over 85 acres including woods and riverside. Central for Oxford, Stratford, Blenheim, Warwick, etc..

BENSON
Benson Waterfront, Benson, Oxon, OX10 6SJ.
Std: 01491 **Tel:** 838304
Nearest Town/Resort Benson/Wallingford
Directions We are situated on the A4074 Oxford to Reading road, Benson Waterfront is opposite the B4009. If travelling from London take the M40 to junction 6 then the B4009.
Open April to October
Access Good **Site** Level
Sites Available ▲ ⊞ ⊞ **Total** 22
Facilities ⨍ 🖪 🚰 ⌢ ⊙ ⌢ 🛇 ☂
🅿 🛇 🛇 🛇 ✕⇥🖪
Nearby Facilities ✓ ⤳
⇌ Didcot/Cholsey
Riverside site for boating, fishing and walking.

BLETCHINGDON
Diamond Farm Caravan & Camping Park, Islip Road, Bletchington, Oxford, Oxon, OX5 3DR.
Std: 01869 **Tel:** 350909
Std: 01869 **Fax:** 350059
Nearest Town/Resort Oxford
Directions A34 from Oxford towards th M40. After 4 miles turn left onto B4027, s is 1 mile on the left.
Acreage 3½ **Open** All Year
Access Good **Site** Level
Sites Available ▲ ⊞ ⊞ **Total** 37
Facilities ⨍ 🏠 📰 🚰 ⌢ ⊙ ⌢ 🛇 ☂
🛇 🛇 🛇 🛇 🛇 🛇 ⊛⇥⊟🖪
Nearby Facilities ⌐ ✓
⇌ Islip
Ideal centre for Oxford, Blenheim Pala and the Cotswolds.

CHARLBURY
Cotswold View Caravan & Camping Site, Enstone Road, Charlbury, Oxfordshire, OX7 3JH.
Std: 0800 **Tel:** 085 3474
Std: 01608 **Fax:** 811891
Email: bookings@cotswoldview.f9.co.uk
Website: www.cotswoldview.co.uk
Nearest Town/Resort Charlbury
Directions From Charlbury take the B402 site is 1 mile on the right. From Enstone ta the B4022, site is 2 miles on the left.
Acreage 10 **Open** April to October
Access Good **Site** Level
Sites Available ▲ ⊞ ⊞ **Total** 125
Facilities ⚹ ⨍ 🏠 📰 🚰 ⌢ ⊙ ⌢ 🛇
🛇 🛇 🛇 🛇⇥⊟🖪 🖪
Nearby Facilities ⌐ ✓ ℛ
⇌ Charlbury
Set in the countryside with many places visit including Woodstock (Blenhe Palace), Oxford, Stratford-upon-Avo Bourton-on-the-Water and Stow-on-th Wold.

CHIPPING NORTON
Camping & Caravanning Club Site, Chipping Norton Road, Chadlington, Chipping Norton, Oxon, OX7 3PE.
Std: 01608 **Tel:** 641993
Website:
www.campingandcaravanningclub.co.uk
Directions Take the A44 or the A361 Chipping Norton. Pick up the A361 Burfo road, turn left at the crossroads and the s is 150 yards. From Burford stay on the A3 and turn right at the sign for Chadlington
Open March to October
Site Lev/Slope
Sites Available ▲ ⊞ ⊞ **Total** 105
Facilities ⚹ ⨍ 📰 🚰 ⌢ ⊙ 🛇 🛇 🛇 🛇 🛇🛇⇥🖪
Nearby Facilities ⌐ ∪

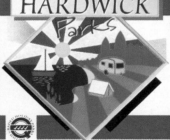

erfect for exploring the Cotswolds. 11 miles
om Blenheim Palace. BTB Graded. Non
embers welcome.

HIPPING NORTON

hurchill Heath Caravan Park, Kingham,
xfordshire, OX7 6UJ.
td: 01608 **Tel:** 658317
earest Town/Resort Stow-on-the-Wold
rections Between Stow-on-the-Wold and
hipping Norton on the B4450.
creage 6 **Open** All Year
ccess Good **Site** Level
tes Available ▲ ⬛ ⬛ **Total** 50
acilities ⨍ ▥ ▣ ⬛ ⌐ ⊙ ⤴ ▱ ◻ ⬛
⬛ ▯⬛ ⛇ ➡⬛
earby Facilities ⌐ ⤢ U
⬥ Kingham
the centre of the Cotswolds.

ENLEY-ON-THAMES

wiss Farm International Camping,
arlow Road, Henley-on-Thames,
xfordshire, RG9 2HY.
d: 01491 **Tel:** 573419
d: 01491 **Fax:** 579934
mail:
quiries@swissfarmcamping.co.uk
ebsite: www.swissfarmcamping.co.uk
earest Town/Resort Henley-on-Thames
rections ½ mile north of Henley on
arlow road A4155.
creage 14 **Open** March to October
ccess Good **Site** Sloping
tes Available ▲ ⬛ ⬛ **Total** 180
acilities ⬛ ⨍ ▣ ▥ ⬛ ⌐ ⊙ ⤴ ▱ ◻ ⬛
⬛ ⨯ ▯ ▥ ▥ ➡ ➡
earby Facilities ⌐ ⤢ ⤢ U
⬥ Henley
eautiful old bridge town famous for its
egatta. Fishing on site.

XFORD

assington Mill Caravan Park, Eynsham
oad, Cassington, Witney, Oxford, OX8
B.
d: 01865 **Tel:** 881081
d: 01865 **Fax:** 884167
mail: cassingtonpark@talk21.com
earest Town/Resort Oxford
rections A40 west of Oxford, 3 miles on
t. A40 east, 1 mile from Eynsham on the
ght.
creage 4 **Open** April to October
ccess Good **Site** Level
tes Available ▲ ⬛ ⬛ **Total** 83
acilities ⬛ ⨍ ▥ ⬛ ⌐ ⊙ ⬛
⬛ ◻ ⬛ ▯➡ ▣ ⬛
earby Facilities ⤢ ⤢
⬥ Oxford
ver, close to Oxford and Blenheim Palace.
oating on site.

WALLINGFORD

ridge Villa Camping & Caravan Park,
rowmarsh Gifford, Wallingford,
xfordshire, OX10 8HB.
d: 01491 **Tel:** 836860
d: 01491 **Fax:** 839103
ebsite: www.oxfordonline.co.uk/
idgevilla
earest Town/Resort Wallingford
rections A4130/500 metres.
creage 4 **Open** 1 February to 31
ecember
ccess Good **Site** Level
tes Available ▲ ⬛ ⬛ **Total** 111
acilities ⨍ ▥ ⬛ ⌐ ⊙ ⤴ ▱ ⬛
⬛ ▯ ▣ ▥ ⬛
earby Facilities ▣ ⤢ ⤢ U ⤴ ℛ
⬥ Cholsey
ithin 400 metres of River Thames.

WITNEY

Hardwick Parks, Downs Road,
Standlake, Nr. Witney, Oxon, OX29 7PZ.
Std: 01865 **Tel:** 300501
Std: 01865 **Fax:** 300037
Email: info@hardwickparks.co.uk
Website: www.hardwickparks.co.uk
Nearest Town/Resort Witney
Directions A415 Witney to Abingdon road,
signposted 4 miles out of Witney on the main
road.
Acreage 40 **Open** April to October
Access Good **Site** Level
Sites Available ▲ ⬛ ⬛ **Total** 250
Facilities ⬛ ⨍ ▥ ⬛ ⌐ ⊙ ⤴ ▱ ◻ ⬛
⬛ ▯ ⬛ ⨯ ▯ ▥ ➡▯ ▣ ⬛
Nearby Facilities ⌐ ⤢ ⤢ U ⤴ ℛ
⬥ Oxford
On the edge of the Cotswolds. Ideal for all
watersports, two lakes on park for fishing,
sailing, boating, jet-skiing and water-skiing.
Parascending.

WITNEY

Lincoln Farm Park, High Street,
Standlake, Nr. Witney, Oxon, OX29 7RH.
Std: 01865 **Tel:** 300239
Std: 01865 **Fax:** 300127
Email: info@lincolnfarm.touristnet.uk.com
Website:
www.lincolnfarm.touristnet.uk.com
Nearest Town/Resort Witney
Directions On the A415 5 miles from Witney
and 9 miles from Abingdon.
Acreage 8 **Open** 1 February to Mid Nov
Access Good **Site** Level
Sites Available ▲ ⬛ ⬛ **Total** 90
Facilities ⬛ ⨍ ▥ ▥ ⬛ ⌐ ⊙ ⤴ ▱ ◻ ⬛
⬛ ▯ ⬛ ⨯ ➡▯ ▣ ⬛
Nearby Facilities ⌐ ⤢ ⤢ ⤴ U ⤴ ℛ
⬥ Oxford
Leisure centre with two indoor swimming
pools, saunas, spa and fitness centre.

RUTLAND

OAKHAM

Wing Caravan & Camping, Wing Hall,
Wing, Oakham, Rutland, LE15 8RY.
Std: 01572 **Tel:** 737283
Std: 01572 **Fax:** 737709
Nearest Town/Resort Oakham
Directions From the A1 take the A47
Peterborough road to Morcott, turn first right
then first left by the White Horse Pub. Go
through the village to the sign Wing, 2½
miles then Wing, 400 yards on the left.
Acreage 9 **Open** All Year
Access Good **Site** Level
Sites Available ▲ ⬛ □ **Total** 45
Facilities ⬛ ▥ ⬛ ⌐ ⬛ ▯➡ ▣ ▣ ⬛
Nearby Facilities ⌐ ⤢ ⤢ ⤴ U ⤴ ℛ
⬥ Oakham
2 miles from Rutland Water for game fishing,
sailing and windsurfing. Bike hire on site.
Course fishing. Limited electric hook-ups.

SHROPSHIRE

BISHOPS CASTLE

Cwnd House Farm, Wentnor, Bishops
Castle, Shropshire.
Std: 01588 **Tel:** Linley 650237
Nearest Town/Resort Church Stretton
Directions Cwnd House Farm is on
Longden Pulverbatch road from Shrewsbury
(13 miles) Bishops Castle is southwest.
From Craven Arms take the A489 to Lydham
Heath, turn right, site is about 1 mile past
the Inn on the Green on the right.

Acreage 2 **Open** May to October
Access Good **Site** Level
Sites Available ▲ ⬛ ⬛ **Total** 10
Facilities ▥ ➡ ⬛
Nearby Facilities ⤢ U
⬥ Church Stretton
Farm site with scenic views, Ideal touring
centre.

BISHOPS CASTLE

The Green Caravan Park, Wentnor,
Bishops Castle, Shropshire, SY9 5EF.
Std: 01588 **Tel:** 650605
Email: info@greencaravanpark.co.uk
Website: www.greencaravanpark.co.uk
Nearest Town/Resort Bishops Castle
Directions Follow brown tourism signs from
the A488 and the A489.
Open Easter to October
Access Good **Site** Level
Sites Available ▲ ⬛ ⬛ **Total** 140
Facilities ⬛ ⨍ ▥ ⬛ ⌐ ⊙ ⤴ ◻ ⬛
⬛ ▯ ⬛ ⨯ ▯ ▥ ➡▯ ▣ ▣
Nearby Facilities ⤢ U ℛ
⬥ Craven Arms
Picturesque, riverside site in an area of
outstanding natural beauty. Superb walking
in the countryside. Excellent birdlife. Central
for touring. David Bellamy Gold Award for
Conservation.

BRIDGNORTH

Stanmore Hall Touring Park, Stourbridge
Road, Bridgnorth, Shropshire, WV15 6DT.
Std: 01746 **Tel:** 761761
Email: stanmore@morris-leisure.co.uk
Website: www.morris-leisure.co.uk
Nearest Town/Resort Bridgnorth
Directions 1¼ miles from Bridgnorth on
A458 to Stourbridge.
Acreage 6 **Open** All Year
Access Good **Site** Level
Sites Available ▲ ⬛ ⬛ **Total** 120
Facilities ⬛ ⨍ ▥ ▥ ⬛ ⌐ ⊙ ⤴ ▱ ◻ ⬛
⬛ ▯ ⬛ ▯➡ ▣ ⬛
Nearby Facilities ⌐ ⤢ ⤢ ⤴ U ⤴ ℛ
⬥ Wolverhampton
Sited around lake and amongst trees, ideal
site for Severn Valley Railway and Iron
Bridge museums. Motorcycles accepted but
families only.

CHURCH STRETTON

Small Batch, Little Stretton, Church
Stretton, Shropshire, SY6 6PW.
Std: 01694 **Tel:** 723358
Nearest Town/Resort Church Stretton
Directions A49 south, 1¼ miles turn right
onto the B4370. Take the second left, at T-
Junction turn right up to site through stream.
Acreage 1½ **Open** Easter to End Sept
Access Good **Site** Level
Sites Available ▲ ⬛ ⬛ **Total** 40
Facilities ▥ ⬛ ⊙ ⬛ ▯➡ ⬛
Nearby Facilities
⬥ Church Stretton
Scenic views and ideal touring.

CLEOBURY MORTIMER

Old Vicarage Activity Centre,
Stottesdon, Nr. Cleobury Mortimer,
Kidderminster, Worcs, DY14 8UH.
Std: 01746 **Tel:** 718222
Std: 01746 **Fax:** 718420
Nearest Town/Resort Cleobury Mortimer/
Bridgnorth
Open All Year
Site Level
Sites Available ▲ **Total** 20
Facilities ⬛ ▥ ⬛ ⌐ ⬛ ▯ ✳ ➡
Nearby Facilities ⤢ U ⤴
⬥ Kidderminster/Ludlow
Quiet farm site attached to a multi-activity
centre.

CLUN

Bush Farm, Clunton, Craven Arms, Shropshire, SY7 0HU.
Std: 01588 **Tel:** 660330
Nearest Town/Resort Clun/Bishops Castle/Ludlow
Directions From the A49 at Craven Arms turn west onto the B4368 signposted Clun, 7 miles into Clunton. Turn left at the Crown Inn, go over a small bridge and turn immediately left. Continue for 500 yards to Bush Farm at the end of the lane.
Acreage 2½ **Open** May **to** September
Access Good **Site** Level
Sites Available A ⊕ ⊜ **Total** 25
Facilities ⚿ ƒ ⅏ ⬚ ⬚ ⅀ ⬚ 🛒 🏪 ╋ ⊟
Nearby Facilities ⌐ ✓ ∪
⚆ Craven Arms
Very peaceful site on the banks of the River Clun. Fishing on site. NO games for children. Ideal base for walking and cycling.

CRAVEN ARMS

Kevindale, Broome, Craven Arms, Salop, SY7 0NT.
Std: 01588 **Tel:** 660326
Nearest Town/Resort Craven Arms
Directions From Craven Arms which is situated on the A49 Hereford to Shewsbury road, take the B4368 Clun/Bishops Castle road in 2 miles take B4367 Knighton road 1¼ miles turn right into Broome Village.
Acreage 2 **Open** April **to** October
Access Good **Site** Level
Sites Available A ⊕ ⊜ **Total** 12
Facilities ⅏ ⬚ ⌐ ⊟ ⅀╋⊟
Nearby Facilities ⌐ ✓ ∪
⚆ Broome
Scenic views, near village inn with good food. Close to Mid Wales Border, ideal walking. Two acre rally field.

ELLESMERE

Fernwood Caravan Park, Lyneal, Nr. Ellesmere, Shropshire, SY12 0QF.
Std: 01948 **Tel:** 710221
Std: 01948 **Fax:** 710324
Nearest Town/Resort Ellesmere
Directions A495 from Ellesmere signposted Whitchurch. In Welshampton, right turn on B5063 signed Wem. Over canal bridge right sign Lyneal.
Acreage 7 **Open** March **to** November
Access Good **Site** Lev/Slope
Sites Available ⊕ ⊜ **Total** 60
Facilities ⚿ ƒ ⅏ ⬚ ⌐ ⊜ ⬚ ⬚ ⅀ ⬚ 🛒 ⅏ ╋ ⊟ ⊟
Nearby Facilities ⌐ ✓ ⚓ ⚆
⚆ Wem
40 acres of woodland open to caravanners. Lake with wildfowl and coarse fishing.

LUDLOW

Westbrook Park, Little Hereford, Ludlow, Shropshire, SY8 4AU.
Std: 01584 **Tel:** 711280
Std: 01584 **Fax:** 711460
Nearest Town/Resort Ludlow
Directions 3 miles west of Tenbury Wells on the A456, enter the village of Little Hereford. Turn left after passing over River Teme bridge, travel 300yds and turn left onto the park.
Acreage 6 **Open** All Year
Access Good **Site** Level
Sites Available A ⊕ ⊜ **Total** 38
Facilities ƒ ⅏ ⬚ ⬚ ⌐ ⊙ ⬚ ⬚ ⬚ ⬚
⅀ ⬚ 🛒 🏪 ⅏ ╋ ⊟ ⊟
Nearby Facilities ⌐ ✓ ∪ ♬
⚆ Ludlow
Well maintained, quality park in a pretty orchard on the banks of the River Teme. ½ a mile of fishing. Short walk to the local inn for good food.

SHREWSBURY

Beaconsfield Farm Holiday Park, Battlefield, Shrewsbury, Shropshire, SY4 4AA.
Std: 01939 **Tel:** 210370
Std: 01939 **Fax:** 210349
Email: mail@beaconsfield-farm.co.uk
Website: www.beaconsfield-farm.co.uk
Nearest Town/Resort Shrewsbury
Directions 1½ miles north of Shrewsbury on the A49.
Acreage 15 **Open** All Year
Access Good **Site** Level
Sites Available ⊕ ⊜ **Total** 60
Facilities ⚿ ƒ ⅏ ⬚ ⬚ ⌐ ⊙ ⊜ ⬚ ⬚ ⬚
⅀ ⬚ 🛒 ✕ ⅏ ⬚ ╋ ⊟ ⊟
Nearby Facilities ⌐ ✓ ⚓ ∪ ♬
⚆ Shrewsbury
5 Star, well landscaped, level park with fly and coarse fishing and a bowling green. ADULTS (Over 25 years) ONLY JULY & AUGUST. 1½ miles to Park & Ride. Ideal base for Shrewsbury and the Welsh border. Holiday homes for sale and hire.

SHREWSBURY

Cartref Caravan & Camping Site, Cartref, Fords Heath, Nr. Shrewsbury, Shropshire.
Std: 01743 **Tel:** 821688
Directions From Shrewsbury bypass A5 trunk road take the A458 Welshpool West. 2 miles to Ford Village, turn south at Ford, follow camp signs. Signposted from the A5 bypass on the Montgomery junction B4386.
Acreage 1½ **Open** Easter **to** October
Access Good **Site** Level
Sites Available A ⊕ ⊜ **Total** 25+
Facilities ⚿ ƒ ⅏ ⬚ ⌐ ⊙ ⬚ ⅀ 🛒 ╋ ⊟ ⊠

Nearby Facilities ⌐ ✓ ⚽
⚆ Shrewsbury
Peaceful countryside. Ideal for touring or an overnight stop.

SHREWSBURY

Oxon Hall Touring Park, Welshpool Road, Bicton Heath, Shrewsbury, Shropshire, SY3 5FB.
Std: 01743 **Tel:** 340868
Email: oxon@morris-leisure.co.uk
Website: www.morris-leisure.co.uk
Nearest Town/Resort Shrewsbury
Directions 1¼ miles from the town centre on the A458, adjacent to Oxon Park and Ride.
Acreage 22 **Open** All Year
Access Good **Site** Level
Sites Available A ⊕ ⊜ **Total** 130
Facilities ⚿ ƒ ⅏ ⬚ ⬚ ⌐ ⊙ ⬚ ⬚ ⬚ ⬚
⅀ ⬚ 🛒 ⅏ ╋ ⊟ ⊟
Nearby Facilities ⌐ ✓ ⚽ ∪ ♬
⚆ Shrewsbury
Well landscaped, level site adjoining local Park and Ride facilities, in a rural situation. Ideal for visiting Shrewsbury and the Welsh border counties. Motorcycles accepted, but families only.

SHREWSBURY

Severn House, Montford Bridge, Shrewsbury, Shropshire, SY4 1ED.
Std: 01743 **Tel:** 850229
Email: severnhouse@netscapeonline.co.uk
Nearest Town/Resort Shrewsbury
Directions 4 miles north west of Shrewsbury on the A5 towards Oswestry and North Wales. At signposts for the site turn off the B4380 and Montford Bridge is ½ mile.
Acreage 2½ **Open** April **to** October
Access Good **Site** Level
Sites Available A ⊕ ⬚ **Total** 25
Facilities ƒ ⅏ ⬚ ⌐ ⊙ ⬚ ⬚ ⅀ 🛒 ╋ ⬚
Nearby Facilities
⚆ Shrewsbury
Graded Park. Riverside site with 30 metres of river for fishing. Dog walk, local shop, pub and meals nearby. Regular bus service.

TELFORD

Camping & Caravanning Club Site, Ebury Hill, Ring Bank, Haughton, Telford, Shropshire, TF6 6BU.
Std: 01743 **Tel:** 709334
Website:
www.campingandcaravanningclub.co.uk
Nearest Town/Resort Shrewsbury
Directions From the A5/A49 take the B5063 signposted Newport, pass Haughmond Abbey and turn left signposted Hadnall. Site is on the left in approx. 1 mile.

creage 18 **Open** March **to** November
ccess Good **Site** Lev/Slope
tes Available ▲ ♨ ♿ **Total** 100
acilities ⚡ 🏕 🗓 🛁 🚿 🍴 🛒 ⊡
earby Facilities 🏕 🗲 ⚓
☀ Shrewsbury

et on an ancient Iron Age hill fort, with anoramic views. Close to Shrewsbury and onbridge Gorge. BTB Graded. Non embers welcome.

ELFORD

evern Gorge Park, Bridgnorth Road, veedale, Telford, Shropshire, TF7 4JB.
d: 01952 **Tel:** 684789
d: 01952 **Fax:** 684789
earest **Town/Resort** Telford
rections From the M54 junction 4, follow gns (A442) for Kidderminster for 1 mile. nen take the A442 signposted dderminster to the first roundabout rockton roundabout 2¾ miles. Follow own Severn Gorge Caravan Park gnposts, 1 mile to the site.
creage 10 **Open** All Year
ccess Good **Site** Level
tes Available ▲ ♨ ♿ **Total** 51
acilities ♿ ⚡ 🗓 🛁 🚿 🍴 🛒 ⊡ ☎
⚡ 🗓 🛁 🚿 ❄ 🍴 ⊡ ⊡
earby Facilities 🏕 🗲 ⚓ ⛳ U ₽
☀ Telford
onbridge, Gorge and museums.

EM

ower Lacon Caravan Park, Wem, hropshire, SY4 5RP.
d: 01939 **Tel:** 232376
d: 01939 **Fax:** 233606
mail: info@llcp.co.uk
ebsite: www.llcp.co.uk
earest **Town/Resort** Wem
irections 1 mile from Wem on the B5065. om the A49 then the B5065, 3 miles.
creage 48 **Open** All Year
ccess Good **Site** Level
tes Available ▲ ♨ ♿ **Total** 270
acilities ♿ ⚡ 🗓 🛁 🚿 🍴 🛒 ⊡ ☎
⚡ 🛒 🗓 🛁 ✕ ♀ 🍴 🛒 ❄ ⊡
earby Facilities 🏕 🗲
☀ Wem

WHITCHURCH
Roden View Caravan & Camping, Roden View, Dobsons Bridge, Whixall, Whitchurch, Shropshire, SY13 2QL.
Std: 01948 **Tel:** 710320
Email: rodenview@talk21.com
Nearest Town/Resort Wem
Directions From Shrewsbury Wem Church turn left after second garage, then turn right for Whixall, at the next T-Junction turn left then immediately right, 2½ miles to the next T-Junction turn right. ½ mile the house is on the right before Dobsons Bridge.
Acreage 4½ **Open** March **to** October
Access Good **Site** Level
Sites Available ♨ ♿ **Total** 5
Facilities ⚡ 🗓 🛁 🚿 🍴 🛒 ⊡ ☎ 🏕 ♀ 🛒 ❄ ⊡
Nearby Facilities 🏕 🗲 ⚓ ⚓
☀ Wem

Near to the Shropshire Union Canal and Whixall Moss. 5 miles from Ellesmere, Shropshire's Lake District. There is a washing machine available for use.

SOMERSET
BATH
Bath Chew Valley Caravan Park, Ham Lane, Bishop Sutton, North East Somerset, BS39 5TZ.
Std: 01275 **Tel:** 332127 **Fax:** 332664
Email: ray@bathchewvalley.co.uk
Nearest Town/Resort Bath
Directions Approaching Bath on the A37 or the A38 Bristol to Wells or Bristol to Taunton roads, take the A368 which links both to Bishop Sutton, turn opposite the Red Lion Pub.
Acreage 2¼ **Open** All Year
Access Good **Site** Level
Sites Available ▲ ♨ ♿ **Total** 33
Facilities ⚡ 🗓 🛁 🚿 🍴 🛒 ⊡ ☎ 🗓 🛁 🚿 ❄ 🛒 ⊡
Nearby Facilities 🏕 🗲 ⚓ ⛳ U ₽ ✗
☀ Bath

ADULTS ONLY PARK. A site for peace and tranquility, set in an area of outstanding natural beauty. Featured on BBC's Gardeners World. ETB 5 Star Graded.

BATH
Bath Marina & Caravan Park, Brassmill Lane, Bath, Somerset, BA1 3JT.
Std: 01225 **Tel:** 428778 **Fax:** 428778
Nearest Town/Resort Bath
Directions 2 miles west of Bath on the A4 at Newbridge, turn left at Capricorn Motors into Brassmill Lane, take the first turning on the right.
Acreage 4 **Open** All Year
Access Good **Site** Level
Sites Available ♨ ♿ **Total** 88
Facilities ♿ ⚡ ♀ 🗓 🛁 🚿 🍴 🛒 ⊡ ☎ ♀ 🗓 🛁 🚿 ❄ 🛒 ⊡
Nearby Facilities 🏕 🗲 ⚓ U ₽
☀ Bath

Alongside a river, picturesque. 3 min walk from park and ride bus.

BATH
Newton Mill Camping & Caravan Park, Newton Road, Bath, Somerset, BA2 9JF.
Std: 01225 **Tel:** 333909
Email: newtonmill@hotmail.com
Website: www.campinginbath.co.uk
Nearest Town/Resort Bath
Directions On the A4 Bath to Bristol road, at the roundabout by the Globe Public House take the exit signposted Newton St. Loe, Park is 1 mile on the left.
Acreage 42 **Open** All Year
Access Good **Site** Level
Sites Available ▲ ♨ ♿ **Total** 195
Facilities ♿ ♀ ⚡ 🗓 🛁 🚿 🍴 🛒 ⊙ 🗓 ♀ 🛒 ✕ ♀ ⊓ ♣ ❄ 🛒 ⊡ ☎
Nearby Facilities 🏕 🗲 U ₽
☀ Bath

A beautiful, idyllic setting in a hidden valley, close to the city centre. Very frequent bus service. Near to the traffic free Bath to Bristol cycle path.

BREAN SANDS
Channel View Caravan Park, Brean Down Road, Brean, Burnham-on-Sea, Somerset, TA8 2RR.
Std: 01278 **Tel:** 751055 **Fax:** 751055
Nearest Town/Resort Brean Sands
Directions Leave the M5 at junction 22 and follow signs to Burnham-on-Sea, Berrow and Brean. Site is ¼ mile past the Brean Down Inn on the left hand side.
Acreage 3 **Open** April **to** Mid Oct

Holiday Resort UNITY

Brean Sands, Somerset TA8 2RB

English Tourism Council

★★★
HOLIDAY PARK

DAVID BELLAMY CONSERVATION AWARD
SILVER

**Call
01278 751235 or
book online
www.hru.co.uk**

*All the facilities
you could
possibly want!*

**Lodges, Caravans,
Villas and Tents for
hire and sale.
Pitches for
Caravans, Tents and
Motorhomes.**

Exclusive Cades Offer

Family of Four - 7 Nights for £35
(hook up £10 extra)

Choose dates to suit you from:
Feb 15th-Mar 28th, April 5th-May 3rd,
May 7th-30th, June 10th-July 19th,
Sept 2nd-Nov 17th

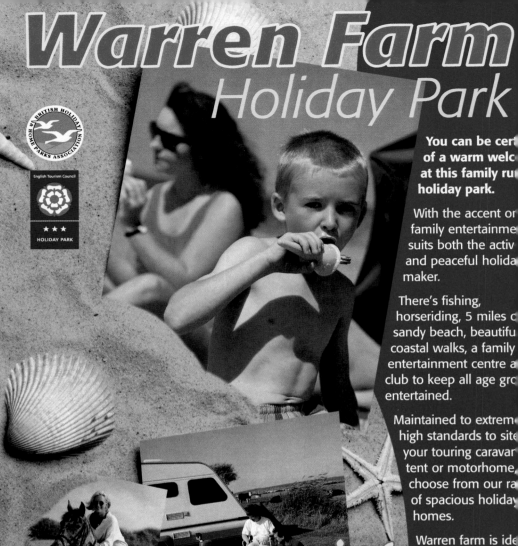

Access Good Site Gentle Slope
Sites Available ▲ ⊕ ⊟ Total 50
Facilities ⑁ ⚡ ⌗ ⊞ ☎ ⌂ ⊙ ⊣ ☕ ☖⊣⊡
Nearby Facilities ⌂ ✓ ⚓ ⤢ ∪
⊁ Highbridge
Quiet and friendly site, on the beach side
overlooking farmland.

BREAN SANDS

Holiday Resort Unity at Unity Farm,
Coast Road, Brean Sands, Somerset, TA8
7RB.
Std: 01278 **Tel:** 751235 **Fax:** 751539
Email: admin@hru.co.uk
Website: www.hru.co.uk
Nearest Town/Resort Burnham-on-Sea
Directions Leave M5 at junction 22. Follow
signs for Berrow and Brean Leisure Park,
then on right 4½ miles from M5.
Acreage 200 **Open** February **to** January
Access Good **Site** Level
Sites Available ▲ ⊕ ⊟ **Total** 800
Facilities ⑁ ⌗ ⊟ ⊞ ☎ ⌂ ⊙ ⊣ ⊿ ⊡ ☕
☖ ⚓ ⅃⊙⊠✕⌷⚑⅄⊹※⊣⊡⊟⊡
Nearby Facilities ⌂ ✓ ⚓ ⤢ ∪ ⊿ ♪ ⊁
⊁ Weston-Super-Mare
200yds from 7 mile beach, own leisure
centre with 30 fun fair attractions, pool
complex with 3 giant water slides, 18 hole
golf course, lake for fishing, horse riding and
10 Pin Bowling. Family entertainment -
Easter to October. Special offers for young
families and OAPs in June and Sept.

BREAN SANDS

Northam Farm Caravan & Touring Park,
Brean, Nr. Burnham-on-Sea, Somerset,
TA8 2SE.
Std: 01278 **Tel:** 751244/751222 **Fax:**
751150
Nearest Town/Resort Burnham-on-Sea
Directions M5 Junction 22. Follow signs to

Brean, ¼ mile past Leisure Park on
righthand side.
Acreage 30 **Open** Easter **to** October
Access Good **Site** Level
Sites Available ▲ ⊕ ⊟ **Total** 350
Facilities ⑁ ⚡ ⌗ ⊞ ☎ ⌂ ⊙ ⊣ ⊿ ⊡ ☕
☖ ⅃⊙⊠✕⌷⚑⊹※⊣⊡⊟
Nearby Facilities ⌂ ✓ ⚓ ⤢ ∪ ⊿
⊁ Weston-super-Mare
Ideal base for seeing Somerset. 200 metres
to sandy beach. Our Seagull Inn with family
entertainment is within easy walking
distance. Excellent facilities and a fishing
lake on park. Café/Take-away food. AA 3
Pennants.

BREAN SANDS

Warren Farm Holiday Park, Brean
Sands, Burnham-on-Sea, Somerset, TA8
2RP.
Std: 01278 **Tel:** 751227 **Fax:** 751033
Email: enquiries@warren-farm.co.uk
Website: www.warren-farm.co.uk
Nearest Town/Resort Burnham-on-Sea
Directions Leave M5 at junction 22, follow
signs to Burnham-on-Sea, Berrow and
Brean on the B3140. Site is 1¼ miles past
the leisure centre.
Acreage 50 **Open** April **to** Mid October
Access Good **Site** Level
Sites Available ▲ ⊕ ⊟ **Total** 500
Facilities ⑁ ⚡ ⌗ ⊞ ☎ ⌂ ⊙ ⊣ ⊿ ⊡ ☕
☖ ⅃⊙⊠✕⅄⚑⌷⊹※⊣⊡⊟
Nearby Facilities ⌂ ✓ ⚓ ⤢ ∪
⊁ Weston-super-Mare
Flat, grassy, family park with excellent
facilities. 100 metres from 5 miles of sandy
beach. Dogs are only allowed with tourers
and campers, not in hire vans.

BRIDGWATER

Currypool Mills, Cannington, Bridgwater,
Somerset, TA5 2NH.
Std: 01278 **Tel:** 671135
Email: currypool.mill@btinternet.com
Nearest Town/Resort Bridgwater
Directions From Bridgwater take the A39
Minehead road, after approx. 5 miles take a
left hand turning signposted Spaxton and
Aisholt. Currypool is approx. ½ a mile on
the left.
Open Easter **to** End October
Access Good **Site** Level
Sites Available ▲ ⊡ **Total** 35
Facilities ⌗ ⊞ ☎ ⌂ ⊣ ⊿ ⊡ ☕
☖ ⊙⊠⅄⊹※⊣⊡
Nearby Facilities ⌂ ✓ ⚓ ⤢ ∪ ♪
⊁ Bridgwater
Quiet location near the Quantock Hills and
Somerset coast. Set amongst streams and
waterfalls. Dog walking fields, putting and
croquet.

BRIDGWATER

Mill Farm Caravan & Camping Park,
Fiddington, Bridgwater, Somerset, TA5
1JQ.
Std: 01278 **Tel:** 732286 **Fax:** 732281
Website: www.millfarm.20m.com
Nearest Town/Resort Bridgwater
Directions Leave the M5 at junction 23 or
24, through Bridgwater, take the A39 west
for 6 miles. Turn right to Fiddington, then
follow camping signs.
Acreage 12 **Open** All Year
Access Good **Site** Level
Sites Available ▲ ⊕ ⊟ **Total** 250
Facilities ⑁ ⌗ ⊞ ☎ ⌂ ⊙ ⊣ ⊿ ⊡ ☕
☖ ⅃⊙⊠⊞⚑⌷⅄⊹※⊣⊡
Nearby Facilities ⌂ ✓ ⤢ ∪ ♪
⊁ Bridgwater

Free boating, canoe and trampoline hire on site. Walking, riding and fishing. Quantock Hills 2 miles. Beach 4 miles. Exmoor, Cheddar Gorge, Wookey Caves within easy reach. Tourist Information Room. Free swimming and paddling pools and luxury indoor heated pools. Children's pony rides on site. Off licence, licensed club in peak season, large sandpit, Splash Pool. Free hot showers and 3 new toilet blocks. Holiday cottage to let.

BRIDGWATER

The Fairways International Touring Caravan & Camping Park, Bath Road, Bawdrip, Bridgwater, Somerset, TA7 8PP.
Std: 01278 **Tel:** 685569 **Fax:** 685569
Email: fairwaysint@btinternet.com
Nearest Town/Resort Bridgwater
Directions 3¼ miles on Glastonbury side of Bridgwater. 1½ miles off M5 junction 23 at junction A39 and B3141.
Acreage 5¾ **Open** 1st March **to** 15th Nov
Access Good **Site** Level
Sites Available A � ♨ **Total** 200
Facilities ♿ ƒ ⊞ ⅏ ♨ ┌ ⊙ ⇃ ♨ ☐ ☎
SⓔⓁ ⓖ ♨ ⓣ ♨ ⋔ ⊛ ➕ ☐
Nearby Facilities ┌ ✓ ⚓ ⟋ ⟋
≠ Bridgwater
Ideal for touring Somerset. Off Licence. Winner of 'Loo of the Year Award' every year from 1994 to 2001.

BRUTON

Batcombe Vale Caravan & Camping Park, Batcombe, Shepton Mallet, Somerset, BA4 6BW.
Std: 01749 **Tel:** 830246
Email: donaldsage@compuserve.com
Website: www.batcombevale.co.uk
Nearest Town/Resort Bruton
Directions Access must be off the B3081

between Bruton and Evercreech from where it is well signed.
Acreage 7 **Open** May **to** September
Access Good **Site** Level
Sites Available A ♨ ♨ **Total** 32
Facilities ƒ ⊞ ⅏ ♨ ┌ ⊙ ⇃ ☎
Ⓛ ⓖ ♨ ➕ ☐
Nearby Facilities ┌ ⚓ ∪
≠ Bruton
Own secluded valley of lakes and wild gardens. Fishing and boating on site. Near Longleat, Stourhead and Glastonbury. All shops are 2 miles away. Jet skiing nearby.

BURNHAM-ON-SEA

Burnham Touring Park, At Burnham-on-Sea Association of Sports Clubs, Stoddens Road, Burnham-on-Sea, Somerset, TA8 1NZ.
Std: 01278 **Tel:** 788355 **Fax:** 751885
Website: www.basc.co.uk
Nearest Town/Resort Burnham-on-Sea
Directions Leave the M5 at junction 22 for Burnham-on-Sea, after 1 mile at roundabout by Tescos turn right and park is 1 mile, entrance over the cattle grid.
Acreage 23 **Open** All Year
Access Good **Site** Level
Sites Available A ♨ ♨
Facilities ♿ ♨ ƒ ⊞ ⅏ ♨ ┌ ⊙ ☎
ⓁⓏ ♨ ♥ ➕ ☐ A
Nearby Facilities ┌ ✓ ⚓ ⟋ ⟋ ℛ
≠ Highbridge
Rallies Only. Good rally site for up to 150 units. Extremely quiet and very spacious. Suits self-contained as toilets are unisex. 1 mile from the beach and shops.

BURNHAM-ON-SEA

Burnham-on-Sea Holiday Village, Marine Drive, Burnham-on-Sea, Somerset, TA8 1LA.
Std: 01278 **Tel:** 783391 **Fax:** 793776
Email: burnham@bourneleisuregroup.co.uk
Website: www.british-holidays.co.uk
Nearest Town/Resort Burnham-on-Sea
Directions Leave the M5 at junction 22, turn left at the roundabout onto the A38 Highbridge. Continue over the mini roundabout and railway bridge, turn next left onto the B3139 to Burnham-on-Sea. Turn left at the Total Garage into Marine Drive and the park is 400 yards on the left.
Acreage 95 **Open** March **to** November
Access Good **Site** Level
Sites Available A ♨ ♨ **Total** 75
Facilities ƒ ⊞ ⅏ ♨ ┌ ⊙ ⇃ ⚑ ☐
Sℛ ⓁⓏ ⓖ ♨ ✗ ♥ ⅏ ♨ ⚑ ✈ ⊛ ☐ ☐
Nearby Facilities ┌ ✓ ⚓ ⟋ ∪ ⟋ ℛ
≠ Highbridge
Near the beach. Fishing, golf and tennis park. Cafe bar and two entertainment venues.

BURNHAM-ON-SEA

Diamond Farm Caravan & Touring Park, Diamond Farm, Weston Road, Brean, Nr Burnham-on-Sea, Somerset, TA8 2RL.
Std: 01278 **Tel:** 751263
Email: trevor@diamondfarm42.freeserve.co.uk
Website: www.diamondfarm.co.uk
Nearest Town/Resort Burnham-on-Sea
Directions M5 junction 22, follow signs Brean, ½ mile past leisure park turn right Lympsham/Weston-super-Mare. Diamond Farm is 800yds on the left hand side.

DIAMOND FARM CARAVAN AND TOURING PARK

WESTON ROAD, BREAN, NR B.O.S, SOMERSET TA8 2RL
TEL: (01278) 751041 / 751263   Website: www.diamondfarm.co.uk

A quiet family site on a working farm alongside the River Axe, and still only 800 yards from 5 miles of beaches at Brean. All modern facilities on a flat site including showers, toilet blocks, laundry, shop and cafe, electric hook-ups and telephone. Free river fishing and many walks along the river are all available on site. An ideal base to enjoy the delights of the countryside, whilst also near enough to all the attractions that Somerset and Brean has to offer. Bungalow by the sea also available for hire.

Acreage 6 **Open** April **to** 15 October
Access Good **Site** Level
Sites Available A ⚑ ⊟ **Total** 100
Facilities & ⚒ ⚐ ⊞ ⚓ ⌐ ⊙ ⊿ 🚿 ⊟ ⚑ ☎
⚒ ⚑ ⊟ ⊠ ✕ ⚑ ⊛ ⊬ ⊟
Nearby Facilities ⌐ ⚑ ⚓ ⚘ ∪ ⊅ ⋇ ⚡
⚡ Weston-super-Mare
A quiet, family site alongside River Axe and only 800yds from the beach. River fishing available on site.

BURNHAM-ON-SEA

Home Farm Holiday Park & Country Club, Edithmead, Burnham-on-Sea, Somerset, TA9 4HD.
Std: 01278 **Tel:** 788888 **Fax:** 780113
Nearest Town/Resort Burnham-on-Sea
Directions M5 Junction 22, follow A38. Home Farm signposted from the B3140 road in to Burnham-on-Sea.
Acreage 44 **Open** All Year
Access Good **Site** Level
Sites Available A ⚑ ⊟ **Total** 800
Facilities & ⚒ ⚐ ⊞ ⚑ ⚑ ⚓ ⌐ ⊙ ⊿ 🚿
⊟
⚒ ⚑ ⊟ ⊠ ✕ ⚑ ⚑ ⚑ ⊛ ⊬ ⊟ ⚑
Nearby Facilities ⌐ ⚑ ⚓ ⚘ ∪ ⊅ ⊅ ⋇
⚡ Highbridge
Outdoor heated swimming pool and fishing lakes on site. Near the beach.

BURNHAM-ON-SEA

Southfield Farm Caravan Park, Brean, Nr. Burnham-on-Sea, Somerset, TA8 2RL.
Std: 01278 **Tel:** 751233
Nearest Town/Resort Burnham-on-Sea
Directions 4 miles north along coast road from Burnham-on-Sea (well signposted). Site is in Brean village.
Acreage 10 **Open** Spring Bank Holiday **to** September
Access Good **Site** Level
Sites Available A ⚑ ⊟
Facilities & ⚒ ⚐ ⚑ ⚓ ⌐ ⊙ ⊿ ☎
⚑ ⚑ ⊟ ⊙ ⚑ ⊬ ⊟
Nearby Facilities ⌐ ⚑ ⚓ ⚘ ∪ ⊅ ⊅ ⚡
⚡ Weston-super-Mare
Adjacent beach, good centre for touring Somerset. Local entertainments nearby.

CHARD

Alpine Grove Touring Park, Forton, Chard, Somerset, TA20 4HD.
Std: 01460 **Tel:** 63479
Email: ask@alpinegrovetouringpark.co.uk
Website: www.alpinegrovetouringpark.co.uk
Nearest Town/Resort Chard
Directions Turn left off the A30 Crewkerne to Chard road onto the B3167 (Axminster). In 1½ miles at the crossroads turn right onto the B3162 signposted Forton. Site is on the

right in about ½ mile.
Acreage 7½ **Open** 1 April **to** End Sept
Access Good **Site** Level
Sites Available A ⚑ ⊟ **Total** 40
Facilities ⚒ ⊞ ⚑ ⚑ ⚓ ⌐ ⊙ ⊿ ⚑ ⚑ ⊙ ⚑ ⚑ ⊛ ⊛ ⊬
Nearby Facilities ⌐ ⚑ ⚓ ⚘ ∪
⚡ Axminster
Pretty woodland site, set amongst oak trees and Rhododendrons. Superb point from which to travel the South and South West coast. Numerous places of interest to visit nearby, only 2 miles from Cricket St Thomas Wildlife Park. Shingle and sandy beach 11 miles. All weather pitches.

CHARD

South Somerset Holiday Park, The Turnpike, Howley, Chard, Somerset, TA20 3EA.
Std: 01460 **Tel:** 62221/66036 **Fax:** 66246
Nearest Town/Resort Chard
Directions 3 miles west of Chard on the A30.
Acreage 7 **Open** All Year
Access Good **Site** Level
Sites Available A ⚑ ⊟ **Total** 110
Facilities & ⚒ ⊞ ⚑ ⚑ ⚓ ⌐ ⊙ ⊿ ⊙ ⚑ ⚑ ⊬ ⊟ ⚑
Nearby Facilities ⌐ ⚑ ∪ ⊅
⚡ Crewkerne
Scenic views and ideal touring. AA 4 Pennants.

WELCOME TO SOMERSET'S ULTIMATE FAMILY DESTINATION

FREE COLOUR BROCHURE

PARK FEATURES...

OPEN ALL YEAR ROUND

☆ AMPLE HOOK UPS
☆ HARD STANDINGS
☆ BATHROOMS & LAUNDERETTE
☆ DISABLED FACILITIES
☆ OPEN AIR SWIMMING POOL (HEATED IN PEAK TIMES)
☆ CABARET CLUB & RESTAURANT
☆ SUPERMARKET
☆ GUESTS WITH PETS AREA
☆ FISHING LAKES
☆ POOL SIDE RESTAURANT & TAKEAWAY (PEAK TIMES)

Set in 44 acres of beautiful parkland **HOME FARM** is one mile from the quaint resort of Burnham-on-Sea which offers miles of golden sand.

HOME FARM HOLIDAY PARK & COUNTRY CLUB
EDITHMEAD, BURNHAM-on-SEA,
SOMERSET TA9 4HD
Telephone: 01278 78 88 88

CHARD

The Beeches, Catchgate Lane, Wambrook, Chard, Somerset, TA20 3PS.
Std: 01460 **Tel:** 66828
Nearest Town/Resort Chard
Directions 1 mile from Chard on the A30 turn right. Pass the bungalow on the left and go up the lane 500 yards, name is on the gate on the right.
Acreage 5 **Open** All Year
Access Good **Site** Level
Sites Available Å ♦ ⊟ **Total** 5
Facilities ☎ ᎒ ⥀
Nearby Facilities ┌ ✔ ⚓ ⥁ ∪ ♫
✈ Axminster/Crewkerne
Unspoilt countryside with lovely walks. Ideal touring. Good food at the pubs in Wambrook, Combe, St Nichols and Wadeford. 30 minute drive to Seaton, Beer, Lyme Regis etc..

CHEDDAR

Broadway House Holiday, Touring Caravan & Camping Park, Cheddar, Somerset, BS27 3DB.
Std: 01934 **Tel:** 742610 **Fax:** 744950
Email: enquiries@broadwayhouse.uk.com
Website: www.broadwayhouse.uk.com
Nearest Town/Resort Cheddar Gorge
Directions Exit 22 (M5) 8 miles. Follow brown tourist signs for Cheddar Gorge. We are midway between Cheddar and Axbridge on the A371.
Acreage 25 **Open** March **to** November
Access Good **Site** Level
Sites Available Å ♦ ⊟ **Total** 400
Facilities & ╢ ⊞ ⅏ ⬜ ㎌ ┌ ⊙ ⌀ ᎒ ▱ ☏ ⊟
⋇ ⊙ ⊗ ✕ ▽ ⓜ ♠ 𝄞 ⊛ ⥁ ▱ ⊟
Nearby Facilities ┌ ✔ ∪ ♫ ⚡
✈ Weston-super-Mare
Centrally situated in wonderful touring area, i.e. Wells, Bristol and Weston-super-Mare.

CHEDDAR

Bucklegrove Caravan & Camping Park, Rodney Stoke, Cheddar, Somerset, BS27 3UZ.
Std: 01749 **Tel:** 870261 **Fax:** 870101
Email: info@bucklegrove.co.uk
Website: www.bucklegrove.co.uk
Nearest Town/Resort Wells/Cheddar
Directions Midway Between Wells and Cheddar on the A371.
Open March **to** January
Access Good **Site** Lev/Slope
Sites Available Å ♦ ⊟ **Total** 125
Facilities & ╢ ⊞ ⅏ ⬜ ㎌ ┌ ⊙ ⌀ ᎒ ▱ ☏ ⊟
⋇ ⊙ ⊗ ✕ ▽ ⓜ ♠ 𝄞 🅿 ▱ ⊟
Nearby Facilities ┌ ✔ ⚓ ⥁ ∪ ♫ ⚡
✈ Weston Super Mare
Friendly, family run park with a free indoor

---

heated pool. Ideal touring centre on the south side of the Mendip Hills with scenic views and walking.

CHEDDAR

Cheddar Bridge Park, Draycott Road, Cheddar, Somerset, BS27 3RJ.
Std: 01934 **Tel:** 743048 **Fax:** 743048
Email: melandsuepike217@aol.com
Nearest Town/Resort Cheddar
Directions On the A371, 100 yards south of Cheddar Village.
Acreage 2 **Open** March **to** October
Access Good **Site** Level
Sites Available Å ♦ ⊟ **Total** 45
Facilities & ╢ ⊞ ⅏ ⬜ ㎌ ┌ ⊙ ⌀ ᎒ ▱ ☏
⋇ ▽ ⅃ ⊙ ⊗ ♠ 🅿 ▱ Å
Nearby Facilities ┌ ✔ ⚓ ⥁ ∪ ♫
✈ Weston-Super-Mare
ADULTS ONLY SITE. NEW park opening in 2002. Riverside location with luxury facilities. Walks to Cheddar Gorge, Mendips and Caves.

CHEDDAR

Froglands Farm Caravan & Camping Park, Froglands Farm, Cheddar, Somerset, BS27 3RH.
Std: 01934 **Tel:** 742058
Nearest Town/Resort Cheddar/Weston-super-Mare
Directions On main A371, 150yds past village church.
Acreage 4 **Open** Easter **to** October
Access Good **Site** Level
Sites Available Å ♦ ⊟ **Total** 68
Facilities ╢ ⊞ ⬜ ㎌ ┌ ⊙ ⌀ ᎒ ▱ ☏
⋇ ▽ ⅃ ⊙ ⊗ ♠ 🅿 ⊟
Nearby Facilities ┌ ✔ ⚓ ⥁ ∪ ♫
✈ Weston-super-Mare
Walking distance, village shops, pubs, Gorge and Caves. AA 3 Pennants.

CHEDDAR

Netherdale Caravan & Camping Site, Bridgwater Road, Sidcot, Winscombe, Somerset, BS25 1NH.
Std: 01934 **Tel:** 843007/843481
Email: netherdale@firmvisual.com
Website: www.firmvisual/netherdale
Nearest Town/Resort Cheddar
Directions From Weston-super-Mare follow A371 to join A38 at Sidcot corner, site ¼ mile south. From Wells and Cheddar follow A371 westwards to join A38 a mile south of site.
Acreage 3½ **Open** March **to** October
Access Good **Site** Lev/Slope
Sites Available Å ♦ ⊟ **Total** 25
Facilities ╢ ⬜ ㎌ ┌ ⊙ ⌀ ᎒
⅃ ⊙ ✕ ♠ 🅿 ⊟
Nearby Facilities ┌ ✔ ⚓ ⥁ ∪ ♫ ⚡
✈ Weston-super-Mare

Excellent walking area, footpath from site to valley and Mendip Hills adjoining. Good views. Ideal touring centre for Somerset. Many historical places and beaches within easy reach of site. Pets welcome on a lead. Only individual motorcycles accepted, not groups. 3 miles from a dry ski slope and a well equipped sports centre.

CHEDDAR

Rodney Stoke Inn, Rodney Stoke, Nr. Cheddar, Somerset, BS27 3XB.
Std: 01749 **Tel:** 870209 **Fax:** 870406
Email: landlord@rodneystokeinn.co.uk
Nearest Town/Resort Cheddar
Directions Take the A371 from Cheddar towards Wells for 3 miles.
Acreage 2 **Open** All Year
Access Good **Site** Level
Sites Available Å ♦ ⊟ **Total** 31
Facilities & ╢ ⬜ ᎒ ┌ ⊙ ⊟
⊗ ✕ ▽ ♠ 𝄞 ▱ ⊟ ⊟
Nearby Facilities ┌ ✔ ⚓ ∪ ♫
✈ Weston-Super-Mare
Central location for Cheddar Gorge and Caves, the City of Wells and Wookey Hole Caves.

CHEDDAR

Splott Farm, Blackford, Near Wedmore, Somerset, BS28 4PD.
Std: 01278 **Tel:** 641522
Nearest Town/Resort Burnham-on-Sea/Cheddar
Directions Leave M5 at junction 22, 2 miles to Highbridge, take B3139 Highbridge/Wells road, about 5 miles.
Acreage 4¼ **Open** March **to** November
Access Good **Site** Gentle Slope
Sites Available Å ♦ ⊟ **Total** 32
Facilities ╢ ⬜ ᎒ ┌ ⊙ ⅃ ▽ ♠ 𝄞 ♫
Nearby Facilities ┌ ✔ ⚓ ⥁ ∪ ♫ ⚡ ⚡
✈ Highbridge
Very peaceful site with views of the Mendip Hills (and Quantocks), very rural area. Ideal touring, Weston-super-Mare, Wells, Cheddar, Burnham-on-Sea, Wookey.

CLEVEDON

Warrens Holiday Village, Colehouse Lane, Clevedon, Somerset, BS21 6TQ.
Std: 01275 **Tel:** 871666
Email: warrensholidays@bigfoot.com
Nearest Town/Resort Weston-super-Mare
Directions M5 junction 20, follow road towards Congresbury for 1 mile.
Acreage 12 **Open** March **to** January
Access Good **Site** Level
Sites Available Å ♦ ⊟ **Total** 150
Facilities & ╢ ⬜ ᎒ ┌ ⊙ ⌀ ᎒ ▱ ⅃ ⅏ ⊗ ✕ ♠ ㎌ ⊟
Nearby Facilities ┌ ✔ ⚓ ⥁ ∪ ♫
✈ Yatton

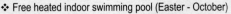

Taste The Real Cheddar!

at BROADWAY HOUSE

Holiday Touring Caravan & Camping Park

- HOLIDAY CARAVANS FOR HIRE
- PREMIER TOURING AND CAMPING PITCHES
- FREE HEATED SWIMMING POOL
- FREE MARVELLOUS ADVENTURE PLAYGROUND/PIXIE AREA
- DISABLED AND BABIES ROOM
- CORNER SHOP WITH THE FRIENDLY SERVICE
- COME AND SEE OUR PET LLAMAS AND PARROT
- FREE ENTRANCE TO "ENGLISH PUB" & FAMILY ROOM
- BARBEQUES FOR YOUR OWN USE
- LAUNDERETTE, SUNBED, AMUSEMENTS, CRAZY GOLF, BOULES, SKATEBOARD RAMP, OUTDOOR TABLE TENNIS
- MOUNTAIN BIKE/CYCLE TANDEM HIRE
- ACTIVITY PROGRAMME ARCHERY, RIFLE SHOOTING, ABSEILING, CAVING, CANOEING, NATURE TRAILS,

SOMERSET, LAND OF THE SUMMER PEOPLE

DAVID BELLAMY CONSERVATION AWARD
GOLD

English Tourism Council
★★★★
HOLIDAY PARK

AA ►►► RAC APPOINTED

BROADWAY HOUSE CHEDDAR, SOMERSET. BS27 3DB

TEL:01934 742610 FAX:01934 744950

Email: enquiries@broadwayhouse.uk.com www.broadwayhouse.uk.com

Fishing.

CONGRESBURY

Oak Farm Touring Park, Weston Road, Congresbury, Somerset, BS49 5EB.
Std: 01934 **Tel:** 833246
Nearest Town/Resort Weston-super-Mare
Directions 4 miles from junc. 21 on M5, on the A370 midway between Bristol and Weston Super Mare.
Open 31st Mar **to** October
Access Good **Site** Level
Sites Available ▲ ⚎ ⚎ **Total** 27
Facilities [⚌] ♿ ₤ ♠ ┌ ⊙ ⌐ ⚑
Nearby Facilities ┌ ✓ ⚐ ⚑ ✕ ∪ ⚐ ⚑
⚓ Yatton
Pub with restaurant. You can also call us on Mobile 07989 319686.

CROWCOMBE

Quantock Orchard Caravan Park, Crowcombe, Nr. Taunton, Somerset, TA4 4AW.
Std: 01984 **Tel:** 618618 **Fax:** 618618
Email: qocp@flaxpool.freeserve.co.uk
Website: www.flaxpool.co.uk
Nearest Town/Resort Minehead
Directions Just off the A358 Taunton to Minehead road, towards Crowcombe Steam Railway Station. 10 miles from the M5 junction 25 Taunton.
Acreage 3½ **Open** All Year
Access Good **Site** Level
Sites Available ▲ ⚎ ⚎ **Total** 75
Facilities ♿ [⚌] ♿ ₤ ♠ ┌ ⊙ ⌐ ⚑ ⚐ ⚑
⚑ ⚌ ⚓ ⚑ ♠ ⚑ ⚐ ⚑ ⚐ ⚑
Nearby Facilities ┌ ✓ ⚐
⚓ Taunton
Located in a designated area of outstanding natural beauty in the Quantock Hills. Close to Exmoor and the coast.

DULVERTON

Exe Valley Caravan Site, Bridgetown, Somerset, TA22 9JR.
Std: 01643 **Tel:** 851432
Nearest Town/Resort Dulverton
Directions Leave the M5 at junction 27 and take the A396 to Dulverton. From the roundabout on the Tiverton by-pass stay on the A396 to Minehead.

Acreage 4 **Open** March **to** October
Access Good **Site** Level
Sites Available ▲ ⚎ ⚎ **Total** 30
Facilities ♿ [⚌] ♿ ₤ ♠ ┌ ⊙ ⌐ ⚑ ⚐ ⚑
⚑ ⚑ ⚌ ⚑ ⚐ ♠ ⚑
Nearby Facilities ┌ ✓ ⚐ ✕ ∪
Most improved site in Exmoor. At the gateway to Exmoor National Park. Free game fishing on site. Newly converted flat in the mill also available.

EMBOROUGH

Old Down Touring Park, Old Down House, Emborough, Radstock, Nr. Bath, Somerset, BA3 4SA.
Std: 01761 **Tel:** 232355 **Fax:** 232355
Email: olddown@talk21.com
Website: www.ukparks.co.uk/olddown
Nearest Town/Resort Midsomer Norton
Directions From Shepton Mallet head north on the A37 towards Bristol. After 6 miles turn right onto the B3139. Old Down Inn is on the left, site entrance is 50 yards along on your right.
Acreage 4 **Open** April **to** November
Access Good **Site** Level
Sites Available ▲ ⚎ ⚎ **Total** 30
Facilities ₤ [⚌] ♠ ┌ ⊙ ⌐ ⚑ ⚐ ⚑
⚑ ⚐ ⚑ ⚐ ⚑ ✕ ⚑ ⚑
Nearby Facilities ┌ ✓
⚓ Bath
Convenient for Bath, Wells and the Mendip Hills.

EXFORD

Westermill Farm, Exford, Minehead, Somerset, TA24 7NJ.
Std: 01643 **Tel:** 831238 **Fax:** 831660
Email: holidays@westermill-exmoor.co.uk
Website: www.exmoorcamping.co.uk
Nearest Town/Resort Exford
Directions Leave Exford on Porlock Road. After ½ mile fork left. Continue for 2 miles past another campsite until 'Westermill' seen on tree, fork left.
Acreage 6 **Open** All Year
Access Good **Site** Level
Sites Available ▲ ⚎ **Total** 60
Facilities ♿ ♠ ┌ ⊙ ⌐ ⚑ ⚐ ⚑
⚑ ⚐ ⚑ ⚑ ✕ ⚑
Nearby Facilities ✓ ∪
⚓ Taunton

Beautiful, secluded site beside a river fo fishing. Fascinating 500 acre farm with Waymarked walks. Centre Exmoor National Park. Log cottages and farmhouse cottage for hire. Holder of the Gold David Bellamy Award for Conservation. Free hot showers

FROME

Seven Acres Touring Caravan & Camping Park, West Woodlands, Frome, Somerset, BA11 5EQ.
Std: 01373 **Tel:** 464222
Nearest Town/Resort Frome
Directions From the Frome by-pass take the B3092 towards Maiden Bradley and Mere. Seven Acres is situated approx. 1 mile from the by-pass.
Acreage 7 **Open** March **to** October
Access Good **Site** Level
Sites Available ▲ ⚎ ⚎ **Total** 32
Facilities ♿ ₤ [⚌] ♿ ♠ ┌ ⊙ ⌐ ⚑
⚑ ⚐ ✕ ⚑ ⚑
Nearby Facilities ┌ ✓ ∪ ⚐
⚓ Frome
Acres of level, landscaped grounds with a stream meandering through. On the outskirts of the Longleat Estate and within easy reach of Stourhead, Cheddar Caves and Stonehenge.

GLASTONBURY

Orchard Camping, c/o Ye Olde Burtle Inn & Restaurant, Catcott Road, Burtle, Somerset, TA7 8NG.
Std: 01278 **Tel:** 722123 **Fax:** 722269
Email: chris@burtleinn.fsnet.co.uk
Website: www.burtleinn.fsnet.co.uk
Nearest Town/Resort Glastonbury
Directions Leave the M5 at junction 22 and take the A38, turn off at Fox & Goose Pub and follow signs for Glastonbury. Situated approx half way between Burnham-on-Sea and Glastonbury.
Acreage 1 **Open** All Year
Access Good **Site** Lev/Slope
Sites Available ▲ ⚎ **Total** 30
Facilities [⚌] ♠ ┌ ⊙ ⌐ ⚑
⚑ ⚐ ⚑ ✕ ⚑ ♠ ⚑ ⚐ ⚑
Nearby Facilities ┌ ✓ ⚐ ✕ ∪ ⚐ ⚑
⚓ Highbridge
Up to half hours drive to Glastonbury Burnham-on-Sea, Cheddar, Street, Weston

super-Mare, Taunton and Bristol. Near to Nature Reserves and peat workings. Blue Bell Cycle Hire. Limited site shop. Licensed Bar.

GLASTONBURY

The Isle of Avalon Touring Caravan Park, Godney Road, Glastonbury, Somerset, BA6 9AF.
Std: 01458 **Tel:** 833618 **Fax:** 833618
Nearest Town/Resort Glastonbury
Directions Leave the M5 at junction 23 and follow the A39. On the approach to Glastonbury there is a B&Q Store on the left, at the roundabout take the second exit signposted Bath, Bristol and Wells. Go straight across next roundabout, turn left at next roundabout and follow caravan signs, 500 yards on the right.
Acreage 8 **Open** All Year
Access Good **Site** Level
Sites Available ▲ ♦ ➡ **Total** 120
Facilities ⅍ ╿ 🅗 🆄 ♨ ┌ ⊙ ⅃ ♨ ▨ ⌨
⅏ ⅃ ⊙ ⴲ🗪⌨
Nearby Facilities ┌ ✔ ⸙
➤ Castle Carey

Ideal for touring. Within walking distance of Glastonbury town, the Abbey and Tor. Close to Clarkes Village, Wells, Wookey Hole, Cheddar Gorge and many other attractions.

GLASTONBURY

The Old Oaks Touring Park, Wick Farm, Wick, Glastonbury, Somerset, BA6 8JS.
Std: 01458 **Tel:** 831437
Email: info@theoldoaks.co.uk
Website: www.theoldoaks.co.uk
Nearest Town/Resort Glastonbury
Directions From Glastonbury take the A361 Shepton Mallet road. In 2 miles turn left signposted Wick 1, site is on the left in 1 mile.
Acreage 2½ **Open** March **to** October
Access Good **Site** Lev/Slope
Sites Available ▲ ♦ ➡ **Total** 40
Facilities ⅍ ╿ 🅗 🆄 ♨ ┌ ⊙ ⅃ ♨ ▨ ⌨
⅏ ⅃ ⊙ ⴲ🗪⌨ ⅃ ▨
Nearby Facilities ✔
➤ Castle Cary

A family run park offering excellent centrally heated facilities in an outstanding environment. Delightfully tranquil with panoramic views, coarse fishing and excellent amenities.

HIGHBRIDGE

Greenacre Place Touring Caravan Park, Bristol Road, Edithmead, Highbridge, Somerset, TA9 4HA.
Std: 01278 **Tel:** 785227
Nearest Town/Resort Burnham-on-Sea
Acreage 1 **Open** March **to** November
Access Good **Site** Level
Sites Available ♦ ➡ **Total** 10
Facilities ╿ 🆄 ♨ ┌ ⊙ ☎ ⅊ ⊙🗪⌨
Nearby Facilities ┌ ✔ ⚓ ∪ ⸙ ♫
➤ Highbridge

Small, peaceful caravan park with easy access. Short drive to sandy beaches. Ideally placed for touring Somerset.

ILMINSTER

Thornleigh Caravan Park, Hanning Road, Horton, Ilminster, Somerset, TA19 9QH.
Std: 01460 **Tel:** 53450 **Fax:** 53450
Email: thewhitethorns@tesco.net
Website: www.ilminster.org/thornleigh
Nearest Town/Resort Ilminster
Directions A303 West Ilminster, take the A358 signposted Chard. ¼ mile turn right signposted Horton and Broadway. Site on the left opposite the church, ¾ mile.
Acreage 1¼ **Open** March **to** October

Access Good **Site** Level
Sites Available ▲ ♦ ➡ **Total** 20
Facilities ⅍ ╿ 🆄 ♨ ┌ ⊙ ⅃ ☎ ⅊ ⊙🗪⌨
Nearby Facilities ┌
➤ Crewkerne

Flat site in a village location, ideal for touring Somerset and Devon. Sauna and solarium on site. ½ hour drive to the south coast. 6 miles to Cricket St Thomas Wildlife Park. National Trust properties nearby. Heated shower block.

LANGPORT

Bowdens Crest Caravan & Camping Park, Bowdens, Langport, Somerset, TA10 0DD.
Std: 01458 **Tel:** 250553 **Fax:** 253360
Email: bowcrest@aol.com
Website: www.scoot.co.uk/bowdens
Nearest Town/Resort Langport
Directions On the A372 Langport to Bridgwater road, 1½ miles out of Langport turn right up the hill as signposted.
Acreage 2½ **Open** 14 Feb **to** 14 Jan
Access Good **Site** Level
Sites Available ▲ ♦ ➡ **Total** 30
Facilities ╿ 🆄 ♨ ┌ ⊙ ⅃ ♨ ▨ ⌨
⅏ ⊙ ⴲ ✗ ♈ 🛆 ⊛🗪⌨ ⊡ ▨
Nearby Facilities ┌ ✔ ♫
➤ Bridgwater

Tranquil countryside site overlooking Somerset levels.

LANGPORT

Thorney Lakes Caravan Site, Thorney Farm, Muchelney, Langport, Somerset, TA10 0DW.
Std: 01458 **Tel:** 250811
Nearest Town/Resort Langport
Directions Turn off the A303 dual carriageway signposted Martock, Ash and Kingsbury Episcopi. Follow signs to Kingsbury Episcopi, at the T-Junction in the village turn right, site is 1 mile on the right.
Acreage 7 **Open** March **to** November
Access Good **Site** Level
Sites Available ▲ ♦ ➡ **Total** 16
Facilities ╿ 🅕 🆄 ♨ ┌ ⊙ ⅃ ☎🗪⌨
Nearby Facilities ┌ ✔
➤ Yeovil/Taunton

Site is an orchard on Somerset Moors. Ideal for walking and cycling. Fishing on site.

MARTOCK

Southfork Caravan Park, Parrett Works, Martock, Somerset, TA12 6AE.
Std: 01935 **Tel:** 825661 **Fax:** 825122
Email: southfork.caravans@virgin.net
Website: www.ukparks.co.uk/southfork
Nearest Town/Resort Martock/Yeovil
Directions Situated 2 miles north west of A303 (between Ilchester and Ilminster). From A303 east of Ilminster, at roundabout take first exit signposted South Petherton and follow camping signs. From A303 west of Ilchester, after Cartgate roundabout (junction with A3088 to Yeovil) take exit signposted Martock and follow camping signs.
Acreage 2 **Open** All Year
Access Good **Site** Level
Sites Available ▲ ♦ ➡ **Total** 30
Facilities ╿ 🅕 🆄 ♨ ┌ ⊙ ⅃ ♨ ▨ ⌨
⅏ ⊙ ⴲ 🛆🗪⌨ ⊡ ▨
Nearby Facilities ┌ ✔ ♫
➤ Yeovil

Set in open countryside near River Parrett. Numerous places of interest nearby for all age groups. Ideal base for touring. 3 static caravans for hire. ETC 5 Star Grading and AA 4 Pennants.

MINEHEAD

Hoburne Blue Anchor, Blue Anchor, Nr. Minehead, Somerset, TA24 6JT.
Std: 01643 **Tel:** 821360 **Fax:** 821572
Email: enquiries@hoburne.com
Website: www.hoburne.com
Nearest Town/Resort Minehead
Directions From A39 at Williton, travel west for 4 miles to Carhampton and turn right onto the B3191 signposted Blue Anchor. Park is 1¼ miles on right.
Acreage 29 **Open** March **to** October
Access Good **Site** Level
Sites Available ♦ ➡ **Total** 103
Facilities ⅍ ╿ 🅗 🆄 ♨ ┌ ⊙ ⅃ ♨ ▨ ⌨
⅏ ⊙ ⴲ ✗ 🛆 ♈ ⊡ ▨
Nearby Facilities ┌ ✔ ⚓ ♫ ∪
➤ Minehead

On waters edge, an ideal base from which to explore Exmoor and this beautiful coastline.

MINEHEAD

Minehead & Exmoor Caravan Park, Porlock Road, Minehead, Somerset, TA24 8SN.
Std: 01643 **Tel:** 703074
Nearest Town/Resort Minehead
Directions 1 mile west of Minehead, official signposts on the A39.
Acreage 3 **Open** 1 March **to** 22 October
Access Good **Site** Level
Sites Available ▲ ♦ ➡ **Total** 50
Facilities ⅍ ╿ 🅗 🆄 ♨ ┌ ⊙ ⅃ ♨ ▨ ⌨
⅊ ⊙ ⴲ🗪⌨
Nearby Facilities ┌ ✔ ⚓ ♫ ∪ ♫
➤ Minehead

1 mile from the centre of Minehead, near the beach and all local attractions.

MINEHEAD

St. Audries Bay, West Quantoxhead, Near Minehead, Somerset, TA4 4DY.
Std: 01984 **Tel:** 632515 **Fax:** 632785
Email: mrandle@staudriesbay.demon.co.uk
Website: www.staudriesbay.demon.co.uk
Nearest Town/Resort Minehead
Directions From Bridgwater follow the A39 towards Minehead. After approx. 12 miles, St. Audries Bay is signposted on the right.
Open May **to** October
Access Good **Site** Level
Sites Available ▲ ♦ ➡ **Total** 22
Facilities ⅍ ╿ 🅗 🆄 ♨ ┌ ⊙ ⅃ ♨ ▨ ⌨
⅏ ⊙ ⴲ ✗ ♈ ♈ 🛆 ⊛ ⊡ ▨
Nearby Facilities ┌ ✔ ⚓ ♫ ∪ ♫
➤ Taunton

Overlooking the sea and close to Quantock Hills (Area of Outstanding Natural Beauty). The centre has full facilities and family entertainment programme.

PORLOCK

Burrowhayes Farm Caravan & Camping Site & Riding Stables, West Luccombe, Porlock, Nr. Minehead, Somerset, TA24 8HT.
Std: 01643 **Tel:** 862463
Email: info@burrowhayes.co.uk
Website: www.burrowhayes.co.uk
Nearest Town/Resort Minehead
Directions 5 miles west of Minehead on A39, left hand turning to West Luccombe, site ¼ mile on the right.
Acreage 8 **Open** 15 March **to** 31 October
Access Good **Site** Lev/Slope
Sites Available ▲ ♦ ➡ **Total** 140
Facilities ╿ 🆄 ♨ ┌ ⊙ ⅃ ♨ ▨ ⌨
⅏ ⅊ ⊙ ⴲ 🛆🗪⌨ ⊡ ▨
Nearby Facilities ┌ ✔ ⚓ ♫ ♫
➤ Taunton

BURROWHAYES FARM

Caravan & Camping Site & Riding Stables
West Luccombe, Porlock, Near Minehead, Somerset TA24 8HC

Between Minehead and Porlock, this family site has a delightful National Trust setting beside the "Horner Water" and is in the heart of the Exmoor National Park. The surrounding moors and woods make it a walkers paradise and children can play and explore safely. Only 2 miles from the coast. Horses & ponies for hire. Sites for touring and motor-caravans (hook-ups), and tents, also modern static caravans for hire.

Tel: (01643) 862463
E-mail: info@burrowhayes.co.uk   www.burrowhayes.co.uk
Prop: Mr. & Mrs. J.C. Dascombe

Real family site set in glorious National Trust scenery on Exmoor. Ideal for walking. Riding stables on site.

PORLOCK

Porlock Caravan Park, Highbank, Porlock, Nr. Minehead, Somerset, TA24 8NS.
Std: 01643 **Tel:** 862269 **Fax:** 862269
Email: adhpcp@aol.com
Website: www.exmoortourism.org/porlockcaravanpark.htm
Nearest Town/Resort Minehead
Directions A39 from Minehead to Lynton, take the B3225 in Porlock to Porlock Weir. Site signposted.
Acreage 3½ **Open** Mid March **to** October
Access Good **Site** Level
Sites Available Å ♛ ⊕ **Total** 40
Facilities ⚡ ☷ & ⌐ ⊙ ⚲ ⊡ ☕
⚲ ⚑ ⊙ ☕ ⊞ ⊟
Nearby Facilities ⌐ ✧ ✗ ∪ ℛ
⇌ Taunton
Scenic views, Ideal touring and walking.

SHEPTON MALLET

Greenacres Camping, Barrow Lane, North Wootton, Nr. Shepton Mallet, Somerset, BA4 4HL.
Std: 01749 **Tel:** 890497
Email: harvie.greenacres@talk21.com
Nearest Town/Resort Wells
Directions From Wells take the A39, turn left at Brownes Garden Centre. Site signposted in the village.
Acreage 4¼ **Open** April **to** October
Site Level
Sites Available Å ⊕ **Total** 30
Facilities ⚡ ☷ & ⌐ ⊙ ⚲ ⊡ ⊞ ⊗ ⊟
Nearby Facilities ⌐ ✧ ∪
⇌ Castle Cary
An award winning family site. Peacefully set within sight of Glastonbury Tor. Some electric hook-ups available.

SHEPTON MALLET

Manleaze Caravan Park, 4 Cannards Grave, Shepton Mallet, Somerset, BA4 4LY.
Std: 01749 **Tel:** 342404
Nearest Town/Resort Shepton Mallet
Acreage 1 **Open** All Year
Access Good **Site** Level
Sites Available Å ⊕ ⊟
Facilities ⚡ ⌐ ⊙ ☕ ⊟
Nearby Facilities ⌐
⇌ Castle Cary

SHEPTON MALLET

Phippens Farm, Stoke St. Michael, Radstock, Somerset, BA3 5JH.
Std: 01749 **Tel:** 840395
Nearest Town/Resort Shepton Mallet
Directions From Bath take the A367 towards Shepton Mallet for 14 miles, turn left in Oakhill, 1 mile. Or from Bristol take the A37, turn left onto the A367 then right in Oakhill.
Acreage 4 **Open** March **to** October
Sites Available Å ⊕ **Total** 20
Facilities ⚡ ☷ ⊞ ⚲
Nearby Facilities
⇌ Castle Cary
Quiet farm site. 2 hard standings available.

SPARKFORD

Long Hazel International Caravan & Camping Park, High Street, Sparkford, Near Yeovil, Somerset, BA22 7JH.
Std: 01963 **Tel:** 440002 **Fax:** 440002
Email: longhazelpark@hotmail.com
Website: www.sparkford.f9.co.uk/lhi.htm
Nearest Town/Resort Yeovil/Sherborne
Directions From Wincanton take the A303 to the end of Sparkford by-pass. At the roundabout turn left into Sparkford Village, site is approx. 400 yards on the left.
Acreage 3½ **Open** March **to** Dec Inc.
Access Good **Site** Level
Sites Available Å ⊕ **Total** 75
Facilities & ⚡ ☷ ☷ & ⌐ ⊙ ⊣ ⚲ ☕
⚲ ⚑ ⊙ ☕ ⊞ ⊗ ⊞ ⊟
Nearby Facilities ⌐ ✧ ∪
⇌ Yeovil/Sherborne/Castle Cary
Full disabled shower unit. Near to an inn and restaurant. Ideal for touring or an overnight halt. Haynes Motor Museum and Fleet Air Arm Museum nearby. 3 static caravans available.

STREET

Bramble Hill Camping Site, Bramble Hill, Walton, Nr. Street, Somerset, BA16 9RQ.
Std: 01458 **Tel:** 442548
Website: www.caravancampingsites.co.uk
Nearest Town/Resort Street
Directions A39 1 mile from Street, 2 miles from Glastonbury.
Acreage 3½ **Open** April **to** September
Access Good **Site** Level
Sites Available Å ⊕ ⊟
Facilities ⚡ ☷ & ⌐ ⊙ ⊣ ⚲ ☕
⚲ ⚑ ⚒ ⊞ ⊞ ⊟
Nearby Facilities ⌐ ✧ ∪
⇌ Castle Cary/Taunton
Quiet site. Caravan storage also available. Dogs are welcome on leads only. Ideal site for visiting Clarks Village - 1 mile. Few seasonal pitches available. Near to Sainsburys, restaurants and swimming pools (1 mile).

TAUNTON

Ashe Farm Caravan & Camp Site, Ashe Farm, Thornfalcon, Taunton, Somerset, TA3 5NW.
Std: 01823 **Tel:** 442567 **Fax:** 443372
Email: camping@ashe-farm.fsnet.co.uk
Nearest Town/Resort Taunton
Directions 4 miles southeast Taunton on A358, turn right at 'Nags Head' towards West Hatch, ¼ mile on right.
Acreage 7 **Open** April **to** October
Access Good **Site** Level
Sites Available Å ⊕ **Total** 30
Facilities ⚡ ☷ ☷ & ⌐ ⊙ ⊣ ⚲ ⊡ ☕
⚲ ⚑ ⊙ ☕ ⚲ ⊞ ⊟
Nearby Facilities ⌐ ✧ ∪ ℛ
⇌ Taunton
Ideal touring centre, easy reach of Quantock and Blackdown Hills.

TAUNTON

Holly Bush Park, Culmhead, Taunton, Somerset, TA3 7EA.
Std: 01823 **Tel:** 421515 **Fax:** 421885
Email: beaumont@hollybushpark.ndo.co.uk
Website: www.hollybushpark.co.uk
Nearest Town/Resort Taunton
Directions From Taunton follow signs for the Racecourse and Corfe on the B3170. 3½ miles from Corfe turn right at crossroads towards Wellington. Turn right at the next T-Junction, site is 200yds on the left.
Acreage 2¼ **Open** All Year
Access Good **Site** Level
Sites Available Å ⊕ **Total** 40
Facilities ⚡ ☷ ☷ & ⌐ ⊙ ⊣ ⚲ ⊡ ☕
⚲ ⚑ ⊙ ☕ ⊞ ⊟
Nearby Facilities ⌐ ✧ ∪ ℛ
⇌ Taunton
Area of Outstanding Natural Beauty.

WATCHET

Doniford Bay Holiday Park, Watchet, Somerset, TA23 0TJ.
Std: 01984 **Tel:** 632423
Website: www.havenholidays.com
Nearest Town/Resort Watchet
Directions Leave the M5 at exit 24. Follow Minehead signs on the A39 until you reach West Quantoxhead. Fork right after St Audries Garage to Doniford Bay, the park is signposted.
Acreage 5 **Open** April **to** End Oct
Site Sloping
Sites Available ⊕ **Total** 46
Facilities & ⚡ ☷ ☷ & ⌐ ⊙ ⊣ ⚲ ⊡ ☕
⚲ ⚑ ⊙ ☕ ✗ ⚒ ↻ ⊞ ⊟
Nearby Facilities ✧ ∪ ℛ
⇌ Taunton
Overlooking the sea. Take-away food available.

WATCHET

Warren Bay Caravan Park, Watchet, Somerset, TA23 0JR.
Std: 01984 **Tel:** 631460 **Fax:** 633999
Nearest Town/Resort Watchet
Directions On the B3191 between Watchet and Blue Anchor. 2 miles from the A39 and 3 miles from Minehead.
Acreage 6 **Open** Easter **to** 30 October
Access Good **Site** Sloping
Sites Available A ⚏ ⛟ **Total** 180
Facilities ✦ 🔟 ♿ ♦ ⌐ ⊙ ⤴ ▢ 🏐
🌣 👁 ⊕ 🛝 ⟊ ⤴ 🛉 ▣
Nearby Facilities ⌐ ✔
⇒ Taunton
We have our own private beach.

WELLINGTON

Gamlins Farm Caravans, Gamlins Farmhouse, Greenham, Wellington, Somerset, TA21 0LZ.
Std: 01823 **Tel:** 672596 **Fax:** 672324
Nearest Town/Resort Wellington
Directions Take the M5 to Wellington then the A38 towards Tiverton and Exeter. Turn right to Greenham, go over two sets of crossroads, round a bend and the site is on the right.
Acreage 3 **Open** Easter **to** September
Access Good **Site** Level
Sites Available A ⚏ ▢ **Total** 25+
Facilities ✦ 🔟 🔟 ♦ ⌐ ⊙ ⤴ ▢ 🏐
🛉 ⤴ ▣
Nearby Facilities ⌐ ✔
⇒ Taunton/Tiverton
Scenic valley setting with a Free coarse fishing lake. Ideal for touring, Exmoor, Quantocks and The Blackdowns.

WELLS

Ebborlands Camping Grounds, Ebborlands Farm, Wookey Hole, Nr Wells, Somerset.
Std: 01749 **Tel:** 672550 **Fax:** 672550
Email: eileengibbs@hotmail.com
Nearest Town/Resort Wells
Directions Wells - Unclassified road to Wookey Hole, approx 2 miles and past caves, on road marked Unsuitable for Charabangs.
Acreage 2 **Open** May **to** October
Access Good **Site** Sloping
Sites Available A ⚏ ⛟ **Total** 20
Facilities 🔟 ⤴ ▣ ⤴ ▣
Nearby Facilities ⌐ ✔ ⚓ ∪ ☔ ✗
⇒ Castle Cary
Near Wookey Hole Caves and Mendip Hills.

WELLS

Haybridge Caravan Park, Haybridge Farm, Haybridge, Wells, Somerset, BA5 1AJ
Nearest Town/Resort Wells
Directions On the main A371 Wells to Cheddar road, just outside the Wells boundary.
Acreage 4 **Open** All Year
Access Good **Site** Lev/Slope
Sites Available A ⚏ ⛟ **Total** 35
Facilities ♿ ✦ ♦ ⌐ ⊙ 🏐 ⤴
Nearby Facilities ⌐ ✔ ∪
⇒ Bristol
Close to Wells and Wookey Hole Caves, ideal touring position.

WELLS

Homestead Park, Wookey Hole, Wells, Somerset, BA5 1BW.
Std: 01749 **Tel:** 673022
Email: homestead.park@virgin.net
Nearest Town/Resort Wells
Directions Leave Wells by A371 towards Cheddar, turn right for Wookey Hole. Site 1¼ miles on left in village.
Acreage 2 **Open** Easter **to** October
Access Good **Site** Level
Sites Available A ⚏ ⛟ **Total** 55
Facilities ✦ 🔟 ♦ ⌐ ⊙ ⤴ 🏐
🛝 👁 ⊕ 🛉 ▣ ▣
Nearby Facilities ⌐ ✔ ∪
⇒ Bristol/Bath
Sheltered on bank of River Axe, Wookey Hole Caves, National Trust Area, Mendip Hills, walking, climbing. Leisure centre nearby.

WELLS

Mendip Heights Camping & Caravan Park, Priddy, Wells, Somerset, BA5 3BP.
Std: 01749 **Tel:** 870241 **Fax:** 870368
Email: cades@mendipheights.co.uk
Website: www.mendipheights.co.uk
Nearest Town/Resort Cheddar/Wells
Directions On A39 north from Wells, turn left at Green Ore crossroads onto B3135 towards Cheddar and follow campsite signs.
Acreage 4¼ **Open** March **to** 15 Nov
Access Good **Site** Level
Sites Available A ⚏ ⛟ **Total** 90
Facilities ✦ 🔟 🔟 ♦ ⌐ ⊙ ⤴ ⤴ ▢ 🏐
🌣 👁 ⊕ 🛝 🛉 ▣ ▣
Nearby Facilities ⌐ ✔ ⚓ ∪ ✗
⇒ Bristol/Bath/Weston-super-Mare
Peaceful, rural park in an area of outstanding natural beauty. Ideal for touring and walking. Near Cheddar, Wookey Hole and Wells. Activities available - see our main advertisement. Pets welcome if kept on leads.

WELLS

Yew Tree Farm, Theale, Near Wedmore, Somerset, BS28 4SN.
Std: 01934 **Tel:** 712475 **Fax:** 712475
Nearest Town/Resort Wells/Cheddar
Directions From Wells take the B3139 Burnham-on-Sea road. From Cheddar follow signs to Wedmore, go through the village and straight on to Theale.
Acreage ½ **Open** All Year
Access Good **Site** Level
Sites Available A ⚏ ▢ **Total** 5
Facilities 🅷 🏐 ✗ 🛉 ▣ ▣
Nearby Facilities ⌐ ✔ ∪ ✗
⇒ Highbridge
Ideal touring.

WESTON-SUPER-MARE

Purn Holiday Park, A370 Bridgwater Road, Bleadon, Weston-super-Mare, Somerset, BS24 0AN.
Std: 01934 **Tel:** 812342 **Fax:** 812342
Email:
gavin@purninternational.freeserve.co.uk
Nearest Town/Resort Weston Super Mare
Directions From North leave M5 at junction 21 take signs for Weston and Hospital. At Hospital roundabout turn left onto the A370, we are on the right in 1 mile, next to the Anchor Inn. From South leave M5 junction 22 take signs for Weston on the left next to the Anchor Inn on A370.
Acreage 11 **Open** March **to** October
Access Good **Site** Level
Sites Available A ⚏ ⛟ **Total** 115
Facilities ✦ 🔟 ♦ ⌐ ⊙ ⤴ ▢ 🏐
🌣 🔟 👁 ⊕ ✗ 🛝 🛉 🌣 ⤴ 🛉 ▣
Nearby Facilities ⌐ ✔ ⚓ ∪ ☔ ✗ ☔
⇒ Weston Super Mare
Nearest Park to Weston, Licensed club with entertainment and dancing. RAC Appointed 4 Ticks and AA 3 Pennants.

WESTON-SUPER-MARE

Slimeridge Farm, Links Road, Uphill, Weston-super-Mare, Somerset, BS23 4XY.
Std: 01934 **Tel:** 641641 **Fax:** 641641
Nearest Town/Resort Weston-Super-Mare
Directions M5 Junction 21, follow A370 to Weston-super-Mare seafront. Follow along with sea on your right. At end turn right signposted Uphill.
Open 1st March **to** 30th October
Access Good **Site** Level
Sites Available A ⚏ ⛟ **Total** 50
Facilities ✦ 🅷 🔟 🔟 ♦ ⌐ ⊙ ⤴ ⤴ ▢ 🏐
🛝 👁 ⊕ 🛉 ▣ ▣
Nearby Facilities ⌐ ✔ ⚓ ∪ ☔ ✗ ☔
⇒ Weston-super-Mare
Quiet site alongside Weston beach. 10 mins walk to town centre.

WESTON-SUPER-MARE

West End Farm Caravan & Camping Park, Locking, Weston-super-Mare, Somerset, BS24 8RH.
Std: 01934 **Tel:** 822529
Directions Leave the M5 at junction 21 and follow signs for Weston-super-Mare, follow the signs for International Helicopter Museum and turn right immediately after Helicopter Museum and follow signs for site.
Access Good **Site** Level
Sites Available A ⚏ ⛟
Facilities ♿ ✦ ✦ 🅵 🔟 ♦ ⌐ ⊙ ⤴ ⤴
▢ 🏐 🌣 🔟 👁 ⊕ 🛝 ⟊ 🛝 🛉 ▣ ▣
Nearby Facilities ⌐ ✔ ⚓ ∪ ☔ ✗
⇒ Weston-super-Mare
Ideal for touring.

WESTON-SUPER-MARE

Weston Gateway Tourist Park, Westwick, Weston-super-Mare, BS24 7TF.
Std: 01934 **Tel:** 510344
Nearest Town/Resort Weston-super-

Exmoor National Park

Small, peaceful park on a working farm for touring Caravans and Tents. Adjacent to the Moor. Spectacular views.
Walkers paradise. Ideal for exploring Exmoor. Winsford 1 mile with shop, garage and thatched Inn.
Quality Heated toilet block with launderette and disabled facilities. Free hot showers.
Electric hook-ups. Children's Monkey Business play area.
Halse Farm, Winsford, Minehead, Somerset TA24 7JL   Tel: (01643) 851259 Fax: (01643) 851592
Website: www.halsefarm.co.uk   E-mail: enquiries@halsefarm.co.uk

Mare
Directions From the M5 junction 21, follow signs for Westwick approx. ¾ miles. From Weston-super-Mare take the A370 to the motorway interchange then follow signs to Westwick.
Acreage 15 **Open** March **to** November
Access Good **Site** Level
Sites Available ▲ ♦ ➤ **Total** 175
Facilities & ∮ ▥ ▤ ⌐ ⊙ ⌐ ▱ ◻ ☂
♨ ⓘ ◻ ⊕ ▣ ♥ Ⅲ ✿ ⚘ ⊛ ➤◻
Nearby Facilities ⌐ ✈ ▲ ⊁ ∪ ♪ ♪ ✗
♒ Weston-super-Mare
Ideal, sheltered park with many famous tourist attractions within easy driving distance. No singles and No commercial vehicles.

WESTON-SUPER-MARE

Weston-super-Mare Rugby Football Club, The Recreation Ground, Drove Road, Weston-super-Mare, Somerset, BS23 3PA.
Std: 01934 **Tel:** 625643 **Fax:** 625643
Email: westonfc@lineone.net
Website: www.weston-warriors/.
Nearest Town/Resort Weston-super-Mare
Directions Leave the M5 at junction 21 and follow the dual carriageway for the town centre. Go straight across 5 roundabouts then turn first left and ground is on the left.
Acreage 2 **Open** All Year
Access Good **Site** Level
Sites Available ▲ ♦ ➤ **Total** 24
Facilities & ∮ ▥ ▤ ⌐ ⊙ ⌐ ☂
♨ ▽ Ⅲ ◻▣
Nearby Facilities ⌐ ✈ ▲ ⊁ ∪ ♪ ♪ ✗
♨ Weston-super-Mare
In Weston town centre. Within walking distance of the beach, pier, Sea Life Centre, swimming pool and many other attractions.

WILLITON

Home Farm Holiday Centre, St. Audries Bay, Williton, Somerset, TA4 4DP.
Std: 01984 **Tel:** 632487 **Fax:** 634687
Nearest Town/Resort Williton / Watchet
Directions Leave M5 at Junction 23, follow A39 towards Minehead for 17 miles. At West Quantoxhead take first right turn after St. Audries Garages (signposted Blue Anchor, Doniford and Watchet) B3191 take first right turning in ½ mile to our drive.
Open All Year
Access Good **Site** Terraced
Sites Available ▲ ♦ ➤ **Total** 40
Facilities & ∮ ▥ ▤ ⌐ ⊙ ⌐ ▱ ◻ ☂
♨ ⓘ ◻ ⊕ ▽ Ⅲ ✿ ➤◻
Nearby Facilities ✈
♨ Taunton
Private beach, good base for touring Exmoor. West Somerset Railway - 2 miles.

WINSFORD

Halse Farm Caravan & Tent Park, Halse Farm, Winsford, Minehead, Somerset, TA24 7JL.
Std: 01643 **Tel:** 851259 **Fax:** 851592
Email: cad@halsefarm.co.uk
Website: www.halsefarm.co.uk
Nearest Town/Resort Dulverton
Directions Signposted from the A396 Tiverton to Minehead road. In Winsford take

small road in front of Royal Oak Inn. 1 mile up hill and over cattle grid, our entrance is immediately on the left.
Acreage 3 **Open** 23 March **to** 31 October
Access Good **Site** Lev/Slope
Sites Available ▲ ♦ ➤ **Total** 44
Facilities & ∮ ▥ ▤ ⌐ ⊙ ⌐ ▱ ◻ ☂
♨ ⓘ ◻ ⊕ ▣ ➤◻
Nearby Facilities ✈ ∪ ♪
♨ Taunton
In Exmoor National Park, on working farm with beautiful views. For those who enjoy peaceful countryside. Quality heated toilet block and FREE showers. David Bellamy Gold Award for Conservation and ETC 4 Star Graded.

WIVELISCOMBE

Waterrow Touring Park, Waterrow, Wiveliscombe, Taunton, Somerset, TA4 2AZ.
Std: 01984 **Tel:** 623464 **Fax:** 624280
Email: taylor@waterrowpark.u-net.com
Website: www.waterrowpark.u-net.com
Nearest Town/Resort Taunton
Directions Leave the M5 at junction 25 and take the A358 signposted Minehead. Then take the B3227 signposted Wiveliscombe, 3 miles after Wiveliscombe you will pass the Rock Pub, the park is on the left within 300 yards.
Acreage 8 **Open** All Year
Access Good **Site** Sloping
Sites Available ▲ ♦ ➤ **Total** 45
Facilities ∮ ▥ ▤ ⌐ ⊙ ⌐ ▱ ◻ ☂
Ⅲ ◻ ⊕ ➤▣◻
Nearby Facilities ⌐ ✈ ▲ ⊁ ∪ ♪
♨ Taunton/Tiverton
EXCLUSIVELY FOR ADULTS. In a peaceful, attractive location alongside the River Tone with a woodland river walk. Good pub nearby. Ideal touring base.

STAFFORDSHIRE

ALREWAS

Woodside Caravan Park, Fradley Junction, Alrewas, South Staffordshire, DE13 7DN.
Std: 01283 **Tel:** 790407
Website: www.ukparks.co.uk/woodside
Nearest Town/Resort Lichfield
Directions From the A38 dual carriageway take the A513 and turn off for Kings Bromley. After 2 miles turn left, 1 mile to canal bridge, turn right along canal bank.
Acreage 7¼ **Open** March **to** October
Access Good **Site** Level
Sites Available ▲ ♦ ➤ **Total** 133
Facilities & ∮ ▥ ▤ ⌐ ⊙ ⌐ ▱ ☂
♨ ⓘ ◻ ⊕ ▣ ♥ ✿ ➤◻
Nearby Facilities ⌐ ✈ ✗ ∪
♨ Lichfield
Situated at the junction of two canals with canal basin, small marina, pub and free fishing. Central for 3 theme parks. Other Web Address: www.ownerships.co.uk/woodside.htm

ALTON

Star Caravan & Camping Park, Nr. Alton Towers, Stoke-on-Trent, Staffordshire, ST10 3DW.
Std: 01538 **Tel:** 702219/702256
Website: www.starcaravanpark.co.uk
Nearest Town/Resort Cheadle
Directions Situated off the B5417, ¾ mile from Alton Towers.
Acreage 50 **Open** 1 Feb **to** 31 Oct
Access Good **Site** Lev/Slope
Sites Available ▲ ♦ ➤ **Total** 188
Facilities & ∮ ▥ ▤ ⌐ ⊙ ⌐ ▱ ◻ ☂
♨ Ⅲ ⓘ ◻ ⊕ ✗ ▱◻▣◻
Nearby Facilities ⌐ ✈ ▲ ∪ ♪ ✗
♨ Stoke
Situated in the centre of beautiful countryside within 9 miles of Leek, Uttoxeter and Ashbourne Town. Within easy reach of the Peak District and Dovedale. Café Restaurant nearby. 6 static caravans for hire please contact Mrs Brindley on 0153_ 702564. Large rally fields always available. Motorcycles are welcome. Pets must be kept on leads at all times. AA 3 Pennants and ETB 3 Star Graded.

BURTON-ON-TRENT

Willowbrook Farm, Alrewas, Burton-on-Trent, Staffordshire, DE13 7BA.
Std: 01283 **Tel:** 790217
Nearest Town/Resort Burton-on-Trent/Lichfield
Directions 6 miles from Burton-on-Trent on the A38 southbound, on the A38 side of the River Trent.
Acreage 5 **Open** All Year
Access Good **Site** Level
Sites Available ▲ ♦ ➤ **Total** 20
Facilities ∮ ▥ ▤ ⌐ ⊙ ⌐ ♥ ➤◻
Nearby Facilities ⌐ ✈
♨ Burton-on-Trent/Lichfield
Alongside the River Trent.

CHEADLE

Quarry Walk Caravan & Camping Park, Coppice Lane, Freehay, Cheadle, Staffordshire, ST10 1RQ.
Std: 01538 **Tel:** 723412
Std: 01538 **Fax:** 723412
Email: quarrywalk@caravanpark.freeserve.co.uk
Website: www.staffordshire-shortbreaks.com
Nearest Town/Resort Cheadle
Directions 1 mile from Cheadle on the A521 towards Upper Tean, turn left at The Crown to Freehay. Stay on this road going up hill for 1¼ miles, go over crossroads and turn right at the roundabout. Park is 1¼ miles on the right.
Acreage 46 **Open** All Year
Access Good **Site** Level
Sites Available ▲ ♦ ➤ **Total** 40
Facilities ∮ ▥ ▤ ⌐ ⊙ ⌐ ◻
♨ ⓘ ◻ ⊕ ▱ ➤▣◻
Nearby Facilities ♪
♨ Stoke-on-Trent
Ideal base for walking, cycling and relaxing. 4 miles from Alton Towers.

EEK

amping & Caravanning Club Site,
ackshaw Grange, Blackshaw Moor,
eek, Staffordshire, ST13 8TL.
td: 01538 **Tel:** 300285
ebsite:
ww.campingandcaravanningclub.co.uk
irections Just 2 miles from Leek on the
53 Leek to Buxton road. The site is located
00 yards past the sign for 'Blackshaw Moor'
n the left hand side.
creage 6 **Open** All Year
te Level
tes Available ∆ ⊕ ⊞ Total 90
acilities ⅏ ⅊ ⅍ ⅌ ⅍ ⅌ ⊙ ⅃ ⅌ ◎ ☎
⅌ ⅒ ◎ ⅍ ⅀ ⅌ ⅌
earby Facilities ⌐ ✎ ☂
⅄ Buxton
n the edge of the Peak District. Ideal for
siting Alton Towers. BTB Graded. Non
embers welcome.

EEK

lencote Caravan Park, Churnet Valley,
ation Road, Cheddleton, Nr. Leek,
affordshire, ST13 7EE.
td: 01538 **Tel:** 360745
td: 01538 **Fax:** 361788
ebsite: www.glencote.co.uk
earest Town/Resort Leek
irections 3¼ miles south of Leek off the
520 (Stone to Leek road).
creage 6 **Open** April to October
te Level
tes Available ⅊ ⊕ ⊞ Total 50
acilities ⅊ ⅍ ⅌ ⅍ ⅌ ⊙ ⅃ ⅌ ◎ ☎
⅌ ◎ ⅍ ⅌ ⅌
earby Facilities ⌐ ✎ ⚓ ⅍ U ℛ ☂
⅄ Stoke-on-Trent
tuated in the heart of Churnet Valley.
team Railway Centre and canalside pub
ose by, near to Alton Towers. David
ellamy Gold Award for Conservation, a
ractical Caravan Top 100 Parks 2001 and
/inner of HETB Caravan Park of the Year
ward 1999.

UGELEY

amping & Caravanning Club Site, Old
outh Hostel, Cannock Chase, Wandon,
ugeley, Staffordshire, WS15 1QW.
td: 01889 **Tel:** 582166
ebsite:
ww.campingandcaravanningclub.co.uk
irections Take the A460 to Hednesford,
rn right at signpost Rawnsley/Hazelslade,
en turn first left, site is ½ mile past the golf
ub.
creage 5 **Open** March to October

Site Sloping
Sites Available ∆ ⊕ ⊞ Total 60
Facilities ⅏ ⅊ ⅍ ⅌ ⅍ ⅌ ⊙ ⅃ ⅌ ◎ ☎
⅌ ◎ ⅍ ⅌ ⅌
Nearby Facilities ⌐ ✎ U ℛ
⅄ Rugeley Town
On the edge of Cannock Chase. 12 miles
from Drayton Manor Park. BTB Graded. Non
members welcome.

RUGELEY

Park View Farm, Little Haywood, Stafford,
Staffordshire, ST18 0TR.
Std: 01889 Tel: 808194
Nearest Town/Resort Rugeley
Directions 3 miles north of Rugeley. Leave
the A51 by-pass to villages of Colwich, Little
and Great Haywood, aite is at the top of the
hill between Little and Great Haywood. Turn
into farm drive adjacent to Jubilee Playing
Field.
Acreage 1 **Open** All Year
Access Good **Site** Level
Sites Available ∆ ⊕ ⊞ Total 11
Facilities ⅌ ⊞ ⅍ ⅌
Nearby Facilities
⅄ Rugeley/Stafford
Within walking distance of Shugborough
Hall. Convenient for Alton Towers.

RUGELEY

Silvertrees Caravan Park, Stafford Brook
Road, Rugeley, Staffordshire, WS15 2TX.
Std: 01889 Tel: 582185
Std: 01889 Fax: 582185
Nearest Town/Resort Rugeley
Directions From A51 take unclassified road
towards Penkridge at traffic lights After two
miles turn right by a white fence, entrance
100 yards on left.
Acreage 10 **Open** April to October
Access Good **Site** Lev/Slope
Sites Available ∆ ⊕ ⊞ Total 50
Facilities ⅊ ⅍ ⅌ ⅍ ⅌ ⊙ ⅃ ⅌ ◎ ☎
◎ ⅍ ⅌ ⅍ ⅌ ⅌ ⊛ ⅍ ⅌
Nearby Facilities
⅄ Rugeley
Set on Cannock Chase, a designated area
of outstanding natural beauty. Tennis on site.
18 miles from Alton Towers.

RUGELEY

Tackeroo - Forest Enterprise, West
Midlands Forest District, Birches Valley,
Rugeley, Staffordshire, WS15 2UQ.
Std: 01889 Tel: 586593
Email: doug.stanley@forestry.gov.uk
Website: www.forestry.gov.uk

Nearest Town/Resort Rugeley
Directions In the centre of Cannock Chase
on the Penkridge to Rugeley road. Join the
A34 Cannock to Stafford road east of
junctions 12 and 13 of the M6. Turn east 1
mile north of Huntingdon for Rugeley, site is
2 miles on the right.
Acreage 3 **Open** All Year
Access Good **Site** Level
Sites Available ∆ ⊕ ⊞ Total 70
Facilities ⅌ ⅌ ⅍ ⅌
Nearby Facilities
⅄ Penkridge
The wide open spaces of Cannock Chase
are ideal for walking, cycling, orienteering
and relaxing. Ideal stopover site, just off the
M6. Note : This site has NO toilets.

STOKE-ON-TRENT

The Cross Inn Caravan Park, Cauldon
Low, Stoke-on-Trent, Staffordshire, ST10
3EX.
Std: 01538 Tel: 308338
Std: 01538 Fax: 308767
Email: adrian_weaver@hotmail.com
Website: www.crossinn.co.uk
Nearest Town/Resort Leek
Directions On the A52 midway between
Stoke-on-Trent and Ashbourne.
Acreage 2 **Open** March to November
Access Good **Site** Level
Sites Available ∆ ⊕ ⊞ Total 30
Facilities ⅏ ⅊ ⅍ ⅌ ⅍ ⅌ ⊙ ⅃ ⅌ ◎ ☎
⅌ ✕ ⅌ ⅍ ⅌ ⅍ ⅌ ⅌
Nearby Facilities ⌐ ✎ ⚓ ⅍ U ℛ ☂
⅄ Stoke-on-Trent
2½ miles from Alton Towers and near the
Peak District National Park.

TRENTHAM

**Trentham Gardens Camping & Caravan
Park,** Trentham Gardens, Trentham,
Stoke-on-Trent, Staffordshire, ST4 8AX.
Std: 01782 Tel: 657519
Std: 01782 Fax: 644536
Email: simon@trenthamgardens.co.uk
Website: www.trenthamgardens.co.uk
Nearest Town/Resort Stoke-on-Trent
Directions 2 minutes from the M6 junction
15, follow signs.
Acreage 35 **Open** All Year
Access Good **Site** Sloping
Sites Available ∆ ⊕ ⊞ Total 250
Facilities ⅏ ⅊ ⅍ ⅌ ⅍ ⅌ ⊙ ⅃ ⅌ ◎ ☎
⅀ ◎ ⅌ ✕ ⅌ ⅍ ⅌ ⅍ ⅌ ⅌
Nearby Facilities ⌐ ✎ U ℛ
⅄ Stoke-on-Trent
Set in 750 acres of ancestral estate and
woodland. Easy travelling distance from
Alton Towers and the Potteries.

SUFFOLK
BECCLES

Beulah Hall Caravan Park, Dairy Lane, Mutford, Beccles, Suffolk, NR34 7QJ.
Std: 01502 **Tel:** 476609
Std: 01502 **Fax:** 476453
Email: carol.stuckey@fsmail.net
Nearest Town/Resort Lowestoft
Directions Halfway between Lowestoft and Beccles on the A146. At T-junction signposted to Mutford take 'New Road', 350 yards to the site.
Acreage 2½ **Open** April **to** October
Access Good **Site** Level
Sites Available A ♦ ♠ **Total** 30
Facilities ƒ ⓌⒺ ♣ ⌐ ⊙ ⇩ ♥ ⓪ ⅂ ⊁ ♥ ⒷⒺ
Nearby Facilities ⌐ ✔ ⚓ ⚘ ∪ ♫
≠ Oulton Broad South
Near to Award Winning beaches and the Broads. Ideal base for touring the area.

BECCLES

Waveney Lodge Caravan Site, Elms Road, Aldeby, Beccles, Suffolk, NR34 0EJ.
Std: 01502 **Tel:** 677445
Email: waveneylodge25@hotmail.com
Nearest Town/Resort Beccles
Directions From Beccles take the A146 towards Norwich, at the first roundabout take the A143 towards Great Yarmouth. After 1 mile take the first turn right, after ¼ mile turn left, site is on the right.
Acreage 1½ **Open** April **to** October
Access Good **Site** Level
Sites Available A ♦ ♠ **Total** 15
Facilities ƒ ⓌⒺ ♣ ⌐ ⊙ ⇩ ♥ ⓪ Ⓜ ♥ ⒷⒺ
Nearby Facilities ⌐ ✔ ⚓ ⚘ ∪ ♫
≠ Beccles
Site enjoys a rural situation, near to the historic market town of Beccles. Close to several excellent beaches. Centrally placed

for enjoying Norfolks and Suffolks unique attractions.

BUNGAY

Outney Meadow Caravan Park, Outney Meadow, Bungay, Suffolk, NR35 1HG.
Std: 01986 **Tel:** 892338
Nearest Town/Resort Bungay
Directions Entrance is signposted from the junction of the A143 and A144 at Bungay.
Acreage 6 **Open** Easter **to** October
Access Good **Site** Level
Sites Available A ♦ ♠ **Total** 45
Facilities ƒ ⊟ ⓌⒺ ♣ ⌐ ⊙ ⇩ 回 ⅃⅄ ⓪ ⊕ ♥ ⒷⒺ
Nearby Facilities ⌐ ✔ ⚘
≠ Beccles
Beside the River Waveney and common.

BURY ST EDMUNDS

The Dell Touring Park, Beyton Road, Thurston, Bury St Edmunds, Suffolk, IP31 3RB
Std: 01359 **Tel:** 270121
Nearest Town/Resort Bury St Edmunds
Directions Take A14 eastbound 6 miles from Bury follow Thurston signs.
Open All Year
Access Good **Site** Level
Sites Available A ♦ ♠ **Total** 100
Facilities & ƒ ⊟ ⓌⒺ ♣ ⌐ ⊙ ⇩ ⅃⅄ ⓪ ⊕ ♥ Ⓜ ♥ ⒷⒺ
Nearby Facilities ✔ ♫
≠ Thurston
Ideal for touring East Anglia. 1 hour from Cambridge, Norwich and coast. New hard standing pitches. New toilet block opening Easter 2002.

DARSHAM

Haw-Wood Farm Caravan & Camping Park, Haw-Wood Farm, Darsham, Saxmundham, Suffolk, IP17 3QT.
Std: 01986 **Tel:** 784248

Nearest Town/Resort Southwold
Directions Turn off the A12 100 yards north of the junction with the A144 at the Little Chef, ¼ mile on the right.
Acreage 7 **Open** April **to** October
Access Good **Site** Level
Sites Available A ♦ ♠ **Total** 90
Facilities ƒ ⓌⒺ ♣ ⌐ ⊙ ⇩ ♥ ⅄ Ⓜ ♥ ⒷⒺ
Nearby Facilities ⌐ ✔
≠ Darsham
5 miles from the beach. Near to a golf club, fishing and clay pigeon shooting.

DUNWICH

Cliff House Holiday Park, Minsmere Road, Dunwich, Saxmundham, Suffolk, IP17 3DQ.
Std: 01728 **Tel:** 648282
Std: 01728 **Fax:** 648996
Nearest Town/Resort Southwold
Directions From A12, at Blythburgh or Yoxford, follow signs to Dunwich Heath.
Acreage 30 **Open** April/Easter **to** End Oct
Access Good **Site** Level
Sites Available ♦ ♠ **Total** 87
Facilities ƒ ⊟ ⓌⒺ ♣ ⌐ ⊙ ⇩ ⌯ ⅃⅄ ⓪ ⊕ ♥ ✕ ♥ Ⓜ Ⓜ ♥ ⒷⒺ
Nearby Facilities ⌐ ✔ ⚓ ⚘ ∪ ♫ ♫
≠ Yoxford
Beach frontage, adjoining National Trust and Minsmere Bird Reserve. Suffolk Heritage Coast. David Bellamy Silver Award for Conservation.

EYE

Honeypot Camp & Caravan Park
Wortham, Eye, Suffolk, IP22 1PW.
Std: 01379 **Tel:** 783312
Std: 01379 **Fax:** 783312
Email: honeypotcamping@talk21.com
Website: www.honeypotcamping.co.uk
Nearest Town/Resort Diss
Directions Four miles south of Diss

Minsmere Road, Dunwich, Saxmundham, Suffolk IP17 3DQ
Tel: 01728 648282
30 acre wooded holiday park on Suffolk's Heritage Coast.
Own beach access. Near Dunwich Heath, Walberswick.
100 lodges/log cabins and holiday caravans, some for sale.
100 touring caravan and tent pitches. Electric hook-ups,
heated showers and a cosy bar and restaurant.

Cliff House Holiday Park
On Suffolk's Heritage Coast

SILVER

---

south side A143, towards Bury St.
munds.
reage 6½ **Open** May to September
cess Good **Site** Level
es Available ▲ ⊕ ⊛ **Total** 35
cilities ⌀ 🔟 ♿ ⌐ ☉ ⌐ 🔟 📺
🔟 🔟 🔟 🔟 🔟 📺 🔟
arby **Facilities** ⌐ ✓
Diss
hly recommended, family run (for over
years), inland touring site, Norfolk/Suffolk
tre. Steam Museum 2 miles. Quiet and
aceful surroundings. Fishing on site.
keside pitches. Free hot water. Free
our illustrated brochure.

ADLEIGH
stead Touring Park, Holt Road,
stead, Near Colchester, Suffolk, CO6
Z.
📞: 01787 **Tel:** 211969
📠: 01787 **Fax:** 211969
arest Town/Resort Hadleigh
ections Between Hadleigh and Boxford
the A1071, opposite 'The Brewers Arms
' (signposted).
reage 3½ **Open** March to October
cess Good **Site** Lev/Slope
es Available ▲ ⊕ ⊛ **Total** 30
ilities ♿ ⌐ 🔟 ♿ ⌐ ☉ 🔟 🔟 🔟 🔟 📺
arby **Facilities** ⌐ ∪
Sudbury
al for touring Constable country.

ALESWORTH
e Garage, St. Lawrence, Beccles,
ffolk, NR34 8LB.
📞: 01986 **Tel:** Ilketshall 781241
arest Town/Resort Halesworth
ections Situated on A144, 3½ miles
rth Halesworth, 5½ miles south Bungay.
reage 1 **Open** March to October
cess Good **Site** Level
es Available ▲ ⊕ ⊛ **Total** 12
cilities 🔟 ⊛ ♿ 🔟 ☉ 🔟 📺
arby **Facilities** ⌐ ✓ ⚓ ✕ ∪
Halesworth
al touring centre. Situated in rural area,
miles coast.

SWICH
w House Touring Caravan Centre,
w House, Bucklesham Road, Foxhall,
wich, Suffolk, IP10 0AU.
📞: 01473 **Tel:** 659437
📠: 01473 **Fax:** 659880
nail: john.e.booth@talk21.com
arest Town/Resort Ipswich/Felixstowe
rections Turn off the A14 Ipswich Ring
ad (South) via slip road onto the A1156
gnposted East Ipswich). In 1 mile turn right
gnposted), in ½ mile turn right signposted
cklesham. Site is on the left in ¼ mile.

Acreage 3½ **Open** All Year
Access Good **Site** Level
Sites Available ▲ ⊕ ⊛ **Total** 30
Facilities ⌀ 🔟 ♿ ⌐ ☉ ⌐ 🔟
🔟 🔟 ☉ ⊛ 🔟 🔟 📺
Nearby Facilities ⌐ ✓ ⚓ ✕ ∪ ♪
✈ Ipswich
Camp in a beautiful garden packed with
ornamental trees and plants, arches and
bower doves, rabbits, bantams and guinea
fowl. Wildlife all around. Ornamental Tree
Walk and Pets Corner. Heated toilet and
shower block. Electric hook-ups available on
ALL pitches. Calor Gas and Camping Gaz
available on site.

IPSWICH
Orwell Meadows Leisure Park, Priory
Lane, Ipswich, Suffolk, IP10 0JS.
Std: 01473 **Tel:** 726666
Std: 01473 **Fax:** 721441
Email: david@orwellmeadows.co.uk
Nearest Town/Resort Ipswich.
Directions From A14 towards Felixstowe
take first exit after Orwell Bridge, at
roundabout turn left and first left again then
follow signs.
Acreage 17
Access Good **Site** Level
Sites Available ▲ ⊕ ⊛ **Total** 80
Facilities ♿ ⌀ 🔟 ♿ ⌐ ☉ 🔟
🔟 🔟 ☉ ✕ 🔟 🔟 ⊹ 🔟 📺
Nearby Facilities ⌐ ✓
✈ Ipswich
A quiet, family run park, ideally situated for
touring beautiful Suffolk. Adjacent to the
Orwell Country Park. Forest and river walks.

IPSWICH
Priory Park, Ipswich, Suffolk, IP10 0JT.
Std: 01473 **Tel:** 727393
Std: 01473 **Fax:** 278372
Email: prioryparkipswich@msn.com
Website: www.priory-park.com
Nearest Town/Resort Ipswich
Directions Travelling east along A14
Ipswich southern by-pass take first exit after
River Orwell Road bridge, turn left towards
Ipswich following caravan/camping signs.
300yards from by-pass on left, follow signs
to Priory Park.
Acreage 100 **Open** Easter to End
October
Access Good **Site** Level
Sites Available ▲ ⊕ ⊛ **Total** 75
Facilities ⌀ 🔟 ♿ ⌐ ☉ 🔟 🔟
🔟 🔟 ☉ ✕ 🔟 🔟 ⊛ 🔟 📺
Nearby Facilities ⌐ ✓ ⚓ ✕ ∪ ♪
✈ Ipswich
Superb historic setting. Frontage onto River
Orwell. Magnificent south facing panoramic
views. 9 hole golf course and hard tennis

court within the park grounds. Club
adventure play area, nature trails, access
to foreshore. NEW toilets, showers and
laundry facilities for 2001. Holiday lodges for
hire. Holiday Homes for sale.

KESSINGLAND
Camping & Caravanning Club Site,
Suffolk Wildlife Park, Whites Lane,
Kessingland, Suffolk, NR33 7SL.
Std: 01502 **Tel:** 742040
Website:
www.campingandcaravanningclub.co.uk
Nearest Town/Resort Lowestoft
Directions From Lowestoft on the A12,
leave at roundabout in Kessingland
following Wildlife Park signs. Turn right
through park entrance.
Acreage 6½ **Open** March to October
Access Good **Site** Level
Sites Available ▲ ⊕ ⊛ **Total** 90
Facilities ♿ ⌀ 🔟 ♿ ⌐ ☉ 🔟 🔟 📺
🔟 ☉ ⊛ 🔟 ⊹ 🔟 📺
Nearby Facilities ⌐ ✓ ♪
✈ Lowestoft
Next to Suffolk Wildlife Park. Set in a quiet
seaside resort, close to Great Yarmouth. 5
miles from Pleasurewood Hills. BTB
Graded. Non members welcome.

LEISTON
Cliff House Caravan Park, Sizewell
Common, Leiston, Suffolk, IP16 4TU.
Std: 01728 **Tel:** 830724
Std: 01728 **Fax:** 830724
Nearest Town/Resort Leiston
Directions Take the A12 to Yoxford then the
B1122 to Leiston. Follow signs to Sizewell
and take a right hand turn before Sizewell
Village to the park.
Acreage 5 **Open** March to November
Access Good **Site** Level
Sites Available ▲ ⊕ ⊛ **Total** 60
Facilities ⌀ 🔟 ♿ ⌐ ☉ 🔟 🔟 📺
🔟 ☉ ⊛ ✕ ☉ 🔟 🔟 📺
Nearby Facilities ⌐ ✓ ⚓ ♪
✈ Saxmundham
Quiet location adjoining the beach. Peaceful
walks in this area of outstanding natural
beauty.

LOWESTOFT
Azure Seas Caravan Park, The Street,
Corton, Lowestoft, Suffolk, NR32 5HN.
Std: 01502 **Tel:** 731403
Std: 01502 **Fax:** 730958
Email: long-beach@fsnet.co.uk
Website: www.norfolkbroads.com/
longbeach
Nearest Town/Resort Lowestoft
Directions From the A12 2 miles north of
Lowestoft, turn east onto Corton Long Lane.
Park is at the junction with The Street.

Acreage 10 **Open** Mid March **to** 5 Nov
Access Good **Site** Level
Sites Available A ⚑ ⚐ **Total** 30
Facilities ☐ ⚹ ⥁ ⚑ ⍨⊙▣⦿▢⚐⚑ A⤏▣▣
Nearby Facilities ⌖ ✈ ⚓ ⤪ ∪
≈ Lowestoft
Adjoining beach. Very convenient for Pleasurewood Hills American Theme Park.

LOWESTOFT

Beach Farm Residential & Holiday Park Ltd., Arbor Lane, Pakefield, Lowestoft, Suffolk, NR33 7BD.
Std: 01502 **Tel:** 572794
Std: 01502 **Fax:** 537460
Email: beachfarmpark@aol.com
Website: www.beachfarmpark.co.uk
Nearest Town/Resort Lowestoft
Directions Main roundabout Kessingland Lowestoft A12 fourth exit, from Lowestoft first exit.
Acreage 5 **Open** March **to** October
Access Good **Site** Level
Sites Available A ⚑ ⚐ **Total** 35
Facilities ☐ ⚹ ⥁ ⚑ ⍨⊙▣⦿⚐⚑⚹▢⍦⚑⤏▣▣⚐
Nearby Facilities ⌖ ✈ ⚓ ⤪ ∪ ℛ
≈ Lowestoft
¼ mile from the beach. Close to all amenities. Club, heated pool and a fast food restaurant on park.

LOWESTOFT

Chestnut Farm Caravan Site, Gisleham, Lowestoft, Suffolk, NR33 8EE.
Std: 01502 **Tel:** 740227
Nearest Town/Resort Lowestoft
Directions 3 miles south of Lowestoft off the A12 at Kessingland (Suffolk Wildlife Park roundabout). Turn west signposted Rushmere/Mutford/Gisleham, take the second left and then the first drive on the left.
Acreage 3 **Open** Easter **to** October

Access Good **Site** Level
Sites Available A ⚑ ⚐ **Total** 20
Facilities ⚹ ⥁ ⚑ ⍨⊙▣⦿▢⚐⚹⤏▣
Nearby Facilities ⌖ ✈ ⚓ ⤪ ∪ ℛ
≈ Oulton Broad/Lowestoft
River fishing on the farm, good cycling area.

LOWESTOFT

Pakefield Caravan Park, Arbor Lane, Pakefield, Lowestoft, Suffolk, NR33 7BQ.
Std: 01502 **Tel:** 561136/511884
Nearest Town/Resort Lowestoft
Directions 2 miles south of Lowestoft off the main A12.
Open April **to** October
Access Good **Site** Level
Sites Available ⚑ ⚐ **Total** 20
Facilities ⚹ ⥁ ⚑ ⍨⊙⊘▢⚑⊙⚐⚹⥂⍦⚑⤏▣▣
Nearby Facilities ⌖ ✈ ⚓ ⤪ ∪ ℛ
≈ Lowestoft/Oulton Broad
Right beside beach yet only minutes walk from main shopping area. Ideal for touring the Broads.

NAYLAND

Rushbanks Farm Caravan & Camping, Bures Road, Wiston, Nayland, Colchester, Essex, CO6 4NA.
Std: 01206 **Tel:** 262350
Nearest Town/Resort Colchester/Clacton
Directions From Colchester take the A134 towards Sudbury. Nayland is 7 miles from Colchester, just across the Suffolk border. Campsite is 2 miles off the A134.
Acreage 5 **Open** May **to** October
Access Good **Site** Level
Sites Available A ⚑ ⚐ **Total** 20
Nearby Facilities ⌖ ✈ ⚓
≈ Colchester
Picturesque and peaceful site on the north banks of the River Stour, ideal for fishing and rowing.

SAXMUNDHAM

Lakeside Country & Leisure Park, Rendham Road, Saxmundham, Suffolk, IP17 2QP.
Std: 01728 **Tel:** 603344
Std: 01728 **Fax:** 603344
Email: lakeside@pgen.net
Website: www.lakesidesuffolk.com
Nearest Town/Resort Saxmundham
Directions From the A12 take the B11▮ west and follow brown tourism signs. T▮ right at sharp hairpin bend signed Kelsa▮
Acreage 46 **Open** 1 May **to** 30 Sept
Access Good **Site** Sloping
Sites Available ⚑ ⚐ **Total** 130
Facilities ⚹ ☐ ⚹ ⥁ ⚑ ⍨⊙⥂▢⚐ ⚑ ⊙
▢⊘⚹ ⌕ ⚑ ⥁ ⊛⤏▣▣
Nearby Facilities ⌖ ✈ ⚓ ∪
≈ Saxmundham
2 fishing lakes. Swimming pool from Spri▮ Bank Hol to the end of August. 7 miles fr▮ the heritage coast.

SAXMUNDHAM

Whitearch Touring Park, Main Road, Benhall, Saxmundham, Suffolk, IP17 1N▮
Std: 01728 **Tel:** 604646
Nearest Town/Resort Saxmundham
Directions Just off the main A12 juncti▮ with the B1121 at the Ipswich end Saxmundham by-pass.
Acreage 14½ **Open** April **to** October
Access Good **Site** Level
Sites Available A ⚑ ⚐ **Total** 40
Facilities ☐ ⚹ ⥁ ⚑ ⍨⊙⥂⊘▢⚑⊛⤏▣
Nearby Facilities ✈ ℛ
≈ Saxmundham
Fishing and tennis on site. Suffolk coa▮ Snape Maltings Concert Hall, Minsmere B▮ Reserve, American Theme Park a▮ castles.

HOTLEY

hotley Caravan Park, Gate Farm Road,
hotley, Suffolk, IP9 1QH.
td: 01473 Tel: 787421
td: 01473 Fax: 400802
mail: p.hammond3@ntlworld.com
earest Town/Resort Ipswich/Felixstowe
irections From Orwell Bridge take exit
l37 and follow the B1456 once in Shotley
0 miles from Ipswich). Go past the Rose
ub on the right and after 1 mile turn left
to Gate Farm Road and go through white
ate.
creage 7 Open March to October
ccess Good Site Lev/Slope
tes Available ⊐ ⊟
acilities ⚓ ⨍ 🛁 🛒 ⬚
earby Facilities ✈ ⚓ ⌄ ♪
⊨ Ipswich
njoy peace and tranquillity in this area of
utstanding natural beauty, with panoramic
ews over the River Orwell. Ideal site for
e over 50's. 9 hole putting green. Tourers/
llies welcome. On site static 25ft 6 berth
ravan with private patio to let. Close to a
arina, restaurants, pubs, fish & chips,
urch, doctors and garage. Easy access
om the A12/A14. You can also telephone
s on Freephone 0800 074 0801.

TOWMARKET

rchard View Caravan Park, c/o
towupland Service Station, Thorney
reen, Stowupland, Stowmarket, Suffolk,
P14 4BJ.
td: 01449 Tel: 612326
earest Town/Resort Stowmarket/
swich
irections ½ mile from the A14 on the
1120 tourist route, in the village of
towupland. Secluded position behind
ervice station.
creage ¾ Open April to September

Access Good Site Level
Sites Available ⚐ ⊟ ⊟ Total 8
Facilities ⨍ 🛁 ⚓ 🛒 ⊙⌄🛒 🛒 SL l🞖 🖨 🔌 🖻
Nearby Facilities ⌐ ✈ ⌄ U
⊨ Stowmarket
Good touring centre for Constable country,
the East coast and Norfolk.

STOWMARKET

Stonham Barns Caravan & Camping
Park, Pettaugh Road, Stonham Aspal,
Stowmarket, Suffolk, IP14 6AT.
Std: 01449 Tel: 711901
Std: 01473 Fax: 890036
Email: enquiries@sbcaravanpark.co.uk
Website: www.sbcaravanpark.co.uk
Nearest Town/Resort Stowmarket/
Ipswich
Directions From the A14 between Ipswich
and Stowmarket take the A140, after 3 miles
turn right onto the A1120, after 2 miles entry
is through Stonham Barns Leisure Complex.
Acreage 5 Open All Year
Access Good Site Level
Sites Available ⚐ ⊟ Total 60
Facilities ⚓ ⨍ 🛁 ⚓ ⌐ ⊙⌄🖥 🖻 🛒
SL 🖨 🔌 🖻 🖻
Nearby Facilities ⌐ ✈
⊨ Stowmarket/Ipswich
Next to a Leisure Complex which has 9 hole
golf, mini golf, driving range, fishing lake,
craft shops, owl sanctuary and a restaurant.

SUDBURY

Willowmere Caravan Park, Bures Road,
Little Cornard, Sudbury, Suffolk, CO10 0NN
Std: 01787 Tel: 375559
Std: 01787 Fax: 375559
Nearest Town/Resort Sudbury
Directions Leave Sudbury on the B1508 to
Bures and Colchester, 1 mile from Sudbury.
Acreage 2 Open Easter to 1 October
Access Good Site Level
Sites Available ⚐ ⊟ ⊟ Total 40

Facilities ⨍ 🛁 ⚓ ⌐ ⊙⌄🖥 🛒 🛒 ⚓🛒
Nearby Facilities ⌐ ✈ ⚓ U ♪
⊨ Sudbury
Quiet, country park near a river.

THEBERTON

Cakes & Ale, Abbey Lane, Theberton,
Suffolk, IP16 4TE.
Std: 01728 Tel: 831655
Std: 01473 Fax: 736270
Nearest Town/Resort Leiston/Aldeburgh
Directions Leave A12 taking B1121
Saxmundham, Benhall, Sternfield in
Saxmundham take B1119 signposted
Leiston proceed for 3 miles then take by-
road left following signs to park.
Acreage 45 Open April to October
Access Good Site Level
Sites Available ⚐ ⊟ ⊟ Total 100
Facilities ⨍ 🛁 🖥 🛁 ⚓ ⌐ ⊙⌄🖥 ⚓ 🖻 🛒
SL 🖨 🔌 🖓 🛁 🗚 ⚓🛒🖻 🖻
Nearby Facilities ⌐ ✈ ⚓ U
⊨ Saxmundham
2 miles best beach in area. Excellent base
for coastal Suffolk, Southwold, Dunwich,
Minsmere, Aldeburgh. Tennis courts, table
tennis, golf driving range and practice nets
and sports field on park.

WOODBRIDGE

Forest Camping, Rendlesham Forest
Caravan Park, Butley, Woodbridge,
Suffolk, IP12 3NF.
Std: 01394 Tel: 450707
Email: admin@forestcamping.co.uk
Website: www.forestcamping.co.uk
Nearest Town/Resort Woodbridge
Directions Take the A1152 off the A12 on
the Woodbridge bypass. Fork left at
roundabout in Bromeswell then straight onto
the B1084 towards Orford. After 4 miles turn
right into forest and follow brown tourism
signs for Rendlesham Forest Centre.

Acreage 7 **Open** April **to** October
Access Good **Site** Level
Sites Available **Total** 90
Facilities
Nearby Facilities
Melton
Near to Orford Castle and Aldeburgh. Cycling in the forest. Open for Easter 2002. AA Recommended Award 1999 and ETB 3 Star Grading.

WOODBRIDGE

St. Margaret's House Caravan & Camping Site, St. Margaret's House, Hollesley Road, Shottisham, Woodbridge, Suffolk, IP12 3HD.
Std: 01394 **Tel:** 411247
Email: ken.norton@virgin.net
Nearest Town/Resort Woodbridge
Directions Turn off the A12 onto the A1152 signposted Bawdsey and Orford). After 1½ miles fork right onto the B1083 signposted Bawdsey. After 3 miles at the T-junction turn left, site is on the left 100 yards past Sorrel Horse Public House.
Acreage 10 **Open** Easter/1 April **to** 31 Oct
Access Good **Site** Level
Sites Available **Total** 25
Facilities
Nearby Facilities
Woodbridge
Situated in an area of outstanding natural beauty. Very quiet site, just birds, rabbits, deer and foxes. 3½ miles from a shingle beach. Large grassy field adjacent for children to play in. Excellent walking and cycling. Swimming pool and bowling within 5 miles. Milk and dairy produce are available from the house. 150 metres from The Sorrel Horse Public House which serves meals, snacks, wine and fine ales.

WOODBRIDGE

The Moon and Sixpence, Newbourne Road, Waldringfield, Woodbridge, Suffolk, IP12 4PP.
Std: 01473 **Tel:** 736650
Email: moonsix@dircon.co.uk
Website: www.moonsix.dircon.co.uk
Nearest Town/Resort Woodbridge
Directions Turn off A12, Ipswich Eastern By-Pass, onto unclassified road signposted Waldringfield, Newbourn. Follow caravan direction signs.
Acreage 5 **Open** April **to** October
Access Good **Site** Level
Sites Available **Total** 75
Facilities
Nearby Facilities
Woodbridge
Picturesque location. Sheltered, terraced site. Own private lake and sandy beach.

SURREY

CHERTSEY

Camping & Caravanning Club Site, Bridge Road, Chertsey, Surrey, KT16 8JX.
Std: 01932 **Tel:** 562405
Website: www.campingandcaravanningclub.co.uk
Directions Leave the M25 at junction 11 and follow the A317 to Chertsey. At the roundabout take the first exit to the traffic lights and go straight across to the next set of traffic lights, turn right and after 400 yards turn left into the site.
Open All Year
Site Level
Sites Available **Total** 200
Facilities
Nearby Facilities
Chertsey
On the banks of the River Thames, fishing on site. Table tennis on site. 4 miles from Thorpe Park. Close to London. BTB Graded and AA 4 Pennants.

EAST HORSLEY

Camping & Caravanning Club Site, Ockham Road North, East Horsley, Surrey, KT24 6PE.
Std: 01483 **Tel:** 283273
Website: www.campingandcaravanningclub.co.uk
Nearest Town/Resort Guildford
Directions Leave the M25 at junction 10 and travel south on the A3, turn left onto the B2039, site is third on the right.
Open March **to** October
Access Good **Site** Level
Sites Available **Total** 135
Facilities
Nearby Facilities
East Horsley
Peaceful site, only 40 minutes from London by train. Fishing lake on site. Non members welcome.

HAMBLEDON

The Merry Harriers, Hambledon, Surrey, GU8 4DR.
Std: 01428 **Tel:** Wormley 682883
Nearest Town/Resort Godalming
Directions Leave Godalming on B2130 and follow Hambledon signs approx. 4 miles.
Acreage 1 **Open** All Year
Access Good **Site** Level
Sites Available **Total** 25
Facilities
Nearby Facilities
Witley
Unspoilt countryside, opposite country pub.

LINGFIELD

Longacres Caravan & Camping Park, Newchapel Road, Lingfield, Surrey, RH7 6LE.
Std: 01342 **Tel:** 833205
Std: 01622 **Fax:** 735038
Nearest Town/Resort East Grinstead
Directions From the M25 junction 6 take the A22 south towards East Grinstead. At Newchapel roundabout turn left onto the B2028 towards Lingfield. Site is on the right in 700yds.
Acreage 18 **Open** All Year
Access Good **Site** Lev/Slope
Sites Available **Total** 60
Facilities
Nearby Facilities
Lingfield
Fishing and tourist information on site. Ideal to visit London, Surrey, Kent and Sussex.

SUSSEX

ARUNDEL

Maynards Caravan & Camping Park, Crossbush, Arundel, West Sussex, BN18 9PQ.
Std: 01903 **Tel:** 882075
Std: 01903 **Fax:** 885547
Nearest Town/Resort Arundel/Littlehampton
Directions ¾ mile from Arundel on A27, turn left into car park of Out & Out Pub & Restaurant going east on Worthing/Brighton road.
Acreage 3 **Open** All Year
Access Good **Site** Level
Sites Available **Total** 70
Facilities
Nearby Facilities
Arundel
Very central for touring. 3 miles to sea, mile to river. Arundel Castle and B Sanctuary. 24 hour shop adjacent.

ARUNDEL

Ship & Anchor Marina, Heywood & Bryett Ltd., Ford, Arundel, West Sussex, BN18 0BJ.
Std: 01243 **Tel:** 551262
Nearest Town/Resort Arundel/Littlehampton
Directions From the A27 at Arundel, foll road signposted to Ford for 2 miles. Site on the left after level-crossing at Ford.
Acreage 12 **Open** March **to** October
Access Good **Site** Level
Sites Available **Total** 160
Facilities
Nearby Facilities
Ford
Beside the River Arun with a public hou on site. 3 miles to beaches. Advan booking is advisable for hook-ups a groups.

BATTLE

Brakes Coppice Park, Forewood Lane, Crowhurst, East Sussex, TN33 9AB.
Std: 01424 **Tel:** 830322
Std: 01424 **Fax:** 830758
Email: brakesco@btinternet.com
Website: www.brakescoppicepark.co.uk
Nearest Town/Resort Battle
Directions Turn right off the A2100 (Bat to Hastings road) 2 miles from Battle. Foll signs to Crowhurst, 1¼ miles turn left i site.
Acreage 3¼ **Open** March **to** October
Access Good **Site** Sloping
Sites Available **Total** 30
Facilities
Nearby Facilities
Crowhurst
Secluded, 11 acre, woodland park with lev pitches. Fishing on site.

BATTLE

Senlac Park Touring Caravan Site, Ma Road, Catsfield, Nr Battle, East Sussex, TN33 9DU.
Std: 01424 **Tel:** 773969
Email: mail@senlacpark.co.uk
Website: www.senlacpark.co.uk
Nearest Town/Resort Battle/Hastings
Directions From Battle take A271, aft about 1½ miles pass the Squirrel Pub House on the left then turn left (B2204). S is on the left hand side.
Acreage 5 **Open** March **to** October
Access Good **Site** Level
Sites Available **Total** 32
Facilities
Nearby Facilities
Battle
20 acre site in an area of outstanding natu beauty. Many historic features nearby. "10 Country". Beach 7 miles. Ideal touring bas

BEXHILL-ON-SEA

Cobbs Hill Farm Caravan & Camping Park, Watermill Lane, Bexhill-on-Sea, East Sussex, TN39 5JA.
Std: 01424 **Tel:** 213460
Nearest Town/Resort Bexhill-on-Sea

rections From Bexhill take the A269, turn
ght into Watermill Lane. Site is 1 mile on
e left.
creage 7 **Open** April **to** October
ccess Good **Site** Level
ites Available ⚠ ⊟ ⊟ **Total** 45
acilities ♿ ∮ 🏠 📷 ⚓ ⌂ ⊙ ⊣ ◻ ▽
◪ ⊙ 🔥 ⚠ ❋⊬⊟
earby Facilities ⌐ ✓ ⚓ ↘ ∪ ♪

≈ Bexhill-on-Sea
uiet countryside, on a small farm. Large
nt field at peak times.

EXHILL-ON-SEA

loofs Caravan Park, Sandhurst Lane,
hydown, Bexhill-on-Sea, East Sussex,
N39 4RG.
td: 01424 **Tel:** 842839
td: 01424 **Fax:** 845669
mail: camping@kloofs.ndirect.co.uk
ebsite: www.kloofs.ndirect.co.uk
earest Town/Resort Bexhill-on-Sea
irections From Bexhill travel west on the
259, at Little Common roundabout turn into
eartree Lane, go up the hill to the
ossroads and turn left.
creage 22 **Open** All Year
ccess Good **Site** Level
ites Available ⚠ ⊟ ⊟ **Total** 50
acilities ♿ ∮ 🏠 📷 ⚓ ⌂ ⊙ ⊣ ◻ ⊟ ▽
◪ ⌐ ⊙ 🏠 ⚠❋⊬⊟ ⊟
earby Facilities ⌐ ✓ ⚓ ↘ ∪
≈ Cooden
l weather, all year. Quiet, rural park only 2
iles from the beach. New centrally heated
ilet and wash block. ETB 5 Star Graded
ark.

ILLINGHURST

imeburners (Camping) Ltd.,
meburners, Newbridge, Billinghurst,
ussex, RH14 9JA.
td: 01403 **Tel:** 782311
mail:
neburnerscampingltd@tinyworld.co.uk
earest Town/Resort Billinghurst
irections 1½ miles west of billinghurst on
272, turn left on B2133 150yds onleft.
pen April **to** October
ccess Good **Site** Level
ites Available ⚠ ⊟ ⊟ **Total** 40
acilities ∮ 📷 ⚓ ⌂ ⊙ ⊣ ▽ ◪ ⌐ ⊙ 🏠❋⊬⊟
earby Facilities ✓ ∪ ♪
ublic house attached, lunch time and
vening food.

BOGNOR REGIS

he Lillies Nursery & Caravan Park,
apton Road, Barnham, Bognor Regis,
ussex, PO22 0AY.
td: 01243 **Tel:** 552081
td: 01243 **Fax:** 552081
mail: thelillies@hotmail.com
ebsite: www.lilliescaravanpark.co.uk
earest Town/Resort Bognor Regis
irections From Bognor Regis take the A29
o Eastergate, turn right at the War Memorial
nto the B2233, 5 miles.
creage 3 **Open** All Year
ccess Good **Site** Level
ites Available ⚠ ⊟ ⊟ **Total** 40
acilities ♿ ∮ 🏠 📷 ⚓ ⌂ ⊙ ⊣ ◻ ⊟ ▽
◪ ◪ ⊙ 🏠 ⚠❋⊬⊟
earby Facilities ⌐ ✓ ⚓ ↘ ∪ ♪
≈ Barnham
uiet, secluded site within walking distance
f Barnham Railway Station where theres a
irect line to all main local attractions.

CHICHESTER

ell Caravan Park, Bell Lane, Birdham,
r. Chichester, Sussex, PO20 7HY.
td: 01243 **Tel:** 512264

Nearest Town/Resort Chichester.
Directions From Chichester take the A286
towards Wittering for approx. 4 miles. At
Birdham turn left into Bell Lane, site is
500yds on the left.
Acreage ¼ **Open** March **to** October
Access Good **Site** Level
Sites Available ⊟ ⊟ **Total** 15
Facilities ∮ 📷 ⚓ ⌂ ⊣ ◻ ▽ ◪ ⊙ 🏠❋⊟
Nearby Facilities ⌐ ✓ ⚓ ↘ ∪ ♪ ⌐
≈ Chichester

CHICHESTER

Camping & Caravanning Club Site, 345
Main Road, Southbourne, Hampshire,
PO10 8JH.
Std: 01243 **Tel:** 373202
Website:
www.campingandcaravanningclub.co.uk
Nearest Town/Resort Chichester
Directions On the A259 from Chichester,
site is on the right past Inlands Road.
Acreage 3 **Open** February **to** November
Access Good **Site** Level
Sites Available ⚠ ⊟ ⊟ **Total** 60
Facilities ♿ ∮ 🏠 📷 ⚓ ⌂ ⊙ ⊣ ◻ ▽
◪ ◪ ⊙ 🏠❋⊬⊟
Nearby Facilities ⌐ ✓ ⚓ ↘ ∪ ♪ ⌐ ✗
≈ Southbourne
500 yards through a footpath to the beach.
Ideal touring, well placed for visiting the
Sussex Downs and south coast resorts.
Close to the City of Portsmouth. BTB
Graded. Non members welcome.

CHICHESTER

Ellscott Park, Sidlesham Lane, Birdham,
Chichester, West Sussex, PO20 7QL.
Std: 01243 **Tel:** 512003
Std: 01243 **Fax:** 512003
Email: angieparks@lineone.net
Website: www.idms.co.uk/ellscottpark
Directions From the A27 Chichester by-
pass turn south onto the A286 towards
Witterings. Travel for approx. 4 miles then
turn left towards Butterfly Farm, site is 500
metres on the right.
Acreage 3 **Open** March **to** October
Access Good **Site** Level
Sites Available ⚠ ⊟ ⊟ **Total** 50
Facilities ♿ ∮ 📷 ⚓ ⌂ ⊙ ⊣ ◻ ▽
◪ ⚠▽⊟⊟
Nearby Facilities ⌐ ✓ ⚓ ↘ ∪ ♪ ⌐
≈ Chichester
The famous West Wittering beach. 1½ miles
from Chichester Harbour for yachting and
boating. Ideal site for walking, cycling and
sight-seeing.

CHICHESTER

Goodwood Caravan Park, Goodwood
Racecourse, Chichester, West Sussex,
PO18 0PS.
Std: 01243 **Tel:** 755033
Std: 01243 **Fax:** 755025
Website: www.goodwood.co.uk
Nearest Town/Resort Chichester
Directions Approx. 4 miles north of
Chichester off the A285 Petworth to
Chichester road, or the A286 Midhurst to
Chichester road.
Open Easter **to** September
Access Good **Site** Level
Sites Available ⚠ ⊟ ⊟ **Total** 62
Facilities ♿ ∮ 🏠 📷 ⚓ ⌂ ⊙|◻⚠▽⊟⊟ ⊟
Nearby Facilities ⌐ ✓ ⚓ ↘ ∪ ♪ ⌐
≈ Chichester
Close to the Cathedral city of Chichester,
Festival Theatre, Roman Villa at Bignor,
Roman Palace at Fishbourne and the open-
air museum at Singleton. Within reach of
Portsmouth and Brighton, also Chichester
Harbour and coastline.

CHICHESTER

Red House Farm, Earnley, Chichester,
West Sussex, PO20 7JG.
Std: 01243 **Tel:** 512959
Std: 01243 **Fax:** 514216
Email: redhousecamping@talk21.com
Nearest Town/Resort Bracklesham Bay
Directions From Chichester take the A286
south to Witterings, after 5 miles turn left
onto the B2198 opposite the garage to
Bracklesham Bay. After 1 mile turn left to
Earnley, site is on the left.
Acreage 4½ **Open** Easter **to** October
Access Good **Site** Level
Sites Available ⚠ ⊟ ⊟ **Total** 100
Facilities ♿ ∮ 📷 ⚓ ⌂ ⊙ ⊣ ◻ ▽
◪ ⊙ 🏠❋⊟
Nearby Facilities ✓ ⚓ ↘
≈ Chichester
Flat and open site on a working farm in a
country area. 1 mile from the village and
beach. No all male/female groups.

CROWBOROUGH

Camping & Caravanning Club Site,
Goldsmith Recreation Ground,
Crowborough, Sussex, TN6 2TN.
Std: 01892 **Tel:** 664827
Website:
www.campingandcaravanningclub.co.uk
Directions Take the A26 turn off into the
entrance to 'Goldsmiths Ground' signposted
leisure centre, at the top of the road turn
right into site lane.
Acreage 13 **Open** February **to** December
Site Lev/Slope
Sites Available ⚠ ⊟ ⊟ **Total** 90
Facilities ♿ ∮ 🏠 📷 ⚓ ⌂ ⊙ ⊣ ◻ ▽
◪ ⊙ 🏠 ✗ ⚠▽⊟⊟
Nearby Facilities ⌐ ✓ ∪ ✗
On the edge of Ashdown Forest. Adjacent
to a sports centre. BTB Graded and AA 4
Pennants. Non members welcome.

EASTBOURNE

**Fairfields Farm Camping & Caravan
Park,** Eastbourne Road, Westham,
Pevensey, East Sussex, BN24 5NG.
Std: 01323 **Tel:** 763165
Email: enquiries@fairfieldsfarm.com
Website: www.fairfieldsfarm.com
Nearest Town/Resort Eastbourne
Directions On B2191, signposted on the
east side of Eastbourne and off the A27 in
the village of Westham.
Acreage 3 **Open** April **to** October
Access Good **Site** Level
Sites Available ⚠ ⊟ ⊟ **Total** 60
Facilities ∮ 📷 ⚓ ⌂ ⊙ ⊣ ◻ ▽ ◪ ⊙❋⊟
Nearby Facilities ⌐ ✓ ⚓ ↘ ∪ ♪
≈ Pevensey/Westham
A clean, well kept site on a small family farm.
Only 2 miles from the sea and 3 miles from
Eastbourne town centre.

GRAFFHAM

Camping & Caravanning Club Site,
Great Bury, Graffham, Petworth, West
Sussex, GU28 0QJ.
Std: 01798 **Tel:** 867476
Website:
www.campingandcaravanningclub.co.uk
Directions From Petworth take the A285,
pass Badgers Pub on the left and the BP
Garage on the right, take the next right turn
signposted Selham Graffham (with brown
camping sign), follow signs to site. From
Chichester take the A285 through Duncton
and turn left signposted Selham Graffham
(with brown camping sign).
Open March **to** October
Site Sloping

Sites Available 𝗔 ⛺ ⛽ Total 90
Facilities ♿ ⚡ 🚾 ⚓ ⚑ ☺ ⛱ ⚒ ▢ ⛽
♨ ⚑ ⚓ 🏪 ⚑ ▢ ⚑
Nearby Facilities ✎ ∪
⚡ Chichester
Set in 20 acres of woodland with many walks. BTB Graded. Non members welcome.

HAILSHAM

Chicheley Farm, Hempstead Lane, Hailsham, East Sussex, BN27 3PR.
Std: 01323 **Tel:** 841253
Std: 01323 **Fax:** 841253
Email: terence-harvey@lineone.net
Nearest Town/Resort Hailsham/Eastbourne
Directions Off the A22 1 mile from Hailsham.
Acreage 2 **Open** Easter **to** End Oct
Access Good **Site** Level
Sites Available 𝗔 ⛺ ⛽ Total 5
Facilities ⚑ 🏪 ▢ ⚑
Nearby Facilities ✎ ⚓ ⚑ ∪ ♪
⚡ Polegate
Hide-away site near 4 acres of bluebell woods. Price £3.00 per night.

HAILSHAM

Peel House Farm Caravan Park,
Sayerlands Lane (B2104), Polegate, East Sussex, BN26 6QX.
Std: 01323 **Tel:** 845629
Std: 01323 **Fax:** 845629
Email: peelhocp@tesco.net
Nearest Town/Resort Hailsham/Eastbourne
Directions Off the A22 at South Hailsham roundabout. Turn right at mini roundabout by the BP Station onto the B2104 signposted Pevensey. We are on the right ½ mile after Cuckoo Trail Crossing.

Acreage 3 **Open** April/Easter **to** End Oct
Access Good **Site** Level
Sites Available 𝗔 ⛺ ⛽ Total 20
Facilities ⚡ 🚾 ⚓ ⚑ ☺ ♨ ⚑ ▢ ⚑
Nearby Facilities ✎ ⚓ ⚑ ∪ ♪
⚡ Polegate
Quiet, rural site with views over the Downs. Footpath and Cuckoo Trail for walking and cycling. Many places to visit nearby. Small shop and garden produce.

HAILSHAM

The Old Mill Caravan Park, Chalvington Road, Golden Cross, Hailsham, East Sussex, BN27 3SS.
Std: 01825 **Tel:** 872532
Website: www.ukparks.co.uk/oldmill
Nearest Town/Resort Hailsham/Eastbourne
Directions 4 miles north west of Hailsham. Turn left off the A22 just before Golden Cross Inn car park. Site is 150yds on the right of Chalvington Road.
Acreage 2 **Open** April **to** October
Access Good **Site** Level
Sites Available 𝗔 ⛺ ⛽ Total 26
Facilities ⚡ 🚾 ⚓ ⚑ ☺ ⚒ ⛽ ⚑ ▢ ⚑
Nearby Facilities ✎ ∪
⚡ Polegate
Ideal touring for beach, downland and countryside. Static holiday caravans sold and sited. Static caravan for hire.

HARTFIELD

St. Ives Farm Caravan Park, St. Ives Farm, Butcherfield Lane, Hartfield, Sussex, TN7 4JX.
Std: 01892 **Tel:** 770213
Nearest Town/Resort East Grinstead
Directions From East Grinstead take the A264 towards Tunbridge Wells, after 6 miles turn right onto the B2026 towards Hartfield.

After 1¼ miles turn right into Butcherfi Lane.
Acreage 8 **Open** March **to** October
Access Good **Site** Level
Sites Available 𝗔 ⛺ ⛽ Total 40
Facilities 🚾 ⚓ ⚑ ☺ ⚑ ▢
Nearby Facilities ✎ ∪ ♪
⚡ East Grinstead
Very pretty rural location, overlooki Ashdown Forest, the home of Winnie Pooh. Adjacent to a network of footpaths

HASTINGS

Shearbarn Holiday Park, Barley Lane, Hastings, East Sussex, TN35 5DX.
Std: 01424 **Tel:** 716474/423583
Std: 01424 **Fax:** 718740
Email: shearbarn@pavilion.co.uk
Website: www.shearbarn.co.uk
Nearest Town/Resort Hastings
Directions From the A259 Hastin seafront travelling towards Rye/Folkesto turn right into Harold Road, right again i Gurth Road and left into Barley La Reception is on the right in ¼ mile.
Acreage 17 **Open** March **to** 15 January
Access Good **Site** Lev/Slope
Sites Available 𝗔 ⛺ ⛽ Total 450
Facilities ♿ ⚡ 🚾 ⚓ ☺ 🔲 ♨ ⚒ ⛽ ⚑ ✕ ♀ ⚑ ⛽
Nearby Facilities ✎ ∪
⚡ Hastings
Good views of the sea and country. Adjace to Hastings Country Park. 20 minute wa to Hastings and the seafront.

HASTINGS

Stalkhurst Camping & Caravan Park,
Stalkhurst Cottage, Ivyhouse Lane, Hastings, Sussex, TN35 4NN.
Std: 01424 **Tel:** 439015
Std: 01424 **Fax:** 445206
Email: stalkhurst@btinternet.com

GREEN, PEACEFUL AND RELAXING

earest Town/Resort Hastings
irections From Hastings take A259
wards Rye, turn left onto B2093. In ½ mile
rn right into Ivyhouse Lane. From the A21
ke the B2093 for 2½ miles, turn left into
yhouse Lane.
creage 2½ Open March to 15 January
ccess Good Site Level
ites Available ▲ ⚲ ⚙ Total 33
acilities ƒ ㎈ ⚒ ┌ ⊙ ⚓ ❤⊡
earby Facilities ┌ ✈ ⚓ ∪ ♠
⚎ Hastings
½ miles to beach. Ideal touring site.

HEATHFIELD

reenviews Caravan Park, Burwash
oad, Broad Oak, Heathfield, East
ussex, TN21 8RT.
td: 01435 Tel: 863531
td: 01435 Fax: 863531
earest Town/Resort Eastbourne
irections 2 miles east of Heathfield on the
orth side of the A265.
pen April to October
ccess Good Site Sloping
ites Available ▲ ⚲ ⚙ Total 10
acilities ƒ ㎈ ⚒ ┌ ⌿ ▬ ⊡ ❤
⚎ ⊙ ⚒ ▽
earby Facilities
⚎ Wadhurst
eally situated for touring, close to
astbourne, Brighton, Hastings, Tunbridge
ells, etc..

HENFIELD

ownsview Caravan Park, Bramlands
ane, Woodmancote, Near Henfield, West
ussex, BN5 9TG.
td: 01273 Tel: 492801
td: 01273 Fax: 495214
mail: phr.peter@lineone.net
earest Town/Resort Brighton
irections Signed off the A281 in the village
f Woodmancote. 2½ miles east of Henfield
nd 9 miles northwest of Brighton centre.
creage 4 Open 1 April/Easter to 31 Oct
ccess Good Site Level
ites Available ▲ ⚲ ⚙
acilities ƒ ㎈ ⚒ ┌ ⊙ ⌿ ▬ ⊡ ❤
⚎ ⌂ ⊙ ⚒ ❤⊡ ❤
earby Facilities ┌ ✈ ⚓ ∪ ♠ ⚓
⚎ Brighton/Hassocks
pecialists in peace and quiet. Near to
righton and South Downs. 2 miles from
staurants etc. NO playgrounds or discos
tc. No Vans or lorries. Waste water hook-
s available. Dogs must be kept on leads.

HENFIELD

armhouse Caravan & Camping Site,
ottington Drive, Small Dole, Henfield,
ussex, BN5 9XZ.
td: 01273 Tel: 493157

Nearest Town/Resort Brighton
Directions Turn first left off A2037 (Henfield/
Upperbeeding). After Small Dole sign into
Tottington Drive, farm at end.
Acreage 4 Open March to November
Access Good Site Level
Sites Available ▲ ⚲ ⚙ Total 35
Facilities ƒ ㎈ ⚒ ┌ ⌿ ⌂ ⚒ ❤⊡
Nearby Facilities ┌ ✈ ∪
⚎ Shoreham
Small farm site near South Downs. Beach
5 miles, Brighton and Worthing 10 miles.

HORAM

Horam Manor Touring Park, Horam, Nr.
Heathfield, East Sussex, TN21 0YD.
Std: 01435 Tel: 813662
Email: horam.manor@virgin.net
Website: www.handbooks.co.uk/horam-
manor
Nearest Town/Resort Heathfield/
Eastbourne
Directions On A267, 3 miles south of
Heathfield, 10 miles north of Eastbourne.
Acreage 7 Open March to October
Access Good Site Sloping
Sites Available ▲ ⚲ ⚙ Total 90
Facilities ⚓ ƒ ㎈ ⚒ ┌ ⊙ ⌿ ▬ ⊡ ❤
⚎ ⌂ ⊙ ❤⊡
Nearby Facilities ┌ ✈ ∪
⚎ Eastbourne
A tranquil rural setting, but with plenty to do
on the estate, and many places to visit.

HORSHAM

Honeybridge Park, Honeybridge Lane,
Dial Post, Nr. Horsham, West Sussex,
RH13 8NX.
Std: 01403 Tel: 710923
Std: 01403 Fax: 710923
Email: enquiries@honeybridgepark.co.uk
Website: www.honeybridgepark.co.uk
Nearest Town/Resort Worthing
Directions 1 mile south of Dial Post on the
A24 (London- Worthing Road). Follow brown
internatioinl signs from the A24 Horsham to
Worthing trunk road, by Old Barn Nursery.
Acreage 15 Open All Year
Access Good Site Level
Sites Available ▲ ⚲ ⚙ Total 100
Facilities ⚓ ƒ ㎈ ⚒ ┌ ⊙ ⌿ ▬ ⊡ ❤
⚎ ⌂ ⚒ ⚓ ⌂ ❤⊡ ❤
Nearby Facilities ┌ ✈ ∪ ♠
⚎ Horsham
A spacious 15 acre park, nestling within the
peace and quiet of an area of outstanding
natural beauty. Heated amenitiy block; free
showers (incl. disabled), washing-up
facilities and laundry. Seasonal pitches and
storage available.

LITTLEHAMPTON

Rutherford's Touring Park, Cornfield
Close, Worthing Road, Littlehampton,
Sussex, BN17 6LD.
Std: 01903 Tel: 714240
Std: 01903 Fax: 714240
Email: rutherford@zoom.co.uk
Website: www.camping-caravaning.co.uk
Nearest Town/Resort Littlehampton
Directions The site is situated on the A259
Worthing to Bognor Regis, between two
Body Shop roundabouts. 3 miles from
Arundel.
Acreage 6½ Open All Year
Access Good Site Level
Sites Available ▲ ⚲ ⚙ Total 80
Facilities ⚓ ƒ ㎈ ⚒ ┌ ⊙ ❤
⚒ ⌂ ⚒ ⚓ ❤⊡ ❤
Nearby Facilities ┌ ✈ ⚓ ⚓ ∪ ♠ ♠
⚎ Littlehampton
1½ to sandy beach. 1 mile to River Arun.

LITTLEHAMPTON

White Rose Touring Park, Mill Lane,
Wick, Littlehampton, West Sussex, BN17
7PH.
Std: 01903 Tel: 716176
Std: 01903 Fax: 732671
Email: snowdondavid@hotmail.com
Nearest Town/Resort Littlehampton
Directions From the A27 take the A284
signposted Littlehampton, site is approx. 1½
miles on the left (first left after Six Bells
Public House).
Acreage 6 Open 15 March to 14 January
Access Good Site Level
Sites Available ▲ ⚲ ⚙ Total 135
Facilities ⚓ ƒ ⌂ ㎈ ⚒ ┌ ⊙ ⌿ ▬ ⊡ ❤
⚒ ⌂ ⚒ ⚓ ❤⊡ ❤
Nearby Facilities ┌ ✈ ⚓ ⚓ ∪ ♠ ♠
⚎ Littlehampton
1½ miles from the beach. Close to Arundel
and South Downs.

NEWHAVEN

Three Ponds Holiday Park, South
Heighton, Newhaven, East Sussex, BN9
0HU.
Std: 01273 Tel: 513530
Nearest Town/Resort Newhaven
Acreage 14½ Open March to October
Access Good Site Level
Sites Available ▲ ⚲□ Total 20
Facilities ƒ ⌂ ㎈ ⚒ ┌ ⊙ ⌿ ▬ ⊡ ❤
⚒ ⌂ ⚒ ⌂ ❤⊡ ❤
Nearby Facilities ┌ ✈
⚎ Newhaven
Fishing lakes on site. Close to Brighton,
Eastbourne and ferry port. Statics also
available for hire.

PEVENSEY BAY

Bay View Caravan & Camping Park, Old Martello Road, Pevensey Bay, Nr. Eastbourne, East Sussex, BN24 6DX.
Std: 01323 **Tel:** 768688
Std: 01323 **Fax:** 769637
Email: holidays@bay-view.co.uk
Website: www.bay-view.co.uk
Nearest Town/Resort Eastbourne
Directions 2 miles from Eastbourne centre off the A259.
Acreage 3¼ **Open** Easter **to** October
Access Good **Site** Level
Sites Available Λ ♨ ⊟ **Total** 49
Facilities ⚡ 🄳 🆄 ♿ 🏦 ⌂ ⊙ 🍴 🌲 🔲 ⚐
⚲ ⚡ 🄲 🏧 🗛 🔲 🍴
Nearby Facilities ⌂ ✈ ⚓ 🎳 ♪
⚐ Pevensey Bay
5 Star Award Winning park, next to the beach. Near to Eastbourne's Sunshine Coast. Gold David Bellamy Conservation Award.

PEVENSEY BAY

Grey Tower Caravan Site, Grey Tower Road, Pevensey Bay, East Sussex, BN24 6DP.
Std: 01323 **Tel:** 762402
Email: greytowercaravansite@pevenseybay.fsnet.co.uk
Nearest Town/Resort Eastbourne
Directions On the coast side of the A259, 1 mile out of Pevensey Bay heading towards Eastbourne.
Acreage 6 **Open** Easter **to** October
Access Good **Site** Level
Sites Available ♨□ **Total** 16
Facilities ⚡ 🄳 🏦 ⌂ 🍴 🌲 🔲 🐾🔲
Nearby Facilities ⌂ ✈ ⚓ 🎳 ♪
⚐ Westham
Park has its own beach. In the heart of historic countryside dating back to the Roman Empire.

ROBERTSBRIDGE

Park Farm Caravan & Camping Site, Park Farm, Bodiam, East Sussex, TN32 5XA
Std: 01580 **Tel:** 830514
Std: 01580 **Fax:** 830519
Nearest Town/Resort Hastings
Directions On the B2244 3 miles south of Hawkhurst and 3 miles north of Sedlescombe.
Acreage 10 **Open April to** October
Access Good **Site** Level
Sites Available Λ ♨ ⊟ **Total** 50
Facilities ⚡ 🄳 🏦 ⌂ ⊙ 🍴 🌲 🐾🔲
Nearby Facilities ✈
⚐ Robertsbridge
Riverside walk to Bodiam Castle and many walks around the farm. Camp fires allowed. Fishing.

RYE

Camber Sands Leisure Park, Lydd Road, Camber, Near Rye, East Sussex, TN31 7RT.
Std: 0870 **Tel:** 442 9284
Std: 01797 **Fax:** 225756
Email: cambersands@gbholidayparks.co.uk
Website: www.gbholidayparks.co.uk
Nearest Town/Resort Rye
Directions From the M25 take the M20 and exit at junction 10. Take the A2070 signposted Brenzett, follow signs to Hastings and Rye. Stay on the A2070 until you see the signs for Rye, 1 mile before Rye turn left for Camber, the holiday park is 3 miles along the road.
Open March **to** November
Access Good **Site** Level
Sites Available Λ ♨ ⊟ **Total** 48
Facilities ⚡ 🄳 🏦 ⌂ ⊙ 🍴 🔲 ⚐
⚲ ⚡ 🄲 🏧 🍴 🗛 ⚓ 🔆 🐾🔲 🍴
Nearby Facilities ⌂ ✈ ⚓ 🎳 ♪
⚐ Rye
Popular touring destination opposite a blue flag sandy beach. Fantastic on-site facilities. Shopping and sightseeing opportunities at Hastings and Canterbury.

RYE

Rother Valley Caravan Park, Station Road, Northiam, East Sussex, TN31 6QT.
Std: 01797 **Tel:** 252116
Std: 01797 **Fax:** 252116
Website: www.rothervalleycamping-bandb.co.uk
Nearest Town/Resort Rye
Directions On the A28 between Tenterden and Hastings.
Acreage 10

Access Good **Site** Lev/Slope
Sites Available Λ ♨ ⊟ **Total** 100
Facilities ⚡ 🄳 🆄 🏦 ⌂ ⊙ 🍴
⚲ ⚡ 🄲 🗛 🍴 🐾🔲 🔲 ⚐
Nearby Facilities ⌂ ✈ ⚓ 🔆 �↺
⚐ Etchingham
Next to East Kent & Sussex Steam Railway 500 metres from the River Rother.

SEAFORD

Buckle Caravan Park, Marine Parade, Seaford, East Sussex, BN25 2QR.
Std: 01323 **Tel:** 897801
Email: holiday@buckle-park.freeserve.co.uk
Website: www.buckle-camping.ukti.co.uk
Nearest Town/Resort Seaford
Directions Take the A259 Newhaven / Seaford coast road, turn right at Abbot Lodge Motor Inn, park is 300 yards on the right.
Acreage 9 **Open** 1 March **to** 2 January
Access Good **Site** Level
Sites Available Λ ♨ ⊟ **Total** 150
Facilities ♿ ⚡ 🄳 🆄 🏦 ⌂ ⊙ 🍴 🔲
⚲ ⚡ 🄲 🗛 🍴 🔲 ⚐
Nearby Facilities ⌂ ✈ ⚓ 🔆 ♪ ↺
⚐ Bishopstone
Adjacent to the beach. Between Brighton and Eastbourne and near to Seven Sisters and South Downs (for walking). Adults on field if required.

SEDLESCOMBE

Crazy Lane Tourist Park, Whydown Farm, Crazy Lane, Sedlescombe, East Sussex, TN33 0QT.
Std: 01424 **Tel:** 870147
Website: www.crazylane.co.uk
Nearest Town/Resort Battle/Hastings
Directions Travelling south on A21, turn left into Crazy Lane, 100 yds past junction A21 B2244, opposite Black Brooks Garden Centre.
Acreage 3 **Open** 1 March **to** 31 Oct
Access Good **Site** Level
Sites Available Λ ♨ ⊟ **Total** 36
Facilities ♿ ⚡ 🄳 🏦 ⌂ ⊙ 🍴 🔲🐾🔲
Nearby Facilities ⌂ ✈ ⚓ 🔆 ♪ ↺
⚐ Battle
Ideal touring, 15 minutes to the beach. Countryside and Hastings.

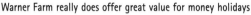
SELSEY

Warner Farm Touring Park, Warner Lane, Selsey, West Sussex, PO20 9EL.
Std: 01243 **Tel:** 604499
Std: 01243 **Fax:** 604499
Email: warner.farm@btinternet.com
Website: www.bunnleisure.co.uk
Nearest Town/Resort Chichester
Directions From the A27 Chichester take the B2145 to Selsey. On entering Selsey turn right into School Lane. Follow signs for Warner Farm Touring Park.
Acreage 10 **Open** March **to** October
Access Good **Site** Level
Sites Available A ⚕ ⚐ **Total** 200
Facilities & ∫ ⚏ ⬚ ⚒ ⌐ ⊙ ⤴ ⚍ ⚑ ⛺ ⚹ ⚐ ⓧ ♈ ⛽ 𝌆 ♨ ⏚ ☆ ⚙ ⤚ ⚏ ⚑
Nearby Facilities ⌐ ✔ ∪ ℛ
⚓ Chichester
Near the beach.

UCKFIELD

Heaven Farm, Furners Green, Uckfield, East Sussex, TN22 3RG.
Std: 01825 **Tel:** 790226
Std: 01825 **Fax:** 790881
Email: butlerenterprises@farmline.uk
Website: www.heavenfarm.co.uk
Nearest Town/Resort Uckfield/Haywards-Heath
Directions On the A275 10 miles north of Lewes and 1 mile south of Danehill. 9 miles from Uckfield and East Grinstead.
Acreage 2 **Open** All Year
Access Good **Site** Lev/Slope
Sites Available A ⚕ ⚐ **Total** 30
Facilities & ∫ ⚏ ⚒ ⌐ ⊙ ⤴ ⚍
⛺ ⚐ ⓧ ⤚ ⚑
Nearby Facilities ⌐ ✔ ⏚ ⚹ ∪
⚓ Haywards Heath
Popular nature trail and tea rooms. Fishing on site. Central for many National Trust gardens etc.. 1 mile from Bluebell Railway.

UCKFIELD

Honeys Green Farm Caravan Park, Easons Green, Framfield, Uckfield, East Sussex, TN22 5RE.
Std: 01825 **Tel:** 840334
Nearest Town/Resort Uckfield/Lewes
Directions Turn off A22 (Uckfield - Eastbourne) at Halland roundabout onto

B2192 signposted Blackboys/Heathfield, site ¼ mile on left.
Acreage 2 **Open** Easter **to** October
Access Good **Site** Level
Sites Available ⚕ ⚐ **Total** 22
Facilities & ∫ ⚏ ⬚ ⚒ ⌐ ⊙ ⤴ ⚍
⛺ ⚐ ⤚ ⚐ ⚑
Nearby Facilities ⌐ ✔ ∪
⚓ Uckfield/Lewes
Small peaceful rural park, coarse fishing lake, walks.

WASHINGTON

Washington Caravan & Camping Park, Riding School & Livery, Old London Road, Washington, West Sussex, RH20 4AJ.
Std: 01903 **Tel:** 892869
Std: 01903 **Fax:** 893252
Nearest Town/Resort Storrington
Directions Situated where the A24 crosses the A283.
Acreage 4 **Open** All Year
Access Good **Site** Sloping
Sites Available A ⚕ ⚐ **Total** 80
Facilities & ∫ ⚏ ⬚ ⚒ ⌐ ⚍ ⚐ ⚑ ⚐ ⚏ ⚑ ⚐
Nearby Facilities ∪
⚓ Pulborough
ETB 4 Star Graded Park. Ideal for touring, South Downs Way, walking, cycling and many places of interest.

WEST WITTERING

Nunnington Farm Camping Site, Nunnington Farm, West Wittering, West Sussex, PO20 8LZ.
Std: 01243 **Tel:** 514013 No Booking
Email:
campingsite@nunningtonfarm.fsnet.co.uk
Nearest Town/Resort Chichester
Directions 7 miles south of Chichester on the A286 - B2179. 200yds before village on left, look for signs.
Acreage 4½ **Open** Easter **to** Mid October
Access Good **Site** Level
Sites Available A ⚕ ⚐ **Total** 125
Facilities & ∫ ⚏ ⬚ ⚒ ⌐ ⊙ ⤴ ⚍
⛺ ⚐ ⚐ ⚑ ⤚ ⚑
Nearby Facilities ✔ ⏚ ⚹ ∪ ℛ
⚓ Chichester
Near the beach.

WEST WITTERING

Scotts Farm Camping Site, Cakeham Road, West Wittering, West Sussex, PO20 8ED.
Std: 01243 **Tel:** 671720 **Fax:** 513669
Website: www.scotts-farm-camping.co.uk
Nearest Town/Resort East Wittering
Directions Take the A27 from Chichester then take the A286 to The Witterings. 7 miles from Chichester.
Acreage 30 **Open** March **to** October
Access Good **Site** Level
Sites Available A ⚕ ⚐ **Total** 700
Facilities & ∫ ⚏ ⬚ ⚒ ⌐ ⊙ ⤴ ⚍ ⚐ ⚑ ⚐ ⚙ ⚏ ⤚ ⚐ ⚑
Nearby Facilities ⌐ ✔ ⏚ ⚹ ∪ ℛ ℛ
⚓ Chichester
5 minutes from the beach, shops, restaurants and pubs.

WEST WITTERING

Wicks Farm Camping Park, Redlands Lane, West Wittering, Chichester, Sussex, PO20 8QD.
Std: 01243 **Tel:** 513116 **Fax:** 511296
Nearest Town/Resort West Wittering/Chichester
Directions From Chichester A286 for Birdham. Then B2179 for West Wittering.
Acreage 2¼ **Open** April **to** October
Access Good **Site** Level
Sites Available A ⚐ **Total** 40
Facilities ∫ ⚏ ⚒ ⌐ ⊙ ⚍ ⚐ ⚹ ⚐ ⚐ ⚙ ⚐ ⚏ ⤚ ⚐ ⚑
Nearby Facilities ⌐ ✔ ⏚ ∪ ℛ
⚓ Chichester

WINCHELSEA

Rye Bay Caravan Park, Pett Level Road, Winchelsea Beach, Sussex, TN36 4NE.
Std: 01797 **Tel:** 226340
Std: 01797 **Fax:** 224699
Nearest Town/Resort Rye
Directions 3 miles west of Rye and 7 miles east of Hastings.
Open March **to** October
Access Good
Sites Available & ⚕ ⚐ **Total** 40
Facilities & ∫ ⚏ ⬚ ⚒ ⌐ ⊙ ⤴ ⚍ ⚐
⚐ ⚙ ⚐ ♈ ⛽ 𝌆 ♨ ⚐ ⤚ ⚑
Nearby Facilities ✔ ⏚ ⚹ ℛ
⚓ Rye
Direct frontage to the beach.

...EEN

... Lane, Wisborough
..., RH14 0EH.
...00313
.../Resort Billinghurst
...From Billinghurst (A29) take the
...st for Petworth. After 2 miles turn
...onto the B2133 for Guildford. Site is 1
...le on the left hand side.
Acreage 3 **Open** All Year
Access Good **Site** Level
Sites Available △ ♠ ♠ **Total** 40
Facilities ⊞ ⅦⒺ ♨ Ր ☉ ☻
⅃⅂ ☺ ♨ ✕ ☖ ⑪ ♠ 朩⊟
Nearby Facilities Ր ✓ ∪ ♪
✦ Billinghurst
Good views, walking and touring. Very close
to a river.

TYNE & WEAR
SOUTH SHIELDS
Lizard Lane Caravan Park, Lizard Lane,
Marsden, South Shields, Tyne & Wear,
NE34 7AB.
Std: 0191 **Tel:** 454 4982
Nearest Town/Resort South Shields
Directions Take the coast road from South
Shields to Marsden and the camp site.
Open March to Last Weekend Oct
Access Good **Site** Sloping
Sites Available △ ♠ ♠ **Total** 70
Facilities ⅍ ⅋ ⅦⒺ ♨ Ր ☉ ⅃ ♨ ☻
⅃⅂ ☺ ♨ 凡 朩⊟
Nearby Facilities Ր ✓ ⚓ ⌇ ∪ ♪ ♪
✦ South Shields
Near the beach. Ideal for touring Scotland,
Yorkshire and the Lakes. Childrens play area
for up to 8 years, new 9 hole Pitch 'n' Putt
and a souvenir shop. 20 new electric hook-
ups (40 in total).

WHITLEY BAY
Whitley Bay Holiday Park, The Links,
Whitley Bay, Tyne & Wear, NE26 4RR.
Std: 0870 **Tel:** 442 9282
Std: 0191 **Fax:** 297 1033
Website: www.leisuregb.co.uk
Nearest Town/Resort Whitley Bay
Directions From north take the A1 south,
just past Morpeth take the A19 signposted
Tyne Tunnel. Then take slip road signed
Whitley Bay and follow caravan park signs.
From south take the A1 north as far as
Washington Services, then take the A19 to
Tyne Tunnel. Go through the tunnel (toll
payable) and take the coast road to
Tynemouth seafront. Turn left at the seafront
and follow signs to St. Mary's Lighthouse.
Open March to 15 Dec

Access Good **Site** Level
Sites Available ♠ ♠ ⅦⒺ **Total** 54
Facilities ⅍ ⅋ ⅃ⅦⒺ ♨ Ր ☉ ⅃ ♨ ☻ ☺
⅍⅂ ⅃⅂ ☺ ♨ ✕ ☖ ⑪ ♨ ∧ ※ 朩⊟ Ⓔ Ⓔ
Nearby Facilities Ր ✓ ∪ ♪
✦ Whitley Bay
Attractive and partly sheleterd park.
Adjacent to the beach and within close
proximity to the popular resort of Whitley
Bay. Ideal holiday park for families, offering
something for all ages.

WARWICKSHIRE
BIDFORD-ON-AVON
Cottage of Content, Barton, Bidford-on-
Avon, Warwicks, B50 4NP.
Std: 01789 **Tel:** 772279
Nearest Town/Resort Bidford-on-Avon
Directions 1 mile from Bidford follow
Honeybourne road for ¾ mile. Turn left at
crossroads signposted Barton, situated on
bend in ¼ mile.
Acreage 2 **Open** March to October
Access Good **Site** Sloping
Sites Available △ ♠ ♠ **Total** 25
Facilities ⅦⒺ ♨ ☉ ⅃ ☻ Ր 凡 朩⊟ Ⓔ Ⓔ
Nearby Facilities Ր ✓ ⚓ ⅃ ∪ ♪ ♪ ⅃
✦ Stratford-upon-Avon

LONG COMPTON
Mill Farm, Long Compton, Shipston-on-
Stour, Warwickshire, CV36 5NZ.
Std: 01608 **Tel:** 684663
Nearest Town/Resort Moreton-on-Marsh
Directions Turn off A3400 west for Barton-
on-the-Heath. Site on right in ½ mile.
Acreage 3 **Open** March to October
Access Good **Site** Level
Sites Available △ ♠ ♠ **Total** 10
Facilities ⅦⒺ ♨ ☉ ⅃ ☻ 朩
Nearby Facilities
✦ Moreton-in-Marsh
Fringe of the Cotswolds.

RUGBY
Lodge Farm, Bilton Lane, Long Lawford,
Rugby, Warwickshire, CV23 9DU.
Std: 01788 **Tel:** 560193
Std: 01788 **Fax:** 550603
Email: alec@lodgefrm.demon.co.uk
Website: www.lodgefarm.com
Nearest Town/Resort Rugby
Directions Take the A428 from Rugby
towards Coventry. After 1½ miles turn left at
Sheaf & Sickle, site is 400 yards on the left.
Acreage 2½ **Open** Easter to End October
Access Good **Site** Level
Sites Available △ ♠ ♠ **Total** 35
Facilities ⅋ ⅦⒺ ♨ Ր ☻ ⅃⅂ ☺ ♨ 朩⊟ Ⓔ Ⓔ
Nearby Facilities Ր ✓ ⚓ ⅃ ∪
✦ Rugby

SOUTHAM
Holt Farm, (N.G. & A.C. Adkins),
Southam, Warwickshire, CV47 1NJ.
Std: 01926 **Tel:** 812225
Directions From Southam By-Pass, follow
camping and caravan signs. Site is 3 miles
from Southam off Priors Marston, Priors
Hardwick Road.
Acreage 1½ **Open** March to End October
Access Good **Site** Level
Sites Available △ ♠ ♠ **Total** 45
Facilities ⅦⒺ ♨ Ր ☉ ☻ ☺ 朩⊟
Nearby Facilities ✓
✦ Leamington Spa
Ideal touring centre for Mid Warwickshire.
Near canal. Dogs must be kept on leads.
You can also call us on Mobile 07790
959638.

STRATFORD-UPON-AVON
Avon Caravan Park, Avon Park, Warwick
Road, Stratford-upon-Avon, Warwickshire,
CV37 0NS.
Std: 01789 **Tel:** 299492 **Fax:** 415330
Email: info@stratfordcaravans.co.uk
Website: www.stratfordcaravans.co.uk
Nearest Town/Resort Stratford-upon-
Avon
Directions From Stratford take the A439 old
Warwick road. Welcome Hotel is on your left,
we are on the right. Only 1 mile from
Stratford.
Acreage 15 **Open** 7 March to 7
December
Access Good **Site** Level
Sites Available △ ♠ **Total** 60
Facilities ⅋ ⊞ ⅦⒺ ♨ Ր ☉ ⅃ ☺ ⅃⅂ ☺ ♨ 朩⊟ Ⓔ Ⓔ
Nearby Facilities Ր ✓ ⅃ ∪ ♪
✦ Stratford-upon-Avon
Only 1 mile from Stratford-upon-Avon.
Courtesy travel to and from Stratford. 1½
miles of Free fishing. Good walks. Central
for Eversham and the Cotswolds. Many
facilities available at the next park.

STRATFORD-UPON-AVON
Dodwell Park, Evesham Road, Stratford-
upon-Avon, Warwickshire, CV37 9SR.
Std: 01789 **Tel:** 204957
Std: 01926 **Fax:** 620199
Nearest Town/Resort Stratford-upon-
Avon
Directions 2 miles southwest of Stratford
on B439 (formerly the A439)- Not the
racecourse site.
Acreage 2 **Open** All Year
Access Good **Site** Lev/Slope
Sites Available △ ♠ ♠ **Total** 50
Facilities ⅋ ⊞ ⅦⒺ ♨ Ր ☉ ⅃ ☺ ☖ ⅃⅂ ☺ ♨ ※ 朩⊟ Ⓔ Ⓔ
Nearby Facilities Ր ✓ ⅃ ∪ ♪
✦ Stratford-upon-Avon
Shakespeare Theatre and Cotswolds.

STRATFORD-UPON-AVON

Island Meadow Caravan Park, Aston Cantlow, Warwickshire, B95 6JP.
Std: 01789 **Tel:** 488273
Std: 01789 **Fax:** 488273
Email:
holiday@islandmeadowcaravanpark.co.uk
Website:
www.islandmeadowcaravanpark.co.uk
Nearest Town/Resort Stratford-upon-Avon
Directions From the A46 or the A3400 follow signs for Aston Cantlow Village. Park is ½ mile west of the village in Mill Lane.
Acreage 3 **Open** March to October
Access Good **Site** Level
Sites Available A ⊕ ⊕ **Total** 34
Facilities & ∱ ⊞ ⅏ ♨ ⌐ ⊙ ⇩ ⬤ ⬛ ☺ ♥
☒ ⬤ ⬛ ❋ ⊬ ⊟
Nearby Facilities ⌐ ✓ ∪
⚓ Wilmcote
Small, quiet island with fishing, adjacent to a picturesque village. Café/Restaurant and childrens play area nearby. Ideal centre for Shakespeare Country.

STRATFORD-UPON-AVON

Riverside Caravan Park, Tiddington Road, Stratford-upon-Avon, Warwickshire, CV37 7AG.
Std: 01789 **Tel:** 292312
Email: info@stratfordcaravans.co.uk
Website: www.stratfordcaravans.co.uk
Nearest Town Stratford-upon-Avon
Directions On the B4086 1¼ miles from the town centre, just before entering Tiddington Village.
Acreage 8 **Open** April to October
Access Good **Site** Lev/Slope
Sites Available A ⊕ ⊕ **Total** 90
Facilities ∱ ⊞ ♨ ⌐ ⊙ ☒ ⅏ ⬤ ⬛ ☺ ✕ ▽ 𝄞 ♠ ⊬ ⊟ ⊟
Nearby Facilities ⌐ ✓ ∪ ⊁ ♪
⚓ Stratford-upon-Avon
Alongside river, close to Shakespeare House.

STUDLEY

Outhill Caravan Park, Outhill, Studley, Warwicks, B80 7DY.
Std: 01527 **Tel:** 852160
Nearest Town Henley-in-Arden
Directions From A435 (Birmingham to Evesham road) turn towards Henley-in-Arden on A4189. Take third turning to the right (approx 1¼ miles), check in at Outhill Farm (first on left).
Acreage 11 **Open** April to October
Access Good **Site** Level
Sites Available ⊕ ⊕ **Total** 15
Facilities ⊞ ⊬
Nearby Facilities
Peace and quiet. Advance booking is essential.

WEST MIDLANDS
HALESOWEN

Camping & Caravanning Club Site, Fieldhouse Lane, Romsley, Halesowen, West Midlands, B62 0NH.
Std: 01562 **Tel:** 710015
Website:
www.campingandcaravanningclub.co.uk
Nearest Town/Resort Halesowen
Directions Travelling northwest on the M5, leave at junction 3 onto the A456. Then take the B4551 to Romsley, turn right at Sun Hotel, take the 5th left turn then the next left and the site is 330 yards on the left hand side.
Acreage 7½ **Open** March to October
Access Good **Site** Sloping
Sites Available A ⊕ ⊕ **Total** 115
Facilities & ∱ ⊞ ⅏ ♨ ⌐ ⊙ ⇩ ⬤ ⬛ ☺ ♥
☒ ⬤ ⬛ 𝄞 ⊬ ⊟ ⊟
Nearby Facilities ✓ ∪
⚓ Bromsgrove
In the heart of the West Midlands. Ideal for walkers and cyclists. BTB Graded and AA 4 Pennants. Non members welcome.

MERIDEN

Somers Wood Caravan & Camping Park, Somers Road, Meriden, North Warwickshire, CV7 7PL.
Std: 01676 **Tel:** 522978
Std: 01676 **Fax:** 522978
Email: enquiries@somerswood.com
Website: www.somerswood.com
Nearest Town/Resort Solihull
Directions Leave the M42 at junction 6, take the A45 to Coventry. Immediately on the left pick up signs for the A452 Leamington. Down to roundabout and turn right onto the A452 signed Leamington/Warwick, at the next roundabout turn left into Hampton Lane. Site is ½ mile on the left hand side.
Acreage 4 **Open** All Year
Access Good **Site** Level
Sites Available A ⊕ ⊕ **Total** 48
Facilities ∱ ⊞ ⅏ ♨ ⌐ ⊙ ⇩ ⬤ ⬛ ☺ ♥
☒ ⬤ ⬛ ✕ ▽ ⊬ ⊟ ⊟ ⬛ A
Nearby Facilities ⌐ ✓ ∪
⚓ Hampton-in-Arden
ADULTS ONLY SITE. Adjacent to a golf course with clubhouse. Approx. 3 miles from the N.E.C. Birmingham. Fishing adjacent.

SUTTON COLDFIELD

Camping & Caravanning Club Site, Kingsbury Water Park, Bodymoor Heath Lane, Sutton Coldfield, West Midlands, B76 0DY.
Std: 01827 **Tel:** 874101
Website:
www.campingandcaravanningclub.co.uk
Directions Leave the M42 at junction 9 and take the B4097 towards Kingsbury. At the roundabout turn left and continue past the main entrance to the water park, go over the motorway and turn next right, follow lane for ½ mile to the site.
Open March to October
Site Level
Sites Available & ⊕ ⊕ **Total** 120
Facilities & ∱ ⊞ ⅏ ♨ ⌐ ⊙ ⇩ ⬤ ⬛ ☺ ♥
☒ ⬤ ⬛ ❋ ⊬ ⊟ ⊟
Nearby Facilities ⌐ ✓ ⊥ ⊁ ♪
⚓ Tamworth
Surrounding the site are the 600 acres of Kingsbury Water Park. BTB Graded. Non members welcome.

WILTSHIRE
BRADFORD-ON-AVON

Church Farm Touring Caravan & Camping Site, Church Farm, Winsley, Bradford-on-Avon, Wiltshire, BA15 2JH.
Std: 01225 **Tel:** 722246 **Fax:** 722246
Email:
book@churchfarmcaravancamping.co.uk
Website:
www.churchfarmcaravancamping.co.uk
Nearest Town/Resort Bradford-on-Avon
Directions On the B3108 between Bradford-on-Avon and Limpley Stoke. Follow Church Farm signs around the outskirts of the village. Bath 5 miles.
Acreage 1½ **Open** All Year
Access Good **Site** Level
Sites Available A ⊕ ⊕ **Total** 20
Facilities ∱ ⊞ ♨ ⌐ ⊙ ⇩ ⬤ ⬛ ☺ ♥
☒ ☺ ⊬ ⊟ ⊟
Nearby Facilities ⌐ ✓ ⊁ ∪
⚓ Bradford-on-Avon
Picturesque site in an area of outstanding natural beauty. 500 metres from the village shop and pub. 5 miles from Bath. ¾ miles from Kennet and Avon Canal for boating, fishing, cycling and walking.

CHIPPENHAM

Piccadilly Caravan Site, Folly Lane West, Lacock, Chippenham, Wiltshire, SN15 2LP.
Std: 01249 **Tel:** 730260
Nearest Town/Resort Chippenham/Melksham
Directions Turn right off A350 Chippenham/Melksham Road, 5 miles south of Chippenham, close to Lacock. Signposted to Gastard (with caravan symbol), site is after the Nurseries.
Acreage 2½ **Open** April to October
Access Good **Site** Level

Sites Available ▲ ⌂ ⊟ Total 40
Facilities � ⊞ ⓌⒸ ♨ ⌐ ☉ ↵ ☖ ☐ ☎
⌦ ⊙ ☕ ⚑⌂☐
Nearby Facilities ⌐ ✎ ∪
⇶ Chippenham
Close National Trust village of Lacock. Ideal
touring centre.

CHIPPENHAM

Plough Lane Caravan Site, Kington
Langley, Chippenham, Wiltshire, SN15
5PS.
Std: 01249 **Tel:** 750795 **Fax:** 750795
Email: ploughlane@lineone.net
Website: www.ploughlane.co.uk
Nearest Town/Resort Chippenham
Directions Well signposted from the A350
north of Chippenham.
Acreage 2 **Open** March **to** October
Access Good **Site** Level
Sites Available ⌂ ⊟ Total 40
Facilities ⓵ ⅃ ⊞ ⓌⒸ ♨ ⌐ ☉ ↵ ☖ ☐ ☎
⌦ ☕⚑⌂A
Nearby Facilities ⌐ ✎ ♞
⇶ Chippenham
ADULTS ONLY SITE.

DEVIZES

Camping & Caravanning Club Site,
Spout Lane, Nr Seend, Devizes, Wiltshire,
SN12 6RN.
Std: 01380 **Tel:** 828839
Website:
www.campingandcaravanningclub.co.uk
Directions Take the A365 from Melksham,
turn right down the lane beside Three
Magpies Public House, site is on the right.
Open All Year
Site Level
Sites Available ▲ ⌂ ⊟ Total 90
Facilities ⓵ ⅃ ⊞ ⓌⒸ ♨ ⌐ ☉ ↵ ☖ ☐ ☎
⊙ ☕⚑⌦⊟☐
Nearby Facilities ✎
Bordering the Kennett & Avon Canal, fishing
on site. BTB Graded. Non members
welcome.

MALMESBURY

Burton Hill Caravan & Camping Park,
Arches Lane, Burton Hill, Malmesbury,
Wiltshire, SN16 0EJ.
Std: 01666 **Tel:** 826880 **Fax:** 823449
Email: burtonhillccp@archesfarm.co.uk
Nearest Town/Resort Malmesbury
Directions ½ mile south of Malmesbury on
the A429, entrance is opposite Malmesbury
Hospital.
Acreage 2 **Open** 1 April/Easter **to**
October
Access Good **Site** Level
Sites Available ▲ ⌂ ⊟ Total 30
Facilities ⓵ ⊞ ♨ ⌐ ☉ ↵ ☖ ☐ ☎ ⊙⚑☐
Nearby Facilities ⌐ ✎ ∫ ⊥ ∪ ♠ ♞
⇶ Chippenham
Good for Malmesbury, the Cotswolds and
Westonbirt Arboretum.

MARLBOROUGH

Hill-View Caravan Park, Oare,
Marlborough, Wiltshire, SN8 4JE.
Std: 01672 **Tel:** 563151
Nearest Town/Resort Marlborough
Directions On A345, 6 miles south of
Marlborough on Pewsey/Amesbury road.
Open Easter **to** September
Access Good **Site** Level
Sites Available ▲ ⌂ ⊟ Total 10
Facilities ⓵ ⊞ ♨ ⌐ ☉ ↵ ☖ ☐ ☎ ⅃⚑☐
Nearby Facilities ✎ ∪
⇶ Pewsey
Place of historic interest and scenic views.
ETB 3 Star Graded. No Statics. SAE for
enquiries. Booking is advisable.

MARLBOROUGH

Postern Hill - Forestry Commission,
Postern Hill, Marlborough, Wiltshire, SN8
4ND.
Std: 01672 **Tel:** 515195
Email: fe.holidays@forestry.gsi.gov.uk
Website: www.forestholidays.co.uk
Nearest Town/Resort Marlborough
Directions 1 mile south of Marlborough on
the A346. Just 10 miles from the M4 junction
15.
Acreage 28½ **Open** Mid Mar **to** End
October
Access Good **Site** Level
Sites Available ▲ ⌂ ⊟ Total 170
Facilities ⓵ ⊞ ♨☉ ☉ ☎ ☕⚑☐☐
Nearby Facilities
⇶ Marlborough
In the heart of Savernake Forest, the ideal
site for exploring historic Wiltshire including
Stonehenge and Salisbury Cathedral.

NETHERHAMPTON

Coombe Caravan Park, Coombe
Nurseries, Race Plain, Netherhampton,
Salisbury, Wilts, SP2 8PN.
Std: 01722 **Tel:** 328451 **Fax:** 328451
Nearest Town/Resort Salisbury
Directions Take A36-A30 Salisbury - Wilton
road, turn off at traffic lights onto A3094
Netherhampton - Stratford Tony road, cross
on bend following Stratford Tony road, 2nd
left behind racecourse, site on right,
signposted.
Acreage 3 **Open** All Year
Access Good **Site** Level
Sites Available ▲ ⌂ ⊟ Total 48
Facilities ⓵ ⊞ ♨ ⌐ ☉ ↵ ☖ ☐ ☎
⌦ ⊙ ☕⚑⌂⊟
Nearby Facilities ⌐ ∪ ♞
⇶ Salisbury
Adjacent to racecourse (flat racing), ideal
touring, lovely views.

ORCHESTON

Stonehenge Touring Park, Orcheston,
Near Shrewton, Wiltshire, SP3 4SH.
Std: 01980 **Tel:** 620304 **Fax:** 621121
Email: julieyoung@vizzavi.net
Website: www.orcheston.freeserve.co.uk
Nearest Town/Resort Salisbury
Directions On A360 11 miles Salisbury, 11
miles Devizes.
Acreage 2 **Open** All Year
Access Good **Site** Level
Sites Available ▲ ⌂ ⊟ Total 30
Facilities ⓵ ⊞ ♨ ⌐ ☉ ↵ ☖ ☐ ☎
⌦ ⊙ ☕✗ ⅃ ⚑⌂☐☐
Nearby Facilities ⌐
⇶ Salisbury
Stonehenge 5 miles, Salisbury plain, easy
reach Bath and the New Forest. Take Away
Food. AA 3 Pennants.

TILSHEAD

Brades Acre, Tilshead, Salisbury,
Wiltshire, SP3 4RX.
Std: 01980 **Tel:** Shrewton 620402
Nearest Town/Resort Salisbury/Devizes
Directions A360, 10 miles to Devizes, 13
miles to Salisbury.
Acreage 1½ **Open** All Year
Access Good **Site** Level
Sites Available ▲ ⌂ ⊟ Total 35
Facilities ⓵ ⊞ ♨ ⌐ ☉ ↵ ☖ ☐ ☎
⌦ ⊙ ☕✗⚑⌂☐
Nearby Facilities ⌐ ✎ ∪ ♞
⇶ Salisbury
Touring for Stonehenge, Salisbury
Cathedral, Wilton and Longleat Houses.
Avebury, Orcheston riding.

WESTBURY

Brokerswood Country Park,
Brokerswood, Nr. Westbury, Wiltshire,
BA13 4EH.
Std: 01373 **Tel:** 822238 **Fax:** 858474
Email: woodland.park@virgin.net
Nearest Town/Resort Westbury/
Trowbridge
Directions 4 miles Westbury, 5 miles
Trowbridge, 5 miles Frome, left off A361
Southwick onto unclassified 1¼ miles on left
turn at Standerwick on A36.
Acreage 5 **Open** All Year
Access Good **Site** Level
Sites Available ▲ ⌂ ⊟ Total 70
Facilities ⅃ ⓵ ⅃ ⊞ ⓌⒸ ♨ ⌐ ☉ ↵
⌦ ⊙ ☕✗⚑⌂☐☐
Nearby Facilities ⌐ ✎ ∪
⇶ Westbury
Site adjoins an 80 acre area of forest open
to the public together with a museum, lake,
Narrow Gauge Railway, etc.

WORCESTERSHIRE
BEWDLEY

Bank Farm Holiday Park, Bank Farm,
Arley, Bewdley, Worcestershire, DY12
3ND.
Std: 01299 **Tel:** 410277
Std: 01299 **Fax:** 404960
Email: bankfarm@tinyworld.co.uk
Website: www.bankfarmholidaypark.co.uk
Nearest Town/Resort Bewdley
Directions From Bewdley take the B4194
to Button Oak, turn right for Arley and fork
left at the New Inn Pub, continue for 1 mile.
Open All Year
Access Good **Site** Level
Sites Available ⌂ ⊟ Total 9
Facilities ⓵ ⅃ ⊞ ⓌⒸ ♨ ⌐ ↵ ☖ ☐ ☎
⌦ ☕⚑⊙ ✵ ⚑⌂☐
Nearby Facilities ⌐ ✎ ♠ ∪ ♞
⇶ Bewdley/Arley
Alongside a river in the Wyre Forest. Very
near to historical town. Horse riding, Pitch
and Putt, tennis, squash and golf.

BROADWAY

Leedons Park, Childswickham Road,
Broadway, Worcestershire, WR12 7HB.
Std: 01386 **Tel:** 852423
Website: www.allenscaravans.com
Nearest Town/Resort Broadway
Directions I mile from Broadway on the
B4632 Cheltenham road, off the A44 for 200
yards and turn right signposted
Childswickham.
Open All Year
Access Good **Site** Level
Sites Available ▲ ⌂ ⊟ Total 300
Facilities ⓵ ⅃ ⊞ ⓌⒸ ♨ ⌐ ↵ ☖ ☐ ☎
⌦ ⊙ ☕✗ⓌⒶ♨ ⟋ ✵ ⚑⌂☐
Nearby Facilities ⌐ ⊥ ∪ ∩
Ideal for touring the Cotswolds.

DROITWICH

**Holt Fleet Farm Camping & Touring
Site,** Holt Fleet, Holt Heath, Worcester,
Worcestershire, WR6 6NW.
Std: 01905 **Tel:** 620512
Std: 01905 **Fax:** 620512
Nearest Town/Resort Droitwich
Directions Leave the M5 at junction 5 and
take the A4133 to Ombersley roundabout,
go straight over and continue for 1¼ miles
turning right at the bottom of the hill.
Acreage 6 **Open** April **to** October
Access Good **Site** Level
Sites Available ▲ ⌂ ⊟ Total 150

acilities ♪ ⅢⒺ ♿ ⌂ ⌃ ☉ 🚻 Ⓛ Ⓐ ☎ ♀ ◄🗐
l/earby Facilities ⌐ ⚲
♣ Droitwich
Quiet site beside the River Severn. Club on
ite. Ideal touring stop over.

EVESHAM

:vesham Vale Caravan Park, Yessell
arm, Boston Lane, Charlton, Near
:vesham, Worcestershire, WR11 6RD.
.td: 01386 **Tel:** 860377
Jearest Town/Resort Evesham
Directions From Evesham take the A44,
fter approx. 1½ miles turn right for Charlton.
'ark is on the left hand side after approx. ¾
nile.
\creage 9 **Open** April **to** October
\ccess Good **Site** Level
'acilities ♪ ⅢⒺ ⌂ ⌃ ☉ 🚻 ▪ ☎
Ⓛ Ⓐ ◄🗐
|earby Facilities ⌐ ⚲ ↘ U ♀
♣ Evesham
)n the Blossom Trail route, near a river for
shing. Central for the Cotswolds, Stratford,
Vorcester, etc..

EVESHAM

Ranch Caravan Park, Station Road,
Honeybourne, Nr. Evesham,
Vorcestershire, WR11 5QG.
td: 01386 **Tel:** 830744
td: 01386 **Fax:** 833503
mail: ranchpark@netscapeonline.co.uk
Vebsite: www.ranch.co.uk
earest Town/Resort Evesham
irections From Evesham take B4035 to
adsey and Bretforton. Turn left to
loneybourne. At village crossroads take
idford direction, site on left in 400 yards.
\creage 48 **Open** March **to** November

Access Good **Site** Level
Sites Available ⚑ 🚃 **Total** 120
Facilities ♪ ⅢⒺ ♿ ⌂ ⌃ ☉ 🚻 ▪ ☎
⚑ Ⓛ Ⓐ ⅋ ♀ ◄🗐 🗐
Nearby Facilities ⌐ ⚲ U
♣ Evesham
Situated in meadow land in Vale of Evesham
on north edge of Cotswolds. Meals available
in licensed club.

GREAT MALVERN

Camping & Caravanning Club Site,
Blackmore Camp Site No. 2, Hanley
Swan, Worcestershire, WR8 0EE.
Std: 01684 **Tel:** 310280
Website:
www.campingandcaravanningclub.co.uk
Nearest Town/Resort Worcester
Directions Take the A38 to Upton-on-
Severn, turn north over the river bridge, turn
second left then first left signposted Hanley
Swan. Site is on the right after 1 mile.
Acreage 17 **Open** All Year
Access Good **Site** Level
Sites Available ⚑ 🚃 **Total** 198
Facilities ⚿ ♪ Ⓜ ⅢⒺ ⌂ ⌃ ☉ 🚻 ▪ Ⓛ ☎
Ⓛ Ⓐ ⅋ 🚻 ◄🗐
Nearby Facilities ⚲ U ♀
♣ Malvern
Close to the River Severn. Situated in the
Malvern Hills, ideal walking country. Close
to the market towns of Ledbury, Tewkesbury
and Evesham. BTB Graded. Non members
welcome.

HARTLEBURY

Shorthill Caravan & Camping Centre,
Crossway Green, Worcester Road,
Hartlebury, Worcestershire, DY13 9SH.
Std: 01299 **Tel:** 250571
Nearest Town/Resort Stourport-on-

Severn
Directions Take the A449 Kidderminster to
Worcester road. At garage island go straight
over, 200 yards to the Little Chef Restaurant,
site is at the rear of the restaurant.
Acreage 3 **Open** All Year
Access Good **Site** Level
Sites Available ⚑ 🚃 🚃 **Total** 50
Facilities ♪ Ⓜ ⅢⒺ ♿ ⌂ ⌃ ☉ 🚻 ▪ ☎
Ⓛ Ⓐ ✕ 🚻 ⅋ 🚻 ◄🗐
Nearby Facilities ⌐ ⚲ ↘ ↘ U ♀ ⚹
♣ Hartlebury
Ideal touring site with outdoor swimming and
paddling pools and a childrens play area.
Inland pleasure/leisure resort, funfair etc.,
3 miles. Secure storage available all year.
Contractors welcome.

MALVERN

Kingsgreen Caravan Park, Berrow, Near
Malvern, Worcestershire, WR13 6AQ.
Std: 01531 **Tel:** 650272
Nearest Town/Resort Ledbury/Malvern
Directions From Ledbury take the A417
towards Gloucester. Go over the M50 then
take the first turning left to Malvern, we are
1 mile on the right. OR M50 Southbound
junction 2, turn left onto the A417, in 1 mile
turn left to the Malverns.
Acreage 3 **Open** 1 March **to** End October
Access Good **Site** Level
Sites Available ⚑ 🚃 🚃 **Total** 45
Facilities ⚿ ♪ ⅢⒺ ♿ ⌂ ⌃ ☉ 🗐 ☎
Ⓛ Ⓐ 🚻 ◄🗐
Nearby Facilities ⌐ ⚲ ↘ ↗ ⚹
♣ Ledbury/Malvern
Beautiful walks on the Malvern Hills and
Malvern with its famous Elgar Route. Historic
Black and White timber towns. Tewkesbury
and Upton-on-Severn. Fishing on site.

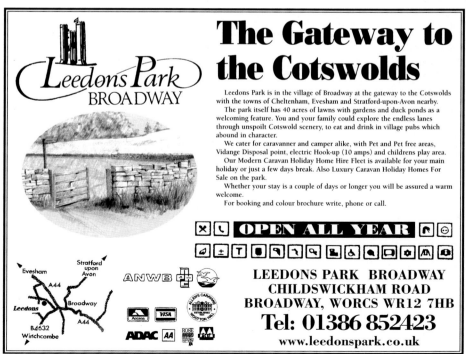

The Gateway to the Cotswolds

Leedons Park BROADWAY

Leedons Park is in the village of Broadway at the gateway to the Cotswolds
with the towns of Cheltenham, Evesham and Stratford-upon-Avon nearby.

The park itself has 40 acres of lawns with gardens and duck ponds as a
welcoming feature. You and your family could explore the endless lanes
through unspoilt Cotswold scenery, to eat and drink in village pubs which
abound in character.

We cater for caravanner and camper alike, with Pet and Pet free areas,
Vidange Disposal point, electric Hook-up (10 amps) and childrens play area.

Our Modern Caravan Holiday Home Hire Fleet is available for your main
holiday or just a few days break. Also Luxury Caravan Holiday Homes For
Sale on the park.

Whether your stay is a couple of days or longer you will be assured a warm
welcome.

For booking and colour brochure write, phone or call.

OPEN ALL YEAR

**LEEDONS PARK BROADWAY
CHILDSWICKHAM ROAD
BROADWAY, WORCS WR12 7HB**

Tel: 01386 852423

www.leedonspark.co.uk

CARAVAN PARK RANCH HOLIDAY CENTRE

NATIONAL CARAVAN COUNCIL LIMITED

* ESTABLISHED FAMILY-RUN PARK
* LOCATED IN THE VALE OF EVESHAM
* TOURERS WELCOME
* MULTI SERVICE PITCHES
* ELECTRIC HOOK-UPS AVAILABLE
* LICENCED CLUB SERVING MEALS
* HEATED OUTDOOR SWIMMING POOL
* SHOP
* LAUNDRY

AA ▶▶

HONEYBOURNE, EVESHAM, WORCS. WR11 7PR

Tel: EVESHAM (01386) 830744

MALVERN

Riverside Caravan Park, Clevelode, Malvern, Worcestershire, WR13 6PE.
Std: 01684 Tel: 310475
Std: 01684 Fax: 310475
Nearest Town/Resort Malvern
Directions Halfway between Worcester and Upton-on-Severn on the B4424.
Acreage 25 **Open** Easter **to** October
Access Good **Site** Lev/Slope
Sites Available ▲ ⊞ ⊟ **Total** 70
Facilities ⨍ 🖃 🖾 ⊞ ⅃ ⌂ ⊙ ⌐ ⥮ ▦ ▢ ⚍
⅀ ☖ ⍨ Π 🕭 ⍾ ⊡
Nearby Facilities Γ ⌿ ⌖ U ℛ
≉ Malvern
On the banks of the River Severn, slipway and a tennis court. NO Fishing for 2001 ONLY. NO Dogs until Foot & Mouth is under control.

MALVERN

The Robin Hood, Castle Morton, Near Malvern, Worcestershire, WR13 6BS.
Std: 01684 Tel: 833212
Nearest Town/Resort Malvern/Ledbury
Directions The B4208 Worcester to Gloucester road.
Open All Year
Access Good **Site** Level
Sites Available ▲ ⊞ ⊟ **Total** 15
Facilities ⊞ ⅃⅂ ╳ ⊡
Nearby Facilities Γ ⌿ ⌖ U ℛ ✕
≉ Malvern/Ledbury
Situated at the foot of the Malvern Hills, ideal for walking, riding and cycling.

MALVERN

Three Counties Park, Sledge Green, Berrow, Nr. Malvern, Worcestershire, WR13 6JW.
Std: 01684 Tel: Birtsmorton 833439
Std: 01684 Fax: 833439
Email: richard.dupont@talk21.com
Nearest Town/Resort Tewkesbury
Directions From Tewkesbury take A438 Ledbury road for 6 miles.
Acreage 2 **Open** April **to** October
Access Good **Site** Level
Sites Available ▲ ⊞ ⊟ **Total** 50
Facilities ⨍ ⊞ 🕭 ⌂ ⊙ ⌐ ⚍ ▦ 🕭 ⥮ ⊡
Nearby Facilities Γ ⌿ ⍨ ⌖ U ⅃
≉ Tewkesbury
Malvern Hills, Rivers Severn and Avon. Walking, boating, and historic sights.

SHRAWLEY

Brant Farm Caravan Park, Shrawley, Worcestershire, WR6 6TD.
Std: 01905 Tel: 621008/620470
Std: 01299 Fax: 827517
Nearest Town/Resort Stourport-on-Severn

Directions On the B4194 between Stourport-on-Severn and Worcester. Near the Rose & Crown Public House.
Acreage 1 **Open** 7 March **to** 31 Oct
Access Good **Site** Level
Sites Available ▲ ⊞ ⊟ **Total** 8
Facilities ⨍ ⊞ 🕭 ⌂ ⊙ ⌐ ⚍ 🕭 ⥮ ⊡
Nearby Facilities ⌿
≉ Kidderminster/Worcester
Near the woods for walking and within 1 mile of the River Severn for fishing.

SHRAWLEY

Lenchford Caravan Park, Shrawley, Worcestershire, WR6 6TB.
Std: 01905 **Tel:** Worcester 620246
Email: michaelbendall@compuserve.com
Nearest Town/Resort Worcester
Directions Take A443 Worcester/Tenbury road. At Holt Heath crossroads, take B4196 to Stourport. Signpost in ¾ mile on right.
Acreage 2 **Open** March **to** December
Access Good **Site** Level
Sites Available ▲ ⊞ ⊟ **Total** 12
Facilities ⚭ ⨍ ⊞ 🕭 ⌂ ⊙ ⌐ ⚍ ▦ ▢ ⚍
⅀ ☖ ⍨ ╳ Π ▦ ⊡
Nearby Facilities Γ ⌿ ⌖ U
≉ Worcester

STANFORD BRIDGE

The Bridge Caravan & Camping Park, Stanford Bridge, Worcestershire, WR6 6RU.
Std: 01886 **Tel:** 812771
Nearest Town/Resort Stourport
Directions From Stourport take the A451 to Great Whitley for 5 miles, then take the B4203 to Stanford Bridge for 2 miles.
Acreage 2 **Open** Easter **to** 30 Sept
Access Good **Site** Level
Sites Available ▲ ⊞ ⊟ **Total** 40
Facilities ⨍ ⊞ 🕭 ⌂ ⅃⅂ ⅂ ⍨ ╳ ⊡
Nearby Facilities Γ ⌿ U
≉ Worcester
On the banks of the River Teme for fishing. Ideal touring.

STOURPORT-ON-SEVERN

Lickhill Manor Caravan Park, Lickhill Manor, Stourport-on-Severn, Worcestershire, DY13 8RL.
Std: 01299 **Tel:** 871041/877820
Std: 01299 **Fax:** 824998
Email: excellent@lickhillmanor.co.uk
Website: www.lickhillmanor.co.uk
Nearest Town/Resort Stourport-on-Severn
Directions From Stourport take the B4195 to Bewdley, at traffic lights on the crossroads follow caravan signs, after ½ mile turn right at the sign.

Acreage 9 **Open** All Year
Access Good **Site** Level
Sites Available ▲ ⊞ ⊟ **Total** 120
Facilities ⅃⅂ ⨍ 🖃 ⊞ 🕭 ⌂ ⊙ ⌐ ⚍ ▢
⅀ ☖ ⍨ ⊛ ⥮ ▦ ▢ ⚍
Nearby Facilities Γ ⌿ ⍨ ⌖ U ℛ
≉ Kidderminster
Alongside river, fishing rights held. Walks through unspoilt Wyre Forest. West Midlands Safari Park, Severn Valley Railway.

STOURPORT-ON-SEVERN

Lincomb Lock Caravan Park, Lincomb Lock, Titton, Stourport-on-Severn, Worcestershire, DY13 9QR.
Std: 01299 **Tel:** 823836
Email: lincomb@hillandale.co.uk
Website: www.hillandale.co.uk
Nearest Town/Resort Stourport-on-Severn
Directions 1 mile from Stourport on A4025 turn right at park signs. Or from A449 join the A4025 at Crossway Green after 1 mile turn left at park signs.
Acreage 1 **Open** 1 March **to** 6 January
Access Good **Site** Level
Sites Available ⊞ ⊟ **Total** 14
Facilities ⨍ 🖃 ⊞ 🕭 ⌂
⅀ ☖ ⍨ Π ▦ ▢ ⚍
Nearby Facilities Γ ⌿ ⌖ U
≉ Kidderminster
Alongside a river. Local attractions to suit all ages including West Midlands Safari Park, Severn Railway, Riverside Amusements, ancient Wyre Forest and local museums.

TENBURY WELLS

Knighton on Teme Caravan Park, Tenbury Wells, Worcestershire, WR15 8NA.
Std: 01584 **Tel:** 781246
Std: 01584 **Fax:** 781246
Email: kotcaravans@talk21.com
Website: www.kotcaravans.co.uk
Nearest Town/Resort Tenbury Wells
Directions From Kidderminster take A456 to Leominster, turn off to Knighton on Teme. Follow green and white signs. Please telephone for a detailed map.
Open Mid March **to** End Dec
Access Good **Site** Sloping
Sites Available ▲ ⊞ ⊟ **Total** 5+
Facilities ⨍ 🕭 ⌂ ⊙ ⅃ ☖ 🕭 ▦ ⍨
Nearby Facilities Γ ⌿
≉ Ludlow
Opposite black and white pub with a bowling green. Fishing and walking in the local area.

WORCESTER

etch Caravan Park, Bath Road,
orcester, Worcs, WR5 3HW.
d: 01905 **Tel:** 820430
earest Town/Resort Worcester
rections Leave the M5 at junction 7 and
low signs for Malvern until you come to
e A38. Turn for Worcester and park
trance is approx. 100 yards on the left.
reage 10 Open April to End October
ccess Good **Site** Level
tes Available ⚠ ⌷ ⌷ **Total** 32
cilities ♿ ⌷ ⌷ ⌷ ⊙ ⌷ ⌷ ⌷ ⌷ ✕ ⌷
earby Facilities ⌷ ⌷ ⌷
Worcester
n the River Severn.

WORCESTER

ll House Caravan & Camping Site,
ll House, Hawford, Worcestershire,
R3 7SE.
d: 01905 **Tel:** 451283
d: 01905 **Fax:** 754143
earest Town/Resort Worcester
rections A449 Worcester to
dderminster.
ereage 8½ **Open** Easter **to** October
ccess Good **Site** Level
tes Available ⚠ ⌷ ⌷ **Total** 150
a c i l i t i e s ♿ ⌷ ⌷ ⌷ ⊙ ⌷ ⌷
⌷ ✕ ⌷ ⌷
arby Facilities ⌷ ⌷ ⌷
Shrubhill/Worcester
ease note motocycles are not allowed into
d. Dogs must be kept on leads.

YORKSHIRE, EAST

BARMBY MOOR

**e Sycamores Camping & Caravan
rk,** Feoffe Common Lane, Barmby
or, East Yorkshire, YO42 4HT.
d: 01759 **Tel:** 388838
ail:
camores@york.camping.freeserve.co.uk
ebsite: www.sycamorescaravans.co.uk
arest Town/Resort York/Bridlington
rections From York take the A1079 (York
Hull road) east for approx. 7 miles, turn
arp left before the Esso Filling Station
inposted Yapham, we are 200 yards on
e right hand side.
reage 3 **Open** March **to** November
ccess Good **Site** Level
tes Available ⚠ ⌷ ⌷ **Total** 36
cilities ♿ ⌷ ⌷ ⌷ ⊙ ⌷ ⌷ ⌷ ⌷ ⌷
arby Facilities ⌷ ⌷ ⌷ U ⌷
York
rk City Centre and a gliding club nearby.

BEVERLEY

keminster Park, Hull Road, Beverley,
st Yorkshire, HU17 0PN.
d: 01482 **Tel:** 882655
d: 01482 **Fax:** 882655
arest Town/Resort Beverley
rections One mile from main Hull to
verley road on the 1174.
en All Year
ccess Good **Site** Level
tes Available ⚠ ⌷ ⌷ **Total** 50
c i l i t i e s ♿ ⌷ ⌷ ⌷ ⊙ ⌷ ⌷ ⌷ ⌷ ⌷
⌷ ✕ ⌷ ⌷ ⌷
arby Facilities ⌷ ⌷ U ⌷
Beverley & Hull
site two ponds well stocked with fish. Bar
h food also takeaway. 14 miles from
rnsea.

BRANDES BURTON

Dacre Lakeside Park, Brandes Burton,
Driffield, East Yorkshire, YO25 8RT.
Std: 01964 **Tel:** 543704
Std: 01964 **Fax:** 544040
Email: dacresurf@aol.com
Website: www.dacrepark.co.uk
Nearest Town/Resort Beverley
Directions From the A1 or M1 take the M62
then the A63 to South Cave. Turn off after
junction 38 onto the A1079. Go by Beverley
onto the A1035, then onto the A165.
Acreage 10 **Open** March **to** October
Access Good **Site** Level
Sites Available ⚠ ⌷ ⌷ **Total** 120
Facilities ♿ ⌷ ⌷ ⌷ ⊙ ⌷ ⌷ ⌷ ⌷ ⌷
⌷ ⌷ ⌷ ⌷ ✕ ⌷ ⌷ ⌷ ✕ ⌷
Nearby Facilities ⌷ ⌷ ⌷ ⌷ U ⌷ ⌷
⌷ Beverley
8 acre lake for fishing, wind surfing and
sailing.

BRANDES BURTON

Fosse Hill, Catwick Lane, Brandes
Burton, East Yorkshire, YO25 8SB.
Std: 01964 **Tel:** 542608
Std: 01964 **Fax:** 543010
Nearest Town/Resort Hornsea
Directions ½ a mile east of the A165.
Open March **to** End Oct
Access Good **Site** Lev/Slope
Sites Available ⚠ ⌷ **Total** 75
F a c i l i t i e s ♿ ⌷ ⌷ ⌷ ⊙ ⌷
⌷ ⌷ ⌷ ✕ ⌷ ⌷ ⌷ ⌷ ⌷ ⌷ ⌷
Nearby Facilities ⌷ ⌷ ⌷ ⌷ ⌷
⌷ Beverley
Lakeside pitches. 3 miles from the beach.
Ideal for touring the Yorkshire Wolds and
York.

BRIDLINGTON

Fir Tree Caravan Park, Jewison Lane,
Bridlington, East Yorkshire, YO16 5YG.
Std: 01262 **Tel:** 676442
Std: 01262 **Fax:** 676442
Email: cadesfirtree@flowerofmay.com
Website: www.flowerofmay.com
Nearest Town/Resort Bridlington
Directions From roundabout on A165 take
B1255 to Flamborough for 2 miles. Jewison
Lane is on the left and site is on the left after
the level crossing.
Acreage 25 **Open** March **to** November
Access Good **Site** Level
Sites Available ⌷ ⌷ **Total** 46
Facilities ♿ ⌷ ⌷ ⌷ ⊙ ⌷ ⌷ ⌷ ⌷
⌷ ⌷ ⌷ ⌷ ⌷ ⌷ ⌷ ⌷ ⌷
Nearby Facilities ⌷ ⌷ ⌷ ⌷ U ⌷ ⌷
⌷ Bridlington
Pets are welcome by arrangement only.

BRIDLINGTON

Old Mill Caravan Park, Bempton,
Bridlington, East Yorkshire, YO15 1EB.
Std: 01262 **Tel:** 673565
Nearest Town/Resort Bridlington
Directions From Bridlington take the B1255
to Flamborough. At Marton turn left into
Jewison Lane signposted Bempton, after
1 mile turn right, site is 500 yards on the
right.
Acreage 2¼ **Open** April **to** October
Access Good **Site** Level
Sites Available ⌷ ⌷ **Total** 55
Facilities ♿ ⌷ ⌷ ⌷ ⊙ ⌷ ⌷ ⌷ ⌷ ⌷
⌷ ⌷ ⌷
Nearby Facilities ⌷ ⌷ ⌷ ⌷ U ⌷
⌷ Bempton
Near to Bempton Bird Sanctuary, two golf
courses and Sewerby Park. Fishing in the
sea and a pond. Heritage coastal walk, Brid
Bay for safe sailing.

BRIDLINGTON

South Cliff Caravan Park, Wilsthorpe,
Bridlington, East Yorkshire, YO15 3QN.
Std: 01262 **Tel:** 671051
Std: 01262 **Fax:** 605639
Website: www.bridlington.net
Nearest Town/Resort Bridlington
Directions 1½ miles south of Bridlington on
the A165.
Open March **to** November
Access Good **Site** Level
Sites Available ⚠ ⌷ ⌷ **Total** 200
Facilities ♿ ⌷ ⌷ ⌷ ⌷ ⌷ ⊙ ⌷ ⌷ ⌷ ⌷
⌷ ⌷ ⌷ ✕ ⌷ ⌷ ⌷ ⌷ ⌷ ⌷
Nearby Facilities ⌷ ⌷ ⌷ ⌷ ⌷ ⌷ ⌷
⌷ Bridlington
Easy access to award winning, sandy
beaches. Special Offers throughout the
season. Holiday homes for hire. Sorry, No
Dogs.

HORNSEA

Cowden Caravan Park, Eelmere Lane,
Cowden, Near Hornsea, East Yorkshire,
HU11 4UL.
Std: 01964 **Tel:** 527393
Nearest Town/Resort Hornsea
Directions On the B1244 east coast road
between Hornsea and Withernsea.
Acreage 19 **Open** 1 March **to** 1 Dec
Access Good **Site** Level
Sites Available ⚠ ⌷ ⌷ **Total** 239
Facilities ♿ ⌷ ⌷ ⌷ ⊙ ⌷ ⌷ ⌷ ⌷ ⌷ ✕ ⌷
Nearby Facilities ⌷ ⌷ ⌷ ⌷ U
⌷ Hull
Near the beach.

HORNSEA

Four Acres Caravan Park, Hornsea
Road, Atwick, Driffield, East Yorkshire,
YO25 8DG.
Std: 01964 **Tel:** 536940
Nearest Town/Resort Hornsea
Directions As you approach Hornsea turn
left at the roundabout, we are approx. 2 miles
along on the right hand side.
Acreage 4 **Open** April **to** October
Access Good **Site** Level
Sites Available ⚠ ⌷ ⌷ **Total** 54
Facilities ♿ ⌷ ⌷ ⊙ ⌷ ⌷ ⌷ ⌷ ⌷ ⌷
Nearby Facilities ⌷ ⌷ ⌷ U
⌷ Bridlington
Near to the beach, local pub, indoor bowls,
swimming baths, shop with Post Office and
a Sunday market.

LITTLE WEIGHTON

Louvain, Rowley Road, Little Weighton,
East Yorkshire, HU20 3XJ.
Std: 01482 **Tel:** 848249
Nearest Town/Resort Beverley
Directions From M62 then A63. At South
cave crossroads turn right (Beverley Road)
keep on this road for approx 3 miles, turn
left at signpost Little Weighton & Rowley.
Acreage 1½ **Open** All Year
Access Good **Site** Level
Sites Available ⚠ ⌷ ⌷ **Total** 20
Facilities ♿ ⌷ ⌷ ⊙ ⌷ ⌷ ⌷ ⌷ ⌷
Nearby Facilities ⌷ ⌷ U
⌷ Hull
Old Town Beverley. Ideal touring.

ROOS

Sand-le-Mere Caravan Park, Seaside
Lane, Tunstall, Roos, Nr. Hull, East
Yorkshire, HU12 0JQ.
Std: 01964 **Tel:** 670403 **Fax:** 671099
Website: www.sand-le-mere.co.uk
Nearest Town/Resort Withernsea
Directions From Hull to Preston heading
north on the A1033. Burton Pidsea, Roos
to Tunstall to the sea.

Acreage 30 **Open** March **to** 31 December
Access Good **Site** Level
Sites Available ▲ ⊞ **Total** 40
Nearby Facilities ↑ ✓ ∪
➤ Hull
Natural slope to the beach. Fresh water fishing. Heated swimming pool and jacuzzi.

SKIPSEA

Far Grange Park Skipsea, Driffield, East Yorkshire, YO25 8SY.
Std: 01262 **Tel:** 468293/468248
Std: 01262 **Fax:** 468648
Email: enquiries@fargrangepark.co.uk
Website: www.fargrangepark.co.uk
Nearest Town/Resort Hornsea
Directions 4¼ miles north of Hornsea on B1242.
Open March **to** October
Access Good **Site** Level
Sites Available ▲ ⊞ **Total** 130
Facilities ⅙ ♿ ∱ 🖪 🚻 🏪 ← ⊙ ➘ ⊿ ◻ ☂
🏧 ◻ ⊖ ✕ ▽ ♠ 🎇 ⊛ 🛒 ◻ ⊟
Nearby Facilities ↑ ✓ ♨ ∪ ℛ
➤ Bridlington
Clifftop location with superb views of Bridlington Bay. Also open Winter weekends.

SKIPSEA

Mill Farm Country Park, Mill Lane, Skipsea, East Yorkshire, YO25 8SS.
Std: 01262 **Tel:** 468211
Nearest Town/Resort Hornsea
Directions The A165 Hull to Bridlington Road, at Beeford take B1249 to Skipsea. At crossroads turn right, then first left up Cross Street which leads on to Mill Lane, site is on the right.
Acreage 6 **Open** 1 March **to** 6 October
Access Good **Site** Level
Sites Available ▲ ⊞ **Total** 56
Facilities ⅙ ∱ 🖪 🚻 🏪 ← ⊙ ☂
🅿 ⊛ 🛒 ◻ ⊟
Nearby Facilities ↑ ✓ ♨ ⤳ ∪ ∂ ℛ
➤ Bridlington
Farm walk, beach nearby. RSPB sites at Bempton and Hornsea. Good centre for many places of local interest. Many facilities nearby including an indoor swimming pool ½ mile away.

SKIPSEA

Skipsea Sands Holiday Park, Mill Lane, Skipsea, East Yorkshire, YO25 8TZ.
Std: 01262 **Tel:** 468210
Std: 01262 **Fax:** 468454
Nearest Town/Resort Hornsea
Directions Off the B1242 Hornsea to Bridlington road. In Skipsea Village follow signs into Cross Street then into Mill Lane, park is 1 mile from the village.

Acreage 8 **Open** March **to** November
Access Good **Site** Level
Sites Available ▲ ⊞ **Total** 90
Facilities ⅙ ∱ 🖪 🚻 🏪 ← ⊙ ➘ ⊿ ◻ ☂
🏧 ◻ ⊖ ✕ ▽ ♠ 🎇 ⊛ 🛒 ◻ ⊟
Nearby Facilities ↑ ✓ ♨ ∪
➤ Bridlington
Coastal park with full facilities for a pleasant family holiday.

SKIPSEA

Skirlington Leisure Park, Low Skirlington, Skipsea, Driffield, East Yorkshire, YO25 8SY.
Std: 01262 **Tel:** 468213/466
Std: 01262 **Fax:** 468105
Email: enquiries@skirlington.com
Website: www.skirlington.com
Nearest Town/Resort Bridlington
Directions 3 miles north of Hornsea on the B1242.
Acreage 30 **Open** March **to** October
Access Good **Site** Level
Sites Available ▲ ⊞ **Total** 300
Facilities ⅙ ♿ ∱ 🖪 🚻 🏪 ← ⊙ ➘ ⊿ ◻ ☂
🏧 🅿 ⊖ ✕ ▽ 🚐 ♠ 🎇 ⊛ 🛒 ◻ ⊟
Nearby Facilities ↑ ✓ ♨ ⤳ ∪ ∂ ℛ
➤ Bridlington
Cliff top site with access to the beach. Family entertainment, Sunday market and fishing.

WILBERFOSS

Fangfoss Old Station Caravan Park, Fangfoss, East Yorkshire, YO41 5QB.
Std: 01759 **Tel:** 380491
Email: fangfoss@pi2000.co.uk
Website: www.ukparks.co.uk/fangfoss
Nearest Town/Resort York
Directions The A1079 towards Hull. 7miles to Wilberfoss, signposted left to Fangfoss.
Acreage 4 **Open** March **to** October
Access Good **Site** Level
Sites Available ▲ ⊞ **Total** 75
Facilities ∱ 🖪 🚻 🏪 ← ⊙ ➘ ⊿ ◻ ☂
🏧 ◻ ⊟ 🛒 ◻ ⊟
Nearby Facilities ↑ ✓ ∪ ℛ
➤ York
Peaceful country park, easy access to Wolds, coast, moors, York etc..

WITHERNSEA

Willows Holiday Park, Hollym Road, Withernsea, East Yorkshire, HU19 2PN.
Std: 01964 **Tel:** 612233
Std: 01964 **Fax:** 612957
Email: info@highfield-caravans.co.uk
Website: www.highfield-caravans.co.uk
Nearest Town/Resort Withernsea
Directions Take the A1033 from Hull to Withernsea. On entering Withernsea Willows Holiday Park is the first holiday park on the left.
Open 4 March **to** 31 October

Access Good **Site** Level
Sites Available ⊞ ◻ **Total** 40
Facilities ∱ 🖪 🚻 🏪 ← ⊙ ◻ ☂
🛒 ◻ ⊖ ▽ ♠ 🚐 ⊟
Nearby Facilities ↑ ✓ ∪
➤ Hull
Only a ten minute walk to the beach. On the edge of the town centre, 15 minute walk.

YORKSHIRE, NORTH

AYSGARTH

Little Cote Site, West Burton, Aysgarth, North Yorkshire, DL8 4JY.
Std: 01969 **Tel:** 663450
Directions From the A684 Aysgarth Northallerton road, 2 miles east of Aysgarth take the B6160 to West Burton, fork left Walden for ¾ mile.
Acreage 2 **Open** March **to** October
Access Good **Site** Lev/Slope
Sites Available ▲ ⊞ **Total** 20
Facilities ☂ ⤳
Nearby Facilities ✓
➤ Northallerton
Small, quiet site alongside a river. Own car essential. Ideal touring.

AYSGARTH

Westholme Caravan & Camping Park, Aysgarth, Leyburn, North Yorks, DL8 3SR.
Std: 01969 **Tel:** 663268
Nearest Town/Resort Leyburn/Hawes
Directions Follow the A684 from Leyburn towards Hawes, turn left in 7½ miles just before Aysgarth.
Acreage 22 **Open** March **to** October
Access Good **Site** Level
Sites Available ▲ ⊞ **Total** 75
Facilities ∱ 🖪 🚻 🏪 ← ⊙ ➘ ◻ 🏧 ◻ ⊖ ✕ ▽ 🚐 ♠ ◻ ☂
Nearby Facilities ✓ ℛ
➤ Darlington
Alongside stream, scenic views, ideal touring centre. Fishing.

BARDEN

Howgill Lodge, Barden, Nr. Skipton, North Yorkshire, BD23 6DJ.
Std: 01756 **Tel:** 720655
Website: www.yorkshirenet.co.uk/stayat/howgill
Nearest Town/Resort Bolton Abbey
Directions Turn off B6160 at Barden Tower, site 1 mile on right.
Acreage 4 **Open** April **to** 31 Oct
Site Terraced
Sites Available ▲ ⊞ **Total** 30
Facilities ⅙ ∱ 🖪 🚻 🏪 ← ⊙ ➘ ◻ 🏧 ◻ ⊖ ✕ 🛒 ⊟
Nearby Facilities ✓ ⤳
➤ Skipton
Beautiful views, ideal for walking or touring. David Bellamy Gold Award for Conservation

BEDALE

Pembroke Caravan Park, 19 Low Street,
Leeming Bar, Northallerton, North
Yorkshire, DL7 9BW.
Std: 01677 **Tel:** 422652
Nearest Town/Resort Bedale
Directions A1 Leeming Services, right onto
A684 to Leeming Bar. Keep left, crossroads
to Leases Road. ½ mile on the right.
Acreage 1¼ **Open** March to October
Access Good **Site** Slight Slope
Sites Available A ⊞ ⊞ **Total** 25
Facilities f ⌂ ♨ ♿ ⌕ ⊙ ⤶ Sᵖ ⊖ ⊛ ⊬ ▣
Nearby Facilities ⌏ ✎ ∪ ♐
⇻ Northallerton
Between the Yorkshire Dales and North
Yorks Moors. Take-away food available.

BENTHAM

Riverside Caravan Park, High Bentham,
Lancaster, Lancashire, LA2 7LW.
Std: 015242 **Tel:** 61272
Std: 015242 **Fax:** 62163
Website: www.riversidecaravanpark.co.uk
Nearest Town/Resort High Bentham
Directions Follow caravan signs off the
B6480 at The Black Bull Hotel in High
Bentham.
Acreage 10 **Open** March to October
Access Good **Site** Level
Sites Available A ⊞ ⊞ **Total** 60
Facilities f ⌂ ♨ ⌕ ⊙ ⤶ ⚑ ▣ ⛽
⊖ ⊛ ♨ ⋀ ⊬ ▣
Nearby Facilities ⌏ ✎ ♐
⇻ High Bentham
Riverside site, great for families.

BOROUGHBRIDGE

Blue Bell Caravan Site, Kirby Hill,
Boroughbridge, North Yorkshire, YO5
2DN.
Std: 01423 **Tel:** 322380
Nearest Town/Resort Ripon
Directions 1 mile from the A1M junction
signposted Boroughbridge.
Acreage 2 **Open** April to October
Site Sloping
Sites Available ⊞ ⊞ **Total** 24
Facilities ⌂ ⌕ ⊙ ⤶ ⚑ ⛽ ⊖ ⊛ ♀ ⊬ ▣
Nearby Facilities ⌏ ✎ ⚓ ⋀ ♐ ✗
⇻ Harrogate

BOROUGHBRIDGE

Camping & Caravanning Club Site, Bar
Lane, Roecliffe, Boroughbridge, North
Yorkshire, YO51 9LS.
Std: 01423 **Tel:** 322683
Website:
www.campingandcaravanningclub.co.uk
Directions From junction 48 aim north and
southbound slip roads, follow signs for Bar
Lane Industrial Estate and Roecliffe Village.
Site entrance is ¼ mile from the roundabout.
Acreage 5 **Open** All Year
Site Level
Sites Available A ⊞ ⊞ **Total** 85
Facilities f ⌂ ♨ ⌕ ⊙ ⤶ ⚑ ▣ ⛽
⊖ ⊛ ♨ ⊬ ▣ ⊖
Nearby Facilities ⌏ ✗ ∪ ♐
⇻ Harrogate
On the banks of the River Ure for fishing,
boat launching facility. Table tennis and pool
table on site. Close to the Yorkshire Dales.
BTB Graded. Non members welcome.

BOROUGHBRIDGE

Boyd Hall Caravan Park, Langthorpe,
Boroughbridge, York, North Yorkshire,
YO5 9BZ.
Std: 01423 **Tel:** 322130
Email: phil.brierley@which.net
Website: www.ghc.org.uk
Nearest Town/Resort Boroughbridge

Directions From Boroughbridge follow the
B6265 towards Ripon (A1), pass the Anchor
Pub on the left hand side, 200 yards further
on turn left to Langthorpe, Skelton and
Newby Hall. Park is second on the right.
Open April to October
Access Good **Site** Level
Sites Available ⊞ ⊞ **Total** 20
Facilities f ⌂ ♨ ⌕ ⊙ ⤶ ⚑ ▣ ⛽
♨ ⊖ ⊛ ⊬ ▣
Nearby Facilities ⌏ ✎ ✗ ∪ ♐
⇻ Knaresborough
Small countryside park. Ideal centre for York,
Harrogate and The Moors.

EASINGWOLD

**Holly Brook Caravan Park - Adults
Only,** Penny Carr Lane, Off Stillington
Road, Easingwold, North Yorkshire, YO61
3EU.
Std: 01347 **Tel:** 821906
Std: 01347 **Fax:** 821906
Email: info@hollybrookpark.co.uk
Nearest Town/Resort York
Directions From York take the A19, as you
enter Easingwold pass the school on your
left and after 50 yards turn right to Stillington,
signposted.
Acreage 2 **Open** March to December
Access Good **Site** Level
Sites Available ⊞ ⊞ **Total** 30
Facilities f ⌂ ⌂ ♨ ⌕ ⊙ ⤶ ⚑ ▣ ⛽
♨ ⊖ ⊛ ⊬ ▣ ⋀
Nearby Facilities ⌏ ✎ ∪ ♐
⇻ York
ADULTS ONLY PARK. Near to York walled
city, stately homes such as Castle Howard,
North Yorkshire Moors, seaside resorts of
Scarborough and Whitby. Herriot Country.

ELVINGTON

Elvington Lake Caravan Park, Lake
Cottage, Elvington, York, North Yorkshire,
YO41 4AZ.
Std: 01904 **Tel:** 608255
Nearest Town/Resort York
Directions From York take the A1079 Hull
road, immediately straight over first
roundabout then turn right onto the B1228,
after 4 miles at the garage on the left, turn
right.
Acreage 3 **Open** All Year
Access Good **Site** Level
Sites Available A ⊞ ⊞ **Total** 15
Facilities ♨ f ⌂ ⌂ ⌕ ⤶ ⚑ ⛽ ⊖ ⋀ ⊬ ▣
Nearby Facilities ⌏ ✎ ∪
⇻ York
The only working windmill water pump. On
the shore of a quality coarse fishing lake.
Award winning park.

FILEY

**Centenary Way Camping & Caravan
Park,** Muston Grange, Filey, North
Yorkshire, YO14 0HU.
Std: 01723 **Tel:** 516415
Nearest Town/Resort Filey
Directions Take the A165 from Bridlington,
at the roundabout turn right onto the A1039,
after 200 yards turn right into Centenary
Way, follow lane to the very end.
Acreage 3½ **Open** March to October
Access Good **Site** Level
Sites Available A ⊞ □ **Total** 100
Facilities f ⌂ ♨ ⌕ ⊙
Sᵖ ⌂ ⊖ ⊛ ⊬ ▣
Nearby Facilities ⌏ ✎ ⚓ ✗ ∪ ♐
⇻ Filey
Just a ten minute walk to the beach and Filey
town. Handy for Scarborough and
Bridlington. 45 minutes to the North
Yorkshire Moors, York and Whitby.

FILEY

Muston Grange Caravan Park, Muston
Road, Filey, North Yorkshire, YO14 0HU.
Std: 01723 **Tel:** 512167
Nearest Town/Resort Filey
Directions On the A1039 south of Filey, site
entrance is on the left 100yds before the
junction with the A165.
Acreage 10 **Open** Late March to October
Access Good **Site** Lev/Slope
Sites Available A ⊞ ⊞ **Total** 220
Facilities ♿ f ⌂ ♨ ⌕ ⊙ ⤶ ⊖ ⊛
Sᵖ ▣ ⊖ ⋀ ⊬ ▣
Nearby Facilities ⌏ ✎ ⚓ ∪
⇻ Filey
Pleasant walk to a five mile stretch of beach,
5 minute walk to a golf course. Ideally
situated for visiting Scarborough, Bridlington
and North Yorkshire Moors.

FILEY

**Orchard Farm Holiday Village &
Cottages,** Stonegate, Hunmanby, Filey,
North Yorkshire, YO14 0PU.
Std: 01723 **Tel:** 891582
Nearest Town/Resort Filey
Directions On the A165 Scarborough to
Bridlington coast road. 3 miles from Filey
towards Bridlington.
Acreage 15 **Open** All Year
Access Good **Site** Level
Sites Available A ⊞ ⊞ **Total** 110
Facilities f ⌂ ⌂ ♨ ⌕ ⊙ ⤶ ⚑ ▣ ⛽
Sᵖ ▣ ⊖ ⊛ ♀ ♨ ⋀ ⊛ ⊬ ▣
Nearby Facilities ⌏ ✎ ⚓ ✗ ∪ ♐ ♐
⇻ Filey/Hunmanby
Near to Award winning beaches. Heated
indoor swimming pool, bar, train and family
room with entertainment.

FILEY

Primrose Valley Holiday Park, Primrose
Valley, Filey, North Yorkshire, YO14 9RF.
Std: 01723 **Tel:** 513730
Std: 01723 **Fax:** 513777
Nearest Town/Resort Filey
Directions From the A64 at Staxton
roundabout take the A165 signposted
Bridlington, park is between Scarborough
and Bridlington.
Open April to October
Access Good **Site** Level
Sites Available ⊞ ⊞ **Total** 65
Facilities f ⌂ ⌂ ♨ ⌕ ⊙ ▣ ⛽
♨ ⊖ ⊛ ✗ ♀ ♨ ⊛ ⊬ ▣
Nearby Facilities ⌏ ⚓ ♐
⇻ Filey
10 minute walk to sandy beaches. Full on
park entertainment and sports facilities.

FILEY

Reighton Sands Holiday Park, Reighton
Gap, Filey, North Yorkshire, YO14 9SJ.
Std: 01723 **Tel:** 890476
Std: 01723 **Fax:** 891043
Website: www.havenholidays.com
Nearest Town/Resort Filey/Scarborough
Directions We are signposted opposite the
garage at Reighton, on the A165 Filey to
Bridlington road, and are located just 1 mile
off this road.
Open Easter to End Oct
Access Good **Site** Lev/Slope
Sites Available A ⊞ ⊞ **Total** 150
Facilities ♿ f ⌂ ⌂ ♨ ⌕ ⊙ ⤶ ⚑ ▣ ⛽
Sᵖ ▣ ⊖ ⊛ ✗ ♀ ▣ ♨ ♨ ⊛ ⊬ ▣ ⊖ ⊖
Nearby Facilities ⌏ ✎ ⚓ ✗ ∪ ♐
⇻ Filey
Near to the beach, Reighton Sands offers
six miles of glorious sandy beaches. Free
sports and leisure facilities, Free Kids Club
and Free entertainment.

GRASSINGTON

Hawkswick Cote Caravan Park, Arncliffe, Skipton, North Yorkshire, BD23 5PX.
Std: 01756 **Tel:** 770226
Std: 01756 **Fax:** 770327
Nearest Town/Resort Skipton
Directions Take the B6265 Skipton to Threshfield road, at Threshfield take the B6160 to Kilnsey, after Kilnsey bear left to Arncliffe. Park is 1½ miles on the left.
Open 1 March **to** 10 November
Access Good **Site** Level
Sites Available ▲ ⊕ ⊜ **Total** 50
Facilities ⓖ ♿ ⅋ ⊞ ⅦⒷ ♨ ⌂ ⊙ ↵ ⇨ ☎
♨ ⊘ ⓖ ⚑ ⊁⊕ �ⓟ ⊟
Nearby Facilities ✔ ✠
⇒ Skipton
Yorkshire Dales walking area and climbing at Kilnsey Crag.

GRASSINGTON

Threaplands Camping & Caravan Park, Threaplands House, Cracoe, Nr. Skipton, North Yorks, BD23 6LD.
Std: 01756 **Tel:** 730248
Nearest Town/Resort Skipton
Directions 6 miles from Skipton on the B6265 to Cracoe. ¼ mile past Cracoe keep going straight on, site is ¼ mile on the left.
Acreage 8 **Open** March **to** October
Access Good **Site** Level
Sites Available ▲ ⊕ ⊜ **Total** 30
Facilities ⅋ ⅦⒷ ♨ ⌂ ⊙ ⇨ ☎ ♨ ⅃⊘ ⓖ ⊕⊟
Nearby Facilities ⌐ ✔ ∪ ✠
⇒ Skipton
Scenic views. Ideal for touring and walking.

GRASSINGTON

Wood Nook Caravan Park, Skirethorns, Threshfield, Skipton, North Yorkshire, BD23 5NU.
Std: 01756 **Tel:** 752412
Std: 01756 **Fax:** 752412
Email: enquiries@woodnook.net
Website: www.woodnook.net
Nearest Town/Resort Grassington
Directions From Skipton take the B6265 to Threshfield, then the B6160 for 50 yards, turn left into Skirethorns Lane and follow signposts.
Acreage 3 **Open** March **to** October
Access Good **Site** Lev/Slope
Sites Available ▲ ⊕ ⊜ **Total** 48
Facilities ⅋ ⅏ ⅦⒷ ♨ ⌂ ⊙ ⇨ ⊠ ⓟ ☎
♨ ⊘ ⓖ ⚑ ⊁⊕ ⓟ ⊟
Nearby Facilities ⌐ ✔ ⚓ ∪ ✠
⇒ Skipton
In the heart of Wharfedale, ideal for walking and touring The Dales.

HARROGATE

Bilton Park, Village Farm, Bilton Lane, Harrogate, North Yorkshire, HG1 4DH.
Std: 01423 **Tel:** 863121
Email: tony@bilton-park.swinternet.co.uk
Nearest Town/Resort Harrogate
Directions On the A59 in Harrogate between the A661 and the A61. Turn at Dragon Inn and site is 1 mile down Bilton Lane.
Acreage 8 **Open** April **to** October
Access Good **Site** Level
Sites Available ▲ ⊕ ⊜ **Total** 25
Facilities ⅋ ⅦⒷ ♨ ⌂ ⊙ ⇨ ☎
♨ ⅃⊘ ⓖ ⚑⊕ ⓟ ⊟
Nearby Facilities ⌐ ✔ ∪
⇒ Harrogate
River. Conference and Exhibition town. Ideal touring.

HARROGATE

High Moor Farm Caravan Park, Skipton Road, Harrogate, North Yorkshire, HG3 2LT.
Std: 01423 **Tel:** 563637
Std: 01423 **Fax:** 529449
Nearest Town/Resort Harrogate
Directions On the A59 4 miles from Harrogate on the left hand side.
Open 1 April/Easter **to** 31 Oct
Access Good **Site** Level
Sites Available ▲ ⊕□ **Total** 300
Facilities ⅋ ⅏ ⅦⒷ ♨ ⌂ ⊙ ⇨ ⊠ ⓟ ☎
♨ ⊘ ⓖ ⚑ ✕ ⊁ ⓟ ⊟
Nearby Facilities ⌐ ✔
⇒ Harrogate

HARROGATE

Ripley Caravan Park, Ripley, Harrogate, North Yorks, HG3 3AU.
Std: 01423 **Tel:** 770050
Std: 01423 **Fax:** 770050
Nearest Town/Resort Harrogate
Directions From Harrogate take A61 towards Ripon, after 3 miles at Ripley roundabout take the B6165 Knaresborough road, site is 300 yards on the left.
Acreage 18 **Open** Easter **to** October
Access Good **Site** Level
Sites Available ▲ ⊕ ⊜ **Total** 100
Facilities ⓖ ♿ ⅋ ⊞ ⅦⒷ ♨ ⌂ ⊙ ⇨ ⊠ ⓟ ☎
♨ ⅃⊘ ⓖ ⚑ ⊁ ⓟ ⊟
Nearby Facilities ⌐ ✔ ⚓ ∪ ♪
⇒ Harrogate
Ideal site for touring Dales, Harrogate and York. A level and quiet family site. David Bellamy Silver Conservation Award, AA 5 Pennants and ETB 5 Star Graded Park.

HARROGATE

Rudding Holiday Park, Follifoot, Harrogate, North Yorkshire, HG2 1JH.
Std: 01423 **Tel:** 870439
Std: 01423 **Fax:** 870859
Email: hpreception@rudding-park.com
Website: www.rudding-park.com
Nearest Town/Resort Harrogate
Directions 3 miles south of Harroga between A61 Leeds/Harrogate road an A661 Wetherby/Harrogate road.
Acreage 30 **Open** March **to** October
Access Good **Site** Level
Sites Available ▲ ⊕ ⊜ **Total** 141
Facilities ⓖ ♿ ⅋ ⊞ ⅦⒷ ♨ ⌂ ⊙ ⇨ ⊠ ⓟ
♨ ⅃⊘ ⓖ ⚑ ✕ ∧ ⚑ ❀ ⊁⊕ ⓟ ⊟ ⊟
Nearby Facilities ⌐ ✔ ∪ ♪
⇒ Harrogate
Set in 50 acres of parkland, peacef Yorkshire countryside. Heated swimmi pool, 18 hole golf course and driving rang

HARROGATE

Shaws Trailer Park, Knaresborough Road, Harrogate, North Yorkshire, HG2 7NE.
Std: 01423 **Tel:** 884432
Website: www.residentialsite.uk
Nearest Town/Resort Harrogate
Directions On the A59, entrance is adjace to Johnsons Cleaners, 50yds south of th Ford garage.
Acreage 11 **Open** All Year
Access Good **Site** Level
Sites Available ▲ ⊕ ⊜ **Total** 77
Facilities ⅋ ⅏ ⅦⒷ ♨ ⌂ ⊙ ⇨ ⊠
⅃⊘ ⓖ ⚑⊕ ⊟
Nearby Facilities ⌐ ✔ ⚓ ∪ ♪
⇒ Starbeck
A quiet and peaceful park. Ideal for touri Yorkshire Dales, spa town of Harrogate mile) and gardens, Knaresborough (4 mile and historic York. Health centre next do and a bus stop at the gateway.

HARROGATE

The Yorkshire Hussar Inn Holiday Caravan Park, Markington, Harrogate, Yorkshire, HG3 3NR.
Std: 01765 **Tel:** 677327
Email: yorkshirehussar@yahoo
Website:
www.yorkshirehussar.homestead.com
Nearest Town/Resort Harrogate/Ripon
Directions 1 mile west of A61 (Harroga Ripon road). Ripon 5 miles. Harrogate miles.
Acreage 5 **Open** April **to** October
Access Good **Site** Level
Sites Available ▲ ⊕ ⊜ **Total** 40
Facilities ⅋ ⊞ ⅦⒷ ♨ ⌂ ⊙ ⇨ ⊠ ⅃ ⓖ ⊠ ⚑⊕
Nearby Facilities ⌐ ✔ ∪ ♪

Nearby Facilities ┏ ✎ ∪ ♫
➤ Harrogate
Ideal touring centre. Site at rear of Inn. Garden setting in village. Ideal touring centre for the Dales. Fountains Abbey 1¼ miles. Holiday vans for hire.

HAWES

Bainbridge Ings Caravan & Camping Site, Hawes, North Yorkshire, DL8 3NU.
Std: 01969 **Tel:** 667354
Website: www.bainbridge-ings.co.uk
Nearest Town/Resort Hawes
Directions Approaching Hawes from Bainbridge on the A684 turn left at the signpost marked Gayle and we are 300yds on at the top of the hill.
Acreage 5 **Open** April **to** October
Access Good **Site** Level
Sites Available ▲ ♦ ➤ **Total** 80
Facilities ⚏ ⊞ ⅏ ⚈ ┏ ⊙⊸ ☎ ⊙ ⌇ ▢ ▣
Nearby Facilities ✎
➤ Garsdale
A quiet, clean, family run site with beautiful views and only ½ mile from Hawes. Motorcycles are accepted but not in groups of more than two.

HAWES

Honeycott Caravan Park, Ingleton Road, Hawes, North Yorkshire, DL8 3LH.
Std: 01969 **Tel:** 667310
Nearest Town/Resort Hawes
Directions ¼ mile out of Hawes on the B6255 Hawes to Ingleton road.
Acreage 2½ **Open** March **to** October
Access Good **Site** Lev/Slope
Sites Available ♦ ➤ **Total** 46
Facilities ⚈ ⊞ ⅏ ⚈ ⚏ ┏ ⊙ ☎ ⚆ ⊙ ⊞ ▣
Nearby Facilities ✎
➤ Garsdale
On the Pennine Way, ideal for walking, fishing, local attractions and touring. Within the Dales National Park area. Short steep hill to park.

HAWES

Shaw Ghyll Farm, Simonstone, Hawes, North Yorkshire, DL8 3LY.
Std: 01969 **Tel:** 667359 **Fax:** 667894
Email: rogerstott@aol.com
Website: www.yorkshirenet.co.uk/accgde/shcotts.htm
Nearest Town/Resort Hawes
Directions 2 miles north of Hawes following the Muker road.
Acreage 2½ **Open** March **to** October
Access Good **Site** Level
Sites Available ▲ ♦ ➤ **Total** 30
Facilities ⚈ ⊞ ⅏ ⚈ ┏ ⊙⊸ ☎ ⚆⊞▣
Nearby Facilities ✎ ⚓ ⅍ ♫ ⚒
Quiet sheltered site, ideal for walks and families, pleasant aspect, river and lovely scenic walks.

HELMSLEY

Foxholme Touring Caravan Park, Harome, Helmsley, North Yorkshire, YO62 5JG.
Std: 01439 **Tel:** 770416 **Fax:** 771744
Nearest Town/Resort Helmsley

Directions A170 towards Scarborough ½ mile turn right to Harome, turn left at church, through village, follow caravan signs.
Acreage 6 **Open** Easter **to** October
Access Good **Site** Level
Sites Available ▲ ♦ ➤ **Total** 60
Facilities ⚈ ⊞ ⅏ ⚈ ┏ ⊙⊸ ☎ ⚆ ▢ ☎
⚏ ⊙ ⚈ ⊞
Nearby Facilities ┏ ∪ ♫
➤ Malton
Ideal touring area. Near National Park, Abbeys, Herriot country. Use of an indoor swimming pool in a hotel in Harome.

HELMSLEY

Golden Square Caravan Park,
Oswaldkirk, York, North Yorkshire, YO62 5YQ.
Std: 01439 **Tel:** 788269
Std: 01439 **Fax:** 788236
Email:
barbara@goldensquarecaravanpark.com
Website:
www.goldensquarecaravanpark.com
Nearest Town/Resort Helmsley
Directions 2 miles south of Helmsley. First right off the B1257 to Ampleforth.
Acreage 10 **Open** 1 March **to** 31 October
Access Good **Site** Level
Sites Available ▲ ♦ ➤ **Total** 110
Facilities ⚏ ⚈ ⊞ ⅏ ⚈ ┏ ⊙⊸ ☎ ⚆ ▢ ☎
⚏ ⊙ ⚈ ⅏ ⊛⊸⚈
Nearby Facilities ┏ ✎ ∪ ♫ ⚒
➤ Thirsk/Malton
Secluded site with magnificent views of North Yorkshire Moors. Regional Winner Loo of the Year Award. De-Lux all service pitches. Seasonal pitches and storage compound. Swimming nearby.

HELMSLEY

Wombleton Caravan Park, Moorfield Lane, Wombleton, Kirbymoorside, North Yorks, YO62 7RY.
Std: 01751 **Tel:** 431684
Website: www.europage.co.uk/wombleton-park
Nearest Town/Resort Kirbymooorside/Helmsley
Directions Leave Helmsley by A170 for 4 miles, turn right for Wombleton go through Wombleton ½ mile on left
Acreage 6 **Open** March **to** October
Access Good **Site** Level
Sites Available ▲ ♦ ➤ **Total** 78
Facilities ⚈ ⊞ ⅏ ⚈ ┏ ⊙⊸ ☎ ⚆ ▢ ☎
⚏ ⊙ ⚈ ⅏ ⊞
Nearby Facilities ┏ ✎ ∪
➤ Malton
Ideal touring, scenic view, near Yorkshire Dales National Parks and Herriot country. Seasonal pitches available.

HELMSLEY

Wren's of Ryedale, Gale Lane, Nawton, North Yorkshire, YO62 7SD.
Std: 01439 **Tel:** 771260
Std: 01439 **Fax:** 771260
Email: dave@wrensofryedale.fsnet.co.uk
Website: www.wrensofryedale.fsnet.co.uk
Nearest Town/Resort Scarborough/York
Directions Leave Helmsley by A170. 2½

---

miles to Beadlam, pass White Horse Inn and church on left, in 50 yards turn right. Site 700 yards down lane.
Acreage 3½ **Open** April **to** October
Access Good **Site** Level
Sites Available ▲ ♦ ➤ **Total** 45
Facilities ⚈ ⊞ ⅏ ⚈ ┏ ⊙⊸ ☎ ⚆ ▢ ☎
⚏ ⊞ ⚈ ⅏ ⚈ ⊞ ▣
Nearby Facilities ┏ ✎ ∪ ♫
➤ Malton
Attractive, quiet, family run site. Situated on edge of Yorkshire Moors National Park. Very good centre for touring.

INGLETON

The Goat Gap Inn, Clapham, North Yorkshire, LA2 8JB.
Std: 015242 **Tel:** 41230
Std: 015242 **Fax:** 41651
Website: www.goatgap.demon.co.uk
Nearest Town/Resort Settle
Directions On the north side of the A65, 1 mile east of Ingleton.
Acreage 10 **Open** All Year
Access Good **Site** Level
Sites Available ▲ ♦ ➤ **Total** 40
Facilities ⚏ ⚈ ⊞ ⅏ ⚈ ┏ ⊙⊸ ☎ ⚆
⚒ ⚓ ⚈ ⊞⊸⚈ ⊞ ▣
Nearby Facilities ┏ ✎ ∪ ⚒
➤ Clapham
Ideal walking and touring. Half way between the Dales and lakes, within sight of three peaks.

INGLETON

The Trees Caravan Park, Westhouse, Ingleton, North Yorkshire, LA6 3NZ.
Std: 015242 **Tel:** 41511
Nearest Town/Resort Ingleton
Directions From Ingleton, travel 1¼ miles along the A65 towards Kirkby Lonsdale (about ¼ mile past the A687 junction - Country Harvest). Turn left at signpost for Lower Westhouse, site is on the left in 50yds.
Acreage 3 **Open** April **to** October
Access Good **Site** Level
Sites Available ♦ ➤ **Total** 29
Facilities ⚒ ⚈ ⊞ ⅏ ⚈ ┏ ⊙⊸ ☎
⚏ ⊙ ⚈ ⊞
Nearby Facilities ┏ ✎ ∪ ♫ ⚒
➤ Bentham
Set in beautiful country scenery. Ideal for walking and touring. Mountains, caves and waterfalls nearby.

KNARESBOROUGH

Allerton Park Caravan Park, Allerton Mauleverer, Nr. Knaresborough, North Yorks, HG5 0SE.
Std: 01423 **Tel:** 330569
Std: 01759 **Fax:** 371377
Email:
enquiries@yorkshireholidayparks.co.uk
Website:
www.yorkshireholidayparks.co.uk
Nearest Town/Resort Knaresborough
Directions A59 York to Harrogate road, ½ mile east of Aim.
Acreage 17 **Open** 1 February **to** 3 January
Access Good **Site** Level
Sites Available ▲ ♦ ➤ **Total** 45

Facilities ⚡ 📶 🚻 ♿ ⚓ ♨ ⊙ ⤵ 🚐 🔲 ☎ 🎱 🛁 🅿 ☕ 🛒
Nearby Facilities ↾ ∪ ⅄
✈ Harrogate
Woodland park with plenty of wildlife and walks. David Bellamy Silver Award for Conservation.

KNARESBOROUGH

Kingfisher Caravan & Camping Park, Low Moor Lane, Farnham, Knaresborough, North Yorks, HG5 9DQ.
Std: 01423 **Tel:** 869411
Nearest Town/Resort Knaresborough
Directions From Knaresborough take the A6055. In 1¼ miles turn left to Farnham Village, in Farnham turn left, park is approx. 1 mile on the left.
Acreage 10 **Open** March to October
Access Good **Site** Level
Sites Available ▲ ⬛ 🚐 **Total** 50
Facilities ♿ ⚡ 🚻 ⚓ ↾ ⊙ ⤵ 🔲 ☎
🎱 🛁 🅿 🛒
Nearby Facilities ↾ ✎ ⚓ ↺ ∪ ☈
✈ Knaresborough
Ideal touring base for the Dales, convenient for Harrogate and York. Adjacent to private fishing and a golf range.

LEYBURN

Constable Burton Hall Caravan Park, Leyburn, Wensleydale, North Yorkshire, DL8 5LJ.
Std: 01677 **Tel:** 450428
Nearest Town/Resort Leyburn
Directions From the A1 take the A684 for 8 miles.
Acreage 10 **Open** April to October
Access Good **Site** Lev/Slope
Sites Available ▲ ⬛ 🚐 **Total** 120
Facilities ♿ ⚡ 🚻 ⚓ ↾ ⊙ ⤵ 🔲 ☎
🛁 🅿 🛒
Nearby Facilities ↾ ✎ ∪
Ideal for walking and touring. Many castles, gardens and historic houses nearby.

MALTON

Castle Howard Caravan & Camping Site, Coneysthorpe, York, North Yorkshire, YO6 7DD.
Std: 01653 **Tel:** 648316
Std: 01653 **Fax:** 648529
Email: fishmanwj@yahoo.com
Website: www.castlehoward.co.uk
Nearest Town/Resort Malton
Directions 15 miles north east of York, off the A64 road to Scarborough. Follow signs to Castle Howard.
Acreage 17 **Open** March to October
Access Good **Site** Level
Sites Available ▲ ⬛ 🚐 **Total** 70
Facilities ⚡ 📶 🚻 ⚓ ↾ ⊙ ⤵ 🔲 🎱 🛁 🅿
Nearby Facilities ✎
✈ Malton
Site is on a private estate with views. Within walking distance of Castle Howard and Great Lake. Near York.

MASHAM

Black Swan Caravan & Camping Site, Rear of Black Swan Hotel, Fearby, Masham, Ripon, North Yorkshire, HG4 4NF.
Std: 01765 **Tel:** 689477
Std: 01765 **Fax:** 689477
Email: blackswanholidaypark@fsmail.net
Website: www.geocities.com/theblackswan_uk/
Nearest Town/Resort Masham
Directions Turn left off A6108 800yds past filling station. Site is 2 miles on the left hand side at the rear of the Black Swan in Fearby.

Acreage 2 **Open** March to October
Access Good **Site** Level
Sites Available ▲ ⬛ 🚐 **Total** 50
Facilities ⚡ 📶 🚻 ⚓ ↾ ⊙ ⤵ 🔲 ☎
🎱 🛁 ✗ 🍴 🛒 ⚓ 🏪 ❄ 🅿 ☕
Nearby Facilities ↾ ✎ ∪ ☈ ⅄
✈ Northallerton
Small site overlooking Burn Valley in beautiful countryside. Ideal for walking.

MUKER

Usha Gap Caravan & Camp Site, Usha Gap, Muker, Richmond, North Yorkshire, DL11 6DW.
Std: 01748 **Tel:** 886214
Email: ushagap@btinternet.com
Nearest Town/Resort Hawes
Acreage 1 **Open** All Year
Access Good **Site** Level
Sites Available ▲ ⬛ 🚐 **Total** 24
Facilities 🚻 🚻 ⚓ ↾ ⊙ ⤵ ☕ 🛒
Nearby Facilities ⅄
✈ Darlington
Alongside a small river. Shops and a pub ¼ mile. Ideal touring and good walking.

NORTHALLERTON

Hutton Bonville Caravan Park, Church Lane, Hutton Bonville, Northallerton, North Yorkshire, DL7 0NR.
Std: 01609 **Tel:** 881416
Nearest Town/Resort Northallerton
Directions 4 miles north of Northallerton on the A167.
Open Easter to October
Access Good **Site** Sloping
Sites Available 🚐 **Total** 5
Facilities ⚡ 🚻 ⚓ ↾ ⊙ 🔲 ☕
🛁 🎱 🛒 🏪 🅿
Nearby Facilities ↾ ✎ ∪
✈ Northallerton

OSMOTHERLEY

Cote Ghyll Caravan Park, Osmotherley, Northallerton, North Yorks, DL6 3AH.
Std: 01609 **Tel:** 883425
Website: www.ukparks.co.uk/coteghyll
Nearest Town/Resort Northallerton
Directions Leave A19 at junction of A684 Northallerton turnoff. Follow Osmotherley signs to village, then caravan signs uphill from village cross. Entrance ½ mile on right.
Open April to October
Access Good **Site** Sloping
Sites Available ▲ ⬛ 🚐 **Total** 77
Facilities ⚡ 🚻 ⚓ ↾ ⊙ ⤵ 🔲 ☕ ⚓ 🏪 🅿
Nearby Facilities
North Yorkshire Moors. Ideal touring. Cleveland Way, Coast to Coast Lyke Wake Walk and National Cycleway all within 1½ miles.
AA 3 Pennants.

PATELEY BRIDGE

Heathfield Caravan Park, Low Wath Road, Pateley Bridge, Harrogate, North Yorkshire, HG3 5PY.
Std: 01423 **Tel:** 711652
Std: 01423 **Fax:** 711652
Nearest Town/Resort Pateley Bridge
Directions From Pateley Bridge take the Low Wath Road, after 1 mile pass the Watermill Inn and turn left, follow signs for ¼ of a mile.
Acreage 8 **Open** 8 March to 31 Oct
Access Good **Site** Sloping
Sites Available ⬛ 🚐 **Total** 4
Facilities ⚡ 📶 🚻 ⚓ ↾ ⊙ ⤵ 🔲 ☕
🎱 🛁 ⚓ 🏪 🅿
Nearby Facilities ✎ ↺ ∪ ☈ ⅄
✈ Harrogate
Secluded wooded valley with a stream and excellent walks.

PATELEY BRIDGE

Westfield, Westfield Farm, Heathfield, Pateley Bridge, Harrogate, North Yorks, HG3 5BX.
Std: 01423 **Tel:** 711880
Nearest Town/Resort Pateley Bridge
Directions From Pateley Bridge 1 mile tu left to Heathfield after 100yds turn left continue on this road through Heathfie caravan site. We are the third site.
Acreage 3 **Open** April to October
Access Single Track. **Site** Lev/Slope
Sites Available ▲ ⬛ 🚐
Facilities ♿ ⚡ 🚻 ⚓ ↾ ⊙ ⤵ ☕ 🅿
Nearby Facilities ✎
✈ Harrogate
Small farm site along stream in quiet Yo shire Dales location.

PICKERING

Overbrook Caravan Park, Malton Gate Thornton-le-Dale, Nr Pickering, North Yorks, YO18 7SE.
Std: 01751 **Tel:** 474417
Nearest Town/Resort Pickering
Directions From A1 follow A64 to A169 miles turn right to Thornton Dale, follow ro for 3½ miles. The site is opposite the villa road sign Thornton Dale, turn right into th railway station.
Acreage 3 **Open** March to October
Access Good **Site** Level
Sites Available ▲ ⬛ 🚐 **Total** 50
Facilities ⚡ 📶 🚻 ⚓ ↾ ⊙ ⤵ 🔲
🎱 🛁 🅿
Nearby Facilities ↾ ✎ ∪ ☈
✈ Malton
In one of North Yorkshires prettiest village Lovely views, Beck runs through the si Ideal for touring and walking. SORRY t park is unsuitable for children.

PICKERING

Rosedale Caravan Park, Rosedale Abbey, Pickering, North Yorkshire, YO18 8SA.
Std: 01751 **Tel:** 417272
Std: 01751 **Fax:** 417272
Email: cadesrosedale@flowerofmay.cor
Website: www.flowerofmay.com
Nearest Town/Resort Pickering
Directions Turn off the A170 towar Rosedale.
Open Easter to End October
Access Good **Site** Level
Sites Available ▲ ⬛ 🚐
Facilities ♿ ⚡ 📶 🚻 ⚓ ↾ ⊙ ⤵ 🛁 🔲
🎱 🛁 🏪 🏪 ❄ 🅿
Nearby Facilities ↾ ✎ ∪
✈ Malton
Idyllic retreat. Ideal for walking and hiki through the beautiful North Yorkshire Moo

PICKERING

Spiers House Caravan & Camping Sit - Forestry Commission, Cropton, Pickering, North Yorks, YO18 8ES.
Std: 01751 **Tel:** 417591
Email: fe.holidays@forestry.gsi.gov.uk
Website: www.forestholidays.co.uk
Nearest Town/Resort Pickering
Directions Take A170 westwards fro Pickering and at Wrelton turn north Cropton, continue from there on t Rosedale Road for 1 mile where site signposted at the edge of Cropton Fores
Acreage 10 **Open** End March to End Se
Access Good **Site** Lev/Slop
Sites Available ▲ ⬛ 🚐 **Total** 150
Facilities ♿ ⚡ 📶 🚻 ⚓ ↾ ⊙ ⤵ 🔲
🎱 🛁 ⚓ 🏪 🏪 🅿 ☕

Nearby Facilities ⌐ U
⇥ Malton
Site located in an extensive open grassland area and there are several way-marked walks in the adjoining forest. An ideal base to explore the surrounding moors and coast.

PICKERING

Sun Inn Caravan Park, Sun Inn, Normanby, Sinnington, North Yorkshire, YO62 6RH.
Std: 01751 **Tel:** 431051
Nearest Town/Resort Pickering
Directions Off the A170.
Acreage ½ **Open** March **to** October
Sites Available ▲ **Total** 6
Facilities ⬓ ♠ ⌐ ⊙ ➡ ✖
Nearby Facilities ⌐ ✔ U
⇥ Malton
Riverside site. Close to the North Yorkshire Moors.

PICKERING

The Black Bull Caravan Park, Malton Road, Pickering, North Yorkshire, YO18 7EA.
Std: 01751 **Tel:** 472528
Nearest Town/Resort Pickering
Directions 1 mile south of Pickering on the Malton road, behind The Black Bull Public House.
Acreage 4 **Open** Easter **to** October
Sites Available ▲ ⊕ ⊟ **Total** 36
Facilities ƒ ⬓ ♠ ⌐ ⊙ ➡ ⬚ ➡
⬚ ⊟ ♠ ⬚ ⊙ ➡ ⬚ ➡
Nearby Facilities ⌐ ✔ U ₽
⇥ Malton
Ideal base for touring the North Yorkshire Moors.

PICKERING

Upper Carr Chalet & Touring Park,
Upper Carr Lane, Malton Road, Pickering, North Yorkshire, YO18 7JP.
Std: 01751 **Tel:** 473115
Std: 01751 **Fax:** 473115
Email: harker@uppercarr.demon.co.uk
Website: www.uppercarr.demon.co.uk
Nearest Town/Resort Pickering
Directions 1½ miles south of Pickering on the A169 Malton road, opposite the Black Bull Pub.
Acreage 6¼ **Open** March **to** October
Access Good **Site** Level
Sites Available ▲ ⊕ ⊟ **Total** 80
Facilities ⬓ ƒ ⬚ ⬓ ♠ ⌐ ⊙ ➡ ⬚ ➡
⬚ ⊟ ♠ ⬚ ❋ ➡ ⬚ ➡
Nearby Facilities ⌐ ✔ U ₽
⇥ Malton
Ideal for Whitby, Scarborough, historic York and North Yorkshire Moors. Golf and tennis opposite. Steam Railway in Pickering. 3 miles from Flamingoland.

PICKERING

Vale of Pickering Caravan Park, Carr House Farm, Allerston, Pickering, North Yorkshire, YO18 7PQ.
Std: 01723 **Tel:** 859280 **Fax:** 850060
Email: tony@valeofpickering.co.uk
Website: www.valeofpickering.co.uk
Nearest Town/Resort Scarborough
Directions From Pickering take the A170 to Allerston, turn right opposite Cayley Arms Hotel, due south 1¼ miles.
Acreage 8 **Open** Mid March **to** End October
Access Good **Site** Level
Sites Available ▲ ⊕ ⊟ **Total** 120
Facilities ⬓ ƒ ⬚ ⬓ ♠ ⌐ ⊙ ➡ ⬚ ➡
⬚ ⊟ ♠ ⬚ ❋ ➡ ⬚ ➡

Nearby Facilities ⌐ ✔ U
⇥ Malton
Superb play area and games area. Extensive improvements to shower blocks. Mobile Fish & Chip van. ETB 5 Star Graded.

PICKERING

Wayside Caravan & Camping Park,
Wrelton, Pickering, North Yorkshire, YO18 8PG.
Std: 01751 **Tel:** 472608
Std: 01751 **Fax:** 472608
Email: waysideparks@talk21.com
Website: www.waysideparks.co.uk
Nearest Town/Resort Pickering
Directions 2½ miles west of Pickering off the A170 at Wrelton, turn right off the by-pass.
Acreage 5 **Open** Easter **to** Early Oct
Access Good
Sites Available ▲ ⊕ ⊟ **Total** 72
Facilities ⬓ ƒ ⬚ ⬓ ♠ ⌐ ⊙ ➡ ⬚ ➡
⬚ ⊟ ♠ ⬚ ➡
Nearby Facilities ⌐ ✔ U
⇥ Malton
Ideal for touring the North Yorkshire Moors. Walks nearby and historic steam railway.

RICHMOND

Brompton-on-Swale Caravan Park,
Brompton-on-Swale, Richmond, North Yorkshire, DL10 7EZ.
Std: 01748 **Tel:** 824629
Std: 01748 **Fax:** 826383
Email:
brompton.caravanpark@btinternet.com
Nearest Town/Resort Richmond
Directions Exit A1 at Catterick A6136. Follow B6271 to Richmond and drive through Brompton-on-Swale. Park on left 1 mile out of Brompton. 1¼ miles south east of Richmond.
Acreage 10 **Open** March **to** End October
Access Good **Site** Level
Sites Available ▲ ⊕ ⊟ **Total** 177
Facilities ⬓ ƒ ⬚ ⬓ ♠ ⌐ ⊙ ➡ ⬚ ➡
⬚ ⊟ ♠ ⬚ ➡ ⬚ ➡
Nearby Facilities ⌐ ⊥ ✹ U ₽
⇥ Darlington/Northallerton
Situated in a peaceful natural setting on the banks of the River Swale which provides fishing and walks. Motor home waste water disposal points. Free heated hot showers.

RICHMOND

Fox Hall Caravan Park, Ravensworth, Richmond, North Yorkshire, DL11 7JZ.
Std: 01325 **Tel:** 718344
Nearest Town/Resort Richmond
Directions From Scotch Corner take the A66 and travel for 5 miles, take the first turning to Ravensworth and park is 400yds on the right.
Acreage 4½ **Open** April **to** October
Access Good **Site** Level
Sites Available ▲ ⊕ ⊟ **Total** 10
Facilities ✗ ƒ ⬚ ⬓ ♠ ⌐ ⊙ ➡ ⬚
Nearby Facilities ⌐ ✔ U ₽
⇥ Darlington
Quiet, wooded site with individual pitches.

RICHMOND

Orchard Caravan Park, Reeth, Richmond, North Yorkshire, DL11 6TT.
Std: 01748 **Tel:** 884475
Nearest Town/Resort Richmond
Directions Approx. 11½ miles from Richmond.
Acreage 3½ **Open** 1 April **to** 31 October
Access Good **Site** Level
Sites Available ▲ ⊕ ⊟ **Total** 56
Facilities ƒ ⬚ ⌐ ⊙ ➡ ⬚ ⊟ ⊙ ➡ ➡

Nearby Facilities ✔
⇥ Darlington
Near a river and hills for walking. Pets are welcome if kept on leads.

RICHMOND

Swaleview Caravan Park, Reeth Road, Richmond, North Yorkshire, DL10 4SF.
Std: 01748 **Tel:** 823106
Nearest Town/Resort Richmond
Directions On A6108, 3 miles west town.
Acreage 4 **Open** March **to** October
Access Good **Site** Level
Sites Available ▲ ⊕ ⊟ **Total** 50
Facilities ƒ ⬚ ⬓ ♠ ⌐ ⊙ ➡ ⬚ ➡
⬚ ⊟ ♠ ⬚ ➡ ➡
Nearby Facilities ⌐ ✔ U ✹
⇥ Darlington
Beautiful area in National Park by side of River Swale. Central for coasts and lakes.

RICHMOND

Tavern House Caravan Park, Newsham, Nr. Richmond, North Yorkshire, DL11 7RA.
Std: 01833 **Tel:** 621223
Nearest Town/Resort Barnard Castle/Richmond
Directions 7 miles west from Scotch Corner on the A66 turn left, 1 mile into the middle of the village, on the right.
Acreage 1½ **Open** March **to** October
Access Good **Site** Lev/Slope
Sites Available ▲ ⊕ ⊟ **Total** 8
Facilities ƒ ⬚ ⬓ ♠ ⌐ ⊙ ➡ ⬚ ➡
⬚ ⊟ ♠ ⬚ ➡ A
Nearby Facilities ⌐ ✔ ✹ U
⇥ Darlington
ADULTS ONLY. Walking, fishing and historic towns.

RIPON

Church Farm Caravan Park, Church Farm, Bishop Monkton, Harrogate, North Yorkshire, HG3 3QQ.
Std: 01765 **Tel:** 677668
Std: 01765 **Fax:** 677668
Nearest Town/Resort Ripon
Directions Left off the Ripon bypass leads straight to Bishop Monkton, camp site is opposite the church.
Acreage 2/3 **Open** March **to** October
Access Good **Site** Level
Sites Available ▲ ⊕ ⊡ **Total** 40
Facilities ⬓ ƒ ⬚ ⬓ ♠ ⌐ ⊙ ➡ ⬚ ➡
⬚ ➡ ⬚ ➡
Nearby Facilities ⌐ ✔ U ₽
⇥ Harrogate
Set in a picturesque village with a stream, two pubs and a shop. Ideal for touring the Yorkshire Dales.

RIPON

Gold Coin Farm, Galphay, Ripon, North Yorkshire, HG4 3NJ.
Std: 01765 **Tel:** 658508
Std: 01765 **Fax:** 658508
Email:
christine@cweatherhead.freeserve.co.uk
Nearest Town/Resort Ripon
Directions 5 miles west of Ripon on the B6265 Pateley Bridge road, after 1 mile turn right to Galphay and the site.
Acreage ½ **Open** April **to** September
Access Good **Site** Level
Sites Available ▲ ⊕ ⊟ **Total** 5
Facilities ⌐
Nearby Facilities
⇥ Harrogate
Near to Fountains Abbey and Lightwater Valley.

RIPON

River Laver Holiday Park, Studley Road, Ripon, North Yorkshire, HG4 2QR.
Std: 01765 **Tel:** 690508
Std: 01765 **Fax:** 698708
Nearest Town/Resort Ripon
Directions ½ mile from Ripon on the B6265 towards Fountains Abbey.
Acreage 5 **Open** 1 March **to** 3 January
Access Good **Site** Level
Sites Available 🚐 🚎 **Total** 50
Facilities ♿ ∮ 🏠 🔽 ♨ ┌ ☺ ⊸ 🍴 💷 🖳 🛢
🏪 ⊙ 🅿 ⛟ 🖃 🖾 🔒
Nearby Facilities ┌ ✓ ♪
➤ Harrogate
Ideal base for the Yorkshire Moors and Dales. Easy access to Fountains Abbey and road network.

RIPON

Riverside Meadows Country Caravan Park, Ure Bank Top (Dept. No. I), Ripon, North Yorkshire, HG4 1JD.
Std: 01765 **Tel:** 602964
Std: 01765 **Fax:** 604045
Email: cadesriverside@flowerofmay.com
Website: www.flowerofmay.com
Nearest Town/Resort Ripon
Directions Leave the A1 onto the A61 north of Ripon town centre, ½ mile.
Acreage 28 **Open** March **to** October
Access Good **Site** Lev/Slope
Sites Available 🚐 🚎 **Total** 400
Facilities ∮ 🏠 🔽 🔽 ♨ ┌ ☺ ⊸ 🍴 💷 🖳 🛢
🏪 ⊙ 🅿 ⛟ 🖃 🏪 ♨ ⛟ 🖃
Nearby Facilities ┌ ✓ ⚓ U
➤ Harrogate
Countryside park alongside a river. Ideal for touring the Yorkshire Dales. NEW bar complex for all the family. Pets are welcome by arrangement.

RIPON

Sleningford Watermill, North Stainley, Ripon, North Yorks, HG4 3HQ.
Std: 01765 **Tel:** 635201
Website: www.ukparks.co.uk/sleningford
Nearest Town/Resort Ripon
Directions 5½ miles N.W. of Ripon (turning at clock tower) onto A6108, between North Stainley and West Tanfield. Or by following Lightwater Valley signs which is 1½ miles along the same road.
Acreage 14 **Open** Easter **to** October
Access Good **Site** Level
Sites Available ▲ 🚐 🚎 **Total** 80
Facilities ♿ ∮ 🔽 ♨ ┌ ☺ ⊸ 🍴 💷 🖳
🏪 🖾 ⊙ 🏪 ♨ ⛟ 🖃
Nearby Facilities ┌ ✓ ⚓ U ♪
Picturesque riverside, fly fishing and canoeing access, quiet rural site, birds, wildflowers etc. Ideal for touring Herriot country and Dales.

RIPON

Winksley Banks Holiday Park, Winksley Banks, Ripon, North Yorkshire, HG4 3NS.
Std: 01765 **Tel:** 658439
Std: 01765 **Fax:** 658439
Email: enquiries@dale-vale-holidays.co.uk
Website: www.dale-vale-holidays.co.uk
Nearest Town/Resort Ripon
Directions Take the B6265 west out of Ripon, after 1 mile turn right to Galphay for 4 miles. Winksley Banks is 1½ miles west of Galphay on the Winksley to Kirkby Malzeard road.
Acreage 2 **Open** 1 March **to** 7 Jan
Access Good **Site** Level
Sites Available ▲ 🚐 🚎 **Total** 6
Facilities ∮ 🔽 ♨ ┌ ☺ ⊸ 🍴 💷 🖳 🛢
🖾 ⊙ 🏪 ⛟ 🖃
Nearby Facilities ┌ ✓ ⚓ ✈ U ♪ ✈

➤ Harrogate
Coarse and trout fishing and a putting green on site. Ideal for touring the Dales.

RIPON

Woodhouse Farm Caravan & Camping Park, Winksley, Nr. Ripon, North Yorkshire, HG4 3PG.
Std: 01765 **Tel:** 658309
Std: 01765 **Fax:** 658882
Email: woodhouse.farm@talk21.com
Website: www.woodhouse-farm.co.uk
Nearest Town/Resort Ripon
Directions Take B6265 from Ripon 3 miles. Right at the Winksley/Grantley sign post. Follow site signs for 2¼ miles.
Acreage 20 **Open** April **to** October
Access Good **Site** Level
Sites Available ▲ 🚐 🚎 **Total** 160
Facilities ∮ 🏠 🔽 ♨ ┌ ☺ ⊸ 🍴 💷
🏪 ⊙ 🏪 🖾 🔽 ♨ ⛟ 🖃 🖃
Nearby Facilities ┌ ✓ U ♪ ✈
➤ Harrogate
An attractive, quiet, country site with excellent facilities. Ideal for touring Yorkshire Dales. On site coarse fishing lake. SAE for Brochure.

SCARBOROUGH

Arosa Caravan & Camping Park, Ratten Row, Seamer, Scarborough, North Yorkshire, YO12 4QB.
Std: 01723 **Tel:** 862166
Std: 01723 **Fax:** 862166
Email:
neilcherry@arosacaravanpark.co.uk
Website: www.mywebpage.inet/arosa
Nearest Town/Resort Scarborough
Directions 4 miles from Scarborough on the A64.
Acreage 4½ **Open** 1 March **to** 4 January

Access Good **Site** Level
Sites Available Total 92
Facilities ♿ ♨ ⊞ 🔥 ⚓ 📞 ⊙ 🍴 🛒 ▢ ☎
♒ ☎ 🛈 🚿 Ⓣ 🎣 🏍 ➷ 🎁 ▣ ⊞
Nearby Facilities ┏ ✔ ⚓ ∪ ⋧ ♫
★ Seamer
Ideal touring.

SCARBOROUGH
Blue Dolphin Holiday Centre, Gristhorpe Bay, Filey, North Yorkshire, YO14 9PU.
Std: 01723 **Tel:** 515155
Std: 01723 **Fax:** 512059
Website: www.havenholidays.com
Nearest Town/Resort Filey
Directions 2½ miles north of Filey off the A165 coast road.
Acreage 5 **Open** 23 March **to** 25 Oct
Access Good **Site** Lev/Slope
Sites Available ▲ ♣ ♨ **Total** 311
Facilities ♿ ♨ ⊞ ⊞ 🔥 ⚓ 📞 ⊙ 🍴
▢
♒ ☎ 🛒 🚿 Ⓧ Ⓣ 🏍 ➷ 🎣 ☀ ♫ ⊞ ▣ ▣
Nearby Facilities ┏ ✔ ⚓ ∪ ⋧ ♫
★ Filey
We are an "All Action" centre. Our tariff does include entertainment passes.

SCARBOROUGH
Brown's Caravan Park, Mill Lane, Cayton Bay, Scarborough, North Yorkshire, YO11 3NN.
Std: 01723 **Tel:** 582303
Website: www.brownscaravan.co.uk
Nearest Town/Resort Scarborough
Directions 3 miles south of Scarborough just off A165.
Acreage ¼ **Open** April **to** September
Access Good **Site** Level
Sites Available ♣ ♨ **Total** 35
Facilities ♨ ⊞ ⚓ 📞 ⊙ ⊙ ▢ ▢ 🛒 Ⓧ 🚿 🎣 🏍 ☀ ⊞

Nearby Facilities ┏ ✔ ⚓ ∪ ⋧ ♫
★ Scarborough
Close to beach. Ideal touring centre for North Yorkshire Moors. ETB 5 Star Grading.

SCARBOROUGH
Cayton Village Caravan Park, D1 Mill Lane, Cayton Bay, Scarborough, North Yorks, YO11 3NN.
Std: 01723 **Tel:** 583171
Email: info@caytontouring.co.uk
Website: www.caytontouring.co.uk
Nearest Town/Resort Scarborough
Directions On the A165, 3 miles south of Scarborough turn inland at Cayton Bay. The park is on the right hand side in ½ mile. From the A64 take the B1261 signposted Filey. At Cayton take the second left at the Blacksmiths Arms onto Mill Lane, the park is on the left hand side.
Acreage 11 **Open** Easter **to** October
Access Good **Site** Level
Sites Available ♣ ♨ **Total** 200
Facilities ♿ ♨ ⊞ ⊞ 🔥 ⚓ 📞 ⊙ 🍴 🛒 ▢ ☎
♒ ☎ 🛈 🚿 ⊞ ☀ ♫ ⊞ ▣
Nearby Facilities ┏ ✔ ⚓ ∪ ⋧ ♫ ⚞
★ Seamer
Sheltered park adjoining Cayton Church, village inns, fish shop and bus service. ½ mile to the beach. 4 acre dog walk. Family bathroom, luxurious shower blocks, central heating and dishwashing. Super Saver and O.A.P. Weeks. Seasonal pitches available. Winter Telephone Number - 01904 624630.

SCARBOROUGH
Crows Nest Caravan Park, Gristhorpe, Filey, North Yorkshire, YO14 9PS.
Std: 01723 **Tel:** 582206
Std: 01723 **Fax:** 582206
Nearest Town/Resort Filey/Scarborough

Directions Off A165 north of Filey, south of Scarborough.
Acreage 12 **Open** March **to** October
Access Good **Site** Lev/Slope
Sites Available ▲ ♣ ♨
Facilities ♿ ♨ ⊞ ⊞ 🔥 ⚓ 📞 ⊙ 🍴 🛒 ▢ ☎
♒ 🛈 ☎ 🚿 Ⓣ 🏍 🎣 ➷ ⊞
Nearby Facilities ┏ ✔ ⚓ ∪ ⋧ ♫
★ Scarborough
AA 4 Pennants and BTA 5 Star Graded.

SCARBOROUGH
Flower of May Holiday Park, Lebberston Cliff, Scarborough, North Yorks, YO11 3NU.
Std: 01723 **Tel:** 584311
Std: 01723 **Fax:** 581361
Email: cadesflower@flowerofmay.com
Website: www.flowerofmay.com
Nearest Town/Resort Scarborough
Directions 3 miles south of Scarborough off A165 signposted at roundabout.
Acreage 13 **Open** Easter **to** October
Access Good **Site** Level
Sites Available ▲ ♣ ♨ **Total** 300
Facilities ♿ ♨ ⊞ ⊞ 🔥 ⚓ 📞 ⊙ 🍴 🛒
▢ ☎ ♒ ☎ 🛈 🚿 Ⓣ 🏍 🎣 ☀ ➷ ⊞
Nearby Facilities ┏ ✔ ⚓ ∪ ⋧ ♫
★ Scarborough
Winner AA Best Holiday Park Northern England 95. Family run park with superb facilities. Exciting playground, luxury leisure centre with indoor pool and golf. Family bars. Supermarket. Pets are welcome by arrangement.

SCARBOROUGH
Jacobs Mount Caravan & Camping Site, Stepney Road, Scarborough, North Yorks, YO12 5NL.
Std: 01723 **Tel:** 361178 **Fax:** 361178

Website: www.jacobsmount.co.uk
Nearest Town/Resort Scarborough
Directions 2 miles west of Scarborough on the A170 Thirsk Road.
Acreage 18 **Open** March to October
Access Good
Sites Available ▲ ⊕ ⊞ **Total** 140
Facilities & ⨍ 🖪 🖩 🗷 ⎐ ◖ ⊿ ⬚ ◉ 🗄
🗜 🖭 ⊟ ⦶ ✕ 🍴 🎾 ⩜ ↦ 🚲 🖳
Nearby Facilities ┌ ✓ ⚓ ≒ ∪ ⟿ ℛ
⚡ Scarborough
Set in Mature woodland in beautiful countryside, yet only 2 miles from Scarborough beaches and attractions. Bar with family room. Touring caravan rallies catered for off-peak. Rose Award RAC Appointed, AA 4 Pennants and Caravan Club Listed. Please see our advertisement.

SCARBOROUGH

Jasmine Park, Cross Lane, Snainton, Scarborough, North Yorkshire, YO13 9BE.
Std: 01723 **Tel:** 859240
Std: 01723 **Fax:** 859240
Email: info@jasminepark.co.uk
Website: www.jasminepark.co.uk
Nearest Town/Resort Scarborough/ Pickering
Directions Turn off the A170 in Snainton Village opposite junior school, ¾ mile signposted.
Acreage 5 **Open** March to December
Access Good **Site** Level
Sites Available ▲ ⊕ ⊞ **Total** 70
Facilities & ⨍ 🖩 🗷 ⎐ ◖ ⊿ ⬚ ◉ 🗄
🗜 🖭 ⊟ ⦶ ↦ 🖳 🖪 🖳
Nearby Facilities ┌ ✓ ⚓ ∪
⚡ Scarborough
Picturesque park in a quiet location. Immaculate facilities. Awards including David Bellamy Gold Award for Conservation and 'In Bloom'. Countryside Discovery member. Personal supervision. SAE for brochure.

SCARBOROUGH

Lebberston Touring Park, Home Farm, Filey Road, Lebberston, Scarborough, North Yorkshire, YO11 3PE.
Std: 01723 **Tel:** 585723
Nearest Town/Resort Scarborough/Filey
Directions From A64 or A165 take B1261 to Lebberston and follow signs.
Acreage 7½ **Open** March to October
Access Good **Site** Lev/Slope
Sites Available ⊕ ⊞ **Total** 125
Facilities & ⨍ 🖩 🗷 ⎐ ◖ ⊿ ⬚ ◉ 🗜 🖭 ◖ ⊟ 🖳
Nearby Facilities ┌ ✓ ⚓ ≒ ∪ ℛ
⚡ Scarborough
Quiet, country park. Well spaced pitches with extensive views over Vale of Pickering and the Yorkshire Wolds. All pets on a lead. Dog area. Trailer tents accepted. AA 3 Pennants.

SCARBOROUGH

Merry Lees Caravan Park, Merry Lees, Staxton, Scarborough, North Yorkshire, YO12 4NN.
Std: 01944 **Tel:** 710080
Std: 01944 **Fax:** 710470
Email: sales@merrylees.co.uk
Website: www.merrylees.co.uk
Nearest Town/Resort Scarborough/Filey
Directions From Scarborough travel south on the A64 towards York, park is 6 miles on the left.
Acreage 7 **Open** March to October
Access Good **Site** Level
Sites Available ▲ ⊕ ⊞ **Total** 60
Facilities ⨍ 🖩 ⎐ ◖ ⊿ ⬚ ◉ 🗜 🖪 🖳
Nearby Facilities ┌ ✓ ⚓ ≒ ∪ ℛ
⚡ Seamer
On the edge of the North Yorkshire Moors and Wolds. 6 miles from the coast.

SCARBOROUGH

Scalby Close Park, Burniston Road, Scarborough, North Yorkshire, YO13 0DA.
Std: 01723 **Tel:** 365908
Nearest Town/Resort Scarborough
Directions 2 miles north of Scarborough's North Bay, signed 400 yards.
Acreage 3 **Open** March to October
Access Good **Site** Level
Sites Available ▲ ⊕ ⊞ **Total** 42
Facilities ⨍ 🖩 🗷 ⎐ ◖ ⊿ ⬚ ◉ 🗜 🖭 🗄 ↦ 🖪 🖳
Nearby Facilities ┌ ✓ ∪
⚡ Scarborough
Sheltered, tree lined, level pitches. Ideal for touring North Yorkshire Moors and the coast. Near to Scarborough.

SCARBOROUGH

Scalby Manor Caravan & Camping Park, Field Lane, Station Road, Scalby, Scarborough, North Yorkshire, YO13 0DA.
Std: 01723 **Tel:** 366212
Nearest Town/Resort Scarborough
Directions Located 2 miles north of Scarborough Town Centre on the coast road to Whitby, A165. Follow signposts to Burniston/Whitby.
Acreage 20 **Open** Easter to October
Access Good
Sites Available ▲ ⊕ ⊞ **Total** 375
Facilities & ⨍ 🖩 🗷 ⎐ ◖ ⊿ ⬚ ◉ 🗜 🖭 🗄 ↦ 🖪 🖳
Nearby Facilities ┌ ✓ ⚓ ≒ ∪ ℛ
⚡ Scarborough
The site offers an ideal touring base for the North Yorkshire National Park and Moors and yet only 2 miles from the resort of Scarborough.

SCARBOROUGH

Spring Willows Touring Park, Main Road, Staxton, Scarborough, North Yorkshire, YO12 4SB.
Std: 01723 **Tel:** 891505
Std: 01723 **Fax:** 891505
Email: fun4all@springwillows.fsnet.co.uk
Website: www.springwillows.co.uk
Nearest Town/Resort Scarborough
Directions Take the A64 towards Scarborough, turn right onto the A1039 to Filey. Entrance is 50 metres on the right.
Acreage 20 **Open** March to Mid Nov
Access Good **Site** Level
Sites Available ▲ ⊕ ⊞ **Total** 184
Facilities & ⨍ ⨍ 🖩 🗷 ⎐ ◖ ⊿ ⬚ ◉ 🗄
🗜 🖭 ⊟ ⦶ ✕ 🍴 🎾 ⩜ ⁂ ↦ 🖪 🖳
Nearby Facilities ┌ ✓ ⚓ ≒ ∪ ℛ
⚡ Seamer
Ideal for touring Yorkshire Moors Scarborough, Whitby and Filey.

SELBY

The Bay Horse Inn, York Road, Barlby, Near Selby, North Yorkshire, YO8 5JH.
Std: 01757 **Tel:** 703878
Std: 01757 **Fax:** 708707
Email: bay-horse@fsbdial.uk
Nearest Town/Resort York
Directions 2 miles north of Selby on the A19 towards York.
Acreage 2 **Open** All Year
Access Good **Site** Level
Sites Available ▲ ⊕ ⊞ **Total** 5
Facilities ⨍ 🖩 🗷 ⎐ ⬚ ◉ 🗜 ⊟ 🖪 🖳
Nearby Facilities ┌ ✓ ⚓ ≒ ∪
⚡ Selby
Ideal for a one night stay.

SETTLE

Knight Stainforth Hall, Stainforth, Settle, North Yorkshire, BD24 0DP.
Std: 01729 **Tel:** 822200
Std: 01729 **Fax:** 823387
Email: info@knightstainforth.co.uk
Website: www.knightstainforth.co.uk
Nearest Town/Resort Settle
Directions A65 Settle/Kendal. Turn opposite Settle High School. 2½ miles along Stackhouse Lane.
Acreage 6 **Open** March to October
Access Good **Site** Sloping
Sites Available ▲ ⊕ ⊞ **Total** 100
Facilities ⨍ 🖩 🗷 ⎐ ◖ ⊿ ⬚ ◉ 🗄
🗜 🖭 ⊟ ⦶ ⁂ ↦ 🖪 🖳
Nearby Facilities ┌ ✓
⚡ Settle
Riverside site, near to potholes. Ideal walking and touring.

The Gateway to the Yorkshire Coast...

Our family run park has been beautifully landscaped around a springwater stream, winding through the beer garden and boardwalk.

Family friendly facilities reflect what you expect of a perfect well deserved holiday. **FREE MODERN HEATED POOL** with luxurious heated toilet and shower rooms including **Sauna, solarium, we have got it all here for you**.

RAC

AA DELUXE

Always wanted to see the world, well...

Step into our New Mexican themed bar, conservatory and entertainment complex and you will never want to go home again.

For even more fun: **Theme Weekends** during off-peak periods are our speciality.

Let your children join **SHARKY'S CLUB** (high season) for a funfilled carefree time.
Sounds good ... it is.

SPRING WILLOWS

TOURING CARAVAN & CAMPING PARK

For more information, please send a S.A.E. to
**SPRING WILLOWS TOURING PARK,
MAIN ROAD, STAXTON, Nr SCARBOROUGH, YO12 4SB**
or ring **01723 891505   Website www.springwillows.co.uk**

English Tourism Council

★ ★ ★ ★ ★
HOLIDAY PARK
EXCELLENT

KNIGHT STAINFORTH CARAVAN & CAMPING PARK
Little Stainforth, Settle, North Yorkshire BD24 0DP   Tel: 01729 822200 Fax: 01729 823387
E-mail: info@knightstainforth.co.uk   Website: www.knightstainforth.co.uk
Situated in the Yorkshire Dales National Park on the banks of the River Ribble. Family run park, catering mainly for families. Facilities include flush toilets, showers, pot washing facilities, launderette, TV & games room and a children's play area. Electric hook-ups are available and some hard standings. Trout and Salmon fishing on site. Booking is advisable for peak periods. No under 18's unless accompanied by adults and no groups of young persons allowed. Last arrivals 9 pm (except by prior arrangement).

SETTLE

Langcliffe Caravan Park, Settle, North Yorkshire, BD24 9LX.
Std: 01729 **Tel:** 822387
Std: 01729 **Fax:** 825072
Email: info@langcliffe.com
Website: www.langcliffe.com
Nearest Town/Resort Settle
Directions Situated just off the B6479 1 mile from the centre of Settle. From the main square take the main road towards Giggleswick, turn right after the railway viaduct.
Acreage 3 **Open** March **to** October
Access Good **Site** Level
Sites Available ▲ ⬥ ⬛ **Total** 69
Facilities ⚐ ⚐ ⬛ ⬛ ⬛ ⬛ ⬛ ⬛ ⬛ ⬛ ⬛
Nearby Facilities ⬥ ✓ ∪ ⚑
⚭ Settle
Situated in a valley close to a river. Many paths and bridleways emerge close to the site making it ideal for exploring the surrounding Yorkshire Dales.

SKIPTON

Eshton Road Caravan Site, Eshton Road, Gargrave, Nr. Skipton, North Yorkshire, BD23 3PN.
Std: 01756 **Tel:** 749229
Std: 01756 **Fax:** 748060
Nearest Town/Resort Skipton
Directions From Skipton take the A65, 4 miles.
Acreage 3 **Open** All Year
Access Good **Site** Level
Sites Available ▲ ⬥ ⬛ **Total** 20
Facilities ⚐ ⬛ ⬛ ⬛ ⬛ ⬛ ⬛
Nearby Facilities ⬥ ✓ ⚑ ⚑
⚭ Gargrave
Alongside the Leeds Liverpool Canal. Ideal for touring the Yorkshire Dales.

SKIPTON

Lower Heights Farm, Silsden, Keighley, North Yorkshire, BD20 9HW.
Std: 01535 **Tel:** 653035
Nearest Town/Resort Skipton
Directions 1 mile from Silsden off A6034.
Acreage 2 **Open** Easter **to** November
Access Good **Site** Level
Sites Available ▲ ⬥ ⬛ **Total** 5
Facilities ⬛ ⬛ ⚑ ⬛
Nearby Facilities ⬥ ⚑
⚭ Steeton
Scenic views. Yorkshire Dales and Bronte Country.

SLINGSBY

Robin Hood Caravan & Camping Park, Green Dyke Lane, Slingsby, North Yorkshire, YO62 4AP.
Std: 01653 **Tel:** 628391
Email: robinhood.caravan@tesco.net
Nearest Town/Resort Malton
Directions From Malton take B1257 westwards 6 miles to Slingsby. Turn right into caravan park.
Acreage 4 **Open** March **to** October
Access Good **Site** Level
Sites Available ▲ ⬥ ⬛ **Total** 48

Facilities ⬥ ⚐ ⬛ ⬛ ⬛ ⬛ ⬛ ⬛ ⬛ ⬛ ⬛
⬛ ⬛ ⬛ ⬛ ⬛ ⬛ ⬛
Nearby Facilities ⬥ ✓ ∪ ⚑
⚭ Malton
In the heart of picturesque Ryedale, this privately owned park offers peace and tranquillity. An ideal centre for York, the Moors, 'Heartbeat' country and the seaside resorts of Scarborough, Whitby and Filey.

TADCASTER

Whitecote Caravan Park, Ryther Road, Ulleskelf, Near Tadcaster, North Yorkshire, LS24 9DY.
Std: 01937 **Tel:** 835231
Nearest Town/Resort York
Open 1 March **to** 28 Feb
Access Good **Site** Level
Facilities ⚐ ⬛ ⬛ ⬛ ⬛ ⬛
⬛ ⬛ ⬛ ⬛ ⬛ ⬛
Nearby Facilities ⬥ ✓
⚭ Ulleskelf

THIRSK

Beechwood Caravan Park, South Kilvington, Thirsk, North Yorkshire, YO7 2LZ.
Std: 01845 **Tel:** 522348
Nearest Town/Resort Thirsk
Directions Take the A61 north from Thirsk, South Kilvington is 1½ miles. Caravan site is on the left on entering the village.
Acreage 1½ **Open** March **to** October
Access Good **Site** Level
Sites Available ⬥ ⬛ **Total** 30
Facilities ⚐ ⚐ ⬛ ⬛ ⬛ ⬛ ⚑ ⬛
Nearby Facilities ⬥ ✓ ∪
⚭ Northallerton
ADULTS ONLY site. Ideal base to explore the Moors and Dales of North Yorkshire. The historic city of York, the spa town of Harrogate and many National Trust sites are within easy reach.

THIRSK

Carlton Miniott Park, Sandhutton Lane, Carlton Miniott, Thirsk, North Yorkshire, YO7 4NH.
Std: 01845 **Tel:** 523106
Std: 01845 **Fax:** 525228
Nearest Town/Resort Thirsk
Directions Situated off the A61 Thirsk to Ripon road. After entering the village take turning to the north signposted Sandhutton (camp site notice under sign). Camp site is then 400 yards on the right hand side.
Open 31 March **to** 31 Oct
Access Good **Site** Level
Sites Available ▲ ⬥ ⬛
Facilities ⚐ ⬛ ⬛ ⬛ ⬛ ⬛
Nearby Facilities ⬥ ✓ ⚑ ∪ ⚑
⚭ Thirsk
Carlton Miniott Park is a private nature reserve covering 27 acres, with 7 acres of deep water lakes for boating and fishing. Excellent facilities. Ideal site for those who seek quiet and picturesque country situations.

THIRSK

Nursery Garden Caravan Park, Baldersby Park, Rainton, Near Thirsk, North Yorkshire, YO7 3PG.
Std: 01845 **Tel:** 577277 **Fax:** 577277
Email: nurserygardencp@talk21.com
Nearest Town/Resort Thirsk
Directions Take the A61 to Ripon, ½ mile from the A1 junction turn left through Baldersby St. James, Park is 2 miles on the left.
Acreage 5½ **Open** March **to** October
Access Good **Site** Level
Sites Available ⬥ ⬛ **Total** 20
Facilities ⚐ ⬛ ⬛ ⬛ ⬛ ⬛ ⬛ ⬛ ⬛
⬛ ⬛ ⬛ ⬛ ⬛ ⬛ ⬛
Nearby Facilities ⬥ ✓ ∪
⚭ Thirsk
Situated within a walled garden with many garden areas. Ideal centre for touring.

THIRSK

Sowerby Caravan Park, Sowerby, Thirsk, North Yorkshire, YO7 3AG.
Std: 01845 **Tel:** 522753
Nearest Town/Resort Thirsk
Directions From Thirsk go through Sowerby towards Dalton, the park is ½ mile south of Sowerby on the right.
Acreage 1½ **Open** March **to** October
Access Good **Site** Level
Sites Available ⬥ ⬛ **Total** 25
Facilities ⚐ ⬛ ⬛ ⬛ ⬛ ⬛ ⬛ ⬛ ⬛ ⬛
⬛ ⬛ ⬛ ⬛ ⬛ ⬛ ⬛
Nearby Facilities ⬥ ✓ ∪
⚭ Thirsk
Alongside a river. Ideal location for touring.

THIRSK

York House Caravan Park, Balk, Thirsk, North Yorkshire, YO7 2AQ.
Std: 01845 **Tel:** 597495
Email: phil.brierley@which.net
Website: www.yhc.org.uk
Nearest Town/Resort Thirsk
Directions From Thirsk take the A19 towards York, after approx. 2 miles take a left turn for Bagby/Balk/Kilburn. Continue through Bagby Village and at the T-Junction turn right, continue down hill for approx 500 yards, park is on the left.
Acreage 14 **Open** April **to** October
Access Good **Site** Level
Sites Available ▲ ⬥ ⬛ **Total** 25
Facilities ⬥ ⚐ ⬛ ⬛ ⬛ ⬛ ⬛ ⬛
⬛ ⬛ ⬛ ⬛ ⬛ ⬛ ⬛ ⬛ ⬛
Nearby Facilities ⬥ ✓ ⚑ ∪
⚭ Thirsk
At the foot of Hambleton Hills, overlooked by White Horse of Kilburn. A stream runs through the park. NEW childrens play area opened in April 1999. Ideal walking location.

WHITBY

Abbot's House Farm Camping & Caravan Site, Abbot's House Farm, Goathland, Whitby, North Yorkshire, YO22 5NH.
Std: 01947 **Tel:** 896270/896026
Email: ivegill@enterprise.net
Website:
www.abbotshousefarm.totalserve.co.uk

Nearest Town/Resort Whitby
Directions From Whitby take the A171 west for approx. 3 miles, turn south onto the A169, after approx. 6 miles turn right signposted Goathland. Turn left opposite Goathland Garage.
Acreage 2½ **Open** Easter to October
Access Good **Site** Level
Sites Available ▲ ⚑ ♠ **Total** 30
Facilities ⬚ ⚐ ⌐ ☎
⬚ ⬚ ⬚ ⬚ ⬚ ⬚ ⬚
Nearby Facilities ⌐ ✗ ⚲ ∪
⚶ Goathland
The North Yorkshire Moors Steam Railway runs through the farm. Yorkshire Televisions 'Heartbeat' country. 9 miles from Whitby, 25 miles from Scarborough and 40 miles from York.

WHITBY

Burnt House Holiday Park, Ugthorpe, Nr. Whitby, North Yorks, YO21 2BG.
Std: 01947 **Tel:** 840448
Nearest Town/Resort Whitby
Directions 8½ miles north of Whitby on A171, towards Guisborough, signposted Ugthorpe Village.
Acreage 7 **Open** March to October
Access Good **Site** Level
Sites Available ▲ ⚑ ♠ **Total** 99
Facilities ⚐ ⬚ ⬚ ⚓ ⌐ ⊙ ◢ ⬚ ☎
⬚ ⬚ ⬚ ⬚ ⬚ ⬚
Nearby Facilities ⌐ ✗ ⚲ ✗
⚶ Whitby
Ideal base for touring coast or countryside, 4 miles to beach. Fully serviced static caravans for sale. Holiday cottage to let.

WHITBY

Grouse Hill Touring Caravan & Camping Park, Fylingdales, Whitby, North Yorkshire, YO22 4QH.
Std: 01947 **Tel:** 880543
Nearest Town/Resort Scarborough/ Whitby
Directions 12 miles from Scarborough and 8 miles from Whitby. Signed off the A171 just north of the Flask Inn.
Open Easter to 1st Tues Oct
Access Good **Site** Lev/Slope
Sites Available ▲ ⚑ ♠ **Total** 198
Facilities ⬚ ✗ ⚐ ⬚ ⬚ ⚓ ⬚ ⬚ ✗ ⬚ ⬚
Nearby Facilities ⌐ ✗ ⚲ ∪
Expansive views of woodland and moorland. Ideal for families. NEW for 2001 - 23 level pitches with electric points. Close to moorland walks. AA 3 Pennants.

WHITBY

Hollins Farm, Glaisdale, Whitby, North Yorkshire, YO21 2PZ.
Std: 01947 **Tel:** 897516

Nearest Town/Resort Whitby
Directions From the A171 turn to Egton, then take the road to Glaisdale. In Glaisdale turn opposite the phone box, continue up around the church for 1½ miles, look for camping sign.
Acreage ½ **Open** All Year
Site Lev/Slope
Sites Available ▲ ⚑ ♠ **Total** 15
Facilities ⬚ ⚓ ⌐ ⊙ ⬚ ⬚ ⬚ ⬚
Nearby Facilities ✗ ∪ ♗
⚶ Glaisdale
Lovely walks and pubs. 8 miles from the beach. Steam railway.

WHITBY

Ladycross Plantation, Egton, Whitby, North Yorkshire, YO21 1UA.
Std: 01947 **Tel:** 895502
Email:
enquiries@ladycrossplantation.co.uk
Website: www.ladycrossplantation.co.uk
Nearest Town/Resort Whitby
Directions Take the A171 Whitby to Teeside road, 5 miles from Whitby turn left signposted Egton, Grosmont, North Yorks Moors Railway and Ladycross.
Acreage 12 **Open** March to October
Access Good **Site** Level
Sites Available ▲ ⚑⬚ **Total** 120
Facilities ⚐ ⬚ ⬚ ⚓ ⌐ ⊙ ◢ ⬚ ☎
⬚ ⬚ ⬚ ⬚ ⬚
Nearby Facilities ✗ ♗
⚶ Egton Bridge
Ideal for exploring national park and the north east coast. David Bellamy Silver Award for Conservation.

WHITBY

Middlewood Farm Holiday Park, Middlewood Lane, Fylingthorpe, Near Whitby, North Yorkshire, YO22 4UF.
Std: 01947 **Tel:** 880414 **Fax:** 880871
Email: info@middlewoodfarm.com
Website: www.middlewoodfarm.com
Nearest Town/Resort Whitby
Directions Signposted. Take the A171 Scarborough to Whitby road, 3 miles south of Whitby take the Fylingthorpe and Robin Hood's Bay road. At Fylingthorpe Post Office turn onto Middlewood Lane, park is 500 yards on the left.
Acreage 7
Access Good **Site** Level
Sites Available ▲ ⚑ ♠ **Total** 150
Facilities ⚐ ⬚ ⚓ ⌐ ⊙ ◢ ⬚ ⬚ ☎
⬚ ⬚ ⬚ ⬚ ✗ ⬚ ⬚
Nearby Facilities ⌐ ✗ ⚲ ♗ ∪ ♗ ♗
⚶ Whitby
A warm and friendly welcome awaits you at this David Bellamy Gold Award winning park. A walkers, artists and wildlife paradise en-

joying magnificent panoramic views. Level, sheltered pitches. Luxury heated facilities. FREE showers/dishwashing. Family bathrooms. Children's adventure playground. Superb Holiday Homes for hire. Twixt the seaside resorts of Whitby and Scarborough.

WHITBY

Northcliffe Holiday Park, High Hawsker, Whitby, North Yorkshire, YO22 4LL.
Std: 01947 **Tel:** 880477
Std: 01947 **Fax:** 880972
Email: enquiries@northcliffe-seaview.com
Website: www.northcliffe-seaview.com
Nearest Town/Resort Whitby
Directions South from Whitby 3 miles, turn left B1447 to Robin Hood's Bay.
Open Mid March to End Oct
Access Good
Sites Available ▲ ⚑ ♠ **Total** 30
Facilities ⚐ ⚐ ⌐ ⬚ ⬚ ⚓ ⌐ ⬚ ⬚ ⬚ ☎
⬚ ⬚ ⬚ ✗ ⬚ ⬚ ⬚
Nearby Facilities ⌐ ✗ ⚲ ∪ ♗
⚶ Whitby
Luxury Award Winning park with panoramic sea views. We're a Double Winner - YTB and ETC. Caravan Holiday Park of the Year 1999. Woodland Shop/cafe/take-away. New childrens play park.

WHITBY

Rigg Farm Caravan Park, Stainsacre, Whitby, North Yorkshire, YO22 4LP.
Std: 01947 **Tel:** 880430
Std: 01947 **Fax:** 880430
Nearest Town/Resort Whitby
Directions Approx. 3 miles from Whitby town. Signposted on the A171 at the junction with Low Hawsker. Also signposted on the B1416 at the junction with Sneatonthorpe.
Acreage 2/3 **Open** 1 March to 31 Oct
Access Good **Site** Level
Sites Available ▲ ⚑ ♠ **Total** 35
Facilities ⚐ ⬚ ⬚ ⚓ ⌐ ⊙ ⬚ ◢ ⬚ ☎
⬚ ⬚ ⬚ ⬚ ⬚ ✗ ⬚
Nearby Facilities ⌐ ✗ ⚲ ∪
⚶ Whitby
Small select caravan park situated in a National Park, yet close to unspoilt, picturesque Whitby Harbour. Ideal for woodland walking. Steam Railway and "Heartbeat" Country within a few miles. Pets are welcome by arrangement.

WHITBY

Sandfield House Farm Caravan Park, Sandsend Road, Whitby, North Yorkshire, YO21 3SR.
Std: 01947 **Tel:** 602660
Email: sandfieldw@aol.com
Nearest Town/Resort Whitby

Directions 1 mile north of Whitby on the A174 coast road.
Acreage 12 **Open** March **to** October
Access Good **Site** Level
Sites Available ⊕ ⊟ **Total** 50
Facilities ⚲ ∮ ⌂ ⓌⒸ ♨ ↑ ⊙ ⊒ ⊡ ☎
℣ ⊙ ⊛ ⊛ ⊬ 🖳
Nearby Facilities ┡ ⟋ ⚓ ⤢ ∪ ♉
⚲ Whitby
Sea views, ¼ mile from a 2 mile long sandy beach. Set in undulating countryside.

WHITBY

Serenity Touring Caravan & Camping Park, High Street, Hinderwell, Whitby, North Yorks, TS13 5JH.
Std: 01947 **Tel:** 841122
Nearest Town/Resort Whitby
Directions Take B1266 off A171 Whitby to Guisborough Moor road. To T-Junction turn left onto A174. 1 mile Hinderwell. Site entrance in village on left signed 'Serenity'.
Acreage 3 **Open** March **to** October
Access Good **Site** Level
Sites Available ⚠ ⊕ ⊟ **Total** 20
Facilities ∮ ⓌⒸ ♨ ↑ ⊙ ☎ ⓁⒺ ⊙ ⊬ 🖳
Nearby Facilities ┡ ⟋ ⚓ ⤢ ∪ ♉ ♉
⚲ Whitby
A very quiet, sheltered and secure. Mainly adult site with lovely country views. ½ mile from the sea. Spectacular coastal, country and moorland walks. Village shops and pubs all nearby.

WHITBY

York House Caravan Park, Hawsker, Whitby, North Yorkshire, YO22 4LW.
Std: 01947 **Tel:** 880354
Nearest Town/Resort Whitby
Directions 3 miles south of Whitby on the A171, signposted.
Acreage 4¼ **Open** March **to** October
Access Good **Site** Lev/Slope
Sites Available ⚠ ⊕ ⊟ **Total** 59
Facilities ∮ ⌂ ⓌⒸ ♨ ↑ ⊙ ⊒ ⊡ ☎
℣ ⓁⒺ ⊙ ⊛ ⊛ ⊬ 🖳
Nearby Facilities ┡ ⟋ ⚓ ⤢ ∪ ♉ ♉
⚲ Whitby
Scenic views of the sea, Whitby and North Yorkshire Moors.

YORK

Acomb Grange, Grange Lane, York, North Yorkshire, YO23 3QZ.
Std: 01904 **Tel:** 781318
Email: peterbrown@acomb-grange.freeserve.co.uk
Website: www.go.to/york
Nearest Town/Resort York
Directions Take the A59 to Harrogate and follow signs to Acomb. Turn into Askham Lane then turn into Grange Lane.
Acreage 2 **Open** All Year

Access Fair **Site** Level
Sites Available ⚠ ⊕ ⊟ **Total** 5
Facilities ∮ ⌂ ⓌⒸ ♨ ↑ ⊙ ⊒ ☎ ⓁⒺ 🖳
Nearby Facilities ┡ ⟋ ♉
⚲ York
Near the City of York, North Yorkshire Moors and Dales. Self Catering accommodation also available.

YORK

Alders Caravan Park, Home Farm, Alne, York, North Yorkshire, YO61 1TB.
Std: 01347 **Tel:** 838722 **Fax:** 838722
Nearest Town/Resort York
Directions 9 miles north of York on the A19, turn left. Or south of Easingwold on the A19, turn right. Alders is 2¼ miles in the centre of the village in Monk Green.
Acreage 6 **Open** March **to** October
Access Good **Site** Level
Sites Available ⊕ ⊟ **Total** 40
Facilities ⚹ ∮ ⌂ ⓌⒸ ♨ ↑ ⊙ ⊙ ☎ ⊬ 🖳
Nearby Facilities ┡ ⟋ ∪
⚲ York
On a working farm, in historic parkland where visitors may enjoy peace and tranquility. York (on bus route), Moors, Dales and coast nearby.

YORK

Cawood Holiday Park, Caravan & Camping Centre, Ryther Road, Cawood, Selby, North Yorkshire, YO8 3TT.
Std: 01757 **Tel:** 268450 **Fax:** 268537
Website: www.ukparks.co.uk/cawood
Nearest Town/Resort Selby/York
Directions From York or the A1 take the B1222 to Cawood traffic lights, turn onto the B1223 signed Tadcaster for 1 mile, park is on the left.
Acreage 8 **Open** 1 March **to** 1 Feb
Access Good **Site** Level
Sites Available ⚠ ⊕ ⊟ **Total** 60
Facilities ⚹ ∮ ⌂ ⓌⒸ ♨ ↑ ⊙ ⊒ ⊡ ☎
℣ ⓁⒺ ⊙ ⚲ ⚹ ⊞ ⚘ ♒ ⊛ ⊬ 🖳 🖳
Nearby Facilities ┡ ⟋ ∪ ♉ ♉
⚲ Selby
Here at Cawood Holiday Park, we have worked hard to create an environment which keeps its natural simplicity to provide a trouble free holiday. Some pitches have views over our fishing lake. A quiet rural park.

YORK

Goosewood Caravan Park, Sutton-on-the-Forest, York, YO61 1ET.
Std: 01347 **Tel:** 810829
Website: www.ukparks.co.uk/goosewood
Nearest Town/Resort York
Directions From the A1237 take the B1363 north. Pass the Haxby-Wigginton junction and in 2 miles take next right and follow signs.

Open All Year
Access Good **Site** Level
Sites Available ⊕ ⊟ **Total** 75
Facilities ∮ ⌂ ⓌⒸ ♨ ↑ ⊙ ⊒ ⊒ ⊡ 🖳
℣ ⊙ ☎ ⊞ ⊬ 🖳 🖳
Nearby Facilities ┡ ⟋ ∪
⚲ York
Set in woodland with our own lake.

YORK

Home Farm Camping & Caravan Park, Moreby, Stillingfleet, York, North Yorkshire, YO19 6HN.
Std: 01904 **Tel:** 728263
Std: 01904 **Fax:** 720059
Nearest Town/Resort York
Directions On the B1222 between the village of Naburn and Stillingfleet. 6 miles south of York City walls.
Acreage 3 **Open** February **to** December
Access Good **Site** Level
Sites Available ⚠ ⊕ ⊟ **Total** 25
Facilities ∮ ⓌⒸ ♨ ↑ ⊙ ☎ ⊙ ⊞ ⊬ 🖳 🖳
Nearby Facilities ⟋ ∪
⚲ York
Alongside the River Ouse. Ideal base to tour York and surrounding Dales and North Yorkshire Moors. 4 miles to the nearest shop or supermarket.

YORK

Moor End Farm, Acaster, Malbis, York, North Yorkshire, YO23 2UQ.
Std: 01904 **Tel:** 706727
Std: 01904 **Fax:** 706727
Email:
moorendfarm@acaster99.fsnet.co.uk
Website: www.ukparks.co.uk/moorend
Nearest Town/Resort York
Directions Off A64 going west turn off a Copmanthorpe and follow symbols and Acaster signs to village.
Acreage 1 **Open** April 1st **to** October
Access Good **Site** Level
Sites Available ⚠ ⊕ ⊟ **Total** 15
Facilities ∮ ⓌⒸ ♨ ↑ ⊙ ☎ ⓁⒺ ⊞ ⊬ 🖳
Nearby Facilities ┡ ⟋ ⚓ ⤢ ∪ ♉
⚲ York
A working farm and small friendly site. Dish washing facilities.

YORK

Moorside Caravan Park, Lords Moor Lane, Strensall, York, North Yorkshire, YO32 5XJ.
Std: 01904 **Tel:** 491865
Nearest Town/Resort York
Directions Take the A1237, then take the Strensall turn and head towards Flaxton.
Open March **to** October
Access Good **Site** Level
Sites Available ⚠ ⊕ ⊟ **Total** 50
Facilities ⚹ ∮ ⌂ ⓌⒸ ♨ ↑ ⊙ ⊒ 🖳 ℣ ⊙ ☎ ⊬⚟

NABURN LOCK CARAVAN & CAMPING PARK
(THE COUNTRY SITE BY THE CITY!)
RAC
★★★★ Naburn Lock Caravan & Camping Park, Naburn, York YO1 4RU. Tel/Fax: (01904) 728697 **AA**
E-mail: nablock@easynet.co.uk Web site: http://www.scoot.co.uk/naburn_lock_caravan/

Sheltered country site only 4 miles from York. From A19 South of York, take B1222 to Naburn. Service Bus & River Bus to York. All facilities. • Ideal for Dales, Moors & Coast • Open March to October **SAE For Brochure**

Nearby Facilities ┌ ✔
⇌ York
NO CHILDREN. Fishing lake on site. Near York Golf Course.

YORK
Mount Pleasant Holiday Park & Park Homes Estate, Acaster Malbis, York, North Yorkshire, YO23 2UA.
Std: 01904 **Tel:** 707078
Std: 01904 **Fax:** 700888
Email: mountpleasant@holgates.com
Website: www.holgates.com
Nearest Town/Resort York
Directions From the A64 York ringroad take the Bishopthorpe/Racecourse exit and head into Bishopthorpe Village. Turn right in the village towards Acaster Airfield, at the next T-Junction turn left and then left again before the boatyard. Park is on the right hand side after 200 metres.
Acreage 20 **Open** 1 March **to** 8 Jan
Access Good **Site** Level
Sites Available ▲ ⊕ ⊟ **Total** 72
Facilities ∮ ⊟ ⊞ ♨ ┌ ⊙ ⇃ ⚍ ▣ ☻
⚙ ☺ ⊛ ⋀⊷⊡ ▣ ☻
Nearby Facilities ┌ ✔ ⊀ ∪
⇌ York
Quiet park with top quality touring pitches and self catering accommodation. Ideally placed for the historical city of York and its many attractions.

YORK
Naburn Lock Caravan & Camping Park, Naburn, York, North Yorkshire, YO19 4RU.
Std: 01904 **Tel:** 728697
Std: 01904 **Fax:** 728697
Email: nablock@easynet.co.uk
Website: www.scoot.co.uk/naburn_lock_caravan/
Nearest Town/Resort York
Directions Take the A19 south from York, before the by-pass turn right onto the B1222, go through Naburn and we are ½ mile on the right.
Acreage 7 **Open** 1 March **to** 6 November
Access Good **Site** Level
Sites Available ▲ ⊕ ⊟ **Total** 100
Facilities ∮ ⊞ ♨⊷⊡ ▣ ☻
⚙ ☺ ⊛ ⊡ ▣ ☻
Nearby Facilities ┌ ✔ ∪ ℛ
⇌ York
Close to historic York, and within easy reach of the Yorkshire Dales, Moors, Wolds and Coast.

YORK
Riverside Caravan & Camping Park, York Marine Services Ltd., Ferry Lane, Bishopthorpe, York, North Yorkshire, YO23 1SB.
Std: 01904 **Tel:** 705812
Std: 01904 **Fax:** 705824
Email: @yorkmarine.co.uk
Website: www.yorkmarine.co.uk
Nearest Town/Resort York
Directions 2 miles south of York.
Acreage 1 **Open** April **to** October
Access Good **Site** Level
Sites Available ▲ ⊕⊟ **Total** 25

Facilities ⚒ ∮ ⊞ ♨ ┌ ⊙ ⇃
▣ ⚙ ⚘ ⚗ ⊠ ✗ ♥ ⋀ ⊛ ⊡ ▣
Nearby Facilities ┌ ✔ ⊿ ⊀ ∪
⇌ York
River, Yorkshire Dales and the seaside resorts of Bridlington, Scarborough and Whitby.

YORK
Swallow Hall Caravan Park, Swallow Hall, Crockey Hill, York, North Yorkshire, YO19 4SG.
Std: 01904 **Tel:** 448219
Std: 01904 **Fax:** 448219
Email: jtscores@hotmail.com
Nearest Town/Resort York
Directions A19, 6-8 miles.
Acreage 5 **Open** Easter **to** October
Access Good **Site** Level
Sites Available ▲ ⊕ ⊟ **Total** 35
Facilities ∮ ⊞ ♨ ┌ ⊙ ☻
⚙ ☺ ⊠ ✗ ♥ ⋀♨
Nearby Facilities ┌ ✔ ∪ ℛ
⇌ York
Golf and tennis on site.

YORK
The Old Post Office Caravan Site, Mill Lane, Acaster Malbis, York, North Yorkshire, YO23 2UJ.
Std: 01904 **Tel:** 702448
Nearest Town/Resort York
Directions From Leeds take the A64 to Copmanthorpe, 2 miles to Acaster Malbis.
Open April **to** October
Access Good **Site** Level
Sites Available ⊕ ⊟ **Total** 12
Facilities ∮ ⊞ ♨ ┌ ⊙ ⚙ ☺ ⊠⊷
Nearby Facilities ┌ ✔ ⊿ ⊀ ∪
⇌ York

YORK
The Ponderosa Caravan Park, East Moor, Sutton-on-the-Forest, Near York, North Yorkshire, YO61 1ET.
Std: 01347 **Tel:** 810744
Std: 01347 **Fax:** 810744
Nearest Town/Resort York
Directions Signposted 800 yards off the B1363 Wigginton to Helmsley road, 6 miles from York.
Acreage 3 **Open** All Year
Access Good **Site** Level
Sites Available ▲ ⊕ ⊟ **Total** 40
Facilities ∮ ⊟ ⊞ ♨ ┌ ⊙ ⇃ ⚍ ▣ ☻
⚙ ⊠ ✗ ♥ ⋀♨
Nearby Facilities ✔
⇌ York
Near to the historic city of York, North Yorkshire Moors and many local attractions.

THANK YOU
FOR USING
CADE'S

YORKSHIRE, SOUTH
BARNSLEY
Greensprings Touring Park, Rockley Lane, Worsbrough, Barnsley, South Yorks, S75 3DS.
Std: 01226 **Tel:** 288298
Std: 01226 **Fax:** 288298
Nearest Town/Resort Barnsley
Directions Junction 36 on M1. A61 to Barnsley, take left turn after ¼ mile signed to Pilley. Site is 1 mile along this road.
Acreage 4 **Open** April **to** October
Access Good **Site** Lev/Slope
Sites Available ▲ ⊕ ⊟ **Total** 60
Facilities ∮ ┌ ⊙ ☻ ⚙ ⚘ ☺ ⊷⊡
Nearby Facilities ┌ ✔ ∪ ⊀
⇌ Barnsley
Country site, well wooded, pleasant walks. Convenient from M1. Ideal location for Sheffield venues. TV Hook-up.

DONCASTER
Waterfront Country Park, The Marina, West Stockwith, Doncaster, South Yorkshire, DN10 4ET.
Std: 01427 **Tel:** 890000
Std: 01427 **Fax:** 890000
Nearest Town/Resort Gainsborough
Directions From Gainsborough travel west on the A631 for 4 miles, then take the A161 for 3 miles to West Stockwith.
Acreage 5½ **Open** All Year
Access Good **Site** Level
Sites Available ⊕ ⊟ **Total** 100
Facilities ⚒ ∮ ⊟ ⊞ ☻
⚙ ⚘ ☺ ⊠ ✗ ♥ ⋀⊷⊡ ▣
Nearby Facilities ┌ ✔ ⊿ ⊀ ∪
⇌ Gainsborough
Tranquil setting adjacent to a marina, river and leisure canal. Waterfront pubs, excellent fishing and boating, lovely walks.

HATFIELD
Hatfield Water Park, Old Thorne Road, Hatfield, Doncaster, South Yorkshire, DN7 6EQ.
Std: 01302 **Tel:** 841572
Nearest Town/Resort Doncaster
Directions Signposted off the A18.
Acreage 10 **Open** All Year
Access Good **Site** Level
Sites Available ▲ ⊕☐ **Total** 75
Facilities ⚒ ∮ ⊞ ♨ ┌ ⊙ ⇃ ⚘ ☺ ⋀ ⊛⊷⊡
Nearby Facilities ┌ ✔ ⊿ ⊀
⇌ Hatfield
Park includes watersports centre situated on our own lake with sailing, wind surfing, canoeing, kayaking and fishing available.

ROTHERHAM
Thrybergh Country Park, Doncaster Road, Thrybergh, Rotherham, South Yorkshire, S65 4NU.
Std: 01709 **Tel:** 850353 **Fax:** 851532
Nearest Town/Resort Rotherham
Directions Thrybergh Country Park is conveniently situated 5 miles from the A1(M) and M1 and 3 miles from the M18 on the main Rotherham to Doncaster road the A630. The entrance is well signposted from both directions.

Acreage 1 Open All Year
Access Good Site Level
Sites Available ▲ ⚌ ⛟ Total 25
Facilities ⛄ ∮ 🛁 🚾 ⌂ ⊡ ☂
🗜🏠⛱✗🅿⊞🔌
Nearby Facilities ⌐ ✓ ⚓ ⚘ ⚲ ☍
⇌ Rotherham
The caravan site forms an integral part of
the country park along with the reservoir
providing fly fishing. A circular walk of 1¾
miles. 24 Hour access to toilets and
showers.

SHEFFIELD

Fox Hagg Farm, Lodge Lane, Rivelin,
Sheffield, South Yorkshire, S6 5SN.
Std: 0114 **Tel:** 230 5589
Nearest Town/Resort Sheffield
Directions Off the A57
Acreage 2 **Open** April to October
Access Good **Site** Level
Sites Available ▲ ⚌ ⛟ **Total** 60
Facilities ∮ 🛁 🚾 ⚡ ⌂ ⊙⊣ ☂ 🗜 ⊞🔌⊡
Nearby Facilities ⌐ ✓ ⚓ ∪ ☍
⇌ Sheffield
Outskirts of Peak District. Ideal touring,
scenic views. Post Office. Nature walks.
Wash room.

YORKSHIRE, WEST
BINGLEY

Harden & Bingley Caravan Park, Goit
Stock Lane, Harden, Bingley, West
Yorkshire, BD16 1DF.
Std: 01535 **Tel:** 273810
Nearest Town/Resort Bingley
Directions From Bingley take the B6429,
at the mini-roundabout in Harden Village
turn left signposted Wilsden, just before the
bridge turn right into Goit Stock Lane.
Acreage 1 **Open** April to October
Access Poor **Site** Lev/Slope
Sites Available ▲ ⚌ ⛟ **Total** 21
Facilities ∮ 🛁 🚾 ⚡ ⌂ ⊙☂ ⊡☂
🗜 🏠 🛒🔌⊡
Nearby Facilities
⇌ Bingley
Quiet, peaceful valley beside a trout beck.
Lovely walks through woodland, Fairy Glen
Waterfall. ETB 4 Star Graded.

HEBDEN BRIDGE

Pennine Camp & Caravan Site, High
Greenwood House, Heptonstall, Hebden
Bridge, West Yorkshire, HX7 7AZ.
Std: 01422 **Tel:** 842287
Nearest Town/Resort Hebden Bridge
Directions From Hebden Bridge take
Heptonstall road then follow tent and
caravan signs.
Open April to October
Site Lev/Slope
Sites Available ▲ ⚌ ⛟ **Total** 50
Facilities ∮ 🚾 ⌂ ⊙ ☂ 🗜 ⊞ ⊡
Nearby Facilities ✓ ∪ ☍
⇌ Hebden Bridge

HOLMFIRTH

Holme Valley Camping & Caravan Park,
Thongsbridge, Holmfirth, West Yorkshire,
HD9 7TD.
Std: 01484 **Tel:** 665819 **Fax:** 663870
Nearest Town/Resort Holmfirth
Directions 5 miles south of Huddersfield,
in the valley bottom off the A6024, halfway
between Honley and Holmfirth.
Acreage 4½ **Open** All Year
Access Good **Site** Level
Sites Available ▲ ∮ ⚌ ⛟ **Total** 62
Facilities ⛄ ∮ 🛁 🚾 ⚡ ⌂ ⊙⊣ ☂
⊡ 🗜 🗜 🏠 ⛱ 🛒⊞⊡⊡

Nearby Facilities ⌐ ✓ ∪ 🅿 ☍
⇌ Brockholes
In a picturesque setting in the heart of 'Last
of the Summer Wine' country, bordering the
Peak District. On-site angling and auto-gas
filling station. Close to local attractions.

KEIGHLEY

Upwood Holiday Park, Blackmoor Road,
Haworth, West Yorkshire, BD22 9SS.
Std: 01535 **Tel:** 644242
Std: 01535 **Fax:** 643254
Email:
caravans@upwoodholidaypark.fsnet.co.uk
Website:
www.upwoodholidaypark.fsnet.co.uk
Nearest Town/Resort Keighley
Directions Situated on the A629 Keighley
to Halifax road. It is recommended that
caravans enter via Flappit Pub. On the
B6144 Blackmoor Road is the first left after
approx. ¾ miles. Upwood is approx. 1 mile
on the left.
Acreage 16 **Open** March to October
Access Good **Site** Lev/Slope
Sites Available ▲ ⚌ ⛟ **Total** 140
Facilities ⛄ ∮ 🛁 🚾 ⚡ ⌂ ⊙⊣ ⊡ ☂
🗜 🏠 ⛱ 🅿 🛒 ⛱ ⊡
Nearby Facilities ⌐ ✓ ⚓ ⚘ ∪
⇌ Oxenhope
Pleasantly situated close to the Yorkshire
Dales National Park. Beautiful, panoramic
views over the surrounding countryside. One
mile from the Bronte Village of Haworth and
Worth Steam Railway.

LEEDS

Glenfield Caravan Park, Blackmoor
Lane, Bardsey, Leeds, West Yorkshire,
LS17 9DZ.
Std: 01937 **Tel:** 574657
Website: www.ukparks.co.uk/glenfieldcp
Nearest Town/Resort Leeds
Directions From Leeds take the A58
towards Wetherby, after approx 8 miles turn
left at Shadwell Harewood sign. After 1 mile
take right hand fork, continue for 1 mile and
site is on the left at the bottom of the hill.
Acreage 4 **Open** All Year
Access Good **Site** Level
Sites Available ▲ ⚌ ⛟ **Total** 30
Facilities ⛄ ∮ 🛁 🚾 ⚡ ⌂ ⊙⊣ ⊡ ☂
🗜 🏠 🛒⊡
Nearby Facilities ⌐ ✓ ∪ 🅿
⇌ Leeds
Beautifully kept park. Lovely walks and
places to eat nearby. Easy access and ideal
touring base. Brand new 5 Star shower block
for 2001.

LEEDS

Moor Lodge Caravan Park, Blackmoor
Lane, Bardsey, Leeds, West Yorkshire,
LS17 9DZ.
Std: 01937 **Tel:** 572424
Nearest Town/Resort Leeds
Directions From Leeds 8 miles along the
A58 Wetherby. Turn left signposted
Shadwell/Harewood, follow lane right fork,
over two crossroads, bottom of hill on right.
Acreage 8 **Open** All Year
Access Good **Site** Level
Sites Available ▲ ⚌ ⛟ **Total** 12
Facilities ⛄ ∮ 🛁 🚾 ⚡ ⌂ ⊙⊣ ⊡ ☂
🗜 🏠 🛒⊞⊡▲
Nearby Facilities ⌐ ✓ ∪ 🅿 ☍
⇌ Leeds
ADULTS ONLY. Immaculate countryside
park.

LEEDS

**Roundhay Park Caravan & Camping
Site,** Elmete Lane, Leeds, West Yorkshire,
LS8 2LG.
Std: 0113 **Tel:** 265 2354
Nearest Town/Resort Leeds
Directions 3 miles from Leeds on the A58
Wetherby road at Roundhay. Site is well
signposted.
Acreage 7 **Open** March to End October
Access Good **Site** Level
Sites Available ▲ ⚌ ⛟ **Total** 60
Facilities ∮ 🛁 🚾 ⚡ ⌂ ⊙⊣ ⊡ ☂
🗜 🗜 🏠 🛒⊞⊡
Nearby Facilities ⌐ ✓ ⚘ 🅿
⇌ Leeds
Secluded, south facing site in part of the 700
acre Roundhay Park Estate. Combines rural
tranquility with city attractions. Convenient
for the Dales, York and Leeds shopping.

OTLEY

St. Helena's Caravan Park, Otley Old
Road, Horsforth, Leeds, West Yorkshire,
LS18 5HZ.
Std: 0113 **Tel:** 284 1142
Nearest Town/Resort Otley/Horsforth/
Leeds
Directions From Leeds take the A660
the A65, then take the A658.
Open April to October
Access Good **Site** Lev/Slope
Sites Available ▲ ⚌ ⛟ **Total** 60
Facilities ⛄ ∮ 🛁 🚾 ⚡ ⌂ ⊙⊡ ☂ 🗜 🛒⊡
Nearby Facilities ⌐ ✓
⇌ Horsforth
Close to the Yorkshire Dales and the market
town of Otley.

OTLEY

Stubbings Farm, Leeds Road, Otley,
West Yorkshire, LS21 1DN.
Std: 01943 **Tel:** 464168
Nearest Town/Resort Otley
Directions Off the A660, 1 mile outside
Otley.
Acreage 3 **Open** All Year
Access Good **Site** Lev/Slope
Sites Available ▲ ⚌ ⛟ **Total** 20
Facilities 🛁 🚾 ⊡
Nearby Facilities ⌐ ✓ ⚓ ⚘ ∪ 🅿 ☍
⇌ Burley-in-Wharfedale
Rural site with beautiful views over the
Wharfe Valley.

SHIPLEY

Dobrudden Caravan Park, Baildon Moor,
Baildon, Shipley, West Yorkshire, BD17
5EE.
Std: 01274 **Tel:** 581016
Std: 01274 **Fax:** 594351
Email: elawr11@aol.com
Nearest Town/Resort Baildon
Directions From the roundabout in Baildon
town centre follow Tourist Information signs.
Acreage 10 **Open** March to December
Access Good **Site** Lev/Slope
Sites Available ▲ ⚌ ⛟ **Total** 20
Facilities ∮ 🛁 🚾 ⚡ ⌂ ⊙⊣ ⊡ ☂
🗜 🗜 🏠 ⛱✗⊞⊡
Nearby Facilities ⌐ ∪ 🅿 ☍
⇌ Baildon
Near to Emmerdale, Haworth Bronte
country, Museum of Photography and steam
railways. Ideal for walking. Pets are welcome
by appointment only.

SILSDEN

Brown Bank Caravan Park, Brown Bank
Lane, Silsden, West Yorkshire, BD20
0NN.
Std: 01535 **Tel:** 653241
Nearest Town/Resort Silsden

Directions From Silsden take the A6034, turn right on the bend into Brown Bank Lane, site is 1½ miles on the right. Also signposted from Addingham on the A6034.
Acreage 12 **Open** April to October
Access Good **Site** Level
Sites Available A ♥ ⊕ **Total** 15
Facilities ⅋ ⒰ ♨ ┌ ⊙ ◔ ▱ ♥
〕 ⊟ ⚁ ⊞ ┡ ⊡ ⊟
Nearby Facilities ┌ ⁄ ∪ ⅄
⚌ Steeton
On the edge of Ilkley Moor with good views and excellent walks. Ideal base for touring. Many attractions within 15 miles.

WAKEFIELD
Nostell Priory Holiday Home Park, Nostell, Wakefield, West Yorkshire, WF4 1QD.
Std: 01924 **Tel:** 863938
Std: 01924 **Fax:** 862226
Nearest Town/Resort Wakefield
Directions A638 Wakefield to Doncaster road, 5 miles from Wakefield, entrance is in the village of Foulby.
Acreage 4 **Open** April to September
Access Good **Site** Level
Sites Available A ♥ ⊕ **Total** 60
Facilities ⅋ ∮ ⒰ ♨ ┌ ⊙ ◔ ▱ ♥
〕 ⊟ ⊞ ┡ ⊡ ⊟
Nearby Facilities ┌ ⁄ ⌂ ⅄
⚌ Fitzwilliam
Nostell Priory Stately Home owned by the National Trust. A lake for fishing (extra charge). Rally field for 150 units also available.

WETHERBY
Maustin Caravan Park, Kearby with Netherby, Nr. Wetherby, West Yorkshire, LS22 4DP.
Std: 0113 **Tel:** 288 6234
Std: 0113 **Fax:** 288 6234
Email: info@maustin.co.uk
Website: www.maustin.co.uk
Nearest Town/Resort Harrogate/ Wetherby
Directions A61 three right turns, after crossing River Wharfe at bottom of Harewood Bank. A1 from Wetherby through Sicklinghall to Kearby.
Acreage 2 **Open** March to October
Access Good **Site** Level
Sites Available A ♥ ⊕ **Total** 13
Facilities ∮ ⒰ ♨ ┌ ⊙ ◔ ♥
〕 ⊟ ⚁ ⚲ ⊞ ⊡ ⊟ A
Nearby Facilities ┌ ⁄ ∪
Quiet site, suits couples. Excellent restaurant/bar open weekends. Flat green bowling. Harewood House nearby. Good touring centre. Holiday homes for hire. Gold Award for Conservation.

WALES
BRIDGEND
PORTHCAWL
Brodawel Camping Park, Brodawel House, Moor Lane, Nottage, Porthcawl, Bridgend, CF36 3EJ.
Std: 01656 **Tel:** 783231 **Fax:** 783231
Nearest Town/Resort Porthcawl
Directions Leave the M4 at junction 37, turn onto the A4229 for Porthcawl for 2 miles, signposted Moor Lane.
Acreage 5 **Open** April to October
Access Good **Site** Level
Sites Available A ♥ ⊕ **Total** 100
Facilities ⅋ ∮ ⒰ ♨ ┌ ⊙ ◔ ▱ ♥
⚲ 〕 ⊟ ⚁ ⊞ ⚘ ⋀ ⊞ ⊡ ⊟
Nearby Facilities ┌ ⁄ ⌂ ⅄ ∪ ≵ ℛ ⅄
⚌ Pyle
Convenient to all beaches, very central for touring area. Off Licence. Designer village Wales 8 miles.

PORTHCAWL
Happy Valley Caravan Park, Wig Fach, Porthcawl, Bridgend, CF32 0NG.
Std: 01656 **Tel:** 782144 **Fax:** 782146
Email: happyvalley@btconnect.com
Nearest Town/Resort Porthcawl
Directions 1 mile south east of Porthcawl on the A4106.
Open April to Sept
Access Good **Site** Level
Sites Available A ♥ ⊕ **Total** 100
Facilities ∮ ⒰ ♨ ┌ ⊙ ◔ ▱ ♥
⚲ 〕 ⊟ ⚲ ⚘ ⋀ ⊞ ⊡ ⊟
Nearby Facilities ┌ ⁄ ⌂ ⅄ ∪ ≵ ℛ ⅄
⚌ Bridgend
Close to the Heritage Coast, ideal for walking.

PORTHCAWL
Kenfig Pool Caravan Park, Kenfig, Near Porthcawl, Bridgend, CF33 4PT.
Std: 01656 **Tel:** 740079
Nearest Town/Resort Porthcawl
Directions 2 miles from Porthcawl. Leave the M4 at junction 37 and go via the village of North Conelly.
Open March to November
Access Good **Site** Level
Sites Available ♥ ⊕ **Total** 6
Facilities ∮ ⒰ ⊟ ⒰ ♨ ┌ ⊙ ◔ ▱
⊡ ⚁ ⊞ ⊡ ⊟
Nearby Facilities ┌ ⁄ ∪
⚌ Bridgend
Adjoining a nature reserve and overlooking Kenfig Pool.

CARDIFF
CARDIFF
Pontcanna Caravan Site, Pontcanna Fields, Off Sophia Close, Pontcanna, Cardiff, CF11 9LB.
Std: 029 **Tel:** 2039 8362 **Fax:** 2039 8362
Nearest Town/Resort Cardiff
Directions Leave the M4 and follow signs for Cardiff City Centre. On reaching the city centre stay in the right hand lane, go over the bridge and to traffic lights, turn right into Cathedral Road. At next traffic lights turn right into Sophia Close and Sophia Gardens, turn left at the Welsh Institute of Sport, the Park is on this road on the left hand side.
Acreage 6 **Open** All Year
Access Good **Site** Level
Sites Available A ♥ ⊕ **Total** 94
Facilities ⅋ ∮ ⒰ ⊟ ⒰ ♨ ┌ ⊙ ◔ ▱ ♥
⚁ ⒰ ⊟ ⊞ ⊡ ⊟
Nearby Facilities ∪ ℛ
⚌ Cardiff Central
Fully equipped for the disabled including specially adapted bikes (available for hire).

CEREDIGION (CARDIGANSHIRE)
ABERAERON
Aeron Coast Caravan Park, North Road, Aberaeron, Ceredigion, SA46 0JF.
Std: 01545 **Tel:** 570349
Email: aeroncoastcaravanpark@aberaeron.freeserve.co.uk
Nearest Town/Resort Aberaeron
Directions Main coastal road A487 on northern edge of Aberaeron. Filling station at entrance.
Acreage 8 **Open** Easter to End October
Access Good **Site** Level
Sites Available A ♥ ⊕ **Total** 50
Facilities ⅋ ∮ ⒰ ♨ ┌ ⊙ ◔ ▱ ♥
⚲ 〕 ⊟ ⚁ ⊞ ⚘ ⋀ ⚙ ⚜ ⚘ ⊞ ⊡ ⊟
Nearby Facilities ┌ ⁄ ⌂ ⅄ ∪ ≵ ℛ
⚌ Aberystwyth
Aberaeron is a recognised beauty spot. Picturesque harbour, coastal and river walks. Tennis court on park. Only 200yds from shops. 4 Star Graded.

ABERAERON
Brynarian Caravan Park, Cross Inn, Llanon, Ceregidion, SY23 5NA.
Std: 01974 **Tel:** 272231
Email: brynariancp@aol.com
Nearest Town/Resort Aberaeron
Directions Take the A487 Aberystwyth to Cardigan road, in Llanrhystud take the B4337 to Cross Inn, turn first right towards Llanon, after 500 yards at the crossroads turn left, park is on the left.
Acreage 2½ **Open** March to October
Access Good **Site** Level
Sites Available A ♥ ⊕ **Total** 20
Facilities ∮ ⒰ ♨ ┌ ⊙ ◔ ▱ ♥
⚁ ⒰ ⊟ ⚁ ⊞ ⊡ ⊟
Nearby Facilities ┌ ⁄ ⌂ ⅄ ∪ ℛ
⚌ Aberystwyth
Very quiet, sheltered site. Central for coast and mountains.

ABERPORTH
Caerfelin Caravan Park, Aberporth, Ceredigion, SA43 2BY.
Std: 01239 **Tel:** 810540
Email: bright@caerfelin.fsbusiness.co.uk
Website: www.caerfelin.co.uk
Nearest Town/Resort Aberporth
Directions Turn off A487 at Blaenannerch onto B433, enter village of Aberporth. Turn right at St. Cynwyls Church, park 200 yards

on left.
Acreage 11½ **Open** Mid March **to** End Oct
Access Good **Site** Lev/Slope
Sites Available ♫ ⚏ **Total** 8
Facilities 🚿 ♨ ♐ ⊙ ⛽ 🛒 💇 🎱 ♨ ⛺
Nearby Facilities ✝ 🏊 ⛵ ⛷ U ♬ ≯
⚏ Carmarthen
Well sheltered site, five minutes walk to sandy beaches and the village of Aberporth.

ABERPORTH

Maes Glas Caravan Park, Penbryn, Sarnau, Llandysul, Ceredigion, SA44 6QE.
Std: 01239 **Tel:** 654268 **Fax:** 654268
Email: enquiries@maesglascaravanpark.co.uk
Website: www.maesglascaravanpark.co.uk
Nearest Town/Resort Llangrannog
Directions Turn off the A487 between Cardigan and New Quay in the village of Sarnau by the old church, signposted Penbryn. Follow the road down for ¾ mile to the telephone box, at next junction bear left and the park entrance is on the right.
Acreage 4 **Open** March **to** October
Access Good **Site** Level
Sites Available ⚏ ♫ ⚏ **Total** 10
Facilities 🚿 ♨ 🛒 ♐ ⊙ 🍴 🛒 ⛽
Nearby Facilities ✝ 🏊 ⛵ ⛷ U
⚏ Aberystwyth
Near Penbryn beach. David Bellamy Gold Award for Conservation.

ABERPORTH

Pilbach Holiday Park, Betws Ifan, Aberporth, Ceredigion, SA44 5RT.
Std: 01239 **Tel:** 851434 **Fax:** 851969

Email: pilbach@fsbdial.co.uk
Nearest Town/Resort Aberporth
Directions From A487 take B4333 Newcaste Emlyn road, turn first left, then first right, then first left.
Acreage 15 **Open** March **to** Mid Nov
Access Good **Site** Level
Sites Available 👤 ♫ ⚏ **Total** 65
Facilities 🚿 🚿 ♨ ♐ ⊙ 🍴 ⛽ 🛒 ⛽ 🎱 ♨ ✕ ♫ 🛒 ♠ ♫ ⚡ ✳ 📶 ⚏ ⚏
Nearby Facilities ✝ ⛷ ⛷ ≯
⚏ Aberystwyth
Dragon Award Park and Bellamy Bronze Award.

ABERYSTWYTH

Aberystwyth Holiday Village, Penparcau Road, Aberystwyth, Ceredigion, SY23 1BP.
Std: 01970 **Tel:** 624211 **Fax:** 611536
Email: enquiries@aberystwythholidays.co.uk
Website: www.aberystwythholidays.co.uk
Nearest Town/Resort Aberystwyth
Directions Take A487 out of Aberystwyth, south ½ mile.
Acreage 30 **Open** March **to** October
Access Good **Site** Level
Sites Available 👤 ♫ ⚏ **Total** 500
Facilities 🚿 🚿 ♨ ♐ ⊙ 🍴 ⛽ 🛒 ⛽ 🎱 ♨ ✕ ♫ 🛒 ♠ ♫ ⚡ ✳ 📶 ⚏ ⚏
Nearby Facilities ✝ 🏊 ⛵ ⛷ U ♬ ♬ ≯
⚏ Aberystwyth
Panoramic views of Aberystwyth, Cardigan Bay and the Rheidol Valley.

ABERYSTWYTH

Glan-Y-Mor Leisure Park, Clarach Bay, Nr. Aberystwyth, Ceredigion, SY23 3DT.
Std: 01970 **Tel:** 828900 **Fax:** 828890
Email: holidays-in-wales@sunbourne.co.uk
Website: www.sunbourne.co.uk

Nearest Town/Resort Aberystwyth
Directions Turn off the A487 following sign for Clarach 1 mile north of Aberystwyth a at Bow Street. Park entrance is on the sea front.
Acreage 20 **Open** March **to** October
Access Good **Site** Lev/Slope
Sites Available 👤 ♫ ⚏ **Total** 160
Facilities 🚿 🚿 ♨ ♐ ⊙ 🍴 ⛽ 🛒 ⛽ 🎱 ♨ ✕ ♫ 🛒 ♠ ♫ ⚡ ✳ 📶 ⚏ ⚏
Nearby Facilities ✝ 🏊 ⛵ ⛷ U ♬ ≯ ≯
⚏ Aberystwyth
Sea front location with many facilities. High quality indoor leisure centre, ten-pin bowling and childrens activities. Pets are welcom but only at certain times. Daffodil Award.

ABERYSTWYTH

Morfa Bychan Holiday Park, Aberystwyth, Ceredigion, SY23 4QQ.
Std: 01970 **Tel:** 617254 **Fax:** 624249
Email: morfa@hillandale.co.uk
Website: www.hillandale.co.uk
Nearest Town/Resort Aberystwyth
Directions Take the A487 south fror Aberystwyth, after ½ mile signposted to th right, but this is NOT suitable for tourin caravans who should continue for 2½ mile and turn right at the second sign. Follov signs for 1½ miles.
Acreage 5 **Open** March **to** October
Access Good **Site** Sloping
Sites Available 👤 ♫ ⚏ **Total** 50
Facilities ♨ 🚿 ♨ ⊙ 🍴 🛒 ⚏ ♐ ⊙ 🍴 🛒 ⚡ ✳ 📶 ⚏ ⚏
Nearby Facilities ✝ 🏊 ⛵ ⛷ U ♬
⚏ Aberystwyth
100 acre park overlooking Cardigan Ba with our own private beach. Heate swimming pool, water hook-ups.

BERYSTWYTH

ean View, North Beach, Clarach Bay,
erystwyth, Ceredigion, SY23 3DT.
d: 01970 **Tel:** 828425
ail: alan@grover10.freeserve.co.uk
ebsite: www.oceanviewholidays.com
arest Town/Resort Aberystwyth
ections Take the A487 Aberystwyth to
chynlleth road. Turn into Bow Street for
arach Bay. Follow road to the beach.
ean View is on the right.
en March **to** October
cess Good **Site** Level
es Available ▲ ⊕ ⊜ **Total** 24
cilities ∱ ⊡ ⅏ ⅏ ♨ ┌ ⊙ ⊿ ⊿ ⊡ ☎
⊡ ⊜ ⋀┱⊡ ⊡
arby Facilities ┌ ⧸ ⚓ ⚲ ∪ ♪ ⤸
Aberystwyth
nall select park, short walk to popular
ach. Glorious views, ideal touring area of
agic Mid-Wales.

ORTH

mbrian Coast Holiday Park, Borth,
redigion, SY24 5JU.
d: 01970 **Tel:** 871233 **Fax:** 871124
nail: holidays-in-
les@sunbourne.co.uk
ebsite: www.sunbourne.co.uk
arest Town/Resort Borth
ections Adjoining the sea front. Turn off
A487 Machynlleth to Aberystwyth road
to the B4353 Borth road. Entrance to the
e is 1¼ miles north of Borth Village.
en March **to** October
cess Good **Site** Level
es Available ▲ ⊕ ⊜
cilities ⧖ ∱ ⊡ ⅏ ⚡ ┌ ⊙ ⊿ ⊿ ⊡ ☎
⊡ ⊜ ⤫ ⚲ ⟊ ♠ ⚶ ♥ ⊛ ⋀┱⊡ ⊡
arby Facilities ┌ ⧸ ⚓ ⚲ ∪ ♪ ⤸

⚓ Borth
Near the beach and adjacent to a golf course
and a nature reserve. Ideal touring base.
Pets are welcome but only at certain times.
Daffodil Award and David Bellamy Award
for Conservation.

BORTH

Glanlerry Caravan Park, Borth,
Ceredigion, SY24 5LU.
Std: 01970 **Tel:** 871413
Email: cath.richards.gcp@talk21.com
Nearest Town/Resort Borth
Open April **to** October
Access Good **Site** Level
Sites Available ▲ ⊕ ⊜
Facilities ⚡ ∱ ⅏ ♨ ┌ ⊙ ⊿ ⊿
⊡ ⅊ ⊙ ⊜ ⋀┱⊡ ⊡
Nearby Facilities ┌ ⧸ ⚓ ∪ ♪
⚓ Borth
Sheltered touring area, alongside a river
bank with spectacular scenery. Beach ½
mile.

BORTH

**The Mill House Caravan & Camping
Park,** Dolybont, Borth, Ceredigion, West
Wales, SY24 5LX.
Std: 01970 **Tel:** 871481
Website: www.ukparks.co.uk/millhousecp
Nearest Town/Resort Borth
Directions On Aberystwyth/Machynlleth
road A487, turn west at Rhydypennau
Garage corner (between Talybont and Bow
Street) onto B4353 through Llandre.
Proceed 1 mile, on Borth B4353 stop under
railway bridge by the white railings, fork right
into Dolybont Village singposted. First right
before hump-back bridge in Village.
Acreage 10 **Open** Easter **to** October
Access Good **Site** Level

Sites Available ▲ ⊕ ⊜ **Total** 40
Facilities ⚡ ∱ ⅏ ♨ ┌ ⊙ ⊿ ☎ ⊙ ⋀┱⊡
Nearby Facilities ┌ ⧸ ⚓ ⚲ ∪ ♪ ⤸
⚓ Borth
Delightful site beside a stream for fishing. 1
mile Borth seaside, safe bathing, rock pools
and sand hills. Please send SAE for
brochure.

BORTH

Ty Mawr Holiday Home & Touring Park,
Ynyslas, Borth, Ceredigion, SY24 5LB.
Std: 01970 **Tel:** 871327
Nearest Town/Resort Aberystwyth/Borth
Directions Take the A487 from Machynlleth
or Aberystwyth, turn onto the B4353 at Tre'r-
Ddol signposted Borth and Ynyslas. After 2
miles Ty Mawr is on the left.
Acreage 4 **Open** March **to** September
Access Good **Site** Level
Sites Available ▲ ⊕ ⊜ **Total** 20
Facilities ∱ ⅏ ♨ ┌ ⊙ ⊿ ⊿ ☎
⅊ ⊙ ⊜ ⋀┱⊡ ⊡
Nearby Facilities ┌ ⧸ ⚓ ⚲ ∪ ♪ ⤸
⚓ Borth
Fabulous views. NO club, just peace and
quiet. Close to a nature reserve and the
beach for safe bathing. David Bellamy
Award for Conservation.

CARDIGAN

Allt-y-Coed, St. Dogmaels, Cardigan,
Ceredigion, SA43 3LP.
Std: 01239 **Tel:** 612673
Nearest Town/Resort Cardigan
Directions Cardigan/St. Dogmaels/Poppit
Sands coast road from Poppit Sands, past
Youth Hostel for 1 mile. Over the cattle grid
and follow coastal footpath signs.
Ordanance Survey Grid Ref : (Sheet 145)
135 495.

Acreage 2 **Open** All Year
Access Good **Site** Level
Sites Available ▲ ⊕ ⊟
Facilities ⑩ ♣ ┌ ⊬
Nearby Facilities ┌ ✔ ⏚ ⊀ ∪ ♗ ♬
⊁ Fishguard
Pembrokeshire coast path goes past the site. Dolphins, seals, falcons, rare birds, wild flowers and panoramic views. Long and short term parking for walks along the coastal path. Ample parking. You can also contact us on Mobile Telephone 07970 221548.

CARDIGAN

Brongwyn Mawr Caravan Park,
Brongwyn Mawr, Penparc, Cardigan, Ceredigion, SA43 1SA.
Std: 01239 **Tel:** 613644 **Fax:** 615725
Email: enquiries@cardiganholidays.co.uk
Website: www.cardiganholidays.co.uk
Nearest Town/Resort Cardigan
Directions 2½ miles north of Cardigan on the A487, turn left at the crossroads in Penparc signed Mwnt and Ferwig. Go straight across the next crossroads and the park is the next lane on the right.
Acreage 2 **Open** March to October
Access Good **Site** Level
Sites Available ▲ ⊕ ⊟ **Total** 20
Facilities ∮ ⊞ ⑩ ♣ ┌ ⊙ ⊣ ⊒ ⊡ ☞
⚑ ⚍ ⚒ ✕ ♨ ⏚ ⊀ ⊬ ⊡ ⊟
Nearby Facilities ┌ ✔ ⏚ ⊀ ∪ ♬
⊁ Aberystwyth/Carmarthen
Secluded park in the countryside. Ideal location to explore, discover and enjoy. Only 2½ miles from a beautiful beach where you can sometimes see the Dolphins.

CARDIGAN

Patch Caravan Park, Gwbert-on-Sea, Cardigan, Ceredigion, SA23 1PP.
Std: 01239 **Tel:** 613241 **Fax:** 615391
Nearest Town/Resort Cardigan
Directions 2 miles from Cardigan on the Gwbert road.
Open Easter to October
Access Good **Site** Level
Sites Available ▲ ⊕ ⊟ **Total** 12
Facilities ⚒ ∮ ⑩ ┌ ⊙ ⊣ ⊒ ⊡ ☞
⚍ ⊬ ⊡ ⊟
Nearby Facilities ┌ ✔ ⏚ ⊀ ∪ ♬
⊁ Carmarthen
In sand dunes right on the sea shore. Superb for sailing.

CARDIGAN

Penralltllyn Caravan Park, Cilgerran, Cardigan, Ceredigion, SA43 2PR.
Std: 01239 **Tel:** 682350
Nearest Town/Resort Cardigan
Directions A484 Cardigan to Carmarthen, Llechryd Bridge (sign on bridge), cross bridge and follow for 1½ miles (no turning off). Large sign on the top of farm lane - camp site.
Acreage ½ **Open** Easter to October
Access Good **Site** Level
Sites Available ▲ ⊕ ⊟ **Total** 20
Facilities ∮ ⑩ ♣ ┌ ⊙ ⚑ ⊬
Nearby Facilities ┌ ✔ ⏚ ⊀ ∪
⊁ CarmarthenHaverfordwest

Quiet site with a pond for canoeing. Farm animals. Plenty of walks, old railway line (closed). Preseli Mountains, various beaches.

DEVILS BRIDGE

Erwbarfe Caravan Park, Devils Bridge, Aberystwyth, Ceredigion, SY23 3JR.
Std: 01970 **Tel:** 890665
Nearest Town/Resort Aberystwyth
Directions Turn off the A44 at Ponterwyd onto the A4120 fro Devils Bridge.
Acreage 5 **Open** March to October
Access Good **Site** Level
Sites Available ▲ ⊕ ⊟ **Total** 20
Facilities ∮ ⊞ ⊞ ⑩ ♣ ┌ ⊙ ⊣ ⊒ ☞
⚑ ⚍ ♨ ✕ ♨ ⊬ ⊡ ⊟
Nearby Facilities ┌ ✔ ∪
Ideal centre for walking.

DEVILS BRIDGE

The Woodlands Caravan Park, Devils Bridge, Aberystwyth, Ceredigion, SY23 3JW.
Std: 01970 **Tel:** 890233 **Fax:** 890233
Email: woodlandscp@btclick.com
Nearest Town/Resort Devils Bridge
Directions 12 miles East of Aberystwyth on A4120 in Devils Bridge village and 300yds from bridge. Or 3 miles south west of Ponterwyd, turn off A44 at Ponterwyd.
Acreage 8 **Open** Easter to October
Access Good **Site** Level
Sites Available ▲ ⊕ ⊟ **Total** 60
Facilities ⚒ ∮ ⑩ ♣ ┌ ⊙ ⊡ ☞
⚑ ⚍ ♨ ♨ ✕ ♨ ⊬ ⊡ ⊟
Nearby Facilities ┌ ✔ ∪
⊁ Devils Bridge
Quiet country site adjoining farm. Ideal for walking, bird watching touring, fishing.

LAMPETER

Hafod Brynog Caravan Park, Ystrad Aeron, Felinfach, Lampeter, Ceredigion, SA48 8AE.
Std: 01570 **Tel:** 470084
Email: amies@hafodbrynog.fsnet.co.uk
Nearest Town/Resort Aberearon
Directions On the main A482 Lampeter to Aberaeron road, 6 miles from both. Site entrance is opposite the church and next to the pub in the village of Ystrad Aeron.
Acreage 8 **Open** Easter to End Sept
Access Good **Site** Lev/Slope
Sites Available ▲ ⊕ ⊟ **Total** 30
Facilities ⚒ ∮ ⊞ ┌ ⊙ ⊣ ⚑ ⚍ ⊡ ☞ ⊬ ⊡
Nearby Facilities ┌ ✔ ⏚ ⊀ ∪ ♗ ♬
⊁ Aberystwyth
A quiet site with beautiful views. 6 miles from Cardigan Bay. Ideal for coastal and inland touring, or just relaxing.

LAMPETER

Moorlands Caravan Park, Llangyby, Nr Lampeter, Ceredigion, SA48 8NN.
Std: 01570 **Tel:** 493543
Email: moorlands@euphony
Website: www.moorlands-caravan-park.co.uk
Nearest Town/Resort Lampeter
Directions 4½ miles approx. on the A485 Lampeter to Tregaron road.

Acreage 2 **Open** Easter to October
Access Good **Site** Level
Sites Available ▲ ⊕ ⊟ **Total** 10
Facilities ∮ ⊞ ⊞ ♣ ┌ ⊙ ⊣ ⊒ ⊡
⚍ ⊙ ⚒ ♡ ⊞ ♨ ⊀ ⊬
Nearby Facilities ┌ ✔ ∪
⊁ Aberystwyth
Ideal touring centre, 12 miles from Cardigan Bay.

LLANARTH

Llain Activity Centre, Llanarth, Ceredigion, SA47 0PZ.
Std: 01545 **Tel:** 580127 **Fax:** 580697
Email:
llain@westwales98.freeserve.co.uk
Website: www.llain.co.uk
Nearest Town/Resort New Quay
Directions Take the A487 south from Aberaeron towards Cardigan. After village of Llwyncelyn take a right hand turn to Cei Bach.
Acreage 1 **Open** March to October
Sites Available ▲ ⊕ ⊟ **Total** 10
Facilities ⑩ ♣ ┌ ⊣ ⊡ ⚒ ♨ ⊀ ❋
Nearby Facilities ✔ ⏚ ⊀ ∪ ♨
⊁ Aberystwyth
On site outdoor activities with qualified staff (May to September).

LLANDYSUL

Camping & Caravanning Club Site, Llwynhelyg, Cross Inn, Llandysul, Ceredigion, SA44 6LW.
Std: 01545 **Tel:** 560029
Website:
www.campingandcaravanningclub.co.uk
Directions From the A487 Cardigan Aberystwyth road, at Synod Inn turn left onto the A486 signposted New Quay. After miles in the village of Cross Inn turn left after the Penrhiwgated Arms Pub, site is on the right after approx. ¾ miles.
Acreage 14 **Open** March to Sept
Site Lev/Slope
Sites Available ▲ ⊕ ⊟ **Total** 100
Facilities ⚒ ∮ ⊞ ⑩ ♣ ┌ ⊙ ⊣ ⊒ ⊡
⚑ ⚍ ⊙ ♨ ❋ ⊬ ⊡ ⊟
Nearby Facilities ✔ ∪ ♬
⊁ Aberystwyth
Near to golden beaches, forests and lakes. 3 miles from horse racing and close to many attractions. BTB Graded. Non members welcome.

LLANON

Woodlands Caravan Park, Llanon, Nr. Aberystwyth, Ceredigion, SY23 5LX.
Std: 01974 **Tel:** 202342
Email: ianlampert@talk21.com
Nearest Town/Resort Aberaeron
Directions 5 miles north of Aberaeron the A487, turn left at the sign.
Acreage 4 **Open** April to October
Access Good **Site** Level
Sites Available ▲ ⊕ ⊟ **Total** 40
Facilities ∮ ⑩ ♣ ┌ ⊙ ⊣ ⊡ ⊙ ⚒ ⊙ ⚑ ⊬ ⊡
Nearby Facilities ┌ ✔ ⊀ ∪ ♬
⊁ Aberystwyth
Tree screened site with a small river. 200 yards from the beach, 300 yards from the main road.

LANRHYSTUD

ngarreg Caravan Park, Llanrhystud,
eredigion, SY23 5DJ.
d: 01974 **Tel:** 202247
ebsite: www.utowcaravans.co.uk
earest Town/Resort Aberystwyth/
beraeron
rections On the A487 in the village of
anrhystud opposite Shell Garage.
creage 7 **Open March to** 2 January
ccess Good **Site** Level
tes Available ⚠ ⊞ ⊟ **Total** 100
acilities ⨍ ⊞ ⊡ ⌐ ⊙ ⊐ ◻ ☕
⌀ ⌂ ⬟ ⊠ ✕ ▽ ⊡ ☂ ⬠ ⌐⊞
earby Facilities ⌐ ⟋ ⚓ ⤳ ∪ ↲
⇺ Aberystwyth
vo touring fields, one on the sea front. A
er runs through the camp for fishing,
ating ramp. 196 acres of scenic hills and
rmland for walking. New toilet block with
sabled toilet.

EW QUAY

ei Bach Country Club, Parc-Y-Brwcs,
ei Bach, Newquay, Ceredigion, SA45
5L.
d: 01545 **Tel:** 580237 **Fax:** 580237
mail: paul@ceibach.freeserve.co.uk
earest Town/Resort New Quay
rections From the A487 take the B4342
r New Quay. Follow the road to Quay-West
d Cambrian Hotel crossroads, take the
ad signed for Cei Bach.
creage 3 **Open** Easter **to** End Sept
ccess Poor **Site** Lev/Slope
tes Available ⚠ ⊞ ⊟ **Total** 60
acilities ⨍ ⊞ ⊡ ⌐ ⊙ ⊐ ◻ ☕
⌀ ⬟ ⊠ ✕ ▽ ⊡ ⬠ ⤳ ⊞⊞⊞
earby Facilities ⌐ ⟋ ⚓ ⤳ ∪ ↲ ♟ ✠
⇺ Aberystwyth
reat views of the coast line, safe sandy
each. Coastal walk to Aberaeron.

EW QUAY

ondeg Caravan Park, Gilfachreda, Nr.
ew Quay, Ceredigion, SA45 9SP.
d: 01545 **Tel:** Llanarth 580491
mail: amies@hafodbrynog.fsnet.co.uk
earest Town/Resort New Quay
rections Take A487 from Aberystwyth to
anarth, then take the B4342 to New Quay
r approx. 1 mile to Gilfachreda Village.
creage 1 **Open** Easter **to** October
ccess Good **Site** Level
tes Available ⊞ ⊟ **Total** 10
acilities ⨍ ⨍ ⊞ ⌐ ⊙ ⊐ ◻ ☕
⌀ ⬟ ⊞⊞
earby Facilities ⌐ ⟋ ⚓ ⤳ ∪ ↲ ♟
⇺ Aberystwyth
uiet, secluded site near a small river
ading to safe, sandy bathing beaches, 10
inutes walk. New Quay harbour town, 2
iles by road.

EW QUAY

ern Mill Camping Site, Gilfachrheda,
ew Quay, Ceredigion, SA45 9SP.
d: 01545 **Tel:** 580699
earest Town/Resort New Quay
rections From Aberystwyth take the A487
a Aberaeron to Llanarth. Gilfachrheda is
cated 1½ miles from Llanarth on the B4342
New Quay road.
creage 2½ **Open** Easter **to** October
ccess Good **Site** Level
tes Available ⚠ ⊞ ⊟ **Total** 50
acilities ⨍ ⊞ ⌐ ⊙ ⊐ ☕
⌀ ⬟ ⤳⊞⊞
earby Facilities ⌐ ⟋ ⚓ ⤳ ∪ ↲ ♟
⇺ Aberystwyth
ery sheltered, family site. ½ mile from two
ndy beaches. Idyllic walks. Ideal centre
r touring Mid Wales.

NEWCASTLE EMLYN

Cenarth Falls Holiday Park, Cenarth,
Newcastle Emlyn, Ceredigion, SA38 9JS.
Std: 01239 **Tel:** 710345 **Fax:** 710344
Email: enquiries@cenarth-holipark.co.uk
Website: www.cenarth-holipark.co.uk
Nearest Town/Resort Newcastle Emlyn
Directions 3 miles west of Newcastle Emlyn
on the A484. Cross Cenarth Bridge and
travel for ¼ mile, turn right at directional
signs for the park.
Acreage 2 **Open** March **to** 9 January
Access Good **Site** Level
Sites Available ⚠ ⊞ ⊟ **Total** 30
Facilities ⬙ ⨍ ⊞ ⊡ ⌐ ⊙ ⊐ ◻ ☕
⌀ ⬟ ⊠ ✕ ▽ ⊡ ☂ ⬠ ⤳ ⊞⊞ ⊡ ⬢
Nearby Facilities ⌐ ⟋ ⚓ ⤳ ∪ ↲
⇺ Carmarthen
Ideal touring location for the coast and
countryside. Near Coastal National Park.
Awarded AA Campsite of the Year for Wales
1997, Daffodil Award, Calor Gas Best Park
in Britain Award 1999 and David Bellamy
Gold Award for Conservation 2000.

PLWMP

Greenfields Caravan Park, Pentregat,
Plwmp, Llandysul, Ceredigion, SA44 6HF.
Std: 01239 **Tel:** 654333 **Fax:** 654333
Nearest Town/Resort Aberaeron
Directions Just off the A487 10 miles south
of Aberaeron and 12 miles north of
Cardigan.
Open 1 March **to** 1 September
Access Good **Site** Sloping
Sites Available ⚠ ⊞ ⊟ **Total** 70
Facilities ⬙ ⨍ ⊞ ⊡ ⌐ ⊙ ⊐ ◻ ☕
⌀ ⊠ ✕ ▽ ⬟ ⊡ ⤳ ⊛ ⤳⊞⊟
Nearby Facilities ⌐ ⟋ ⚓ ⤳ ∪ ↲
⇺ Aberystwyth
Rural site within easy reach of several good
beaches. Ideal touring.

SARNAU

Brynawelon Touring & Camping Park,
Sarnau, Llandysul, Ceredigion, SA44
6RE.
Std: 01239 **Tel:** 654584
Nearest Town/Resort Cardigan
Directions Travelling north on A487 take a
right turn at Sarnau crossroads, site is
550yds on the left.
Acreage 2 **Open** April **to** September
Access Good **Site** Level
Sites Available ⚠ ⊞ ⊟ **Total** 30
Facilities ⨍ ⨍ ⊞ ⊡ ⌐ ⊙ ⊐ ☕
⌀ ⬟ ⬠ ⤳⊞
Nearby Facilities ⟋ ⤳ ∪
⇺ Carmarthen
Quiet family site with rural surroundings. 2
miles to Penbryn Beach.

SARNAU

Dyffryn Bern Caravan Park, Penbryn,
Sarnau, Llandysul, Ceredigion, SA44
6RD.
Std: 01239 **Tel:** 810900
Email: enquiries@dyffryn.com
Website: www.dyffryn.com
Nearest Town/Resort New Quay/
Cardigan
Directions Off the A487.
Acreage 14 **Open** March **to** December
Access Good **Site** Sloping
Sites Available ⚠ ⊟ **Total** 50
Facilities ⨍ ⊞ ⌐ ⊙ ⊡ ◻ ▽ ⬠ ⤳⊟
Nearby Facilities ⌐ ⟋ ⚓ ⤳ ∪ ↲ ♟ ✠
⇺ Aberystwyth/Carmarthen
Near the beach with splendid sea views.
Fishing lake.

SARNAU

Manorafon Caravan Park, Sarnau,
Llandysul, Ceredigion, SA44 6QH.
Std: 01239 **Tel:** 810564 **Fax:** 810564
Email: manorafon@ukgateway.net
Nearest Town/Resort Cardigan
Directions Take the A487 north from
Cardigan for 7 miles to Tanyagroes, go
through the village, second road on the left
signed Penbryn/Tresaith. After ½ mile take
the first right, after ¾ mile turn second left,
we are 200 yards on the right.
Acreage 1½ **Open** Easter **to** October
Access Average **Site** Sloping
Sites Available ⚠ ⊞ ⊟ **Total** 15
Facilities ⨍ ⊞ ⌐ ⊙ ☕ ⊡ ⬟ ⊠ ⊡ ⬢
Nearby Facilities ⌐ ⟋ ⚓ ⤳ ∪ ↲
⇺ Aberystwyth
Set in a wooded valley, good for families. ¾
mile from Penbryn beach. Ideal camping and
touring for birdwatchers, golfers and
walkers.

SARNAU

Talywerydd Touring Caravan Park,
Penbryn Sands, Sarnau, Ceredigion,
SA44 6QY.
Std: 01239 **Tel:** 810322
Website: www.caravan-sitefinder.co.uk
Nearest Town/Resort Cardigan
Directions From Cardigan take the second
Penbryn turn off the A487. From
Aberystwyth take the second Penbryn turn
off the A487. Talywerydd is 500yds on the
left.
Acreage 4 **Open** March **to** End October
Access Good **Site** Level
Sites Available ⚠ ⊞ ⊟ **Total** 40
Facilities ⨍ ⊞ ⊞ ⊡ ⌐ ⊙ ⊐ ◻ ☕
⌀ ⬟ ⊠ ✕ ▽ ⊡ ☂ ⬠ ⤳⊞⊟
Nearby Facilities ⌐ ⟋ ⚓ ∪
⇺ Aberystwyth
Family site with scenic views over Cardigan
Bay. 2 miles from Penbryn Beach. Covered
heated swimming pool.

SARNAU

Treddafydd Farm, Treddafydd, Sarnau,
Llandysul, Ceredigion, SA44 6PZ.
Std: 01239 **Tel:** 654551
Nearest Town/Resort Cardigan
Directions On the A487 in the village of
Sarnau turn by the church then first left.
Acreage 2 **Open** Easter **to** October
Access Good **Site** Lev/Slope
Sites Available Total 15
Facilities ⨍ ⊞ ⌐ ⊙ ⊐ ◻ ◻ ⬢
Nearby Facilities ⌐ ⟋ ⚓ ∪
⇺ Aberystwyth
1 mile from sandy Penbryn beach.

TREGARON

Aeron View Caravan Park, Blaenpennal,
Aberystwyth, Ceredigion, SY23 4TW.
Std: 01974 **Tel:** 251488
Email: aeronview@hotmail.com
Website: www.aeronview.com
Nearest Town/Resort Aberystwyth
Directions Leave Aberystwyth on the A487,
after approx. 2 miles turn left onto the A485
to Tregaron. After 12 miles turn right onto
the B4577 to Blaenpennal.
Acreage 2 **Open** March **to** October
Access Good **Site** Level
Sites Available ⚠ ⊞ ⊟ **Total** 6
Facilities ⨍ ⊞ ⊞ ⊡ ⌐ ⊙ ⊐ ◻ ☕
⌀ ⬟ ⤳⊞
Nearby Facilities ⟋
⇺ Aberystwyth
Quiet, inland site set in the picturesque
Aeron Valley which is famous for the Red
Kite. Prime fishing area. Ideal touring.

CARMARTHENSHIRE

CARMARTHEN

Coedhirion Farm Parc, Coedhirion, Llanddarog, Carmarthen, Carmarthenshire, SA32 8BH.
Std: 01267 **Tel:** 275666
Nearest Town/Resort Carmarthen
Directions 9 miles west of the M4 junction 49, just off the A48 dual carriageway, 6 miles east of Carmarthen.
Acreage 5 **Open** Easter **to** Christmas
Access Good **Site** Level
Sites Available Å ♥ ⊖ **Total** 20
Facilities ∮ ⊞ ⅏ ⅍ ♪ ⊙ ☻
⌖ ┃ ⊘ ⊛ ┿ ⊡ ⊟
Nearby Facilities ┌ ✓ ⚓
≉ Carmarthen
Quiet, convenient, woodland site. 5 minutes from the National Botanical Garden of Wales.

CLYNDERWEN

Derwenlas, Clynderwen, Carmarthenshire, SA66 7SU.
Std: 01437 **Tel:** 563504
Nearest Town/Resort Narberth
Directions 3 to 3½ miles north of Narberth on the A478.
Open April **to** September
Access Good **Site** Level
Sites Available Å ♥ ⊖ **Total** 8
Facilities ∮ ⅏ ⅍ ♪ ⊙ ⊶ ⊡ ☻
⌖ ┃ ⊘ ⊛ ┿ ⊡
Nearby Facilities ┌ ✓ ⚓ ⅃ ∪
≉ Clynderwen

KIDWELLY

Carmarthen Bay Touring & Camping, Tanylan Farm, Kidwelly, Carmarthenshire, SA17 5HJ.
Std: 01267 **Tel:** 267306
Email: tanylanfarm@aol.com
Website: www.tanylanfarmholidays.co.uk
Nearest Town/Resort Kidwelly
Directions In Kidwelly turn left at the Spar Supermarket, take the coastal road to Ferryside for approx. 1 mile and turn left at the duck pond.
Acreage 4 **Open** Easter **to** End Sept
Access Good **Site** Level
Sites Available Å ♥ ⊖ **Total** 50
Facilities ♿ ∮ ⅏ ⅍ ♪ ⊙ ⊶ ☻
⌖ ⅏ ⊘ ⊛ ⊞ ⊡ ⅍
Nearby Facilities ┌ ✓ ∪ ♪
≉ Kidwelly
Level ground on this working dairy farm. 200 yards from the beach. Membership to Haven Holidays available.

LAUGHARNE

Ants Hill Caravan Park, Laugharne, Carmarthenshire, SA33 4QN.
Std: 01994 **Tel:** 427293 **Fax:** 427293
Email:
antshillcaravanpark@tinyworld.co.uk
Nearest Town/Resort Carmarthen
Directions From the M4 to Carmarthen, follow the A40 towards St Clears. Turn off onto the A4066 for Laugharne and Pendine, site is the first turning left before the signpost for Laugharne.
Acreage 6½ **Open** Easter **to** October
Access Good **Site** Level
Sites Available Å ♥ ⊖ **Total** 60
Facilities ∮ ⅏ ⅍ ♪ ⊙ ⊶ ⊡ ☻
⌖ ⌖ ┃ ⊘ ⊛ ✕ ▽ ⅏ ⅍ ⎟ ┿ ⊡ ⊟
Nearby Facilities ┌ ✓ ∪
≉ Carmarthen
Ideal for inland and coastal touring. Historic township with its Circa 12th Castle and Dylan Thomas' Boat House. Near the famous sands of Pendine.

LLANDDEUSANT

Blaenau Farm, Llanddeusant, Llangadog, Carmarthenshire, SA19 9UN.
Std: 01550 **Tel:** 740277
Nearest Town/Resort Llandovery
Directions Approx. 20 miles from the M4.
Open Easter **to** October
Access Poor
Sites Available Å ♥ ⊖
Facilities ⅏ ☻
Nearby Facilities ✓ ⚓
≉ Llangadog
Extensive mountain farm site.

LLANDDEUSANT

The Black Mountain Caravan & Camping Park, Llanddeusant, Llangadog, Carmarthenshire, SA19 9YG.
Std: 01550 **Tel:** 740621/740217 **Fax:** 740621/740217
Email:
blackmountain@mapsweet.force9.co.uk
Website: www.breconbeacons-holidays.com
Nearest Town/Resort Llandovery
Directions Take the A40 to Llangadog then the A4069 signposted Brynaman. Turn left at a disused pub (Three Horseshoes) and continue for 3½ miles to Cross Inn.
Acreage 6½ **Open** All Year
Access Good **Site** Lev/Slope
Sites Available Å ♥ ⊖ **Total** 50
Facilities ∮ ⊞ ⅏ ⅍ ♪ ⊙ ⊶ ⊡ ☻
⌖ ⊘ ┿ ⊡ ⊟
Nearby Facilities ┌ ✓ ∪
≉ Llandovery
Ideal for walking, fishing and caving.

LLANDOVERY

Erwlon Caravan & Camping Park, Erwlon, Llandovery, Carmarthenshire, SA20 0RD.
Std: 01550 **Tel:** 720332
Email: peter@erwlon.fsnet.co.uk
Nearest Town/Resort Llandovery
Directions ½ mile east of Llandovery on the A40 towards Brecon.
Acreage 5 **Open** April **to** October
Access Good **Site** Level
Sites Available Å ♥ ⊖ **Total** 40
Facilities ♿ ∮ ⊞ ⅏ ⅍ ♪ ⊙ ⊶ ⊡ ☻
⌖ ┃ ⊘ ⊛ ⅏ ┿ ⊡
Nearby Facilities ✓ ∪ ♪
≉ Llandovery
Alongside a river. Convenient for Brecon Beacons, South Wales valleys and coastline. Ideally located for touring South Wales.

LLANDOVERY

Galltyberau, Rhandirmwyn, Llandovery, Carmarthenshire, SA20 0PH.
Std: 01550 **Tel:** 760218
Nearest Town/Resort Llandovery
Directions From Llandovery take the Rhandirmwyn road for 7 miles, after the village turn second left by the concrete bridge.
Acreage 3 **Open** March **to** October
Access Good **Site** Level
Sites Available Å ♥ ⊖ **Total** 20
Facilities ☻
Nearby Facilities ✓
≉ Llandovery
Riverside site in beautiful countryside with special scientific value. Bird reserve nearby.

LLANGADOG

Abermarlais Caravan Park, Nr Llangadog, Carmarthenshire, SA19 9NG.
Std: 01550 **Tel:** 777868
Website: www.ukparks.co.uk/abermarlais
Nearest Town/Resort Llandovery
Directions 6 miles west of Llandovery a 6 miles east of Llandeilo on the A40.
Acreage 16 **Open** 15 March **to** 1 Nov
Access Good **Site** Lev/Slope
Sites Available Å ♥ ⊖ **Total** 88
Facilities ∮ ⊞ ⅏ ⅍ ♪ ⊙ ⊶ ☻
⌖ ┃ ⊘ ⊛ ┿ ⊡ ⊟
Nearby Facilities ✓ ∪ ⅋
≉ Llangadog
Alongside river with scenic views.

LLANWRDA

Maesbach Caravan Park, Ffarmers, Llanwrda, Carmarthenshire, SA19 8EX.
Std: 01558 **Tel:** 650650
Email: hugh.t.thomas@talk21.com
Website:
www.maesbachcaravanpark.com
Nearest Town/Resort Lampeter
Directions Turn off the A40 (Llandello Llandovery road) onto the A482 to Lampet Turn right to Ffarmers, north of Pumpsa turn right at Drovers Inn in Ffarmers.
Acreage 4½ **Open** March **to** October
Access Good **Site** Lev/Slope
Sites Available Å ♥ ⊖ **Total** 20
Facilities ∮ ⊞ ⅏ ⅍ ♪ ⊙ ⊶ ☻
⌖ ⊘ ┿ ⊡ ⊟
Nearby Facilities ┌ ✓ ∪
≉ Llanwrda
Local walking and bird life.

NEWCASTLE EMLYN

Afon Teifi Caravan & Camping Park, Pentrecagal, Newcastle Emlyn, Carmarthenshire, SA38 9HT.
Std: 01559 **Tel:** 370532
Nearest Town/Resort Newcastle Emlyn
Directions On the A484 2 miles east Newcastle Emlyn.
Acreage 6½ **Open** All Year
Access Good **Site** Level
Sites Available Å ♥ ⊖ **Total** 110
Facilities ♿ ∮ ⊞ ⅏ ⅍ ♪ ⊙ ⊶ ⊡ ⊟
⌖ ┃ ⊘ ⊛ ⅏ ⊛ ┿ ⊡
Nearby Facilities ┌ ✓ ⅋
≉ Carmarthen
Situated by the River Teifi in the beaut Teifi Valley. Only 20 minutes from numero Cardigan Bay beaches. Ideal touring cent

NEWCASTLE EMLYN

Dolbryn Farm, Capel Iwan Road, Newcastle Emlyn, Carmarthenshire, SA 9LP.
Std: 01239 **Tel:** 710683
Nearest Town/Resort Newcastle Emlyn
Directions Turn left off the A4 Carmarthen to Cardigan road at Newcas Emlyn signposted leisure centre swimming pool. Follow camping signs 1½ miles.
Acreage 4 **Open** Easter **to** October
Access Good **Site** Lev/Slope
Sites Available Å ♥ ⊖ **Total** 40
Facilities ♿ ∮ ⊞ ⅍ ♪ ⊙ ⊶ ▽ ⊛ ┿ ⊡
Nearby Facilities ┌ ✓ ∪
≉ Carmarthen
Idyllic country site with stream, lakes, hi etc..

NEWCASTLE EMLYN

Moelfryn Caravan & Camp Park, Pant-Bwlch, Newcastle Emlyn, Carmarthenshire, SA38 9JE.
Std: 01559 **Tel:** 371231 **Fax:** 371231
Email: moelfryn@tinyonline.co.uk
Nearest Town/Resort Newcastle Emlyn
Directions From Newcastle Emlyn take t B4333, pass the BP Garage and contin for 3 miles, at the telephone kiosk on yo right turn right, site is approx. 500 yards.
Acreage 3 **Open** 1 March **to** 10 Jan

...creage 3 **Open** 1 March **to** 10 Jan
...ccess Good **Site** Level
...ites Available ▲ ⊕ ⊞ **Total** 25
...acilities ∮ ⬚ ♨ ⌐ ⊙ 🟉 🏠 🖃 🅿
...earby Facilities ⌐ ✔ ↘ ∪
🚌 Carmarthen
...ituated in a tranquil, rural setting with
...anoramic views for relaxation. Perfect base
...r exploring the beauty of West Wales.

...UMPSAINT

...enlanwen, Pumpsaint, Llanwrda,
...armarthenshire, SA19 8RR.
...td: 01558 **Tel:** 650667
...earest Town/Resort Lampeter
...irections 7 miles northwest of Llandovery,
...ke A40, turn right onto A482 at Llanwrda, past
...ridgend Inn on left and look for site signs. From
...ampeter take A482 for 8 miles to Pumpsaint.
...creage 3 **Open** All Year
...ccess Good **Site** Level
...ites Available ▲ ⊕ ⊞ **Total** 20
...acilities ⬚ ♨
...earby Facilities ∪
🚌 Llandovery
...cenic views, guided tour of gold mines with
...afe and shop. Pony trekking, ideal for families.

...T. CLEARS

...fon Lodge Caravan Park, Parciau Bach,
...t. Clears, Carmarthenshire, SA33 4LG
...td: 01994 **Tel:** 230647
...mail: yvonne@afonlodge.f9.co.uk
...ebsite: www.fp.afonlodge.f9.co.uk
...earest Town/Resort St. Clears
...irections From St. Clears traffic lights take
...lanboidy Road. In a 100 yards fork right,
...en first right, first right.
...creage 5 **Open** March **to** 9 January
...ccess Good **Site** Lev/Slope
...ites Available ▲ ⊕ ⊞ **Total** 35
a c i l i t i e s ∮ 🔲 ⬚ ♨ ⌐ ⊙ ⌿ 🖃 🔲 ⛟
🟉 🏠 🔀 🏐 ♨🚻🖃
...earby Facilities ⌐ ✔ ⚓ ↘ ∪
🚌 Whitland
...eautiful tranquil site, ideal touring. T.V.
...ook-up.

...AVERNSPITE

...outh Carvan Caravan Park,
...avernspite, Whitland, Carmarthenshire,
...A34 0NL.
...td: 01834 **Tel:** 831451
...earest Town/Resort Whitland
...irections From St. Clears take A477 to
...enby at Red Roses turn right 1¾ miles
...own road into village of Tavernspite.
...creage 15 **Open** April **to** October
...ccess Good **Site** Level
...ites Available ▲ ⊕ ⊞ **Total** 65
...🚲🖃 ∮ ⬚ ♨ ⌐ ⊙🔲 🔀 ❄ 🔀 🏐 ♨ 🚻 🖃
...earby Facilities ✔ ∪
🚌 Whitland
...ide screen colour TV in the bar.

...HITLAND

...ld Vicarage Caravan Park, Red Roses,
...hitland, Carmarthenshire, SA34 0PG.
...td: 01834 **Tel:** 831637
...earest Town/Resort Saundersfoot/Tenby
...irections From Carmarthen take the A40
...en the A477 St. Clears to Tenby road on
...o Red Roses. Park is on the left opposite
...porting Chance Pub.
...creage 3 **Open** 1 March **to** 2 January
...ccess Good **Site** Level
...ites Available ▲ ⊕ ⊞ **Total** 40
a c i l i t i e s ⬚ ♨ ⊙ ⌿ 🖃 🔲 ⛟
🔲 🔀 ♨ 🏐 🔀 ♨🖃
...earby Facilities ⌐ ✔ ⚓ ↘ ∪
🚌 Whitland
½ miles from Pendine beach. Fishing
...cally. Ideal for touring South West Wales.

CONWY

ABERGELE

Henllys Farm Camping & Touring Site,
Towyn Road, Towyn, Abergele, Conwy,
LL22 9HF.
Std: 01745 **Tel:** 351208
Nearest Town/Resort Rhyl
Directions On A548 south side, near
Towyn.
Acreage 11 **Open** Whitsun **to** September
Access Good **Site** Level
Sites Available ▲ ⊕ ⊞ **Total** 280
Facilities ⊞ ∮ ⬚ ♨ ⌐ ⊙ ⌿ 🖃 🔲 ⛟
🔲 🏠 🔀 🏐 🖃 🅿
Nearby Facilities ⌐ ✔
🚌 Rhyl
½ mile from the beach.

ABERGELE

Millers Cottage Caravan Park, Gaingc
Road, Towyn, Abergele, Conwy, LL22
9HS.
Std: 01745 **Tel:** 832102 **Fax:** 833053
Email:
millerscaravans@netscapeonline.co.uk
Nearest Town/Resort Abergele/Rhyl
Directions From the A55 take the Towyn
turn-off and follow signs for Towyn. At Towyn
crossroads traffic lights go straight across
and turn left at the bottom of the road.
Open 21 March **to** 30 Oct
Access Good **Site** Level
Sites Available ⊕ **Total** 8
Facilities ⬚ ∮ 🔲 ⬚ ♨ ⌐ ⊙ ⌿ 🖃 🔲 ⛟
🔀 🔀 ♨ 🏐 🔀 ♨🖃
Nearby Facilities ⌐ ✔ ⚓ ↘ ∪ ⚲ 🏌 🔀
🚌 Abergele/Rhyl
Next to the beach and close to major
attractions of North Wales.

ABERGELE

Roberts Caravan Park, Waterloo Service
Station, Penrefail Cross Roads, Abergele,
Conwy, LL22 8PN.
Std: 01745 **Tel:** 833265
Nearest Town/Resort Abergele
Directions From Abergele take the A548
Llanrwst road for 2 miles, at the crossroads
of the B5381 turn left towards St. Asaph,
site is 100 yards on the right of the junction.
Open Mid March **to** End Oct
Access Good **Site** Lev/Slope
Sites Available ⊕ ⊞ **Total** 40
F a c i l i t i e s ∮ 🔲 ⬚ ♨ ⌐ ⊙ ⌿ 🖃
🔀 🔲 ♨🖃
Nearby Facilities ⌐ ✔ ↘ ∪ ⚲ 🏌
🚌 Rhyl
A quiet, tidy site with a well stocked shop.
Near the beach and within easy reach of the
Snowdonia mountain range.

BETWS-Y-COED

Camp Snowdonia, Tan Aeldroch Farm,
Near Betws-y-Coed, Conwy, LL25 0LZ.
Std: 01690 **Tel:** 750225
Nearest Town/Resort Betws-y-Coed
Directions From Betws-y-Coed take the
A470 to Dolwyddelan, pass under the railway
arch and site is ½ a mile on the left.
Acreage 6 **Open** April **to** October
Access Poor **Site** Level
Sites Available ▲ ⊕ ⊞ **Total** 20
Facilities ⊙ ⌿ 🖃 ⛟
Nearby Facilities ⌐ ✔ ↘ ∪ 🔀
🚌 Pont-y-Pant
Peaceful and tranquil riverside setting. No
music or radios.

BETWS-Y-COED

Hendr Farm, Betws-y-Coed, Conwy, LL24
0BN.
Std: 01690 **Tel:** 710950

Nearest Town/Resort Betws-y-Coed
Directions ½ mile west of the village of
Betws-y-Coed.
Acreage 2 **Open** 14 March **to** 31 Oct
Access Good **Site** Level
Sites Available ▲ ⊕ ⊞ **Total** 60
Facilities ⬚ ⬚ ♨ ⌐ ⊙ ⌿ ⛟ 🔲 🏠 ♨🖃
Nearby Facilities ⌐ ✔ ∪
🚌 Betws-y-Coed
River, hill, country and mountain walks.

BETWS-Y-COED

Riverside Caravan & Camping Park, Old
Church Road, Betws-y-Coed, Conwy,
LL24 0BA.
Std: 01690 **Tel:** 710310 **Fax:** 710826
Email: markh.01@genie.co.uk
Nearest Town/Resort Betws-y-Coed
Directions Enter Betws-y-Coed over
Waterloo Bridge. Take first right after
passing "Little Chef" Filling Station.
Acreage 3¼ **Open** 14 March **to** October
Access Good **Site** Level
Sites Available ▲ ⊕ ⊞ **Total** 120
Facilities ⬚ ⬚ ∮ ⬚ ♨ ⌐ ⊙ ⌿ 🖃 ⛟ ⛟
🏠 🔀🖃
Nearby Facilities ⌐ ✔ ∪ 🔀
🚌 Betws-y-Coed
Alongside river, adjacent to golf course.
Ideally based as centre for touring
Snowdonia.

BETWS-Y-COED

Rynys Farm Camping Site, Rynys Farm,
Near Betws-Y-Coed, Llanrwst, Conwy,
LL26 0RU.
Std: 01690 **Tel:** 710218
Email: carol@rynys.fsnet.co.uk
Website: www.rynys.fsnet.co.uk
Nearest Town/Resort Betws-y-Coed
Directions 2 miles south of Betws-y-Coed
Left by Conway Falls, 200yds from A5.
Acreage 6 **Open** All Year
Access Good **Site** Level
Sites Available ▲ ⊕ ⊞
Facilities ⬚ ♨ ⌐ ⊙ ⛟ 🖃
Nearby Facilities
🚌 Betws-y-Coed
Very scenic and peaceful site with excellent
clean facilities. Central for touring.

BETWS-Y-COED

Tyn Rhos Caravan Park, Tyn Rhos Farm,
Pentrefoelas, Betwys-y-Coed, Conwy,
LL24 0LN.
Std: 01690 **Tel:** 770655 **Fax:** 770655
Email: tudur.jones@farming.co.uk
Nearest Town/Resort Betws-y-Coed
Directions 4½ miles from Betws-y-Coed
along the A5, in the village of Pentrefoelas.
Open April **to** October
Access Good **Site** Level
Sites Available ⊕ **Total** 5
Facilities ∮ ♨🔀
Nearby Facilities ⌐ ✔ ⚓ ∪ 🔀
🚌 Betws-y-Coed
Ideal for Snowdonia's mountains and
walking. Ideal for touring North Wales.

COLWYN BAY

Bron-Y-Wendon Touring Caravan Park,
Wern Road, Llanddulas, Colwyn Bay,
Conwy, LL22 8HG.
Std: 01492 **Tel:** 512903 **Fax:** 512909
Email: bron-y-wendon@northwales-
holidays.co.uk
Website: www.northwales-holidays.co.uk
Nearest Town/Resort Colwyn Bay
Directions Follow the A55 into North Wales
and take the Llanddulas junction (A547).
Follow the tourist information signs to the
park.
Acreage 8 **Open** 21 March **to** 30 October

Access Good **Site** Lev/Slope
Sites Available ⌂ ⚏ **Total** 130
Facilities ♿ ⚑ ∮ 🚻 🚿 ♨ ⌂ ⊙ ⊿ 🛒 ◫ ☎ ⚏ ⊗ ⚡ ♦ 🚮 🗜
Nearby Facilities ┌ ✓ ⚓ ⌇ U ⊅ 🏇 ≯
≋ Colwyn Bay

All pitches have coastal views. Just a short walk to the beach. Site is ideal for seaside and touring. 5 Star Graded Park and Daffodil Award.

COLWYN BAY

Dinarth Hall, Rhos-on-Sea, Colwyn Bay, Conwy, LL28 4PX.
Std: 01492 **Tel:** 548203
Nearest Town/Resort Rhos on Sea
Directions A55 to Rhos-on-Sea then B5115.
Acreage 4 **Open** Easter **to** October
Access Good **Site** Level
Sites Available ⌂ ⚏ ⚏ **Total** 90
Facilities ∮ 🚿 ♨ ⌂ ⊙ ⊿ 🛒 ◫ ☎ ⚏ ⊗ 🚮 🗜
Nearby Facilities ┌ ✓ ⚓ ⌇ U ⊅ ≯
≋ Colwyn Bay

Close to sea and within reach of Snowdonia.

CONWY

Conwy Touring Park, Conwy, LL32 8UX.
Std: 01492 **Tel:** 592856 **Fax:** 580024
Website: www.conwytouringpark.com
Nearest Town/Resort Conwy
Acreage 70 **Open** Easter
Access Good **Site** Level
Sites Available ⌂ ⚏ ⚏ **Total** 300
Facilities ♿ ⚑ ∮ 🚻 🚿 ♨ ⌂ ⊙ ⊿ 🛒 ◫ ☎ ⚏ ⊗ ⚡ ♦ 🚮 🗜
Nearby Facilities ┌ ✓ ⚓ ⌇ U ⊅ 🏇 ≯
≋ Conwy

Scenic views, ideal for touring Snowdonia. Special Offers. Storage available.

CONWY

Tyn Terfyn Touring Caravan Park, Tal Y Bont, Conwy, LL32 8YX.
Std: 01492 **Tel:** 660525
Email: glentynterfyn@tinyworld.co.uk
Nearest Town/Resort Conwy
Directions From Conwy travel 5 miles (approx) on the B5106 until road sign for Tal-y-Bont. First house on the left after sign.
Acreage 2 **Open** 14 March **to** October
Access Good **Site** Level
Sites Available ⌂ ⚏ ⚏ **Total** 15
Facilities ♿ ∮ 🚿 ♨ ⌂ ⊙ ⊿ 🛒 ☎ ⚏ ⊗ 🚮 🗜
Nearby Facilities ┌ ✓ ⚓ ⌇ U ⊅ 🏇 ≯

Scenic views, good walking, fishing and boating. Ideal touring location.

LLANRWST

Bodnant Caravan Park, Nebo Road, Llanrwst, Conwy Valley, LL26 0SD.
Std: 01492 **Tel:** 640248
Email: ermin@bodnant-caravan-park.co.uk
Website: www.bodnant-caravan-park.co.uk
Nearest Town/Resort Llanrwst
Directions Entrance on the 30 mile limit on Nebo Road. From Betws-y-Coed (A470). Sharp right at first crossroads to the B5427 Nebo road opposite leisure centre.
Acreage 4 **Open** March **to** October
Access Good **Site** Level
Sites Available ⌂ ⚏ ⚏ **Total** 58
Facilities ∮ ⊟ 🚿 ♨ ⌂ ⊙ ⊿ ☎ ⚏ ⊗ ♦ 🚮 🗜
Nearby Facilities ┌ ✓ ⚓ ⌇ U ⊅ ≯
≋ Llanrwst

Lovely scenery, small, quiet, clean site. Ideal touring centre. 26 times Winner of Wales in Bloom. 8 multi service pitches. 2 holiday caravans for hire.

LLANRWST

Glyn Farm Caravans, Trefriw, Nr. Llanrwst, Conwy, LL27 0RZ.
Std: 01492 **Tel:** 640442
Nearest Town/Resort Llanrwst
Directions Follow the A470 to Llanrws[t] over hump bridge onto the B5106 Betws-Coed to Conwy road. Trefriw is 1¼ mile[s] from Gwydir Castle. Turn right oppos[ite] woollen mills, site 200yds.
Open March **to** October
Access Good **Site** Level
Sites Available ⚏ **Total** 28
Facilities ∮ 🚿 🚻 ♨ ⌂ ⊙ ⊿ ☎ ⚏ 🛒 ♦ 🚮[
Nearby Facilities ┌ ✓ ⌇ U ⊅ 🏇 ≯
≋ Llanrwst

Very centrally situated for Snowdonia a[nd] the sea. Beautiful country, lovely walks a[nd] ideal touring. Small family run site.

PENMAENMAWR

Trwyn Yr Wylfa Farm, Trwyn Yr Wylfa, Penmaenmawr, Conwy, LL34 6SF.
Std: 01492 **Tel:** 622357
Nearest Town/Resort Penmaenmawr
Directions Leave A55 at roundabout f[or] Penmaenmawr. Turn by Mountain Vie[w] Hotel, farm is ¼ mile east.
Acreage 10 **Open** Spring Bank Holiday [to] End Aug
Site Level
Sites Available ⌂ ⚏ **Total** 100
Facilities ⚑ 🚿 ⌂ ⊙ 🚮
Nearby Facilities ┌ ✓ ⚓ ⌇ U ⊅ ≯
≋ Penmaenmawr

Secluded site in Snowdonia National Par[k]

PENMAENMAWR

Tyddyn Du Touring Park, Conwy Old Road, Penmaenmawr, Conwy, LL34 6RE
Std: 01492 **Tel:** 622300 **Fax:** 622300

ebsite: www.ukparks.co.uk/tyddyndu
earest Town/Resort Penmaenmawr
irections 1 mile east of Penmaenmawr.
ake the A55 from Conwy and turn right
e roundabout after the Little Chef and
arp left again. Site access is on the right
ter Legend Inn.
creage 5 **Open** 21 March **to** 31 Oct
ccess Good **Site** Lev/Slope
ites Available ⚠ 🚐 🚙 **Total** 100
acilities ⚒ ⨍ 🆅 🏧 ⌐ ⊙ ☕ ▭ 🍴
▯ 🏧❋⊡🅱
earby Facilities ⌐ ✈ ⚓ ❧ ∪ ↯
⚞ Penmaenmawr
te overlooks Conwy Bay to Llandudno and
nglesey. Close to the A55 so ideal for
uring Snowdonia.

ENMAENMAWR

oodlands Camping Park, Pendyffrin
all, Penmaenmawr, Conwy, LL34 6UF.
td: 01492 **Tel:** 623219
earest Town/Resort Penmaenmawr/
onwy
irections 200yds off A55 expressway
etween Conwy and Penmaenmawr.
creage 9 **Open** March **to** October
te Level
ites Available ⚠ 🚐 🚙 **Total** 100
acilities ⚒ ⨍ 🆅 🏧 ⌐ ⊙ ☕ ▭ 🍴
▮ 🅱 ▯ 🅿 🅱
earby Facilities ⌐ ✈ ⚓ ❧ ∪ ↯ ✗ ❧
⚞ Penmaenmawr
amilies and couples only. Situated in 96
cres of private parkland and woodlands
thin Snowdonia National Park. Just a short
alk to the beach. Ideal touring centre.
A.E. for details.

REFRIW

las Meirion Caravan Park, Gower
oad, Trefriw, Conwy, LL27 0RZ.
td: 01492 **Tel:** 640247 **Fax:** 640247
ebsite: www.4snowdoniaholidays.co.uk
earest Town/Resort Betws-y-Coed
irections On the B5106 Betws-y-Coed to
onwy road, in Trefriw turn directly opposite
'oollen Mill, site is 300 metres on the left.
creage 2 **Open** Easter **to** End October
ccess Good **Site** Level
ites Available ⚠ 🚐 🚙 **Total** 5
acilities ⨍ 🆅 🏧 ⌐ ⊙ ☕ 🍴 ▯ 🅿 🅱
earby Facilities ✈ ❧ ∪ ❧
⚞ Llandudno Junction
uiet, family run site in an attractive garden
etting.

Y-NANT

lan Ceirw Caravan Park, Ty Nant,
orwen, Conwy, LL21 0RF.
td: 01490 **Tel:** 420346
mail:
anceirwcaravanpark@tinyworld.co.uk
ebsite: www.ukparks.com/glanceirw
earest Town/Resort Corwen/Betws-y-
oed
irections Between Corwen and Betws-y-
oed just off the A5. Coming from Betws-y-
oed take the second right after
errigydrudion over a small bridge and
00yds along the lane. From Corwen turn
ft after Glan Ceirn signs over a small
idge, 300yds on the left.
creage 1 **Open** March **to** October
ccess Good **Site** Level
ites Available ⚠ 🚐 🚙 **Total** 10
acilities ⨍ 🆅 🏧 🆅 🏧 ⌐ ⊙ ☕ ▯ 🍴
▮ 🅱 ▯ 🅿 🏧 ❋❧🅱
earby Facilities ✈ ⚓ ❧ ❧
⚞ Ruabon
icturesque site bordering Snowdonia
ational Park. Trout fishing on site. Ideal for
uring North and West Wales.

DENBIGHSHIRE
CORWEN

Hendwr Caravan Park, Llandrillo,
Corwen, Denbighshire, LL21 0SN.
Std: 01490 **Tel:** 440210
Nearest Town/Resort Corwen/Bala
Directions From Corwen (A5) take the
B4401 for 4 miles, turn right at sign Hendwr.
Site is on the right in ¼ mile. From Bala take
the A494 for 1½ miles, turn right onto the
B4401 via Llandrillo. Site is 1 mile north of
the left.
Acreage 2¼ **Open** April **to** October
Access Good **Site** Level
Sites Available ⚠ 🚐 🚙 **Total** 60
Facilities ⨍ 🆅 🆅 🏧 ⌐ ⊙ ☕ ▭ 🍴
🆇 🍴 🅱 ❋❧🅱
Nearby Facilities ⌐ ✈ ⚓ ❧ ∪ ↯
⚞ Ruabon
Alongside a river, good walking, pony
trekking and fishing. Wonderful views and
an excellent touring centre for North Wales.

DENBIGH

Station House Caravan Park, Bodfari,
Denbigh, Denbighshire, LL16 4DA.
Std: 01745 **Tel:** 710372 **Fax:** 710372
Nearest Town/Resort Denbigh
Directions From the A541 Mold to Denbigh
road, turn onto the B5429 in the direction of
Tremeirchion. Site is immediately on the left
by cream house.
Acreage 2 **Open** April **to** October
Access Good **Site** Level
Sites Available ⚠ 🚐 🚙 **Total** 26
Facilities ⨍ 🆅 🏧 ⌐ ⊙ ☕ 🍴
🆇 🅱 🏧 🍴 🅱
Nearby Facilities ⌐ ✈ ∪
⚞ Rhyl
Attractive site with scenic views. Ideal
touring centre. Offa's Dyke path 400yds.
Close to two inns (400yds).

LLANGOLLEN

Ddol Hir Caravan Park, Pandy Road,
Glyn Ceiriog, Llangollen, Denbighshire,
LL20 7PD.
Std: 01691 **Tel:** 718681
Website: www.ukparks.com
Nearest Town/Resort Llangollen
Directions Turn off the A5 at Chirk onto the
B4500, park is on the left approx. 6 miles,
just through the village of Glyn Ceiriog.
Acreage 6 **Open** March **to** October
Access Good **Site** Level
Sites Available ⚠ 🚐 🚙 **Total** 25
Facilities ⨍ 🆅 ⌐ ⊙ ☕ 🍴 🆇 🅱 🏧❋🅱
Nearby Facilities ⌐ ✈ ∪ 🅿 ❧
⚞ Chirk
Riverside site in a scenic valley with
mountain views. Trout fishing and pony
trekking. Within walking distance of shops
and pubs.

LLANGOLLEN

Pontbell Caravan Park, Glan Llyn, Glyn
Ceiriog, Llangollen, Denbighshire, LL20
7AB.
Std: 01691 **Tel:** 718320
Email: jeff.bell@micro-plus-web.net
Nearest Town/Resort Wrexham
Directions Take the Wrexham bypass to
Chirk, in Chirk turn right by the church on
the left, then turn right to Glyn Ceiriog. Follow
road for 6 miles and Park is on the left hand
side.
Open Easter **to** End Sept
Access Good **Site** Level
Sites Available ⚠ 🚐 🚙 **Total** 7
Facilities 🆅 🏧 ⌐ ⊙ ☕ 🆇❧
Nearby Facilities ⌐ ✈ ∪ ❧
⚞ Chirk

Set amidst lovely countryside, nice and
quiet. Good walking. Close to the town for
shopping and not far from Llangollen.

LLANGOLLEN

Ty-Ucha Caravan Park, Maesmawr
Road, Llangollen, Denbighshire, LL20
7PP.
Std: 01978 **Tel:** 860677
Nearest Town/Resort Llangollen
Directions 1 mile east of Llangollen on the
A5, 200 yards signposted.
Acreage 5 **Open** Easter **to** October
Access Good **Site** Level
Sites Available 🚐 🚙 **Total** 40
Facilities ⚒ ⨍ 🆅 🏧 ⌐ ⊙ ☕ 🅱 🏧🅱
Nearby Facilities ⌐ ✈ ∪ ❧
⚞ Ruabon
Quiet site with outstanding panoramic views.
Ideal for walking and touring.

PRESTATYN

Nant Mill Farm Caravan & Tenting Park,
Nant Mill, Prestatyn, Denbighshire, LL19
9LY.
Std: 01745 **Tel:** 852360
Email: nantmilltouring@aol.com
Nearest Town/Resort Prestatyn
Directions ½ mile east of Prestatyn on A548
coast road.
Acreage 5 **Open** Easter **to** October
Access Good **Site** Lev/Slope
Sites Available ⚠ 🚐 🚙 **Total** 150
Facilities ⨍ 🆅 🏧 ⌐ ⊙ ☕ ▭ 🍴
🆇 🅱 🍴 🆅 ❋❧🅱
Nearby Facilities ⌐ ✈ ⚓ ❧ ∪ 🅿
⚞ Prestatyn
Near town shops. ½ mile beach, ideal to tour
north Wales. Hotel bar meals 200yds.

PRESTATYN

Presthaven Sands Holiday Park, Shore
Road, Gronant, Prestatyn, Denbighshire,
LL19 9TT.
Std: 01745 **Tel:** 856471 **Fax:** 886646
Website: www.havenholidays.com
Nearest Town/Resort Prestatyn/Rhyl
Directions Take the A548 out of Prestatyn
towards Gronant. The park is signposted left,
then entrance is ½ mile further on the right.
Acreage 12 **Open** Easter **to** Oct
Access Good **Site** Level
Sites Available ⚠ 🚐 🚙 **Total** 97
Facilities ⨍ 🆅 🆅 🏧 ⌐ ⊙ ☕ 🍴
🆇 🅱 🆅 ✗ 🆇 ⚓ ❋❧🅱🅱
Nearby Facilities ⌐ ✈ ⚓ ❧ ∪ ↯ 🅿
⚞ Prestatyn/Rhyl
Alongside 2 miles of beaches and sand
dunes.

RUTHIN

Allt Gymbyd Caravan Park, Llanarmon-
Yn-Ial, Near Mold, Denbighshire, CH7
4QU.
Std: 01824 **Tel:** 780647 **Fax:** 780647
Nearest Town/Resort Mold
Directions From Mold take the A451
Wrexham road for 4 miles, at crossroads
opposite the Bridge Inn turn right onto the
A5104 Corwen road. Continue to Liver turn
right and follow signs.
Open March **to** October
Access Good
Sites Available ⚠ 🚐 🚙 **Total** 30
Facilities ⨍ 🆅 🆅 🆅 🏧 ⌐ 🍴 🅱
🅱 🆅 🏧🅱
Nearby Facilities ⌐ ✈ ❧ ∪ ❧
⚞ Wrexham
Overlooking Clwydian Range. Golf course
on the park.

CONWY, FLINT, GWYNEDD

RUTHIN

Dyffryn Ial Caravan Site, Troell Yr Alun, Llanarmon-yn-Ial, Mold, Denbighshire, CH7 4QU.
Std: 01824 **Tel:** 780286 **Fax:** 780286
Nearest Town/Resort Mold/Ruthin
Directions From Chester take the A494 towards Ruthin, turn onto the B4931 for Llanarmon-Yn-Ial. After 1 mile pass the closed old quarry and site is right by the river.
Acreage ½ **Open** April **to** September
Access Good **Site** Level
Sites Available � ⊕ **Total** 18
Facilities ⚿ ⓌⒸ ⚲ ୮
Nearby Facilities ୮ ✓ Ս
➤ Wrexham/Chester/Rhyl
Quiet, scenic site alongside a river. Near Offa's Dyke footpath and over 100 other footpaths in the area. Ideal for touring North Wales. Close to the mediaeval town of Ruthin and Clwydian Hills.

RUTHIN

Parc Farm Caravan Park, Llanarmon-Yn-Ial, Near Mold, Denbighshire, CH7 4QW.
Std: 01824 **Tel:** 780666 **Fax:** 780700
Email: evansparc@aol.com
Website: www.parcfarm.co.uk
Nearest Town/Resort Ruthin
Directions From Mold take the A494 towards Ruthin for approx. 5 miles, turn left onto the B5430 Llanarmon-Yn-Ial road. After 2½ miles passing the sign for the village, Parc Farm is the next turning on the right and is signposted at the entrance. Or approaching from Chester via the A5104 Corwen road for approx. 12 miles, turn right onto the B5430 then as above.
Acreage 2 **Open** March **to** November
Access Good **Site** Lev/Slope
Sites Available ⊕ ⊕ **Total** 20
Facilities ∫ ⓁⒸ ⚲ ୮ ⊙ ⚌
ⓈⓁ ⓁⒼ ⓐ ✕ ⊡ ⛱ ⛛ ⛘ ⊡
Nearby Facilities ୮ ✓ Ս ℛ
➤ Penyffordd
Privately owned, family run park set in 46 acres of wooded park and in the heart of the Clloydian Mountains. Beautiful scenery, good walks. Central location.

FLINTSHIRE

GRONANT

Greenacres Caravan Park, Shore Road, Gronant, Flintshire, LL19 9SS.
Std: 01745 **Tel:** 854061 **Fax:** 887898
Nearest Town/Resort Prestatyn
Directions 2 miles from Prestatyn off the main A548 coast road.
Open 1 March **to** 14 January
Access Good **Site** Level
Sites Available ⊕□ **Total** 40
Facilities ⚿ ∫ ⓁⒸ ⚲ ୮ ⊡ ⚌
ⓈⓁ ⓐ ✕ ♉ ⊡ ⛱ ⛛ ⛘ ⊡
Nearby Facilities ୮ ℛ
➤ Prestatyn
500 yards from the beach. Two licensed premises with live entertainment. Health suite and swimming pool.

MOLD

Fron Farm Caravan & Camping Site, Fron Farm, Hendre, Mold, Flintshire, CH7 5QW.
Std: 01352 **Tel:** 741217
Nearest Town/Resort Mold/Holywell
Directions A541 between Denbigh and Mold, take sign for Rhes-Y-Cae. Fron Farm is the third turning on the right including farm lanes.
Acreage 5 **Open** April **to** October

Access Good **Site** Lev/Slope
Sites Available ⊕ ⊕ **Total** 25
Facilities ∫ ⓁⒸ ⚲ ୮ ⊙ ⊙ ⓐ ⊡ ⛛
Nearby Facilities ✓ Ս
➤ Flint/Chester
Farm site with animals to see and scenic views. Lovely walks. Ideal touring. No need to book.

MOLD

MOLD

Pantymwyn Caravan Park, Erw Goed, Pantymwyn, Mold, Flintshire, CH7 5EF.
Std: 01352 **Tel:** 740365
Nearest Town/Resort Mold/Rhyl
Directions 3 miles from Mold town towards Mold Golf Club.
Acreage 29 **Open** April **to** October
Access Good **Site** Sloping
Sites Available ⊕ ⊕ **Total** 160
Facilities ⚿ ⚲ ୮ ⓁⒸ ⊙ ⚌ ⊡ ⚌
ⓂⓁ ⓁⒼ ⓐ ⓐ ⊛ ⛛ ⛘ ⊡
Nearby Facilities ୮ ✓ Ս ℛ ⛛
➤ Buckley
Quiet, country site surrounded by mature trees and farmland. Ideal for touring and walking.

QUEENSFERRY

Greenacres Farm Park, Mancot, Deeside, Flintshire, CH5 2AZ.
Std: 01244 **Tel:** 531147
Nearest Town/Resort Queensferry/Hawarden
Directions From Queensferry roundabout follow signs for 'Farm Park'.
Acreage 3 **Open** February **to** October
Access Good **Site** Level
Sites Available ♉ ⊕ ⊕ **Total** 55
Facilities ⚿ ∫ ⓁⒸ ⚲ ୮ ⊙ ⚌ ⚌
ⓁⒼ ✕ ⛛ ⛘ ⊡
Nearby Facilities ୮ Ս ℛ
➤ Hawarden/Shotton
Adjacent to Farm Park tourist attraction. 7 miles from Chester.

GWYNEDD

ABERDARON

Brynfynnon Caravan Park, Rhoshirwaun, Rhydlios, Near Aberdaron, Pwllheli, Gwynedd, LL53 8LP.
Std: 01758 **Tel:** 730643
Nearest Town/Resort Pwllheli
Directions Approx. 14 miles from Pwllheli.
Acreage 2½ **Open** March **to** October
Access Good **Site** Level
Sites Available ♉ ⊕ ⊕ **Total** 15
Facilities ∫ ⓁⒸ ⚲ ୮ ⊙ ⚌ ⓐ ⛛ ⛘ ⊡
Nearby Facilities ୮ ✓ ⚓ ⛛ Ս ⛛ ⛛
➤ Pwllheli
Near to several pleasant beaches. Ideal site for children. Good for family touring. Separate field for tents.

ABERDARON

Mur Melyn Camping Site, Mur Melyn, Aberdaron, Pwllheli, Gwynedd, LL53 8LW.
Std: 01758 **Tel:** 760522
Nearest Town/Resort Pwllheli
Directions Take A499 west from Pwllheli, then fork onto to B4413 at Llanbedrog about 3 miles before Aberdaron take Whistling Sand road. Turn left at Pen-y-Bont House to site ½ mile.
Acreage 2½ **Open** Whitsun **to** September
Access Good **Site** Level
Sites Available ♉ ⊕ ⊕ **Total** 60
Facilities ⓁⒸ ୮ ⊙ ⚌ ⛘ ⛛
Nearby Facilities ✓ ⚓ ⛛ Ս
➤ Pwllheli
Near beach, scenic views, ideal touring, river nearby, ideal for Wales.

ABERDARON

Tir Glyn Caravan Park, Tir Glyn Farm, Uwchmynydd, Aberdaron, Pwllheli, Gwynedd, LL53 8DA.
Std: 01758 **Tel:** 760248
Nearest Town/Resort Aberdaron/Abersoch
Directions Pwllheli to Abersoch road, take the B4413 at Llanbedrog to Aberdaron. I Aberdaron Village turn right on the bridge signed Uwchmynydd, keep left then turn firs left, we are first farm on the left.
Acreage 3 **Open** May **to** October
Access Good **Site** Lev/Slope
Sites Available ♉ ⊕ ⊕ **Total** 30
Facilities ⚿ ∫ ⓁⒸ ୮ ⊙ ⚌ ⓁⒼ ⊙ ⛛
Nearby Facilities ୮ ✓ ⚓ ⛛ Ս
➤ Pwllheli
Surrounded by National Trust land overlooking the sea for scenic views. Nea beaches.

ABERSOCH

Beach View Caravan Park, Bwlchtocyn, Abersoch, Gwynedd, LL53 7BT.
Std: 01758 **Tel:** 712956
Nearest Town/Resort Abersoch
Directions Drive through Abersoch an Sarn Bach, go over small crossroads the bear left signposted Bwlchtocyn. Continu past the Post Office, chapel and follow sign for Porthtocyn Hotel and beach. Beach Vie is on the left hand side.
Acreage 8 **Open** Mid March **to** Mid October
Access Good **Site** Level
Sites Available ♉ ⊕ ⊕ **Total** 50
Facilities ⚿ ∫ ⓁⒸ ⚲ ୮ ⊙ ⚌ ⊡ ⛛
ⓁⒼ ⊙ ⛛ ⛘ ⊡
Nearby Facilities ୮ ✓ ⚓ ⛛ Ս ⛛ ⛛
➤ Pwllheli
6 minute walk to the beach. Ideal centre fo touring, walking, sailing and all other wate sports.

ABERSOCH

Bryn Bach Camping & Caravan Park, Tyddyn Talgoch Uchaf, Bwlchtocyn, Abersoch, Gwynedd, LL53 7BT.
Std: 01758 **Tel:** 712285 **Fax:** 712285
Email: brynbach.abersoch@virgin.net
Website: www.abersochholidays.co.uk
Nearest Town/Resort Abersoch
Directions From Abersoch take the road fo Sarnbach, after approx. 1 mile turn le signposted Bwlch Tocyn. Stay on this roa and Bryn Bach is approx. 1 mile on the lef
Acreage 2 **Open** March **to** End October
Access Good **Site** Lev/Slope
Sites Available ♉ ⊕ ⊕ **Total** 45
Facilities ⚿ ∫ ⓁⒸ ⚲ ୮ ⊙ ⚌ ⓁⒼ ⛛ ⛘ ⊡
Nearby Facilities ୮ ✓ ⚓ ⛛ Ս ⛛
➤ Pwllheli
Magnificent views. Only a short walk to tw sandy beaches. Near a golf course an many other activities.

ABERSOCH

Bryn Cethin Bach Caravan Park, Lon Garmon, Abersoch, Gwynedd, LL53 7UL.
Std: 01758 **Tel:** 712719 **Fax:** 712719
Nearest Town/Resort Abersoch
Directions Take the A499 to Abersoch, for right at Abersoch Land & Sea Garage, par is ½ mile up the hill on the right.
Acreage 4 **Open** Easter **to** End October
Access Good **Site** Level
Sites Available ⊕ ⊕ **Total** 24
Facilities ⚿ ∫ ⓁⒸ ⚲ ୮ ⊙ ⚌ ⓐ ⊡ ⊡
⊙ ⓐ ⊛ ⛛ ⛘ ⊡ ⊡
Nearby Facilities ୮ ✓ ⚓ ⛛ Ս ⛛
➤ Pwllheli

TYN-Y-MUR
Touring & Camping Park
Lon Garmon
Abersoch Tel: (01758) 712328
"The perfect family holiday!"
Tyn-Y-Mur is situated on the hill above the village of Abersoch (10 min. walk). Modern toilets and launderette, showers and dishwashing room with FREE HOT WATER. Baby changing facilities. Children's play area. Panoramic views of Cardigan Bay and Bardsey Island. Ideal for all beach and country pursuits.
For Colour Brochure Send To:
Tyn-Y-Mur, Lon Garmon, Abersoch, Gwynedd LL53 7UL

wo lakes stocked with fish, no charge for residents.

ABERSOCH
euccoh Camping & Touring Site, Sarn ach, Abersoch, Pwllheli, Gwynedd, LL53 _D.
td: 01758 **Tel:** 713293
earest Town/Resort Abersoch
irections Take Sarn Bach road out of bersoch, continue on main road to Sarn ach. Turn right in the square.
creage 5 **Open** March **to** October
ccess Good **Site** Level
ites Available ▲ ➡ ⊞ **Total** 68
acilities ⓓ ⨍ ☐ ⓘ ♨ ↾ ☉ ⌣ ⌴ ☒ ⍟
☖ ⎅ ☐ ⍟
earby Facilities ↾ ⏚ ⬥ ✦ ∪ ⅃ ⅄
⇻ Pwllheli
ear the beach, ideal touring and scenic ews. Dogs are allowed on leads. Cafe/ staurant, public telephone and licensed ub nearby.

ABERSOCH
easide Camping Site, Lon Golff, bersoch, Gwynedd, LL53 7EU.
td: 01758 **Tel:** 712271
earest Town/Resort Abersoch
irections Take the A499 Pwllheli to bersoch road, turn left at Sarn Bach illage, site is approx. ½ mile from the main ad.
creage 3 **Open** May **to** September
ites Available ▲ ⊡ **Total** 70
acilities ⨍ ⓘ ♨ ↾ ☉ ⌣ ⍟ ☖ ⍟ ☐
earby Facilities ↾ ⏚ ⬥ ∪ ⅃
⇻ Pwllheli
nly 400 metres from a safe, sandy beach nd a golf course.

ABERSOCH
an-y-Bryn Farm, Tan-y-Bryn, Sarn Bach, bersoch, Gwynedd, LL53 7DA.
td: 01758 **Tel:** 712093
earest Town/Resort Abersoch
irections From Abersoch take the road to arn Bach turn left at the

ABERSOCH
rem Y Mor (Seaview), Glaswen, Sarn ach, Abersoch, Gwynedd, LL53 7DA.
td: 01758 **Tel:** 712052 **Fax:** 713243
ebsite: www.tggroup.co.uk
earest Town/Resort Abersoch
irections From Abersoch take the road to arn Bach. In Sarn Bach turn left at the

square, 200 metres on the right.
Acreage 6 **Open** March **to** October
Access Good **Site** Lev/Slope
Sites Available ▲ ⊡ ⊞ **Total** 70
Facilities ⓓ ⨍ ☐ ⓘ ⓤ ♨ ↾ ☉ ⌣ ⌴ ☒ ⍟
⍟ ⓘ ⎅ ⎅ ⍟ ↾ ☐ ⍟
Nearby Facilities ↾ ⏚ ⬥ ✦ ∪ ⅃ ⅄ ✦
⇻ Pwllheli
10 minute walk from the beach, golf, horse riding, sailing and water sports.

ABERSOCH
Tyn-y-Mur Camping Site, Abersoch, Gwynedd, LL53 7UL.
Std: 0175 871 **Tel:** 2328
Nearest Town/Resort Abersoch
Directions A499 Pwllheli to Abersoch, on approaching Abersoch turn right at Land & Sea Services Garage, is then 1 mile on lefthand side.
Acreage 3 **Open** March **to** October
Access Good **Site** Level
Sites Available ▲ ⊡ ⊞ **Total** 90
Facilities ⨍ ⓘ ⓤ ♨ ↾ ☉ ⌣ ⌴ ☒ ⍟
⍟ ⎅ ⎅ ☐ ⍟
Nearby Facilities ↾ ⏚ ⬥ ✦ ∪ ⅃ ⅄
⇻ Pwllheli
Superb, uninterrupted panoramic coastal views of Abersoch Bay and Hell's Mouth. Only allowed 1 pet per unit.

ARTHOG
Garthyfog Camping Site, Garthyfog Farm, Arthog, Gwynedd, LL39 1AX.
Std: 01341 **Tel:** Fairbourne 250338
Email: garthyfog@tinyworld.co.uk
Nearest Town/Resort Barmouth/ Dolgellau
Directions A493, 6 miles from Dolgellau, left by Village hall, look for signs on righthand side.
Acreage 5 **Open** All Year
Site Lev/Slope
Sites Available ▲ ⊡ ⊞ **Total** 20
Facilities ⓤ ↾ ☉ ⌣ ⍟
Nearby Facilities ↾ ⏚ ⬥ ✦ ∪ ⅃ ⅄ ✦
⇻ Morfa Mawddach
2 miles from Fairbourne, safe bathing, sandy beach and shops. Beautiful scenery, panoramic views. 300 yards from main road, sheltered from wind. Mains cold water. Plenty of room for children to play around the farm, rope-swing, little stream, etc. 2 static caravans and a log cabin to let.

ARTHOG
Graig-Wen, Arthog, Gwynedd, LL39 1BQ.
Std: 01341 **Tel:** 250482/250900 **Fax:** 250482
Email: graig-wen@supanet.com
Website: www.graig-wen.supanet.com

Nearest Town/Resort Fairbourne
Directions Between Dolgellau and Fairbourne on the A493.
Acreage 42
Access Good **Site** Lev/Slope
Sites Available ▲ ⊡ ⊞
Facilities ⓤ ⓓ ↾ ☉ ⌣ ⍟ ⍟ ⓘ ☖ ↾ ☐ ⍟
Nearby Facilities ↾ ⏚ ⬥ ✦ ∪ ⅃ ⅄ ✦
Land reaching down to estuary with scenic views, woodlands and pastures. Ideal for bird watchers, nature lovers, walkers, cyclists and outdoor pursuits.

BALA
Bryn Gwyn Farm Caravan & Camping Park, Godre'r Aran, Llanuwchllyn, Bala, Gwynedd, LL23 7UB.
Std: 01678 **Tel:** 540687
Nearest Town/Resort Bala
Directions Bryn Gwyn is ½ mile off the A494 near Llanuwchllyn Village signposted Trawsfynydd. Drive straight through Bala and travel along lakeside for 5 miles, on the right.
Acreage 5 **Open** Easter **to** End Oct
Access Good **Site** Level
Sites Available ▲ ⊡ ⊞ **Total** 20
Facilities ⨍ ⓓ ⨍ ⓤ ♨ ↾ ☉ ⌣ ⍟
⎅ ⍟ ⍟ ↾ ☐ ⍟
Nearby Facilities ↾ ⏚ ⬥ ✦ ✦
⇻ Wrexham
Small, peaceful, riverside park with wonderful views of the Aran mountains. Free fishing. Within easy walking distance of the village inn. Ideal touring centre for the coast and Snowdonia. Refurbished toilet block to a higher standard in 2000.

BALA
Camping & Caravanning Club Site, Crynierth Caravan Park, Cefn-Ddwysarn, Bala, Gwynedd, LL23 7LN.
Std: 01678 **Tel:** 530324
Website:
www.campingandcaravanningclub.co.uk
Nearest Town/Resort Bala
Directions From the A5 turn onto the A494 to Bala. At signpost Cefn-Ddwysarn turn right before the red phone box, site is 400 yards on the left.
Acreage 4 **Open** March **to** October
Access Good **Site** Level
Sites Available ▲ ⊡ ⊞ **Total** 50
Facilities ⓓ ⨍ ⓤ ♨ ↾ ☉ ⌣ ⌴ ☒ ⍟
⍟ ⍟ ⓘ ⎅ ☖ ↾ ☐ ⍟
Nearby Facilities ↾ ⏚ ⬥ ✦ ∪ ⅃
⇻ Ruabon
Situated on the edge of Snowdonia National Park. 4 miles from Bala Lake. Good for watersports. Ideal touring site. Non members welcome.

BALA

Glanllyn-Lakeside Caravan & Camping Park, Bala, Gwynedd, LL23 7ST.
Std: 01678 **Tel:** 540227
Email: iinfo@glanllyn.com
Website: www.glanllyn.com
Nearest Town/Resort Bala
Directions 3 miles south west of Bala on the A494, situated on the left alongside Bala Lake.
Acreage 14 **Open** Easter **to** October
Access Good **Site** Level
Sites Available ▲ ⌂ ⊞ **Total** 100
Facilities ⌀ 🔢 🚿 ┌ ⊙ ⌄ ⊒ ◻ ▣
🔲 🏠 🛒 ⊞ ┌◻ ▣
Nearby Facilities ┌ ✔ ⚓ ⤢ ∪ ♫ ⚡
⇌ Wrexham
Level parkland with trees. Alongside a lake and river, large launching area for sailing.

BALA

Pen Y Bont Touring & Camping Park,
Llangynog Road, Bala, Gwynedd, LL23 7PH.
Std: 01678 **Tel:** 520549 **Fax:** 520006
Email: penybont@aol.com
Website: www.penybont-bala.co.uk
Nearest Town/Resort Bala
Directions ½ mile from Bala on B4391 to Llangynog.
Acreage 6 **Open** March **to** October
Access Good **Site** Level
Sites Available ▲ ⌂ ⊞ **Total** 85
Facilities ⌀ ┌ ⊞ 🔢 🔢 🚿 ┌ ⊙ ⌄ ⊒ ◻ ▣
🔲 🏠 🛒 ⊞ ┌◻ ▣
Nearby Facilities ┌ ✔ ⚓ ⤢ ♫ ⚡
⇌ Ruabon
Nearest park to Bala (10 minute walk) and next to a sailing club. Free showers, separate vanity cubicles and washing areas all under cover. 4 Star Excellent Grading and AA 4 Pennants.

BALA

Pen Y Garth Caravan & Camping Park.
Bala, Gwynedd, LL23 7ES.
Std: 01678 **Tel:** 520485 **Fax:** 520401
Email: stay@penygarth.co.uk
Website: www.penygarth.co.uk
Directions Take B4391 Bala to Llangynog road. 1 mile from Bala fork right at sign to Rhos-Y-Gwaliau, site in 600yds.
Acreage 20 **Open** March **to** October
Access Good **Site** Level
Sites Available ▲ ⌂ ⊞ **Total** 63
Facilities ⌀ 🔢 🚿 ┌⊙⌐◻○⌂🔲 🔲🏠🛒⊞┌◻▣
Nearby Facilities ┌ ✔ ⚓ ⤢ ∪ ♫ ⚡
⇌ Ruabon
Picturesque setting with superb views, within Snowdonia National Park. Short walk from Bala Lake, 1 mile from the town. Within easy reach of numerous attractions, Snowdon,

lakes, coast, etc.. Wealth of wildlife, safe for children. 4 Star Graded Park, AA 4 Pennants and Dragon Award for holiday caravans (for hire).

BALA

Ty-Isaf Camping Site, Llangynog Road, Bala, Gwynedd, LL23 7PP.
Std: 01678 **Tel:** 520574
Nearest Town/Resort Bala
Directions 2½ miles southeast of Bala on the B4391, near the telephone kiosk and post box.
Acreage 2 **Open** April/Easter **to** Oct
Access Good **Site** Level
Sites Available ▲ ⌂ ⊞ **Total** 30
Facilities ⌀ ⌀ ┌ 🔢 🚿 ┌ ⊙ ⌄ ⊒ ⊞
🔲 🏠 🛒 ◯⊞┌◻
Nearby Facilities ┌ ✔ ⚓ ∪ ♫ ⚡
⇌ Ruabon
Working farm alongside a stream. Ideal touring.

BALA

Tyn Cornel Camping & Caravan Park,
Frongoch, Bala, Gwynedd, LL23 7NU.
Std: 01678 **Tel:** 520759 **Fax:** 520759
Website: www.tyn-cornel.co.uk
Nearest Town/Resort Bala
Directions Leave Bala on the A4212 Porthmadog road, turn left after 4 miles over river bridge.
Acreage 1¼ **Open** Mid March **to** End Oct
Access Good **Site** Level
Sites Available ▲ ⌂ ⊞ **Total** 37
Facilities ┌ 🔢 🚿⊙◻⌐ ◻○⊞┌◻
Nearby Facilities ┌ ✔ ⚓ ⤢ ∪ ⚡
⇌ Llangollen
Next to National White Water Centre on the River Tryweryn. Canoeing and white water rafting available.

BANGOR

Dinas Farm Camping Site, Dinas Farm, Halfway Bridge, Bangor, Gwynedd, LL57 4NB.
Std: 01248 **Tel:** 364227
Nearest Town/Resort Bangor
Directions Take the A5 from the A55 roundabout towards Bethesda, 3 miles south of Bangor turn right at Halfway Bridge towards Tregarth, first farm on the left. 2 miles north of Bethesda.
Acreage 4 **Open** Easter **to** October
Access Good **Site** Level
Sites Available ▲ ⌂ ⊞ **Total** 35
Facilities ⌀ 🔢 🚿 ┌ ⊙ ⌄ ⊞
🔲 🏠 🛒 ◯⊞┌◻
Nearby Facilities ┌ ✔ ⚡
⇌ Bangor
Alongside the River Ogwen for salmon and trout fishing. Centrally situated for mountains and beaches.

BARMOUTH

Bellaport Touring Park, Bellaport, Talybont, Nr. Barmouth, Gwynedd, LL43 2BX.
Std: 01341 **Tel:** 247338
Nearest Town/Resort Barmouth
Directions 4 miles north of Barmouth, turn right at 40mph limit sign and our sign leaving Talybont.
Acreage 2 **Open** March **to** October
Access Good **Site** Level
Sites Available ⌂ ⊞ **Total** 20
Facilities ✗ ┌ 🔢 ┌ ⊞ ⌄ ⊞
Nearby Facilities ┌ ✔ ⚓ ⤢ ∪ ♫ ⚡
⇌ Talybont
A quiet park in the Snowdonia National Park where the mountains run down to the sea. Booking is advisable in peak periods. No cycles, no scooters and no roller blades.

BARMOUTH

Benar Beach Camping & Touring Site,
Talybont, Barmouth, Gwynedd, LL43 2AR.
Std: 01341 **Tel:** 247001
Nearest Town/Resort Barmouth
Directions From Barmouth take the A496 north for 5 miles, turn off by Llanddwywe Church in Talybont, site is by the beach.
Acreage 9 **Open** March **to** October
Access Good **Site** Level
Sites Available ▲ ⌂ ⊞ **Total** 270
Facilities ⌀ ┌ ⊞ 🔢 🚿 ┌ ⊙ ⌄ ⊒
🔲 ◯⊞┌◻▣
Nearby Facilities ┌ ✔ ⚓ ⤢ ∪ ⚡ ♫ ⚡
⇌ Dyffryn Ardudwy
100 yards from a safe beach with miles of golden sand. Spectacular scenery of Snowdonia. Naturist area and 1 mile south of a naturist beach. ½ mile from public telephone, café/restaurant and licensed club.

BARMOUTH

Hendre Mynach Touring Caravan & Camping Park, Barmouth, Gwynedd, LL42 1YR.
Std: 01341 **Tel:** 280262 **Fax:** 280586
Email: mynach@lineone.net
Nearest Town/Resort Barmouth
Directions ¼ mile north of Barmouth on the A496 Barmouth to Harlech road.
Acreage 10 **Open** 1 March **to** 9 January
Access Good **Site** Level
Sites Available ▲ ⌂ ⊞ **Total** 245
Facilities ┌ 🔢 🚿 ┌⊙◯🔲⌂ 🔲🏠⊞✗⊞┌◻▣
Nearby Facilities ┌ ✔ ⚓ ⤢ ∪ ⚡ ♫ ⚡
⇌ Barmouth
100yds from a safe, sandy beach, 15 minutes walk down the promenade to Barmouth town centre. An excellent base for estuary and mountain walks. Pub nearby with childrens room, 15 minute walk.

HENDRE MYNACH
BARMOUTH TOURING CARAVAN AND CAMPING PARK
BARMOUTH, GWYNEDD LL42 1YR
"AWARDED AA BEST CAMPSITE IN WALES 2001"

FOR BROCHURE AND FURTHER INFORMATION
TEL: (01341) 280262   Fax: (01341) 280586   E-mail: mynach@lineone.net

* Shop & Off-Licence
* Showers
* Parent & Baby Room
* Children's Play Area
* Launderette
* Dishwashing
* Heated Toilets
* Hard Standings available
* Hair Dryers
* Mains Electric, TV and Water Hook-ups
* Pets Welcome
* Dog Walk on Site

Short walk to two local family pubs, with games room and bar food. Barmouth town centre is a safe and pleasant 15 minute walk along the promenade. Ideal site for families and as a base for estuary and mountain walks. Many local amenities within easy walking distance. Train and bus stops close by.

AA ⏩
CAMPING NEAR THE MOUNTAINS AND
WITHIN 100 YARDS OF A SAFE SANDY BEACH

RAC

BARMOUTH

Moelfre View Caravan Park, Talybont, Nr. Barmouth, Gwynedd, LL43 2AQ.
Std: 01341 **Tel:** 247100
Nearest Town/Resort Barmouth
Directions 4 miles from Barmouth on the A496 Harlech road.
Open 1 March to 14 January
Access Good **Site** Level
Sites Available ▲ ⌖ ⊟ **Total** 45
Facilities 🚿 ♿ ⚡ 🅿 ▢ ⌂ 🍴 🔌 ◨ ♨
🕴 ⊙ 🛒 ▦ ▣ ⊞
Nearby Facilities ⊢ ⟋ ⚓ ∪ 🎠 🏇
🚲 Talybont
Just a two minute walk from a safe sandy beach.

BARMOUTH

Parc Isaf Farm, Dyffryn Ardudwy, Gwynedd, LL44 2RJ.
Std: 01341 **Tel:** 247447 **Fax:** 247447
Nearest Town/Resort Barmouth
Directions From Barmouth take the A496 north for 5 miles, go through the small village of Talybont, ¼ mile on opposite the church on the left there is a right hand turn through pillar gateway. Second farm on the right, signposted.
Acreage 3 **Open** March to October
Access Good **Site** Lev/Slope
Sites Available ▲ ⌖ ⊟ **Total** 30
Facilities 🚿 ⚡ 🅿 🔌 ⊙ ♨ ⌂ ♨
Nearby Facilities ⊢ ⟋ ⚓ ∪ 🎠
🚲 Dyffryn Ardudwy/Talybont
Overlooking Cardigan Bay. Plenty of mountain and woodland walks, Harlech Castle and Portmeirion (Italian village).

BARMOUTH

Sunnysands Holiday Park, Talybont, Nr. Barmouth, Gwynedd, LL43 2LQ.
Std: 01341 **Tel:** 247301 **Fax:** 242637
Email: enquiries@sunnysands.co.uk
Website: www.sunnysands.co.uk
Nearest Town/Resort Barmouth
Directions 3½ miles from Barmouth on the seaward side of the A496. 7 miles from Harlech.
Acreage 1½ **Open** 1 March to 16 November
Access Good **Site** Level
Sites Available ⌖ ⊟ **Total** 25
Facilities 🚿 ⚡ 🅿 🍴 ▢ ⌂ 🔌 ⊙ ♨ ⌂ ♨
🕴 ⊙ 🛒 ♿ ▦ ▣ ⊞ ▣ ⊞
Nearby Facilities ⊢ ⟋ ⚓ 🎠 ∪ 🏇 🎣
🚲 Barmouth
Situated on the edge of a safe, sandy beach, recently awarded the Blue Flag. Ideal base for exploring Snowdonia National Park, and only 7 miles from Harlech with its castle and other attractions.

BEDDGELERT

Beddgelert - Forestry Commission, Beddgelert, Gwynedd, LL55 4UU.
Std: 01766 **Tel:** 890288
Email: fe.holidays@forestry.gsi.gov.uk
Website: www.forestholidays.co.uk
Nearest Town/Resort Beddgelert
Directions 2 miles north of Beddgelert Village on the A4085.
Acreage 23½ **Open** 1 January to 19 November
Access Good **Site** Level
Sites Available ▲ ⌖ ⊟ **Total** 280
Facilities 🚿 ⚡ 🅿 🔌 ⊙ ♨ ⌂ ♨
🕴 ⊙ 🛒 ♿ ▣ ⊞
Nearby Facilities ⟋ ∪ 🎣

In the heart of Snowdonia, within walking distance of Snowdon itself. Walking, cycling and canoeing also nearby. SITE RE-OPENS 20 December 2002.

BETHESDA

Ogwen Bank Caravan Park, Bethesda, Gwynedd, LL57 3LQ.
Std: 01248 **Tel:** 600486 **Fax:** 600559
Email: info@ogwenbank.co.uk
Website: www.ogwenbank.co.uk
Nearest Town/Resort Bangor
Directions Follow the A5 signposted for Betwys-y-Coed. Park is situated on the right just after the village of Bethesda.
Open March to October
Access Good **Site** Lev/Slope
Sites Available ⌖ ⊟
Facilities 🚿 ⊟ 🅿 ♿ ⚡ 🔌 ⊙ ♨ ⌂ ▢ ♨
🕴 🕴 ⊙ 🛒 ♿ ⚔ ▦ 🏇 ♨ ▣ ⊞
Nearby Facilities ⊢ ⟋ ⚓ ∪ 🏇 🎣
🚲 Bangor
Set in ancient woodlands, alongside a river and waterfalls. All individual pitches are level.

CAERNARFON

Bryn Gloch Caravan & Camping Park, Betws Garmon, Caernarfon, Gwynedd, LL54 7YY.
Std: 01286 **Tel:** 650216 **Fax:** 650591
Email: eurig@easynet.co.uk
Website: www.bryngloch.co.uk
Nearest Town/Resort Caernarfon
Directions 4½ miles south west of Caernarfon on A4085. Site on right opposite Betws Garmon church.
Acreage 12 **Open** All Year
Access Good **Site** Level
Sites Available ▲ ⌖ ⊟ **Total** 150
Facilities 🚿 ⚡ ⊟ 🅿 ♿ 🔌 ⊙ ♨ ⌂ ▢ ♨
🕴 🕴 🕴 ⊙ 🛒 ♿ ⚔ ▦ 🏇 ♨ ⊛ ♨ ▣ ▣ ⊞

Nearby Facilities ⌐ ✓ ⚓ ⟍ ∪ ♫ ⚲
≈ Bangor
Fishing, scenic views, ideal touring centre. Family owned and operated. AA 4 Pennants. Award winning site.

CAERNARFON

Challoner Camping Site, Erw Hywel, Llanrug, Caernarfon, Gwynedd, LL55 2AJ.
Std: 01286 **Tel:** 672685
Nearest Town/Resort Caernarfon
Directions A4086 from Caernarfon, 3 miles to Llanberis ½ mile west of Llanrug.
Acreage 2 **Open** 1 March **to** 12 January
Access Good **Site** Level
Sites Available ▲ ⊕ ⊟ **Total** 35
Facilities ⨍ ⊞ ⌐ ⊙ ❄ ⚲ ⛬ ⌷ ⊟
Nearby Facilities ⌐ ✓ ⚓ ⟍ ∪ ♫ ⚲
≈ Bangor
Flat dry, touring, view of Anglesey. Quiet, flat site, very central for Snowdonia Mountains and the sea.

CAERNARFON

Dinlle Caravan Park, Dinas Dinlle, Caernarfon, Gwynedd, LL54 5TW.
Std: 01286 **Tel:** 830324 **Fax:** 831562
Website: www.thornleyleisure.co.uk
Nearest Town/Resort Caernarfon
Directions From Caernarfon take the road towards Pwllheli, after 3 miles turn right for Dinas Dinlle and Caernarfon Airport, along the coast for 300 yards and turn right.
Acreage 22 **Open** March **to** November
Access Good **Site** Level
Sites Available ▲ ⊕ ⊟ **Total** 175
Facilities & & ⨍ ⊞ ⌐ ⊙ ⊶ ⛲ ⊡ ⊠ ▯ ♀ ⍩ ♠ ⋂ ⟍ ☀ ⊶⊟ ⊡ ⊟
Nearby Facilities ⌐ ✓ ⚓ ⟍ ∪ ♫
≈ Bangor
Near the beach.

CAERNARFON

Glan Gwna Holiday Park, Caeathro, Caernarfon, Gwynedd, LL55 2SG.
Std: 01286 **Tel:** 673456 **Fax:** 673456
Email: touring@glangwna.com
Website: www.glangwna.com
Nearest Town/Resort Caernarfon
Directions 1¼ mile from Caernarfon on A4085.
Acreage 5 **Open** Easter **to** October
Access Good **Site** Lev/Slope
Sites Available ▲ ⊕ ⊟ **Total** 100
Facilities ⨍ ⊞ ⌐ ⊙ ⊶ ⛲ ⊡ ⊠ ⚲ ⊙ ♠ ✕ ▽ ⋂ ⊶⊟
Nearby Facilities ⌐ ✓ ⚓ ⟍ ∪ ♫ ⚲
≈ Bangor
Lakes and a river for fishing.

CAERNARFON

Llyn-y-Gele Caravan Park, Pontllyfni, Caernarfon, Gwynedd, LL54 5EL.
Std: 01286 **Tel:** 660283/660289
Nearest Town/Resort Caernarfon
Directions Take the A487 out of Caernarfon for 3 miles, onto the A499 for 4 miles. Entrance to the site is the first right by garage and shop in the village of Pontllyfni.
Acreage 4 **Open** Easter **to** October
Access Good **Site** Level
Sites Available ▲ ⊕ ⊟ **Total** 30
Facilities ⨍ ⊞ ⌐ ⊙ ⊶ ⛲ ⊙ ⋂ ⊶⊟ ⊟
Nearby Facilities ⌐ ✓ ⚓ ⟍ ∪ ♫
≈ Bangor
Panoramic views of Snowdonia range. 7 minute walk to a beach with safe bathing. Fishing ¼ mile. Ideal location for touring Snowdonia.

CAERNARFON

Plas Gwyn Caravan Site, Plas Gwyn, Llanrug, Caernarfon, Gwynedd, LL55 2AQ.
Std: 01286 **Tel:** 672619 **Fax:** 672619
Email: info@plasgwyn.co.uk
Website: www.plasgwyn.co.uk
Nearest Town/Resort Caernarfon
Directions 3 miles from Caernarfon on the A4086, signposted on right.
Acreage 4 **Open** March **to** October
Access Good **Site** Level
Sites Available ▲ ⊕ ⊟ **Total** 35
Facilities ⨍ ⊞ ⊠ ⌐ ⊙ ⊡ ⊟ ⚲ ⊙ ♠ ⊶⊟ ⊟
Nearby Facilities ⌐ ✓ ⚓ ⟍ ∪ ♫ ⚲
≈ Bangor
Small, peaceful park. 3 miles from Snowdonia Mountains and 5 miles from the beach. Award winning hire caravans. Ensuite bed and breakfast available in the house.

CAERNARFON

Rhyd-y-Galen Caravan Park, Rhyd-y-Galen, Bethel, Caernarfon, Gwynedd, LL55 3PS.
Std: 01248 **Tel:** 670110
Nearest Town/Resort Caernarfon
Directions Signposted 1½ miles east of Caernarfon on the B4366.
Acreage 3 **Open** Easter **to** October
Access Good **Site** Lev/Slope
Sites Available ▲ ⊕ ⊟ **Total** 35
Facilities ⨍ ⊞ ⌐ ⊙ ⊡ ⛲ ⚲ ⊙ ⋂ ⊶⊟ ⊟
Nearby Facilities ⌐ ✓ ⚓ ⟍ ∪ ♫ ⚲
≈ Bangor
Ideal touring site for North Wales. Outdoor pursuit centre within 1½ miles. Beaches, mountains and forest within low mileage.

CAERNARFON

Riverside Camping, Seiont Nurseries, Pontrug, Caernarfon, Gwynedd, LL55 2BB.
Std: 01286 **Tel:** 678781/672524 **Fax:** 677223
Email:
sales@seiontnurseries.freeserve.co.uk
Nearest Town/Resort Caernarfon
Directions 2 miles out of Caernarfon on the righthand side of the A4086 (Llanberis road).
Acreage 4½ **Open** Easter **to** October
Access Good **Site** Level
Sites Available ▲ ⊕ ⊟ **Total** 55
Facilities & ⨍ ⊞ ⊠ ⌐ ⊙ ⊶ ⛲ ⚲ ⋂ ⊶⊟ ⊟
Nearby Facilities ⌐ ✓ ⚓ ⟍ ∪ ♫ ⚲
≈ Bangor
The campsite is bordered on two sides by a lovely river which is suitable for paddling and bathing. An ideal area for touring. Dogs on leads at all times. You can also E-mail us on - brenda@riversidecamping.freeserve.co.uk

CAERNARFON

Talymignedd Camping Site, Talymignedd, Nantlle, Caernarfon, Gwynedd, LL54 6BT.
Std: 01286 **Tel:** 880374
Nearest Town/Resort Caernarfon/Porthmadog
Directions On the B4418 Rhyd-ddu to Penygroes road.
Open March **to** October
Access Good **Site** Level
Sites Available ▲ ⊕ ⊟ **Total** 10
Facilities ⊞ ⊠ ⌐ ⊙ ⊡
Nearby Facilities ⌐ ✓ ⟍ ∪ ♫
≈ Porthmadog
Plenty of walking space. Fishing in a river

or lake. Ideal for touring Snowdonia and Llyn Peninsula. 20 minute drive to the nearest beach. Central for Caernarfon, Pwllheli and Porthmadog.

CAERNARFON

Tyn Rhos Farm Caravan Site, Tyn Rhos Farm, Saron, Llanwnda, Caernarfon, Gwynedd, LL55 5UH.
Std: 01286 **Tel:** 830362
Nearest Town/Resort Caernarfon
Directions From Caernarfon take the A487, after passing Tesco go straight on at the roundabout, turn first right to Saron Llanfaglan, entrance is 3 miles on the left.
Acreage 2 **Open** March **to** October
Access Good **Site** Level
Sites Available ▲ ⊕ ⊟ **Total** 20
Facilities ⨍ ⊞ ⊠ ⌐ ⊙ ⊶ ⛲
Nearby Facilities ⌐ ✓ ⚓ ⟍ ∪ ♫ ⚲
≈ Bangor
3 miles from Dinas Dinlle beach, 15 miles from Snowdonia and within easy reach of Anglesey and Lleyn Peninsula.

CAERNARFON

Tyn-y-Coed Farm Caravan Park, Llanrug, Caernarfon, Gwynedd, LL55 2AQ.
Std: 01286 **Tel:** 673565 **Fax:** 673565
Nearest Town/Resort Caernarfon
Directions From Caernarfon take the A4086 towards Llanberis, 3½ miles from Caernarfon.
Acreage 1 **Open** May **to** September
Access Good **Site** Sloping
Sites Available ▲ ⊕ ⊟ **Total** 20
Facilities ⨍ ⊞ ⊠ ⌐ ⊙ ⊶ ⛲ ⊙ ⋂ ⊶⊟ ⊟
Nearby Facilities ⌐ ✓ ⚓ ⟍ ∪ ♫ ⚲
≈ Bangor
Walking on secluded country foot paths. Pets are welcome on a lead. Electric hookups to tourers and tents if required.

CAERNARFON

Tyn-yr-Onnen Mountain Farm Caravan & Camping Park, Waunfawr, Caernarfon, Gwynedd, LL55 4AX.
Std: 01286 **Tel:** 650281 **Fax:** 650043
Nearest Town/Resort Caernarfon
Directions A4085 Caernarfon (A487) to Beddgelert, left at Waunfawr village church/chip shop, signposted from that point.
Acreage 4¼ **Open** 1st May Holiday **to** Sept
Access Good **Site** Lev/Slope
Sites Available ▲ ⊕ ⊟ **Total** 60
Facilities ⨍ ⊞ ⊠ ⌐ ⊙ ⊶ ⛲ ⊡ ⊠ ⚲ ⍩ ♠ ☀ ⊶⊟ ⊡ ⊟
Nearby Facilities ⌐ ✓ ⚓ ⟍ ∪ ♫ ⚲
≈ Bangor
A working farm at the foot of a mountain, secluded and peaceful, ideal touring and walking base. Colour brochure only on receiving a S.A.E.. AA 3 Pennants and WTB 3 Star Graded.

CAERNARFON

White Tower Caravan Park, Llandwrog, Caernarfon, Gwynedd, LL54 5UH.
Std: 01286 **Tel:** 830649
Email: whitetower@supanet.com
Website: www.whitetower.supanet.com
Nearest Town/Resort Caernarfon
Directions From Caernarfon follow the A487 Porthmadog road for approx ¼ mile, go past the Tesco Supermarket, straight ahead at the roundabout and take the first turning on the right. We are 3 miles on the right.
Acreage 3 **Open** March **to** October
Access Good **Site** Level
Sites Available ▲ ⊕ ⊟ **Total** 52

Glan Gwna Country Holiday Park

**Caeathro, Caernarfon, Gwynedd,
North Wales LL55 2SG**
Warden: (01286) 676402 (Summer Months On...
Reception: (01286) 673456

E-mail: touring@glangwna.com
Website: www.glangwna.com

Set in sheltered
rural surroundings,
yet just 2 miles from
the Royal Town of
Caernarfon lies the
magnificient family
run holiday park -
'Glan Gwna'.

Being located between
Snowdonia National Park
and the golden beaches of
the Lleyn Peninsula,
the park is ideally situated
to allow easy access to all
the pleasures this beautiful
region has to offer.

BOOKING ESSENTIAL BANK HOLIDAYS & SUMMER MONT...

FACILITIES ON THE PARK

- Outdoor heated swimming pool
- Gildas Bar - evening entertainment
- Poolside Bar - catering for meals and snacks
- Launderette
- Supermarket
- Take-Away
- Hair Salon
- Children's Play Area
- Coarse & game fishing
- Holiday home accommodation for hire and sale

Glan Gwna has excellent touring facilities for caravans, tents and motor homes with resident site wardens, and offers both riverside and parkland pitches.

DIRECTIONS TO PARK - 1½ miles from Caernarfon on A4085

IN THE HEART OF SNOWDONIA

LLANDWROG, CAERNARFON
GWYNEDD LL54 5UH
TEL: 01286 830649
WEB: www.whitetower.supanet.com
E-MAIL: whitetower@supanet.com

Quiet, rural setting with splendid views of Snowdon. Electric hook-ups, heated toilet and shower facilities, baby room, washing up area, launderette with ironing facilities, fresh water points and separate facilities for the disabled. Outdoor heated swimming pool (Mid May to Mid Sept), Calor Gas, Camping Gaz, lounge bar with family room, children's play area, TV and Games room. Please note that some of the facilities may be limited during low season. Approximately 3 miles south of Caernarfon and 2½ miles from Dinas Dinlle beach. Supervised continuously by the resident proprietors to a very high standard and offers an ideal choice for your family holiday.

Facilities ♿ ⚡ ⚑ 📶 ⚓ ☐ ⊙ ⌿ ⚐ ☒ ⊞ ☐ ☎ ♨ ⚑ 📶 ⚑ ⚘ ⚒ ⚘ ⚘ ⊞ 🛈 🛝 ⛱
Nearby Facilities ⌐ ⚲ ⚓ ⚓ ∪ ∌ ℛ ⚐
⚐ Bangor
2½ miles beach, 3¼ miles Caernarfon. Splendid views of Snowdon. Central for touring Llyn Peninsula, Anglesey and Snowdonia.

CHWILOG

Tyddyn Heilyn, Chwilog, Pwllheli, Gwynedd, LL53 6SW.
Std: 01766 **Tel:** 810441 **Fax:** 810441
Nearest Town/Resort Criccieth
Directions From the A497 take the B4354, in Chwilog Village turn right opposite Madryn Arms, second site on the right, signpost at entrance.
Acreage 1 **Open** April **to** September
Access Good **Site** Level
Sites Available Å ♥ ⚐
Facilities ⚡ ⚑ 📶 ⚓ ⌐ ⊙ ⚑ ☒ ⚑ ⊞ A
Nearby Facilities ⌐ ⚲ ⚓ ⚓ ∪ ∌ ℛ ⚐
⚐ Criccieth
Shady site on the Lleyn Peninsula at the edge of Snowdonia National Park. Near to shops and a choice of good beaches. River and tree-lined walks through farmland. Ideal for Portmeirion, Porthmadog and Pwllheli marinas.

CLYNNOG FAWR

Aberafon Camping Site, Gyrn Goch, Caernarfon, Gwynedd, LL54 5PN.
Std: 01286 **Tel:** 660295 **Fax:** 660582
Email: hugh@maelor.demon.co.uk
Website: www.maelor.demon.co.uk/aberafon.html
Nearest Town/Resort Caernarfon
Directions From Caernarfon take the A499 towards Pwllheli. 1 mile after Clynnog Fawr on the right hand side.
Acreage 15 **Open** April **to** October
Access Poor **Site** Level
Sites Available Å ♥ ⚐ **Total** 65
Facilities ⚑ 📶 ⚓ ⌐ ⊙ 🛒 🛈 ⚑ 📶 ⚑ A↦☐
Nearby Facilities ⌐ ⚲ ⚓ ⚓ ∪ ∌ ℛ ⚐
⚐ Pwllheli
Private beach. Boat launching available. Take-away food.

CRICCIETH

Cae-Canol Caravan & Camping, Criccieth, Gwynedd, LL52 0NB.
Std: 01766 **Tel:** 522351
Nearest Town/Resort Criccieth
Directions Take the B4411 from Criccieth, 2 miles. Also 2½ miles from the A487 towards Criccieth.
Acreage 3 **Open** April **to** October
Access Very Good **Site** Level
Sites Available Å ♥ ⚐ **Total** 25

Facilities ⚡ ⚑ 📶 ⚓ ⌐ ⊙ ⚑ 🛈 ⊞ ☒
Nearby Facilities ⌐ ⚲ ⚓ ⚓ ∪ ℛ ⚐
⚐ Criccieth
Sheltered, grassy site. Private trout fishing available for caravanners and campers. Delightful riverside walk nearby. Ideal for touring.

CRICCIETH

Camping & Caravanning Club Site, Tyddyn Sianel, Llanystumdwy, Criccieth, Gwynedd, LL52 0LS.
Std: 01766 **Tel:** 522855
Website: www.campingandcaravanningclub.co.uk
Nearest Town/Resort Criccieth
Directions From Criccieth take the A497 and turn second right signposted Llanstumdwy, site is on the right.
Acreage 4 **Open** April **to** October
Access Good **Site** Sloping
Sites Available Å ♥ ⚐ **Total** 60
Facilities ⚑ 📶 ⚓ ⌐ ⊙ ⚑ ⚑ ⊞ ☐ ☒
🛈 ☐ ⚑↦⊞ ☐
Nearby Facilities ⌐ ⚲ ∪ ℛ
⚐ Criccieth
Situated just outside Criccieth with scenic coastal views. Nearby attractions include Ffestiniog Railway and Snowdonia National Park. BTB Graded. Non members welcome.

CRICCIETH

Eisteddfa Caravan & Camping Site, Eisteddfa Lodge, Pentrefelin, Criccieth, Gwynedd, LL52 0PT.
Std: 01766 **Tel:** 522696
Email: karen@eisteddfa.fsnet.co.uk
Website: www.eisteddfa.fsnet.co.uk
Nearest Town/Resort Criccieth
Directions On the A497 Porthmadog to Criccieth road, 1½ miles north east of Criccieth. Entrance is at the west end of Pentrefelin beside the Plas Gwyn Nursing Home.
Acreage 11 **Open** March **to** October
Access Good **Site** Lev/Slope
Sites Available Å ♥ ⚐ **Total** 145
Facilities ⚑ 📶 ⚓ ⌐ ⊙ 🛒 🛈 🛈 ☐ ⚑ ✕ ⚑↦☐
Nearby Facilities ⌐ ⚲ ⚓ ⚓ ∪ ∌ ℛ ⚐
⚐ Criccieth

CRICCIETH

Muriau Bach, Rhoslan, Criccieth, Gwynedd, LL52 0NP.
Std: 01766 **Tel:** 530642
Nearest Town/Resort Criccieth
Directions Coming from Porthmadog on the A487, turn left onto the B4411. Fourth entrance on the left over a cattle grid, with a drive leading up to the site.
Acreage 1¼ **Open** March **to** October
Access Good **Site** Level

Sites Available Å ♥ ⚐ **Total** 30
Facilities ⚑ 📶 ⚓ ⌐ ⊙ ⚑ 🛈 ☐ ♨↦
Nearby Facilities ⌐ ⚲ ⚓ ⚓ ∪ ∌ ℛ ⚐
⚐ Criccieth
Attractive, clean, level site, near to the sea and mountains and central to all places of interest. Commanding the best views in the area, nice walks nearby. Cycle track nearby that leads to Caernarfon. Concessions for pensioners (off peak season) free hot water. Pets welcome but strictly on a lead. Rock climbing at Tremadog. Bowling green, highland railway and two leisure centres all within easy reach.

CRICCIETH

Mynydd-Du Caravan & Camping Site, Mynydd-Du, Criccieth, Gwynedd, LL52 0PS.
Std: 01766 **Tel:** 522533
Nearest Town/Resort Criccieth
Directions On the A497, 3 miles west of Porthmadog and 1 mile east of Criccieth.
Acreage 5½ **Open** April **to** October
Access Good **Site** Level
Sites Available Å ♥ ⚐ **Total** 80
Facilities ⚑ ⌐ ⊙ ⚑ ⊞ ☐
Nearby Facilities ⌐ ⚲ ⚓ ⚓ ∪ ∌ ℛ ⚐
⚐ Criccieth
Superb views of the Snowdonia range of hills and Cardigan Bay. 1 mile from the beach. Central for places of interest including castles.

CRICCIETH

Plymouth Farm, Criccieth, Gwynedd, LL52 0PS.
Std: 01766 **Tel:** 522327
Nearest Town/Resort Criccieth
Open Easter **to** October
Access Good **Site** Level
Sites Available ♥ ⚐ **Total** 16
Facilities ⚑ 📶 ⚓ ⌐ ⊙ ⚑ ☒ ⚑
Nearby Facilities ⌐ ⚲ ⚓ ⚓ ∪ ℛ ⚐
⚐ Criccieth
Beach, tennis court and bowling green. Central for Porthmadog and Pwllheli.

CRICCIETH

Tyddyn Morthwyl, Criccieth, Gwynedd, LL52 0NF.
Std: 01766 **Tel:** 522115
Nearest Town/Resort Criccieth
Directions 1½ miles north of Criccieth on B4411 main road to Caernarfon.
Acreage 6 **Open** March **to** October
Access Good **Site** Level
Sites Available Å ♥ ⚐ **Total** 40
Facilities ⚑ 📶 ⚓ ⌐ ⊙ ⚑ ♨ ⊞ ☐ ☒
Nearby Facilities ⌐ ⚲ ⚓ ⚓ ∪ ∌ ℛ ⚐
⚐ Criccieth
Central for mountains of Snowdonia and beaches of Lleyn Peninsula. Level and sheltered with mountain views.

NAS DINLLE

orfa Lodge Caravan Park, Dinas Dinlle,
ear Caernarfon, Gwynedd, LL54 5TP.
d: 01286 **Tel:** 830205 **Fax:** 831329
nail: info@morfalodge.co.uk
ebsite: www.morfalodge.co.uk
earest Town/Resort Caernarfon
rections From the A487 south from
aernarfon which leads onto the A499. 7
les from Caernarfon turn for Dinas Dinlle,
n right at the far end of Beach Road.
:reage 15 **Open** March to October
:cess Good **Site** Level
tes Available ▲ ⊕ ➾ **Total** 145
:ilities ♿ ∮ 🖩 🅗 🆄 ♨ ♏ ⌁ 🔲 ☎
🏢 🅛 ✕ 🐕 ⌖ 🅰 ⑇ ☀ ⌘ 🔛 🔲 🅑
earby Facilities ┏ ✔ ⚓ ⌄ ∪ ✈ ♪ ✗
  Bangor
mile from Dinas Dinlle beach, central for
uring Snowdonia, Anglesey and Lleyn
:ninsula.

NAS MAWDDWY

nypwll Caravan Site, Dinas Mawddwy,
achynlleth, Gwynedd, SY20 9JF.
d: 01650 **Tel:** 531326
earest Town/Resort Machynlleth
rections From the A470 turn right in
allwyd, Dinas Mawddwy is 1 mile
gnposted, turn right by the Red Lion Inn
d site is first on the left by the bridge.
:reage 2 **Open** March to End October
:cess Good **Site** Level
tes Available ▲ ⊕ ➾
cilities ∮ 🖩 🅰 ♏ 🅐 🔲 🅐 ✈
earby Facilities ✔ ⚓ ✗ ✈
  Machynlleth
verside site with lovely scenery and
rrounded by rhododendrons. 17 miles
m the beach. Lovely walks. Near to
rmouth, Dolgelley and Aberdovey.

DOLGELLAU

Dolgamedd Camping & Caravan Site,
Dolgamedd, Bontnewydd, Dolgellau,
Gwynedd, LL40 2SH.
Std: 01341 **Tel:** 422624 **Fax:** 422624
Nearest Town/Resort Dolgellau
Directions 3 miles from Dolgellau towards
Bala, turn right for Brithdir and continue over
the bridge and we are 30 yards on the left.
Acreage 6 **Open** Easter/1 April to End Oct
Access Good **Site** Level
Sites Available ▲ ⊕ ➾ **Total** 65
Facilities ∮ 🅗 🆄 🅰 ♏ ⊙ ⌁ 🔛 🔲 🅑
Nearby Facilities ┏ ✔ ⚓ ✗ ∪ ⑇ ♪ ✗
  ✈ Machynlleth/Barmouth
Sheltered, level site alongside the River
Wnion, good for Salmon fishing and
swimming. Way-marked riverside and
woodland walks. Picnic tables, camp fires
and BBQ sites.

DOLGELLAU

Dolserau Uchaf, Dolgellau, Gwynedd,
LL40 2DE.
Std: 01341 **Tel:** 422639
Nearest Town/Resort Dolgellau
Directions 3 miles from Dolgellau on the
A494.
Acreage 1 **Open** Easter to October
Access Good **Site** Level
Sites Available ▲ ⊕ ➾ **Total** 20
Facilities ♨ 🅗 🅰 ♏ ⊙ ⌁ 🔛 🔲
Nearby Facilities ┏ ✔ ∪
  ✈ Barmouth
Quiet site with open views of the Cader Idris
Range.

DOLGELLAU

Llwyn-Yr-Helm Farm, Brithdir, Dolgellau,
Gwynedd, LL40 2SA.
Std: 01341 **Tel:** 450254
Nearest Town/Resort Dolgellau

Directions Take minor road at telephone
kiosk off the B4416 which is a loop road from
A470 to A494, Dolgellau 4 miles.
Acreage 2½ **Open** Easter to End October
Site Level
Sites Available ▲ ⊕ ➾ **Total** 25
Facilities ∮ 🅛 🅰 ♏ ⊙ ☎ 🆂 🔛 🔲
Nearby Facilities ┏ ✔ ⚓ ✗ ∪ ⑇ ♪ ✗
  ✈ Machynlleth
Friendly, quiet small farm site with scenic
views, ideal for walking, touring and sandy
beaches. Milk and eggs available. Well
behaved pets welcome.

DOLGELLAU

Pant-y-Cae, Arthog, Gwynedd, LL39 1LJ.
Std: 01341 **Tel:** 250892 **Fax:** 250892
Nearest Town/Resort Fairbourne
Directions Take the A493 Tywyn to
Dolgellau road. From Dolgellau after Arthog
Village sign turn next left for Cregennan
Lakes, then turn second left.
Acreage 4 **Open** All Year
Access Good **Site** Lev/Slope
Sites Available ▲ ⊕□ **Total** 56
Facilities 🅛 🅰 ♏ 🅘 🔛 🔲 🅑
Nearby Facilities ┏ ✔ ⚓ ∪ ✗
2 miles from the beach, horse riding, fishing,
walking and climbing, launderette, shop and
gas supplies.

DOLGELLAU

Tanyfron Camping & Caravan Park,
Arran Road, Dolgellau, Gwynedd, LL40
2AA.
Std: 01341 **Tel:** 422638 **Fax:** 421251
Email: rowlands@tanyfron.freeserve.co.uk
Nearest Town/Resort Dolgellau
Directions From Welshpool take A470, turn
for Dolgellau by Hanson Depot. ¼ mile on
left - Dolgellau straight on ½ mile from site.
Acreage 3¼ **Open** 1 March to 7 Jan

"... in the very heart of North Wales"

snowdon view caravan park

Snowdon View is a most attractive caravan and camping park. Set amongst beautiful Snowdonia scenery, it is perfectly situated for exploring all the magnificence of the area, and is ideal for short or long stays. The Park facilities include indoor heated swimming pool, delightful cottage pub providing bar meals, adventure playground, launderette, dog walk, Free showers, ample supply of water points and electric hook-ups. Well maintained grounds.

Snowdon View Caravan Park, Brynrefail, Nr. Llanberis, Caernarfon, Gwynedd LL55 3PD
Telephone: 01286 870349

Access Good **Site** Level
Sites Available ▲ ⌖ ⊟ **Total** 43
Facilities ∮ ⚐ ⛳ ⓌⒷ ♨ ℝ ⊙ ⌿ 🚽 ◨ ⬚ ☎ ⌖ ⚑ ⚙ ⚒ ⧈ 🅿
Nearby Facilities ┏ ✔ ⚓ ✈ U ♀ ⚡
≈ Barmouth
10 miles beach, scenic views, walking, touring, fishing, walking distance of town. TV hook-ups to touring pitches. En-suite B&B available. WTB 5 Star Graded Park and 2000 Wales in Bloom Award Winners.

DOLGELLAU
Tyddyn Farm, Islawrdref, Dolgellau, Gwynedd, LL40 1TL.
Std: 01341 **Tel:** 422472
Nearest Town/Resort Dolgellau
Directions From Dolgellau take the Cader road, 2½ miles up for Cader Idris Mountain.
Acreage 3 **Open** All Year
Access Good **Site** Sloping
Sites Available ▲ ⌖ ⬚ **Total** 15
Facilities ☎ ✚ 🅿
Nearby Facilities ┏ ✔ U ⚡
≈ Machynlleth
River, mountains and lovely walks.

DOLGELLAU
Vanner Abbey Farm Caravan Park, Vanner Farm, Llanelltyd, Dolgellau, Gwynedd, LL40 2HE.
Std: 01341 **Tel:** 422854
Email: enquiries@vanner.co.uk
Website: www.vanner.co.uk
Nearest Town/Resort Dolgellau
Directions From Dolgellau take the A470 north for 1½ miles, follow Cymer Abbey signs to the site.
Acreage 3 **Open** Easter to End October
Access Good **Site** Level
Sites Available ▲ ⌖ ⊟ **Total** 30
Facilities ⚒ ∮ ⓌⒷ ♨ ℝ ⊙ ☎ ⌖ ⚙ ⚒ 🅿
Nearby Facilities ┏ ✔ U ♀ ⚡
≈ Barmouth
Quiet site set alongside a river.

DYFFRYN ARDUDWY
Dyffryn Seaside Estate, Dyffryn Ardudwy, Gwynedd, LL44 2HD.
Std: 01341 **Tel:** 247220 **Fax:** 247622
Nearest Town/Resort Barmouth
Directions From Barmouth take the A496 north, after 5 miles turn left at the church just north of Talybont.
Acreage 11 **Open** Easter to September
Site Level
Sites Available ▲ **Total** 250
Facilities ☎ ∮ ⓌⒷ ♨ ℝ ⊙ ⌿ 🚽 ⬚ ◨ ⬚ ☎ ⚡ ⌖ ⚙ ⚒ ✕ ▽ 🅟 ⋔ ⚏ ❀ ℙ ⬚
Nearby Facilities ┏ ✔ ⚓ ✈ U ⚡ ⚡
≈ Dyffryn Ardudwy
Near the beach. Mountain walks.

DYFFRYN ARDUDWY
Murmur-yr-Afon Touring Caravan & Camping Site, Dyffryn Ardudwy, Gwynedd, LL44 2BE.
Std: 01341 **Tel:** 247353 **Fax:** 247353
Email:
mills@murmuryrafon25.freeserve.co.uk
Nearest Town/Resort Barmouth
Directions Take the A496 coast road from Barmouth towards Harlech. Site entrance is 100yds from the Power Garage in Dyffryn Village on the right hand side.
Acreage 4 **Open** March to October
Access Good **Site** Level
Sites Available ▲ ⌖ ⊟ **Total** 47
Facilities ⚒ ∮ ⚐ ⓌⒷ ♨ ℝ ⊙ ⌿ 🚽 ⬚ ◨ ⬚ ☎
⧈ ⚙ ⚒ ⬚ 🅿
Nearby Facilities ┏ ✔ ⚓ ✈ U ♀ ♀ ⚡
≈ Dyffryn
1 mile from beach. Set in sheltered and natural surroundings, 100yds from village and shops, petrol stations and licensed premises.

FFESTINIOG
Llechrwd, Maentwrog, Blaenau Ffestiniog, Gwynedd, LL41 4HF.
Std: 01766 **Tel:** Maentwrog 590240
Directions On the A496. Blaenau Ffestiniog 3 miles, Porthmadog 8 miles.
Acreage 5 **Open** Easter to October
Access Good **Site** Lev/Slope
Sites Available ▲ ⌖ ⊟
Facilities ∮ ⓌⒷ ♨ ℝ ⊙ ☎ ⊙ ⚒ 🅿
Nearby Facilities ┏ ✔ U ⚡
≈ Blaenau Ffestiniog
Riverside camp.

HARLECH
Woodlands Caravan Park, Harlech, Gwynedd, LL46 2UE.
Std: 01766 **Tel:** 780419 **Fax:** 780419
Email: grace@woodlandscp.fsnet.co.uk
Website: www.woodlandscp.fsnet.co.uk
Nearest Town/Resort Harlech
Directions Leave A496 at Harlech railway crossing, site signposted at crossing at foot of castle.
Acreage 2 **Open** March to October
Access Good **Site** Level
Sites Available ⌖ ⊟ **Total** 37
Facilities ∮ ⚐ ⓌⒷ ♨ ℝ ⊙ 🚽 ◨ ⬚ ☎
⚒ ⊙ ⚒ 🅿
Nearby Facilities ┏ ✔ ⚓ ✈ U ⚡ ⚡
≈ Harlech
Near beach, shops and golfcourse. Harlech Castle adjacent. Swimming pool nearby. Centrally heated shower and toilet building. Ideal touring.

LLANBEDROG
Bolmynydd Touring & Camping Park, Contact Address: Refail, Llanbedrog, Pwllheli, Gwynedd, LL53 7NP.
Std: 01758 **Tel:** 740511
Email: refail.llanbedrog@ukonline.co.uk
Nearest Town/Resort Llanbedrog
Directions Follow the A499 from Pwllheli to Llanbedrog for 3½ miles. Continue towards Abersoch (on the A499) for ½ mile and take the first left lane after Llanbedrog Riding Centre (by the red post box). Site ½ mile on the left.
Acreage 2 **Open** Easter to End September
Access Fair **Site** Level
Sites Available ▲ ⌖ ⊟ **Total** 48
Facilities ∮ ⓌⒷ ♨ ℝ ⊙ ⌿ 🚽 ⬚ ◨ ☎
⧈ ⊙ ⚒ ⬚ 🅿
Nearby Facilities ┏ ✔ ⚓ ✈ U ⚡
≈ Pwllheli
5 minutes walk to the beach and nearest pub. Adjacent to 500 acres of moorland with beautiful hill and coastal footpath Panoramic views of Llyn Peninsula, Snowdonia and coast. New facilities with central heating. WTB 4 Star Graded.

LLANBEDROG
Refail Touring & Camping Park, Refail, Llanbedrog, Pwllheli, Gwynedd, LL53 7NP.
Std: 01758 **Tel:** 740511
Email: refail.llanbedrog@ukonline.co.uk
Nearest Town/Resort Llanbedrog
Directions Follow A499 from Pwllheli to Llanbedrog turn right onto B4413 to LLanbedrog, site situated 500 metres on the right hand side.
Acreage 2 **Open** Easter to 30 Sept
Access Good **Site** Level
Sites Available ▲ ⌖ ⊟ **Total** 33
Facilities ⚒ ∮ ⚐ ⓌⒷ ♨ ℝ ⊙ ⌿ 🚽 ⬚ ◨ ☎
⧈ ⧈ ⚙ 🅿 ⬚
Nearby Facilities ┏ ✔ ⚓ ✈ U ♀ ⚡
≈ Pwllheli
Small, friendly park for an ideal family holiday. Beautiful beach, pub and bistro within a five minute walk. Lovely coastal and country walks. Excellent facilities with heated modern shower block, launderette and dishwashing room. WTB 4 Star Graded.

LLANBEDROG
Wern Newydd Caravan & Camping Park, Llanbedrog, Pwllheli, Gwynedd, LL53 7PG.
Std: 01758 **Tel:** 740810/740220 **Fax:** 740810
Nearest Town/Resort Abersoch
Directions From Pwllheli take the A499 towards Abersoch, in Llanbedrog turn right

Garreg Goch Caravan Park

Black Rock Sands, Morfa Bychan, Porthmadog, Gwynedd LL49 9YD
Telephone: (01766) 512210

Garreg Goch Caravan Park is a small, quiet, select park catering for families.
The park is situated within six minutes walk from the famous Black Rock Sands
which is a two mile long firm sandy beach.

✳ *Children's Play Area* ✳ *Park Shop* ✳ *Launderette* ✳ *Showers and Toilets*
✳ *Pitches for Tourers and Tents* ✳ *Electric hook-up.*

Morfa Bychan is a quiet village situated about two miles west of Porthmadog with
easy access to the beach, golfing, sailing and Snowdonia National Park.

---

nto the B4413 signposted Aberdaron.
ontinue through the village and turn right
y the newsagents onto an unclassified
oad, site is 700 yards on the right.
creage 2½ **Open** March **to** October
ccess Good **Site** Level
ites Available ⚠ ⛺ ⛺ **Total** 30
acilities ⚿ ⚡ Ⓦ ⚓ ⌂ ☉ ⚐ ⛟ ☎
⚑ ⚑ ❄ 🄿
earby Facilities ⌲ ⚓ ⚓ ⚓ ∪ ⚓
⚑ Pwllheli/Bangor
eaceful, secluded park on the beautiful
eyn Peninsula. Just a five minute walk to
e village of Llanbedrog with its shops,
opular country inns and several good
aces to eat. It also boasts a popular, safe,
andy beach for swimming wind-surfing and
oating. 10 minute walk to the beach and 2
iles from Abersoch.

LANBERIS
nowdon View Caravan Park, Brynrefail,
r. Llanberis, Caernarfon, Gwynedd, LL55
PD.
td: 01286 **Tel:** 870349 **Fax:** 870349
earest Town/Resort Caernarfon
irections Located on the B4547 Bongor
 Caernarfon road.
pen 1 March **to** 12 December
ccess Good **Site** Lev/Slope
ites Available ⚠ ⛺ ⛺
ds ⚿ Ⓦ ⚓ ☉ ⚐ 🄿 ⛟ 🄿 🄿 ⚓ 🄿 🄿 🄿
earby Facilities ⌲ ⚓ ⚓ ∪ ⚓
 Bangor

MORFA NEFYN
raeanfryn Farm, Morfa Nefyn,
wynedd, LL53 6YQ.
td: 01758 **Tel:** 720455 **Fax:** 720485
mail: ian.jan.harrison@tinyworld.co.uk
earest Town/Resort Pwllheli
irections From Pwllheli take the A497 for

5 miles, at the roundabout turn left and then
turn next left. Entrance to the site is 50 yards
on the right.
Acreage 1 **Open** All Year
Access Good **Site** Level
Sites Available ⚠ ⛺ ⛺ **Total** 12
Facilities ⚿ Ⓦ ⚓ ⚐ ⛟ ⚐ 🄿
Nearby Facilities ⌲ ⚓ ⚓ ⚓ ∪ ⚓
⚑ Pwllheli/Bangor
Rural location, 1 mile from the beach.
Barbecue area. Café/Restaurant nearby.
Camping and Caravan Club Site.

PORTHMADOG
**Black Rock Sands Camping & Touring
Park,** Morfa Bychan, Porthmadog,
Gwynedd, LL49 9YD.
Std: 01766 **Tel:** 513919
Nearest Town/Resort Porthmadog
Directions From Porthmadog take the road
to Morfa Bychan, turn right just before the
beach.
Acreage 9 **Open** March **to** October
Access Good **Site** Level
Sites Available ⚠ ⛺ ⛺ **Total** 140
Facilities ⚿ Ⓦ ⚓ ⌂ ☉ ⚐ ⚐ ⚐ ⛟
⚑ ⚑ ⚓ ⚐ ⚐ ❄ 🄿 🄿
Nearby Facilities ⌲ ⚓ ⚓ ⚓ ∪ ⚓ 🄿
⚑ Porthmadog
Adjacent to a 7 mile sandy beach.

PORTHMADOG
Garreg Goch Caravan Park, Black Rock
Sands, Morfa Bychan, Porthmadog,
Gwynedd, LL49 9YD.
Std: 01766 **Tel:** 512210
Nearest Town/Resort Porthmadog
Directions Turn off A487 in Porthmadog,
at Woolworths, follow signs for Morfa
Bychan for 2 miles, turn left at sign for park.
Acreage 5 **Open** March **to** October
Access Good **Site** Level

Sites Available ⚠ ⛺ ⛺ **Total** 24
Facilities ⚿ ⚡ Ⓦ ⚓ ⌂ ☉ ⚐ ⚐ ⛟
⚑ ⚑ ⚐ ⚐ ⚐ ❄ 🄿 🄿
Nearby Facilities ⌲ ⚓ ⚓ ⚓ ∪ ⚓ 🄿 🄿
⚑ Porthmadog
Near sandy beach, scenic views. Ideal for
touring places of interest.

PORTHMADOG
Glan-Y-Mor Camping Park, Morfa
Bychan, Porthmadog, Gwynedd, LL49 9LD.
Std: 01766 **Tel:** 514640
Nearest Town/Resort Porthmadog
Directions From Porthmadog take the road
to Morfa Bychan, continue to the beach,
entrance is on the left.
Acreage 5 **Open** May **to** September
Site Level
Sites Available ⚠ **Total** 60
Facilities Ⓦ ⚓ ⌂ ⛟ ⚐ 🄿
Nearby Facilities ⌲ ⚓ ⚓ ⚓ ∪ ⚓ 🄿 🄿
⚑ Porthmadog
Adjacent to a 7 mile sandy beach.

PORTHMADOG
Greenacres Holiday Park, Black Rock
Sands, Morfa Bychan, Porthmadog,
Gwynedd, LL49 9YB.
Std: 08457 **Tel:** 125931 **Fax:** 512084
Website: www.british-holidays.co.uk
Nearest Town/Resort Porthmadog
Directions After going over the toll bridge
at Porthmadog, go along the high street and
turn between the Post Office and
Woolworths. ¼ mile on through the village
of Morfa Bychan, take the right fork to Black
Rock Sands, Greenacres is about 2 miles.
Open March **to** October
Access Good **Site** Level
Sites Available ⛺ ⛺ **Total** 52
Facilities ⚿ ⚡ ⚿ Ⓦ ⚓ ⚐ ⚐ ⚐ ⛟
⚑ ⚑ ⚐ ⚐ ❄ 🄿 🄿 🄿 ❄ ❄ ⚐ 🄿 🄿

TYDDYN LLWYN CARAVAN PARK
Morfa Bychan Road, Porthmadog, Gwynedd LL49 9UR

Situated in a delightful, secluded, wooded valley but close to the town. An ideal centre from which to tour Snowdonia and North Wales. Good facilities and local attractions.

For Brochure Tel: (01766) 512205
Fax: (01766) 514601
Web Site: www.tyddynllwyn.com

Nearby Facilities ⌐ ✔ ⚓ ∪ ♫ ⚡
⚓ Porthmadog
Near the beach with scenic views. New sport and leisure facilities including bike hire, bowling and Pitch & Putt. Kids Club and a full family entertainment programme. Ideal touring. Dragon Award.

PORTHMADOG
Gwyndy Caravan Park, Black Rock Sands, Morfa Bychan, Porthmadog, Gwynedd, LL49 9YB.
Std: 01766 **Tel:** 512047 **Fax:** 512047
Email: martin@gwyndy.globalnet.co.uk
Nearest Town/Resort Porthmadog
Directions In Porthmadog turn at Woolworths to Black Rock Sands follow the road into the village of Morfa Bychan past the petrol station and Spar, turn first left and then second right into road leading into caravan park, exactly 2 miles from Porthmadog.
Acreage 5 **Open** March to November
Access Good **Site** Level
Sites Available ▲ ⊞ ⚘ **Total** 24
Facilities ✦ ⒰ ⚒ ⌐ ⊙ ⚘ ⚘ ▣ ☎
⚲ ⓘ ⓖ ⚘ ⊟
Nearby Facilities ⌐ ✔ ⚓ ⚓ ∪ ♫ ⚡
⚓ Porthmadog
Select family run park, just a few minutes from the beach, with backdrop of mountain views. Ideal for touring the Snowdonia area. All super pitches.

PORTHMADOG
Ty Bricks Caravan Site, Porthmadog, Gwynedd, LL49 9PP.
Std: 01766 **Tel:** 512597
Nearest Town/Resort Porthmadog
Acreage 4 **Open** March to October
Access Good **Site** Level
Sites Available ⊞ ⚘ **Total** 18
Facilities ✦ ⒰ ☎ ⊙ ⊬ ▣
Nearby Facilities ⌐ ✔ ⚓ ⚓ ∪ ♫ ⚡
⚓ Porthmadog
Small, quiet site with very scenic views.

PORTHMADOG
Tyddyn Adi Camping Park, Morfa Bychan, Porthmadog, Gwynedd, LL49 9YW.
Std: 01766 **Tel:** 512933
Nearest Town/Resort Porthmadog
Directions From Porthmadog take the Morfa Bychan road 2¼ miles. Follow to the end of village and there is a large red sign on the right.
Acreage 28 **Open** Easter to October
Access Good **Site** Level
Sites Available ▲ ⊞ ⚘ **Total** 200
Facilities ✦ ⒰ ⚒ ⌐ ⊙ ▣ ⚘
⚲ ⓖ ⚘ ⓜ ⚘ ✳ ⊬ ⊟
Nearby Facilities ⌐ ✔ ⚓ ⚓ ∪ ♫ ⚡

⚓ Porthmadog
Close to Porthmadog attractions and ¼ mile from Black Rock Sands. Ideal for touring.

PORTHMADOG
Tyddyn Llwyn Caravan Park & Campsite, Black Rock Road, Porthmadog, Gwynedd, LL49 9UR.
Std: 01766 **Tel:** 512205 **Fax:** 512205
Email: info@tyddynllwyn.com
Website: www.tyddynllwyn.com
Nearest Town/Resort Porthmadog
Directions On high street turn by the Post Office signposted golf course and Black Rock Sands. Park is on the right in under ¼ mile. Verge signs on left.
Acreage 52 **Open** March to October
Access Good **Site** Lev/Slope
Sites Available ▲ ⊞ ⚘ **Total** 153
Facilities ✦ ⒰ ⚒ ⚘ ⌐ ⊙ ⚘ ⚘ ⚘ ⚘
⚲ ⓖ ⚘ ✳ ▽ ⓜ ♣ ⊬ ▣ ⊟
Nearby Facilities ⌐ ✔ ⚓ ⚓ ∪ ♫ ⚡
⚓ Porthmadog
Only 2 miles from Black Rock Sands. In a sheltered valley beneath Moel Y Gest mountain with beautiful wooded scenery. AA Graded.

PWLLHELI
Bodfel Hall Caravan Park, Bodfel Hall, Pwllheli, Gwynedd, LL53 6DW.
Std: 01758 **Tel:** 612014
Email: caravan@bodfel.com
Website: www.bodfel.com
Nearest Town/Resort Pwllheli
Directions West out of Pwllheli, turn right onto the A497, 2½ miles turn right after the entrance to Bodfel Hall Adventure Park and follow signs.
Acreage 2½ **Open** March to October
Access Good **Site** Level
Sites Available ⊞ ⚘ **Total** 50
Facilities ⒰ ⌐ ⊙ ⓖ ⚘ ⚘ ♣ ⊬ ▣
Nearby Facilities ⌐ ✔ ⚓ ⚓ ∪ ♫ ⚡
⚓ Pwllheli
Situated in the centre of Lleyn Peninsula with all beaches and golf courses within easy reach.

PWLLHELI
Bodwrog Farm, Bodwrog, Llanbedrog, Pwllheli, Gwynedd, LL53 7RE.
Std: 01758 **Tel:** 740341
Nearest Town/Resort Pwllheli/Abersoch
Directions From Pwllheli take the A499 to Llanbedrog, turn right opposite Glyn-Y-Weddw Pub on the B4413. After 1 mile site is the third opening on the left after the Ship Inn, cattle grid inside entrance.
Acreage 2 **Open** Easter to Late Autumn
Access Good **Site** Lev/Slope
Sites Available ▲ ⊞ ⚘ **Total** 20
Facilities ✦ ⒰ ⚒ ⌐ ⊙ ☎ ⓖ ▣ ⊟

Nearby Facilities ⌐ ✔ ⚓ ⚓ ∪ ⚡
⚓ Pwllheli
Superb coastal views. 1½ miles from sandy, sheltered beach. Quiet, scenic walk. Local restaurants and pubs within 1 mile. New shower and toilet block Very good television reception.

PWLLHELI
Caer Odyn Caravan Park, Lon Llan, Edern, Pwllheli, Gwynedd, LL53 8YS.
Std: 01758 **Tel:** 720846 **Fax:** 721488
Nearest Town/Resort Nefyn
Directions From the north west on the M55, A55, A487 or the A499.
Acreage 10 **Open** 1 March to 5 January
Access Good **Site** Level
Sites Available ⊞ ⚘ **Total** 6
Facilities ⚘ ✦ ⒰ ⚘ ⚒ ⌐ ⊬ ⚘ ⚘
⓪ ⚘
Nearby Facilities ⌐ ✔ ⚓ ⚓ ∪ ♫ ⚡
⚓ Pwllheli
Quiet, family owned site. 1 mile from a sandy beach and a 27 hole golf course.

PWLLHELI
Hirdre Fawr, Tudweiliog, Pwllheli, Gwynedd, LL53 8YY.
Std: 01758 **Tel:** 770278 **Fax:** 770278
Nearest Town/Resort Pwllheli/Nefyn
Directions From Nefyn take the B44 towards Aberdaron, site is on the right half side halfway between Edern and Tudweiliog villages.
Open May to September
Access Good **Site** Level
Sites Available ⊞ ⚘ **Total** 20
Facilities ⒰ ⌐ ⊙ ⚘ ⓘ ✳ ⊬
Nearby Facilities ⌐ ✔ ∪
⚓ Pwllheli
Family site, 1 mile from the beach. 6 miles from Abersoch and 22 miles from Snowdon.

PWLLHELI
Porthysgaden Site, Porthysgaden, Tudweiliog, Pwllheli, Gwynedd, LL53 8PF.
Std: 01758 **Tel:** 770206
Nearest Town/Resort Pwllheli
Directions Follow the B4417 and turn right after the village of Tudweiliog then turn first right to the farm.
Acreage 4 **Open** April to October
Access Good **Site** Level
Sites Available ▲ ⊞ ⚘ **Total** 40
Facilities ⒰ ⚒ ⌐ ⊙ ⊬ ▣ ⓘ ✳ ⊬
Nearby Facilities ⌐ ✔ ⚓ ⚓ ∪ ♫ ⚡
⚓ Pwllheli
¼ mile from the beach, sea, rocks and slipway for boats. Good fishing.

ᵥLLHELI

osfawr Nurseries Touring Caravan & ᵐping Park, Rhosfawr, Y Ffor, Pwllheli, ᵧnedd, LL53 6YA.
ᵭ: 01766 Tel: 810545
ᵃil: jkcamping@aol.com
arest Town/Resort Pwllheli
ᵉctions 2 miles from Y Ffor on the B4354
ᵧn road, telephone box on the left, we
ᵉ just a bit further along on the right.
ʳeage 2 Open March to End October
ᶜess Good Site Level
ᵉs Available ⅄ ⬠ ⌂ Total 20
ᶜilities ⓖ ⨍ Ⓜ ⓐ ⌐ ⊙ ☻ ♁↦⊟ ⬚
  Pwllheli
ᵘated in the centre of the beautiful Llyn
ᵉninsula. Ideal for touring. Tea room.

ᴸLSARNAU

ʳcdy Touring Caravan & Camping
ʳk, Talsarnau, Gwynedd, LL47 6YG.
ᵭ: 01766 Tel: 770736
ᵃil: anwen@barcdy.idps.co.uk
ᵇsite: www.croeso-cynnes-wales.co.uk
arest Town/Resort Harlech.
ʳections From Bala A4212 to
ᵃwsfynydd. A487 to Maentwrog. At
ᵃentwrog left onto A496, signposted
ᵃrlech. Site 4 miles.
ʳeage 12 Open April to October
ᶜess Good Site Lev/Slope
ᵉs Available ⅄ ⬠ ⌂ Total 78
 cilities ⨍ Ⓜ ⓐ ⌐ ⊙ ⌐ ⧠ ⬚ ☻
         ♁⊟⬚⬚ ☻
arby Facilities ⌐ ↗ ⬟ ↘ ∪ ⚡
  Talsarnau.
ᵃlks from site to nearby mountains and
ᵉs. Ideal touring Snowdonia.

ᵞWYN

ᵉthle Caravan Park, Caethle, Aberdyfi
ᵃd, Tywyn, Gwynedd, LL36 9HS.
ᵭ: 01654 Tel: 710587 Fax: 710587
arest Town/Resort Tywyn/Aberdovey
ʳections On the A493 coast road, 1½
ᵉs from Tywyn and 2 miles from Aberdyfi.
ʳeage 4 Open April/Easter to End Oct
ᶜess Good Site Level
ᵉs Available ⅄ ⬠ ⌂ Total 30
 ᵃcilities ⨍ Ⓜ ⓐ ⌐ ⊙ ⌐ ☻
       ⓘ☻↦⊟⬚
arby Facilities ⌐ ↗ ⬟ ↘ ∪ ⚡ ⚡ ⚡
  Tywyn/Aberdyfi
ᵗuresque, uncommercialised site within
ᵉ Snowdonia National Park. Near the
ᵃch, leisure centre and narrow gauge rail-
ᵧ.

ᵞWYN

ᵛmrhwyddfor Campsite, T. D. Nutting,
ᵧllyn, Tywyn, Gwynedd, LL36 9AJ.
ᵭ: 01654 Tel: 761286/761380
arest Town/Resort Dolgellau
ʳections Situated on the A487 between
lgellau and Machynlleth, at foot of Cader
is mountain, right at the bottom of Talyllyn
ss, a white house under the rocks.
ʳeage 6 Open All Year
ᶜess Good Site Level
ᵉs Available ⅄ ⬠ ⌂ Total 30
 ᵃcilities ⨍ ⒣ Ⓜ ⓐ ⌐ ⊙ ⌐ ☻
       ☻✕ⓣ↦⊟⬚
arby Facilities ⌐ ↗ ⬟ ↘ ∪ ⚡ ⚡
  Machynlleth
ʳy central for Tywyn, Aberdovey,
ʳmouth. The site runs alongside a stream.
ᵃl for the mountains and sea. All kept very
ᵃn, excellent reputation. TV reception on
ᵉ. Public telephone and Cafe/Restaurant
ᵃry. Prices on application.

TYWYN

Dôl Einion, Tal-y-Llyn, Tywyn, Gwynedd, LL36 9AJ.
Std: 01654 Tel: 761312
Nearest Town/Resort Dolgellau
Directions From Dolgellau take the A470 for 2 miles, turn right onto the A487 and continue for 4 miles. Turn right onto the B4405, site is 300 metres.
Acreage 3 Open All Year
Access Good Site Level
Sites Available ⅄ ⬠ ⌂
Facilities ⨍ ⒣ Ⓜ ⓐ ⌐ ⊙ ☻ ⓘ⚡↦
Nearby Facilities ↗ ∪ ⚡
 ⇌ Machynlleth
Flat, grassy site with a stream. At the start of the popular Minffordd path to the summit of Cader Idris. Fly fishing ½ mile, narrow gauge railway 3 miles and beach 11 miles. Café/ Restaurant and Public Telephone nearby.

TYWYN

Glanywern, Llanegryn, Tywyn, Gwynedd, LL36 9TH.
Std: 01654 Tel: 782247
Nearest Town/Resort Tywyn/Aberdovey
Directions 5 miles north of Tywyn.
Acreage 4 Open April to End Oct
Access Good Site Level
Sites Available ⅄ ⬠⬚ Total 20
Facilities ⨍ Ⓜ ⓐ ⌐ ⊙ ☻
Nearby Facilities ⌐
 ⇌ Tywyn
Alongside the River Dysynni.

TYWYN

Llabwst Farm, Rhoslefain, Tywyn, Gwynedd, LL36 9NE.
Std: 01654 Tel: 711013
Nearest Town/Resort Tywyn
Directions From Tywyn take the A493 for 4½ miles, in Rhoslefain turn right opposite the white cottage, farm is 400 yards.
Acreage 2 Open Spring Bank Hol to Oct
Access Fair Site Lev/Slope
Sites Available ⅄ ⬠⬚
Facilities Ⓜ↦
Nearby Facilities ⌐ ↗
 ⇌ Tywyn
On a quiet farm site with sea and mountain scenery. Central for all the area, Cardigan Bay and Snowdonia. Ideal touring.

TYWYN

Tynllwyn Caravan & Camping Park, Bryncrug, Tywyn, Gwynedd, LL36 9RD.
Std: 01654 Tel: 710370 Fax: 710370
Email: pspsmc@aol.com
Nearest Town/Resort Tywyn
Directions Leave Tywyn on the A493, after approx. 2½ miles turn right onto the B4405, turn first right by the grass island and go up the lane.
Acreage 7 Open March to October
Access Good Site Level
Sites Available ⅄ ⬠ ⌂ Total 68
Facilities ⨍ Ⓜ ⓐ ⌐ ⊙ ⌐ ⧠ ⬚ ☻
       ⓢⓘ ☻↦⊟⬚
Nearby Facilities ⌐ ↗ ⬟ ∪ ⚡ ⚡
 ⇌ Tywyn
Narrow gauge steam train runs alongside the site. Luxury static caravans also available for hire. Ideal touring.

TYWYN

Waenfach Caravan Site, Waenfach, Llanegryn, Tywyn, Gwynedd, LL36 9SB.
Std: 01654 Tel: Tywyn 710375
Nearest Town/Resort Tywyn
Directions 3 miles north of Tywyn on the A493.

Open Easter to October
Access Good
Sites Available ⅄ ⬠ ⌂ Total 20
Facilities ⨍ Ⓜ ⓐ ⌐ ⊙ ⌐ ⬚ ☻
       ⓘ ⓞ ☻↦⊟
Nearby Facilities ⌐ ↗ ⬟ ↘ ∪ ⚡ ⚡ ⚡
 ⇌ Tywyn
Small site on a working farm. 3 miles from the sea.

TYWYN

Ynysymaengwyn Caravan Park, The Lodge, Tywyn, Gwynedd, LL36 9RY.
Std: 01654 Tel: 710684 Fax: 710684
Email:
rita@ynysymaengwyn.freeserve.co.uk
Nearest Town/Resort Tywyn
Directions Take the A493 from Tywyn to Dolgellau, we are the second caravan park on the left.
Acreage 4 Open April to October
Access Good Site Level
Sites Available ⅄ ⬠ ⌂ Total 80
Facilities ⨍ Ⓜ ⓐ ⌐ ⊙ ⌐ ⧠ ⬚ ☻
       ⓜⓘ ⓞ ☻↦⊟
Nearby Facilities ⌐ ↗ ⬟ ↘ ∪ ⚡ ⚡
 ⇌ Tywyn
In the grounds of an old manor house with a river at the bottom of the site for fishing. Near to the beach and shops. Woodland walks. Welsh Tourist Board 4 Star Grading and AA 3 Pennants.

ISLE OF ANGLESEY

AMLWCH

Plas Eilian, Llaneilian, Amlwch, Anglesey, LL68 9LS.
Std: 01407 Tel: Amlwch 830323
Nearest Town/Resort Amlwch
Directions Follow coastal road from Bangor for about 18 miles. Turn right by garage, continue straight until you reach the church.
Acreage 3 Open April to October
Access Good Site Level
Sites Available ⅄ ⬠ ⌂ Total 18
Facilities Ⓜ ⌐ ⊙ ☻ ⓘ ☻↦
Nearby Facilities ⌐ ↗ ⬟ ↘ ∪ ⚡ ⚡
 ⇌ Bangor
Pets are welcome on a lead.

AMLWCH

Point Lynas Caravan Park, Llaneilian, Amlwch, Anglesey, LL68 9LT.
Std: 01407 Tel: Amlwch Fax: 853832
Email: peter@pantysaer.freeserve.co.uk
Nearest Town/Resort Amlwch
Directions Turn off the A5025 at Anglesey Mowers towards the sea. Follow signs for Llaneilian/Porth Eilian. Pass the phone box, entrance is 300yds on the left.
Acreage 1¼ Open Late March to October
Access Good Site Level
Sites Available ⅄ ⬠ ⌂ Total 15
Facilities ⓖ ⨍ Ⓜ ⓐ ⌐ ⊙ ⌐ ⬚ ☻
       ⓞ ☻↦⊟⬚
Nearby Facilities ⌐ ↗ ↘ ⚡
 ⇌ Bangor
200yds from Porth Eilian Cove.

AMLWCH

Tyn Rhos, Penysarn, Amlwch, Anglesey, LL69 9AD.
Std: 01407 Tel: 830574
Nearest Town/Resort Amlwch
Directions A5025 turn off bypass to village of Penysarn. Take the first right after Y Bedol Public House and cross the cattle grid. 100yds up the drive.
Acreage 2 Open Easter to September
Access Good Site Level
Sites Available ⅄ ⬠ ⌂ Total 30

Facilities ⚡ 🚾 ♿ 📞 ⊙ ☕ 🍴 🛒 ⚓ ▣
Nearby Facilities ┏ 🚲 ⚓ ⌕ ⛵ ⚲ 🏇
⇌ Bangor
Near the village shops, post office and inn. Sports centre, beaches and swimming all 2 miles. Cafe/restaurant and licensed club within 200yds. 6 berth caravan available for hire, all mod cons.

BEAUMARIS

Kingsbridge Caravan Park, Llanfaes, Beaumaris, Anglesey, LL58 8LR.
Std: 01248 **Tel:** 490636
Nearest Town/Resort Beaumaris
Directions 1¼ miles past Beaumaris Castle. At crossroads turn left, 400yds to the site.
Acreage 14 **Open** March to October
Access Good **Site** Level
Sites Available ▲ 🚐 ⊞ **Total** 48
Facilities ⚡ 🚾 ♿ 📞 ⊙ ☕ 🍴
🏊 🎮 ⊙ ⊠ ▥ 🍴 ▣
Nearby Facilities ┏ 🚲 ⚓ ⌕ ∪ ⚲ 🏇
⇌ Bangor
Fishing, scenic views, historical sites. Ideal for touring and bird watching. Brochure sent on request.

BENLLECH

Ad Astra Caravan Park, Brynteg, Nr. Benllech, Anglesey, LL78 7JH.
Std: 01248 **Tel:** Tynygongl 853283
Email: brian@brynteg53.fsnet.co.uk
Website: www.adastracaravanpark.co.uk
Nearest Town/Resort Benllech
Directions Turn left up the hill from Benllech Village square on B5108. Drive 1½ miles to California Inn, turn left onto B5110. Park is 500 yards on right hand side.
Acreage 3 **Open** March to October
Access Good **Site** Level
Sites Available ▲ 🚐 ⊞
Facilities ♿ ⚡ 🎮 🚾 ♿ 📞 ⊙ ☕ ☕
🎮 ⊙ ☕ ▣
Nearby Facilities ┏ 🚲 ⚓ ⌕ ∪ ⚲ 🏇
⇌ Bangor
Scenic views, ideal base for touring.

BENLLECH

Bodafon Caravan & Camping Park, Bodafon, Benllech, Anglesey, LL74 8RU.
Std: 01248 **Tel:** 852417
Nearest Town/Resort Benllech Bay
Directions A5025 through Benllech, ¼ mile on left going through 30mph signs.
Acreage 5 **Open** March to October
Access Good **Site** Lev/Slope
Sites Available ▲ 🚐 ⊞ **Total** 50
Facilities ⚡ 🎮 🚾 ♿ 📞 ⊙ ☕ ☕
⊙ ☕ ☕ ▣
Nearby Facilities ┏ 🚲 ⚓ ⌕ ∪ ⚲
⇌ Bangor
Near to beach (¾ mile), good views, quiet family site. Ideal touring.

BENLLECH

Bwlch Holiday Park, Tynygongl, Benllech Bay, Anglesey, LL74 8RF.
Std: 01248 **Tel:** Tynygongl 852914
Email: lloyd.caravans@virgin.net
Nearest Town/Resort Benllech Bay
Directions Take the A5025 Menai Bridge to Benllech road for 8 miles, turn left onto the B5108, 1 mile.
Acreage 12 **Open** March to October
Access Good **Site** Level
Sites Available ▲ 🚐 ⊞ **Total** 12
Facilities ♿ ⚡ 🎮 🚾 ♿ 📞 ⊙ ☕ 🎮 ⊙
⊠ ☕ ☕ ▣
Nearby Facilities ┏ 🚲 ⚓ ⌕ ∪ ⚲ 🏇
⇌ Bangor
Near beach, ideal touring, golf, riding

BENLLECH

Golden Sunset Holidays, Tyn-Y-Gongl, Benllech, Anglesey, LL74 8TB.
Std: 01248 **Tel:** 852345
Nearest Town/Resort Benllech
Directions Turn right off the A5025 in the centre of Benllech and turn immediately left into site entrance.
Acreage 10 **Open** May to Sept Inc.
Access Good **Site** Lev/Slope
Sites Available ▲ 🚐 ⊞ **Total** 120
Facilities ⚡ ⚡ 🚾 ♿ 📞 ⊙ ☕ ☕ 🍴 ⊙ ☕ ▣
Nearby Facilities ┏ ⚲
⇌ Bangor
Close to the village and beach.

BENLLECH

Nant Newydd Caravan Park, Brynteg, Near Benllech Bay, Anglesey, LL78 7JJ.
Std: 01248 **Tel:** 852842 **Fax:** 852281
Website: www.nantnewydd.co.uk
Nearest Town/Resort Benllech Bay
Directions From Britannia Bridge take the A5025 to Benllech. Turn left at the square and take the B5108. Turn left onto the B5110 and site is 1 mile on the right.
Open March to October
Access Good **Site** Level
Sites Available ▲ 🚐 ⊞
Facilities ⚡ ⚡ 🎮 🚾 ♿ 📞 ⊙ ☕
🏊 🎮 ⊙ ⊠ ▥ 🍴 ⊛ ☕ ▣
Nearby Facilities ┏ 🚲 ⚓ ⌕ ∪ ⚲ 🏇
⇌ Bangor
A small, select, family-run, country park with beautiful gardens and water falls. Within 3 miles of sandy beaches. Baby changing room, tennis court and five-aside football.

BENLLECH

Plas Uchaf Caravan & Camping Park, Benllech Bay, Benllech, Anglesey, LL74 8NU.
Std: 01407 **Tel:** 763012
Nearest Town/Resort Benllech
Directions ¼ mile from Benllech, signposted just after fire station on the B5108.
Acreage 9 **Open** March to October
Access Good **Site** Level
Sites Available ▲ 🚐 ⊞ **Total** 80
Facilities ♿ ⚡ 🎮 🚾 ♿ 📞 ⊙ ☕ ☕ 🍴
🏊 ☕ 🍴 ⊛ ☕ ▣
Nearby Facilities ┏ 🚲 ⚓ ⌕ ∪ ⚲
⇌ Bangor
Well sheltered, family park, under a mile from the beach. Tarmac roads, close mown grass, picnic tables, street lighting, freezers etc..

BENLLECH

St. David's Park, Red Wharf Bay, Isle of Anglesey, LL75 8RJ.
Std: 01248 **Tel:** 852341 **Fax:** 852777
Email: paul@stdavidspark.com
Website: www.stdavidspark.com
Nearest Town/Resort Benllech
Directions On the A5025 1 mile south of Benllech.
Acreage 3 **Open** March to October
Site Sloping
Sites Available ▲ 🚐 ⊞ **Total** 130
Facilities ♿ ⚡ 🚾 ♿ 📞 ⊙ ☕ ☕ 🍴
🏊 🎮 ⊙ ⊠ 🍴 ▥ 🍴 ⊛ ☕ ▣
Nearby Facilities ┏ 🚲 ⚓ ⌕ ∪
⇌ Bangor
Private beach, fully licenced bars and entertainment.

BENLLECH

Ty Newydd Leisure Park, Llanbedrgoch, Isle of Anglesey, LL76 8TZ.
Std: 01248 **Tel:** 450677 **Fax:** 450711
Email: tynewyddcc@aol.com
Website: www.members.aol.com/tynewyddcc
Nearest Town/Resort Benllech
Directions From Britannia Bridge take A5025 Amlwch road, after passing through Pentraeth Village bear left at lay-by. Site ¾ miles on the right hand side.
Acreage 9 **Open** March to End Oct
Access Good **Site** Level
Sites Available ▲ 🚐 ⊞ **Total** 40
Facilities ♿ ⚡ 🎮 🚾 ⚡ 📞 ⊙ ☕ 🍴 ▣
🏊 🎮 ⊙ ⊠ 🍴 ▥ 🍴 🍴 🍴 ⊛ ☕ ▣ ☕
Nearby Facilities ┏ 🚲 ⚓ ⌕ ∪ ⚲ 🏇
⇌ Bangor
Near the beach with views of Snowdonia

BRYNSIENCYN

Fron Caravan & Camping Site, Brynsiencyn, Anglesey, LL61 6TX.
Std: 01248 **Tel:** 430310 **Fax:** 430310
Email: froncaravanpark@brynsiecyn.fsnet.co.uk
Nearest Town/Resort Llanfairpwllgwyn
Directions At start of Llanfairpwllgwyn turn left onto A4080 to Brysiencyn follow road through village site is on the right ¼ mile after village.
Acreage 5¼ **Open** Easter to September
Access Good **Site** Level
Sites Available ▲ 🚐 ⊞ **Total** 70
Facilities ⚡ 🚾 ♿ 📞 ⊙ ☕ ☕ ☕
🏊 🎮 ⊙ ⊠ 🍴 ▥ 🍴 ⊛ ☕ ▣
Nearby Facilities ┏ 🚲 ⚓ ⌕ ∪ ⚲ 🏇
⇌ Bangor
Ideal for touring Anglesey and North Wales. Wales Tourist Board 4 Star Grading.

LLANFAIRPWLL

Plas Coch Caravan & Leisure Park, Llanedwen, Llanfairpwll, Anglesey, LL61 6EJ.
Std: 01248 **Tel:** 714346
Nearest Town/Resort Menai Bridge
Directions Turn off the A5 onto the A4080 after approx. 2 miles turn left at first crossroads.
Acreage 40 **Open** April to October
Access Good **Site** Level
Sites Available ▲ 🚐 ⊞ **Total** 40
Facilities 🚾 ♿ 📞 ⊙ ☕ ☕
🍴 ⊙ ⊠ ▥ 🍴 🍴 ⊛ ☕ ▣ ☕
Nearby Facilities ┏ 🚲 ⚓ ⌕ ∪ ⚲ 🏇
⇌ Llanfairpwll/Bangor
½ mile frontage on the Menai Straits for fishing and all watersports. Close to a golf course in an area of outstanding natural beauty. 200 acres of park and farmland.

MOELFRE

Tyddyn Isaf Camping & Caravan Park, Lligwy Bay, Dulas, Anglesey, LL70 9PQ.
Std: 01248 **Tel:** 410203 **Fax:** 410667
Email: enquiries@tyddynisaf.demon.co.uk
Website: www.tyddynisaf.demon.co.uk
Nearest Town/Resort Benllech
Directions Take the A5025 from Britannia Bridge, go through Benllech approx. 8 miles continue to Moelfre Island via left stay on the main road to Brynrefail Village. Turn right opposite the telephone box and International camping sign, we are ½ mile on the right down the lane.
Acreage 16 **Open** March to October
Access Good **Site** Sloping
Sites Available ▲ 🚐 ⊞ **Total** 80
Facilities ⚡ 🎮 🚾 ♿ 📞 ⊙ ☕ ☕ ☕
🏊 🎮 ⊙ ⊠ 🍴 ▥ 🍴 🍴 ▣
Nearby Facilities ┏ 🚲 ⚓ ⌕ ∪ ⚲ 🏇

Bangor
amily run park with a private footpath to a
...e, sandy beach. "Loo of the Year" Winner,
...5 Pennant Premier Park, Welcome Host
...ward, Dragon Award and WTB 5 Star
...raded.

MOELFRE

...n Rhos Caravan Park, Moelfre,
...glesey, LL72 8NL.
...d: 01248 **Tel:** 852417 **Fax:** 852417
...earest Town/Resort Benllech
...rections From Benllech proceed along
...e A5025 to the roundabout, turn left to
...oelfre and at MDM Design turn left for 2
...les, site is on the right.
...creage 10 **Open** March **to** October
...ccess Good **Site** Sloping
...acilities ♦ ⊞ ♨ ▯ ⊙ ⌿ ◰ ⊚ ☎
⊙ ⊟⊠⊟
...earby Facilities ↑ ⋌ ⚓ ⋋ ∪ ♠
Bangor
...ear Lligwy Beach. Surrounded by
...merous footpaths, including coastal path,
...hing and an ancient monument.

NEWBOROUGH

...welfryn Caravan Park, Newborough,
...glesey, LL61 6SG.
...d: 01248 **Tel:** 440230
...earest Town/Resort Bangor
...rections On the A4080 from Britannia
...idge take a left by a tall column, and follow
...e A4080 through to Newborough. Turn left
...t the crossroads for Beach Road, site is on
...e left after ¼ mile.
...creage 2 **Open** 1 April/Easter **to** 30 Sept
...ccess Good **Site** Lev/Slope
...tes Available ♦ ♩ ⊞ **Total** 24
...cilities ♦ ⊞ ⌿ ⋋ ∪ ⊹
...earby Facilities ⌿ ⋋ ∪ ⌿
Bangor
...eauty spot on the edge of Forestry
...ommission land. 1½ miles from the beach.
...anddwyn Island.

PENTRAETH

...ai Mawr Caravan Park, Pentraeth,
...glesey, LL75 8DX.
...d: 01248 **Tel:** 450467 **Fax:** 450467
...earest Town/Resort Benllech/Llangefni
...rections From Bangor take the A5025
...rough Pentraeth and up the hill, after The
...ull Pub take the third turning on the right
...gned Clai Mawr Caravan Park.
...creage 1½ **Open** March **to** October
...ccess Good **Site** Lev/Slope
...tes Available ♩ ⊞ **Total** 8
...cilities ♦ ⊞ ▯ ♨ ▯ ⊙ ⌿ ◰ ⊚ ☎
⊙ ⊟⊠⊹⊟⊟
...earby Facilities ↑ ⋌ ⚓ ⋋ ∪ ⌿
Bangor
...uiet, family run site overlooking Red Wharf
...ay and the Snowdon Mountains.

PENTRAETH

...hos Caravan Park, Rhos Farm,
...ntraeth, Anglesey, North Wales, LL75
...DZ.
...d: 01248 **Tel:** 450214
...earest Town/Resort Red Wharf Bay
...rections Through Pentraeth on A5025
...ain road. Site entrance on left 1 mile north
...Pentraeth.
...creage 6 **Open** March **to** October
...ccess Good **Site** Level
...tes Available ♦ ♩ ⊞ **Total** 40
...acilities ♦ ⊞ ♨ ▯ ⊙ ⌿ ⊚ ☎
⊙ ⊟ ♨ ⊹⊟⊟
...earby Facilities ↑ ⋌ ⚓ ⋋ ∪ ⌿
Bangor
...ear beach and central location for
...glesey, good views of Snowdonia.

RHOSNEIGR

Plas Caravan Park, Llanfaelog,
Rhosneigr, Anglesey, LL63 5TU.
Std: 01407 **Tel:** 810234 **Fax:** 811052
Email: gail@plascaravanpark.co.uk
Website: www.plascaravanpark.co.uk
Nearest Town/Resort Rhosneigr
Directions On the A5 go through
Gwalchmai, turn left onto the A4080.
Continue until you reach the village of
Llanfaelog, turn right at the Post Office and
general stores, park is ½ mile on the right
hand side.
Open Mid-March **to** End October
Access Good **Site** Level
Sites Available ♦ ♩ ⊞ **Total** 17
Facilities ♦ ▯ ⊞ ♨ ▯ ⊙ ⌿ ⊚ ☎
⊠ ⊟⊠⊟
Nearby Facilities ↑ ⋌ ⚓ ⋋ ∪ ⌿
⇌ Rhosneigr
Sheltered site in a rural setting, within
walking distance to the beach.

RHOSNEIGR

Shoreside Camp & Caravan Park,
Station Road, Rhosneigr, Anglesey, LL64
5QX.
Std: 01407 **Tel:** 810279
Website: www.caravancampingsites.co.uk
Nearest Town/Resort Rhosneigr
Directions A4080 Rhosneigr, opposite the
golf club.
Acreage 6 **Open** Easter **to** October
Access Good **Site** Lev/Slope
Sites Available ♦ ♩ ⊞ **Total** 100
Facilities ♦ ⊞ ♨ ▯ ⊙ ⌿ ☎
▯⊙ ♨ ⊹⊟⊟
Nearby Facilities ↑ ⋌ ⚓ ⋋ ∪ ⌿ ♠ ⋋
⇌ Rhosneigr
Riding centre on site, bowling and tennis.
Near the beach and opposite a golf club. 10
miles from Holyhead, day trips to Dublin.

RHOSNEIGR

Ty Hen, Station Road, Rhosneigr,
Anglesey, LL64 5QZ.
Std: 01407 **Tel:** 810331 **Fax:** 811261
Email: bernardtyhen@hotmail.com
Website: www.ukparks.co.uk/tyhen
Nearest Town/Resort Rhosneigr
Directions Take the A55 across Anglesey,
turn left onto the A4080 for Rhosneigr. Turn
right at Llanfaelog Post Office, Ty Hen is next
to the Railway Station, up the drive ½ mile.
Acreage 50 **Open** April **to** October
Access Good **Site** Level
Sites Available ♦ ♩ ⊞ **Total** 41
Facilities ♦ ▯ ⊞ ♨ ▯ ⌿ ◰ ⊚ ☎
⊙⊠♠⊟⊛⊟
Nearby Facilities ↑ ⋌ ⚓ ⋋ ∪ ⌿ ♠ ⋋
⇌ Rhosneigr
On the banks of a 65 acre lake, good for
fishing. Five Seaside Award beaches. Golf
and sub-aqua. David Bellamy Gold Award
for Conservation.

RHOSNEIGR

Tyn Llidiart Camping Site, Tywyn
Trewan, Bryngwran, Anglesey, LL65 3SW.
Std: 01407 **Tel:** 810678
Email: alice@awoolleson.freeserve.co.uk
Website: www.5van.co.uk
Nearest Town/Resort Rhosneigr
Directions Turn off the A5 at Bryngwran
Post Office, at second crossroads turn right,
continue down the lane and take the right
hand fork, site is on the left.
Acreage 1 **Open** All Year
Access Poor **Site** Level
Sites Available ♦ ♩ ⊞ **Total** 5
Facilities ♦ ⊞ ▯ ⊙ ☎ ▯⊹⊟
Nearby Facilities ↑ ⋌ ⚓ ⋋ ∪ ⌿
⇌ Rhosneigr

Camping & Caravanning Club Certified Site.
Ideal touring centre for Anglesey and North
Wales.

TREARDDUR BAY

Tyn Rhos Camping Site, Ravenspoint
Road, Trearddur Bay, Holyhead, Anglesey,
LL65 2BQ.
Std: 01407 **Tel:** 860369
Nearest Town/Resort Holyhead
Directions Follow the A55 across Anglesey.
Leave the A55 at Caergeiliog junction, follow
signs (A5) for Valley. Turn left at Valley onto
the B4545 for Trearddur Bay. After the
Beach Hotel turn left onto Ravenspoint
Road, ¾ miles to the shared entrance, take
left hand branch.
Acreage 20 **Open** March **to** October
Access Good **Site** Lev/Slope
Sites Available ♦ ♩ ⊞ **Total** 200
Facilities ♦ ⊞ ♨ ▯ ⊙ ⌿ ◰ ⊚ ☎
⊠ ▯ ⊙ ♀ ♨ ⊹⊟⊟
Nearby Facilities ↑ ⋌ ⚓ ⋋ ∪ ⌿ ⋋
⇌ Holyhead
Well established family run site, rural
location with modern facilities. Views of
Snowdonia, coastal walks, sandy beaches
(Blue Flag Award) 10 minutes. Ideal touring
base, Holyhead port town to Ireland - 3
miles. Separate rally field also available.

VALLEY

Bodowyr Caravan Park, Bodowyr,
Bodedern, Anglesey, LL65 3SS.
Std: 01407 **Tel:** 741171
Email: bodowyr@yahoo.com
Nearest Town/Resort Holyhead
Directions From Holyhead take the A55,
turn off at the Bodedern exit and turn left for
Bodedern. Bodowyr is the first turning on
the left. Site has international camping signs
from the A5 junction.
Open March **to** November
Access Good **Site** Level
Sites Available ♦ ♩ ⊞ **Total** 30
Facilities ▯ ⊞ ♨ ▯ ⊙ ⌿ ◰ ☎
▯⊠✕⊟ ♨ ⊹⊟
Nearby Facilities ↑ ⋌ ⚓ ⋋ ∪ ⌿ ♠ ⋋
⇌ Valley
Very handy for ferries to Ireland. Close to
beaches and a wide range of sporting
facilities.

VALLEY

Pen-Y-Bont Farm Caravan & Camping,
Four Mile Bridge, Valley, Near Holyhead,
Anglesey, LL65 3EY.
Std: 01407 **Tel:** 740481
Nearest Town/Resort Valley
Directions Follow the new A55 to within 4
miles of Holyhead, branch off at sign for
Valley, roundabout, turn left at Valley
crossroads and straight on to the B5250. We
are 1½ miles from the crossroads.
Access Good **Site** Level
Sites Available ♦ ♩
Facilities ⌿ ⊞ ☎ ▯
Nearby Facilities ↑ ⋌ ⚓ ⋋ ∪ ⌿ ⋋
⇌ Valley
Ideal for sailing, canoeing, wind surfing,
fishing, bathing, bird watching, etc.. Shops,
Post Office, café and market nearby.

WALES
CONTINUES
ON THE
NEXT PAGE

MERTHYR TYDFIL

MERTHYR TYDFIL

Grawen Caravan & Camping Park, Cwm-Taf, Cefn Coed, Merthyr Tydfil, CF48 2HS.
Std: 01685 **Tel:** 723740 **Fax:** 723740
Nearest Town/Resort Merthyr Tydfil
Directions Easy access along the A470 Brecon Beacons road, 2 miles from Cefn Coed and 4 miles from Merthyr Tydfil. 2 miles off the A465 Heads of the Valleys road, ¼ mile from the reservoir.
Acreage 3½ **Open** April **to** 30 October
Access Good **Site** Level
Sites Available ⚠ ⊕ ⊜ **Total** 50
Facilities ⨍ ⊟ ⊞ ⓦ ⚓ ⌐ ⊙ ⌿ ◻ ☕
⚲ ⓘⓩ ♨ ⌂ ⊁⊟◻⊟
Nearby Facilities ⌐ ✚ ⚠ ⚓ ♉ ⊙ ⌿ ☈ ⇗
⇻ Merthyr Tydfil
Picturesque mountain, forest and reservoir walks inside the Brecon Beacons National Park. A wealth of history can be found in the town of Merthyr Tydfil and the Valleys.

MONMOUTHSHIRE

MONMOUTH

Bridge Caravan Park & Camping Site, Dingestow, Monmouth, Monmouthshire, NP25 4DY.
Std: 01600 **Tel:** 740241
Nearest Town/Resort Monmouth
Directions 4 miles west of Monmouth.
Acreage 4 **Open** Easter **to** October
Access Good **Site** Level
Sites Available ⚠ ⊕ ⊜ **Total** 123
Facilities ⨍ ⊟ ⊞ ⓦ ⚓ ⌐ ⊙ ⌿ ◻ ☕
ⓘⓩ ☺ ⚓ Ⓜ ⊁⊟ ◻⊟
Nearby Facilities ⌐ ✚ ⊙ ☈
⇻ Abergavenny
Riverside site with free fishing. Easy access.

MONMOUTH

Glen Trothy Caravan Park, Mitchel Troy, Monmouth, Monmouthshire, NP25 4BD.
Std: 01600 **Tel:** 712295 **Fax:** 712295
Website: www.glentrothy.co.uk
Nearest Town/Resort Monmouth
Directions From north M5, M50 then A40 taking the left turn after the traffic lights and before reaching road tunnel. From East Gloucester, A40 Ross on Wye, A40 Monmouth. From south and southeast M4 Severn Bridge, A466 Chepstow, Tintern and Monmouth turning left at traffic lights onto A40.
Acreage 6½ **Open** 1 March **to** 31 October
Access Good **Site** Level
Sites Available ⚠ ⊕ ⊜ **Total** 130
Facilities ⚓ ⨍ ⊟ ⓦ ⚓ ⌐ ⊙ ⌿ ☺
◻ ⓘ ☺ ⚲ Ⓜ
Nearby Facilities ⌐ ✚ ⊙ ☈
⇻ Abergavenny
Alongside a river for fishing. Ideal touring. No arrivals before 2pm.

MONMOUTH

Monmouth Caravan Park, Rockfield Road, Monmouth, Monmouthshire, NP5 3BA.
Std: 01600 **Tel:** 714745 **Fax:** 716690
Email:
mail@monmouthcaravanpark.co.uk
Website:
www.monmouthcaravanpark.co.uk
Nearest Town/Resort Monmouth
Directions Take the B4233 Rockfield Road, we are ¼ mile, opposite the fire and ambulance station.
Acreage 3¾ **Open** March **to** October
Access Good **Site** Level
Sites Available ⚠ ⊕ ⊜ **Total** 40
Facilities ⚓ ⨍ ⊟ ⓦ ⚓ ⌐ ⊙ ⌿ ☕
⚲ ⓘⓩ ☺ ✕ ⌿ ⚓ ⊟ ◻⊟
Nearby Facilities ⌐ ✚ ♉ ⊙ ☈ ⇗
⇻ Hereford
Set in an area of outstanding natural beauty. Ideal touring.

MONMOUTH

Monnow Bridge Caravan Site, Drybridge Street, Monmouth, Monmouthshire, NP5 3AD.
Std: 01600 **Tel:** 714004
Nearest Town/Resort Monmouth
Directions On the edge of town, 5 minutes from the town centre.
Acreage 1½ **Open** All Year
Access Good **Site** Level
Sites Available ⚠ ⊕ ⊜
Facilities ⨍ ⊟ ⓦ ⚓ ⌐ ⊙ ⌿ ☕ ⓘⓩ ◻ ⊟
Nearby Facilities ⌐ ✚ ♉ ☈ ⇗
⇻ Newport
On the banks of the River Monnow and on Offas Dyke Path. Ideal for touring Wye Valley and the Forest of Dean.

NEWPORT

NEWPORT

Pentre-Tai Farm, Rhiwderin, Newport, South Wales, NP10 8RQ.
Std: 01633 **Tel:** 893284 **Fax:** 893284
Email: george@pentretai.f9.co.uk
Nearest Town/Resort Newport
Directions Leave the M4 at junction 28 and take the A467, at the next roundabout take the A468 for approx. 1 mile. Turn right immediately after 'Rhiwderin Inn' and go straight through the village and on down lane. Farm is on the left.
Acreage 5 **Open** March **to** October
Access Good **Site** Lev/Slope
Sites Available ⚠ ⊕ ⊜ **Total** 5
Facilities ⨍ ⓦ ⊙ ⌿ ☕ ⓘⓩ
Nearby Facilities ⌐ ✚ ⊙ ☈
⇻ Newport
Ideal for visiting Cardiff and the Welsh castles. Useful stopover for Irish ferry. Good pub nearby. B&B also available (WTB 2 Star).

PEMBROKESHIRE

AMROTH

Little Kings Park, Ludchurch, Amroth, Pembrokeshire, SA67 8PG.
Std: 01834 **Tel:** 831330 **Fax:** 831161
Website: www.littlekings.co.uk
Nearest Town/Resort Amroth/ Saundersfoot
Acreage 17 **Open** Easter then 27 April to 30 Sept
Access Good **Site** Level
Sites Available ⚠ ⊕ ⊜ **Total** 100
Facilities ⚓ ⨍ ⊟ ⓦ ⚓ ⌐ ⊙ ⌿ ⚓ ◻
⚲ ⓘⓩ ☺ ♈ ⚲ ✱ ☀ Ⓜ ⊟ ◻⊟
Nearby Facilities ⌐ ✚ ⚠ ⚓ ⊙
⇻ Narberth
1¼ miles from the beach. Ideal for walking the Pembrokeshire coastal path.

AMROTH

Meadow House Holiday Park, Amroth, Pembrokeshire, SA67 8NS.
Std: 01834 **Tel:** 812438
Nearest Town/Resort Saundersfoot
Directions From Carmarthen take the A477 past Folly Cross, turn left at the signpost to Amroth and Wisemans Bridge. Pass Summerhill Village and park is on the left hand side.
Acreage 25 **Open** March **to** October
Access Good **Site** Level
Sites Available ⚠ ⊕ ⊜ **Total** 60
Facilities ⨍ ⓦ ⚓ ⌐ ⊙ ⌿ ⚓ ◻ ☕
ⓘⓩ ☺ ✕ ⊙ ⚓ ☀ ⊟
Nearby Facilities ⌐ ✚ ⚠ ⚓ ⊙ ☈ ⇗
⇻ Kilgetty
Overlooking the sea. Coastal footpath Amroth and Wisemans Bridge beaches.

AMROTH

Pantglas Farm, Tavernspite, Whitland, Pembrokeshire, SA34 0NS.
Std: 01834 **Tel:** 831618
Email: steve@pantglasfarm.com
Website: www.pantglasfarm.com
Nearest Town/Resort Amroth
Directions A477 towards Tenby take the B4314 at Red Roses crossroads Tavernspite 1¼ miles, take the middle road at the village pump. Pantglas is ½ mile down on the left.
Acreage 8 **Open** Easter **to** October
Access Good **Site** Level
Sites Available ⚠ ⊕ ⊜ **Total** 75
Facilities ⚓ ⨍ ⊟ ⓦ ⚓ ⌐ ⊙ ⌿ ⚓ ◻
ⓘⓩ ☺ ⚓ Ⓜ ⊟ ◻⊟
Nearby Facilities ⌐ ✚ ⚠ ⚓ ⊙ ☈
⇻ Whitland
A quiet, secluded, family run caravan and camping park. Super play area for kids. High standard toilet and shower facilities. Caravan storage available for £2.50 weekly. Easy reach of Tenby, Saundersfoot and Amroth.

ANGLE

Castle Farm Camping Site, Castle Farm, Angle, Nr. Pembroke, Pembrokeshire, SA71 5AR.
Std: 01646 **Tel:** 641220
Nearest Town/Resort Angle
Directions Approx. 10 miles from Pembroke.
Acreage 2 **Open** April to October
Access Good **Site** Sloping
Sites Available ⚠ ⬛ ⬛ **Total** 25
Facilities ⬛ ⬛ ⬛ ⬛ ⬛ ⬛ ⬛ ⬛
Nearby Facilities ✓ ⬛ ⬛ U ⬛ ⬛
⬛ Pembroke
Near a safe, sandy beach.

BROAD HAVEN

Creampots Touring Caravan & Camping Park, Broadway, Broad Haven, Haverfordwest, Pembrokeshire, SA62 3TU.
Std: 01437 **Tel:** 781776
Website: www.creampots.co.uk
Nearest Town/Resort Broad Haven
Directions Take B4131 Broad Haven road from Haverfordwest to Broadway (5 miles). Turn left and Creampots is the SECOND site on the right (600yds).
Acreage 7 **Open** Easter to October
Access Good **Site** Level
Sites Available ⚠ ⬛ ⬛ **Total** 72
Facilities ⬛ ⬛ ⬛ ⬛ ⬛ ⬛ ⬛ ⬛ ⬛ ⬛
⬛ ⬛ ⬛ ⬛ ⬛
Nearby Facilities ⬛ ✓ ⬛ ⬛ U
⬛ Haverfordwest
Ideal touring base, 1½ miles from safe, sandy beach and coastal path at Broad Haven.

FISHGUARD

Fishguard Bay Caravan Park, Garn Gelli, Fishguard, Pembrokeshire, SA65 9ET.
Std: 01348 **Tel:** 811415 **Fax:** 811425
Email: neil@fishguardbay.com
Website: www.fishguardbay.com
Nearest Town/Resort Fishguard
Directions Take the A487 Cardigan road from Fishguard for 1½ miles, turn left at sign.
Acreage 5 **Open** March to December
Access Good **Site** Lev/Slope
Sites Available ⚠ ⬛ ⬛ **Total** 50
Facilities ⬛ ⬛ ⬛ ⬛ ⬛ ⬛ ⬛ ⬛ ⬛
⬛ ⬛ ⬛ ⬛ ⬛ ⬛ ⬛
Nearby Facilities ⬛ ✓ ⬛ ⬛ U ⬛ ⬛
⬛ Fishguard
Superb cliff top location offering excellent views and walks along this 'Heritage' coast of Pembrokeshire.

FISHGUARD

Rosebush Caravan & Camping Park, Rhoslwyn, Rosebush, Narberth, Pembrokeshire, SA66 7QT.
Std: 01437 **Tel:** 532206
Nearest Town/Resort Fishguard
Directions From the A40 take the B4313 near Narberth to Fishguard. 1 mile from the B4329 Haverfordwest to Cardigan road.
Acreage 15 **Open** March to October
Access Good **Site** Level
Sites Available ⚠ ⬛ ⬛ **Total** 45
Facilities ⬛ ⬛ ⬛ ⬛ ⬛ ⬛ ⬛ ⬛
⬛ ⬛ ⬛ ⬛ ⬛
Nearby Facilities ⬛
⬛ Clynderwen
In the centre of Pembrokeshire, 800ft above sea level. 3 acre lake for coarse fishing. Mountain walks. David Bellamy Gold Award for Conservation.

FISHGUARD

Tregroes Touring Park, Fishguard, Pembrokeshire, SA65 9QF.
Std: 01348 **Tel:** 872316
Nearest Town/Resort Fishguard
Directions Turn off the A40 1 mile south of Fishguard onto an unclassified road signposted Manorowen and caravan sign.
Acreage 5 **Open** April to October
Access Good **Site** Level
Sites Available ⚠ ⬛ ⬛ **Total** 45
Facilities ⬛ ⬛ ⬛ ⬛ ⬛ ⬛ ⬛
⬛ ⬛ ⬛ ⬛ ⬛
Nearby Facilities ⬛ ✓ ⬛ ⬛ U ⬛ ⬛
⬛ Fishguard
Attractive farm site. Adjacent to a national park and near the coast for watersports and bathing etc.. 1 mile from Fishguard. Nearest park to the Irish ferry.

HAVERFORDWEST

Brandy Brook Caravan & Camping Site, Rhyndaston, Hayscastle, Haverfordwest, Pembrokeshire, SA62 5PT.
Std: 01348 **Tel:** 840272
Nearest Town/Resort Haverfordwest
Directions From Haverfordwest take the A487 west towards St. Davids, turn right at Roch Hotel, signposted.
Acreage 5 **Open** Easter to October
Access Poor **Site** Lev/Slope
Sites Available ⚠ ⬛ ⬛ **Total** 46
Facilities ⬛ ⬛ ⬛ ⬛ ⬛ ⬛ ⬛
⬛ ⬛ ⬛ ⬛
Nearby Facilities ⬛ ✓ ⬛ ⬛ U ⬛ ⬛
⬛ Haverfordwest

HAVERFORDWEST

Broad Haven Holiday Park, Broad Haven, Haverfordwest, Pembrokeshire, SA62 3JD.
Std: 01437 **Tel:** 781277 **Fax:** 781088
Email: bhhp@btinternet.com
Website:
www.broadhavenholidaypark.com
Nearest Town/Resort Broad Haven
Directions From Haverfordwest take the road to Broad Haven, as you enter Broad Haven site is on the right at the bottom of the hill.
Acreage 3 **Open** 20 May to 5 September
Site Lev/Slope
Sites Available ⚠ **Total** 35
Facilities ⬛ ⬛ ⬛ ⬛ ⬛ ⬛ ⬛ ⬛
⬛ ⬛ ⬛ ⬛ ⬛ ⬛ ⬛ ⬛
Nearby Facilities
⬛ Haverfordwest
In the heart of the Pembrokeshire Coast National Park, alongside Broad Haven's safe sandy beach.

HAVERFORDWEST

Dunston Hill, Pelcomb, Haverfordwest, Pembrokeshire, SA62 6ED.
Std: 01437 **Tel:** 710525 **Fax:** 710525
Nearest Town/Resort Haverfordwest
Directions Take the A487 for St. Davids.
Open May to November
Access Good **Site** Gentle Slope
Sites Available ⚠ ⬛ ⬛
Facilities ⬛ ⬛ ⬛ ⬛ ⬛ ⬛ ⬛
Nearby Facilities ⬛ ✓ ⬛ ⬛ U ⬛
⬛ Haverfordwest
Beach and cliff top walks. 25 minutes to St. Davids, Britain's smallest city. Central for many places.

HAVERFORDWEST

Foxdale Camping Park, Glebe Lane, Marloes, Haverfordwest, Pembrokeshire, SA62 3AY.
Std: 01646 **Tel:** 636243
Email: foxdale.guest.house@totalise.co.uk

Web: www.foxdale.guest.house.8m.com
Nearest Town/Resort Haverfordwest
Directions From Haverfordwest take the B4327 Dale road, approx. 1½ miles before Dale Marloes is signposted to the right. On entering Marloes turn right at the church into Glebe Lane.
Acreage 2 **Open** March to October
Site Level
Sites Available ⚠ ⬛ **Total** 60
Facilities ⬛ ⬛ ⬛ ⬛ ⬛ ⬛ ⬛ ⬛ ⬛ ⬛ ⬛ ⬛
Nearby Facilities ⬛ ✓ ⬛ ⬛ U ⬛
⬛ Haverfordwest/Milford Haven
Surrounded by beautiful beaches, wonderful walking. Pembrokeshire cliff path. Bird islands of Skomer, Skokholm and Grassholm. Bird watching, fishing, windsurfing, diving etc..

HAVERFORDWEST

Nolton Cross Caravan Park, Nolton, Haverfordwest, Pembrokeshire, SA62 3NP.
Std: 01437 **Tel:** 710701 **Fax:** 710329
Email: noltoncross@nolton.fsnet.co.uk
Website: www.noltoncross-holidays.co.uk
Nearest Town/Resort Haverfordwest
Directions Take the A487 from Haverfordwest towards St Davids, after 5 miles at Simpson Cross turn left for Nolton, follow for 1 mile to the next crossroads and turn left, entrance is 100 yards on the right.
Acreage 1½ **Open** March to December
Access Good **Site** Level
Sites Available ⚠ ⬛ ⬛ **Total** 15
Facilities ⬛ ⬛ ⬛ ⬛ ⬛ ⬛ ⬛ ⬛ ⬛ ⬛ ⬛
Nearby Facilities ✓ U
⬛ Haverfordwest
Set in open countryside. 1½ miles from the coast.

HAVERFORDWEST

Pelcomb Cross Caravan Park, Pelcomb Cross, Haverfordwest, Pembrokeshire, SA62 6AB.
Std: 01437 **Tel:** 710431
Email: @justpembrokeshire.co.uk
Website: www.justpembrokeshire.co.uk
Nearest Town/Resort Haverfordwest
Directions From Haverfordwest take the A487 to St. Davids for 2 miles, site is second on the right past the Pelcomb Inn.
Acreage 4 **Open** March to October
Access Good **Site** Level
Sites Available ⚠ ⬛ ⬛ **Total** 30
Facilities ⬛ ⬛ ⬛ ⬛ ⬛ ⬛ ⬛ ⬛ ⬛
⬛ ⬛ ⬛ ⬛ ⬛
Nearby Facilities ⬛ ✓ ⬛ ⬛ U ⬛ ⬛
⬛ Haverfordwest
Very scenic, family run park. Close to coastal paths and beaches. Children and pets welcome.

HAVERFORDWEST

Scamford Caravan Park, Keeston, Haverfordwest, Pembrokeshire, SA62 6HN.
Std: 01437 **Tel:** 710304 **Fax:** 710304
Email: scamfordcaravanpark@talk21.com
Website: www.scamford-caravan-holidays.co.uk
Nearest Town/Resort Newgale
Directions From Haverfordwest take the A487 towards St. Davids. In approx. 4¼ miles turn right at Keeston, then follow signs for Scamford Caravan Park.
Open April to October
Access Good **Site** Level
Sites Available ⬛ ⬛ **Total** 5
Facilities ⬛ ⬛ ⬛ ⬛ ⬛ ⬛ ⬛ ⬛
⬛ ⬛ ⬛ ⬛ ⬛
Nearby Facilities ⬛ ✓ ⬛ ⬛ U ⬛ ⬛ ⬛

⚊ Haverfordwest
Ideal location for many beaches, coast path, Preseli Hills, Milford Haven Waterway, etc..

HAVERFORDWEST

The Rising Sun Inn, St. David's Road, Pelcomb Bridge, Haverfordwest, Pembrokeshire, SA62 6EA.
Std: 01437 **Tel:** 765171
Nearest Town/Resort Haverfordwest
Directions From Haverfordwest take the A487 road to St Davids. After approx. 1¼ miles at Pelcomb Bridge turn left, site is on the corner.
Acreage 2½ **Open** Easter **to** October
Access Good **Site** Lev/Slope
Sites Available ⚊ ⚊ ⚊ **Total** 25
Facilities ⚊ ⚊ ⚊ ⚊ ⚊ ⚊ ⚊ ⚊ ⚊ ⚊ ⚊ ⚊
Nearby Facilities ⚊ ⚊ ⚊ ⚊
⚊ Haverfordwest
5/7 miles from many lovely beaches. Ideal centre for touring, bird watching, golf, etc..

KILGETTY

Ryelands Caravan Park, Ryelands Lane, Kilgetty, Pembrokeshire, SA68 0UY.
Std: 01834 **Tel:** 812369
Nearest Town/Resort Saundersfoot/Tenby
Directions Turn left after railway bridge in Kilgetty into Ryelands Lane. Site in ½ mile on the right.
Acreage 5 **Open** March **to** 30 October
Access Good **Site** Lev/Slope
Sites Available ⚊ ⚊ ⚊ **Total** 45
Facilities ⚊ ⚊ ⚊ ⚊ ⚊ ⚊ ⚊ ⚊ ⚊
Nearby Facilities ⚊ ⚊ ⚊ ⚊
⚊ Kilgetty
Set in open countryside with views to the west, north and east.

LITTLE HAVEN

Howelston Caravan & Camping Site, Littlehaven, Haverfordwest, Pembrokeshire, SA62 3UU.
Std: 01437 **Tel:** 781253
Nearest Town/Resort Haverfordwest
Directions Off B4327 6 miles S.W. of Haverfordwest, turn right at Hasgaurd crossroads and right again in ¼ mile. Site on left in ½ mile.
Acreage 5 **Open** April **to** September
Access Good **Site** Lev/Slope
Sites Available ⚊ ⚊ ⚊ **Total** 60
Facilities ⚊ ⚊ ⚊ ⚊ ⚊ ⚊ ⚊ ⚊ ⚊
Nearby Facilities ⚊ ⚊ ⚊ ⚊ ⚊ ⚊ ⚊
⚊ Haverfordwest
1 mile from nearest beach. Site overlooking St. Brides Bay. Freezing and dish washing facilities. Cafe nearby.

LITTLE HAVEN

Redlands Touring Caravan Park, Little Haven, Haverfordwest, Pembrokeshire, SA62 3SJ.
Std: 01437 **Tel:** 781300 **Fax:** 781300
Email: nancy.whitby@virgin.net
Website: www.redlandstouring.co.uk
Nearest Town/Resort Little Haven
Directions 6½ miles southwest of Haverfordwest, on B4327 Dale Road.
Acreage 5 **Open** Easter **to** End Sept
Access Good **Site** Level
Sites Available ⚊ ⚊ ⚊ **Total** 60
Facilities ⚊ ⚊ ⚊ ⚊ ⚊ ⚊ ⚊ ⚊ ⚊
⚊ ⚊ ⚊ ⚊
Nearby Facilities ⚊ ⚊ ⚊ ⚊ ⚊ ⚊
⚊ Haverfordwest
Small well run site in Pembrokeshire National Park, within easy reach of coastal path and superb sandy beaches. Also open Winter months by arrangement.

LITTLE HAVEN

South Cockett Caravan & Camping Park, Broadway, Little Haven, Haverfordwest, Pembrokeshire, SA62 3TU.
Std: 01437 **Tel:** 781296/781760 **Fax:** 781296
Nearest Town/Resort Broad Haven
Directions From Haverfordwest take B4341 road for Broad Haven for about 6 miles, turn left at official camping signs, site 300yds.
Acreage 6 **Open** Easter **to** October
Access Good **Site** Level
Sites Available ⚊ ⚊ ⚊ **Total** 75
Facilities ⚊ ⚊ ⚊ ⚊ ⚊ ⚊ ⚊ ⚊ ⚊ ⚊
⚊ ⚊ ⚊ ⚊
Nearby Facilities ⚊ ⚊ ⚊ ⚊
⚊ Haverfordwest
Scenic views, ideal touring, near beach, coastal path nearby.

LLANDISSILIO

Llandissilio Caravan Park, Clynderwen, Pembrokeshire, SA66 7TT.
Std: 01437 **Tel:** 563408 **Fax:** 563747
Nearest Town/Resort Tenby/Saundersfoot
Directions Take the A478 Tenby to Cardigan road, then take the A40 at Narberth.
Acreage 8½ **Open** March **to** October
Access Good **Site** Level
Sites Available ⚊ ⚊ ⚊ **Total** 50
Facilities ⚊ ⚊ ⚊ ⚊ ⚊ ⚊ ⚊ ⚊ ⚊ ⚊
⚊ ⚊ ⚊ ⚊ ⚊ ⚊ ⚊ ⚊ ⚊ ⚊ ⚊ ⚊ ⚊ ⚊
Nearby Facilities ⚊ ⚊ ⚊
⚊ Narberth
Indoor heated pool, sauna and jacuzzi. Bar. Lovely walks.

MANORBIER

Park Farm Caravans, Manorbier, Tenby, Pembrokeshire, SA70 7SU.
Std: 01834 **Tel:** 871273 (Site Office)
Nearest Town/Resort Tenby
Directions 5 miles west of Tenby on A4139 take second turning left for Manorbier.
Acreage 7 **Open** Easter **to** October
Access Good **Site** Level
Sites Available ⚊ ⚊ ⚊ **Total** 70
Facilities ⚊ ⚊ ⚊ ⚊ ⚊ ⚊ ⚊ ⚊ ⚊
⚊ ⚊ ⚊ ⚊ ⚊
Nearby Facilities ⚊ ⚊ ⚊ ⚊ ⚊ ⚊ ⚊ ⚊
⚊ Manorbier
Footpath to beach. For ENQUIRIES please telephone 01646 672583.

MARLOES

East Hook Farm, Marloes, Haverfordwest, Pembrokeshire, SA62 3BJ.
Std: 01646 **Tel:** 636291
Nearest Town/Resort Haverfordwest
Open All Year
Access Good **Site** Level
Sites Available ⚊ ⚊ ⚊ **Total** 30
Facilities ⚊ ⚊ ⚊ ⚊ ⚊ ⚊ ⚊ ⚊ ⚊
Nearby Facilities ⚊ ⚊ ⚊ ⚊
⚊ Haverfordwest
Within walking distance of two beaches. Cream teas available on site. The Boat to Skomer and Skokholm nearby.

MILFORD HAVEN

Sandy Haven Caravan Park, Herbrandston, Nr. Milford Haven, Pembrokeshire, SA73 2AL.
Std: 01646 **Tel:** 698844
Nearest Town/Resort Milford Haven
Directions Take the Dale Road from Milford Haven, turn left at Herbrandston School and follow the village road down to the beach.
Acreage 3½ **Open** Easter **to** September

⚊ Milford Haven
Very quiet and uncommercialised site, alongside a beautiful beach and sea estuary. Ideal family holidays, boating, windsurfing, canoeing, etc.. You can also call our Answerphone on 01646 698844.

MYNACHLOG-DDU

Trefach Country Pub & Caravan Park, Mynachlog-Ddu, Clynderwen, Pembrokeshire, SA66 7RU.
Std: 01994 **Tel:** 419225 **Fax:** 419221
Email: trefach@bigfoot.com
Website: www.bigfoot.com/~trefach
Nearest Town/Resort Crymmych
Directions 1½ miles off A478 at Glandy Cross Inn.
Acreage 18 **Open** March **to** October
Access Good **Site** Lev/Slope
Sites Available ⚊ ⚊ ⚊ **Total** 70
Facilities ⚊ ⚊ ⚊ ⚊ ⚊ ⚊ ⚊ ⚊ ⚊ ⚊
⚊ ⚊ ⚊ ⚊ ⚊ ⚊ ⚊ ⚊ ⚊ ⚊ ⚊ ⚊ ⚊ ⚊
Nearby Facilities ⚊ ⚊
⚊ Clynderwen
In the Preseli Hills, good walking and pony trekking. Central for touring West Wales.

NARBERTH

Allensbank Caravan Park, Narberth, Pembrokeshire, SA67 8RF.
Std: 01834 **Tel:** 860243 **Fax:** 861622
Nearest Town/Resort Narberth
Directions 1 mile south of Narberth on the A478 Tenby road.
Acreage 5 **Open** Easter **to** October
Access Good **Site** Level
Sites Available ⚊ ⚊ ⚊ **Total** 10
Facilities ⚊ ⚊ ⚊ ⚊ ⚊ ⚊ ⚊ ⚊
⚊ ⚊ ⚊ ⚊ ⚊ ⚊ ⚊ ⚊
Nearby Facilities ⚊ ⚊ ⚊ ⚊ ⚊ ⚊ ⚊ ⚊
Ideal touring situation.

NARBERTH

Dingle Caravan Park, The Dingle, Jesse Road, Narberth, Pembrokeshire, SA67 7DP.
Std: 01834 **Tel:** 861806 **Fax:** 860482
Nearest Town/Resort Narberth
Directions 2 miles from the A40.
Open Easter **to** October
Access Good **Site** Level
Sites Available ⚊ ⚊ ⚊ **Total** 30
Facilities ⚊ ⚊ ⚊ ⚊ ⚊ ⚊ ⚊ ⚊
⚊ ⚊ ⚊ ⚊ ⚊
Nearby Facilities ⚊ ⚊ ⚊ ⚊ ⚊ ⚊
⚊ Narberth
Central location. 6 miles from the nearest beach.

NARBERTH

Noble Court Caravan Park, Redstone Road, Narberth, Pembrokeshire, SA67 7ES.
Std: 01834 **Tel:** 861191 **Fax:** 861484
Nearest Town/Resort Narberth
Directions ½ mile north of Narberth on B4313 road and ½ mile south of A40 on B4313.
Acreage 20 **Open** March **to** November
Access Good **Site** Lev/Slope
Sites Available ⚊ ⚊ ⚊ **Total** 92
Facilities ⚊ ⚊ ⚊ ⚊ ⚊ ⚊ ⚊ ⚊ ⚊ ⚊
⚊ ⚊ ⚊ ⚊ ⚊ ⚊ ⚊ ⚊ ⚊ ⚊ ⚊ ⚊ ⚊ ⚊
Nearby Facilities ⚊ ⚊ ⚊ ⚊
⚊ Narberth
Conveniently situated for travel to all Pembrokeshire beaches and countryside also Pembrokeshire National Park. Quiet family caravan park with amenities for all ages. Fishing on site.

LLWYNGWAIR MANOR HOLIDAY PARK
NEWPORT, PEMBS. SA42 0LX

55 acres of beautiful parkland in Pembrokeshire National Park.
Alongside the River Nevern. 1 mile from the sea.
Tennis court, fishing and licensed bars. Electric hook-ups for tourers.
Self catering apartments and caravans for rent.

TELEPHONE: (01239) 820498

NEWPORT
Llwyngwair Manor, Newport, Pembrokeshire, SA42 0LX.
Std: 01239 **Tel:** 820498
Email: plowe10456@aol.com
Nearest Town/Resort Newport
Directions 1 mile from Newport on the A487 to Cardigan.
Open March **to** November
Access Good **Site** Level
Sites Available ▲ ⊕ ⊟ **Total** 80
Facilities ⬙
Nearby Facilities ⬙ ⬙ ⬙ ⬙ ⬙ ⬙
➤ Fishguard
1 mile from sandy beach. 55 acres of wood and parkland in Pembrokeshire Coast National Park, alongside the River Nevern. Tennis on site.

NEWPORT
Morawelon, Parrog, Newport, Pembrokeshire, SA42 0RW.
Std: 01239 **Tel:** 820565
Nearest Town/Resort Fishguard/ Cardigan
Directions A487 from Fishguard, 7 miles to Newport. A487 from Cardigan, 12 miles to Newport. Turn down road signposted Parrog Beach or Parrog at the western end of town. Morawelon is the last house at the end of the road by the quay wall.
Acreage 5 **Open** Easter **to** Mid Oct
Access Good **Site** Lev/Slope
Sites Available ▲ ⊕ ⊟ **Total** 85
Facilities ⬙ ⬙ ⬙ ⬙ ⬙ ⬙ ⬙ ⬙ ⬙ ⬙ ⬙ ⬙
Nearby Facilities ⬙ ⬙ ⬙ ⬙ ⬙ ⬙
➤ Fishguard
Direct access to the beach and sea, scenic views over the bay, ideal centre for Windsurfers, sailing etc. Salmon river fishing and coastal path walking. All accessable from the site. Boat park by the quay wall. Tourist Board Verified.

NEWPORT
Tycanol Farm Camp Site, Newport, Pembrokeshire, SA42 0ST.
Std: 01239 **Tel:** 820264
Nearest Town/Resort Newport
Acreage 6 **Open** All Year
Access Good **Site** Level
Sites Available ▲ ⊕ ⊟ **Total** 40
Facilities ⬙ ⬙ ⬙ ⬙ ⬙ ⬙ ⬙ ⬙ ⬙ ⬙ ⬙ ⬙ ⬙ ⬙ ⬙
Nearby Facilities ⬙ ⬙ ⬙ ⬙ ⬙ ⬙
➤ Fishguard
Situated on a coastal path with easy access to beaches and the town. FREE barbecue nightly.

PEMBROKE
Windmill Hill Caravan Park, Windmill Hill Farm, Pembroke, Pembrokeshire, SA71 5BT.
Std: 01646 **Tel:** 682392
Nearest Town/Resort Pembroke
Directions Situated approx. 1 mile from Pembroke town on the B4319 towards Castlemartin.
Acreage 6 **Open** March **to** October
Access Good **Site** Level
Sites Available ▲ ⊕ ⊟ **Total** 60
Facilities ⬙ ⬙ ⬙ ⬙ ⬙ ⬙ ⬙ ⬙
Nearby Facilities ⬙ ⬙ ⬙ ⬙ ⬙ ⬙
➤ Pembroke
Numerous excellent beaches, famous climbing area. 3 miles from the Irish ferry terminal.

REYNALTON
Croft Holiday Park, Reynalton, Kilgetty, Pembrokeshire, SA68 0PE.
Std: 01834 **Tel:** 860315 **Fax:** 860510
Nearest Town/Resort Saundersfoot
Directions From Narberth take the A478 following signs for Tenby. In Templeton turn second right at the Boars Head towards Yerbeston, turn second left to Reynalton and the park is ½ mile on the right hand side.
Open March **to** November
Access Good **Site** Level
Sites Available ▲ ⊕ ⊟ **Total** 55
Facilities ⬙ ⬙ ⬙ ⬙ ⬙ ⬙ ⬙ ⬙ ⬙ ⬙ ⬙ ⬙
Nearby Facilities ⬙ ⬙ ⬙ ⬙ ⬙ ⬙
➤ Kilgetty
Close to the seaside resorts of Tenby and Saundersfoot, and Pembrokeshire National Park.

SAUNDERSFOOT
Hill Park Caravans, Pentlepoir, Saundersfoot, Pembrokeshire, SA69 9BH.
Std: 01834 **Tel:** 811288 **Fax:** 811288
Email: dai.cope@ic24.net
Nearest Town/Resort Saundersfoot/ Kilgetty
Directions On the main A478 Tenby road, opposite the B4316 turning for Saundersfoot.
Acreage 1½ **Open** April **to** October
Access Good **Site** Level
Sites Available ▲ ⊕ ⊟ **Total** 25
Facilities ⬙ ⬙ ⬙ ⬙ ⬙ ⬙ ⬙ ⬙ ⬙ ⬙ ⬙ ⬙
Nearby Facilities ⬙ ⬙ ⬙ ⬙ ⬙ ⬙
➤ Saundersfoot/Kilgetty
Next door to the village pub. Conveniently situated for all attractions: 1 mile from Saundersfoot and beaches; Oakwood and Folly Farm tourist attractions.

SAUNDERSFOOT
Mill House Caravan Park, Pleasant Valley, Stepaside, Saundersfoot, Pembrokeshire, SA67 8LN.
Std: 01834 **Tel:** 812069
Email: holiday@millhousecaravan.demon.co.uk
Website: www.millhousecaravan.demon.co.uk
Nearest Town/Resort Saundersfoot
Directions 12 miles west of St. Clears on the A477 turn left signposted Stepaside. After crossing the bridge turn sharp left then immediately left again signed Pleasant Valley. Site is approx. 300 metres on the left hand side.
Acreage 2½ **Open** March **to** October
Access Good **Site** Level
Sites Available ▲ ⊕ ⊟ **Total** 12
Facilities ⬙ ⬙ ⬙ ⬙ ⬙ ⬙ ⬙ ⬙ ⬙ ⬙ ⬙ ⬙ ⬙
Nearby Facilities ⬙ ⬙ ⬙ ⬙ ⬙ ⬙
➤ Kilgetty
Beautiful and sheltered setting in a wooded valley, next to an old water mill. 15 minute walk to the beach and coastal path. Good pub just a 5 minute walk. Holiday caravans for hire.

SAUNDERSFOOT
Moreton Farm Leisure Park, Moreton, Saundersfoot, Pembrokeshire, SA69 9EA.
Std: 01834 **Tel:** 812016
Email: moretonfarm@btconnect.com
Website: www.moretonfarm.co.uk
Nearest Town/Resort Tenby/ Saundersfoot
Directions From St. Clears o the A477, turn left onto A478 for Tenby. Site is on left 1¼ miles, opposite chapel.
Acreage 12 **Open** March **to** October
Access Good **Site** Level
Sites Available ▲ ⊕ ⊟ **Total** 60
Facilities ⬙ ⬙ ⬙ ⬙ ⬙ ⬙ ⬙ ⬙ ⬙ ⬙ ⬙ ⬙ ⬙
Nearby Facilities ⬙ ⬙ ⬙ ⬙ ⬙ ⬙
➤ Saundersfoot
1 mile of safe golden beach. Dragon Award.

SAUNDERSFOOT
Moysland Farm Camping Site, Tenby Road, Saundersfoot, Pembrokeshire, SA69 9DS.
Tel: Saundersfoot 812455
Nearest Town/Resort Saundersfoot
Directions Leave the M4 and take the A48 and A40 to St. Clears, turn onto the A477 to Kilgetty then take the A478 to Tenby. Site is on right hand side of road before New Hedges roundabout.

Acreage 3 **Open** Whitsun **to** September
Access Good **Site** Level
Sites Available ▲ ⊕ ⊟ **Total** 20
Facilities ⚡ 🚽 ♿ 🏪 ⊙ 🛏️ ❄️ 🖂 🏧
Nearby Facilities 🏌️ 🚣 ⚓ 🎣 ∪ ♒ 🏇
🚣 Tenby
Beach ¼ mile, ideal centre for touring. Tents
for hire. Please send S.A.E. for details.

SAUNDERSFOOT

Trevayne Farm, Saundersfoot,
Pembrokeshire, SA69 9DL.
Std: 01834 **Tel:** 813402
Nearest Town/Resort Saundersfoot/
Tenby
Directions A40 to St. Clears A477 to
Kilgetty. A478 towards Tenby, approx 2½
miles from Tenby turn left for Saundersfoot,
right for New Hedges and left again for
Trevayne ¾ mile.
Acreage 7 **Open** Easter **to** October
Access Good **Site** Level
Sites Available ▲ ⊕ ⊟ **Total** 100
Facilities ⚡ ♿ 🚽 ♿ ⊙ 🛏️ ❄️ 🖂
Nearby Facilities 🏌️ 🚣 ⚓ 🎣 ∪ 🏇 🏇
🚣 Tenby
Situated on coast with lovely sandy beach
and scenery. 60 electricity hook-ups
available for touring and motor caravans and
campers.

ST. DAVIDS

Glan-Y-Mor Camp Site, Caerfai Road, St.
Davids, Pembrokeshire, SA62 6QT.
Std: 01437 **Tel:** 721788 **Fax:** 721988
Email: clive@divewales.com
Website: www.divewales.com
Nearest Town/Resort St. Davids
Directions Turn left at the Information
Centre in St. Davids.
Site Level
Sites Available ▲ **Total** 55
Facilities ♿ 🚽 ⊙ ♿ 🗶 ❄️ 🖂
Nearby Facilities 🏌️ 🚣 ⚓ 🎣 ∪ 🏇
🚣 Haverfordwest
4 minute walk to the beach and a 5 minute
walk to St. Davids town centre.

ST. DAVIDS

Lleithyr Farm Caravan Park,
Whitesands, St. Davids, Pembrokeshire,
SA62 6PR.
Std: 01437 **Tel:** 720245 **Fax:** 720245
Email: james@lleithyr.catchtrust.org
Website: www.whitesands-stdavids.co.uk
Nearest Town/Resort St. Davids
Directions From St. Davids take the
Whitesands road, turn right at the
crossroads, then turn next left.
Open Easter **to** Nov
Access Good **Site** Level
Sites Available ▲ ⊕ ⊟
Facilities ⚡ ♿ 🚽 🏪 ⊙ 🖳 🏧 ♿ 🛏️ ❄️ 🖂

Nearby Facilities 🏌️ 🚣 ⚓ 🎣 ∪ ♒ 🏇
🚣 Haverfordwest
National Parks Coastal Path runs through
the farm. Unlimited pitches. ½ mile from a
championship surfing and canoeing beach.
¼ mile from a 9 hole golf course.

ST. DAVIDS

Nine Wells Caravan & Camping Park,
Nine Wells, Solva, Nr. Haverfordwest,
Pembrokeshire, SA62 6UH.
Std: 01437 **Tel:** 721809
Nearest Town/Resort Haverfordwest
Directions From Haverfordwest take A487
to Solva. ¼ mile past Solva turn left at Nine
Wells. Site clearly signposted.
Acreage 4½ **Open** Easter **to** October
Access Good **Site** Lev/Slope
Sites Available ▲ ⊕ ⊟ **Total** 70
Facilities ⚡ ♿ 🚽 ⊙ 🖳 ♿ 🖂 🏧
Nearby Facilities 🏌️ 🚣 ⚓ 🎣 ∪ 🏇
🚣 Haverfordwest
Sandy beach ¾ mile. Walk the coastal
footpath to Solva. About 5 minute walk to
cove and coastal footpath and Iron Age Fort,
down National Trust Valley.

ST. DAVIDS

Park Hall Camping Park, Maerdy Farm,
Penycwm, Haverfordwest, Pembrokeshire.
Std: 01437 **Tel:** 721606/721282 **Fax:**
721606
Nearest Town/Resort Haverfordwest
Directions 12 miles from Haverfordwest on
the A487 and 6 miles from St. Davids. Turn
at the 14th Signal Regiment Brawdy.
Acreage 7 **Open** March **to** October
Access Good **Site** Level
Sites Available ▲ ⊕ ⊟ **Total** 100
Facilities ⚡ 🖳 🛏️ ♿ 🚽 ⊙ 🖳 ♿ 🖂
Nearby Facilities 🏌️ 🚣 ⚓ 🎣 ∪ ♒ 🏇
🚣 Haverfordwest
Near beach, scenic views. Ideal touring,
fishing on private lake.

ST. DAVIDS

Prendergast Caravan & Camping Park,
Cartlett Lodge, Trefin, Haverfordwest,
Pembrokeshire, SA62 5AL.
Std: 01348 **Tel:** 831368
Nearest Town/Resort St. Davids/
Fishguard
Directions From Haverfordwest take A40
towards Fishguard, until Letterston. Turn left
on B4331 until you reach A487. Turn left for
St. Davids in about 2½ miles. Turn right by
sign for Trefin.
Acreage ½ **Open** April **to** September
Access Good **Site** Lev/Slope
Sites Available ▲ ⊕ ⊟ **Total** 12
Facilities ♿ ⚡ 🚽 ⊙ 🖳 ♿ 🖳 🖂
Nearby Facilities 🏌️ 🚣 ⚓ 🎣 ∪ ♒ 🏇
🚣 Haverfordwest

Lovely walks along a coastal path.

ST. DAVIDS

Rhosson Farm, St. Davids,
Haverfordwest, Pembrokeshire, SA62
6PY.
Std: 01437 **Tel:** 720335/6
Nearest Town/Resort St. Davids
Directions Take the road to the lifeboat
station and past the cathedral, Rhosson
Farm is approx. 2 miles down this road on
the left, signposted.
Acreage 8 **Open** Easter **to** October
Access Good **Site** Lev/Slope
Sites Available ▲ ⊕ ⊟
Facilities ⚡ 🚽 🏪 ⊙ 🖳 ♿ 🛏️ ❄️ 🖂
Nearby Facilities 🏌️ 🚣 ⚓ 🎣 ∪ 🏇
🚣 Haverfordwest
Sea and coastal views. Just minutes away
from the beautiful Pembrokeshire coast and
beaches. You can also contact us on Mobile
07967 139132.

ST. DAVIDS

Rhos-y-Cribed, St. Davids,
Haverfordwest, Pembrokeshire, SA62
6RR.
Std: 01437 **Tel:** 720336
Nearest Town/Resort St. Davids
Directions Take the Porthclais road out of
St Davids down to the harbour. Farm is
signposted near the car park.
Access Good **Site** Level
Sites Available ▲ ⊕ ⊟
Facilities ♿ ♿ 🚽 ⊙ 🖳 🛀 ❄️ 🖂
Nearby Facilities 🏌️ 🚣 ⚓ 🎣 ∪ 🏇
🚣 Haverfordwest
Views of St Davids, the cathedral and St
Brides Bay. Near the harbour and coastal
path. You can also contact us on Mobile
07967 139132.

TENBY

Buttyland, Manorbier, Tenby,
Pembrokeshire, SA70 7SN.
Std: 01834 **Tel:** 871278
Email: buttyland@tesco.net
Website: www.buttyland.co.uk
Nearest Town/Resort Tenby
Directions Take the A4139 west from Tenby
for 6 miles. Turn right by Chapel with red
cross, 400yds down the road on the right
hand side.
Acreage 10 **Open** Easter **to** End
September
Access Good **Site** Level
Sites Available ▲ ⊕ ⊟ **Total** 53
Facilities ⚡ ♿ 🚽 🏪 ⊙ 🖳 🛒 ♿ 📷 🖂
♿ 🗶 ⊛ ❄️ 🖂
Nearby Facilities 🏌️ 🚣 ∪ 🏇
Manorbier Beach and the Blue Flag beach
of Tenby. Ideal touring.

ENBY

rackwell Holiday Park, Penally, Tenby,
embrokeshire, SA70 7RX.
d: 01834 Tel: 842688 Fax: 842626
nail: crackwell@thebelgravehotel.co.uk
earest Town/Resort Tenby
rections 2 miles west of Tenby on the
4139 coastal road, between Tenby and
dstep Haven.
creage 8 Open April to October
ccess Good Site Lev/Slope
tes Available ⚑ ⚑ Total 100
cilities ⚏ ⌂ ▥ ⌖ 🚿 ⊙ ◔ 🍴 ⊡ 🛒
⚒ 🏪 🕂 ▣ ☎
earby Facilities ⌖ ↗ ⚓ ⤢ U ⤾ ♫ ⚐
⚑ Penally
ear the beach.

ENBY

oss Park Holiday Centre, Broadmoor,
getty, Tenby, Pembrokeshire, SA68 0RS
d: 01834 Tel: 811244 Fax: 814300
nail:
quiries@crossparkholidaycentre.co.uk
ebsite:
ww.crossparkholidaycentre.co.uk
earest Town/Resort Tenby
rections At Kilgetty roundabout follow the
477 west for 1 mile to Broad Moor, turn
ht at the Cross Inn Pub and we are 150
rds along on the left.
creage 11 Open 28 March to October
ccess Good Site Level
tes Available ⚑ ⚑ Total 50
cilities ⚏ ⌂ ▥ ⌖ 🚿 ⊙ ◔ 🍴 ⊡ 🛒
⚒ ⊙ ⚒ ✕ ▽ 🏪 🕂 ➔ 🕂 ▣ ☎
earby Facilities ⌖ ↗ ⚓ ⤢ U ⤾ ♫
⚑ Tenby
acres of landscaped gardens and lawns
rrounded by mature trees and colourful
rubs. Excellent on-site facilities.

TENBY

Hazelbrook Caravan Park, Sageston, Nr.
Tenby, Pembrokeshire, SA70 8SY.
Std: 01646 Tel: 651351 Fax: 651595
Website:
www.hazelbrookcaravanpark.co.uk
Nearest Town/Resort Tenby
Directions Turn off the A477 in the village
of Sageston turning onto the B4318 for
Tenby. Caravan park is 300 yards on the
right, 60 foot entrance.
Acreage 7½ Open 1 March to 9 January
Access Good Site Level
Sites Available ▲ ⚑ ⚑ Total 70
Facilities ⚏ ⌂ ▥ ⌖ 🚿 ⊙ ◔ 🍴 ⊡ 🛒
⚒ ⊙ ⚒ 🏪 🕂 ▣ ☎
Nearby Facilities ⌖ ↗ ⚓ ⤢ U ♫
⚑ Tenby
1 mile from Carew Castle and Mill, 2 miles
from Dinosaur Park and 7 miles from
Oakwood Theme Park.

TENBY

Kiln Park Holiday Centre, Marsh Road,
Tenby, Pembrokeshire, SA70 7RB.
Std: 08457 Tel: 433433
Website: www.british-holidays.co.uk
Nearest Town/Resort Tenby
Directions Follow the A478 to Tenby,
signposted from Tenby.
Acreage 150 Open March to September
Access Good Site Level
Sites Available ▲ ⚑ ⚑ Total 300
Facilities ♿ ⚏ ⌂ ▥ ⌖ 🚿 ⊙ ◔ 🍴 ⊡ 🛒
⚒ ⊙ ⚒ ✕ ▽ 🏪 ⤢ ➔ ✫ 🕂 ▣ ☎
Nearby Facilities ⌖ ↗ ⚓ ⤢ U ⤾ ♫ ⚐
⚑ Tenby
5 minutes walk from sandy beach. Tenby has
usual resort amusements. Childrens Club
and a full family entertainment programme.
Burger King and cafe on park.

TENBY

Lodge Farm Caravan & Camping Park,
Lodge Farm, New Hedges, Tenby,
Pembrokeshire, SA70 8TH.
Std: 01834 Tel: 842468
Nearest Town/Resort Tenby/
Saundersfoot
Directions Approaching Tenby on A478,
turn left at New Hedges roundabout, first
right, through village, Lodge farm entrance
opposite minimarket.
Acreage 10 Open April to October
Access Good Site Level
Sites Available ▲ ⚑ ⚑ Total 65+
Facilities ⚒ ⚏ ▥ ⌖ 🚿 ⊙ ⊡ 🛒 ☎
▣ ⊙ ▽ 🏪 🕂 ❋ 🕂 ▣
Nearby Facilities ⌖ ↗ ⚓ ⤢ U ⤾ ♫ ⚐
⚑ Tenby
Near beaches. Sky Television in club.
Camping and Caravan Club Listed Site and
AA 2 Pennants.

TENBY

Manorbier Bay Caravanserai, A4139,
Near Tenby, Pembrokeshire, SA70 7SR.
Std: 01834 Tel: 871235
Nearest Town/Resort Tenby
Directions From Tenby take the A4139
heading west towards Pembroke, ½ mile
east of Jameston Village.
Open March to October
Access Good Site Level
Sites Available ⚑▢ Total 19
Facilities ⚏ ▥ ⌖ 🚿 ⊡ 🛒 ☎
▣ ⊙ 🏪 🕂 ▣
Nearby Facilities ⌖ ↗ ⤢ U ⤾
⚑ Manorbier
Manorbier beach is accessible by a public
footpath.

TENBY

Manorbier Country Park, Station Road, Manorbier, Tenby, Pembrokeshire, SA70 7SN.
Std: 01834 **Tel:** 871952 **Fax:** 871203
Email: enquiries@countrypark.co.uk
Website: www.countrypark.co.uk
Nearest Town/Resort Tenby
Open March to October
Access Good **Site** Level
Sites Available ▲ ⬛ ⬛ **Total** 50
Facilities ⟨symbols⟩
Nearby Facilities ⟨symbols⟩
⚲ Manorbier

TENBY

Masterland Farm Touring Caravan & Tent Park, Broadmoor, Kilgetty, Pembrokeshire, SA68 0RH.
Std: 01834 **Tel:** 813298 **Fax:** 814408
Email: bonsermasterland@aol.com
Website: www.ukparks.co.uk/masterland
Nearest Town/Resort Tenby
Directions After Carmarthen take main A40 to St. Clears, then take the A477 to Broadmoor. Turn right at Cross Inn Public House, Masterland Farm is 300yds on your right.
Acreage 8 **Open** 1 March to 7 January
Access Good **Site** Level
Sites Available ▲ ⬛ ⬛ **Total** 38
Facilities ⟨symbols⟩
Nearby Facilities ⟨symbols⟩
⚲ Kilgetty
Ideal touring, close to leisure parks etc..

TENBY

Milton Bridge Caravan Park, Milton, Nr. Tenby, Pembrokeshire, SA70 8PH.
Std: 01646 **Tel:** 651204 **Fax:** 651204
Email: miltonbridge@lineone.net
Nearest Town/Resort Tenby
Directions Half way between Kilgetty and Pembroke Dock on the A477.
Acreage 3 **Open** March to October
Access Good **Site** Lev/Slope
Sites Available ⬛ ⬛ **Total** 15
Facilities ⟨symbols⟩
Nearby Facilities ⟨symbols⟩
⚲ Lamphey
Small, friendly park situated on a tidal river. Ideal base for exploring the many attractions in the area.

TENBY

Red House Farm, Twy Cross, Tenby, Pembrokeshire, SA69 9DP.
Std: 01834 **Tel:** 813918
Nearest Town/Resort Tenby

Directions Situated just off the A478, 1½ miles from both Tenby and Saundersfoot. Regular bus service.
Acreage 2 **Open** May to September
Access Good **Site** Lev/Slope
Sites Available ▲ ⬛□ **Total** 10
Facilities ⟨symbols⟩
Nearby Facilities ⟨symbols⟩
⚲ Tenby
Very quiet, small site. Most appreciated by those seeking peace rather than entertainment. Not suitable for small children. Sorry No pets.

TENBY

Rowston Holiday Park, New Hedges, Tenby, Pembrokeshire, SA70 8TL.
Std: 01834 **Tel:** 842178 **Fax:** 842178
Nearest Town/Resort Tenby/Saundersfoot
Directions 1 mile north of Tenby, in the village of New Hedges.
Acreage 20 **Open** April to November
Access Good **Site** Lev/Slope
Sites Available ▲ ⬛ ⬛ **Total** 120
Facilities ⟨symbols⟩
Nearby Facilities ⟨symbols⟩
⚲ Tenby
Just a two minute walk to the pretty village of New Hedges with Londis Store, Post Office, garage and tavern providing meals and entertainment in high season. No dogs Mid July/August.

TENBY

Sunnyvale Holiday Park, Valley Road, Saundersfoot, Pembrokeshire, SA69 9BT.
Std: 01348 **Tel:** 872462 **Fax:** 872351
Website: www.howellsleisure.co.uk
Nearest Town/Resort Tenby
Directions Take the A478 to Tenby, proceed through Pentlepoir and take a left turn into Valley Road, Sunnyvale is 300 yards down on the left hand side.
Acreage 5 **Open** March to October
Access Good **Site** Lev/Slope
Sites Available ▲ ⬛ ⬛ **Total** 50
Facilities ⟨symbols⟩
Nearby Facilities ⟨symbols⟩
⚲ Saundersfoot
Near Tenby, Saundersfoot and numerous golden sandy beaches. Clubhouse with Free nightly live entertainment for adults and children. Pitches from just £4 per night.

TENBY

Tudor Glen Caravan Park, Jameston, Nr. Tenby, Pembrokeshire, SA70 7SS.
Std: 01834 **Tel:** 871417 **Fax:** 871832
Email: info@tudorglencaravanpark.co.uk

Website: www.tudorglencaravanpark.co.uk
Nearest Town/Resort Tenby
Directions From Tenby take the A41 Coast Road west for 6 miles. Site is on t right before entering village of Jameston.
Acreage 6 **Open** March to October
Access Good **Site** Lev/Slope
Sites Available ▲ ⬛ ⬛ **Total** 46
Facilities ⟨symbols⟩
Nearby Facilities ⟨symbols⟩
⚲ Manorbier
Family run site, ideal touring base.

TENBY

Well Park Caravans, Tenby, Pembrokeshire, SA70 8TL.
Std: 01834 **Tel:** 842179
Email: enquiries@wellparkcaravans.co.
Website: www.wellparkcaravans.co.uk
Nearest Town/Resort Tenby
Directions On righthand side of main Ter (A478) road 1 mile north of Tenby.
Acreage 10 **Open** April to October
Access Good **Site** Lev/Slope
Sites Available ▲ ⬛ ⬛ **Total** 100
Facilities ⟨symbols⟩
Nearby Facilities ⟨symbols⟩
⚲ Tenby
A family run site, situated in pleasa surroundings. Excellent facilities. Ve central and convenient for the beauti beaches and places of interest along Pembrokeshire coast. Wales in Blo Award Winning Park, Daffodil Award and 4 Pennants.

TENBY

Whitewell Camping Park, Lydstep Beach, Penally, Tenby, Pembrokeshire, SA70 7RY.
Std: 01834 **Tel:** 842200
Website: www.huntingtonsguide.co.uk
Nearest Town/Resort Tenby
Acreage 13 **Open** April to September
Access Good **Site** Level
Sites Available ▲ ⬛ ⬛ **Total** 120
Facilities ⟨symbols⟩
Nearby Facilities ⟨symbols⟩
⚲ Tenby
½ mile Lydstep Beach, green countrysi on all sides.

TENBY

Windmills Camping Park, Narberth Road, Tenby, Pembrokeshire, SA70 8TJ
Std: 01834 **Tel:** 842200
Website: www.huntingtonsguide.co.uk
Nearest Town/Resort Tenby
Acreage 4 **Open** Easter to September

e Lev/Slope
es Available ▲ ⊕ ⇎ **Total** 40
cilities ⸙ ▯ ⓌⒸ ♨ ╒ ☺ ⌿ ⮝ ☏
▦ 𝄞⊞
arby Facilities ╒ ⸜ ⚓ ↘ ∪ ⇥ ♂ ♀
Tenby
a views, ¾ mile Tenby town centre.

⦂ENBY

od Park Caravan Park, New Hedges,
nby, Pembrokeshire, SA70 8TL.
d: 01834 **Tel:** 843414
nail: info@woodpark.co.uk
ebsite: www.woodpark.co.uk
arest Town/Resort Tenby
rections From Tenby take the A478 north
2 miles, at roundabout go straight on
vards Tenby, turn second right then right
ain.
reage 2 **Open** April **to** October
ccess Good Site Lev/Slope
es Available ▲ ⊕ ⇎ **Total** 60
cilities ⸙ ⓌⒸ ♨ ╒ ☺ ⌿ ⮝ ☏
⊙ ♀ ▦ ▯ 𝄞
arby Facilities ╒ ⸜ ⚓ ↘ ∪ ⇥ ♂ ♀
Tenby
iet, family park ideally situated between
nby and Saundersfoot.

OWYS

⦂ECON

chorage Caravan Park, Bronllys,
econ, Powys, LD3 0LD.
d: 01874 **Tel:** 711246
arest Town/Resort Brecon
rections On the A438, 8 miles north east
Brecon on the west side of Bronllys
age.
reage 8 **Open** All Year
ccess Good Site Lev/Slope
es Available ▲ ⊕ ⇎ **Total** 110
cilities ⚒ ⸙ ▯ ⓌⒸ ♨ ╒ ☺ ⌿ ⮝ ☏
🅿 ⊙ ▦ ☏ ▯ 𝄞
arby Facilities ╒ ⸜ ⚓ ↘ ∪ ⇥ ♂ ♀
Abergavenny
erlooking the Brecon Beacons National
rk. Ideally situated for touring and walking
d and South Wales. Baby bath. 4 Star
aded Park and AA 3 Pennants.

⦂ECON

shops Meadow Caravan Park, Hay
ad, Brecon, Powys, LD3 9SW.
d: 01874 **Tel:** 610000 **Fax:** 614922
nail: www.bishops-meadow.co.uk
ebsite: www.bishops-meadow.co.uk
arest Town/Resort Brecon
rections On the B4602 1 mile from
econ.
reage 5 **Open** March **to** October
ccess Good Site Lev/Slope
es Available ▲ ⊕ ⇎ **Total** 80
cilities ⚒ ⸙ ▯ ⓌⒸ ♨ ╒ ☺ ⌿ ⮝ ☏
⊙ ♨ ✕ ▦ ☏ ▯
arby Facilities ╒ ⸜ ↘ ∪ ⇥
Merthyr Tydfil

⦂ECON

ynich Caravan Park, Brecon, Powys,
3 7SH.
d: 01874 **Tel:** 623325 **Fax:** 623325
nail: brynich@aol.com
ebsite: www.brynich.co.uk
arest Town/Resort Brecon
rections 1 mile east of Brecon on A470.
0 yards from A40/A470 roundabout.
reage 20 **Open** Easter **to** October
ccess Very Easy **Site** Level
es Available ▲ ⊕ ⇎ **Total** 130

Facilities ⚒ ⸙ ▯ ⓌⒸ ♨ ╒ ☺ ⌿ ⮝ ☏
𝄞 ▯ ⊙ ♨ ▦ ⊛ ☏ ▯ 𝄞
Nearby Facilities ╒ ⸜ ⚓ ↘ ∪ ⇥ ♂ ♀
⇥ Abergavenny/Merthyr Tydfil
Ideal centre for touring and discovering the
many scenic views of central Wales. Large
pitch sizes. Calor Award for Most Improved
Park in Wales 1998, AA 3 Pennent, AA Best
Campsite in Wales 1999 and RAC
Appointed. Adventure playground, excellent
facilities including two heated shower blocks
with free hot water, two disabled shower
rooms. Baby room with bath. Recreation
field and dog exercise field.

BRECON

Lakeside Caravan & Camping Park,
Llangorse Lake, Llangorse, Brecon,
Powys, LD3 7TR.
Std: 01874 **Tel:** 658226 **Fax:** 658430
Email: holidays@lakeside.zx3.net
Website: www.lakeside-holidays.zx3.net
Nearest Town/Resort Brecon
Directions From Brecon take the A40 east
for 2 miles, take left hand turn signposted
Llangorse, follow signs for 4 miles, turn right
for the lake.
Acreage 14 **Open** 31 March **to** 31
October
Access Good **Site** Level
Sites Available ▲ ⊕ ⇎ **Total** 40
Facilities ⸙ ⓌⒸ ♨ ╒ ☺ ⌿ ⮝ ☏
𝄞 ▯ ⊙ ♨ ✕ ♀ ▦ ↘ ☏ ▯ 𝄞
Nearby Facilities ⸜ ⚓ ↘ ∪ ⇥ ♂
⇥ Abergavenny
The area teems with wildlife, the scenery is
outstanding and our welcome is warm. Very
near to Llangorse Lake.

BRECON

Pencelli Castle Caravan & Camp Park,
Pencelli Castle, Pencelli, Brecon, Powys,
LD3 7LX.
Std: 01874 **Tel:** 665451 **Fax:** 665452
Email: pencelli.castle@virgin.net
Website: www.pencelli-castle.co.uk
Nearest Town/Resort Brecon
Directions Leave Brecon on the A40
heading east, after 2 miles turn onto the
B4558 signposted Pencelli. We are on the
outskirts of the village.
Acreage 10 **Open** All Year
Access Good **Site** Level
Sites Available ▲ ⊕ ⇎ **Total** 80
Facilities ⚒ ⸙ ▯ ⓌⒸ ♨ ╒ ☺ ⌿ ⮝ ☏
𝄞 ▯ ⊙ ♨ ▦ ⊛ ▯
Nearby Facilities ╒ ⸜ ⚓ ↘ ∪ ⇥ ♂ ♀
Calor Gas Best Park in Wales 2001 and 5
Star Grading. In the heart of the Brecon
Beacons National Park. Within walking
distance of the highest peaks. Adjoining
Brecon Canal. Village pub 100 yards.

BUILTH WELLS

Goblaen House Caravan Site,
Rhosgoch, Painscastle, Builth Wells,
Powys, LD2 3JY.
Std: 01497 **Tel:** 851654
Nearest Town/Resort Hay-on-Wye
Directions From Hay-on-Wye to Clyro, on
to Painscastle then Rhosgoch.
Acreage 1 **Open** March **to** October
Access Good **Site** Level
Sites Available ▲ ⊕⸏ **Total** 10
Facilities ⸙ ⓌⒸ ╒ ☺ ⌿ ▦ 𝄞 ⊛ ↘ ▯
Nearby Facilities ╒ ⸜ ⚓ ↘ ∪ ♂ ⇥
⇥ Builth Wells
Stream running through the site and a 3 hole
golf course on site, pony trekking.

BUILTH WELLS

Irfon Caravan Park, Upper Chapel Road,
Garth, Builth Wells, Powys, LD4 4BH.
Std: 01591 **Tel:** 620310
Nearest Town/Resort Builth Wells
Directions 500 yards along the B4519 out
of Garth (Garth is 6 miles west of Builth Wells
along the A483).
Acreage 6½ **Open** Easter **to** October
Access Good Site Lev/Slope
Sites Available ▲ ⊕ ⇎ **Total** 24
Facilities ⸙ ▯ ⓌⒸ ♨ ╒ ☺ ⌿ ⮝ ☏
🅿 ⊙ ▦ ☏ ▯
Nearby Facilities ╒ ⸜ ∪ ♂
⇥ Garth
Now under new ownership. Quiet site
alongside a river, fly fishing available. Scenic
views, ideal touring in the beauty of the
mountains and forest.

CLYRO

Forest Park, Clyro, Hay-on-Wye,
Herefordshire, HR3 5SG.
Std: 01497 **Tel:** 820156 **Fax:** 821653
Nearest Town/Resort Brecon/Hereford
Directions From Hereford take the A438
towards Brecon, at the village of Clyro follow
the road to Painscastle and signs to the park
for approx. ¾ miles, park is on the right hand
side.
Acreage 10 **Open** All Year
Access Good **Site** Sloping
Sites Available ▲ ⊕ ⇎ **Total** 29
Facilities ⸙ ▯ ⓌⒸ ♨ ╒ ☺ ⌿ ▦ ☏
🅿 ⊛ ☏ ▯
Nearby Facilities ╒ ⸜ ↘ ∪
⇥ Hereford
Two golf courses, Salmon and Trout fishing,
walking on the Black Mountains, Offa's Dyke
Path, Brecon Beacons and the Town of
Books Hay-on-Wye.

CRICKHOWELL

Riverside Caravan & Camping Park
New Road, Crickhowell, Powys, NP8 1AY.
Std: 01873 **Tel:** 810397
Nearest Town/Resort Crickhowell
Directions Between the A40 and the A4077
at Crickhowell.
Acreage 3½ **Open** March **to** October
Access Good **Site** Level
Sites Available ▲ ⊕ ⇎ **Total** 65
Facilities ⸙ ▯ ⓌⒸ ♨ ╒ ☺ ⊙ ▦ ▯A
Nearby Facilities ╒ ⸜ ∪ ⇥
⇥ Abergavenny
ADULTS ONLY, No children under 18 years,
over 18 years at owners discretion. Near river,
mountain and canal walks, pony trekking and
fishing. Town 5 mins walk, in National Park.
New improved toilet, shower block with
laundry (with drying facilities). A.A. 3
Pennants. No hang gliders and paragliders.

LLANBRYNMAIR

Cringoed Caravan & Camping Park,
Llanbrynmair, Powys, SY19 7DR.
Std: 01650 **Tel:** 521237
Email: cringoedcaravan.park@virgin.net
Nearest Town/Resort Newtown
Directions Take the A470 from Newtown
to Llanbrynmair for 18 miles, turn onto the
B4518 for 1 mile, site is on the right.
Acreage 5 **Open** March **to** January
Access Good **Site** Level
Sites Available ▲ ⊕ ⇎ **Total** 50
Facilities ⸙ ▯ ⓌⒸ ♨ ╒ ☺ ⌿ ⮝ ☏
🅿 ⊙ ▦ ☏ ▯
Nearby Facilities ╒ ⸜ ⚓ ∪ ⇥
⇥ Machynlleth
Ideal base by the river for touring the many
beaches, railways, castles, slate mines,
nature reserves and the Alternative
Technology Centre.

LLANDRINDOD WELLS

Bryncrach Caravan Site, Bryncrach, Hundred House, Llandrindod Wells, Powys, LD1 5RY.
Std: 01982 **Tel:** 570291
Nearest Town/Resort Builth Wells
Directions Hundred House is on the A481 between Builth Wells and the A44. Turn left signposted Franks Bridge immediately before the public house, after 250 yards turn left into farm road.
Acreage 1¾ **Open** All Year
Access Good **Site** Level
Sites Available ▲ ⬛ ⬛ **Total** 15
Facilities ⨍ 🏠 📖 ⬛ ♨ ⬛
⬛ 🛒 ⬛
Nearby Facilities ┌ ✓ ∪ ♪
≉ Llandrindod Wells
Quiet site with splendid views and walks. Fishing and riding can be arranged. River nearby.

LLANDRINDOD WELLS

Dalmore Caravan Park, Howey, Llandrindod Wells, Powys, LD1 5RG.
Std: 01597 **Tel:** 822483 **Fax:** 822483
Email: peter.speake@freeuk.com
Nearest Town/Resort Llandrindod Wells
Directions 2 miles south of Llandrindod off the main A483, towards Builth Wells.
Acreage 2 **Open** March to October
Access Good **Site** Lev/Gentle Slope
Sites Available ▲ ⬛ ⬛ **Total** 20
Facilities ⨍ 📖 ⬛ ♨ ⬛
⬛ 🛒 ⬛
Nearby Facilities ┌ ✓ ⚓ ∪ ♪
≉ Llandrindod
Ideal base for hiking and touring Mid Wales, scenic views.

LLANDRINDOD WELLS

The Park Motel, Crossgates, Llandrindod Wells, Powys, LD1 6RF.
Std: 01597 **Tel:** 851201
Email: lisa@theparkmotel.freeserve.co.uk
Website:
www.theparkmotel.freeserve.co.uk
Nearest Town/Resort Llandrindod Wells
Directions 3 miles north of Llandrindod Wells. Follow the A483 to Crossgates, turn left at the roundabout onto A44 (Rhayader). Park is ¼ mile on the left.
Acreage 1 **Open** March to October
Access Good **Site** Level
Sites Available ▲ ⬛ ⬛ **Total** 15
Facilities ⨍ 📖 ⬛ ♨ ⬛
⬛ 🛒 ⬛ 📖 ⬛
Nearby Facilities ┌ ✓ ⚓ ∪ ♪
≉ Penybont
Set in 3 acres of beautiful Mid-Wales countryside yet conveniently situated on the A44. Ideal for touring.

LLANFYLLIN

Henstent Caravan Park, Llangynog, Nr. Oswestry, Powys, SY10 0EP.
Std: 01691 **Tel:** 860479
Nearest Town/Resort Bala
Directions Situated on the B4391. Follow signs for Bala from Oswestry. 18 miles from Oswestry, 12 miles from Bala.
Acreage 1 **Open** March to October
Access Good **Site** Sloping
Sites Available ▲ ⬛ ⬛ **Total** 35
Facilities ⨍ 📖 ⬛ ♨ ⬛
⬛ 🛒 ⬛
Nearby Facilities ┌ ✓ ⚓ ∪ ⚲
≉ Gobowen
Views of Berwyn Mountains. Alongside River Tanat, fishing and walking. Heated toilet block.

LLANGAMMARCH WELLS

Riverside Caravan Park, Llangammarch Wells, Powys, LD4 4BY.
Std: 01591 **Tel:** 620465/620629
Website: www.caravancampingsites.co.uk
Nearest Town/Resort Builth Wells
Directions From Builth take A483 towards Garth, signposted in Garth Llangannarch 2 miles.
Acreage 3 **Open** April to October
Access Good **Site** Level
Sites Available ▲ ⬛ ⬛ **Total** 25
Facilities ⨍ ⨍ 📖 ⬛ ♨ ⬛
📖 ⬛ ⬛ ⬛ ✳ 🛒 ⬛
Nearby Facilities ┌ ✓ ∪ ♪
≉ Llangammarch Wells
Alongside river, scenic views, ideal touring. Cafe/restaurant nearby.

LLANIDLOES

Dol-Llys Touring Site, Dol-Llys Farm, Llanidloes, Powys, SY18 6JA.
Std: 01686 **Tel:** 412694
Nearest Town/Resort Llanidloes
Directions From Llanidloes take the B4569, past hospital, fork right onto the Oakley Park Road, Dol-Llys is the first farm on the right.
Acreage 2 **Open** April to October
Access Good **Site** Level
Sites Available ▲ ⬛ ⬛
Facilities ⨍ 📖 ⬛ ♨ ⬛ 🛒 ⬛
Nearby Facilities ┌ ✓ ⚓ ♪
≉ Caersws
Alongside the banks of the River Severn.

LLANIDLOES

Glandulas Caravan Park, Swn-y-Buarth, Llanidloes, Powys, SY18 6RE.
Std: 01686 **Tel:** 412862
Nearest Town/Resort Llanidloes
Directions Just off the A470 signposted Sports Centre.
Acreage ¼ **Open** 1 April to 15 October
Access Good **Site** Level
Sites Available ▲ ⬛ **Total** 4
Facilities 🏠 📖 ⬛ ♨ 🛒 ⬛
Nearby Facilities ┌ ✓ ⚓ ∪ ♪
≉ Caersws
Situated on a small farm, overlooking a river. Within walking distance (½ mile) to a pleasant, friendly, market town. Walking, fishing and sailing are popular in the area. 40 minutes to the coast.

LLANSANTFFRAID

Bryn-Vyrnwy Caravan Park, Llansantffraid-Ym-Mechain, Powys, SY22 6AY.
Std: 01691 **Tel:** 828252
Nearest Town/Resort Oswestry/Welshpool
Directions From Oswestry take the A483 to Welshpool, at Llynclys take the A495 for 3 miles.
Acreage 3 **Open** April to October
Access Good **Site** Level
Sites Available ▲ ⬛ ⬛
Facilities ⨍ 📖 ⬛ ♨ ⬛ 📖 ⬛ ⬛
Nearby Facilities ┌ ✓ ∪
≉ Welshpool
On the banks of the River Vyrnwy. Near to excellent golf courses and famous Wales tourist attractions.

LLANSANTFFRAID

Vyrnwy Caravan Park, Llansantffraid-Ym-Mechain, Powys, SY22 6SY.
Std: 01691 **Tel:** 828217 **Fax:** 828669
Nearest Town/Resort Oswestry/Welshpool
Directions Take the A483 then the B4393. 8 miles from Oswestry and 8 miles from Welshpool.

Open April to October
Access Good **Site** Level
Sites Available ▲ ⬛ ⬛ **Total** 40
Facilities ⨍ 📖 ⬛ ♨ ⬛ ⬛ ⬛ 🛒 ⬛
Nearby Facilities ┌ ✓ ⚲ ∪
≉ Gobowen
Alongside a river.

LLANWDDYN

Fronheulog, Lake Vyrnwy, Via Oswestry, Powys, SY10 0NN.
Std: 01691 **Tel:** Llanwyddyn 870662
Nearest Town/Resort Lake Vyrnwy
Directions 2 miles south of Lake Vyrnwy on B4393. 8 miles from Llanfyllin, Bala miles.
Acreage 2 **Open** March to October
Access Good **Site** Level
Sites Available ▲ ⬛ ⬛ **Total** 22
Facilities ⨍ 📖 ⬛ 📖 ⬛ 🛒 ⬛
Nearby Facilities ✓
ADULTS ONLY. Pre-booking necessary. RSPB reserve nearby. Ideal centre for touring. Cold water tap. Price Guide £2.00 per person per night.

MACHYNLLETH

Morben Isaf Holiday & Touring Park, Derwenlas, Machynlleth, Powys, SY20 8SR.
Std: 01654 **Tel:** 781473
Nearest Town/Resort Machynlleth
Directions 2½ miles south of Machynlleth on the A487 Aberystwyth road.
Acreage 42 **Open** March to October
Access Good **Site** Level
Sites Available ▲ ⬛ ⬛ **Total** 26
Facilities ⨍ 🏠 📖 ⬛ ♨ ⬛ ⬛ ⬛
📖 ⬛ 🛒 ⬛
Nearby Facilities ┌ ✓ ⚓ ⚲ ∪ ♪ ✕
≉ Machynlleth

MIDDLETOWN

Bank Farm Caravan Park, Middletown, Welshpool, Powys, SY21 8EJ.
Std: 01938 **Tel:** 570526
Email: gill@bankfarmcaravans.fsnet.co.uk
Nearest Town/Resort Welshpool
Directions On A458 5½ miles east of Welshpool and 13¼ miles west of Shrewsbury
Acreage 2 **Open** March to October
Access Good **Site** Lev/Slope
Sites Available ▲ ⬛ ⬛ **Total** 20
Facilities ⚬ ⨍ 📖 ⬛ ♨ ⬛ ⬛ ⬛
📖 ⬛ 🛒 ⬛
Nearby Facilities ┌ ✓ ∪
≉ Welshpool
Scenic views, touring area.

MONTGOMERY

Bacheldre Watermill, Churchstoke, Montgomery, Powys, SY15 6TE.
Std: 01588 **Tel:** 620489 **Fax:** 620105
Email: bacheldremill@onetel.het.uk
Nearest Town/Resort Bishops Castle
Directions Head north west on the B4385 for 5 miles. Turn left at the crossroads on the A489, continue for ½ mile then turn left.
Acreage 2 **Open** Easter to October
Access Good **Site** Level
Sites Available ▲ ⬛ ⬛ **Total** 25
Facilities ⨍ 📖 ⬛ ♨ ⬛ ⬛ 📖 🛒 ⬛ ⬛
Nearby Facilities ┌ ✓ ∪
≉ Welshpool
Ideal for touring and walking.

NEWTOWN

Llwyn Celyn Holiday Park, Adfa, Nr. Newtown, Powys, SY16 3DG.
Std: 01938 **Tel:** 810720
Nearest Town/Resort Newtown
Directions Bypass round Welshpool on the A483, take turn to Berriew on the B4390

ollow to Newmills, ¼ mile turn right for Adfa,
rough Adfa Village and first left. Park is
n the left.
creage 14 **Open** Wk Before Easter **to**
ct
ccess Good **Site** Level
ites Available ▲ ⚏ ⚌ **Total** 16
acilities ⚒ ⚙ ⛊ ⚓ ⌐ ☉ ⚐ ◻ ☎
⚑ ⚉ ⚊ ⚘ ⚏ ⛫ ⊟
earby Facilities ⌐ ✔ ∪ ⚹
⚓ Welshpool
cenic views, good walking and bird
atching.

NEWTOWN

mithy Caravan Park, Abermule,
ewtown, Powys, SY15 6ND.
td: 01584 **Tel:** 711280 **Fax:** 711460
earest Town/Resort Newtown
irections Leave the A483 3 miles north
ewtown and enter the village of Abermule.
urn down the lane opposite the village shop
nd Post Office.
creage 4 **Open** All Year
ccess Good **Site** Level
ites Available ▲ ⚏ ⚌ **Total** 30
acilities ⚒ ⚙ ⛊ ⚓ ⌐ ☉ ⚐ ◻ ☎
⚑ ⚉ ⚊ ⚘ ☀ ⛫ ⊟ ⊟
earby Facilities ⌐ ✔ ∪ ♫
⚓ Newtown
utstanding quality park, maintained to the
ighest standards. 2 miles of fishing on the
iver Severn. Bowling and tennis courts
earby.

NEWTOWN

ynycwm Camping & Caravan Site,
ynycwm, Aberhafesp, Newtown, Powys,
Y16 3JF.
td: 01686 **Tel:** 688651
earest Town/Resort Newtown
irections 7 miles north west of Newtown
a A489 to Caersws, then B4569 north sign-
osted Aberhafesp, cross B4568 ignore sign
r Aberhafesp and continue to next
rossroads. Turn left signposted Bwlch y
arreg. Farm and site 1 mile on right.
creage 3 **Open** May **to** October
ccess Good **Site** Level
ites Available ▲ ⚏ ⚌ **Total** 50
acilities ⚙ ⛊ ⚓ ⌐ ☉ ⚐ ⚊ ☎
⚉ ⚘ ⛫ ⊟
earby Facilities ⌐ ✔ ⚓ ⚹ ∪
⚓ Caersws
cenic views, pony trekking close, farm site.
ou can also contact us on Mobile 07711
97424.

PENYBONTFAWR

arc Farm Caravan Park, Penybontfawr,
owys, SY10 0PD.
td: 01691 **Tel:** 860204
earest Town/Resort Oswestry/
Velshpool
irections On the B4391 from Llanfyllin
wards Bala.
creage 5 **Open** Easter **to** End Oct
ccess Good **Site** Level
ites Available ⚏ ⚌ **Total** 65
acilities ⚒ ⚙ ⛊ ⚓ ⌐ ☉ ⚊ ◻ ☎
⚑ ⚘ ⚊ ⊟
earby Facilities ⌐ ✔ ⚓ ⚹ ∪ ⚹
⚓ Welshpool

Situated by a river. Ideal touring.

PRESTEIGNE

Rockbridge Park, Presteigne, Powys,
LD8 2NF.
Std: 01547 **Tel:** 560300
Email: roy.deakins@lineone.net
Nearest Town/Resort Presteigne
Directions 1 mile west of Presteigne on the
B4356 Llanbister road.
Acreage 6 **Open** April **to** September
Access Good **Site** Level
Sites Available ▲ ⚏ ⚌ **Total** 30
Facilities ⚒ ⚙ ⛊ ⚐ ⚓ ⌐ ☉ ⚊ ◻ ☎
⚑ ⚉ ⚊ ⊟
Nearby Facilities ⌐ ✔ ∪ ♫
⚓ Knighton
In peaceful surroundings on the upper
reaches of the River Lugg.

PRESTEIGNE

Walton Caravan Site, Court Cottage,
Walton, Presteigne, Powys, LD8 2PY.
Std: 01544 **Tel:** 350259
Nearest Town/Resort Kington
Directions On the A44 Kington to
Aberystwyth road, in the village of Walton
opposite the Crown Hotel.
Acreage 7 **Open** All Year
Access Good **Site** Level
Sites Available ▲ ⚏ ⚌ **Total** 30+
Facilities ⚙ ⛊ ⌐ ☉ ⚊ ⚑ ⚉ ⚊ ⚘ ☓ ⛫ ⊟ ⊟
Nearby Facilities ⌐
⚓ Knighton
Many walks and rides into the hills. The
Crown Hotel (opposite) is excellent for its
restaurant.

RHAYADER

Gigrin Farm, South Street, Rhayader,
Powys, LD6 5BL.
Std: 01597 **Tel:** 810243 **Fax:** 810357
Email: kites@gigrin.co.uk
Website: www.gigrin.co.uk
Nearest Town/Resort Rhayader/
Llandrindod Wells
Directions Just off the A470 ½ mile south
of Rhayader.
Acreage 2 **Open** All Year
Access Good **Site** Level
Sites Available ▲ ⚏ ⚌ **Total** 15
Facilities ⚒ ⚙ ⛊ ⚓ ⛫ ⊟
Nearby Facilities ⌐ ∪ ♫
⚓ Llandrindod Wells
Situated in a beautiful area surrounded by
hills. Leisure centre in Rhayader. Red Kite
feeding daily. Ideal for walking and cycling
in Elan Valley.

RHAYADER

Wyeside Caravan & Camping Park,
Llangurig Road, Rhayader, Powys, LD6
5LB.
Std: 01597 **Tel:** 810183 **Fax:** 810183
Email: info@wyesidecamping.co.uk
Website: www.wyesidecamping.co.uk
Nearest Town/Resort Rhayader
Directions On the A470 north of Rhayader.
Acreage 8 **Open** February **to** Nov
Access Good **Site** Level
Sites Available ▲ ⚏ ⚌ **Total** 140
Facilities ⚒ ⚙ ⛊ ⚐ ⚓ ⌐ ☉ ⚊ ⚊ ◻ ☎
⚑ ⚉ ⚊ ⚘ ⛫ ⊟

Nearby Facilities ⌐ ✔ ∪ ♫
⚓ Llandrindod Wells
Set along the banks of the River Wye with
excellent facilities. 5 minutes walk to the
town centre and 3 miles from Elan Valley.

TALGARTH

Riverside International Caravan Park,
Bronllys, Talgarth, Nr Brecon, Powys, LD3
0HL.
Std: 01874 **Tel:** 711320 **Fax:** 712064
Email:
riversideinternational@bronllys1.freeserve.co.uk
Website: www.wiz.to/riverside/
Nearest Town/Resort Brecon
Directions Leave Brecon on A438 8 miles
to Bronllys, turn right in the village for
Talgarth, site ¼ mile on right - opposite
Bronllys Castle.
Acreage 9 **Open** Easter **to** October
Access Good **Site** Lev/Slope
Sites Available ▲ ⚏ ⚌ **Total** 85
Facilities ⚒ ⚙ ⛊ ⚐ ⚓ ⌐ ☉ ⚊ ⚊ ◻ ☎
⚑ ⚉ ⚊ ☓ ⚐ ⛫ ⊟ ⊟
Nearby Facilities ⌐ ✔ ⚓ ⚹ ∪ ♫ ⚹
⚓ Abergavenny
Edge of Brecon Beacon National Park. Free
freezer service and ice packs.

WELSHPOOL

Henllan Caravan Park, Llangyniew,
Welshpool, Powys, SY21 9EJ.
Std: 01938 **Tel:** 810554
Email: sue@henllancp.fsnet.co.uk
Website: www.ukparks.co.uk
Nearest Town/Resort Welshpool
Directions 6 miles from Welshpool on the
A458.
Acreage ½ **Open** March **to** December
Access Good **Site** Level
Sites Available ▲ ⚏⚌ **Total** 10
Facilities ⚙ ⛊ ⚐ ⚓ ⌐ ☉ ⚊ ⚊ ◻ ☎
⚑ ⚉ ⚊ ☓ ⚐ ⚉ ⚊ ⚘ ⛫ ⊟
Nearby Facilities ⌐ ✔ ∪ ♫
⚓ Welshpool
Alongside the River Banwy. Ideal touring, 9
hole golf course and bowling green.

SWANSEA

LLANGENNITH

Hillend Camping Park, Hillend,
Llangennith, Gower, Swansea, SA3 1JD.
Std: 01792 **Tel:** 386204 **Fax:** 386204
Nearest Town/Resort Swansea
Directions Exit M4 junction 47, follow the
A483 (Swansea), A484 (Llanelli), B4296
(Gower), B4295 (Gower) to Llangennith,
then signposts to Hillend.
Acreage 14 **Open** April **to** October
Access Good **Site** Level
Sites Available ▲ ⚏ ⚌ **Total** 250
Facilities ⛊ ⚓ ⌐ ☉ ⚊ ◻ ☎
⚑ ⚉ ⚊ ⚘ ☀ ⊟
Nearby Facilities ⌐ ✔ ∪ ♫ ⚹
⚓ Swansea
100yds from Rhossilli Bay in Britain's first
area of outstanding natural beauty. Ideal for
surfing, canoeing, walking, fishing,
windsurfing, bathing and hang gliding.

LLANMADOC

Llanmadoc Caravan & Camping Park, Llanmadoc, Gower Coast, Swansea, SA3 1DE.
Std: 01792 **Tel:** 386202
Nearest Town/Resort Swansea
Directions M4 come off at junction 47 A483, signposted to Gower left at traffic lights Gorseinon, right at Gonerton.
Acreage 11 **Open** April to October
Access Good **Site** Lev/Slope
Sites Available Δ ⊕ ⊕ **Total** 230
Facilities ⌂ ▢ ⌕ & ⌐ ⊙ ⌿ ⊜
♨ ⌕ ⊙★□
Nearby Facilities ⌐ ✓ ⌣ ∪ ∌ ⊁
✈ Swansea
Adjoining sandy beach and a National Trust and nature conservancy. Area of outstanding natural beauty. Electric hook-ups on request.

OXWICH

Oxwich Camping Park, Oxwich, Gower, Swansea, SA3 1LS.
Std: 01792 **Tel:** 390777
Nearest Town/Resort Swansea
Directions A4118 from Swansea, 10 miles turn left. 1¼ miles turn right at crossroads, ¼ mile on right hand side.
Acreage 10 **Open** April to September
Site Lev/Slope
Sites Available Δ ⊕ **Total** 180

PORT EYNON

Bank Farm, Horton, Gower, Swansea, SA3 1LL.
Std: 01792 **Tel:** 390228 **Fax:** 391282
Email: bankfarmleisure@cs.com
Website: www.bankfarmleisure.co.uk
Nearest Town/Resort Swansea
Directions Take the A4118 from Swansea towards Port Eynon, turn left for Horton 1 mile before Port Eynon, turn right at the site entrance after 200 yards.
Acreage 80 **Open** March to 15 November
Access Good **Site** Sloping
Sites Available Δ ⊕ ⊕ **Total** 230
Facilities ⌂ ▢ & ⌐ ⊙ ⌿ ⊜
♨ ⌕ ⊙ & ✗ ⌕ ⌧ ★ ⌂ ⊡ ⊟
Nearby Facilities ⌐ ✓ ∪ ∌ ⊁
✈ Swansea
Overlooking the beach. Heated swimming pool.

RHOSSILI

Pitton Cross Caravan & Camping Park, Rhossili, Swansea, SA3 1PH.
Std: 01792 **Tel:** 390593 **Fax:** 391010

Facilities ▢ & ⌐ ⊙ ⌿ ⌂ ⊜
♨ ⌕ ⊙ & ✗ ⌕ ⌧ ★ ⌂ ▷ ⊟
Nearby Facilities ⌐ ✓ ⌣ ∪ ∌ ⊁
✈ Swansea
Near sandy beach. Water sports and nature reserve.

PORT EYNON

(see above)

Email: rogerbuttonmm@tesco.net
Website: www.pittoncross.co.uk
Nearest Town/Resort Swansea
Acreage 6 Open April to October
Access Good Site Level
Sites Available Δ ⊕ ⊕ Total 100
Facilities ⅙ ⌿ ⌂ ▢ & ⌐ ⊙ ⌿ ⊜ ⌂ ⊜
♨ ⌕ ⌧ ▢ ⊙ & ⌧ ★ ⌂ ⊡ ⊟
Nearby Facilities ⌐ ✓ ⌣ ∪ ∌ ⊁
✈ Swansea
Quiet site.

SWANSEA

Riverside Caravan Park, Ynysforgan Farm, Morriston, Swansea, SA6 6QL.
Std: 01792 **Tel:** 775587
Nearest Town/Resort Swansea
Directions Direct access to site from roundabout under motorway junction 45 of M4.
Acreage 7 **Open** All Year
Access Good **Site** Level
Sites Available ⊕ ⊕ **Total** 120
Facilities & ⅙ ⌂ ▢ & ⌐ ⊙ ⌿ ⊜ ⌂ ⊜
♨ ⌕ ⌧ ⊙ & ⌕ ⌧ ★ ⌂ ⊡ ⊟
Nearby Facilities ⌐ ✓ ⌣ ∪ ∌ ⊁
✈ Swansea
Alongside river, ideal touring, flat level grassy site. Indoor swimming pool and jaccuzi. Television room. Dogs are welcome (no dangerous breeds) only by arrangement.

SWANSEA

Three Cliffs Bay Caravan Site, North Hills Farm, Penmaen, Gower, Swansea, SA3 2HB.
Std: 01792 **Tel:** 371218
Nearest Town/Resort Swansea
Directions Take the A4118 from Swansea, site is signposted in the village of Penmaen.
Acreage 5 **Open** Easter **to** October
Access Good **Site** Lev/Slope
Sites Available A ⊕ ⊖ **Total** 95
Facilities ⨍ ⓋⒺ ♨ ⌐ ⊙ ᵔ ⌑ ⌾
⌻ Ⓘ ⊕ ⌸
Nearby Facilities ⌐ ✓ ⚐ ↘ ∪ ⚇ ♪ ✗
≠ Swansea
Overlooking Three Cliffs Bay.

VALE OF GLAMORGAN

BARRY

Vale Touring Caravan Park, Port Road (West), Barry, Vale of Glamorgan, CF62 3BT.
Std: 01446 **Tel:** 719311
Nearest Town/Resort Barry Island
Directions The park is located 2 miles west of Barry on the A4226. When you reach the roundabout with sculpture arrows turn left, park is on your right.
Acreage 2 **Open** March **to** December
Access Good **Site** Level
Sites Available ⊕ ⊖ **Total** 40
Facilities ⨍ ⓋⒺ ♨ ⌐ ⊙ ᵔ ⌑
Ⓘ ⊕ Ⓜ ⊕ ⌸ ⌾
Nearby Facilities ⌐ ✓ ⚐ ↘ ∪ ⚇
≠ Barry
Ideal touring, beach 2 miles away.

LLANTWIT MAJOR

Acorn Camping & Caravanning, Rosedew Farm, Hamlane South, Llantwit Major, Vale of Glamorgan, CF61 1RP.
Std: 01446 **Tel:** 794024 **Fax:** 794024
Email: acorncampsite@aol.com
Website:
www.camping+caravansites.co.uk
Nearest Town/Resort Llantwit Major
Directions From M4 junction 33 follow signs Cardiff Airport then B4265 for Llantwit Major. Approach the site from Beach Road or via Ham Lane East through Ham Manor Park.
Acreage 4 **Open** February **to** 8 December
Access Good **Site** Level
Sites Available A ⊕ ⊖ **Total** 90
Facilities ⚙ ⨍ ⓋⒺ ♨ ⌐ ⊙ ᵔ ⌑ ⌾
⌻ Ⓘ ⊕ ♨ Ⓜ ⊕ ⌸ ⌾
Nearby Facilities ⌐ ✓ ∪ ⚇
≠ Barry
1 mile from beach, 1 mile from town, coastal walks, ideal base for touring. Take-away food available. Holiday hire caravans available, one suitable for wheelchair. David Bellamy Silver Award for Conservation.

PENARTH

Lavernock Holiday Estate, Fort Road, Penarth, Vale of Glamorgan, CF64.
Std: 029 **Tel:** 2070 7310 **Fax:** 2070 0509
Email: sales@lavernockpoint.com
Website: www.lavernockpoint.com
Nearest Town/Resort Penarth
Directions From the B4267 turn left into Fort Road, opposite Cosmeston Lakes.
Acreage 5 **Open** May **to** September
Site Lev/Slope
Sites Available A ⊕ ⊖ **Total** 120
Facilities ⨍ ⓋⒺ ⌐ ⊙ ᵔ ⌑ ⌾
⌑ ⌻ ⊕ ⋇ ⛝ Ⓜ ⌾ ⚟
Nearby Facilities ⌐
≠ Penarth
Near the beach.

WREXHAM

RUABON

James' Caravan Park, Llangollen Road, Ruabon, Wrexham, LL14 6DW.
Std: 01978 **Tel:** 820148 **Fax:** 820148
Email: ray@carastay.demon.co.uk
Nearest Town/Resort Wrexham/Llangollen
Directions Situated on the A539 west of the junction with the A483.
Acreage 6 **Open** All Year
Access Good **Site** Lev/Slope
Sites Available ⊕ ⊖ **Total** 40
Facilities ⚙ ⨍ Ⓜ ⓋⒺ ♨ ⌐ ⊙ ᵔ
⊕ ♨ ⊕ ⌸ ⌾
Nearby Facilities ⌐ ✓
≠ Ruabon
An attractive park with mature trees. Old farm buildings house the owners collection of old and original farm machinery, carefully restored and maintained, adding charm and interest to the park. 10 minute walk to the village. Near to Ellesmere, Llangollen and Chester.

WREXHAM

Cae Adar Farm, Bwlchgwyn, Wrexham, LL11 5UE.
Std: 01978 **Tel:** 757385
Nearest Town/Resort Wrexham
Directions On the A525 Wrexham to Ruthin road.
Acreage 2 **Open** May **to** October
Access Good **Site** Level
Sites Available A ⊕ ⊖ **Total** 12
Facilities ⨍ ⓋⒺ ♨ ⌐ ⊙
Nearby Facilities ⌐ ✓
≠ Wrexham

WREXHAM

Camping & Caravanning Club Site, c/o The Racecourse, Overton Road, Bangor-y-Coed, Wrexham, LL13 0DA.
Std: 01978 **Tel:** 781009
Website:
www.campingandcaravanningclub.co.uk
Directions From the A525 follow racecourse and international camping signs through the village. Turn left immediately opposite the Buck Hotel signposted racecourse, site is approx. 1 mile on the right hand side.
Acreage 6 **Open** March **to** October
Site Lev/Slope
Sites Available A ⊕ ⊖ **Total** 100
Facilities ⚙ ⨍ ⓋⒺ ♨ ⌐ ⊙ ᵔ ⌑ ⌾ ⌾
⌻ ⊕ ♨ ⊕ ⌸ ⌾
Nearby Facilities ⌐
≠ Wrexham
Located on the racecourse. Just 5 miles from Wrexham and Erddig House. Non members welcome.

WREXHAM

The Plassey Touring Caravan & Leisure Park, Eyton, Wrexham, LL13 0SP.
Std: 01978 **Tel:** 780277 **Fax:** 780019
Email: jbrookshaw@aol.com
Website: www.theplassey.co.uk
Nearest Town/Resort Wrexham
Acreage 10 **Open** 1 March **to** 7 Nov
Access Good **Site** Level
Sites Available A ⊕ ⊖ **Total** 120
Facilities ⚙ ⚡ ⨍ ⊟ Ⓜ ⓋⒺ ♨ ⌐ ⊙ ᵔ ⌑
⌑ ⌻ Ⓘ ⊕ ♨ ⋇ ⛝ ⚟ Ⓜ ♨ ⊛ ⌸ ⊟ ⌾
Nearby Facilities ∪ ⚇
≠ Wrexham
On site facilities include a 9 hole golf course, fishing, a craft centre with 16 workshops and boutiques, garden centre, hair and beauty studio, restaurant and coffee shop. Tuition on ceramics and decoupage.

SCOTLAND

ABERDEENSHIRE

BANCHORY

Campfield Caravan Park, Glassel, Banchory, Aberdeenshire, AB31 4DN.
Std: 01339 **Tel:** 882250 **Fax:** 882250
Nearest Town/Resort Banchory
Directions On the A980 5 miles north of Banchory.
Acreage 2 **Open** April **to** September
Access Good **Site** Sloping
Sites Available A ⊕ ⊖
Facilities ⨍ ⊟ ⓋⒺ ⌐ ⊙ ᵔ ⌑ ⌻ ⊕ ♨ ⌸
Nearby Facilities ⌐ ✓ ∪ ⚇ ♪
≠ Aberdeen

BANCHORY

Feughside Caravan Park, Strachan, Banchory, Aberdeenshire, AB31 6NT.
Std: 01330 **Tel:** 850669
Nearest Town/Resort Banchory
Directions Take B974 to Strachan, 3 miles. Continue straight on B976, 2 miles to Feughside Inn. Site is directly behind Inn, turn right directly after Inn.
Open April **to** Mid October
Access Good **Site** Level
Sites Available A ⊕ ⊖ **Total** 20
Facilities ⨍ ⊟ Ⓜ ⓋⒺ ♨ ⌐ ⊙ ᵔ ⌑ ⌻
⊕ ♨ ⊕ ⌸ ⌾
Nearby Facilities ⌐ ✓ ∪ ♪ ✗
Scenic views. Near river. Ideal touring area. Good walks. Family site in country. Fishing nearby Trout Loch, hotel 100 yards, pitch and putt nearby.

BANCHORY

Silver Ladies Caravan Park, Strachan, By Banchory, Aberdeenshire, AB31 6NL.
Std: 01330 **Tel:** 822800 **Fax:** 825701
Nearest Town/Resort Banchory
Directions 1 mile south of Banchory on left of B974 Fettercairn road.
Acreage 7 **Open** April **to** October
Access Good **Site** Level
Sites Available A ⊕ ⊖ **Total** 17
Facilities ⨍ ⊟ Ⓜ ⌐ ⊙ ᵔ ⌑ ⌾ ⌻ ⌾
⊕ ♨ ⊕ ⋇ ⊕ ⌸ ⌾
Nearby Facilities ⌐ ✓ ∪ ⚇ ♪ ✗
Near River Dee, scenic views. Ideal base for exploring Royal Deeside.

BANFF

Banff Links Caravan Park, Banff Links, Swardanes, Banff, Aberdeenshire, AB45 2JJ
Std: 01261 **Tel:** 812228
Nearest Town/Resort Banff
Directions From Banff take the A98 west for approx. 1000 metres. On the outskirts of Banff.
Open 1 April **to** 28 October
Access Good **Site** Level
Sites Available A ⊕⌑ **Total** 133
Facilities ⚙ ⨍ ⊟ Ⓜ ⓋⒺ ♨ ⌐ ⊙ ᵔ ⌑ ⌾ ⌻
⌑ ⌻ ⊕ ♨ ⋇ ⊕ ⌸ ⌾
Nearby Facilities ⌐ ✓ ⚐ ↘ ∪
On the beach. Ideal touring.

CRUDEN BAY

Craig Head Caravan Park, Cruden Bay, Peterhead, Aberdeenshire, AB42 0PL.
Std: 01779 **Tel:** 812251
Nearest Town/Resort Peterhead
Directions From Peterhead take the A90 south for approx. 9 miles, signposted on the left.
Acreage 5 **Open** All Year
Access Good **Site** Level
Sites Available A ⊕ ⊖ **Total** 15
Facilities ⨍ Ⓜ ⓋⒺ ♨ ⌐ ⊙ ᵔ ⌑ ⌾ Ⓘ ⌾
⊕ ♨ ⋇ ⊕ ⌸ ⌾
Nearby Facilities ⌐ ✓ ⚐ ↘ ∪ ⚇ ♪ ✗

JOHNSHAVEN

Wairds Park, Beach Road, Johnshaven, Nr. Montrose, Aberdeenshire, DD10 0HD.
Std: 01561 **Tel:** 362616
Nearest Town/Resort Montrose
Directions 10 miles north of Montrose on the A92.
Acreage 6 **Open** 1 April **to** 15 October
Access Good **Site** Level
Sites Available ⌂ ⊞ **Total** 20
Facilities ⅙ ∮ ⬛ ⬛ ⚍ ſ ⊙⌁ ⅃ ⚑ ⬛ ⚋ ⊛ ⚍⊟
Nearby Facilities ſ ✔
⚓ Montrose
Coastal site in a quiet setting. Easy access to tourist routes.

KINTORE

Hillhead Caravan Park, Kintore, Aberdeenshire, AB51 0YX.
Std: 01467 **Tel:** 632809 **Fax:** 633173
Email: enquiries@hillheadcaravan.co.uk
Website: www.hillheadcaravan.co.uk
Nearest Town/Resort Kintore
Directions From south leave the A96 at Broomhill roundabouts third exit. From north stay on the A96 past Kintore (DO NOT enter Kintore), leave at Broomhill roundabouts first exit. Follow brown and white caravan signs onto the B994, in ¼ mile turn left onto the B994 signposted Kemnay. After 2 miles turn right signposted Kintore and Hillhead Caravan Park is 1 mile on the right.
Acreage 1½ **Open** All Year
Access Good **Site** Level
Sites Available ⌂ ⌂ ⊞ **Total** 29
Facilities ⅙ ∮ ⬛ ⬛ ⚍ ſ ⊙⌁ ⅃ ⚌
⚋ ⬛ ⚍⊟⬛
Nearby Facilities ſ ✔ ⚲
Quiet, sheltered park. Easy access to Castle and Malt Whisky Trails, Aberdeen and Royal Deeside.

PORTSOY

Sandend Caravan Park, Sandend, Portsoy, Aberdeenshire, AB45 2UA.
Std: 01261 **Tel:** 842660
Nearest Town/Resort Portsoy
Directions 3 miles from Portsoy on the A98.
Acreage 4½ **Open** April **to** 4 October
Access Good **Site** Level
Sites Available ⌂ ⌂ ⊞ **Total** 52
Facilities ⅙ ∮ ⬛ ⬛ ⚍ ſ ⊙
⌁ ⬛ ⚍ ⚋⚍⊟
Nearby Facilities ſ ✔ ⚲ ✆
In a conservation village overlooking a sandy beach. Ideal for touring and The Whisky Trail.

ST. CYRUS

East Bowstrips Holiday Park, St. Cyrus, Nr Montrose, Aberdeenshire, DD10 0DE.
Std: 01674 **Tel:** 850328 **Fax:** 850328
Email: tully@bowstrips.freeserve.co.uk
Website: www.ukparks.co.uk/ eastbowstrips
Nearest Town/Resort Montrose
Directions Approx 6 miles north of Montrose. Follow A92, enter village of St. Cyrus, first left after Hotel, second right.
Acreage 4 **Open** April **to** October
Access Good **Site** Lev/Slope
Sites Available ⌂ ⌂ ⊞ **Total** 30
Facilities ⅙ ∮ ⬛ ⬛ ⚍ ſ ⊙⌁ ⬛ ⚍
⚋ ⬛ ⚋ ⬛ ⚍⊟⬛
Nearby Facilities ſ ✔
Quiet, family park by the coast. Ideal touring base. Excellent facilities. Beautiful sandy beach and nature reserve approx 1 mile. Special facilities for disabled visitors including adapted caravan for hire. Tourist Board 5 Star Graded and AA 4 Pennants.

STONEHAVEN

Queen Elizabeth Caravan Park, Cowie Village, Stonehaven, Aberdeenshire, AB39 2RD
Std: 01569 **Tel:** 764041
Nearest Town/Resort Stonehaven
Directions Follow the A957 through Stonehaven heading north, then follow signs for Cowie Village.
Open 29 March **to** 29 October
Access Good **Site** Lev/Slope
Sites Available ⌂ ⊞ **Total** 112
Facilities ⅙ ∮ ⬛ ⬛ ⚍ ſ ⊙⌁ ⬛ ⬛
⚋ ⬛ ⚌ ✆ ⚍⊟⬛
Nearby Facilities ſ ✔ ⚓ ⚲
Just a short walk to the beach, amusements, leisure centre, outdoor swimming pool and childrens play area. 5-10 minute walk to the town centre for shops, bars, restaurants, etc.. 15-20 minute drive to Aberdeen City.

TURRIFF

East Balthangie Caravan Park, East Balthangie, Cuminestown, Turriff, Aberdeenshire, AB53 5XY.
Std: 01888 **Tel:** 544921 **Fax:** 544261
Email: ebc@4horse.co.uk
Nearest Town/Resort Turriff
Directions Take the A92 from Aberdeen to Ellon, turn onto the B9107 to Cuminestown. After New Deer turn right to New Byth, caravan park is 3 miles on the right.
Acreage 5 **Open** March **to** October
Access Good **Site** Level
Sites Available ⌂ ⌂ ⊞ **Total** 12
Facilities ∮ ⬛ ⬛ ⚍ ſ ⊙ ⚍ ⚋⚌ ⬛ ⚋⚍⊡⬛
Nearby Facilities ſ ✔ ⚓ ⟳
⚓ Aberdeen
Good base for touring.

WESTHILL

Mains of Keir Caravan Site, Mains of Keir, Skene, Westhill, Aberdeenshire, AB32 6YA
Std: 01224 **Tel:** 743282
Nearest Town/Resort Aberdeen
Directions From Aberdeen take the A944 for 7 miles, then take the B979 signposted Kirkton of Skene, follow signs.
Acreage 1½ **Open** April **to** October
Access Good **Site** Sloping
Sites Available ⌂ ⊞☐ **Total** 10
Facilities ∮ ⬛ ⬛ ⚍ ſ ⊙⌁ ⚌ ⬛ ⚋⚍⊟
Nearby Facilities ſ ✔
⚓ Aberdeen
Small, peaceful, country site. Near to squash courts, golf course and a swimming pool. Castle Trail, Whisky Trail and Royal Deeside. Ideal for touring the north east of Scotland.

WESTHILL

Skene Caravan Park, Skene, Westhill, Aberdeenshire, AB32 6YA.
Std: 01224 **Tel:** 743282
Nearest Town/Resort Aberdeen
Directions From Aberdeen take the A944 to Elrick Village, after ¼ mile take the road on the right and follow caravan signs.
Acreage 1½ **Open** April **to** October
Access Good **Site** Sloping
Sites Available ⌂ ⊞☐ **Total** 10
Facilities ſ ⬛ ⬛ ⚍ ſ ⊙⌁ ⚌ ⬛ ⚋ ⬛
Nearby Facilities ſ ⚲
⚓ Aberdeen
Ideal for touring the north east of Scotland.

ANGUS

ARBROATH

Elliot Caravan Park, Dundee Road, Arbroath, Angus, DD11 2PH.
Std: 01241 **Tel:** 873466

Nearest Town/Resort Arbroath
Directions On the A92, ½ mile from town
Acreage 2 **Open** April **to** September
Access Good **Site** Level
Sites Available ⌂ ⊞ **Total** 8
Facilities ⅙ ∮ ⬛ ⚍ ſ ⊙⌁ ⬛ ⚌ ⚋ ⬛ ⚍⊟
Nearby Facilities ſ ✔ ⟳ ⚓ ⚲
⚓ Arbroath
Near the beach, across from a golf club. Ideal for touring and sea fishing.

ARBROATH

Red Lion Caravan Park, Dundee Road, Arbroath, Angus, DD11 2PT.
Std: 01241 **Tel:** 872038
Email: redlion@perthshire-caravans.co.u
Website: www.perthshire-caravans.co.uk
Nearest Town/Resort Arbroath
Directions From Dundee take the A92 when entering Arbroath the park is on the left past the first mini roundabout.
Acreage 4 **Open** March **to** October
Access Good **Site** Level
Sites Available ⌂ ⊞ **Total** 40
Facilities ⅙ ∮ ⬛ ⬛ ⚍ ſ ⊙⌁ ⬛ ⚌ ⬛ ⚋
✕ ✔ ⬛ ⚍⊟⬛
Nearby Facilities ſ ✔ ⟳ ⚲
Adjacent to the seaside and beach.

BRECHIN

Glenesk Caravan Park, Edzell, Brechin, Angus, DD9 7YP.
Std: 01356 **Tel:** 648565
Website: www.angus_glens.co.uk
Nearest Town/Resort Edzell
Directions Take the B966 Edzell t Fettercairn road. 1½ miles north of Edze take an unclassified road signposte Tarfside and Glenesk, park entrance is mile from the junction on the right hand side.
Acreage 8 **Open** April **to** October
Access Good **Site** Level
Sites Available ⌂ ⌂ ⊞ **Total** 45
Facilities ∮ ⬛ ⬛ ⚍ ſ ⊙⌁ ⬛ ⚌ ⬛ ⚋
⬛ ⚋ ⚍ ⊛ ⚍⊟
Nearby Facilities ſ ✔ ⟳
Set in a natural birch woodland around small fishing loch. Ideally situated for access to the Glens or the historic towns an coastline of North Angus.

CARNOUSTIE

Woodlands Caravan Park, Newton Road, Carnoustie, Angus, DD7 6GR.
Std: 01241 **Tel:** 854430
Nearest Town/Resort Carnoustie
Directions Off the A92 Dundee to Arbroat road signed Carnoustie with carava symbol. After 1 mile turn right into Newton Road and follow signs.
Acreage 4½ **Open** March **to** Mid October
Access Good **Site** Level
Sites Available ⌂ ⊞ **Total** 120
Facilities ⅙ ∮ ⬛ ⬛ ⚍ ſ ⊙⌁ ⬛
⬛ ⚌ ⚋ ⬛ ⚋⚍⊟
Nearby Facilities ſ ✔ ⟳ ✕ ⚓ ⚲
½ mile from the beach and sea front, ope golf course and leisure facilities. Ideal fo touring the glens of Angus and the wildlif trails on the local cliffs.

FORFAR

Lochlands Caravan Site, Dundee Road, Forfar, Angus, DD8 1XF.
Std: 01307 **Tel:** 463621 **Fax:** 463621
Nearest Town/Resort Forfar
Directions From Dundee take the A9 towards Aberdeen. After 12 miles take th A932 to Forfar, site is first turn right (approx 150 yards).
Acreage 3 **Open** April **to** October
Access Good **Site** Level
Sites Available ⌂ ⊞☐ **Total** 25

...cilities ⚠ ⓕ 🏠 📶 ⚡ ⌂ 🅿 ⚡ ✕ 🚐 ▣
...arby Facilities ⌐ ⟋ ∪
Dundee
...ideal base for touring Angus, from ...roath and Carnoustie on the coast to ...e Glens. Many attractions in the area ...cluding Glamis Castle.

...ONIFIETH

...verview Caravan Park, Marine ...ive, Monifieth, By Dundee, Angus, ...05 4NN.
...d: 01382 Tel: 535471 Fax: 535375
...arest Town/Resort Dundee
...rections A92 Dundee to Arbroath ...ad, after 3 miles turn right into ...onifieth, site is well signposted.
...creage 5½ Open April to October
...ccess Good Site Level
...acilities ⚠ ⓕ 🏠 📶 ⚡ ⌂ ⊙ ⌣ ⚿
⚡ ▣ ⓞ ⚿ ✕ 🚐 ▣
...earby Facilities ⌐ ⟋ ⚓ ⤳ ∪ ⅃
Dundee
...rivate access to a sandy beach. ...agnificent views. Supermarket, village ...ops and two golf courses within a 5 ...inute walk.

...ONIFIETH

...ayview Caravan Park, Marine Drive, ...onifieth, Dundee, DD5 4NN.
...d: 01382 Tel: 532837
...mail: dockie@icscotland.net
...earest Town/Resort Monifieth
...irections Take the A92 towards ...rbroath then follow camping signs ...rough Monifieth. As you go under the ...ilway line you will go past Riverview ...aravan Park, Tayview is next.
...pen April to October
...ccess Good Site Level
...ites Available ⚠ ⌑ ⚿ Total 45+
...acilities ⚠ ⓕ 📶 ⚡ ⌂ ⊙ ⚿ ▣ ⓞ ⚿ 🚐 ▣
...earby Facilities ⌐ ⟋ ⚓ ⤳ ⅃ ⅄
= Dundee
...djoining the beach and River Tay. 5 ...inute walk to the local shops.

...RGYLL & BUTE

...RROCHAR

...rdgartan - Forestry Commission,
...rdgartan, Arrochar, Argyll & Bute, G83 7AR
...td: 01301 Tel: 702293
...mail: fe.holidays@forestry.gsi.gov.uk
...ebsite: www.forestholidays.co.uk
...earest Town/Resort Arrochar
...irections 2 miles west of Arrochar on the ...83 Glasgow to Inverary road.
...creage 17 Open End March to End Oct
...ccess Good Site Level
...ites Available ⚠ ⌑ ⚿ Total 200
...acilities ⚠ ⓕ 🏠 📶 ⚡ ⌂ ⊙ ⌣ 🔲 Ⅺ
⚡ ▣ ⚿ 🅿 ▣
...earby Facilities ⟋ ⚓ ⤳ ⅄
...n the shores of Loch Long, surrounded by ...e magnificent mountain scenery of Argyll ...orest Park. Ideal for outdoor activities.

...RROCHAR

...lenloin House, Arrochar, Argyll & Bute, ...83 7AJ.
...td: 01301 Tel: 702239
...earest Town/Resort Helensburgh
...pen 1 March to 1 Nov
...ccess Good Site Level
...ites Available ⚠ ⌑▢ Total 30
...acilities ⓕ 🏠 📶 ⚡ ⌂ ⊙ ⌣ 🔲 Ⅺ
⚡ ▣ ⌂ ✕ ▣
...earby Facilities ⟋ ⚓ ⤳ ⅄
...eal for hill walking, fishing and touring ...est Highlands.

BALMEANACH

Balmeanach Park, Balmeanach, Fishnish, Isle of Mull, Argyll & Bute, PA65 6BA.
Std: 01680 Tel: 300342 Fax: 300342
Website: www.holidaymull.org/members/ balmeanach.html
Nearest Town/Resort Tobermory
Directions From Oban take the ferry crossing to Craignure. Turn right onto the A849 for 5 miles then follow signs for Balmeanach Park.
Acreage 15 Open April to October
Access Good Site Lev/Slope
Sites Available ⚠ ⌑ ⚿ Total 12
Facilities ⓕ 🏠 📶 ⚡ ⌂ ⊙ ⌣ ⚿ ⚿ ⚿
⅃ ▣ ⓞ ⚿ ✕ ⚡ ▣
Nearby Facilities ⌐ ⟋ ∪ ⅃
⚓ Oban
Very peaceful site, ideal for bird watching. Good location for touring the Isle of Mull.

CAMPBELTOWN

Peninver Sands Holiday Park, Peninver, By Campbeltown, Argyll & Bute, PA28 6QP
Std: 01586 Tel: 552262 Fax: 552262
Nearest Town/Resort Campbeltown
Directions From Campbeltown take the B842 north for 4½ miles. Park is on the right as you enter Peninver.
Acreage 2½ Open April to October
Access Good Site Lev/Slope
Sites Available ⚠ ⌑ ⚿ Total 25
Facilities ⓕ 🏠 ⚡ ⌂ ⊙ ⌣ 🔲 📶 ⓞ ⚿ 🚐 ▣
Nearby Facilities ⌐ ⟋ ⚓ ⤳ ∪ ⅃
⚓ Oban
Near the beach. Ideal base for touring Kintyre.

CARRADALE

Carradale Bay Caravan Park, Carradale, Kintyre, Argyll & Bute, PA28 6QG.
Std: 01583 Tel: 431665
Email: enquiries@carradalebay.abelgratis.com
Website: www.carradalebay.com
Nearest Town/Resort Campbeltown
Directions From Campbeltown B842, turn right onto the B879 (signposted Carradale). In ¼ mile at caravan park sign turn right onto a single track road. Site entrance within ¼ mile.
Acreage 12 Open Easter to September
Access Good Site Level
Sites Available ⚠ ⌑ ⚿ Total 65
Facilities ⓕ 📶 ⚡ ⌂ ⊙ ⌣ 🔲 ⚿ 🚐 ▣ ▣
Nearby Facilities ⌐ ⟋ ⤳
Situated on a safe, sloping, sandy beach with a river running alongside.

DUNOON

Stratheck Country Park, Loch Eck, By Dunoon, Argyll & Bute, PA23 8SG.
Std: 01369 Tel: 840472 Fax: 840472
Website: www.stratheck.co.uk
Nearest Town/Resort Dunoon
Directions 7 miles north of Dunoon on the A815.
Open March to October
Access Good Site Level
Sites Available ⚠ ⌑ ⚿ Total 50
Facilities ⚠ ⓕ 🏠 📶 ⚡ ⌂ ⊙ ⌣ 🔲 ⚿
Ⅺ ▣ ⓞ ⚿ ▼ ⚿ ⚿ 🚐 ▣
Nearby Facilities ⌐ ⟋ ⚓ ⤳ ∪ ⅃
⚓ Greenock
Lochside site, adjacent to Younger Botanic Gardens. Ideal outdoor pursuits area.

GLENBARR

Killegruer Caravan Site, Woodend, Glenbarr, Tarbert, Argyll & Bute, PA29 6XB
Std: 01583 Tel: 421241
Nearest Town/Resort Campbeltown
Directions 12 miles north of Campbeltown

on the A83.
Acreage 1¼ Open April to September
Access Good Site Level
Sites Available ⚠ ⌑ ⚿ Total 25
Facilities ⚠ ⓕ 🏠 ⚡ ⌂ ⊙ ⅃ ⓞ ⚿ ⚿ 🚐 ▣
Nearby Facilities ∪
⚓ Oban
Overlooks a sandy beach with views of the Inner Hebrides and the Mull of Kintyre. Site facilities have recently been upgraded. Hair dryers available. Close to ferry link to Northern Ireland and the Inner Hebrides.

GLENDARUEL

Glendaruel Caravan Park, Glendaruel, Argyll & Bute, PA22 3AB.
Std: 01369 Tel: 820267 Fax: 820367
Email: mail@glendaruelcaravanpark.co.uk
Website: www.glendaruelcaravanpark.co.uk
Nearest Town/Resort Tighnabruaich
Directions 13 miles south Strachur on A886 or by ferry to Dunoon and then on the B836. B836 not recommended for touring caravans - 1 in 5 gradient.
Acreage 6 Open April to October
Access Good Site Level
Sites Available ⚠ ⌑ ⚿ Total 45
Facilities ⓕ 📶 ⚡ ⌂ ⊙ ⌣ 🔲 Ⅺ ⓞ ⚿ ⚿
Ⅲ ⚿ 🚐 ▣
Nearby Facilities ⌐ ⟋ ⚓ ⤳ ∪ ⅃ ⅄ ⅃
⚓ Gourock
Peaceful secluded site within a 22 acre country park. Kyles of Bute 5 miles. Adult bicycles for hire. Ideal centre touring and walking. Dogs are welcome, strictly on leads. Sea trout and Salmon fishing. Winner of the Calor Environmental Award 'Most Improved Park in Scotland'. Best Caravan & Camping Park in Argyll the Isles Loch Lomond, Stirling & Trossachs Tourist Board and Antartex Tourism Award.

INVERUGLAS

Loch Lomond Holiday Park, Inveruglas, Near Tarbet, Argyll & Bute, G83 7DW.
Std: 01301 Tel: 704224 Fax: 704206
Email: enquiries@lochlomond.caravans.co.uk
Web: www.lochlomond.caravans.co.uk
Nearest Town/Resort Tarbet
Directions 3 miles north of Tarbet on the A82.
Acreage 1 Open March to October
Access Good Site Level
Sites Available ⌑ ⚿ Total 18
Facilities ⚠ ⓕ 🏠 📶 ⚡ ⌂ ⊙ ⌣ 🔲 Ⅺ ⓞ ⚿ Ⅲ
⚿ Ⅲ ⚿ 🚐 ▣
Nearby Facilities ⌐ ⟋ ⚓ ⤳ ∪ ⅃ ⅄
⚓ Tarbet
Own beach in a superb location. Ideal for hill walking and touring.

ISLE OF MULL (CRAIGNURE)

Shieling Holidays, Craignure, Isle of Mull, Argyll & Bute, PA65 6AY.
Std: 01680 Tel: 812496
Email: graciemull@aol.com
Website: www.shielingholidays.co.uk
Nearest Town/Resort Craignure
Directions From Craignure Ferry turn left on A849 to Iona for 400 metres, then left again at church.
Acreage 7½ Open April to October
Access Good Site Level
Sites Available ⚠ ⌑ ⚿ Total 42
Facilities ⓕ 🏠 📶 ⚡ ⌂ ⊙ ⌣ 🔲 Ⅺ ⓞ ⚿ Ⅲ
⚿ Ⅲ ⚿ 🚐 ∪
Nearby Facilities ⌐ ⟋ ⚓ ⤳ ∪
⚓ Oban
Enchanting location by the sea. Boats and canoes. Hostel beds.

KILBERRY

Port Ban Holiday Park Port Ban, Kilberry, Tarbert, Argyll & Bute, PA29 6YD.
Std: 01880 **Tel:** 770224 **Fax:** 770246
Email: portban@aol.com
Website: www.portban.com
Nearest Town/Resort Tarbert
Directions Lochgilphead, pass through Ardrishaig 2 miles.
Open March **to** October
Access Poor **Site** Lev/Slope
Sites Available A ⬠□ **Total** 30
Facilities ⌁ 🚻 ⛺ 🅿 ⬠ 🔥 ⬚ 📵 ⬛
⬠ ⑆ 🝢 ✕ ⬚ 🄰 ⬚⊣🄿
Nearby Facilities ⌁ ✓ ⚓ ⬚ U ₰
⇌ Oban
Next to the beach in a remote area, site of special scientific interest.

LOCHGILPHEAD

Lochgilphead Caravan Park, Bank Park, Lochgilphead, Argyll & Bute, PA31 8NX.
Std: 01546 **Tel:** 602003 **Fax:** 603699
Nearest Town/Resort Lochgilphead
Directions Close to the junction of the A83 and the A816.
Acreage 7 **Open** April **to** October
Access Good **Site** Level
Sites Available A ⬠ ⛺ **Total** 70
Facilities ⌁ 🚻 ⬚ 🅿 ⬚ 🔥 ⬠ 🝢 📵 ⬛
⬚ 🄾 ⬚ ⬚⊣🄿🄴
Nearby Facilities ⌁ ✓ ⚓ ⬚ U ₰
⇌ Oban
Adjacent to Loch Fyne, Crinan Canal and the town.

LUSS

Camping & Caravanning Club Site,
Luss, Loch Lomond, Nr. Glasgow, Argyll & Bute, G83 8NT.
Std: 01436 **Tel:** 860658
Website:
www.campingandcaravanningclub.co.uk
Nearest Town/Resort Luss
Directions Take the A82 from the Erskide Bridge and head north towards Tarbet. Ignore first signpost for Luss. After the bagpipe and kiltmakers workshop take the next turn right signposted Lodge of Loch Lomond and international camping sign, site approx. 200 yards.
Acreage 12 **Open** March **to** October
Access Good **Site** Level
Sites Available A **Total** 90
Facilities ⬚ ⌁ 🚻 ⬚ 🅿 ⊙⊣🄾 🅿🄲 ⬠ ⬚⊣🄿🄴
Nearby Facilities ⌁
⇌ Balloch
On the banks of Loch Lomond with good views of Ben Lomond. Fishing (permit required) and watersports on site. CLUB MEMBER CARAVANNERS & MOTORHOMES ONLY. AA 4 Pennants and BTB Graded.

OBAN

Oban Divers Caravan Park,
Glenshellach Road, Oban, Argyll & Bute, PA34 4QJ.
Std: 01631 **Tel:** 562755 **Fax:** 562755
Email: obandivers@tesco.net
Website: www.obandivers.co.uk
Nearest Town/Resort Oban
Directions From north go through Oban to the traffic island, take ferry and caravan signs into Albany Street then first or second left. take the first right, then first left signposted caravans/tents. Glenshellach Road is 1½ miles.
Acreage 4 **Open** Easter **to** End Sept
Access Good **Site** Lev/Slope
Sites Available A ⬠ ⛺ **Total** 45
Facilities ⬚ ⌁ 🚻 ⬚ 🅿 ⬚ 🔥 ⊙⊣ 🝢 📵 ⬛
⬠ 🅿🄲 ⬚ ⬚ 🄿 ⬛

Nearby Facilities ⌁ ✓ ⚓ ⬚ U ₰ ⌀
⇌ Oban
Quiet, scenic park on different levels with a stream running through. Member of Countryside Discovery. Limited facilities only during March and October.

SOUTHEND

Machribeg Caravan Site, Southend, By Campbeltown, Argyll & Bute, PA28 6RW.
Std: 01586 **Tel:** 830249
Nearest Town/Resort Campbeltown
Directions Take the B843 from Campbeltown for 10 miles. Site is situated 250yds through Southend Village on the left by the beach.
Acreage 4 **Open** Easter **to** September
Access Good **Site** Sloping
Sites Available A ⬠ ⛺ **Total** 80
Facilities 🚻 ⬚ 🅿 ⊙⊣ ⬚ 📵 ⬛
🄾 🅿🄲 ⬚ ⬚⊣🄿
Nearby Facilities ⌁ ✓ ⚓ ⬚ U ⌀
Near the beach with good views, very quiet location. 18 hole golf course.

TAYNUILT

Crunachy Caravan & Camping Park,
Bridge of Awe, Taynuilt, Argyll & Bute, PA35 1HT.
Std: 01866 **Tel:** 822612
Nearest Town/Resort Oban
Directions Alongside main A85 Tyndrum to Oban 14 miles east of Oban outside the village of Taynuilt.
Acreage 9 **Open** March **to** November
Access Good **Site** Level
Sites Available A ⬠ ⛺ **Total** 80
Facilities ⬚ ⌁ 🚻 ⬚ 🅿 ⊙⊣ 📵 ⬛
⬠ ⑆ 🝢 ✕ 🄰 ⬚⊣🄿🄴
Nearby Facilities ⌁ ✓ ⚓ U ⌀
⇌ Taynuilt
Alongside the River Awe at the foot of Ben Cruachan.

TIGHNABRUAICH

Carry Farm Holiday Park, Ardlamont, Tighnabruaich, Argyll & Bute, PA21 2AH.
Std: 01770 **Tel:** 811717 **Fax:** 811717
Email: tssargyll@ecosse.net
Website: www.carryfarm.co.uk
Nearest Town/Resort Dunoon
Directions Leave Dunoon heading towards Strachur, after Sandbank turn left, after 15 miles at the T-Junction turn right, after 1 mile turn left, 8 miles to Tighnabruaich.
Open April **to** October
Access Good **Site** Level
Sites Available A ⬠ ⛺ **Total** 4
Facilities ⌁ 🚻 ⬚ 🅿 ⊙⊣ 🝢 🅿🄲 ⬠ 🄰⊣
Nearby Facilities ⌁ ✓ ⚓ ⬚ U ₰
⇌ Gourock
Beautiful scenery. Plenty of attractions and activities.

AYRSHIRE, EAST

NEW CUMNOCK

Glen Afton Park, Afton Road, New Cumnock, East Ayrshire, KA18 4PR.
Std: 01290 **Tel:** 332251 **Fax:** 332251
Email: premiereleisure@netscape.net
Nearest Town/Resort Ayr
Directions From the A76 Dumfries to Ayr road, at New Cumnock take the B741 to Dalmellington, then turn immediate first left onto Afton Road. Park is 3 miles on the right.
Acreage 10 **Open** All Year
Access Good **Site** Level
Sites Available A ⬠□ **Total** 15
Facilities ⌁ 🚻 🚻 ⬚ ⌁ ⊙⊙ 🅿🄲 ⬠ ✕
⌀ 🄰 🝢 ⬚ ⬛
Nearby Facilities ⌁ ✓ U
Beautiful Burns countryside. Close to a river. Good walking route.

PATNA

Carskeoch House Caravan Park, Patn East Ayrshire, KA6 7NR.
Std: 01292 **Tel:** 531205
Nearest Town/Resort Ayr
Directions From Ayr take the A713 Cas Douglas road.
Acreage 13 **Open** March **to** October
Access Reasonable **Site** Sloping
Sites Available A ⬠ ⛺ **Total** 50
Facilities ⌁ 🚻 ⬚ 🅿 ⊣ 🄾 📵 ⬛ ⬠ 🝢 🄲 ⌀
Nearby Facilities ⌁ ✓
⇌ Ayr

AYRSHIRE, NORTH

IRVINE

Cunningham Head Estate Caravan Park, Cunningham Head, Nr. Kilmarnocl North Ayrshire, KA3 2PE.
Std: 01294 **Tel:** 850238
Nearest Town/Resort Irvine
Directions From Irvine take A736 Glasgc road at Stanecastle roundabout turn e onto B769 Stewarton road. Park is 2 mil on left.
Acreage 20 **Open** April **to** September
Access Good **Site** Level
Sites Available A ⬠ ⛺ **Total** 90
Facilities ⌁ 🚻 ⬚ 🅿 ⊙⊣ 📵 ⬛ ⬠ 🄲⊣🄿
Nearby Facilities ⌁ ✓ ⚓ ⬚ U ₰
On grounds of mansion house (now gon Ideal for touring Burns Country and th coast resorts. Near Magnum Leisure Cent NEW for 2000 "The Big Idea" Nob Experience.

SALTCOATS

Sandylands Holiday Park, Auchenharv Park, Saltcoats, North Ayrshire, KA21 5J
Std: 01294 **Tel:** 469411 **Fax:** 467823
Email: sandylands@gbholidayparks.co.
Website: www.gbholidayparks.co.uk
Nearest Town/Resort Saltcoats
Directions Follow signs for Kilmarnock an then Irvine. Follow the A78 signs Stevenson, go through Stevenson, past th Auchenharvie Leisure Centre and th holiday park is on the left.
Open March **to** October
Access Good **Site** Level
Sites Available A ⬠ ⛺ **Total** 20
Facilities ⬚ ⌁ 🚻 ⊙ ⌱🅿🄲 ⬚⊙🄸🝢🄰⑆🝢🄿⬛
Nearby Facilities ⌁ ✓ ⌀
⇌ Saltcoats
Relaxing seaside destination offering gre facilities and outstanding views. Gre location for visiting beautiful Arran ar charming Scottish towns.

SKELMORLIE

Skelmorlie Mains Caravan & Camping Site, Skelmorlie Mains, Skelmorlie, North Ayrshire, PA17 5EU.
Std: 01475 **Tel:** 520794 **Fax:** 520794
Nearest Town/Resort Largs
Directions ½ mile from A78 south c Skelmorlie.
Acreage 4 **Open** April **to** October
Access Good **Site** Sloping
Sites Available A ⬠ ⛺ **Total** 100
Facilities ⌁ 🚻 ⬚ 🅿 ⊙⊣ 📵 ⬛ 🄼 🄰✕🝢⬛
Nearby Facilities ⌁ ✓ ⚓ ⬚ U ₰ ⌀
⇌ Wemyss Bay
Scenic view of Cumbrae, Arran, Bute Island and Firth of Clyde.

AYRSHIRE, SOUTH

AYR

Heads of Ayr Leisure Park, Dunure Road, Ayr, South Ayrshire, KA7 4LD.
Std: 01292 **Tel:** 442269 **Fax:** 500298

SANDYLANDS HOLIDAY PARK
Scottish Hospitality on the Ayrshire Coast

A warm welcome awaits you on this lively, happy and friendly park. Sandylands is set in a relaxing seaside holiday destination with great Scottish scenery. It's a fantastic location for visiting beautiful Arran or one of the charming Scottish towns.

- Indoor heated swimming pool • Family and adult club • Beach access
- Amusements • Entertainment • Mini-market • Adjacent to a golf course

Fantastic rates available - Phone 01294 469411 for details
Visit our website www.gbholidayparks.co.uk
Sandylands Holiday Park, Auchenharvie Park, Saltcoats, Ayrshire KA2 5JN

Nearest Town/Resort Ayr
Directions 5 miles south of Ayr on the A719.
Acreage 9 **Open** March **to** October
Access Good **Site** Level
Sites Available A ⚑ ♛ **Total** 160
Facilities f ⊞⅃⊞ ⚓ ♜⊙⌕Ⅎ◍⚒✗♥�♠⋀⊛↦⊡
Nearby Facilities ┍ ✓ ⚓ ∪ ℛ
≉ Ayr
Just a 10 minute walk to the beach.

AYR
Middlemuir Holiday Park, Tarbolton, Nr. Ayr, South Ayrshire, KA5 5NR.
Std: 01292 **Tel:** 541647 **Fax:** 541647
Email: middlemuir@yahoo.co.uk
Nearest Town/Resort Ayr
Directions From Ayr take the B743 towards Mauchline, after approx. 5 miles turn left at the third turning for Tarbolton. Park is on the right after approx. 400 yards.
Open March **to** October
Access Good **Site** Level
Sites Available ⚑ ♛ **Total** 25
Facilities f ⊞⅃⊞ ⚓ ♜⊙⌕◍ Ⅎ ⊙ ⚒ Ⅶ
♠ ⋀ ⊛↦⊡
Nearby Facilities ┍ ✓ ⚓ ∪
Quiet, rural setting, yet close to all amenities. Ideal for touring Ayrshire.

BARRHILL
Queensland Holiday Park, Barrhill, Girvan, South Ayrshire, KA26 0PZ.
Std: 01465 **Tel:** 821364 **Fax:** 821364
Email: queenslandhp@yahoo.com
Nearest Town/Resort Girvan
Directions 10 miles south east of Girvan on the A714.
Acreage 1 **Open** March **to** October
Access Good **Site** Level
Sites Available A ⚑ ♛ **Total** 15
Facilities ⚿ f ⊞⅃⊞ ⚓ ♜⊙⌕◍ ⊙
♠ ⋀ ⊛↦⊡
Nearby Facilities ┍ ✓
Ideal location for walking and cycling in Galloway Forest, or for touring South Scotland. Good local rivers.

GIRVAN
Bennane Shore Holiday Park, Lendalfoot, Girvan, South Ayrshire, KA26 0JG.
Std: 01465 **Tel:** 891233 **Fax:** 891233
Nearest Town/Resort Girvan
Directions 8 miles south of Girvan on the A77 Stranraer to Glasgow trunk road.
Acreage 7 **Open** March **to** October
Access Good **Site** Level
Sites Available A ⚑ ♛ **Total** 25
Facilities f ⊞⅃⊞ ⚓ ♜⊙⌕◍ Ⅎ ⊙ ⚒↦⊡
Nearby Facilities ┍ ✓ ⚓ ⚓ ∪ ✈ ℛ ⚓
≉ Girvan
Beach front, scenic views. Private slipway for the boating enthusiasts. Ideal touring.

GIRVAN
Carleton Caravan Park, Carleton Lodge, Lendalfoot, Girvan, South Ayrshire, KA26 0JF.
Std: 01465 **Tel:** 891120
Nearest Town/Resort Girvan
Directions Off A77 Girvan/Stranraer road at Lendalfoot village. 800 yards on unclassified road.
Acreage 9 **Open** March **to** October
Access Good **Site** Terraced
Sites Available A ⚑ ♛ **Total** 10
Facilities ⊞⅃ ⚓ ♜⊙⌕↦⊡
Nearby Facilities ┍ ✓ ⚓ ⚓
≉ Girvan
Small quiet site, near sea, ideal touring area.

MAYBOLE
Walled Garden Caravan Park, Kilkerran Estate, Crosshill, Maybole, South Ayrshire, KA19 7SL.
Std: 01655 **Tel:** 740323
Email: walledgardencp@clara.co.uk
Website: www.walledgardencp.clara.co.uk
Nearest Town/Resort Ayr
Directions From Maybole take the B7023 to Crosshill. Turn right at the war memorial towards Dailly, after 1½ miles turn left at caravan park signs and follow local signs.
Acreage 4 **Open** April **to** October
Access Good **Site** Lev/Slope
Sites Available A ⚑□ **Total** 90
Facilities f ⊞⅃⊞ ⚓ ♜⊙⌕◍ Ⅎ ⊙ ⚒
Ⅶ ♠⋀↦⊡⊡
Nearby Facilities ┍ ✓ ∪
Walled garden set in beautiful woodland, very well sheltered. Nice walks, superb wildlife and fishing locally.

PRESTWICK
Prestwick Holiday Park, Prestwick, South Ayrshire, KA9 1UH.
Std: 01292 **Tel:** 479261
Website: www.ukparks.co.uk/prestwick
Nearest Town/Resort Prestwick/Ayr
Directions Signposted off the A79 1 mile north of Prestwick.
Acreage 11 **Open** March **to** October
Access Good **Site** Level
Sites Available A ⚑ ♛ **Total** 186
Facilities ⚿ f ⊞ ⚓ ♜⊙⌕
◍ Ⅎ ⊙ ⚒ Ⅶ ♥ Ⅶ ♠ ⋀ ⊛↦⊡
Nearby Facilities ┍ ✓ ⚓ ⚓ ∪ ℛ
≉ Prestwick
Ideal for the beach, towns and touring.

TROON
St. Meddans Caravan Site, Low St. Meddans, Troon, South Ayrshire, KA10 6NS.
Std: 01292 **Tel:** 312957
Nearest Town/Resort Troon
Acreage 1 **Open** 1st Fri March **to** Last Sun Oct
Sites Available ⚑ ♛ **Total** 25
Facilities f ⚓ ♜⊙⌕ ♥ ⅊ ⊙
Nearby Facilities ≉ Troon
Just a 5 minute walk from beaches, golf courses and the town centre.

DUMFRIES & GALLOWAY
ANNAN
Galabank Caravan & Camping Site, North Street, Annan, Dumfries & Galloway, DG1 2SB.
Std: 01556 **Tel:** 503806
Nearest Town/Resort Annan
Open May **to** Early Sept
Access Good **Site** Level
Sites Available A ⚑ ♛ **Total** 30
Facilities f ⊞ ⚓ ♜⊙⌕ ♥ ⅊↦⊡
Nearby Facilities ✓ ℛ
≉ Annan
Alongside a river with river walks. Putting in the adjacent park. Swimming pool nearby. Ideal touring. Dogs are welcome if kept on leads.

AUCHENMALG
Cock Inn Caravan Park, Auchenmalg, Nr. Glenluce, Newton Stewart, Dumfries & Galloway, DG8 0JT.
Std: 01581 **Tel:** 500227
Website: www.cockinncaravanpark.co.uk
Nearest Town/Resort Stranraer
Acreage 6½ **Open** March **to** October
Access Good **Site** Lev/Slope
Sites Available A ⚑ ♛ **Total** 70
Facilities ⚿ f ⊞⅃⊞ ⚓ ♜⊙⌕◍ ⅊
⊙ ⚒✗⋀↦⊡⊡
Nearby Facilities ┍ ✓ ⚓ ⚓ ∪ ⚓
Near the beach.

BORGUE
Brighouse Bay Holiday Park, Borgue, Kirkcudbright, Dumfries & Galloway, DG6 4TS
Std: 01557 **Tel:** 870267 **Fax:** 870319
Email: cades@brighouse-bay.co.uk
Website: www.gillespie-leisure.com
Nearest Town/Resort Kirkcudbright
Directions From Kirkcudbright take the A755 signposted Gatehouse of Fleet, west over river. On outskirts of town take B727 signposted Borgue. After 4 miles turn left at Brighouse Bay sign. Park is on the left, behind trees, in 2 miles.
Acreage 25 **Open** All Year
Access Good **Site** Lev/Slope
Sites Available A ⚑ ♛ **Total** 180
Facilities ⚿ f ⊞ ⊞⅃⊞ ⚓ ♜⊙⌕◍ ⊙
⅊ ⊙ ⚒✗ ♥ Ⅶ ♠⋀ ✈ ⊛↦⊡⊞⊞
≉ Dumfries

Beautifully situated on a quiet peninsula with its own sandy beach and working farm, family park with exceptional on-site recreational facilities including an indoor pool complex, members lounge, spa facilities, fitness room, quad and mountain bikes, pony trekking centre, 18 hole golf course and driving range, fishing, nature trails, boating and slipway.

CAIRNRYAN

Cairnryan Caravan Park, Cairnryan, Stranraer, Dumfries & Galloway, DG9 8QX.
Std: 01581 **Tel:** 200231 **Fax:** 200207
Nearest Town/Resort Stranraer
Directions 5 miles north of Stranraer on the A77. Directly opposite the P&O Ferry terminal.
Acreage 9 **Open** March to October
Access Good **Site** Lev/Slope
Sites Available ⚠ ⬛ ⬛ **Total** 15
Facilities ⫽ 🏠🔵 ⬛ ℾ ⊙⬛ ⬛ ⬛ ⬛
🔦⬛⬛🔶⬛⬛⬛⬛🔵⬛
Nearby Facilities ℾ ✓ ⚓ ⬛ ∪
⇌ Stranraer
Overlooking the sea.

CASTLE DOUGLAS

Lochside Caravan & Camping Site, Lochside Park, Castle Douglas, Dumfries & Galloway, DG7 1EZ.
Std: 01556 **Tel:** 502949
Nearest Town/Resort Castle Douglas
Directions Well signposted in town centre of Castle Douglas.
Acreage 6 **Open** Easter to October
Access Good **Site** Level
Sites Available ⚠ ⬛ ⬛ **Total** 161
Facilities ⚙ ⫽ 🏠🔵 ⬛ ℾ ⊙⬛
⬛ ⬛ ⬛ ⬛ 🔶⬛
Nearby Facilities ℾ ✓ ⚓ ✦ ₰

Beside Loch, ideal touring. Nearby squash courts, putting, swimming pool and bowling green. Dogs are welcome if kept on leads.

CREETOWN

Creetown Caravan Park, Silver Street, Creetown, Dumfries & Galloway, DG8 7HU
Std: 01671 **Tel:** 820377 **Fax:** 820377
Email: beatrice.mcneill@btinternet.com
Website: www.creetown-caravans.co.uk
Nearest Town/Resort Newton Stewart
Directions 6 miles east of Newton Stewart on the A75, in the village of Creetown.
Acreage 3½ **Open** March to October
Access Good **Site** Level
Sites Available ⚠ ⬛ ⬛ **Total** 20
Facilities ⫽ 🔵 ⬛ ℾ ⊙⬛ ⬛ ⬛ ⬛ ⬛
🔦⬛⬛🔶⬛🔵⬛
Nearby Facilities ℾ ✓ ₰
⇌ Barrhill
Adjacent to the village.

CREETOWN

Ferry Croft Caravan Site, Creetown, Dumfries & Galloway, DG8 7JS.
Std: 01671 **Tel:** 820502
Email: doncook@pgen.net
Nearest Town/Resort Newton Stewart
Directions 6 miles from Newton Stewart on the A75, turn off for Creetown. When reaching the clock tower turn up the hill following the signs for Ferry Croft Caravan Site.
Acreage ½ **Open** Easter to End Sept
Access Good **Site** Level
Sites Available ⚠ ⬛ ⬛ **Total** 8
Facilities ⫽ 🔵 ⬛ ℾ ⊙⬛ 🔦🔶◨⬛
Nearby Facilities ℾ ✓ ∪ ₰ ✦
⇌ Stranraer
ADULTS ONLY SITE. Small, quiet, attractive site at the edge of the village of Creetown. Close to the coast and hills, within easy reach of good beaches, golf, fishing and forest walks. Ideal touring.

CROCKETFORD

Park of Brandedleys, Crocketford, Dumfries & Galloway, DG2 8RG.
Std: 01556 **Tel:** 690250 **Fax:** 690681
Email: brandedleys@holgates.com
Website: www.holgates.com
Nearest Town/Resort Dumfries
Directions Turn left off A75 Dumfries/Castle Douglas road on edge of Crocketford village onto unclassified road. Site on right 150 yards
Acreage 20 **Open** All Year
Access Good **Site** Lev/Slope
Sites Available ⚠ ⬛ ⬛ **Total** 80
Facilities ⚙ ⫽ 🏠🔵 ⬛ ℾ ⊙⬛ ⬛ ⬛
🔦⬛⬛🔶☓⬛⬛⬛⬛⊛⬛🔵⬛
Nearby Facilities ℾ ✓ ⚓ ✦ ∪ ₰
⇌ Dumfries
Ideal touring centre, set in beautiful countryside overlooking loch and hills. Sauna. Caravans for sale. Caravans, chalet, log cabins and cottage for hire. Calor Award Best Park in Scotland 1995"

DALBEATTIE

Islecroft Caravan & Camping Site, Mill Street, Dalbeattie, Dumfries & Galloway, DG5 4HE.
Std: 01556 **Tel:** 610012
Nearest Town/Resort Dalbeattie
Directions Adjacent to Colliston Park, off Mill Street in the centre of Dalbeattie.
Acreage 3¼ **Open** Easter to September
Access Good **Site** Level
Sites Available ⚠ ⬛ ⬛ **Total** 30
Facilities ⫽ 🔵 ⬛ ℾ ⊙⬛ ⬛ 🔦⬛⬛🔶◨⬛
Nearby Facilities ℾ ✓ ⚓ ✦ ∪ ₰
⇌ Dumfries
Ideal position for touring inland and coastal areas of the region. Dogs are welcome if kept on leads.

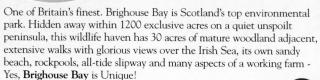

PARK OF
BRANDEDLEYS

Experience our quality accommodation, set in a peaceful
location, with superb views of loch and surrounding hills.
Ideal for sight-seeing, shopping, golf and fishing.
Relax and enjoy our new Bar & Restaurant with Family Room.
Indoor and outdoor heated swimming pools, sauna, tennis,
badminton, play area, games arcade, etc..
Luxury Holiday homes for sale.

CROCKETFORD, DUMFRIES DG2 8RG
TELEPHONE: 01556 690250   FAX: 01556 690681
www.holgates.com   brandedleys@holgates.com

DALBEATTIE

Sandyhills Bay Leisure Park, Sandyhills,
Dalbeattie, Dumfries & Galloway, DG5 4NY
Std: 01387 **Tel:** 780257
Email: cades@sandyhills-bay.co.uk
Website: www.gillespie-leisure.com
Nearest Town/Resort Dalbeattie
Directions On A710 coast road from
Dumfries to Dalbeattie, next Sandyhills
Village and Colvend Golf Course.
Acreage 6 **Open** 1st April **to** 31st October
Access Good **Site** Level
Sites Available A ⌂ ⊕ **Total** 60
Facilities ⸾ Ⓦ ⚲ ⌒ ⊙ ⌁ ⎕ ⛴
⎔ ⚱ ⊕ ⊁ ⎆ ⎆
Nearby Facilities ⌇ ⟋ ⚓ ⊁ ∪
A unique park only yards from a fabulous
sandy beach with golf, riding, fishing and
eating out within ¼ mile. Magnificent coastal
walks. Take-away food. Thistle Commended
holiday caravans. For Bookings please
telephone 01557 870267.

DUMFRIES

Barnsoul Farm, Irongray, Dumfries,
Dumfries & Galloway, DG2 9SQ.
Std: 01387 **Tel:** 730249 **Fax:** 730249
Email: barnsouldg@aol.com
Website: www.barnsoulfarm.co.uk
Nearest Town/Resort Dumfries
Directions Leave Dumfries on the A75,
travel 6 miles in the direction of Stranraer.
Turn right at the sign for "Shawhead" and
"Barnsoul Farm 2½ Miles". Go into
Shawhead Village turn right then left
following signs for Barnsoul.
Acreage 200 **Open** April **to** October
Access Good **Site** Lev/Slope
Sites Available A ⌂ ⊕ **Total** 20
Facilities ⸾ Ⓦ ⚲ ⌒ ⊙ ⌁ ⎕ ⛴ ⎔
⎆ Ⓦ ⊛ ⊁ ⎆
Nearby Facilities ⌇ ⟋ ⚓ ⊁ ∪ ⊁ ⟀
Very scenic inland site, woods and fields.
Hire caravans, chalets, touring pitches and
wigwam/sheiling bothies. AA 2 Pennants.

DUMFRIES

Mouswald Place Caravan Site,
Mouswald Place, Mouswald, Dumfries,
Dumfries & Galloway, DG1 4JS.
Std: 01387 **Tel:** 830226 **Fax:** 830226
Nearest Town/Resort Dumfries
Directions From Dumfries take the A75 for
2½ miles. Take the right fork to Mouswald
and Caravan Park, ¾ mile on the right.
Acreage 5½ **Open** March **to** October
Site Lev/Slope
Sites Available A ⌂ ⊕ **Total** 30
Facilities ⚲ ⸾ Ⓦ ⚲ ⌒ ⊙ ⌁ ⎕
⛴ ⎆ ⚱ Ⓦ ⎆
Nearby Facilities ⌇ ⟋ ⚓ ⊁ ∪
Small, quiet, woodland park.

ECCLEFECHAN

Cressfield Caravan Park, Ecclefechan,
Nr Lockerbie, Dumfries & Galloway, DG11
3DR.
Std: 01576 **Tel:** 300702 **Fax:** 300702
Nearest Town/Resort Lockerbie
Directions Leave A74(M) at Ecclefechan -
junction 19 (5 miles south of Lockerbie, 8
miles north of Gretna). Follow the B7076 for
½ mile to south side of village.
Acreage 15 **Open** All Year
Access Good **Site** Level
Sites Available A ⌂ ⊕ **Total** 115
Facilities ⚲ ⸾ ⎕ Ⓦ ⚲ ⌒ ⊙ ⌁ ⎕ ⛴ ⎔
⎆ ⚱ ⊛ ⎆ ⎆
Nearby Facilities ⌇ ⟋ ⚓ ∪
Peaceful country park with excellent
facilities, just north of the border. Ideal
touring base or night halt.

ECCLEFECHAN

Hoddom Castle Caravan Park, Hoddom,
Lockerbie, Dumfries & Galloway, DG11 1AS
Std: 01576 **Tel:** 300251
Nearest Town/Resort Lockerbie
Directions Exit A74/M74 at Ecclefechan
(junction 19). At church in village turn west
on the B725 (Dalton). 2½ miles to entrance
at Hoddom Bridge.
Acreage 24 **Open** April **to** October
Access Good **Site** Lev/Slope
Sites Available A ⌂ ⊕ **Total** 180
Facilities ⚲ ⸾ ⎕ Ⓦ ⚲ ⌒ ⊙ ⌁ ⎕ ⛴ ⎔ ⊕
⊁ ⚱ ⎆ ⎔ ⎆ ⎆
Nearby Facilities ⌇ ⟋ ⟀
Quiet site in parkland of a castle. Nature
trails and woodland walks on land adjoining
park. 9 hole golf course on site.

GATEHOUSE OF FLEET

Anwoth Holiday Park, Garden Street,
Gatehouse of Fleet, Dumfries & Galloway,
DG7 2EX.
Std: 01557 **Tel:** 814333 **Fax:** 814333
Nearest Town/Resort Gatehouse of Fleet
Directions In the village of Gatehouse of Fleet.
Acreage 7 **Open** March **to** October
Access Good **Site** Level
Sites Available A ⌂ ⊕ **Total** 66
Facilities ⚲ ⚲ ⸾ Ⓦ ⚲ ⌒ ⊙ ⌁
⎕ ⎆ ⊛ ⎆ ⎆ ⎆
Nearby Facilities ⌇ ⟋ ⚓ ∪ ⊁ ⟀ ⟀
Within walking distance of village amenities.
Ideal touring.

GATEHOUSE OF FLEET

Mossyard Caravan Park, Mossyard,
Gatehouse of Fleet, Castle Douglas,
Dumfries & Galloway, DG7 2ET.
Std: 01557 **Tel:** 840226
Nearest Town/Resort Gatehouse of Fleet
Directions 4 miles west of Gatehouse of
Fleet on the A75. Turn left at Mossyard sign.

Acreage 6½ **Open** Easter **to** End Oct
Access Good **Site** Lev/Slope
Sites Available A ⌂ ⊕ **Total** 55
Facilities ⸾ Ⓦ ⚲ ⌒ ⊙ ⌁ ⎕ ⛴ ⎔ ⎆ ⎆
Nearby Facilities ⌇ ⟋ ⟀
⊁ Dumfries
A working farm in a coastal location with
direct access to sandy beaches.

GLENLUCE

Glenluce Caravan Park, Glenluce
Village, Dumfries & Galloway, DG8 0QR.
Std: 01581 **Tel:** 300412
Email: peter@glenlucecaravan.co.uk
Website: www.glenlucecaravan.co.uk
Nearest Town/Resort Stranraer
Directions 10 miles east of Stranraer on
A75 Dumfries/Stranraer road. Entrance to
park at telephone kiosk in centre of village
opposite the Inglenook Restaurant.
Acreage 5 **Open** March **to** October
Access Good **Site** Lev/Slope
Sites Available A ⌂ ⊕ **Total** 40
Facilities ⸾ ⎕ Ⓦ ⚲ ⌒ ⊙ ⌁ ⚲ ⎆ ⎕ ⎆
⛴ ⎔ ⎆ ⚱ ⟀ ⊛ ⎆ ⎆ ⎆
Nearby Facilities ⌇ ⟋ ⚓ ∪ ⟀
⊁ Stranraer
Secluded sun trap park in the private
grounds of a former estate mansion house.
Near to the beach and golf, with bowling,
pony trekking, fishing and superb walks all
within 1 mile. Luxury spa and indoor
swimming pool.

GLENLUCE

Whitecairn Farm Caravan Park,
Glenluce, Newton Stewart, Dumfries &
Galloway, DG8 0NZ.
Std: 01581 **Tel:** 300267 **Fax:** 300434
Website: www.whitecairncaravans.co.uk
Nearest Town/Resort Stranraer
Directions 1½ miles north of Glenluce
village.
Acreage 4 **Open** March **to** Oct
Access Good **Site** Level
Sites Available A ⌂ ⊕ **Total** 30
Facilities ⸾ ⎕ Ⓦ ⚲ ⌒ ⊙ ⌁ ⛴
⛴ ⎔ ⎆ ⎆ ⎆
Nearby Facilities ⌇ ⟋ ⚓ ∪
Central location for touring Wigtownshire.
Very peacful park, away from the main road.
2 miles from A75.

GRETNA

The Braids Caravan Park, Annan Road,
Gretna, Dumfries & Galloway, DG16 5DQ.
Std: 01461 **Tel:** 337409 **Fax:** 337409
Website: www.gretnawedding.com
Directions From the M6 run straight onto
the A74. Take the A75 signposted Dumfries/
Stranraer. In 1 mile take the second left for
Gretna (B721), park is 600yds on the left.
Acreage 5 **Open** All Year

Access Good **Site** Lev/Slope
Sites Available ▲ ⊕ ☻ **Total** 84
Facilities ⚭ �ℹ 🚽 🔥 ⓦ ♨ ⓡ ☺⌁ ▣ ⓠ ☎
🏪 🅿 ☉ ⊜ 🛒 ⊬ 🎣 🍴
Nearby Facilities ⌐ ✔ ∪
⚦ Gretna
Ideal touring centre, advice given. Fishing
can be arranged. Good area for bird
watching. On board tank waste disposal
point. Small rallies welcome, rally building
available. STB 4 Star Graded Park.

ISLE OF WHITHORN
Castlewigg Caravan Park, Whithorn,
Newton Stewart, Dumfries & Galloway,
DG8 8DP.
Std: 01988 **Tel:** 500616 **Fax:** 500616
Email: castlewigg@southernmachars.com
Nearest Town/Resort Newton Stewart
Directions From roundabout at Newton
Stewart turn onto the A714 to Wigtown. Just
before Wigtown take the A746 to Whithorn.
3 miles after Sorbie site on the right.
Acreage 4¼ **Open** All Year
Access Good **Site** Level
Sites Available ▲ ⊕ ☻ **Total** 15
Facilities ℹ 🚽 ⓦ 🔥 ⓡ ☺⌁ ▣ ⓠ ☎
🏪 🅿 ☉ ⊜ 🛒 ⊬ 🎣 ▣ ⊡
Nearby Facilities ⌐ ✔ ∪ ⚑
⚦ Stranraer
Quiet, country site in a central location with
scenic views. Beaches nearby. Excellent
fishing. Award winning gardens.

KIPPFORD
Kippford Caravan Park, Kippford,
Dalbeattie, Dumfries & Galloway, DG5 4LF
Std: 01556 **Tel:** 620636 **Fax:** 620607
Email: info@kippfordholidaypark.co.uk
Website: www.kippfordholidaypark.co.uk
Directions From Dumfries take the A711
to Dalbeattie, then turn left onto the A710
signposted Colvend Coast. The park
entrance is on the main road in 3½ miles,
200yds after the branch road to Kippford.
Acreage 18
Access Good **Site** Sloping
Sites Available ▲ ⊕ ☻ **Total** 184
Facilities ℹ 🚽 ⓦ 🔥 ⓡ ☺⌁ ▣ ⓠ 🏪
☉ ⊜ 🛒 ⊬ 🎣 ▣ ⊡
Nearby Facilities ⌐ ✔ ∆ 🎣 ∪
David Bellamy Gold Award for Conservation,
STB 5 Star Graded and Thistle Award. Just
a 15 minute stroll to the beautiful seaside
village of Kippford. Hilly, part wooded coastal
walks. Adventure and Junior playgrounds.
Adjacent to a shop, fishing and golf. Free
marquee for mini rallies. Level pitches,
terraced on sloping ground in small groups.

KIRKCOWAN
Three Lochs Holiday Park, Balminnoch,
Kirkcowan, Newton Stewart, Dumfries &
Galloway, DG8 0EP.
Std: 01671 **Tel:** 830304 **Fax:** 830335
Email: info@3lochs.junglelink.co.uk
Website: www.3lochs.co.uk
Nearest Town/Resort Newton Stewart
Acreage 15 **Open** Easter **to** October
Access Good **Site** Level
Sites Available ▲ ⊕ ☻ **Total** 80
Facilities ⚭ ℹ ⓦ 🔥 ⓡ ☺⌁ ▣ ⓠ ☎
🏪 🅿 ☉ ⊜ 🛒 ⊬ 🎣 ▣ ⊡

Nearby Facilities ⌐ ✔ ∆ 🎣 ∪
Three Lochs for coarse or trout fishing and
sailing. Full size snooker.

KIRKCUDBRIGHT
Seaward Caravan Park, Dhoon Bay,
Kirkcudbright, Dumfries & Galloway, DG6
4TS.
Std: 01557 **Tel:** 331079
Email: cades@seaward-park.co.uk
Website: www.gillespie-leisure.com
Nearest Town/Resort Kirkcudbright
Directions Take A755 signposted Gatehouse
of Fleet, west from Kirkcudbright. On outskirts
turn left onto the B727 signposted Borgue.
Park is on the right in 2 miles.
Acreage 6¼ **Open** 1st March **to** 31st
October
Access Good **Site** Level
Sites Available ▲ ⊕ ☻ **Total** 50
Facilities ⚭ ℹ 🚽 ⓦ 🔥 ⓡ ☺⌁ ▣ ⓠ 🏪 ☉ ⊜
♨ 🛒 🎣 ♨ 🍴 ▣ ⊡
Nearby Facilities ⌐ ✔ ∆ 🎣 ∪ ⚑
An exclusive park beautifully situated with
exceptional views over Kirkcudbright Bay.
Many on-site amenities plus all the activities
at nearby Brighouse Bay. NEW indoor
complex. 9 hole golf course. Sea adjacent
for angling and sandy beach ¼ mile away.
Thistle Commended caravans for hire. For
Bookings please telephone 01557 870267.

KIRKCUDBRIGHT
Silvercraigs Caravan Site, Silvercraigs
Road, Kirkcudbright, Dumfries & Galloway,
DG6 4BT.
Std: 01557 **Tel:** 330123
Nearest Town/Resort Kirkcudbright
Directions Turn left from St. Mary's Street
to St. Mary's Place, follow Barrhill Road and
Silvercraigs Road, site on left.
Acreage 5¼ **Open** Easter **to** October
Access Good **Site** Sloping
Sites Available ▲ ⊕ ☻ **Total** 50
Facilities ⚭ ℹ 🚽 ⓦ 🔥 ⓡ ☺⌁ ▣ ⓠ 🏪 🅿 ☉ ⊜ 🛒 ⊬
Nearby Facilities ⌐ ✔ ∆ ∪ ⚑
Ideal touring, near sea. Laundry facilities
available. Wildlife Park nearby. Pets
welcome if kept on leads.

KIRKPATRICK FLEMING
**King Robert the Bruce's Cave Caravan
& Camping Site,** Cove Lodge, Kirkpatrick
Fleming, By Lockerbie, Dumfries &
Galloway, DG11 3AT.
Std: 01461 **Tel:** 800285
Nearest Town/Resort Gretna
Directions Turn off A74 M74 at Kirkpatrick
Fleming, then in Kirkpatrick follow all signs
to Bruces Cave.
Acreage 80 **Open** All Year
Access Good **Site** Level
Sites Available ▲ ⊕ ☻ **Total** 40
Facilities ⚭ ℹ 🚽 ⓦ 🔥 ⓡ ☺⌁ ▣ ⓠ ☎
♨ 🅿 ☉ ⊜ 🛒 ✖ 🎣 ⊬ 🍴 ▣ ⊡
Nearby Facilities ⌐ ✔ ∆ 🎣 ∪ ⚑
⚦ Annan
In grounds of 80 acre estate, peacefull and
quiet and secluded, famous ancient
monument of King Robert the Bruce's cave
in grounds of site, free fishing on 3 mile
stretch of river for Trout, Sea Trout, Salmon.
New disabled toilet block and laundry room.

LANGHOLM
Ewes Water Caravan & Camping Park,
Milntown, Langholm, Dumfries &
Galloway, DG13 0DH.
Std: 01387 **Tel:** 380386 **Fax:** 381670
Email: jim.balmer@zoom.co.uk
Nearest Town/Resort Langholm
Directions On the A7 ½ mile north of
Langholm and 23½ miles north of Carlisle
Acreage 1 **Open** April **to** September
Access Good **Site** Level
Sites Available ▲ ⊕☐ **Total** 23
Facilities ⚭ ℹ ⓦ 🔥 ⓡ ☺⌁ ▣ ⓠ
☻ 🅿 ☉ 🛒 ⊬ ▣ ⊡
Nearby Facilities ⌐ ✔ ∪
Alongside a river with mapped local walks.
Ideal for touring Borders, Edinburgh,
Glasgow and the Lake District (30 miles).

LANGHOLM
Whitshiels Caravan Park, Langholm,
Dumfries & Galloway, DG13 0HG.
Std: 01387 **Tel:** 380494
Nearest Town/Resort Langholm
Directions 200 yards north of Langholm on
the A7.
Acreage ½ **Open** All Year
Access Good **Site** Level
Sites Available ▲ ⊕ ☻ **Total** 10
Facilities ℹ 🚽 ⓦ 🔥 ⓡ ☺⌁ ▣ ✖ 🏪⊡
Nearby Facilities ⌐ ✔ ∆ ∪ ⚑ ⚑
⚦ Carlisle
Ideal area for fishing, golf, Hadrians Wall,
Gretna Green, Borders region and
Armstrong Clan Museum. Scenic route to
Edinburgh.

LOCHMABEN
Halleaths Caravan Park, Halleaths,
Lochmaben, Lockerbie, Dumfries &
Galloway, DG11 1NA.
Std: 01387 **Tel:** 810630 **Fax:** 810005
Nearest Town Lochmaben/Lockerbie
Directions From Lockerbie on M74, take
A709 to Lochmaben. ½ mile on the right after
crossing the River Annan.
Acreage 8 **Open** March **to** November
Access Good **Site** Level
Sites Available ▲ ⊕ ☻ **Total** 70
Facilities ℹ 🚽 ⓦ 🔥 ⓡ ☺⌁ ▣ ⓠ ☎
♨ 🅿 ☉ ⊜ 🛒 ⊬ 🎣 ▣ ⊡
Nearby Facilities ⌐ ✔ ∆ 🎣 ∪ ⚑ ⚑
⚦ Lockerbie
Bowling, tennis, yachting, boating, golf and
both coarse and game fishing, all within 1
mile of park.

LOCHMABEN
Kirkloch Caravan & Camping Site,
Kirkloch Brae, Lochmaben, Dumfries &
Galloway.
Std: 01556 **Tel:** 503806
Nearest Town/Resort Lochmaben
Acreage 1½ **Open** Easter **to** October
Access Good **Site** Level
Sites Available ▲ ⊕ ☻ **Total** 30
Facilities ℹ 🚽 ⓦ 🔥 ⓡ ☺⌁ ▣ ⓠ 🏪 ▣ ⊡
Nearby Facilities ⌐ ✔
⚦ Dumfries
Beside a loch and adjacent to a golf course.
Ideal touring. Dogs are welcome if kept on
leads.

LOCHNAW

Drumlochart Caravan Park, Lochnaw, Leswalt, By Stranraer, Dumfries & Galloway, DG9 0RN.
Std: 01776 **Tel:** 870232 **Fax:** 870276
Email: office@drumlochart.co.uk
Website: www.drumlochart.co.uk
Nearest Town/Resort Stranraer
Acreage 22 **Open** March **to** October
Access Good **Site** Level
Sites Available ⌀ ⛺ **Total** 30
Facilities ⚡ ⌂ ⅏ ♨ ⌿ ⊙ ♨ SI
⬚ ⬚ ⬚ ⌁ ⬚⊡
Nearby Facilities ⌿ ✎ ⚓ ⛳ U
Woodland setting with a 10 acre loch for rowing boats and free fishing.

MONREITH

Knock School Caravan Park, Monreith, Newton Stewart, Dumfries & Galloway, DG8 8NJ.
Std: 01988 **Tel:** 700414/700409
Email: heywoodsimon@hotmail.com
Nearest Town/Resort Port William
Directions 3 miles south on A747 at crossroads to golf course.
Acreage 1 **Open** Easter **to** October
Access Good **Site** Lev/Slope
Sites Available ⚑ ⌀ ⛺ **Total** 15
Facilities ⚡ ⌿ ⌂ ⅏ ♨ SI ⌁⊡
Nearby Facilities ⌿ ✎ U
Near sandy beaches and golf. One hard standing pitch available.

MONREITH

Monreith Sands Holiday Park, Newton Stewart, Dumfries & Galloway, DG8 9LJ.
Std: 01998 **Tel:** 700218
Nearest Town/Resort Port William
Directions 2 miles south of Port William.
Acreage 2
Access Good **Site** Lev/Slope
Sites Available ⚑ ⌀ ⛺ **Total** 20
Facilities ⅏ ♨ ⌿ ⊙ ♨ SI ⅏ Ⅸ ⬚ ⌁⊡
Nearby Facilities ⌿ ✎ ⚓ ⛳ U ♪
⚓ Stranraer
Beach 200 yards, quiet site. Golf 1 mile.

NEWTON STEWART

Glentrool Holiday Park, Glentrool, Nr. Newton Stewart, Dumfries & Galloway, DG8 6RN.
Std: 01671 **Tel:** 840280
Email: glentroolpark@freeuk.com
Website: www.glentroolpark.freeuk.com
Nearest Town/Resort Glentrool
Directions Situated off the A714, 9 miles north of Newton Stewart, ½ mile south of Glentrool Village.
Acreage 7½ **Open** March **to** October
Access Good **Site** Level
Sites Available ⚑ ⌀ ⛺ **Total** 17

Facilities ⚓ ⚡ ⌂ ⅏ ♨ ⌿ ⊙ ⬚⊡
Nearby Facilities ⌿ ✎ U ♪
⚓ Barhill
On edge of forest, ideal touring. Fly fishing on site.

PALNACKIE

Barlochan Caravan Park, Palnackie, By Castle Douglas, Dumfries & Galloway, DG7 1PF.
Std: 01556 **Tel:** 600256
Email: cades@barlochan.co.uk
Website: www.gillespie-leisure.com
Nearest Town/Resort Dalbeattie
Directions From Dalbeattie take the A711 west. Turn left at the T-Junction (traffic lights), park is on the right in 2 miles.
Acreage 8 **Open** April **to** October
Access Good **Site** Lev/Slope
Sites Available ⚑ ⌀ ⛺ **Total** 80
Facilities ⚓ ⚡ ⅏ ♨ ⌿ ⊙ ♨ SI ⬚ ⬚
⬚ ⅏ ⌁⊡
Nearby Facilities ⌿ ✎ ⚓ U
Quiet, terraced park overlooking a river estuary. Own coarse fishing loch (free). Thistle Award holiday caravans to let. Ideal touring base. For Bookings please telephone 01557 870267.

PORTPATRICK

Galloway Point Holiday Park, Portree Farm, Portpatrick, Stranraer, Dumfries & Galloway, DG9 9AA.
Std: 01776 **Tel:** 810561 **Fax:** 810561
Nearest Town/Resort Portpatrick
Directions A75 from Dumfries. A77 from Glasgow and Stranraer. ½ mile south of Portpatrick.
Acreage 17 **Open** Easter **to** Mid October
Access Good **Site** Lev/Slope
Sites Available ⚑ ⌀ ⛺ **Total** 100
Facilities ⚡ ⅏ ♨ ⌿ ⊙ ♨ Ⅸ Ⅸ ⬚
⬚⚕ ⬚ ⅏ ⌁⊡
Nearby Facilities ⌿ ✎ ⚓ U ♪ ♪ ♪
Overlooking Irish Sea. Only ten minutes walk to fishing village of Portpatrick. Botanical gardens nearby. David Bellamy Silver Award for Conservation, AA 3 Pennants and RAC Appointed.

PORTPATRICK

Sunnymeade Caravan Park, Portpatrick, Nr. Stranraer, Dumfries & Galloway, DG9 8LN
Std: 01776 **Tel:** 810293 **Fax:** 810293
Email: info@sunnymeade98.freeserve.co.uk
Website: www.sunny-meade.co.uk
Nearest Town/Resort Portpatrick
Directions A77 to Portpatrick. First left on entering village, park is ¼ mile on the left.
Open Easter **to** October
Access Good **Site** Lev/Slope
Sites Available ⚑ ⌀ ⛺

Facilities ⚡ ⌂ ⅏ ♨ ⌿ ⊙ ♨ Ⅸ ⬚ ⬚ ⅏ ⬚⊡
Nearby Facilities ⌿ ✎ ⚓ U ♪
⚓ Stranraer
Overlooking Irish Sea. Private fishing pond on the park. Near golf, beach, bowling, fishing .

PORTWILLIAM

West Barr Caravan Park, West Barr, Portwilliam, Newton Stewart, Dumfries & Galloway, DG8 9QS.
Std: 01988 **Tel:** 700367
Nearest Town/Resort Portwilliam
Directions 1½ miles north of Portwilliam on the A747.
Open April **to** October
Access Good **Site** Level
Sites Available ⚑ ⌀ ⛺ **Total** 6
Facilities ⚡ ♨ ⅏ ♨ ⊙ ⬚ ⬚ ⬚⊡
Nearby Facilities ⌿ ✎ ⚓ U ♪
⚓ Stranraer
Small site on the shores of Luce Bay. Ideal for touring Galloway.

ROCKCLIFFE

Castle Point Caravan Park, Rockcliffe by Dalbeattie, Dumfries & Galloway, DG5 4QL.
Std: 01556 **Tel:** 630248
Email: kce22@dial.pipex.com
Nearest Town/Resort Rockcliffe
Directions In Dalbeattie take A710. 5 miles turn right to Rockcliffe. Sign for park in 1 mile near entrance to village.
Acreage 5 **Open** March **to** October
Access Good **Site** Level
Sites Available ⚑ ⌀ ⛺ **Total** 55
Facilities ⚡ ♨ ♨ ⅏ ♨ ⊙ ⬚ ⬚⊡ ⬚
Nearby Facilities ⌿ ✎ ⚓ ⛳ U
Overlooking sea and Rockcliffe Bay, (shore 200yds). Very quiet and well kept park with a lovely view. Website: http://homepage.mac.com/castle_point_site/personalpage3.html

SANDHEAD

Sands of Luce Caravan Park, Sandhead, Stranraer, Dumfries & Galloway, DG9 9JR.
Std: 01776 **Tel:** 830456 **Fax:** 830456
Email: sandsofluce@aol.com
Website: www.sandsofluce.co.uk
Nearest Town/Resort Stranraer
Directions From Stranraer follow the A77 to the A716. Site entrance is 1 mile south of Stoneykirk Village at the junction of the A716 and the B7084.
Acreage 12 **Open** Mid March **to** October
Access Good **Site** Lev/Slope
Sites Available ⚑ ⌀ ⛺ **Total** 90
Facilities ⚓ ⚡ ♨ ⅏ ♨ ⊙ ⬚ SI Ⅸ ⬚ ⬚ ⅏ ⌁⊡ ⬚
Nearby Facilities ⌿ ✎ ⚓ U ♪
Site extends directly onto a wide sandy beach. Ideal for children and watersports.

SANQUHAR

Castleview Caravan Site, Townfoot, Sanquhar, Dumfries & Galloway, DG4 6AX
Std: 01659 **Tel:** 50291
Nearest Town/Resort Sanquhar
Directions On the A76 at the south end of Sanquhar, within 30mph.
Acreage 2 **Open** March **to** October
Access Good **Site** Level
Sites Available ▲ ⊞ ⊟ **Total** 15
Facilities ⨍ ⬚ ⊞ ⬚ ⬚ ⊡⬚⬚ ⬚⬚ ⬚⬚ ⬚⬚
Nearby Facilities ⬚ ✓ ∪ ⬚
  ⬚ Sanquhar

STRANRAER

Aird Donald Caravan Park, Stranraer, Dumfries & Galloway, DG9 8RN.
Std: 01776 **Tel:** 702025
Email: airddimman@u-net.com
Website: www.aird-donald.co.uk
Nearest Town/Resort Stranraer
Directions Off A75 entering Stranraer. Signposted.
Acreage 12 **Open** All Year
Access Good **Site** Level
Sites Available ▲ ⊞ ⊟ **Total** 100
Facilities ⬚ ⨍ ⬚ ⬚ ⬚ ⬚⬚⬚ ⬚ ⬚ ⬚⬚⬚
Nearby Facilities ⬚ ✓ ⬚ ⬚ ∪ ⬚ ⬚ ⬚
  ⬚ Stranraer
Only 1 mile east of Stranraer town. Ideal touring. Also tarmac hard standing for touring caravans in wet weather. Ideal site for ferry to Ireland. New toilet and shower block. Leisure centre nearby.

THORNHILL

Penpont Caravan & Camping Park, Penpont, Thornhill, Dumfries & Galloway, DG3 4BH.
Std: 01848 **Tel:** 330470
Email: penpont.caravan.park@ukgateway.net
Nearest Town/Resort Thornhill
Directions 2 miles west of Thornhill on A702, on the left just before Penpont Village.
Acreage 1¾ **Open** April **to** October
Access Good **Site** Lev/Slope
Sites Available ▲ ⊞ ⊟ **Total** 40
Facilities ⨍ ⬚ ⬚ ⬚⬚⬚ ⬚ ⬚⬚ ⬚⬚⬚
Nearby Facilities ⬚ ✓ ∪
  ⬚ Dumfries
Quiet and peaceful park in lovely countryside. Ideal touring centre. Cycling, walking, fishing and bird watching. AA Graded.

DUNBARTONSHIRE, WEST

BALLOCH, LOCH LOMOND

Lomond Woods Holiday Park, Tullichewan, Balloch, Loch Lomond, West Dunbartonshire, G83 8QP.
Std: 01389 **Tel:** 755000 **Fax:** 755563
Email: lomondwoods@holiday-parks.co.uk
Website: www.holiday-parks.co.uk
Nearest Town/Resort Balloch
Directions Follow international direction signs from A82 onto the A811 to Balloch.
Acreage 13 **Open** All Year
Access Good **Site** Level
Sites Available ▲ ⊞ ⊟ **Total** 140
Facilities ⬚ ⨍ ⬚ ⬚ ⬚ ⬚ ⬚⬚⬚ ⬚ ⬚ ⬚⬚⬚⬚⬚⬚⬚
Nearby Facilities ⬚ ✓ ⬚ ⬚ ∪ ⬚ ⬚ ⬚
  ⬚ Balloch
Premier family park. Next to Lomond Shores Visitor Attraction. Ideal for touring Loch Lomond, Trossachs and the West Highlands. Close to Glasgow.

FIFE

CRAIL

Ashburn House Caravan Site, St Andrews Road, Crail, Fife, KY10 3UL.
Std: 01333 **Tel:** 450314
Nearest Town/Resort Crail
Directions A917 coast road to St Andrews.
Acreage 3 **Open** March **to** October
Access Good **Site** Level
Sites Available ▲ ⊞ ⊟ **Total** 65
Facilities ⨍ ⬚ ⬚ ⬚ ⬚ ⬚⬚⬚
  ⬚⬚ ⬚ ⬚⬚⬚
Nearby Facilities ⬚ ✓ ⬚ ⬚ ∪ ⬚ ⬚
Near beach and coastal walks. Ideal for touring and golf.

ELIE

Shell Bay Caravan Park, Kincraig Hill, Elie, Fife, KY9 1HB.
Std: 01333 **Tel:** 330283 **Fax:** 330008
Nearest Town/Resort Leven
Directions On the A917 2 miles from Elie.
Open 21 March **to** 31 October
Access Good **Site** Level
Sites Available ▲ ⊞□ **Total** 120
Facilities ⨍ ⬚ ⬚ ⬚ ⬚ ⬚⬚⬚ ⬚ ⬚ ⬚ ⬚ ⬚
  ⬚⬚ ⬚ ⬚ ⬚ ⬚ ⬚ ⬚ ⬚ ⬚ ⬚⬚⬚⬚
Nearby Facilities ⬚ ✓ ⬚ ⬚ ∪ ⬚ ⬚ ⬚
  ⬚ Kirkcaldy
On the beach with a children's club and Free entertainment.

KIRKCALDY

Dunnikier Caravan Park, Dunnikier Way, Kirkcaldy, Fife, KY1 3ND.
Std: 01592 **Tel:** 267563
Web: www.dunnikiercaravanpark.co.uk
Nearest Town/Resort Kirkcaldy
Directions Leave the M90 at junction 2A and take the A92. Leave the A92 at Kirkcaldy West and take the road to Kirkcaldy. At the retail park roundabout take the third exit and follow the road for 1¼ miles, site is on the left.
Acreage 7¾ **Open** 1 March **to** 31 Jan
Access Good **Site** Level
Sites Available ▲ ⊞ ⊟ **Total** 60
Facilities ⬚ ⨍ ⬚ ⬚ ⬚ ⬚ ⬚⬚⬚ ⬚ ⬚
  ⬚ ⬚ ⬚ ⬚⬚⬚
Nearby Facilities ⬚ ✓ ⬚ ⬚ ∪ ⬚ ⬚
Within easy reach (by road or rail) of Edinburgh and Dundee.

LEVEN

Letham Feus Caravan Park, Cupar Road, Leven, Fife, KY8 5NT.
Std: 01333 **Tel:** 351900 **Fax:** 351900
Email: slcar@freenetname.co.uk
Nearest Town/Resort Leven
Directions On the A916 2 miles north east of Kennoway.
Acreage 3 **Open** April **to** September
Access Good **Site** Gently Sloping
Sites Available ▲ ⊞ ⊟ **Total** 21
Facilities ⨍ ⬚ ⬚ ⬚ ⬚⬚⬚ ⬚ ⬚ ⬚ ⬚
  ⬚ ⬚⬚⬚⬚
Nearby Facilities ⬚ ✓ ⬚ ⬚ ∪ ⬚
Small, peaceful site with wonderful sea views of Firth of Forth. 5 minutes from Letham, 3 minutes from East Neuk and golf courses galore. Ideal for St Andrews. Holiday Home hire and sales.

LEVEN

Woodland Gardens Caravan & Camping Park, Woodland Gardens, Blindwell Road, Lundin Links, Leven, Fife, KY8 5QG.
Std: 01333 **Tel:** 360319
Email: woodlandgardens@lineone.net
Website: www.woodland-gardens.co.uk
Nearest Town/Resort Leven
Directions On the A915 Kirkcaldy, Leven and St. Andrews road, 3 miles east of Leven at the east end of Lundin Links turn north, signposted.
Acreage 1 **Open** April **to** October
Access Good **Site** Level
Sites Available ▲ ⊞ ⊟ **Total** 20
Facilities ⨍ ⬚ ⬚ ⬚ ⬚⬚⬚ ⬚ ⬚ ⬚⬚ ⬚ ⬚ ⬚ ⬚ ⬚⬚⬚
Nearby Facilities ⬚ ✓ ⬚ ⬚ ∪ ⬚ ⬚
  ⬚ Kirkcaldy
Small, exclusive, quiet site. Ideal for golfing walking or relaxing around East Fife. Close to a sandy beach. Within easy reach of Edinburgh.

ST. ANDREWS

Craigtoun Meadows Holiday Park, Mount Melville, St. Andrews, Fife, KY16 8PQ
Std: 01334 **Tel:** 475959 **Fax:** 476424
Email: craigtoun@aol.com
Website: www.craigtounmeadows.co.uk
Nearest Town/Resort St. Andrews
Directions 1½ miles west of St. Andrews on the Craigtoun road.
Acreage 32 **Open** March **to** October
Access Good **Site** Lev/Slope
Sites Available ▲ ⊞ ⊟ **Total** 70
Facilities ⬚ ⨍ ⬚ ⬚ ⬚ ⬚ ⬚⬚⬚ ⬚ ⬚
  ⬚ ⬚ ⬚ ⬚ ⬚ ⬚⬚⬚⬚
Nearby Facilities ⬚ ✓ ⬚ ⬚ ∪ ⬚
  ⬚ Leuchars
Rural, landscaped park. Ideal base for exploring Fife.

ST. MONANS

St. Monans Caravan Park, St. Monans, Fife, KY10 2DN.
Std: 01333 **Tel:** 730778 **Fax:** 730466
Nearest Town/Resort St. Andrews
Directions Park is on the A917 at east end of St. Monans.
Acreage 1 **Open** 21 March **to** October
Access Good **Site** Level
Sites Available ▲ ⊞ ⊟ **Total** 18
Facilities ⨍ ⬚ ⬚ ⬚⬚⬚ ⬚ ⬚ ⬚ ⬚ ⬚ ⬚⬚⬚
Nearby Facilities ⬚ ✓ ⬚ ⬚ ∪ ⬚ ⬚
  ⬚ Leuchars
Small, quiet park, near the sea and small villages with harbours.

HIGHLAND

ACHARACLE

Resipole Farm Caravan & Camping Park, Loch Sunart, Acharacle, Highland, PH36 4HX.
Std: 01967 **Tel:** 431235 **Fax:** 431777
Email: info@resipole.co.uk
Website: www.resipole.co.uk
Nearest Town/Resort Fort William
Directions From Fort William take the A82 south for 8 miles, across Corran Ferry, then take the A861 to Strontian and Salen. Site is 7¼ miles west of Strontian on the roadside.
Acreage 6 **Open** April **to** October
Access Good **Site** Level
Sites Available ▲ ⊞ ⊟ **Total** 60
Facilities ⬚ ⨍ ⬚ ⬚ ⬚ ⬚ ⬚⬚⬚ ⬚ ⬚
  ⬚ ⬚ ⬚ ⬚ ⬚ ⬚⬚⬚⬚
Nearby Facilities ⬚ ✓ ⬚ ⬚ ∪
  ⬚ Fort William
Loch side, roomy site with scenic views. Central to the area. Golf on site.

ARISAIG

Gorton Sands Caravan Site, Gorton Farm, Arisaig, Highland, PH39 4NS.
Std: 01687 **Tel:** 450283
Nearest Town/Resort Arisaig
Directions A830 Fort William/Mallaig road, 2 miles west of Arisaig, turn left at sign 'Back of Keppoch', ¾ mile to road end across cattle grid.
Acreage 6 **Open** April **to** September
Access Good **Site** Level
Sites Available ▲ ⊞ ⊟ **Total** 45

Facilities ⚡ ! ⏣ ⓌⒸ ⚓ ⌒ ⊙⌐ ▭ ◻ ☎
⬚ ⏢ ⊕ ➔⬚ ⬚
Nearby Facilities ⌐ ✚ ⚓ ↘ ∪ ⚐
 ⚑ Arisaig
On sandy beach, views of Isles of Skye, Eigg and Rhum. Boat trips to Isles, hill walking, ideal for bathing or boating.

ARISAIG
Invercaimbe Caravan & Camp Site, Arisaig, Highland, PH39 4NT.
Std: 01687 **Tel:** 450375 **Fax:** 450375
Email: joycew@madasafish.com
Nearest Town/Resort Fort William
Directions From Fort William take the A830 or 38 miles. Site is 1½ miles past Arisaig Village, first turning on the left after the bridge.
Acreage 1½ **Open** Easter **to** End Oct
Access Good **Site** Level
Sites Available ⚑ ⊞ ⊕ **Total** 26
Facilities ! ⓌⒸ ⌐ ⊙⌐ ☎ ♨ ⌕➔⬚
Nearby Facilities ⌐ ✚ ⚓ ↘ ⚑
 ⚑ Arisaig
On the beach, next to the sea and a river. Trips to all the islands locally.

ARISAIG
Portnardoran Caravan Site, Arisaig, Highland, PH39 4NT.
Std: 01687 **Tel:** 450267 **Fax:** 450267
Nearest Town/Resort Mallaig
Directions 2 miles north of Arisaig village, on Fort William - Arisaig road A830.
Acreage 2 **Open** Easter **to** October
Access Good **Site** Level
Sites Available ⚑ ⊞ ⊕ **Total** 40
Facilities ! ⓌⒸ ⚓ ⌐ ⊙⌐ ◻ ♨ ⌕ ⚑ ⬚ ⌐➔⬚
Nearby Facilities ⌐ ✚ ⚓ ↘ ✚ ⚑
 ⚑ Arisaig
Beside silver sands, scenic views of inner Hebrides, safe for swimming.

ARISAIG
Silverbeach Caravan & Camping, Silverbeach, 5 Bunnacaimbe, Arisaig, Highland, PH39 4NT.
Std: 01687 **Tel:** 450630
Nearest Town/Resort Arisaig
Directions 2 miles north of Arisaig Village on the A830 Fort William to Mallaig road.
Acreage 2 **Open** May **to** September
Access Good **Site** Lev/Slope
Sites Available ⚑ ⊞ ⊕ **Total** 10
Facilities ! ⓌⒸ ⚓ ⌐ ⊙⌐ ☎ ⌐➔⬚
 ⚑ Arisaig
On the shoreline of a beautiful, sandy beach with views of the Isles of Eigg, Rum and Skye. Ideal for young families.

ARISAIG
Skyeview, Arisaig, Highland, PH39 4NJ.
Std: 01687 **Tel:** 450209
Nearest Town/Resort Arisaig
Directions 1 mile north of Arisaig just off the A830.
Acreage 1 **Open** April **to** October
Access Good **Site** Sloping
Sites Available Total 10
Facilities ! ⓌⒸ ⚓ ⌐ ⊙⌐ ⬚ ⌐➔
Nearby Facilities ⌐ ✚ ⚓ ↘ ∪
 ⚑ Arisaig
Panoramic views of Skye and the Inner Hebrides. Ideal for hill walking, fishing, golfing and boat trips.

AVIEMORE
Aviemore Mountain Resort Caravan Park, Aviemore, Highland, PH22 1PF.
Std: 01479 **Tel:** 810751 **Fax:** 811473
Nearest Town/Resort Aviemore
Directions Entrance to the park is off the main A9 at the south end of Aviemore.

Acreage 6 **Open** December **to** October
Access Good
Sites Available ⚑ ⊞ ⊕ **Total** 90
Facilities ! ⓌⒸ ⚓ ⌐ ⊙⌐ ⌦⌦➔⬚⬚ ⬚
Nearby Facilities ⌐ ✚ ⚓ ↘ ∪ ⚐ ⚑
 ⚑ Aviemore
Within walking distance of bars, restaurants and shops. Good for walking, fishing and ski-ing.

AVIEMORE
Glenmore - Forestry Commission, Glenmore, Near Aviemore, Highland, PH22 1QU.
Std: 01479 **Tel:** 861271
Email: fe.holidays@forestry.gsi.gov.uk
Website: www.forestholidays.co.uk
Nearest Town/Resort Aviemore
Directions From the A9 turn onto the B9152 south of Aviemore. At Aviemore turn right onto the B970, site is 5 miles.
Acreage 20 **Open** Mid Dec **to** End Oct
Access Good **Site** Level
Sites Available ⚑ ⊞ ⊕ **Total** 220
Facilities ! ⓌⒸ ⚓ ⌐ ⊙⌐ ⬚ ⬚⬚ ⬚ ⬚ ▭➔⬚⬚
Nearby Facilities ✚ ⚓ ↘ ∪ ⚑
In the heart of The Cairngorms. Near to Loch Morlich with its sandy beaches. Ideal for walking, cycling, mountaineering and winter sports. Near ski slopes.

AVIEMORE
High Range Touring Caravan Park, Grampian Road, Aviemore, Highland, PH22 1PT.
Std: 01479 **Tel:** 810636 **Fax:** 811322
Email: info@highrange.co.uk
Website: www.highrange.co.uk
Nearest Town/Resort Aviemore
Directions Off the B9152 at the south end of Aviemore, directly opposite the B970.
Acreage 2 **Open** 1 Dec **to** 31 Oct
Access Good **Site** Level
Sites Available ⚑ ⊞ ⊕ **Total** 44
Facilities ! ⓌⒸ ⚓ ⌐ ⊙⌐ ◻ ⬚ ☎ ✚ ⚐ ⌦➔⬚⬚
Nearby Facilities ⌐ ✚ ⚓ ↘ ∪ ⚐ ⚑
Splendid view of Craigellachie Nature Reserve, the Lairig Ghru Pass and the peaks and ski runs of the Cairngorms.

AVIEMORE
Rothiemurchus Camp & Caravan Park, Coylumbridge, Nr. Aviemore, Highland, PH22 1QU.
Std: 01479 **Tel:** 812800 **Fax:** 812800
Email:
lizsangster@rothiemurchus.freeserve.co.uk
Website: www.ukparks.com
Nearest Town/Resort Aviemore
Directions From Aviemore take the ski road towards Glenmore. Park on right in 1¼ miles.
Acreage 4 **Open** All Year
Access Good **Site** Level
Sites Available ⚑ ⊞ ⊕ **Total** 39
Facilities ! ⓌⒸ ⚓ ⌐ ⊙⌐ ☎ ⬚♨ ⬚ ⬚ ⊕➔⬚⬚
Nearby Facilities ⌐ ✚ ⚓ ↘ ∪ ⚐ ⚑
Environmentally friendly park alongside a river, in a pinewood setting. Close to Aviemore, ideal for ski-ing, boating, walking et cetera.

BALMACARA
Reraig Caravan Site, Balmacara, Kyle of Lochalsh, Highland, IV40 8DH.
Std: 01599 **Tel:** 566215
Website: www.reraigcs.co.uk
Nearest Town/Resort Kyle of Lochalsh
Directions On the A87, 1¾ miles west of junction with A890.

Acreage 2 **Open** Mid April **to** September
Access Good **Site** Level
Sites Available ⚑ ⊞ ⊕ **Total** 45
Facilities ! ⓌⒸ ⚓ ⌐ ⊙⌐ ☎ ⬚➔⬚⬚
Nearby Facilities
 ⚑ Kyle of Lochalsh
Hotel adjacent to site. Dishwashing sinks, hairdryers. Forest walks adjacent to site. No bookings by telephone. No large tents. No awnings during July and August.

BEAULY
Lovat Bridge Caravan Park, Lovat Bridge, Beauly, Inverness-shire, IV4 7AY.
Std: 01463 **Tel:** 782374
Email: allanlymburn@beauly782.fsnet.co.uk
Website: www.lovatbridge.fsnet.co.uk
Nearest Town/Resort Beauly
Directions 1 mile south of Beauly on the old A9.
Acreage 12 **Open** 15 March **to** 15 Oct
Access Good **Site** Level
Sites Available ⚑ ⊞ ⊕ **Total** 40
Facilities ! ⓌⒸ ⊕ ✄ ⓌⒸ ⚓ ⌐ ⊙⌐ ◻ ⊕ ⬚ ☎ ⬚
♠ ⬚ ⊕➔⬚⬚
Nearby Facilities ⌐ ✚ ⚓ ↘ ∪ ⚐ ⚑
Sheltered site alongside a river. Ideal touring.

BETTYHILL
Craigdhu Caravan & Camping, Bettyhill, Nr. Thurso, Highland, KW14 7SP.
Std: 01641 **Tel:** 521273
Nearest Town/Resort Thurso
Directions Main Thurso/Tongue road.
Acreage 4½ **Open** April **to** October
Access Good **Site** Lev/Slope
Sites Available ⚑ ⊞ ⊕ **Total** 90
Facilities ! ⓌⒸ ⚓ ⌐ ⊙⌐ ☎ ⬚ ⬚➔⬚⬚
Nearby Facilities ✚ ⚓ ∪ ⚐ ⚑
 ⚑ Kinbrace
Near beautiful beaches, river, fishing. Scenic views. Ideal touring. Rare plants. New swimming pool, telephone, cafe/restaurant and licensed club nearby.

BROADFORD
Campbell's "Cullin View" Caravan & Camping Site, Breakish, Isle of Skye, Highland, IV42 8PY.
Std: 01471 **Tel:** Broadford 822248
Nearest Town/Resort Broadford
Directions 6 miles from Skye Bridge ferry at side of garage.
Acreage 4 **Open** April **to** October
Access Good **Site** Lev/Slope
Sites Available ⚑ ⊞ ⊕
Facilities ⊕ ⚡ ! ⓌⒸ ⚓ ⌐ ⊙⌐
⬚ ⊕ ⬚➔⬚⬚
Nearby Facilities ⌐ ✚ ⚓ ↘ ∪ ⚐ ⚑
Scenic views.

BRORA
Green Park Caravan & Camping Site, Dalchalm, Brora, Highland, KW9 6LP.
Std: 01408 **Tel:** 621513
Nearest Town/Resort Brora
Directions 1 mile north of Brora on the A9.
Acreage 2½+ **Open** May **to** September
Access Good **Site** Level
Sites Available ⚑ ⊞ ⊕ **Total** 30
Facilities ! ⓌⒸ ⌐ ⊙⌐ ☎ ⬚ ⊕➔⬚⬚
Nearby Facilities ⌐ ✚ ⚓ ↘ ⚐
 ⚑ Brora
Close to Brora Golf Course, ¼ mile from a sandy beach and near the River Brora and Loch for fishing.

DINGWALL
Camping & Caravanning Club Site, Jubilee Park Road, Dingwall, Highland, IV15 9QZ.
Std: 01349 **Tel:** 862236

Website:
www.campingandcaravanningclub.co.uk
Nearest Town/Resort Dingwall
Directions From the northwest on the A862 in Dingwall turn right into Hill Street (past the Shell Filling Station), turn right into High Street then turn first left after the railway bridge, site is ahead.
Acreage 6½ **Open** March to Nov
Access Good **Site** Level
Sites Available A ⊕ ⊟ **Total** 85
Facilities ⅃ ⌂ ⌂ ⌂ ⍾ Γ ⊙ ⊣ ⌷
⌂ ⦿ ⌂ ⊣ ⌷ ⌷
Nearby Facilities Γ ✔ ⚓ ⅄
Central for touring the Highlands. Train and ferry links to the Isle of Skye. Close to the city of Inverness. BTB Graded. Non members welcome.

DORNIE

Ardelve, Dornie, Kyle, Highland, IV40 8DY
Nearest Town/Resort Kyle of Lochalsh
Directions Just off A87, Invergarry/Kyle road.
Acreage 2 **Open** May to September
Access Good **Site** Sloping
Sites Available A ⊕ ⊟
Facilities ⌂ ⌂ Γ ⊙⌂⊣⌷
⊭ Kyle of Lochalsh
Ideal for touring Skye. Near Eilan Donan Castle. Static caravans for hire.

DORNOCH

Dornoch Caravan & Camping Park, The Links, Dornoch, Highland, IV25 3LX.
Std: 01862 **Tel:** 810423 **Fax:** 810423
Email: info@dornochcaravans.co.uk
Website: www.dornochcaravans.co.uk
Nearest Town/Resort Dornoch
Directions From A9, 6 miles north of Tain, turn right into Dornoch. Turn right at the bottom of the square.
Acreage 25 **Open** April to 22nd October
Access Good **Site** Level
Sites Available A ⊕ ⊟ **Total** 130
Facilities ⅃ ⅃ ⌂ ⌂ Γ ⊙⌂ ⊣ ⌷ ⌷ ⦿
⌢ ⅊ ⌂ ⌂ ⊙ ⌂ ⦿⊣⌷⌷
Nearby Facilities Γ ✔ ⚓ ⅄
⊭ Tain
Beach, championship golf course, cathedral town. Scenic views, ideal touring.

DORNOCH

Seaview Farm Caravan Park, Hilton, Dornoch, Highland, IV25 3PW.
Std: 01862 **Tel:** 810294
Nearest Town/Resort Dornoch
Directions In Dornoch turn left at Tourist Office for 1½ miles.
Acreage 3½ **Open** Easter to October
Access Good **Site** Level
Sites Available A ⊕ ⊟ **Total** 24
Facilities ⅃ ⌂ ⌂⊙⌂⊣ ⌷ ⌂ ⌂⊣⌷
Nearby Facilities Γ ✔ ⅊ ⅄
⊭ Tain
Just a 10 minute walk to a pleasant beach. Adjacent to Royal Dornoch Golf Course. Near to Dornoch Cathedral and Dunrobin Castle.

DRUMNADROCHIT

Bearnock Campsite, Glenurquhart, Drumnadrochit, Highland, IV63 6TN.
Std: 01456 **Tel:** 476353/476296
Nearest Town/Resort Drumnadrochit
Directions On the A831 midway between Drumnadrochit and Cannich.
Open March to October
Access Good **Site** Level
Sites Available A ⊕ ⊟ **Total** 15
Facilities ⌂ ⊟ ⌢ ⅊ ✗ ⌂⊣⌷
Nearby Facilities ✔ ⅄ ⊙ ⅄
⊭ Inverness
Alongside a river for fishing. Ideal for touring and climbing.

DRUMNADROCHIT

Borlum Farm Caravan & Camping Park, Drumnadrochit, Highland, IV63 6XN.
Std: 01456 **Tel:** 450220 **Fax:** 450358
Email: info@borlum.com
Website: www.borlum.com
Nearest Town/Resort Drumnadrochit
Directions Take A82 from Drumnadrochit towards Fort William site is on right.
Acreage 2 **Open** April to October
Access Good **Site** Lev/Slope
Sites Available A ⊕ ⊟ **Total** 25
Facilities ⅃ ⌂ ⌂ ⌢ Γ ⊙⌂ ⌂⊣⌷ ⌷
Nearby Facilities ✔ ⊙ ⅊
⊭ Inverness
Overlooking Loch Ness, Ideal touring centre.

DUNDONNELL

Badrallach Bothy & Camp Site, Croft 9, Badrallach, Dundonnell, Highland, IV23 2QP
Std: 01854 **Tel:** 633281
Email: michael-stott2@virgin.net
Website: www.badrallach.com
Nearest Town/Resort Ullapool/Gairloch
Directions Off the A832, 1 mile east of the Dundonnell Hotel take a left turn onto a single track road to Badrallach, 7 miles to lochshore site.
Acreage 1 **Open** All Year
Access Poor **Site** Level
Sites Available A ⊕ ⊟ **Total** 15
Facilities ⅃ ⌂ ⌂ Γ ⊣ ⌂ ⌂ ⅊ ⊣ ⌷ ⌷
Nearby Facilities ✔ ⚓ ✓ ⅄
⊭ Garve/Inverness
Lochshore site on a working croft, overlooking Anteallach on the Scoraig Peninsular. Bothy, peat stove. Otters, porpoises, Golden Eagles and wild flowers galore. Total peace and quiet - Perfect! Caravans by prior booking only.

DURNESS

Sango Sands Caravan & Camping Site, Durness, Sutherland, Highlands, IV27 4PP
Std: 01971 **Tel:** 511262/511222 **Fax:** 511205
Nearest Town/Resort Durness
Directions On the A838 in the centre of Durness Village.
Acreage 12 **Open** April to 15 October
Access Good **Site** Level
Sites Available A ⊕ ⊟ **Total** 82
Facilities ⅃ ⌂ ⌂ Γ ⊙⌂ ⌂ ⌷ ⌢ ⌂ ⅊ ⌂
✗ ⌂ ⌂⊣⌷
Nearby Facilities Γ ✔ ⚓ ✓ ⅄
Overlooking Sango Bay.

EDINBANE

Loch Greshornish Caravan & Camp Site, Borve, Arnisort, Isle of Skye, Highland, IV51 9PS.
Std: 01470 **Tel:** 582230 **Fax:** 582230
Email: info@greshcamp.freeserve.co.uk
Website: www.greshcamp.freeserve.co.uk
Nearest Town/Resort Portree
Directions On entry to Portree turn left onto the A850 to Dunvegan. Follow this road for approx. 12 miles, campsite is located on the right hand side.
Acreage 5 **Open** 1 April to 15 October
Access Good **Site** Level
Sites Available A ⊕ ⊟ **Total** 130
Facilities ⅃ ⌂ ⌂ Γ ⊙⌂ ⌢ ⅊ ⌂⊣
Nearby Facilities Γ ✔ ✓ ⊙ ⅊
⊭ Kyle of Lochalsh
Alongside a loch with mainly level pitches and an open outlook. Quiet yet close to the village of Edinbane (1 mile).

EVANTON

Black Rock Caravan & Camping Park, Evanton, Highland, IV16 9UN.
Std: 01349 **Tel:** 830917 **Fax:** 830917

Email: relax@blackrockscot.fsnet.co.uk
Nearest Town/Resort Dingwall
Directions A9 north from Inverness for 1? miles. Turn left for Evanton B817, procee? for ¾ mile.
Acreage 4½ **Open** April to October
Access Good **Site** Level
Sites Available A ⊕ ⊟ **Total** 67
Facilities ⅃ ⌂ ⌂ ⌂ Γ ⊙⌂ ⌂⊣ ⌷ ⌷
⌂ ⦿ ⌂ ⊛ ⌂⊣⌷
Nearby Facilities Γ ✔ ⚓ ✓ ⊙ ⅊ ⅄
⊭ Dingwall
Centrally situated for touring the Highland? Bordered on one side by River Glass. ? bed hostel on site.

FORT AUGUSTUS

Fort Augustus Caravan & Camping Park, Market Hill, Fort Augustus, Highland, PH32 4DS.
Std: 01320 **Tel:** 366618/366360 **Fax:** 366360
Nearest Town/Resort Fort Augustus
Directions ¼ mile south of Fort Augustu? on the A82.
Acreage 3½ **Open** Mid April to Sept
Access Good **Site** Level
Sites Available A ⊕ ⊟ **Total** 50
Facilities ⅃ ⅃ ⌂ Γ ⊙⌂⊣ ⌂ ⦿
⌂ ⌂ ⌂⊣⌷
Nearby Facilities Γ ✔ ⚓ ✓ ⊙ ⅊ ⅄
⊭ Spean Bridge
Ideal touring alongside golf course, ne? Loch Ness, scenic views and hill walking.

FORT WILLIAM

Linnhe Lochside Holidays, Corpach, Fort William, Highland, PH33 7NL.
Std: 01397 **Tel:** 772376 **Fax:** 772007
Email: holidays@linnhe.demon.co.uk
Website: www.linnhe-lochside-holidays.co.uk
Nearest Town/Resort Fort William
Directions On the A830, 1 mile west ? Corpach village, 5 miles from Fort Willia?
Acreage 14 **Open** 15th Dec to 31st Oct
Access Good **Site** Level
Sites Available A ⊕ ⊟ **Total** 65
Facilities ⅃ ⌂ ⌂ ⌂ Γ ⊙⌂⊣ ⌂ ⦿
⌢ ⅊ ⌂ ⦿ ⌂ ⌂⊣⌷
Nearby Facilities Γ ✔ ⚓ ✓ ⊙ ⅊ ⅄
⊭ Corpach
Practical Caravan 'Best in Region 2000' an? Calor/STB Best Park in Scotland 199? Award. Magnificent scenery from this to? quality park with a private beach and bo? slipway. Mains serviced pitches availabl? Toddlers play room. Holiday chalets an? caravans for hire.

GAIRLOCH

Gairloch Holiday Park, Strath, Gairloch, Highland, IV21 2BX.
Std: 01445 **Tel:** 712373
Email: info@gairlochcaravanpark.com
Website: www.gairlochcaravanpark.com
Nearest Town/Resort Gairloch
Directions Turn off the A832 at Auchtercai? onto the B8021. In approx. ¼ mile turn rig? by Millcroft Hotel then immediately right in? the site.
Acreage 6 **Open** Easter to Mid October
Access Good **Site** Level
Sites Available A ⊕ ⊟ **Total** 75
Facilities ⅃ ⌂ ⌂ ⌂ Γ ⊙⌂⊣ ⌂ ⦿
⌂ ⅊ ⌂ ⌂⊣⌷ ⌷
Nearby Facilities Γ ✔ ⚓ ✓ ⊙ ⅄
⊭ Achnasheen
Near the beach. In the village centre fo? shops, hotels and restaurants. STB 4 Sta? Graded Park and AA 3 Pennants.

GAIRLOCH

Sands Holiday Centre, Gairloch,
Highland, IV21 2DL.
Std: 01445 **Tel:** 712152 **Fax:** 712518
Email: litsands@aol.com
Website:
www.highlandcaravancamping.co.uk
Nearest Town/Resort Gairloch
Directions Turn west off the A832 onto the
B8012. Site 3 miles on, beside sandy beach.
Acreage 55 **Open** April to October
Access Good **Site** Lev/Slope
Sites Available ▲ ♠ ⊞ **Total** 250
Facilities ✚ 🏠 ⬚ ⬚ ⬚ ⬚ ⬚ ⬚
⬚ ⬚ ⬚ ⬚ ⬚ ⬚ ⬚
Nearby Facilities ⬚ ⬚ ⬚ ⬚ ⬚ ⬚ ⬚
‡ Achnasheen
Site is near beach, scenic views, river, loch
fishing and launching slip. Tennis and
climbing wall in Gairloch Leisure Centre.

GLENCOE

Invercoe Caravan & Camping Park,
Glencoe, Ballachulish, Highland, PA49 4HP
Std: 01855 **Tel:** 811210 **Fax:** 811210
Email: invercoe@sol.co.uk
Website: www.invercoe.co.uk
Nearest Town/Resort Fort William
Directions Heading north on the A82 turn
right at Glencoe crossroads onto the B863.
Acreage 5 **Open** Easter to October
Access Good **Site** Level
Sites Available ▲ ♠ ⊞ **Total** 60
Facilities ♿ ✚ 🏠 ⬚ ⬚ ⬚ ⬚ ⬚ ⬚
⬚ ⬚ ⬚ ⬚ ⬚
Nearby Facilities ⬚ ⬚ ⬚
Lochside site with beautiful scenery. Ideal
centre for touring West Highlands. No
advanced bookings.

GLENCOE

Red Squirrel Campsite, Leacantuim
Farm, Glencoe, Highland, PA49 4HX.
Std: 01855 **Tel:** 811256
Nearest Town/Resort Fort William
Directions Off the main A82 in Glencoe
village, follow signs.
Acreage 20 **Open** All Year
Site Lev/Slope
Sites Available ▲ ♠
Facilities 🏠 ⬚ ⬚ ⬚ ⬚ ⬚ ⬚ ⬚
Nearby Facilities ⬚ ⬚ ⬚ ⬚ ⬚ ⬚
‡ Fort William
Casual and very different site. River for
swimming and centre of the mountains. 500
yards from a public telephone.

GRANTOWN-ON-SPEY

Grantown-on-Spey Caravan Park,
Seafield Avenue, Grantown-on-Spey,
Highland, PH26 3JQ.
Std: 01479 **Tel:** 872474
Website: www.caravansscotland.com

Nearest Town/Resort Grantown-on-Spey
Directions From Aviemore come into
Grantown high street, through the traffic
lights and turn left at the Bank of Scotland,
site signposted.
Acreage 27½ **Open** End March to Oct
Access Good **Site** Level
Sites Available ▲ ♠ ⊞ **Total** 150
Facilities ✚ 🏠 ⬚ ⬚ ⬚ ⬚ ⬚ ⬚ ⬚
⬚ ⬚ ⬚ ⬚ ⬚ ⬚ ⬚
Nearby Facilities ⬚ ⬚ ⬚ ⬚
‡ Aviemore
Quiet park, central for touring the Highlands
and the Whisky Trail. Good fishing, walking
and golf.

INVERGARRY

Faichem Park, Ardgarry Farm, Faichem,
Invergarry, Highland, PH35 4HG.
Std: 01809 **Tel:** 501226 **Fax:** 501307
Email: ardgarry.farm@lineone.net
Website: www.campsitesscotland.co.uk
Nearest Town/Resort Invergarry
Directions From the A82 at Invergarry take
the A87, continue for 1 mile. Turn right at
Faichem signpost, bear left up hill, first
entrance on the right.
Acreage 2 **Open** April to October
Access Good **Site** Lev/Slope
Sites Available ▲ ♠ ⊞ **Total** 30
Facilities ✚ 🏠 ⬚ ⬚ ⬚ ⬚ ⬚ ⬚ ⬚
Nearby Facilities ⬚ ⬚ ⬚ ⬚ ⬚ ⬚
‡ Spean Bridge
Panoramic views across Glengarry.

INVERGARRY

Faichemard Farm Camp Site,
Faichemard Farm, Invergarry, Highland,
PH35 4HG.
Std: 01809 **Tel:** 501314 **Fax:** 501314
Email: a&dgrant@fsbdial.co.uk
Nearest Town/Resort Fort William
Directions Take A82 to Invergarry (25
miles) travel west on A87 for 1 mile, take
side road on right at sign for Faichem, go
past Ardgarry Farm and Faichem Park
Camp Site to signpost A & D Grant.
Acreage 10 **Open** April to October
Access Good **Site** Lev/Slope
Sites Available ▲ ♠ ⊞ **Total** 40
Facilities ✚ 🏠 ⬚ ⬚ ⬚ ⬚
⬚ ⬚ ⬚ ⬚ ⬚ ⬚
Nearby Facilities ⬚ ⬚ ⬚ ⬚ ⬚ ⬚
Hill walking, bird watching, space and quiet.
Pitch price £5-£7, every pitch has its own
picnic table.

INVERMORISTON

Loch Ness Caravan & Camping Park,
Easter Port Clair, Invermorriston,
Highland, IV3 6YE.
Std: 01320 **Tel:** 351207 **Fax:** 351207
Nearest Town/Resort Inverness

Directions Main A82 road between Inverness
and Fort William. 35 miles either way.
Acreage 8 **Open** End Mar to End Oct
Access Good **Site** Level
Sites Available ▲ ♠ ⊞ **Total** 85
Facilities ✚ 🏠 ⬚ ⬚ ⬚ ⬚ ⬚ ⬚ ⬚
⬚ ⬚ ⬚ ⬚ ⬚ ⬚ ⬚
Nearby Facilities ⬚ ⬚ ⬚ ⬚ ⬚ ⬚ ⬚
Loch side site with scenic views. Ideal touring.
Pets are welcome with caravans only.

INVERNESS

**Auchnahillin Caravan & Camping
Centre,** Daviot East, Inverness, Highland,
IV2 5XQ.
Std: 01463 **Tel:** 772286 **Fax:** 772282
Email: info@auchnahillin.co.uk
Website: www.auchnahillin.co.uk
Nearest Town/Resort Inverness
Directions Drive south on the A9 from
Inverness for 5 miles, turn left onto the
B9154. Park is 1 mile from this junction in
Daviot East.
Acreage 12 **Open** Easter to October
Access Good **Site** Level
Sites Available ▲ ♠ ⊞ **Total** 100
Facilities ✚ 🏠 ⬚ ⬚ ⬚ ⬚ ⬚ ⬚ ⬚
⬚ ⬚ ⬚ ⬚ ⬚ ⬚ ⬚
Nearby Facilities ⬚ ⬚ ⬚ ⬚
touring area to discover grandeur of
Highlands. Scenic views.

INVERNESS

Bught Caravan Park, Bught Lane,
Inverness, Highland, IV3 5JR.
Std: 01463 **Tel:** 236920 **Fax:** 712850
Nearest Town/Resort Inverness
Directions On the A82 to town centre,
approx. 2 miles.
Acreage 4½ **Open** April to September
Access Good **Site** Level
Sites Available ▲ ♠ ⊞ **Total** 172
Facilities ♿ ✚ 🏠 ⬚ ⬚ ⬚ ⬚ ⬚ ⬚
⬚ ⬚ ⬚ ⬚
Nearby Facilities ⬚ ⬚ ⬚
Adjacent to a river, sports centre, aquadome,
golf course, Floral Hall, large play area
including a boating pond and mini railway.

INVERNESS

Scaniport Caravan & Camping Park,
Scaniport, Inverness, Highland, IV2 6DL.
Std: 01463 **Tel:** 751226
Email: sylviaphilip@aol.com
Nearest Town/Resort Inverness
Directions From Inverness take the B862
southwest towards Dores for approx. 4
miles.
Acreage 2 **Open** Easter to September
Access Good **Site** Level
Sites Available ▲ ♠ ⊞ **Total** 30
Facilities 🏠 ⬚ ⬚ ⬚ ⬚ ⬚ ⬚ ⬚
Nearby Facilities ⬚ ⬚
‡ Inverness

JOHN O'GROATS

John O'Groats Caravan & Camping Site, John O'Groats, Nr. Wick, Highland, KW1 4YS.
Std: 01955 **Tel:** 611329
Nearest Town/Resort John O' Groats
Directions End of A99 beside last house.
Acreage 4 **Open** April **to** October
Access Good **Site** Level
Sites Available ▲ ♦ ⊕ **Total** 90
Facilities &
Nearby Facilities ✓
On sea shore with clear view of Orkney Islands. Day trips to Orkney by passenger ferry, jetty nearby. Hotel and snack bar within 150 yards. Cliff scenery and sea birds 1½ miles.

JOHN O'GROATS

Stroma View Huna, Wick, Highland, KW1 4YL.
Std: 01955 **Tel:** 611313
Website: www.google.com/stromaview
Nearest Town/Resort John O'Groats
Directions Take the A99 to John O'Groats, turn left at the Sea View Hotel and follow the A836 Thurso road for 1½ miles. Site is on the left opposite the Island of Stroma. Well signposted.
Acreage 1 **Open** April **to** October
Access Good **Site** Level
Sites Available ▲ ♦ ⊕ **Total** 30
Facilities
Nearby Facilities ✓
Near beach, sand. Views of Stroma, Orkney Isles. Dairy produce on site. Seal colony at Gills Bay, 1½ miles west of site. Ferry from Jog to Orkney daily. Free showers. Fast offshore sea cruises and fishing trips, weather permitting, on 105 "Tiger Lilly". 2-6 Berth caravans. All mod cons. Other Web Site: www.yell.com/ukcaravanparks

LAIDE

Gruinard Bay Caravan Park, Laide, Highland, IV22 2ND.
Std: 01445 **Tel:** 731225 **Fax:** 731225
Email: gruinard@ecosse.net
Website: www.highlandbreaks.com
Nearest Town/Resort Gairloch
Directions On the A832 5 miles north of Gairloch.
Acreage 3½ **Open** April **to** October
Access Good **Site** Level
Sites Available ▲ ♦ ⊕ **Total** 35
Facilities
Nearby Facilities
Beach front location with superb views to the mountains and islands. Ideal for walking, fishing and relaxing.

LAIRG

Dunroamin Caravan & Camping Park, Main Street, Lairg, Sutherland, IV27 4AR.
Std: 01549 **Tel:** 402447 **Fax:** 402784
Email: enquiries@lairgcaravanpark.co.uk
Website: www.lairgcaravanpark.co.uk
Nearest Town/Resort Lairg
Directions 300yds east of Loch Shin on the A839 on Main Street Lairg.
Acreage 4 **Open** April **to** October
Access Good **Site** Level
Sites Available ▲ ♦ ⊕ **Total** 40
Facilities
Nearby Facilities
Ideal centre for touring, fishing and sight seeing. Close to Loch Shin and all amenities.

LAIRG

Woodend Caravan & Camping Park, Woodend, Achnairn, Lairg, Highland, IV27 4DN.
Std: 01549 **Tel:** 402248 **Fax:** 402248
Nearest Town/Resort Lairg
Directions A836 from Lairg onto A838 and follow site signs.
Acreage 4 **Open** April **to** September
Access Good **Site** Lev/Slope
Sites Available ▲ ♦ ⊕ **Total** 45
Facilities
Nearby Facilities ✓
≠ Lairg
Overlooking Loch Shin, fishing and scenic views. Campers Kitchen is a small building where campers can take their cooking stores to prepare food, with table, chairs and a dish washing area. Ideal touring centre for north west. AA 3 Pennants. Gold Award for Quality & Service from International Caravan & Camping Guide.

LOCHALINE

Fiunary Caravan & Camping Park, Morvern, Highland, PA34 5XX.
Std: 01967 **Tel:** 421225
Nearest Town/Resort Fort William
Directions Turn off the A82 8 miles south of Fort William for the Car Ferry at Corran. 5 minute crossing to Ardgour. Take the A884 and follow signposts to Lochaline, then take the B849 to the site.
Acreage 5 **Open** May **to** September
Access Good **Site** Lev/Slope
Sites Available ▲ ♦ ⊕
Facilities
Nearby Facilities ✓
≠ Fort William
Own beach. Forest walks commence from the site. Convenient for the Isle of Mull car ferry.

LOCHINVER

Clachtoll Camp Site, Near Lochinver, Highland, IV27 4JD.
Std: 01571 **Tel:** 855229
Nearest Town/Resort Inverness/Dingwall
Directions 7 miles north of Lochinver on the B869.
Open May **to** October
Access Good **Site** Level
Sites Available ▲ ♦ ⊕ **Total** 40
Facilities
Nearby Facilities
≠ Lairg
Near the beach. Sea and loch fishing. Climbing and hill walking.

MELVICH

Halladale Inn Caravan Park, Melvich, Highland, KW14 7YJ.
Std: 01641 **Tel:** 531282 **Fax:** 541282
Email: jack@melvich.demon.co.uk
Website: www.melvich.demon.co.uk
Nearest Town/Resort Thurso
Directions 17 miles west of Thurso on the A836 north coast road.
Open April **to** October
Access Good **Site** Level
Sites Available ▲ ♦ ⊕ **Total** 14
Facilities
Nearby Facilities
≠ Thurso/Forsinard
Sandy beaches and sea fishing, wild brown trout and salmon fishing. Bird watching, surfing and diving.

NAIRN

Spindrift Caravan & Camping Park, Little Kildrummie, Nairn, Highland, IV12 5QU.
Std: 01667 **Tel:** 453992
Email: camping@spindriftcaravanpark.freeserve.co.uk
Website: www.spindriftcaravanpark.freeserve.co.uk
Nearest Town/Resort Nairn
Directions From Nairn take the B9090 south for 1¼ miles. Turn right at sharp left hand bend signposted Little Kildrummie onto unclassified road and the entrance is 400yds on the left hand side.
Acreage 3 **Open** 1st April **to** 31st October
Access Good **Site** Level
Sites Available ▲ ♦ ⊕ **Total** 40
Facilities
Nearby Facilities
≠ Nairn
A quiet grassy site, sheltered by trees overlooking the River Nairn. Fishing permit available from reception. STB 4 Star Graded. Park and AA 4 Pennants.

NEWTONMORE

Invernahavon Caravan Site, Glentruim, Newtonmore, Inverness-shire, PH20 1BE
Std: 01540 **Tel:** 673534/673219 **Fax:** 673219
Nearest Town/Resort Newtonmore
Directions 2 miles south of Newtonmore on the A9 turn right onto Glentruim road, site is 400 yards on the right.
Acreage 12 **Open** 29 March **to** 7 October
Access Good **Site** Level
Sites Available ▲ ♦ ⊕ **Total** 85
Facilities &
Nearby Facilities
≠ Newtonmore
Near a river and the mountains.

POOLEWE

Camping & Caravanning Club Site, Inverewe Gardens, Poolewe, Achnasheen, Highlands, IV22 2LF.
Std: 01445 **Tel:** 781249
Website: www.campingandcaravanningclub.co.uk
Directions Site entrance is on the A832 north of the village of Poolewe.
Acreage 3 **Open** March **to** October
Site Level
Sites Available ▲ ♦ ⊕ **Total** 55
Facilities &
Nearby Facilities
≠ Achnasheen
Close to Inverewe Gardens and Loch Ewe. National Trust Ranger Walks ¼ mile. BTB Graded. Non members welcome.

PORTREE

Torvaig Caravan & Camping Site, Torvaig, Staffin Road, Portree, Isle of Skye, Highland, IV51 9HU.
Std: 01478 **Tel:** 612209
Nearest Town/Resort Portree
Directions 1 mile north of Portree on main Staffin road A855.
Acreage 3 **Open** April **to** October
Access Good **Site** Sloping
Sites Available ▲ ♦ ⊕ **Total** 90
Facilities
Nearby Facilities
≠ Kyle of Lochash
Scenic views and ideal base for touring Skye.

OY BRIDGE

veroy Caravan Park, Roy Bridge,
ghland, PH31 4AQ.
d: 01397 **Tel:** 712275
mail: renee@rbarberis.co.uk
ebsite: www.fort-william.net/
neecaravans
earest Town/Resort Fort William
rections 12 miles from Fort William on
e A82 and the A86.
pen All Year
ccess Good **Site** Level
tes Available ▲ ⊞ ⊞
acilities ⸙ ▯ ▥ ⸙ ⌐ ⊙⊣ ⚊ ▢ ❤ ▯⤧
earby Facilities ⌐ ✔ ↘ ∪ ⤸ ♉ ⚹
⚹ Roy Bridge
atic caravans also available for hire.

PEAN BRIDGE

ronaba Caravan & Camping Site,
ronaba Farm, Spean Bridge, Highland,
┤34 4DX.
d: 01397 **Tel:** 712259
earest Town/Resort Spean Bridge
rections On the main A82 Fort William
Inverness road. 2¼ miles north of Spean
idge, on the left hand side just beyond AA
one box.
creage 4 **Open** Easter **to** October
ccess Good **Site** Lev/Slope
tes Available ▲ ⊞ ⊞ **Total** 25
acilities ⸙ ▯ ▥ ⸙ ⌐ ⊙ ❤ ▯⤧▢
earby Facilities ⌐ ✔ ↕ ↘ ∪ ⤸ ♉ ⚹
⚹ Spean Bridge
cenic views, ideal touring. Gas, telephone
d cafe/restaurant all within 2¼ miles. Site
as a flat area.

TAFFIN

affin Caravan & Camping Site, Staffin,
e of Skye, Highland, IV51 9JX.
d: 01470 562 **Tel:** 213
earest Town/Resort Portree
rections South side of Staffin village.
creage 1½ **Open** April **to** September
ccess Good **Site** Lev/Slope
tes Available ▲ ⊞ ⊞ **Total** 80
acilities ⸙ ⸙ ▯ ▥ ⸙ ⌐ ⊙⊣ ▯⤧ ⌂▢
earby Facilities ✔ ↕ ↘ ∪ ⤸ ⚹
⚹ Kyle
andy beaches 1 mile. Site overlooking
affin Bay. Free hot showers. Public
lephone ½ mile, local cafe/restaurant.

TRATHPEFFER

verside Caravan Park, Contin, By
rathpeffer, Ross-shire, IV14 9ES.
d: 01997 **Tel:** 421351
earest Town/Resort Dingwall
rections From Dingwall take the A835
est towards Ullapool for 7 miles.
pen All Year
ccess Good **Site** Level
tes Available ▲ ⊞ ⊞ **Total** 30
acilities ⸙ ▥ ⸙ ⌐ ⊙⊣ ⚊ ⸑ ⌂ ❤
earby Facilities ⌐ ✔ ∪ ⚹
⚹ Dingwall
verside site with nice scenery. Ideal for
uring, fishing, shooting, golf and walking.

TRONTIAN

lenview Caravan Park, Strontian,
ghland, PH36 4HZ.
d: 01967 **Tel:** 402123 **Fax:** 402123
mail: glenview58@lineone.net
ebsite: www.glenviewcp.com
earest Town/Resort Fort William
rections On the A52 Glencoe to Fort
illiam road take the Corran Ferry across
ch Linnhe. Follow signs to Strontian and
rn right at the Police Station.
creage 3½ **Open** March **to** January
ccess Good **Site** Level

Sites Available ▲ ⊞ □ **Total** 29
Facilities ⸙ ▯ ▥ ⸙ ⌐ ⊙⊣ ⚊ ▢ ❤
▯⤧ ⊙⤧▢ ▢
Nearby Facilities ⌐ ✔ ↕ ⚹ ⚹
⚹ Fort William
Quiet, peaceful park behind a village. Two
shops, Post Office and three hotels within
walking distance. Ideal for touring the west
coast.

THURSO

Thurso Caravan Park, Smith Terrace,
Thurso, Highland, KW14 7JY.
Std: 01847 **Tel:** 805514
Nearest Town/Resort Thurso
Directions On the A9 within Thurso town
boundary.
Acreage 4½ **Open** May **to** September
Access Good **Site** Sloping
Sites Available ▲ ⊞ ⊞ **Total** 117
Facilities ⸙ ▯ ▥ ⸙ ⌐ ⊙⊣ ⚊ ▢ ❤
▯ ⊟ ✕ ▯ ⚹ ⌂┥
Nearby Facilities ⌐ ✔ ↕
⚹ Thurso
Near the beach.

UIG

Uig Bay Camping & Caravan Site, 10
Idrigill, Uig, Isle of Skye, Highland, IV51 9XU
Std: 01470 542714 **Fax:** 542714
Nearest Town/Resort Uig
Directions From Portree take the A850
towards Uig, turn onto the A856 and travel
towards Uig Ferry Terminal. Turn right just
before the pier to site.
Acreage 2¼ **Open** March **to** October
Access Good **Site** Level
Sites Available ▲ ⊞ ⊞ **Total** 50
Facilities ⸙ ⸙ ▯ ▥ ⸙ ⌐ ⊙⊣ ⚊ ▢ ❤
▯ ⊟❤▢ ▢
Nearby Facilities ✔ ∪ ⚹
⚹ Fort William
Close to a pebble beach. Near ferry terminal
to the Western Isles. Ideal for touring the
Highlands. Cycle hire locally.

ULLAPOOL

Ardmair Point Caravan Site, Ullapool,
Highland, IV26 2TN.
Std: 01854 **Tel:** 612054 **Fax:** 612757
Email: p.fraser@btinternet.com
Website: www.ardmair.com
Nearest Town/Resort Ullapool
Directions 3½ miles north of Ullapool on
A835.
Acreage 3½ **Open** May **to** September
Access Good **Site** Level
Sites Available ▲ ⊞ ⊞ **Total** 45
Facilities ⸙ ⸙ ▯ ▥ ⸙ ⌐ ⊙⊣ ▢ ❤
⚹ ⊙ ⊟ ✕ ▯❤▢ ▢
Nearby Facilities ⌐ ✔ ↕ ↘ ∪ ♉ ⚹
⚹ Garve
Beautiful location with outstanding views
from the site over sea to 'Summer Isles'.
Boating centre, hire of boats.

ULLAPOOL

Broomfield Holiday Park, Shore Street,
Ullapool, Highland, IV26 2SX.
Std: 01854 **Tel:** 612020 **Fax:** 613151
Email: sross@broomfieldhp.com
Website: www.broomfieldhp.com
Nearest Town/Resort Ullapool
Directions Turn right past Ullapool Harbour.
Acreage 11 **Open** Easter **to** September
Access Good **Site** Level
Sites Available ▲ ⸙ ⊞ ⊞ **Total** 140
Facilities ⸙ ⸙ ▥ ⸙ ⌐ ⊙⊣ ⚊ ▢ ❤
▯ ⊟❤✕▯⤧ ┥
Nearby Facilities ⌐ ✔ ↘ ∪ ♉ ⚹
⚹ Garve
On the sea front. Beside a cafe/restaurant
and adjacent to a golf course.

WICK

Central Caravans, Oldhall, Watten,
Highland, KW1 5XL.
Std: 01955 **Tel:** 621215
Nearest Town/Resort Wick/Thurso
Directions On the A882 midway between
Wick and Thurso.
Acreage ½ **Open** April **to** October
Access Good **Site** Level
Sites Available ▲ ⊞ ⊞ **Total** 15
Facilities ⸙ ▥ ⸙ ⌐ ⊙⊣ ⚊ ▢ ⊟❤▢
Nearby Facilities ✔ ⚹
⚹ Wick/Thurso
Situated by Loch Watten which is famous
for its brown Trout fishing. Boating also on
the loch.

LANARKSHIRE, NORTH
GLASGOW

Craigendmuir Caravan Park,
Craigendmuir Park, Stepps, Nr. Glasgow,
North Lanarkshire, G33 6AF.
Std: 0141 **Tel:** 779 4159 **Fax:** 779 4057
Email: info@craigendmuir.co.uk
Website: www.craigendmuir.co.uk
Nearest Town/Resort Glasgow
Directions Take the A80 to Cumbernauld
and exit at Stepps, Buchanaw Business
Park, Cardowan Road, follow signs.
Acreage 2 **Open** All Year
Access Good **Site** Level
Sites Available ▲ ⊞ ⊞ **Total** 40
Facilities ⸙ ⸙ ▯ ▥ ⸙ ⌐ ⊙⊣ ⚊ ▢ ❤
⚹ ▯ ⊙ ⊟❤▢ ▢
Nearby Facilities
⚹ Stepps
Close proximity to Glasgow and near all
major roads.

MOTHERWELL

Strathclyde Country Park, 366 Hamilton
Road, Motherwell, North Lanarkshire, ML1
3ED.
Std: 01698 **Tel:** 266155 **Fax:** 252925
Email: strathclyde@northlan.gov.uk
Nearest Town/Resort Motherwell
Directions From north or south leave the
M74 at junction 5. From Motherwell head
south down the A72 and the park entrance
is on the right at the traffic lights.
Open April **to** October
Access Good **Site** Level
Sites Available ▲ ⊞ ⊞ **Total** 250
Facilities ⸙ ⸙ ▯ ▥ ⸙ ⌐ ⊣ ⚊ ▢ ❤
⚹ ▯ ⊙ ✕ ▯ ⊛❤▢
Nearby Facilities ⌐ ✔ ↕ ↘ ∪ ⤸ ♉
⚹ Motherwell
Watersports Centre with formal courses and
fun boats. Innkeepers Fayre and Theme
Park. Walking, fishing, Visitor Centre and
land train. Programme of special events.

LANARKSHIRE, SOUTH
DOUGLAS

Crossburn Caravan Park, 56 Ayr Road,
Douglas, South Lanarkshire, ML11 0QA.
Std: 01555 **Tel:** 851029
Nearest Town/Resort Lanark
Directions 1½ miles west of the M74, on
the A70 Edinburgh to Ayr road in Douglas
Village.
Acreage 4 **Open** All Year
Access Good **Site** Level
Sites Available ▲ ⊞ ⊞ **Total** 50
Facilities ⸙ ▯ ▥ ⸙ ⌐ ⊙⊣ ⚊ ▢ ❤
⚹ ▯ ⊙ ✕ ▯❤▢
Nearby Facilities
⚹ Lanark

LANARK

Clyde Valley Caravan Park,
Kirkfieldbank, Nr. Lanark, South
Lanarkshire, ML11 9JW.
Std: 01555 **Tel:** 663951 **Fax:** 357684
Nearest Town/Resort Lanark
Directions Leave the M74 onto the A73 for
Lanark, ½ mile north to Kirkfieldbank.
Acreage 5 **Open** April **to** October
Access Good **Site** Level
Sites Available Λ ⊕ ⇔ **Total** 50
Facilities ⅗ ⫪ ⅏ ▥ ⬧ ⌐ ☉ ⟜ ◫ ⬤
⍨ ◌ ⊁ ⊟
Nearby Facilities ⌐ ⟋ ⟰ ∪
⇌ Lanark
Two fishing river run past the site.

LANARK

Newhouse Caravan & Camping Park,
Ravenstruther, Lanark, South Lanarkshire,
ML11 8NP.
Std: 01555 **Tel:** 870228
Email: newhousepark@btinternet.com
Website: www.ukparks.co.uk/newhouse
Nearest Town/Resort Lanark
Directions On A70 Edinburgh road from
Lanark, 3 miles east on left.
Acreage 8 **Open** 1 April **to** End Sept
Access Good **Site** Level
Sites Available Λ ⊕ ⇔ **Total** 45
Facilities ⅗ ⫪ ⅏ ▥ ⬧ ⌐ ☉ ⟜ ◣ ◫ ⬤
⍨ ⍨ ◌ ⊟ ◭ ⊛ ⟜ ⊟
Nearby Facilities ⌐ ⟋ ⟰ ∪ ℛ ⊁ ⚡
Ideal touring, near Clyde Valley, 40 minutes
from Edinburgh and Glasgow. Near New
Lanark Conservation Village.

LOTHIAN, EAST

DUNBAR

Camping & Caravanning Club Site,
Barns Ness, Dunbar, East Lothian, EH42
1QP.
Std: 01368 **Tel:** 863536
Website:
www.campingandcaravanningclub.co.uk
Directions On the A1 approx. 6 miles south
of Dunbar (near the Power Station) you will
see signs for Barns Ness and Skateraw, turn
right at camp site sign towards the
lighthouse and take in the views of the sea.
Acreage 10 **Open** March **to** October
Access Poor **Site** Level
Sites Available Λ ⊕ ⇔ **Total** 80
Facilities ⅏ ▥ ⬧ ⌐ ☉ ⟜ ◫ ◌ ◣ ◣
◭ ⟜ ⊟ ⊟
Nearby Facilities ⟋ ⇥ ∪
⇌ Dunbar
Close to the town of Dunbar, on the Scottish
coast. BTB Graded. Non members
welcome.

DUNBAR

Thorntonloch Caravan Park, Innerwick,
Dunbar, East Lothian, EH42 1QS.
Std: 01368 **Tel:** 840236
Nearest Town/Resort Dunbar
Directions 6 miles south of Dunbar on the A1.
Open March **to** October
Access Good **Site** Level
Sites Available Λ ⊕□ **Total** 10
Facilities ⌐ ⅏ ▥ ⬧ ⌐ ☉ ⟜ ◫ ⍨ ⫧
◌ ◣ ⟜ ⊟ ⊟
Nearby Facilities ⌐ ⟋ ⇥
⇌ Dunbar
Quiet site on the beach.

DUNBAR

Thurston Manor Holiday Home Park,
Innerwick, Dunbar, East Lothian, EH42
1SA.
Std: 01368 **Tel:** 840643 **Fax:** 840261
Email: mail@thurstonmanor.co.uk
Website: www.thurstonmanor.co.uk
Nearest Town/Resort Dunbar
Directions 4 miles south of Dunbar on the A1
take the Innerwick sign. Park is ½ mile on the
right. Tourist signs can be seen from the A1.
Acreage 250 **Open** 1 March **to** 31
October
Access Good **Site** Level
Sites Available Λ ⊕ ⇔ **Total** 100
Facilities ⅗ ⫪ ⅏ ▥ ⬧ ⌐ ☉ ⟜ ◣ ◫ ⬤
⍨ ◌ ◣ ⅄ ⊠ ⬧ ◭ ⟜ ⟜ ⊟
Nearby Facilities ⌐ ⟋ ⟰ ∪ ℛ ⊁
⇌ Dunbar
5 Star facilities and our own woodland valley
of great natural beauty. Ideal touring park.

HADDINGTON

The Monks' Muir, Haddington, East
Lothian, EH41 3SB.
Std: 01620 **Tel:** 860340 **Fax:** 861770
Nearest Town/Resort Haddington
Directions Direct access from the main A1
road, between Haddington and East Linton.
Very well signposted.
Acreage 7½ **Open** All Year
Access Good **Site** Level
Sites Available Λ ⊕ ⇔ **Total** 85
Facilities ⫪ ⅏ ▥ ⬧ ⌐ ☉ ⟜ ◫ ⍨
◌ ◣ ✕ ◭ ⟜ ⊟
Nearby Facilities ⌐ ⟋ ⟰ ⇥ ∪ ℛ ℛ
⇌ Dunbar/Drem
In the heart of East Lothian, close to the
Museum of Flight, Myreton Motor Museum,
The Scottish Seabird Centre and 15 minutes
from Edinburgh or the beach.

NORTH BERWICK

Gilsland Caravan & Camping Park,
Grange Road, North Berwick, East
Lothian, EH39 5JA.
Std: 01620 **Tel:** 892205
Email: bmacnair@gilnbscot.freeserve.co.uk

LOTHIAN, WEST

BLACKBURN

Mosshall Farm Caravan Park, Mosshall
Farm, Blackburn, West Lothian, EH47 7D
Std: 01501 **Tel:** 762318
Directions Leave the M8 at junction 4 ai
take the road for Whitburn. At T-Junctic
A705 take a left turn towards Blackburn, v
are 300 yards on the right.
Acreage ¾ **Open** All Year
Access Good **Site** Level
Sites Available Λ ⊕ ⇔ **Total** 25
Facilities ⅗ ⫪ ⅏ ▥ ⬧ ⌐ ☉ ⍨ ⫧
Nearby Facilities ⌐ ⟋ ⟰ ∪ ℛ
⇌ Bathgate
Situated half way between Edinburgh ai
Glasgow.

EAST CALDER

Linwater Caravan Park, West Clifton, E
East Calder, West Lothian, EH53 0HT.
Std: 0131 **Tel:** 333 3326 **Fax:** 333 1952
Email: linwater@supanet.com
Website: www.ukparks.co.uk/linwater
Nearest Town/Resort Edinburgh
Directions At Newbridge junction of the M
M9/A8 take the B7030. Continue for 2 mil
then turn right at signpost for East Calde
park is through West Clifton on the right.
Acreage 5 **Open** March **to** October
Access Good **Site** Level
Sites Available Λ ⊕ ⇔ **Total** 60
Facilities ⅗ ⫪ ▥ ⬧ ⌐ ☉ ⟜ ◫ ⍨
◌ ◣ ⟜ ⊟ ⊟
Nearby Facilities ⌐ ⟋ ⟰ ∪ ℛ ⊁
Ideal for visiting Edinburgh, Royal Highlan
Showground and touring.

LINLITHGOW

**Beecraigs Country Park Caravan &
Camping Site,** The Park Centre, Nr.
Linlithgow, West Lothian, EH49 6PL.
Std: 01506 **Tel:** 844516 **Fax:** 846256
Email: mail@beecraigs.com
Website: www.beecraigs.com
Nearest Town/Resort Linlithgow
Directions Follow the signs for Beecrai
Country Park taking you approximately
miles up Preston Road. At the top of the I
road turn left following signs for Beecrai
Loch and Restaurant. Take the first rig
restaurant is reception area.
Acreage 6½ **Open** All Year
Access Good **Site** Level
Sites Available Λ ⊕ ⇔ **Total** 54
Facilities ⅗ ⫪ ⅏ ▥ ⬧ ⌐ ☉ ⟜ ◫ ⍨
◣ ✕ ◭ ⟜ ⊟
Nearby Facilities ⌐ ⟋ ⟰ ⇥ ∪ ℛ ⊁
Within a 913 acre Country Park which offe
a wide range of leisure and recreation
interests - fishing, outdoor activities, pl
area, Red Deer Farm and woodland walk

The Monks' Muir
Set in rural tranquility
on Edinburgh's doorstep
Haddington, East Lothian EH41 3SB
Tel: (01620) 860340   Fax: (01620) 861770

Friendly, tasteful and relaxing, in an area of great beauty: broad beaches, rich farmland, lonely hills, delightful villages and challenging golf courses. "Five-Star" grading, "Thistle" Award, David Bellamy GOLD, Green Organisation "Green Apple" and 1999 Finalist for " Best Park in Scotland"!

MORAY

ABERLOUR

Aberlour Garden Caravan Park, Aberlour-on-Spey, Moray, AB38 9LD.
Std: 01340 **Tel:** 871586 **Fax:** 871586
Email: abergard@compuserve.com
Website: www.ourworld.compuserve.com/ homepages/abergard
Directions Turn off the A95 midway between Aberlour and Craigellachie, site signposted 200 yards. Vehicles over 10' 6" high should use the A941 to Dufftown, site signposted.
Acreage 5 **Open** April **to** October
Access Good **Site** Level
Sites Available ▲ ♉ ♊ **Total** 56
Facilities ⬥ ⨍ ▣ ▥ ♨ ℾ ⊙ ➔ ▢ ⎗
▮ ▤ ▨ ✦ ▤ ▣ ▣
Nearby Facilities ↾ ⟋ ∪ ♈
Close to Speyside Way and on the malt whisky and castle trail.

BURGHEAD

Burghead Beach Caravan Park, Station Road, Burghead, Moray, IV30 5RP.
Std: 01343 **Tel:** 830084 **Fax:** 821291
Nearest Town/Resort Burghead
Directions 4 miles west of Elgin.
Acreage 5 **Open** April **to** October
Access Good **Site** Level
Sites Available ▲ ♉ ♊ **Total** 80
Facilities ⬥ ⨍ ▥ ♨ ℾ ⊙ ➔ ▢
▨ ♉ ➔ ▣
Nearby Facilities ↾ ⟋ ⛱ ✦
Near an excellent beach.

BURGHEAD

The Red Craig Hotel & Caravan & Camping Park, Masonhaugh, Burghead, Moray, IV30 5XX.
Std: 01343 **Tel:** 835663 **Fax:** 835663
Email: reception@redcraig-hotel.co.uk
Website: www.redcraig-hotel.co.uk
Nearest Town/Resort Elgin
Directions Turn off the A96 Elgin to Inverness road onto the A9013 Burghead road. Turn right just before the village onto the B9040, site is 300 yards on the left.
Acreage 4 **Open** April **to** October
Access Good **Site** Level
Sites Available ▲ ♉ ♊ **Total** 38

Facilities ⨍ ▣ ▥ ♨ ℾ ⊙ ➔ ▢ ℗ ▣ ▩
✕ ♈ ▥ ✦ ➔ ▣ ▣
Nearby Facilities ↾ ⟋ ⛱ ✦ ∪ ♉ ♈
Panoramic views across the Moray Firth. Live music every second and last Saturday of the month.

FINDHORN

Findhorn Sands Caravan Park, Findhorn, Moray, IV36 0YZ.
Std: 01309 **Tel:** 690324
Nearest Town/Resort Elgin
Directions Turn off the main A96 onto the B9011 to Kinloss at Forres roundabout. Turn left to Findhorn Village, site is on the beach.
Open April **to** October
Access Good **Site** Level
Sites Available ▲ ♉ ♊ **Total** 45
Facilities ⬥ ⨍ ▥ ♨ ℾ ⊙
➔ ▢ ℗ ▣ ▩ ▤ ➔ ▣
Nearby Facilities ↾ ⟋ ⛱ ✦ ♉ ♈
Near a sandy beach and only 100 yards from the village of Findhorn. STB 5 Star Graded Park.

FOCHABERS

Burnside Caravan Park, Keith Road, Fochabers, Moray, IV32 7ET.
Std: 01343 **Tel:** 820511 **Fax:** 820511
Nearest Town/Resort Fochabers
Directions On the A96 at Fochabers.
Acreage 10 **Open** April **to** October
Access Good **Site** Level
Sites Available ▲ ♉ ♊ **Total** 110
Facilities ⬥ ⨍ ▥ ♨ ℾ ⊙ ➔ ▢ ℗
▣ ▩ ▤ ▨ ➔ ▣ ▣
Nearby Facilities ↾ ⟋ ∪ ♈
On site sauna and spa. Central touring position.

FORRES

Old Mill Caravan Park, Brodie, Moray, IV30 0TD.
Std: 01309 **Tel:** 641244
Nearest Town/Resort Forres
Directions 3 miles east of Forres on the A96.
Acreage 6 **Open** April **to** September
Access Good **Site** Level
Sites Available ▲ ♉ ♊ **Total** 74
Facilities ⨍ ▣ ▥ ♨ ℾ ⊙ ➔ ▢ ℗ ▣ ▩ ✕
▨ ➔ ▣ ▣

Nearby Facilities ↾ ⟋ ⛱ ✦ ∪ ♉ ♈
Sheltered park with modern facilities. Adjacent to the grounds of Brodie Castle with its lake and woodland walks.

HOPEMAN

Station Caravan Park, Hopeman, Nr. Elgin, Moray, IV30 5RU.
Std: 01343 **Tel:** 830880 **Fax:** 830880
Email: stationcaravanpark@talk21.com
Website: www.ukparks.co.uk/station
Nearest Town/Resort Elgin
Acreage 13 **Open** March **to** November
Access Good **Site** Level
Sites Available ▲ ♉ ♊ **Total** 37
Facilities ⬥ ⨍ ▥ ♨ ℾ ⊙ ➔ ▢ ℗ ▣ ▩
▥ ▤ ➔ ▣ ▣
Nearby Facilities ↾ ⟋ ⛱ ✦ ∪ ♉ ♈
On a beach on Moray Firth coast.

LOSSIEMOUTH

Lossiemouth Bay Caravan Park, East Beach, Lossiemouth, Moray, IV31 6NW.
Std: 01343 **Tel:** 813980 **Fax:** 821291
Nearest Town/Resort Lossiemouth
Directions 5 miles from Elgin on the A96.
Acreage 10 **Open** April **to** October
Access Good **Site** Level
Sites Available ▲ ♉ ♊ **Total** 80
Facilities ⬥ ⨍ ▥ ♨ ℾ ⊙ ➔ ▢ ℗ ▣ ▩ ➔ ▣
Nearby Facilities ↾ ⟋ ⛱ ✦ ∪ ♉
At the beach and close to local facilities

LOSSIEMOUTH

Silver Sands Leisure Park, Covesea West Beach, Lossiemouth, Moray, IV31 6SP
Std: 01343 **Tel:** 813262
Email: holidays@silversand.freeserve.co.uk
Website: www.travel.to/silversands
Nearest Town/Resort Lossiemouth
Directions Elgin/Lossiemouth A941, turn left 1 mile before Lossiemouth continue 1¼ miles, past R.A.F. camp, turn left, site beside lighthouse.
Acreage 14 **Open** April **to** October
Access Good **Site** Level
Sites Available ▲ ♉ ♊ **Total** 140
Facilities ✕ ⨍ ▣ ▥ ♨ ℾ ⊙ ➔ ➔ ▢ ♉ ▩
▥ ▣ ▩ ✕ ♈ ▥ ♨ ▥ ▨ ➔ ▣ ▣
Nearby Facilities ↾ ⟋ ⛱ ✦ ∪ ♉ ♈ ♈
Beautiful unspoilt golden beach next to park, no roads to cross. Ideal touring area for fishing villages, castles and distilleries.

DRUM MOHR CARAVAN PARK   *Near Edinburgh*

East Lothian's premier touring park for caravanners and campers. A secluded, well landscaped site on the edge of East Lothian's beautiful countryside, yet only 20 minutes from Princes Street, Edinburgh.

120 pitches (most with electric hook-up and a few fully serviced), children's play area, well stocked shop, plus Tourist Information at reception. Facilities are of an exceptionally high standard, the toilet blocks include showers, laundry room, dishwashing area and chemical waste disposal.

Send for a brochure to: **Drum Mohr Caravan Park**
Levenhall, Musselburgh, Nr. Edinburgh EH21 8JS
Tel: 0131 665 6867   Fax: 0131 653 6859
E-mail: bookings@drummohr.org   Website: www.drummohr.org

PERTH & KINROSS

ABERFELDY

Glengoulandie Deer Park,
Glengoulandie, Foss, By Pitlochry, Perth & Kinross, PH15 6NL.
Std: 01887 **Tel:** 830261
Nearest Town/Resort Aberfeldy
Directions B846 road from Aberfeldy to Kinloch Rannoch for 8 miles, on left hand side.
Acreage 3 **Open** April **to** 1 Nov
Access Good **Site** Level
Sites Available A ⊕ ⊕ **Total** 10
Facilities ⓌＲ⊙ＳＯ♠➔⊡
Nearby Facilities ┏╱⚓┶Ｕ⚲Ｒ⚹
➤ Pitlochry
Adjoining a wildlife park.

ABERFELDY

Kenmore Caravan & Camping Park,
Aberfeldy, Perth & Kinross, PH15 2HN.
Std: 01887 **Tel:** 830226 **Fax:** 830211
Email: info@taymouth.co.uk
Website: www.taymouth.co.uk
Nearest Town/Resort Aberfeldy
Directions 6 miles west on A827 from Aberfeldy to Killin.
Acreage 14 **Open** April **to** October
Access Good **Site** Level
Sites Available A ⊕ ⊕ **Total** 160
Facilities ♿ ✦ ⓇＲ Ｗ ♠ ┏⊙♨ ♠ ⊡ ♥
Ｓ℞ Ｉ℞ ☺ ➌ ✕ ⓈⓇ ♠ ➔⊡
Nearby Facilities ┏╱⚓┶Ｕ⚲Ｒ⚹
➤ Pitlochry
By river near loch. Touring centre. All outdoor pursuits and water sports. Excellent par 70 golf course on site. AA 5 Pennants.

AUCHTERARDER

Auchterarder Caravan Park, Nether Coul, Auchterarder, Perth & Kinross, PH3 1ET.
Std: 01764 **Tel:** 663119 **Fax:** 663119
Email: nethercoul@talk21.com
Nearest Town/Resort Auchterarder/Perth
Directions Situated between the A9 and the A824 east of Auchterarder Village, 1½ miles from the main road. Reached by turning onto the B8062 (Dunning) from the A824.
Acreage 5 **Open** All Year
Access Good **Site** Level
Sites Available A ⊕ ⊕ **Total** 23
Facilities ♿ ✦ ⓇＲ Ｗ ♠ ┏⊙♨ Ｓ℞ Ｉ℞
☺ ➌ ♠➔⊡
Nearby Facilities ┏╱⚓┶Ｕ⚲Ｒ
Bordered by Pairney Water with private fishing. Ideal central location in the heart of Perthshire. Self catering chalets and B&B also available. You can also telephone us on Mobile 07979 370894.

BLAIR ATHOLL

Blair Castle Caravan Park, Blair Atholl, Pitlochry, Perth & Kinross, PH18 5SR.
Std: 01796 **Tel:** 481263 **Fax:** 481587
Email: mail@blaircastlecaravanpark.co.uk
Web: www.blaircastlecaravanpark.co.uk
Nearest Town/Resort Pitlochry
Directions Follow A9 north past Pitlochry, after 6 miles turn off following signs to Blair Atholl. After 1¼ miles turn right into caravan park.
Acreage 35 **Open** April **to** Late Oct
Access Good **Site** Level
Sites Available A ⊕ ⊕ **Total** 283
Facilities ♿ ✦ ⓇＲ Ｗ ♠ ┏⊙♨ ☺ Ｓ℞
Ｉ℞ ☺ ➌ ✕ ♠ ➔⊡
Nearby Facilities ┏╱┶Ｕ⚹
➤ Blair Atholl
Blair Castle, Bruar Falls and the picturesque town of Pitlochry.

BLAIRGOWRIE

Ballintuim Caravan Park & Hotel,
Ballintuim, By Blairgowrie, Perth & Kinross, PH10 7NH.
Std: 01250 **Tel:** 886276
Nearest Town/Resort Blairgowrie
Directions From Blairgowrie take the A93 towards Braemar, turn left onto the A924 towards Pitlochry for 3 miles.
Acreage 18 **Open** All Year
Access Good **Site** Lev/Slope
Sites Available A ⊕ ⊕ **Total** 20
Facilities ✦ ⓇＲ Ｗ ♠ ┏⊙♨ ♠ ⊡
Ｉ℞ ☺ ➌ ✕ Ⓨ ♠➔⊡
Nearby Facilities ┏╱Ｕ⚹
➤ Perth
Set on a hillside, near a river, in a Perthshire valley. Picnic by the pond on site.

BLAIRGOWRIE

Beech Hedge Caravan Park, Cargill, Perth & Kinross, PH2 6DU.
Std: 0125 0883 **Tel:** Meikleour 249
Nearest Town/Resort Blairgowrie
Directions 8 miles north of Perth on A93 Breamar road.
Acreage 2 **Open** March **to** October
Access Good **Site** Level
Sites Available A ⊕ ⊕ **Total** 20
Facilities ⓇＷ ♠ ┏⊙♨ ♠ ⊡ ♥ ☺➔⊡
Nearby Facilities ┏╱Ｕ⚲Ｒ
➤ Perth
Scenic views, ideal touring centre.

BLAIRGOWRIE

Blairgowrie Holiday Park, Rattray, Blairgowrie, Perth & Kinross, PH10 7AL.
Std: 01250 **Tel:** 872941 **Fax:** 874535
Email: blairgowrie@holiday-parks.co.uk
Website: www.holiday-parks.co.uk
Nearest Town/Resort Blairgowrie
Directions 1 mile north of Blairgowrie town centre off the A93. Turn right past Keathbank

Mill and the petrol station. Park is on the left in 250yds following international signs.
Acreage 15 **Open** All Year
Access Good **Site** Level
Sites Available A ⊕ ⊕ **Total** 30
Facilities ✦ ⓇＲ Ｗ ♠ ┏⊙♨ ♠ ⊡ ♥
Ｓ℞ ☺ ➌ ♠ ➔⊡ ♥
Nearby Facilities ┏╱Ｕ⚲Ｒ⚹
➤ Perth
Beautiful landscaped, family park. Ideal centre for touring Perthshire, Angus, Glens and Royal Deeside. Local swimming pool. Pine lodges and caravans available for hire all year round.

BLAIRGOWRIE

Nether Craig Caravan Park, By Alyth, Blairgowrie, Perth & Kinross, PH11 8HN.
Std: 01575 **Tel:** 560204 **Fax:** 560315
Email: nethercraig@lineone.net
Nearest Town/Resort Alyth
Directions At roundabout south of Alyth join the B954 signposted Glenisla. Follow caravan signs for 4½ miles (DO NOT go into Alyth).
Acreage 4 **Open** 15 March **to** 31 October
Access Good **Site** Level
Sites Available A ⊕ ⊕ **Total** 40
Facilities ♿ ✦ ⓇＲ Ｗ ♠ ┏⊙♨ ♠ ⊡ ♥
Ｓ℞ ☺ ➌ ♠➔⊡
Nearby Facilities ┏╱Ｕ⚲Ｒ⚹
➤ Dundee
Peaceful, rural, touring park with unspoilt views. Ideal country pursuits and touring.

BRIDGE OF CALLY

Corriefodly Holiday Park, Bridge of Cally, Perth & Kinross, PH10 7JG.
Std: 01250 **Tel:** 886236
Email: corriefodly@holiday-parks.co.uk
Website: www.holiday-parks.co.uk
Nearest Town/Resort Blairgowrie
Directions From Blairgowrie take A93 north for 6 miles. Turn onto A924 Pitlochry road, site approx 200yds from junction of A93 & A924.
Acreage 17½ **Open** All Year
Access Good **Site** Level
Sites Available A ⊕ ⊕ **Total** 165
Facilities ✦ ⓇＲ Ｗ ♠ ┏⊙♨ ♠ ⊡
Ｉ℞ ☺ ➌ ✕ ♠ ♠➔⊡ ♥
Nearby Facilities ┏╱Ｕ⚲Ｒ⚹
➤ Perth
Riverside setting with scenic views. Level hardstanding pitches and grass. Private fishing on site. Lounge bar and TV lounge. Ideal touring base.

COMRIE

Twenty Shilling Wood Caravan Park, St Fillans Road, Comrie, Perth & Kinross, PH6 2JY.
Std: 01764 **Tel:** 670411 **Fax:** 670411
Email: alowe20@aol.com

Access Good **Site** Level
Sites Available ▲ ⚏ ⊟ **Total** 164
Facilities ∮ 🚽 ♿ ⌐ ⊙⊶ ▣ ℞ 🅿️
🄐 🛆 🄿 🄳 🄶
Nearby Facilities ⌐ ✔ ⚓ ∪ ⅄
Off-road activity centre, fishing and hill walking. Near to golf courses, clay pigeon shooting and pony trekking.

INCHTURE

Inchmartine Caravan Park, Dundee Road, Inchture, Perth & Kinross, PH14 9QQ
Std: 01821 **Tel:** 670212 **Fax:** 670266
Email: enquiries@perthshire-caravans.co.uk
Website: www.perthshire-caravans.co.uk
Nearest Town/Resort Dundee
Directions Situated just off the A90 northbound, 12 miles north of Perth and 10 miles south of Dundee.
Acreage 8 **Open** April **to** October
Access Good **Site** Level
Sites Available ▲ ⚏ ⊟ **Total** 45
Facilities ∮ 🚽 ♿ ⌐ ⊙⊶ ℞ 🄰 🅿️
Nearby Facilities
⚓ Dundee
A rural setting.

PITLOCHRY

Milton of Fonab Caravan Site, Bridge Road, Pitlochry, Perth & Kinross, PH16 5NA
Std: 01796 **Tel:** 472882 **Fax:** 474363
Email: info@fonab.co.uk
Website: www.fonab.co.uk
Nearest Town/Resort Pitlochry
Directions ½ mile south of Pitlochry, opposite Bell's Distillery.
Acreage 15 **Open** End March **to** Beginning Oct
Access Good **Site** Level
Sites Available ▲ ⚏ ⊟ **Total** 154
Facilities & 🚿 ∮ 🚽 ♿ ⌐ ⊙⊶ ▣
℞ 🄰 🛒 ⊷🅿️
Nearby Facilities ⌐ ✔ ∪
On the banks of the River Tummel. 5 minute walk to Pitlochry Festival Theatre and a 10 minute walk to Dam and Fish Ladder.

ST. FILLANS

Loch Earn Caravan Park, South Shore Road, St. Fillans, Perth & Kinross, PH6 2NL
Std: 01764 **Tel:** 685270
Email: lochearn@perthshire-caravans.co.uk
Website: www.perthshire-caravans.co.uk
Directions From Perth take the A85 and turn off signed South Loch Earn. Before entering St. Fillans turn left over the hump back bridge, Park is 1 mile.
Acreage 4 **Open** 31 March **to** 31 October
Access Good **Site** Level
Sites Available ⚏ ⊟ **Total** 40
Facilities & ∮ 🚽 🚽 ♿ ⌐ ⊙⊶ ▣
℞ 🄰 🛒 ✖ 🛒 🄰 🅿️ 🄶
Nearby Facilities
⚓ Perth
Lochside park with boating and fishing.

ST. FILLANS

St. Fillans Caravan Park, Station Road, St. Fillans, Perth & Kinross, PH6 2NE.
Std: 01764 **Tel:** 685274
Nearest Town/Resort Crieff
Directions Travel 12 miles west on the A85.
Open April **to** October
Access Poor **Site** Level
Sites Available ⚏ ⊟
Facilities ∮ 🄵 🄷 🚽 ♿ ⌐ ⊙⊶ ⊷
℞ 🄰 🄼 🄰
Nearby Facilities ⌐ ✔ ⚓ ∪ ⅄ ⅄ ✗
⚓ Perth
Near a loch. Walking, golf, touring, fishing and all water sports.

SCOTTISH BORDERS

COCKBURNSPATH

Chesterfield Caravan Park, The Neuk, Cockburnspath, Borders, TD13 5YH.
Std: 01368 **Tel:** 830459 **Fax:** 830394
Email: arfindla@aol.com
Web: www.chesterfieldcaravanpark.co.uk
Nearest Town/Resort Eyemouth
Directions From the A1 bypass, follow signs to Abbey St. Bathans. Caravan park is situated ½ mile on the left from this junction.
Open April **to** Mid October
Access Good **Site** Level
Sites Available ▲ ⚏ ⊟
Facilities ∮ 🚽 ♿ ⌐ ⊙⊶ ▣ ℞ 🄰
🛒 🄰 ⊷🅿️
Quiet, tidy, clean, country site with scenic views. Within easy reach of the A1, Scottish Borders, Edinburgh, Berwick-on-Tweed. Nearest beach 3 miles.

COCKBURNSPATH

Pease Bay Holiday Park, Pease Bay, Cockburnspath, Borders, TD13 5YP.
Std: 01368 **Tel:** 830206 **Fax:** 830663
Email: info@peasebay.co.uk
Website: www.peasebay.co.uk
Nearest Town/Resort Dunbar
Directions 9 miles on the A1.
Acreage 40 **Open** 1 March **to** 31 January
Access Good **Site** Lev/Slope
Sites Available ▲ ⚏☐ **Total** 309
Facilities ∮ 🄵 🄷 🚽 ♿ ⌐ ⊙⊶ ⊷ 🛒 🄰 🅿️
℞ ℞ 🄰 🛒 ✖ 🛒 🄰 ※⊷🅿️🄶
Nearby Facilities ⌐ ✔ ⚓ ∪ ⅄ ✗
⚓ Dunbar
Beach front.

COLDINGHAM

Crosslaw Caravan Park, School Road, Coldingham, Borders, TD14 5UA.
Std: 01890 **Tel:** 771316 **Fax:** 226410
Nearest Town/Resort Coldingham/Eyemouth
Directions Take the A1 north to Reston, turn right for Coldingham and follow brown tourism signs.
Acreage 22 **Open** 15 March **to** 15 Nov
Access Good **Site** Sloping
Sites Available ▲ ⚏☐ **Total** 50
Facilities & 🚿 ∮ 🄵 🄷 🄷 🚽 ⌐ ⊙⊶ ▣
🄰 🛒⊷🅿️
Nearby Facilities ⌐ ✔
⚓ Berwick-upon-Tweed
Sloping site with level pitches and tremendous views. 1 mile from the beach.

COLDINGHAM

Scoutscroft Holiday Centre, St Abbs Road, Coldingham, Eyemouth, Borders, TD14 5NB.
Std: 01890 **Tel:** 771338 **Fax:** 771746
Email: holidays@scoutscroft.co.uk
Website: www.scoutscroft.co.uk
Nearest Town/Resort Eyemouth
Acreage 16 **Open** March **to** October
Access Good **Site** Level
Sites Available ▲ ∮ ⚏ ⊟ **Total** 180
Facilities & ∮ 🄵 🄷 🄷 🚽 ♿ ⌐ ⊙⊶ ⊷ 🛒 🄰 🅿️
℞ ℞ 🄰 🛒 ✖ 🛒 🄰 ※⊷🅿️ 🄶 🄶
Nearby Facilities ⌐ ✔ ⚓ ∪ ⅄ ⅄
⚓ Berwick-on-Tweed
¾ miles from Coldingham Bay.

ETTRICK

Honey Cottage Caravan Park, Hope House, Ettrick Valley, Borders, TD7 5HU.
Std: 01750 **Tel:** 620246
Web: www.honeycottagecaravanpark.co.uk
Nearest Town/Resort Selkirk
Directions On the B709 Langholm road. 30 minutes from Selkirk on the B7009 and Hawick (B711).

---

bsite: www.ukparks.co.uk/
ntyshilling
arest Town/Resort Crieff
ections ¼ mile west of Comrie on A85.
reage 10¼ Open Late March to 20 Oct
cess Good Site Level
es Available ⚏ ⊟ Total 16
cilities 🚿 ∮ 🄷 🚽 ♿ ⌐ ⊙⊶ ⊷ 🛒 🄰 🅿️
🄰 🄰 🄿 🄳 🄶
arby Facilities ⌐ ✔ ⚓ ∪ ⅄ ⅄ ✗
Perth
mily run, spotless all season, peaceful
ltered park in woodlands visted by deer
d many woodland birds. Individual
hes. Pets permitted. David Bellamy Gold
ard for Conservation.

OMRIE

st Lodge Caravan Park, Comrie,
th, PH6 2LS.
l: 01764 Tel: 670354 Fax: 670354
arest Town/Resort Comrie
ections On A85, 5 miles from Crieff. 1
e east of Comrie.
reage 3 Open 1 April to 31 October
cess Good Site Level
es Available ▲ ⚏ ⊟ Total 20
ilities ∮ 🄷 🚽 ♿ ⌐ ⊙⊶ ▣ ℞ 🄰 ⊷🅿️🄶
arby Facilities ⌐ ✔ ⚓ ∪ ⅄ ⅄
Perth
ltered friendly site, ideal for touring, set
eautiful country area. Caravans for hire
htly or weekly.

RIEFF

eff Holiday Village, Turret Bank,
eff, Perth & Kinross, PH7 4JN.
l: 01764 Tel: 653513 Fax: 655028
ail: info@crieff-holidayvillage.co.uk
bsite: www.crieff-holidayvillage.co.uk
arest Town/Resort Crieff
ections Follow A85 Crieff/Comrie road,
n left ¼ mile from Crieff at first crossroads.
e 300 yards on left, well signposted.
reage 2 Open All Year
cess Good Site Level
es Available ▲ ⚏ ⊟ Total 45
cilities ∮ 🄷 🚽 ♿ ⌐ ⊙⊶ ⊷ 🛒 🄰 🅿️ 🄰
🄰 ⊙ 🛒 🄼 🄰 🄰⊷🅿️🄶
arby Facilities ⌐ ✔ ⚓ ∪ ⅄ ⅄ ✗
Gleneagles
autifully situated, bounded by River
rret. Adjacent to public parks. Ideal touring
ntre.

UNKELD

vermill Farm Caravan Park, Inver,
nkeld, Perth & Kinross, PA8 0JR.
d: 01350 Tel: 727477 Fax: 727477
ail: invermill@talk21.com
arest Town/Resort Dunkeld
rections From the A9 turn onto the A822
nposted Crieff, turn immediately right
owing signs to Inver.
reage 5 Open End March to Mid/End Oct
cess Good Site Level
es Available ▲ ⚏ ⊟ Total 65
cilities & ∮ 🄷 🚽 ♿ ⌐ ⊙⊶ ▣ 🄰 ⊷🅿️🄶
arby Facilities ⌐ ✔ ⚓ ∪ ⅄ ⅄ ✗
Dunkeld
verside setting. 1 mile from Dunkeld which
s many tourist attractions along with
lking, fishing, golf and cycling.

LENDEVON

endevon Park, Glendevon, By Dollar,
rth & Kinross, FK14 7JY.
d: 01259 Tel: 781208 Fax: 781208
ail: info@glendevonestate.co.uk
ebsite: www.glendevonestate.co.uk
arest Town/Resort Dollar
rections On the A823 midway between
nfermline and Crieff.
creage 15 Open April to October

Open All Year
Access Good **Site** Level
Sites Available ⚠ ⊕ ⊕ **Total** 30
Facilities ⌁ 🄷 🆄🄱 ♨ ⌐ ⊙⊸🔲 🅂🅴 🄾 🚿
🄰🍴🄿🄱🄴
Nearby Facilities ⌐ ✔ 🛈 ⚓ 🛥 🚴 ⚡
Ettrick water right outside pitches. Beautiful
Ettrick Hills for walkers and climbers. Quiet
roads for cyclists. Ideal for touring the
Scottish Borders. Restaurant 1 mile.

EYEMOUTH
Eyemouth Holiday Park, Fort Road,
Eyemouth, Berwickshire, TD14 5BE.
Std: 01890 **Tel:** 751050 **Fax:** 751462
Email: lawson@oceaneye.demon.co.uk
Nearest Town/Resort Eyemouth
Acreage 50 **Open** 20 March **to** 20 Nov
Access Good **Site** Level
Sites Available ⊕ ⊕ **Total** 16
Facilities ⌁ ⌁ 🄵 🄷 🆄🄱 ♨ ⌐ ⊙⊸🔲 🄾 🚿
🄾🄰✗🍴🄼🄰🄿🄱🄴
Nearby Facilities ⌐ ✔ 🛈 ⚓ 🛥 🚴 ⚡
Cliffside location with superb views of the
sea. Private beach, sea angling and a
marine reserve.

GREENLAW
Blackadder Touring Park, Greenlaw
Caravan Park, Greenlaw, Berwickshire,
TD10 6XX.
Std: 01361 **Tel:** 810341
Email: chris@greenlawcaravanpark.co.uk
Website: www.scottishcaravanpark.com
Nearest Town/Resort Duns
Directions Signposted in the village of
Greenlaw.
Acreage 6 **Open** April **to** October
Access Good **Site** Level
Sites Available ⚠ ⊕🄾 **Total** 25
Facilities ⌁ 🄵 🄷 🆄🄱 ♨ ⌐ ⊙⊸🔲 🄸🄵 🄾
🄰🄰🍴🄴🄱🄴
Nearby Facilities ⌐ ✔ 🛈 🚴 ⚡
An attractive riverside setting situated in a
natural valley.

JEDBURGH
Camping & Caravanning Club Site,
Elliot Park, Jedburgh, Borders, TD8 6EF.
Std: 01835 **Tel:** 863393
Website:
www.campingandcaravanningclub.co.uk
Nearest Town/Resort Jedburgh
Directions On the A68 Newcastle to
Edinburgh road, on the northern side of
Jedburgh, entrance lies directly opposite the
Edinburgh & Jedburgh Woollen Mills.
Acreage 3 **Open** April **to** October
Access Good **Site** Level
Sites Available ⚠ ⊕ ⊕ **Total** 55
Facilities ⌁ 🆄🄱 ♨ ⌐ ⊙⊸🔲 🄸🄵 🄾 🄰🍴🄿🄱🄴
Nearby Facilities ⌐ ⚡ 🚴

⚓ Berwick-upon-Tweed
Quiet, secluded site bounded by the River
Jedburgh for fishing. Ideal touring base for
the Scottish Borders. 1 mile from Mary
Queen of Scots' House. Disabled toilet and
shower only. BTB Graded. Non members
welcome.

JEDBURGH
Jedwater Caravan Park, Jedburgh,
Borders, TD8 6PJ.
Std: 01835 **Tel:** 840219 **Fax:** 840219
Email: jedwater@jedburgh.com
Website: www.jedburgh.com
Nearest Town/Resort Jedburgh
Directions 4 miles south of Jedburgh on the
A68.
Acreage 10 **Open** Easter **to** October
Access Good **Site** Level
Sites Available ⌁ ⊕ ⊕ **Total** 45
Facilities ⌁ 🄷 🆄🄱 ♨ ⌐ ⊙🔲 🅂🅴 🄾 🄰🄱🄼🍴
🄰 ❈🍴🄱🄴
Nearby Facilities ⌐ ✔ 🛈 ⚡ 🚴
Sheltered park alongside a river. Ideal spot
for visiting historical Border towns.

KELSO
Springwood Caravan Park, Kelso,
Borders, TD5 8LS.
Std: 01573 **Tel:** 224596 **Fax:** 224033
Email: admin@springwoodestate.co.uk
Website: www.springwoodestate.co.uk
Nearest Town/Resort Kelso
Directions 1 mile from Kelso. Take the A699
south of the river.
Acreage 24½ **Open** End March **to** Mid Oct
Access Good **Site** Lev/Slope
Sites Available ⚠ ⊕ ⊕ **Total** 35
Facilities ⌁ 🄵 🄷 🆄🄱 ♨ ⌐ ⊙⊸🔲 🄾 🚿
🅂🅴 🄸🄵 🄾 🄰🍴🄰🄱🄴
Nearby Facilities ⌐ ✔ 🛈 ⚡
⚓ Berwick-upon-Tweed
Good walking and cycling.

PEEBLES
Crossburn Caravan Park, Edinburgh
Road, Peebles, Borders, EH45 8ED.
Std: 01721 **Tel:** 720501 **Fax:** 720501
Email: enquiries@crossburncaravans.co.uk
Website: www.crossburncaravans.co.uk
Nearest Town/Resort Peebles
Directions ½ mile north of Peebles on the
A703.
Acreage 6 **Open** 1 April/Easter **to** Oct
Access Good **Site** Level
Sites Available ⚠ ⊕ ⊕ **Total** 50
Facilities ⌁ 🄵 🄷 🆄🄱 ♨ ⌐ ⊙⊸🔲 🄾 🚿
🅂🅴 🄾 🄰🍴🄰🄱🄴
Nearby Facilities ⌐ ✔ 🛈
⚓ Edinburgh

River nearby. Ideal touring base.

PEEBLES
Rosetta Caravan & Camping Park,
Rosetta Road, Peebles, Borders, EH45 8
Std: 01721 **Tel:** 720770 **Fax:** 720623
Nearest Town/Resort Peebles
Directions 1 mile from Peebles, v
signposted from all main roads.
Acreage 27 **Open** April **to** October
Access Good **Site** Level
Sites Available ⚠ ⊕ ⊕ **Total** 130
Facilities ⌁ 🄷 🆄🄱 ♨ ⌐ ⊙⊸ ♫ 🄾
🅂🅴 🄸🄵 🄾 🄰🍴 🄼 🄰🍴🄱🄴
Nearby Facilities ⌐ ✔ 🛈 🚶 ⚡
⚓ Edinburgh
Scenic views. Fishing on the River Twe
Adjacent to a golf course. Ideal touring.

WESTERN ISLES
HARRIS
Laig House Caravan Site, 10 Drinnis
Hadder, Harris, Western Isles, HS3 3D✗
Std: 01859 **Tel:** 511207
Website: www.caravansite.co.uk
Nearest Town/Resort Tarbert
Directions 4½ miles south of Tarbert on
east coast.
Acreage 2½ **Open** April **to** October
Access Good **Site** Level
Sites Available ⚠ ⊕ ⊕ **Total** 20
Facilities ⚿ ⌁ 🄵 🄷 🆄🄱 ♨ ⌐ ⊙⊸🔲 🄾
🄼🄾 🄸🄵 🄾 🄰🍴🄰 ❈🍴🄱🄴
Nearby Facilities ⌐ ✔ 🛈 ⚓ 🚶 ⚡ 🚴 ⚡
⚓ Kyle of Lochalsh
Ideal touring, free fishing on coast.
walking and excellent beaches.

HARRIS
Minch View Caravan Site, 10
Drinishader, Isle of Harris, Western Isles
HS3 3DX.
Std: 01859 **Tel:** 511207
Website: www.caravansite.co.uk
Nearest Town/Resort Tarbert
Directions South east of Tarbert along
A859 (5 miles). Turn off the A859
Drinishader road end. From car ferry t
left at all junctions.
Acreage 3 **Open** April **to** October
Access Good **Site** Level
Sites Available ⚠ ⊕ **Total** 26
Facilities ⌁ 🄷 🆄🄱 ♨ ⌐ ⊙⊸🔲 🄾
🄼🄾 🄸🄵 🄾 🄰🍴🄰🄱🄴
Nearby Facilities ⌐ ✔ 🛈 ⚓ 🛥 🚶
⚓ Kyle of Lochalsh
Alongside the sea and a fresh water lc
with scenic views. Ideal touring.

ADULTS ONLY!
The following is a list of Parks who have specifically informed us that they cater purely for adults and d**o**
not accept children. We have listed them by *County* and then by *Town*. Simply find one to suit you**r**
chosen destination and then refer to the particular *County* in the main section of the guide for details.

ENGLAND
CHESHIRE
CHESTER Netherwood Touring Site,
CORNWALL
NEWQUAY Resparva House Touring Park,
NEWQUAY Sunnyside Holiday Park,
POLZEATH South Winds Camping & Caravan Park,
POLZEATH Tristram Caravan & Camping Park,

TRURO Chacewater Camping & Caravan Park,
CUMBRIA
MEALSGATE The Larches Caravan Park,
DERBYSHIRE
AMBERGATE, The Firs Farm Caravan & Camping Park,
DEVON
CHAGFORD, Woodland Springs Touring Park,
TIVERTON, Zeacombe House Caravan Park,

ORSET
RIDPORT, Binghams Farm Touring Caravan Park,
WANAGE, Cauldron Barn Farm Caravan Park,

AMPSHIRE
NGWOOD, Tree Tops Touring Caravan Park,

ANCASHIRE
LACKPOOL Sunset Park,

INCOLNSHIRE
OSTON Pilgrims Way Camping Park,
PALDING Delph Bank Touring
aravan & Camping Park,

ORFOLK
TTLEBOROUGH Oak Tree Caravan Park,
ROMER, Little Haven Caravan & Camping Park,
NGS LYNN, Gatton Water Touring
aravan & Camping Site,
ORTH WALSHAM, Two Mills Touring Park,

XFORDSHIRE
BINGDON, Bridge House Caravan Site,
ANBURY Bo Peep Farm Caravan Park,

OMERSET
ATH Bath Chew Valley Caravan Park,
URNHAM-ON-SEA Burnham Touring Park,
HEDDAR Cheddar Bridge Park,
ULVERTON Exe Valley Caravan Site,
LASTONBURY The Old Oaks Touring Park,
IVELISCOMBE Waterrow Touring Park,

USSEX
ATTLE Senlac Park Touring Caravan Site,

WEST MIDLANDS
MERIDEN Somers Wood Caravan & Camping Park,

WILTSHIRE
CHIPPENHAM Plough Lane Caravan Site,

YORKSHIRE (EAST)
WITHERNSEA Willows Holiday Park,
EASINGWOLD Holly Brook Caravan Park - Adults Only,

YORKSHIRE (NORTH)
RICHMOND Tavern House Caravan Park,
THIRSK Beechwood Caravan Park,
YORK, Moorside Caravan Park,

YORKSHIRE (WEST)
LEEDS, Moor Lodge Caravan Park,
WETHERBY, Maustin Caravan Park,

WALES
GWYNEDD
CHWILOG Tyddyn Heilyn,
POWYS
CRICKHOWELL Riverside Caravan & Camping Park
LLANWDDYN Fronheulog,
MONTGOMERY Bacheldre Watermill,

SCOTLAND
ABERDEENSHIRE
TURRIFF East Balthangie Caravan Park,
DUMFRIES & GALLOWAY
CREETOWN Ferry Croft Caravan Site,

FISHING ON SITE

Here for the very first time, we have endeavoured to cater for the fisherman by listing alphabetically parks featuring *'fishing on site'* or *'lakes'* in the attraction section of their entry. We have listed them by *County* and then by *Town*. Simply find one to suit your chosen destination and then refer back to that particular *County* in the guide for details.

ENGLAND

CAMBRIDGESHIRE
ST. IVES, Crystal Lakes Touring & Fishing Site,
WISBECH, Virginia Lake & Caravan Park,
CHESHIRE
KNUTSFORD, Woodlands Park,
CORNWALL
BOSCASTLE, St. Tinney Farm Holidays,
NEWQUAY, Newperran Tourist Park,
NEWQUAY, Trebellan Park,
NEWQUAY, Trencreek Holiday Park,
NEWQUAY, Trevella Park,
NEWQUAY, Trevornick Holiday Park,
NEWQUAY, White Acres Country Park,
PERRANPORTH, Perran Springs Touring Park,
ST. AUSTELL, Trencreek Farm Holiday Park,
TRURO, Camping & Caravanning Club Site,
CUMBRIA
LONGTOWN, Oakbank Lakes,
WINDERMERE, Limefitt Park,
DERBYSHIRE
ASHBOURNE, Callow Top Holiday Park,
MATLOCK, Merebrook Caravan Park,
DEVON
COMBE MARTIN, Newberry Farm,
CREDITON, Yeatheridge Farm Caravan Park,
EXETER, Haldon Lodge Farm Caravan & Camping Park,
ILFRACOMBE, Mill Park Touring Site,
MORTEHOE, Warcombe Farm Camping Park,
OKEHAMPTON, Culverhayes Camping Park,
TAVISTOCK, Dartmoor Country Holidays,
DORSET
WEYMOUTH, Osmington Mills Holidays Ltd.,
DURHAM
MIDDLETON-IN-TEESDALE, Mickleton Mill Caravan Park,
ESSEX
ST. OSYTH, The Orchards Holiday Village,
WEELEY, Weeley Bridge Caravan Park,
GLOUCESTERSHIRE
GLOUCESTER, Red Lion Caravan & Camping Park,
TEWKESBURY, Camping & Caravanning Club Site,
HAMPSHIRE
HAYLING ISLAND, Fishery Creek Caravan & Camping Park,
HEREFORDSHIRE
LEOMINSTER, Nicholson Farm,
ROSS-ON-WYE, Broadmeadow Caravan Park,
ISLE OF WIGHT
SANDOWN, Village Way Caravan & Camping Park,
YARMOUTH, The Orchards Holiday Caravan & Camping Park,
LANCASHIRE
GARSTANG, Claylands Caravan Park,
GARSTANG, Smithy Caravan Park,
KIRKHAM, Whitmore Fisheries & Caravan Park,
ORMSKIRK, Hurlston Hall Country Caravan Park,
LINCOLNSHIRE
CLEETHORPES, Thorpe Park Holiday Centre,
HORNCASTLE, Ashby Park,
HORNCASTLE, Horncastle Golf & Country Club,
INGOLDMELLS, Country Meadows Holiday Park,
MABLETHORPE, Grange Farm Leisure Ltd.,
MABLETHORPE, Willows Caravan Park,
MARKET DEEPING, The Deepings Caravan Park,
SKEGNESS, Herons Mead Fishing Lake & Touring Park,
SKEGNESS, Hill View Fishing Lakes & Touring Caravan Park,
SKEGNESS, Manor Farm Caravan Park,
SKEGNESS, Skegness Water Leisure Park,
SLEAFORD, Woodland Waters,
SPALDING, Lake Ross Caravan Park,
TATTERSHALL, Willow Holt Caravan & Camping Park,
WAINFLEET ALL SAINTS, Swan Lake Caravan Park,
NORFOLK
CAWSTON, Haveringland Hall Park,

NORFOLK
FAKENHAM, The Old Brick Kilns,
HARLESTON, Little Lakeland Caravan Park,
HARLESTON, Waveney Valley Lakes.
KINGS LYNN, Gatton Water Touring Caravan & Camping Site,
NORWICH, Camping & Caravanning Club Site,
NORTHUMBERLAND
HALTWHISTLE, Camping & Caravanning Club Site,
HAYDON BRIDGE, Poplars Riverside Caravan Park,
NOTTINGHAMSHIRE
NEWARK, Milestone Caravan Park,
NOTTINGHAM, Moor Farm Holiday & Home Park,
OXFORDSHIRE
HENLEY-ON-THAMES, Swiss Farm International Camping,
SHROPSHIRE
BISHOPS CASTLE, Walcot Caravan & Camp Site,
BRIDGNORTH, Woodend Farm,
CLUN, Bush Farm,
SOMERSET
BREAN SANDS, Northam Farm Caravan & Touring Park,
BURNHAM-ON-SEA, Home Farm Holiday Park & Country Club,
DULVERTON, Exe Valley Caravan Site,
LANGPORT, Thorney Lakes Caravan Site,
WELLINGTON, Gamlins Farm Caravans,
SUFFOLK
EYE, Honeypot Camp & Caravan Park
SAXMUNDHAM, Lakeside Country & Leisure Park,
STOWMARKET, Stonham Barns Caravan & Camping Park,
SURREY
CHERTSEY, Camping & Caravanning Club Site,
EAST HORSLEY, Camping & Caravanning Club Site,
SUSSEX
BATTLE, Brakes Coppice Park,
HASTINGS, Spindlewood Country Holiday Park,
NEWHAVEN, Three Ponds Holiday Park,
UCKFIELD, Heaven Farm,
UCKFIELD, Honeys Green Farm Caravan Park,
WILTSHIRE
DEVIZES, Camping & Caravanning Club Site,
WORCESTERSHIRE
EVESHAM, Weir Meadow Holiday & Touring Park,
MALVERN, Kingsgreen Caravan Park,
YORKSHIRE (NORTH)
ELVINGTON, Elvington Lake Caravan Park,
KNARESBOROUGH, Lido Caravan Park,
RIPON, Woodhouse Farm Caravan & Camping Park,
YORK, Cawood Holiday Park,
YORK, Moorside Caravan Park,
YORK, Poplar Farm Caravan Park,
YORK, Wigman Hall,

WALES

CAERPHILLY, BARGOED, Parc Cwm Darran Caravan & Camp Site,
CEREDIGION
CARDIGAN, Blaenwaun Farm,
NEW QUAY, Pencnwc Holiday Park,
SARNAU, Dyffryn Bern Caravan Park,
TREGARON, Hendrewen Caravan Park,
CONWY
TY-NANT, Glan Ceirw Caravan Park,
GWYNEDD
BALA, Bryn Melyn Country Holiday Park,
PEMBROKESHIRE
NARBERTH, Noble Court Caravan Park,
ST. FLORENCE, New Minerton Leisure Park,

SCOTLAND

DUMFRIES & GALLOWAY
NEWTON STEWART, Glentrool Holiday Park,
PERTH & KINROSS
BRIDGE OF CALLY, Corriefodly Holiday Park,
STIRLING
DRYMEN, Camping & Caravanning Club Site,

CADE'S   FIFTY PENCE

CAMPING, TOURING & MOTOR CARAVAN SITE GUIDE 2002

PRESENT THIS VOUCHER TO THE SITE OPERATOR WHEN PAYING TO RECEIVE FIFTY PENCE DISCOUNT PER VOUCHER, PER NIGHT. SEE CONDITIONS OVERLEAF. VALID UNTIL 31-12-02.

CADE'S   FIFTY PENCE

CAMPING, TOURING & MOTOR CARAVAN SITE GUIDE 2002

PRESENT THIS VOUCHER TO THE SITE OPERATOR WHEN PAYING TO RECEIVE FIFTY PENCE DISCOUNT PER VOUCHER, PER NIGHT. SEE CONDITIONS OVERLEAF. VALID UNTIL 31-12-02.

CADE'S   FIFTY PENCE

CAMPING, TOURING & MOTOR CARAVAN SITE GUIDE 2002

PRESENT THIS VOUCHER TO THE SITE OPERATOR WHEN PAYING TO RECEIVE FIFTY PENCE DISCOUNT PER VOUCHER, PER NIGHT. SEE CONDITIONS OVERLEAF. VALID UNTIL 31-12-02.

CADE'S   FIFTY PENCE

CAMPING, TOURING & MOTOR CARAVAN SITE GUIDE 2002

PRESENT THIS VOUCHER TO THE SITE OPERATOR WHEN PAYING TO RECEIVE FIFTY PENCE DISCOUNT PER VOUCHER, PER NIGHT. SEE CONDITIONS OVERLEAF. VALID UNTIL 31-12-02.

CADE'S   FIFTY PENCE

CAMPING, TOURING & MOTOR CARAVAN SITE GUIDE 2002

PRESENT THIS VOUCHER TO THE SITE OPERATOR WHEN PAYING TO RECEIVE FIFTY PENCE DISCOUNT PER VOUCHER, PER NIGHT. SEE CONDITIONS OVERLEAF. VALID UNTIL 31-12-02.

CADE'S   FIFTY PENCE

CAMPING, TOURING & MOTOR CARAVAN SITE GUIDE 2001

PRESENT THIS VOUCHER TO THE SITE OPERATOR WHEN PAYING TO RECEIVE FIFTY PENCE DISCOUNT PER VOUCHER, PER NIGHT. SEE CONDITIONS OVERLEAF. VALID UNTIL 31-12-02.

CADE'S   FIFTY PENCE

CAMPING, TOURING & MOTOR CARAVAN SITE GUIDE 2002

PRESENT THIS VOUCHER TO THE SITE OPERATOR WHEN PAYING TO RECEIVE FIFTY PENCE DISCOUNT PER VOUCHER, PER NIGHT. SEE CONDITIONS OVERLEAF. VALID UNTIL 31-12-02.

CADE'S   FIFTY PENCE

CAMPING, TOURING & MOTOR CARAVAN SITE GUIDE 2002

PRESENT THIS VOUCHER TO THE SITE OPERATOR WHEN PAYING TO RECEIVE FIFTY PENCE DISCOUNT PER VOUCHER, PER NIGHT. SEE CONDITIONS OVERLEAF. VALID UNTIL 31-12-02.

CADE'S   FIFTY PENCE

CAMPING, TOURING & MOTOR CARAVAN SITE GUIDE 2001

PRESENT THIS VOUCHER TO THE SITE OPERATOR WHEN PAYING TO RECEIVE FIFTY PENCE DISCOUNT PER VOUCHER, PER NIGHT. SEE CONDITIONS OVERLEAF. VALID UNTIL 31-12-02.

CADE'S   FIFTY PENCE

CAMPING, TOURING & MOTOR CARAVAN SITE GUIDE 2001

PRESENT THIS VOUCHER TO THE SITE OPERATOR WHEN PAYING TO RECEIVE FIFTY PENCE DISCOUNT PER VOUCHER, PER NIGHT. SEE CONDITIONS OVERLEAF. VALID UNTIL 31-12-02.

MONEY OFF VOUCHERS

CONDITIONS OF USE

Vouchers will only be redeemed by those sites featuring a ◪ symbol in the *facilities* line of their County entry. Presentation of this voucher to the Site Operator at the time of paying your balance will entitle you to a fifty pence discount per voucher, per night. (Only one voucher per night). Vouchers may be used in multiples i.e. five vouchers presented for a five night stay will entitle you to a discount of £2.50.

A CADE'S CAMPING, TOURING & MOTOR CARAVAN SITE GUIDE 2002 EDITION must be presented at the time of payment. Vouchers are valid for accommodation only. Vouchers may not be exchanged for cash. May not be used with any other offer. Valid until 31-12-02.

CONDITIONS OF USE

Vouchers will only be redeemed by those sites featuring a ◪ symbol in the *facilities* line of their County entry. Presentation of this voucher to the Site Operator at the time of paying your balance will entitle you to a fifty pence discount per voucher, per night. (Only one voucher per night). Vouchers may be used in multiples i.e. five vouchers presented for a five night stay will entitle you to a discount of £2.50.

A CADE'S CAMPING, TOURING & MOTOR CARAVAN SITE GUIDE 2002 EDITION must be presented at the time of payment. Vouchers are valid for accommodation only. Vouchers may not be exchanged for cash. May not be used with any other offer. Valid until 31-12-02.

CONDITIONS OF USE

Vouchers will only be redeemed by those sites featuring a ◪ symbol in the *facilities* line of their County entry. Presentation of this voucher to the Site Operator at the time of paying your balance will entitle you to a fifty pence discount per voucher, per night. (Only one voucher per night). Vouchers may be used in multiples i.e. five vouchers presented for a five night stay will entitle you to a discount of £2.50.

A CADE'S CAMPING, TOURING & MOTOR CARAVAN SITE GUIDE 2002 EDITION must be presented at the time of payment. Vouchers are valid for accommodation only. Vouchers may not be exchanged for cash. May not be used with any other offer. Valid until 31-12-02.

CONDITIONS OF USE

Vouchers will only be redeemed by those sites featuring a ◪ symbol in the *facilities* line of their County entry. Presentation of this voucher to the Site Operator at the time of paying your balance will entitle you to a fifty pence discount per voucher, per night. (Only one voucher per night). Vouchers may be used in multiples i.e. five vouchers presented for a five night stay will entitle you to a discount of £2.50.

A CADE'S CAMPING, TOURING & MOTOR CARAVAN SITE GUIDE 2002 EDITION must be presented at the time of payment. Vouchers are valid for accommodation only. Vouchers may not be exchanged for cash. May not be used with any other offer. Valid until 31-12-02.

CONDITIONS OF USE

Vouchers will only be redeemed by those sites featuring a ◪ symbol in the *facilities* line of their County entry. Presentation of this voucher to the Site Operator at the time of paying your balance will entitle you to a fifty pence discount per voucher, per night. (Only one voucher per night). Vouchers may be used in multiples i.e. five vouchers presented for a five night stay will entitle you to a discount of £2.50.

A CADE'S CAMPING, TOURING & MOTOR CARAVAN SITE GUIDE 2002 EDITION must be presented at the time of payment. Vouchers are valid for accommodation only. Vouchers may not be exchanged for cash. May not be used with any other offer. Valid until 31-12-02.

CONDITIONS OF USE

Vouchers will only be redeemed by those sites featuring a ◪ symbol in the *facilities* line of their County entry. Presentation of this voucher to the Site Operator at the time of paying your balance will entitle you to a fifty pence discount per voucher, per night. (Only one voucher per night). Vouchers may be used in multiples i.e. five vouchers presented for a five night stay will entitle you to a discount of £2.50.

A CADE'S CAMPING, TOURING & MOTOR CARAVAN SITE GUIDE 2002 EDITION must be presented at the time of payment. Vouchers are valid for accommodation only. Vouchers may not be exchanged for cash. May not be used with any other offer. Valid until 31-12-02.

CONDITIONS OF USE

Vouchers will only be redeemed by those sites featuring a ◪ symbol in the *facilities* line of their County entry. Presentation of this voucher to the Site Operator at the time of paying your balance will entitle you to a fifty pence discount per voucher, per night. (Only one voucher per night). Vouchers may be used in multiples i.e. five vouchers presented for a five night stay will entitle you to a discount of £2.50.

A CADE'S CAMPING, TOURING & MOTOR CARAVAN SITE GUIDE 2002 EDITION must be presented at the time of payment. Vouchers are valid for accommodation only. Vouchers may not be exchanged for cash. May not be used with any other offer. Valid until 31-12-02.

CONDITIONS OF USE

Vouchers will only be redeemed by those sites featuring a ◪ symbol in the *facilities* line of their County entry. Presentation of this voucher to the Site Operator at the time of paying your balance will entitle you to a fifty pence discount per voucher, per night. (Only one voucher per night). Vouchers may be used in multiples i.e. five vouchers presented for a five night stay will entitle you to a discount of £2.50.

A CADE'S CAMPING, TOURING & MOTOR CARAVAN SITE GUIDE 2002 EDITION must be presented at the time of payment. Vouchers are valid for accommodation only. Vouchers may not be exchanged for cash. May not be used with any other offer. Valid until 31-12-02.

CONDITIONS OF USE

Vouchers will only be redeemed by those sites featuring a ◪ symbol in the *facilities* line of their County entry. Presentation of this voucher to the Site Operator at the time of paying your balance will entitle you to a fifty pence discount per voucher, per night. (Only one voucher per night). Vouchers may be used in multiples i.e. five vouchers presented for a five night stay will entitle you to a discount of £2.50.

A CADE'S CAMPING, TOURING & MOTOR CARAVAN SITE GUIDE 2002 EDITION must be presented at the time of payment. Vouchers are valid for accommodation only. Vouchers may not be exchanged for cash. May not be used with any other offer. Valid until 31-12-02.

CONDITIONS OF USE

Vouchers will only be redeemed by those sites featuring a ◪ symbol in the *facilities* line of their County entry. Presentation of this voucher to the Site Operator at the time of paying your balance will entitle you to a fifty pence discount per voucher, per night. (Only one voucher per night). Vouchers may be used in multiples i.e. five vouchers presented for a five night stay will entitle you to a discount of £2.50.

A CADE'S CAMPING, TOURING & MOTOR CARAVAN SITE GUIDE 2002 EDITION must be presented at the time of payment. Vouchers are valid for accommodation only. Vouchers may not be exchanged for cash. May not be used with any other offer. Valid until 31-12-02.

CADE'S FIFTY PENCE **CAMPING, TOURING & MOTOR CARAVAN SITE GUIDE 2002** PRESENT THIS VOUCHER TO THE SITE OPERATOR WHEN PAYING TO RECEIVE FIFTY PENCE DISCOUNT PER VOUCHER, PER NIGHT. SEE CONDITIONS OVERLEAF. VALID UNTIL 31-12-02.	CADE'S FIFTY PENCE **CAMPING, TOURING & MOTOR CARAVAN SITE GUIDE 2002** PRESENT THIS VOUCHER TO THE SITE OPERATOR WHEN PAYING TO RECEIVE FIFTY PENCE DISCOUNT PER VOUCHER, PER NIGHT. SEE CONDITIONS OVERLEAF. VALID UNTIL 31-12-02.
CADE'S FIFTY PENCE **CAMPING, TOURING & MOTOR CARAVAN SITE GUIDE 2002** PRESENT THIS VOUCHER TO THE SITE OPERATOR WHEN PAYING TO RECEIVE FIFTY PENCE DISCOUNT PER VOUCHER, PER NIGHT. SEE CONDITIONS OVERLEAF. VALID UNTIL 31-12-02.	CADE'S FIFTY PENCE **CAMPING, TOURING & MOTOR CARAVAN SITE GUIDE 2002** PRESENT THIS VOUCHER TO THE SITE OPERATOR WHEN PAYING TO RECEIVE FIFTY PENCE DISCOUNT PER VOUCHER, PER NIGHT. SEE CONDITIONS OVERLEAF. VALID UNTIL 31-12-02.
CADE'S FIFTY PENCE **CAMPING, TOURING & MOTOR CARAVAN SITE GUIDE 2002** PRESENT THIS VOUCHER TO THE SITE OPERATOR WHEN PAYING TO RECEIVE FIFTY PENCE DISCOUNT PER VOUCHER, PER NIGHT. SEE CONDITIONS OVERLEAF. VALID UNTIL 31-12-02.	CADE'S FIFTY PENCE **CAMPING, TOURING & MOTOR CARAVAN SITE GUIDE 2001** PRESENT THIS VOUCHER TO THE SITE OPERATOR WHEN PAYING TO RECEIVE FIFTY PENCE DISCOUNT PER VOUCHER, PER NIGHT. SEE CONDITIONS OVERLEAF. VALID UNTIL 31-12-02.
CADE'S FIFTY PENCE **CAMPING, TOURING & MOTOR CARAVAN SITE GUIDE 2002** PRESENT THIS VOUCHER TO THE SITE OPERATOR WHEN PAYING TO RECEIVE FIFTY PENCE DISCOUNT PER VOUCHER, PER NIGHT. SEE CONDITIONS OVERLEAF. VALID UNTIL 31-12-02.	CADE'S FIFTY PENCE **CAMPING, TOURING & MOTOR CARAVAN SITE GUIDE 2002** PRESENT THIS VOUCHER TO THE SITE OPERATOR WHEN PAYING TO RECEIVE FIFTY PENCE DISCOUNT PER VOUCHER, PER NIGHT. SEE CONDITIONS OVERLEAF. VALID UNTIL 31-12-02.
CADE'S FIFTY PENCE **CAMPING, TOURING & MOTOR CARAVAN SITE GUIDE 2001** PRESENT THIS VOUCHER TO THE SITE OPERATOR WHEN PAYING TO RECEIVE FIFTY PENCE DISCOUNT PER VOUCHER, PER NIGHT. SEE CONDITIONS OVERLEAF. VALID UNTIL 31-12-02.	CADE'S FIFTY PENCE **CAMPING, TOURING & MOTOR CARAVAN SITE GUIDE 2001** PRESENT THIS VOUCHER TO THE SITE OPERATOR WHEN PAYING TO RECEIVE FIFTY PENCE DISCOUNT PER VOUCHER, PER NIGHT. SEE CONDITIONS OVERLEAF. VALID UNTIL 31-12-02.

MONEY OFF VOUCHERS

CONDITIONS OF USE

Vouchers will only be redeemed by those sites featuring a ⊠ symbol in the *facilities* line of their County entry. Presentation of this voucher to the Site Operator at the time of paying your balance will entitle you to a fifty pence discount per voucher, per night. (Only one voucher per night). Vouchers may be used in multiples i.e. five vouchers presented for a five night stay will entitle you to a discount of £2.50.

A CADE'S CAMPING, TOURING & MOTOR CARAVAN SITE GUIDE 2002 EDITION must be presented at the time of payment. Vouchers are valid for accommodation only. Vouchers may not be exchanged for cash. May not be used with any other offer. Valid until 31-12-02.

CONDITIONS OF USE

Vouchers will only be redeemed by those sites featuring a ⊠ symbol in the *facilities* line of their County entry. Presentation of this voucher to the Site Operator at the time of paying your balance will entitle you to a fifty pence discount per voucher, per night. (Only one voucher per night). Vouchers may be used in multiples i.e. five vouchers presented for a five night stay will entitle you to a discount of £2.50.

A CADE'S CAMPING, TOURING & MOTOR CARAVAN SITE GUIDE 2002 EDITION must be presented at the time of payment. Vouchers are valid for accommodation only. Vouchers may not be exchanged for cash. May not be used with any other offer. Valid until 31-12-02.

CONDITIONS OF USE

Vouchers will only be redeemed by those sites featuring a ⊠ symbol in the *facilities* line of their County entry. Presentation of this voucher to the Site Operator at the time of paying your balance will entitle you to a fifty pence discount per voucher, per night. (Only one voucher per night). Vouchers may be used in multiples i.e. five vouchers presented for a five night stay will entitle you to a discount of £2.50.

A CADE'S CAMPING, TOURING & MOTOR CARAVAN SITE GUIDE 2002 EDITION must be presented at the time of payment. Vouchers are valid for accommodation only. Vouchers may not be exchanged for cash. May not be used with any other offer. Valid until 31-12-02.

CONDITIONS OF USE

Vouchers will only be redeemed by those sites featuring a ⊠ symbol in the *facilities* line of their County entry. Presentation of this voucher to the Site Operator at the time of paying your balance will entitle you to a fifty pence discount per voucher, per night. (Only one voucher per night). Vouchers may be used in multiples i.e. five vouchers presented for a five night stay will entitle you to a discount of £2.50.

A CADE'S CAMPING, TOURING & MOTOR CARAVAN SITE GUIDE 2002 EDITION must be presented at the time of payment. Vouchers are valid for accommodation only. Vouchers may not be exchanged for cash. May not be used with any other offer. Valid until 31-12-02.

CONDITIONS OF USE

Vouchers will only be redeemed by those sites featuring a ⊠ symbol in the *facilities* line of their County entry. Presentation of this voucher to the Site Operator at the time of paying your balance will entitle you to a fifty pence discount per voucher, per night. (Only one voucher per night). Vouchers may be used in multiples i.e. five vouchers presented for a five night stay will entitle you to a discount of £2.50.

A CADE'S CAMPING, TOURING & MOTOR CARAVAN SITE GUIDE 2002 EDITION must be presented at the time of payment. Vouchers are valid for accommodation only. Vouchers may not be exchanged for cash. May not be used with any other offer. Valid until 31-12-02.

CONDITIONS OF USE

Vouchers will only be redeemed by those sites featuring a ⊠ symbol in the *facilities* line of their County entry. Presentation of this voucher to the Site Operator at the time of paying your balance will entitle you to a fifty pence discount per voucher, per night. (Only one voucher per night). Vouchers may be used in multiples i.e. five vouchers presented for a five night stay will entitle you to a discount of £2.50.

A CADE'S CAMPING, TOURING & MOTOR CARAVAN SITE GUIDE 2002 EDITION must be presented at the time of payment. Vouchers are valid for accommodation only. Vouchers may not be exchanged for cash. May not be used with any other offer. Valid until 31-12-02.

CONDITIONS OF USE

Vouchers will only be redeemed by those sites featuring a ⊠ symbol in the *facilities* line of their County entry. Presentation of this voucher to the Site Operator at the time of paying your balance will entitle you to a fifty pence discount per voucher, per night. (Only one voucher per night). Vouchers may be used in multiples i.e. five vouchers presented for a five night stay will entitle you to a discount of £2.50.

A CADE'S CAMPING, TOURING & MOTOR CARAVAN SITE GUIDE 2002 EDITION must be presented at the time of payment. Vouchers are valid for accommodation only. Vouchers may not be exchanged for cash. May not be used with any other offer. Valid until 31-12-02.

CONDITIONS OF USE

Vouchers will only be redeemed by those sites featuring a ⊠ symbol in the *facilities* line of their County entry. Presentation of this voucher to the Site Operator at the time of paying your balance will entitle you to a fifty pence discount per voucher, per night. (Only one voucher per night). Vouchers may be used in multiples i.e. five vouchers presented for a five night stay will entitle you to a discount of £2.50.

A CADE'S CAMPING, TOURING & MOTOR CARAVAN SITE GUIDE 2002 EDITION must be presented at the time of payment. Vouchers are valid for accommodation only. Vouchers may not be exchanged for cash. May not be used with any other offer. Valid until 31-12-02.

CONDITIONS OF USE

Vouchers will only be redeemed by those sites featuring a ⊠ symbol in the *facilities* line of their County entry. Presentation of this voucher to the Site Operator at the time of paying your balance will entitle you to a fifty pence discount per voucher, per night. (Only one voucher per night). Vouchers may be used in multiples i.e. five vouchers presented for a five night stay will entitle you to a discount of £2.50.

A CADE'S CAMPING, TOURING & MOTOR CARAVAN SITE GUIDE 2002 EDITION must be presented at the time of payment. Vouchers are valid for accommodation only. Vouchers may not be exchanged for cash. May not be used with any other offer. Valid until 31-12-02.

CONDITIONS OF USE

Vouchers will only be redeemed by those sites featuring a ⊠ symbol in the *facilities* line of their County entry. Presentation of this voucher to the Site Operator at the time of paying your balance will entitle you to a fifty pence discount per voucher, per night. (Only one voucher per night). Vouchers may be used in multiples i.e. five vouchers presented for a five night stay will entitle you to a discount of £2.50.

A CADE'S CAMPING, TOURING & MOTOR CARAVAN SITE GUIDE 2002 EDITION must be presented at the time of payment. Vouchers are valid for accommodation only. Vouchers may not be exchanged for cash. May not be used with any other offer. Valid until 31-12-02.

MAP SECTION

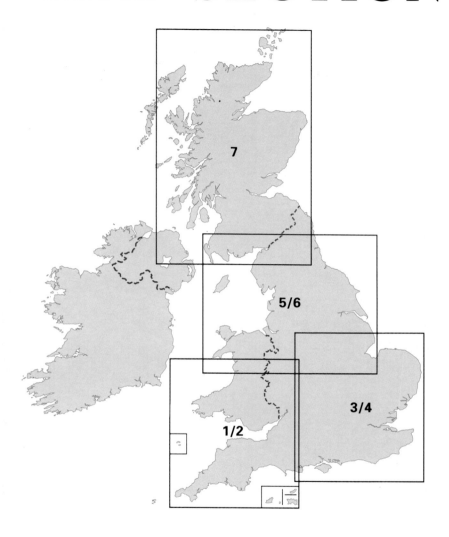

7

5/6

3/4

1/2

Maps designed and produced by GEOprojects (UK) Ltd., Reading, Berkshire. RG1 4QS. © GEOprojects (UK) Ltd.

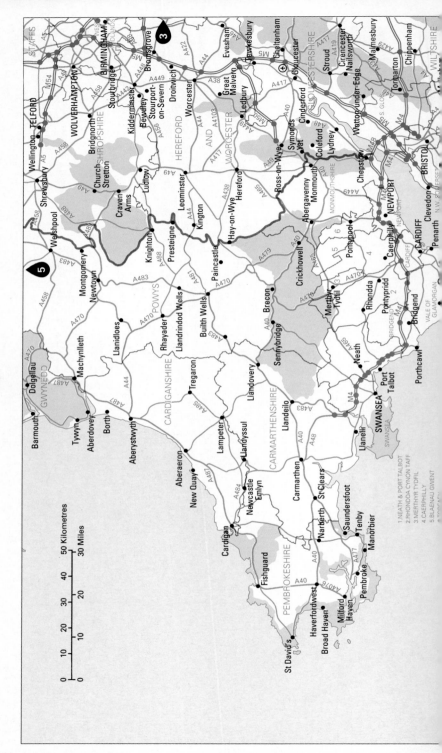

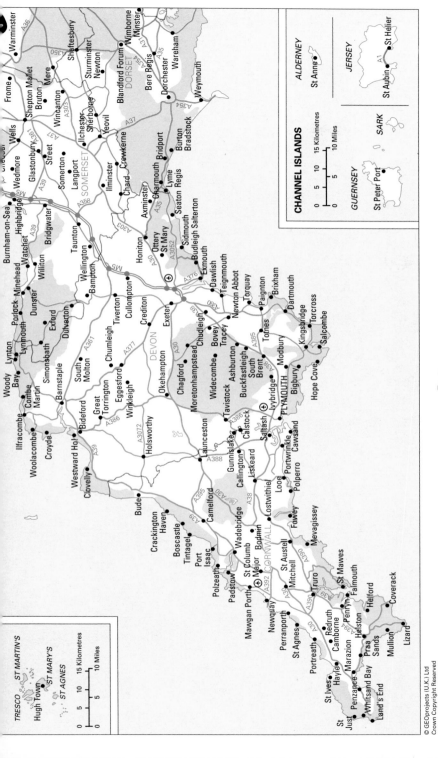

2

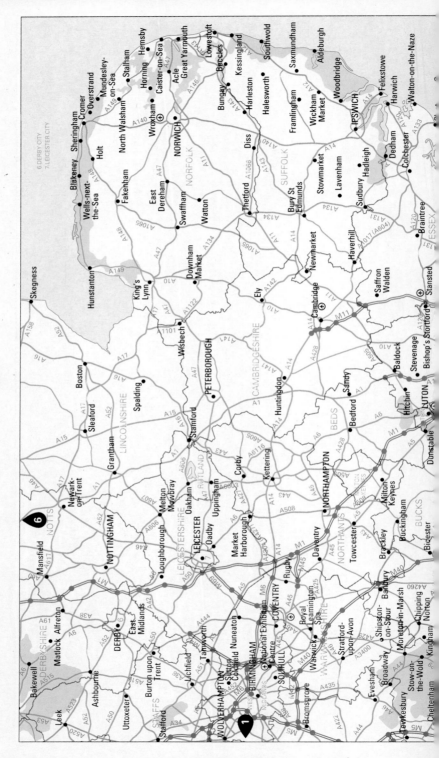

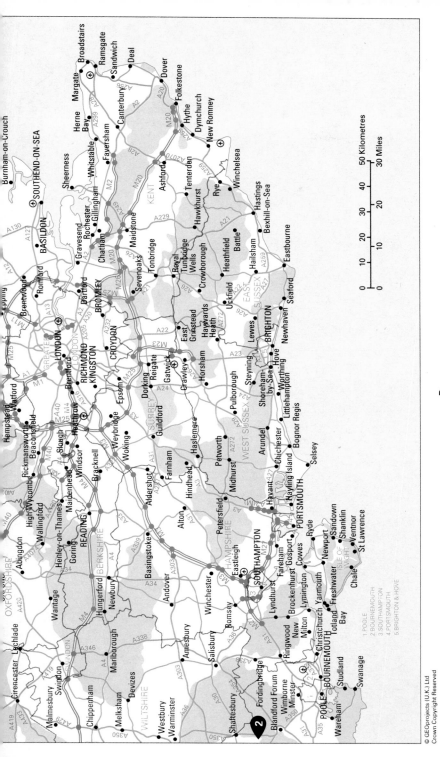

4

Langholm
Lockerbie
Bellingham

New Galloway
DUMFRIES AND GALLOWAY
Dumfries
Gretna
Longtown
Greenhead

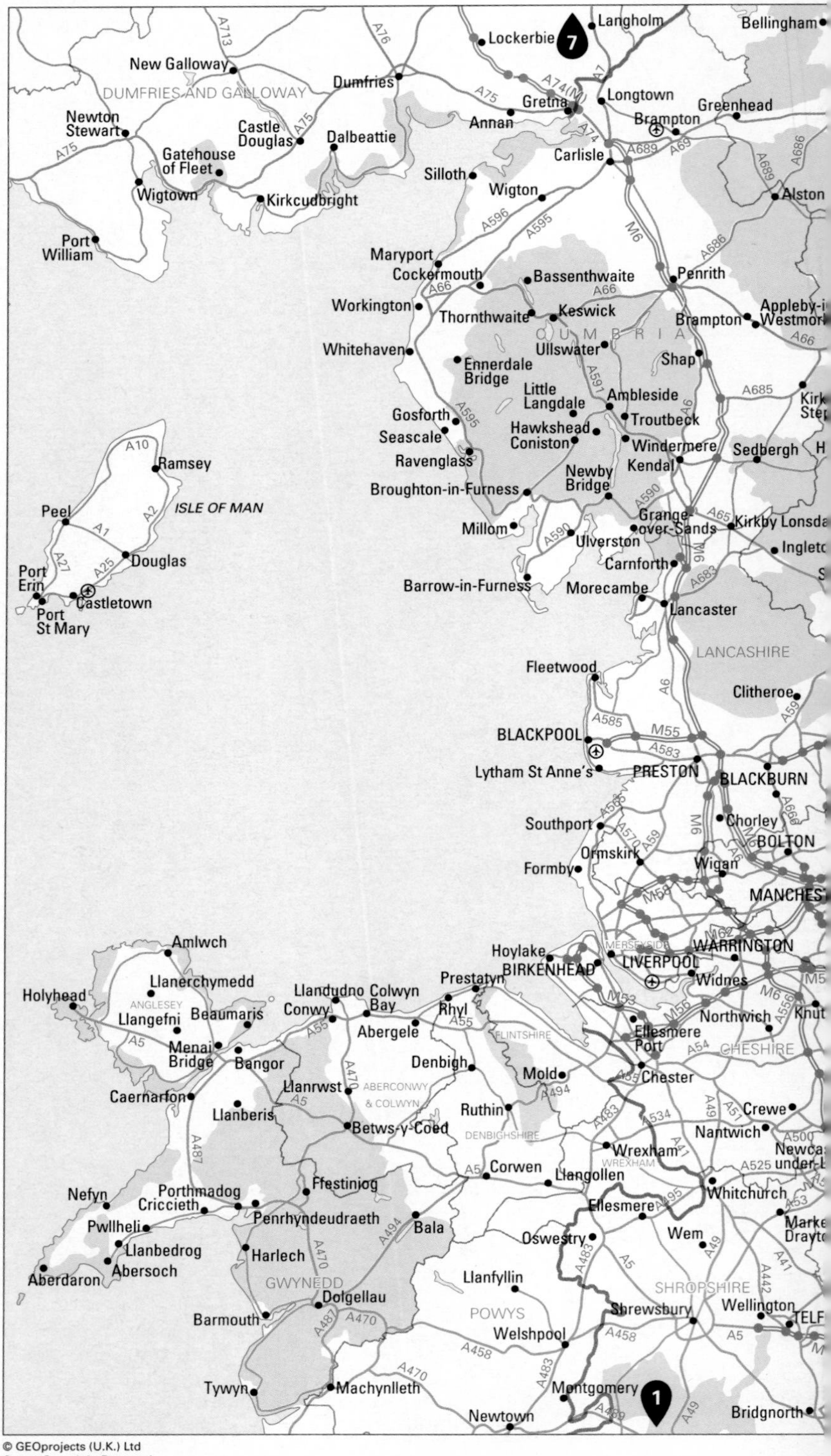

Newton Stewart
Castle Douglas
Dalbeattie
Annan
Brampton
Carlisle

Gatehouse of Fleet
Wigtown
Kirkcudbright
Silloth
Wigton
Alston

Port William
Maryport
Cockermouth
Penrith
Appleby-i
Westmor

Workington
Bassenthwaite
Thornthwaite
Keswick
Brampton
A66

Whitehaven
Ullswater
CUMBRIA
Shap

Ennerdale Bridge
Little Langdale
Ambleside
Kirk
Step

Gosforth
Hawkshead
Troutbeck

Seascale
Coniston
Windermere
Sedbergh
H

Ravenglass
Newby Bridge
Kendal

Broughton-in-Furness
Grange-over-Sands
Kirkby Lonsda

Millom
Ulverston
Ingleto

Barrow-in-Furness
Carnforth
Morecambe
Lancaster

ISLE OF MAN

Ramsey
Peel
Douglas
Port Erin
Castletown
Port St Mary

5

Fleetwood
LANCASHIRE
Clitheroe

BLACKPOOL
PRESTON
BLACKBURN

Lytham St Anne's
Southport
Chorley
BOLTON

Formby
Ormskirk
Wigan

MANCHES

Amlwch
WARRINGTON

Llanerchymedd
Hoylake
BIRKENHEAD
LIVERPOOL
Widnes

Holyhead
ANGLESEY
Beaumaris
Llandudno
Colwyn Bay
Prestatyn
Northwich
Knut

Llangefni
Conwy
Rhyl
Ellesmere Port
CHESHIRE

Menai Bridge
Bangor
Abergele
Denbigh
Mold
Chester

Caernarfon
Llanrwst
ABERCONWY & COLWYN
Ruthin
Crewe
Nantwich
Newca
under-L

Llanberis
Betws-y-Coed
DENBIGHSHIRE
Corwen
Wrexham
WREXHAM

Nefyn
Porthmadog
Ffestiniog
Llangollen
Whitchurch

Criccieth
Penrhyndeudraeth
Bala
Ellesmere
Wem
Marke
Drayto

Pwllheli
Oswestry

Llanbedrog
Llanfyllin
SHROPSHIRE

Aberdaron
Abersoch
Harlech
GWYNEDD
Dolgellau
POWYS
Shrewsbury
Wellington
TELF

Barmouth
Welshpool

Tywyn
Machynlleth
Montgomery

Newtown
Bridgnorth

286

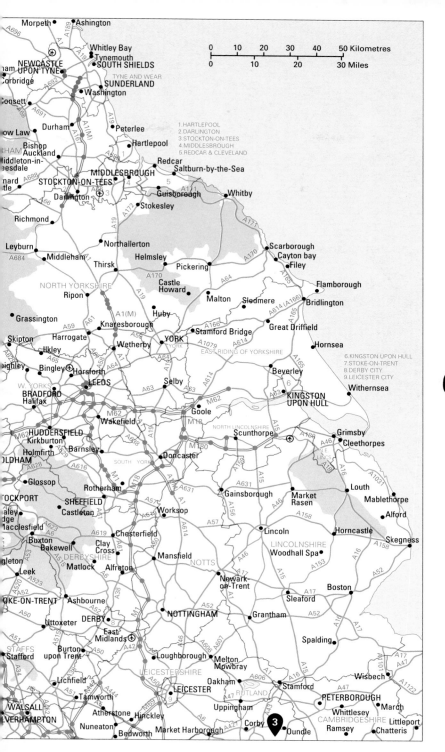

0   10   20   30   40   50 Kilometres

0   10   20   30 Miles

Morpeth • Ashington
Whitley Bay
ham • Tynemouth
NEWCASTLE • SOUTH SHIELDS
UPON TYNE
Corbridge
TYNE AND WEAR
SUNDERLAND
onsett • Washington

Durham • Peterlee
Bishop
Auckland • Hartlepool
iddleton-in-
eesdale
Redcar
STOCKTON-ON-TEES • Saltburn-by-the-Sea
nard • MIDDLESBROUGH
tle • Darlington • Guisborough • Whitby
Stokesley

1.HARTLEPOOL
2.DARLINGTON
3.STOCKTON-ON-TEES
4.MIDDLESBROUGH
5.REDCAR & CLEVELAND

Richmond

Leyburn • Northallerton • Scarborough
Middleham • Helmsley • Cayton bay
Thirsk • Pickering • Filey

NORTH YORKSHIRE
Castle
Howard • Flamborough

Grassington • Ripon • Malton • Sledmere • Bridlington

Skipton • Huby
Knaresborough • Great Driffield
Harrogate • Stamford Bridge
Ilkley • Wetherby • YORK • Hornsea
ighley • Bingley • Horsforth
EAST RIDING OF YORKSHIRE
LEEDS • Selby • Beverley
W. YORKS
BRADFORD • Goole
Halifax • Wakefield • KINGSTON
UPON HULL
HUDDERSFIELD • Withernsea
Kirkburton • NORTH LINCOLNSHIRE
Holmfirth • Barnsley • Scunthorpe • Grimsby
OLDHAM • Doncaster • Cleethorpes

6.KINGSTON UPON HULL
7.STOKE-ON-TRENT
8.DERBY CITY
9.LEICESTER CITY

6

Glossop • Rotherham • Gainsborough • Market • Louth
Rasen • Mablethorpe
OCKPORT • SHEFFIELD • Worksop
aley • Castleton • Alford
dge • Lincoln • Horncastle
acclesfield • Chesterfield • Skegness
Buxton • Clay • LINCOLNSHIRE
Bakewell • Cross • Mansfield • Woodhall Spa
gleton • DERBYSHIRE
Leek • Matlock • Alfreton • Newark- • Boston
on-Trent
KE-ON-TRENT • Ashbourne • NOTTS • Sleaford
Uttoxeter • DERBY • NOTTINGHAM • Grantham
East • Spalding
STAFFS • Midlands
Stafford • Burton • Loughborough
upon Trent • Melton
Lichfield • Mowbray • Wisbech
LEICESTERSHIRE
WALSALL • Tamworth • Oakham • Stamford • March
Atherstone • LEICESTER • RUTLAND • PETERBOROUGH
VERHAMPTON • Hinckley • Uppingham • Whittlesey • Littleport
Nuneaton • CAMBRIDGESHIRE
Bedworth • Market Harborough • Corby **3** • Ramsey • Chatteris
Oundle